MICHAEL COLLINS

MICHAEL COLLINS

The Man Who Made Ireland

TIM PAT COOGAN

ROBERTS RINEHART PUBLISHERS

*For Barbara, her mother Mabel, my father Eamon Coogan,
who worked for Collins, and my mother Beatrice*

Contents

List of Illustrations

Acknowledgements

It is a measure of Michael Collins' standing in the eyes of his countrymen, not a race noticeable for an excess of charity towards the reputations of their fellow men, that I can truly say that of all the books and research projects I have undertaken, this was the one for which I received the most unstinted and widespread assistance with material and information.

One great tragedy darkened this bright landscape of friendship and helpfulness. Before this American edition appeared, a motor accident had claimed the life of the person who was my greatest single source of encouragement, editorial and psychological support from the time I first began researching to the moment the last proof went to the printers: Barbara Hayley, Professor of English at St. Patrick's College, Maynooth. A wonderful human being, an inspired teacher, her contribution to this work was an illustration of the meaning of the latin word "educare", from which "education" is derived: to draw out. Barbara was the one who drew out this book.

The Collins family were unfailingly courteous and co-operative. I must particularly thank Mr Michael Collins, Mr Liam Collins, Col Pat Collins, Gen Sean Collins-Powell, Ms Nancy Hurley and Ms Mary-Clare O'Malley, for all the information and material they provided. The Collins' family friend and historian, the late Mr Liam O'Donnadcha, also provided invaluable notes and guidance. The historian, the late Leon O'Broin, was a tower of strength and inspiration before his health failed. The first-hand reminiscences of Vinnie Bryne, Sr Margaret Mary and Ms Eileen O'Donovan were not only valuable but fascinating. Mr Eamonn de Barra provided me with both reminiscences and some extremely valuable documents. Lord Longford placed his unrivalled knowledge of the Treaty negotiations and of Irish affairs generally at my disposal. Heavy debts of gratitude are also owed to Ms Maire Molloy, for allowing me to reproduce the letters of Michael Collins to her mother and to Liam Tobin's daughters, Ms Ann Thornton and Ms Marie Tobin, for entrusting me with their father's papers and those of his close comrade, Frank Thornton; to Mr Felix Cronin for giving me unpublished letters of Collins to his mother (Kitty Kiernan), also to Professor Edith Sagarra for the file on exchanges between Churchill and Collins.

I cannot say enough about the kindness and assistance rendered by the staffs and directors of the various libraries and archives which I consulted. Though I single out a number of names for especial mention, I can truly say that I met with an almost universally helpful response. My thanks go to Mr Donal MacCartney and to Mr Seamus Helferty at University College Dublin, and Ms Kerry Holland of the Archives Department for making available to me the invaluable Mulcahy and O'Malley collections and other papers; at Dublin University, Dr Bernard Meehan, Keeper of Manuscripts, and Ms Felicity O'Mahony were unfailingly helpful; as were the staff of the National Library of Ireland, in particular Mr Gerry Lyne. My thanks too to the Director of National Archives, Dr David Craig, and his courteous and knowledgeable staffs in The State Paper Office and the Public Records Office; to Mr John Toolin and Mr Patrick Long at the Kilmainham Museum; Former Minister for Defence, Mr Brian Lenihan, Minister for Justice, for providing me with Department of Defence material; Mr Gregoir O'Duill for his assistance with Department of Finance Archives; Mr John Teehan of the National Museum of Ireland for facilitating my inspection of Collins memorabilia at a time when the museum was undergoing renovation; Mr David C. Sheehy, Diocesan Archivist to the Archdioces of Dublin, for his help with the immensely valuable Archbishops' Byrne and Walsh Collections; Mr Trevor Parkhill for his assistance at the Public Record Office of Northern Ireland; Ms Hilary Jones, her colleagues at the Public Records Office, London, and John and Angela Heuston, who all combined to make my sojourn at Kew both enjoyable and enlightening; Mr Nicholas B. Scheetz for his helpfulness in guiding me through the Shane Leslie papers at Georgetown University; Lady Leslie for granting me permission to consult the collection; Dr Margaret O'Donoghue for allowing me to make use of the Florrie O'Donoghue collection in the National Library of Ireland; to Mr Paddy Cooney, BL TD, for granting me permission to inspect the MacEoin papers in the Franciscan Archives, Killiney; Cannon John Brennan for giving me the unpublished memoirs of Kathleen Napoli McKenna; Archbishop Ryan of Perth for assistance with the history of the Dr Clune peace mission; to Faber & Faber for allowing me to quote from Louis MacNeice's poem 'Dublin'.

For their kind permission to reproduce the illustrations in this book, I must also thank Joe Cashman; the Collins family; Felix Cronin, the Hulton-Deutsch Collection; Kilmainham Jail Historical Museum; George Morrison; the National Library of Ireland; the National Museum of Ireland; Ms Eileen O'Donovan; Ms Essie Driscoll; Dr C. O'Reilly; Popperfoto; and the State Paper Office, Dublin. I am especially grateful to Kenneth Griffith for his expert help in the compilation of the pictures.

For overall guidance as to source material and assistance with proof-reading I am more indebted than I can say to Dr Michael Hopkinson, Mr John O'Mahony, and to Brid and Michael O'Siadhail, who rendered most useful assistance in these spheres. Mr Uinseann MacEoin, Mr Harold O'Sullivan, Dr Maurice O'Connell, Dr Dermot Keogh and Fr F. X. Martin also contributed invaluable guidance and material. Help came also from Professor J.B. Lyons; Mrs Sinead Derrig (née Mason), Dr Martin Gilbert, Dr Eamonn Phoenix, Dr John Dalat, Mr Liam MacAndrews, Mr Liam Flynn and Mr Liam Moher. The warmest of thanks to Lord Longford, the author of the classic study of the Treaty negotiations, *Peace By Ordeal*, for his advice and encouragement. Mr Rory Brady B.L. was kind enough to provide the invaluable service of reading the book from a legal standpoint and Ms Carmel Frawley came to my assistance with typing at a critical juncture. I should also like to record with pride and gratitude the research assistance rendered by those two fine journalists, my daughter Jackie and my son Tom.

I wish to express my sincere thanks to Frank Delaney for helping to get this book started and, in particular, to Richard Cohen of Hutchinson for his tactful and enlightened encouragement through first the writing, and then the editing stage—and here I speak as one who was himself an editor for twenty years—before handing over to Annelise Evans who proved herself a model of everything a good editor should be.

Last, but far from least, I wish to express my appreciation for the very Irish solution which presented itself to the even more Irish problem of dealing with the fact that de Valera's papers, in the Franciscan Archives, Killiney, are closed to researchers until cataloguing is completed in some years' time. Until the eleventh hour it appeared that this ban might prevent me gaining access to the Sean MacEoin papers held there also, but at the eleventh hour, while this book was going through the printers, thanks to the good offices of Fr Benignus Millet OFM, Mr Liam O'Lonargain and Mr Brendan MacGiolla Choille and his wife Eilis, I was given access to the MacEoin collection. Mr MacGiolla Choille, a former Keeper of the Public Records, also gave me the benefit of his unrivalled personal insights into matters concerning de Valera. I had earlier had the benefit of two major sources of assistance, one mysterious, but welcome, the anonymous gift of photostats of some interesting de Valera letters, 'from an admirer', after I had appeared on a television documentary about Collins; the other more substantial, and even more welcome—the continued provision of advice, documents and original manuscripts of his own writings on de Valera from Dr T.P. O'Neill, de Valera's official biographer. Dr O'Neill manfully contributed valuable help all through the writing of this book although we disagree profoundly about de Valera's role in the events described. His continuing supportive friendship, and that of his wife, Marie, is an indication that though ideas may contend, men need not. Would that his example was followed in other parts of our country.

Preface to The American edition

America's loss was to be Ireland's gain. For if Michael Collins had taken his brother Pat's advice, the Republic of Ireland might not exist today. Watching the storm clouds of World War I gather over Europe, Pat had written to Michael from Chicago urging his young brother to leave his job in a London stockbroker's office and come to join him in America. Had they teamed up, one is tempted to speculate that one of the all-time great Pat-and-Mike success stories might have resulted. But twenty-six-year-old Michael agonized over the decision while walking the docks of London, seeing the ships leave for the New World. War was imminent; a call up would surely follow, bringing with it an unthinkable choice: either become a conscientious objector or don a British uniform and fight for the Crown.

Eventually Collins solved the problem in his own inimitable way. He put on an Irish uniform and went to fight for Ireland, in the 1916 Easter Rebellion in Dublin. That searing week of flame and folly claimed the lives of some of the people he most admired: Tom Clarke, James Connolly, Sean Hurley, Sean MacDiarmida, Joseph Plunkett. Their names, and the parts they played in his career, will figure in subsequent pages. With their deaths, there also died his faith in conventional methods of fighting for Ireland's freedom. He still believed in fighting. But in the parliamentary game as played at Westminster the rules were so arranged that the outnumbered Irish nationalists always lost. Now he understood that static warfare—seizing a stronghold, be it a building such as Dublin's General Post Office, in which he fought during the rebellion, or a mountain top, and then slugging it out with rifles and shot guns against an adversary who possessed heavy artillery—would continue to provide the Irish with heroes and martyrs, and the British with victories.

Instead Collins evolved a new concept of guerilla warfare that in time would be copied by guerilla leaders all over the globe from Mao to Shamir. The Collins philosophy was based not on the capture of enemy bricks and mortar, but of its information. Traditionally Dublin Castle, the seat of British administration in Ireland, had used a network of spies and informers to infiltrate and then snuff out movements directed at securing Irish independence.

Collins perfected a system of spying on the spies. Every important branch of the Castle system, whether it was banking, policing, the railways, shipping, the postal service—whatever—was infiltrated by his agents. These were not highly-trained, CIA-style operatives, but ordinary men and women, little people whom nobody had ever taken notice of before. Collins gave them a belief in themselves, a courage they did not know they possessed, and they in return gave him a complete picture of how their masters operated.

A secretary in Military Intelligence saw to it that Collins had a copy of the Colonel's orders to the Captain before he received the originals. A railway porter carried dispatches, the docker smuggled in revolvers, the detective told him who the informers were—and the Squad used the revolvers to deal with those informers. For the first time in their history the Irish had a team of assassins trained to eliminate informers. Collins demoralized the hitherto invincible Royal Irish Constabulary, the armed police force that operated from fortified barracks and held Ireland for the Crown. Inevitably more generalized warfare broke out all over the country as the British introduced new men and new methods in a vain effort to counter the guerilla tactics of Collins's Active Service Units and the Flying Columns of Volunteers, which lived on the run, eating and sleeping where they could.

Held back from making a full scale use of their Army by the force of world opinion—largely Irish-American opinion—the British tried to fight a "police war" carried on by hastily-formed forces of ex-service men and officers troubled by little discipline and less conscience. The Black and Tans and the Auxiliaries wrote new chapters of horror in the bloodstained story of the Anglo-Irish relationship. Reprisals for the activities of Collins and his colleagues included the burning of homes and creameries, random murder and the widespread use of torture. Through it all Collins lived a "life on the bicycle." The most-wanted man in Europe, he smiled his way through a hundred hold-ups never wearing a disguise, never missing an appointment, never certain where he would spend the night.

In addition to his campaign of warfare, he ran a national loan, which was banned by the British so that either its advertisement or sale became illegal. Yet the loan was fully subscribed, and every subscriber got a receipt. He was president of the omnipresent secret society, the Irish Republican Brotherhood, which regarded him as the real president of the Irish Republic, and he was Minister for Finance in the *Sinn Fein* cabinet. In addition he was Director of Intelligence of the Irish Republican Army. Any one of those jobs would have consumed the energy of an ordinary man, but Collins combined them all efficiently and effectively.

He had little formal education (that part of his development ceased when he passed his junior-grade civil service examinations at the age of sixteen), but he was an omnivorous reader and combined a mind like a laser beam with a hawk-like eye for detail. Nothing escaped his attention. Everything attracted his interest: Shaw's latest play, the way the Swiss organized a Citizen Army, Benjamin Franklin's proposals for dealing with loyalists, or the latest edition of Popular Mechanics. An article in that journal in November of 1920 led to the first use in warfare of the Thomson gun. Collins saw the article on the recently-invented weapon and had enquiries made about this "splendid thing,"* which led to the Irish-American leader Joseph McGarrity of Philadelphia buying five hundred of the weapons. Two Irish-American ex-officers were sent to Ireland to train the I.R.A. in the use of the weapons. Only a handful got through the American customs, but these were duly used in a number of Dublin ambushes.

Tough and abrasive with his male, and sometimes female, colleagues, Collins was gentle and playful with children and old people. Throughout the eighteen months that Eamon de Valera was in America on a propaganda and fund-raising mission, Collins risked his life to call each week to his absent chief's family, bringing them money and companionship. Eventually the war effort Collins had spearheaded drove the British to a conference table and a settlement as foreseeable as it was unpalatable to many Irishmen and women; a partitioned Irish Free State that would owe allegiance to the Crown. It was a deal that had been foreshadowed to de Valera in four days of talks between himself and Lloyd George, the British Prime Minister, in London during July 1921. De Valera did not want to be the man who faced up to the implications of that deal. Instead he repaid the kindness Collins had shown his family in Machiavellian fashion. He stayed away himself from the opprobrious negotiations but manipulated Collins into going to London as part of the delegation that signed the Anglo-Irish Treaty of December 6th, 1921, the constitutional foundation document of modern Ireland. Collins took the leading part in the Treaty's negotiation. Subsequently, he became Chairman of the Executive Council (in effect, the Government) of the Irish Free State that emerged, and later Commander-in-Chief of the Army.

The Treaty did not yield the Republic he had hoped for but it provided what Collins prophetically termed a "stepping stone" to today's Irish Republic. All the other stepping stones to the tragedy of today's Northern Ireland situation were part of that negotiation too. In a very real sense Collins' premature death was caused by the forces that still rage about the Northeastern corner of the land

and people for whom he fought. The story of his life explains tomorrow's news from Belfast. Would he have brought fire or prosperity to his country had he lived? Or would he have died of drink or disillusionment at the effects of the civil war that broke out over the terms of the Treaty?

We don't know. What we can be sure of is that this Irish Sigfried kept his Appointment in Samarra a couple of months short of his thirty-second birthday in a remote Cork valley known as *Beal na mBlath,* The Mouth of Flowers. He died, not far from where he was born, in an ambush laid by a former comrade in arms, a man who had undergone sadistic tortures at the hands of British Intelligence Officers rather than betray his boyhood friend, Michael Collins. Collins' career is a paradigm of the tragedy of modern Ireland: the suffering, the waste of talent, the hope, the bedeviling effect of history and nomenclature whereby one man's terrorist is another man's freedom fighter. Like Prometheus, Collins stole fire. Like Prometheus, he paid for his feat and much of what he set about doing remains undone. But his name burns brightly wherever the Irish meet. Michael Collins was the man who made Ireland possible.

*Described by Sean Cronin in *The McGarrity Papers,* Anvil Books, Tralee, Co. Kerry, 1978, p.98.

Prologue

Dublin, May 1916. A line of prisoners marches along the quays towards a boat that is going to take them to jail somewhere in England. Not the most pleasant of prospects, but at least they've come safely out of the fighting that has left the centre of the city in ruins and none of them was picked out to face a firing squad. Some of their friends were not so lucky. In fact quite a number of the people they pass on the street think they have got off too lightly. Here and there a man calls out a jeer or an oath. He might have a brother or a son at the front. Generally it is the women who are most vituperative. These are 'separation women'. Their only income is the separation allowance they are paid by the British Government while their husbands are away fighting for the rights of small nations. Their comments express both their disgust at the destruction and killing caused by the week-long rebellion and their fears that the Government may react by cutting off their livelihood.

'Bleedin' bastards, my husband's out in the war fightin' for you bowsies and yiz go and yiz stab them in the back.' 'Yiz are too cowardly to fight, and too lazy to work.' One lady with a shawl yells something about her two fine sons and runs along the line of soldiers guarding the prisoners to call out, 'Everyone of yiz should get a dose of capital punishment, and a bloody good kick up the arse after.'

But here and there the prisoners get an occasional word of encouragement too. From the top of the tram a respectable looking man in a bowler hat calls out, 'God save ye, lads – up the Republic.' Another man wearing an apron and covered in flour, obviously a baker, breaks through the soldiers to thrust fistfuls of chocolate and cigarettes into the hands of a prisoner who is so surprised that he can only think to shout his thanks a few seconds after the stranger has dropped back into the crowd. As the column passes the ruins of Liberty Hall shelled into rubble by the gunboat *Helga* during the

fighting, a good-looking, well-dressed young woman, Nancy
O'Brien, at last catches up with the prisoner she's been searching for,
her cousin.

A few weeks ago, he and his friend Sean MacDiarmada had taken
part in the Easter Rising, and her cousin had marched out of Liberty
Hall in his new Volunteer's uniform, to fight. For a week she had gone
to the top of Howth Head to listen to the shelling and watch the flames
rise from the Post Office. At least part of her prayer had been
answered. Although MacDiarmada had been condemned to death her
cousin Michael had emerged safely from the conflagration, even if he
was going off into captivity.

Slightly breathless from having to jog to keep up, she called over a
soldier's head, 'What will you do now?' 'Do?' asked the tall, mocking
young man with a West Cork accent nearly as broad as his shoulders.
'Do? Sure I'll get ready for the next round, of course. I've got some of
the names taken down already,' he said, waving a diary, 'the besht of
min.' Nancy was flabbergasted. 'But . . . what? . . . How are you
going to train them?' she called out finally, just as the column neared
the cattle-boat waiting for the prisoners. 'Sure won't His Majesty's
Government train them for me?'

1

The Little Fella

'One day he'll be a great man. He'll do great work for Ireland.'

Michael Collins Senior, on his deathbed

Dear Sirr,
Lord Edward Fitzgerald will be this evening in Watling St. Place a watch in Watling St two houses up from Usher's Island and another towards Queen's Bridge, a third in Island St, the rear of the stables near Watling St which leads up to Thomas St and Dirty Lane at one of three places Lord Edward will be found – he wears a wig and will have one or two more with him – they may be armed.

Dublin Castle, 18 May 1798.[1]

Anyone who might have seen the young Michael Collins in a loft on a sunny summer day on the family farm at Woodfield in West Cork a hundred years after the foregoing letter was written would have found it very hard to credit that he would ever survive to march into captivity – or live to smash the system of informers and intelligence-gathering that enabled Major Sirr to be in the right place at the right time to capture Lord Edward Fitzgerald. For, as he crawled across the loft which his sister had covered in blooms, the little boy was very obviously in the wrong place at the wrong time. In creating the floral carpeting his sisters had inadvertently left the trap door unbolted and the child suddenly disappeared through the treacherous blooms.[2] Terrified at what they might see sprawled beneath them the two girls rushed to the opening to discover their youngest brother unhurt, his fall broken by a pile of hay. On this occasion Michael Collins had escaped the jaws of *bael na mblath*, the mouth of flowers. Ironically, however, when death did come for him nearly thirty years later it would find him in a little Cork valley called – Bael na mBlath. Before that he would have become a legend in his lifetime and would have had a variety of escapes which made his safe emergence from the 1916 Rebellion seem like child's play.

Much of Collins' life's work was directed at destroying not only Dublin Castle's intelligence system, but the legislative Union of Great Britain and Ireland which it maintained. This Union came into being as a result of the 1798 Rebellion which was broken by the capture of Lord Edward Fitzgerald and by that of Theobald Wolfe Tone, the daring Republican theoretician who had succeeded in prising a French fleet from the Directory in the unfulfilled hope of driving the British out of Ireland. The Union meant that Ireland's parliament in Dublin was subsumed into the British parliament at Westminister. Dublin, Ireland's capital, had declined after the legislative shot-gun marriage and with the decay of Dublin there followed a parallel decline in the Irish economy leading to heavy emigration, famine, sporadic rebellion and the creation of a Protestant landlord class which increasingly absented itself from Ireland. Irish estates, viewed too often merely as sources of rent, not responsibility, were inefficiently managed, and uneconomically divided amongst tenants who if they fell behind in their rents could be evicted at will, or if they improved their holdings have their rents increased. The Clonakilty district of West Cork in which Michael Collins grew up[3] had more than its share of the land agitations which convulsed Ireland in the late nineteenth century. Two of the great onslaughts against landlordism took place on the Bence Jones and Smith-Barry estates near Clonakilty, under what was known as the Plan of Campaign. This combined the withholding of rent with boycotting, a refusal to have any dealings whatsoever with the object of the boycott. A landlord placed under this interdiction could not be traded with, worked for, or even spoken to. Both landlordism and the reaction of boycotting which it provoked were to leave their marks on the Collins family.

Two of Michael's uncles had once come to blows with two members of the landlord class who came roistering through the Woodfield crops on horseback. The Collinses used the trespassers' own riding whips to drive them off and spent a year in Cork jail for their pains. Michael's father made a day-long journey on horseback each month to visit them. Within the ranks of landlordism there was of course a responsible minority who cared for their estates and their tenantry. But that could give rise to problems too. One local landlord, a Protestant clergyman, was kind to one of Michael's sisters, treating her for burns she sustained at Woodfield through the carelessness of a servant girl. However when Michael senior sought to repay his goodness in a small way, by obliging the cleric with the loan of a winnowing machine, he was beaten up by another member of the Collins clan, a cousin.[4] The clergyman might have been kindly, but he was one of 'them', a landlord who at the time was being boycotted. He bravely lent the winnowing machine to the clergyman the day after he was beaten but escaped further embarrassment by building a new barn and concreting the contentious machine into the floor so that no one could borrow it again! Michael Senior was equally hard to shift when a local merchant dunned him for the bill which he claimed to have paid he allowed the man to take him to law so that he could publicly get the better of him, triumphantly producing his receipt in open court.[5] The Plan of Campaign was actually ruined by the opposition of a group of Unionist landlords under the resolute leadership of Arthur Smith-Barry. The Plan leaders, including William Smith O'Brien and John Dillon, who were also two of the leaders of the Irish Parliamentary Party, were summoned to court but failed to turn up, and disappeared for several weeks into a cloud of national gossip and excitement. It was afterwards noted[6] that the first time they were seen again in public was in Paris on the day that Michael Collins was born, 16 October 1890.

The case against the fleeing Irish leaders had been gathered efficiently by the principal force on the side of landlordism and the British connection, the Royal Irish Constabulary, a force built on a lengthy tradition of spies and informers, radiating out from Dublin Castle. The RIC's Register of Informants[7] describes the nature of these sources whose identities were carefully guarded, being entered only under 'Cognomen of Informant'. Around the time Collins was born, in the years 1889–90, the Register, which covered the whole country, contained many references to people and movements that would affect his life such as The Gaelic Athletic Association, The Gaelic League, The Irish Republican Brotherhood, the Labour movement, and to specific agitations such as the Smith-Barry affair.

Even in far-away County Armagh there was 'Easer', described as an 'old IRB man, friend of O'Donovan Rossa, gives information about IRB'. 'Steam' of Cork was 'well in with the boys', and a member of the IRB. 'Jennings', a recognised synonym for treachery, was 'one of our oldest and most reliable men' in Cork City. 'Charon' was 'most useful, with regard to Trades and Labour Unions'. 'H' was trustworthy as to 'state of district. Plots to assassinate and contemporary outrages as to infernal machines'. Many of the payments recorded were quite small, a pound or two over a year, so one can only speculate as to the place in society and the services rendered to the crown by 'Nero' who was described as being 'worth any money' and was paid £205. The standard of morality engendered by the 'Informant' system may be gauged by the fact that many of the entries stressed that the spies were 'sworn IRB men'.

The greatest 'sworn IRB man' of them all, Michael Collins, was born into the O'Coileain clan, formerly the lords of Ui Chonaill, known today as Upper and Lower Connelloe in County Limerick. The O'Coileains have their roots in both the bardic and warrior traditions of Ireland. Sean O'Coileain was a celebrated eighteenth-century poet and the O'Coileains' prowess in warfare is recalled in the ancient topographical poem by Giolla na Naomh O hUidhrin:

> The Ui Chonaill of the battalion of Munster
> Ample is the gathering
> A great family with whom it is not fitting
> to contend
> Is the battle-trooped host of the O'Coileains.

The Collinses were people of some consequence in the district and Collins' childhood was exceptionally happy, but the spores of memory, an interweaving of dispossession, of the consciousness of being a member of the *Duainaire* (the Dispossessed), of landlordism, of the famine, hung in his folk-consciousness with all the virulence of the potato blight. For example one of the local ballads which the Collins children learned to sing was a 'come-all-ye' ballad on the Bence Jones affair.[8] It was poor stuff, but potent:

> Come all ye noble Land Leaguers
> I hope you will draw near
> And drop a tear of sympathy around Billy
> Jones' bier
> He died last night in Brighton
> From land-leaguing and boycotting and all
> such landlord woe.

The Collinses did not suffer unduly from 'landlord woes'. Life was hard but by the standards of the Catholic farmers of the time the family was comfortably off, living on a holding of 90 acres with eight children to help with the work. These were Margaret, John, Johanna (or Hannie as she was always called), Mary, Helena, Patrick and Kate. Michael, the youngest, was pampered and spoiled by everyone.

One of the most significant factors in Collins' background was the age of his parents. His father, Michael senior, was seventy-five years old when Michael was born. He died at eighty-one when Michael was six, leaving the boy with a reverence for old people which he never lost. But his father's death also had the result of leaving an impressionable boy without fatherly control and susceptible to outside influences, in particular those of a nationalist-minded teacher, Denis Lyons, and an equally nationalist-inclined blacksmith, James Santry, both of whom as we shall see may be said to have guided his feet along the road to rebellion.

Michael John Collins was in his sixtieth year when he married Marianne O'Brien, a local girl of twenty-three. The seventh son of a seventh son, he had a reputation as a healer of animals, with in addition a knowledge of French, Latin and Greek. He was apparently also a gifted mathematician, was widely read and had a phenomenal memory. He received the basis of his unusual education from a cousin on his mother's side, Diarmuid O'Suillibhain, a hedge schoolmaster, one of the itinerant schoolteachers who defied the penal laws in the era before Catholic Emancipation (1829) to teach their pupils, sometimes literally under hedges. O'Suilleabhain was said to have studied at a Belgian university and to have been a friend of Wolfe Tone's. His father had also joined the Irish Republican Brotherhood, popularly named the Fenians, though he does not seem to have taken part in the aborted Fenian rising of 1865. Thus in the person of his father, Michael Collins in his childhood had a not insignificant link with the founder of Irish Republicanism.

That a man of such ability should wait so long before taking a wife speaks volumes for the uncertainties and conservatism created by the conditions of the Irish rural economy. When weighing up the normal pros and cons of marriage one had to add to the cons the thought of having to leave with one's offspring for the insecurity of America or, worse, see them die of famine or its infections. Some of course saw the situation differently, as an Irish toast of those years shows: '*Sláinte go saol agat, páiste gach bliadhan agat agus bás in Eirin.*' It means 'Health and life to you, a child every year to you, and death in Ireland.' The child every year was the parents' insurance against accident or old age, and death in Ireland meant one would be spared the pangs of emigration.

Marianne O'Brien's life was a demonstration of the last two wishes coming true. She had had to care for her many brothers and sisters from her middle teens when her father was killed and her mother injured after their horse shied, throwing them out of their trap as they returned one evening from a funeral. Obviously she regarded the courtship of Michael John Collins and his ninety acres as being preferable to her situation at home. But at Woodfield, she soon had a very large household to cope with again. When she moved there, apart from Michael John she had to care for his three brothers, Maurice, Tom and Paddy. Children duly arrived with the rapidity demanded by the Catholic church of the time.

Woodfield was almost completely self-supporting. And it was principally Marianne who supported the farmstead.[9] Carding the wool from their own sheep. Milking the twelve cows, curing the bacon from their own pigs. Baking, cleaning, sewing, ironing, making butter, making clothes, making babies. So good with money that she built a new house on the farm after Michael John died, despite the fact that a thief began the work by stealing the workmen's wages. So hospitable, that in an area noted for hospitality she was described as 'a hostess in ten thousand'.[10] Certainly on a perceived, obvious level, Marianne Collins left a powerful force of example behind her.

Though her busy life did not leave her with much time for any revolutionary branch of nationalism, she nevertheless had a sturdy sense of Irishness that manifested itself at an extraordinarily early age. There is a well-attested story in the Collins family[11] of how she took part when she was seven in a ceremony organised by the school at Lisavaird, then run by a Miss Collins, no relation, in honour of the local Big House family, the Freakes. The children had to recite a verse containing the line 'Thank God I am a happy English child'. But Marianne suddenly piped up, in front of the dignitaries, 'Thank God I am a happy *Irish* child!' She was badly beaten and sent to Coventry as a result. In later life Marianne also learned Latin and Greek from a hedge schoolmaster, an alcoholic priest.

Her daughter Mary recalled the night before Michael was born:

My mother carried the heaviest burden (of work) and at this time suffered greatly from pain in a broken ankle which I suppose was never properly set. I remember the night before Michael was born – I was then nine – I held the strainer while she poured the milk, fresh from the cow, from very heavy pails into the pans for setting the cream. She moaned occasionally and when I asked her was she sick she said she had a toothache and would go to bed when the cakes were made for tomorrow. I said nothing as in those days children were to be seen but not heard. The next morning there was the miracle of the baby. No doctor. No trained nurse and mother and baby well and comfortable! To say that we loved this baby would be an understatement – we simply adored him. Old Uncle Paddy said as soon as he saw him, 'Be careful of this child for he will be a great and mighty man when we are all forgotten.'[12]

One is entitled to wonder how 'comfortable' in reality was Marianne O'Brien. What tumult of the blood and of the intellect did that vibrant, loving young woman quench within herself as she was turned on the Woodfield lathe into that archetypical figure of self-sacrificial Irish motherhood? All contemporary records stress the happiness of the marriage despite the disparity in ages. The father was so vigorous that his children did not think of him as old. 'My father never had an old age', wrote Mary, and this seems to have been a generally accepted verdict.

But '*uisce fé talamh*' (literally: water under the ground) is an old Irish saying to describe secret currents, hidden matters. If 'beauty born of murmuring sound' was held to infuse the personality of Lucy in the Wordsworth poem one wonders what deep, unspoken discordancies and intimations did the discrepancies of age and the strain of Marianne's labours cause her to pass on to her son along with her love of reading and of flowers? The buoyant personality that swung so easily from elation to despair and back again? The cloud-burst temper? The demanding energy that achieved impossible tasks and still had strength left over for exuberant wrestling matches? The bluff, the courage, the love of children and of old people. And somewhere inside, hidden, *uisce fé talamh*, stone in the peach of West Cork charm and personality, the relentless mind that tore down the RIC's Judas tapestry. Where did these qualities come from?

Katie told a curiously prophetic anecdote of those days concerning his choice of reading. Starting with Lamb's tales, the young Michael worked his way through Shakespeare and, in the fashion of literary minded young patriots of the day, through a combination of English classics and sentimental historical Irish novels and ballads. Out of this medley it emerged that his favourite work was *The Mill on the Floss*. He told Katie, who was closest to him at the time, 'We're like Tom and Maggie Tulliver.' Katie replied that he could never be cruel like Tom. After a moment's silence Collins said, 'I could be worse. . . .'[13]

From his earliest days Michael seems to have wanted to be the leader in everything that went on around him. His cousin Michael O'Brien wrote of him[14] in their childhood days that Collins would always 'insist on running the show at Woodfield when we were kids, even to holding the pike (fork) when we endeavoured to spear salmon'. (There were only small trout in the river.) The family history abounds with doting anecdotes of the young Collins. Celestine, going away to be a nun in England, recalls the little boy waving goodbye until the pony and trap took her around a bend and out of sight. Mary tells of being left to look after the household for a day of drudgery during which she forgot to dig the potatoes until evening. Wearily forcing herself to the kitchen garden she was met by her three-year-old brother dragging behind him a bucket of potatoes that he had somehow managed to dig up by himself. Johnny remembers his prowess with horses, in particular, being found one day while still a baby curled up fast asleep in a stable between the hoofs of a notoriously vicious animal. His father on his deathbed told his grieving family to mind Michael because, 'One day he'll be a great man. He'll do great work for Ireland.'[15] Michael was six years old at the time.

Such are the stories told about him. But many of the stories told *to* him were products of hatred, not love. These grew out of the history of his race and place and they had a powerful, formative influence on his imagination. For pikes of a sort other than those used in efforts to spear fish had traditionally been fashioned at what in Collins' childhood was the neighbourhood place of enchantment, the forge at nearby Lisavaird, run by the blacksmith, James Santry. Santry's grandfather had fought in 1798 and his grandfather had made pikes for two of the revolutions which Tone's teachings had helped to inspire in the subsequent century, 1848 and 1865. In a very literal sense the sparks of revolution were fanned into life for Michael Collins in James Santry's old forge. Close by in Lisavaird National School what was begun by Santry was continued by the local schoolmaster, Denis Lyons, an active member of the Irish Republican Brotherhood, the

IRB, which had set off the Fenian revolt of 1865. Lyons' rule was harsh. He could never be accused of spoiling any child through sparing the rod, but his excellent results made the community overlook both his methods and his dangerous politics.

Collins never seems to have held any grudge about Lyons' severity and he revelled in the doctrines of Wolfe Tone's physical force republicanism which the teacher imparted along with the three Rs:

To subvert the tyranny of our execrable Government, to break the connection with England, the never failing source of all our political evils, and to assert the independence of my country – these were my objects. To unite the whole people of Ireland, to abolish the memory of all past dissensions, and to substitute the common name of Irishman in place of the denomination of Protestant, Catholic and Dissenter – these were my means.[16]

Later in life, during a period of self-analysis[17], Collins gave a friend an assessment of the importance of Santry and Lyons to the development of his political thinking which shows how highly he rated their influence:

In Denis Lyons and James Santry I had my first tutors capable of – because of their personalities alone – infusing into me a pride of the Irish as a race. Other men may have helped me along the searching path to a political goal. I may have worked hard myself in the long search, nevertheless Denis Lyons and James Santry remain to me my first stalwarts. In Denis Lyons especially his manner, although seemingly hiding what meant most to him, had this pride of Irishness that has always meant most to me.

Woodfield is a lightly wooded hill, overlooking a fertile, picturesque valley with a river that the Collins children fished and played in. Although naturally athletic, Michael, like most Irish boys of his and many subsequent generations, never learned to swim, a commentary on the education and attitudes of a sea-girt society whose once valuable fishing trade had been wiped out and which viewed the sea as a phenomenon that either created employment in the British Navy or was one's means of emigration. Only a small percentage of the population had a tradition of earning a dangerous living, usually in small open boats, from the fertile but furious coastline. 'What the sea gives it takes back' is an old Irish saying. And part of Collins' life's work would be to try to get his countrymen to take back from the sea the harvest they once reaped. The sea is only a few miles away from his birthplace, the beaches, cliffs and fjords of West Cork being punctuated to the east by the thriving town of Clonakilty four miles away and three miles to the west by the cliff-crowned village of Rosscarbery where one of Collins' heroes was born: O'Donovan Rossa, the Fenian leader, who actually visited Lisavaird School while the Collins children were there. At Rosscarbery the children heard stories of Cliodhna, the queen of the Munster fairies. A favourite Sunday trip was to the cliffs above Cliodhna's rock. Here, Collins' friend Piaras Beaslai tells us, 'Michael heard many a wonderful tale of Cliodhna's enchantments, of wrecks and perils, and drownings and treasure trove.'[18]

The tales were not all of enchantment. The sufferings of O'Donovan Rossa in English prisons were recounted. Of Skibbereen a few miles west of Rosscarbery where at that time all the principal shops were still owned by Protestants and the history of eviction and emigration is commemorated by the ballad 'Old Skibbereen', in which a father tells his orphaned son how they came to be in America:

> Oh, well do I remember the bleak December day,
> The landlord and the sheriff came to drive us all away;
> They set my roof on fire with their cursed English spleen.
> And that's another reason that I left old Skibbereen.

Collins himself would live to experience his own roof set on fire, and during his childhood a familiar sight to him, off the coast near Skibbereen, was the awesome Fastnet Rock lighthouse. It owes its existence to a disaster which occurred at the height of the famine. In November 1847 the US-registered *Stephen Whitney* laden with men, women and children escaping to the new world was wrecked on the Fastnet during a gale.

His early years were crisscrossed by such contrasting strands of joy and horror, myth and reality, love and hate, in a way that seems to foreshadow his later life. Sam's Cross, his native hamlet near Woodfield, is named after Sam Wallace, a highwayman, who is said to have robbed the rich to feed the poor. The major attraction of the crossroads is The Four Alls, a pub owned by a member of the Collins clan. It doesn't display photographs of its most famous patron: 'Some of our customers mightn't like them.' And even today the signpost on the main road from Clonakilty pointing to Collins' birthplace is sometimes vandalised: 'Ah sure you wouldn't know who'd do these things', is the customary explanation of locals, delivered in a tone that suggests the speaker knows exactly who does such things.

At home Collins received a gentler, more complex, but nevertheless complementary vision of history and politics, from that taught by Santry and Lyons. Unlike his family and neighbours his father never sang rebel songs. Yet he had lived through the famine and joined the Fenians and told his children that he thought the land should be owned by the people, in other words their people, the Catholics. The last eviction in the district had occurred while the owner of the farm lay on his deathbed. An enraged son had reacted by driving a fork into the agent's eye. That stopped the eviction, it was said locally. 'The only thing they understand is violence', was the corollary. It was a corollary Michael Collins agreed with. He told his cousin Sean

Hurley, as they passed the home of a once notorious evicting landlord: 'When I'm a man we'll have him and his kind out of Ireland.'[19]

The talk around the Collins fireside frequently turned as it did at the firesides of their neighbours to landlords and their methods, 'hanging gales', rack-renting, and the occasional exercise of the *droit de seigneur*, for Wolfe Tone's vision had not been fulfilled. Protestant and Catholic had not united in the common name of Irishmen and the big estates and big businesses, what there were of them, were generally held by Protestants. Any time the Collinses wished to go to Cork they had to pass through the town of Bandon. This solidly Protestant oasis in the ever-encroaching desert of Catholicism at the time of Collins' boyhood was still infused with the spirit of its builder, Richard Boyle, Earl of Cork, who thanked Almighty God that there was not an Irishman nor a Papist in the place.[20] But this fact never created any anti- Protestant feeling at Woodfield. Marianne died attended by Protestant neighbours and there was a large concourse of Protestants at her funeral.

There is no evidence at any stage in his life, even when he was at the height of his disagreements with Northern Ireland's Protestant leadership, that Michael Collins ever uttered a sectarian sentiment. A celebrated liberal Presbyterian, the Rev. J. B. Armour, came from Northern Ireland to study in Cork University not long before Collins was born, and wrote: 'There seems to be none of that bigotry with regard to religious principle which is all too evident in Belfast.'[21] But though Armour was correct in his observation that Catholics and Protestants were closer together in Cork than they were in Belfast, where the holders of the land were concerned it was the closeness of apartness, never more savagely described than by a Protestant poet from Northern Ireland, Louis MacNeice:

> The mist on the Wicklow Hills
> Is close, as close
> As the peasantry were to the landlord
> As the Irish to the Anglo-Irish,
> As the killer is close one moment
> To the man he kills.[22]

What the Protestant-Catholic divide did mean in practice was that when the Anglo-Irish war started it was to Protestants, as Loyalists, that the British automatically turned for their sources of intelligence whereas Collins drew his mainly, though not exclusively, from Catholics, and the IRA would be largely a Catholic force.

Two other influences which Michael John and Marianne also passed on to their children were a strongly held Catholic faith and a love of Nationalist literature and songs. Helena, the innocent cause of the winnowing-machine controversy, walked for the first time after the burning when she was five, following a pilgrimage made by Marianne to the shrine of St Fachtna, a local saint, an event which was probably a contributory factor in Helena's becoming a nun. Michael always had a deeply felt religious sensibility, though he did pass through the usual Republican anti-clerical period when he lived in London.

His sister, Mary Collins, played her part in helping to heighten her young brother's interest in the Nationalist struggle and in guerrilla warfare. While at school in Edinburgh she developed a sympathy with the Boers and on her return for holidays to Woodfield would tell Michael of her fights at school with 'pro-jingoists'. It was from Mary that Michael heard 'how the gallant Boer farmers used to leave their work, take part in an ambush and return perhaps to milk the cows the next morning.'[23] De Wet became one of Collins' heroes.[24] Mary Collins Powell quotes a ballad of the time, 'which, no doubt, left a lasting impression on Michael's young mind':

> Great faith I have in moral force
> Great trust in thought and pen
> I know the value of discourse
> To sway the minds of men
> But why should words my frenzy whet
> Unless we are to strike
> Our despot lords who fear no threat
> But reverence the pike
> Oh, do be wise, leave moral force
> The strength of thought and pen
> And all the value of discourse
> To lily-livered men
> But if you covet not to die
> Of hunger in a dyke
> If life we prize is liberty
> A Pike – A Pike – A Pike.

In its own unsophisticated way that ballad may be said to have done more than leave a 'lasting impression' on Collins' mind. It summed up the Santry and Lyons arguments and policy he advocated throughout his short, turbulent life. The condition of Ireland could only be improved by the use of force.

The young Michael devoured the writings of Thomas Davis, the nationalist philosopher and propagandist of the Young Ireland movement which led to the revolt of 1848, the songs and Fenian tales of A. M. and T. D. Sullivan, the songs and poetry of Thomas Moore. The novels of Banim and Kickham, set against a background of tenant strife, landlordism, oppression and emigration, stirred him deeply. He was found weeping one day over the sufferings of the peasantry in Kickham's *Knocknagow*.

His contemporary and biographer, Frank O'Connor says: 'If I had recorded all the occasions when he wept I should have given the impression that he was hysterical. He wasn't; he laughed and wept as a child does (and indeed as people in earlier centuries seem to have done) quite without self-consciousness.'[25]

One force which moved him early on in life, though not to tears, was Arthur Griffith's *United Irishman*, whose editorials he began studying when he was twelve years of age. He wrote at this time: 'In Arthur Griffith there is a mighty force afoot in Ireland. He has none of the wildness of some I could name. Instead there is an abundance of wisdom and an awareness of things that ARE Ireland.'[26] By contrast he was totally dismissive of the Irish Parliamentary Party: those 'slaves of England' were nothing but 'chains around Irish necks'.[27]

Denis Lyons, for whom he wrote the foregoing in an essay, and who probably introduced him to Griffith, must have been pleased with his pupil. Along with Griffith's separatism, illustrations of how England had systematically suppressed Irish trade, and doctrines of Irish national self-development, he took aboard the preachings of another editor, D. P. Moran of *The Leader*, which advocated an 'Irish Ireland'. Both writers sought to promote a heightened consciousness of being Irish across a broad spectrum, encouraging support for Irish goods, games, art, literature, music and language. Collins' parents spoke Irish, but only when they didn't want their children to understand them. For like many patriotic Irish parents of the time they feared that the Irish language would be a barrier to their children's prospects of advancement in the English-speaking world.

As a boy Michael was popular, but regarded as somewhat 'wild'. Galloping about on the Collinses' white mare, Gypsy. Playing football and hurling, and the popular Cork sport of 'bowling', throwing an iron ball along the country roads, with more enthusiasm than skill but with plentiful explosions of temperament. Skylarking with his close companion, Sean Hurley, a cousin of the same age who shared his interest in sport and, increasingly, in the political situation. Marianne was worried that if he stayed at home he might fall into bad company. 'He is head of his class and I am afraid he will get into mischief', she told his sisters[28]. By now the only man at Woodfield was his eldest brother Johnny, twelve years older than Michael. Employment opportunities in the district were limited. The RIC and the Services were unattractive to someone of his outlook. Watching her youngest in his teens as her health began to fail, Marianne decided that his future lay in London.

There was a tradition in the area that when a male child was born in Clonakilty the neighbours would say, 'Musha, God bless him. It's the fine sorter he'll make'.[29] His sister Johanna, 'Hannie', was already in London working for the post office, and Michael was sent to

Clonakilty to study for the post office examinations and live with his sister Margaret, whose husband P. J. O'Driscoll owned the *West Cork People*, a local newspaper which was founded through the 'kindly aid' of Marianne. Here Collins developed an interest in newspapers which never left him. He learnt to type, acted as a copyboy, and wrote up sporting events.

After a year and a half in Clonakilty, he passed the Post Office examination and was given a job in the Post Office Savings Bank in West Kensington. In July 1906, Collins moved to London at the age of fifteen to live with Hannie at 5 Netherwood Road, West Kensington, which, his family believes, was his home for the next nine years, though the plaque on the house, erected by the Hammersmith authorities, only records his last year there, 1914–15, the period for which evidence of his occupancy appears on the voters' lists.[30]

Marianne died of cancer the following year, showing 'Christian fortitude' after a 'lingering and torturing illness . . . cold water . . . her food and drink for seven weeks previous to her happy release'. On her death, 'one who knew her' wrote a poem which was reproduced in the *West Cork People*.[31] It contained the following:

> Friend and stranger at her smiling board
> Found a welcome ever warmly stored;
> In her pulse the quickening rush
> Spoke the bosom's generous flush.
> An honest pleasure beamed in her eye;
> At her home 'twas ever so –
> Those who came were loath to go;
> Hers was Irish hospitality.

Collins preserved it in an envelope which also contained Marianne's mass card.[32] It gives her age as '54 years'. Underneath the figure, Collins, ever sentimental, ever meticulous, simply wrote, in tiny script, '52'. He did not cross out the wrong age, nor is it likely that in either his memory or his character, very much of Marianne was ever crossed out. One's seventeenth year is an impressionable age at which to see your mother follow the father you hardly knew into the grave.

Given the ideological baggage which he took with him to London, it is not surprising that Collins threw himself into the Irish rather than the English world of that city. Though Collins was taken out of West Cork, West Cork was never taken out of him. His closest friend in London was his closest friend in Clonakilty, his cousin Sean Hurley. He joined the Gaelic Athletic Association, playing football and hurling and, as he grew physically, developed into a fine athlete, particularly in hurling and the long jump. Though he played fair, his hair-trigger temperament meant that if a row developed on the field he was generally either its cause or a participant. Off the field when Collins was about eighteen there was a major row over GAA members playing soccer, one of the four games proscribed by the Association. (The others were rugby, hockey and cricket.) Collins was one of those who objected vigorously to 'garrison games'[33] which he saw as aiding 'the peaceful penetration of Ireland'. There should be 'no soccer for gaels'.

The London GAA split over the issue, several clubs breaking up so that only three remained, one of them Collins', the Geraldines, of which he became treasurer. Collins' report for the second half of 1909 reads:

An eventful half year has followed a somewhat riotous general meeting. Great hopes instead of being fulfilled have been rudely shattered. . . . Our internal troubles were saddening but our efforts in football and hurling were perfectly heartbreaking. In no single contest have our colours been crowned with success. . . . In hurling . . . we were drawn to play five matches but disgraceful to say in only one case did we field a full team. If members are not prepared to act more harmoniously together and more self-sacrificingly generally . . . the club will soon have faded into inglorious and well-deserved oblivion.[34]

The Collins approach worked and the Geraldines grew and prospered. His career in London's Irish world[35] was a combination of logical progression from the ideas and attitudes imparted at the Woodfield fireside, in forge and school at Lisavaird, by his reading of Irish history and by his own determination, in Michael O'Brien's words, 'to insist on running the show', whatever that show might be. He was involved in further controversy during 1909 because of his then pronounced anti-clericalism. The year before he had come to London, 1905, Arthur Griffith had founded a political party, Sinn Fein ('We Ourselves'), as a vehicle for his *United Irishman* ideas.

Invited by a Sinn Fein club to read a paper on 'The Catholic Church in Ireland', Collins delivered a broadside against the church's attitude to Irish nationalism, concluding with the recommendation that the way to deal with the Irish hierarchy was 'to exterminate them'. The most significant step Collins took that year was attended not by controversy, but by total secrecy, which paradoxically is commemorated annually today by unwitting but enthusiastic crowds at Ireland's premier sporting event, the All-Ireland Gaelic Football Final. In November 1909, at Barnsbury Hall, Michael Collins was sworn in as a member of the Irish Republican Brotherhood by his fellow post office worker, Sam Maguire. Maguire, who died in obscurity, is commemorated by the trophy awarded to the winning All-Ireland team, the Sam Maguire Cup. In the Irish world Collins went on to become both treasurer of the IRB for London and the South of England and treasurer of the London GAA.

In the outer, commercial world he moved to positions of less authority, though he was building up a knowledge of financial dealings and of organisation that blossomed when he needed it, in a way that suggests that he may have deliberately set out to acquire such skills. This would certainly have been in accordance with the IRB's policy of infiltrating every possible branch of activity likely to be of use to the Brotherhood. For, though an understanding of financial affairs came easily to him, and it appears obvious that he could have become a wealthy man with comparative ease, he seems to have had an inner dissatisfaction, an 'other' directed sense, where ordinary career values were concerned. He once wrote:

However happy I happen to be in a particular job, the thought is always with me that my future is otherwise than among the facts and figures of money. Yet I do not really dream of greater things . . . only the thought is always there.[36]

He afterwards wrote of himself:

The trade I know best is the financial trade, but from study and observation I have acquired a wide knowledge of social and economic conditions and have specially studied the building trade and unskilled labour. Proficient in typewriting, but have never tested speed. Thorough knowledge of double-entry system and well used to making trial balances and balance sheets.[37]

He also seems to have known enough about agriculture to win an agricultural scholarship in 1913 which, had he had the financial backing, would have brought him a training course in Athlone. His sister Mary regarded this as one of his most extraordinary achievements as he had no agricultural science textbooks apart from a national school handbook.

He remained at the Savings Bank until 1910 when he moved to a firm of stockbrokers, Horne and Co., 23 Moorgate St, where he was put in charge of messengers.

He had taken evening classes at the King's College to prepare for civil service examinations and left Horne's to join the Board of Trade as a clerk on 1 September 1914. The pay scale may have something to do with his brief stay there. It was £70–£150. There was also a pressure from the family to get him away from the approaching war and over to his brother Pat in Chicago. This is usually cited by his family and biographers as the cause of his moving to the Guaranty Trust Company of New York's London branch in Lombard St in May 1915. As we shall see later, however, there may have been other reasons connected with his inner, IRB world.

Insofar as his outer, cultural and social worlds were concerned, Hannie encouraged him to broaden his nationalist readings. An omnivorous reader, he developed an appetite for a wide variety of authors – Hardy, Meredith, H. G. Wells, Arnold Bennett, Conrad and Swinburne, as well as Wilde, Yeats, Padraig Colum and James

Stephens. He was a keen theatre-goer, Shaw being his first favourite in the London theatre, Barrie second. He took pride in being able to declaim tracts of Synge, Wilde and Yeats. In a judgement which underlines the tragedy of his early death Frank O'Connor says: 'Collins' studiousness was the mental activity of a highly gifted country lad to whom culture remained a mysterious and all powerful magic. Though not one for everyday use.'[38]

Perhaps not 'everyday use'. In the theatre of Michael Collins' life what stage performance could hold his attention against the dramas that filled many of his ordinary days? But in a moment of reflection, quarried out of the hurly-burly of a prison camp he would write to a friend in a natural way that showed that he found theatre neither remote from him nor mysterious:

Glad you liked Widower's Houses: Does this mean that you approved of all the unpleasant things as well, if my memory doesn't trick me that episode about the Duke of W and the letters is in it, the my Dear Jenny – publish and be damned thing. Somehow that has always struck me as being particularly tickling. I think you'll like Candida too, but Marie O'Neill doesn't strike me as being the correct thing for the name part, all the Abbey taught players were and are very narrow, excluding Fay or the much admired Sara who are the men? By the way Shaw himself has written a most excellent skit on Candida – perhaps you've read it. 'How she lied to her husband.' Oh lovely! It's in the volume containing John Bull and Major Barbara.[39]

Who knows to what 'everyday use' he might have devoted his powers had he lived or what his breadth of culture might have been.

Hannie increasingly disapproved of his political activities. She shared their mother's fears that these might 'get him into mischief' and, in effect, both by advice and the provision of alternative reading material, provided a counterbalancing influence to her sister Mary's nationalist promptings. She also introduced him to her wide circle of English friends, though obviously, before he ever left Cork, Collins' mind had been firmly cast in the Fenian tradition and no sisterly urgings would break that mould.

All Collins' family admired and respected him. But the difference between Hannie and Mary, for example, lay in the fact that Hannie, who never married, lived in London and made a successful, lifelong, career in the British postal service. Mary lived in Ireland, in Cork, and actively helped Collins in his work in any way she could. Her son, Sean Collins-Powell, ultimately became Chief of Staff of the National Army founded by his famous uncle. Why two people from the same family and background so often go in such different directions is a question which frequently puzzles observers of Ireland. A chief of the Irish Special Branch told me once that after he had arrested certain young IRA men, and established their identity, he could immediately tell what teacher had influenced them into joining the movement. But what influenced the teacher? And why did the IRA men's older or younger brothers not join? These are questions which will continue to be asked as long as the Anglo-Irish difficulty is unresolved and British uniforms remain in Ireland.

Collins had a tendency to rise to the bait of any anti-Irish slur, real or inferred. After his death, his Guaranty Trust supervisor wrote that 'the staff, who were privileged to know him, will never believe that he could do an unworthy act'.[40] But he also noted that: 'Only on very rare occasions did his sunny smile disappear, and this was usually the result of one of his fellow clerks making some disparaging and, probably unthinking, remark about his beloved Ireland. Then he would look as though he might prove a dangerous enemy.'

The fact that Collins, who prevented an unfortunate Irish soldier in British uniform from watching a hurling match, and who, in later life, would frequently have cause to write in despatches of the English as the Enemy, never developed any knee-jerk anti-British sentiment was probably helped by entrée to Hannie's social circle. She certainly helped him financially. His wages when he came first to Netherwood Road were fifteen shillings a week. And she added to her role of friend and elder sister by attempting to exercise a maternal influence where drink and sex were concerned. He certainly drank, but not to excess like many of his contemporaries in the Irish community, and Frank O'Connor solemnly assures us that he was 'shrewd enough'[41] to know about the evils of prostitution 'only at second hand through the works of Tolstoy and Shaw'. But P. S. O'Hegarty, one of his greatest admirers, gives a more believable picture of a strong-willed adolescent boy, with normal healthy urges, who had been reared without a father and was now living in a big city with no surveillance save that of his eldest sister:

Everybody in Sinn Fein circles knew him, and everybody liked him, but he was not a leader. He had strong individuality, clearly-held opinions, and noticeable maturity even as a boy of seventeen when he made his appearance in Irish circles in London. But his place was rather as the raw material of a leader than as a leader. When he came to London as a mere boy, he fell into spasmodic association with a hard-drinking, hard-living crowd from his own place, and their influence on him was not good. During most of his years in London he was in the 'blast and bloody' stage of adolescent evolution, and was regarded as a wild youth with plenty of ability, who was spoiled by his wildness. Not that his wildness was any deeper than the surface. Behind it his mind grew and his ideas enlarged.[42]

His second cousin Nancy O'Brien who also worked in the post office said of him at this time: 'All the girls were mad about him. He'd turn up at the ceilidhe with Padraic O'Conaire and would not give them a "reck".' He was the sort of man that women either empathise with or seek to pull down. Generally in his London years

women of his own class found him 'cheeky', his 'Big Fellow'
sobriquet indicating swollen- headedness as much as height, just
under six feet. They were attracted to his energy, his athletic build, the
dark brown hair, the square-jawed truculent look that could change so
suddenly to a boyish grin. But in the battle of the sexes, the strong-
minded Irish Catholic women have always displayed to a high degree
the sexual combativeness of the peer group. They can be generous
with love but niggardly with understanding. The women that Collins
was to find generous in both respects as his hero-reputation grew had
no impulse towards competitiveness, being of a different class and out
of his range through marriage and circumstances: Moya Llewelyn
Davies and Lady Lavery. These we will meet later, at the point where
they exerted an influence on the Collins story. In their positions they
could be helpful and supportive without being competitive.

Another who was apparently helpful, though hardly supportive,
would be Lady Londonderry. Collins was not being condescending to
the type of girl he met at the ceilidhes but he had a shyness that took
refuge in a pose of indifference in public and could come out as an
awkward stiltedness when he was corresponding with someone he
cared for.

In the 1914–18 period of his life that 'someone' was Susan Killeen,
from County Clare, who later, curiously enough, went to live in
Granard, County Longford, where the girl he later became engaged
to, Kitty Kiernan, came from. Even in the midst of other pre-
occupations revolutionaries have traditionally found time for women,
and Collins was far from being an exception. Women were strongly
attracted to him and he appears to have had several girlfriends. Susan,
who for some reason appears to have escaped the notice of other
biographers, was a highly intelligent girl, who secured her education
through scholarships. She also worked in the London Post Office and
was active in the same Irish-Ireland social circles in which Collins
moved and in which they met. From Collins' correspondence with
her it is obvious that they had a number of close friends in common.
Nancy O'Brien shared digs with her in Dublin, for instance, and she
worked in P. S. O'Hegarty's bookshop in Dawson St after she had
returned to Ireland at the outbreak of the First World War rather than
give her allegiance to England. She and Collins remained friendly,
though their correspondence had tapered off, until after his engagement to Kiernan was announced in 1922. By then she was becoming
politically as well as romantically estranged from him. Yet she
preserved his letters. Or rather, most of them, because not long before
she died, she spent a day in the attic going through the correspondence, and her family feel that she may have destroyed some on that
occasion. Those that survive provide an insight into less complicated
days, before the Anglo-Irish relationship had descended to its bloodier
depths or civil war was even thought of.

The following letter[43] from Collins was written as his time in London was drawing to a close and it is illuminating as an indication of how he felt as the strands of his private and public lives began to draw together, as well as of his relationship with Susan:

5, Netherwood Rd
West Kensington.
19–10–15

A cara dilis,

Beleive [sic] me I don't remember ever being more disappointed in my life than I was on Saturday week, when I found on calling at the A.D. that you were on leave and would not be back before I left Dublin although indeed I had feared that some such ill-luck was coming my way as I didn't hear from you before leaving London. It appears I must regard it as a punishment for not writing – but I really do hate letter-writing, and I'm not good at it and can't write down the things I want to say – however don't think that because I don't write I forget.

Well how did you enjoy your holiday? Do you think it worth the after feeling? And of course the keener the enjoyment of a holiday the more miserable the after-feeling. I'm trying to make myself beleive [sic] that if one was in Dublin it wouldn't be so bad but I suppose that's because I'm selfish and want to think I'm the only one in the world's [sic] who's lonely and despondent. But London is a terrible place, worse than ever now – I'll never be happy until I'm out of it and then mightn't either.

Will you please tell Dolly Brennan that I'm very sorry I wasn't able to call at the office on Saturday morning but something else turned up and I was taken out to Lucan.

When you write, as I'm sure you will, I hope you will tell me about all the interesting things you did on the 'Hills of Clare'. Have you that poem off by heart yet?

With fondest rememberances,
do cara go deo
Miceal O'Coileain

The poem Collins was referring to was 'The Hills of Clare' by Thomas Hayes, a typically sentimental exile's lament. He had copied out its seven verses and sent it to Susan. It includes the following:

Ah yes I've been to many lands
I've climbed the Himalay . . .

I've been to where La Plata flows,
By Argentina's plains,
To western isles where beauty grows,
To India's mosques and fanes,
But still I hoped 'twould be my lot
One day the hearth to share
With those I loved and ne'er forgot
Upon the hills of Clare.

Michael Collins was never destined to see either the Himalay or Argentine plains. His world would be bounded by London and Liverpool, Dublin and West Cork. Other cities and places he would know only by correspondence. But one thing he did know and share with Irishmen scattered across the world in such places: what it was to have a burning sense of race and place but through exile to be denied contact with it except for occasions such as language classes, which by now had at least given him the proficiency to write his name in Irish. Once near the end of his life he told his friend P. S. O'Hegarty what it was he fought for. Struggling for words to express his feelings properly, he said, with many pauses and hesitations:

I stand for an Irish civilisation based on the people and embodying and maintaining the things – their habits, ways of thought, customs – that make them different – the sort of life I was brought up in . . . Once, years ago, a crowd of us were going along the Shepherd's Bush Road when out of a lane came a chap with a donkey – just the sort of donkey and just the sort of cart they have at home. He came out quite suddenly and abruptly and we all cheered him. Nobody who has not been an exile will understand me, but I stand for that.[44]

When he wrote to Susan Killeen, Collins' term of exile was drawing to a close. Part of his feeling that 'London was a terrible place – worse than ever now' was to do with his dislike of the threat facing him of having either to fight for England or to become a conscientious objector, both courses being abhorrent to his way of thinking. But part was due to the tension and uncertainty caused by the fact that he knew that the Nationalist tradition which had formed him was about to break out in rebellion once more against the British and Unionist alliance. The Irish Republican Brotherhood was planning another uprising. This time the issue was not about land, but about freedom.

By 1915 the land question in Ireland had largely been settled through a series of ameliorative Acts which, culminating in the Wyndham Act of 1903, created a system of tenant purchase. Collins' angst was caused by the fact that though landlordism and 'hanging gales' were passing away, the other great dream of Irish Nationalists, Home Rule, still hung in the balance. It was on the Statute Book, at last, but postponed until after the end of the war.

The demand had been first formulated by the parliamentary strain of Irish self-assertion beginning with Daniel O'Connell, the nineteenth-century inventor of today's mass, peaceful civil rights demonstrations. It continued with Isaac Butt who founded the Irish Home Rule League in 1870 and led an Irish Home Rule party at Westminster. His attempts at ameliorating conditions in Ireland by normal parliamentary methods were systematically frustrated.

Twenty-eight Bills aimed at improving the lot of the Irish peasantry, in other words staving off famine, were blocked between 1870 and 1880.[45] As a result he adopted the tactic of obstructionism: 'They block our bills, we'll block theirs.' His tactics were developed and amplified by Charles Stewart Parnell (1846–1891), the 'uncrowned king of Ireland', who used the Irish MPs to make and unmake British governments so as to force them to concede a parliament of their own to the Irish. Parnell and his party were destroyed by the O'Shea divorce case, but as the First World War approached the Irish political leadership of William O'Brien, John Dillon and John Redmond had managed, devotedly and painfully, to put the parliamentary pieces together. Hampered at Westminster by a lack of finance and, at best, a lack of understanding of the Irish situation on the part of their hearers, at worst by a positive anti-Irish prejudice, they had nevertheless manoeuvred so successfully that the House of Lords veto had been smashed and their efforts, combined with changes in British electoral outlook, had for the first time forced a Home Rule measure through both the Commons and the Lords. Compared to the mountainous opposition it had aroused, it was a fairly mouse-like proposal. There was to be a two-chambered parliament in Dublin, but Westminster was to retain both wide legislative powers and an Irish representation; hardly Wolfe Tone's 'breaking of the link', yet sufficient nevertheless to give rise to three traditions that continue to bedevil Anglo-Irish relationships and the peace of Ireland itself, even today.

The first was of course the resistance of the Anglo-Irish and, particularly potent in the north-east, their Scots-Irish Presbyterian supporters, to any attempt either to dilute their cherished union with Great Britain, or to thrust them under an All-Ireland parliament, which they saw as threatening to drown them in Popery. More particularly they saw an end to the union as giving flesh and blood, the latter being more likely, to the proposition that behind every Protestant land-holder there loomed the brooding spectre of a vengeful dispossessed Catholic.

The second was the calculated decision by a succession of Tory leaders, beginning with Randolph Churchill, to use Ulster sentiment on the Home Rule issue for political gain in England. It was a dangerous and a discreditable ploy. By the time Gladstone moved the first Home Rule Bill in 1886 there was already a long and bloody history of sectarian bloodletting in Northern Ireland stemming from the widespread 'plantation' of Protestants in the area begun under James I at the beginning of the seventeenth century. Insurrection by dispossessed Catholics had provoked Protestant backlashes under both Cromwell and William of Orange, whose victory at the Battle of the Boyne in 1690 continues to be one of the more significant dates in contemporary Irish history. It left Ulster with most of the land

securely in Protestant hands, many of them specially imported Scots
Presbyterian 'planters', and a desire on the part of Protestants to
commemorate and continue with that scheme of things, symbolised
by the para-military Orange Order formed a hundred years later.

The parts of the province where the Protestants failed to triumph
were left with an equally blood-drenched Catholic tradition of
withstanding the Orangemen. Here is what a prominent IRA man of
Collins' day, John McCoy, wrote of an area that is still a no-go area to
British troops as this is being written:

The natives killed and, in some cases mutilated, the new settlers, their wives
and families. One family in the centre of the valley were overpowered and
their tongues cut out. The husband was a school teacher and the fear that he
would be able to write the names of his attackers prompted the cutting off of
his hands. This man lived to write the names of the men he knew . . . with a
pen between his toes and several of them were hanged from the shafts of a
cart. Such methods broke the efforts to plant the area and in my day the
mountain districts stretching in Southern Armagh from Newry to Cross-
maglen near the Monaghan border contained a concentrated area composed
of the old Gaelic people unmixed with foreign blood.[46]

Orangism, combined with the industrial revolution, meant that the
province emerged into the Home Rule era with a red-bricked,
Mancunian capital, Belfast, and a surrounding countryside that
looked like the Scottish lowlands, peopled by a hard-working, hard-
fighting breed who took their Presbyterianism from the narrower
versions of the covenanting tradition and kept their powder as dry as
their pawky sense of humour. In the cities the landscape of the mind
had been equally blood-drenched. In Derry by the hardship of the
defenders before the eventual triumph of the Williamites in the siege.
In Belfast by the several outbreaks of ferocious communal rioting that
marked the scramble of Catholic and Protestant workers for the
crumbs, the jobs, which fell from the tables of the rich millowners and
shipbuilders. The fortunes of the latter grew as their workers
combined against each other rather than their employers in outbursts
of sectarian passion that restricted growth in either trade unions or
wages, but not in profits.

Thus it was against a lowering orange-hued background of bigotry,
pogrom and privilege that Gladstone set about introducing the first
Home Rule Bill. He was moved by a combination of genuine
conviction that the Irish question should be settled and by the fact that
he was dependent on the Irish vote at Westminster to remain in power.
Churchill shared neither compulsion. He told a friend, 'I had decided
some time ago that if the GOM went for home rule, the Orange Card
would be the one to play. Please God it may turn out the ace of trumps
and not the two.'[47] It was an ace, for the Tories. Churchill played his
hand with duplicitous finesse, winning over a great audience of

Unionists at the Ulster Hall in Belfast where he began his campaign by revealing to them that he had had an ancestor who had been a General on the side of William of Orange – but not that he had also served under James II. He coined the slogan 'Ulster will fight and Ulster will be right.'[48] As another Randolph Churchill, his grandson, observed many years later, 'that pithy phrase contains the reason Ulster is part of the United Kingdom today.' More immediately it also contained the reason why Gladstone was driven from office on the Home Rule issue.

The second Home Rule attempt also went down before the same combination of Ulster Unionist obduracy and high placed Tory incitement to extra-parliamentary resistance. In 1893 as the Unionists prepared for fresh battle with Gladstone, once more in office and espousing Home Rule as the price for Irish nationalist parliamentary support, the exhortations came from the Prime Minister himself, Lord Salisbury.[49]

A third significant delivery of highly charged, highly placed, Tory rhetoric took place in 1912 at an event described as 'the wedding of Protestant Ulster with the Conservative and Unionist party'. It was to prove a blood wedding, though the occasion itself passed off peacefully, impressively. More than 100,000 people, including a platform party that included some seventy English, Scottish and Welsh MPs, gathered at Belfast's Balmoral show grounds under 'the largest Union Jack ever woven' to hear Bonar Law, the Conservative leader, warn them, in imagery drawn from the siege of Derry, against Asquith's Home Rule proposals:

Once more you hold the pass, the pass for the Empire. You are a besieged city. The timid have left you; your Lundys have betrayed you; but you have closed your gates. The Government have erected by their Parliamentary Act a boom against you to shut you off from the help of the British people. You will burst that boom. That help will come, and when the crisis is over men will say to you in words not unlike those used by Pitt – you have saved yourselves by your exertions, and you will save the Empire by your example.[50]

Bonar Law's Balmoral speech brings us to the third factor in the triad of misfortunes that continue to disrupt Anglo-Irish relationships in our day. For the unionist 'marriage' oratory with its evocation of a combination of what we know in our time as the 'Falklands spirit', references such as 'the pass for the Empire', and the menacing exhortation to Unionists to prepare for 'exertions' confirmed the belief of Michael Collins and those who thought like him that democracy as practised from Westminster was a sham. No matter what the ballot box said in Ireland, in London its findings would always be ignored by the politicians. Certainly he had historical precedent for this belief. Apart from the Home Rule controversies mentioned above, nationalist and Catholic Ireland had been trying unsuccessfully since the days of O'Connell to undo the Union by parliamentary methods. But the particular tragedy of the Home Rule controversies for constitutional nationalists was that they provided conclusive proof that although in successive elections Ireland as a whole voted for Home Rule, and sent sufficient MPs to London to get it for them, such democratic majorities did not count at Westminster where the Irish were submerged, as the Act of Union intended them to be, into a one-to-five minority of the total membership. Even though over the period of Home Rule agitation the percentage of pro-Home Rule Irish MPs did not materially change from the first result in 1886, of eighty-six for to seventeen opposed, in the end the rule of law would always come down to Bonar Law, or someone like him.

Sterner methods were called for. These would result in the destruction of the Irish Parliamentary Party, destruction most un-gratefully hailed by Frank O'Connor in words which Collins nevertheless would certainly have applauded: 'The Parliamentary Party, heavy with sleep and sin, simply disappeared; rarely has any democratic country known such a sweeping up of reactionaries.'[51] A harsh, unjust judgement, but as George III once observed, 'If you want to baste an Irishman you can easily get an Irishman to turn the spit.'[52] The hand that turned the third Home Rule Bill on the spit, even more fervently than did Law, was that of an Irishman, the Dublin-born lawyer Edward Carson. It was he who first read the terms of the Ulster Covenant, based on the old Scottish Covenant, to the world on the steps of Craigavon, the mansion on the outskirts of Belfast owned by James Craig, the millionaire inheritor of a whiskey fortune who would one day lead Ulster in Carson's stead. The Covenant contained the following:

Being convinced in our consciences that home rule would be disastrous to the material well-being of Ulster as well as the whole of Ireland, subversive of our civil and religious freedom, destructive of our citzenship, and perilous to the unity of the empire, we . . . loyal subjects of His Gracious Majesty King George V . . . do hereby pledge ourselves in solemn covenant . . . to stand by one another in defending for ourselves and our children our cherished position of equal citzenship in the United Kingdom, and in using all means which may be found necessary to defeat the present conspiracy to set up a home rule parliament in Ireland . . . and mutually pledge ourselves to refuse to recognise its authority.[53]

By now, on their third assault against Home Rule, the Unionists were so well organised that they were eventually able to collect 471,414 signatures to this document in and outside Ulster, chiefly in. And behind the signatures there stood various groupings of some 90,000 men, soon to be reorganised and formed into the Ulster Volunteer Force (UVF). Carson was the leader of a formidable movement. He had come to prominence as part of the process known as 'killing Home Rule by kindness'. A carrot-and-stick method of attempting to pacify the country by resolving the land crisis – by a benign approach that ultimately resulted in the Wyndham Land Act – and at the same time employing coercion to damp down extremism in the pursuit of either land or political objectives. The stick was never more assiduously wielded than in the combination of Arthur Balfour as Chief Secretary of Ireland and Edward Carson as his crown prosecutor. As Balfour told his niece afterwards:

I made Carson and he made me. I've told you how no one had courage. Everyone right up to the top was trembling. Some of the RMs were splendid, but on the whole it was an impossible state of affairs. Carson had nerve, however. I sent him all over the place, getting convictions, we worked together.[54]

Not everyone thought so highly of Carson. When he prosecuted William O'Brien for Plan of Campaign activities in 1887, three years before Collins was born, in Mitchelstown, County Cork, police shot and killed a number of stone-throwers in an episode often recalled around the Collins fireside. At the hearing O'Brien's defence counsel told Carson: 'You are low, mean and contemptible, venal and corrupt. You think by this display you will get some position from the Tory Government, for whom you are doing this job.'[55] Carson certainly did attain 'some position', becoming one of the top earners at the English Bar, a Unionist MP for Trinity, and a member of the British wartime Coalition Cabinet. More importantly, where Ireland was concerned, he also became leader of the Unionists in their coalition with the Tories in pre-war resistance to Home Rule. Fears that that resistance might get to the point of civil war were heightened by what Asquith termed 'reckless rodomontade' at a huge demonstration at Blenheim Palace on 24 July 1912 where Bonar Law spelled out where he and his party stood in relation to opposition to Home Rule and the Liberals and support for the Unionists:

We regard the government as a revolutionary committee which has seized upon despotic power by fraud. In our opposition to them we shall not be guided by the considerations or bound by the restraints which would influence us in an ordinary constitutional struggle . . . I can imagine no length of resistance to which Ulster can go in which I should not be prepared to support them, and in which, in my belief, they would not be supported by the overwhelming majority of the British people.[56]

Law was moved by a number of considerations such as the fact that his party had been out of office for several years, and that Ulster seemed to offer a means of getting back in again. There was also his Scots-Canadian, Presbyterian ancestry and his own experience of Ulster, based on his memories of his father's time there as a minister, and the hospitality bestowed on him by his political hostess Lady

Londonderry. After his Blenheim 'rhodomontade', Irish nationalists were further embittered, but not surprised, when the 'Curragh Incident' of March 1914 seemed to indicate that that 'overwhelming majority' included the British Army. A group of officers stationed at the Curragh in County Kildare, the Army's major centre in Ireland, made known their reluctance to proceed against their fellow Conservatives, the Ulster anti-Home Rulers. The 'mutiny' ended not with courts martial but with the return in triumph to Ireland from the War Office of the officers' spokesman, Brigadier-General H. P. Gough, with a document drafted by a man whom Michael Collins later had shot, the Director of Military Operations, General (later Field Marshal) Sir Henry Wilson. It ended, in Gough's own handwriting: 'I understand the reading of the last paragraph to be that that the troops under our command will not be called upon to enforce the present Home Rule Bill on Ulster, and that we can so assure our officers.'[57] The usefulness of this document to the Unionists was underscored a month later when under the eyes of police and customs officials the Ulstermen, in flagrant defiance of the law, ran in three hundred tons of rifles to the province from Germany.[58] The Ulster Unionists now had a strong Ulster Volunteer Force (UVF), guns to put in their hands, and the support or more probably the acquiescence, of every property-owning or decision-taking Protestant of consequence in the province. In England, apart from Law and his party rank and file, they drew aid and comfort from figures of the eminence of Lord Milner, Waldorf Astor, Lord Rothschild, Lord Iveagh and the Duke of Bedford, Sir Edward Elgar and Rudyard Kipling.

War brought down the curtain on this particular phase of the Home Rule saga. Asquith was able to introduce Home Rule to law on 18 September 1914 and to accompany this step with an Amending Bill to suspend its operation until after the war. By this time partition had been added to the nomenclature of the debate, Law having suggested exclusion of the six north-eastern counties of Antrim, Armagh, Tyrone, Down, Fermanagh and Tyrone at an all-party conference convened by the King at Buckingham Palace on 21 July.[59] John Redmond was bitterly opposed to this and would only advocate the county option in which the wishes of the nationalists could be considered. Knowing the Liberals, and some Tories, favoured the county option, Carson adroitly avoided criticism on grounds of obduracy by arguing that the greater the number of Catholics included, the greater would be the pressure for ultimate unification – and he held out for all nine counties of Ulster.

Watching the drama unfold from Dublin the prophet of Irish nationalism, Padraig Pearse 1879–1916 had once declared, 'Personally I think the Orangeman with the rifle is a much less ridiculous figure than the Nationalist without a rifle.'[60] Pearse was a distinguished

educationalist, who had founded his own school, St Enda's, to impart
a distinctively Irish system of education. He wrote with equal facility
in both Irish and English. The son of an Irish mother and an English
father, he qualified as a barrister but, unlike Carson, devoted his
oratorical gifts to the IRB rather than the Bar and the Unionist cause.
There were many who agreed with him, particularly in the ranks of
the [Irish] Volunteers formed by a professor of Gaelic, Eoin MacNeill,
at a meeting in the Rotunda in Parnell Square, Dublin, on 25
November 1913, with the intention of defending Home Rule should
force be used against it.

Five months later to the day, 25 April 1914, Michael Collins was
enrolled[61] into the No. 1 Company of the London Volunteers by his
cousin, Sean Hurley. Thereafter the pair, with another friend, Padraic
O'Conaire, the Gaelic writer, would drill each week in the German
gymnasium at King's Cross, using hired, sawn-off Martini-Henry
rifles, while they put aside weekly contributions against the day when
rifles of their own would become available.

Unknown to MacNeill, the Volunteers were infiltrated[62] and
largely controlled by the IRB from the time of their inception. They
were intent not on defence, but offence, and were in touch with the
American wing of the Brotherhood, Clan na nGael, from whom
money was sent, through the Clan leader, John Devoy, an associate of
O'Donovan Rossa's, to help fund an uprising.[63] At the same time the
Wolfe Tone/J. B. Armour/Parnell strain of Irish Protestantism that
had traditionally allied itself to Catholic claims for independence and
civil rights began to assert itself. The month before the Volunteers'
formation at the Rotunda a meeting of Protestants opposed to
Carson's activities was held, appropriately enough, in J. B. Armour's
town of Ballymoney. Those present included a hero of the relief of
Ladysmith, Captain Jack White, who had already helped the workers
of Dublin to drill in the Irish Citizen Army.

Another celebrated figure was Roger Casement, who as a member
of the British Consular Service had earned a knighthood and world-
wide fame for his courage and humanity in exposing the Belgians' ill-
treatment of their colonial subjects in the Belgian Congo and
Putumayo. By 1914 he had increasingingly espoused the Irish cause
and was well-known as a writer and publicist in the Nationalist
interest. The attendance included the historian Alice Stopford Greene
and Mary Spring-Rice, a daughter of Lord Monteagle. Following
the Ballymoney meeting, a Committee, which included the three
last-named, was set up in London to arrange for the purchase and
shipment of arms to the Irish Volunteers.

In Washington, Devoy was heavily involved with Count Von
Bernstorff, the German Ambassador who, like most foreign
observers, regarded the Home Rule crisis as a potentially priceless

sapping of Great Britain's strength in the event of war. And so, in July 1914, a week before the Great War did break out, Erskine Childers, an Englishman, with Mary Spring-Rice amongst his crew, sailed his yacht, the *Asgard*, into Howth Harbour and history with a cargo of German rifles aboard. The difference in the authorities' view of those who ran 35,000 rifles into Ulster to oppose Home Rule and those who smuggled 1,500 into Dublin in support of it was underscored on the evening of the landing when troops fired on a Dublin crowd and killed three people. Three more arguments in favour of the revolutionaries and against those who favoured 'due process'.

Was Collins present at the gun-running? That question helped to start me thinking of writing this book. I was prevented from attending the State funeral for Childers' son, also called Erskine, who had become President of Ireland, by the need to attend the funeral of a colleague of my own which took place near Howth, and afterwards went for a walk around the harbour. Here I met two old men who had spent the morning watching the planes fly overhead bringing in foreign dignitaries for the President's funeral. 'You know,' said one of them, 'I was here the day his father sailed in the guns. Michael Collins put me up on his shoulder so as I could see.' I had never heard that Collins had taken part in the gun-running and was disposed to argue with him. It must have been someone else. 'No. I knew him well,' the old man said. 'He used to stay up there sometimes with some of the lads. There was a house up there,' he said, gesticulating, 'and there was good-looking girls living in it. The lads used to be after them. He was a fine-looking fellow himself, God rest him.'

Subsequently I read all the accounts of the gun-running I could find, but came across no mention of Collins. I realised that this in itself proved nothing one way or the other, as despite his 'Big Fellow', swash-buckling, side Collins could shun publicity when he wanted to, and working in England, involved with the IRB, this might have been such an occasion. At all events my interest in Collins eventually led to this book and during my research I came across Susan Killeen. She lived around this time at 1 Island View, Howth, lodging with a Mrs Quick along with a number of other girls whom Collins frequently enquired after in his letters to Susan. The letters also contain references to Howth and his yearnings to be there.

He may have also had yearnings to be somewhere else. It is established that Collins was in direct contact with John Devoy after the 1916 Rising. But there could have been either direct or indirect contact before that. Biographers speak of Collins after the outbreak of war, and before returning to Ireland, walking the docklands of London, looking at the ships and wondering if he should go to America and make a new life away from the calls of Ireland and possibly conscription. At this stage Devoy and the German Embassy in Washington had arranged that Sir Roger Casement should go to Germany, both to get arms and to try to enlist Irish prisoners of war in an Irish Brigade which would fight the British in Ireland. It is a matter of speculation as to how different subsequent Irish history might have been had Casement succeeded in his mission. In the event the arms didn't get in, the Brigade idea failed also and Casement was captured and hanged in 1916. The following telegram was sent from the German Embassy in Washington to the Foreign Office, Berlin. It is dated 1 September 1914 and reads: 'An Irish priest (sic) named Michael Collins and Sir Roger Casement are going to Germany in order to visit the Irish prisoners.'[64]

That '(sic)' is revealing. Whoever that 'priest' was intended to be it is not unreasonable to assume that (a) he did not take holy orders and (b) may have spoken with a rich West Cork accent. In fact Casement took with him a Norwegian sailor called Christiansen, and Collins never got to Germany. He gave in his notice to the Guaranty Trust Company, saying that he was going 'to join up', for which he received an extra week's pay which he donated to the Brotherhood, and on the following day, 15 January 1916, he crossed to Ireland. The IRB had put an end to his uncertainties by telling him that a rising was definitely planned.

When he told Hannie that he was going back to Dublin to join his friends in the coming fray she was aghast. 'They'll let you down Michael. They'll let you down',[65] she told him prophetically. But Collins was impervious to entreaty. The gospel of historical continuity had ruled that it was time for a pike, a pike . . . and so, with a toss of his head and a jut to his jaw, to Dublin he went.

2

Easter 1916

'No man has a right to fix the boundary
to the march of a nation.'

Charles Stewart Parnell

Collins was now twenty-six. Such reputation as he had was largely based amongst the London Irish. His enemies saw a bossy, hot-tempered character given to outbursts of fury and intolerance, his friends, a generous, outgoing man capable of great kindness, interested in the affairs of the day, particularly anything to do with Ireland.

A good athlete, of lithe movement and sudden gesture, he was an attractive but not remarkable figure. Of his life and struggles in London, P. S. O'Hegarty wrote: '. . . there was very little of the Mick Collins of those days to give promise of the man who was to come'. Yet O'Hegarty noted:

he was always on the right side in the many battles, on the many platforms, in which Sinn Fein fought. In its own organisation, in the Gaelic League, in the Gaelic Athletic Association, and finally in the Irish Volunteers . . . He was well-read in modern literature and drama and keen to talk about them, and in the great years of the Court Theatre, and in the weeks when the Manchester Repertory Company came to the Coronet, you would find him constantly in the gallery. He was growing and deepening in those years in body and mind, reaching out . . . towards every quickening and ennobling thing in life.[1]

Collins was well enough thought of within the IRB to be kept fairly near to the centre of the action. His first job in Dublin was, as he described it, 'financial advisor' to Count Plunkett for three days a week. The job brought him £1 a week and his lunch at the Plunkett home at Larkfield, Kimmage. It also brought him into touch with 'the refugees', the group of Irish camping at Larkfield, who like himself had come over to Dublin to get away from conscription and to take part in the rumoured uprising. At least one member of the Plunkett family obviously had more in mind for Collins than the family book-keeping. This was Joseph Plunkett, the tubercular poet and an organiser of the 1916 Rising, who was literally to lean on Collins' shoulder when the fighting started. It was he who lent Collins the book that was to colour his whole approach to the subsequent Anglo-Irish War, Chesterton's *The Man Who Was Thursday*, in which the head anarchist makes the point, 'If you don't seem to be hiding, nobody hunts you out.' Collins also found another job to augment his income from the Plunketts, with the accountancy firm of Craig Gardiner and Co., Dawson St, and after an interlude staying with relatives got himself lodgings at 16 Rathdown Road.

During this short spell in Dublin Collins became a member of the Keating Branch of the Gaelic League. It would be difficult to overstress the importance of the Irish language to Collins. It was bound up in his mind with the necessity of shaking off the colonial shackles and of creating a distinctively Irish mode of thought and self-development. He deemed the formation of the Gaelic League to revive the Irish language and culture, in 1893, as the most important event of 'not only the nineteenth century, but in the whole history of our nation'. He later studied the language intensively and began signing his name, in its Irish form, Miceal O'Coileain, expecting others, including his fiancée, to address him that way. The heritage of the Clan O'Coileain he descended from was a very real thing to him.

Cultural and economic well-being had a correlation, in a distinctively Sinn Fein, 'we ourselves' context which he would sum up as follows:

Millionaires can spend their surplus wealth bestowing libraries broadcast upon the world. But who will say that the benefits accruing could be compared with those arising from a condition of things in which the people themselves . . . were prosperous enough to buy their own books and to put together their own local libraries in which they could take a personal interest and acquire knowledge in proportion to that interest?[2]

In the Gaelic League, he associated with men who, apart from becoming leaders in the struggles that lay ahead, were to become his closest allies and bitterest enemies. These included Richard Mulcahy, Gearoid O'Sullivan, Cathal Brugha and Rory O'Connor. Mulcahy, known as 'the tic tac man' from his habit of tracing invisible patterns in the air with his fingers as he spoke, was a slim, blue-eyed aesthetic figure, who gave up his medical studies at University College Dublin to become a full-time revolutionary. He would eventually became Chief of Staff of the IRA, working closely with Collins and succeeding him as Commander-in-Chief of the Irish Army. O'Sullivan, a cousin of Collins', was a fellow Corkman. In a very real sense he hoisted the flag of rebellion over Dublin, because, being the youngest officer in the General Post Office which became the rebels' HQ in the Rising, he was given the honour of raising the tricolour over the GPO. He would later be one of Collins' closest allies in his role of Adjutant General of the IRA. Cathal Brugha, whom Mulcahy described as being 'as brave and as brainless as a bull', grew to hate Collins in a feud that was to be a causal factor in creating civil war.[3] The director of a firm of church candle-makers, he was also President of the Keating Branch.

His enthusiasm for the Irish language led him to change his name to Cathal Brugha from its English form, Charles Burgess. O'Connor, who had been working as engineer in Canada had, like Collins, returned to Dublin to take part in the Rising. He and Collins were close friends during the Anglo-Irish war, in which O'Connor became Director of Engineering and for a time Director of Operations in England, but were destined to die on opposite sides in the subsequent civil war.

Rory O'Connor said of Collins at this period: 'There was no one at Kimmage to equal him.' O'Connor at that stage was assisting the refugees' chief instructor in bomb-making, Dr Thomas Dillon. Collins is remembered as getting materials for the devices but, characteristically, along with iron washers and such-like, he is also recalled for supplying secondhand clothes to the more impoverished Volunteers.[4] Two other figures with whom Collins would not have time to establish a lasting relationship, but whom he admired greatly, were Sean MacDiarmada and Tom Clarke. MacDiarmada, a man with a light, pleasing personality, had travelled all over the country, sometimes on foot or on bicycle despite the fact that an attack of polio had left him practically a cripple. Clarke was the movement's link with the Fenians, an old dynamiter who had somehow kept his sanity through penal servitude in England, made his way to America, and then returned to Dublin to set up a little shop in the ironically named Great Britain St, which dispensed tobacco and revolutionary doctrines that struck more deadly sparks than any of his matches. Collins, with his equal regard for age and for Fenianism, revered Clarke in particular.

The economic conditions of the Dublin of the day mirrored the indifference of London to political initiative. Appalling slums, high infant mortality and unemployment[5] had driven workers to militant, but unsuccessful, trade union activity in what became known as the great Dublin lock-out of 1913. The workers were defeated and one of their two principal leaders, James Larkin, left for America. The other, James Connolly, remained at the head of the tiny Citizen Army formed to protect the workers from police brutality during 1913. Connolly had come to believe that social amelioration could only come in the wake of political independence. The IRB shared this view but feared that his war-like manoeuvrings would bring the British down on them before they were ready to strike.[6] Accordingly he was co-opted into the Brotherhood's inner circle and took part in the planning of the proposed rebellion. Thus separatism and socialism forged a hard cutting edge to their grievances. But it was still only a very small blade.

John E. Redmond had forced a measure of control on the original Volunteer force formed at the Rotunda in response to the Carsonites. However, on 20 September 1914, after the outbreak of war, he made a recruiting speech at Woodenbridge in County Wicklow and the Volunteers split, leaving Redmond with the larger section, under the name of National Volunteers, and the IRB with the re-christened smaller, but more militant, Irish Volunteers, which Collins supported. At a Volunteer meeting in the St George's Hall in Southwark, a speaker proposed a Redmondite Man of Prudence for office with the recommendation, 'I'd go to hell and back with him.' Collins called out from the back of the hall, 'Don't mind about the return half of the ticket.'[7]

Redmond spoke both believing in the cause Britain said it was fighting the war for, the rights of small nations, and hoping that his own particular small nation would benefit at war's end through having shown loyalty to the Empire. But as Easter 1916 approached Redmond was coming to acknowledge, as the physical force school had traditionally claimed, that in Anglo-Irish affairs altruism on the part of an Irish nationalist leader was the sword of self-immolation.[8] The Orangemen, 'the Kaiser's Irish friends', who had but lately been threatening to take up arms against the British, had been rewarded by being allowed to form their own regiments but Nationalists, including Redmond's son, were refused commissions. Kitchener personally vetoed a scheme which envisaged using the Volunteers for coastal defence.[9] He had a particular animus against Irish nationalists, and ordered that a green banner emblazoned with a harp, designed by patriotic ladies for an Irish regiment that never materialised, be taken away, but that a similar banner adorned by the Red Hand of Ulster be proudly displayed. Lloyd George reckoned that this 'sinister order constituted the first word in a new chapter of Irish history'.[10] The relationship of Redmond to the Irish Parliamentary Party is symbolised today by the positioning of his bust at Westminster: he is recognised in bronze – but stands outside the Members' Bar.

A threat of enforced conscription hung over Ireland with Carson and Bonar Law in the Cabinet and Redmond out of it. Redmond and his long-term colleague, John Dillon, became estranged and the drift in his influence was such that the Chief Secretary for Ireland, Augustine Birrell[11], feared that Home Rule had been finished by the elevation of Carson to the Cabinet. 'Ireland', said the Chief Secretary, 'is in a rotten state – ripe for a row, without leadership'.

Though he lacked details Birrell was completely correct in the substance of his judgement. Ireland was 'ripe for a row'. The minority within the IRB had been in contact with the Germans through John Devoy in New York. Joseph Plunkett was received at the Foreign Office by Von Bethmann Holweig early in 1915 and it was arranged that a shipload of arms and ammunition would be sent to Ireland the following spring. An Irish uprising timed to coincide with a German offensive on the Western Front would benefit the Germans. The Devoy–Plunkett faction within the IRB then formed a Military Council some time in June 1915 to further these plans. The Council came to consist of Pearse, Plunkett, Eamonn Ceannt, a Gaelic Leaguer and traditional musician, Tom Clarke and Sean MacDiarmada. Connolly was added in January 1916 and Thomas MacDonagh in April of that year, only a few days before the date planned for the Rising, Easter Sunday. He too had seemingly been kept in ignorance of the Council's aims and existence until that time even though he was a close friend of Pearse's and taught with him in St Enda's, the Irish-Ireland school founded and run by Pearse at Rathfarnham, County Dublin. The secrecy paid off almost to the end insofar as the two major sources of expected opposition were concerned. One was Dublin Castle, the centre and symbol of British rule in Ireland, the other Eoin MacNeill and those who thought like him in the Volunteers. The MacNeillites believed that the corps should remain in being only to help prevent any attempt to frustrate Home Rule's introduction at the end of the war.

These included ironically enough a man without whom there would have been no IRB, Bulmer Hobson, who with Dinny McCullough had founded the Dungannon Clubs in Belfast and used the Clubs to revive the Brotherhood which was at the time practically moribund. It was Hobson and McCullough[12] who with P. S. O'Hegarty had co-opted Tom Clarke onto the Supreme Council of the IRB and appointed Sean MacDiarmada as full-time organiser, on a salary of thirty shillings a week. Now Clarke and MacDiarmada arranged that Hobson should be kidnapped lest he get word of their plans to MacNeill. A third source however dealt their plans a near fatal blow. Captain Hall's celebrated cypher centre, Room 40 at the Admiralty in London, had both intercepted and decoded the transmissions between Devoy/Bernsdorff and Berlin. As a result the German ship bringing the arms was intercepted off the Kerry coast on Good Friday and subsequently scuttled by her captain. Roger Casement got ashore from a U-boat in a half-drowned condition and was captured. The arms seizure clearly signalled that the Rising had lost whatever chance of success it might have had. In addition MacNeill learned of the Council's plans and, horror-struck at the duplicity and projected loss of life, sent officers round the country countermanding all Volunteer activities for the weekend, placing an advertisement to this effect in the *Sunday Independent* also. But the plotters decided to go ahead nevertheless. They had two reasons for proceeding. First, they reckoned that if they did not strike now it would soon be impossible because the Castle had to be on the verge of a round-up. Secondly, they believed a protest in arms was necessary because the general sense of nationality had sunk so low as to require a blood sacrifice to revive it. They expected to fail, and to pay for the failure with their lives, but they felt it was their historical duty to continue in the footsteps of Wolfe Tone and the tradition of a rising in every generation. And so on Easter Monday, 24 April 1916, the hopeless uprising began.

Nancy O'Brien must have been extraordinarily well-trusted by Michael, because he met her with MacDiarmada during Holy Week[13] and both he and MacDiarmada openly discussed the prospects of the coming rising with her in a Dublin cafe. They also met on Holy Saturday and shook hands on O'Connell Bridge. Nancy would normally have gone home to Sam's Cross for the Easter break, but made an excuse to Collins for not going, claiming that she was supposed to be at the Post Office the following Tuesday. With his usual instinct for trying to joke his way out of a serious moment Collins replied laughingly, 'Ah you'll have longer than that.' Nancy did have longer, an agonised week longer, much of which she spent on Howth Head watching the flames grow over Dublin. But Collins was afterwards remembered by friends who met him that day as being 'jocular and fooling about as usual'.[14]

But on the Monday morning he was sombre and tense. The accountancy side of his nature that dealt in practicalities was at war with the high heroic side that gloried in following in the footsteps of Rossa. On Good Friday he had dispatched Colm O'Lochlainn to Kerry as part of the German arms plot. Apart from its miscarrying, three of the five members of O'Lochlainn's party were drowned and Collins had a shrewd suspicion that these would be far from being the last of the casualties involved in the course he was following. At the Metropole Hotel he found he could well have been amongst the first of them.

Plunkett's throat had been operated on for tuberculosis in Switzer-land and during Good Friday Collins had to transfer him to the Metropole so that he would be within easy reach of the GPO on the morning of the insurrection. In his room Plunkett warned Collins and another aide-de-camp, Commandant Brennan Whitmore, that they might be stopped on their way out of the hotel by a small dark-haired man. He gave Collins the key to a trunk in which there were three automatics which were to be used in the event of this happening. At the foot of the stairs they found the dark-haired man waiting. The lobby of the hotel was full of British officers preparing to depart for Fairyhouse Races. Hands closed on the pocketed automatics. But the dark-haired one offered them nothing beyond a greeting: 'Good-day to you gentlemen'.[15] Perhaps he belonged to that not inconsiderable body of British opinion which believed that insurrections do not happen after midday.

Collins was present at the final colloquy which had guaranteed that this one would. It took place in a shabby room at Liberty Hall, headquarters of the Irish Transport and General Workers' Union, between Connolly, Pearse and Plunkett. After it these three lined up at the head of their men outside Liberty Hall. Just before twelve o'clock, with Collins, one of the few to possess one, resplendent in his Volunteer's uniform, a couple of paces behind his leader, the thin, ragged column marched towards destiny. Much of their weaponry accompanied them in a handcart – obsolete German rifles (landed at Howth), shotguns, revolvers. The original plans for the rebellion, drawn up mainly by Connolly and Plunkett, called for risings at various centres throughout the country. But apart from some sieges and ambushes in north County Dublin, and Counties Galway, Wexford, Meath and Cork, fighting was confined to Dublin city around the centres which the divided and weakened rebels could hold. These formed a ring around the heart of Dublin.

Despite the splits and the setbacks they might have captured Dublin Castle because the citadel was practically undefended, though the spirit of Major Sirr had not entirely departed. The Permanant Under Secretary, Sir Matthew Nathan, and the Military Intelligence Officer, Major Ivor Price, were inside planning a widespread round-up of rebels, assisted in arranging the commandeering of telephone and telegraph facilities by the Secretary of the Post Office, Sir Arthur Hamilton Norway. But apart from some messengers and a few unarmed police that was all. The insurgents overcame the military guard at the gate and then withdrew, believing themselves too weak to do otherwise. One of the few places the Volunteers were to be found in any strength was in Norway's place of work, the General Post Office, which they took over a few minutes after he had left the building to go to the Castle to help deal with the threatened insurrection. The GPO, one of the handful of strong points which the Volunteers seized throughout the city, would be an inferno before the week was out. It was the rebels' headquarters.

That was where Padraig Pearse read the proclamation of the Republic to a bemused and, initially, amused Dublin crowd. The previous year he had delivered the oration over the grave of Collins' boyhood hero, O'Donovan Rossa. He spoke for Collins when he described Rossa's vision of Ireland: 'not free merely, but Gaelic as well: not Gaelic merely but free as well.' And he articulated the self-sacrificial philosophy of their revolution of plotters and poets when he finished the oration by declaring:

Life springs from death: and from the graves of patriot men and women spring living nations. The Defenders of this Realm have worked well in secret and in the open. They think they have pacified Ireland. They think that they have purchased half of us and intimidated the other half. They think they have foreseen everything; but the fools, the fools, the fools! – they have left us our Fenian dead, and while Ireland holds these graves, Ireland unfree shall never be at peace.[16]

By signing the proclamation Pearse guaranteed that his own grave would shortly be added to those of the Fenian dead. So did James Connolly, whose weaponry had been delivered to the GPO on a handcart. So did the other signatories. Plunkett, MacDonagh, MacDiarmada, Ceannt and Tom Clarke, given the honour of heading the list of signatories.

Apart from the GPO the rebels seized St Stephen's Green, Jacob's biscuit factory, the College of Surgeons, The Four Courts, the North and South Dublin Unions, Marrowbone Lane Distillery, Boland's Mill and outposts on Lower Mount St. However it's not the size of the dog in the fight that counts so much as the size of the fight in the dog. There may have been as many as 1,200 insurgents, including the Fianna, the IRB's militant counter-version of Baden-Powell's Boy Scouts. Though initially taken off-balance, the British, between forces in Dublin barracks and near to hand at the Curragh, were immediately able to call on some 6,000 officers and men. Later in the week reinforcements poured in from England and from Belfast, a source from which one notable gesture of assistance was refused. Carson, whose activities had done so much to the propel the lethal handcart across the cobblestones of Dublin, was not taken up on his offer of 50,000 UVF volunteers. The British, having co-operated with him in delaying the passage of Home Rule, now intended to be prompt and single-handed in dealing with the crisis that co-operation had produced.

Collins made a mark for himself as soon as he entered the GPO. He poured two tierces of stout down the drain[17] while making an observation (sanitised), to the effect that the rebels of 1798 had been condemned for drinking but that wouldn't happen to these Volunteers! He then took part in trussing up an English officer who had blundered into their midst to buy a stamp and reassured the man that he needn't worry, 'we don't shoot prisoners'. Most of his duties lay in the operations room where the leaders laid out maps and plans, the unreality of which were heightened as the week progressed by the glow cast on them by the ever-encircling fires. He sorted out a row involving the London Irish and Desmond Fitzgerald, his future Chief of Propaganda, over Fitzgerald's refusal to issue rations to the men because they hadn't chits! Fitzgerald later recorded how

Michael Collins . . . strode in one morning with some of his men who were covered with dust and had been demolishing walls and building barricades, and announced that these men were to be fed if it took the last food in the place. I did not attempt to argue with him, and the men sat down openly rejoicing that I had been crushed . . . But while they were eating, those of our most regular and assiduous customers who appeared at the door of the room were told to disappear quickly or they would be dealt with.[18]

Fitzgerald described Collins as 'the most active and efficient officer in the place'. He made an attempt to note the names and addresses of the combatants and generally speaking, his spirit and sense of humour held up throughout the week. When someone remarked to him, 'Terrible destruction, Mick,' he looked out over Dublin's rubble-strewn main street and replied, 'Don't worry, you old cod, we'll rebuild it, and the whole city, in ten years – if necessary.' And after a particularly furious fusillade he and Gearoid O'Sullivan went up to Pearse and asked would he mind if they popped out for a bit – they had a date with two girls they didn't like disappointing.

Later he would describe his feelings during the week to a friend in a stiff-upper-lip near-propagandist style that doesn't do him justice:

Although I was never actually scared in the GPO I was – and others also – witless enough to do the most stupid things. As the flames and heat increased so apparently did the shelling. Machine-gun fire made escape more or less impossible. Not that we wished to escape. No man wished to budge. In that building, the defiance of our men, and the gallantry, reached unimaginable proportions.[19]

Collins was no simpleton. He possessed more courage than ten, but he also had the crucifying gift we know as imagination. With his extraordinary facility for not only being able to see but to do there came the unnerving ability to foresee, to know the dangers involved. From the crucible of Easter Week there emerge two vivid descriptions of Collins and the man with whom his name is ever linked in comradeship and contest, Eamon de Valera, that paint both our Irish Danton and his Robespierre not in poster colours but in more human tints. They too had their agony in the garden.

De Valera was eight years older than Collins. He was born in New York on 14 October 1882, of a Spanish father and an Irish mother. The difference in the two men's characters is summarised in their early upbringing. Collins was doted on by his mother and sisters, secure and confident in his surroundings – so secure that he became cocky and wanted to be 'the Big Fellow' in all that was done. De Valera's mother wanted to have as little to do with him as possible. She had been left by his father not long after her son was born and she had him reared from infancy with her people in Limerick, while she remained in America and married again. Even when she had a new home and family she did not take him back and he seems to have preferred life in boarding school to life with his mother's relations.

A teacher of mathematics by profession, de Valera's interest in the Irish language had led him to join the Volunteers at the force's inception. During the Rising he commanded Boland's Mill, on the Grand Canal Basin in the eastern part of the city where the Grand Canal links up with the Liffey. The post also commanded a stretch of railway line running back into Dublin to Westland Row station and its outposts in Mount St dominated the main Dublin–Dun Laoghaire road. He also knew very well going into the fight that with the collapse of the German shipment the thing was a foredoomed failure.

The Easter after the rising de Valera was safely in prison but writing to his wife Sinead he relived his feelings during Easter 1916:

It is Easter Saturday and my mind naturally reverts to this and tomorrow's festival a year ago. How I thank God that you have not the agonies before you this year which I foresaw at the corresponding time last year. I could not tell you then the feelings that were rending my heart on your account. But sweetheart I know you will believe me – I know you will not think it was selfishness or callous indifference or senseless optimism that made me so calm when I was about to offer up you and the children as a sacrifice. If you could have seen my heart on that terrible day of anxiety for you, Easter Sunday, you would have known – when I called to see you and found that the strain had been too much for you, I only found what I had anticipated all the day long. Could you have seen me that night when I stooped over you to give you that parting kiss you would know that though I gave it lightly as if we were to meet again in the morning it was simply to save you, to give you some sixteen hours' respite; for in my heart I believed it was the last kiss I would give you on earth.[20]

Not surprisingly, de Valera didn't sleep very much either in the nights before or after the Rising's commencement. Strained, a tall, gangling figure with red socks, he ran around the rail line at night, having trenches dug and forgetting the password so that he nearly got shot. One of his men went mad and shot a comrade, being cut down himself in retaliation. A Volunteer wrote afterwards, 'You had a feeling that your comrades might go mad – or, what was even worse, that you might go mad yourself.'[21]

When one of his subordinates, Lt Fitzgerald, tried to make him sleep de Valera replied, 'I can't trust the men – they'll leave their posts or fall asleep if I don't watch them.' Only when Fitzgerald promised to sit beside him and wake him if anything happened did he lie down. Sleep hit him immediately, but turned to nightmare. He started to sweat and toss about and suddenly, 'His eyes wild, he sat bolt upright and in an awful voice, bawled, "Set fire to the railway! Set fire to the railway!" '

He insisted that papers dipped in whiskey be used to set fire to waiting rooms and rolling stock but another officer, Captain John McMahon, 'eventually persuaded de Valera to listen to reason and the fires were put out. De Valera quickly recovered his composure.'[22]

One of the many remarkable examples of the loyalty extended to de Valera is the way his contemporaries consistently remained silent about his crack-up in 1916. Years later, when they were in Ballykinlar Internment Camp together, Captain Michael Cullen, one of those placed in charge of him at the time, approached a fellow prisoner, Dr Tom O'Higgins, and, warning him first that he would shoot him if he ever mentioned the story to anyone, told him what had happened and asked him for a medical opinion on de Valera's condition.[23] By then (1920) de Valera was publicly quarrelling with the Clan na nGael leader, John Devoy, in America, and Cullen was worried that he might again have lost his reason.

De Valera was responsible for one of the most talked-of episodes of the entire week. After the British had begun shelling his position he ordered that a green flag be placed at the top of an empty tower a few hundred yards from his command post. The ruse worked and fire concentrated on the old tower thereafter, not on the mill. Subsequently there was controversy as to who actually hoisted the flag. One authoritative account[24] says that de Valera ordered Captain Michael Cullen and three volunteers to carry out the hoisting. But his own official biography states that he tied the flag to a pike and placed it in a corner of the tower himself. Whatever is the truth about this and whoever tied the flag, after the Rising the episode burnished a reputation already glittering by virtue of another circumstance, the fact that it was at a position some distance from Boland's Mill but occupied by Volunteers under his command that the 'Irish Thermopylae' occurred: No. 25 Northumberland Rd.

Here Captain Michael Malone and his men inflicted the heaviest casualties of the week on the British troops whose officers continuously urged them up an open road under his Mauser. Malone was shot by a trigger-happy soldier after the ceasefire and his automatic eventually passed into de Valera's possession. He kept it all his life, as well he might. In a very real sense de Valera's power grew out of the barrel of that gun. The fact that de Valera's was an isolated post, the last to act on Pearse's order to call a ceasefire, meant that though condemned to death, he was not included with the first batch of prisoners to be executed. The respite gave his mother time to produce evidence of his American citizenship and so have his sentence commuted to imprisonment from which he emerged a hero, the last Commandant to surrender during Easter Week.

The gunboat *Helga* came up the Liffey and its shelling, combined with sustained machine-gun and rifle fire, had Sackville Street in flames by Friday, the GPO being the epicentre of the holocaust. It had to be evacuated, first by tunnelling through shops alongside and then by making a dash across the bullet-swept street into Moore St and the temporary shelter of more tunnelled shops. Revolver in hand, his britches singed by burning debris, Collins led his men across, shouting encouragement at them. They got as far as No. 16, a grocery shop, but could go no further. Troops had the area sealed off. The London Irish had decided not to surrender but rather than be conscripted, and probably killed, for England, to fight to the end in Dublin. Collins knew that whatever slim chance of survival the leaders now had, protracted hostilities would guarantee their deaths. He tried to talk the Londoners out of fighting, one of the few occasions in his life when he ever argued such a course. Failing to move them he then went for MacDiarmada who for the last time exercised his extraordinary power of leadership. All he said was, 'We'll die. You'll escape. No one will try to conscript you.'[25] But the desperate London Irish laid down their arms. Though Collins had begun the revolution by pouring away porter he ended it with whiskey. Somehow he had managed to lay hands on a bottle and it helped to ease the misery of the last hours before surrender for himself and two friends, Fionan Lynch, who would one day serve in an Irish Government with Collins, and Jim Ryan, a young doctor from Wexford who had acted as medical officer to the Volunteers in the GPO. Thoughts of forming a government were far from the minds of the three men as the last action in the fight neared. Collins presented a brooding figure. Desmond Ryan, Pearse's literary executor, who fought alongside both of them in the GPO, drew this picture of him:

Michael Collins sat in a corner, a look of horror in his eyes, a pallor spreading over his face. Disjointed words told Harding that O'Rahilly's eviscerated corpse and the riddled civilians on the blood-clogged cobbles had come to life in one man's imagination, straining his control to breaking point. Moans escaped him and he huddled into his corner at every far-away sound. Macken went swiftly to Michael Collins and spoke to him in cheerful undertones . . . Collins looked up, and back, stoical and impassive, with the rest of the doomed Volunteers, waiting for the end.[26]

Apart from the obvious reasons of defeat and surrender, there may have been another reason for Collins' depression in those last hours depicted by Ryan. One of those killed in the final, unsuccessful attempts to break through the encircling British barricades around the GPO was his best friend since boyhood days, Sean Hurley. Something of what the death of Hurley must have meant to Collins can be gleaned from an appraisal of his cousin which Collins gave in a letter to a friend:

He has the sharpness of wit to see my own particular mood. We think the

same way in Irish matters. We have walked London's streets on many a
night, silently, because our thinking was elsewhere . . . I appreciate him
because his mind seems compact whereas mine fritters away hours in idle
thought. At worst he is a boon companion, at best there is no one else I would
have as a friend.[27]

Hurley would not be the last friend Collins was to lose along the path
to freedom. Many more such deaths lay in the future.

At 4 pm on Saturday 9 April there was a ceasefire and Pearse issued
an order declaring an unconditional surrender, 'in order to prevent the
further slaughter of Dublin citizens, and in the hope of saving the lives
of our followers now surrounded and hopelessly outnumbered.'

After the surrender took effect the Volunteers were marched down
O'Connell St, between rows of troops with fixed bayonets to Parnell
Square, Collins remarking as he marched off with a backwards look at
the GPO, 'Well at least the flag's still flying.'[28] At that moment there
wasn't much else to take comfort from. Parnell had tried to restore
Home Rule. He had failed. His statue now stood at the bottom of the
square, inscribed 'No man has the right to set a boundary to the
onward march of a nation.' At that moment in 1916 it would have
been hard to know which was the more appropriate piece of
symbolism, the fact that Parnell was pointing towards the Rotunda
maternity hospital, or the fact that he had his back turned on the
prisoners. Part of the Rotunda complex had been the scene of the
formation of the Volunteers Collins had fought with. They had failed.
Tom Clarke's little shop fifty yards from where they now huddled in
the open was being used as a British operations centre. Overlooking
the Square was Vaughan's Hotel. One day Collins would use it as an
operations centre. But such a thought was far from his mind at that
point. He was more concerned with the treatment that some of the
prisoners, in particular Tom Clarke, were receiving from the officer in
charge, a Captain Lee-Wilson.[29]

There had been some atrocities on the part of the British troops
during the fighting. Fifteen innocent civilians were deliberately killed
around the King Street area, and one officer, Captain Bowen
Colthurst,[30] shot six people in cold blood, including the pacifist,
Sheehy-Skeffington. But in general the troops behaved decently after
the surrender. Looking at the Howth rifles and their bullets in awe
rather than in anger, they talked of the wounds these had made. And
the cheery word, and even the cup of tea, was not unknown,
particularly when an Australian unit relieved the Royal Irish Rifles
from Belfast. But Lee-Wilson, in classical bad apple fashion, lowered
the tone considerably, ill-treating Collins amongst others when he
found him trying to slip some malted milk tablets to a comrade.

Liam Tobin, then a slim twenty-two-year-old from Cork,
apprenticed to the hardware trade, who would later develop an

uncanny skill in intelligence-gathering, has left this account of his activities:

He wore a smoking cap with a fancy tassel hanging out of it. He kept walking round and round, stopping now and again to speak to his soldiers, saying, 'Whom do you consider worst, the Boches or the Sinn Feiners?' and of course they always answered that we were the worst. With the number of us lying in the small area of grass we were cramped for space, and it was damp and uncomfortable so that I got a bad cramp in my legs. As Lee-Wilson was passing, Piaras Beaslai, said to him, 'There's a young fellow here who is not well', explaining what was wrong and asking if I could stand up. Lee-Wilson said, 'No, let the so and so stay where he is.' Those of us who wanted to relieve ourselves had to do it on the grass lying alongside our comrades; we had to use the place where we lay.[31]

But what really enraged the prisoners was Lee-Wilson's practice of taking some of the prisoners, among them Clarke, to the steps of the Rotunda Hospital where he stripped them naked, apparently for the benefit of nurses looking out of the windows. Clarke suffered a good deal from an old wound to his elbow which made it difficult for him to bend his arm. However Lee-Wilson disregarded this and ripped off his jacket so that the wound opened. Tobin writes: 'I looked up at him and I vowed that I would deal with him some time in the future.' He did.

Some years later, the Collins intelligence network, developed with the aid of Tobin and another 1916 man, Frank Thornton, discovered that Lee-Wilson was acting as a District Inspector of the RIC in County Wexford. He was shot dead.

As Thornton's lot of prisoners were being marched off to Richmond Barracks in Inchicore, in the western part of the city, for screening, he says, 'If it weren't for the fact that we were so strongly guarded by British troops, we would have been torn asunder by the soldiers' wives in the area.'[32] These 'separation women' simply gave more extreme expression to the anger felt by most Dubliners at the destruction of life and property, and the effects of a week of terror, food shortages and looting as the slum dwellers poured out of the back streets to take their one chance in a lifetime of sampling the wares of the city's best shops. More civilians were killed and wounded than the combined total of British and Irish military casualties. Civilian casualties were 256 killed and some two thousand wounded. Sixty-two of the rebels had been killed outright and sixteen were executed subsequently. Piaras Beaslai gives this account of how the retribution process began:

On Sunday morning the prisoners were brought to Richmond Barracks. They were placed sitting on the floor of the gymnasium, and the political detectives of the 'G' Division of the Dublin Police came like a flock of carrion crows to pick out 'suspects' for court martial. I was one of the first to be picked out, and for the rest of the day could watch the detectives passing to and fro among the two thousand prisoners studying their faces for victims for the firing squad. Anybody who had seen that sight may be pardoned if he felt little compunction at the subsequent shooting of these same 'G' men.[33]

Of the men picked out by the 'G' men for court martial, those who did not merit death sentences were condemned to penal servitude in British prisons like Dartmoor or Portland. Those who received death sentences, subsequently commuted to life imprisonment as a result of public opinion, were also sent to hard labour in England. It was in Richmond Barracks that Collins had one of the luckiest escapes of his life. The 'G' men initially selected him for inclusion amongst those severely dealt with, but after Collins had been some time with the selected batch of prisoners, he heard his name being called from the further end of the building. Looking, he could not see who was calling him. After two or three attempts to locate the caller he grew impatient and decided to risk a walk across the room. And once there, he stayed. It was for him probably the luckiest escape of his career.[34] And, it may be added, one of the worst blunders the police ever made. For, as Frank O'Connor observed, the detectives, 'left behind them the one really dangerous man, the man who in a few short years would kill off the craftiest of them and render the rest so impotent that he would be able to walk the streets of Dublin undisguised'.[35]

Sean MacDiarmada very nearly survived the screening process also, but at the last moment one of the detectives, Hoey, whom Collins would later have eliminated, spotted him and dragged him out of the line of lesser offenders which was forming up to march to the ship taking them to prison in England. He was court-martialled at Richmond Barracks and sentenced to be shot in Kilmainham Jail. Frank Thornton, who was court-martialled along with him, describes their last interlude together:

Sean . . . walked with difficulty with the aid of a stick . . . and one of the first acts of our escort when we were ordered to fall-in for our march to Kilmainham, was to take away that stick, and immediately Harry Boland came to his rescue, and put his arm around him, Gerald Crofts doing likewise for myself, as my right leg by this time had got very stiff and sore from congealed blood. We were marched along the road to Kilmainham Jail, and with every yard there were indications of the changed attitudes of the people.

The open trams passing by always brought a cheer from somebody, even though rifles were pointed at the offender on every occasion. Old men stood at the street corners and saluted, despite being pushed around. Finally, reaching Kilmainham, Sean MacDermott turned round to the three of us, shook hands and said: 'I'll be shot, and it will be a bad day for Ireland that I'm not. You fellows will get an opportunity, even if in years to come, to follow on where we left off.' Well poor Sean was shot, as he felt he would be.[36]

But Michael Collins was safe, and because of his uncanny luck, well-placed, in the principal 'Republican University', to give vent to his burning determination to follow on in MacDiarmada's footsteps.

The 'Republican University'[37] which Irish revolutionaries have traditionally attended has many constituent colleges, the jails and internment camps of Ireland and England. Felons do not 'graduate' from these in the accepted sense – they are hammered out on the anvils of circumstance. Apart from the deadening effect of confinement and prison routine (and the correspondingly unduly enlivening effect of sexual deprivation), they have to survive the abrasion of the relationship between the authorities and themselves, an amalgam of the results of mutual prejudice, and a desire on the one side to be regarded as political prisoners, on the other to consider them as ordinary criminals. There is also the attrition of being thrust into the company of a collection of men with sharply contrasting personalities, economic, social and cultural backgrounds. One can emerge from this process either broken and disillusioned, or deepened in one's convictions and knowledge by the time and opportunity to study books, men and movements in a continuously testing environment wherein one learns more about oneself than about others. Collins was destined to graduate at the head of the class from his particular course which began at Stafford Detention Barracks on 1 May 1916.

The course was short but intensive, lasting from the beginning of May until Christmas week, 1916. The first three weeks were spent in solitary confinement from which communication with the outside world was established with difficulty. But obviously word of the executions had seeped through; when letters were allowed, on 16 May, Collins wrote to Hannie:

Positively you have no idea of what it's like, the dreadful monotony, the heart-scalding eternal brooding on all sorts of things, thoughts of friends dead & living, especially those recently dead, but above all the time, the horror of the way in which it refuses to pass . . . it is only with the utmost effort that I can concentrate my thoughts or be at all rational – you see I seem to have lost acquaintance with myself and with the people I knew. Wilde's 'Reading Gaol' keeps coming up. You remember 'All that we know who be in gaol . . .'[38]

But even in that dark night of the soul he looked forward, asking Hannie for 'a few good (& long) novels in cheap editions, and if still at the flat, Heath's *Practical French Grammar* or some such text book . . .'

He perked up greatly as soon as prison conditions eased, being remembered at Stafford for revealing, if contradictory, facets of his personality: Collins the butt of horse-play jokes, Collins the reflective, Collins the outgoing personality who could get unlikely people to work for him. Under the first heading his temper got him baited unmercifully. The prisoners had a rough game, a version of leapfrog called 'weak horses' whose ostensible aim was for two teams to compete in leaping over each others' backs until someone broke and became the 'weak sister'. In reality most of the fun was derived from riling Collins. The teams were picked so that the heaviest men, Jim Ryan, who had been the doctor in the GPO, Mort O'Connell and Denis Daly, were always on the team opposing Collins' and would deliberately set out to break him so that he would fly into one of his rages. The writer Desmond Ryan[39], however, noted that of all the men in the camp it was Collins who was attracted to a book he was reading and commented on it intelligently and sensitively. The acute Hannie observed[40] when she visited him that he seemed to have gained such control over one of the warders that the man couldn't do enough for him. Warders were to figure large in Collins' subsequent planning.

As soon as letter-writing was allowed he wrote to Susan, Sioban or Sheevaun as he called her, probably because he was beginning to study Irish and was experimenting with its forms. His letters show his restrained awkwardness in expressing himself to members of the opposite sex, his kind-heartedness and his eye for detail, even detail he disliked. He was listed under his Rathdown Rd address as 'Irish Prisoner 48F', a form of depersonalisation which irked him. 'Is one expected to lose one's identity, one's humanity, to become instead a numbered nonentity?' he asked[41]; but when Susan managed to get a parcel through to him he wrote back underlining '48F not 46F' at the head of his letter:

My dear Sioban,
    Today I was called away to recieve [sic] a parcel, which on examination I found to contain many very delightful articles, and in the writing on the wrapper, I think I discerned 'the fine touch of your claw'. It was very kind and thoughtful of you and I am very grateful indeed, my friends altogether have been most kind – a greater deal kinder than I deserve or have any right to expect.
    As you were fortunate enough to be away from the scene of our little 'shemozzle', it is profoundly to be hoped that you didn't stare 'upon the hills of Clare', as did I understand other of our friends 'Upon the Hill of Howth'. If our performance will only teach the housekeepers of Dublin to have more grub in reserve for the future it will surely not have been in vain, but seriously I'm afraid there must have been a lot of hardship and misery which must continue for many a day and which all our sympathy cannot soften.
    Life here has not been so ghastly since communications from the outer world have been allowed, and since we've been allowed reading matter and to write letters (this last concession being used by myself solely for the purpose of begging things). Also we are allowed to smoke, but no amount of privileges could compensate for the one thing which any of us haven't got in this or similar places. And the thoughts – I saw poor Pearse's last letter in the *Daily News* this day and it didn't make me exactly prayerful. However I

suppose things might be worse which, no less than ever, is something to be thankful for itself into the eternal question of what fate is thine unhappy Isle?

Well goodbye, the circumstances absolve me from the necessity of apologising for being uninteresting. Give my kindest regards to the friends I have among your colleagues. Tell Dolly I'd like to hear from her. Also an account from Nancy of her Howth experience would be most enlivening, because I'm sure she didn't lose her sense of humour unless she was very badly off. May I be looking forward to a letter from you? Really I cannot say how grateful I am to you for your kindness to me and that you should remember me.
> Love
> Michael Collins

Four days later a letter from Susan evidently got through in the wake of her parcel, and his reply to her[42], while characteristically somewhat stilted, also shows his essential kindheartedness and concern for others:

My dear Sheevaun,
Indeed was glad to get your letter – in spite of the effort at disparagement. I have already written you and no doubt you've received that precious document ere this. What impels me to this fresh effort is the following chiefly. Could you get in touch with some of the CmBan people and ask them to look up Mrs Kirwan of Maynooth whose husband is here. They have five or six children who are not I am afraid being attended to at all. Also Mrs Little, 31, The rear of Upper Clanbrassil St, more or less similarly placed. If you could get hold of a Miss Kearney she might be able to help . . .

Conditions have improved wonderfully during the last week. We are now allowed to communicate freely with each other so that I know all the other fellows' troubles. As for myself – a good deal changed, but do my level best to keep up appearances. Ghastly still at times. Well goodbye. 'See you again before the resurrection.' With all the thanks in the world for your kind thoughtfulness.
> Love
> Michael

Between 1 May and 16 June the British deported to England a total of 2,519 prisoners, many of them totally unconnected with the Volunteers or the Rising. These were initially scattered around the British penal landscape: Aylesbury, Glasgow, Knutsford, Lewes, Perth, Reading, Stafford, Wakefield, Wandsworth, Woking. But a degree of centralisation was thought necessary and a German prisoner-of-war camp at Frongoch, a remote beauty spot three miles from the town of Bala in Merionethshire, North Wales, was given over to the Irish, receiving its first contingent on 9 June. By the end of June, Collins knew that he would be transferred there. Writing to Susan from Stafford on 27 June he expressed little enthusiasm for the move:

. . . regarding our transfers. Removal instructions have been served on about 120 or 130 men and they'll be off tomorrow. . . . You will see in my letter to Dolly what the place is likely to be like. I shan't like the one letter a week in the very least. You have no idea of the number of letters I've been writing, especially for the past few weeks. I'm afraid I've lost my keen sense of the ridiculous, as in ordinary life I'd have the knowledge that they weren't fit to send anybody. But I can see myself writing the first letter in the camp and choking it full of requests just as I did my first one here. And my poor sister the victim. In spite of concessions, etc. one gets plenty of time to think here and my thoughts are often self-accusing goodness knows. I can't tell you how small I feel sometimes. Tis all very fine for writers to talk about the sublime thoughts which enter into people when they are faced by death – once, when I was in a pretty tight corner, what struck me was, how much nicer I might have been to the people who had a regard for me. You were one of them although I had no right to suppose, etc. Well I'm in that sort of mood again today – don't know why.

Glad to hear that you are all enjoying Howth. Sorry though that the weather isn't more suitable. But think of the 80 degree or 90 degree or something of November and how we'll all enjoy it. You on Howth we on Bala. Beannact leat [in English: A blessing on you].
Fondest love.

Frongoch, which was divided into two camps, North and South, had been a distillery. Apart from the prison complex formed around the old buildings dominated by a high brick chimney and the nearby railway siding, there was no sign of habitation. Collins wrote to Susan:

. . . It's situated most picturesquely on rising ground amid pretty Welsh hills. Up to the present it hasn't presented any good points to me, for it rained all the time . . . so that all the ground around and between the huts is a mass of slippery, shifting mud. We sleep 30 in an 'ut (this is the regulation name) the dimensions being 60 long, 16 wide and 10 foot high in the middle. Not too much room to spare! Of course when we've made roads etc. the place will be much better. But the cold at present is – well not pleasant even now, but I cheer them all up by asking them – what'll they do when the winter comes?[43]

Nethertheless the place had some amenities. In addition to a jail and the censor's office, the distillery also housed a hospital, an artists' shed, a cookhouse, a barber's shop and facilities for tailoring and shoe-making, as well as a carpenters' and an engineers' workshop. Collins wrote in another letter:

Prating about home, friends and so on doesn't alter the fact that this is Frongoch, an internment camp. There is only one thing to do while the situation is as it is. . . . make what I can of it.[44]

One of the best ways of dissipating pent-up tensions in a prison camp is sport. Collins is remembered at Frongoch for excelling at a number of sports.[45] He won the 100 yards during the camp sports on 8 August, overtaking M. W. O'Reilly with the amiable observation,

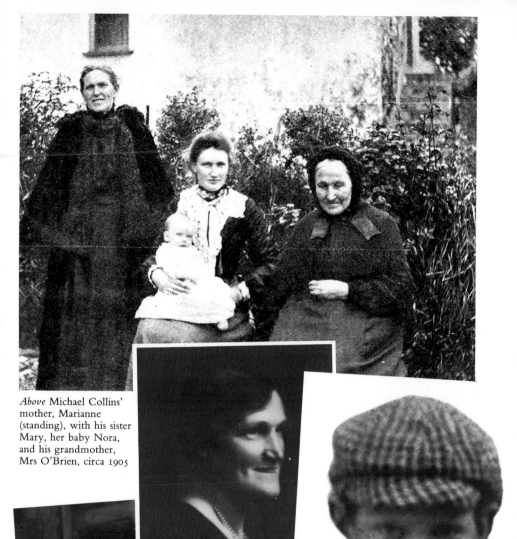

Above Michael Collins'
mother, Marianne
(standing), with his sister
Mary, her baby Nora,
and his grandmother,
Mrs O'Brien, circa 1905

Michael Collins, aged six; and his sisters
Hannie (*above*), with whom he lived for
nine years in London, and Helena (*left*),
later Sister Mary Celestine

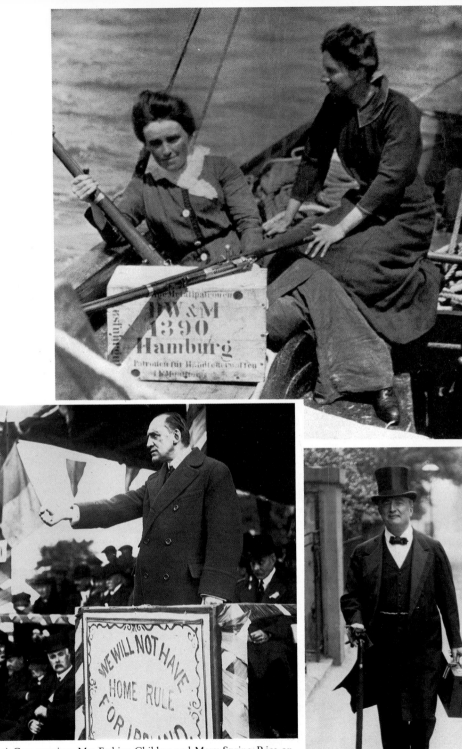

(*Top*) Gun-running: Mrs Erskine Childers and Mary Spring-Rice on board the *Asgard*, 1914
(*Right*) Irish Parliamentary Party leader John Redmond
(*Above*) Carson addressing an anti-Home Rule meeting, 1913

The Easter Rising, 1916: (*top*) a barricade in Talbot Street; (*above*) the shelled ruins of Liberty Hall – a few days earlier, Collins had marched out of the Hall to take part in the Rising; Collins' heroes, Sean MacDiarmada (*far left*) and James Connolly (*left*), who were executed for their part in the Rising

Collins in Stafford Jail (marked with an arrow)

(Above) Eamon de Valera under arrest before his court martial
(*Right*) Collins on release from Frongoch internment camp, December 1916 – his hand is on his knee to hide a hole in his trousers

'Ah, you whore, you can't run,' and was runner-up to his friend Sean Hales, the Munster champion, in the 56-lb weight-throwing competition. He was particularly fond of wrestling, but his opponents can't have been too fond of him. Apart from his custom of claiming a 'bit of ear', biting the ear of a victim after he had overpowered him, he tended to lose his temper during bouts:

He would go into a bout with a friendly determination. Grimness would begin to rise later, particularly if he were closely matched, and the contest would end in a heated and often bloody fracas. [46]

He generated a wide force field, impressing himself on the camp staff as much as on his companions. Robert J. Roberts, a sixteen-year-old canteen assistant at Frongoch wrote later:

Hut 32 was the noisiest in Camp North with ceaseless activity close to the Camp 2 canteen. Collins was always dressed in very good clothing, but rarely wore a collar or tie and his boots were army boots unpolished. The North Camp was far superior to the South as far as hygiene was concerned, but frightfully cold and wet even in June and no roads in the camp except very rough ones from the entrance and to the cookhouse. Mud everywhere, deep liquid mud. An effort to repair them by using boiler house clinkers manhandled and moved in an old waggon by the prisoners at threepence an hour, that is how I came in contact with Michael Collins, coming into the canteen covered in mud with the crowd, and we objected and told them to wash their boots at the water taps outside. He just laughed. He had a great sense of humour but was a very stern disciplinarian. [47]

The prisoners took advantage of Roberts' youth to steal cherry-wood pipes from a box which he placed on the counter, before allowing himself to be called away to the end of the counter. He says:

. . . when I returned there were only very few pipes in the box and no payments for other goods missing. I reported what was going on and we complained to the senior prisoner, who was Michael Collins. He arranged to assist us by locking the canteen door and searching each prisoner. If a prisoner had one pipe or box of matches he was given the benefit of the doubt. Otherwise stolen goods were returned.

Roberts was a classic example of the person in a seemingly lowly, but in fact highly useful position, whom Collins was later to win over in great numbers and use to such devastating effect. He decided that he wanted to study Welsh, and persuaded Roberts, on his day off from the camp, to get hold of some dictionaries and elementary alphabet cards, leaflets and some chalk. 'Michael Collins paid for all. He was never short of money,' Roberts recalls. 'Collins must have told his mother about me, because she sent me a small present of a tie-pin in the pattern of the shamrock inlaid with green Connemara stone for my kindness to her son.' Of course Collins' mother had died nine years earlier, but he obviously used her name to impress on Roberts how much he thought of him. This use of psychology by Collins was so successful that over half a century later Roberts would write:

Michael Collins was very highly respected, especially by the civilian canteen staff. The manager used to remark that whenever we took a problem to him he always listened logically. He used to be one of the first to the morning Mass and one of the first at the breakfast table, the best meal of the day . . . He was a heavy smoker but would go without, proving that he was more self-willed than the rest . . . wonderfully fit, he could out-walk everyone on the route marches into the Welsh hills and would arrive back in camp none the worse for wear while some of the guards fell by the wayside.[48]

Frongoch was infested with rodents: the prisoners rechristened the place in a pun on the Irish word for rat, 'frangach'. In one of his letters to Susan, Collins notes: 'Had a most exciting experience myself the other night – woke up to find a rat between my blankets – didn't catch the blighter either.'[49]

But Collins at this time was a more sombre person than the jocosity would indicate. For him the GPO had been the crucible of a great, dangerous experiment. Frongoch was the laboratory where the results were analysed, not without some pain to himself, although character-istically he sought to leaven his broodings with humour. Writing to Susan on 27 July 1916 he said:

Oh! Yes, I got those papers quite alright. And I'm very much obliged for them. 'Pon my word but I get a queer feeling often – in spite of my selfishness – when I think of the trouble I'm putting people to. I do hope to repay in some small way though. Just at present I'm in good form over the smashing of the H R proposals. Anything but a divided Ireland – you understand of course that I mean geographically divided. From the letters and accounts I get the country seems to be very sound – I imagine there will be better material than ever in Ireland for the next European war, that at any rate is something to be thankful for.

'The next European war' – the next round. Collins was thinking ahead, in one sense. But in terms of Republican theology, thinking back, to Wolfe Tone and his teaching that England's difficulty was Ireland's opportunity. But was it the correct approach? Within a few days of his writing to Susan, word reached the camp of Roger Casement's execution,[50] heightening Collins' depressions and his questionings. A brave man had died. For what? Casement had in fact become disillusioned by the Germans,[51] their lack of commitment to an Irish uprising, and his submarine return to Ireland had been for the purpose of calling off the Rising. In the camp with Collins was the one surviving member of the party that had been sent down to Kerry to pick him up, the driver of the car that had gone over the pier. More tragic bungling, added to by the failure to signal to the *Aud* as she cruised fruitlessly off the Kerry coast instead of being brought into

Fenit harbour where transport had been provided for her cargo. And the whole thing was compounded by the local Volunteer commander, Austin Stack, finally deciding to call at the RIC barracks where Casement was held to find out what was happening – and getting himself arrested!

Stack, who worked in a solicitor's office, and had some legal training, was a famous Kerry Gaelic All-Ireland footballer and Commandant of the Kerry Brigade of the Irish Volunteers. After his arrest he was sentenced to death. This was then commuted to twenty years' penal servitude. In jail he built up a national reputation for his leadership of revolts against attempts to impose criminal status on Volunteers. His courage was unquestionable, but his judgement left something to be desired.

No wonder MacNeill had sent the O'Rahilly around vetoing the plans. The wonder lay in O'Rahilly's fatal gallantry in joining the doomed uprising after expending himself in trying to spare others its horrors. Collins didn't blame the men or the movement which had brought him to Frongoch. But by now he had too many first-hand impressions and reports of the Rising and its aftermath to be able to accept what had happened uncritically – or unmoved. His particular leader, Joseph Plunkett, had married Grace Gifford on the morning of his execution, fifteen soldiers with fixed bayonets lining the cell as an officer ticked off the seconds of the ten minutes bride and bridegroom were given together before the groom was taken out to be shot.[52] He had heard how Connolly, in such pain that he had to be given morphine to make him sleep, had then been woken up to be told he would be shot at dawn: but that he had composed himself sufficiently to pat his sobbing wife on the head and say, 'Don't cry, Lillie, you'll unman me.'[53] How Pearse had told the court martial that sentenced him to death, 'When I was a child of ten I went down on my knees by my bedside and promised God that I should devote my life in an effort to free my country. I have kept that promise.' With his belief in historical continuity he would have found himself largely in agreement with Pearse's concluding remarks to the court martial: 'You cannot extinguish the Irish passion for freedom. If our deed has not been sufficient to win freedom, then our children will win it by a better deed.'[54] But he had no intention of leaving the 'better deed' to the next generation and he had no great opinion of the planning of the Rising as he made clear in a letter to Kevin O'Brien:

It is so easy to fault the actions of others when their particular actions have resulted in defeat. I want to be quite fair about this – the Easter Rising – and say how much I admired the men in the ranks and the womenfolk thus engaged. But at the same time – as it must appear to others also – the actions of the leaders should not pass without comment. They have died nobly at the hands of the firing squads. So much I grant. But I do not think the Rising week was an appropriate time for the issue of memoranda couched in poetic phrases, nor of actions worked out in a similar fashion. Looking at it from the inside (I was in the GPO) it had the air of a Greek tragedy about it, the illusion being more or less completed with the issue of the before-mentioned memoranda. Of Pearse and Connolly I admire the latter the most. Connolly was a realist, Pearse the direct opposite. There was an air of earthy directness about Connolly. It impressed me. I would have followed him through hell had such action been necessary. But I honestly doubt very much if I would have followed Pearse – not without some thought anyway.

I think chiefly of Tom Clarke and MacDiarmada. Both built on the best foundations. Ireland will not see another Sean MacDiarmada.

These are sharp reflections. On the whole I think the Rising was bungled terribly, costing many a good life. It seemed at first to be well-organised, but afterwards became subjected to panic decisions and a great lack of very essential organisation and co-operation.[55]

Collins resolved that the vehicle for that 'very essential organisation and co-operation' should be the IRB.

And it may have been in Frongoch that the first glimmering of another method of warfare, along the lines of de Wet's approach, may have presented itself. It is known that there was considerable debate within the camp about the merits or demerits of 'static warfare'. In fact, before surrendering, one of the executed leaders, Major John MacBride, who had fought for the Boers in South Africa, had addressed his men and warned them never again to allow themselves to be locked up in buildings confronting an enemy who could easily subdue them with the aid of superior man- and fire-power. Collins was to become the supreme architect of the 'hit-and-run' ambush technique which effectively countered this superiority.

In that noticeable pattern of his life in which he formed friends easily with either youth or age the counterpoint to the youthful Roberts in Frongoch was Henry Dixon, a seventy-year-old solicitor, disciple of Arthur Griffith and a member of the IRB, who served as camp librarian – a useful position for establishing contact throughout the camp.[56] Outside the camp, contact was established with Mrs Kathleen Clarke, Tom's widow, and sister of Edward Daly, who was also executed for his part in the Rising, and the threads were also picked up in the other prisons where 1916 men had been incarcerated throughout England and, chiefly in Reading and Lewes, where de Valera was beginning to make a name for himself as the prisoners' leader. The IRB was organised on a cell system[57] wherein only the cell or circle leader knew who all the members were or how to make contact with the circle above him. The President of the Supreme Council was the controller, the chief of the entire Brotherhood. Michael Collins was elected Head Centre of the Frongoch outfit. Thus when the Frongoch gates swung open he was in a position to ensure that the

spores of revolutionary violence blasted into the air above the GPO in
Easter Week would be wafted into every corner of Ireland.

Another scheme which Collins helped to originate in Frongoch was
the formation of what later became one of Ireland's largest insurance
businesses, the New Ireland Assurance Company. This was born out
of a desire to keep in Irish hands a portion of the large amount of
money being sent out of the country to English insurers. It also
provided a useful cover later on for IRB activities. Some of its
principal figures, including M. W. O'Reilly and Denis McCullough,
were Frongoch men.

Within Frongoch itself the great fear hanging over the prisoners was
that they would be conscripted, and to avoid this they gave false
names and confused the authorities in any way they could. Collins
played a leading part in this form of defiance. He refused to co-operate
with the authorities, insisting on the prisoners drawing up their own
lists of names and addresses, even when these were only needed to buy
tickets for the prisoners' correct home destinations. But it was
remarked that he carefully noted the prisoners' identities for his own
purposes. He had a capacity for being able to weave details into a
useful pattern. For instance Brennan-Whitmore one day laughingly
told a comrade how, as a result of the authorities' black propaganda to
the effect that the prisoners were rich with German gold, a guard had
wistfully enquired whether he was 'one of the boys with all the
money'[58] – and Whitmore found himself hauled before an IRB meeting as a result. Collins wanted to be told everything he could about the
soldier. A short time later the man became one of the conduits through
which letters and information were smuggled out of the camp.

Such channels became vitally necessary as tensions built up, against
the back-drop of the prisoners' desire to maintain their prisoner-of-
war status at all costs. The proposals that they should work in nearby
quarries and should provide scavenging and cinder removal services
for the soldiers were refused. As a result, relationships within the
camp soured. The route marches were introduced and parcels and
letters were stopped. After the 'ash-pit incident', as it became known,
up to a hundred men were confined to cells with loss of all privileges.
The food was another bone of contention. Collins does not seem to
have been exaggerating when he wrote:

With the exception of Friday when we get uneatable herrings, the food never
varies, frozen meat quite frequently and dried beans are the staple diets. The
potato ration is so small that one hardly notices it.[59]

Collins concluded that letter by saying, 'Mind you I'm not grumbling
in the strict sense!' However the prisoners grumbled in other senses,
and a great deal of propaganda was generated as they fought for
prisoner-of-war status. The authorities sought to counter the unrest

by transfers, and courts martial aimed at removing the trouble-makers
to more controllable and more overtly criminal surroundings such as
Reading jail.

But criminalisation was something Collins loathed with every fibre
of his being. After being taken from Stafford to Frongoch, Collins
was one of those removed from the camp a few days later and brought
to London for screening by the Advisory Committee on the
Internment of Rebels set up after the Rising in a vain attempt to
apportion blame and find out who the real leaders of the revolutionary
movement were. Before being returned to Frongoch, Collins wrote
to Susan Killeen expressing his detestation of the criminalisation
process:

This morning I was able to see through the open pane of my window the
convicts at exercise. It was the most revolting thing I have ever seen. Each
convict seems to have cultivated a ghastly expression to match the colour of
his turf-ash-grey garb. Broad arrows everywhere. As the man walked round
and round the ring – those wretched arrows simply danced before the eyes.
That awful convict dress is one horror we're saved at any rate.[60]

Imbued with this spirit he rejected all suggestions of compromise or
moderation, writing a reasoned rationale for his stance: 'Sit down –
refuse to budge – you have the British beaten. For a time they'll raise
war – in the end they'll despair. Method, but unorthodox, has them
beaten the whole time',[61] but articulating it in a most unreasoning
hectoring way to anyone who showed what he considered faint
heartedness: 'Coward', 'Bloody lousers', 'ould cods'.[62] This inability
to show to his peers in speech the restraint he displayed to the young
and the old, or when he took a pen in hand, was to make many a
dangerous enemy for Collins. But his policy paid dividends. Certainly
the ploy of concealing their identities kept prisoners from being
conscripted. Probably the propaganda engendered by their protest,
particularly in America, got them home for Christmas. But not
without cost.

Two hundred of the prisoners went on a three-day hunger strike on
2 November, and the prison commandant, Col Heygate-Lambert,
declared that he would have discipline in the camp even though it was
filled with nothing but dead bodies.[63] One prisoner, Eamonn
Tierney, who had a fear of conscription, went mad after this. Four
others cracked up in the foetid, confined conditions and died the
following year. Many others suffered from sickness of various kinds.
The two camp doctors followed instructions in not attending to
patients who refused to give their names. But one of them, Dr Peters,
'worried by statements concerning the treatment of prisoners', broke
under the strain and drowned himself in the River Tryweryn, near
Bala.[64]

Michael Collins' statements concerning the battle of wills in the camp found their mark in a celebrated exposé in William O'Brien's *Cork Free Press* on 11 November, and in a number of other papers, notably the *Manchester Guardian*, later in the month. They detonated in America and on the floor of the House of Commons to such good effect that an amnesty was finally declared on 21 December by the Chief Secretary for Ireland, Henry Duke.

Collins exploded into freedom and Dublin on Christmas morning with Gearoid O'Sullivan. They went to see Joe O'Reilly, another Stafford and Frongoch graduate who, like Collins, was a Corkman, but a far gentler one. The pair burst through the door of the room O'Reilly was sharing with a friend, extracted 'a piece of ear' that left both his ears bleeding, 'pinched and savaged him',[65] poured what they could of a bottle of port down his throat and left O'Reilly to explain to his traumatised room-mate that it was only Collins having a bit of fun. Collins continued to roister round Dublin all that day until the evening when 'he was lifted on to a sidecar and, drunk as a lord, bundled by his friends into the Cork train'.[66]

3

Kicking Down a Rotten Door

'Put him in to get him out.'

Slogan on prisoner's election poster, 1917

The first visit home after Frongoch was anti-climactic. To begin with Christmas affected transport arrangements so that Collins had to walk from Clonakilty to Woodfield through December's darkness and chills. The good cheer with which he had departed Dublin further evaporated on arrival at the news that his grandmother had just died. An innocent old lady, her life bounded by her family and the small hills of Sam's Cross, she had greeted the news that Michael was involved in the Easter rebellion with the observation, 'I suppose that Michael is fighting for William O'Brien and James O'Brien is fighting for Mr Redmond. [William O'Brien was the old opponent of Collins's childhood ogre, Smith-Barry; O'Brien had become estranged from Redmond on the Home Rule issue. James O'Brien was another grandson.]

During his holiday Collins was to find a good deal of that lack of comprehension – coupled with a degree of fear that he might be the cause of bringing grief to the area. He obviously sensed something of this after calling on Sean Hurley's mother and wrote to Hannie: 'I think poor Sean Hurley's mother felt his loss more keenly when I came home than at any other time.' But he wasn't prepared to extend the same sensitivity to the generality of those he met. The First World War had brought unwonted prosperity to the farmers of the district, as it had to other parts of the country, and their reception of the returned firebrand may be gauged from his comments to 'Shiobhain a Cushla' (Susan my sweetheart). He had earlier met a mutual friend and apologised for being able to spend 'only a minute with her'. He said:

I was quite unable to talk to anyone and I didn't feel at all well; some kind of reaction was setting in and I was rapidly giving way. Better now but not very much. Lots of trouble here. Poor old grandmother was dead when I came home, and then that brother of mine and his wife were both very unwell. However think they're improving so I probably will have a decent rest next week and then go back to Dublin to thank you for all the kindnesses which have been bestowed on me.

It seems that the spirit prevailing here anyway is very poor. The people are much, much too careful and I've sustained myself principally on rows since returning.[1]

Accordingly, after three dispiriting weeks spent 'drinking Clonakilty wrastler on a Frongoch stomach', as he put it himself in a letter to Hannie, Collins returned to Dublin one step ahead of the RIC who came to his family seeking him in connection with a brawl in Cork. His relations say that the police visit was only an attempt at intimidation and that he had nothing to do with the fight in Cork. But of course! Who could imagine Michael Collins mixed up in a brawl! At all events he gave the police the slip, not for the last time in his career, and returned to Dublin. Here he found the 'national spirit' a good deal better. As he had written to Susan with unintentional prescience, 'some kind of reaction' was indeed setting in. The reaction manifested itself in two ways. One was a tremendous outpouring of support and sympathy for the insurgent Aprilists, now mistakenly all lumped together in the public's mind as 'Sinn Feiners', through an unselective use of the term by the British media and military, after the Rising. The other was a corresponding outburst of prejudice. The sympathy was engendered by the effect of the executions of the leaders coming against a backdrop of the frustration of the green constitutional traditions' hopes of Home Rule, which they had democratically expressed, by the undemocratic action of the Orange and Tory conspiracy. The execution of Roger Casement, which came in August, long after it was abundantly clear that all threat to Britain from the Rising was well past, summed up the different treatment meted out to Orange and Green. The man who successfully sought the death penalty for Casement was F. E. Smith, who later became Lord Birkenhead. He had told an audience at Ballyclare, County Antrim[2] that in resisting Home Rule he would be prepared to 'risk the collapse of the entire body politic to prevent this monstrous crime.' During his trial Casement had said, 'the Unionists' champion had chosen a part they felt would lead to the Woolsack, while I went a road that I knew must lead to the dock. And the events proved both were right.' Listening to this oration as he lolled back on the prosecutor's bench, F. E. Smith smiled and commented, 'And quite right too!' It seemed unlikely at the time that of all men he and Michael Collins would ever become friendly, but incredibly enough the conflicting currents swirling through Ireland in that January of 1917 were destined to throw the two men together and, out of their encounter, friendship would emerge.

Irish-American reaction to the immediate post-Rising executions was intense. A huge relief fund was set up. Dr Thomas Addis Emmet, a descendant of Robert Emmet's brother, became its president and there were scores of bishops and archbishops amongst its patrons. Well over a hundred thousand dollars was sent to Ireland as a result. This at a time when President Woodrow Wilson was telling Washingtonians: '. . . every people has a right to choose the sovereignty under which they shall live . . . small states . . . have a right to enjoy the same respect for their territorial integrity that great and powerful nations expect and insist on . . .'[3]

This at a time when Britain was being exhausted by Jutland and Verdun and needed American aid to survive but was being told by her Washington Ambassador, Sir Cecil Spring Rice, that it was 'most unfortunate that it has been found necessary to execute the Rebels'. He said:

I do not think we can count on American help, perhaps not even on American sympathy . . . the attitude towards England has been changed by recent events in Ireland . . . If we are able in some measure to settle the Home Rule question at once, the announcement will have a beneficial effect here, although I do not think that anything we can do would conciliate the Irish here. They have blood in their eyes when they look our way . . . Our cause for the present among the Irish here is a lost one . . .'[4]

With an American presidential election looming in November the British Cabinet knew it had to find some way of addressing the Irish question, but the method it chose was not to heed the electoral call for Home Rule but to go instead for a Lloyd George manoeuvre which would ensure that Irish nationalists would acquire even more 'blood in their eyes'. The deal in effect took Partition from the realms of debate, as it had been during the pre-war Buckingham Palace conference, and inscribed it on the Irish political agenda, albeit in Janus-faced, Lloyd-Georgian fashion.

At the end of May 1916 both Redmond and Carson received Home Rule proposals whereby the postponed 1914 Home Rule Act was to be brought into operation immediately for twenty-six counties only, the six north-eastern counties (Antrim, Down, Armagh, Derry, Fermanagh and Tyrone) being excluded for an undeclared period which was described as follows:

The Bill to remain in force during the continuance of the war and a period of twelve months thereafter; but, if Parliament has not by that time made further and permanent provision for the Government of Ireland, the period for which the Bill is to remain in force is to be extended by Order in Council for such time as may be necessary in order to enable Parliament to make such provision.

Initially at least, John Redmond thought he was quite clear as to its interpretation. At a meeting of Six-County Nationalists in Belfast on 23 June when he dealt with a report in that day's *Irish Times* concerning a promise that Lloyd George was supposed to have given Carson to the effect that Partition would be permanent, a voice in the audience cried 'never'. Redmond said: 'I entirely re-echo that cry of "never". That statement is an absolute lie . . . The proposals are temporary and provisional. If they were not I would oppose them.'

Alas for Redmond's trust in Lloyd George. Unknown to the unfortunate Irish parliamentarian, the 'Welsh wizard' had sent with Carson's copy of the draft proposal this note:

> Whitehall Place
> May 29th, 1916.
>
> My dear Carson,
>   I enclose Greer's draft propositions.
>   We must make it clear that at the end of the provisional period Ulster does not, whether she wills it or not, merge in the rest of Ireland.
> Ever sincerely,
> D. Lloyd George.
> P.S. Will you show it to Craig?

In the circumstances that 'Ever sincerely' is a nice touch, though understandably the nicety was rather lost on a John Redmond who was rapidly going down in a tide of post-Rising sentiment. When he discovered what had happened, under outraged pressure from his increasingly disillusioned supporters, he withdrew his assent on 24 July and the Government temporarily abandoned the scheme. These were the Home Rule proposals the news of whose 'smashing' had left Collins exultant in Frongoch, as he told Susan Killeen. He had also written to Nancy O'Brien on the same day (27 July) saying: 'I'm glad to see that this particular business has been dropped. Surely John E. & Co must be discredited now, although there's a lot of damn fools knocking about.'

But his exultation was premature. For as William O'Brien realised afterwards, that Lloyd George draft, as *realpolitik*, was a Magna Carta of Sir Edward Carson's Six Counties, an 'unhappy instrument' to which 'must be traced the responsibility for all the years of disappointment, bloodshed, and devastation that were to follow'.[5] They still follow as this is being written.

So much for the temper of the post-Rising Irish nationalists and the proposals made by the Government in London to deal with their ardour. As Michael Collins returned to Ireland in January 1917, to continue from Woodfield the assault on the system which he had begun the previous Easter, the country was being run by an Irish Executive, or Government, as it was equally known. It consisted of a Lord Lieutenant, a Chief Secretary and an Under Secretary, the first two being politicians, the third a civil servant. The military and naval establishments were directed from London, though the Lord

Lieutenant was supposed to be in charge of both. However, as at the time of the Rising the Chief Secretary was in the Cabinet, often absent from Dublin, and the Lord Lieutenant was not, the day-to-day running of the administration devolved upon the Under Secretary. As John Redmond, the leader of the Irish Parliamentary Party, also had to be in London, near to the Chief Secretary, the House of Commons was the effective source of Irish decision-making. Britain's influence was exercised through Dublin Castle where the offices of the Chief Secretary and the Under Secretary were located, as were those of the law officers who formed part of the Executive or Government. It was from the Castle also that the two police forces, the Royal Irish Constabulary and the Dublin Metropolitan Police, were controlled. The influence of the Castle on Ireland was such that to this day Dublin's major banking, insurance and administrative centres, including the Central Bank and the City Hall buildings, are all within a stone's throw of the pile, the former nerve centre of a great, colonial, civil and military bureaucracy. But in January 1917 the nerves were bad, and destined to get even worse. Augustine Birrell, the witty and cultivated Chief Secretary at the time of the Rising, had been made its political scapegoat and reshufflings and demoralisation had followed his fall. This process was to continue as the political situation deteriorated, in part under hammer blows inflicted by Michael Collins, until a report by Sir Warren Fisher to the British Government three years later would state:

The Castle Administration does not administer. On the mechanical side it can never have been good Irish Govt in relation to policy . . . it simply has no existence. The prevailing conception of the post of Under Secretary, who should be the principal permanent advisor of the Irish Government in Civil Affairs appears to be that he is a routine clerk . . . The Chief Secretary is entirely unconcerned with the exploration or settlement of the problems which the Irish administration exists to solve . . . with the Chief Secretary skied on Olympus and his top permananent official hewing wood in the remotest valley the natural expectation is that essentials will suffer . . . the heads of the RIC and DMP respectively seem to be mediocrities, and while the morale of the former force is getting shaken the latter force has apparently lost it entirely . . . the office under its present management has lost its grip on the country.[6]

The report, while accurate in many respects, nevertheless only dealt with the symptoms of the Irish disease, not its causes. For instance the reason for the impotence of the Under Secretary, Sir James MacMahon, was at least in part his religion. He was a Catholic, and the Castle was riven by sectarianism and by Freemasonry. What Sir Warren Fisher was talking about was not merely bad administration; he was in fact describing the outcome of a political vacuum. The population of Ireland had voted in successive elections by majorities of the order of five to one for Home Rule. The ballot box was unambiguous in its verdict. But that verdict did not count against the manoeuvrings of the Tory/Orange caucus at Westminster.

The electoral vacuum was to be demonstrated yet again within days of Collins' return to Dublin from Woodfield. On 20 January Count Plunkett, the father of his old leader in the GPO, Joseph Plunkett, was formally expelled from the Royal Dublin Society because of his family's connection with the Rising (his other two sons George and John were at the time still undergoing penal servitude in England), an action which caused a good deal of resentment outside the *ancien régime* circles of the RDS itself. The Count announced his intention of standing in a by-election that had arisen in North Roscommon. Collins saw the possibility of using the campaign to do more than test public reaction to the attitudes of the RDS. North Roscommon could be a platform from which both to deliver a rebuff to the Irish Parlimentary Party and to derive some nationwide publicity for the aims of the physical force school. He travelled to Roscommon and campaigned vigorously for the Count. Collins and those who thought like him were quite clear as to where they stood. What they were not clear about was where Plunkett stood on the great issue of abstention. If elected, would he take his seat in Westminster, or would he abstain? There was a good reason for the uncertainty. Plunkett himself had not made up his mind and did not declare for abstention until a meeting of his supporters was held in Boyle after the election result was announced and it was found that he had defeated his Irish Parliamentary Party opponent by 3,022 votes to 1,708.[7]

As Collins himself wrote afterwards, his decision

was not received very enthusiastically by some of the most energetic of his supporters. They had returned a man, it was said, who did not intend to represent them anywhere . . . there was at this stage no unity of opinion on the policy of abstention among the various elements which formed the opposition, which was joined together only in opposition to the Redmondites.

On 19 February Collins became Secretary to the Irish National Aid Fund. The Fund had been set up by Mrs Kathleen Clarke to alleviate distress amongst the dependants of those killed or imprisoned as a result of the Rising. It was funded both by public subscription and by money from the Clan na nGael in America. The Christmas release of internees and the less heinously regarded prisoners from Reading, including Arthur Griffith, meant that suddenly a great deal more work became attached to the post so it was decided to make it salaried, at the princely sum of £2 10s a week. Collins was the favourite candidate. When I interviewed Mrs Clarke,[8] she spoke warmly of 'Mick's' drive and efficiency which reminded her of Sean

MacDiarmada. She obviously took pride in having done well by her executed husband's and brother's memories in passing on their contacts and any secrets she held for them to Collins. His IRB friends also campaigned for him though without his knowledge or consent, and he got the job after a pro-forma interview during which he showed himself so certain of the outcome that throughout it he sat not at, but on, a desk swinging his legs, 'altogether too cocksure', sniffed one of the lady interviewers. However the cocky one was to prove himself one of the all-time great administrators in a field in which the Irish have tradition-ally excelled, relief dispensation, wherein industry and efficiency have to be tempered with humanity and an ability to empathise with the aid recipients, whether these be in a third-world country or a Dublin back street. And with that extraordinary point–counterpoint nature of his, wherein humanity and generosity ran side by side with the most ruthless militarism and political chicanery, it was the National Aid Association, with its network of friends and contacts, that put Collins into a position of national influence only nine months after he had lain out in the open all night in Parnell Square, trying to keep Tom Clarke alive. Apart from running the National Aid Association with great efficiency, Collins took an active part in the reorganisation of the Volunteers, the IRB and Sinn Fein, and established strong links with Clan na nGael through John Devoy in New York. He also began making trips to various centres in England such as London, Liverpool and Manchester, setting up the arms-smuggling network which was later to work so spectacularly well. In London his main agent was his old friend Sam Maguire. In Liverpool it was another Frongoch friend, Neil Kerr, who apart from having a key position as a purser in a transatlantic shipping line, was also Head Centre of the IRB there, and in Manchester, Patrick O'Donoghue, whose large house in a comfortable suburb he would one day use to hide the Marchmont children whose kidnapping would gain him a priceless source of military intelligence. Even more importantly, as time pro-gressed, he made secret contact with figures who as we shall see later, would be of crucial importance in the coming onslaught on Dublin Castle – four of its trusted detectives, Joe Kavanagh, James MacNamara, David Neligan and above all, Ned Broy.

Most of this activity was hidden from the public. What people saw was a powerfully built, extraordinarily efficient young man with a big heart and sometimes, a big mouth. One description of the time says:

It was a joy to watch Collins at his work. He was most methodical in everything; had an extraordinary aptitude for detail; always knew exactly what he wanted to do, and disposed of each particular task without a moment's hesitation.

He never missed an appointment. Never lost a file, or a piece of paper. Kept meticulous accounts and, most important of all, the fund's beneficiaries were treated like heroes of the revolution, not objects of charity. It was in the National Aid Association's offices in 10 Exchequer St that, building on his GPO and and Frongoch reputations, his mythic status began to emerge. One fatal lineament of that outline, a disregard for menacing firearms, showed itself the day a man flourished a revolver at the Association's president, Alderman Corrigan. Collins bore down on the gunman and kicked him down the stairs. His only comment as he threw down the gun and picked up his pen again was 'those bloody fellows'.

Insofar as the public was concerned, the banner under which Collins and his cohorts marched was that of Arthur Griffith's Sinn Fein. But as Wolfe Tone Republicans they supported only part of the Sinn Fein policy; abstention and self-sufficiency were acceptable, but two of Griffith's cardinal principles were not: his belief in the superiority of moral, as opposed to physical, force, and his recognition of the British Crown. Nor was his opposition to the Rising properly understood. Griffith, who feared that the country had not the physical or mental resources to withstand an unsuccessful attempt at insurrection, had in fact made his way to the GPO at the outbreak of the rising. Here he had spoken with Sean MacDiarmada who, as part of the general IRB policy of infiltration of all potentially useful organisations, had become business manager of Griffith's paper, *Nationality,* and who advised him to return home. Griffith would be needed in the Ireland that would emerge from the ruins of the Rising. The public thought increasingly highly of this gifted journalist and patriot who chose to live in poverty in Ireland for most of his life, rather than leave for America and a lucrative offer of a career in journalism. Hitherto he had been little known outside a relatively restricted circle of writers and intellectuals through his various newspapers, The *United Irishman, Eire, Nationality* and even, when the censor struck, his accurately named publication, *Scissors and Paste.* Now, in the wake of the Rising, a re-issued *Nationality* did reach a wider audience as MacDiarmada foresaw. Influenced in economic philosophy by Frederick List, who advocated protectionism and tariffs behind which to build up industry, Griffith added an Irish gloss to these doctrines, preaching that Ireland was a separate nation and must develop all the best resources of that nation whether these be in literature, language, afforestation or manufacturing, acceptable ideas whose hour had struck. Hundreds of Sinn Fein Clubs were springing up around the country and his theories were much discussed. He had been putting forward the idea of a dual monarchy for Ireland since 1904 when his great work, *The Resurrection of Hungary,* was first serialised in the *United Irishman* and later published in book form. Ironically, at the time it was the Fenians who thought that the people would never support his central theory, that Irishmen should do as the Hungarians had done in Vienna – withdraw from the Imperial Parliament and set up their own parliament and subordinate bodies. The type of parliament he was aiming at, representative of 'the King, Lords and Commons of Ireland', was based on that extinguished by the Act of Union which followed Wolfe Tone's rebellion. Now in 1917, after their own rising, it was the Fenian standard-bearers who objected to his proposal that the King should be retained in an independent Ireland so as to reassure loyalists, particularly Northern loyalists.

In an effort to resolve these differences and chart a new policy, Count Plunkett convened a meeting of public bodies and interested parties on 19 April in the Mansion House. Plunkett proposed to start a new organisation which would scrap all the existing national organis-ations, including Sinn Fein. Griffith suggested that each group should keep its identity but that a joint executive be formed which would include Sinn Fein, Labour, the Volunteers, and Plunkett's followers, on a programme of abstention and appealing to the Peace Conference after the war, which America had just entered. This was defeated, and he announced that Sinn Fein would continue as it was. Then, as a split loomed, a private session was held and in Collins' words: '. . . the divergence of opinion was so great that, to avoid a split, it was announced that there should be no greater union than a loose co-operation.'[9] The 'loose co-operation' was applied almost immediately to one of Collins' current projects, the winning of another by-election on 9 May 1917, this time in Longford where he was backing the candidacy of a 1916 prisoner in Lewes jail, Joseph McGuinness, a member of a well-liked Longford family.

The by-election had more significance for Collins than the election of McGuinness. For it was during the campaign that he stayed in The Greville Arms, run by the Kiernans – 'four beautiful sisters and their brother . . . lovely glamorous girls . . . had all the right ideas'.[10] According to Sean MacEoin Collins fell in love with one of the girls, Helen, who chose to marry a solicitor, Paul McGovern. Frank O'Connor claims 'on the night before her wedding he went to her hotel and pleaded with her not to go through with the marriage' and that during the speeches he was so agitated he shredded his handker-chief. Collins transferred his affections to another sister, Kitty, whom Harry Boland was already in love with, a fact which may have had a bearing on his subsequent relationship with Collins. (A third sister, Maud, was courted by the tragic Thomas Ashe.)

McGuinness was advised not to stand by the prisoners' leader, Eamon de Valera, who wrote: 'As regards the contesting of elections question, it is so extremely dangerous from several points of view that most of us here consider it unwise.'[11] This was the first occasion on record that Collins decided not to be bound by de Valera's wishes. It would not be the last. De Valera's stated attitude was based on a doctrinaire separatism that refused to acknowledge the British Parliament, and on fears of a loss of face for the men of 1916 if the candidate were defeated. He promptly forgot such arguments later when a candidate himself. Collins went ahead without McGuinness' permission in a campaign whose message was summed up by a poster showing a man in prison uniform with a caption saying: 'Put him in to get him out'. It succeeded, but only just. On the first count the Irish Parliamentary Party candidate, Patrick MacKenna, was declared elected. However, as Beaslai puts it, 'a bundle of uncounted votes was then discovered' and McGuinness won by thirty-seven votes.

Many years later, Alasdair MacCaba, by then the much-admired Chairman of the Irish Educational Building Society, gave me his version of how the discovery came about. 'I jumped up on the platform, put a .45 to the head of the returning officer, clicked back the hammer and told him to think again.' Whatever the worth of MacCaba's intervention, Lloyd George now most certainly had to think again. Count Plunkett, with the benefit of a sympathy vote, had been a blow to the Irish Parliamentary Party. Joseph McGuinness, a common criminal serving a jail sentence, was a blow to a British Government constrained by the circumstances of the war to be mindful of Irish-American opinion.

There is a well-established British tradition for dealing with such problems. Buy time, be seen to be doing something, set up a tribunal, a commission, a forum, an assembly, a convention. The history of Ireland is strewn with such milestones. Lloyd George chose the convention option. It met on 25 July, allegedly representative of all shades of Irish opinion to 'recommend a settlement of the Irish problem'. In fact, however, the Convention members were nominated by the British Government. It was the political equivalent of an expedient normally reserved for Irish political trials, the packed jury. Sinn Fein were allocated 5 per cent of the membership, but Griffith declined to attend unless the delegates were elected by the Irish people. So although the Convention might have been represented in a good light in America, in Ireland, where Sinn Fein support was rising by the hour, it was doomed from the start. However it was accompanied by another move which was to have far-reaching effects. With a view to 'creating a favourable atmosphere for the Irish Convention' Bonar Law announced on 15 June that the remainder of the 1916 prisoners still in England were to be released unconditionally.

The prisoners held in Lewes Jail had been agitating for prisoner-of-war status. A huge protest meeting on their behalf in Beresford Place, the site of the *Helga*-blasted Liberty Hall, which the British had proscribed, had gone ahead anyhow on 10 June, resulting in the first death of a member of the crown forces since 1916, a police inspector killed by a blow from a hurley stick. Both Cathal Brugha and Count Plunkett were arrested as a result. Consequently when the Lewes men landed back in Dublin they received a tumultuous welcome. The cheerful pugnacity of Frank Thornton's account of the triumphant journey home reads very differently from that of his post-Rising departure from Dublin. He says:

The British had issued us with 3rd class tickets. However feeling in a first-class mood, Eamon de Valera decided that we should all travel first class . . . the ordinary passengers [gave us] plenty of moral support. The Captain, concluding that discretion was the better part of valour, decided to leave us there . . . Having won our point we spent our journey . . . with a crowd of British Tommies trying to teach children 'The Soldiers Song'. . . there was a terrifically enthusiastic crowd on the pier at Dunlaoghaire . . . We were escorted to our carriages on the train and when we arrived at Westland Row our real trouble started . . . the crowd nearly tore us asunder. Every man was trying to carry some other man out to the coaches outside. . . . We were carried out to the open brakes outside Westland Row and escorted though the city by a huge crowd of people up to Flemings Hotel in Gardiner Place. Here a royal feast awaited us . . . we were back in Dublin with a determination. The surrender of 1916 was only a breathing space between that and the commencement of war proper for the freedom of the country . . .

The first shot in that campaign was fired on the afternoon of the prisoners' return. At a meeting in Exchequer Hall, Exchequer St, they found a linen scroll prepared for their signatures. It was addressed to the President and Congress of the United States and contained a quotation from Wilson's recent statement to Russia, 'The right of each people to defend itself against external aggression, external influence, etc. . . .' After signature it was immediately taken to the United States by a member of the IRB, Dr Patrick MacCartan. The second shot was the selection of Eamon de Valera to contest a by-election in East Clare caused by the death in action in France of Major William Redmond, brother of the Irish Parliamentary Party leader.

De Valera made such an impact on the voters of East Clare that he was to hold the seat for nearly forty years. His appeal has never adequately been defined. His grasp of the Irish psychology, particularly in the days before TV or widespread education brought more sophistication to the electorate, his study of Machiavelli's doctrines, and his 1916 reputation formed a formidable political arsenal. This was added to, rather than detracted from, by his studied aloofness and his actual self-confidence, his harsh Limerick accent and his striking appearance. Over six feet tall, angular, with staring eyes, he had a prison-pale complexion that he often deliberately accentuated by wearing a black cloak. People voted for him out of a spirit summed up by the true story of his meeting with an old man during a Clare election campaign in the twenties.[12] Seeing the old man at the side of a road, de Valera stopped the car and attempted to engage him in conversation. 'Are you one of them political gentlemen come down for the election?' the old man asked suspiciously. De Valera replied that he supposed one could say that such was the case, whereupon the old man spat on the ground and walked off saying, 'You're wasting your time. We're all for de Valera down here.'

De Valera's victory, on 10 July by 5,010 votes to 2,035, over P. J. Lynch, the Parliamentary Party candidate, was significant for two reasons. Firstly it marked his emergence into a leading role on the national political stage. Secondly, for the first time since the rising, the Volunteers appeared as an open, disciplined force, wearing uniforms, acting as election workers, and, most importantly in a contest in which feelings ran high, maintaining order, at both candidates' meetings, albeit armed only with sticks.

With the return to Ireland of the Lewes men the cast was now complete. To the names that have already flitted across these pages were now added figures like William T. Cosgrave, who had fought alongside Cathal Brugha during 1916 and was also given life imprisonment after the Rising, who won another by-election in August of that year, in Kilkenny, and later went on to become the country's prime minister for ten years, and Piaras Beaslai, journalist and polemicist, who later was Collins' biographer. Curiously enough Collins did not take part in the Clare campaign. It may be that as Beaslai says, the return of the 122 prisoners 'most of whom had to be provided for' created a new work-load which kept him in Dublin. But in view of his intense involvement in other by-election campaigns, one is tempted to regard it as a significant omission. Collins' normal attitude to work was summed up in an observation to Terence MacSwiney: 'It is my experience that people who are very busy are never so busy that they cannot do something extra.'

And certainly, in mid-summer 1917, Collins was 'very busy'. He transferred his offices to 32 Bachelor's Walk and continued to use these premises, relatively unscathed, until the end of the Anglo-Irish war some four years later. His fellow Committee member Diarmuid Lynch said Collins did 90 per cent of the drafting of the revision of the Volunteer Constitution and records that '. . . very few changes were made in the draft as submitted by him.'

These were swirling, reckless days. Friendships were made and enmities formed. After Frongoch Collins' closest friends were the three Corkmen Gearoid O'Sullivan, Diarmuid O'Hegarty, and 'the medieval page', Joe O'Reilly. O'Hegarty, an acknowledged administrator, played a vital part in organising the IRB while Collins was still in Frongoch. He was later to become Secretary to the first native Irish Government, set up at least in part as a result of his efforts.

O'Reilly, from Bantry, County Cork, had known Collins in London and had been with him in Stafford and Frongoch. Collins bumped into him in Dublin about six months after their release and immediately ordered – not offered – him a job as his assistant. O'Reilly's devotion to Collins was legendary. Frank O'Connor wrote that 'no one except O'Reilly himself could do justice to it or to the strange flavour of romance that surrounds it and makes one think of a mediaeval tale. He was courier, clerk, messenger boy, nurse and slave.'

After Lewes Collins added Thomas Ashe and Harry Boland to the friends. Ashe, a brave and steadfast man of strong religious feeling, was the second officer of the Dublin Brigade in seniority, after de Valera, to survive the Rising. He had played a leading role in the Asbourne engagement outside Dublin, where a party of police were ambushed and overwhelmed in the sort of attack which was to form the pattern of the future. Ashe had one of the Volunteers' few successes, and had supported Collins against de Valera in the Lewes debates over McGuinness' candidature. Outside prison he was one of the first to proclaim Collins a man of unusual ability and formed a strong, if short-lived friendship with him. Harry Boland, a tailor by trade, was simply Collins' partner in crime. They were two of a kind, brave, energetic, unscrupulous, jolly buccaneers. Boland had considerable political talent of the 'vote early vote often' variety. As Frank O'Connor observed, when the pair of them got their hands on a list of candidates for an executive or an election panel there was little danger of moderation showing its hideous fangs. Without their partnership the Sinn Fein effort would have collapsed.

However these friendships and others, like that with Liam Tobin, were heavily offset through Collins incurring the wrath of Cathal Brugha. Given the differences in their attitudes to almost everything that mattered Collins would inevitably have had to clash with the formulaic, rule-book approach of the older man. Brugha was a 'static warfare' man. He still thought of fighting in GPO terms. It's doubtful if he ever seriously believed they could win the war. For him, carrying on the fight was the important thing, keeping faith with the men who had raised the standard in other generations. He opposed Collins over ambushing. Their military differences were compounded by Collins' unfortunate tendency to bait people, particularly fish that rose to the fly, and he, O'Sullivan and O'Hegarty used to delight in maddening the older man at occasions such as Gaelic League meetings with nit-picking questions about accounts. In a very literal sense Brugha would one day settle accounts with Collins. A man of 'adamantine simplicity' he had been hit by rifle fire, bomb fragments and bullets from a Colt automatic during his defence of the South Dublin Union in 1916 but refused either to die or to surrender. Instead, the squat little long-lipped man propped himself up against a wall after his colleagues had retreated and punctuated bursts from his 'Peter the Painter' revolver with the chorus from A. M. Sullivan's 'God Save Ireland':

> 'God save Ireland!' said the heroes;
> 'God save Ireland!' said they all.
> 'Whether on the scaffold high
> Or the battlefield we die,
> O, what matter when for Erin dear we fall!'

Hearing him sing his comrades returned and fought beside him until the surrender. He escaped a firing squad because he was thought to be dying anyhow. But the fitness engendered by Volunteer training and earlier years of swimming and boxing saved him. After the Rising, as the Volunteers started to reorganise, a meeting of some fifty representatives from different parts of the country was held in Flemming's Hotel. Brugha turned up on crutches and presided over the gathering which hailed him as a 'modern Cuchullain'.

Cuchullain too propped himself up *in extremis*, his enemies knowing it was safe to approach only when a raven had perched on the dead warrior's shoulder. Brugha, after the failure of 1916, detested the IRB and, despite his fearsome reputation, viewed the Volunteers as a defensive, not an offensive, body, but one which should be used only if the British made an attack on the population such as an attempt to enforce conscription. He didn't think the organisation had the capacity to initiate a successful campaign.

De Valera made common ground with Brugha over the IRB issue, arguing unsuccessfully with prominent IRB men like Harry Boland and Austin Stack that they should leave the Brotherhood. He claimed that his objections were based on the church's teachings regarding secret societies. Later, as the struggle progressed, both men did become supporters of his.

In that first week of release from prison de Valera displayed two of the enduring traits of his career. One was an ability to wrestle with his conscience and win. He had only barely arrived home to be reunited with his family, before, despite his scruples over MacGuinness contesting elections, he was on his way to Clare. Secondly he demonstrated his talent for bringing divergent viewpoints together. He insisted that Eoin MacNeill, the man who had opposed the Rising, should be on his election platforms, thus ensuring support not only from the Volunteers, but from the wide circle of academic and Gaelic League intellectuals who admired the polymath MacNeill. Even Pearse, in his 1916 statement of surrender, had gone out of his way to note that 'both Eoin MacNeill and we have acted in the best interests of Ireland'.

However by the end of that year of aftermath and regrouping de Valera had also demonstrated another vitally important facet of his

character. He would be a unifying force only when he was in control
of whatever movement it was required unifying. In October 1917 the
two largest and most important bodies were Sinn Fein and the Irish
Volunteers. The Volunteers' aim was the Republic contained in the
Proclamation of 1916 but Sinn Fein stood for Griffith's 'restoration of
the King, Lords and Commons.' If the two organisations were not to
go in separate directions a compromise was obviously necessary.

De Valera and Griffith met over coffee in a Grafton St café a week
before the Sinn Fein Convention was due to be held in the Mansion
House on 25 October. De Valera insisted that he should control Sinn
Fein as he had the Volunteers and the IRB behind him. He urged
Griffith not to contest his nomination for the presidency, saying that if
there was a contest he, de Valera, would win in any case. This was
very far from being the case as the ballot for the Executive
subsequently proved. Griffith's supporters headed the list and the
IRB-supported candidates came in at the bottom of the poll, Collins
himself being the last to be elected.

However there was one essential difference between Griffith and de
Valera. Griffith wanted influence, de Valera wanted power. Despite
the fact that Sinn Fein had suddenly mushroomed into a huge
organisation which showed every sign of achieving the results he had
hitherto only dreamed of, when the Convention met Griffith
announced that he was retiring in favour of de Valera, 'a soldier and a
statesman'. Plunkett then withdrew his candidacy also. Griffith
became Vice- President and, secure in office, de Valera stated 'we are
not doctrinaire republicans' and obtained support from both the Sinn
Fein and Volunteer camps for the following policy declaration:

Sinn Fein aims at securing the international recognition of Ireland as an
independent Irish Republic. Having achieved that status, the Irish people
may, by referendum, freely choose their own form of government.

The other important decision taken at this open Ard Fheis, or
convention, was that at the next general election every seat would be
contested and that any Sinn Feiners elected would form themselves
into a new national Assembly, Dail Eireann. When these political
deliberations concluded a secret convention of Volunteers was held on
27 October at the Gaelic Athletic Association's ground at Jones's
Road, Drumcondra. The IRB dominated these proceedings, securing
de Valera's election as President of the Volunteers, Collins' as Director
of Organisation and placing two important IRB men Diarmuid Lynch
and Sean MacGarry, in the key posts of Director of Communication
and General Secretary respectively. Lynch, a member of the IRB's
Supreme Council, had been sentenced to death for his part in 1916, but
his American citizenship saved him. McGarry, also a Supreme
Council man, had reorganised the IRB with Hobson and McCullough.

The Dublin Executive of the reorganised Volunteers was also taken over by the IRB. One Volunteer post which the Brotherhood did not win was that of Chief of Staff; Cathal Brugha was elected on his Cuchullain reputation. Subsequently de Valera again refused to join the Brotherhood, remarking darkly that he suspected Collins was 'organising more than the Volunteers'. De Valera had made a calculation that his best road forward was on the high public ground of his 1916 popularity. The secret routes of the IRB would not advance his ambitions. Nor did it please him to see anyone working to improve those routes. 'Curse all secret societies,' he exclaimed once. In effect that meant 'curse Michael Collins' too.

Electorally, 1917 was a triumphant year for Sinn Fein. Apart from taking seats from the Irish Parliamentary Party by way of by-election, they were actually presented with one when Laurence Ginnell, who had been a stalwart champion of the Frongoch men in their agitations, added to the excitements of Clare and Kilkenny by resigning and later becoming treasurer of Sinn Fein.

But behind the cheering at the hustings it was brought home to Collins that there was a harsher side to the power struggle. It was an aspect of this that first brought him to the public's attention. To counter the growing disaffection in the country the authorities made copious use of the Defence of the Realm Act (DORA) which amongst other provisions allowed for deportations, and trial by court martial for offences such as illegal drilling or making speeches likely to cause disaffection. In August three prominent Sinn Feiners, Thomas Ashe, Austin Stack and Fionan Lynch, were arrested on the latter charge. Collins was friendly with all three, particularly Ashe, with whom he shared public platforms and private IRB activity, and Lynch, who lived with him at 44 Harcourt St.

The Ashe trio followed the increasingly common practice of refusing to recognise the court and received sentences of a year, eighteen months and two years respectively. However, the relatively light sentences masked that fundamentally serious issue which erupts so continuously on to the Anglo–Irish legal landscape, the question of political status. As the trio saw it they had been tried under a particular Act, before a particular type of court, charged with a particular type of offence, yet as soon as the jail gates closed on them they were classed as common criminals.

There were already about forty DORA victims in Mountjoy. It was mutually agreed that they would all go on hunger strike for political status. Austin Stack was elected leader and the strike began on 20 September. As this was a breach of prison discipline the authorities retaliated by taking away the prisoners' beds, bedding and boots.

After five or six days of lying on a cold stone floor the prisoners were subjected to forcible feeding. On 25 September Fionan Lynch saw Ashe being carried off to receive this treatment and called out to him, 'Stick it Tom boy.' Ashe called back, 'I'll stick it, Fin.' It was the last time they spoke to each other. Ashe was carried back, blue in the face and unconscious. He was removed to the Mater Misericordiae Hospital where he died within a few hours.

A combination of spontaneous feeling and IRB organisation made his death the subject of a national demonstration of mourning and protest. Clad in a Volunteer uniform, the shirt of which had been given to him by Collins, the body lay in state while some 30,000 people visited the hospital to pay their respects. Public bodies from all over the country were represented at his gigantic funeral. It was the Volunteers' greatest show of strength since the Rising. For a short time, as they marshalled the crowds, and marched in the funeral procession wearing their Volunteer uniforms, the Dublin Brigade, under the command of Dick McKee, took over the city. McKee, for a period was, after Collins, arguably the most important man in the Volunteers until his death in 1920. A printer by trade, he is spoken of as having natural leadership qualities and, following his release from Frongoch, he played a vital role in reorganising the Volunteers all over the country. Under him the Dublin Brigade became the most formidable in the country.

At the graveside three volleys were fired and then Collins, in Volunteer uniform, stepped forward and made a short and revealing speech in Irish and English. His English words were: 'Nothing additional remains to be said. That volley which we have just heard is the only speech which it is proper to make above the grave of a dead Fenian.'

He was observed weeping bitterly afterwards, but soon dried his tears. For a very great deal that was 'additional' remained to be said. The inquest for instance, on 1 November, censured the Castle authorities, the prison authority, spoke of 'inhuman punishment' and condemned forcible feeding. As it had taken three weeks to reach this verdict during the public hearing of a variety of witnesses, including Lynch and Stack, the impact on public opinion was considerable. The immediate official reaction to Ashe's death was that the Mountjoy prisoners were first awarded a special category status and then, after they had been transferred to Dundalk, giving rise to another hunger strike, released on 17 November.

A more lasting effect was created by the circulation of thousands of copies of 'The Last Poem of Thomas Ashe'. Written in Lewes Jail, its grace notes of sacrifice, sentiment and religion struck a sharp and powerful chord in the unsophisticated Catholic Ireland of 1917:

Let me carry your Cross for Ireland, Lord!
My cares in this world are few,
And few are the tears will fall for me
When I go on my way to you. . .

Let me carry your Cross for Ireland, Lord!
For Ireland weak with tears,
For the aged man of the clouded brow,
And the child of tender years.
For the empty homes of her golden plains,
For the hopes of her future, too!
Let me carry your Cross for Ireland, Lord!
For the cause of Roisin Dhu.

Nevertheless, despite the fact that widespread outcry at the manner
of Ashe's death belied his prophecy that 'few are the tears that will fall
for me', 1918 began with a reversal of Sinn Fein's electoral fortunes.
The party lost two by-elections for a change. One was in South
Armagh on 1 February where the Parliamentary candidate was backed
by the Ancient Order of Hibernians and helped by the fact that the
Unionist candidate stood down in his favour. The other was in
Waterford on 22 March. This vacancy, which was filled by his son,
was caused by the death of the Irish Parliamentary Party leader, John
Redmond, earlier in the month. A broken and disillusioned man, his
biographer truly said of his life that it 'will stand for ever as a symbolic
tragedy of a greatly gifted and disinterested statesman, who trusted
overmuch in the efficacy of Parliamentary agitation.'

Michael Collins did not trust that form of agitation 'overmuch'.
That fateful March he made a contact which, more than any other,
made the form of 'agitation' he did have faith in, physical force, a
reality. At No. 5 Cabra Rd, Dublin, the householder, Michael Foley,
introduced him to the celebrated detective Eamonn Broy. Three and a
half years later in London as the British and Irish delegations met for
negotiations which, in no small measure, his information helped to
bring about, this is how Broy appeared to one observer:

. . . a strongly-built, broad-shouldered, stiff-backed man entered the room. I
found it difficult to believe that this gauche, ill-at-ease, obsequious person
was Ned Broy, the famous 'G' man who had turned traitor and wilily
double-crossed his British masters. But not for long: soon I was convinced
that his hard, cruel, green eyes were indicative of his character.

Some fifty years later after he had retired following a controversial
but highly successful career, during which he became Commissioner
of Police under de Valera, I asked the still superficially deferential
Broy why he had acted as he did and he told me:

I come from Kildare. We were reared in a grimmer tradition than most. We
remembered '98, the Yeomanry and what they did. There was a church once

near where I was born and the Yeos rounded up the women and children, locked them in and set fire to the church. We remembered that, the pitch-capping and the flogging. And we talked about Wolfe Tone and the Fenians. The Fenians were riddled with informers. After 1916 I felt it was time we learned the lesson.

Collins thought so too. Before meeting Broy he and Harry Boland had talked with the old parliamentarian, Tim Healy, who had represented the Mountjoy prisoners at the Ashe inquest, and Healy had told them that their ideas of physical force were 'stark mad', though at the same time he conceded that 'there wasn't the ghost of a chance of getting anything out of the British Parliament.'[13] Broy, however, frankly told Collins that the RIC would 'have to be dealt with. You'll have to shoot.' Collins received this intelligence without demur. Since the Rising, Broy had been passing on information to Sinn Fein, via the O'Hanrachain family who had had a son executed and he thought that therefore he 'could rely on them to be bitter'. But nothing seemed to come of his efforts.

Of the other three Castle detectives who helped Collins significantly, two, Joe Kavanagh and David Neligan, had the same experience as Broy in that their initial offers of help were turned down before Collins got to hear of them. Joe Kavanagh had first tried to help the prisoners after the 1916 Rising, offering to take messages for them, or to do any kindness he could, but he was spurned in the belief that he was simply another 'G' man using different methods to get results. However he was friendly with a Sinn Fein sympathiser who ultimately put him in touch with Collins. This was Thomas Gay, the librarian of the Dublin corporation library in Capel St. Kavanagh was married, with a family, and his actions took unusual courage. Collins realised his worth when Kavanagh, through Gay, sent a message corroborating a warning Broy had given concerning what became known as the 'German Plot' swoop which, as we shall see, was of crucial importance to Sinn Fein.

Kavanagh worked for Collins for about a year before dying, of natural causes. But by then he had recruited another detective to take his place, James MacNamara, whose family were prominent loyalists, and who was regarded by the Castle authorities as one of their most trusted men, being brave, tough and a dead shot. He informed for Collins until almost the end of the war until, one day, he was suddenly sacked without reason. Prudently he did not seek one. As Collins said to him on hearing the news of his dismissal, 'You're lucky. If they had anything on you you'd have been shot outright.'

David Neligan made up for the loss of both Kavanagh and MacNamara. One of the most remarkable figures of the period, he was drawing five pensions when I first met him in the sixties – an old IRA pension, one from the RIC, the Irish Police force, the Irish civil service – and the British Secret Service.[14] He had sent offers of help to Sinn Fein through Patrick Sheehan, who became secretary to de Valera, but Sheehan returned with the dispiriting advice that he should resign from the force as his brother Maurice, a trade union organiser, was advising him to do at the time, May 1920.

Neligan duly resigned, but then Collins, who had not been told of his offer, got to hear what had happened and sent word to him in Tralee, County Kerry, where he lived, asking him to come to see him in Dublin where he asked him to rejoin. Neligan, who hated the Castle, offered to help by joining a flying column instead but Collins replied: 'We have plenty of men for columns, but no one can fill your place in the Castle.' Reluctantly, Neligan agreed, arranging that he be sent bogus threatening letters which he showed to the authorities, as the reason for his change of mind. After a few months working for Collins as a 'G' man he took advantage of the British shortage of knowledgeable personnel to apply to the Secret Service and was accepted, remaining undetected until after the British left Southern Ireland.

Initially Collins kept his contacts so compartmented that they did not know each other. He used to meet Kavanagh and MacNamara in Thomas Gay's house in Clontarf unknown to Tobin who fed the documents and information they provided into his system without knowing where they came from. But, as the war progressed and personnel changed, this proved more difficult to do. Neligan came into contact with Tobin immediately. By then the strain had changed Tobin from the light-hearted young man who once accompanied Collins on a hair-brained mission to Westminster Abbey, to see if they could steal the Stone of Scone, to a figure whom Neligan described wonderingly:

Tall, gaunt, cynical, with tragic eyes, he looked like a man who had seen the inside of hell. He walked without moving his arms and seemed emptied of energy. Yet this man was, after Collins, the Castle's most dangerous enemy.[15]

Collins, in the midst of the horrors, however, struck Neligan as having:

. . . a winning smile, a ready laugh and cheerful manner. He had a trick of turning his head swiftly and then the resolute line of his jaw showed. He was a friendly man with the fortunate manners of putting one at ease.[16]

Broy had a similarly good first impression of Collins. Like Broy himself, Collins 'was athletic. He was light on his feet. You could see he was fit'. This appealed to the non-drinking, non-smoking Broy. Between his views on the RIC and on sport Collins immediately struck Broy as 'the man I was looking for'. Although he claims that he did say to 'Mick', who was dressed in breeches and leggings,

'you'll have to change your clothes.' Collins accepted the advice. 'After
that he dressed like a company director. This had a tremendous effect, a
psychological effect on lads from the country. They felt everything was
all right if a man wore a clean collar and tie!' So, it may be remarked, did
the average member of the British security forces. One reason Collins
got away from so many checkpoints subsequently was simply because
the troops didn't think that terrorists dressed in neat grey suits.

Collins was of course quite clear on the central role of the police in
the British system. What Broy brought to him, however, was a
detailed, inside knowledge not only of how the system worked in its
political aspects but how the men involved were trained, thought and
felt. By 1918 he had been a policeman for seven years. At that time the
DMP oath still included: 'I swear I will not belong to any secret
society, the Society of Freemasons excepted.' The police force was
divided into six divisions, 'A' to 'F'. 'G', the political wing, had three
sections, political, ordinary crime, carriage supervision. 'G' Division
was directed at all national movements. Anyone suspected of being
disloyal to the British connection had an 'S' placed after their name.
There were 'G' men at all boats and railway stations and the
movements of all 'S' people were watched while in the city, and the
relevant RIC barracks were notified as to their movements and whom
they met. Back at home the movements of 'S' persons were similarly
monitored and the details forwarded to Dublin. Each 'G' man had his
own notebook and its contents were transferred at night to 'a very
large book'. In 1915 Broy had been appointed a confidential clerk in
the headquarters of 'G' Division, Gt Brunswick St Police Station,
now Pearse St. This meant that for a large part of each working day he
was alone with the 'very large book'. A copy of every secret report
crossed his desk. By the time he met Collins the flood of reports was
less than it had been because, following the Rising, the authorities had
been cutting down on the normal complement of some forty 'G' men
thinking that the executions had successfully cowed would-be rebels.
As Collins saw immediately, 'The British could replace a detective.
But he couldn't step into the dead man's shoes and his knowledge.'
Also, as Broy pointed out to him, while, after three weeks' training 'a
big change came over the simple country lad', the recruit was still Irish
and susceptible to an appeal to patriotic instincts. In the depot and at
mealtimes these men discussed politics honestly and openly and
showed themselves quite nationalistic on the Home Rule issue and on
topics like the latitude allowed to the Ulstermen to drill and arm.
Later, as the struggle developed, it was this factor properly used, as
much as intimidation, that accounted for the number of 'Good night,
Mick's or 'Good day, Mr Collins's with which DMP men passed
unhindered the most wanted man in Ireland. The myth of Collins,
'The man they couldn't catch', was born in No. 5 Cabra Rd.

Collins being a different man to so many different people, it was probably inevitable that descriptions of him vary greatly. Though he was fair-complexioned and brown-haired, Beaslai notes with puzzlement: 'A great many people who saw him received the impression that his hair was black or very dark.'[17] Beaslai gives a description of a man 'about five foot eleven inches in height . . .', with a face

intensely mobile and expressive, changing rapidly from a scowl of anger to a broad grin of enjoyment, now showing scorn or defiance and now the sunniest good humour. His restless energy showed itself in a series of abrupt jerky movements, and in an explosive brusquerie of manner which often offended the pompous and pretentious, and those sedate persons who disliked hurry. He always dressed well, and was particularly neat and tidy in his habits. His suits were generally of dark grey.

He had a funny patois of his own that he sometimes used with close friends, broadening his West Cork brogue so that 'eggs' came out something like 'ogs'.

Frank O'Connor describes a figure of raw genius, whose behaviour ranged through that of business tycoon, military expert, compassionate charmer, especially where children, the downtrodden, or old people were concerned, to that of a hooligan whose antics could sometimes resemble those of berserkers at play.

A network was set up so that Broy could pass messages to Collins undetected and vice versa. At Kingsbridge Station there was Pat Treacy, a relation of Broy's. In Capel St there was Thomas Gay. Broy could call there quite innocently in the evenings. Just as during the mornings he could drop in for a healthful glass of buttermilk to a little dairy in Parnell Square where the circuit between himself and Collins could be closed unsuspectedly, appropriately enough by passing on messages to Sean Duffy, who travelled all over the city in his job as an electrician.

Dairies were a particular feature of Dublin at the time and one of the most important intelligence and weaponry clearing houses in the city was Phil Sheerin's 'Coolevin Dairies', situated under the loopline bridge in Amiens St, close to the railway station. Couriers from Belfast, generally railway employees, could drop messages there without difficulty and it was also conveniently near the docks for sailors or dockers bringing in arms. Collins had one of his offices in the back rooms. The place was raided several times, but nothing was ever found and Sheerin survived unscathed throughout the war. Messages were also left in Harry Boland's tailoring shop in Middle Abbey St and in 'The Bookshop' in Dawson St where the studious Miss Susan Killeen had taken a job. The Bookshop became a veritable Collins post office as indeed did many another shop around the city. Broy commented, 'I felt my own little office surrounded by police to

Clontarf and all the streets and places shown on this map formed part of Michael Collins's daily round in his life on a bicycle.

CLONTARF
(approx 1½ mls) →

CLONLIFFE ROAD

Croke Park

Mater Misericordiae Hospital

Barry's Hotel

Denmark St

Gaelic League

Parnell Square

Mountjoy St

Rabbiati's

Vaughan's Hotel

Rotunda

Kirwan's Pub

Devlin's Pub

Gresham Hotel

Talbot Street

Amiens St

Coolevin Diaries

Liberty Hall

GPO

Hotel Métropole

Abbey St

Custom House

RIVER LIFFEY

KIRWAN ST

PHOENIX PARK

BRUNSWICK ST

Capel Street

Four Courts

Bank of Ireland

Kilmainham Jail

Clarence Hotel

Crow St

Dame Street

Trinity College

Kidd's Back Pub

Lincoln Pl

Dublin Castle

Wicklow Hotel

Grafton St

Dawson St

Kildare St

Kildare Street Club

Merrion Square

Boland's Bakery

Mansion House

Mount Street

Harcourt Street

Mespil Road

Beggar's Bush Barracks

Crumlin Road

Richmond Barracks

Cullenswood House

RANELAGH

Brendan Road

DUBLIN 1916

0   ½
mile

DONNYBROOK

↓ RATHGAR

protect me was a kind of base for penetrating the British Government. Always they boasted of their informers. Now we could think of our informers.'

Collins was able to destroy Castle rule because the system was far less secure than it appeared. One of his principal agents in the Castle, Thomas Markham, a senior civil servant, prepared a report for him which gave a an insider's account of 'how it really worked':

The British system was based on:
(a) The grasp of human weakness and vanity.
(b) A correct appreciation of the value and use of duplicity and Pecksniffian-ism.
(c) A clear conception of the truth that success in governing depends on well-contrived antagonisms in the economic and social structure of the state.
A new Chief Secretary is powerless to alter the system fundamentally, or even 'materially'. Yet all departures [in policy] went to him. All staff are vetted by the police with exhaustive descriptions of family tree in all its hues and activities.
Belfast staff is very carefully selected as to loyalty. Numerical strength makes it a Staff-in-Waiting prepared to work for the whole Irish service if and when the opportunity arises.
Dealing with police and politics were the pivotal props of the system. . . . The Royal Irish Constabulary, organised in Counties, Districts . . . During his training his vanity, ignorance and intelligence were each subjected to the treatment designed to make the British Government his servant and his God. The RIC had something to do with every phase of governmental activity.
The constable records everything in his diary. What he frightens from the child and coaxes from the cailín. What he hears, sees, infers. The sergeant transfers the constable's report, never abbreviating. It is not his part to select. The policeman moves in a social atmosphere, he writes down everything, gossipy servants, what the RIC pensioner says. A 'someone' whose name is never written down. He's a 'reliable source'. He could be the publican. The rail spy could be the inspector. He frequently is.
The road to the Castle is paved with anonymous letters, deriving from the besetting Irish sin, jealousy. The depth and widespread nature of this treachery would make a good Irishman despair. The local loyalist could have a good post and be merely a disreputable spotter . . . what was said at a Volunteer meeting; where arms were kept; the eavesdropping prison warder; the opening of letters in the post.
Ambiguity and elasticity are the marked features of the system enabling the Administration to sanction in Belfast what it refused in Dublin. The exact standard of Irish morality, public and private, was taken, and rule measured in accordance. Ideology was ignored.[18]

Ideology was certainly ignored in the case of the recruitment of one of the most startling additions to the Collins network, his cousin

Nancy O'Brien. One day Nancy was sent for by Sir James MacMahon and told that in view of the worsening situation it was imperative that the Castle's most secret coded messages be in safe hands and that he was putting her in charge of handling these messages for him! Collins' first reaction on hearing of his cousin's new job was to exclaim, 'In the name of Jasus how did these people ever get an empire?!' His second was to ensure that Nancy's new role was exploited to the full, unmercifully, until the end of the struggle.

Nancy was one of the unsung heroines of the time. She had a good deal of Collins' intelligence and daring, though not his temper. In view of the demands he made on her she could hardly have worked with him if she had. Many of her lunch hours were spent in the GPO lavatory copying out decoded messages which she then smuggled out to him in her bodice. During her working hours she would frequently get disconcerting messages to check on something which might entail a hurried journey up steep stairs through the GPO labyrinth seeking information in some office where she had no right to be. When she complained to him that the climbing and the lack of lunch was wearing her out his reaction was to give her a pinch and say, 'Yerrah, ye can well afford to lose a bit of that.'

Her flat in Glasnevin was used as post office and staging post by everyone from members of the active service units to warders from Mountjoy. Often after the former's visits, she would have to pick up bullets that had dropped on a carpet or had been left lying on a dressing table – evidence every bit as incriminating as the guns she had hidden. Her looks and personality once attracted assistance with heavy luggage from a friendly British officer on a train to Cork, he not realising that the weight of her baggage came from the rifles she was ferrying.

On one occasion Collins subjected her to an inquisition over an important letter he thought she should have received. She denied having seen it; the only message she had recently seen had been some gibberish from an unknown admirer referring to 'Angelus bells and the light glinting in her hair.' He blew up. 'What sort of a Gligeen ejit are you anyway? That's the message I'm looking for. The warders change at six o'clock and our man will be in his room when the light goes on!' Nancy broke down in tears and told him where and how to deal with his messages in future.

That night 'well after midnight' Nancy was awakened by stones thrown at her window. There was Collins, in defiance of the curfew, standing in the front garden beckoning her down. 'Listen,' he told her, 'I'm sorry for what happened. I shouldn't have said it. I'm under the most terrible strain. Here's a little present for you,' he said, placing something on the garden wall. With that, the most wanted man in Europe disappeared into the darkness leaving behind him – a bag of bullseyes.[19]

Another vitally important agent was Lily Merin, a cousin of Beaslai's, who worked in the Castle as a WAAC typist. Collins' first test query to her was did she know a 'ginger-haired typist'?[20] A letter written on stolen Dail Eireann notepaper which gave indications of the existence of a death squad operating from the Castle had fallen into Collins' hands. The only clue as to the identity of one of its members was a sentence in the letter which said, 'X has a ginger-haired typist. Ginger for short.' After learning the officer's name, with subsequent fatal consequences for him, Collins briefed Merin on intelligence details such as the fact that carbon paper can be deciphered.

He then gave her the key to a house in Clonliffe Road used by one of his intelligence officers and she used to visit it regularly over a period of two years, letting herself in, going to a specified room and using the typewriter there to make her reports, which were placed in sealed envelopes and left on the typing table to be picked up by Collins. In all the time she used the house she never saw any of the other occupants, nor did the intelligence officer ever meet her or even know of her existence.

As the war intensified Dame St and Grafton St swarmed with British agents of all sorts, many of them Army Intelligence Officers dressed in mufti. Merin used to walk up and down the streets, ostensibly window-shopping on the arm of either Frank Saurin or Tom Cullen, identifying these agents for the Squad. She also provided Collins with the names and addresses of several officers who lived out of barracks in civilian digs while engaged in under-cover operations. She survived undetected until the ending of hostilities, but was suddenly dismissed without explanation after the Truce came into operation, an indication of how the British were able to breach IRA security once the Volunteers came into the open and of how the Collins network would have been dealt with had hostilities recommenced.

The British were also responsible for placing another woman, Josephine Marchmont, in a position where Collins was able to mastermind an extraordinary scheme which resulted in her being turned into an IRA agent.[21] She was employed at the HQ of the 6th Division in Cork Military Barracks with the rank of a foreman clerk, as confidential secretary to a Captain Webb who was the principal staff officer to the commander of the division, Major General Sir Peter Strickland. Strickland controlled the key areas of Cork, Kerry, Waterford, Wexford, South Tipperary and Kilkenny.

She was trusted implicitly. Her father had been a Head Constable in the RIC. Her husband had been killed in the First World War. But one day an orderly in the canteen, noticing that she appeared to be depressed, asked what was wrong and discovered that she was pining for her children, two little boys, who were in the custody of her mother-in-law, a formidable lady apparently, at Barry, South Wales.

This information was passed on to the alert Adjutant of the Cork No. 1 Brigade of the IRA, Florrie O'Donoghue, who in later life would become a noted commentator on the period, and one of the greatest collectors of its military history. He in turn informed Collins and as a result of this slight piece of intelligence Josephine Marchmont was eventually made an offer she could not refuse. She would be reunited with her children if she agreed to work for the IRA.

Collins oversaw the arrangements whereby O'Donoghue and a prominent Volunteer called Sean Phelan, who was later killed in an attack on a train at Upton, County Cork,[22] organised the kidnapping of the children, with the help of Patrick O'Donoghue of Manchester (no relation) and got them safely to Cork, where they were reunited with their mother and lodged with the families of friendly farmers. Marchmont's subsequent information alerted the IRA to the details of impending troop movements, such as raids and sweeps, and enabled the IRA to plan many a successful ambush, execute spies, and weed out 'stool pigeons' placed in internment camps amongst captured Volunteers. She came under suspicion following the killing of three British Intelligence officers in November 1920, but an act of kindness she had done saved her from exposure.

A soldier whom she had assisted in 'subbing' his pay tipped her off one lunchtime that all female staff were to be searched that evening on their way home, most particularly herself. She promptly returned the copied documents she had intended bringing out with her and escaped detection. Though her activities were curtailed after that she continued to supply information throughout the war, at the end of which she married – Florrie O'Donoghue.

Proposing a vote of sympathy to O'Donoghue on Josephine's death in 1966, which was seconded by the Lord Mayor of Cork, Alderman Sean Casey, TD, Dr Seamus Fitzgerald paid tribute to Josephine's 'significant part in the national struggle' but indicated that even at that stage the nature of the dead woman's contribution was still such a delicate subject that he could 'only leave references to her important activities in this field to those in higher authority'.[23]

In the spring of 1918 the struggle, though still comparatively mild in comparison with what was to come, had taken a turn that brought Collins two brushes with the police. Sinn Fein, both as part of its general muscle-flexing and because of folk memory of famine, became concerned at the war's acceleration of the flow of food out of the country and took a number of steps to reduce it. In the west, cattle were driven off grazing land and the ground was parcelled out for tillage by the local Sinn Fein Clubs. The rents were then passed on to the landlords; at least that was the theory of the thing. The cattle-driving and ground-breaking were occasions of great local excitement, often accompanied by bands and marching Volunteers. The

Volunteers were controlled from Dublin by a General Headquarters Staff (GHQ), which included Cathal Brugha, Chief of Staff, Richard Mulcahy, Deputy Chief of Staff, Collins, in a variety of roles, and Dick McKee. Slightly disturbed by the socialistic whiff of these activities GHQ issued a directive that they were 'neither of a national nor a military character'. However, coupled with the arms raiding which some Volunteers were also engaging in, the drives produced a response of a military nature. It was forbidden to carry arms in Tipperary, Galway or Clare, and Clare was declared a fully-fledged military area on 27 February. Persons wishing to enter or leave the county were issued with passports. The *Clare Champion* was suppressed. Extra troops were drafted in and mail and telegrams were subjected to miltary censorship.

In Dublin, Diarmuid Lynch, the Sinn Fein 'Food Director', ordered that the herd of pigs en route to England be impounded at the North Wall, slaughtered and sold to local butchers. The proceeds were handed over to their owners, but Lynch, an American citizen, was arrested and sentenced to deportation. He wanted to get married before being deported so as to assist his fiancée with her passport application but the authorities refused him permission. However while held in Dundalk Jail he was married in his cell by a priest who had ostensibly paid him a routine visit in the company of his fiancée and some friends.

The jail wedding created a sensation and to compound the publicity his bride accompanied him on the train to Dublin and deportation. The Lynches were met at Amiens St Station by a huge crowd and followed to the Bridewell by a party of friends, including Collins, who coolly entered the jail and spent a long time talking with Lynch, arranging communication routes between Ireland and America. A few days later he was in jail himself. He was arrested outside his Bachelor's Walk office on 3 April by 'G' men. At first he resisted fiercely, to the cheers of a large and sympathetic crowd. But another IRB man, Joe McGrath, turned up and negotiated with the police to such good effect that he and Collins were allowed to walk together over O'Connell Bridge to Brunswick St Station with the 'G' men following behind. From Brunswick St he was brought to Longford, charged at the Assizes with making a speech 'likely to cause disaffection' at Legga, near Granard and remanded to Sligo Jail.

From Sligo he wrote to Hannie on 10 April: '. . . Sad! Sad! Sad! . . . Before me the prospect of a long holiday . . . I'm very anxious to know what Lloyd George has done about Conscription for this country. If he goes for – well he's ended . . .'.

Lloyd George did go for conscription and thereby unleashed forces which meant that from the time of the so-called 'German Plot' arrests on 17 May 1918 until the summer of 1919, Boland and Collins, principally Collins, were the main motor forces in the Irish revolutionary situation. Both men were tough, intelligent, unusually energetic and courageous plotters. Between them, they achieved a great deal. But it was a tragedy for them, and for Ireland, that decisions taken elsewhere meant inevitably that most of their achievement was to lie in the realm of violence. The bloodshed they became involved in was made inevitable by the political warfare that broke out at a committee table they probably knew very little about. This was the Irish Committee of the British Government which, following a decision of the Cabinet to set it up on 11 April, met only four days later on Monday 15 April 1918 to draw up 'as soon as possible' a Home Rule Bill for Ireland. Alas, the speed at which the committee came into being was not to be paralleled by the speed with which it followed its instructions. In the world of politics wherein a week can be a long time, 'as soon as possible' turned out to be a very long time indeed. It wasn't for want of 'clout'; practically all the stars of the British firmament took part in its deliberations from the time of its first meeting, under the chairmanship of Walter Long. On the first day those present included Lord Curzon and General Smuts. The following day Austen Chamberlain joined the Committee and before the Irish tragedy bled itself to a temporary halt figures such as Balfour, Birkenhead, Churchill and Lloyd George would all have worried at the bone. The proceedings were sometimes clouded in such secrecy that no minutes were issued for months at a time.[24] The Committee issue which preoccupied Balfour and Churchill was the problem already outlined, the interaction of Unionist and Tory sentiment.

The dilemma of the Coalition Government, which was, of course, dependent on Unionist support, is perfectly highlighted in the contrasting views of Viscount Grey, the British Foreign Secretary, and Arthur Balfour, one of the Unionists' principal spokesmen. Viscount Grey cabled from Washington:

A real amelioration of American feeling may result from a policy of self-government for Ireland on good lines. I continue to take the line that Unionists have given up Unionism and Home Rulers have come to recognise that the Protestant area of Ulster must have separate treatment and that a fresh start is to be expected.

Some of the feeling of America arises from the belief that the Irish policy of the Government is directed by Carson. An important member of the administration told me the other day what this point of view was. They regard it as unfair that Carson should have been allowed to import arms into Ulster from Germany. Arms which were to have been used against the policy of the British government. They regard it as very unfair that these arms should not have been seized or molested, while arms used by Nationalists are seized. . . . They also point to the fact that Carson has twice been taken into the Cabinet . . . and that the other day the first announcement in the American papers that the Cabinet was considering a new Irish policy contained the statement that Carson had been called into consultation with the Cabinet.[25]

However 'a settlement on good lines' was anathema to the Balfour faction. Balfour submitted a markedly different viewpoint:

I admit that for many reasons, amongst which the British party system is not the least important, the Unionist policy has not succeeded . . . The only really workmanlike alternative to preserving the Union is the excision from it of the south and west of Ireland. . . . I gathered, however, that the Cabinet, while agreeing with the Committee that Ireland as a whole may have Dominion status, if she wants it, are unalterably averse to granting independence from any of its parts . . . had strong exception to the doctrine that Ireland, all Ireland, has a separate national existence . . . as a single, undivided political unit . . . On the one hand, they make it as easy as possible for Ulster to join itself with the rest of Ireland in forming a 'dominion' state. On the other hand, they give it no power whatever to remain what it is, and as I think ought to be, an integral part of the UK.

. . . is it tolerable that we should take by force from our loyal fellow countrymen for no better reason than that they should live in the same island with those who proclaim their disloyalty in every quarter of the world?[26]

On the conscription issue the underlying approach of the Government was summed up in October 1917 when the Cabinet was told that with Europe 'in anguish', Ireland 'had no real grievances', but that 'actual rebellions and seditious acts were being promulgated'.[27] The proceedings of the Irish Committee, as it were the Cabinet's private instrument for the introduction of Home Rule, the Convention, its public evidence of activity, and the bedevilling factor of conscription produced a hopeless thrombosis of policy. What was missing at the Committee table (and, indeed, at the Cabinet table, if one exempts Unionists from Northern Ireland who were mainly concerned with frustrating the Government's plans for Southern Ireland) was any sense of empathy with or real understanding of the position in Ireland. While maintaining the fiction that what was being discussed was an integral part of the United Kingdom, none of the elected representatives present ever seems to have reflected on the irony of the fact that of all the views and arguments put forward, none was prefaced by the simple expression 'my constituents . . .'. In France the British Army was under fierce pressure along a fifty-mile front. In London Lloyd George was under almost equally fierce pressure from Sir Henry Wilson not to allow an estimated 150,000 'recalcitrant Irishmen' to shirk the responsibilities being borne by the two and a half million strong army then engaged in several different theatres of war. Sir Henry won the argument. Despite warnings from President Wilson himself of the possible effects on American public opinion the Cabinet decided to bracket the introduction of the Military Service Act to Ireland with the publication of the Convention's report, hoping that the latter would meet the American difficulty.

In fact it solved nothing. The Convention reported on 5 April 1918, proposing a version of Home Rule whereby Ireland would get a parliament which would have no control over the Army and Navy, or over the postal services, customs and excise until the British Parliament decided it should have them. All matters concerning the Crown, peace and war were fully reserved to the Imperial Parliament and 40 per cent of the seats in the lower house were to be given to Unionists. There was also a Minority Report which proposed to concede a watered-down form of 'Dominion Home Rule' which in effect would have given Ireland less than the autonomy enjoyed by the existing Dominions.

It wasn't much of a signpost along the long and bloody road to Home Rule at the best of times. In the perfervid condition of the country at that moment, to include conscription in the directions meant that it pointed inevitably to disaster. However the Government pushed the Military Service Bill through the House on 16 April. The Irish Parliamentary Party withdrew in protest, never to return. A chapter in the British/Irish relationship of 118 years duration, stretching back to the Act of Union, was now irrevocably closed.

Two days after the withdrawal a huge meeting was convened in Dublin at the Mansion House by the Lord Mayor, Laurence O'Neill. Every strand of Irish Nationalist opinion, including Labour, was represented. The meeting agreed the terms of two statements drawn up by de Valera. The first was an anti-conscription pledge for signature at church doors the following Sunday:

Denying the right of the British Government to enforce compulsory service in this country, we pledge ourselves solemnly to one another to resist conscription by the most effective means at our disposal.

The second, a declaration for immediate publication, affirmed the call to resistance and foreshadowed the form that resistance would take by saying flatly: 'The passage of the Conscription Bill by the British House of Commons must be regarded as a declaration of war on the Irish nation.'

The meeting also appointed a deputation including representatives from Sinn Fein, The Irish Parliamentary Party and Labour to call on the Catholic Bishops, who were meeting at Maynooth Seminary on the same day, to issue a statement on conscription. The Bishops did so in terms somewhat less fire-eating than de Valera's:

We consider that conscription forced in this way upon Ireland is an oppressive and inhuman law which the Irish people have a right to resist by every means that are consonant with the law of God.

However their Lordships' statement had an enormous impact throughout the country. The Mansion House pledge was signed at every Catholic church door in the country. The day after the Mansion House meeting the Irish Parliamentary Party withdrew its candidate in a by-election in County Offaly and the Sinn Fein candidate was returned unopposed. This was a dramatic reversal of the trend in Sinn Fein's electoral fortunes which, only two weeks earlier, had seen yet another Sinn Fein candidate, Sean Milroy, defeated by his Parliamentary Party rival in East Tyrone. The week after the Offaly by-election Labour declared a one-day general strike and the whole country, with the exception of Belfast, closed down on 25 April.

During the conscription turmoil the Volunteers' Executive met in secret to decide its response to the crisis and took a number of decisions that were to have lasting implications for Collins. The British were trying to square the circle of keeping trouble out of the prisons while keeping trouble-makers out of the way by employing what was known as the 'cat and mouse' Act. Prisoners were released only to be pounced on again. A short while after Collins was picked up, Fionan Lynch and Austin Stack, for example, were re-arrested in this way, to finish serving their sentences, even though they had been freed after their hunger strike at the time of Ashe's death.

It was no time for dogma and the Volunteers' GHQ decided that the policy of not recognising the courts was playing into the enemy's hands. Collins was too valuable to be left in prison. He was told to give bail and did so, driving first to Granard where the streets were lined with people to welcome him to freedom. On his return to Dublin he persuaded another young man who was holding out against recognition to give bail also and installed him in his office at Bachelor's Walk. This was Tom Cullen, a captain in the Wicklow Volunteers who, with Thornton and Tobin, completed the intelligence team which broke the Castle's spy system.

In March the Volunteers had decided on a very drastic method of responding to conscription which necessitated a reorganisation of GHQ. Cathal Brugha, who had been Chief of Staff, went to England to link up with figures like Neil Kerr in Liverpool and Sam Maguire in London in drawing up contingency plans for assassinating members of the British Cabinet. So far as GHQ was concerned, if conscription were foisted on an unwilling people it would be tantamount to a massacre of civilians, justifying similar retribution on its authors' heads. Prior to the Executive meeting which confirmed the new Chief of Staff, Dick Mulcahy, another IRB man, Mulcahy and Collins conferred as to which of them should take the post. It was decided that it should go to Mulcahy as he had worked in Dublin for several years

prior to the Rising and knew the city, whereas Collins had only
arrived there in January 1916. However in addition to being Director
of Organisation, Collins also became Adjutant General. Dick McKee
commented on the arrangement, to Collins, 'You'd be too impetuous
for a Chief of Staff.'

Yet it was Collins' caution that saved the emerging nationalist
movement two months later. Lloyd George, realising that strong
measures would be needed to carry conscription through, began by
putting in strong men to execute them. The Irish Executive, or
Government, had been going through a period of changing times
since the Rising. Now it was shuffled once more to weed out any
vestige of weakness or pro-nationalist sentiment. The Lord Lieutenant, Lord Wimborne, was replaced by Field Marshal Lord French with
the new title of 'Lord Lieutenant-General and General Governor of
Ireland'. The Chief Secretary, Henry Duke, was replaced by Edward
Shortt, Sir Bryan Mahon went from the Military Command in favour
of General Sir Frederick Shaw and other changes were made down the
line.

According to Sir Henry Wilson, 'Lloyd George impressed on
Johnny the necessity of putting the onus for first shooting on the
rebels.'[28] Throughout the summer every conceivable use was made
of DORA to further this aim. Apart from banning drilling and the
carrying of arms, manifestations of Irishism such as language classes,
football matches, dancing competions and athletic meetings were also
prohibited. A major crack-down on Sinn Fein began with the
'German Plot' arrests of 17 May. The pretext for these was the capture
of one Joseph Dowling, a member of Casement's ill-fated Irish
Brigade, on an island off Galway on 12 April. The Germans had
landed him from a submarine on their own initiative, hoping that he
would set up links with Sinn Fein. No one on the Sinn Fein Executive
had ever heard of him, though Collins and some of the other GHQ
staff knew of the approach. However on Wednesday 15 May Broy got
a list of prominent Sinn Feiners to Collins warning him that everyone
on the list and many others, were due to be arrested shortly, probably
the following Friday. On that day, from the Castle, Kavanagh
corroborated the rumour; a series of raids was being planned for that
night.

There was a meeting of the Volunteer Executive at 44 Parnell
Square that night, and Collins, who had earlier circulated the arrest
rumours to those on the list, warned everyone present, including de
Valera, not to go home. De Valera vacillated for a time but eventually
did go home and was arrested in Greystones. Most of the Sinn Fein
leadership was also picked up during the night, Arthur Griffith,
Darrell Figgis, Count Plunkett, William Cosgrave, Mrs Tom Clarke
and Countess Markievicz. Markievicz, a member of a famous

Anglo-Irish family the Gore-Booths, who had married a Polish count, had also taken part in the 1916 Rising. Collins with Harry Boland and Eamonn Duggan had called in at Vaughan's Hotel and stayed until after midnight, thus getting to their homes after the raiders had called. Realising what was happening, Collins cycled out to Clontarf to warn the General Secretary of the Volunteers, Sean MacGarry. Finding that the Secretary had already been arrested he decided that lightning would not strike twice and slept in MacGarry's house. He woke up to begin his 'life on the bicycle'. The British Government felt that a good day's work had been done in carrying out the swoops, even though it was agreed that the evidence on which these were carried out, supplied by Admiral Hall, proved German intention rather than action. Looking at the situation caused by the 'German Plot' crack-down, and the subsequent sorry showing of British Intelligence during the ensuing war, one can understand why a leading British civil servant, Sir Mark Beresford Sturgis, confided to his diary after listening to Hall on another occasion: '. . . it would be more alarming if the pink paper prophecies had produced a winner or two in the past of which I cannot remember a single instance.'[29]

In the event Ireland saw neither Home Rule nor conscription. Throughout the summer and autumn of 1918 the Government hesitated over introducing either in the general climate of unrest. The signing of the Armistice removed conscription from the Irish agenda, though not the effect that its threat produced, but the Home Rule issue remained as pressing as ever. On Armistice Day itself the Cabinet received a telegram from the Washington Embassy containing a serious warning from Cardinal O'Connell, the 'dominant figure among Irish Americans'.[30] The Cardinal said that 'all Irish-Americans were in a state of ebullition which would soon break out into hostile utterances against England unless some definite action were taken about Home Rule.' A principle of self-determination had been recognised by all. England could not refuse it to Ireland, the Cardinal said. By way of underlining the Cardinal's warning, the 'state of ebullition' in Dublin took the form not of 'hostile utterances', but of real hostilities towards the Armistice celebrations which were attacked by the Volunteers acting under orders from GHQ. Collins subsequently described the outcome to Stack in rather callous terms:

As a result of the various encounters there were 125 cases of wounded soldiers treated at the Dublin hospitals that night. . . . Before morning, 3 soldiers and 1 officer had ceased to need any attention and one other died the following day. A policeman too was in a very precarious condition up to a few days ago when I ceased to take any further interest in him. He was unlikely to recover. We had a staff meeting and I wasn't in any of it . . .[31]

The German Plot swoops and the outcry over conscription created a situation which Collins and Boland manipulated to the full. They went over with a fine toothcomb the list of candidates chosen to represent Sinn Fein at the General Election on 14 December which followed the Armistice to ensure that only those who favoured a 'forward policy' were selected. This short-term success would plague Collins in the long term, because the voice of moderation was muted in the National Assembly when he desperately needed it in support for the Anglo-Irish Treaty. But that day lay ahead. For the moment the country was so grateful for the defeat of conscription that it obliterated the Irish Parliamentary Party and gave Sinn Fein a majority in all but four counties, Antrim, Derry, Armagh and Down. Sinn Fein won 73 out of 105 seats. The Irish Parliamentary Party was reduced from 80 to 6 seats. The Unionists, whose voices sounded so loud at the Council Chambers of the mighty in London, made a fainter sound in Ireland, securing 315,394 votes out of a total of 1,526,910. But this was not the customary four-fifths majority for Home Rule. In this election, the electorate had cast their votes for a party that said it stood for an All-Ireland Irish Republic, sovereign and independent of England. Collins, for example, told the electors of South Cork:

You are requested by your votes to assert before the nations of the world that Ireland's claim is to the status of an independent nation, and that we shall be satisfied with nothing less than our full claim – that, in fact, any scheme of government which does not confer upon the people of Ireland the supreme, absolute and final control of all this country, of all the affairs of the country, external as well as internal, is a mockery and will not be accepted.[32]

Interestingly, Collins' address never mentioned the word 'Republic'. He was unequivocal in stating that if elected he would not attend the British Parliament, believing attendance there would be 'wrong in principle, in practice a ghastly failure' which had 'wellnigh landed us in disaster until sixteen of the noblest men that this or any generation in Ireland produced, by their calm and unflinching self-sacrifice redeemed the national situation.' He concluded his appeal with the ringing declaration that he accepted Wolfe Tone's dictum:

To subvert the tyranny of our execrable Government, to break the connection of England – the unfailing source of all our ills – and to assert the independence of my native country . . . these were my objects.[33]

And Collins wound up by saying, 'Today these are my objects.' Unquestionably, therefore, the people of South Cork and of Ireland got a clear indication of the intentions of Collins, the fiery patriot. But Collins was pragmatist as well as patriot. Though he broke out his flag on the highest possible campsite nearest to the stars, he was prepared, when it came to it, to camp somewhere lower down the mountain once he was assured of a secure base from which to proceed further at a later date. However, to those who thought like Cathal Brugha the

Republic proclaimed by 'sixteen of the noblest men' had to be fought for, literally to the death.

Where the British Cabinet was concerned, the eruption of a crowd of ravening Sinn Fein Republicans on to the Imperial political landscape immediately raised the issue of whether or not to permit the opening of the Parliament which the Sinn Feiners proposed to set up for themselves in Dublin, not whether or not to grapple finally with the Irish problem. In fact, they long-fingered all of these. One of Chief Secretary Shortt's most trusted Irish appointees was the Right Hon. Justice O'Connor[34], to whom he wrote in the New Year: 'I am afraid that while the Peace Conference is sitting it will be impossible to get Lloyd George to appreciate the situation . . .' And he gave a fairly broad hint that his own ability to do anything in the Prime Minister's absence was severely limited. 'Obstruction, jealousy, stabs in the back all contribute to make the life of a Chief Secretary a rather heart-rending business.'

Shortt proved an accurate prophet. The opening of the post-war Great Power Peace Conference in Paris effectively took Lloyd George's mind off the Irish issue for several crucial months in 1919, during which the initiative passed from the British Cabinet table into the hands of the Irish revolutionaries and, in particular, Michael Collins.

4

The Twelve Apostles

'I am the Lord of the dance, said he,
And I'll lead you all, wherever you may be.'

From hymn by Sydney Carter

Michael Collins, in 1918–19, was responsible for a number of initiatives: the setting-up of two underground newspapers, the building of an intelligence network, an arms smuggling route, the organisation of a national loan, the creation of his elite hit unit, the 'Squad', a bomb-making factory, and a variety of other schemes.

Merely to get around to all his offices each day on a bicycle would have taxed the strength of most men, but when Collins got to his offices, or to Vaughan's Hotel at night, he would in a normal day deal with anything up to a hundred letters to and from all parts of the country. It was not unusual for a colleague to get as many as five or six communications from him in the course of one day. The people and projects he dealt with included everything from smuggling in coke for the bomb factories, to shooting spies. From organising a by-election campaign, to getting a few rounds of ammunition or a rifle or two for a hard-pressed country unit. From ensuring that loan receipts were sent promptly to making intelligence contacts with people whose identities will probably never be known.

Kevin O'Shiel, his friend and legal advisor, has left an unpublished account[1] of an incident which occurred after hostilities had ceased which sheds light on how the underworld war was fought. Collins and O'Shiel had been involved in meetings with Lloyd George and Churchill and Collins had sent O'Shiel ahead to Euston with instructions to (a) procure a bottle of Jameson's whiskey and (b) ensure that they had a compartment to themselves. O'Shiel was guarding the door of the compartment when a 'spruce, well-groomed fellow' approached him and told him to inform Collins that 'Major Shore (or Shaw) of the Auxiliaries was next door'. Despite O'Shiel's protestations that Collins was seeing no one the Major replied 'with great cocksureness', 'Oh, he'll see me alright.'

When O'Shiel told Collins someone wanted to see him 'he was

mad' – at first. For when he heard the name he picked up the bottle and said, 'Yes, we'll certainly see him.' There followed 'one of the most interesting nights' O'Shiel ever spent. The major, who had also provided himself with a bottle of whiskey, turned out to have been one of Collins' principal adversaries. The anecdote which lodged with O'Shiel most strongly concerned one of the several informants which it emerged both had employed as double agents. Neither had trusted the man in question. 'That fellow was your man always', said Collins. 'No,' said the major, 'he was yours. He tried to lead us into an ambush one night.' The spy had told the officer that if he raided the home of the woman Austin Stack later married, in Lansdowne Terrace, he would get 'the whole Sinn Fein Cabinet'.

Collins asked the major for the date, and after consulting his diary told him 'after a chuckle' that had he come that night he would have 'collared the whole Cabinet and IRA chiefs as well.' 'My God,' exclaimed the major, 'What a miss! I might be Sir Shaw [or Shore] now!' Collins told the major that he always trusted the judgement of the man who had warned him against the double agent, but that after hearing his story he now trusted him a hundredfold. Later he told O'Shiel who it was that had given the warning – Liam Tobin.

That true story helps to explain why Collins used to mark certain files 'DBI', meaning Don't Butt In. Woe betide an associate who disobeyed the instruction, but he himself cheerfully crashed through everyone else's sphere of operation. Still 'running the show', as in his boyhood days at Woodfield.

He had little foibles like hating the use of pencils or rubber stamps, but he never forgot an appointment, or a promise. He kept a mass of detail in his head, from the time friendly warders came on duty, when a co-operative postman made his rounds, exactly when and where a parcel might be collected. He made up his mind instantly and an order, once given, was rarely changed. In the midst of the vortex he forced himself to study politics, literature, other countries' methods of economic development, anything which might benefit the country once he reached his objectives. Particularly in his last few years of life he continually worked to develop a philosophy for himself. And, throughout all this, he made it a point to visit friends or helpers who had been wounded or fallen ill. As the pressure intensified he tried to train himself to do without sleep and made a point of giving up smoking and drinking. 'I'll be a slave to nothing,' he boasted.

Collins' demoniacal energy can be said to explain how he managed to bring his extraordinary gifts of concentration and intelligence to bear when he got to his various work centres, while the daily brushes with death which he experienced en route probably go a long way to explain also the dreadful bouts of horseplay he engaged in like a pressure cooker giving off steam. British propaganda, which continually portrayed him as a hulking thug, probably played a part in saving his life. The young tommy who turned to his mate on Newcomen Bridge, after Collins had greeted him cheerily, and said, "'E's a decent sort, wished me good dye 'e did', wasn't programmed for the broad smile and friendly word that got 'the decent sort' through without being searched. Nor was the officer at a road block who was engaged in sympathetic conversation by a fine-looking young man who got out of his car to keep him company while the other passengers were being searched. Had he had the charming conversationalist frisked he would have found documents on him which would have hung Collins. On another night he stepped out of a car which also contained Neligan, MacNamara and Broy, with whom he had been conferring at Thomas Gay's house, and while they showed their detective passes, commiserated with the officer in charge on 'these dreadful ambushes'. Broy called to him, 'Step in, Sergeant' and 'Sergeant' Collins got back in the car bearing documents, passed over to him earlier that evening, which would have accounted not only for him, but for the other three as well.

Joseph Plunkett's extraordinary legacy of the idea that if he didn't think of himself as being on the run, then he wasn't a fugitive, worked for him time and again. Michael Collins moved through his various worlds – including making trips to England – like a businessman, not a spy. The only indication of espionage activities I ever came across in his papers was a set of tiny envelopes which he used for sending messages. At the time of writing few people are left who knew him well, but one of these, Pat Murphy, like Collins a West Cork man, but one of Ascendancy background, singles out the 'no-fugitive' quality as being one of his outstanding characteristics. The other was his extraordinary quality of making allies of people within seconds of meeting them.

Murphy was at the time working for *Freeman's Journal* as a night reporter. He met 'a big fellow with a West Cork accent' in a doorway near the *Freeman's Journal* where both were sheltering because a tender full of Tans was prowling the street. Murphy invited 'Carroll', as he called himself, back to the office for Bovril. But the *Freeman* was raided almost immediately and Murphy was given the job of showing a search party round the office in pursuit of 'a big fellow of about thirty, called Carroll, who is known to be on the premises'. No one was found and Murphy returned to his Bovril thinking that his visitor had managed to leave the building.

As he poured out the boiling water he heard a noise behind him and turned to find 'the big fellow' stepping onto his desk from a skylight. 'Thanks for the Bovril,' he said. 'If I ever make any money I'll leave you some shares in Bovril.' Murphy had grown to know 'Carroll' quite well over the next few weeks before he discovered who he was.[2]

One of Collins' and McKee's ploys was to hold 'Irish classes' around the country. The effect of these camps was to bring young country lads into touch with the leadership from Dublin and to give Collins and the others an estimate of who the good men were. At the Coosan camp near Athlone, for instance, Terence MacSwiney distinguished himself and in his memoirs Mulcahy recalled Austin Stack did not.[3] At Glandore in County Cork, Liam Deasy was impressed by the 'incredible example' of Dick McKee, who in six days turned 'raw amateurs into trained guerrillas'. These 'amateurs' had to be trained to make the leap of the imagination necessary to conceive of actually taking on the RIC and, behind this force, the British Army, in a heavily garrisoned area, poorly armed themselves, and with the tradition of viewing both the police and the army as not only omnipresent, but omnipotent.

Volunteers were unemployed and depended for food, shelter and clothing on the local population, and it was remarkable how this support held up right through the war, despite the pressures of incessant raids by the military and the activities of the inevitable informers. It was this spirit more than the IRA's armaments, or even the tactics of guerrilla warfare, which brought the IRA whatever success it achieved. Neither Collins nor the Volunteers would have survived without the country-wide network of women supporters who acted as intelligence agents, couriers, secretaries, providers of meals, shelter and nursing services. One must take note of the Trojan work done by women who never talked and were known only to a relatively small circle. Peig, the family maid at Woodfield, was a courier, adviser and nurse, who saved many a life, carried many a message, helped to plan many an ambush even. It was only after her death, while still in the service of the Collins family, when from all over the country famous figures from the fight for independence came to her funeral, that her story came to be more generally told.[4]

Sinead Mason, Collins' intelligence secretary, worked a twelve-hour day for him throughout most of the war and holds secrets for him no one can even guess at (she was still alive as this book was being written). For a time it was thought by friends such as the O'Connors and Nancy O'Brien that he might marry Sinead,[5] who was described by Sister Margaret Mary as being 'a merry, pretty girl, and very sensible'. Sinead Mason lived near the O'Connors with her aunt at 23 Brendan Rd. Collins sent her down to Woodfield for a holiday when the strain of war began to tell on her. A celebrated story of the period had Tom Cullen waltzing around the office with Sinead one day when suddenly Collins' footstep was heard outside. Sinead was promptly hurled into a chair and Cullen buried himself in a newspaper. Wasting time was a mortal sin in Collins' eyes. But wasting it with Sinead Mason . . .

Another major concern of Collins was the importance of jail and jail-breaking to the Republican tradition. The most sensational prison escape was that of de Valera from Lincoln Jail on 3 February 1919, which was to have important consequences for the course of Irish history, as we shall see later. But a number of other break-outs, from Mountjoy, Strangeways, Usk (in Wales) and Cork, had a significant bearing on developments also.

Collins organised the escape of Robert Barton from Mountjoy Jail, Dublin on 16 March 1919. He smuggled him in a file with which to saw through the bars of his ground-floor cell and arranged for a party of volunteers to throw a rope ladder over the twenty-foot prison wall and then catch him in a blanket when he jumped from the top. Barton was then brought to safety to the home of Collins' friend, Batt O'Connor.

Barton, a County Wicklow landowner, was a cousin of Erskine Childers. He had distinguished himself in Collins' eyes by his kindness to prisoners and their relatives in the aftermath of 1916, while he was an officer in the British Army. Later, when the Dail set up a land-bank, Barton became its Director[6], working closely with Collins whom he subsequently accompanied to Downing Street to negotiate the Anglo-Irish Treaty. When Batt O'Connor exulted over the escape, Collins replied: 'That's only the beginning. We're going to get Beaslai and Fleming out next.'

Beaslai, a Gaelic scholar, poet and playwright, was useful, both as a public speaker and as editor of *An tOglach*. Fleming was in a different category, a hero of jail resistance in the O'Donovan Rossa mould. Collins wanted him out, both for his publicity value and as a token of recognition for the struggle he had put up in jail. He had been sent to Maryborough Jail (now Portlaoise Jail) for five years by a court martial on a trumped-up charge on 9 March 1917.[7] He was christened 'Samson' because it took so many warders to put the prison uniform on him each day.[8] Eventually he was given political status and transferred to Mountjoy, having somehow managed, not only to break up his cell, but also systematically to destroy the 'muffs', a type of straitjacket used for insane prisoners, with which he was habitually spancelled by teams of warders, who also used iron manacles and leather belts to truss him up so tightly that his stomach could not accept food. Once he literally burned the straitjacket off his body by first using the manacles to smash the thick glass on his gas jet and then tearing off the pieces of the 'muff' as they burned.

For Beaslai's escape a rope ladder was again favoured, and, this time, eighteen other prisoners followed Beaslai and Fleming over the top, while on the ground below, Paddy Daly, later Commander of Collins' elite 'Squad', called out the names of the men who were to escape and five other prisoners with their hands in their pockets clutching what appeared to be revolvers kept the warders at bay. The 'revolvers' were, in fact, spoons, which added hugely to the public's enjoyment of the escapade when the news broke.

Collins himself broke into a fit of laughter when O'Reilly, whom he had stationed outside the jail with three bicycles, a measure of the total he expected to escape, rushed into the Wicklow Hotel to tell him: 'The whole jail is out.' Later that evening, as he worked at Cullenswood House, he was seen to throw down his pen several times to chuckle over the escape.[8]

Beaslai would give him further cause for amusement the following October when, having been picked up again in May, he made another escape, this time from Strangeways Prison in Manchester. Austin Stack was one of those who made up the party of six escapees on this occasion.

Stack and some of his companions had been transferred to Strangeways following another jail drama, the great riot in Crumlin Road Jail the previous Christmas. This almost touched off a sectarian riot outside the jail in Belfast as 'Orange' mobs gathered during the Republicans' defiance which lasted for the best part of two weeks. It began on 22 December 1918, when Stack ordered that a Volunteer, John Doran, who had just been tried, be taken by his colleagues into the Republicans' wing, and not the criminal section where the authorities wanted to place him. It continued until it was unofficially agreed that Doran would be considered 'political' after sentence. Stack had planned the protest with care, and prior to the seizing of Doran the prisoners had laid in food and were able to resist efforts to break them such as denying them provisions and shutting off the gas. The only breaking which occurred was of prison property.

The Strangeways breakout on 25 October 1919 was a particularly audacious affair. Collins himself crossed over to talk to Stack about the arrangements beforehand, using an assumed name. Prominent GHQ personnel like Rory O'Connor and Peadar Clancy also took part in the final breakout which necessitated having volunteers from Liverpool and Manchester holding up the traffic while six prisoners climbed down a ladder propped up against the outside of the prison wall.

Collins was also behind the escape of Denis MacNeilis from Cork Jail the previous year, on Armistice Day, 11 November 1918. MacNeilis was one of the first Volunteers to take a shot at a policeman and was in jail for wounding an RIC man, an activity of which Collins approved mightily.[10] However, he was correspondingly aghast at the unexpected escape of four 'German Plot' detainees from Usk on 21 January 1919. He feared, needlessly as it turned out, that the escape would interfere with a far greater coup he was planning, freeing de Valera.

In jail, de Valera had succeeded in getting another prisoner, Sean Milroy, to draw a postcard showing a drunken man with a huge key outside his hall door saying, 'I can't get in'. On the other side of the card a year later the same man was shown, in jail, looking through a carefully drawn keyhole saying 'I can't get out'. To avoid suspicion the card was sent out in the name of a third prisoner, Sean MacGarry. Both key and keyhole were replicas of the actual lock and master key. De Valera had got the wax impression of the key for Milroy by borrowing the chaplain's master key from the sacristy while the priest was saying Mass. De Valera, who was serving the Mass, had earlier melted down the stumps of altar candles, and he warmed the wax thus obtained with the heat of his body and took impressions of the key. In Dublin a key was fashioned from Milroy's drawing by Gerry Boland, Harry's brother, and smuggled back into the jail in a cake. The first key didn't work, but a second key and cake later, on the evening of 3 February, de Valera, MacGarry and Milroy were able to unlock every gate they came to without difficulty until they arrived at the outer wall of the prison, where they encountered disaster.

Collins had brought a duplicate key with him. When he fitted it in the outside of the door it broke in the lock. So near and yet so far. De Valera and the others were now on one side of the door; Collins and Boland, who had had to cut through the barbed wire of an outer, perimeter fence to get to the last obstacle, were on the other. Beaslai gives an interesting account of what happened next:

Boland, in describing the scene to me, dwelt on the feeling of utter despair which seized on him at that juncture. Collins said, in a heart-broken tone, 'I've broken a key in the lock, Dev.' De Valera uttered an ejaculation and tried to thrust his own key into the lock from the other side. By an extraordinary piece of luck, he succeeded in pushing out the broken key with his own and opening the gate.[11]

And so the prisoners were freed, completing their escape by Boland wrapping his fur coat around the gangling de Valera, putting his arm around him, as though they were a courting couple, and passing several genuinely courting British soldiers and their girlfriends from a nearby military hospital with cheery good wishes. Fortunately for the escapees, collective passion appears to have been such as to render the couples oblivious to the fact that the burly Boland, the supposed 'woman' had a remarkably deep voice. Curiously, in his official biography, compiled at a time when, of course, both Collins and Boland were long dead, de Valera plays up the role of Boland and Brugha in organising it, and says it was Boland who broke the key in the lock.[12] He does not refer at all to a far more important detail – the controversy over his decision to go to America immediately after his escape.

Leaving de Valera hidden in Manchester, MacGarry and Milroy in Liverpool, Collins went to London, spent a day there meeting contacts and, after thirty-six hours without food, returned to Liverpool, meaning to spend the night with Neil Kerr. Finding there was a boat leaving for Dublin, he immediately forgot about food and sleep and set out for Dublin where he reported to GHQ on de Valera's intentions. Beaslai describes the reaction:

The statement was received by all of us with dismay. We felt that de Valera's departure would be a fatal mistake, that the country would misunderstand his motives and regard it as a selfish, or even cowardly, desertion. When this view was expressed, Collins replied, 'I told him so, but you know what it is to try to argue with Dev. He says he had thought it all out in prison and that he feels that the one place where he can be useful to Ireland is in America.' The meeting took the view that the place for an Irish leader was in Ireland wherein the strength of the fight put up would determine the support in America, and it was decided to send Brugha to England to urge de Valera either not to go at all or, failing that, to show himself first in Ireland so that the publicity value of his escape should not be dissipated. [13]

Beaslai says, 'Brugha accordingly went to England and succeeded in persuading de Valera not to go straight to America, but first to return to Ireland.'

De Valera's version of the visit is that Brugha 'stayed from Friday, 7 February until the following Sunday, bringing him up-to-date with the progress made to establish an Irish legislature and conditions in Ireland.' De Valera would have us believe that it was subsequent to Brugha's visit and his weighing up of the chances of getting a hearing at the Peace Conference in Paris that he began to think that the place in which he could best work for Ireland was the USA where he could bring pressure to bear on President Wilson. [14] In any event his American decision shows how his priorities changed since he wrote feelingly to Sinead from jail telling her that he was memorising Merriman's lengthy erotic love poem, 'The Midnight Court', in Irish, so that they could read it together:

I am getting the 'Cuirt an Meadón Oidce' all off by heart. . . . If you read it I know you would like it. It is the nicest poem I have met in Irish. One of the principal pleasures I have in doing Irish poetry is to be able to read it with you when we are together. [15]

Even a few months before he was sprung from Lincoln, de Valera was protesting how much he wanted to be with his wife and children:

I cannot tell you how I feel being unable to be at your side just now. I am ever thinking of you . . . one of my resolutions . . . was that I would strive to be more with you and the children than in the past, but these matters are in God's hands. [16]

He was certainly more lyrical in prose style than Collins, but less direct in either style or action. In fact he left the resolution of the question of how he spent his freedom on release from Lincoln Jail not 'in God's hands', but in those of Michael Collins, who was charged with getting him to America.

Padraig O'Keefe, a particularly abrasive Corkonian[17], also told a story about de Valera's American trip which conflicts with the Authorised Version. De Valera pulled him aside one day in the Sinn Fein offices, shortly before he departed and, according to O'Keefe, said to him, 'Paddy, did you hear they're sending me to America.'

'Bejasus they are not', replied O'Keefe. 'It's your own [sanguinary] idea to get over there out of the trouble.'

Collins arranged for de Valera to be brought back to Dublin aboard the *Cambria* from Liverpool on 20 February and found him a hiding place in the Gate Lodge of the Archbishop of Dublin's house in Drumcondra, where he occupied himself for much of March drafting a statement for the Peace Conference in Paris. Collins, meanwhile, busied himself by arranging a public welcome for him at the end of the month, embroiling himself in general controversy as a result. An announcement was published that Sinn Fein were organising a reception for de Valera's return. It was proposed that he would be met by the Lord Mayor and presented with the keys of the city at his springboard to fame – the bridge at Mount Street which had been defended by Michael Malone in 1916. The keys to the city were an honour normally reserved for royalty. De Valera liked the idea and prepared a suitably fiery speech.[18]

O'Keefe also said that during this period Collins had turned over his own office to de Valera. Not knowing this callers continued to come asking for the 'Big Fella'. De Valera flounced out angrily one afternoon asking, 'What's all this about a Big Fella?' That evening there was a Sinn Fein meeting at which a chair was left vacant for de Valera as Chairman. When Collins asked him to take it he replied, 'Let the Big Fella take the Chair'.

De Valera's fiery speech was never delivered and this brought into the open the difference between those in Sinn Fein who, like Collins, espoused a 'forward' policy, and those who, like Darrell Figgis, were in favour purely of passive resistance and the efficacy of moral force. At the previous Sinn Fein Convention in October, it had been decided that so many of the Executive were in prison that an election should be held in which the candidature would be confined to persons at liberty, and to hold another election if and when the prisoners were released. The October decision resulted in the selection of an executive which was too pacifist for Collins' liking, 'moderates' generally receiving more votes than Volunteers. Ironically, it was Cathal Brugha's poor showing which aroused Collins' greatest wrath:

Cathal Brugha is a white man. There he is half crippled with English bullets, away from the meeting because he is doing work that they would never dare to think of, and they vote for Mr X and Mrs Y and leave Cathal near the bottom of the list. [Brugha was absent in England making arrangements to assassinate members of the British Cabinet if conscription was introduced.][19]

De Valera's escape, and the publicity bombshell it set off, interacted with the effects of the great influenza epidemic which swept through jails, as it did through the rest of Europe at the time. One of those whose life it claimed was a prominent Sinn Feiner, Pierce MacCan, from Tipperary, who came of a good family and was liked by everyone who knew him. His death caused great ill-feeling in Ireland. The prison doctor at Gloucester Jail urged that the entire prison be evacuated and the authorities reacted with unwonted measures of alacrity and clemency to his suggestion. Another factor in the decision may have been the fact that amongst those who contracted the illness, but recovered, was Arthur Griffith. At all events, the prisoners were returned to Ireland and Griffith presided over the meeting called to discuss the Sinn Fein reception issue. Darrell Figgis led the charge by demanding the minutes of the Executive which decided to honour de Valera. Figgis describes what happened next.

Michael Collins rose. Characteristically, he swept aside all pretences, and said that the announcement had been written by him, and that the decision to make it had been made not by Sinn Fein, though declared in its name, but by the 'proper body, the Irish Volunteers'. He spoke with much more vehemence and emphasis, saying that the sooner fighting was forced and a general state of disorder created through the country (his words in this connection are too well printed in my memory ever to be forgotten) the better it would be for the country. Ireland was likely to get more out of the state of general disorder than from a continuance of the situation as it then stood. The proper people to make decisions of that kind were ready to face the British military, and were resolved to force the issue and they were not to be deterred by weaklings and cowards. For himself, he accepted full responsibility for the announcement and he told the meeting with forceful candour that he held them in no opinion at all, that, in fact, they were only summoned to confirm what the proper people had decided. He had always a truculent manner, but in such situations he was certainly candour itself. As I looked on him as he spoke, for all the hostility between us, I found something refreshing and admirable in his contempt for us all. His brow was gathered in a thunderous frown, and his chin thrust forward, while he emphasised his points on the back of a chair with heavy strokes of his hand. He was a great foeman when he fought thus – a worthier foeman than when he manipulated organisations. But, by his contempt of his audience, he had touched the combative in Griffith.[20]

Griffith declared himself strongly opposed to the reception pro-posal, but said that he would accept the decision of the meeting and of 'no other body'.[21] The meeting adjourned while Griffith conferred with de Valera and, ultimately, a letter was published from de Valera in which he said:

I think you must all agree with me that the present occasion is scarcely one on which we would be justified in risking the lives of citizens. I am certain it would not . . . We who have waited know how to wait. Many a heavy fish is caught even with a fine line if the angler is patient.

Michael Collins was no patient angler. He wrote to Austin Stack:

. . . it is bad and very bad. The chief actor was very firm on the withdrawal, as indeed was Cathal. I used my influence the other way, and was in a practical minority of one. It may be that all arguments were sound, but it seems to me that they have put up a challenge which strikes at the fundamentals of our policy and our attitude.[22]

In a nutshell, Collins was willing to go to war, but as Griffith, de Valera and Figgis correctly divined, the public was not, and it would take several more months of repression and British policy blundering before the shooting of detectives and officials could be countenanced. Ironically, one of Collins' victims would be a brother of the doctor who had got the prisoners evacuated from Gloucester Jail – the Examining Magistrate, Alan Bell.

The Mount Street reception having been cancelled, a meeting of the first Dail was held on 10 April 1919 to enunciate Sinn Fein policy. Some of the Dail's principal architects were absent, organising the Lincoln Jail escape when 'the first Parliament of the Republic of Ireland' was set up in Dublin in the Lord Mayor's official residence, the Mansion House.[23] Presided over by Cathal Brugha, it met in an atmosphere of great dignity and make-believe. The roll call of members deemed to have been elected to the parliament, or 'First Dail', as it is more generally known, included the Unionists who had been returned to Westminster in the 'Khaki' election the previous December, figures like Edward Carson, Colonel Sir J. Craig and E. M. Archdale. These were declared to be 'as lathair' (absent), a not unreasonable relationship for them to have with a Sinn Fein assembly, one would have thought. Nor would one have been surprised at the lack of response from Irish Parliamentary figures such as Captain W. Redmond or Joseph Devlin. Of the Sinn Fein representation, some forty were either 'ar dibirt at gallaib' (deported by the foreigner) or 'fe glas ag gallaib' (jailed). In fact, of the 104 names called, only 28 were 'i lathair' (present). Nevertheless this quorum proceeded determinedly with the business of the First Day.

Some high-minded declarations were promulgated: A Message to the Free Nations of the World, a Declaration of Independence, and a Democratic Programme. Fraught and swirling words were uttered in French, Irish and English. The Declaration of Independence, for instance, contained the following:

We the elected representatives of the ancient Irish people in the National Parliament assembled do, in the name of the Irish nation, ratify the establishment of the Irish Republic and pledge ourselves and our people to make this Declaration effective by every means at our command.

We ordain that the elected representatives of the Irish people alone have power to make laws binding on the people of Ireland, and that the Irish Parliament is the only Parliament to which that people will give its allegiance.

We solemnly declare foreign government in Ireland to be an invasion of our national right which we will never tolerate, and we demand the evacuation of our country by the English Garrison.

The foregoing was, of course, no more and no less than a declaration of war, but lest there be any doubt remaining abroad as to what the insurgents' intentions were a Message to the Free Nations of the World was also read stating that Ireland was calling

upon every free nation to uphold her national claim to complete independence as an Irish Republic against the arrogant pretensions of England founded in fraud and sustained only by an overwhelming military occupation and demands to be confronted publicly with England at the Congress of Nations in order that the civilised world, having judged between English wrong and Irish right, may guarantee to Ireland its permanent support for the maintenance of her national independence.

There is no record that Collins ever found fault with any of these sentiments, but he did take exception to parts of the Democratic Programme as being 'too socialistic'.[24] Amongst the Programme's provisions was a declaration that 'all right to private property must be subordinated to the public right and welfare'. 'Every citizen' was to have 'an adequate share of the produce of the Nation's labour'.

The proceedings were conducted in a dignified fashion undoubtedly, but one wonders at the wit of *The Times* correspondent who wrote: 'The proceedings throughout were orderly and dignified, not a word being uttered that could produce ill-feeling.' Goblet, the French historian, was a more realistic analyst. He wrote: 'A new epoch was beginning, and one that would be terrible.'[25] As if to underscore his words, while the Dail was sitting, a party of Volunteers, imbued with the spirit of Collins rather than of Figgis, held up a party of RIC escorting a load of gelignite at Soloheadbeg, County Tipperary, and cold-bloodedly shot two of them dead. In their way, the killings, which were unsanctioned by Volunteer HQ, were literal translations of what the words uttered in the Mansion House actually meant.

It was after the sitting of the First Dail that, with an instinctive appositeness, the public began to refer to the Volunteers as the Irish Republican Army, soon shortening the term to IRA. Sean Treacy, the Tipperary IRA leader, and another firebrand, Michael Brennan of Clare, both of whom had served terms under the Defence of the Realm Act, DORA, had met earlier in the month and decided that whatever happened they were not going to spend any more time in prison. They would carry weapons and fight to resist arrest. Treacy warned Brennan that they were in fact declaring war on the British Empire by this policy and that they had better check their finances first. Brennan had one shilling and sixpence, Treacy fourpence.[26] Nevertheless Treacy, watching the Volunteer numbers dwindle as the threat of conscription receded, decided to go to war anyway. He echoed Collins' view as he marched into captivity after 1916: 'We'll have to get the British to organise us. We'll have to shoot.' Accordingly he took part in what is generally regarded as the firing of the first premeditated shots from the Volunteer side.

Collins attended all the April Dail sittings, although he was now on the run and hotly pursued, a warrant having been issued for his arrest a few days earlier as a result of his failure to turn up in court after giving bail. Efforts were made to arrest him as the Dail sat, but he was forewarned by Broy and got away. De Valera was elected President of Dail Eireann, or Priomh Aire, in Irish, First Minister in English. Later during his tour of America, he allowed himself to be described as 'President of the Irish Republic', a concession to American nomeclature which had important political and psychological implications for him later. Collins was appointed by de Valera as Minister for Finance in an eight-man Ministry: Arthur Griffith, Home Affairs; W. T. Cosgrave, Local Government; Countess Markievicz, Labour; Eoin MacNeill, Industries; and Robert Barton, Agriculture. The Dail also gave its blessing to the opening of 'embassies' in France and Washington, under Sean T. O'Kelly and Dr Pat MacCartan respectively. These appointments, and the proceedings which followed on 10 April, at a subsequent meeting of the Dail, were characterised by a good deal of waffle, mutual admiration and unreality.[27] Nevertheless, as with all functionings of this national parliament, decisions were taken which had severely practical results.

De Valera proposed that, 'members of the police forces acting in this country as part of the forces of the British occupation and as agents of the British Government be ostracised socially by the people'.[28] The motion was seconded by Eoin MacNeill who said that, 'the police in Ireland are a force of spies. The police in Ireland are a force of traitors, and the police in Ireland are a force of perjurers.' It was carried unanimously.[29] De Valera made another important announcement that day:

'It is obvious that the work of our Government cannot be carried out without funds. The Minister for Finance is accordingly preparing a prospectus which will shortly be published for the issue of a loan of one million pounds sterling – £500,000 to be offered to the public for immediate subscription, £250,000 at home and £325,000 abroad, in bonds and such amounts as to meet the needs of the small subscriber.[30]

Collins was to do more than 'issue a prospectus'. He was to be responsible for the entire organisation of the loan, its advertising, collection and the issue of receipts. The British declared the loan to be illegal but, despite continual harassment, Collins carried through the project successfully at a time when he was holding down four major positions in a full-scale guerrilla war, of which he was the main architect. His diligence seems all the more remarkable in view of the fact that he evidently disliked much of the loan work. Writing to Boland a year after de Valera's announcement, on 19 April 1920, he said:

I append a draft statement of the loan results in a general way up to date. These figures are the figures received at the Head Office only. The enterprise will certainly break my heart if anything ever will. I never imagined there would be so much cowardice, dishonesty, hedging, insincerity, and meanness in the world, as my experience of this work has revealed.

He had another experience during the April 1919 sittings which aroused considerably more enthusiasm in him, though it was also highly revealing of 'cowardice, dishonesty, insincerity and meanness'. Broy smuggled him into Detective Headquarters in Brunswick Street, where he spent the night going through the 'G' Division records. As with many of the turning points in his life, he approached the escapade in a light-hearted fashion. Encountering his old Frongoch companion, Sean Nunan, en route, he impulsively brought him along 'for the crack'. Nunan, who later became a director of the *Irish Press*, told me about the Brunswick St visit on more than one occasion. His abiding memory was the fright he got during the small hours of the morning when a drunk broke a window in their wing, and he feared that the police would come to inspect the damage. However, they dealt with the offender, a soldier, without coming near Broy's sanctum. Nunan remembered Collins chuckling over the contents of his own file which began, 'He comes of a brainy Cork family.' But the Brunswick St experience was no laughing matter. Collins had had the entire *modus operandi* of the RIC's intelligence system laid out before him. He saw both what he was up against and how to combat his enemy, the first Irish revolutionary to do so. Initially, he gave no sign of the importance of the discovery, turning up at the following day's Dail sitting 'with no great sign of fatigue considering his busy, sleepless night'.[31]

Then, on 9 April, he took the first steps towards implementing the lessons of Brunswick St. Acting on his orders, a number of 'G' men were accosted by Volunteers and warned against an excess of zeal. 'G' men who did not comply would pay for their stubborn courage with their lives, thus inaugurating a new and bloodier phase of the Anglo-Irish struggle. For the moment, Sinn Fein policy was largely directed towards a peaceful goal, the Peace Conference between the great powers who had fought in the First World War then meeting in Paris.

Collins had been active on the Peace Conference front, as he was in every other phase of Sinn Fein activity. In the New Year, he had been part of a delegation which went to London hoping to see President Wilson as he passed through on his way to Paris. When it was pointed out to him that his chances of seeing Wilson were slim, he replied with characteristic insouciance: 'If necessary we can buccaneer him.'[32] Wilson was not for buccaneering and he went on to Paris without seeing the Irishmen.

Undaunted, Collins accompanied O'Kelly and Gavan Duffy, who had defended Casement and had an extensive law practice in London, to a house in Kensington to draw up a submission to the American President. It was the home of a couple with whom Collins was to have a significant relationship thereafter, Crompton and Moya Llewelyn Davies. Moya, who was Irish-born, 'made some helpful suggestions' to the draft.[33]

Kathleen Napoli MacKenna was friendly with Moya Llewelyn Davies who spent a good deal of time during the Anglo-Irish war living in Furry Park House in Killester, north County Dublin, an eighteenth-century mansion which in those days was entirely surrounded by trees and fields running down to the extensive sand dunes and slob-lands fringing the sea at Clontarf. In a letter to Kathleen about evenings in her London home where, amongst others, her husband Crompton – Solicitor-General to the British Post Office and a former ally of Lloyd George's in land reform and other social issues – was in the habit of entertaining distinguished guests such as Bertrand Russell, Moya said:

The Irish trait is very strong in me, and when I moved in the highest circles, intellectually, in England, and had the greatest living philosopher and greatest living mathematician to dinner, in the course of the evening I would escape to the kitchen, and sit by the fire and talk to Ellie, the cook from Tipperary.[34]

Moya's 'Irish trait' caused her to involve herself in Irish affairs in many ways – writing pamphlets and articles, studying Irish, and later translating the classic tale of island life, *Twenty Years a Growing*, into English. Furry Park, with its sweeping staircases and panelled halls, its marbled fireplaces and gracious drawing rooms, must have been a place of enchantment in those days. A romantic vantage point from which a young wife surveyed the revolution sweeping through her country while her cultivated, studious, and older, Welsh husband attended to his duties in London.

Napoli MacKenna describes how Moya looked one night when she arrived unexpectedly at Furry Park with a message. Collins, whom

Napoli MacKenna likened to 'Siegfrid, the personification of joyous, powerful youth', was in the grounds watching for a 'tout' he had spotted. In anything but joyous mood Siegfrid let himself in the back door and left Kathleen standing in the rain at the hall door.

Moya herself, tall, thin, agile, extremely elegant in a brown, gold-brocaded tight-fitting frock with long clinging sleeves, carefully-groomed, her well-chiselled head Eton cropped, a cigarette in a long holder between her slender tapering fingers opened the door . . . calling me Caitlin . . . I admired her wide-open, wonder-filled eyes that shone like stars . . .

The friendship which formed between Collins and the Llewelyn Davieses gave rise to controversy on the grounds of both politics and sex. Politically, it was alleged by Republican critics that the Davieses and Sir James Barrie[35] were part of a British Intelligence plot, because both Barrie and John Chartres, whom Collins also saw at the Llewelyn Davieses' house, had been in Intelligence during the war. Chartres became part of the Irish team during the Anglo-Irish Treaty negotiations on Collins' invitation and he also assisted Collins with drafting advice.

It was also freely rumoured that Collins and Moya became lovers, an impression which Moya, as we shall see, appeared keen to further, although her first impressions of Collins do not appear to have been overwhelming. He appeared to her to be 'pasty' and too much given to smoking and bombast.[36] Nevertheless, she was to show herself prepared to do a lot more for Collins and the Irish situation than was President Wilson.

Wilson was not insensitive to the Irish issue. Irish-American leaders had begun to lift their heads up over the parapet again immediately the war ended, freeing them from the taint of helping Germany with their agitations. Wilson sent an emissary to Ireland to investigate matters, George Creel, who talked to Boland and Collins, amongst others. The President also gave ear to the views of Sir Shane Leslie and was in touch personally with Sir Horace Plunkett in the latter's capacity as Chairman of the Irish Convention. But he was not prepared to quarrel with his war-time allies over seating Ireland at the Peace Conference, as the Irish-Americans so stridently demanded. He needed British support in many areas, not least for the League of Nations which, *inter alia*, he hoped to use to advance Ireland's case. But many Irish-Americans were suspicious of the League, with its commitment, as they saw it, to involvement in foreign wars, and they were unenthusiastic about the Treaty of Versailles which gave neither promise of a new world order, nor restoration of the old.

Creel reported to Wilson on 1 March on his Irish visit, saying that an

Irish settlement was imperative in view of the Irish-American lobby. He thought Home Rule was no longer an option and that an offer of Dominion status would be accepted. But he warned against the British Prime Minister's bona fides over Ireland and that delay would mean 'that sentiment in Ireland and America will harden in favour of an Irish Republic'. It would indeed.

Three days after Wilson got Creel's report a resolution (which Wilson opposed) in the name of Thomas Gallagher of Illinois was passed by the House of Representatives by 261 votes to 41. It read as follows:

That it is the earnest hope of the Congress of the United States of America that the Peace Conference now sitting at Paris and passing upon the rights of various peoples will favourably consider the claims of Ireland to self-determination.

The importance of the resolution was widely oversold in Irish circles, so much so that a de Valera historian[37] would write later, 'The American people had instructed their President to support Ireland's claim.' In fact, nothing of the sort had occurred. The resolution was passed too late to be dealt with by the Senate and so did not have the full approval of Congress. Yet it was a shot across Wilson's bows. He got another that evening when a delegation appointed at an Irish Race Convention in Philadelphia the previous month saw him in New York to present him with resolutions passed at the Convention (held on 22 and 23 February). The meeting took place in a poor atmosphere. Wilson only agreed to it finally on condition that the Clan na nGael leader, Judge Cohalan, withdrew from the delegation. His German contacts at the time of 1916 and prior to America's ending the war were still not forgiven. The President told the delegation that he was unable to intervene in the domestic policy of other governments. He did, however, take a more supportive attitude to another of the Race Convention's decisions – the appointment of a three-man delegation to the Peace Conference to attempt to secure a hearing for Ireland.

On 12 April 1919, Collins proposed a motion, which was seconded by W. T. Cosgrave and passed by the Dail:

The elected Parliament and Government of the Irish Republic pledge the active support of the Irish Nation in translating into deed the principles enunciated by the President of the US at Washington's Tomb on 4 July, 1918, and whole-heartedly accepted [by America]. We are eager and ready to enter a World League of Nations based on equality of rights, in which the guarantees exchanged neither recognise nor imply a difference between big nations and small, between those that are powerful and those that are weak. We are willing to accept all the duties, responsibilities and burdens which inclusion in such a League implies.

In this motion Collins was signalling the general implicit recognition by his colleagues of an Irish Republic; his party's faith in Wilson's declaration of support for the aspirations of 'small nations'; and Sinn Fein's opposition to Article 10 of the Covenant of the League of Nations:

The High Contracting Powers undertake to respect and preserve against external aggression the territorial integrity and existing political independence of all State members of the League. In case of any such aggression the Executive Council shall advise upon the means by which this obligation shall be fulfilled.

This could be taken as recognising the territorial status quo of League members and it certainly posed a very large question as to how a self-proclaimed Irish Republic, which Great Britain did not recognise, might hope to find itself at the Paris negotiating table confronting 'the arrogant pretensions of England'. That confrontation could only come about if England, which at the time regarded all Ireland as an integral part of her imperial status quo, gave her permission for it to happen. The unlikelihood of this occurring did not worry Collins greatly. He had a number of other successes on his mind. The day after he successfully moved the motion, he wrote on 13 April to his sister, Helena:

The week that has passed has been a busy one for us – perhaps it has been a historical one for very often we are actors in events that have more meaning and consequence than we realise. At any rate – permanent or not – last week did, I feel, mark the inception of something new. The elected representatives of the people have definitely turned their backs on the old order and the developments are sure to be interesting. Generally the situation is working out to the satisfaction of Ireland – that is the foreign countries. At home we go from success to success in our own guerrilla way. Escapes of prisoners, raids against the enemy etc.[38]

The last session of the Dail which de Valera attended before he departed for America was held on 9 May in honour of the three-man American delegation appointed by the Irish Race Convention, which visited Ireland en route for Paris. During the proceedings Collins greatly impressed the Irish-Americans, both with his power of oratory and as an escapologist. They were already somewhat over-whelmed by their kaleidoscopic Irish visit which lasted for ten days, beginning on 3 May. Everywhere they went, they were treated to traditional Irish hospitality. Apart from being invited to address the Dail, they attended several civic receptions, including one at which they received the Freedom of the City of Limerick. The only rebuffs they got occurred in the north, where the Lord Mayor of Belfast refused to see them. Their speeches along the way greatly heartened nationalists, but they so infuriated the decision-takers in London that even the King wanted Lloyd George to demand from Wilson 'a disavowal of the action of these American citizens'.

Wilson's own view of the trio was that they had:

behaved in a way which so inflamed British public opinion that the situation has got quite out of hand, and we are utterly at a loss how to act in the matter without involving the Government of the United States with the Government of Great Britain in a way which might create an actual breach between the two.

The three were in no way wide-eyed or visionary. Frank P. Walsh, a Kansas City lawyer, was a former Joint President of Wilson's War Labour Conference Board. Edward F. Dunne was a former Mayor of Chicago and Governor of Illinois, and Michael J. Ryan was a successful Philadelphia lawyer. But a combination of their empathy with the land of their forebears and their and Wilson's differing interpretations of what they were meant to be doing in Ireland put paid to any lingering hopes which may have existed for a Sinn Fein presence at the Peace Conference. The Senate had passed a resolution on 6 June asking that the Irish be admitted to 'present the case of Ireland'. Further, the Senate expressed sympathy with the aspirations of the Irish people 'for a government of their own choice'. This resolution, which was also hailed by the Nationalists, was largely a sham.

The Irish Committee was informed[39] by a telegram from the British Embassy in Washington three days later that the influential Senator Lodge had informed the Embassy that he was 'certainly not' in favour of an independent Ireland. The resolution was, in fact, an attack on Wilson and the League of Nations.

Accordingly, when the trio met Wilson in Paris on 11 June and pressed him on his celebrated war-time aim of self-determination for small nations, he made the heartfelt reply: 'You have touched on the great metaphysical tragedy of today'. By then he was suffering from the pressures of having to crush the hopes aroused by his words in places as far removed as Africa and Korea. The 'revolutionary situation' prevailing in the country, which the delegation described to the President, can be understood by a study of the table[40] compiled by Arthur Griffith the month before the Americans toured Ireland:

	1917	1918
Arrests	347	1107
English raids	11	260
Meetings suppressed	2	32
Deportations	24	91
Courts martial	36	62
Bayonet or baton charges	18	81
Sentences	269	973
Death from prison treatment	5	1
Newspapers suppressed	–	12

The figures were compiled with propagandist intent, but they were accurate and contrasted with Assizes Judges' comments at the time about the lack of ordinary crime in the country. All the foregoing offences related to speech-making, military display, having or issuing papers likely to cause 'disaffection' and so on. One person was jailed for 'whistling derisively at the police'.[41]

The Dail, meeting in honour of the American delegation, was surrounded by armed soldiers looking for Collins just after he had made a lengthy and powerful speech detailing the extent of British financial malpractice and over-taxation in Ireland. (This contained ideas for reparation which found expression first in the Anglo-Irish Treaty negotiations and later, ironically enough, in de Valera's successful prosecution of an 'economic war' against Britain in the 1930s that led to the abolition of some of the objectionable clauses which Collins was forced to concede in the Treaty.) When the proceedings concluded, the soldiers and detectives, led by Detective Daniel Hoey, entered the Mansion House looking for him, but he escaped via a ladder provided by O'Reilly. After a three-hour wait in a dusty building nearby he emerged in a filthy condition. Showing an instinct for publicity he sent O'Reilly to fetch his Volunteer uniform. Resplendent in this, he turned up at the reception for the Americans, the only man not in mufti, and created a sensation. The Most Wanted Man appearing in uniform! The creation of the Collins legend was well under way.

'Actors in events that have more meaning and consequence than we realise . . .' The letter which Collins had written to his sister, Helena, was truer than he knew. De Valera's decision to go to America still stood, and it was decided that Boland would go over in advance to make arrangements for him. It meant a parting of the ways for the hitherto inseparable friends. Boland would go with de Valera in more ways than one.

A factor which could be overstressed, but hardly overlooked, in assessing the reasons for Boland and Collins' estrangement is the fact that both fell in love with the same girl, Kitty Kiernan. She eventually preferred Collins and although, before she made her choice, Boland said he was sure the 'triangle' as he termed it (see page 281) would never spoil their friendship, he would hardly have been human if he had not felt some resentment afterwards. Indeed, it seems to have been confidently expected at one stage that it was Boland, not Collins, she planned to marry. Boland's mother seems to have been so certain of this that she actually wrote[42] to congratulate Kitty who, it appears, had not told.Boland that it was Collins she loved. Boland, who at that stage was going on another lengthy trip to America, was still talking of honeymoon plans to Kitty.

In many ways the Boland/Collins relationship is symbolised by

Mrs Batt O'Connor's reminiscence[43] of seeing their two heads on the pillow, fast asleep in the moonlight. The Roland and Oliver image is limned by the knowledge that she could see them only because the bedroom door had been left open in case of a raid, and that Collins' bare arm rested on a bedside table – between two revolvers.

Beaslai, who shared a room with them in Vaughan's, recalled an argument in which Boland took the unexpected position that the use of force in pursuit of a principle lowered its value. Collins agreed with Beaslai who quoted Shaw's Armourer: 'Nothing is ever done in this world unless men are prepared to kill one another, if it is not done.' But Boland held to the precept that to live by the sword was to perish by it. They had another memorable night in Vaughan's to mark Boland's departure for the US and Boland enthusiastically joined in the applause for Collins' rendition of 'Kelly and Burke and Shea', the final verse of which is:

> 'Oh, the fighting races don't die out
> If they seldom die in bed,
> For love is the first in their heart, no doubt,'
> Said Burke, then Kelly said:
> 'When Michael the great Archangel stands
> The angel with the sword,
> And the battle's dead from a hundred lands
> Are arranged in one big horde,
> One line that for Gabriel's trumpet waits,
> Will stretch three-deep that day
> From Jehoshaphat to the Golden Gates,
> Kelly and Burke and Shea.'
> 'Well, here's thank God for the race and the sod,'
> Said Kelly and Burke and Shea.

Today it is easier to laugh at such doggerel than to comprehend its meaning for the men in Vaughan's Hotel that night. For Kelly and Burke and Shea, one could read Beaslai and Boland and Collins. They were of the 'fighting races' and they knew the line 'they seldom die in bed' could apply to them. It did. Beaslai was arrested the day after Boland left for America, but of the three he was the only one who lived to write about the night in Vaughan's. The real tragedy of the gascons was that they died on opposite sides, Boland forgetting to leave his bedroom door open, Collins, too, neglecting elementary precautions.

The preparations being made for smuggling de Valera to the US aboard a liner by two of Collins' agents, were such that very little notice could be given. De Valera was actually at home in Greystones, preparing to celebrate his wife's birthday, when Collins and one of the agents, Dick O'Neill, appeared to tell him that he'd have to leave that night, Sunday 1 June 1919.

(*Left*) Nancy O'Brien, Collins' cousin and subsequent collaborator – she smuggled decoded messages from the Castle to Collins in her hair

(*Below*) Kitty Kiernan, Collins' fiancée

(*Left*) Hazel, Lady Lavery

(*Far left*) Edith, Lady Londonderry

FACING PAGE

Life on a bicycle: two leading players in Collins' undercover war were his Dublin Castle 'mole', Dave Neligan (*far left*), and British Intelligence Officer Captain Hardy (*below left*), whom Collins called a 'notorious murderer'

(*Foot*) Key men in the Volunteers, Seamus Robinson, Sean Treacy, Dan Breen and Michael Brennan

THIS PAGE

(*Above*) 'Apostles' Joe Slattery, Joe Dolan (second and third left) and William Stapleton (second right), Dublin Brigade members Joe Leonard (far left) and Charlie Dalton (far right), and Adj. Gen. Gearoid O'Sullivan (standing)

(*Below*) The infamous Cairo Gang (the two on the extreme left and the one in the middle are Irish)

Proving it more
potent to endure
than to inflict:
Thomas Ashe,
Kevin Barry (top
right), Terence
MacSwiney (below
right); a woman
with her child
outside Mountjoy
Jail while her
husband is hanged,
1921

De Valera and O'Neill made the Holyhead crossing together. He was recognised aboard by a Fr McCarthy who had been a prison chaplain in 1916. He wanted to bring de Valera to a stateroom to meet another traveller, Sir James MacMahon, the Under Secretary for State for Ireland. De Valera knew MacMahon. They were both members of the same confraternity of St Vincent de Paul in Blackrock, but he decided this was no time to be discussing the corporal works of mercy and declined the invitation. They were followed by detectives at Holyhead but shook them off and de Valera was safely smuggled aboard the liner *Celtic*.

And so, stowed away and seasick, to New York went the 'President of the First Republic', pausing only to write a reassuring note to the long-suffering Sinead:

A Cuisle – I hope you were not too anxious yesterday. It may be the beginning of that birthday gift you prayed for.

I have made arrangements with S. Nunan to put to your account whatever is left after certain payments are made, with the exception of £25.

I trust you will not allow yourself to be lonely. It will be but for a short time.

I have only a minute or two. Kiss the children.
Dev
Le gradh mo croidhe[44]

In fact, de Valera spun out that 'short time' for eighteen months and, during his absence, Collins' reputation acquired heroic proportions. He too became a President shortly after de Valera departed, though not a publicly announced one. The IRB do not announce the results of their elections. Sometime during June or July Collins was elected President of the Supreme Council of the IRB.[45]

The departure of Boland initially widened the breach between Collins and Sinn Fein. Boland's nominee for his position as Joint Honorary Secretary was spurned. Collins wrote to Stack in a fury:

The position is intolerable – the policy now seems to be to squeeze out any-one who is tainted with strong fighting ideas, or I should say I suppose ideas of the utility of fighting. Of course, any of the Dail Ministers are not eligible for the Stan. Cttee. and only 1/3 of the entire numbers may be members of the Dail. The result is that there is a Standing Committee of malcontents, and their first act is to appoint a pacifist secretary and announce the absence of H.B. Our own people give away in a moment what the Detective Division has been unable to find out in five weeks.[46]

Next day, still simmering at the disclosure of Boland's whereabouts, he again wrote to Stack:

. . . it seems to me that official Sinn Fein is inclined to be ever less militant and ever more political and theoretical . . . There is I suppose the tendency of all revolutionary movements to divide themselves up into their component parts. Now the moral force department have probably been affected by British propaganda.

But having said the position was 'disheartening' and had him 'awfully fed up', Collins characteristically concluded with one of his favourite quotations from Wolfe Tone, ''Tis in vain for soldiers to complain.' All he learned about British police methodology, all his own sources of information drove Collins to a realisation that if he wanted to put his knowledge to use then there was a grim logic to the situation.

Collins formally faced up to the implications of that logic with the formation of the 'Squad', which was officially founded on 19 September 1919 (though by that time it had been operative for two months and members of the Squad had two killings to their credit) at 46 Parnell Square, the meeting place of the Keating branch of the Gaelic League. The Squad was a group of assassins, a specially selected hit-squad directly under Collins' orders. The first recruits were warned by Dick McKee that their work would not be suitable for anyone with scruples about taking life, so they had no illusions as to what they were going into. Collins impressed on the Squad members that no organisation in Irish history had had a unit to deal with spies and the members of the Squad regarded themselves as being part of an elite. Its first leader was Mick McDonnell, a former Frongoch man, who was later succeeded by Paddy Daly.[47]

The first members of the Squad were Joe Leonard, Sean Doyle, Jim Slattery, Bill Stapleton, Pat McCrae, James Conroy, Ben Barret and Daly. Then in January 1920 Collins added Tom Keogh, Mick O'Reilly and Vincent Byrne. The expanded Squad became popularly known as the 'Twelve Apostles'.

Vinnie Byrne told me:

We were all young, twenty, twenty-one. We never thought we'd win or lose. We just wanted to have a go. We'd go out in pairs, walk up to the target and do it, then split. You wouldn't be nervous while you'd be waiting to plug him, but you'd imagine everyone was looking into your face. On a typical job we'd use about eight, including the back-up. Nobody got in our way. One of us would knock him over with the first shot, and the other would finish him off with a shot to the head.

Collins was a marvel. If he hadn't done the work he did, we'd still be under Britain. Informers and drink would have taken care of us. But our movement was temperate. Collins would meet us from time to time and say, 'You're doing great work, lads.' There was no formality about him. I remember after the Irish Government was set up I was on guard duty at Government Buildings, and he was Commander-in-Chief. He saw me and came over to me and put his arm around me and said, 'How are you going on, Vinny?'[48]

As explained earlier, the lynchpin of the British Intelligence system was the 'G' Division. When Collins began killing off its members, he paralysed the service.

Collins was very careful about the shooting of policemen. Once an order was given he was ruthless. It had to be carried out. Vinnie Byrne told me: 'You got your orders. He was your target. That was your job and it was up to you to see that it was done however you went about it.' But Collins 'went about it' cautiously. Broy remembered that 'Collins would always work out how the public would react to the shooting of a 'G' man first. And then he'd hang back for a while before he'd have another one shot. He tried to warn them off first without killing them.'[49]

Within two days (9 April 1919) of being shown the secret of Brunswick St, Collins began warning off detectives. One, Detective Sergeant Halley, was called on by a party of Volunteers at his home. Another, Constable O'Brien, was gagged and tied to the railings at Brunswick St Police Station. The 'G' man emerged unhurt from his ordeal, and, according to Broy, afterwards remarked that merely being warned was 'damned decent' of Sinn Fein. He took no further active role against the Volunteers. However, others were not so amenable. 'The Dog' Smith, for example, was a courageous man, as the son of a man sent to warn him told me afterwards: 'He told Dad that he appreciated him coming to tell him to lay off. He knew he was doing it because we were neighbours, but he said, "I'm not letting any young scuts tell me how to do my duty".'

The 'young scuts' were Boland and Collins who had tried unsuccessfully to get him to drop charges against Beaslai who had been arrested in possession of incendiary articles for *An tOglach*. The Squad waited for him for several nights before managing to waylay him near his home in Drumcondra, on 30 July 1919. A running battle developed, with Smith firing on his attackers and succeeding in getting in through his own front door even though hard hit. The Squad members were amazed to see him keep running. Collins did not merely weigh up the reaction to the subsequent death from wounds of the unfortunate Smith; he analysed the reasons why the detective 'kept running', and from then on the Squad was armed not with .38 but .45 revolvers.

The authorities responded to Smith's shooting by banning Sinn Fein and thereby creating a fertile climate for Collins' extremism. The Dail was banned on 12 September and Sinn Fein HQ at No. 6, Harcourt was raided. Collins reacted by having another detective shot, Hoey, a deeply religious man, who had, however, picked MacDiarmada out for the firing squads after 1916.

The Squad took a pride in its work. Daly remembers arguing with Collins on his positioning in a stake-out of one important quarry, (Assistant Commissioner Redmond, see page 129). It seemed that neither Daly nor his companions Leonard and Doyle were to go any-where near their intended victim and that other members of the Squad would account for him. ' "Are we to wait for the Stop Press?" I asked him,' Daly recalled. 'Collins replied: "The goal-man often gets more of the ball than the rest of the team . . .".' Actually as events turned out, it was Daly who felled Redmond with a single shot to the head. Even a glimpse of some of the detail of the Squad's activities as recounted by Daly still makes chilling reading today in a world accustomed to the horrors of war on a far greater scale: '. . . As he went down I heard him say, "What have I done to deserve this treatment" . . . Tom Keogh spotted Brooks at Westland Row station by accident and got him . . . Hugh said, "Kells is up there if you want him? . . ." "Where?" "On the footpath." "The fellows who went after Sergeant Revill will do a bit of crowing tonight".' (This last said of the team which had apparently hit another target successfully; in fact he lived.)

The obvious ruthlessness of the killings was balanced by strict instructions to the Squad that no one was to be shot except under orders or in self-defence when on active service. For instance, Daly's wife died the year the Squad was formed and he was left to raise a family which included a daughter with a deformed hand. A neighbour, an RIC man, maltreated the girl during a search of the Daly home and it was said afterwards, wrongly, that Daly intended to shoot the policeman. Collins heard the story and sent for Daly in a rage. 'What's this? Any man who has revenge in his heart is not fit to be a Volunteer.'

Not only was the Squad absolutely convinced of the rightness of their actions, they were soldiers fighting a far stronger enemy by the only means at their disposal; others, sometimes in highly significant places, shared this view. Byrne, for example, remembered going to confession to 'a great priest, Father Moriarty of South William Street. I told him: "I shot a man, Father." "Did you think you were doing right? Had you no qualms about it?" he asked me. I told him I didn't have any qualms, I thought I was doing right, and he said, "Carry on with the good work," and gave me absolution.'

Other helpers the Squad were able to count on were figures like 'Ninepence O'Connor' (so nicknamed because he was 'only as tall as ninepence worth of coppers'), who used to hide guns for Dick McKee behind a church altar. And there was also a well-known figure, 'the Black Man', a former boxer who perpetually walked the streets of Dublin. After a job the Squad would drop their guns in his pockets as they ran past. One inevitability of the Collins strategy was war, because as the police system crumbled, the British were forced to replace it with a military one.

As the war developed and grew in intensity, so too did the demand for the deadly ministrations of the Apostles increase, and their ranks grew also.

By 6 November 1919 the Irish Committee finally issued a report[50] (with an accompanying request for special secrecy) that contained the bones of the settlement which the British actually came to in 1921. Had the Report been acted on promptly and in the spirit it advocated, 'that the Government should make a sincere attempt to deal with the Irish situation once and for all', Ireland would have been spared a great deal of agony. The Committee agreed that:

. . . in view of the situation in Ireland itself, of public opinion in the Dominions, and in the United States of America, they cannot recommend the policy either of repealing or of postponing the Home Rule Act of 1914. In their judgement it is essential, now that the war is over, and the peace Conference has dealt with so many analogous questions in Europe, that the Government should make a sincere attempt to deal with the Irish question once and for all.

The Committee found two problems:

On the one hand the Government was committed against any solution which would break with the unity of the Empire. On the other, it was committed that Ulster must not be forced under the rule of an Irish parliament against its will. The first condition therefore excludes any proposal for allowing Ireland, or any part of Ireland to establish an independent Republic. The second again precludes them from again attempting what has so often failed in the past, the establishment of a single parliament for all Ireland on the lines of the Home Rule Acts of 1886, 1893 and 1914.

The stipulations in the last paragraph obviously made it inevitable that the type of Home Rule which would be agreeable to Britain was going to be very far short of the All-Ireland Republic which the Sinn Feiners had declared for themselves at the beginning of the year. The logic of the thing was clearly a separate state for 'Ulster', apart from any limitations as to the precise form of Home Rule which would be offered to the Southern nationalists. And on 24 November the Committee duly recommended to the Cabinet that two parliaments be set up in Ireland, linked by a Council of Ireland. The powers reserved included the Crown, Foreign Affairs, the conferring of dignities and questions of treason. A large measure of autonomy it clearly was not, nor was it intended to be. Discussing the Committee's Report two weeks earlier, on 11 November, Lord Birkenhead, the then Lord Chancellor, said:

I assent to this proposed Bill as effecting an ingenious strengthening of our tactical position before the world. I am absolutely satisfied that the Sinn Feiners will refuse it. Otherwise in the present state of Ireland I could not even be a party to making the offer, for I believe the Sinn Feiners, if they accept their parliament, would use it only for the purpose of forwarding separation.[51]

Birkenhead was a cynical but accurate prophet. The Cabinet was given a knowledgeable assessment of their Irish handiwork by Chief Justice O'Connor in a letter dated 24 December 1919:

I am sorry to say I can hear no good word for the Home Rule scheme . . . a parliament for the Nine instead of Six Counties would be less objectionable than the scheme as outlined, but even the changes will not make it acceptable, nor have I much hope that it will be honestly worked, if passed. I wish I could give you a more favourable view for all the decent people in this country (who I believe form the majority of the population) and all they want is peace.[52]

But peace did not come to Ireland.

5

The Year of Terror

'We have murder by the throat.'

Lloyd George

The year 1920 is remembered in Ireland as the Year of the Terror, the year the dreaded Black and Tans came. It was the year when the phase of daring escapades, of raids and rallies, gave way to the inevitable grimmer phase when the implications of the war began to strike home to everybody. On the one hand the Irish began to prove the truth of the assertion that successful revolutions are in fact no more than the kicking down of an already rotted door. The tiny handful of Volunteers – probably no more than three or four thousand strong countrywide – with their revolvers and shotguns began to paralyse the entire British system, or so it seemed. What in fact happened was that the British position was so untenable morally that they could not use their Army properly and were never able to put forth their full military might. Like a powerful wrestler whose own strength is used against him by a smaller opponent in judo, Lloyd George was forced to forgo his big battalions and attempt to combat Collins in his own underground world of Intelligence. And in that world Collins had something more important than weaponry, or even his ferocious drive and initiative. Behind his handful of detectives, his porters and clerks and postmen and warders and train drivers, his Tobins and his Cullens, he had the spirit of the people. Florrie O'Donoghue summed it up after a visit he paid to his native district in Cork to inspect the aftermath of British reprisals. Writing to the woman who had become his wife in extraordinary circumstances, he spoke in awed terms of what might be termed the Mujahadeen factor.

The calm undaunted fate of those people looking at the ruins of their own homes. I am not referring to my own people merely. I saw and spoke to them all, and I am convinced that there was something supernatural in the unshakable courage and olden Gaelic simplicity of these people. Truly the hills of Ireland could be levelled to the ground and all her children driven out upon the seas of the world before England can conquer us while we have such faith and courage.[1]

In Dublin the same spirit prevailed. Thornton expressed it in less high-flown language:

> . . . the ordinary 'five–eight' common citizen was marvellous. Time after time when our men were watching houses, watching individuals, or watching for ambushes, men and women came along and quietly told them to look out that there was somebody watching them from a door or a street corner, and even after ambushes, we had women who were out shopping virtually grabbing grenades and revolvers from men who were in danger of being captured and coolly walking through the enemy lines. This spirit prevailed right throughout the country, but here in this citadel of British Imperialism the assistance given by the ordinary man and woman was simply marvellous and was responsible in the main for the success of our fighting services.

Put another way, what both O'Donoghue and Thornton were saying in effect was: because of her history, subversion in Ireland can only successfully be dealt with through military methods by the Irish, never by the British. But it was largely by military means that Lloyd George sought to proceed: nasty means at that. The British too had their 'squads'. Each side used the other's terminology: 'murder gangs'.

During 1919, the more active IRA leaders throughout the country had been itching for a fight. In Clare the leader of what was probably the first, and certainly one of the most successful, of the Flying Columns[2], Michael Brennan, was hauled over the coals 'very roughly'[3] by Mulcahy for unauthorised militarism. Tomas MacCurtain, head of the Volunteers in Cork, and Terence MacSwiney, his second-in-command, backed the idea of a 'revolving rising',[4] seizing a strongpoint in Cork one week, in Galway the next and so on throughout the country, holding out for as long as they could before going down to a glorious defeat which would have the effect of arousing the populace of the various areas, as 1916 had done. The 'static warfare' approach of course conflicted with Collins' ideas. But as 1919 ended GHQ felt that the Volunteers had grown sufficiently in strength to be allowed to go on the offensive. MacSwiney and MacCurtain were given instructions to attack a number of barracks in their area, and to be back at work the next morning 'as though a dog hadn't barked'.[5] Accordingly, on 1 January 1920 three barracks in the Cork area were successfully attacked, thus inaugurating a new phase of the struggle. Similar activities spread in the succeeding days to other parts of the country and Wexford, Waterford and Kilkenny were placed under martial law. In the midst of this uproar municipal elections were held under the authority of the Castle on 15 January. Sinn Fein repeated its triumph of the 'Khaki elections' to Westminster. The party's victories in Northern Ireland were particularly significant. Even the reduced Six-County area which the unionists were now resignedly seeking to agree on for exclusion from Home Rule showed Sinn Fein majorities in two counties, Fermanagh and Tyrone. Most disturbingly for the membership and organisers of the old Ulster Volunteer Force, Derry, the Covenanters' 'Maiden City', returned a Catholic Mayor, H. C. O'Doherty. In all, out of a total of 206 councils, Ireland gave 172 to Sinn Fein. As we shall see, this election result was an important factor in turning the militant Ulster Protestants from ballot to bullet as a means of holding their position.

But for the moment the point to note is that these councils promptly began cutting their links with the Castle and declaring their allegiance to the Dail. Many of the new councillors were IRA men. Amongst them was Tomas MacCurtain, who was elected Lord Mayor of Cork; Terence MacSwiney was appointed his deputy. A few days later, on 20 January, a policeman was shot in Thurles and that night, in a pattern that was to become all too familiar throughout the year, police and military shot up the town in reprisal. The editorial reaction of Lloyd George's own newspaper, the *Daily Chronicle*, was ominously significant:

Nobody can fail to deplore such occurrences, but equally obviously nobody can wonder at them. Indeed it is obvious that, if these murderous clubs pursue their course much longer, we may see counter clubs springing up, and the lives of prominent Sinn Feiners becoming as unsafe as prominent officials.

Reprisals had made their appearance; counter-insurgency 'murder clubs' as the *Chronicle* called them were on the way. Through one of his post office agents Collins was given sight of a letter written by a British Intelligence officer (in the St Andrew's Hotel, Dublin, on 2 March) to a colleague in the War Office who was about to join him. It contained the following:

Have duly reported and found things in a fearful mess, but I think I will be able to make a good show. Have been given a free hand to carry on, and everyone has been very charming. Re our little stunt, I see no prospects until I have got things on a firmer basis, but still hope and believe there are possibilities.[6]

MacCurtain received a threatening letter on 16 March: 'Thomas MacCurtain prepare for death. You are doomed.' It was written on Dail Eireann notepaper, seized in a police raid on 76 Harcourt St. A number of similar death notices were sent to other prominent Sinn Feiners, apparently with a view to making it appear that the rebels were now murdering each other. Four nights later, after a policeman had been shot dead near Cork, police cordoned off an area around MacCurtain's home. Around 1 am a party of armed men with blackened faces forced their way into his house and shot him dead in the presence of his wife. IRA intelligence subsequently established the fact that a group of civilians entered King St RIC barracks shortly afterwards. One of the group was further identified as looking suspiciously like the man in a photograph which Crow St provided of the officer to whom the 'little stunt' letter was written.

Collins was hard-hit by the death. He wrote to MacSwiney, 'I have not very much heart in what I am doing today thinking of poor Tomas. It is surely the most appalling thing that has been done yet.'[7] It was also a thing which would have far-reaching consequences in another highly sensitive part of the country, Northern Ireland. Collins took no retaliatory action until after the inquest which was in effect a trial of British policy. Despite efforts by Lord French and Lloyd George to claim that MacCurtain was murdered by his own extremists the jury, which had been selected by the police, brought in a verdict that was a comprehensive indictment of both Westminster and Dublin Castle:

We find that Alderman Tomas MacCurtain, Lord Mayor of Cork, died from shock and haemorrhage, caused by bullet wounds, and that he was wilfully wounded under circumstances of the most callous brutality: and that the murder was organised and carried out by the RIC officially directed by the British Government.

We return a verdict of wilful murder against David Lloyd George, Prime Minister of England; Lord French, Lord Lieutenant of Ireland; Ian MacPherson, late Chief Secretary of Ireland; Acting Inspector General Smith of the RIC, Divisional Inspector Clayton of the RIC; DI Swanzy and some unknown members of the RIC.[8]

They didn't stay unknown very long. When he was sworn in to succeed MacCurtain, MacSwiney said, 'We do not abrogate our function to demand and see the evildoers and murderers are punished for their crimes.'

Neither the death of MacCurtain nor the awful vengeance for his death which followed put a stop to the murdering of Lord Mayors. In Limerick the following year, on 6 March 1921, three leading citizens with nationalist sympathies, Joseph O'Donoghue, George Clancy and Michael O'Callaghan, were murdered during curfew hours in circumstances identical with MacCurtain's killing. Clancy was the Mayor at the time and O'Callaghan had preceded him in 1920. The killings were so outrageous that General Gough, of Curragh mutiny fame, wrote: 'Law and order have given way to a bloody and brutal anarchy . . . England has departed further from her own standards, and further from the standards even of any nation in the world, not excepting the Turk and Zulu, than has ever been known in history before.'[9]

While these events were taking place Britain was changing its team in Ireland. In March a new Commander-in-Chief was appointed, General Sir Nevil Macready, son of the famous actor, with experience behind him as Commissioner of the Metropolitan Police in London, of ruthlessness against miners in Tonypandy in Wales, and of service in Belfast during the Ulster gun-running crisis. None of this left him with a predisposition to win friends and influence the people of Ireland in his new posting, by other than approved methods of military efficiency. He was shortly to be joined by General Hugh Tudor as head of a reconstituted police force. The Cabinet was well aware from · the time of the Fisher report that efficiency was sadly lacking in Dublin Castle. Lord French, who 'skied on Olympus' in the viceregal lodge, also made sure that the Government was kept continually aware of the position.[10]

Accordingly, in April, one of England's most distinguished civil servants, Sir John Anderson (later Viscount Waverley), was sent to take over the administration with two able lieutenants, Mark Beresford Sturgis and, most significantly, a Lloyd George man, Alfred (Andy) Cope, a former customs detective whose talents the Prime Minister had discovered in, of all places, the Ministry of Pensions. More importantly, Cope had helped to draw up the Fisher Report. During this exercise he had met Sir James MacMahon, the Catholic Under Secretary of under-utilised talents and, more importantly to Cope, of under-utilised contacts in Nationalist circles. While both open and undercover military methods were employed to crush Sinn Fein, covertly Cope sought to find a political path for Lloyd George out of the Irish morass. Not for nothing did the Welsh wizard sleep under a framed, embroidered text from the Book of Job: 'There is a path which no fowl knoweth and which the eye of the vulture hath not seen.'[11] Under the new men MacMahon was treated with greater respect[12] and it was probably he who ultimately put Cope on the road to meeting Collins. With the administrative and military wings taken care of, Lloyd George made political alterations also. Sir Hamar Greenwood was appointed Chief Secretary in place of MacPherson. A hard job called for a hard man and certainly few political figures of the time could have stood over the activities of the next actors to enter the scene as brazenly as did Hamar Greenwood whose name was to pass into Irish folklore – 'telling a Hamar' – as a synonym for lying. The actors, who also earned an unenviable niche in Irish history, were the specially raised corps known as the Black and Tans and the Auxiliary Cadets.

The former owed their existence to a combination of the increasing ineffectiveness of the RIC under the weight of the Sinn Fein moral and physical onslaught; the shakiness of Britain's moral position in the eye of world opinion; and the influence of Sir Henry Wilson, zealous for the reputation of the Army as Chief of the Imperial General Staff and a rabid Unionist. The Cabinet listened to his urging 'with all my force the necessity for doubling the police and not employing the military'.[13]

From the end of 1919 advertisements were placed in English papers for men willing to undertake 'a rough and dangerous task'. The task was to carry out the 'shoot-to-kill' policy outlined by Lt Colonel Smyth (see p. 150). From around March, when the first successful respondents to the ads began arriving in Ireland, the Tans carried out the Smyth policy with the full rigour of the lawless in two particular regards: the assuaging of their collective thirsts, and of the itch in their trigger fingers. Frank Thornton was in Limerick in March, with his comrade Joe Dolan, when the Tans made their debut in the city in a manner that was typical of their behaviour all over the country:

They arrived in a string of lorries and proceeded to shoot up the city, left, right and centre. Both Dolan and I were staying in the Glentworth Hotel, which is on the main road to the railway station. Just past the Glentworth stands Tate's Clock, standing at least 120 ft high and brilliantly illuminated at night. We were awakened by shooting at about 12.30 to 1 am and on looking through the window we saw thirty or forty Black and Tans all lying on the road and having a cockshot at Tate's Clock with their rifles.
    After a bit they were organised by someone in control and they proceeded to shoot in regular relays at the clock. Getting tired of this after a bit, they then forced their way into the Glentworth and insisted on the management opening up the bar . . . after carousing downstairs for about an hour they made their departure.

The Tans were not, as was said, the scourings of the jails of England, they were merely encouraged to behave as if they were. They were ex-servicemen, generally unemployed, to whom the official offer of ten shillings a day and the unofficial assurance that they would be given a free hand in making Ireland a 'hell for rebels' were attractive baits. They owed the 'Black and Tan' description to the unattractive black and brown combination of khaki and police clothing provided for them by the British by way of uniform, resulting in the Irish giving them the nickname after a famous pack of hounds.
    To ensure that the Tans' morale kept up, and to counter the effect of the *Irish Bulletin*, the Castle published the *Weekly Summary* from 5 May. In an editorial headed 'Black and Tans' published on 27 August the *Summary* said:

They did not wait for the usual uniform. They came at once. They were wanted badly, and the RIC welcome them. They know what danger is. They have looked Death in the eyes before, and did not flinch. They will not flinch now.
    They will go on with the job – the job of making Ireland once again safe for the law-abiding, and an appropriate hell for those whose trade is agitation, and whose method is murder.

Suffice it to say that the Tans, as the Tate's Clock episode indicates, made Ireland safe neither for the law-abiding nor for anyone else for that matter, but made of the country a most inappropriate hell for an entire population.

Churchill is credited with thinking up the second force, the Police Auxiliary Cadets, who were mostly ex-officers, with a view to both bolstering the RIC and controlling the Black and Tans while at the same time avoiding the appearance of all-out military conflict. In the event the Auxiliaries, who were paid £1 a day as befitted their status as officers and gentlemen, were set up and maintained as an autonomous force, wearing a distinctive blue uniform with a Glengarry cap and, generally, the even more notably distinguishing trademark of a brace of revolvers worn strapped to the hip, wild-west style. The 'Auxis', as they were popularly known, were more formidable than the Tans, a tough, ruthless, energetic and courageous force who showed themselves ready, willing and able to use those guns. 'Time and time again the Volunteers testified to their bravery, but too often the mangled corpse of a woman or an old man did as much for their savagery'.[14] Walter Long accurately informed the House of Commons (3 June 1920) when he said that there was no foundation for the suggestion that the Irish police were not allowed to shoot. He was 'glad to say that the police had not only shot, but had shot with extremely good effect, and he hoped they would do it again'. They did. Several towns and villages were shot up by the police, including Limerick, Fermoy, Thurles, Killmalock, Kilcommon and Lismore. Curfew was imposed and khaki became the predominant colour in cities like Cork and Dublin.

Kathleen Napoli MacKenna described how Dublin looked one Sunday morning in July, a time when the streets would normally be more or less empty save for Mass-goers:

. . . citizens were thronging to hear Mass through streets filled with British Regulars carrying rifles with fixed bayonets, Auxiliary Cadets, Black and Tans and, here and there, broad-shouldered plainclothes men distinguishable as members of the 'G' Division of the Dublin Metropolitan Division engaged in political espionage. A tank was ambling along Bachelor's Walk, military lorries, filled with armed-to-the-teeth troops, their rifles at the ready, were racing through O'Connell St, and military cordons were drawn with barbed wire around the entrances to Grafton St from Nassau St and College Green.[15]

Along with this visible menace there were the hidden dangers of the British Secret Service and its attendant squads of assassins.

One of the agents sent against Collins was described by Sir Basil Thompson as 'one of the best and cleverest Secret Service men that England ever had'.[16] Plump, sharp-featured, middle-aged, of average height, his knee-length boots were the only distinguishing thing about the man known as Jameson, though he was apparently born Burns, the son of a police officer from Limerick. He had worked in intelligence in India before the First World War and during it somehow managed to elude detection in Germany. Afterwards he had been an *agent provocateur* during the London police strike. In Dublin his cover story was that he was a salesman of musical instruments with an interest in bird-watching. He began by infiltrating Irish circles in London by posing as one of the fiery communist speakers whose podium adjoined the Irish Self-Determination League's platform at Speakers' Corner in Hyde Park. As the communists supported the Irish revolution these Sunday morning occasions were friendly affairs through which Jameson had easily become acquainted with Sean McGrath and Art O'Brien. The consequences may be gauged from a despatch of Collins' to O'Brien: 'Jameson: has duly arrived and has been interviewed by 3 of us. I shall report developments later on.'[17]

The 'developments' were intended to centre on two of Jameson's stated objectives, firstly to provide the IRA with arms, as he had earlier done through O'Brien as evidence of good faith, and secondly to foment mutiny in the British Army and Navy, in both Ireland and England. In fact things fell out in fatally different fashion from what was expected. Jameson's visit was to cost England the lives of two of her best agents, that of Jameson himself and that of Assistant Commissioner Redmond, mentioned earlier in Chapter 4.

The Jameson incident gives another glimpse of Collins' extra-ordinary network of agents. The story shows that Collins had penetrated right into the heart of the British Secret Service. Collins had him watched in London as well as Dublin and one day in January sent a warning to Art O'Brien:

Jameson: What I have to say with regard to him will probably be somewhat of a thunderbolt to you. I believe we have the man or one of them. I have absolutely certain information that the man who came from London met and spoke to me, and reported that I was growing a moustache to Basil Thompson. I may get some more information. In the meantime will you get in touch with him somehow and show him my paragraph on himself in the other memo.[18]

The other paragraph was a decoy written in the tone of Collins' note to O'Brien on Jameson of December. Hand-written on the memo is a message asking O'Brien to 'find out from Jameson what addresses I gave him so that I can warn. I am not quite certain as my note is not very clear.' So obviously Jameson had succeed in prising some information out of Collins before he was unmasked. But the really remarkable thing is that Collins had obviously succeeded in placing someone close to Basil Thompson himself.

Collins at first took to Jameson and had him introduced to members of GHQ who also seemed to find nothing wrong with him. For no apparent reason, however, Tom Cullen took an immediate dislike to the agent and described him as a 'crooked English bastard', perhaps sensing that he and Jameson were in the same line of work. This feeling transmitted itself to Thornton and Tobin and they decided to lay a trap for Jameson. Meanwhile Jameson was also setting traps for Collins, traps which very nearly succeeded in their objective.

Collins brought him to lunch at Mrs O'Connor's, to have her vet him. He relied on her instinct and judgement so much that he adjudged it worth while exposing her to the risk of identification as one of his agents, for a detective had been posted outside at a safe distance.[19] Seeing Jameson come out again with another man, he cycled off to alert a waiting contingent of detectives and police. Incredibly he misinformed them, telling them that the bird had flown, not knowing that the bird was still in the house where Mrs O'Connor was telling him that she did not like her visitor. The man with Jameson was Liam Tobin. Collins was soon informed of the detective's mistake; one of the men in the police party had been MacNamara.

MacNamara had also been present in the Castle the previous day when Redmond, an able man who had been brought down from Belfast to reorganise the demoralised detective division, made what proved to be a fatal remark while dressing down subordinates: 'You were supposed to be looking for Collins. You have been after him for months and never caught sight of him, while a new man, just over from England, met him and talked to him after two days.'

However it was one thing to know that Redmond was a force to be reckoned with. It was another thing to identify that force. Collins sent Thornton to Belfast[20] where he linked up with the Belfast equivalent of Broy, a Sergeant Matt MacCarthy from Kerry, who operated from one of the most strongly loyalist centres in Ireland, Chichester St Barracks. Describing Thornton as his cousin, McCarthy installed him in the barracks for the night, the occasion of the police boxing championships. Every policeman who could was attending, including the District Inspector. Thornton was able to enter his office and remove a photograph of Redmond from his files. The photograph was in Collins' hands next day.

This Sergeant McCarthy helped Collins out of a tight corner in Kirwan's one night. He had come down from Belfast to hand over the latest police codes to Collins when the place was raided. His police pass caused the Auxiliary to relax and offer the pair a drink – without searching Collins, who had the codes on him. The barman put away the .45 he was preparing to use on the Auxiliary and poured a round of pints. Redmond had led a raid on Mrs O'Connor's house after which he had assured her that he would not trouble her again. He spoke truer than he knew. Paddy Daly was to shoot him dead three days later, outside the Standard Hotel in Harcourt St which he was due to vacate shortly for the safety of rooms which were almost ready for him in the Castle. One of the unfortunate Redmond's last acts of police work was to spend the night of the raid on O'Connor's staking out the house in a futile vigil for Collins in the company of another detective – MacNamara. On his death the Castle offered a reward of £10,000 for information leading to convictions in what was by then a total of fourteen dead DMP and RIC. The toll would go higher, but the reward would not be claimed.

Meanwhile Jameson returned to England where Collins was able to secure a report on his briefing to Sir Basil Thompson. With extraordinary courage the spy then returned to Dublin and contacted Crow St, which now proceeded to lay a trap for him. The spy arranged to hand over a portmanteau of revolvers to Thornton at 56 Bachelor's Walk, Dublin, the home of both the New Ireland Assurance Company and of a famous Dublin tobacconist, Knapp and Peterson's Ltd. Thornton accepted the revolvers, but instead of going up to the New Ireland offices, which were frequently used to plan activities that the British would certainly have wished to insure against, he went downstairs to Knapp and Peterson's basement while Tobin took Jameson away. Then Thornton sprinted down to the quartermaster-general's stores, run by Sean MacMahon at 32 Bachelor's Walk. The strain of trying to keep the underground army supplied had turned MacMahon's hair white by the time he was thirty. To him bullets were as precious as diamonds. When he read a newspaper account of some soldiers being 'riddled with bullets' he was furious. 'Riddled! Blast them, where do they think we'll get them.'[21] The revolvers were naturally warmly welcomed and should have guaranteed Jameson's bona fides. However, Thornton had earlier asked MacNamara to let him know if any special raids were planned by the Castle that day. A few hours after the revolvers were handed over word came that 56 Bachelor's Walk was to be raided at three o'clock.

It was, watched from across the river by Tobin, Thornton and Cullen. All the raiders found in the basement was a Volunteer's cap which convinced them that they were on the right track. After midnight they returned and dug up floors and knocked down walls looking for secret passages. Not surprisingly Jameson again went back to the drawing-board. He returned to London to report, and, showing remarkable courage, went back to Dublin yet again, still trying to see Collins.

Joe O'Reilly told Jameson that his wish to meet Collins was about to be granted.[22] He was collected by two of the 'apostles', Paddy Daly and Joe Dowling, and brought by tram to the back entrance of the Albert College in Ballymun. Here Paddy Daly told him that he was a spy and that he was doomed. There are differing accounts of what Jameson said in reply but all agree that he stood to attention and clicked his heels while the hammers of the .45s cocked. As Daly was 'close . . . as the killer is close one moment to the man he kills', I give his recollection of the agent's last words: 'That's right. God bless the

King. I would love to die for him.' An iron cross he had given Tobin was hung in his memory on the walls in Crow St alongside pictures of other agents who had either shared or, it was hoped, would share his fate.

One of the most important of these was an Irishman, H. Quinlisk, a former corporal in the Royal Irish Regiment, who, as a German prisoner of war, had enrolled in Casement's Brigade. It was probably Quinlisk who first gave the Castle an accurate idea of the extent of Collins' influence. On his return to Ireland he received assistance from Sinn Fein and from Collins who gave him money, bought him a new suit and got him a place in his lodgings at Miss MacCarthy's, 44 Mountjoy St, which by then he generally only used to keep his clothes in. Quinlisk apparently reciprocated by having the place raided. Collins put it down to happenstance. Apparently he thought that Quinlisk's knowledge of German and his military experience could be put to some use by the Volunteers. That wasn't what Quinlisk had in mind.

On 11 November 1919 he wrote to 'The Under Secretary, Dublin Castle' telling him that he had decided to tell 'all I know' of Sinn Fein and of 'that scoundrel Michael Collins' who had 'treated me scurvily'. The letter resulted in an interview in Brunswick St, an account of which was given to Broy to type and a copy sent along to Collins. Quinlisk lived like a caricature of a Greene/Le Carré portrait of an agent manipulated for some three months before his end. Unknown to him, his treachery was widely known. Kathleen Napoli MacKenna recalls seeing

a well-dressed young man [at 6 Harcourt St], with frank open countenance and nonchalant air sitting smoking, his legs dangling, on a console-table in the inner hall. I noticed the colours of his regimental tie. Fitzie[23] stopped to talk to him; I walked on to the hall-door and as I awaited her I could hear their chatter and laughter.

'Darn nice lad, that: pity he's up to no good in here', Fitzie remarked carelessly when she joined me. 'Who's he?' I enquired. 'Quinlisk, an ex-member of Casement's Irish Brigade on the make for blood money.'

MacKenna thought no more of the incident, imagining Anna FitzSimons meant something to do with recompensing Quinlisk for his Brigade activities. But the following February FitzSimons asked her if she remembered the day in the hall and told her Quinlisk had just been found shot dead in Cork. Collins had sent him on a false trail, letting him believe that he was going to be in Wren's Hotel, Cork. The result was that a message in code went to the RIC District Inspector in Cork from the Castle instructing him to surround Wren's Hotel and arrest Michael Collins. Quinlisk himself travelled to Cork and made a beeline for Wren's so as to be on the scene to collect the £10,000 offered after Redmond's shooting. Instead the Cork IRA found him and he was discovered dead in a ditch on 18 February 1920. Napoli MacKenna wrote:

The event impressed me deeply and threw a new light on the bitterness of the struggle in which I was now taking my part. From it I realised . . . how ruthless Collins could be when necessary. He had played up to, and trapped, this Irish Judas who for hard cash was prepared to betray one of Ireland's most valuable leaders.

It would be impossible to chronicle the individual killings carried out by each side as the war intensified but a few other examples of that 'ruthlessness' which suddenly dawned on Napoli MacKenna may be noted to indicate the nature of the war. Before doing so it is necessary to understand the importance of the Dublin institution known as 'Kidd's Back'.

As we saw, Neligan had managed to get himself accepted as a member of the British Secret Service. He then proceeded to introduce Tobin, Thornton and Cullen to his Secret Service colleagues. They generally met either at the Rabbiatti Saloon in Malborough St or in 'Kidd's Back', a famous bar off Grafton St at the back of what is now the Berni Inn in Nassau St. The British *modus operandi* was to have each member of the Secret Service surround himself with a number of touts, or minor informers. Some must have been worse than useless to their employers. They were generally English and completely at sea. One day in Rabbiatti's, Cullen and Thornton found themselves sharing a table with a group of them, one of whom suddenly exclaimed wonderingly: 'Gor blimey, how did you learn the Irish brogue. We're here in Dublin for the last twelve months and we can't pick any of it up. You fellows have it perfect.' The Irishmen solemnly explained that there was an art in such matters.

The more senior British Intelligence officers patronised Kidd's Back, and Willie Beaumont and Neligan introduced Cullen, Saurin and Thornton to some of them, pretending the three Irishmen were their touts. (Collins literally charmed Beaumont into joining the British Secret Service. He induced Beaumont's brother, Sean, to arrange a meeting between the ex-British officer, who had publicly announced his intention of 'getting' Collins, and himself. Beaumont was 'so impressed . . . that he offered his services to us.') The three became habitués of this mecca of British Intelligence. As Thornton says, 'a lot of our information was picked up by taking a very big risk.' Some of the most dangerous men in Europe met in that bar, from both sides. One day some of the British agents were chatting with the three Irishmen when an officer suddenly said to Cullen: 'Surely you fellows know Liam Tobin, Frank Thornton and Tom Cullen. These are Collins' three officers and if you get those fellows we should locate Collins himself.' That conversation in Kidd's was a tribute to the effectiveness of the campaign Collins and his men were waging against the Castle's hitherto invincible intelligence system. At least one of the battles in that campaign was fought out in Kidd's.

Liam Tobin used to drink with Fergus Brian Mulloy, a sergeant in the British Army who worked for Colonel Hill Dillon, Chief Intelligence Officer at Parkgate St. Neither he nor Dillon suspected Lily Merin, who was working as Dillon's secretary! Mulloy also met Thornton and Cullen and whether through the snobbery of the British officer system, or the confusion and rivalry between the various British forces, he never succeeded in fingering his new acquaintances to the representatives of the units who shared the bar with him. Auxiliaries, Secret Service, Military Intelligence, police officers, all sat drinking within arm's reach as Mulloy drank with Tobin.

Yet Mulloy seems to have been under no illusion as to whom or what he was dealing with. After his death it became known that he had written to his sister in America that if he were murdered 'a man named Tobin' would have been responsible. His cover story was that he intended joining the British Secret Service in order to help the IRA and he promised to get arms and an army pass for Tobin and company. These never materialised and he eventually proposed that Thornton and Cullen should accompany him into the Castle one night and he would make it possible for them to copy out secret documents. The pair had a shrewd notion that if they got into the Castle they stood a very poor chance of getting out again and counter-proposed that Mulloy assist them in shooting Colonel Hill Dillon who lived outside Parkgate in civilian quarters. The Colonel promptly disappeared into safer lodgings.

Then, in another well-known Dublin rendezvous, the Café Cairo, Mulloy suggested that Tobin give him some information to show his superiors to prove that he was achieving something – perhaps the names and addresses of some Sinn Feiners who were prominent but whose removal to jail would not seriously damage the movement, say, Countess Markievicz or Count Plunkett? 'Write the addresses and I'll be trusted with more secrets', he said, handing Tobin a sheet of captured Dail Eireann notepaper. Tobin had an apocalyptic vision of one of both of the two being found murdered with a sheet of Dail Eireann notepaper beside them containing the handwriting of Michael Collins' right-hand man. It would enable the British to make the sort of claims Lloyd George and French had come out with after MacCurtain's murder four days earlier. The interview terminated and that evening, going up the stairs of Vaughan's, Tobin was heard to say to Collins, 'We'll have to shoot that fellow.' Collins replied simply: 'Well shoot him so.' Mulloy died on the pavement of Wicklow St on the following evening, 25 March 1920.

Collins also discovered that the hall porter of the Wicklow Hotel,

William Doran, was an informer. Joe Dolan described what happened:

The Squad made several attempts to get him but were unsuccessful. At last Mick Collins sent a dispatch to Liam Tobin to hurry it up, as he was doing a lot of damage. Tobin asked me to do it as I knew him. Dan McDonnell and myself entered the Wicklow Hotel one morning about nine o'clock, shot him dead in the hall, and walked away. I was back there at 1 pm having my lunch.

Not knowing who had had him shot, his destitute widow applied to the Sinn Fein for a pension. For the sake of the children, Collins directed that she should be paid.

Amongst assassins on the other side the names of Captain Hardy and Igoe stand out. Hardy was the liaison officer between Dublin Castle and Special Intelligence Office, Scotland Yard. He was involved with the UVF in ways that even today the Northern Ireland authorities wish to keep secret.[24] These schemes included a plot to kidnap Arthur Griffith. Collins himself described Hardy as a 'notorious murderer'.[25] Crow St had a long list of killings to debit to Igoe and his men. Torture was added to the scale of horrors awaiting anyone who fell into such hands. Watching the forces pile up against him Collins summed up the position in a memorable letter: '. . . to my mind it is now a question of our nerves. There is no doubt a great deal of punishment ahead of us. It is a question of the body wearing longer than the lash.'[26]

The punishment did come, but so did a great deal of assistance in bearing it, from all sorts of unexpected quarters. One such was a publican, Liam Devlin, who had returned from Scotland to buy a pub in Parnell Square, directly opposite the Rotunda. Devlin, who had been active in Sinn Fein in Scotland and was put in touch with Collins through the IRB, now offered a means of protection to Collins, the use of his pub as an office and meeting place. It was an ideal cover, centrally situated in a busy part of Dublin, so that Collins and his contacts were able to come and go unremarked. Devlin's became

Mick's unofficial headquarters. 'We used Devlin's extensively and every night Mick, Gearoid O'Sullivan, Liam Tobin, Dermot O'Hegarty, Piaras Beaslai, Frank Thornton, Tom Cullen and Joe O'Reilly met there, the events of the day were discussed and plans were made for the following day. Any particular Column leader or Brigade Officer arriving in town was generally instructed to report to Devlin's. . . . Mrs Devlin acted in the capacity of a very generous hostess. Visitors from the country never left without getting a meal and in quite a large number of instances a bed for the night.[27]

The Devlins wanted Collins to use a large comfortable room at the front of the house, but he preferred to sleep at the back, where he could hear the sound of horses in a nearby stable.[28] Possibly the sound of breaking furniture was less audible from the back of the pub also! In exercise Collins would push the sofa at an opponent, throw the wash jug, the basin – 'a broken lock meant as little to him as a broken vessel'. The Devlins gave Collins an ordinary furnished room. As O'Connor notes,

within a month it was a wreck. There was scarcely a chair with a back to it; the delph had disappeared, yet when one of the gang, hearing a tumble and thunder from the sitting room in which Collins was lashing out with a chair, apologised to the Devlins, they merely smiled and said: 'It eases his mind'. They spoke with the understanding of love, for it was in this savage lashing and straining that all the accumulated anxiety was released.

The rollings on the floor with Liam Tobin, Gearoid O'Sullivan and Tom Cullen were roisterings between men who were taking life and knew that at any second their own could be snuffed out. The heaving mass on the floor striving for 'a bit of ear' was after all the hunted Leadership of the Irish Republican Army.

One of Collins' worst faults was his habit of baiting people, most notably O'Reilly and Tom Cullen. Once, in the emotional firestorm he always experienced before or after the carrying out of one of his killings, or 'jobs' as those involved always referred to them, he was so outrageous to O'Reilly that the unfortunate man broke down and wept, and said that he could take no more, he was going home. Collins snarled at him: 'All right, take some despatches for me on your way', and the selfless O'Reilly, worn out from sleepless nights and ceaseless Trojan work for Collins, took the despatches to the girl for whom they were intended. He had obviously been crying, and when she asked him why, he broke down again and gave her the reason, at which she flew into such a rage that she went immediately to Collins and read him the Riot Act for insensitivity to the amount of work O'Reilly did.

Collins stormed back at her, 'You mind your own fucking business. I know how O'Reilly works', and poor O'Reilly was back at work the following morning for some more of the same treatment, which so enraged at least one observer that years later Ernie O'Malley would write:

He had a habit of baiting Tom Cullen . . . and a few of the Dublin men that I hated. I could understand, take or make use of a tell-off, but the prodding got on my nerves. One day I told Collins and left the room in a rage. He never baited anyone in my presence afterwards.[30]

Joe O'Reilly once uncannily recreated both the horror that gripped Collins on the eve of a 'job' and the hold he exerted on O'Reilly's imagination. It happened when Frank O'Connor and Dr Richard Hayes were interviewing him one evening a dozen years after Collins was killed. By then O'Reilly had matured from a harassed drudge into the polished, golf-playing man who became ADC to W. T. Cosgrave, then President of the Executive Council (effectively the Prime Minister), and an important official in the Board of Works. After some hours O'Connor asked him, 'How did Collins behave when he had to have someone shot?' O'Reilly 'seemed to collapse . . . Something had gone wrong with him . . .' Seemingly some kind of auto-hypnotism occurred for he suddenly went into the Collins war-spasm. O'Connor writes:

. . . he suddenly jumped up, thrust his hands into his pockets and began to stamp about the room, digging his heels in with a savagery that almost shook the house. Finally he threw himself onto a sofa, picked up a newspaper, which he pretended to read, tossed it aside after a few moments and said in a coarse country voice, 'Jesus Christ Almighty, how often have I to tell ye . . . ?' It was no longer Joe O'Reilly who was in the room. It was Michael Collins, and for close on two hours I had an experience that must be every biographer's dream, of watching someone I had never known as though he were still alive. Every gesture, every intonation was imprinted on O'Reilly's brain as if on tape.[31]

The depth of the imprintation shocked O'Connor almost as much as it did O'Reilly. He said, 'You could see not only Collins, but also the effect he was having upon a gentle, sensitive boy, and it made you want to intervene between a boy who was no longer there and a ghost. I did it even at the risk of breaking the record.' At one point in the hypnosis, O'Reilly began recreating the scene when the girl-next-door stormed into Collins to protest at his cruelty. O'Reilly was beginning to describe Collins' response in normal tones when, O'Connor writes, 'suddenly Collins was back in the room again: "I know his value better than you do. He goes to Mass for me every morning. Jesus Christ, do you think I don't know what he's worth to me?"'

Generally when O'Connor writes of Collins, a sense of affection, of love almost, emerges, but he concludes his account: 'When O'Reilly left, the handsome, sprightly young man had disappeared. In his place was an elderly, bewildered man, and you could see what he would be like if Collins had lived.'

Against this description of Collins' methods one must balance that of another contemporary who, like O'Malley, later fought against Collins: Oscar Traynor, who succeeded Dick McKee as OC of the Dublin Brigade during some of the fiercest fighting of the Anglo-Irish war. To Traynor,

it was like a breath of fresh air to meet him or to talk to him. He was always full of ideas. His ideas were good too. You got the impression of eventual success. This man wasn't beaten. This fellow didn't think we were finished, nor did he give the impression of being finished himself. Mick Collins was very easy on men. He'd talk nicely to them, even if he didn't think much of them. After raging he'd come back and apologise.[32]

These methods maintained discipline on a force of young men

bound together more by idealism than training. Unpunctuality, for instance, sent him into a fury in which he would swing his watch so violently as he enquired why the —— he had been kept waiting that recipients of this treatment feared they were going to be struck by the timepiece. The point was that split-second timing was essential for the successful carrying out of his raids, meetings and ambushes. Even though he went about Dublin deliberately refusing to wear disguise, or to allow the ever-increasing strength of the enemy to interfere with his movements, he was at risk every second of the day. The solicitor Michael Noyek, called to a meeting with Collins in Kirwan's pub in Parnell St one day, received the usual indication of his whereabouts, an imperceptible nod of the head and a movement of the eyes to indicate where Collins sat in the snug, and there was the most wanted man in Europe 'sitting calmly, working away in a crowd of dealers'.[33]

That little anecdote is a testimonial to Collins' success. Those stallholders from nearby Moore St knew perfectly well who Collins was, but not one of them, in a class not normally associated with aversion to turning a quick penny, thought of betraying him, and, business with Noyek finished, Collins was apt to come up suddenly behind someone in the street and invite him to join him immediately in blowing up a barracks! Apart from the sudden shock of such a practical joke on an already strained Volunteer, there was the fact that they never knew when he might be serious.

Collins' personality was such that some of his practical-joking side rubbed off even on the gentle O'Reilly. Knowing that Sean Nunan and Frank Kelly, both friends of Collins, were looking for a flat in the Howth area, O'Reilly took time off from the revolution to concoct an advertisement offering rooms at a dream rent, and stipulating that the tenants would have to care for a parrot. Nunan and Kelly boned up on parrot-lore and then had a long, fruitless cycle, trying to locate a non-existent address. O'Reilly was suitably consoling when they returned muttering inadvisabilities about 'that stupid bitch of a landlady and her parrot'.[34]

On one occasion, Collins got word that Lord French would be passing through College St a little later and he got himself a gun, rounded up anyone who happened to be nearby, and set off to lead an ambush,[35] his extraordinary magnetism being such that he was joined on that hare-brained occasion by men who could hardly hold a weapon, never mind know anything about ambush techniques. Another time a friend rushed in to Devlin's to tell him that Mulcahy and Diarmuid O'Hegarty were trapped by police at a meeting in Parnell Square. 'I'll get Tobin and some of the boys and we won't be long getting them away', was Collins' reaction. Then he ran upstairs, whistling, to get his gun, and he and the friend headed up the square without waiting for Tobin. The case was less grievous than reported.

Mulcahy and O'Hegarty were coming down the square towards them. 'Can ye bloody children not look after yourselves yet?' was his salutation. As the four of them strolled down O'Connell St on a Sunday morning a policemen, who obviously knew who they were, looked up as they passed. 'Good morning boys.' Collins burst out laughing. 'The comic war', he said.[36]

Liam Deasy, one of the leading Cork IRA men, put his finger on one of the major reasons for Collins' success – his accessibility to, and concern for, men who came up from the country with some problem. He could be generous in time and effort to make either the humblest recruit or the most senior officer feel that his efforts were appreciated, albeit in his own alarming fashion. Deasy, who had come to Dublin on IRA business after a period of intense, savage, guerrilla warfare, recalls a memorable Easter with Collins.[37] Collins met him at Devlin's and ordered a taxi in which he took Frank Thornton, Gearoid O'Sullivan and Deasy to the Phoenix Park races.[38] In the grandstand enclosure they met a thunderstruck colleague who enquired incredulously on seeing them, 'Are ye mad?' Collins replied, 'We'll show ye country fellows how to work and enjoy yourselves,' and they spent the afternoon shoulder to shoulder with British officers, Intelligence agents, civil servants and loyalist supporters of Dublin Castle, who would cheerfully have joined in hanging all four of them. Before they left, Collins paid their bookies' debts.

At Vaughan's Hotel that night, Collins was warned that it would be curfew time in twenty minutes, and he replied, 'To hell with curfew and them that enforce it.' 'We finished our business twenty-five minutes after curfew and the two of us walked along an empty Parnell Square to Devlin's, the awestruck Deasy recalled. The next morning, Easter Sunday, Deasy went with Collins from Devlin's on foot right across Dublin to Harcourt St, where they had a meeting with James MacNamara. After this, Collins had some business to transact in the Commercial Buildings in O'Connell St from whence the pair went back to Devlin's at a 'four miles an hour walk'. From Devlin's they took a taxi to Rathmines. They were stopped at a checkpoint and a suspicious policeman ran his fingers through Collins' hair, twisting his head around in an effort to recognise him, but they were let go and proceeded on to lunch with Mrs O'Donovan where Collins' contribution to the talk of his escape was to tell his friend Tadgh O'Sullivan, 'You bloody country fellows are too careful.' Then he hired a horse and sidecar and took O'Sullivan with himself and Deasy out to the well-known hostelry on the foothills of Dublin, the Lamb Doyle's at Sandyford, where he had a small sherry. The sidecar dropped them off at Palmerston Park, Rathgar, where there followed four hours of serious discussion of the IRB's role in shaping events. After this, everyone who had attended the meeting was tired and most of the participants went to bed. 'They may as well have stayed up,' Deasy recalls, 'Collins went to every room and started a pillow fight. By four o'clock when he at last dropped off from sheer exhaustion, there was nothing to be seen in any room but feathers from floor to ceiling.' Sean Dowling has left another impression of Collins:

I knew Maureen Power, who was high in the movement. She was at a meeting attended by Sean Treacy shortly before he was shot. . . . Collins was going full pelt with the language. Treacy jumped up. 'How dare you go on like that in front of a lady.' It stopped him; he recoiled at once and apologised to both of them.[39]

This was the same Collins who, when Batt O'Connor was knocked down by a car, called at the house every evening to comfort his wife and family through a period when it seemed that Batt might not live. 'We saw the real man then,' said Sister Margaret Mary. His weekly visits to the de Valera family at Greystones, bringing money and solace, meant that the family were not split up as they had been after the 1916 Rising. Collins, the man who was seen in Greystones playing with the de Valera children, not the pillow-fighting hooligan, was the man the O'Connors saw in their hour of need.

The most peculiarly Irish form of weapon used in the conflict was that of hunger-striking. Long before the British came to Ireland there was a custom whereby a man would sometimes retaliate on a powerful enemy by starving himself outside his door. It was inevitable therefore that the tactic of hunger-striking would be employed in a struggle between two such unequal protagonists. Apart from the strikes involving Ashe and Stack mentioned earlier, there were major strikes at Mountjoy Jail in Dublin and at Wormwood Scrubs in England. The Mountjoy strike began on 5 April 1920 for a familiar Republican demand, the right to be recognised as prisoners of war, or failing that, for release. Because of the relatively unknown nature of hunger-striking the affair mushroomed into a state of national anxiety over what was universally believed to be the prisoners' imminent demise. Labour leaders called the general strike on 12 April and it was so widely observed that the prisoners were released unconditionally, three days later. Victory celebrations were held throughout the country, their impact on public opinion being sharply heightened by the action of police and military in Miltown Malbay in County Clare who shot up a bonfire crowd without warning, killing three people and wounding nine. A military inquiry was held but the results were never published. The second hunger-strike broke out amongst the Sinn Fein prisoners in Wormwood Scrubs less than a week after the Mountjoy men were set free. Their strike began on 21 April and continued until release was secured eighteen days later. This strike too was marked by violence. London mobs attacked the Irish crowds praying and demonstrating outside the jail. The police did not interfere.

A number of bodies wore out very quickly under 'the lash' of the Terror. As Sean Lemass noted:

. . . the time the Black and Tan War became active the numbers began to shrink very rapidly. The enormous companies that we commanded during the conscription period began to dissipate very quickly when it became a different type of operation. Some of them had quite conscientious objections to the type of work we were engaged in and dropped out for that reason.[40]

The 'type of work' the Volunteers were engaged in was killing people, notably spies and informers. For though there was very evidently a war in full swing in Ireland from the end of 1919, intensifying throughout 1920 and reaching a crescendo prior to the Truce of 1921, it was rarely a pitched battle affair. The Irish engaged the British successfully on two fronts, propaganda and intelligence and held them to a draw in the military field, largely through the use of their 'flying columns'. These columns, very poorly armed and generally numbering no more than fifteen to twenty men, lived 'on their keeping', staging an ambush here, a barracks raid there, perhaps after a night, or nights, spent out in the open, 'laying on', that is waiting to set up an ambush. Very often afterwards they would strike out in the depths of an Irish winter, through fog and bog, to a billet in a barn or a farm, perhaps twenty miles away. Denied the status of belligerents, the Volunteers knew that they fought in the likelihood of execution if captured under arms, or even without them, depending on whose hands they fell into. But they put up such a fight, particularly in Cork, Clare, Tipperary, Longford, Limerick and Mayo, that they tied up well over 50,000 troops and drove the RIC out of all but the most strongly fortified barracks in the larger towns.

The Cork IRA was certainly up against some formidable military opponents. There was Brigade Major Montgomery, later Field Marshal Montgomery of El Alamein, who wrote of his Irish experiences: 'My whole attention was given to defeating the rebels. It never bothered me a bit how many houses were burned.'[41] He told his father: 'Any civilian or Republican soldier who interferes with any officer or soldier is shot at once.' Montgomery set up a special 'Cork City Intelligence Unit' and prepared a special manual on how to deal with the rebels – sanguinarily – but his intelligence efforts were not in Collins' class, one Josephine Marchment being worth a score of his best intelligence agents, while his heavy-footed Western Front methodology could never hope to combat the fast-moving flying columns with their advantages not only of mobility, but also of motivation and local support.

THE YEAR OF TERROR

Of course, had the British Army been used in a more all-out fashion, concentration camps, air raids, artillery bombardments and the rest of it, the result might have been different. But Lloyd George never felt secure enough to adopt such a policy and place the various forces in Ireland under a unified command as both the generals and the revamped Irish Executive demanded. In vain did Sir Henry Wilson plead for the introduction of methods such as drawing up lists of prominent Republicans and 'shooting by roster'. He felt that if the Sinn Feiners were to be murdered the government should be seen to do the murdering. But as he recorded in his diary Lloyd George 'fairly danced' when it was proposed to him that the government should take responsibility for reprisals.[42] He felt that no government could take responsibility for such activities. The dogs were only to be allowed off the leash in the murky underground of the war between two secret services that developed from the time Collins began having agents shot. But even in this limited arena, on the face of it, the British would appear to have had the advantage. Practitioners of what Kipling termed 'the Great Game', espionage, with all the resources of empire at their disposal, they were confronted by a group of country lads, led by a twenty-nine-year-old ex-post office clerk, 'from a brainy Cork family'. But Collins won, notwithstanding the combination of national spirit, his associates' talents, his own gift for intelligence work and all the rest of it, by his ability not only to endure, but to inflict, as an unpublished account by Sergeant Mannix, one of his principal contacts in the Dublin Metropolitan Police recalls:

I also attended a number of meetings at Williamstown, Booterstown, and at Rathgar Avenue which were convened for the purpose of passing the death sentence on a number of spies. The death sentence was passed on 9 or 10 informers for a date not fixed. The following are the names of those who sat at that meeting. . . . Michael Collins, Frank Thornton, Mr M. Byrne, Mr James Sullivan and myself . . . I also secured information pertaining to a cheque which was being received from the British Secret Service by 'Andrew Knight' who was employed as a Tram Inspector on the Dalkey line . . . he was taken off a tram car, taken out to Killiney Golf Links and shot.[43]

Collins took no pleasure in killing. There are in fact well-authenticated stories, in addition to O'Reilly's vision, of the tension and horror that gripped him before a 'job' was to be carried out. But with his knowledge of the Castle regime he realised that one spy was more dangerous to him than a regiment of soldiers. So too, according to Flor Begley, the Assistant Brigade Adjutant of Cork No. 3 Brigade, did the men in the field.[44] In theory the shooting of spies was supposed to be authorised by GHQ. Cathal Brugha, as Minister for Defence, wanted documentary proof of guilt to be provided beforehand so as to be able to satisfy an international commission (which he visualised being set up after hostilities had ended) that the Volunteers had acted correctly. In Cork however, Volunteers, hunted from pillar to post, felt this an inappropriately bureaucratic procedure which if carried out would allow a certain spy to continue his work while Brugha was deliberating. They appealed to Collins saying that they felt sure of their ground and the spy should be shot out of hand. According to Begley, Collins replied, 'Shoot him and say nothing about it.' 'No use, must let would-be spies know of it', was the reply. Collins agreed. 'Shoot him and label him if ye want to.' This provided further friction between Collins and Brugha, but it was the method which was adopted. Tom Barry calculated that his brigade shot some sixteen spies in this fashion.[45] The calibre of these wretches may be gauged from the fact that one was a man found drunk in a ditch by Volunteers. Befuddled by the spoils of his blood money he babbled on to them after being woken up, in the belief that they were British soldiers, until he realised too late that he was talking himself into another, longer, sleep.

One of the bedevilling factors of the Volunteer campaign was land hunger, a desire on the part of some unscrupulous people to profit from the disorders of the time. A letter to Collins from a priest in Rosmuck, in Connemara, in the west, for instance, dated 10 March 1920, spoke of widespread agrarian outrage and of intimidation on the part of locals styling themselves Volunteers and 'pressing young fellows into the Volunteers', thus getting the movement a bad name and costing some £1,000 in lost loan subscriptions. The same considerations were present in urban areas too, of course. One of the reasons the Belfast 'confetti' (rivets) was bespattered around with such energy was the fact that the expelled Catholic workers had their jobs taken by unemployed Protestant ex-servicemen.

Brugha continued to run his candle-making business during the war, and rarely came in contact with the rank and file and the realities of their existence. Liam Deasy was one of those who attended a significant meeting, presided over by Brugha, on 1 August 1920 in Dublin to discuss the IRA's tactics.[46] The attendance included Collins, Mulcahy, MacSwiney, McKee and a Catholic priest, Father Dick MacCarthy, representing the OC of West Limerick, Sean Finn. Ambushing was one of the main items on the agenda. Brugha argued against ambushes, preferring what Deasy termed 'straight fights'. He wanted the ambushers to call on the Auxiliaries or Tans to surrender before fire was opened. The Cork OCs pointed out that if they did this they would be robbed of their principal weapon, surprise, which they badly needed against a numerically superior and more heavily armed enemy. GHQ's initial plan for dealing with the Auxiliaries, who were quickly identified as a more dangerous foe than the Tans, was to confine them in towns by the use of overlapping formations of Volunteers. Terry MacSwiney pointed out that they didn't have the guns for this and it was decided to leave decisions on ambush methodology in the hands of the local OCs. A few days later, on 23 August the result of this decision was seen in a trend-setting ambush at Macroom in which six police were shot and a quantity of rifles seized.

But Brugha never got over his antipathy towards ambushing. It became a grisly joke in Volunteer circles. Oscar Traynor told Ernie O'Malley that he became particularly upset when a woman, the mother of three children, was accidently killed in crossfire while she was shopping.[47] He tried to have it laid down that ambushes would henceforth be banned on Saturdays, shopping day for most Dublin families. The only result, however, was that some wits in the Dublin Brigade began to inform their colleagues solemnly that 'the Saturday ambush has been postponed until Monday.' It was a miracle of either luck or marksmanship on both sides that civilian casualties were not far higher. Ambushes became so frequent in parts of Dublin that an area of Camden St was christened the Dardanelles. The Tans and Auxiliaries tore about the city in lorries seated back to back with their loaded guns pointing outwards. Neither they, nor the citizenry, knew when something nasty might suddenly be propelled from, or into the lorries. Joe Leonard, a member of the Squad, described how the IRA found a

partial cure for their greater activity, in the number 9 bomb manufactured in our National Munition Factory at Denzil Lane and which some of our 'Littlers' were very adept at introducing into their tenders causing the Tans to leave same in a state of undress.[48]

Sean MacBride, one of the 'littlers', showed me over his own company area of Pearse St and Westland Row one night and described how he operated:

We'd walk up and down on opposite sides of the street. And when we'd see a patrol or a lorry coming along we'd fire on it, or lob a bomb and fire on them when they'd jump out. Then we'd run like hares, dump the revolvers and I'd get back to college. The professors weren't too keen on what we were doing, but it didn't matter. So long as I got back quickly to Earlsfort Terrace I could pretend I was attending classes when the ambush took place. I remember one evening myself and another Volunteer were pinned down on the railway line by Tans firing on us. I could see the sparks from the bullets striking the tracks. I noticed blood coming from my friend's head and suddenly I realised he was dead. I had to see his parents and go to the wake and that sort of thing. It was my first experience of death. I was about sixteen at the time.[49]

At a Cabinet meeting held in Downing St on 31 May 1920, the Cabinet began holding its cloak over a form of reprisals policy, a 'plan whereby Irishmen were made to feel the effect of the campaign of murder and arson along economic channels'. The meeting sought recommendations from the Irish Executive on 'the best method of imposing fines on Irishmen in an affected area' and on the 'best method of interfering with the everyday facilities of an affected area'.[50] Policy calmly formulated in public-school accents behind closed doors can manifest itself in very raucous and savage proceedings when translated into action. The 'best method' turned out to be burning creameries, bacon factories and mills. One of the largest creameries destroyed – by uniformed RIC men – at Knocklong, County Limerick, on 22 August, was owned by Sir Thomas Cleeves, a Unionist.

'Telling a Hamar' probably reached its highest point in October after a bad day's work in Tubercurry, County Sligo. This began with the shooting of a popular RIC Officer, DI Brady, with, it was claimed, expanding bullets. Following the killing the RIC went berserk, shooting up the town and burning down the local creamery. The reprisal created such outrage that the Castle took the hitherto unprecedented step of issuing a communiqué which admitted that the men had 'broken out of hand' and that:

Reprisals continued till early in the morning, despite the efforts of the officers. The men were eventually got into the police lorries, and while final instructions were been given by the officer, the lorries moved off, and a creamery in the neighbourhood was burned.[51]

The outrage spread to England. There was a debate in the House of Commons on a censure motion put down by Arthur Henderson, Deputy Leader of the Labour Party, who wanted an official investigation into the reprisals policy. What he got was a full-blooded defence of the policy from Greenwood. He did admit that there had been a reprisal but with justifiable provocation. 'They knew him, they loved him. Soldiers and policemen trained under the British flag love their officers.' However, despite the Castle's communiqué, reluctantly based on the first-hand accounts of its own agents, he denied the creamery burning. In fact he said he had 'never seen a tittle of evidence to prove' that the security forces had ever done any such thing, leaving his hearers to marvel at the nationwide tendency towards spontaneous combustion in Irish dairy produce.

Greenwood had more to defend to Henderson and the world than creamery destruction. Britain's entire policy was on the line. He was clearly identifying himself with the concept of police war as envisaged by Lloyd George and Churchill. He had predicted on 20 September: 'we'll win out quickly if we pursue our firm and consistent policy.'[52] That night the doctrine of firm consistency was to be demonstrated in the north County Dublin town of Balbriggan in spectacular fashion. Greenwood told the House that it was 'impossible' to find out who was responsible for either shootings or burnings amongst the 150 men who broke out from the nearby Black and Tans' encampment, following a brawl in a pub in which two Tans were shot. But it was easy enough to see what they did. The Tans burned a hosiery factory, forty-nine houses and four public houses and killed two local people during hours of drunken looting and indiscriminate firing. The following day the reprisals policy had another airing in County Clare. As a reprisal for an IRA ambush the police shot up the towns of Ennistymon, Lahinch and Miltown Malbay, killing four people and destroying Lahinch Town Hall and a score of other buildings. In the south, the towns of Fermoy, Thurles, Lismore and Mallow were amongst those sacked. Sir Henry Wilson noted in his diary for 23 September:

At Balbriggan, Thurles and Galway yesterday the local people marked down certain SFs as in their opinion the actual murderers or instigators and then coolly went out and shot them without question or trial . . . Winston saw very little harm in this but it horrifies me.[53]

The execution of this economic policy was accompanied by a parallel destruction of human life. According to one authority[54] over 200 unarmed persons were killed by Crown forces in 1920. These included women and children. 'Sixty-nine were persons deliberately killed in the streets or in their own homes; thirty-six were men killed while in custody, the rest were the victims of indiscriminate firing by military and police'.[55] Some of the individual cases reverberate even today.[56] At Bantry a hunchback boy was shot after Tans failed to find his father in a raid. Ellen Quinn of Kiltartan, County Galway, was killed sitting on her garden wall holding a child in her arms when a policeman took a pot shot from a passing lorry. Two priests were shot. A young curate in Galway, Fr Griffin, was fished out of a bog hole with a bullet in his head, apparently because he had been imprudent in showing his Volunteer sympathies. Canon Magner, of Dunmanway, County Cork, got a note from the Tans telling him to toll his bell on Armistice Day or else. He refused and the bell tolled for him on a quiet road near Bandon on 15 December. An Auxiliary shot one of the two men he had been talking to as the Auxiliary lorry approached. Then the canon was asked for his name and having given it was immediately shot dead by the same Auxiliary. The third man was left shocked but otherwise unharmed as the bodies were dragged into a ditch and robbed. He, however, was a Resident Magistrate who insisted on an inquiry, with the result that the murderous Auxiliary was found guilty – but insane.

Six Volunteers captured, unarmed, by Black and Tans at Kerry Pike near Cork City were identified by their clothes only when their bodies were handed over to their relatives. One had had his heart cut out, another his skull battered in, a third his nose cut off, a fourth his tongue. I have seen pictures[57] of the bodies of the two Loughnane

brothers, Patrick and Henry, from Gort, County Galway, after they had
been pulled out of a pond. All I will say is I hope the fire which destroyed
the lower parts of their bodies was not started before they died.

Apart from random savagery, arising from a controlled lack of
discipline, torture was systematically employed to extract information from prisoners. The 'intelligence room' at Dublin Castle became
a place of horror in Volunteers' imaginations.[58] But the horror was
not confined to Dublin Castle, as Tom Hales and Pat Harte found out
to their cost when they were surprised and captured by Major Percival
of the Essex Regiment on 26 July 1920 near Bandon. Percival, who
later rose to be a general and lived to experience the humiliation of
surrendering Singapore to the Japanese, was also in charge of the
raiding party that later burned Collins' home in Woodfield. He had a
habit of driving about the countryside in the mornings in an open
touring car so that he could 'have cockshots at farmers working in the
fields'.[59] On capturing Hales and Harte he first ordered that they be
stripped and beaten.[60] After this he had them dressed, bound with
leather straps and caused a charge of guncotton to be placed on their
backs. The detonators failed to go off and the prisoners were made to
run while being prodded with bayonets. They were then thrown into
a lorry and on the way to Bandon Barracks were again beaten with
rifle butts, Harte receiving a particularly severe blow to the temple
from which he apparently never recovered.

At the barracks they were handed over to the Intelligence Officer,
Captain Kelly, an Irishman, who ordered a firing squad and had the
prisoners stood against a wall. He told Hales to hold up a Union Jack
and 'salute it at the peril of your life'. Hales refused and was beaten
unconscious. As he recovered he saw Harte receiving the same
treatment, ultimately holding the flag just long enough for another
officer to take a photograph. Another beating followed and they were
thrown into a room, still strapped and bleeding, at 6.30 pm. Hales said
that 'until ten o'clock there was a continual howl for our blood.' At ten
o'clock he was taken upstairs to a room where there were six officers
seated around a table, including Kelly and Percival. He was again
stripped and bound and Kelly, who referred to him as a 'murdering
bastard', instructed two of the other officers to beat him with canes,
which they did, one standing on each side, until they 'drove blood out
through him'. Then pliers were used on his lower body and to extract
his finger nails, so that Hales says, 'My fingers were so bruised that I
got unconscious.'

On regaining consciousness he was questioned about prominent
figures including Michael Collins. He gave no information and two
officers took off their tunics and punched him until he fell on the floor

with several teeth either knocked out or loosened. Finally he was pulled by the hair to the top of the stairs and thrown to the bottom, where he was again beaten before being dragged to a cell. Hales recovered. Harte, however, suffered brain damage and died in hospital, insane.

There are two points worth noting about the Hales incident. One, the supreme irony of the fact that having endured such punishment to protect Collins he later played a prominent role in encompassing his death. Secondly that he, like O'Malley, held out. Others who could not were then put in peril from their comrades. A typical case was Vincent Fourvargue, a member of the Third Battalion of the Dublin Brigade. Under duress he gave away the names of some of his unit. The British responded by staging a fake ambush in Dublin's South Circular Rd which allowed him to escape. He then made his way to England, but Collins wasn't fooled and had him shot in London, on 3 April 1921.

In the case of Harte and Hales, Collins also showed the Avenging Angel/Angel of Mercy sides of his character. His correspondence to Art O'Brien[61] contains several enquiries after Harte's health and suggestions for medical treatment and, when he was subsequently in London for the ordeal of the Treaty negotiations, he made time to visit him in Pentonville Prison. But he also tried to have Percival killed. Finding that he could not be got at in Cork, he sent a hit squad to follow him to England when he went on holiday in March 1921. Percival, however, remained out of reach in a military barracks. On 16 March he arrived at Liverpool St Station in London at 3 pm but the waiting Squad members were forced to pull out a few minutes beforehand when Sam Maguire turned up to warn them that Scotland Yard was on the way. Percival's luck continued. The following month, in Cork, on 19 April, a raiding party led by him killed one of the men Collins placed outside the station, Tadhg O'Sullivan.

As we have seen, Collins' special genius for intelligence work lay in the speed with which he could evaluate and act on any possibility of making contact with potential allies. RIC Sergeant Gerry Maher of Naas, County Kildare, was a typical example. Sean Kavanagh, then the newly appointed Intelligence Officer for County Kildare, had heard that Maher had passed on a warning to local Volunteers that their homes were about to be raided.[62] He mentioned this to his friend, Michael Staines, who told Collins. Kavanagh promptly found himself summoned to the Gaelic League HQ at 46 Parnell Square to meet Collins, who explained to Kavanagh that Maher could be of immense use in his job as County Inspector's Chief Clerk. As Confidential Clerk, Maher had access to the key of a new police code, the circulation of which was restricted below County Inspector rank. That evening, after dark, Kavanagh called on Maher and told him frankly what his mission was. Maher's reply was, 'You're the man I've been waiting for for years', and, says Kavanagh, he 'went on to explain that he had tried to establish contact but that nobody had tried to get in touch with him.' Maher duly turned over the key to the code then in use and Collins provided him with wax so that he could take an impression of the actual key used by the County Inspector to open the safe in his office. Kavanagh brought this to Collins and in a few days Maher had his own key to the safe. Kavanagh's subsequent description of how his own and Maher's operations worked is a perfect illustration of how the Collins network worked, not only in Naas, but all round the country.

Kavanagh visited Maher's house two or three times a week, always at night, either to collect Maher's information or to pass on queries from Collins. A railway courier system was established by which written messages to or from Collins could be sent via the ticket collector at nearby Sallins within a few hours. The collector handed letters to one of four sympathetic guards on mainline trains which were then delivered to Sean O'Connell, a clerk at Kingsbridge Station, Dublin.

The code was changed periodically, RIC sergeants being sent all round the country with a new cipher to each County Inspector. In Kildare the County Inspector's messenger was met at Sallins, and almost invariably a copy of the new cipher passed to Collins via Maher and Kavanagh. Maher was able to recruit another RIC man, Constable Paddy Casey, who took over Maher's duties whenever the latter was absent on leave, or through illness. During all the time the Maher–Kavanagh network operated Kavanagh was under orders from Collins to have no dealings with the local IRA. The only man who knew officially of his work was the local Battalion OC, Tom Harris. Kavanagh reported directly to Collins at Vaughan's Hotel.

How all these snippets of information which Collins received bore fruit may be judged from some memos concerning the MacCurtain killings. Item No. 8 in a list of dispatches to the Adjutant of the Cork No. 1 Brigade (O'Donaghue) on 20 July read: 'Enclosed is a memo regarding Constable Ashe. Please let me have your observations.' The memo (signed by Mulcahy using the Irish form of his name Risteard Ua Maolcatha) read as follows:

D/Information.

With regard to the report of Brig. Com. Wexford that Const. Ashe who is now at Gorey is probably one of those who was on the MacCurtain job – he states that this information was given him by John MacCarthy, Strand St, Kanturk.

R. ua M.

Another report about a second police officer, chilling for the implications of what even a child's remark can lead to in wartime, reached Collins towards the end of the month. It came from Monaghan on 30 July:

Head Constable Cahill came to Monaghan about 3 weeks after the murder of Thos. MacCurtain. He came from King's St Barracks, Cork and was escorted by 4 armed police men. One of his guard remarked to one of the older men in Monaghan Bk, He, (meaning Cahill) is a good man. He is not afraid of them (meaning the Volunteers). One of his children (about 10 years of age) remarked in the Barrack a short time after they came, 'When I grow up I won't murder Lord Mayors.'

He passed various remarks to the other men and Sergeant Faughan about what way to suppress sedition, and said that the proper way to do so, was to shoot them down.

From this and various remarks he made he gave me the impression he had to do with the murder of Thos. MacCurtain.[63]

The most terrible repercussions of all, literally on a national scale, followed the unearthing of DI Swanzy whom Collins traced via Belfast, through Sergeant Matt MacCarthy, who located Swanzy in the predominantly Orange town of Lisburn to which he had been transferred immediately after the MacCurtain killing. It was a point of honour with the Cork No. 1 Brigade to avenge their Commandant and members of the Brigade vied with each other to be sent north on the mission. This was turned down on the grounds of impracticability because the Cork accents would have been an instant giveaway. Instead, one Cork Volunteer, Sean Culhane, Intelligence Officer of the Brigade, who knew Swanzy, was sent north with MacCurtain's gun to link up with Belfast Volunteers who accompanied him to the assassination scene in a taxi on Sunday 22 August 1920. Culhane picked Swanzy out from a large crowd of churchgoers and was given the honour of firing the first shot. Swanzy went down and Culhane and one of his escort jumped back into the taxi. The second man, Roger McCorley, was so keen to take a hand in the killing that he was almost left in Lisburn:

I was the last to leave the spot where Swanzy fell as I delayed long enough to put another shot into him. The taxi started off before I reached it . . . but as they opened the door opposite to that on which I was running I was forced to grab the handle of the door on my side, open the car and throw myself in. As I still had my finger on the trigger of my gun and as I landed in a heap on the floor I accidentally fired a shot in the car.[64]

McCorley was luckier than most of the Catholic population of Lisburn. A UVF revival begun in the wake of the municipal election results enabled Protestant outrage at the Swanzy shooting to be translated into an organised pogrom in the town. Banbridge had also experienced prolonged anti-Catholic rioting during the previous month because of an IRA shooting, that of Lieutenant Colonel Bruce

Smyth VC, a native of Banbridge and Divisional Commissioner of the RIC for Munster.

Colonel Smyth's death, like that of MacCurtain, has to be understood against the larger, though hidden, backdrop of the British policy response to the IRA's growing strength. The Colonel's killing was brought about through his spelling out of part of that policy to an RIC garrison in Listowel on 19 June 1920. A sworn statement of his remarks on that occasion was given to Arthur Griffith by one of his hearers and published in the *Irish Bulletin*. Kathleen Napoli MacKenna reproduced part of it in her memoir:

Well, men I have something to tell you, something I am sure you would not want your wives to hear. Sinn Fein has had all the sport up to the present and we are going to have it now . . . We must take the offensive and beat Sinn Fein at its own game. Martial Law, applying to all Ireland, is to come into operation immediately. In fact we are to have our scheme of amalgamation completed on 21 June. I am promised as many troops from England as I require, thousands are coming in daily . . .

If a police barracks is burnt, or if the barracks already occupied is not suitable, then the best house in the locality is to be commandeered, the occupants thrown out into the gutter. Let them lie there, the more the merrier. Police and military will patrol the country at least five times a week. They are not to confine themselves to the main roads, but make across the country, lie in ambush and when civilians are seen approaching shout 'Up hands'. Should the order not be obeyed at once shoot and shoot to kill. If the persons approaching carry their hands in their pockets, or are in any way suspicious-looking, shoot them down. You may make mistakes occasionally, and innocent persons may be shot, but that cannot be helped, and you are bound to get the right person sometime.

The more you shoot the better I shall like you and I assure you that no policeman will get into trouble for shooting a man.

Hunger-strikers will be allowed to die in gaol – the more the better. Some of them have already died and a damn bad job they were not all allowed to die. As a matter of fact some them have already been dealt with in a manner their friends will never know about.

An emigrant ship left an Irish port for a foreign one lately with lots of Sinn Feiners on board: I assure you men it will never reach port.

We want you to carry out this scheme and wipe out Sinn Fein. Any man who is not prepared to do this is a hindrance, and had better leave the job at once.

One sequel to this address which may be noted illustrates the quite fiendish nature of some of the undercover operations of the period. The 'emigrant ship' of whose doom the Colonel apparently had foreknowledge was apparently the *Viknor* whose fate was also alluded to in a highly significant despatch from the British Admiralty which the Collins network captured. It is addressed to Sir Charles Cooke and signed by the celebrated intelligence expert Captain R. C. Hall. It says: 'I am afraid the *Viknor* has gone down. She had some very important prisoners aboard and I badly wanted their papers.'[65]

That was the underground background to the Smyth address. As the Napoli MacKenna memoir notes, the public sequel to this address was as 'unique, dramatic, and seemingly impossible as would have been a mutiny in the King's bodyguard'. The Colonel asked one of the men if he was prepared to co-operate, which was the signal for the men's previously chosen leader to step forward. Napoli MacKenna describes what the constable said and did:

'By your accent I take it you are an Englishmen, and in your ignorance you forget you are addressing Irishmen.' The Constable removed his cap, belt and arms and laid them on the table saying: 'These too are English. Take them and go to hell with you, you murderer.'

Worse was to follow for Colonel Smyth. When he ordered the arrest of the mutineer he was informed by the other men that if a hand were laid on their comrade 'the room would run red with blood.' A month later, in the County Club of Cork, an IRA Volunteer walked up to Smyth and said, 'Your orders were to shoot on sight. You are in sight now. So make ready.'[66] The Colonel tried to escape but was shot dead. In the wake of the MacCurtain, Smyth and Swanzy killings, the existence of a strong, well-organised force of Ulster Protestants emerged once again as a factor in the struggle between Irish Catholic Nationalists and the British Empire.

Mutinous Irishmen emerged in another part of the British Empire nine days after the Smyth speech. At Jullundur, in the Punjab, on 28 June, 250 men of the First Battalion of the Connaught Rangers also laid down their arms in protest against the news from Ireland.[67] The affair created a sensation. Sixty-two Rangers were court-martialled and death sentences plentifully bestowed; though ultimately only one soldier, James Daly, was actually executed, many underwent penal servitude until long after the Anglo-Irish war ended.

During October 1920 Collins' admiration for fighting men involved him in one of the grimmest incidents of the war. He had encouraged the Soloheadbeg men, Dan Breen and Sean Treacy, to stay around Dublin a good deal rather than in their native Tipperary. They assisted the Squad on various jobs which suited Collins and Treacy in particular because he had a girlfriend in the city. But it was a highly dangerous place for two such wanted countrymen; since Soloheadbeg, both were scarcely less sought after than Collins himself. They were sleeping in the home of a Professor Carolan in Whitehall in north Dublin on the night of 11 October 1920 when British Intelligence located them.

Somehow, even though they were found in bed, Breen and Treacy fought their way out, killing two of the undercover men in the process. One of these subsequently turned out to be associated with a number of shootings of the Lynch type (see page 157). Major Smyth, brother of the colonel who caused the RIC mutiny in Listowel, was serving in the Middle East. He came back to avenge his brother and was himself killed. Breen was badly cut in falling through a glass conservatory roof, and finally had to take his chances in knocking on the door of a strange house and asking for sanctuary, because he was suffering from loss of blood. Luckily for him, the occupants, though not in sympathy with Sinn Fein, adhered to the Irish tradition of shielding the fugitive and he was transferred to the Mater Misericordiae Hospital where the nuns ensured that he recovered safely by wheeling him into the maternity ward during raids. Treacy too got away but Professor Carolan was put up against a wall of his house, shot through the head and left for dead. The raiders put out a story that he had been killed by one of Breen's bullets. The Professor however recovered long enough to tell what had really happened.

Collins had been informed that top British military personnel like Generals Macready and Tudor were to walk in Smyth's funeral procession and the Squad, including Sean Treacy, were placed in readiness. However the generals thought better of attendance and the Squad dispersed harmlessly but Treacy, who apparently actually had gone to the funeral to pray for the man he had shot, was recognised in the doorway of the 'Republican outfitters', Peadar Clancy's shop in Talbot St. There was another raid, which missed Dick McKee, but netted Joe Vize, Collins' Director of Purchases, head of arms smuggling, a loss which would later cost Collins dear. Treacy and one of the British Intelligence officers were killed.

Two RIC sergeants who knew the Tipperary men were brought to Dublin to identify the corpse and to assist in searching the hospitals for Breen. Neligan told Collins of this and one of them, a Sergeant Roche, was actually shot dead by the Squad as he was chatting with Neligan on a Dublin quay. Neligan told me, nearly fifty years later, that he still prayed for Roche every night. The other detective was also shot dead. Neligan came under suspicion, because another policeman had seen him talking to the Squad men just prior to the Roche shooting, a particularly horrific affair. Joe Dolan described the shooting thus: 'I fired six shots into him. Tom Keogh and Jim Slattery fired a few more into him for luck.' Neligan was able to discredit the badly shocked policeman's story, but subsequently he found that he was being followed by a suspicious detective. One night, after curfew, the shadowing stopped in a dark alley. Neligan shot and killed his colleague.

The ending of the Breen/Treacy saga is described by Breen himself in his colourful book.[68] He had been removed from the Mater

Misericordiae Hospital to a safe house when Collins got word that his hideout was surrounded by soldiers and Black and Tans. He called out the Squad to lead a rescue attempt personally, which in the circumstances would have been almost certainly suicidal. Breen saw him from a window standing outside the cordon with 'a few of the boys':

Their services were not needed. The soldiers raided almost every house in the locality, including the house next door, but never came into the house where I was. All the same I felt grateful to Mick. As I have already explained, he was the only member of GHQ who stood by us consistently.

While the major IRA effort was of course confined to Ireland, Cathal Brugha's urgings that the war should be carried to England resulted in some spectacular operations in the UK, particularly in Liverpool, where seventeen warehouses were burned on the night of 28 November 1920. Burnings also took place in various other UK centres under the direction of Rory O'Connor. Collins produced a list of the home addresses of Black and Tans and some of these were also attacked and destroyed by fire. O'Connor drew up somewhat unrealistic plans for incendiary attacks in London, Birmingham, Sheffield, Newcastle, Manchester and Liverpool, the destruction of railways, tube stations, reservoirs, the Ministry of Pensions and the homes of figures like General Tudor and Lord FitzAlan. By way of evaluating the IRA's capability to carry out this programme, however, it should be noted that his proposals were accompanied by a report on the state of the IRA in London which said:

I find that things are in a very serious way. Owing to the unemployment, in many cases our men have had to sleep on the Embankment, and in one case, one of the men has only been able to have four dinners per week . . . various Irish societies have apparently done nothing towards relief of distress . . . the QM practically extracted money from the members of the G.A.A.[69]

Several key figures in the Collins network were picked up just before the November burnings, including Neil Kerr and Steve Lanigan in Liverpool and Paddy O'Donoghue in Manchester, and the Brugha/O'Connor offensive had a damaging effect on the arms-smuggling routes Collins had built up. But by the following May he had repaired the damage to the extent that he was arranging for a ton of potassium chlorate per week to be sent from Liverpool under the guise of bread soda.[70] In fact had a raid not driven Mulcahy to escape across the roof-tops of his hideout in Longwood Avenue, leaving his papers behind, seconds ahead of the Auxiliaries, very large-scale operations would have taken place in Liverpool and Manchester during April 1921. These would have included the destruction of all British shipping in Liverpool and of Manchester's electricity supply. But the capture of the Mulcahy papers alerted the authorities and created a sensation in England when they were released to the press, not so much for the revelations about IRA strength and ruthlessness as for the fact that included in the papers was a proposal made by an eccentric for infecting horses' feed with glanders. This was taken up by the press as evidence of a fiendishness on a far greater scale than merely blacking out a city and destroying a shipping fleet!

One of the most tragic aspects of the struggle was the execution by both sides of prisoners and hostages who were often people of quite remarkable calibre. Collins, who played such a notable part in bringing about and conducting the war, was keenly aware of his role in these events. On the Irish side the religious fervour of some of the prisoners executed was such that it had a bearing on changing papal policy in Rome (see Chapter 7) To this day one of the most popular Irish rebel ballads is 'Kevin Barry', describing the capture, torture and hanging of Barry, an eighteen-year-old student.

Barry was captured after a raid on a British Army party who were collecting bread from a bakery in Church St, Dublin on 20 September 1920. Learning that the raid was to take place at 11 am he calculated that he would have plenty of time to take part and still attend his medical examinations at University College Dublin which were scheduled for 2 pm. The intention was merely to hold up the tommies and take their rifles. But shooting broke out and three of the soldiers died. Barry was subsequently captured and sentenced to hang. Because of his youth the case attracted enormous attention. Collins saw to it that it received the maximum publicity. In the Fenian days men had frequently been executed with no word from their leaders and little outside protest. Moya Llewelyn Davies coined a memorable phrase for Collins to describe the campaign to have Barry reprieved. He declared that there would be 'no more lonely scaffolds in our time'.[71] But despite widespread protests at the fact that Barry had been maltreated after capture and pleas for mercy, a Conference of Ministers presided over by Lloyd George in Bonar Law's rooms in the House of Commons on 28 October decided that they could not recommend any commutation of the death penalty.[72]

Amongst those taking part in the Conference was Sir Hamar Greenwood, so it need not surprise us that 'it was pointed out . . . that it was precisely young and irresponsible men of this type who were the main cause of the present disturbances in Ireland.' Barry had made an altar in his cell at which he received two Masses on the morning of his execution.[73]

Outside the jail a crowd of some 5,000 said the rosary and sang hymns, watched over by soldiers and armoured cars. The crowds were a causative factor in Collins' last desperate hopes of a rescue attempt being abandoned. This would have involved the use of explosives to blow a hole in the jail wall. Barry's guards were under instruction to shoot him if any rescue attempt was made, so the

attempt, had it been made, was fairly certain to have ended unsuccessfully and in bloodshed anyhow. Collins realised this all along. 'His
intense, painful ability to enter the victim's mind placed him under
intolerable strain.'[74] The night before the execution the gathering in
Vaughan's Hotel saw Collins in a state of depression. He remained
brooding the whole night, taking no part in the conversation, the only
words he uttered being: 'Poor Kevin Barry'. Frank O'Connor says
'his face was drawn with agony, his long lock of hair drooping.'

Along with the Barry execution another moral turning-point of the
period was the last great hunger-strike of the time, that involving
Terence MacSwiney. When he was sworn in to succeed MacCurtain
the previous year, MacSwiney had made the prophetic statement: 'It is
not those who can inflict the most, but those that can suffer the most
who will conquer.' He began to demonstrate the meaning of that
utterance on 12 August 1921, having been arrested at City Hall, Cork,
presiding over an IRA meeting. Having refused to recognise his court
martial (for possession of documents likely to cause disaffection), he
went on hunger-strike for release and was transferred to Brixton
prison. The ten Volunteers arrested with him also went on hunger-
strike in Cork Jail. Like the other members of GHQ,[75] Collins was
uneasy at the strike-for-release policy, though he had no objection to a
strike for political status or for the remission of grievances, but he felt
release was too dangerously large a demand. In the case of the
Wormwood Scrubs' prisoners the men had only been held on
suspicion. MacSwiney was too big a figure for the British to give way
easily. Nor did they. The Cabinet agreed with Balfour at a meeting
held in Downing St on 23 July[76] that the release of MacSwiney would
be a fatal blow to the policy of coercion to which the government was
committed.

MacSwiney endured until 25 October before dying, a fast of
seventy-four days. One of the Cork ten, Michael Fitzgerald, had
already died on 17 October; another, Joseph Murphy, died a few
hours after MacSwiney. The other eight acceded to Arthur Griffith's
request that they should come off the protest at that stage. These
sacrifices had an incalculable effect on world opinion. The transfer of
MacSwiney to Brixton focused world opinion on the Lord Mayor and
elevated the Sinn Fein cause to a moral plane higher than much of what
was happening in Ireland would ever have done. Londoners lined the
streets to pay their respects as the body was taken through the city
accompanied by a guard of honour of Volunteers wearing their illegal
uniforms. Robed bishops and priests accompanied them. Sir Henry
Wilson, however, spoiled the last stage of the journey by persuading
Lloyd George to have MacSwiney's brothers and sisters removed
from the boat train at Holyhead and to divert the coffin to Cork, so as
to forestall Sinn Fein's plans to derive political advantage from a huge

public reception for the remains in Dublin. But the Field Marshal was unable to prevent the country practically closing down in answer to Dail decree that the day of MacSwiney's burial, 31 October, should be observed as a day of national mourning.

MacSwiney's burial, coupled with the execution of Kevin Barry the following day, might be taken as ending a phase of endurance. Such happenings moved Eoin MacNeill to compose a much quoted epigram:

> In prison we are their jailers;
> On trial their judges,
> Persecuted their punishers,
> Dead their conquerors.

Lloyd George made speeches at Caernarvon, on 9 October, and at the Guildhall Banquet, on 9 November, which clearly backed the policy of reprisal and hanging. At the Guildhall he summed it up by saying:

There is no doubt that at last their [the police] patience has given way and there has been some severe hitting back . . . let us be fair to these gallant men who are doing their duty in Ireland . . . it is no use talking about this being war and these being reprisals when these things are being done [by the IRA] with impunity in Ireland.

We have murder by the throat . . . we had to reorganise the police. When the Government was ready we struck the terrorists and now the terrorists are complaining of terror.

In Ireland it was realised that 'murder by the throat' meant throats like Barry's. Michael Collins also interpreted Lloyd George's speech differently from the Guildhall audience. He knew why the Prime Minister felt his murder gang policy was working and he was laying plans to prove him wrong.

6

The Sky Darkens

'It is not those who can inflict the most, but those that can suffer the most who will conquer.'

Terence MacSwiney

That winter of 1920–21 was to see some of the most horrific deeds of the entire war on what became known ever afterwards as 'Bloody Sunday', 21 November 1920. As the 'Kidd's Back' war intensified Collins began to realise that the British were improving their intelligence network in Dublin. Hitherto the British approach had been somewhat amateurish, as some of the spy episodes recounted will have indicated. Captain Hardy himself, 'the notorious murderer',[1] who afterwards became a novelist, wrote that for all the hope the various agents initially sent over had of remaining undetected at their Dublin addresses they 'might as well have worn uniforms'. But from 11 May onwards things had begun to improve on the British intelligence front. Colonel Ormonde d'Epée Winter, code-named 'O', arrived in Dublin. Mark Sturgis described him as looking 'like a wicked little white snake . . . probably entirely non-moral'. David Neligan however described him as being 'a decent old fellow'. And Collins welcomed him to town by having him ambushed in Thomas St as he drove to pay his first call on the Viceregal Lodge. Appropriately enough the attackers waited in a butcher's shop but only succeeded in wounding him in the hand.[2] However, though in the end Collins defeated Winter, 'O's arrival did do something for British counter-insurgency operations, hampered as they were by poor information and internecine rivalry between the hydra-headed British security efforts.

A group of intelligence officers, known as the 'Cairo Gang' because of their Middle-Eastern experience, rather than the fact that some of them frequented a Dublin haunt known as the Cairo Café, began to augment their spying activities by carrying out shootings in Dublin. Collins was particularly annoyed by the death of John Lynch of Killmallock, County Limerick, who was shot in his bed at 2 am in the Exchange Hotel, Dublin, on 23 September. The Castle's cover story was that he had resisted arrest and fired on police. In fact Lynch never carried a gun. He may have been mistaken for Liam Lynch, the Cork IRA leader, but he was not a Volunteer and was unconnected with the IRA beyond the fact that he was a Sinn Fein loan organiser and had come to Dublin to hand over some £23,000 to Collins.

By 5 October Collins had compiled a report on the shooting for Arthur Griffith which included the following:

At 1.35 am on the morning of the murder a 'phone message was received by Captain Baggelly, General Staff, Ship St Barracks . . . to send a car. A car was sent . . . members of the RIC force picked up a small party of military . . . and proceeded to the Royal Exchange Hotel.

At 2.15 am a 'phone message passed from the Headquarters of the Dublin District to College Street Station, giving the information that the RIC had been to the Royal Exchange Hotel and shot a man named Lynch.

There is not the slightest doubt that there was no intention whatever to arrest Mr Lynch.

Captain Baggelly was one of those whose fate would illustrate the danger of being mentioned in dispatches by Michael Collins. The Cairo Gang, though they made mistakes like those over Lynch, were getting closer. October saw all three of Collins' top intelligence agents picked up and released after questioning, Thornton being held for ten days before being released. Tobin and Cullen also got away with a grilling after being detained in Vaughan's. Collins knew that it was only a matter of time before they and he were finished. But just as the Gang were closing in on him he was closing in on them.

Information had come from various sources which showed that the British had set up an intelligence network working on 'proper continental lines with a Central Headquarters and other houses forming minor centres scattered all throughout the city'.[3] Here the sister of an IRA man had told her brother that some of the gentlemen in the house where she worked spoke with English accents, went out after curfew, and kept odd hours. Then one of Lynch's killers got a fit of conscience in drink and told a girl what he had done. Sergeant Mannix of the DMP station at Donnybrook was particularly valuable. In his own words he 'secured names and addresses of British Secret Service Officers who were shot on "Bloody Sunday"'. As a result Collins was able to get an IRA hall porter placed in one of the houses and hall door and room keys were obtained for all the others. Detailed reports were prepared on each agent. Thornton's job was to collate the information. He also got:

the very unenvious [sic] job of presenting my full report to a joint meeting of the Dail Cabinet and Army Council, at which I had to prove that each and every man on my list was an accredited Secret Service man of the British Government.

At the head of his list were the Gang's leaders, Colonel Aimes and Major Bennett, two men with whom he had become 'great friends' in Kidd's Back. The joint meeting sealed their fate and that of the others on Thornton's list. Sunday 21 November was decided on both for speed and because there was a big football match on in Croke Park that day and Dublin would be unusually crowded.[4] On the night of the 20th Collins went to the Gaiety Theatre with a group which included Dave Neligan. He happened to speculate as to what sort of men they were whom he had consigned to doom the next day. Neligan told him to look into the next box where he could see some of them for himself. After the show Collins went to Vaughan's where a meeting was held to put the finishing touches to the plans for the next day. Amongst those present were Peadar Clancy, Dick McKee and a young Gaelic scholar from Clare called Conor Clune who had nothing to do with the Volunteers but had come to the hotel to see Beaslai about Irish language projects. There was a raid by Auxiliaries – all the IRA men got away safely, but the raiders took Clune with them. Clancy and McKee were asleep in their hideout in nearby Gloucester St when it too was raided later in the night. Both were captured, McKee barely having time to destroy the list of intended victims before the raiders burst into the room. Captain Hardy would have one of the greatest triumphs of the British undercover war effort. McKee, Clancy and the innocent Clune would pass one of the most hellish nights imaginable. For Clune there was the terror of the uninitiated, for the others, the horror of the too-well-informed. They were in the hands of the torturers and the plans they had helped to formulate would give their captors an added incentive for brutality.

Next morning, shortly after eight o'clock, groups of Volunteers, members of the Squad augmented by the Dublin Brigade, converged on eight different addresses in Dublin. Nineteen soldiers, one or two of them probably not agents, were roused from their sleep and shot, some in the presence of their wives, and girlfriends, some in bed, others standing against a wall. One was 'shot in his pyjamas in the back garden'.[5] Captain Baggelly, who died at 119 Lower Baggot St, never knew that one of the three-man party which shot him would be a future Irish Taoiseach, Prime Minister Sean Lemass.[6] The killers were all young men, generally of religious sensibility, and most of them didn't find their work easy. One, Mick O'Hanlon, recalled, 'When we got in we found our man had a girl and that he was covering the door and the landing . . . none of us fired as she was in bed with him and she covered him with her arms . . .'[7] But this moment soon passed. Following the hesitation O'Hanlon notes simply, 'Mick Flanagan shot him.'[8]

Some didn't hesitate. O'Hanlon also recalled that one of the victims, 'an old major', had a meal prepared. 'Mick White ate the breakfast.' Joe Dolan was so disgusted at finding that one prime target, Major King, a colleague of Hardy, was missing when he burst into his room, that he took revenge by giving his half-naked mistress 'a right scourging with a sword scabbard', and setting fire to the room afterwards.[9] But in general the spirit of the morning was accurately summed up by Charlie Dalton:

In the hall three or four men were lined up against the wall, some of our officers facing them. Knowing their fate I felt great pity for them. It was plain they knew it too. As I crossed the threshold the volley was fired . . . the sights and sounds of that morning were to be with me for many days and night. . . . I remembered I had not been to Mass. I slipped out, and in the silence before the altar, I thought over our morning's work and offered up a prayer for the fallen.[10]

There would be further reason for prayer before the day was out. The Volunteers got away from most of the death sites without incident but those involved in the Mount St and Pembroke Road areas had to fight their way through encircling Auxiliaries in a series of running battles. Somehow they managed to do this successfully and despite being greatly outnumbered and out-gunned, got away with their wounded. Only one member of the entire operation was captured, Frank Teeling, and Collins would soon engineer his escape. He sat in Devlin's waiting for news as O'Reilly cycled round the city collecting reports. The city was filled with horrific accounts of what had happened. At Masses priests advised their congregations to go straight home and remain indoors for the rest of the day.

Collins was 'white and defiant with no expression of pleasure'[11] as O'Reilly reported. He asked, 'Any casualties?' and, Teeling's capture not being known at the time, was told 'no'. His reaction to this was, 'there'll be no football match today', and he sent O'Reilly to warn the Gaelic Athletic Association that the afternoon's game between Dublin and Tipperary should be called off. The GAA sent back word that it was too late. Crowds would be congregating in the area of Croke Park whether a match was played or not. As the morning progressed Collins began to get uneasy about the whereabouts of McKee and Clancy. They had helped to wind up this particular clock. Why weren't they in Devlin's to hear how it struck? O'Reilly was sent to find out. Nearing their lodgings he was met by a boy who told him he had a message for Collins: 'They were captured last night.'

When Collins heard the news he sank back in his chair and exclaimed, 'Good God. We're finished now. It's all up.' When he recovered, frantic messages were sent to MacNamara and Neligan to locate the captured men. MacNamara heard that two men resembling them had been taken into the Bridewell. Collins ordered Neligan to go down and check and Neligan showed extraordinary courage in obeying. He went through every cell in the place, telling the sergeant on duty he was looking for a cousin. Had they been there the Squad might have got them out. But eventually their location in the Castle became known and Collins realised they were beyond hope. He went for his usual Sunday lunch at O'Donovans', cycling back and forth across the terror-filled city as he normally did. He had to sit with what was in effect a *memento mori* during the meal, for not knowing what had happened Mrs O'Donovan had set Dick McKee's customary place. Meanwhile the Auxiliaries and Tans made arrangements to surround Croke Park while the match was in progress, ostensibly to search the crowd for known Sinn Feiners. Later it was claimed in their defence that IRA men in the crowd fired first. But it is not denied that the security forces opened up on both crowd and playing field with rifles and machine-guns causing bloodshed and panic. Fourteen people died and hundreds were injured, none of them Tans or Auxiliaries. The stand in which each year the Sam Maguire cup is presented is named after one of the dead, Hogan, the Tipperary player who was shot on the playing field.

That night most of the prisoners held in Dublin Castle were transferred to Beggar's Bush. Clancy, Clune and McKee were left in the guardroom beside the canteen where, MacNamara reported, the Auxiliaries were 'drunk and thirsting for vengeance'. Later that night the three were 'shot while attempting to escape'. Neligan and the other friendly detectives reported to Collins that all three had been tortured and that, when their bodies were being loaded on to a lorry, the officer responsible had battered their faces with his torch.

Collins was beside himself at the news. Contemporary accounts speak of him swaying in anguish as he relived the tortures, continually repeating that all was over. He caused uproar by insisting that the bodies be dressed in Volunteer uniforms. Even the bravest of men thought he was mad and some refused to accompany him to the mortuary chapel in the pro-cathedral. However he pushed his way through the small crowd of detectives and spies who were hanging around the gate to see who would turn up and stood in the chapel as doctors opened the coffins to examine the bodies. The stories had been so awful that the investigators were almost glad at what was revealed. Badly battered faces certainly, and bayonet thrusts, and bullet wounds, but not the mutilations expected. He took part in dressing his comrades in Volunteers' uniforms and accepted the verdict of the clergy that the coffins should be closed again because of the condition of the faces. Next morning he also attended the funeral Mass and, with no one present knowing from one moment to the next whether the Auxiliaries might suddenly burst upon the scene, made his last gestures of friendship and defiance. First, wearing a trenchcoat, he stepped out of the crowd, which, because of the threat of the Auxiliaries, was unusually small for such an occasion and pinned an 'in memoriam' message on the coffin: 'In memory of two good friends – Dick and Peadar – and two of Ireland's best soldiers. Miceal O'Coileain, 25/11/20.' Then he helped to carry the coffins. An *Evening Herald* photographer got a picture which appeared in the early edition, but the Squad visited the paper and the block was taken out for later editions. Copies were bought up around the city and the Castle missed getting a good picture of their chief enemy. He went to Glasnevin for the burial also and was recognised by a woman. 'There's Mick Collins,' she exclaimed. He turned round and snarled at her, 'You bloody bitch.'[12] It was the same date as that on which, in London, the men Collins, Clancy and McKee had had shot the previous Sunday were laid to rest. Years later, in his novel *Never in Vain*, J. L. Hardy[13] had his hero, Andrew Kerr, receive another note: 'Andrew Kerr. This is to warn you that you have been sentenced to death for the brutal murder of Clancy, McKee.' Hardy wasn't writing fiction. In the copy of the novel Liam Tobin, the man who sent him the original of the death threat, at Collins' instigation, has written: 'Hardy on arrival in Dublin lived in Harcourt St. He was responsible for many murders including those at Drumcondra and McKee, Clune, Clancy.'

In the aftermath of Bloody Sunday, quite a number of people either felt like sending death threats or sensed that they were under threat. The immediate reaction was for the agents who had escaped, and despite all the planning a number were missed, to pour into the Castle seeking sanctuary. Within hours of the shootings the various small houses and apartments within the Castle's walls were filled with shocked men and hysterical women who had barely paused to fill a suitcase before seeking shelter. Collins might be coming for them next. The O'Connor children discovered that a neighbour of theirs, the father of one of their playmates, 'a boy called Percy Smith',[14] had been shot. A Protestant, and a loyalist, his house, No. 117 Morehampton Rd, had been the scene of two shootings (a Captain McClean and a man known as 'Caldron'). Emerging from a downstairs room at the sound of the shots, Smith was killed because the gunmen thought he was trying to prevent their escape. British propaganda made what it could from the death, trying to elicit sympathy for the dead army men, not mentioning that they were spies, glossing over Croke Park and putting the number of officers shot at a reduced figure, generally fourteen or less. Thornton, however, gives twenty names in his memoir, including one who escaped. In each case he gives the officer's name, rank and the address at which the shooting took place. Sir Henry Wilson was furious at the fate of 'the poor murdered officers' and said after the funeral that he wondered that Churchill, Greenwood and Lloyd George 'did not hang their heads in shame'.[15] Interestingly, in his diary for 25 November, Erskine Childers talked of the funeral of the 'murdered officers'.[16] The account given to the Cabinet of the events of Bloody Sunday, not for the first time in the Anglo-Irish war, makes one wonder how much the Government were kept informed by the military of what was really happening in Ireland:

The motive for these terrible crimes . . . is hard to explain, but the fact that several of the murdered officers were engaged on work connected with the preparation of cases for courts martial suggests an endeavour on the part of desperate criminals to strike back at the men who were thought to be specially concerned in bringing them to justice.[17]

No indication was given by Greenwood that the men were an elite, undercover 'hit' unit. Croke Park was passed off as a search operation intended to capture

men belonging to the Tipperary units of the Irish Republican Army . . . most desperate characters in that organisation [Tipperary were of course playing]. The police were fired upon by armed Sinn Fein pickets at the entrance to the field . . . the police returned the fire . . . there is no doubt that some of the most desperate criminals in Ireland were amongst the spectators. The responsibility for the loss of innocent lives must rest with those men, and not with the police or military who were forced to fire in self-defence and used no unnecessary violence . . . a civilian and a boy of ten were . . . shot in the streets of Dublin . . . and three prisoners who were being detained in a guard room at the entrance to Dublin Castle were shot while trying to escape.

Churchill subsequently stated at a Cabinet meeting[18] that no reprisals had taken place after the Dublin murders. However the initiated amongst the ranks of British decision-takers knew that Collins had probably struck the most damaging blow of the entire undercover war. The Cairo Gang had had one instruction, to locate and destroy Collins and his organisation.[19] They had failed and the implications of that failure were well understood.

It was Collins' most testing hour. The atmosphere in Dublin was so terrible that many trusted agents and couriers feared to leave their homes. William Cosgrave, one of the steadiest men ever to come into Irish public life, was so intimidated that he donned a soutane and took refuge for a period in a Borstal run by the Christian Brothers in Glencree in the Dublin Mountains. Cosgrave was not acting unwisely. Anything might have happened. General Boyd, GOC of the Dublin District, ordered Arthur Griffith arrested without consulting the Chief Secretary. Lloyd George was angered by this but Boyd justified his action by saying that if he hadn't arrested Griffith there might have been more murders, because there was such feeling amongst the regimental officers.[20] He felt it advisable to be seen to be cracking down on prominent Sinn Feiners as a result. However the man in the eye of the storm, Michael Collins, refused to let himself be cowed. When couriers' nerves failed he got on his bicycle and went himself to pick up despatches or to get the latest news from the friendly sources in the Castle and the DMP. If change may be said to be effected by a combination of will and circumstances then in that ghastly November, with the memory of the battered faces of McKee and Clancy before him to remind him of what lay in wait for himself, Collins both showed the former and created the latter. He later described the elimination of the Cairo Gang in the following terms:

My one intention was the destruction of the undesirables who continued to make miserable the lives of the ordinary decent citizens. I have proof enough to assure myself of the atrocities which this gang of spies and informers have committed. Perjury and torture are words too easily known to them.

If I had a second motive it was no more than a feeling such as I would have for a dangerous reptile.

By their destruction the very air is made sweeter. That should be the future's judgement on this particular event. For myself, my conscience is clear. There is no crime in detecting and destroying in wartime the spy and the informer. They have destroyed without trial. I have paid them back in their own coin.[21]

A week after Bloody Sunday, on 28 November, there came the news of the Kilmichael ambush by Tom Barry and his flying column. The Auxiliaries had suffered their greatest losses to date, seventeen killed in the attack. Sean Collins (equally known as Johnny), Collins' brother, had played a part in its planning. Collins' depression lifted. The fighting races had not died out.

The year ended with the most spectacular reprisal of all, that on portions of the city of Cork on 11 December. Following an ambush, shops were looted, civic buildings set alight, including the City Hall and half of the principal street of the city, St Patrick St, was gutted. Two brothers named Delaney were murdered in their beds for good measure. Hamar Greenwood gave a virtuoso performance in the House of Commons – 'there was no evidence that the fires were started by the Crown Forces.' He said that the City Hall had been destroyed after flames spread to it from St Patrick St. To do this the fires would have had to spread for half a kilometre, crossing the River Lee and leaving the intervening streets untouched. A more convincing verdict on the Cork example of the 'police war' policy and of the utilisation of such a policy generally comes from within the ranks of the Auxiliaries themselves. It gives a good idea of the difficulties experienced by those in the front line who had to operate the policy:

16.12.20   Aux. Division, RIC,
                                           Dunmanway,
                                           Co. Cork.

My darling Mother,
. . . we came here from Cork and are billeted in a workhouse – filthily dirty.

Half of us are down with bronchitis. I am at present in bed . . . recovering
from a severe chill contracted on Saturday night last during the burning and
looting of Cork in which I took a reluctant part. We did it all right never mind
how much the well intentioned Hamar Greenwood would excuse us. In all
my life I have never experienced such orgies of murder, arson and looting as I
have witnessed during the past 16 days with the RIC Auxiliaries. It baffles
description. And we are supposed to be officers and gentlemen. There are
quite a number of decent fellows and likewise a lot of ruffians.

On our arrival here from Cork one of our heroes held up a car with a priest
and a civilian in it and shot them through the head without cause or
provocation. We were very kindly received by the people but the consequences of this cold-blooded murder is that no one will come within a mile of
us now and all shops are closed. The brute who did it has been sodden with
drink for some time and has been sent to Cork under arrest for examination
by experts in lunacy. If certified sane he will be court-martialled and shot.
The poor old priest was 65 and everybody's friend.

The burning and sacking of Cork followed immediately on the ambush of
our men. I, as orderly sergeant had to collect 20 men for a raid and then left the
barracks in the motor cars. I did not go for I was feeling seedy. The party had not
got 100 yards from barracks when bombs were thrown at them over a wall. One
dropped in a car and wounded eight men, one of whom has since died.

Very naturally the rest of the Co. were enraged. The houses in the vicinity
of the ambush were set alight. And from there the various parties set out on
their mission of destruction. Many who witnessed similar scenes in France
and Flanders say, that nothing they had experienced was comparable to the
punishment meted out to Cork. I got back to barracks at 4 am.

Reprisals are necessary and loyal Irishman agree but there is a lot which
should not be done . . .[22]

While Collins' daily routine was a chapter of near escapes, some
stand out as being particularly hair-raising. His 'life on the bicycle' had
given him severe stomach trouble, necessitating special food, and
Eileen O'Donovan, then a girl of fourteen, was up before dawn on
Christmas Eve, 1920, to prepare his breakfast of curds and whey. That
evening, for the first and only time in her life, she saw him drunk on
raw whiskey. His condition had been brought on, not by Christmas
spirit, but by the Auxiliaries. He always enjoyed Christmas and the
day was a busy one with a myriad of visits and present-giving to a long
list of people ranging from friendly sailors to hostesses who had fed
him and his men during the year. Poor O'Reilly nearly had the pedals
worn off his bicycle going around the city delivering them all. Collins
decided to stand a dinner in the Gresham Hotel, in O'Connell St, one
of the best-known places in Ireland. Too well known. Neligan nearly
had a seizure when he was invited and turned down the invitation with
a few appropriate comments on the subject of suicide.

When the party arrived at the Gresham, they discovered that all the
private rooms were taken as Collins would surely have reckoned on

beforehand, had his normal foresight and instinct for danger not gone
on Christmas holiday. They sat at a table in the public dining room,
Collins, Rory O'Connor, Gearoid O'Sullivan, Tobin and Cullen; the
Castle could not have imagined a more welcome Christmas present. It
was very nearly delivered. A party of Auxiliaries raided the hotel.
Collins was searched and a bottle of whiskey discovered in his hip
pocket. 'For his landlady', he said. Less convincing was his explanation for one of the entries in a notebook which was also discovered.
'Rifles', said the Auxiliary. 'Refills', said Collins. Understandably,
after that exchange he felt a need to relieve himself and was taken to the
lavatory under escort. When he didn't return Tobin became alarmed
and went looking for him. He found him held under one of the bright
hand-basin lights while an Auxiliary officer tousled his hair and
compared his likeness with a photograph of Collins he held in his
other hand. Collins had despairingly made up his mind to make a grab
for the officer's revolver when suddenly he was released and he and
Tobin were allowed to return to the table. It was still touch and go.
Collins whispered to Tobin to 'be ready to make a rush for it.' But in
his absence his whiskey bottle had helped to ease the atmosphere.
O'Connor had offered the Auxiliaries a drink and a second bottle of
whiskey was ordered into the bargain. John Jameson spread a benign
glow over the Auxiliaries and they departed without the Castle's
five-man Christmas present. The Castle might have taken some small
comfort from the episode had they known of the cosmic hangovers
the five proceeded to inflict on themselves. They finished the whiskey
– and their wine – and then repaired to Vaughan's. Diarmuid
O'Hegarty, who had not been at the Gresham either, was horror-
stricken at the prospect of a raid on Vaughan's and implored them to
go home, with conspicuous lack of success. Delayed reaction, and
John Jameson's, had taken over and there were wrestling matches and
tumblers of whiskey before the warriors were decanted into a car and
poured into some of Mrs O'Donovan's beds for the night.

On New Year's Eve, 'O' struck Collins a more serious blow than
the fright of Christmas Eve had been. One of the most prominent Sinn
Fein women, Eileen MacGrane, a lecturer in the National University,
was in her bath, in her flat in Dawson St, when 'O's men burst in.
Collins was furious at their subsequent behaviour. Writing to Art
O'Brien later he said . . . 'gallant British officers bandied her name
around with every low suggestion, please do everything possible.'[23]
It wasn't only Eileen MacGrane's modesty that suffered. Some of
Collins' most valuable files were captured in a room in her flat which
he rented. These included documents that eventually led to the arrest
of Broy. In his book, Neligan criticises Collins for not being careful
enough in protecting his sources.[24] This is the incident he is referring

to. In fact Collins was extraordinarily careful and secretive in his protection of people, but his work method involved keeping such detailed records for checking and cross-checking that he left himself open to a discovery of this sort. Eileen MacGrane had a rough time of it in jail in England, but Broy would have been tortured and killed had his role been even guessed at. Though he was arrested on suspicion, as some of the documents found had obviously been typed by him (Collins had also kept the day-book he took from Brunswick St) it proved possible to muddy the waters.

Firstly he sent a warning to Broy's superior officer who, not wishing to appear on Collins' hit list as Broy's accuser, destroyed any incriminating evidence he could lay his hands on. Next Collins got another detective, who shared Broy's office, to disappear suddenly out of the country, partly through inducement, partly by threat, which automatically deflected suspicion on him. (Collins saw to it that this man was sent a return ticket when the Truce was signed.) Finally he wrote and signed a letter which he sent into the Castle, arranging for its discovery. It purported to be an inquiry to an unnamed contact asking what was behind the fuss about this man Broy who had never been any good and was always an enemy of the IRA. These stratagems and the coming of the Truce saved Broy's life. But the MacGrane raid[25] meant that Collins found out for himself just how true was his own saying that the British could replace a detective, but not his knowledge. Although Neligan continued to operate successfully Broy was irreplaceable.

Broy's seizure initiated an era during which Collins, even by his own standards, was incredibly lucky to escape capture. The common factor which saved him in each case was loyalty. The night Broy was caught, Christy Harte, the hall porter at Vaughan's, was taken to the Castle. After several bad days he was put in a darkened room and told that if he betrayed Collins he would be given £5,000 and a new start in life anywhere in the world. However Harte, a poor man, continued to maintain that he did not know Collins. Eventually he was released – to make a full report to Collins.

A little later the military raided a house in Brendan's Rd close to O'Connor's where Collins was staying. An officer rummaged through the love letters of the occupant, a girl, and was so abashed when she berated him for his lack of chivalry that he dropped the list of the addresses he was supposed to be raiding. He rang up the Castle to be given the addresses of the houses he had yet to raid, but was told that such information was not for transmission over the telephone and to return at once to the Castle. Next morning the girl found the list and gave it to Batt O'Connor; the only house on the list still unraided was No. 23, where Collins had spent the night.

He had an even nearer miss some weeks later, on Friday 1 April, when one of his helpers, Eileen Hoey, made an April Fool out of a party of Tans and detectives at No. 5 Mespil Rd, which was one of his intelligence centres. Hoey talked her way out of an incriminating revolver find by blaming it on a mythical lodger in the house. Then, after a gruelling in the Castle, she was driven back in the small hours of the morning to Mespil Rd where the Tans proceeded to set up a week-end-long stake-out for Collins who, unknown to the Tans, had been due at nine o'clock that Saturday morning.

But after saying the Rosary for inspiration, Hoey got her mother to fake a heart attack and persuaded the Tans to accompany her to a neighbouring doctor, whom she never attended, but who was preferable to her mother's loyalist physician. The doctor, correctly divining *Uisce fé Talamh* (water under the ground), came to the house, 'treated' the mother in private and agreed to get a message to Collins who was duly stopped by a scout within an ace of Mespil Rd. The stake-out produced a valuable haul of papers for the Castle and landed Hoey in jail where she was subjected to 'shocking ill-treatment'[26] but released after the Truce.

The raid on his papers hit Collins hard. He said afterwards, 'The raid was much worse than I thought. Practically the entire record is gone.'[27] His methodology, which incensed Neligan, necessitated keeping so many records that their discovery was inevitably damaging. Nevertheless his incredible resilience showed itself yet again. By now even the British were coming to admire him. Lloyd George's right-hand man, Cabinet Secretary Tom Jones, wrote to Bonar Law at this stage: 'The tenacity of the IRA is extraordinary. Where was Michael Collins during the Great War? He would have been worth a dozen brass-hats.'[28] Collins recovered sufficiently to take part in a notable 'first' the following month (May 1921), the first use of the Thompson sub-machine gun in warfare.

Clan na nGael had organised the purchase of a large consignment which the US Customs seized on 16 June 1921, underlining the difficulty of smuggling large-scale supplies of armaments to Ireland undetected by Britain or her allies. However a few dozen had got through the previous month. Two Irish-American ex-American Army officers from Chicago, Captain Cronin and Major Dineen, also arrived safely and conducted Thompson training sessions. Collins was delighted with the new toy and so enthusiastically tested one in the grounds of the Christian Brothers at Marino, County Dublin, that a Brother came out to warn him that the noise would attract the enemy.[29] The guns were actually used in a number of Dublin ambushes and had a psychological effect, but did not materially affect the war.[30]

Tom Barry, one of the men Collins introduced to the Thompson, recalls that the sound of the weapon was not the only danger to accrue from Collins' behaviour at the time. He wrote about an occasion when Collins acted drunk and succeeded in bluffing both of them safely out of a death trap.

One night we ran into a hold-up by about fifty Auxiliaries. . . . I was next to Collins and he put up such a fine act, joking and blasting in turn that he had the whole search party of terrorists in good humour in a short time.[31]

After a perfunctory search they got through safely, but Barry berated Collins for not having scouts out in front of them. The reaction he got was:

Mick as usual guffawed and chaffed me about being a windy West Cork buggar . . . Failing to see the joke, I told him crossly that it was quite true, I was a windy beggar, as I had a wholesome regard for my neck.[32]

Barry in fact was one of the bravest men in the war and probably the most successful field commander. Apart from his victory at Kilmichael he achieved a spectacular success at Crossbarry, County Cork, on 19 March 1921. In a day-long engagement, encouraged by the traditional pipes of Flor Begley, Barry and a force of about a hundred men broke through a more heavily armed British encircle-ment of ten times that number and got away safely, inflicting heavy casualties as they went. Barry bore Collins no grudge but the same combination of Collins' style and the difficulties created by another unsuccessful attempt at large-scale arms shipments, this time from Italy, did create a good deal of hostility towards Collins in other circles both during, and indeed long after, the Thompson period.

The long-running Italian arms saga, which actually began in 1920, was finally abandoned a year later, in 1921. Apart from illustrating the kind of difficulties Collins' style brought on him, it conclusively proved the impossibility of getting any large-scale arms shipment through British Intelligence. The Rector of the Irish College in Rome, Monsignor Hagan, and Monsignor M. J. Curran, Vice Rector, had introduced Donal Hales and a colleague to Italian War Office officials, possibly even the War Minister. Collins' subsequent letter to Hales indicated that:

The reports were so satisfactory that the Trade Department say they are sending another friend out shortly, who is interested in the same business, but has new ideas to develop . . . the new visitor hopes the way will be well-paved for him when he gets there.[33]

Collins had been involved in the Italian affair for several months before he told the Cork IRA what he had in mind. He acknowledged to Hales on 13 August 1920 that he had received:

. . . the important communication on the subject of Italian Cabinets and such antiques in this country. This is a matter which requires very careful organisation so that there may be no loss. You will understand that although the finances are not exactly limited yet a loss would render further dealings uninviting.[34]

One of his September despatches to Art O'Brien read as follows:

ITALIAN FURNITURE: Joe Vize is away at the moment, so I cannot give you any details, also I have not yet gone into the matter quite fully with Liam. I am doing so however. You will be fully advised as to how things go ahead.[35]

But as far as Liam Deasy and Florrie O'Donoghue were concerned the Italian gun-running idea had only taken shape at a meeting with Collins in Barry's Hotel, Dublin months later, on 16 December 1920. Deasy and O'Donoghue were impressed and, in view of the importance of the project, O'Donoghue suggested a man 'we could ill spare' as a pilot, Mick Leahy, Vice OC Cork No. 1 Brigade, because he had qualified as a marine engineer.

It was decided that Leahy, the 'new visitor' Collins mentioned to Hales would be sent to Italy and that arrangements for the actual landing would be placed in the hands of the Vice-OC of the Skibbereen Brigade, Patrick O'Driscoll. A site screened from the sea was picked out not far from where Collins grew up, the channel inside Rabbit Island, about 400 yards off Myross Strand. Dumps were constructed. A flotilla of small boats was arranged and special boxes provided with ropes bound round them so that they could be filled with arms and then lowered from the Italian ship into the boats and thus brought ashore. Meanwhile all the roads and lanes leading to the landing beaches were to be guarded by a strong force of Volunteers.

Leahy was suitably impressed when he was instructed by his OC Sean O'Hegarty, to go to Dublin on 2 January 1921, in order to make arrangements with Collins for a passport to Italy. He was to become progressively less impressed.[36] In Dublin he met Gearoid O'Sullivan, at that stage Adjutant General, and was taken on a 'very lengthy journey through many streets, and eventually fetched up at Devlin's in Parnell St 'only the length of O'Connell St from where we started. . . . I had the feeling it was all done to impress me, the boy from the country.' Worse was to follow. Leahy goes on:

When we entered Devlin's pub, I was surprised to find nearly all the GHQ Staff assembled and a merry party in progress, this despite Gearoid's protestations that Dublin was a dangerous place for the likes of him. My choice of lemonade when whiskey was being pressed did not go down too well with Michael Collins who seemed to be master of the revels. Dick Mulcahy was in Devlin's, but was quiet in comparison to a number of them and left early . . .

The Devlin's affair had been Tom Cullen's stag party and Leahy was put out to find that no one took any interest in his mission until after the wedding breakfast next day. Then, having being sent to

London by Collins to get a British passport, he found that he was expected to make the arrangements himself. He finally found his way over the Swiss border into Italy, at Modane, on 28 March.

He linked up with Donal Hales, who taught at Genoa University and was married to an Italian. Hales was friendly with both d'Annunzio and Mussolini, and introduced Leahy to d'Annunzio before bringing him to the gun-running ship, the *Stella Maris*, a four-masted barque, with a 'ballast' of rifles, machine-guns, revolvers and ammunition. But the money for the shipment failed to arrive from Dublin, and Leahy's own money began running out. Collins wrote to Hales on 7 March:

The arrangement made for the transfer of the money was a bad one, as of course it would be obvious what it was meant for – I have a better plan if I can work it out properly. It is to pay the amount for the credit of the Branch – not for any individual. You could then make application at your end.[37]

The money never got through. In desperation Leahy set out for Paris and Sean T. O'Kelly, who suggested that Leahy make his way to London where Art O'Brien would have more direct contact with Collins. All O'Brien could get for Leahy was an instruction to return home, which he did on 23 April 1921.

Collins gave him no satisfaction. He said he had got his messages but that the project was out of the question. 'The British knew all about it.' Tom Hales said:

. . . failure remained a mystery to my brother for a long time . . . in my view members of the Cabinet, not Collins, were not too hot about the under-taking, and as time went by, on to April 1921 all possibly became worried about the success of this undertaking. It may also be governed by a third factor, you remember when the ease off was suggested . . .[38]

Hales, one of the most knowledgeable men about IRA affairs of this period in the country, was almost certainly putting his suggestions in a deliberately tentative fashion – it's a celebrated Cork characteristic! Both he and O'Donoghue knew that the 'ease off' reference referred to de Valera's proposal on his return from America (see Chapter 7). But Leahy himself probably contributed to the aborting of the mission inadvertently, possibly through being identified by British Intelligence. Collins sent Hales a cheque for his expenses in the matter on 7 July 1921 with a letter which said:

The business, I think, should be kept in view, but unfortunately it has not been found practicable. We were not very satisfied with our messenger in the latter stages of the procedings, and we consequently had to change plans temporarily at any rate. You should be very reticent in any reference you make to this . . .[39]

Hales was duly 'reticent'; so was Collins himself, and his silence, combined with his flamboyance at the Cullen party, injured his reputation in some circles for many years.

One consequence of the increasing intensity of the war was that some seventy persons were found shot as spies between January and April. Though all were labelled, 'spies and informers beware', or somesuch, it is very doubtful if the IRA did in fact execute them all. Some were the work of criminals, some of the 'Dirty Tricks Brigade', units like the Igoe gang and others. The IRA did however carry out some executions which Collins regretted. In Cork, an elderly loyalist landowner, a Mrs Lindsay, gave away an ambush. Six Volunteers were captured and sentenced to death as a result. Cork No. 1 Brigade kidnapped Mrs Lindsay and her chauffeur and sent word to the British that she would die if the Volunteers did. The Volunteers were executed and the Cork men shot the old lady and her driver without sanction from GHQ. The usual thing in such cases was to burn the informant's house. One captive of the period who had a happier experience was General Lucas who was captured by a party of Volunteers under Liam Lynch in July 1920, while fishing on the Blackwater. He was moved around for almost a month before his last custodian, Michael Brennan, the Commander of the East Clare Brigade, engineered his escape. Brennan,[40] who liked Lucas otherwise, got tired of buying the General his daily bottle of whiskey, out of his own pocket. Moreover it was impossible to mount attacks on British patrols while at the same time guarding a British general in secrecy.[41] To keep fit Lucas played tennis and made hay while in captivity. Collins' network saw to it that letters to and from his wife were delivered. The only time Lucas expressed fear was when his captors offered to take him salmon poaching on the River Shannon one night. The thought of being found 'stroke hauling' salmon by the bailiffs worried him greatly. He was both relieved and astounded to find that his IRA boatman on the poaching trip was the Chief Bailiff. Lucas' troops shot up Fermoy and a number of other towns in reprisal for his capture. After escaping he lectured them for 'an over-zealous display of loyalty'. Displeased at his allowing himself to be captured, the Army authorities made no use of Lucas' services thereafter.

Collins was said to be opposed to the shooting of women. Even in one case very close to him, a neighbour of Batt O'Connor's, a Mrs Maud Walsh, escaped with her life despite activities of a more serious nature than those which claimed the lives of other spies.

This does not appear to have been his attitude always, to judge from a story concerning my father. According to this he and another Volunteer were sent out by Collins to shoot two young women, who had been consorting with British soldiers and had apparently given away information. But my father decided that the girls 'were very young and very beautiful' and made up his own and his companion's mind that they should not be shot. For once Collins does not appear to have been too concerned about the non-fulfilment of a 'job'. My father was promoted to more congenial duties concerned with intelligence and the operations of the underground Sinn Fein Courts. But the ferocity of the struggle in Cork militated against kindly feelings.

In February 1921 a group of Volunteers were given away by an informer at Clonmult and surrounded by Tans, Auxiliaries and regular troops. After a two-hour fight the thatch on the cottage they were sheltering in was set alight and they surrendered on being promised fair treatment. However when the Volunteers emerged with their hands up the Auxiliaries fell on them 'like wild beasts' and nine were battered to death.[42] The six who survived, through the intervention of a regular officer, were subsequently executed by order of a court martial. The Cork No. 1 Brigade again seized and shot a hostage, a Major Compton Smith, a man whose character greatly impressed his captors. His last letters were sent to Collins, who wrote to Art O'Brien after Greenwood had made capital out of the shooting in the House of Commons urging him to publicise the fact that Compton Smith in his last letter to his wife said that he had been treated 'far better than Englishmen would treat an Irishman in the same circumstances'.[43] His final letter to General Strickland urged that there be no reprisals, and he said that the men who captured him were no murder gang, but men filled with a sense of high duty.

Collins' sister Mary described the morning the Clonmult prisoners were shot in Cork City. Tomas MacCurtain's widow had erected an altar outside the barracks wall and the women, including the mothers of the condemned men, prayed there under the shadow of a tank. They heard a volley and prayed until an ambulance emerged:

and just as we were about to disperse we heard another volley of shots . . . instead of shooting the six they had arranged to kill them one by one. In another 15 minutes there was another volley . . . was again repeated after an interval . . .

I cannot describe the wonderful patience and heroism, almost to the point of elation, displayed by these bereaved mothers. . . . The reaction, no doubt, came later but that day they each felt it a privilege to have raised a son for God and Ireland.[44]

Reaction of a different sort did come that day. Mary Collins-Powell describes hearing that afternoon that:

there had been six British soldiers shot in various parts of the city as reprisals for the morning executions. Some of them were mere children with gooseberries and sweets in their pockets, a few walking with the colleens . . . I was sorely stricken with sympathy for those boys and also for the very young Volunteers . . . who got orders to shoot unarmed men . . . Freedom, what crimes are committed in thy name.

While these tragedies were occurring in the foreground of Collins' life, in the background he had to contend with a vendetta that Brugha conducted against him and which de Valera literally presided over. It was so intense that it caused him to think seriously about quitting his highly successful underground war in Dublin and taking to the hills with the Cork IRA.

Brugha at this stage, March 1921, was pursuing Collins over what he described as irregularities in the Scot accounts for arms purchase. His allegation seems to have been, not so much that Collins was embezzling money, but that he was using IRA funds for IRB purposes. For once Collins was not able to produce his usual meticulously prepared accounts. Tom Cullen had left a bag of papers with a friend who was raided and the papers seized. They had included the accounts Brugha was now querying almost a year later. Collins wrote to Michael Staines[45] in Mountjoy, who with Eamonn Duggan was one of the prisoners' principal leaders, on 16 March, unaware that Brugha had already carried his campaign into the prison, which with executions taking place within its walls, was an unlikely venue wherein to conduct a squabble about petty cash. Collins' letter gives an indication of his pressures and thoughts that week:

There was a Dail meeting on Friday and consequently I was rushing all day on Thursday. Then there was a lot of men from the country on Saturday and Sunday, so I had not the slightest opportunity of writing you a word. You don't know how I feel for you all. It is dreadful to think of you remaining in your cells and just thinking and brooding when the poor lads were being taken to their deaths. May God help every man to bear it as they bore it . . .

Enclosed is a letter from Cathal. He is making an awful fuss and rumpus generally about accounts. It is so intolerable that I am thinking seriously of getting away to Cork No. 3. I would get a run for my money there anyway . . .

Staines replied the next day, 17 March 1921:

. . . I enclose . . . a note from . . . C. [Brugha] If I could have a chat with Cathal I am sure I would be able to satisfy him that everything is alright but it is a different matter putting my thoughts on paper. If I say what I think I will probably get his rag out and we cannot afford that at the present critical juncture. As he is such a crank and you know exactly how the a/cs stand I would be glad if you will suggest the wording of my reply.

As you are aware I know practically nothing about the a/cs now and T.C. [Tom Cullen] didn't lodge the money with my knowledge except in this way that he was my assistant for a certain time and during that time had the right to act for me. I don't remember signing cheques for any of this money. Since we were appointed treasurers you always kept the a/cs and during that time I was satisfied that all the money was accounted for and I am satisfied still.

Above all things I will depend on you not to let Cathal know that I sent you his letter. Did T.C. lodge the money in No. 1 joint a/c or did he open a social account for it?

It was terrible here on Sunday looking at the Boy's (*sic*) friends coming to say their last goodbye, but when the visits were over our sorrowful feelings gave way to a feeling of pride that they were facing death so bravely and we kept up communication practically all night. They sent us messages for their friends in this world and so sure were they that they were going straight to heaven that we gave them messages for our friends there. Their last message to the boys was 'carry on the fight we will watch over you and pray for you in heaven'. . . .

. . . For goodness sake get that Cork No. 3 idea out of your head. You are required where you are at present. Don't take C. too seriously and rub him the right way an odd time . . .

Collins's reply is dated the 21st:

Yours of the 17th reached me on the morning of the 19th or rather late on the 18th. There was not an opportunity of sending in a reply since, although I was very anxious to reply to that particular communication of yours . . .

Yes the lads were great weren't they. A fellow prisoner of yours . . . in a letter to me, put the thing in the following beautiful way: 'Monday morning was very terrible, but pride afterwards took the sadness away, and they were so certain of heaven that death became not only unfeared but desired. They one and all stepped across the threshold joyfully.'

. . . Enclosed is a little statement which will help you in replying to Cathal. In replying to him it would be well to point out the difficulty of getting anything more than general details in view of the seizures of books etc. This is the thing that has nettled me most in reality – he expects every sixpence to be accounted for, nothwithstanding all we have gone through in the way of raids, etc.

Collins pointedly does not reply to Staines' admonition about his 'Cork No. 3' idea. This may be because Staines had given him an opportunity of drafting a reply which temporarily deflected Brugha. The intensity of Brugha's hatred may be gauged from the mere fact that he would send such a request in to Staines during the octave of the execution of men who, in Mother Dodd's words, were 'strong in the conviction that the fight for country was a fight for Faith'.[46]

Sean Dowling summed it up tellingly:

Cathal Brugha hated Collins like poison. It was pathological . . . Brugha was Minister for Defence but he never did anything. He was not able, but he was never on the run. He continued to work as manager for Lalor's candle factory on Ormond Quay . . . Collins was so energetic that he had usurped many of Brugha's functions: he sure was hated by him. . . .[47]

Brugha's hatred for Collins actively interfered with the war effort. Payments for arms were held up, as letters from Collins to P. G. O'Daly in Liverpool show: 'I am very sorry about the matter of funds.

That is not my fault. I thought the little man had arranged to send you on what you required. I shall mention the matter to him.'[48]

Next day he wrote again:

You will understand that I could forward you some money for your own use, but the way things are going here at present I don't like doing that. It is up to these people who are making so much fuss to attend to things. Nothing like it happened when I was in charge of a certain number of details. It should not happen now either.

The same shortages occurred elsewhere. Mulcahy wrote to the Director of Purchases, Liam Mellowes, complaining that: 'in the hearing of the QMG's staff, just returned from Scotland, 9,000 rounds of .303 offered for sale were refused for lack of money . . . we would be lynched down the country if this were known.'[49] Mulcahy was not exaggerating. At the time 'men were dying for lack of the few rounds of ammunition to defend themselves'.[50] But Mellowes, who had been in America with de Valera, was inclined to take sides against Collins. He wrote back:

It is quite possible that the situation reported to you by QMG as existing in G [Glasgow] is quite correct. In fact I am so informed myself. As the M/D has stated relative to London and Manchester . . . he will debit me with amounts unless I can show goods on hand and I was not, and am not, going to put myself in the position of adding to the Glasgow muddle by making further disbursements until I saw my way clear.[51]

That particular round in the Brugha-Collins feud was brought to a close by means of a highly embarrassing inquiry presided over by de Valera. Dowling described the scene:

Collins came, he brought books and receipts and was able to account for all of it except maybe a hundred pounds . . . Austin Stack told me the story afterwards in Waterford. He found it very embarrassing. Collins was so upset by the accusation that he openly wept. 'Now,' said de Valera, 'it is quite clear that these charges are groundless.' Brugha arose without a word and left the room. Stack rushed after him: 'Come in, shake hands'. But Brugha angrily turned from him; 'You'll find him out yet,' he spat. He stamped out.[52]

Ultimately Brugha's dislike of Collins came down to simple jealousy. De Valera remarked to Mulcahy that it was a great pity that a man with Brugha's many fine qualities should be guilty of 'a dirty little vice like jealousy',[53] as though he were immune from it himself. Collins had taken such a grip on the British imagination that the first question raiding parties often asked on entering a house was, 'Where's Michael Collins?' Frequently different raiding parties at opposite ends of the city would smash into homes yelling, 'Where is he? We know he's here.' Other men too had hair's-breadth escapes, indeed all the leading figures in Sinn Fein and the Volunteers were constantly harried, but Collins was the one who most caught the popular imagination, and Brugha resented press labels on Collins such as 'the Irish de Wet'. *He* was the Minister for Defence; Collins he saw as a mere subordinate manipulating press coverage to gain an undeserved notoriety.

Collins' notoriety was such that while Auxiliaries were tearing houses apart looking for him in Dublin, he was said to be involved in escapades in other parts of the country. In one such, a shoot-out at Burgatia House, near Rosscarbery, on 2 February 1921, he was supposed to have taken part mounted on a white horse and to have been killed. Commenting on the *Daily Sketch* report of this, he wrote to Celestine:

Yes indeed, the English papers have been giving me plenty of notoriety – a notoriety one would gladly be rid of, but they must make a scapegoat. The *Daily Sketch* had a gorgeous thing one time – 'Mike', the super hater, dour, hard, no ray of humour, no trace of human feeling. Oh lovely! The white horse story was an exaggeration. I have not ridden a white horse since I rode 'Gipsy', and used her mane as a bridle.[54]

Collins had other things to worry him during this period (March/ April 1921). As part of the reprisal policy the security forces broke up fairs and destroyed the agricultural machinery and farm buildings of suspects. Collins' old home, Woodfield, at the time occupied by his brother Johnny's large family, was amongst those which were razed. Collins' own account of the burning has survived:

Col Commandant Higginson, the Commanding Officer of a brigade at the Cork City Headquarters of the 6th Division ordered the destruction as an official reprisal for the attack on Rosscarbery. It should be understood that my brother's place was four miles from Rosscarbery. The enemy force came bringing with them several of the neighbouring civilians as hostages – some of the civilians were forced at the point of the bayonet to bring hay and straw into the house. The hay and straw were then sprinkled with petrol (also forced). On arrival of the English forces the house was occupied by a maiden lady, a maid and eight little children (ages from twelve years downwards to a little child of less than twelve months). It should also be explained that quite a short time prior to the burning the mother of the children had died.

She had been in bad health for nearly twelve months and, no doubt, a succession of raids by British forces contributed to hasten her untimely end. My brother, the father of all the children, was attending a County Council meeting in Cork and was not present at the time of the burning. The little children were without anyone to protect them. The English forces proceeded to throw them out of the house and having done this proceeded with the burning.

The dwelling house itself, and every out-office (with the exception of one stable) were completely destroyed. The hayshed which contained some hay, was likewise destroyed. A farmhand was ploughing in a field near the house – the English forces went to the horses, took the harness off them and threw it into the fire. The net result therefore was that eight young children were left homeless and there was no person or nothing left to carry on the ordinary work of the farm, so that of course production suffered.

To complete the story my brother, himself, was arrested on his arrival at the Railway Station at Clonakilty – the timing of the arrest practically coincided with the burning of his house.

He is at present at Spike Island, was visited on Friday last and is likely to lose the use of his right hand as a result of medical neglect. The above are the details – there were in fact other, minor, points of brutality which cannot be told until all the evidence is available. The important thing is that the case is no exception.

My brother was over military age, but he had always been an advanced Irishman. He was a member of the Cork County Council. Being over military age he devoted himself to this work and to general Local Reconstruction.[55]

Collins was right. The case was no exception; four other houses were burned in the same area that night (16 April 1921) alone and hundreds were burned throughout the country, but his letter is remarkably dispassionate considering the impact the burning had on him. 'They knew where they could hurt me most,' he said and went into one of his black moods for days. With no home or family of his own, Woodfield had always been his anchor. Now he brooded on an old forecast that around the beginning of the Twentieth Century there would be no Collinses at Woodfield, and on the new and more pressing realities of how to cope with the burning's aftermath. Johnny's family had to be farmed out amongst neighbours and in the terror of the time it was hard enough to get all the children placed for fear of further reprisals. Liam Collins, the baby mentioned, suffered ill-health all his life as a result of the hardships of those days. Johnny did not lose his hand, which had been injured in an accident on the farm, but due to the absence of medical facilities at Spike Island Prison, or, it was suspected, the unwillingness to provide any, the hand did suffer permanent damage and he had to give up farming and leave Woodfield. So the old prophecy came true. However neither Collins nor the country at large had much time to ponder such things.

The IRA countered the farm-burnings by destroying the homes of loyalists. Sean Hales, whose Brigade operated in the Woodfield area, summed up the counter-burning policy to the seventy-year-old Lord Bandon – whom he had surprised in bed with a young lady not his wife – as he prepared to sprinkle the petrol: 'You burned my castle last week. Now I'll burn yours.'[56] The Hales treatment repeated throughout the country caused such reaction from loyalists that the reprisals policy was abandoned by the Cabinet. In order to save face Army officers were instructed to tell their subordinates that the decision was not 'because of the vapourings of some insignificant member of the House of Commons', but, 'largely due to His Majesty's influence, so that in that case we can all be perfectly happy about the decision.'[57]

Throughout the burnings period Collins was attempting to use his influence to make a friend of his, Sean MacEoin, 'perfectly happy'.[58] The lengths to which he was prepared to go to get men out of jail were never better exemplified than in the case of MacEoin. Few fighting men excited Collins' admiration to the extent Sean MacEoin did. A blacksmith, from Ballinalee, County Longford, he took charge of the Longford brigade at Collins' request. Amongst his exploits was a reprisal upon a reprisal party of Auxiliaries and Black and Tans who looted and burned several shops and houses in Granard, County Longford on 5 November 1920 after the IRA had carried out an ambush a few days earlier. On the way home from the reprisal, the Auxiliaries and Tans, who outnumbered the IRA by five to one, were attacked by MacEoin and twenty Volunteers who created terrible slaughter amongst the drunken reprisalists. As many as twenty deaths and several times that number of injured are believed to have been inflicted, but the exact casualties were never given. MacEoin had a reputation for chivalry. When he was surrounded in a cottage near Ballinalee the following January, he came out of the shelter of the house to make his stand because there were women inside. Once outside he killed the police officer in charge and put the rest of the party to flight. In another ambush in February, he and his column forced a larger party of Auxiliaries to surrender after a hard-fought engagement. He congratulated the surviving Auxiliaries on their courage, and did what he could for the wounded before sending them back to base in one of the captured lorries. Three of the Auxiliary party paid tribute to him at his court martial in June of that year. The court martial came about as a result of one of Cathal Brugha's obsessions.

From the first, Brugha had wanted to counter the reprisal policy by bringing the war to England, first by assassinating members of the British Cabinet and then by actions such as machine-gunning cinema queues. Collins had blocked the assassination scheme, pointing out that England could always replace a Cabinet, and telling Brugha flatly, 'You'll get none of my men for that.' Brugha had replied icily: 'That's all right *Mister* Collins, I want none of your men. I'll get men of my own.'

He didn't find them that easy to get. The Donegal Commandant, Joe Sweeney, told Mulcahy that he found Brugha's proposal 'completely immoral'. Eventually, around the beginning of March 1921, Brugha sent for MacEoin who could hardly find his way around Dublin, never mind London, and arranged that he would remain in Dublin under Brugha's direct command. Emerging from the interview however he bumped into Collins and there were emissions of sulphur before Collins managed to arrange with Mulcahy, as Chief of Staff, to countermand the orders of the Minister for Defence, and repoint the blacksmith in the direction of Balinalee.

However MacEoin had been identified in Dublin, by the RIC. He was taken off the train at Mullingar and, in an attempt to escape, was shot through the lung and beaten with rifle butts. As a doctor only gave him an hour to live, a party of Black and Tans decided they had better make the best use possible of the time available and beat him up savagely. Various efforts to rescue him miscarried.

In one, Collins had smuggled in a change of clothes, a watch and a hacksaw, soap and oil. MacEoin used his gifts to work all one Thursday night and Friday morning, cutting through the bars of his downstairs cell and obliterating the marks of his handiwork in preparation for an escape on Friday evening.

Recovering from wounds as he was, MacEoin had driven his temperature sky-high by his sawing exertions and when the prison doctor put in an unexpected appearance he attributed MacEoin's fever to the damp of the ground floor cell and ordered him moved immediately.

Next, Collins attempted to make use of the fact that every morning a British armoured car drove to the Dublin abattoir to collect meat. He decided to have the crew held up and the car used in an attempt on Mountjoy Jail. Emmet Dalton and a group from the Squad were entrusted with the rescue. Each morning Dalton's younger brother Charlie sat in a window overlooking the abattoir watching the armoured car. Nearby, personally checked each time by Collins himself, the rescue party, dressed in army fatigues, waited for the signal that would show all the tommies had come out of the car. One morning they did emerge. Dalton lifted the blind, the tommies were surrounded and their vehicle commandeered. Emmet Dalton and Joe Leonard, dressed as British officers, climbed in, Dalton carrying an official-looking letter marked OHMS. At the jail gate Dalton, who had been an officer in the British Army during the war, gave the correct salutes, waved his OHMS envelope and in imperious fashion demanded entry on important business. Once inside, the driver, Pat McCrea, managed to turn the armoured car in the narrow passageway so that it blocked both inner gates, while Dalton and Leonard headed for the Governor's office, where it was hoped MacEoin would be waiting. But on this particular morning the changing of the guard was late and he was informed that he would have to wait.

Dalton's cover story, and the written authorisation in the letter, was that he had been sent by the Castle to collect MacEoin. He was arguing with a suspicious Governor and staff that he should be allowed to proceed to his cell with the Chief Warder to collect the prisoner when, outside, a sentry opened fire.

The rescue team kept their heads. One, Tom Keogh, shot the sentry, and then coolly held up an approaching party of soldiers as a machine-gun mounted high up in the gate turret rained bullets down on the armoured car. Leonard and Dalton tied up the Governor and his staff with their own ties. The raiders remounted the armoured car despite the machine-gun fire and made off safely through an approaching party of soldiers who were misled by the sight of the officers' uniforms.

Collins' next attempt was still-born. He planned to get a revolver in to MacEoin so that during his court martial he could hold up the officers of the court and throw himself out of a window of City Hall, beside the Castle, where the court martial was to be held. Michael Noyek, MacEoin's solicitor, was perfectly willing to do the smuggling, and MacEoin was prepared to try for the window, though the fall would very likely have killed him, but Collins abandoned the idea when Noyek pointed out that all the court martial officers were armed. He finally got MacEoin out, as we shall see, by refusing to stop the war until the British released him.

MacEoin was luckier than one of Kevin Barry's prison friends, a Volunteer called Frank Flood who, a few months after Barry was executed (on 14 March 1921) told a nun, Mother Patricia Dodd, of Barry's last wish for him. 'He wanted me to have a long and prosperous life – here I am again.'59 'Here' was a condemned cell. Flood was one of a number of Volunteers sentenced to death by court martial for the 'Bloody Sunday' killings. As so often happens in such cases none of the accused was in any way involved. The one man who had taken part in the shootings, Frank Teeling, escaped with Ernie O'Malley and Simon Donnelly from Kilmainham. Collins, who had planned the escape, wanted a Volunteer called Paddy Moran to accompany them, but knowing he was innocent and not wanting to make trouble for those who had given evidence on his behalf, Moran refused to breakout, believing he was sure to be acquitted. The court martial decided otherwise however. On the eve of his execution he invited Mother Dodd to come and stay with him and his comrades in heaven in which, like his comrades, he felt assured of the 'highest, highest place', as the nun described it. The one note of regret she seems to have encountered was struck by Volunteer Bernard Ryan who spoke of his young wife whom he had 'loved for years and only married now when he could keep her'. By contrast another Volunteer, Tommy Whelan, informed her: 'I have just told my mother that just as a priest starts a new life at ordination so on Monday I will start a new life that will last for ever.'

But apart from eliciting a sigh from the tender-hearted over the Karma of the British and Irish peoples, which so often apparently dooms them to torture each other, the manner in which these men met their deaths had a most important historical consequence, at the critical time when the Anglo-Irish Treaty was hanging in the balance.

Paddy Daly was appointed as OC of the Squad and the corps was expanded. So did its work, as the British began sending in fresh undercover agents to replace the shattered Cairo Gang. A member of the Squad also disposed of one of their existing agents, Shankers Ryan, the man who betrayed McKee and Clancy to Hardy's clutches. He was shot not long after their deaths as he sat drinking close to the place they were captured in Gloucester St.

After the Cairo Gang one of the Squad's principal enemies was the Igoe Gang, an effort to meet like with like run by a Head Constable from Mayo. Igoe, who would have made an ideal member of the Squad himself, was held to be responsible for several deaths. He and his men, RIC personnel drawn from different parts of the country, patrolled the streets of Dublin in plain clothes, looking for wanted men. Igoe developed a simple but very effective trick of doubling back on his tracks so that scouts who had gone ahead to alert the Squad to ambush him almost invariably lost him. On one such occasion the Squad, including members of GHQ, were stationed in St Stephen's Green waiting for Igoe to come up Grafton St when he and his men suddenly wheeled into Dame St. Here they chanced on two Volunteers, Charlie Dalton and Sweeney Newell of Galway, neither of whom was carrying a gun. Dalton they let go, not knowing of his role in Bloody Sunday or the fact that, while still only seventeen, he had taken on an entire patrol of rifle-carrying British tommies single-handed and put them to flight, wounding two of them with his revolver. Newell, however, they held on to for a time, releasing him unharmed from the Bridewell later that afternoon. But as he walked along the unusually deserted streets congratulating himself on his luck he was 'fired on from all sides'.[60] He was taken to hospital, where he hung between life and death for a long time, eventually recovering, though lame in one leg, which, it was subsequently discovered, had had a large safety pin sewn into it.

On one occasion the Squad was on the point of opening up on Igoe and his men in Thomas St when a patrol of soldiers appeared up a side street behind the Squad and advanced towards them in extended order. Vinnie Byrne, a typical Dubliner, though the occasion called for an appropriate song and began to sing, 'Do I want to see my mammy anymore? Do I? Yes I do.' The Squad leader agreed that if fighting started the chances of any of his men seeing their 'mammies' again were slim and the .45s remained undrawn. The only time that the Squad and Igoe's men met face to face the Squad got the better of the encounter, which took place in Parliament St, 'where a running fight took place in which three of the gang were shot, the rest running away. For some reason or another, after this incident at Parliament St, we saw less of Igoe's gang on the streets', Thornton writes.

But the lack of visibility does not appear to have indicated a lack of activity on Igoe's part. When he appeared before a Whitehall tribunal seeking compensation for his services in Ireland the tribunal gave

. . . considerable attention to Head Constable Igoe's case. Col. Winter gave evidence on Igoe's behalf and emphasised the H/C's loyalty and devotion to duty and his quite exceptional danger which may involve him in frequent removals from one part of the globe to another. The tribunal also saw Igoe himself: he created a favourable impression. One feature of hardship is that Igoe will never be able to return to a 43-acre farm in Ireland to which he had hoped to retire when he left the RIC. Col. Winter considers £1500 the least that Igoe deserves. He suggests annuity and lump sum.[61]

The most spectacular, though less sanguinary, aborted operation of the whole period involved Lloyd George personally. The Auxiliaries and Tans responded to the 'littlers' campaign of bombing their lorries by having posts erected in the vehicles to which they tied captured Sinn Fein TDs (*Teachtarai Dail*, or Dail Deputies). 'Bomb us now,' they called cheerily as they careered about with the terrified hostages aboard. By way of retaliation Collins decided for once to fall in with Brugha's oft-expressed wish to carry the war to England. While Lloyd George, Hamar Greenwood, Bonar Law, Balfour and the rest of them were debating in the House of Commons whether or not to introduce martial law to Ireland in the wake of Bloody Sunday, Collins was planning to kidnap and hold twelve members of the Government including, if possible, some of the men mentioned above, as hostages against the hostage-taking in Ireland. Three top men were sent to London early in 1921 to liaise with Sam Maguire and Reggie Dunne: George Fitzgerald, Sean Flood and Frank Thornton.

Thornton describes the job as being 'colossal'. The movement of every member of the Government had to be checked so as to be able to say with certainty who did what at regular time each night. This process threw up 'some very interesting sidelights on the private lives of members of the British Government'. It also provided the names of not twelve, but twenty-five MPs 'who did a regular thing on the same night every week'. Each of the twenty-five was then pointed out to IRA men in London so that they would know whom to swoop on when the time came. Everything was in readiness – men, transport and intelligence – when for some reason the practice of hostage-carrying ceased in Ireland and the London kidnappings were called off.

During the planning stage Thornton and Flood were involved in an episode which shows what notions of security were in those days. They were going to Acton to check up on some of their arrangements and entered the Westminster tube station to find the lift gates just closing. Flood challenged Thornton to race him to the platform and the pair set off at top speed, Flood in front. Then:

around the second-last bend I heard a terrific crash and on coming round the corner I fell over two men on the ground, one of whom was Sean Flood. We picked ourselves up and both assisted to his feet the man whom Sean Flood had knocked down. To our amazement two other men who were with him ordered us to put our hands up.

We more or less ignored them and started to brush down the man and apologise to him when to our amazement we discovered that the man we had knocked down was Lloyd George, Prime Minister of England.

Lloyd George told the guards to put their guns away which they were loath to do, pointing out that he had obviously been felled by Irishmen. Lloyd George replied, 'Well, Irishmen or no Irishmen, if they were out to shoot me I was shot long ago.' Profuse in their apologies, Thornton and Flood took a tube in the opposite direction to Acton and spent the next few hours looking over their shoulders to check that they really were not being followed.

Another slaughter was avoided on the eve of the truce. Collins had made preparations which would have put Bloody Sunday in the shade. This time he had the names and addresses of some sixty fresh agents whom the British had been pouring into Dublin in increasing desperation and, in addition, there were plans to wipe out the Kidd's Back confraternity and the groups which habitually patrolled Grafton St. Throughout Dublin, groups of Black and Tans and Auxiliaries had all been targeted for being mown down when, half an hour before the operation was due to begin, it was called off. Lloyd George had sent word that he wanted peace.

7

Peace Comes Dropping Slow

'At 8.00 pm we held up four soldiers and searched them,
but found no arms. We took them to a field in our area
where they were executed before 9.00 pm.'

Report of OC, H Co., Cork No. 1 Brigade,
on eve of Truce, 10 July 1921.

Peace moves continued intermittently throughout 1921 until a truce was arranged in July. Many of the initiatives were either English or English-inspired. Art O'Brien's Irish Self-Determination League pricked some consciences. Others were stirred by the activities of Lord Henry Cavendish-Bentinck's 'Peace with Ireland Council' formed amongst English Catholics. And writers of the stature of Belloc, Chesterton and Shaw added their voices to the chorus of protest raised by some influential newspapers, including *The Times*, but most frequently by the *Manchester Guardian* and the *Daily Herald*, the organ of the Labour Party. The Labour Party-sponsored British Labour Commission presented a report on Irish conditions to a Conference at Caxton Hall on 29 December which said that the Auxiliaries and Black and Tans were 'compelling the Irish people – men women and children – to live in an atmosphere of sheer terrorism'. The Conference called for negotiations, echoing a previous resolution passed by the Labour Party on 11 November, and endorsed by the Irish Labour Congress on 16 November. Independent Liberals, including Asquith, also added their voices to the chorus expressing disquiet about the trend of British policy in Ireland.

None of these public initiatives of themselves bore any fruit, though they helped to set the scene for a private attempt that stimulated further movement. Brigadier General Cockerill MP drew up a memorandum for Lloyd George suggesting that the Irish problem

could be solved only by a Conference of fully accredited plenipotentiaries, representing Ireland and Great Britain, equal in number, and untrammelled by restrictive instructions and empowered by means of negotiation to make the best peace possible. . . . Pending the negotiation there should be a truce and amnesty. Once the provisions of the new Constitution were agreed, they should be submitted for final acceptance or rejection, but no amendment, to the parliaments of the contracting peoples.[1]

The Brigadier also sent a letter to *The Times* outlining these proposals on the day on which he sent his memo to Lloyd George. His letter appeared on 8 October 1920 and aroused considerable interest. Publicly, Arthur Griffith welcomed the idea of direct negotiations with no preconditions. Privately, a contact of Griffith's, Patrick Moylette, a London-based Irish businessman, got in touch with Cockerill on 21 October to tell Lloyd George that 'he could have peace with Sinn Fein, whenever he wished', on the lines of Cockerill's letter. Cockerill made a note of the substance of his message:

. . . accommodation could be had on the various contentious points. A new Constitution could be agreed between the parties which would be acceptable in Ireland with peril neither to the authority of the Crown nor the security of the British Isles nor the liberties of Ulster. The word Republic should be interpreted with understanding. What other word could be used to express the idea of a revolt from the existing form of Constitution. Ireland had always been a kingdom – they had not looked elsewhere for a king and had never uttered a word of disloyalty to the crown. If Ulster would join with them in a spirit of conciliation to seek a settlement by consent there was practically no limit to the concessions they would be prepared to make . . . As regards the question of the Army and Navy, Sinn Fein had no ambitions in those directions. Ireland could not afford such luxuries.[2]

Cockerill duly passed all this on to Lloyd George with an addition which sounds more as though it came from Moylette than either Griffith or Collins. 'He agreed with me that Ireland should retain, as at present, some share of control over the direction of the armed forces of the Crown. Her own safety demanded it.' Moylette may either have been giving his own opinion on military matters or quoting only what he thought was Griffith's view, for certainly Collins would never have given up the chance of setting up the first standing Irish Army. But Moylette was correct in telling Cockerill that he could stress to Lloyd George that the chief merit to Sinn Fein of Cockerill's Conference proposal was 'its spirit. If there is ever to be a true union of the four nations, its terms of peace must be negotiated, not directed'. All this was a far cry from the sort of settlement which the Irish Committee in its deliberations argued about *conferring* on Ireland. The Cockerill parameters were largely those within which the Treaty settlement was finally agreed. But the Cockerill initiative was significant in two other ways. By the introduction of Moylette to the dialogue it opened up the principle of talking to Sinn Fein. This, though subsequently temporarily abandoned in favour of a resumption of the policy of frightfulness, meant that the unthinkable became first thinkable and then ultimately do-able. The second consequence of the Cockerill memorandum lay in the introduction of the Roman Catholic Church to the peace process which, though initially unsuccessful, ultimately resulted in Collins' character being brought to the Pope's attention in a manner which, as we shall see, proved highly advantageous to the Irish at a crucial juncture.

As Lloyd George was well aware, Moylette was by no means a centre-stage figure in Sinn Fein councils. Moreover there was a strong body of opinion in the Cabinet against contact with Sinn Fein. Reacting to Tory hostility to Cope's activities in Dublin, the Irish Committee had decided that 'no person serving in the Irish Government should in any circumstances be permitted to hold communication with Sinn Fein'.[3] Nevertheless, Lloyd George saw Moylette, even on the day after Bloody Sunday, to discuss a letter from Griffith on the 16th, agreeing to a truce 'unhampered by preliminary conditions'. Surprised that Lloyd George did see him, in the circumstances, Moylette's first words to the Prime Minister were, 'Well, I suppose this ends all further hope?' To which Lloyd George replied, 'Not at all, they got what they deserved – beaten by counter-jumpers.'[4] At the time, Lloyd George was also using Alfred Davies MP and John Steele, the London Correspondent of the *Chicago Tribune*, to send signals through to Sinn Fein. Word was sent to Griffith, in the aftermath of Bloody Sunday, not to break off the contacts and to 'keep his nerve'. In the circumstances Griffith might well have felt that Lloyd George was the one with nerve, seeing that it was Lloyd George's men who had locked him up. Nevertheless he sent back word, via Steele, that he would do what he could to reduce the level of violence but that the British would have to taper off the reprisals.[5] Either was easier said than done, but Lloyd George was serious about wanting talks and was genuinely annoyed at Griffith's unauthorised arrest, which he saw as an intrusion of the military arm into the area of political prerogative.[6] He told George Russell (AE)[7] that it would be impossible for him politically to talk to either Collins or Brugha but that he was prepared to negotiate 'anything short of a Republic'. As we shall see, his opportunity to do so arose at a lunch party held in London the next day, 30 November 1920. But before examining the further course of peace negotiations it is time to pick up the threads of the progress of another main player in Anglo-Irish events who has been absent from these pages for some time, but who is shortly to make a significant re-entry, Eamon de Valera.

De Valera's lengthy stay in the US (from June 1919 to December 1920) was a spectacular combination of success and failure. His activities were summed up by the historian Francis M. Carroll as follows:

De Valera spoke before State legislatures, conferred with Governors, was given the freedom of several cities, and received two honorary doctorates . . . always, he addressed large public audiences . . perhaps de Valera's travels throughout America, more than any other event since the 1916 Rising, dramatised for the American people the dimensions of the Irish struggle.[8]

But there were hidden costs to this triumphal progress. De Valera concerned himself with four issues during his protracted stay in America: the raising of money; the securing of recognition of the Irish Republic; the defeat of the League of Nations; and the recognition of himself as the supreme spokesman and arbiter of policy on Ireland by the leaders of the existing Irish-American organisations. He succeeded best in the first objective, and probably deserves to be regarded as one of the first 'junk-bond' salesman. So-called 'bond-certificates' were issued from January 1920, the name being decided on after Franklin D. Roosevelt had been consulted on the law against issuing regular 'bonds' in the name of a Government not recognised by the US. Irish-Americans whom the *Wall Street Journal* (4 February 1920) scornfully described as 'Irish domestic servants, and others of like or lower standards of intelligence',[9] subscribed a total of $5,123,640 to the bond-certificates. De Valera only allowed something over half of this to come to Ireland, the rest remaining in American banks from which source he eventually succeeded in getting control of sufficient funds to found what became his family's newspaper empire, the Irish Press Group. Why he did not send all the money on to the Ministry of Finance in Dublin, or pass it on to the American White Cross, must necessarily remain a matter of conjecture. One would have thought Alan Bell's fate said all that was required about Collins' determination to safeguard loan funds. The British brought Bell, a senior police official, out of retirement to find out how and where Collins was depositing the loan's proceeds. Bell set up a kind of Star Chamber for bank managers in Dublin Castle which seriously threatened the loan until one spring morning in 1920. Collins ordered the Squad to take him off the tram bringing him to work, and to shoot him dead in front of the horrified commuters. Nevertheless Boland wrote to Collins from New York on 22 September 1920:

The Chief . . . is particularly anxious that you at home be satisfied that you can safeguard the money. There is roughly speaking three million dollars available for dispatch to Ireland. . . . will you in your next dispatch assure him that you can safeguard the funds . . .

De Valera's fund-raising attempts in the States were hampered by diversions amongst the Irish-American organisations, both those which he helped to create and those which existed before his arrival. The linked issues of the German Peace Treaty and the League of Nations were of course useful for focusing anti-British, Irish-American sentiments. But these issues were targeted by many other groups in the United States, the Republicans, for example, finding them a handy stick with which to beat the Democrats. And though the Senate defeated the ratification of the German Peace Treaty as early as March 1920 it was July 1921 before a truce obtained in Ireland. Yet in his first public report to the Dail on his return from America, de Valera claimed that Article 10, which was represented as committing the US to defending the territorial status quo of its allies, specifically that of the British in Ireland, had been his prime objective in the US. He allowed speakers to praise him as though he had forced America to adopt the League only on condition that Ireland was a consenting party. He completely failed to secure recognition of the Irish Republic at either the Democratic or Republican Convention, in large part because of his last failure, that of getting himself recognised as the sole leader of the Irish-American opinion. He wrote to one of his rivals:

I am answerable to the Irish people for the proper execution of the trust with which I have been charged. I am definitely responsible to them, and I alone am responsible. It is my obvious duty to select such instruments as may be available for the task set me. It is my duty to superintend every important step in the execution of that task. [10]

His two principal adversaries were Judge Cohalan, the head of the Friends of Irish Freedom, the most important of the open Irish-American organisations, and John Devoy, editor of the *Gaelic American*. Devoy was the man behind such notable episodes in Fenian history as the rescue by the whaler *Catalpa* of Irish prisoners from Western Australia on Easter Monday 1876 and the even more spectacular gesture of defiance in Dublin on Easter Monday of 1916. They were formidable opponents. Cohalan, a judge of the New York Supreme Court was closely associated with Tammany Hall (the notoriously corrupt headquarters of the Democrats in New York) and Devoy was renowned as a 'difficult' man. They came from a background of 'Bossism', the tough, brawling world of Irish-America, formed, in the New World, by deprivation and the antagonism of nativist and Wasp groupings, and in the Old, by attitudes summed up in two sayings that were part joke, part precept: 'If there's a government, I'm against it' and 'Look after your own'. Questions of personality aside, Devoy and Cohalan favoured a policy of working for Irish independence as Americans and through the American system. They had seen how the taint of being pro-German had weakened the Irish-American movement during the war. They wanted no suspicion of un-American activity attaching to their post-war agitations. Collins, who had considerable dealings with Devoy on IRB matters, was under no illusions as to the character of the two men, and was aware of differences of approach within the Irish-American firmament even before de Valera arrived on the scene. But he favoured co-operating rather than feuding with the Irish-American leaders. He wrote to Sean Nunan at a relatively early stage in the personality clash, 6 October 1919:

From the very beginning and indeed prior to anybody going out I knew very well what to expect from the people in command in the U.S.A. However, the best not the worst must be made of them, and there is little doubt that eventually things will be all right.

'Eventually', however, things became far from 'all right'. De Valera said of Cohalan, '. . . big as the country is, it was not big enough to hold the Judge and myself'.[11]

At an early stage in the De Valera tour one Irish-American leader, watching the tensions build up, commented that the best thing to do with de Valera was, 'turn everything over to him. He will make a failure of it, but a failure is better than a split. And a split is certain unless De Valera can have his way.'[12] Events certainly bore out the truth of the statement. The internal power struggle came into the open during February over an interview De Valera gave to the *Westminster Gazette*. He likened the position of Cuba *vis-à-vis* America to that of Ireland in relation to England and suggested that a British version of the Monroe doctrine would both concede Irish independence and guarantee British security. As Americans understood the reality of Cuba's position to be that of a political slum, dominated by the US, de Valera's analogy was badly received. John Devoy attacked the interview in the *Gaelic American*, arguing that de Valera was falling prey to moderation and abandoning the claim for an Irish Republic. In March de Valera sent MacCartan back to Dublin to put his side of the case before the Sinn Fein decision-takers. He also wrote to Cohalan saying that 'to ignore the article in the *Gaelic American* would result in injury to the cause I have been sent here to promote'.[13] Cohalan replied telling him that he was not responsible for Devoy's opinions and pointing out that freedom of opinion was one of America's 'fundamental liberties. We have no law of *lèse-majesté* here.'[14] De Valera thought it wiser not to reply to Cohalan after that but he sent a highly charged letter to Griffith, timed to coincide with MacCartan's lobbying effort on his behalf:

A deadly attempt to ruin our chances for the bonds, and for everything we came here to accomplish, is being made. If I am asked for the ulterior motives I can only guess what they are. 1) To drive me home – jealousy, envy, resentment of a rival – some devilish cause I do not know what prompts. 2) To compel me to become a rubber stamp for somebody.[15]

In fact the 'purpose' cannot have been too 'deadly'. The bonds raised some $600,000 in New York, Cohalan and Devoy's power base. De Valera himself said the dispute was not about fundamentals. 'The trouble is purely one of personalities. I cannot feel confidence enough in a certain man to let him have implicit control of tactics here, without consultation and agreement with me.' A month later de Valera also sent Boland home to explain his position. He arrived on 27 May and Collins and he greeted each other as cordially as at any other time, Collins not suspecting that in America Boland had surrendered to de Valera's charisma and now gave allegiance to him. In the circumstances, forced to choose between Cohalan and Devoy and their own elected President, both Griffith, who had stood down for him, and Collins, who had arranged for him to get into the States, backed de Valera over the Cuban interview, even though Brugha, Count Plunkett and Countess Markievicz were prepared to repudiate him at that stage. But Griffith and Collins persuaded the others to accede to de Valera's request that Boland should bring back to America a 'declaration of solidarity with de Valera'.

The cost of de Valera's ego became disastrously clear during the Presidential Conventions of the Republican and Democratic parties. De Valera led his own delegation to the Republican Convention in Chicago where the Resolutions Committee turned down by eleven votes to one a 'plank' approval by him calling for recognition of an Irish Republic, adopting one proposed by Cohalan, calling for 'recognition of the principle that the people of Ireland have the right to determine freely, without dictation from outside, their own governmental institutions, and their international relations with other states and peoples'. This resolution was accepted by a majority of seven votes to six. But de Valera said he wanted a Republican plank or nothing. Nothing is what he got. Faced with two delegations and two planks the Resolutions Committee decided to have no plank at all. De Valera felt his pride demanded no other course. He wrote to Griffith saying that he had undermined the Cohalan initiative lest people assume that the judge was 'the power behind our movement – the man to whom they would have to go. Were I to allow myself to appear thus as a puppet, apart from any *personal pride*, the movement would suffer a severe blow.' It seems to have escaped his attention that the movement *had* suffered a severe blow. Undeterred he moved on to the Democratic Convention, held a few weeks later at the end of June in San Francisco. Here he completed a double by failing to get the Democrats to adopt a resolution. The cost of the Convention fiascoes in money terms may be guessed at from the fact that on 29 June 1920 the Dail voted de Valera a 'sum not exceeding $500,000 as he may require in connection with the election campaign for the Presidency of the United States of America', and 'a sum not exceeding $1,000,000 to obtain the recognition of the Irish Republic by the Government of the United States'. None of the million-dollar vote was to be spent 'unless the recognition was assured'. Nevertheless these sums make the figure of $1,000,000 voted to the Ministry of Defence actually to fight the war seem paltry. De Valera's antagonism towards Devoy and Cohalan cost the services of at least two good men. Diarmuid Lynch, the National Secretary of the Friends of Irish Freedom, resigned both his secretaryship and his Dail seat in disgust. He followed James O'Mara who had already given up his work for the National Loan in America through finding it impossible to work with de Valera.

In both these cases Collins sided with de Valera. He wrote to Griffith showing a typical concern for detail: 'I wonder if you have stopped the *Bulletin* going to him [Lynch]. I think this is absolutely essential. It will give them a power out there to use against the President.'[16] O'Mara's defection hit Collins particularly hard. He wrote to Harry Boland grieving both at the loss of one of the best financial brains to come into the Sinn Fein orbit and at such petty feuding when issues of, quite literally, life and death were being fought out all round him. This supportive attitude, which makes a stark contrast to that shown by de Valera, was no isolated matter for Collins.

Though he thought Boland 'mad to put the idea in Sinead's head', Collins saw to it that Sinead de Valera's wish to join her husband in America was granted within a few days because 'she's had a bad time'. The only warning he issued before smuggling her across the Atlantic concerned her habit of praising him: 'Don't take any notice of her, she's so grateful'.[17] Sinead may have been motivated to join her husband by the spate of rumours circulating in Dublin concerning an alleged affair between de Valera and his secretary, Kathleen O'Connell, who was travelling with him in the States. However, to judge from the friendly tone of correspondence between Sinead and Kathleen after Sinead landed in America, she found no evidence of an affair and Kathleen remained de Valera's respected secretary for several decades. But the visit was not a success. Sinead missed her children and did not like either the boredom of hotel life or the razzmatazz of American public life. She returned home in September 1920 after about six weeks, leaving the biographer to speculate whether the attention Collins gave de Valera's family would have been seen by that student of Machiavelli as cause for gratitude, or as a source of suspicion that Collins was attempting to gain some influence with him via his family circle.

In the month of Sinead's arrival in America, August 1920, Devoy invoked Collins' name in his feud with de Valera. Collins had given an interview to the syndicated columnist Carl W. Ackerman in which he had said, 'there will be no compromise and no negotiations with any British Government until Ireland is recognised as an Independent Republic'. Pressed by Ackerman as to whether he would consider accepting Dominion Home Rule as an 'instalment', Collins replied:

I see you think we have only to whittle our demand down to Dominion Home Rule and we shall get it. This talk about Dominion Home Rule is not prompted by England with a view to granting it to us, but merely with a view to getting rid of the Republican movement. England will give us neither as a gift. The same effort that would get us Dominion Home Rule will get us a Republic.[18]

Devoy, anxious to make the comparison between Collins risking his life in Ireland while de Valera toured America in luxury, used this interview in the *Gaelic American* to praise Collins. On one occasion a large picture of Collins appeared on page one captioned 'Ireland's Fighting Chief'; on another he printed an editorial entitled 'Michael Collins speaks for Ireland.'[19] Collins wrote to both Boland and de Valera condemning the publicity.

Collins and Boland used to write to each other using the noms de plume of W. Field (Collins) and J. Woods (Boland). In November Mr Field in Dublin told Mr Woods now back in New York that the Supreme Council would abide by any decisions which Mr Woods took in the dispute.[20] Armed with this carte blanche Boland took the extremely radical step of breaking with the American wing of the IRB a few weeks before Bloody Sunday. He made the break public by writing to the *Gaelic American* and other sections of the Irish-American press, a step Collins was decidedly unhappy with. His conspirator's soul revolted at the thought of a secret society airing its differences with a powerful ally in the press while locked in a vicious war with an even more powerful opponent.[21] Nevertheless, he loyally stood by de Valera, writing to Boland only two days before Bloody Sunday, 'Practically everybody here had accepted in the face of recent developments the inevitability of the steps taken.' His attitude, despite his unhappiness over the publicity, was still what he had written to Devoy two months earlier: 'Every member of the Irish Cabinet is in full accord with President de Valera's policy. When he speaks to America he speaks for us all.'[22]   Collins later apologised to Devoy for taking this position. He sent him a message[23] saying:

Our idea was to have some sort of a world-wide Irish federation, each separate part working through the Government, and in accordance with the laws of the country where it had its being, but all joined by common ties of blood and race. Unfortunately some of those we sent to America did not understand the vital principle of that idea.

De Valera finally decided that the answer to 'the *Gaelic American* difference' was to set up his own Irish-American organisation which he did at a meeting in Washington on 16 November 1920, The American Association for the Recognition of the Irish Republic. He was fully aware that American politicians were not going to concede recognition to an Irish Republic. Indeed he said as much to the Dail on his return: 'If I were President of the United States I could not, and would not, recognise Ireland as a Republic.'[24] But still smarting from having left himself open to a charge of being 'soft' on the Republic, de Valera was determined to stake out the most extreme position possible to safeguard himself from further attack. Then, leaving his newly formed organisation feuding merrily with those led by Cohalan and Devoy, much to the detriment of concentration on the struggle in Ireland, he arranged to have Collins smuggle him home so as to be in on the peace moves then gathering force.

The peace moves owed their origin to the lunch party referred to earlier (page 187). The lunch was given in London on 30 November for the Clare-born Archbishop of Perth, Joseph Clune. It was to afford Lloyd George an opportunity of furthering the peace process but more importantly to lead to a sort of moral turning-point insofar as the Vatican's view of Ireland was concerned. Clune had been Chaplain General to the Australian Army during the war but he was also an uncle of Conor Clune who was done to death in the Castle after Bloody Sunday. The Archbishop had been staying with Bishop Fogarty in Ennis when the Black and Tan reprisal occurred in Lahinch and his account of what transpired so appalled the guests at the lunch that one of them, Joe Devlin, the Nationalist MP, arranged for him to meet Lloyd George, which he did the next day, to give him the details. Lloyd George professed himself shocked at these happenings, denounced all reprisals and asked the Archbishop to act as a mediator if Cabinet sanction could be obtained.

There followed what the Archbishop later described to his secretary, Father John MacMahon,[25] as a 'Gilbertian situation'. Lloyd George informed him the next day that although he had obtained the approval of a majority of his Cabinet, over the strong objections of a minority, the difficulty now arose as to how the Archbishop's safety in Ireland could be guaranteed. Father MacMahon said:

So completely had the Auxiliaries been given a free hand to do what they liked . . . that neither the Government nor the ordinary military command in Ireland could control this irresponsible and undisciplined corps of truculent adventurers. Mr Lloyd George admitted the situation to the Archbishop and quoted the advice received from the official military officials in Dublin that they could not guarantee the safety of Archbishop Clune if it became public that he was going to Ireland to interview the Sinn Fein leaders. Never for a moment would they consent to a safe conduct for the Sinn Fein leaders to meet the Archbishop.

At this stage a further element of farce entered the proceedings. At that stage the worst clerical thorn in the side of the British establishment was Dr Daniel Mannix, the Archbishop of Melbourne, whom the Government had sent a destroyer to intercept on the high seas to prevent him landing in Ireland. He had led the MacSwiney funeral cortege through London and was unrelenting in his denunciation of British policy in Ireland. He too was in London at the time and Clune consulted him about furthering Lloyd George's request. Mannix put him in touch with Art O'Brien, who gave him a letter for Collins and Mannix himself telegraphed Bishop Fogarty in Ennis: 'Archbishop Clune crossing to Dublin tonight. Meet him Gresham Hotel on important business.' That telegram saved Fogarty's life.

Clune stayed as 'Dr Walsh' in the home of Sir John O'Connell, a leading Dublin Catholic lawyer. Mannix's advice to contact Art

O'Brien bore fruit in the form of meetings with Joe O'Reilly which resulted in an appointment to meet Collins on 7 December at the home of Dr Farnan in Merrion Square. Collins had sent O'Reilly cycling the ten miles to hilly Killiney with a letter for Clune. O'Reilly noticed detectives in the area of the house and entered by a back way. He warned Clune about the detectives. 'This upset his Grace a bit,' O'Reilly noted. 'He realised the danger to which he was exposing Michael Collins and he discussed whether it was worth the risk to continue his mission. I remained silent until he made his own decision.' The next day O'Reilly again met Clune in the Gresham, and gave him Dr Farnan's address. O'Reilly warned Clune about being followed and told him not to go near the Castle to try calling the detectives off. The value of Collins' capture to the authorities would outweigh the worth of any promise he might get.

Meanwhile Bishop Fogarty had had cause to be thankful for the Clune mission. When he got Mannix's telegram he decided at first not go to Dublin. He telegraphed Clune accordingly, prepaying the reply. Clune intended to tell him not to worry about coming up but forgot to send the prepaid wire. Getting no reply, Fogarty set off for Dublin, feeling that Clune must have some good reason for contacting him. That night a party of Auxiliaries with blackened faces and drawn revolvers came to his house looking for him. They refused to believe he was not at home and searched thoroughly, even looking under the beds. No damage was caused, other than a bad fright for the servants and the loss of some papers and whiskey.

The attempt on Fogarty's life was one of the reasons the head of the Auxiliaries, Brigadier General Crozier, resigned his command. He later wrote:

At Killaloe I received further evidence the hidden hand was still at work and was told in confidence that instructions had been received to kill the Roman Catholic Bishop of Killaloe, Dr Fogarty, by drowning him in a sack from the bridge over the River Shannon so as to run no further risk of detection by having his body found.[26]

Clune, too, had several near escapes from violence during his visit. On one occasion he was upstairs in Farnham's house talking with Collins when a lorry-load of Auxiliaries drew up outside and there was a knock on the door. It turned out that one of the Auxiliaries had a message from his wife for Farnan, a leading gynaecologist. A second lorry passed by another day as Collins and the Archbishop came down the stairs while Farnan hailed a taxi for Clune from across the road. Collins stepped behind the open hall door, drew his revolver, closed the door and got out the back as the lorry turned. He picked up his bicycle from the tobacconist's in Merrion Road, where he always left it during the negotiations, and cycled away safely, leaving the lorry patrolling up and down outside Farnan's house.

Ironically the least-interrupted negotiations Clune had in Dublin were conducted in the lowering atmosphere of Mountjoy Jail where he handed over Mannix's letter to Griffith. Cope made the necessary arrangements for Fogarty and Clune to see not only Griffith, but also MacNeill and Staines. Griffith was the most enthusiastic of the three for a truce and Cope impressed the Bishops with his enthusiasm for a settlement also. Fogarty subsequently told MacMahon that 'alone among the die-hards in Dublin Castle, he kept Lloyd George's interest in the truce alive'. At his suggestion Clune drew up proposals for a truce and forwarded them to the Castle. The terms were not well received. There were two major sticking points. One was the fact that the IRA proposed holding on to their weapons and the second was immunity for Collins and Mulcahy during the truce. There was a third reason for the military heads not wanting a truce – they thought they had the IRA and Sinn Fein on the run. A party of them crossed from Dun Laoghaire on the mailboat to put this view to Lloyd George. Clune, who was on the same boat, only discovered their mission when Cope materialised on deck and pointing to a group of officers said very dejectedly:

I don't like to see these fellows crossing in such strong numbers. They have convinced themselves that they have the boys in the hills beaten and they want no talk of Truce to interfere with them now. But the Prime Minister may not listen to them. Who knows? I still have hopes of that Truce.

His hopes were not realised. Apart from the Castle contingent, the weight of the Conservative wing of the coalition and the ever-present influence of Sir Henry Wilson, another factor now entered the equation – an apparent willingness on the part of significant sections of Sinn Fein to sue for peace, or as the British saw it, to cave in. A letter from Roger Sweetman, the Sinn Fein Deputy for Wexford North, which appeared in the press on 30 November, proposed a conference of public bodies to formulate truce proposals. Six of the thirty-two members of Galway County Council not in jail or on the run, met on 3 December and discussed, though did not pass, a resolution calling on the Dail to negotiate a truce. A telegram was sent to Lloyd George from Fr. O'Flanagan, the Vice-President of Sinn Fein, who had accompanied the Chief Justice, James O'Connor, on the latest of his peace attempts to London that very week, saying: 'You state you are willing to make peace at once without waiting till Christmas. Ireland is also willing to make peace. What first steps do you propose?'

Collins himself described what happened next:

the intermediary . . . returned to the Prime Minister of England, and the latter had three things in his hand (the letter, resolution and telegram). 'Now Dr Clune,' he said, 'this is the white feather and we are going to make these fellows surrender.' The first time he [Lloyd George] saw Dr Clune he did not know of the letter to the press . . . it was when he went back that he was confronted with these things. He did not want to suggest for one moment that Lloyd George was sincere. Indeed, when Dr Clune came back Lloyd George made the excuse that he could not control his Cabinet . . . but it was wrong to give him the chance to bolster up his actions by the ill-timed actions of persons who ought to have hesitated before they leaped.[27]

One of the statements which surfaced in the press of the time was that if negotiations did take place Collins' own safety was to be guaranteed. Collins issued a statement saying that Fr. O'Flanagan had acted without authority and that so far as he was concerned himself: 'No person in Ireland or anywhere else, had any authority to use my name. My personal safety does not count as a factor in the question of Ireland's rights. I thank no one for refraining from murdering me.'

Another suggestion was that Griffith arranged to be arrested so that he could negotiate more freely and safely. Collins dealt with this in a second statement which the *Independent* was afraid to publish having received a visit from revolver-brandishing Auxiliaries after publishing the previous statement (on 6 December).[28] He asked: 'Does anyone think that Mr Griffith would be so foolish as to negotiate with anybody from behind prison bars, away from his followers and from his movement?' Griffith was neither caving in nor asking for a truce. If one was offered he would not reject it, but he had not initiated the truce suggestions. 'Everyone in Ireland,' Collins wrote, 'has reason to be mistrustful of English politicians of all schools and we have learned to be more distrustful of their promises than their threats.' It was in this statement that he first publicly used the phrase that became his hallmark, 'Let us drop talking and get on with our work.'[29]

Clune told Collins that Lloyd George's main interest seemed to lie in meeting the amazing escapologist 'Mick' as he always referred to him. He took a mischievous delight in the rage of 'the Castle contingent' at their inability to lay hands on Collins when the Archbishop could apparently see him at will. However, behind the Welsh charm and puckishness there lay the steel that had carried Lloyd George through the First World War. He sent Clune back to Dublin on 11 December with a message to say that the Dail would be permitted to meet openly to discuss peace terms but, and it was a very big but, neither Collins nor Mulcahy could attend and arms would have to given up. On hearing the terms Collins wrote to Griffith:

It seems to me that no additional good can come from further continuing these discussions. . . . We have clearly demonstrated our willingness to have peace on honourable terms. Lloyd George insists on capitulation. Between these two there is no mean; and it is only a waste of time continuing.[30]

The pacific Griffith agreed with him. He told Clune that the terms amounted to surrender and that 'there would be no surrender, no matter what frightfulness was used'.[31] The burning of Cork had occurred during the course of the Clune initiative and both Griffith and Collins were concerned that the British were using the talks as a smoke screen behind which they stepped up their campaign. Clune believed that Lloyd George was more circumscribed by Cabinet restraint than did Collins. He wrote to Art O'Brien that this view was 'too credulous'. He said:

My own feeling about Lloyd George is that we should not allow him to disassociate himself from his public actions, as head of his cabinet. Particularly on this side, there is too great a tendency to believe that Lloyd George is wishful for peace, and that it is only his own wild men that prevent him from accomplishing his desires.[32]

Nevertheless he was anxious to go as far as possible along the road to peace. After Clune had had further talks with Lloyd George and the Castle administration he obtained from Griffith a draft peace formula which the Archbishop and he went over at a lengthy meeting on 18 December before Clune returned to London to see Lloyd George for the last time. The final draft of the Irish proposals was:

The British Government undertakes that during the truce, no raids, arrests, pursuits, burnings, lootings, demolitions, courts martial or other acts of violence will be carried out by its forces, and there will be no enforcement of the Martial Law Proclamations. We on our side undertake to use all possible means to ensure that no acts whatever of violence will occur on our side during the period of the truce. The British Government on their part and we on ours, will use our best efforts to bring about the conditions above mentioned, with the object of creating an atmosphere favourable to the meeting together of the representatives of the Irish people with a view to the bringing about of a permanent peace.

The proposal foundered, not on its prose, but on something it did not contain, the question of the surrender of arms. At their final meeting, in Downing St, on 21 December, Lloyd George upheld the military viewpoint that arms must be handed in. He told Clune that the military were confident of mopping up the IRA, 'some hundreds of men on the hills', and saw no reason for giving Sinn Fein a new lease of life by declaring a truce during which they would be allowed to hold on to their weapons.

Lloyd George met his Cabinet on Christmas Eve[33] and reported on Clune's mission. He told them that, after the Archbishop had interviewed various leaders, 'he found Michael Collins the only one with whom effective business could be done'. Collins, he reported, wanted peace but the stumbling block on his part was the handing in of arms and, on theirs, the fact that Collins was the organiser of murder. Surprisingly, the Cabinet was also informed that arms were being surrendered 'in some quantities'. The report stiffened the Cabinet's resolve to 'do nothing to check the surrender of arms' and it was decided to hold a major review of the Irish situation, with all the Irish Executive present, as soon as possible after Christmas. Clune was asked to stay in London for the outcome of the meeting.

The meeting,[34] which went on over two days (29 and 30 December), was more instructive of how the military perceived the situation in Ireland, and filtered information accordingly, than for an insight into the state of Irish public opinion. General Tudor admitted that drink was a problem with the Auxiliary Divisions but said that 'anyone who has seen the Black and Tans on parade must admit that their discipline was very fine'. When Lloyd George brought up the bad effect on public opinion of steps such as the arrest of Arthur Griffith after Bloody Sunday the Cabinet Record notes that: 'Mr Churchill interposed that it was fair to remember that no reprisals had taken place after the Dublin murders.' Nobody mentioned Croke Park, though it was stated that publication of the report into the burning of Cork 'would be disastrous for the Government's whole policy in Ireland'. The consensus amongst generals Boyd, Macready, Strickland and Tudor was that another four months at the present rate of favourable progress would bring victory but that a truce would give Sinn Fein a chance to re-group, particularly in the intelligence field. Sir Henry Wilson, present in his capacity as CIGS, drew the meeting's attention to 'the decent peasant', who was nearly on the Government's side but who would go over to Sinn Fein if a truce were declared. He felt that if military law were applied to the whole of Ireland, in six months perhaps 90 per cent of the people would be on the side of the Government. Macready thought that if an election were held in the forthcoming three to four months, under the terms of the Government of Ireland Act, 'there would be a general boycott, at the point of a pistol, on the word of Michael Collins'. To which Lloyd George replied feelingly that if Michael Collins could stop three million people using their vote, it did not say much for the success of the policy they were pursuing. But in the circumstances it was not surprising that Clune was not asked to continue his efforts and the Cabinet decided on the military option. However there was one point at which the Archbishop's influence was to have an effect not guessed at by the men around the table.

Sir John Anderson said everything would depend on 'the line it was possible to get the Church to take.' The question of the Church's influence was a not unfamiliar theme in Cabinet. Various efforts had been made either to enlist the aid of the Vatican directly in support of the British position, or to silence critical clerics, most noticeably Mannix. The Cabinet's main preoccupation was to secure from the Pope a condemnation of the Irish insurgents and Curzon exerted considerable pressure on the British representative in Rome, Count de Salis, to secure this. The Count enlisted the support of two influential cardinals for the British initiative, Merry Del Val, Secretary to the Congregation of the Holy Office and Gasquet, Archivist to the Holy Roman Church. As a result a Papal condemnation was prepared. Not knowing this, Clune summed up the position, in a letter to Fogarty, on New Year's Day 1921, describing a visit to him by Sir Philip Kerr, Lloyd George's Private Secretary. He told Fogarty that the Government:

. . . had come to the conclusion that it was better to see the thing through as was done in the American and South African wars unless meanwhile the Sinn Feiners surrender their arms and publicly announce the abandonment of violent measures; that the Government felt sanguine that the new Home Rule Bill when studied and understood would be worked . . . He then added a few gracious compliments from the Prime Minister. My first comment was that I felt sure that the Holy Ghost had nothing to do with such a decision which sent him off exploding with laughter. What is the source of this strange optimism about all classes working the Home Rule Bill in harmony within a few months I can't make out.

The Government's determination to carry on the policy of frightfulness to the bitter end may be bluff. I think it is not; and hence I believe that the position needs further reconsideration in the light of this considered declaration of policy on their part. The secretary incidentally mentioned that from my conversations the Prime Minister had a higher idea of the gunmen . . . through the working of the Home Rule Act practically every English official could be sent out of Ireland in a few months, etc, etc . . . ought our boys to allow themselves to be butchered to make a Saxon holiday? Ought they not rely on passive resistance?

The Archbishop had indeed given high praise to Sinn Fein in Lloyd George's presence, a fact which led to world headlines. Sean T. O'Kelly, the Dail's Representative in Paris, gave a lunch for Clune as he passed through en route for the Vatican. At this Clune told journalists that he 'admired the courage' of the Sinn Feiners. He then went on:

During the negotiations, when my taxi would stop before the house where I was to meet one of the leaders I was exposing him to certain death. I never saw one of them tremble. When Mr Lloyd George, the Prime Minister, in my presence spoke of them as 'assassins' I corrected him, saying; 'No sir, not assassins but the cream of their race.'

The phrase 'the cream of their race', went round the globe and Clune went on to Rome. He was deeply torn by the calls of race and his outrage as a churchman at the taking of human life. Like Fogarty, he had been chilled by the psychological impact of Mountjoy 'where so many of our brave boys were held'. He had been reassured in meeting Collins, Mulcahy, O'Higgins, Fitzgerald and the others, as to the calibre of those leading the Irish struggle. However this was not the view of certain other members of the Irish Church. Such a one was Dr Cohalan, the Bishop of Cork, who pronounced a decree of excommunication on 12 December 1920. In fact the Bishop was extremely even-handed and judicious in his condemnation of violence. His quite lengthy exposition of the circumstances leading up to his decree contained the following:

We are face to face with the crimes of individuals and with Government crimes. The crimes of the Government in Ireland are on a different plane and are infinitely greater than the crimes of a private military organisation, because it is the duty of the Government, through its servants, to protect the lives and property of the citizens, especially the innocent, unoffending citizens.

But it was the statement's concluding paragraph which the British fastened on and which, *inter alia*, has made the Bishop's name execrated by the IRA ever since. It said:

Besides the sinfulness of the acts from their opposition to the law of God, anyone; be he a subject of this diocese or an extern, who, within the diocese of Cork, shall organise or take part in ambushes or kidnappings, or shall otherwise be guilty of murder or attempted murder, shall incur by the very fact the censure of excommunication.

Clune arrived in Rome in the wake of the publicity over this decree and a growing belief, fostered by the British, that some priests were preaching that it was not a sin to shoot policemen. In fact the British were not entirely wide of the mark as the following letter to Florrie O'Donoghue, on Cohalan's edict, from the Chaplain to the Brigade shows:

An excommunication . . . may be inflicted only for the external and grievous (or mortal) violation of the law (Canon 2242) . . . kidnapping, ambushing and killing obviously would be grave sins or violation of the law. And if these acts were being performed by the I.V. as private persons (whether physical or moral) they would fall under the Excommunication.

But they are doing them by and with the authority of the State – the Republic of Ireland. And the State has the right and duty to defend the lives and property of citizens and to punish even with death those who are aiming at the destruction of the lives or property of the citizens or itself. It has moreover a right and duty to protect by every means in its power the liberty of the State and its citizens against the Army of Occupation of a Foreign Power unjustly present in the country.

Hence these acts performed by the I.V. the Army of the Republic are not only not sinful but are good and meritorious. And therefore the Excommunication does not affect us. There is no need to worry about it. Let the boys keep going to Mass and Confession and Communion as usual. There is no necessity for telling a priest in Confession that you went to Mass on

Sunday so there is no necessity to tell him one is in the I.R.A. or that one took part in an ambush or killing etc.

My love and blessing to all the Brigade staff. God keep and protect you all.

DOC

Bde Chapn.

For their part some Protestant clergymen were equally staunch in their support of the forces of the Crown. I have a copy of a list of informants in Ireland drawn up by Captain Hall[35] which includes the names of several Protestant clergymen. *Guns in Ulster*, a sympathetic study of the B-Specials by Wallace Clarke, singles out a number of clergymen for special praise because of their work in organising and openly patrolling with the Specials. But such pre-ecumenical considerations were absent from the minds of the Irishmen as they prepared to meet the Pope. They were unaware that since the previous summer, when Balfour had visited Rome, British pressure for a Vatican condemnation of IRA violence had been growing.

The day after the Cabinet chose the hard-line option, an instruction to de Salis to make 'more pressing and insistent representations' was sent in which he was to be mindful of the recent example of Dr Cohalan who had called for excommunication.[36] Sir John Anderson's words had borne fruit. When Clune met Pope Benedict he discovered that a Papal condemnation of all violence in Ireland had been drawn up in terms that would fall most heavily upon Sinn Fein. The Pope specifically mentioned the rumour about priests preaching it no sin to shoot policemen. His interpreter was Father Patrick Murray, the Superior General of the Redemptorists, the order to which Clune had belonged before becoming an Archbishop. A man used to the emollient language of Vatican diplomacy, Murray, as he afterwards told MacMahon, was amazed by the plain-spoken way Clune reacted to this news:

He told the Holy Father amongst other things that such a pronouncement would be a disaster for the Church, not only in Ireland, but in every country where there were descendants of the Irish race. In fact his language was so strong that when I, as his interpreter, translated it into Italian, I had to excuse him for speaking so strongly as the matter was so grave. His reasons seemed to make a great impression on his Holiness.[37]

So great an impression in fact that the condemnation was shelved. Mrs Gavan Duffy, wife of the Sinn Fein representative in Rome, sent Art O'Brien an account of what happened. When she arrived to see the Archbishop off he 'had very grave news':

He then told me that a condemnation had been drawn up and that his audience alone had postponed its publication. One justification was the lie about priests preaching that it is not a sin to kill policemen and I should imagine that Cohalan of Cork was another . . . From many different sources

I have heard that the Pope was immensely impressed by Dr Clune, the murder of his young nephew, his admiration for our leaders, in particular Mick Collins, his testimony of the religious faith of the Republicans – all made a very deep impression on Benedict . . . Roger's supposed diary [Casement's diary, depicting homosexual activity] has been sent over here to show the Vatican the type of leader we follow.[38]

When Collins passed this dispatch on to de Valera, who by this stage had arrived back in Dublin, he made one significant omission, his own name, and made a joke about being all right now in the care of the Holy Father. He had already learned in the few weeks since de Valera's return that praise of 'The Big Fellow' was not welcome to 'The Long Fellow'. Clune's opposition to the threatened condemnation was strongly supported. The secretary of the Irish Hierarchy, Dr O'Doherty, issued a very broad hint to the Vatican 'that Ireland will not stand another Parnell pronouncement'[39], that is, no Papal Rescript and, amongst other protests, the American Archbishop Hayes warned that taking sides against 'our people would be like a spark applied to the American powder magazine'.[40] Accordingly, when Mannix also saw the Pope a month later, the Pope, far from dressing him down, took his advice that he should make a public contribution to the White Cross, an American charitable relief organisation active in Ireland, accompanied by a letter for publication.

The White Cross organisation was a highly reputable body which disbursed some five million dollars collected by the American Committee for Relief in Ireland in the spring and summer of 1921, far more than de Valera's efforts at the time resulted in. It was strictly non-partisan. Collins personally ensured that the White Cross' work remained aloof from politics, issuing strict orders that the IRA should not benefit from White Cross funds.[41] The Relief Committee acquired such stature in the US that, despite hostile reports from the pro-British Consul in Dublin, Dumont, Warren Harding wrote approvingly to its Chairman, Judge Morgan J. O'Brien: 'It was powerful boost that lent a degree of credibility and official approval which the Irish movement had never enjoyed in the United States.[42] It was also to have some significant implications for Anglo-American relations.[43] Collins was later to call on the assistance of the White Cross in drawing up Ireland's first Constitution. The Pope went on to ask Mannix to submit a draft of the type of letter he felt should be issued. Having passed through many hands it duly appeared on 22 May with the basic Mannix hand still discernible:

We are most especially concerned about the condition of Ireland. Unflinching even to the shedding of blood in her devotion to the ancient Faith and in her reverence for the Holy See she is subjected today to the indignity of devastation and slaughter . . . neutrality . . . by no means prevents us from wishing . . . that a lasting peace . . . may take the place of this terrible enmity

. . . we do not perceive how this bitter strife can profit either of the parties, when property and homes are being ruthlessly and disgracefully laid waste, when villages and farmsteads are being set aflame, when neither sacred places nor sacred persons are spared, when on both sides a war resulting in the deaths of unarmed people, even of women and children, is carried on. We exhort English as well as Irish to calmly consider . . . some means of mutual agreement.

This missive, the first time the Pope had spoken on the Irish question, was highly unwelcome to the British. Curzon thought it 'just the sort of casuistic performance that might have been expected from the Vatican'. Collins was correspondingly delighted. Efforts to get a similar pronouncement from the Irish hierarchy had proved fruitless.[44] He immediately wrote to de Valera:

I was specially informed that it would be a good thing for you to write to His Holiness acknowledging his beneficent remarks about Ireland thanking Him for His subscription. I know this will strike yourself, but it's a message that came directly from Dr Mannix immediately he had finished his audience with His Holiness. It might be as well if our representative in Rome specially delivered this communication of yours.

The British delivered a 'communication' of their own to the Vatican making a vigorous protest at the Pope's not only failing to condemn the IRA but actually making a partisan statement which 'put HMG and the Irish murder gang on a footing of equality'. The Vatican riposted by offering the services of Cardinal Gaspari, the Secretary of State, as a mediator. But the British, although uneasily aware that the military men's 'four months' was up with no end in sight to the policy of 'frightfulness' which had disturbed Benedict, had had enough of clerical mediators for the time being. The next time a priest was called upon it was to introduce an Englishman to de Valera.

Collins had had de Valera met by Tom Cullen and Batt O'Connor[45] when his ferry docked at the Customs House Dock. The meeting set the tone for much of what happened subsequently. De Valera asked Cullen how things were going. 'Great,' replied Cullen with more enthusiasm than caution, 'the Big Fellow is leading us and everything is going marvellous'. De Valera reacted by slapping his hand on the guard rail and exclaiming, 'Big Fellow! We'll see who's the Big Fellow.'[46] Cullen took him to Dr Farnan's house, where Brugha was his first visitor. Collins did not meet him until 5 am the next morning, Christmas Eve 1920, the day that nearly ended so disastrously for him in the Gresham. It is not being unduly fanciful to see a certain symbolism in that sequence of visits, for de Valera's first major initiative on returning to Ireland was to try to get Collins out of the country, to America. He sent Collins a lengthy letter on 18 January outlining a variety of tasks which he wanted Collins to carry out in the US. One of these was to 'see to the building up of a system of communications through which despatches and material can be sent with increased safety at regular intervals between the two countries'. As de Valera had first-hand experience of the efficiency of Collins' existing system of communication, having been safely smuggled back and forth across the Atlantic himself, this desideratum seems a trifle odd. But no more so than point 'F' which was:

to examine the possibilities of the US from the point of view of supplying material to the Minister of Defence. To make a report and recommendations to the Minister on this head and as far as possible to execute any commissions which that Minister may give in relation to his own Department.

In other words to take orders from Brugha.

Not surprisingly, Collins was both angered and hurt at de Valera's suggestion. 'The long whore won't get rid of me that easily', was his original reaction according to Frank O'Connor,[47] but both Broy and Oscar Traynor told O'Malley that he was deeply wounded by the attempt. Broy described him as being practically in tears and Traynor thought the idea disastrous. 'I know it's all bullsology,' Collins told him, 'but if I'm ordered I'll have to go.' No order came. De Valera found that his proposal met with a hostile reaction from everyone apart from Brugha and the Minister for Home Affairs, Stack. Collins had come to symbolise the entire struggle to the fighting men, including the British fighting men. The British made such an ogre figure out of him that he came to have a correspondingly heroic stature in the minds of the Volunteers. Collins' larger-than-life personality magnified his deeds so that they outshone everyone else's. De Valera made it abundantly clear however that he wasn't going to let Collins outshine him. Even though Collins had been Acting President while he was in America, on his return he appointed Stack as his President-designate.[48] But de Valera was not only virtually demoting Collins, he was doing so for a man of far lesser capacity. Stack was viewed as a 'dud', a by-word for inefficiency in the underground ministry.[49] His want of ability sometimes jeopardised the lives of Volunteers.[50] By not having a separate police force to call on the active Volunteers in the flying columns were often put at risk through trying to fit in police duties, such as supervising fairs, or guarding courts when they should have been lying low between staging raids and ambushes. Stack's proposal to meet this difficulty was that 'Collins' intelligence agents should be used to distribute circulars about district courts'.[51]

In addition to these drawbacks Stack apparently felt that he suffered in GHQ's eyes for the sins of a close friend of his, another prominent Kerry IRA man, Paddy Cahill, the Commander of the Kerry No. 1 Brigade. Because Cahill tended to concentrate his efforts on his own area, the Tralee, Castlegregory district, Mulcahy made a memorably scathing comment on his conduct of the war: 'Paddy took his column up Sliabh Mis and stayed there.'[52] De Valera's nomination of Stack as President-designate thus seems to have been a calculated rebuff for Collins.

De Valera arranged with Collins to preside over his first meeting of the Dail on 21 January 1921. But Brugha argued that it might result in everyone being captured and, despite Collins' feelings to the contrary, the meeting was deferred for four days. When it was held, differences of approach on the military front immediately surfaced between Collins and de Valera. De Valera proposed a formula which, if accepted, would have contained two conflicting proposals: that they should have no public change, continue as they had been and try to keep their people together, and that they should try to ease off as far as possible, consistent with showing the country that they were in the same position as before.

Collins took issue with the 'ease off' approach which to him smacked too much of the sort of policy which was also advocated at the same meeting by Roger Sweetman. He said:

the enemy were repeating the very same things they had practised in Ireland in other days. It was not in the strong places the deepest terror was, but in the weak places. Where the fight was carried on hardest, except in Cork, these were the safest areas . . . it would be better work to give the Volunteers the necessary moral support than to be finding fault with the men carrying on fighting against odds never before known.[53]

Collins' force and eloquence carried the day but de Valera wanted to exert his authority, to prove that he was back in charge. He continued to develop his theories of a different form of warfare, one fought with an eye to public relations. He felt it would be better to change from hit and run guerrilla tactics to having a series of battles with the British. The one operation of this nature in which de Valera did get his way was, both a publicity success and a military débâcle, the burning of the Custom House on 25 May 1921. Urban guerrillas used to blazing off six shots (at best) at an enemy before disappearing into a crowd could not easily be metamorphosed into a standing army. The account given by Joe McGuinness of the ASU (see page 209), a survivor of the Custom House attack, makes this abundantly clear. That morning he and his comrades were told:

the 2nd Battalion under Tom Ennis would enter the building and destroy it by fire . . . the ASU would act as a covering party on the outside, in conjunction with the Squad . . . We were further instructed that we were not to fire on any British lorries unless they fired on us first. We were given a revolver, four or five rounds of ammunition each.

What McGuinness did not know as he was being briefed was that

Michael Collins was deeply unhappy about the 'static warfare' operation. 'It remained a Dublin Brigade Affair and "Collins' outfit" kept out of it, though the Squad and the Active Service Unit were reluctantly allowed to lend a hand *outside* the building.'[54] However, disapproving or not, Collins was not a man to let his men go into battle unremarked. McGuinness notes: 'As we were about to leave our mobilisation place at Strand St, Michael Collins came to the doorway on a bicycle and wished us luck.'

The reasons for Collins' apprehensions can readily be deduced from McGuinness' description of what followed:

We saw the blaze starting . . . at about this time . . . an armoured car crossed O'Connell Bridge . . . it was followed by three or four armoured Lancia cars . . . this party opened machine-gun fire on the windows of Liberty Hall [the Volunteers were still inside] . . . another party of Black and Tans who were stationed in a hotel on the quays, came towards the Customs House at the double . . . we opened fire on them . . . I threw my hand grenade at a lorry. The Tans opened fire on us . . . other lorries arrived almost immediately . . . when our ammunition was used up we withdrew.

The operation yielded a world-wide propaganda success. Not only was the finest building in Dublin destroyed, local government administration and the collection of income tax were paralysed. However, from the military point of view, it was a disaster. Six Volunteers were killed, twelve wounded and some seventy of the best IRA fighters of the time were captured. The attack also served to erode Collins' power base somewhat because a few days later, ostensibly to make up for the losses, the ASU, Intelligence and the Squad were all amalgamated into the Dublin Brigade, which gave Brugha and de Valera more control over 'Collins' outfit'.[55]

De Valera's theories of warfare were completely inapplicable to the situation. Even the flying columns in the most successful rural districts didn't know what it was to have more than thirty rounds of rifle ammunition per man.[56] One of the outstanding countrymen, Ernie O'Malley, has left a vivid picture of the impression de Valera made with his theories and of the tensions which these unleashed:

de Valera was tall, his lean, stringy build over-emphasised his height . . . He looked worn. He smiled with his eyes. The lines on his face broke as if ice had cracked. His voice rumbled from the depth with harsh, but not a hard dryness . . . there was a sense of sternness about him, dignity, a definite honesty and a friendly way of making one feel at ease . . .

I pointed out posts and barracks, outlined our battalions' areas, gave, as far as I could remember, our armaments and told him the support the people gave us. He had not the human qualities of Collins, 'The Big Fellow'. 'Dev' was more reserved, the scholarly type. He was cold and controlled. Collins might solve a problem boisterously by improvisation, solve it by its own development. The talk lasted for nearly three hours. He shook hands . . .

I sat in a smaller room with Mulcahy and Collins. 'What did you think of the interview?', asked Collins. 'He did not know much about the army in the south,' I said. Both laughed as if amused. Collins mentioned some of the questions the President had asked. They laughed again. I felt uncomfortable. Dev was the President. After all, I thought, how could he be expected to know the military situation thoroughly? Cathal Brugha the Minister for Defence, did not know his senior officers well. He worked as a traveller, whilst his deputy was paid his salary. The desire to work without pay was understandable, but his position as MD needed all his energies. Many members of the GHQ staff did not know the country . . . I resented their jokes at the expense of 'The Long Fellow'.[57]

As 'Big Fellow' and 'Long Fellow' began moving towards their inevitable estrangement, the Ireland de Valera was familiarising himself with was beginning to suffer the results of Lloyd George's choice between two men 'on the spot'. One was James O'Connor, the Chief Justice, who wrote to the Prime Minister saying:

you may compel Ireland to pass under the Caudine Forks, but I put it to you that it is not wise. The people are stubborn – I wish they were sagacious for, if so, they might accept your suggestions of working the Act and asking for extensions – and they are suspicious, for which there is warrant enough in the history of both countries.[58]

There would be further warrant. O'Connor was in fact an extremely well-informed observer whose opinions deserved to be treated with respect.[59] But Lloyd George opted to accept the advice of another correspondent from Ireland, Hamar Greenwood, the Chief Secretary. Greenwood was disturbed by the fact that O'Connor's friend Fr O'Flanagan was trying to get peace talks going. He wrote to Lloyd George:

In my opinion, you ought not to see de Valera . . . I urge you not to be rushed into negotiations that are certain at this stage to be abortive. Leave things to me I am here on the spot . . . the tide has turned against Sinn Fein.[60]

Lloyd George decided to continue on the basis of Greenwood's analysis, part of which was based on the fact that the Chief Secretary thought it a good sign that some twenty Sinn Feiners were then facing death sentences – readers will have gained an insight in Chapter 6 as to what the effects of these were on Sinn Fein support. From the burning of Cork, the British instituted a system of official reprisals. The army began formally to destroy houses in the wake of IRA activities. Seven houses were destroyed in Midleton, County Cork, on 1 January 1921 after three RIC men were killed in an ambush. This policy was rigorously enforced in what was known as the 'Martial Law' area, the province of Munster and Leinster counties of Kilkenny and Wexford. The policy boomeranged badly on the British when the IRA began destroying Loyalist property in retaliation.

In the general escalation of hostilities, a new 'Active Service Unit' (ASU) was formed early in 1921, comprising some fifty members of the Dublin Brigade. Like the Squad these were full-time operatives and were paid between four and five pounds a week. The ASU was the hit-unit of the Brigade in the same way that the Squad carried out the Intelligence Department's 'jobs'. Both the Squad and the ASU were amalgamated shortly before the Truce in July 1921, becoming known as the 'Guard'. When a National Army was formed, the 'Guard' became the 'Dublin Guards', the first regular unit of the Irish Army. The Volunteers began attacking trains and troop lorries in the street. Many civilian casualties were caused this way. One of these casualties was the Moylette/Steele peace initiative. The way of the peacemaker is hard in any land, but particularly so in Ireland. In a memo to de Valera, O'Hegarty described their efforts in disparaging terms: 'The impression I gathered from Moylette was that he was the paw, that Steele was the cat and that Sir Philip Kerr was the monkey. In other words, that Steele is a tool of Lloyd George. I think M. C. has somewhat the same opinion.'[61]

The 'Irish Businessmen's Conciliation Committee', which struggled through the thorns from March to 21 May, had little better luck. The committee was composed of a group of leading Unionist businessmen, including Andrew Jameson, Sir William Goulding, Sir Walter Nugent and a number of other people with a stake in the country, like Major Bryan Cooper.

A more tenacious, more successful entrant in the peace lists was the unlikely figure of Andy Cope, who extended himself so thoroughly on Lloyd George's behalf that Mark Sturgis wrote in his diary: 'GHQ regard Andy as a complete "Shinner" and believe him no more or less than they would believe Michael Collins, so anything he says they regard as ipso facto, something to be resisted and yielded, if at all, only after a struggle.' Where and how Cope met Collins is still a subject of controversy, but it may have a bearing on a curious correspondence that took place between Sir John Anderson and General Macready in March and April of 1920.

One of the legends about Michael Collins is that he had a price of £10,000 on his head. But this does not appear to have been the case. Macready wrote to Anderson on 5 March 1921[62] suggesting that:

rewards should be offered for Michael Collins and certain other people. The following is suggested:

	£
Charles Burgess (otherwise Cathal Brugha)	10,000
Michael Collins	10,000
Richard Mulcahy	10,000
William Cosgrave	3,500

Gerald O'Sullivan	3,500
Austin Stack	3,500
Joseph McDonagh	3,500

De Valera's name does not appear on this list because, realising that he was less of a problem politicking in relative freedom than languishing a martyr in jail, the British had directed that he was not to be arrested on his return from America. Anderson replied on 9 March objecting on three grounds: 1. Rewards do not make a difference. 2. They make heroes. 3. What about state servants? (meaning why should a state servant be paid for turning someone in in the line of duty). He went on to make the following significant observation: 'You may not be aware that it has already been made known quietly in what seemed like likely quarters that liberal reward, though not on such a scale as your letter indicates, would be given for valuable information leading to definite results.'

Seemingly someone failed to bring this reply to the general's attention for Macready tried again on 8 April:

My Dear Jonathan,
You have never replied to the query I put to you some time ago about offering 'head money' for Michael and others. I do not suppose for a moment it will be done, but what about it?

To which Anderson replied:

I put the question immediately to Ministers, but they were not disposed to move for reasons such as I indicated to you in my letter of March 9.

There may have been more reasons than Anderson indicated for not putting a public price on Collins' head. Lloyd George was playing a very deep game at the time trying either to best or cajole Sinn Fein to the conference table in his public 'Hamar-and-olive-branch' stance, but privately Cope was clearly being encouraged to go further than the Tudor Tories and the militarists would have wished. Hypersensitive, highly intelligent, and a workaholic, he had Lloyd George's complete confidence. Everything Cope did was done with official but unacknowledged sanction.[63]

As a result of Cope's activities Collins was forced to confront charges such as 'Collins is a drunkard and spent the time during the truce boozing with Cope.'[64] Sean T. O'Kelly denied making the allegation but admitted that he had 'joined with others' in telling pre-truce Collins–Cope stories, including one in which Collins 'on one occasion carried him to bed'.[65] Angered, Collins replied: 'I don't know who told you that I met Cope before the Truce and I should like to meet the man who says it, or repeats it, and I may say that I consider the man who repeats it just as bad as the man who said it.'[66]

However Mrs Larry Nugent, a prominent Sinn Feiner, met Cope at

Judge O'Connor's and, surprised to find that he seemingly wanted only to meet de Valera, Stack and Brugha asked, 'Do you not want to meet Michael Collins?' According to Mrs Nugent he replied: 'No. I meet Michael every night.'[67] Mrs Nugent later put a date of 3 May on a subsequent meeting with Cope. Even this later date was more than two months before the Truce. From all we know of Collins' life and his method of operation it seems quite possible that he and Cope could have got together. They seem to have been kindred spirits insofar as lack of formality was concerned. A month after the Truce we find Sturgis sniffing into his diary:

I cursed Andy for avoiding the Royal Box at the Horse Show – he goes down the main drain, not only for business, but for pleasure; spends most of his evenings with 'shinners' of various sorts and seems to dislike all other society. They remember, if he seems to forget sometimes, that he is a highly placed British official with much of the dignity of England in his hands and I worry sometimes that his sympathies will encourage them to think they will get through him all they can.[68]

The peace offensive quickened throughout April and May. Collins was interviewed again by Ackerman and again turned down Dominion Home Rule:

When I saw you before I said the same effort which would get us Dominion Home Rule would get us a Republic. I am still of that opinion and have never had so many peace moves as we have had since last autumn. Our Army is becoming stronger every day, its morale is improving and its efficiency is increasing.[69]

The IRA was in fact in very straitened circumstances. However, it was still making such inroads into the military prong of Lloyd George's 'peace-and-war' double approach that he had a Liverpool priest, a Father James Hughes, contacted in a further peace initiative which had the result of putting Lord Derby in touch with de Valera on 21 April in Dublin. Though these talks yielded nothing of substance they had the effect of encouraging Lloyd George in two other initiatives. In one he gave an interview to New York's *Herald Tribune* on 11 May 1921 in which he said: 'I will meet Mr de Valera or any of the Irish leaders without conditions on my part and without asking promises from them. It is the only way a conclusion can be reached.' In the other he gave his blessing to Cope to set up a meeting in Dublin between de Valera and Sir James Craig. Nothing came of it. Craig afterwards told Emmet Dalton, who brought him to the talks, that de Valera was 'impossible'.[70]

The elections called for by 'The Better Government of Ireland Act' were held on 24 May. In an effort to sweeten the atmosphere, Lloyd George replaced Lord French as Viceroy by a Catholic, James Talbot, Lord FitzAlan, the first in Irish history, as hitherto Catholics were debarred from representing the Crown in Ireland. However the general reaction to this would-be conciliatory gesture was 'We would as soon have a Catholic hangman.' As early as January of that year Collins, anticipating the elections,[71] had sent a very detailed memo[72] to de Valera on the subject of elections. He analysed the returns for Parliamentary, County Council, Rural and Urban District Council and Board of Guardian polls and said: 'It is my opinion that candidates should be put forward, and put forward in every division. The programme will be abstentionist from the Northern Parliament and Assembly with their colleagues.'

Sinn Fein did adopt the abstentionist policy. De Valera entered into a pact with the Nationalist Party, led by John Dillon in the South and Joe Devlin in the North, whereby each contested the election on a ticket of abstention and self-determination and, under PR, each gave its first vote to its own side and second vote to the other. Nationalists returned included Collins, de Valera, Griffith, Sean O'Mahony, Sean Milroy and Eoin MacNeill. There would have been a greater Nationalist return but for the gerrymander of constituencies. The elections in the North were marked by ferocious violence, personation and gerrymandering by the Unionists, who won forty seats.

A number of other points may be made about the election's outcome. Firstly the election, which made Craig the Six Counties' first Prime Minister (Carson had relinquished the leadership due to his age) had the more important long-term result of definitely and unmistakably releasing the scent of Partition into the Irish electoral air. Secondly, though the Unionists gained a large majority, the orange cloak would henceforth have to hang most uncomfortably over some spots of green. Armagh, for instance gave two of its four seats to anti-Partitionist candidates. Thirdly, in the South, Sinn Fein recorded an even larger victory than it had done in 1918 in the wake of the Rising. After years of warfare and terror the electorate declared itself unequivocally in favour of Sinn Fein. The party won 124 seats unopposed and the four seats allocated to the National University went to Sinn Feiners also. Southern Ireland's pro-Unionist support consisted solely of four Trinity College seats and two senators.

Although there was as yet no line on a map to mark a border the country was *de facto* partitioned, the division in the country was unmistakable – as were its challenges and opportunities.

Lloyd George was faced with the simplest and most complex of choices, war or peace. He was now assured by Macready and Wilson that full-blooded Martial Law would be necessary to crush Sinn Fein. The four months was conveniently forgotten. If victory were not quickly assured it would be necessary by October to relieve most of the troops then in Ireland. For Martial Law to succeed all normal life would have to be suspended. Banks, post offices, newspapers, transport, even bicycles, all would have to come under the control of the military who would then, with the rebels immobilised, have to carry out a 'foul job for any soldier'. It was an even fouler one for any statesman who had to reckon with public opinion. Nevertheless Churchill urged Lloyd George to go for 'a tremendous onslaught'.[73] Chamberlain, who had succeeded the fatally ill Bonar Law as leader of the Conservatives, agreed with Churchill but felt that a new offer of peace should be made on the basis of a larger form of self-government for the South than had been contained in the Act which had caused the election.

If this did not work the way was clear for 'the most unlimited exercise of rough-handed force', as Churchill put it. The Cabinet decided on 26 May that if the Southern Parliament was not in operation by 12 July then Martial Law was to be proclaimed throughout the South.

Then, to use a most abused phrase, fate took a hand in the person of a man bearing a name one might not have expected to find taking part in negotiations involving the British and the Irish – Tom Casement, brother of Roger. As he says in his diary, 'I had kept in touch with my old friend General Smuts, Prime Minister of the Union of South Africa and had promised to meet him on his arrival in London for the Imperial Conference.' On 13 June 1920 Casement left Galway to travel via Dublin to London to meet Smuts at the Savoy Hotel. In Dublin he was met by de Valera. Casement notes:

de Valera rode up on a bicycle and introduced himself. He asked me why I was going to London to see Smuts and that I had no authority from him or any official message from him. That was understood but he told me he would like Smuts to know what was required and that he would meet him if I could arrange a meeting . . . during our talk I told him that Smuts could not stand for an Irish Republic, as he was Prime Minister of a Dominion, de Valera frankly told me that a Republic was out of the question. All he wanted was a Treaty between two nations. I saw that point and told him that I would put it before Smuts.

That diary entry throws an interesting light on de Valera's psychology. Years later Casement sent de Valera a copy of his diary and after the entry for 14 June 1921 de Valera wrote:

this is not accurate. I might have said that I was aware that it was out of the question to demand that Smuts should accept the Republican position as a condition precedent to seeing me. It is probable that I indicated that the line to be pursued in seeking a settlement was that of a treaty between the two countries.[74]

It is curious, in view of the fact that the note was obviously written for the historical record, that de Valera in his authorised biography did not advert at all either to Casement or to the differing interpretation of

his remarks. Smuts is introduced to the scene with the comment:
'After much preliminary spadework initiated by de Valera, Smuts and
his secretary arrived in Dublin on July 5th.' In fact the spadework had
been initiated by King George V himself and had borne fruit on the
day that Casement met de Valera when, unknown to either of them,
Smuts sent what turned out to be an historic letter to Lloyd George.
Smuts had been invited to Windsor on 12 June by the King who was
disturbed by happenings in Ireland. He had been invited by Craig to
open the new parliament in Belfast but he feared that to do so 'might
look like a deliberate affront to the South'.[75]

Smuts realised that, as the King had never opened a subordinate
parliament before, to do so at that juncture could appear partisan, but
he suggested that the King might do more than 'open a small
parliament. He might address all Ireland – address a message of peace
to all Ireland – and to the Dominions too.' The King liked the idea and
suggested that Smuts put his thoughts on paper. Smuts did so and sent
a copy to Lloyd George who invited him to a Cabinet meeting on 17
June to discuss the King's speech. The occasion was stage-managed
superbly by Lloyd George who explained Smuts' presence by saying
the latter had written him an interesting letter on Ireland. According
to his biography Smuts found that the draft submitted by Lord
Stamfordham, the King's Secretary, was the speech he had written at
Windsor. However, 'nothing was said about my being the author.
They innocently consulted me and I innocently answered them. But
imagine the interesting position'. Smuts centred his arguments on the
need to produce an appeal to the Irish in America because 'the real
solution of our defence problem, which was now a Pacific problem,
was to draw the United States and Japan closer together'.[76] He
impressed his hearers by pointing out that the forthcoming Imperial
Conference was concerned with this matter and a settlement in Ireland
would produce a good climate both in the Conference and between
the Conference members and the Americans. The line of reasoning
influenced the meeting towards his draft rather than towards one
prepared by Balfour. A newspaper report adverted to by Smuts'
biographer described this as a 'bloodthirsty document amounting to a
declaration of war against the South'. However when the King spoke,
on the 22nd, his speech, although it retained some Balfourisms also
contained the following:

I speak from a full heart when I pray that my coming to Ireland today may
prove to be the first step towards the end of strife among her people,
whatever their race or creed.

In that hope I appeal to all Irishmen to pause, to stretch out the hand of
forbearance and conciliation, to forgive and forget, and to join in making for
the land they love a new era of peace, contentment and goodwill.

It is my earnest desire that in Southern Ireland, too, there may, ere long, take place a parallel to what is now passing in this hall; that there a similar occasion may present itself, and a similar ceremony be performed. For this the Parliament of the United Kingdom has in the fullest measure provided the powers. For this the Parliament of Ulster is pointing the way . . .

The divisions and contradictions in British policy-making and execution almost wrecked the good effect this speech created. For on the same day that King George spoke, British troops arrested de Valera. They did not know who he was initially. When Cope found out he had him transferred from jail to officers' quarters while he fought to have him released. He succeeded a day later. Meanwhile, in London, Casement had seen Smuts and the South African delegation. He told them that he could arrange a meeting with de Valera, but that a truce was essential. Smuts, who was said by his delegation to be 'raising hell with Lloyd George',[77] passed this on to the Prime Minister. Various intense Cabinet meetings followed including one to which all the relevant civil servants and military were summoned and Cope was called upon to give his advice and opinions. He confided to Sturgis afterwards that the 'sweat poured off him' as he stood before this formidable array and argued so forcibly for peace that Hamar Greenwood interrupted him to tell him to 'curb his Sinn Fein tendencies'.[78] But the days of the Greenwood analysis were numbered. Lloyd George sent a public appeal to de Valera proposing a peace conference so that 'the King's appeal for reconciliation, for peace in Ireland shall not have been made in vain'. He proposed that de Valera should bring any colleague he wished with him under safe conduct and proposed a meeting in London with Sir James Craig. De Valera temporised, replying on 28 June that 'we most earnestly desire . . . a lasting peace, but see no avenue by which it can be reached if you deny Ireland's essential unity and set aside the principle of self-determination.' Five days later, on 30 June 1921, Casement crossed again to Ireland with Captain Lane, Smuts' Private Secretary, whom he introduced to de Valera at the Mansion House. Casement suggested to Cope that Griffith, Barton, and MacNeill should be released to help the negotiations. The three, along with Eamonn Duggan and Michael Staines, were released and when Casement met them, at Farnan's house, 'they all appeared happy . . . a good sign.' The reason for the gathering at Farnan's house was a visit by Smuts to whom de Valera explained his ideas. Significantly, in view of what was to come. Collins was not amongst those present.

De Valera began his talks with Smuts by stating that his demand was for a Republic. If a Republic were forthcoming the Irish would give the English any guarantees they sought as to defence. If Ireland was only offered Dominion Status she would not be prepared to limit herself by such defence stipulations. When Smuts argued that it would be a mistake to seek a Republic de Valera's response gave him grounds for hope. He said, 'If the status of a Dominion is offered to me I will use all our machinery to get the Irish people to accept it.'

A rash of peace-making broke out on both sides of the Irish Sea. The Southern Irish Unionists were brought into the process. The Earl of Midleton, Sir Maurice Dockrell, Sir R. Wood and Andrew Jameson met Lloyd George in London and de Valera and Griffith in Dublin. But not the Northern Unionists; Craig was conspicuous by his absence. He told Sturgis that he would 'sit on Ulster like a rock. Let the PM and Sinn Fein settle it. He was satisfied with what he'd got.' The military men on both sides were brought into the conference, Macready being cheered by a Dublin crowd as he turned up at the Mansion House. He and Colonel Brind negotiated truce terms with Duggan and Barton:

1. No incoming troops, RIC and auxiliary police and munitions. No movements for military purposes of troops and munitions, except maintenance drafts.
2. No provocative display of forces, armed or not armed.
3. It is understood that all provisions of this Truce apply to the Martial Law area equally to the rest of Ireland.
4. No pursuits of Irish officers, or men, or war material, or military stores.
5. No secret agents, noting descriptions or movements, and no interference with the movements of Irish persons, military or civil and no attempt to discover the haunts or habits of Irish officers and men.

Note there are other details concerning courts, motor transport etc. to be dealt with later.

On the Irish side it was agreed:

1. Attacks on Crown Forces and civilians to cease.
2. No provocative display of force, armed or unarmed.
3. No interference with British Government or private property.
4. To discountenance and prevent any action likely to cause disturbance of the peace which might necessitate military interference.

There were differing interpretations of the Truce on both sides, but it meant in practice that the IRA retained their weapons and the right to drill and train, a major advance on the 'surrender weapons' policy of seven months earlier. The IRA were secretly circulated by Mulcahy with an instruction, dated 9 July 1921, that 'active operations by our troops will be suspended as from noon, Monday 11 July'. Collins took no chances. On 8 July the *Freeman's Journal* carried a House of Commons report denying that any reward had ever been offered for Collins. He cut it out and wrote under it, 'Tudor offered £4,000 to any of his men who'd bring me in dead. Even up to 12.30 tomorrow I'm sure the offer will be honoured.' Certainly the IRA kept up the offensive to within minutes of that noontide.[79] On some it had a galvanic effect. Knowing that retribution could not occur after the

11th, many literally eleventh-hour warriors now took the field. For others, used to hard fighting, the harshness engendered by war was summed up by the matter-of-fact cold-bloodedness of this IRA report: 'At 8.00 pm we held up four soldiers (2 Royal Engineers; 2 Staffs) and searched them, but found no arms. We took them to a field in our area where they were executed before 9.00 pm.[80]

The men who had undergone that harshness were not all overjoyed to hear of the Truce. Liam Deasy, OC Cork No. 3 Brigade, described his feelings when a meeting he was presiding at was suddenly interrupted by the arrival of the *Cork Examiner* bearing news of the coming truce:

The news was received in silence. There was no enthusiasm. The feeling seemed to be that this was the end of an epoch and that things would never be the same again. Even in retrospect, after more than fifty years, I well remember that my personal feeling was one of disappointment and I must admit I foresaw defeat and trouble ahead.[81]

It was not in Collins' nature to foresee defeat but he could certainly see trouble coming. He told Moya Llewelyn Davies that the Truce was 'only the first move. The days ahead are going to be the truly trying ones and we can only face them with set faces and hearts full of hope and confidence.'[82] He had had sight of the British plans for Martial Law and he had been sufficiently impressed by them to send de Valera an accurate warning (on 27 June) that Martial Law would be 'of the most rigorous kind and . . . will be supported by three times the present military strength.'

Had the Truce not come into effect Collins had retaliatory plans of his own drawn up. Apart from the wholesale shooting of agents and Auxiliaries mentioned in Chapter 5 he outlined a ruthless scheme to de Valera on 26 June which the Cabinet subsequently adopted but did not implement.[83] Collins advocated 'a regular all-round, thought-out onslaught on all the departments which operate on behalf of foreign Governments in Ireland. In my opinion, the proper way to start this, and the proper basis to start it on is legislation.' Collins suggested that once his proposals were adopted notices should be issued to 'all parties concerned that it was illegal for anyone to support or dispense English law in this country. After a fixed date . . . they would be liable to certain penalties . . . no English connection should be tolerated . . .' The fact that the Cabinet would adopt such a sanguinary policy during the period of Truce and peace talks indicates the extent of the doubts on the Irish side concerning the prospects for peace. Collins in particular had good reason for taking a sombre view of the future. He commented, 'once a truce is agreed, and we come out in the open, it is extermination for us if the truce should fail . . . We shall be like rabbits coming out from their holes.' He knew better than anyone else in the country what the real strengths and weaknesses of the IRA were. Even Dorothy Macardle, a historian favoured by de Valera, has conceded that the state of the Volunteers at the coming of the Truce was parlous in the extreme.[84]

In Collins' own immediate sphere of activity just before the Truce the Dublin Brigade had suffered a body blow in the Custom House operation. He suffered one himself immediately after it. De Valera agreed to go London on 12 July to see Lloyd George, but he deliberately left Collins out of the delegation he took with him. Collins protested but got no satisfaction. Griffith, Stack, Barton, Childers and Plunkett were to accompany the President to London, but not Michael Collins. De Valera later told his biographers that his reason for excluding Collins was that he did not want the British to obtain photographs of him. We are not told how he squared this reasoning with the fact that if Collins had gone to America as he had wished several months earlier, the British would have had unrivalled opportunities for taking pictures. (They could also have obtained the picture of Collins published in the *Gaelic American* as a result of de Valera's feud with Devoy.) But we can readily understand Collins' mood as he penned this note sitting in his Harcourt St office in Dublin while de Valera prepared to meet Lloyd George in London the next day:

Agreement is a trifling word or so I have come to look on it as such. At this moment there is more ill-will within a victorious assembly than ever could be found anywhere else except in the devil's assembly. It cannot be fought against. The issue and persons are mixed to such an extent as to make discernibility an utter impossibility except for a few.[85]

Collins' depression was totally at variance with the mood of the rest of the country. Indeed, as Frank O'Connor commented, there was 'far too great a feeling of confidence'.[86] O'Connor, who lived through those days, understood why this should have been so. The British had sued for peace. Their officers had had to treat with Volunteer officers. 'Terrorised by landlords, bullied by policemen, magistrates and soldiers, shipped like cattle to the American boats, the people had never known their veins to run with pride before'.[87] Now as in the first days of the French Revolution it was 'bliss . . . to be alive'. The Thermidorian reaction lay around the corner unseen as parties, marriages, heroes' welcomes greeted the return home of the men on the run. As one warrior I have knowledge of put it rather ruefully, 'My wife, an angel, was one of the many young ladies who developed a condition for which marriage was the only cure.' Egos popped like champagne corks. Even the Black and Tans joined in the general relaxation that glorious summer. They could be seen here posing for a souvenir photo with a former adversary in the Volunteers, there 'scurrying about, still in their cages, but with towels framed all around the railings to show they were on pleasure bent. The sun warmed us and the sun of freedom was rising on the horizon, warming our hearts.'[88]

But it rose too slowly. One of the tragedies of that summer was the amount of time let slip before a treaty was concluded. On the one hand the belief took hold that peace was now secure. There would be no return to war. On the other, the numbers in the Volunteers mushroomed. Guns poured into the country, expectations of what could be won from the British soared. And, of course, Collins and his associates became visible and traceable to their opponents, 'rabbits, out from their holes'. O'Connor could well have been right in his judgement that 'there was only one hope: negotiation broad and brief'. But with de Valera, one of the great procrastinators of Irish history, a speedy settlement was impossible.

Lloyd George made one fundamental miscalculation throughout the early part of 1921. He continued to regard Collins as the extremist and de Valera as the more moderate of the two. In fact Dr T. Ryle Dwyer has the evidence of history on his side when he judges that: 'Unlike the President who tended to portray a moderate public image while privately advocating a more hardline approach, Collins tended to do the opposite. Privately he was much more moderate than was generally believed.'[89]

De Valera met the hard-line approach by appearing to sound conciliatory so as to make it appear in the eyes of the world that it was the British, not the Irish, who were the hard-liners. He talked, not about an Irish Republic, but about self-determination, for which America and England had fought in the First World War. 'If England should concede that right there would be no further difficulties, either with her or with the Ulster minority. If Ulster should claim autonomy, we would be willing to grant it.' He showed himself willing to accept Dominion status, quoting Bonar Law to show that the Dominions had 'control of their whole destinies . . . We are thoroughly sane and reasonable people, not a coterie of political doctrinarians, or even party politicians, Republican or other.'[90] He told Harry Boland:

In public statements our policy should be not to make it easy for Lloyd George by proclaiming that nothing but so and so will satisfy us. Our position should be simply that we are insisting on only one right, and that is the right of the people of this country to determine for themselves how they should be governed. That sounds moderate but includes everything.[91]

It did indeed 'sound moderate' to the British, especially in view of the tough-line utterances Collins made to Ackerman. Just as the British tried to keep de Valera in a position where he might become of use to them there appear to have been two strands to their approach to Collins. On the one hand he would certainly have been killed, with or without torture, had he fallen into the hands of one segment of the Castle's forces, those referred to by Griffith as 'the Camerilla', in an article in the *Bulletin* on 11 December 1919:

There is a 'Camerilla' in Dublin Castle directing the present outrages against the Irish people. The organ of the Camerilla in the English Press is the London *Daily Express* which prints, day after day, from its Dublin correspondent, a series of concocted falsehoods forged in Dublin Castle. Two of the members of the Camerilla were formerly employed under Arthur Balfour in 1888 as secret agents to sustain the Piggott forgeries against Parnell . . . the members of the Camerilla, together with a couple of members of the British Cabinet, have as object the provocation of the Irish people into an armed uprising.

The hawkish element which in 1921 had an equally hawkish Chief Secretary to turn to would certainly have used their Hardys and their Igoes to dispose of Collins. But the 'Peace Party', headed by Anderson, Cope, MacMahon and Wylie, the Law Officer, who were responsive to Lloyd George's anxiety for a settlement, may have preferred to see him alive and in a position to 'deliver' on a solution to the Irish problem. To some extent this judgement has to be a matter of conjecture. To this day the Irish files are amongst the most closely guarded of the British State papers. Hundred-year rules hang over the papers of key figures like Colonel Winter. Not only mysteries, but more importantly in Ireland, a land of long memories and long-tailed families, names remain to be revealed.

It is a matter of record that Lloyd George and his circle thought highly of Collins during the war, ironically, more highly then they came to do during the peace. Worthington Evans expressed his admiration of Collins' military genius to Wilson at a dinner, and the two nearly came to blows as a result.[92] Lloyd George's feelings were of course not based on abstract admiration. His concern was how best to make use of Collins' position which he was able to gauge with some accuracy from the information passed on by the various British moles and listening posts. He told the Cabinet on 27 April that 'de Valera and Michael Collins have quarrelled'. Years later de Valera would allow his biographers to admit that it was from April 1921 that 'Collins did not accept my view of things as he had done before and was inclined to give public expression to his own opinions even when they differed from mine.'

Lloyd George was wrong in his assessment of the reasons for the quarrel. He told the Cabinet, Collins 'carries a gun and makes it impossible to negotiate. De Valera cannot come here and say he is willing to give up Irish Independence, for if he did he might be shot.'[93]

Lloyd George had no moral objections to meeting Collins: 'No doubt he is the head and font of the movement. If I could see him a settlement might be possible.' The question for Lloyd George was political: 'Whether the British people would be willing for us to negotiate with the head of a band of murderers.'[94] He had not made up his mind on the issue a few weeks later when he told Cabinet that his information was that de Valera was opposed to 'the gun business', but was in the grip of the militants led by Collins.

And so the British political and military machine remained poised before the Sinn Fein mouseholes like a giant cat that knew where the mice were, even if it wasn't quite sure what each of them was doing, but was afraid either to pounce or to let them go because of the conflicting pressures coming from those in favour of an Irish settlement and 'Tudor Toryism'.

Though he had brought a strong team with him de Valera began his July meetings with Lloyd George by insisting on meeting him alone. The Prime Minister, who apparently discovered, like many another man before and after him, that de Valera could be disarmingly likeable when he chose, subsequently reported to his Cabinet:

After three [there were actually four in all] interviews with Mr de Valera, aggregating several hours, I found it difficult to see exactly where the Irish leader stood . . . What he wanted was a Republic, but this the Prime Minister had said was impossible, being inconsistent with the Monarchy. Mr de Valera, however had not admitted this inconsistency . . . as the conversation progressed, it became increasingly clear that Ulster was the real difficulty.[95]

De Valera made a show of keeping Collins informed from London. He wrote to him on 15 July saying 'the meetings have been between us two alone as principals . . . you will be glad to know that I am not dissatisfied with the general situation . . . the proposal will be theirs – we will be free to consider it without prejudice'. Collins wrote back the next day saying that 'things and people here are splendid – everything going on magnificently, fine spirit, fine confidence, and although there was a little more relaxation than I should have liked, everybody is working *fairly* hard again.'

Eventually, Lloyd George told the Cabinet, de Valera had said that he had to consult his own Cabinet, as only two members of it were with him in London and asked for a draft of the British proposals to bring back to Ireland with him. Lloyd George said that he had given de Valera 'a very serious warning' that if the talks broke down the resumed war

would bear an entirely different character, as Britain's reduced military commitments around the world meant that more troops were available to be sent to Ireland where a great military concentration would take place, with a view to the repression of the rebellion and the restoration of order.

The draft which Lloyd George drew up, in consultation with Balfour and Chamberlain, offered the twenty-six Southern Counties a type of Dominion status in which Ireland could have an army, but no navy. Britain was to have whatever facilities she might require in time of need. There was to be free trade between Britain and Ireland but partition was to be acknowledged. The twenty-six county State was to allow for full recognition of the existing powers and privileges of the Parliament of Northern Ireland which could not be 'abrogated except by their own consent'.

There had already been a skirmish in London the day before over partition, as Craig had publicly announced that 'it now merely remains for Mr de Valera and the British people to come to terms regarding the area outside of which I am Prime Minister. I go back to Ireland to carry on the practical work of Government.'

De Valera wrote immediately to Lloyd George complaining that the claim that he only spoke for the area outside of the North was 'wholly inadmissible' and saying that before going on with any further talks he wanted a 'definite statement as to whether your Government is in agreement with Sir James Craig and intends to support his view'. Lloyd George replied: 'I am responsible neither for Sir James Craig's statement to the Press, to which you refer, nor for your statement to which Sir James's purports to be a reply.'

On 19 July de Valera wrote: 'Things may burst up here suddenly, so all should be prepared.' Collins was seemingly unperturbed and proceeded to give de Valera a description of a two-day trip he had just made through Cork.

The spirit animating the enemy in Cork City and in the parts of the County I visited is arrogant and provocative. They are trying to regard the position not as a truce but as a surrender on our part. For instance, the car in which I was travelling was held up in Clonakilty by regular troops although they have no power whatever to undertake such action. I was not in it at the time . . . The first exciting incident I had was a few minutes after leaving Cork City, going southwards. We very nearly ran into one of our own trenches. I said to the driver that if anything happened it would be the irony of fate.

I would like you to know that while I was down in Cork yesterday we intercepted messages from Bandon – that's the CI's office – DIs, Macroom, Bantry, Clonakilty, Castletownbere and Skibbereen. The purport of the message was as follows: 'Submit return at once of rough estimate of No. of males between ages of 16 and 50 in your district.' Skibbereen said, '7,000 males'. Bantry and Clonakilty replied, 'letter by next train'. Macroom replied '3,000 males'. Castletownbere replied, 'roughly 1,500 males'. I can't judge what this could mean, unless it is an enquiry with a view to arrangements for a round-up. I think it well that you should know this. That wire was handed in at Bandon at midday yesterday.

Wires have also been issued to the effect that in the event of negotiations breaking down the enemy forces would be confined to barracks, and will get a further cipher as to the next step. Generally speaking, I fancy the idea is to have preparations made to attack us the moment they decide to finish their offers. I don't know whether anything really tangible has been referred to up to the present, but I should say that in the final result it would be worthwhile stipulating that no matter how bad the terms are they would be submitted to a full meeting. You will know my object in this.

De Valera and Lloyd George continued their shadow-boxing, with de Valera pretending that he was so shocked by the British proposals when he had sight of them that he at first refused to take them back to Dublin. Then he sent a messenger for them, but let it be thought in Dublin that the British had forwarded them. Behind the shadow-boxing however there now lay one ineluctable truth which Collins more than anyone else would have reason to ponder bitterly. After his lengthy tête-à-têtes with Lloyd George, Eamon de Valera knew better than any man alive how slim was the prospect of a Republic and what sort of a settlement he and his colleagues were likely to get.

Collins had correctly analysed the mood of the British military and the steps being taken to resume hostilities. The Cork preparations were replicated in every county in the country and the members of the Cabinet had to consider very firmly whether or not their acceptance or rejection of British proposals meant peace or war, not just horse-trading. If it had to be either, it was important that the Dail was shown to be informed and united on the issues. But Collins also wanted a 'full meeting' in order to secure the release of imprisoned Deputies, amongst whom was Sean MacEoin. He visited Mountjoy Jail himself to see MacEoin, on 14 July, using the name James Gill. He also walked out of a Cabinet meeting in fury after de Valera had stated his reluctance to jeopardise the Truce for one man. The British announced that they would release all prisoners, except MacEoin, on 6 August but Collins promptly broke into print with a statement in the *Irish Times* on 8 August saying flatly: 'There can and will be no meeting of Dail Eireann until Commandant Sean MacEoin is released. The refusal to release him appears to indicate a desire on the part of the English Government to terminate the Truce.'

Much as he disliked being upstaged, de Valera had no option but to follow Collins' initiative and say that he could go no further with the negotiations until MacEoin was set free. MacEoin was released that evening and must have wondered, at least temporarily, if he were not better off in jail. As he started up the steps of the hotel where Collins was waiting for him Collins, forgetting about his wounds, made a welcoming dive at him and the pair fetched up in a heap on the floor. MacEoin survived to deliver a speech in Irish which Collins had written out for him, proposing de Valera as 'President of the Irish Republic' when the Dail met to consider the British proposals.

Nevertheless, a despatch which Art O'Brien sent to Collins, on 20 August, was nearer the mark than O'Brien evidently realised at the time: 'Attached another cutting from the *Daily Express* about Dev. You will see at the end that they tried to work in the old stunt of divisions in the ranks.' The *Express* may have been actuated by malice in its report about divisions but it was not without accuracy.

A step taken by de Valera at this stage is worth noting since it shows how acquiescent the Dail was towards him. He formally rejected Lloyd George's offer on 10 August after consulting with the Cabinet. He wrote, 'on the occasion of our last interview I gave it as my judgement that Dail Eireann could not, and that the Irish people would not, accept the proposals of your Government. I now confirm that judgement.' In fact, the Dail did not meet until almost a week after that letter went to Lloyd George and then its function was merely to rubber-stamp de Valera's action.

Collins seemingly saw little wrong in this for he wrote to Art O'Brien on the 17th saying:

I think we may still be pleased enough with ourselves. Although LG's words looked big you will notice a few peculiarities in his statement – peculiarities which do not look as if he felt himself very happy about the thought of resuming, his insistence on the Dominion status offer is peculiar also . . . it may mean that by constantly repeating Dominion Home Rule he may reconcile his people to it.

De Valera was attempting similar reconciliation at the time. Having met Lloyd George he obviously realised that partition might have to be accepted. He told the Dail on 22 August, 'they had not the power, and some of them had not the inclination, to use force with Ulster'. He did not think that policy would be successful. They would be making the same mistake with that section as England had made with Ireland. He would not be responsible for such a policy . . . for his part, if the Republic were recognised he would be in favour of giving each county power to vote itself out of the Republic. Otherwise they would be compelled to use force. This went even further than he had gone in his 10 August rejection of the British proposals in which he had said: 'We do not contemplate the use of force . . . if your Government stands aside, we can effect a complete reconciliation. We do agree with you that no common action can be secured by force.' He was now conceding to Ulster sufficient autonomy and recognition to allow it to opt out of the state he was hoping to set up. If the use of force was eschewed there was no other possible means of bringing Belfast under Dublin rule. The following day de Valera made another highly significant statement. He pointed out that the title 'President of the Republic', though accepted, had 'never been constitutionally created'. As a matter of fact the President was President, not of the Republic, but of the Ministry of Dail Eireann. This point, which never seems to have troubled him in his travels to the United States, did not stop him allowing Collins and MacEoin to co-operate in proposing him for the position, which he seems to have seen as a kind of political blank cheque. He told the Dail on 23 August: 'I am no longer to be looked on as a party leader. I am representing the nation and I shall represent the whole nation if I am elected to office and I shall not be bound by any section whatever of the nation.' The real significance of his assumption of the 'Presidency of the Irish Republic', prior to the start of negotiations which he knew from his talks with Lloyd George were highly unlikely to yield a Republic, only emerged later. It was a classic example of how de Valera outmanoeuvred his closest colleagues without their being aware of it. In the minds of an electorate predisposed towards 'follow-my-leader' the title naturally had a bearing subsequently on the widespread support he attracted to his views.

The diplomatic sparring continued right throughout September with de Valera and Lloyd George exchanging more than a dozen letters and telegrams. One of those hit a snag on 9 September when Lloyd George refused to accept de Valera's assertion that 'our nation has formally declared its independence and recognises itself as a sovereign State. It is only as the representatives of that State, and as its chosen guardians, that we have any authority or powers to act on behalf of our people.' Harry Boland and Joe McGrath went with this missive to the Gareloch in Scotland where Lloyd George was on holiday, despite Collins' warning that 'you might as well stay where you are'. He was proved right. Lloyd George immediately cancelled the arrangements which had been proceeding for a conference. As Lloyd George had already told de Valera that he could not entertain any claim to enter into negotiations on the basis that Ireland was 'an independent and sovereign State', this reply cannot have been unexpected. The British never abandoned that position in subsequent exchanges of letters and telegrams. For example, on 18 September Lloyd George specifically stated that unless a paragraph in another letter of de Valera's (dated 12 September) affirming independence as an independent State was withdrawn, 'conference between us is impossible'. He pointed out that de Valera had made no such condition when he came to see him in July, but had come as 'the chosen leader of the great majority in Southern Ireland', and continued:

From the very outset of our conversation I told you that we looked to Ireland to own allegiance to the Throne, and to make her future as a member of the British Commonwealth. That was the basis of or proposals, and we cannot alter it. The status which you now claim in advance for your delegates is, in effect, a repudiation of that basis.

De Valera tried to head off the inevitable on 19 September by trying to slip into conference with the plea:

We have had no thought at any time of asking you to accept any conditions precedent to a conference. We would have thought it as unreasonable to expect you, as a preliminary, to recognise the Irish Republic, formally, or informally, as that you should expect us, formally, or informally, to surrender our national position . . . We request you, therefore, to state whether your letter of 7 September is intended to be a demand for a surrender on our part, or an invitation to a conference free on both sides and without prejudice should agreement not be reached. If the latter, we readily confirm our acceptance of the invitation and our appointed delegates will meet your Government's representatives at any time in the immediate future that you designate.

Lloyd George's reply was ten days in coming and contained no give whatever on the recognition issue. It said:

His Majesty's Government . . . cannot enter a conference upon the basis of this correspondence. Notwithstanding your personal assurance to the contrary, which they much appreciate, it might be argued in future that the acceptance of a conference on this basis had involved them in a recognition which no British Government can accord. On this point they must guard themselves against any possible doubt . . . The position taken up by His Majesty's Government is fundamental to the existence of the British Empire and they cannot alter it. My colleagues and I remain, however, keenly anxious to make in co-operation with your delegates another determined effort to explore every possibility of settlement by personal discussion . . . We, therefore, send you herewith a fresh invitation to a conference in London on 11 October, where we can meet your delegates as spokesmen of the people whom you represent with a view to ascertaining how the association of Ireland with the community of nations known as the British Empire may best be reconciled with Irish national aspirations.

It was obvious that the self-recognition game was up although de Valera's reply of 30 September, which Griffith drafted for him, was posed as merely a letter of acceptance rather than one of capitulation:

We have received your letter of invitation to a Conference in London on October 11th 'with a view to ascertaining how the association of Ireland with the community of nations known as the British Empire may best be reconciled with Irish national aspirations.'

Our respective positions have been stated and are understood, and we agree that conference, not correspondence, is the most practical and hopeful way to an understanding. We accept the invitation, and our Delegates will meet you in London on the date mentioned 'to explore every possibility of settlement by personal discussion'.

Collins later judged that

the communication of Sept. 29th from Lloyd George made it clear that they were going into a conference not on the recognition of the Irish Republic . . . if we all stood on the recognition of the Irish Republic as a prelude to any conference we could very easily have said so, and there would have been no conference . . . it was the acceptance of the invitation that formed the compromise.[96]

Robert Barton, one of those who took part in the conference with him, and fell out with him over its outcome, nevertheless agreed with this assessment. He said:

in these preliminaries the English refused to recognise us as acting on behalf of the Irish Republic and the fact that we agreed to negotiate at all on any other basis was possibly the primary cause of our downfall. Certainly it was the first milestone on the road to disaster.[97]

It was a milestone certainly, but one has to go back in time to decide whether the formation of the UVF or the failure to concede Home Rule were the real culprits. One thing is certain however. The day of reckoning was at hand. On 20 August 1921, he held a long argumentative session with Collins (at which Harry Boland was present) about who should go to London for the continuation of the peace process. Having left Collins at home while he teased out from Lloyd George what was on offer, he now, having found out, began to steer Collins towards the negotiating table in Downing St. The man who had felt his place was in America during most of the Tan war felt he must stay in Dublin during the coming diplomatic offensive in London. Collins, who thought of himself as a soldier, not a politician, resisted bitterly. He wanted de Valera to go. So did Griffith and Cosgrave, but Barton, Brugha and Stack backed de Valera who then used his casting vote in the Cabinet to get his way over staying at home. It took more than a casting vote to get Collins to go. Pointing out that he was universally regarded as the epitome of the Republican gunman he argued that if he stayed at home this reputation would be of value because the delegates who did go would be able either to seek concessions on the pretext of placating him, or at worst buy time by saying they would have to refer back to him.

In dealing with de Valera this was the worst possible line he could have taken because in the 'Long Fellow's' view there was only one figure in Ireland to whom all must defer, himself. Collins compounded the error by pleading with de Valera 'for three hours one night after the decision had been made to send the delegation to London' that:

for several years (rightly or wrongly made no difference) the English had held me to be the one man most necessary to capture because they held me to be the one man responsible for the smashing of their Secret Service Organisation and for their failure to terrorise the Irish people with their Black and Tans . . . the important fact was that in England as in Ireland, the Michael Collins legend existed. It pictured me as mysterious active menace, elusive, unknown, unaccountable, and in this respect I was the only living Irishman of whom it could be said . . . Bring me into the spotlight of a London conference and quickly will be discovered the common clay of which I am made. The glamour of the legendary figure will be gone.[98]

If de Valera had any doubts about either the morality or the practicality of what he was doing those were not the arguments to reinforce them. In the end it was not de Valera but Batt O'Connor, whom de Valera instructed to convince Collins, who in fact persuaded him to go. Obviously there were very few people still alive as this book was being written who had first-hand knowledge of this aspect of the story, but a daughter of Batt O'Connor's, Sister Margaret Mary, was one such. A member of the enclosed order, the Carmelites, whom I had to get special permission to visit, she was a girl of twelve when Collins arrived at her home for the fateful colloquy. She was sleeping in a downstairs room in Brendon Rd, because of an ankle injury which ruled out stair-climbing. Collins and her father were next door.

Daddy brought out the bottle and they talked for hours and hours. I could hear Mick's light voice arguing. Mick didn't think it right that he should go, because he was a soldier. De Valera should go, he kept saying. It's not my place. He sounded terribly upset. But daddy kept arguing 'You'll have to go Mick. It's the one chance you'll get. Think of how it will look in America if you miss this opportunity. Think of what this could do for Ireland. It's your duty. It's a great opportunity. Think of what you can lose if you don't go.'

Batt O'Connor himself painted a similar picture:

I will never forget his agony of mind. He would not sit down, but kept pacing up and down the floor, saying that he should not be put in that position. It was an unheard-of thing that a soldier who had fought in the field should be elected to carry out negotiations. It was de Valera's job, not his.[99]

It was the worst single decision of de Valera's life, for himself and for Ireland. Instead of the experience and prestige of the most revered political figure on the Irish side being made available to parley against the English, de Valera's full force was ultimately to be turned against his fellow countrymen. The consequence of his decision was to drive him to an extremist position in which he helped to unleash a hurricane of violence and destruction on Ireland. He knew that any agreement brought back from London would be a compromise. He admitted to the Dail when announcing his decision to stay in Dublin that 'he knew fairly well from his experience over in London how far it was possible to get the British Government to go'.[100] Even as he took part in those Dail proceedings he had had the implications of his letter of agreement to enter into conference spelled out to him. Mary MacSwiney stated forcefully that unless the British received the Irish on their terms the alternative was war:

a settlement within the Empire . . . was impossible. Association with a community of nations known as the British Empire might be reconciled with Irish aspirations outside but not inside that Empire. An association that would involve any allegiance direct or indirect to the British Crown – that was one point on which they could never give in . . . Their allegiance was to the Irish Republic. They had taken an oath to the Irish Republic . . . they had no *arrière-pensée* when taking that oath, they meant a Republic not a Dominion inside the Empire.

With Brugha and Stack standing balefully in the wings ready to denounce anything that Collins signed, de Valera knew that if dissent was to be kept to a minimum his signature would be an essential to any Treaty document. Even a rejection of terms would have been more palatable to the public if he were part of the team which did the rejecting.

De Valera later gave several different reasons why he did not go. Amongst these, he made the claim that his staying at home was 'generally accepted' and only became an issue when the Treaty was signed.[101] This is not true. Cosgrave formally proposed a motion that the President should go with the delegation, as Chairman, because of his 'extraordinary' experience in negotiations, and the advantage of being in touch recently (with Lloyd George).[102] The British would have their Head of State on their delegation, yet the Irish were sending over a team 'leaving their ablest player in reserve'. Collins also said he felt the President should go and said bluntly that he did not want to go himself and would very much prefer not to have been chosen.

It is not unduly fanciful to imagine the shade of Machiavelli nodding approval at his pupil's elbow as de Valera proceeded to scuttle these arguments. Insofar as Collins' objections were concerned he declared that from the personal contact he had with him he felt and he knew the Minister for Finance was a man for that team. He was absolutely vital to the delegation. He said that he himself would go if he were not the President, the 'symbol of the Republic'. The 'symbol' should be kept 'untouched' . . . not compromised by any arrangements which it might be necessary for plenipotentiaries to make. He was sure the Dail realised the task they were giving to them – to win 'what a mighty army and navy might not be able to win for them'. It was not a shirking of duty, but he realised the position and how necessary it was 'to keep the Head of State and the symbol untouched and that was why he asked to be left out'. Left out he duly was. Cosgrave's motion was defeated. Collins must have thought dark thoughts about what his few words of Irish for Sean MacEoin had helped to bring about. 'You might say the trap is sprung',[103] he wrote later to Joe O'Reilly. The Presidency of the Republic was indeed being used to ensure that the President was not going to be bound by any sector of the nation.

The Dail then unanimously passed a motion put down by Liam de Roiste: 'that if plenipotentiaries for negotiations be appointed, either by the Cabinet or the Dail, such plenipotentiaries be given a free hand in such negotiations and duly to report to the Dail'. De Valera made it quite clear to the Dail that he fully supported de Roiste's contention that the plenipotentiaries should go without their hands being 'tied in any way'. But he later tried to override the Dail motion by attempting to limit the plenipotentiaries' freedom of action by issuing them with letters of instruction which said:

1. The plenipotentaries have full powers as defined in their credentials.
2. It is understood before decisions are finally reached on a main question, that a despatch notifying the intention to make these decisions will be sent to members of the Cabinet in Dublin, and that a reply will be awaited by the plenipotentiaries before final decision is made.
3. It is also understood that the complete text of the draft treaty about to be signed will be similarly submitted to Dublin, and a reply awaited.
4. It is understood the Cabinet in Dublin will be kept regularly informed of the progress of the negotiations.

The plenipotentiaries, apart from Collins, were Griffith, Barton, Duggan and George Gavan Duffy. Erskine Childers was the official Secretary to the Delegation. Brugha and Stack were invited to go but refused and, unlike Collins, were not subject to any pressure to reconsider. De Valera later admitted to Joe McGarrity 'for your eyes only' that he had deliberately built division into the negotiating team in his selection process. He told McGarrity[104] that he had expected that Collins and Griffith would ultimately accept the Crown. However he reckoned that Barton and particularly his cousin, Childers, 'an intellectual Republican',[105] would oppose them on this. Duffy and Duggan he said were mere padding, chosen for their legal training; both were solicitors. Brugha he had not chosen because he would have caused wasteful rows and he knew that Griffith and Collins would not work with Stack. That sort of *divide et emperor* reasoning, a balancing of opposites, might work in Cabinet selection, under a strong leader. To send such a delegation overseas while the leader stayed at home was not merely inviting, it was guaranteeing trouble. But de Valera told McGarrity that he had intended that 'the Cabinet at home should hang on to the delegation's coattails', leaving everything safe for a final 'tug of war'. That final 'tug of war', according to the de Valera grand design, was to come not by, with or from a Republic, but on an idea of de Valera's, the External Association formula.

In return for recognition by Great Britain and the Commonwealth of an independent Irish State, Ireland was to become an external associate of the British Commonwealth. According to Barton the delegates had 'only a hazy conception of what it would be in its final form' but were said to be clear that 'no vestige of British authority would remain in Ireland. The compromise would be as regards our foreign relations.'[106] Griffith, who was supposed to be the leader of the plenipotentiaries, gave a celebrated account of how he first heard of External Association to P. S. O'Hegarty:

The first I heard of External Association was when Dev was pressing me to go over as a plenipotentiary. I went in to him one day and found him with Cathal and Austin at his desk, all three sitting. I was standing. He told me he wanted me to go to London. I said to him; 'You are my Chief, and if you tell me to go, I'll go. But I know, and you know, that I can't bring back a Republic.' Then he produced this External Association idea – the first I ever heard of it – and after half-an-hour's persuasion, Cathal gave a reluctant consent to it. Stack said nothing, but sat there, sullen. I said nothing. Then the other two left, and left me alone with him. I said, 'Look here Dev, what is the meaning of this External Association idea? What are you getting at with it?' He replied by getting a pencil and paper and drew the line thus: [At this point Griffith too produced paper and pencil and drew a line AB at a sixty degree angle.] 'That,' said he, 'is me, in the straightjacket of the Republic. I must get out of it.' Then he drew another line, a curved line [from A] AC. 'That,' said he, 'is External Association. The purpose of it is to bring Cathal along.' Then he drew another straight line. [Here Griffith drew the line AD] 'That,' said he, 'is where we'll eventually get to.' Then I was satisfied, and said no more about it.[107]

De Valera in fact had first embodied the External Association idea in a memorandum he prepared, but did not send, to Lloyd George after his return from the July talks. He gave it to the plenipotentiaries as Draft Treaty A, not to be confused with Draft Treaty B which he also gave them, in an equally unfinished state. The idea behind B was to use it for propaganda purposes if the negotiations broke down, as containing the terms which Ireland was prepared to accept. What exactly the plenipotentiaries were to accept was not spelt out. They were expected to produce that draft themselves. 'We must depend on your side for the initiative after this', de Valera wrote to Griffith.[108] It was understandable in the circumstances that it was another remark de Valera made at the time which lodged more weightily with Collins than the details of External Association: 'We must have scape-goats.'[109] Wearily Collins told Sean O'Muirthle, 'Let them make a scapegoat, or anything they wish of me. We have accepted the situation, as it is, and someone must go.'[110] He was quite clear that he was enmeshed in a web of intrigue and hostility. Shortly after the Truce was signed, not realising that his old friend had, in America, become a member of the de Valera camp, he wrote to Harry Boland warning him that things had changed for the worse in Dublin:

I don't intend to dwell overmuch on what to me are issues more vital than truces. But I think it right that you should be warned of the changes here. There's something about which I don't like, and I have the impression that the whole thing is pressing on me. I find myself looking at friends as if they were enemies – looking at them twice just to make sure that they really are friends after all, I mention no names. After all it may be a wrong impression that's got into me. Frankly, though, I don't care for things as they are now.[111]

That was in July. Later that month, on the 29th, Brugha seized on another opportunity to embarrass Collins. He raised with the Cabinet the fact that Tom Cullen had caused an Englishman called Robbie to be expelled from the country as a suspected British agent. Collins, obviously feeling that Cullen may have been in the wrong, wrote to Tobin:

Will you please caution Tom that he is not to be making use of sweeping remarks in places where they may be taken up wrongly . . . not slightest particle of real evidence . . . reports must be submitted by my staff to you. We've seen what results of talking to other Departments has been.[112]

In September Brugha made a serious attempt to embarrass both Collins and Mulcahy. He tried to appoint Stack as Deputy Chief of Staff to Mulcahy. When Mulcahy objected, Brugha tried to sack him, sending him a letter reeking of animus towards both him and Collins:

Before you are very much older my friend, I shall show you that I have as little intention of taking dictation from you as to how I should reprove inefficiency or negligence on the part of yourself or the D/I [Collins, Director of Intelligence] as I have of allowing you to appoint a Deputy Chief of Staff of your own choosing.[113]

Mulcahy immediately sent the file to de Valera 'to draw your attention to the attitude of the Minister for Defence to myself and to at least one other member of the General Staff'. This produced a meeting between Brugha, Mulcahy and de Valera[114] which ended as unsatisfactorily as the meeting in the spring over the Glasgow accounts. Brugha burst into tears and walked out exclaiming that he 'could do no wrong'.[115]

In fact in August Brugha had returned to the charge over the accounts. Stack backed him saying 'a serious charge had been made which should be probed to the bottom'. De Valera managed to do nothing in a way which indicated to Collins that if he were to be a target for mud-slinging de Valera, while he might not join in throwing, would do nothing to obstruct the throwers.[116] Collins admitted later that he had acted against good advice, from Tim Healy amongst others, in going. 'I was warned more times than I can recall about the ONE. And when I was caught for this delegation my immediate thought was of how easily I had walked into the preparations. But having walked in, I had to stay.'[117] One could hardly imagine a worse background of suspicion and mistrust against which to begin negotiations of any sort, let alone talks of such historic importance.

Well might Collins and Griffith agree when they got to London, that they did not know 'whether they were being instructed or confused from Dublin'.[118] They also agreed that Collins would become the *de facto* leader of the delegation. Years of overwork, poverty, strain and imprisonment had taken their toll of Griffith, now in his fiftieth year.[119] Knowledgeable contemporaries[120] have left descriptions of Griffith in his last years, having to borrow a pound to take a guest to lunch; of sitting in his office in his stockinged feet while his boots were repaired; of being so abstracted that he used to ruin Kathleen Napoli MacKenna's hair, while dictating his *Bulletin* articles. He had a habit of standing behind her, smoothing down her hair while he concentrated, his eyes on the middle distance, which caused Desmond Fitzgerald to joke that 'when Kathleen washes her hair there is enough copying ink in the water for another day's *Bulletin*'. Winston Churchill summed him up as having the appearance of a 'tired scholar'. Accordingly Collins took on a major share of the negotiating donkey-work. Apart from wearing drafting and side conference sessions with his own colleagues he took part in seven plenary sessions, nine meetings of the sub- committees set up by the Plenary Conference and almost all of the twenty-four meetings of the sub-conferences to which the plenary sessions gave way after 24 October. In addition there were various informal meetings with Tom Jones, Secretary of the Cabinet. Apart from conference business, he continued to discharge a good deal of his normal workload.

It is quite clear that though Collins was negotiating for peace, he was also making certain to do what he could to prepare for war. One note[121] shows him arranging a meeting of the English centres of the IRB, another[122] puts Paddy Daly in touch with a Liverpool police sergeant because he can 'tell you of the instructions that have been issued regarding the protection of houses of relatives of Black and Tans here', and there were many other such missives. Another example of Collins' activities during the talks is recorded in a 'note' in an important compilation of Treaty documents I have had access to.[123] There is a widespread belief in Ireland, which I have frequently heard expressed, that once the delegation landed in London, there was little or no contact with Dublin until the Treaty was signed and presented as a *fait accompli*, thus helping to bring about the civil war. In fact as the 'note' states with regard to the 'Instructions to Plenipotentaries':

These were adhered to rigidly so far as the delegation as a whole was concerned.

Until the date of the signing of the Treaty every week one or more delegates returned to Dublin and reported to members of the Cabinet. Michael Collins returned almost every weekend.

Collins is known to have met de Valera on several of these visits[124] and to have kept in touch with the IRB. In fact Collins secured the IRB's prior approval for the wording of the Oath[125] which he eventually assented to in the Treaty.

In London Collins stayed in 15 Cadogan Gardens, while Griffith and the other delegates stayed in 10 Hans Place. It was generally assumed at the time that he wanted to be on his own so that he could receive his intelligence agents in privacy, but in fact he had a large household. The publicity department was housed at Cadogan Gardens, as was Diarmuid O'Hegarty, one of the secretaries to the delegation and other prominent figures such as Joe MacGrath, Dan MacCarthy and Sean Milroy. Collins did have his own intelligence agents and bodyguard with him. Liam Tobin, Tom Cullen, Emmet Dalton, Ned Broy, Joe Guilfoyle and Joe Dolan all accompanied him, which would have effectively ended both the anonymity and the usefulness of the Crow St team, had hostilities recommenced. In fact this was thought such a likely outcome that Dalton arranged for an aeroplane to be purchased by friends with a Canadian Air Force background ostensibly 'to inspect forests', in reality to fly Collins out in an emergency. One key agent whose cover remained intact was Dave Neligan whom the British brought to London in his Secret Service capacity to spy on Collins and company, all of whom travelled separately from the Hans Place contingent. This included Griffith, Barton, Childers, Duggan, Gavan Duffy, their wives and two of the assistant secretaries to the delegation, Fionan Lynch and John Chartres. The secretarial assistants included Lily Brennan, the Lyons sisters, Alice and Ellie, and Kathleen Napoli MacKenna. When they arrived at Euston by special train a huge crowd waited for them – the King and Queen had just passed through and the Irish spectators and the royalists combined to cheer, and chair, the party to their cars, which were preceded all the way to Hans Place by a pipe band.

Kathleen Napoli MacKenna painted an equally animated picture of the day the negotiations opened, Tuesday 11 October 1921:

The precincts of Downing St presented an impressive scene with men, women and children kneeling in prayer across the thoroughfares. The paths were lined along the route with Irish exiles, including nuns and clergymen, reciting the rosary, singing hymns, exclaiming good wishes, pouring blessings on the difficult undertaking. There were tricolours, banners, flags, lengths of cloth and cardboard with wishes and slogans in Gaelic and English.

But there was a darker side to the picture which Napoli MacKenna, a keen chessplayer, also captured. She struggled through the crowds 'just in time to see my little "pawns" – taut, rigid, serious – entering the Battle Field . . . Liam Tobin . . . near to the railings of No. 10, and Emmet Dalton . . . handsome as a Wild West cinema star, the butt of a

service rifle [sic] peeping from his hip pocket, standing all alert.'
Though she intended no irony, in the circumstances in which the Irish
delegation was chosen, Napoli MacKenna's 'pawns' is a not inappropriate description. They were 'standing all alert' inside Downing St
too. The credentials which the Irishmen were issued by de Valera read
as follows:

TO ALL WHOM THESE PRESENTS COME, GREETINGS
In virtue of the authority vested in me by Dail Eireann, I hereby appoint:
Arthur Griffith, TD   Minister for Foreign Affairs.
                                        CHAIRMAN
Michael Collins, TD   Minister of Finance
Robert Barton, TD   Minister of Economic Affairs
Eamonn J. Duggan, TD
George Gavan Duffy, TD
as Envoys Plenipotentiary from the Elected Government of The REPUBLIC OF
IRELAND to negotiate and conclude on behalf of Ireland with the represent-
atives of His Britannic Majesty, George V, a Treaty or Treaties of
Settlement, Association and Accommodation between Ireland and the
community of nations known as the British Commonwealth.
IN WITNESS WHEREOF I hereunto subscribe my name as President.

With this remarkable document de Valera was trying to recover
both the self-recognition of the Republic which he had lost in agreeing
to the negotiations in the first place, and to have it tacitly accepted that
the delegates' business was to come to an accommodation with the
Commonwealth, not to sign a Treaty agreeing to take an oath of
loyalty to the Crown. Lloyd George reacted by killing it and two
other birds with the same stone. There had been some fears of
awkwardness on the British side about 'shaking hands with murder',
that is, Michael Collins, and on the Irish at having to take the hand of
Hamar Greenwood. Lloyd George solved the problem by greeting the
Irishmen individually at the door of the conference room and then
escorting them to their side of the large table across which he
introduced them to their opposite numbers so that handshakes and the
production of credentials were rendered equally superfluous. The
'Welsh Wizard' had begun as he intended to continue.

8

Settling This Old Strife

'Blessed are the Peacemakers.'

Gospel according to St Matthew, V, ix

Michael Collins was thirty years of age when, at eleven o'clock on the morning of 11 October 1921, he sat down to negotiate with one of the most formidable political teams that England ever assembled. Facing him were David Lloyd George, Lord Birkenhead, Austen Chamberlain and Winston Churchill. Alongside them were Sir Gordon Hewart, the Attorney General, Sir Lamington Worthington Evans, the Conservative Secretary for War and Sir Hamar Greenwood, the Chief Secretary for Ireland. Though not of the calibre of the Big Four, these three alone would have constituted a useful team in their own right. Taken together, the English negotiators, backed up inside the chamber by two of the most brilliant public servants of the century, Lionel Curtis and Tom Jones, and outside it by the resources of an imperial civil service, presented an obstacle of Himalayan proportions to Irish Republican aspirations.

Collins established an extraordinary friendship with one of his adversaries during the struggle to surmount that obstacle, courageous, fractious, noble, and foredoomed as the attempt was.[1] Apart from his affinity to Collins by virtue of their shared realism, audacity and courage, Birkenhead was in his heyday a great athlete and visitors to his estate were exposed to a daily routine of golf, riding and tennis. Like Collins (as we shall see in Chapter 9) Birkenhead loved women, and social drinking – though he seems to have eschewed the bottle for most of the negotiations – and one could well imagine the pair, had Birkenhead been younger at the time, enthusiastically fighting, and biting, for 'a bit of ear'. Birkenhead, like Collins, had an 'X' factor behind the ruthlessness, the patronising, baiting, put-down demeanour which he carried like a weapon. The factor in both cases was patriotism, a patriotism which so often seems to be the Karma of the Anglo-Irish relationship that the one appears as the obverse of the other's medal: freedom-fighter/terrorist; law-giver/oppressor.

Austen Chamberlain afterwards wrote that Birkenhead had managed to 'enter Michael Collins' mind, won his sympathy and secured his confidence. The very fact that to him life was a gallant adventure created a link between him and Michael Collins without which we might never have reached agreement.' It was an extraordinary turn-around for 'Galloper Smith', who as the rising lawyer and Tory politician, F. E. Smith, had acted as Carson's 'galloper' at the great anti-Home Rule rallies in Ulster. Whether he had come to his new position through expediency, because it was the way the compass of empire was now set, or for any other reason, Birkenhead's conversion was so complete that in the Treaty debates on Ireland he became Carson's principal, and most successful, adversary in the House of Lords.

Lloyd George was described by Lord Longford as being able to:

talk to perfection the jargon of nationalist aspiration. . . . He believed in the paramount necessity of settling the Irish question . . . but . . . he was a politician, not a philanthropist or international philosopher . . . His own reputation was endangered anyway by negotiations. It would be blackened inevitably by the consequences of another recourse to war, but it would be destroyed once and for all by any surrender that Parliament judged one of principle, say for Ireland to retain her Republic.

Austen Chamberlain of course was the son of Joseph Chamberlain, a man whose name in Irish history will be forever synonymous with opposition to Irish Home Rule. He had followed in his father's footsteps where Ireland was concerned for much of his political career and even to agree to confer with Irishmen on Dominion Status was a major departure for him. But concession on any form of Irish Republic, whether internally, or Externally Associated, would not have been a mere alteration of policy, it would have been an abandonment of principle. 'And when principle was touched, he would yield to no Irishman in devotion.'[2] However he had one friendly connecting link with the Irish delegation. Arthur Chamberlain, his cousin, was chairman of a firm called Kynoch's, a munitions factory which was the largest employer in the County Wicklow town of Arklow. Arthur had met Griffith as early as 1907 and had impressed the founder of Sinn Fein as having a genuine interest in furthering Irish industrialisation. By the time the negotiations were over 'Austen Chamberlain came to have a great admiration for Arthur Griffith'.[3]

Finally, of the Big Four, there was the Great Warlord himself, W. S. Churchill, the archetypal representative of the Officer and Gentlemen class who could understand and defend war fought along conventional lines with uniformed battalions and thundering heavy guns. Organised slaughter, conducted by people who had the status of belligerents, was one thing. But he could never bring himself to empathise with the ideals and aspirations of peasants who fought out of uniform and shot men in their beds. Yet though the gulf between Chartwell and Woodfield was practically unbridgeable, Churchill's cousin, Shane Leslie,[4] who himself played an honourable and constructive role in trying to bring about a settlement of the Irish issue, has written that without Churchill there could have been no Anglo-Irish Treaty. Certainly it was Churchill who piloted the Treaty through the House at several junctures when storms across the Irish seas seemed certain to wash it away. But much of Churchill's work on the Treaty to which Leslie refers took place away from the conference table, in private meetings with Collins at the home of Sir John Lavery, the painter, in Cromwell Place, and there is, of necessity, an element of speculation surrounding its evaluation. There can be no doubt that he, after Lloyd George, was the man whom the Irish viewed with most suspicion. His espousal of the Auxiliaries, his pre-war Home Rule speeches and his floor-crossing from the Conservative to the Liberal Party in opposition to Balfour and the Free Trade issue were dubious credentials for entrusting him with negotiations with Irish rebels seeking to dismember the British Empire.

The secretaries of the two delegations were almost as interesting as their principals. On the Irish side, Erskine Childers is the best-remembered, as much for the doom which the Treaty brought on him, as for his manifold qualities as a writer, draftsman, and highminded human being – the man who gave England the book *The Riddle of the Sands*, and Ireland the Howth gun-running. But Diarmuid O'Hegarty, Fionan Lynch and John Chartres were outstanding men also. The first two we have met before, helping Collins to revivify the IRB after 1916. Chartres was Collins' protégé. A barrister, Collins had him brought to London from Germany. Republican mythology has subsequently tended to cast him as 'the mystery man of the Treaty',[5] who may have been a British spy.[6]

Chartres came to Dublin in 1916 to do business with the Kynoch factory for the British War Office and apparently, fired with post-1916 Irish nationalism, contacted Griffith in 1917, subsequently becoming an important *Nationality* contributor, writing leaders and articles under the pseudonym HI (Haud Immemor, 'Let them not be forgotten'). It is said that none of the Irish leaders, including de Valera, was aware of his *Who's Who* entry which contained the following:

Chartres, John; son of late Surgeon-Major Chartres, M.D. 8th Hussars . . . m. Anne Vivanti. . . . Educated Wellington College, Germany, University of London; Barrister of Middle Temple (Powell Prizeman in Common Law); Chief of Intelligence Section of War Office Armaments Output Committee, 1915 transferred to Ministry of Munitions same year; organised and for nine years directed the Intelligence Departments of *The Times* . . .

In fact Collins was well aware of the entry and what it portended.[7]

The 'intelligence work' for the Armaments Committee consisted of circulating information concerning its work throughout the War Office and the *Times* job consisted of re-organising the Library. His wife, Madame Annie Vivanti, a Piedmontese, also worked for Sinn Fein. Collins described her as 'this brilliant writer,' who 'has been a great accession to our cause in France as well as her native Italy.'[8] Chartres himself worked for four years with Collins prior to the Treaty:

> Whatever he asked of John Chartres was done without argument or fuss, whether it was to convey a machine gun to Dublin, to obtain plans of certain offices in Dublin Castle, or to live in an hotel resorted to by Auxiliaries for the purpose of picking an acquaintance with them and their friends and acquiring scraps of information for the IRA Intelligence Department . . . John Chartres . . . could be trusted absolutely and whose abilities were as great as they were varied.[9]

In fact the irony of Chartres is that he was unhappy with certain aspects of the Treaty and after Collins' death felt that his successors were lacking in Republican philosophy, so much so that he was dismissed from an Irish Government post in Berlin over a strongly Republican article, published on 27 July 1922, by a contributor to an official journal he was responsible for.[10]

The fact that allegations against Chartres persist to this day indicates something of the intensity of feeling caused by the rifts in Dublin, interacting with the profound philosophical differences which arose amongst the Irish during and after the Treaty negotiations. For example, Moylette, the businessman who helped to initiate the Clune peace attempt, told me once that Childers was 'an improver' sent in by the British to 'improve' a revolutionary situation to the point where it would explode prematurely to the detriment of the revolutionaries. 'They did it all the time in India,' he told me solemnly. Curtis and Childers had been to the same school, Haileybury, and had fought against the Boers. But there, except in ability, the resemblance ended. Curtis stood for the ennobling qualities of the British Empire, Childers for the oppressed struggling to be free. Curtis was the spirit behind the *Round Table* journal, Childers animated the *Irish Bulletin*. The other English Principal Secretary, Tom Jones, animated everything. He was the Cope of the negotiations (Cope himself was also hovering in attendance throughout the talks), the go-between between Lloyd George and Griffith and Collins. He knew Ireland well, having first been Barrington Lecturer travelling the entire thirty-two counties, and subsequently Professor of Economics at Queen's University, Belfast. If it could not be said that he used his knowledge to mislead the Irish delegation, it can certainly be shown that he used it to lead them in the direction Lloyd

George wanted them to go. There was another ally on the British side, tradition, the conscious use of pomp, psychology and setting as an adjunct in negotiation. As they trod the corridors of power in Downing St, or the richly carpeted warrens of the Houses of Parliament, adorned by bookcase and portrait recalling great deeds and personages of the past, the effect on that small handful of Irishmen, contesting with the heads of an empire at the height of its power, must have been awesome. Robert Barton recorded:

It was clear from the start that the English interest was centred on Michael Collins. We Irishmen were nervous and ill at ease, it was our first introduction to Diplomacy. The English were at home and confident in surroundings where they had met and out-manoeuvred or intimidated their opponents in a hundred similar struggles. On the walls hung portraits of past prime ministers, the builders of Britain's Empire. Opposite to me was the portrait of Sir Robert Walpole and beneath it sat Winston Churchill.[11]

Formidable psychological pressures indeed for an Irish delegation that would soon be torn by internal dissension, and weakened by the need to refer and, in Collins' case, to travel incessantly back to Ireland. He above all of them would have to cope with a growing certainty of enmity and suspicion of treachery in Dublin. The British also had a reasonably good grasp of the state of public opinion in Ireland, and of the disunity in the Irish camp, as is made clear by an intelligence report which was circulated to the British negotiators a little after the Conference opened:

The Sinn Fein Party, or moderate section of Dail Eireann, as represented at the Conference by Arthur Griffith, fear that during the 'Truce', British politicians may possibly become acquainted with the real feeling of the Irish people on the Irish question, and realise they are most anxious to have peace. They also fear that British public opinion will assert itself and induce the P.M. to withdraw part of the offer already made.

. . . They will boggle considerably at taking the Oath of Allegiance to the Crown, but will take it if the Government will not give way. They feel that the people as a whole will compel them to accept the compromise.

They fear that we know much more about their domestic troubles than we actually do, as the possession of this information might induce the British Government to reduce the offer to them.

They are doing their utmost to prevent people talking about the many subjects of disunion, as they fear that if it gets to the ears of the Conference it will weaken the hands of their own delegates.[12]

As to the calibre of those delegates, the British reckoned that Collins was 'the strongest personality of the party'. Griffith, 'more clever than de Valera, but not so attractive, is the real power in Sinn Fein'. George Gavan Duffy was 'vain and self-sufficient, likes to hear himself talk'. Eamonn Duggan was 'completely under the influence of Michael Collins', but it was at least conceded that he 'recognises that he is not one of the strong men'. Poor Barton on the other hand was dismissed out of hand for having 'no outstanding quality'.[13]

Barton, so summarily dismissed in this profile, has left a good picture of the opening of the proceedings.[14] Lloyd George began with a general review of the situation, stressing the importance of the negotiations for both countries and emphasising England's desire to conclude a peace treaty, but acknowledging that both sides had limitations beyond which they could not go. 'If these limitations prove insuperable, then the responsibility for failure will rest, not with those at the council table, but with *others*.'[15] From the outset the Prime Minister was using the tactics of dividing the delegation from those at home, the 'others', the impossibilists. Griffith replied, unemotionally, but impressively, that 'England's policy in the past has been to treat Ireland as a conquered and subject country. If there is a change in the policy of subordinating Ireland to English interests, then there appears to be a possibility of peace.'[16] He then went on to follow the line which the Irish delegates hoped to focus on. Barton said:

I was struck at this time and on many others by the adroit manner in which he succeeded in making the discussion pivot upon Ulster and the relationship of the 6 Counties to the rest of Ireland and keeping the relationship of Ireland to the Crown in the background . . . his determination to . . . find the possible points of agreement before we touched at all upon the points of the Crown and allegiance.

Away from the conference table, another pattern, a cleavage in the delegation, was established that day. Barton and Duffy were rebuked by Griffith for 'being too emphatic and creating the wrong atmosphere' in exchanges with Lloyd George, Churchill and Birkenhead over trade and neutrality. Overall however Griffith was pleased and wrote to de Valera:

The meeting today has left on my mind the impression that the English Government is anxious for peace and also that this question of naval defence re the coasts of Ireland is a fixed idea of theirs – that they believe it vital to their lives.

The question of the Crown and Ulster did not arise. When they do, the sailing will be rough. Today they were amiable and both sides were quite polite to each other. The report herewith states what occurred. But, of course, the discussion had very many minor points of interest, amusement and instruction. Ll. G. is a remarkably suave and astute man, but on the whole we have scored today, although the most difficult part has yet to be discussed.

Barton commented on this letter: 'poor Griffith! He always scored when he fell for the baited trap.' Collins did not feel that anyone had a particular advantage. Thinking of his colleagues and opponents in London, his adversaries in Dublin, he wrote, on the night of the first

day of talks, to one man he knew he could trust, the faithful Joe
O'Reilly:

You know the way it is. Either way it will be wrong. Wrong because of what
has come to pass. You might say the trap is sprung. This could be a good
thing. Enough has been said to put behind as waste the strife of other days.
But that's the way it is. Neither I nor anyone else can end or mend it.

At this stage a certain amount of, if not quite speculation, then at
least reconstruction becomes necessary. Between 11 and 24 October
seven Plenary Sessions took place. Somewhere in this period it
appears that Collins decided that he and Griffith would have to go it
alone in making the best deal they could. Dominion status was as far as
he could hope to go. Face-to-face contact with the British leaders had
confirmed this view. He also knew the limits of the support or
direction he could expect from Dublin. A set of letters he wrote[17]
during the talks gives an indication both of his thinking and of the
problems he and Griffith faced in negotiating:

(4 November) . . . Not much achieved, principally because P.M. [Lloyd
George] recognises our over-riding difficulty – Dublin. Plays on that. On the
other hand we fight every word, recognising that to betray ourselves would
mean disaster for us.
    G [Griffith] said, 'What do we accept?'
    Indeed what do we accept? If we accept at all it will be inferred as a gross
betrayal or a similar act of treachery. What have we come for? I ask myself
that question a dozen times a day.

(15 November) . . . I do believe it is L.G.'s ambition to kill two birds with
one stone (G & me). If so, he didn't succeed. I looked at G. and he looked at
me. We nodded and then plunged into the fray. I prefer Birkenhead to anyone
else. He understands and has real insight into our problems – the Dublin one
as much as any other. Dublin is the real problem. They know what we are
doing, but I don't know exactly the state of their activities. No turning back
now.

(Also November, undated) . . . Rather the years that have gone before with
all their attendant risks than the atmosphere that is part of this conference.
Who should one trust – even on my own side of the fence? Griffith. Beyond
Griffith no one. As for C [Childers] it would be better that he led the
delegation. He is sharp to realise how things will have due effect in Dublin –
and acts accordingly.
    To go for a drink is one thing. To be driven to it is another.

(Undated) G and I had a lonely meeting – a house almost empty of customers
– and talked and talked.
    He confessed that he was far from well and asked me to assume leadership
of our party, even if unofficial. He and I recognise that if such a thing were
official it would provide bullets for the unmentionables.
    I agreed G is in poor health and further burdens will do no more than
grossly worsen his condition.

We came to the topic for the thousandth time of the Dublinites. I have often said that Brugha commanded respect and I still say the same. I respect a fighter and B. is one. Only he is misguided. Yet even in enmity he is capable of sincerity – which is more than I can say of the others.

Several writers, amongst them, from opposing perspectives, the uniquely well-placed Lord Longford and Barton, tend to portray the Treaty negotiations as being the inevitable outcome of superior British statecraft. Of course this factor did have a marked bearing on the outcome of the talks, but the two factors above had an even greater bearing. British diplomacy defined the parameters of the agreement. It was Collins' decision to have an agreement at all that prevented the talks from breaking down.[18]

I believe that the record, particularly that concerning Northern Ireland, bears the interpretation that in deciding to conclude a treaty Collins had more radical long-term strategic goals in view than either his colleagues or the British suspected. He decided to go for the maximum degree of independence he could achieve through negotiation and then, once he got control of an army and saw the British safely out of Dublin Castle, he would set about removing any restrictions imposed by the Treaty – by fair means or foul. My reasons for advancing this thesis will become clearer in Chapter 11 on Northern Ireland.

So far as the bulk of the Irish delegation was concerned, a procedural change was proposed from the British side when the seventh session was reached which had the effect of transferring the main business of the negotiations to sub-conferences.[19] The Irish in London and in Dublin reluctantly accepted the proposal although very soon critical voices would be raised against it. Barton said: 'from the moment Griffith and Collins met Lloyd George and Chamberlain alone their power to resist weakened. They became almost pro-British in their arguments with us and Duffy and I often felt that we had to fight them first and the English afterwards.'

In fact Barton, Lord Longford and the rest of the Irish team were misled as to the source of the sub-conference proposal. The real authors of the proposal, Griffith and Collins, were only named[20] when Tom Jones' Diaries were published, long after everyone concerned was dead. By now Collins and Griffith had an interest in common with the British. Both sides wanted to get rid of Childers. Griffith mistrusted him and thought that as an Englishman he had had far too much trust reposed in him. Collins disliked his pre-occupation with detail and his theoretical approach generally. On 13 October 1922 he and Childers were engaged with Churchill and Admiral Beatty on a sub-conference on defence which Childers opened with the remarkable statement: 'Now, Gentlemen, I mean to demonstrate that Ireland is not only no source of danger to England, but from the military standpoint is virtually useless.' Churchill and Beatty exchanged glances and the following dialogue occurred:

Childers: 'Take the matter of Irish bases for English submarine chasers. From the viewpoint of naval expediency Plymouth is a far better base than any port on the Irish coast.'
Beatty: 'You really think so?'
Childers (having stood by the claims of Plymouth): 'For instance (tapping the map) supposing Ireland was not there at all . . .'
Beatty (smiling): 'Ah, but Ireland *is* there . . .'
Churchill (very definitely *not* smiling):'And how many times have we wished she were *not!*'

To compound the emotions generated by these proceedings Collins also discovered that Childers was sending back secret reports to de Valera.[21] Quite possibly the British may have done so too, but certainly they regarded him as a fanatical opponent of any settlement along Dominion lines and a 'renegade Englishman'.[22] And it was true that, insofar as their influence really counted, Worthington Evans and Greenwood were unsympathetic to Irish aspirations. Thereafter Childers was excluded from all but one meeting of the sub-conferences, Barton attended four, and Gavan Duffy three. Collins and Griffith, whether separately or together, attended all twenty-four sub-conferences, various meetings with Birkenhead, Lloyd George and Churchill and at least nine 'informal meetings' with Tom Jones. Thus, however one views their achievement, Michael Collins and Arthur Griffith have to be regarded as the two Irishmen most responsible for contemporary Ireland's political architecture.

As Collins' correspondence shows, he and Griffith felt that they faced worse problems with Dublin than across the conference table. While at this remove it might appear to be axiomatic that a delegation from a small country entering crucial negotiations with the world's largest empire needed all the expert help it could get, de Valera did not act as though this was his view. He behaved as if the paramount requirement was that his needs, and his lines of authority, should be met and obeyed. Within a few days of talks opening he was telling Griffith that he 'would be very glad'[23] if Diarmuid O'Hegarty were sent back to Dublin. 'Please do not keep him an hour longer than is necessary.' Three days later he was writing[24] to make a complaint on Brugha's behalf that military advisers had not been chosen through the Minister for Defence. Collins had brought over Eoin O' Duffy, Emmet Dalton and Ginger O'Connell. Brugha and de Valera were at the time engaged in reorganising the Volunteers for their own purposes, as we shall see shortly, and Brugha had earmarked O'Connell for a role in this process. Two points might be noted here on the question of experts. One, de Valera had already made a suggestion that Stack be invited to London to help the delegation in a wrangle that developed with the British (during the session on 13 October) over the functioning of Sinn Fein courts.[25] Stack had refused to join the delegation in the first place and Collins and Griffith did not take up the suggestion which would have had the effect of installing one of Collins' most bitter critics at the talks in a position of power without responsibility. The second point is that Griffith had already tried, and failed, to get de Valera to send him over an expert of his own choosing, his friend and ally Darrell Figgis.[26]

But while de Valera demanded that the delegates should act in consultation with him he had no compunction in acting without consultation with them, even when they were directly involved in the consequences of his action. On 20 October 1921 he deliberately engaged in a controversy with the Pope in a manner which may have been the final straw in deciding Collins and Griffith to adopt the sub-conference option. The next day, on the morning of the Sixth Plenary Session, 21 October 1921, the text of a telegram from de Valera to Pope Benedict appeared in the press criticising the Pope for remarks he had made in a congratulatory telegram to King George V:

We rejoice at the resumption of the Anglo-Irish negotiations and pray to the Lord with all our heart that He may bless them and grant to your Majesty the great joy and imperishable glory of bringing to an end the agelong dissension.

The King's reply was:

I have received the message of your Holiness with much pleasure and with all my heart I join in your prayer that the Conference . . . may achieve a permanent settlement of the troubles in Ireland and may initiate a new era of peace and happiness for my people.

In his telegram de Valera said:

The people of Ireland . . . are confident that the ambiguities in the reply sent in the name of King George will not mislead you into believing that the troubles are in Ireland, or that the people of Ireland owe allegiance to the British King. The independence of Ireland has been formally proclaimed . . . The trouble is between England and Ireland and its source that rulers of Britain have endeavoured to impose their will upon Ireland.

British press reaction to this communication may be gauged from the leading article in *The Times*; 'Towards the Pope himself it is an act of impertinence; and towards the King it is unmannerly to the point of churlishness.' De Valera conceded to Griffith that his telegram was 'somewhat disconcerting' but he went on to make a remarkable statement:

We cannot expect the Vatican to recognise us, but we have a right to expect that it will not go out of its way to proclaim its denial of recognition as it did by *addressing King George alone* as if he were the common father, so to speak, of both disputant nations . . . the Vatican recognised the struggle between Ireland and Britain as purely a domestic one for King George.[27]

In plain language, de Valera was resurrecting the self-recognition issue and insulting the British King into the bargain at a time when Collins and Griffith were engaged in sensitive negotiations with the British Prime Minister.

When the Sixth Session opened Lloyd George allowed the Irish to make a complaint about British military occupation of County Council offices in Sligo and then launched into a tremendous attack over the telegram, armed with the timely discovery of two major Irish attempts at gun-running. The German police had impounded a shipload of weapons at Hamburg and the British police had aborted a Brugha–Mellowes plot to bring in armaments by an arrest at Cardiff which promised to yield some embarrassing evidence. The Truce was being taken advantage of, Lloyd George claimed, to 'accumulate destructive stores' in a manner which was having a 'serious effect' on Parliament. De Valera's telegram, 'offensive to the King', and the gun-running were combining to 'make our task almost impossible'.

Few negotiators in history can have had a more awkward corner to argue their way out of. But somehow Griffith and Collins managed it. Griffith began[28] by dealing with the arms issue: 'My conception of the Truce does not mean that your military forces should prepare . . . for the end of it and that we should not.' He argued that de Valera was *compelled* to take note of the phrase in the King's message referring to 'troubles in Ireland'. The trouble 'is not a trouble in Ireland, but is one between Ireland and Great Britain'. A sturdy defence for a man who privately disapproved of the telegram.

Collins went one better. He had the audacity to argue that the fault in Cardiff lay in the fact that the British police force 'took advantage of a condition which did not exist prior to the Truce'. Understandably puzzled Lloyd George asked, 'In what way?' To which Collins replied, '*Because our people took less precautions!*' On Hamburg he refused to accept that the ship was destined for Ireland at all because the British had issued a similar false report on 24 April 1918 (the 'German Plot' affair) to the effect that two submarines loaded with arms from Germany were on their way to Ireland. 'Unfortunately there was no truth in that.' But he had the documents in his possession. Somewhat dazedly, one guesses, the British negotiators then turned to a document Collins had earlier submitted on defence. Churchill found it 'of marked ability'. The only problem was that it was also a 'reasoned and deliberate refusal of every article which we made out for the defence of our security'! And so, between the concentration on defence and interpretations of the Truce, the Irish managed to sidle away from the implication of the telegram during that session.

After it, Collins took action on the Hamburg and de Valera fronts.

He sent Sean MacBride[29] to Hamburg. MacBride, who was still in his teens, found the ship under guard, but managed to have the arms transferred to another ship. He told me that he accomplished this near-impossible feat because of anti-British feeling amongst the German police. However Collins had less luck with de Valera. He returned to Dublin after the Sixth Session to ask him to join the delegation, but was refused. The sub-conference procedure was adopted the following week.

Griffith sent de Valera an important report of a conversation with Lloyd George and Chamberlain after the Seventh Plenary Session, on 24 October, in which, interestingly enough, he did not mention the sub-conference arrangement, stressing the significance the British attached to the Crown:

They pressed me to say that I would accept the Crown provided we came to other agreements. It was evident they wanted something to reassure themselves against the Die-hards. I told them I had no authority. If we came to an agreement on all other points I could recommend some form of Association with the Crown . . . I told them the only possibility of Ireland considering Association of any kind with the Crown was in exchange for essential unity – a concession to Ulster . . . They always fell back on the impossibility of peace except on acceptance of the Crown.

After his tête-à-têtes with Lloyd George the contents of the letter can hardly have surprised de Valera but his reply certainly surprised Collins and Griffith. More importantly it angered them. The first paragraph contained the following:

We are all here at one that there can be no question of our asking the Irish people to enter an arrangement which would make them subject to the British King. If war is the alternative, we can only face it, and I think the sooner the other side is made to realise it the better.

It created a scene when it arrived in London. Collins was furious and told the full delegation that he was going home. Dublin was trying to put him in the wrong and 'get me to do the dirty work for them'.[30] Griffith also threatened to go home unless his hands were left free. It was decided to send a letter of protest to de Valera signed by all the delegates. Collins refused to sign this at first, probably because the letter offered de Valera a way out of coming to London 'to do his own dirty work', by suggesting that he should only come over if he could do so without publicity, which was clearly impossible. On Collins' refusal Duffy and Barton also refused to sign, saying that it would appear that everyone except Collins was prepared to give allegiance. 'Eventually,' says Barton, 'Griffith induced Collins to make his protest by signing instead of returning home'.[31] The incredibly hidden nature of the Collins–de Valera power struggle is underscored by Barton's final word on the episode: 'I do not today quite understand what was the cause of Collins' extraordinary outburst.' It was the comment of an honest, intelligent man, albeit something of a political innocent, who through being in prison had been away from the unfolding of most of the drama which followed de Valera's return from America.

When de Valera got the delegation's letter he obviously realised he had gone too far and sent a temporising reply which mollified those in London, but left his position on Association unchanged. The delegates had stated that they considered that his letter was 'tying their hands in discussion and inconsistent with the powers given them on their appointment . . . it is obvious that we could not continue any longer in the conference and should return to Dublin immediately if the powers were withdrawn.'

De Valera replied:

There can be no question of tying the hands of the plenipotentiaries beyond the extent to which they are tied by their original instructions. Of course a Cabinet decision cannot be withdrawn or varied except by the Cabinet as a whole . . . the delegation must understand these memos of mine, except I explicitly state otherwise, are nothing more than an attempt to keep you in touch with the views of the Cabinet here on the various points as they arise. I think it most important that you should be kept aware of these views, for when the delegation returns there will be a question of a Cabinet decision as a policy.

Where at least one of his Cabinet colleagues was concerned Collins had little need of memos to find out how he felt. While the talks were moving exhaustively, and exhaustingly, towards their climax he was involved with Cathal Brugha in no less than three distracting controversies during the month of November. The first was bound up with the question of the Courts and manifestations of Sinn Fein activity during the Truce, in this case the continuation of the IRA practice of collecting levies from the public to maintain the Volunteers. The British had agreed to turn a blind eye to the substance provided the style was changed. 'Levies' would cease; 'collections of money' would continue. However the wording of Brugha's circular instructing officers that 'levies' were now illegal created fears that officers who had been collecting levies hitherto were now considered to have been acting illegally. Mulcahy suggested that retrospective approval be granted. Brugha refused saying:

If the local Officers send us a full list of the monies received and the manner of its expenditure we will credit the subscribers with having contributed to the National Exchequer and take the sums into account as a set-off in calculating the amounts due from them in the case of further taxation, or refunding the amount as may be decided.[32]

Mulcahy then consulted Collins, as Minister of Finance. Collins immediately wrote back vetoing Brugha's scheme: 'It is a proposition which would be wholly impracticable [and] raises a tremendous question, so far as the liability for levies by the Government goes.'[33]

The second incident was a bungled IRA arms raid on Windsor Barracks on 23 November in which an Irish Guardsman, a Sergeant Roche, was found to be implicated. For a moment both Truce and talks trembled. The British thought Collins was responsible. Collins thought Brugha had planned the raid so as to embarrass him. He nearly went berserk and instituted an inquiry which found that Brugha had not being trying to undermine him.

Brugha had given Michael Brennan, OC of the 1st Western Division, £1,000 to buy arms. Brennan selected Michael Hogan and Ned Lynch, who had lived in London for years, to make the purchases. Brennan said:

We knew there were many agents in London who would sell anything for cash and the only problem was how to get in touch with them. Lynch was certain he could make the necessary contacts through his acquaintances . . . In justice to Cathal Brugha . . . there wasn't even a suggestion of getting arms anywhere except by purchase.[34]

Hogan and Lynch bumped into Roche, a fellow Clare man, in a pub. He offered to place the resources of Windsor Barracks at their disposal. Scotland Yard intervened and in Brennan's words: 'my first news of their scheme was the newspaper reports of their arrest. Neither Brugha nor I had any knowledge of the scheme to get the arms of a military barracks . . .' On hearing this Collins cooled down. Not only did he succeed in convincing the British that no one except those directly involved in the raid knew about it beforehand, he subsequently managed to secure the release of Hogan, Lynch and Roche. The raid, however, had occurred on the eve of the last act in a long-running plot by de Valera and Brugha[35] to undermine the influence Collins exercised on the Army through the IRB, going back to the previous March. Having tried to tighten his hold on the Army by every means possible, de Valera finally attempted a 'surrender and re-grant' policy towards both officers and men that brought him into direct conflict with the GHQ staff on 25 November.

Prior to this there had been friction over Brugha's attempt to have Austin Stack appointed Deputy Chief of Staff. Mulcahy wrote on 1 November 1921 that he would take no responsibility for 'any position' if Stack was appointed Deputy Chief of Staff. Mulcahy admired Collins whom he regarded as the 'outstanding leader with all the qualifications for the only system of war which could beat the British' and as Chief of Staff, and he had helped to blunt Brugha's attacks on Collins. As a result Brugha made two unsuccessful attempts during the Truce to sack Mulcahy using issues such as the Robbie affair and the O'Connell appointment.

De Valera did not study Machiavelli merely for enjoyment. He was adept at concealing his moves from public view – there is no mention of the O'Connell and New Army controversies in his authorised biography – and the Brugha–Stack animosity to Collins was so well-established as to be accepted as part of the normal order of things so far as the senior members of the IRA and IRB were concerned.

To judge from various anecdotes preserved in the Collins family,[36] Collins had a great respect for de Valera, deriving in part from his respect for teachers going back to his Denis Lyons days and in part from the soldier's respect for authority. He had certainly shown this earlier in the year, in March, when the curtain went up on the first act of the Army reorganisation drama, the taking over of Army control by the Dail. Without Collins' influence the IRB would never have amended its Constitution so as to cede to the Dail the Government powers of the Supreme Council. This meant in effect that Collins as President of the IRB handed over power to de Valera. Now, in November, as the battle for the Treaty raged in London, de Valera persuaded the Dail to agree to a scheme of offering all officers fresh commissions subject to them and their men taking an oath of loyalty to the Dail.

The real reason for reorganising the 'New Army' at that juncture was obscured by pointing out that 25 November was 'the anniversary of the founding of the Volunteer force in 1913'. However, though Collins undoubtedly respected de Valera and found him, in Mulcahy's term, 'disarming', there was a limit to how disarming he would allow him to be. He wrote to Mulcahy on 23 November in terms which both demonstrate the power he could exert when he wished and the fact that he did keep his IRB colleagues generally informed throughout the Treaty negotiations:

I have heard from Mr Griffith that the Cabinet has been summoned for the 25th to meet the GHQ Staff of the Old Army (it reminds me of Napoleon). The members of the Cabinet at present in London have been asked to be present. I think *we ought to have a meeting of the GHQ Staff very early Friday morning* [author's italics]. I would strongly suggest that we should have associated at that meeting Directors of the Staff who operated for a certain time in the Old Army. I mean Directors who really did operate, not nominal Directors . . . Staines, Hegarty . . . wide knowledge of the Staff and the things that were done during the days when it was hard work to organise and to run the Old Army

Enclosed I am sending you a copy of a letter which was written yesterday by Mr Griffith [Giving details of Lloyd George's and Birkenhead's reception of the Irish proposals for a Treaty] to the President. You will *treat this in the usual fashion.*[37]

The fruits of that letter were seen two days later. Mulcahy had proposed that before the 'Old Army' was disbanded the GHQ staff should be brought in, thanked for their past services, and told what was in prospect. This ceremony was delayed for several hours while Collins and Griffith explained to the Cabinet in Dublin what was on the table in London. They had actually left on the tiring boat and train journey back to London when de Valera called in the waiting officers. He had suggested to Mulcahy that he could have his choice for Deputy Chief of Staff, Eoin O'Duffy, provided that Stack also be appointed so as to be 'Brugha's ghost on the staff'. But not one member of the GHQ staff found the reshuffling and the 'New Army' proposals acceptable. Ginger O'Connell summed up the way he and his colleagues felt. They were he said 'a band of brothers'. He thought no change was necessary. Neither did Eoin O'Duffy who said he found the proposals personally insulting. De Valera realised he was being checkmated. Collins might not be present in the room, but his influence was. The President interrupted O'Duffy: 'Rising excitedly, he pushed away the table in front of him and, half screaming, half-shouting said: "Ye may mutiny if you like, but Ireland will give me another army," and dismissed them all from his sight.'[38] But even a man with de Valera's ego had to acknowledge, if only to himself, that with the Truce hanging in the balance, it would be lunacy to proceed with an attempt to reorganise the GHQ staff against its wishes. He let it be known a few days later that there would be no 'New Army', but that the new commissions should be accepted. This took the heat out of the army controversy, but it can have done little to cool Collins' suspicions of his leader. These Dublin-based pressures playing about Collins and Griffith may fairly be regarded as part of the 'why' of signing the Treaty, the text of which can be examined in the appendix. An insight into the 'how' may be gained from the sonorous language of a British memorandum[39] of 27 October 1921:

1. THE CROWN . . . The Crown is the symbol of all that keeps the nations of the Empire together. It is the keystone of the arch in law as well as in sentiment . . . The British Government must know definitely whether or not the Irish Delegates are prepared that Ireland should maintain its ancient allegiance to the Throne, not as a state subordinate to Great Britain, but as one of the Nations of the Commonwealth, in close association with the Realm of England, Scotland and Wales.
2. COMMON CITIZENSHIP . . . No man can be a subject of two States. He must be either a subject of the King or an alien, and the question no more admits of an equivocal answer than whether he is alive or dead. The essence of common citizenship is that all who enjoy it are at peace or at war together . . . it is not compatible with neutrality in any form . . . His Majesty's Government must therefore know whether or not the Irish Delegates will acknowledge this common citizenship and the full partnership in the fortunes of the fraternity of nations known as the British Empire which it entails.
3. DEFENCE . . . Of supreme importance . . . Ireland will have no Navy

and no Air Force, and it is manifest that Great Britain, to whom will belong the vital task of Naval and Air Defence, must have, for that definite and limited purpose, and by agreement beforehand, such facilities of access and the like as are required for the competent discharge of that task.

4. TRADE & COMMERCE . . . Neither side shall impose protective duties or other restrictions upon the flow of transport, trade and commerce between all parts of these islands. [The British sought a 'definite assurance' on this point.]

5. FINANCE . . . Ireland shall assume responsibility for a share of the present debt of the United Kingdom and of the liability for pensions arising out of the Great War.

The Irish reply, dated 29 October, 'accepted the principle that the naval and air defence of the Irish coasts would be a matter of common concern to Ireland and to the British Commonwealth'.[40] This was in line with de Valera's thinking on such matters as revealed in his controversial Cuban interview with the *Westminster Gazette*. But he made no comment on defence, concentrating instead on the proposal in the final paragraph of the reply from the Irish delegation which became known as 'The Chartres Crown':

The unimpaired unity of Ireland is a condition precedent to the conclusion of a Treaty of Association between Ireland and the Nations of the British Commonwealth. Subject to this, and . . . agreements on . . . other issues the Irish Delegates are prepared to recommend that the elected Government of a free and undivided Ireland, secured in absolute and unfettered possession of all legislative and executive authority, should, for the purposes of the association recognise the Crown as symbol and accepted head of the combination of signatory states.

De Valera wrote to Griffith: 'We are not quite certain what exactly the last three lines may involve, and accordingly refrain from making any comment. You know the views here from my despatch No. 7.' This was the letter which had provoked the all-delegation complaint about the attempt to curtail their powers. So with a stroke of the pen de Valera had both managed to maintain his hard-line position without drawing any further remonstrance from the delegation and, as Collins suspected, stitched it into the record that, whatever anyone else might commit themselves to, *he* was not countenancing any retreat from the Republic.

It is important to remember that throughout this period, as Longford notes,[41] there was serious discontent in the pro-Unionist, Die-hard, or extreme right-wing, section of the Conservative party, which was appalled at the prospect of the Government talking to Sinn Fein and had a motion of censure down for debate in the House of Commons on 31 October 1921, the night before Collins and Griffith were unexpectedly invited to meet Lloyd George at Churchill's house at 9.30 pm.[42] Longford describes the talk which ensued as one of the most important of the entire negotiation; 'some would say the most important in the whole negotiation'. It was explained that the Prime Minister was preparing his speech for the Die-hards and wanted to elucidate the Irish reply of the previous day to the British proposals. At Churchill's house the British immediately suggested a division of forces.

Accordingly Griffith had 'about three-quarters of an hour' with Lloyd George upstairs; downstairs Birkenhead and Churchill saw Collins alone and subsequently all five talked together. One historian has described the evening as 'something of a turning point for Collins'.[43] What exactly was said we shall never know, but the upshot of the night, in Griffith's words, was that Lloyd George said 'the bias of his speech had to be peace or war with Ireland'.[44] If Griffith would give him 'personal assurances' on the Crown, *free partnership* with the British Empire and coastal naval facilities he would 'smite the Die-hards' and would 'fight on the Ulster matter to secure essential unity'. Lloyd George duly smote the Die-hards, the censure motion was easily defeated and Griffith then moved to give form to the assurances Lloyd George sought. He called a meeting of the delegates and told them he intended to send the Prime Minister a letter which contained the following:

Provided I was otherwise satisfied I was prepared to recommend a recognition of the Crown . . . the formula to be arrived at in a similar discussion at a later stage . . . I similarly agreed to recommend free partnership with the British Commonwealth, the formula . . . to be arrived at . . . later . . . the British Navy should be afforded facilities for coastal defence . . . mutual obligations our common security . . . this attitude of mine conditional on the recognition of the essential unity of Ireland . . . on no account would I recommend any association with the Crown of Empire, if the unity of Ireland were denied in word or fact.

Griffith made the significant observation that he intended the letter to be a personal one 'because he was very anxious to shield Collins from attacks that might be made on him at home as a result of its being sent'.[45] The letter caused uproar. Barton did not know whether Collins had seen the letter before the rest of the delegation but he was suspicious and angry. 'It was in our opinion stating a false case. Going much further than either we or the Cabinet at home were prepared to go.'[46] After 'ugly scenes', in which Griffith is said to have used some 'very abusive language', Duffy, Barton and Childers 'decided that in no circumstances would we permit this letter to be sent as a personal letter, or in the form submitted to us'.[47] Duffy got up specially early the next morning to prepare a memo to Griffith expressing the dissidents' objections:

That letter will necessarily be read by Lloyd George as indicating a weakening from the last memorandum of the delegates [that of 29 October]. We had in the last memorandum very carefully limited the recognition of the British Crown that we would recommend, your letter abandons that nor have we yet made any fight at the Conference against entertaining it.[48]

Duffy, who obviously did not realise that the sub-conference had become permanent, went on to argue that until they got an answer from Lloyd George to their memorandum it was wrong to send him a letter, very likely for use in Washington as well as with Craig and company, which 'cuts up that memorandum'. Griffith bowed to the pressure; the letter was re-drafted and signed by Griffith as Chairman. Then, on the morning of 2 November, Collins and Griffith took the letter down to the House of Lords where they met Birkenhead, who tried without success to get the Irish to accept alterations in the Crown and Empire references. Another conference on the document took place in Downing St that afternoon, involving Collins and Griffith, Lloyd George, Chamberlain and Birkenhead. Further changes were proposed from the British side and Collins and Griffith argued with their colleagues until these were accepted 'very reluctantly' and, around midnight, the final draft was sent to Downing St. It now contained this passage:

I was prepared to recommend a free partnership of Ireland with the other States associated within the British Commonwealth, the formula defining the partnership to be arrived at in a later discussion. I was, on the same condition, prepared to recommend that Ireland should consent to a recognition of the Crown as head of the proposed association of free States.

This was of course contingent on 'essential unity' being secured. But 'within the British Commonwealth', went further than the draft that the delegates had objected to in the first place. That had merely recognised a partnership 'with the British Commonwealth'. Within meant *within the British Empire*. Despite Duffy's legalism, confusion and mistrust, arising out of the problems with Dublin, had done their work. Barton commented afterwards: 'In my opinion, these Conferences between the English and Griffith and Collins on 30 October, 1 November and 2 November sealed the doom of the Republic.'[49] The Republic was probably doomed from the moment de Valera accepted the invitation to send Barton and the others to London. But Barton would have felt confirmed in his view, had one other detail been known to him at the time he was arguing with Griffith. He thought, as did Childers and Duffy, that Griffith had drafted the 'assurances' letter in the first place, which was bad enough. But had they known that it was, in fact, drawn up by Tom Jones[50] before Collins and Griffith even met Lloyd George in Churchill's home they would probably have gone home there and then. In fact Collins and Griffith were well aware of the agenda *before* it was called. The letter may be seen as a by-product of the sub-conference methodology. It eventually proved to be the hinge on which the entire Treaty swung, and its genesis is therefore of historic importance. Significantly, there is no record of any meeting with Tom Jones entered in the official log of 'Informal Meetings with the Cabinet Secretary' until 8 November, almost two weeks after he gave Griffith and Collins the draft. Collins and Griffith did not falsify the record, they simply did not record all of it. The Treaty could well have been voted down if the full circumstances of the letter and the sub-conferences were known.[51] The reason that Jones' handing over of the missive to Collins and Griffith does not appear in the listing of sub-conferences is that he did not give it to them – he passed it over to Duggan. Most writers on the Treaty tend to write Duggan off as a mere cipher of Collins' but in the background he did what he had done in Ireland, liaison work. Cope, who does not figure in the sub-conferences either, also worked hard behind the scenes, only occasionally showing up – albeit as a figure of influence – in Longford's pages, for instance. Sturgis in his diaries, however, recorded during the negotiations that the word from London concerning 'Andy' indicated that he was doing Trojan work, but he does not indicate its nature. There was a great deal more going on in London than Brugha, de Valera or Stack knew.

The letter, in Jones' writing and initialled by him read as follows:

Dear P.M.,
You can appreciate the difficulty of conducting negotiations by means of written documents, which in the event of a breakdown, might be made public and be used by one side against the other. For that reason it is natural that the formal reply which we have sent you today may seem to be couched in terms of such diplomatic caution, as to conceal our genuine desire for peace. We therefore give you this personal assurance that in essence the meaning of our reply is that we are prepared to be free partners in the British Commonwealth, to recognise the golden limit [?link] of Crown as its head and to have unity of control in all matters of the naval defence of these islands. All this to be subject to our securing the unity of Ireland as a condition precedent or incorporated in whatever Treaty is made.

At its head Jones had written 'Draft of private letter of assurance which I suggested to Mr Duggan that Arthur Griffith might give to Prime Minister. T.J.'. By coincidence I happened to read the document an hour or so before I lunched with a friend in the House of Lords. As I walked down the corridors, thinking of Griffith and Collins being shown into Birkenhead's room to argue over the letter, Barton's description of the British at the start of the talks seemed particularly apt, 'at home and confident in surroundings where they had met and outmanoeuvred or intimidated their opponents in a hundred similar struggles'.

But, for all its appositeness, Barton's comment only illuminates part of the picture. Incontestably Collins wanted the best deal he could get for Ireland. He did not trust Lloyd George or his associates, as a letter of his makes clear:

This is a real nest of singing birds. They chirrup mightily one to the other – and there's the falseness of it all, because not one trusts the other. Lloyd George's attitude I find to be particularly obnoxious. He is all comradely – all craft and wiliness – all arm around shoulder – all the old friends' act. Not long ago he would joyfully have had me at the rope's end. He thinks that the past is all washed out now – but that's to my face. What he thinks behind my back makes me sick at the thought of it.[52]

But, as he said to C. P. Scott, whom Lloyd George had sent along to try to soften him up two days before the meeting in Churchill's home, 'surely it would be a discredit to us all if after coming together in conference we did not manage to agree.'[53] Hence the willingness to give Lloyd George the 'assurances' letter. And hence Griffith's willingness to be accommodating in the next decisive step of the Die-hards saga, the Unionist Party Conference at Liverpool on 17 November 1921. Collins and Griffith came to the conclusion that decisions had to be taken and that it was up to them to take them. Here is the political balance sheet which both men drew up in London:

M.C.: What will be the outcome if the present talks break down. 1, a declaration of war by the British. 2, Cessation of hostilities on our part. We have, mistakenly, put all our cards on the table; we have laid ourselves open to the British. 3, Perhaps a continuation of efforts by the British to find a solution. This because world opinion is with us – proving that the British dare not engage us in full scale war.

Comment by Griffith: No declaration of war by the British. Point number three is the most likely.

M.C.: How best to reconcile our ideas with the fixed ideas at present held by certain members of the Cabinet? I will not agree to anything which threatens to plunge the people of Ireland into a war – not without their authority. Still less do I agree to being dictated to by those not embroiled in these negotiations . . . If they are not in agreement with the steps we are taking, and hope to take, why then did they themselves not consider their own presence here in London? Example: Brugha refused to be a member of the delegation.

Comment by Griffith: It is not so much a question of who dictating to whom. It is a question of powers invested in us as representatives of our country. Sooner or later a decision will have to be made.

Comment by Collins: Exactly. What are our powers? Are we to commit our country one way or the other, yet without authority to do so?

M.C.: The advantages of Dominion status to us, as a *stepping stone* [author's italics] to complete independence are immeasurable.

Comment by Griffith: Agreed, but with one question. How far can we trust the signatures of the British delegation in this matter? Once signed we are committed. But are they?

M.C.: No we are not committed – not until both the Dail and Westminster ratify whatever agreement is made.

Comment by Griffith: Ratification by the Dail means what precisely? That a certain amount of power is still in the hands of those we know will be against anything which treats of Empire status.

M.C.: I agree in part to the above. Supposing, however, we were to go back to Dublin tomorrow with a document which gave us a Republic. Would such a document find favour with everyone? I doubt it.

Comment by Griffith: So do I. But sooner or later a decision will have to be made and we shall have to make it – whatever our position and authority.[54]

Three points about that exchange of views are worth noting. One, Collins, the man who more than any other impelled his country into war, is now setting his face against a repetition of that course, despite de Valera's 'we can only face it'. Collins knew with certainty, however, that he would be a marked man, his intelligence service was laid bare and armaments to carry on the fight were in very short supply as the Italian episode demonstrated. Sean MacEoin reckoned that he now had 4,000 men, but only one rifle for every fifty men, about enough ammunition to keep them supplied for 'about fifty minutes per rifle'.[55] Though they inclined to the third option, Collins and Griffith felt that if they could rely on their British counterparts, the way forward was onto Collins' 'stepping stone'. It might carry them to Ulster which, combined with their uncertainty about Dublin, is inextricably bound up in the next decisive step taken in the treaty negotiations where once again Tom Jones enters the picture.

For a brief moment after Griffith had managed to get Jones' brainchild – a brainchild that was certainly well baptised by Lloyd George before Duggan saw it – returned to the British under the guise of his own 'assurances' letter, all was sweetness and light. Collins and Griffith paid another visit to the House of Lords at Birkenhead's invitation where they were informed that the letter was greatly appreciated as a 'document upon which they could deal with Craig'.[56] So much so that in fact the British were prepared to resign if Ulster proved unreasonable and, as Griffith wrote to de Valera, in such a case 'no English Government is capable of formation on a war policy against Ireland'. He went on:

The tactical course I have followed has been to throw the question of Ulster against the questions of Association and the Crown. This is now the position. The British Government is up against Ulster and we, for the moment, are standing aside. If they secure 'Ulster's' consent we shall have gained essential unity and the difficulty we shall be up against will be the formula of association and recognition. You will observe my wording, which they accept, is consistent with external association and external recognition.[57]

But, as readers will remember, Griffith's phrase in his letter to Lloyd George, which was the basis for this hopeful analysis, spoke of association 'within the British Commonwealth' which was hardly 'consistent' with external association. More inconsistencies showed up in the next five days. Carson and Bonar Law were not dissuaded from opposition and Craig, who was continually in touch with his 'Tudor' advisers, refused to budge. He had his Six-County area. Dublin and London could come to any arrangement they wished, so long as they left him out of it. Thus the Prime Minister was confronted not only with an impasse in the Irish negotiations but with his own promise to resign. He escaped from his dilemma with a classical piece of Welsh wizardry. Jones met Collins and Griffith at an 'informal meeting' in the Grosvenor Hotel to tell them that unless the Ulster Government accepted Lloyd George's proposal that they hold their Six-County area, but under an All-Ireland Parliament, he would resign and undoubtedly be replaced by a militarist government, hostile to Ireland. Then, giving it as his own idea, Jones suggested the following:

Supposing the Twenty-Six Counties of the South were to be given all the powers under discussion, and suppose Ulster were to be not only restricted to existing powers, but also submitted to a Boundary Commission set up to 'delimit' her area? How would that strike them?[58]

It struck them that, as Griffith wrote to de Valera next day, it would give them 'most of Tyrone and Fermanagh, and part of Armagh, Londonderry, Down etc.' However he adopted the attitude that it was 'their look-out for the moment'. But Jones obviously gathered from his meeting that there was some enthusiasm for the Boundary Commission in the Irish camp because he returned the next day with a further gloss on the idea. Craig 'had become far more intractable as a result of certain interviews in London.'[59] But rather than go out of office, if Ulster refused the Boundary Commission, as Jones and the Irish agreed they probably would, and so expose beloved Ireland to the horrors of Bonar Law, Lloyd George would stay in office and call a full Cabinet meeting to get the backing he would need in order to rally public opinion against Ulster, which would be made to appear 'utterly unreasonable in insisting [on coercing] areas that wished to get out'.[60]

Jones expressly asked if the delegation would support such a move.

Griffith replied that the proposal would be a British, not an Irish one and was therefore not binding, but said 'we realised its value as a tactical manoeuvre and if Lloyd George made it we would not queer his position'.[61] The big Unionist Conference in Liverpool was approaching and Lloyd George wanted to make sure that no one else queered it either, before that date. He had a voluminous correspondence with Craig which yielded one important proposal from the Ulster man on 11 November, as a 'lesser evil than being included in an all-Ireland Parliament'[62] namely that the Northern state should have the same powers *as those proposed for the South*. In effect, though the term was not used, 'They proposed Ulster should be formed into a Dominion and pay none except voluntary contribution to England.'[63] Dominion status was certainly beginning to peep above the negotiating horizon. Significantly Lloyd George showed this letter to Griffith at a meeting on 12 November in Sir Philip Sassoon's house in Park Lane at which he again sought and received reassurances that Griffith would not repudiate him if he proceeded according to the Jones formula, which now seemed even more coercive of the Ulstermen through stipulating that the part that remained after the Boundary Commission had done its work would have to 'bear the same taxation as England'.

Taken together with the assurances given by Griffith in his earlier letter, and on the night he talked with Lloyd George in Churchill's house, after Jones had revealed what was on the table, we have now come to the real turning point in the whole Treaty negotiation saga. For Lloyd George interpreted the assurances as meaning that if he confronted Ulster along the lines suggested, Griffith as a quid pro quo would not subsequently break off the negotiations on Ulster. Jones drew up a memorandum on the British proposals which he showed to Griffith the following evening, appropriately enough, the 13th. Griffith is thought not to have given them much attention on that occasion. He 'briefly indicated his assent'[64] to the memo's contents. Collins was not present at the time, but the overriding shared belief of Collins and Griffith that they could not look to Dublin for guidance and that it was up to them to make a settlement, coupled with the Boundary Commission proposal, meant that in practice from then on the Irish delegation could not break on Ulster. If they did so Griffith, though he wrote nothing down himself, could be accused of reneging on written proposals. Longford holds that in this phase of the negotiations the Irish were manoeuvred towards committing themselves into giving partition *de jure* as well as *de facto* status. Were they in fact manoeuvred, one wonders, or did they bow to the inevitable, as they saw it, and, in a sense, connive at a set-up? In any event Chamberlain and the other Unionist leaders accepted Lloyd George's interpretation and, thus fortified, went on to defeat the Die-hards at

Liverpool. The Conference turned down Colonel Gretton's motion of censure – for parleying with Sinn Fein at all – in favour of an amendment which said:

That this Conference expresses its earnest hope that consistent with the supremacy of the Crown, the security of the Empire and the pledges given to Ulster and the safeguarding of the interests of the minority in the South of Ireland, a solution of the Irish difficulties may be found in the Conference now in progress which will bring peace to Great Britain and Ireland, and strength to the Empire.

And so the talks went on. Was there ever any possibility of their conceding to Irish nationalists either a united Ireland or one delimited by a Boundary Commission, as Jones and Lloyd George indicated? Almost none, I should say. The strength of Unionist sentiment in England at the time may be gauged from three happenings in the week that Griffith was manoeuvred into or, possibly, acquiesced in giving his assurances to Lloyd George.

In a secret meeting Birkenhead induced the Liverpool Unionist leader, Salvidge,[65] to sponsor the amendment which defeated Gretton, by assuring him that 'a settlement was almost reached' which would involve no coercion of Ulster if she refused to co-operate in Dominion Home Rule, but which would guarantee the Crown, British naval interests and keep Ireland within the Empire.

Secondly, neither Lloyd George's promises to resign nor talk of Cabinet backing for a 'strong position' against the Ulstermen were practical politics. The 'full Cabinet meeting' which Jones spoke to Griffith about was held on 10 November. The record contains no hint whatever that he ever contemplated resignation. But what it does say is that [author's italics] *'emphasis was laid upon the importance of exercising the greatest patience in the conduct of the negotiations with the Cabinet of Northern Ireland'.*[66]

Thirdly, very powerful figures in decision-taking England were actively conniving at steps to ensure that the Six Counties would be strong enough militarily to frustrate any moves towards a united Ireland. On the very day of the Liverpool Conference the *Irish Bulletin* carried a report of a highly significant circular issued by Colonel Wickham to senior officers of the Ulster Special Constabulary.

Away from the rarefied atmosphere of Cabinet and Conference, the circular dealt with the unacknowledged, but all too real interaction of the supposedly illegal loyalist para-militaries of Northern Ireland with the forces of 'law and order' that set off the historical chain-reaction which in our day led, amongst other things, to the formation of the Provisional IRA. It said:

Owing to the number of reports which have been received as to the growth of unauthorised loyalist defence forces, the government have under consideration the desirability of obtaining the services of the best elements of these organisations.

They have decided that the scheme most likely to meet the situation would be to enrol all who volunteer and are considerable in Class C of the USC and to form them into regular military units . . .

The force is intended to be a military one only, to be called out in grave emergency to act in a military capacity. They will not of necessity be utilised for local defence but may be drafted to any theatres of operation within the Six Counties. It is not intended that this force should interfere with or replace Class B Special Constabulary who remain as a local force for local protection . . .

The 'C' scheme therefore applies mostly to towns and cities where there is a population surplus to 'B' requirements. The most suitable class for this force are ex-soldiers . . . what is required is to ensure that every unit recommended for formation can be constituted from a reliable section of the population.

The circular, which was of course yet another illustration of the doctrine 'Ulster will fight and Ulster will be right', was a clear breach of the Truce. The seriousness of the incident, coming at a time of delicately poised negotiations, may be gauged from Sir John Anderson's wire to the Chief Secretary:

Matter seems to me most serious. Wickham, while an officer of the Imperial Government, has not only constituted himself the instrument of another authority in a most delicate matter involving big political issues but has done so in terms which suggest that in so acting he was carrying out instructions of the Government which employed him. I cannot understand how any British officer could get into such a position and can only suppose that he received assurances on which he relied that the action he was taking would not be disapproved.[67]

Wickham was in fact acting on instructions from Sir Henry Wilson and Worthington Evans. Despite a flurry of indignation and dis- avowal from Lloyd George, Wickham went on to become head of a new force recommended by Wilson, The Royal Ulster Constabulary, partly because the RIC was deemed to contain too many Catholics.[68] Worthington Evans was one of those who counselled 'patience' with the 'Ulster Government' at the Cabinet meeting of 10 November. The meeting expressed 'satisfaction with the results which had been achieved in the negotiations with Sinn Fein'. But there was very little 'satisfaction' on the Sinn Fein side. The one limited area in which progress was made lay in quelling some Southern Unionist fears. On the eve of the Liverpool Conference, Griffith saw a delegation consisting of Lord Midleton, Dr Barnard and Andrew Jameson. He gave them assurances on land purchase and income tax and on the provision of a Senate in the proposed Irish Parliament to allow their voices to be heard. Though he would not discuss Ulster with them, Griffith told de Valera 'we parted on cordial terms'.[69] But there was little cordiality and much bickering and suspicion in the Irish camp. Griffith's health was not good. As the talks neared their end Collins wrote: 'More and more responsibility rests with me. What responsibility it is.'[70]

He had just come through an especially bad patch. In Dublin he was faced with the 'New Army' manoeuvre, and in London there had been a furious row and Duffy had been sent home to complain about the way the leaders of the delegation were conducting the negotiations. The Irish had had to put on paper their reply to the British proposals, which were now based on Dominion status within the Empire, on the lines of Canada, with an Oath of Allegiance to the King and guarantees on defence.

A memorandum by Childers had been submitted to Collins and Griffith in Barton's name, 'owing to the animosity which Mr Griffith had shown to any proposals put forward by Childers'.[71] On 22 November the whole delegation met, reworked the Barton–Childers formula and sent it to the British, calling it a 'Memorandum by the Irish Representatives'.

This 'Memorandum', the first formal statement of the Irish claim to be submitted, reflected the ambiguity of the position of the Six Counties in its preamble which stated that the proposals were put forward 'upon the *assumption* that the essential unity of Ireland is maintained'. Legislative and executive authority were to be derived 'exclusively from the Elected Representatives of the Irish people'. Ireland would agree to be 'associated with the British Commonwealth for all purposes of common concern, including defence, peace, war, and political treaties; and to recognise the British Crown as Head of the Association.' To mark that recognition Ireland proposed to make an annual contribution to the King's personal revenue.

Barton described the British as being 'bitterly disappointed' with this document and as having 'the dogs of war ready to unleash' as a result.[72] That was their public face; privately they unleashed Jones and somehow yet another conference was arranged to bridge the divide between the British minimum requirement of Dominion status and the Irish demand for External Association. This meeting, on the 23rd, at Downing St, resulted in a further conference being arranged with Birkenhead, Collins and Griffith on the basis of the 2 November letter of assurances from Griffith, ostensibly to prevent what Lloyd George called 'the tragedy' of a break-up 'on any verbal or technical misunderstanding'. But by so limiting the conversation the parties involved managed to exclude the voice of de Valera – Barton, who was present at the Downing St meeting. Birkenhead's suggestion that they bring a constitutional lawyer with them meant that Chartres, not Childers, accompanied Collins and Griffith to the meeting, in Birkenhead's room in the House of Lords on 24 November.

Chartres argued that in Ireland the Crown would not function, but that externally it would be recognised as the head of the aggregate of states. The Irish required a symbolism acceptable to themselves. However Birkenhead stipulated that the British also had their own symbolism. It was made clear that failure to recognise the Crown would mean war. Birkenhead did come to one momentous agreement on nomenclature with Griffith. Griffith proposed that the British might prefer to translate *Saorstat Eireann* as 'Free State', rather than as 'Republic'. Birkenhead agreed that the title Free State would go into the Treaty.

External Association therefore had been fully aired with the British and had been found unacceptable to them. What next for Collins and Griffith? They decided to return to Dublin to consult their Cabinet colleagues. All the Cabinet could come up with was to approve unanimously that Ireland 'should recognise the British Crown for the purposes of Association, as symbol and accepted head of the combination of associated states', and to repeat the offer of an annual subscription to the civil list. In the de Valera camp Childers held that Dominion status on the Canadian model was out because in Canada, though the law said otherwise, the fact was that distance made Canada independent of her nominal subordination to England. In Ireland the law would be the fact because of Ireland's proximity to England. Griffith and Collins both vigorously argued this contention but, having handed in Dublin's reiteration of External Association on Monday, 22 November 1922, and, predictably, found it unacceptable to the British, they were favourably inclined towards a compromise proposal which emanated from Lloyd George following upon the rejection, but which may have initially come from Collins.

Throughout the negotiations, Collins had been studying authorities on Dominion status: Duncan Hall, Berridale Keith, Josiah Wedgwood and Jan Smuts (probably under the tutelage of Crompton Llewelyn Davies). To him Dominion status represented the only possibility of compromise between the Crown and the Republic. He developed his ideas in a 'personal and unofficial memorandum' that in view of the Lloyd George offer now appears highly significant. Collins' memorandum said:

The Colonies as full-grown children are restive under any appearance of parental restraint, though willing to co-operate with the parent on an equal footing in all family affairs. Ireland, as a separate nation, would be also restive under control from the neighbouring nation, but equally willing to co-operate in free association on all matters . . . of common concern . . .

The problem on both sides can only be solved by recognising without limitation the complete independence of the several countries, and only on that basis can they all be associated by ties of co-operation and friendship. The only association which it will be for Ireland to enter will be based, not on the present technical legal status of the Dominions, but on the real position they claim, and have in fact secured.

It is essential that the *de facto* position should be recognised *de jure*, and that all its implications as regards sovereignty, allegiance and constitutional independence should be acknowledged. An association on the foregoing conditions would be a novelty in the world. But the world is looking for such a development.

Chamberlain's comment on this memorandum to Birkenhead was: 'extraordinarily interesting though sometimes perverse and sometime Utopian. Who outside our six [the British delegation] would guess the name of the writer?'[73]

However if Collins' Dominion status ideas were merely 'perverse' to Chamberlain, to Lloyd George de Valera's External Association proposal was 'impossible'. He said that 'any British Government that attempted to propose to the British people the abrogation of the Crown would be smashed to atoms'. But on Dominion status he introduced a most important 'sweetener'. The Irish could insert in the Treaty 'any phrase they liked which would ensure that the position of the Crown in Ireland should be no more in practice than it was in Canada or in any other Dominion'. As Griffith wrote to de Valera the next day this effectively 'knocked out my argument on the document they sent in – that the Crown in the Dominions was merely a symbol but that in Ireland it would be a reality'.[74] That offer in fact became the cornerstone of all subsequent Irish Dominion constitutional advancement.

The following day an important meeting was held in Downing St, to which Duggan was brought, but not Barton. The Downing St meeting confirmed the Chequers offer about the Canadian analogy in the Treaty and came to one crucial decision, namely that Griffith would get the final draft of the British proposals before Craig got his copy. Longford suggests that the Irish 'did themselves a disservice by this policy'.[75] His argument is that without it Collins and Griffith 'would have been in the same position as was de Valera towards the terms handed him in July. There would have been no ultimatum. There would have been plenty of time to discuss the terms in Dublin and reach a decision there.' But did Collins and Griffith believe that a 'decision' was possible in Dublin? Or rather did they believe it possible to get a decision they could agree with? From what has passed so far I believe it is not unreasonable to speculate that the 'the ultimatum' could well have suited them because it gave them the opportunity of producing a *fait accompli*, as opposed to further hair-splitting and politicking in Dublin which they feared would only result in losing Ireland an historic opportunity.

On 1 December Downing St was a-hum with people coming and going as further meetings and sub-conferences ensured that various

changes were embodied in the draft. These included a stipulation that
the Oath only imposed allegiance to the Crown 'as head of the State
and Empire' and that naval defence would only be an exclusively
British prerogative 'until an arrangement has been made whereby . . .
the Free State undertakes her own coastal defence', a highly significant
concession which introduced the principle that Britain's defence stake
in Ireland would not be permanent and made possible Ireland's
neutrality in the Second World War. The tension and bitterness which
the Treaty was to cause in Ireland is foreshadowed in Childers' diary
description of the final document:

It is July 20th 'in practice' minus army recruiting, and plus Boundary
Commission. Impossible to accept [Oath as before] . . . point by point
discussion of clauses . . . Griffith . . . flared out at me with some vague
charge . . . I protested at such vague nonsense. M.C. instead of backing me
up said he thought I implied a wider criticism. Refused to withdraw . . .
M.C. made a ghost of a suggestion of an apology after the meeting. A.G. in
favour of going to Dublin 'to carry out instruction to ask Cabinet before a
grave decision was made.'

Childers was unimpressed:

They don't understand the meaning of half of them [points] the English
worked on these skilled draughtsmen . . . Cope urged me to support peace
. . . I thought of the fate of Ireland being settled hugger-mugger by ignorant
Irish negotiators and A.G. in genuine sympathy with many of the English
claims.

When the final English draft arrived at Hans Place, Childers
comments: 'A.G. muzzy with whiskey, succeeded in getting some
copies from him . . . Bitterly dissatisfied. Went to bed at 2 am. What a
day!'

'Muzzy' or not, Griffith was en route for Ireland at 8.30 am that
morning (2 December). Collins stayed back for a final discussion at
the Treasury on financial matters with the Chancellor of the
Exchequer, Sir Robert Horne, and Lionel Curtis. Childers accompanied him. Later in the day there was a second Treasury meeting
attended by Lloyd George and R. G. Hawtrey of the Treasury, an
economist described by Longford as being 'already competent to
dazzle and befog beyond the common run of economists'. Collins
attended this meeting alone.

Childers's diary indicates why:

when shown British draft on income tax for Ulster I blew the whole thing to
pieces by pointing out not only the gross impropriety of a provincial fund but
the grotesque results which might follow Ulster receiving too much from
central funds. Horne's answer was 'Ulster would not come in without that
clause.' M.C. did not understand the subject or only imperfectly.

Apart from their mutual tensions, fate too worked against Collins and Childers. As they were returning to Dublin with Duffy for the vital Cabinet meeting on the British terms, the mailboat collided with a trawler in the Irish Sea at 3.30 am. By the time the mailboat recrossed the Irish Sea and berthed at Dun Laoghaire it was 10.15 am.

The wracking night coming at the end of the exhausting negotiations was the worst possible preparation for a fractious Cabinet meeting that began at 11 am, less than an hour after the boat had docked. In Collins' case the effect of the night was particularly severe. He had to contend with the effects of not one meeting but two.

Collins had intended to see O'Muirthle, the man who had played a key role in organising the IRB in and after Frongoch, and other members of the Supreme Council of the Brotherhood, before entering the arena with Brugha, de Valera and Stack, so that he could acquaint the IRB with the details of the British offer. As matters turned out he had to phone O'Muirthle from the Mansion House to arrange for him to pick up a copy.[76] O'Muirthle then consulted with the IRB during the morning and Collins and he met during the lunchtime adjournment of the Mansion House conclave. The IRB's objections may be summarised as centring around the Oath, for which an alternative form of wording was proposed; defence, and the provisions governing the Six Counties.

These reservations can hardly have been either surprising to, or welcomed by, Collins, embattled as he was at the time, but they were at least based on the document's merits. However, two words may be used to sum up the seven hours in the Mansion House: acrimony and confusion.

Brugha asked who had been responsible for the sub-conference arrangement – having done nothing when Duffy reported on it to Dublin weeks earlier – and on being told 'the British', remarked that they 'selected their men'. Collins contained himself well[77] while Griffith stalked over to where Brugha was sitting and demanded that he retract the allegation. Collins' comment was, 'If you are not satisfied with us, get another five to go over.' It was Barton's sense of honour that saved the day. Although he had strongly disapproved of the sub-conference idea, he intervened to say that he refused to have the private proceedings of the delegates discussed and pointed out that Collins and Griffith had gone to the sub-conferences with the delegation's full knowledge and consent. Duggan interjected to say that there had been meetings afterwards at which proceedings were reported. Childers notes in his diary, 'Nobody contradicted this.' Brugha subsequently asked that the remark be withdrawn. Childers commented: 'It was an unpleasant scene.'

This was one of the most important Cabinet discussions ever

conducted by any Irish political party but, remarkably, no proper record was taken.[78] Colm O'Murchadha, the acting secretary to the Cabinet, Childers, Stack and Barton made some notes but the public's main source of information came from subsequent Dail debates during which various people gave accounts of what they said they had said. De Valera took pride in this. At pains to show the Dail that he was not in any way responsible for the Treaty's signing he said: 'I did not give, nor did the Cabinet give, any instructions to the delegation as to any final document which they were to put in.'[79]

In fact there was particular confusion over what de Valera said, or intended. He clearly objected to the Oath and Ulster clauses, but thought that with amendments the document could be acceptable. Without them the delegation, whom he conceded had done their utmost, should show the British 'they were prepared to face the consequences, war or no war.'[80] However Collins subsequently thought that 'de Valera had proposed an oath consistent with Dominion status.' Childers noted that he had said, 'King of the Associated States'.[81] De Valera later claimed that he had said Association, not Associated States. O'Murchadha's official note of the Oath the President proposed was:

I . . . do solemnly swear true faith and allegiance to the constitution of the Irish Free State, to the Treaty of Association and to recognise the King of Great Britain as Head of the Associated States.

On top of this de Valera subsequently gave two more differing versions of the Oaths he proposed.[82] Given the circumstances of the time it certainly explains the irritation Collins and Griffith expressed over being unable to tell whether they were being instructed or confused from Dublin. They were expected to face-down the British, 'war or no war', for the sake of hair-splitting. Later, nearing the close of the meeting, Childers asked de Valera if scrapping the Oath in the draft meant scrapping also the first four clauses in the Treaty, those dealing with Dominion status. 'Yes', replied de Valera. This bit of by-play, which would of course have meant aborting the entire agreement, later caused trouble between Collins, who had not heard it, and Childers, who wanted to implement the President's wishes.

Griffith said that he didn't like the document[83] but that he did not think it dishonourable. It practically gave a Republic. The first allegiance was to Ireland. If it were to be rejected the people were entitled to know what the alternative was. The country would not fight on the question of allegiance. There would be a split. He would not recommend the Government to accept, but thought the pleni-potentiaries should sign and leave it to the President and the Dail to reject. According to Stack's memoir[84] a significant exchange then occurred.

Brugha interrupted: 'Don't you realise that if you sign this thing, you will split Ireland from top to bottom?'

Griffith pondered this and replied, 'I suppose that's so. I'll tell you what I'll do. I'll not sign the document, but I'll bring it back and submit it to the Dail and if necessary to the people.' This exchange is said to have persuaded de Valera not to join the delegation. Certainly, he later told the Dail that he would 'probably' have gone but for it.[85] But in the afternoon session O'Murchadha records Griffith as saying that he would not take the responsibility of breaking on the Crown; that when as many concessions as possible were extracted, and when accepted by Craig ['Accepted' was obviously misheard, or uttered unthinkingly] he would go before the Dail. The Dail was the body to decide for or against war.

The most eloquent statement of the day was embodied in Collins' silence. As Childers notes in his diary, 'M.C. difficult to understand. Repeatedly pressed by Dev but I really don't know what his answer amounted to.' O'Murchadha however noted that he said that the non-acceptance of the Treaty would be a gamble, as England could arrange a war in Ireland within a week. He thought the sacrifices to North East Ulster justified for the sake of essential unity. He felt further concessions could be obtained on trade and defence. The Oath of Allegiance would not come into force for twelve months, the question therefore was – was it worth taking the twelve months and seeing how it would work? He would recommend the Dail should go to the country on the Treaty but would recommend rejection of the Oath. He obviously threw in enough question-marks and savers to prevent de Valera bringing his thoughts into the open. Duggan followed his lead. Duffy and Barton were unequivocally opposed.

The divisions at the meeting were underlined when the delegates went back to London on separate boats, Collins and Griffith from Dun Laoghaire, Barton, Duffy and Childers from Dublin. They also went with separate ideas as to what they were supposed to be doing. O'Murchadha records the meeting as deciding that the delegates were to carry out their original instructions with the same powers. The existing Oath could not be subscribed to and the Cabinet was prepared to face war as a result; Griffith was to say the document could not be signed and to try to break on Ulster. Childers noted that amendments to the trade and defence clauses were not mandatory but merely 'suggestions'. A majority of the Cabinet, including de Valera, but not Brugha and Stack, were in favour of the delegation trying to see Craig in London. And it was stitched into the record that de Valera was not joining the delegation 'at this stage of the negotiations'.

The general air of unreality and lack of a sense of proportion that hung over this day of bickering is symbolised by the fact that the delegates were being sent back to create a risk of war, not over the dismemberment of their country, but on the wording of the Oath. The British very soon became aware of this folly and it played its part in the enshrinement of partition.

En route to London, Barton's party encountered Cope and Tim Healy.[86] Barton gave Cope no information but, with Diarmuid O'Hegarty, had a two-hour conversation with Healy, who was aghast at the prospect of war, strongly in favour of the terms on offer, and was meeting Lloyd George the next day. After seeing the Prime Minister Healy had a 'long interview' with Collins, after which he told Barton that Collins was 'the only sensible man amongst us'. He had probably given the same opinion to Lloyd George, and perhaps more besides, for a Cabinet meeting, the following Monday, was informed that 'Mr Arthur Griffith and Mr Michael Collins were greatly disappointed at the rejection of the British proposals. The latter appeared to be not unwilling to accept paragraphs 1, 2 and 3 (Dominion status) though he would have preferred an immediate decision on Ulster and would have remitted the question of Ulster safeguards for discussion between representatives of Ulster and the rest of Ireland.'[87]

Before that meeting was held the Irish had again quarrelled amongst themselves over what to put in the document summarising their position as a result of the Dublin Mansion House meeting. Collins was of course beside himself at the thought of going back to Downing St yet again with External Association. 'I did not go to this conference for the reason that I had in my own estimation fully argued all points.'[88] Eventually Griffith, who had been as enraged as Collins at the proposals, decided to accompany them so as to lessen the appearance of dissension.

For someone totally out of sympathy with his mission Griffith 'played up like a man and fought as hard as we did', Barton noted afterwards. It was 'one of his greatest efforts in debate. Considering that a few minutes before he had been refusing to come at all his force and conviction were astounding.'[89] Trying all the time to keep the break point centred on Ulster he asked, in view of his own promise concerning Association in relation to 'essential unity', for a similar letter on 'essential unity' from Craig. The British told him that there would be no letter. Craig would refuse the proposals, nevertheless they would persevere with them, hand over Dublin Castle, withdraw their troops, pass a ratifying act in the next few days . . . glittering vistas were opening up and then Duffy intervened to say: 'We should be as closely associated with you in large matters as the Dominions, and in the matter of defence still more so, but our difficulty is coming into the Empire.' That was the slip the British were waiting for. 'That ends it,' cried Chamberlain and he was on his feet as he spoke. With that appearance of spontaneity which only orchestration can bring, his colleagues joined him. They would send the final proposals tomorrow and inform Craig that the talks had broken down. The journey back to Hans Place was enlivened for Gavan Duffy by Griffith's informing him of matters concerning his ancestry he had not previously been aware of. The result of his support for Barton and Duffy had been the loss of his opportunity to break on Ulster. The night of Sunday 4 December 1921 was not a pleasant one in Hans Place.

Then 'in the early hours of the morning' Jones re-entered the picture yet again.[90] He claims that he found Griffith 'labouring under a deep sense of crisis'. Griffith is said to have told him that he and Collins would accept the Treaty, but something fresh was needed to get it through the Dail, even a 'conditional recognition of Irish unity, however shadowy, in return for the acceptance of the Empire by Sinn Fein'. For this, Jones says, Griffith would give 'Ulster' any safeguards required, including scrapping the Boundary Commission. They agreed that Collins would see Lloyd George later that morning. The meeting took place at 9.30, fifteen minutes later than arranged because, we are told,[91] Collins' objections to going were only overcome at the last moment. According to Collins' own record[92] of what transpired he told Lloyd George that he was 'perfectly dissatisfied' with the British proposals for the Six Counties. He repeated Griffith's argument of the previous day, saying that Craig should state his terms for either rejecting or accepting unity, in writing.

Lloyd George's reaction to this, says Collins, was to counter-attack. The Prime Minister said:

I myself pointed out on a previous occasion that the North would be forced economically to come in. I assented but I said that the position was so serious owing to certain recent actions that for my part I was anxious to secure a definite reply from Craig and his colleagues, and I was as agreeable to a reply rejecting as accepting. In view of the former we would save Tyrone, and Fermanagh, parts of Derry, Armagh and Down by the Boundary Commission, and thus avoid such things as the raid on the Tyrone County Council and the ejection of the staff. [Since the end of November the Craigites had been cracking down on Sinn Fein-controlled county councils which were disputing the authority of the new 'Ulster' Government.] Another such incident would, in my view, inevitably lead to a conflict, and this conflict, in the nature of things (assuming for instance that some of the Anglo-Northern police were killed or wounded), would inevitably spread through Ireland. Mr Lloyd George expressed a view that this might be put to Craig, and if so the safeguards would be a matter for working out between ourselves and Craig afterwards.

Lloyd George also expressed willingness to show some flexibility on financial, trade and defence matters and to consider a new oath – if the Irish accepted Dominion status. Says Collins:

The conversation ended with Lloyd George saying that if Clauses 1 and 2 of the Treaty were accepted (Dominion status) he would be in a position to hold up any action until we had, if we desired to do so, submitted the matter to Dail Eireann and the country. I left it at that saying that unless I sent word to the contrary some members of the delegation would meet him at 2 o'clock.

Thus, although there was nothing new of substance produced from Lloyd George's side, Collins effectively got the talks restarted. The Conference duly entered its last phase that afternoon. Significantly Collins and Griffith brought Barton, the most resolutely Republican of the team, on this penultimate visit to Downing St. The generally accepted account of what happened there is that Griffith was confronted with his pledges given prior to the Liverpool Conference. The Conference adjourned, there was an anguished debate amongst the Irish who eventually agreed to sign the Treaty, and the fate of Ireland was decided in the small hours of 6 December. This interpretation is true insofar as it goes. But, as these pages should have by now made clear, this appears to be only part of the story. From the time de Valera accepted the invitation to negotiate in September, both Collins and Griffith seem to have decided that compromise was inevitable. They realised they would not be supported by de Valera in facing that inevitability and, having explored the British offer, they then embarked on the sub-conference route to settlement.

The confusions of 3 December in the Mansion House and the subsequent differing interpretations in preparing for the following day's meeting with the British could only have confirmed them in the view they were being 'confused not directed'. The seeming breakdown of Sunday over Gavan Duffy's blunder may not have been all it seemed. It was certainly portrayed as a most serious crisis in all the London papers that mattered on the 5th and 6th. But, significantly, Lloyd George's own mouthpiece, the *Daily Chronicle*, carried headlines and comment (6 December) which said: 'Irish Crisis, chances of getting round it – if the negotiators are still unable to sign a compact let them adjourn their negotiations for a fixed period of weeks.' Moreover just as it was generally believed that the sub-conference idea emanated from the British not the Irish, it was also widely believed[93] that it was the British who asked Collins to have the morning meeting with Lloyd George which put the conference back on the rails. In fact, as Jones' diaries revealed long afterwards, it was Griffith who asked Jones to arrange the meeting.[94]

According to Collins' memorandum on the meeting with Lloyd George, the Prime Minister opened by telling him that he was informing his colleagues later in the day that the conference had ended. The *Daily Chronicle* that morning (5 December) had carried a report headlined 'Grave Irish outlook — little hope of settlement now entertained'. The headline next day indicates that both paper and Prime Minister received new information between one edition and the next.

Certainly there is no indication of breakdown in the Cabinet record of the meeting Lloyd George had with his colleagues after seeing Collins. Two highly significant things were said however:

1. . . . there were indications that the division of opinion which had manifested itself among the Irish Representatives in London, also existed in the Irish Cabinet . . . a majority of the members of that Cabinet had rejected the terms and submitted counter-proposals.

2. Attention was drawn . . . to the fact that the document contained no counter-proposals regarding Ulster, from which it would appear that no Sinn Fein objection would be forthcoming to the proposals regarding Ulster.[95]

Thus the British were fully aware of the divisions in the Irish ranks and could fine-tune the last moves accordingly. Furthermore the document produced from the shambles of the Mansion House, containing the distilled wisdom of the allegedly most extreme All-Ireland, Republican wing of the Nationalist movement, indicated that the British could, in real terms, disregard further protestations about Irish unity.

Whether they needed any encouragement to do so is a moot point, but they certainly adopted that policy when on the afternoon of 6 December 1922, Arthur Griffith started off on the familiar path about further progress being contingent on learning Craig's intentions concerning Irish unity. He was promptly accused of going back on his promises not to let Lloyd George down over the Boundary Commission. Collins then took up the running. He pointed out[96] that the delegation's fighting position would be surrendered if they agreed to sign without Craig's agreement on unity and recalled that every document ever given to the British on Association with the Commonwealth was contingent on unity. While Collins was speaking Lloyd George administered the *coup de grace*.

He had left the room for a few moments to rummage amongst his suits for the document Jones had shown Griffith the previous month outlining the Boundary Commission proposals. On finding the correct pair of trousers he returned with both the document and a real or simulated show of anger at what he characterised as the Irish attempt to break on Ulster whereas their real problem lay in Dublin. Barton, who of course had never heard of the memorandum, had no idea what was going on and he whispered to Collins: 'What is this letter?'

'I don't know what the hell it is,' was the reply.

Lloyd George rubbed salt into the wounds. 'Do you mean to tell me, Mr Collins, that you never heard of this document from Mr Griffith?'

Collins said nothing and Lloyd George went on to say that he had assumed that both were party to the memorandum. 'I took the risk of breaking my party. You in Ireland often bring against us in England the charge of breach of faith. Now it is for you to show that Irishmen know how to keep faith.'

At that Griffith capitulated: 'I said that I would not let you down on that and I won't', he replied. Further argument on the Six Counties was now denied him, but he did remonstrate that it was unfair to tie his colleagues to his promise. The conversation then switched to trade, defence and the Oath, the very topics Collins had indicated at the Mansion House that movement might be forthcoming on. There was movement on all of them, almost as if he guessed or knew, possibly from Birkenhead or Cope, that there would be. The Oath which Collins had prepared after his IRB consultations was accepted with insignificant changes. Collins also secured agreement, over Lloyd George's objections, to a reduction in the period allowed to the Six Counties within which to decide for or against joining the Free State. He thought a year was too long and got it reduced to a month because he felt a year would allow life to be made impossible for the Nationalists. To prove this contention he cited both loyalist outrages and instances of partisanship on the part of the British Army towards loyalists and of corresponding bias against Nationalists. Reluctantly Lloyd George accepted the 'Ulster month'.

Britain no longer sought the exclusive right to defend Irish coastal waters and Ireland was to be permitted to build and maintain vessels for revenue and fisheries protection. Furthermore the two governments were to meet after five years to review the 'undertaking by Ireland of a share in her own coastal defence'. Finally, Lloyd George proposed that if the Irish agreed to sign the Treaty he would drop Britain's demand for free trade.

Griffith again repeated that he would sign, but said again that it was unfair to ask the others to do so before they knew Craig's position. Lloyd George replied: 'Do I understand, Mr Griffith, that though everyone else refuses, you will nevertheless agree to sign?'[97] There was a pause as Griffith no doubt struggled with a vision of the contumely his answer would bring upon him, and then he replied simply, 'That is so, Mr Prime Minister.' Austen Chamberlain said afterwards, 'A braver man than Arthur Griffith I have never met.'[98]

As we have seen, Lloyd George knew that Collins was in favour of signing. Barton, who had been invited to make a rare appearance in sub-conference that now seems more than coincidental, was thus the one to convince. Ultimatum time had arrived. Lloyd George bent all his formidable array of psychological weaponry on him. 'That is not enough, if we sign we shall sign as a delegation and stake the life of our government on our signature. Is the Irish delegation prepared to do the same?'

Barton's report says: 'He particularly addressed himself to me and said very solemnly that those who were not for peace must take the full responsibility for the war that would immediately follow refusal by any delegate to sign the Articles of Agreement.' Having let that sink in the Welsh Wizard continued to weave his spell in a manner more theatrical than ethical. 'I have to communicate with Sir James Craig tonight,' he said, holding up two envelopes.

Here are the alternative letters which I have prepared, one enclosing the Articles of Agreement reached by His Majesty's Government and yourselves, and the other saying that Sinn Fein representatives refuse the Oath of allegiance and refuse to come within the Empire. If I send this letter, it is war – and war within three days. Which letter am I to send? Whichever letter you choose travels by special train to Holyhead, and by destroyer to Belfast. The train is waiting with steam up at Euston. Mr Shakespeare is ready. If he is to reach Sir James Craig in time we must have your answer by ten pm tonight. You can have until then but no longer to decide whether you will give peace or war to your country.[99]

That was some weight of responsibility to have deposited on the shoulders of a young man, by the leader of what was then still the world's largest empire. Lloyd George was of course bluffing for Barton's benefit. He had promised to give Collins more time to consider just that morning and he was only committed to sending Craig a copy of the proposals, nothing else hung on their despatch. But getting the Treaty through Dublin hinged on getting all the delegates to sign in London.

Barton was not the only one with a load on his shoulders. No one knew better than Michael Collins himself that he was going to have to carry the burden of the Treaty with his countrymen. Churchill's famous description of Collins recalls his agony at that moment: 'Michael Collins rose looking as though he were going to shoot someone, preferably himself. In all my life I have never seen so much pain and suffering in restraint.'[100] He had kept his cards so close to his chest that when, on the way back to Hans Place, he told Barton that he intended to sign, Barton was astounded. But he acknowledged Collins' motives in taking the step. 'He knew that physical resistance, if resumed, would collapse, and he was not going to be the leader of a forlorn hope.'[101] Forlorn or no, Barton would not give in easily. For hours he and Duffy held out, bolstered by Childers.

Griffith spoke 'almost passionately for signing'[102] and there was much putting on of coats and threats of departing to Downing St with or without Barton and Duffy. A remark of Collins' lodged with Barton and helped to tip the scales. Collins had pointed out how few active Volunteers there had been. 'Do you want to send them out to be slaughtered?' he asked. Duggan had added to this by saying: 'Barton, you will be hanged from a lamppost in Dublin if your refusal to sign causes a new war in Ireland.' And then, suddenly, Duggan broke down and began recalling the deaths of Moran, Flood and the others.

He described Mountjoy, on the morning 'when I saw the hangman who was to hang our young lads there'. Childers records: 'There was long and hot argument about committing our young men to die. Die for nothing. What could G.D. (Gavan Duffy) get better? G.D. assented quietly. Bob was shaken. Asked me out and I said it was principle.' And here Childers inadvertently gave the scales of decision the final touch. He added, 'and I felt Molly was with us'. This had the opposite effect on Barton to what was intended. The idea of resolving his tumult of conscience on the basis of what Childers' American wife had to say about the situation angered Barton. He replied, 'Well I suppose I must sign.'

Judging from Kathleen Napoli MacKenna's reminiscences Collins had gone to Cadogan Gardens while most of this discussion was in progress. She was told to go to Hans Place and set off there with Broy. There was an air of menace about that was not due only to the fog:

We were conscious that figures were sheltering everywhere in the shadows . . . three or four thugs stepped out unexpectedly before us and, without uttering a syllable, blocked our way. One flashed an electric torch in Broy's face, and by its light I could see pistols glinting. They scrutinised Broy thoroughly, passing the torch over his head, face and body, then slunk silently away.[103]

Collins came to Hans Place with Tobin and Cullen. Outside, says Napoli MacKenna:

the vicinity was bristling with Scotland Yard men. Mick was irritated to find the other delegates had not as yet come down to the hall. He stalked nervously up and down the dining room, his attache case in his left hand, his old mackintosh dangling untidily over it . . . Tom poured him out a sherry . . . he sent Eddie upstairs to tell the others he was waiting . . . outside Diarmuid O'Hegarty, Desmond Fitzgerald, Eamonn Broy . . . were waiting in the cars . . .

Collins was informed that the discussion upstairs 'gave no sign of terminating.'. . . Like a wild beast in a cage he paced up and down the room, morose, silent and sullen; then plumped down in a dining-room chair that happened to be placed in line with that part of the stairs down which those who were to join him would have to come . . . he fell into a short profound sleep. Poor 'Big Fellow!' As I gazed my heart ached with anguish at the thought of what his mental torture must be. I appreciated the weight of responsibility placed by events beyond his control on his young generous shoulders . . . suddenly those going to Downing St came down the stairs.

In Dublin detectives and Auxiliaries had suddenly reappeared on the streets also. They stopped pedestrians and searched them. Memories of the pre-truce terror flooded back. Was it war again? In Downing St the same question was asked. 'We had doubts as to whether we would see them again', said Lloyd George. He thought they would, 'provided that Michael Collins has as much moral courage as he has physical courage . . . but moral courage is a much higher quality than physical courage and it is a quality that brave men often lack.'[104] Suddenly a message came that the Irish were on their way back. Pulse rates increased sharply. The Irishmen marched in. It was

clear from their faces that they had come to a great decision after a prolonged struggle. As before they were superficially very calm and quiet. There was a long pause, or seemed to be; then Mr Griffith said: 'Mr Prime Minister, the delegation is willing to sign the agreements.'

At 2.30 am they did so after a final frenzy of last-minute argument, redrafting and re-typing.

Birkenhead turned to Collins after putting his name to the document and said, 'I may have signed my political death-warrant tonight.' The younger man replied, 'I may have signed my actual death-warrant.'

9

Fighting the Waves

'For forms of government let fools contest.'

Alexander Pope

Now the waking nightmare began. Cathleen ni Houlihan, Yeats' synonym for Ireland, would show herself as an envious, strident, venomous bitch throughout the Treaty debates conducted both in and outside the Dail. One of the mildest epithets hurled at the delegates was 'traitors'. Griffith and Collins were reckoned to have been drugged or drunk when they signed the Treaty,[1] but Collins was singled out for special treatment, on the grounds of both drink and sex. Countess Markievicz regaled the Dail with a rumour that Collins had broken up a royal romance![2] She said that the Governor Generalship, 'the centre of English immorality and divorce', had been earmarked for a member of the royal family until Collins came along. As a result 'Princess Mary's wedding is to be broken off . . . the Princess Mary is to be married to Michael Collins who will be appointed first Governor.'

This nonsense came at a particularly bad moment. Collins had fallen in love and planned to marry Kitty Kiernan. She had visited him in London during the talks but the strain and uncertainty of his position, and her Catholic conscience, seem to have made the visit a stormy one. She wrote to him saying:

. . . why not marry the one I really love, and what a cowardly thing of me to be afraid to marry the one I really want, and who loves me just as well as any of the others I thought of marrying.

Then London came. I should not have gone. It gave rise to such talk. People got to know about it and I thought it better from a girl's very conventional and narrow point of view that we had better have something definite, and so we have drifted . . . now don't think by this that I want a row or want you to end it. Not likely. I want you only not to think bad of me when we had those scenes.[3]

Collins wrote back on 5 and 6 December sending her a two-part letter. The first part said:

If the question were of no interest at all to me surely I could not blame you for having concern for your own future and your lifelong happiness. When it does so very closely concern you I cannot blame you more. This is really my straightforward and genuine point of view.

He was interrupted then by the alarms and excursions attendant on the signing of the Treaty and resumed the letter to express hopes doomed to be unfulfilled:

To bed about five, and up to go to Mass and didn't (need I say it) forget your candle. My plans in regard to home are as yet uncertain. I don't know how things will go now but with God's help we have brought peace to this land of ours – a peace which will end this old strife of ours for ever.

He met the Countess Markievicz's charge in typically Collins fashion, cutting through the rumours and uncertainties to make his engagement public knowledge, while still safeguarding his fiancée's identity. His statement of rebuttal delivered with stilted, old-world courtesy drew loud applause:

I do not come from the class the Deputy for the Dublin Division comes from; I come from the plain people of Ireland. The lady whose name was mentioned is, I understand, betrothed to some man. I know nothing of her personally, I know nothing of her in any way whatsoever, but the statement may cause her pain and may cause pain to the lady who is betrothed to me (Hear! Hear!). I just stand in that plain way, and I will not allow without challenge any Deputy in the assembly of my nation to insult any lady either of his nation or of any other nation. (Loud applause.)

He rounded this off by sending Kitty an express letter that evening (3 January 1921):

My Dearest Kitty,
    This will reach you before the letters I sent today. My dear, dear Kitty, see the references to yourself and Princess Mary of England.
                    My betrothed,
                    My fondest love,
                    Michael.

Incredibly enough, 'Princess Mary' type accusations, however understandable amidst the hopes and hates of revolution, were still being levelled at Collins as this book was being written. So much so that Dr T. Ryle Dwyer came to the defence of his reputation, pointing out that pursuing 'a piece of ear' rather than 'a piece of ass' did not make a man either a homosexual or a 'rampant philanderer'.[4] Sharing beds with other men, or staying at the homes of single women was a necessary concomitant of a life on the run in which a bed anywhere was a prize. Both Collins and associates like Tobin and Cullen knew what it was to spend nights in the open, literally within seconds of death. In one raid on Vaughan's Tobin and Cullen escaped by hanging by their fingertips from a window ledge. In another, Collins and other Vaughan's habitués got out ahead of a raiding party but were trapped inside a cordon and had to spend the night in the meagre shelter afforded by the buttresses of a nearby church. As they shrank back against the cold stone, armed sentries walked up and down within feet of them. Sanctuary, not sex, was the priority in such conditions.

In the film Cathal O'Shannon made of his life, Emmet Dalton, then an old man,[5] said of Collins, 'I loved him. I use no other word. I loved him as a man loves another man, with pure love.' Dalton, Tobin, McKee, all Collins' close companions had the close bonding of men in war. That did not make them homosexual. Yearnings for women must have been overwhelming at times – after leaving the arena gladiators traditionally sought release – and I know from contemporary testimony[6] that some men on active service needed to have a woman after a 'job'. But that did not make them womanisers. The majority of Volunteers afterwards settled down to the strictly observed Catholic marriages of the time.

Nevertheless the rumours about Collins' sexual activities had gained fresh currency the year before Dr T. Ryle Dwyer's book was published (1989) following the screening of an important, two-hour-long, award-winning documentary on Collins for RTE (Radio Telefis Eireann) in 1989, which subsequently became a best-selling video.[7] Amongst those who took part was Mr Eoghan Harris who had written a film script which gave rise to stories about Collins being homosexual. Mr Harris said amongst other things that Collins was 'cruel, calculating, devious, two-timed a lot of women and was probably hypocritical in the sense that he went to Communion a lot while carrying on an affair with two women at the same time.'

He based these statements on a large file, 'the best American money can buy. Every person he ever spoke to, every document, diaries, bits of paper he left around, they're all here, all the facts.' This collection, said Mr Harris, was 'compiled by Mr Arthur Schlesinger Jnr, great historian, and may be sixteen others.'

As Arthur Schlesinger[8] is the only one of the seventeen scholars referred to at this point, I got in touch with him. He told me he was 'surprised'[9] and wrote: 'I would never dream of posing as an authority on Michael Collins . . . I have never said or thought that Collins was a hypocrite and a womaniser who received Holy Communion while taking advantage of different women.' In fact Dr Schlesinger was so horrified at the idea of being associated with such a theory that he authorised me to 'deny these statements', and made a similar rebuttal on behalf of Alexandra [his wife, the expert on Collins in the family].[10] The interest generated by Mr Harris' remark is an example of the way in which myths about Collins are generated today.

Women did play an important part in the Anglo-Irish war, much more so than the role they were accorded in the political life of the state they helped to create. Collins was constantly in the company of courageous, passionate women, some of them very beautiful, his cousin Nancy for example. She was doubly related to him.[11] Nancy told Liam O'Donnachadcha, also a cousin, 'All the girls were mad about him.'[12] Was Nancy 'mad' about Collins? Some members of the family think so, but his affections turned elsewhere and in 1922 she married his brother, Johnny, and reunited the large family scattered after the burning of Woodfield. Nancy's calibre may be gauged from her attitude towards the youngest stepson, Liam, who suffered a multiplicity of illnesses as a result of hardships sustained while still an infant after the Woodfield break-up, amongst them bad eyesight. When he got older he wanted to be a lawyer, but couldn't read the text books. Nancy sat up 'every night for four hours and in her beautiful, Civil Service, copperplate handwriting she copied out every single book'.[13] Liam became a solicitor and built up one of the largest practices in Cork.

It is certain that by the time the Treaty negotiations began, insofar as women in Ireland were concerned, everyone else, including Susan Killeen, had faded from the centre of Collins' affections in favour of Kitty Kiernan. He was still friendly with Susan but, as the following letter[14] indicates, hardly intimate:

Madam,
    None of your impudence. I want to know what I asked about No. 9. Keep in touch and see if the place is raided. I gave you 4/6 for that damned ticket you sent me but I don't suppose I'll go. Other people are like cats too but not because of the number of their lives.
Do dtuigeann tu bas me [Trans: do you want to kill me?]
                    Miceal

There is a story in Susan's family that she told Collins that he didn't want a wife, he wanted someone to cook and sew for him. She disagreed with Collins over the Treaty and of course about Kitty Kiernan. It is part of the family folklore that when Collins was agonising over whether or not to declare war on those who were defying him on the Treaty some of their mutual friends came to her and asked her to advise him. 'Why should I tell him what to do?' she is said to have replied. 'If he wants advice, let him ask Kitty Kiernan!' Susan was however destined to be happier than Kitty Kiernan and, ironically enough, in Granard, Kitty's home town, where she went to live with her bank manager husband and large family.

Kitty Kiernan was to experience tragedy and unhappiness for most of her life, civil war claiming the lives of two men who loved her and illness ruining her later days. She must have caused some unhappiness too, judging from the tone of a letter Harry Boland wrote to her before setting off for America:

Pulse of my heart . . . How I can leave you even at the order of 'the Chief' [de Valera]. I do not know, and I'm asking myself all the time if I have not made a great mistake in leaving you behind . . . I would just love to have you come to America where we will spend our honeymoon in perfect bliss!

Mick and I spent the last night together. He saw me home at 2 am, and as I had to catch the 7.35 am I bade him goodbye – only to find him at Kingsbridge as fresh as a daisy to see me off. I need not say to you how much I love him, and I know he has a warm spot in his heart for me, and I feel sure in no matter what manner our Triangle may work out, he and I shall be always friends.[15]

The triangle was to 'work out' in death. Although in America Boland's first reaction on hearing the news was to welcome the Treaty, he soon swung behind the de Valera line and on 15 December 1921 telegraphed the Dail, in his capacity as a Deputy for Roscommon-Mayo, rejecting the Treaty. However his distancing himself from Collins in this way appears to have been politically, not romantically motivated. Kitty does not appear to have told him about her engagement plans. This news seems to have come from Collins himself on Boland's return from America to take part in the Treaty debates. A note from Boland to Kitty[16] on the subject contrasts markedly with his lyrical letter on departure:

Kitty,
    I want to congratulate you. M. told me of your engagement, and I wish you long life and happiness,
                    Ever yours,
                    H. Boland

Collins and Kitty appear to have talked about marriage during the London negotiations. They made a pact that they would write to each other every day and the lovers' letters literally fill a book, named after the phrase that appears in most of his, *In Great Haste*. As his life entered its last turbulent phase many of the letters he wrote to Kitty contain things like: 'I read over all your letters again last night and I started writing to you sitting up in bed but I had to give it up. Positively I was too worn out to write legibly,'[17] and 'I'm so tired that I can scarcely remain awake. This is just a line to tell you so.'[18] Kitty however wrote passionately and open-heartedly at times: 'I almost shudder at the thought of the strength of my love, what I do believe I am capable of feeling and that without you, life held nothing for me. Nobody mattered to me, not even myself, if you were not with me.'[19] She writes about wishing that she could be near him so that she could make 'sacred and profane love'[20] to him and apparently got her wish later in the month when she recalls a night of passion:

Last night was a real wedding night for you and me. Didn't you feel that way too, but couldn't put it into words? I *wanted* to run away with you. That must be the feeling with people who do run away like that. We had it last night. That was our night. Glad today, *for both you and me*, that I did not go.[21]

Kitty did not hesitate to put intimate thoughts on paper. She describes going to bed early and lying awake thinking of him:

. . . madly passionately in love with you, to use your own words . . . I found myself promising you faithfully that I'd never had a real row, nor fall out with you at all, no matter what you did, 'if' first, you are sympathetic to me (now don't laugh, because I'm real serious), if you are not too rough, and don't hurt me when we are just playing, just fooling and a few other little ifs.[22]

By contrast his letters are guarded, stilted, the work of a man who is constantly aware of how easily ones innermost thoughts can fall into the hands of others. His letter to Kitty on the night of the Markievicz attack, restrained though it was, was one of his most expressive. Collins, the world's expert on interrupting the mails, is now hoist with his own petard. He warns her about the need to take care with their correspondence, urging her to put a letter into an inner envelope, marked personal, and worries that some of her letters are falling into the hands of his enemies on the anti-Treaty side.[23]

Another reason for this hesitancy to express himself may have been her lack of interest in politics, except insofar as they involved following his doings in the newspapers. For example when she heard of his military appointment during the civil war, after they had been apart by force of circumstance for some three weeks, she wrote: 'You are C. in Chief now. What does this mean? More trouble I suppose. Will it ever end? But God is good. I wish that we were already married, and that the very next time we'd meet was on our honeymoon.'[24]

An overview of the correspondence gives one an impression of a want of intellectual communication between them. There is little doubt that he reciprocated her passion, as references like the night 'you really wanted me', make clear but his suspicions about tampering with his mail – which, as we shall see, were to have fatal consequences for one suspect, Noel Lemass – confined his mode of address to 'dear' rather than Harry Boland's lyricism. Kitty talks of being ill a good deal. There are also frequent references to rows and misunderstandings. A combination of her natural hot temper and her edginess, caused possibly by Bright's disease, from which she seems to have died ultimately, would certain explain these.

Sister Margaret Mary told me that she and her sisters all thought that he was going to marry Sinead Mason. 'She was very nice, but he was a great ladies' man.' They were filled with curiosity about Kitty when she was suddenly introduced to their circle. A story is told of a shopping expedition on which Kitty bought a large hat which she asked him to carry. His reaction to this was 'blasth ye, woman, I'm not going to be seen carrying *that*!' And Kevin O'Shiel said that Collins' comment when Kitty put on the hat was: 'The cartwheel's bigger than the cart!'[25] After Collins' death her life became something of an emotional wasteland. She read and re-read his letters and when she finally married, to Felix Cronin, then Quartermaster General in the Army, installed his portrait in her living room and called the second of her two children Michael Collins Cronin.[26] She died in 1945, the years preceding her death punctuated by stays in nursing homes.

Both Collins and Kiernan were deeply religious. *In Great Haste* contains several references to prayer and attendance at Mass and Communion. Her last letter to him[27] mentions the possibility of going together to make the severe Lough Derg pilgrimage, which involves sleeplessness, bare feet, fasting and continuous prayer over a three-day period. During a period of great difficulty with the English in May 1922 his piety made such an impression on a Passionate Order priest giving a mission in Greystones that the Missioner, Ignatius CP, wrote after Collins' death to his sister Lena:

Michael was very busy in Dublin, worked and worried almost beyond endurance. He got to Greystones one night very late, and very tired . . . He got up next morning as early as 5.30 am, came to the church and made a glorious General Confession, and received Holy Communion. He said to me afterwards, 'Say the Mass for Ireland and God bless you, Father.' He crossed an hour or so later to London.[28]

On the one hand Collins' defenders have traditionally argued that this piety preserved him from any female entanglements, on the other his critics say it renders him a hypocrite if he did yield to the urgings of the flesh. It's a very Irish type of debate, though less common now than it used to be, and one that shows a very superficial understanding of human sexuality.

Much is revealed in Collins' response to a letter from a parish priest which included this advice:

Will you attend Mass and receive Holy Communion every morning as long as the Conference lasts? You will I am sure, when you know you have not only Ireland's temporal destiny but her spiritual one as well in your hands. That is a dreadful responsibility remember. Beware too of English hospitality, live retired after conference in your hotel. Remember there is a danger and pardon me for pointing it out. You will be watched and criticised and your every smallest action shall be held up before the world and it may possibly happen that a set shall be put on your track and lead you astray and spy upon you. Be on your guard.[29]

Collins was very struck by this letter. The points about temporal and spiritual destiny and the phrase 'dreadful responsibility' are underlined in blue pencil, that about 'English hospitality' in red. After acknowledging the letter through his secretary, Collins himself wrote thanking the priest for his information about British intentions and saying:

You will remember the other advice you gave me. Believe me, I know fully the English method in these matters; I didn't live so long among them without finding it out. The other part of your advice is being attended to also though not – for certain essential reasons – quite fully. You needn't worry, I will tell you the whole story some time.[30]

The 'not quite fully' could refer to either receiving the sacraments daily or accepting British hospitality. As we know he did make an effort to attend the sacraments with some frequency, it is more likely that he was giving an explanation – before he might be asked for one – as to why he would be attending certain houses outside the strictly Irish-Ireland circle that the rest of the delegation confined themselves to. Even on a visit to Chequers, Griffith would not accept hospitality. His drinking was confined to Hans Place or the homes of Irish friends. The houses Collins visited were those of the Laverys and the Llewelyn Daviesses.

Collins' friendship with the Llewelyn Davies family caused them great anguish in the months before the Truce. In March 1921, through no fault of Collins but because of what he called a 'frightful example of carelessness and thoughtlessness'[31] premises were hired for the propaganda department under a false name, Moya's, and when the premises were inevitably raided this fact highlighted Collins' relationship with Moya. She was arrested and imprisoned and her husband was promptly dismissed, losing an income of £2,500 a year.[32] She was in some respects lucky, because at the time of the raid there were no guns in the house. She normally kept them in open hat-boxes, concealed only by scarves or underclothing. On top of this, either because of Crompton's friendship with Lloyd George, or possibly because the Government simply found the affair embarrassing, there was very little publicity about the dismissal. It was not raised in Parliament until just after the Truce had come into effect[33] and only rated one paragraph in the Irish papers the next day.

Collins obviously took the arrests and dismissal to heart. He made repeated efforts to get Crompton employed by the Dail as a legal expert in terms which are indicative as much of his concern for the future as for his friend:

It seems to me that we have to take things now on a permanent basis. This is a time when precedents are being made and when much thinking ahead is necessary. Establishments that at the moment may look threatening are in my opinion going to have a permanent character. Therefore it is important that right lines are laid down at the start.[34]

There was some resistance. Art O'Connor agreed that it would be 'worth many thousands a year in order to get the foundation of our land system and policy right',[35] but went on to say that 'some of their colleagues' might regard the appointment as 'a needless expenditure'. Crompton, who was 'a bit broken up',[36] ultimately found himself a partnership in a London firm of solicitors specialising in international law. He did in fact help Collins considerably with research and drafting during the Treaty negotiations and with speech writing thereafter.[37]

In Dublin, Collins used his network of warders to see to it that everything possible was done to make prison life easier in Mountjoy for Moya and her two companions, his helpers Eileen MacGrane and Patricia Hoey. 'Mick saw to it that little comforts such as woollen rugs, good books, food, China tea, which she preferred, sweetmeats were smuggled into her and her companions,' writes Kathleen MacKenna. Collins himself said, 'I'm in very close touch. She keeps in tip-top form . . . I fancy it could easily be arranged [if Crompton went to work on 'certain liberals'] that she might be released quietly.'[38] All three were released soon after the Truce and 'Moya went immediately to her husband and children in London.'[39] The next time Kathleen and Moya met was in Cadogan Gardens, Collins' headquarters during the Treaty negotiations. But were Collins and Moya lovers? Does it matter? One might well ask in 1990, but in 1921 the question could sometimes carry with it insinuations of espionage and conspiracy concerning the Treaty's signing and it therefore has to be addressed. There is strong, but not conclusive, circumstantial evidence that Collins and Moya were indeed lovers. Two anecdotes about now-vanished manuscripts certainly point in that direction. Both are redolent of the atmosphere of menace and conspiracy that accompanied so many of Collins' activities.

The first was related to me by Valentine Iremonger, the distinguished poet, playwright, translator of Irish literature and former diplomat.[40] Iremonger, who during the mid-1950s was Counsellor to the Irish Embassy in London, paid a visit to Rex Taylor in Lancashire while he was writing his biography of Collins.[41] Taylor showed him research material, which included Collins' diaries and day-books and a collection of Moya Llewelyn Davies' letters, some of which indicated a love affair. Taylor agreed to send 'small parcels at a time' to the Embassy so that Iremonger could have them copied and place the copies in the National Library with a thirty-year prohibition on publication. But following a subsequent conversation on an open telephone line, 'two men in bowler hats, acting for the firm of solicitors who represented the Llewelyn Davieses, showed up with authorisation to repossess the documents and took them away'.

The second anecdote came from Sister Margaret Mary, Batt O'Connor's daughter. Moya, who had helped Batt O'Connor with the publication of his book on Collins, showed the manuscript of her autobiography to Batt and his wife. Mrs O'Connor was aghast to read her account of her relationship with Collins and decided something must be done. She summoned some of his closest associates, including Liam Tobin and Frank Thornton, to a reading. It was generally agreed that the book contained material concerning their dead leader that should not be printed. They decided to send the unfortunate Moya an anonymous death threat. The crude censorship worked, the book never appeared and the manuscript has been lost sight of.

Poor Moya never suspected the conspirators. She recalled: 'it was put up to Mick that he should allow the Army to be canvassed as the other side was doing, and he refused. His attitude in that first week was that if the people didn't want the Treaty he had no wish whatever to force it upon them. They could take it or leave it.'[42] Moya believed that Collins had made 'no attempt to persuade you' [Thornton] or any of 'his extremists of the IRB'. She recalled the enormous satisfaction that Collins got from receiving a letter signed by Tobin, Cullen, Thornton and the others telling him they were 'with him' in that first uncertain week after the Treaty was signed. Collins' pleasure was of course quite genuine. Moya clearly did not realise that Collins had kept the IRB suitably informed before signing the Treaty.

Obviously, therefore, for all his genuine solicitude for Moya and her husband during her imprisonment, whatever their degree of intimacy was (the Sunday Press of 23 August 1987 discussed a rumour that Collins and she had a child) it did not allow her either to share his thoughts fully or to understand the fierce, primitive, clannishness that surrounded him.

Collins' reputation has also suffered because of his friendship with Sir James Barrie at whose house it was wrongly believed that he first met John Chartres. Kathleen Napoli MacKenna has left an account of the Llewelyn Davies connection which, though affectionate, nevertheless clearly shows how the suspicions arose. Moya brought Kathleen to meet Crompton, 'Bertrand Russell, Sir James Barrie and other intellectuals' and told her something of their background:

In his youth Jimmy Barrie loved a girl named Sylvia with a spiritual love similar to that of Dante for Beatrice. Sylvia married a Llewelyn Davies and, on her early demise, Barrie took care of the education of her two sons, and wrote for them the tales of Peter Pan and Wendy . . . In turn Jimmy Barrie was the confidant and bosom friend of 'The Welsh Wizard' Lloyd George who, when a Liberal taking his first steps on the road to political fame, was sponsored by Crompton. In the evenings Lloyd George visited Barrie's flat where, according to himself, 'he let his nerves relax and drew completely aside the curtain of his soul', disclosing plans, tactics, opinions, comments and so on! Naturally wily Lloyd George knew all about Moya's political associations, and of Barrie's friendship with Moya's husband.[43]

Some republicans to this day believe that the entire Barrie/Llewelyn

Davies/Chartres connection were spies who kept 'Ireland's principal war leader . . . dangling upon a line held firmly from Downing St.'[44]

The sheer importance of the Treaty for Ireland, would of course account in part for the explosion of myth and gossip. But there was also the Lilliputian factor. The impact of emerging out of the cabins and the small houses, the world wherein their soldiers were not accorded belligerent rights, into the world of the denizens of the big houses, was such that it inevitably expressed itself in the tones of envy and small-mindedness. The houses where the delegates stayed were not especially grand by London standards but consider the effects of the following description of a party at Hans Place (on 10 November 1921) on the imaginations of flying-column men who slept fifteen or twenty to a room in wet clothes – and made sure they broke nothing and, if they could, paid for everything before they left.

When the feast was at its height Mick with Liam Tobin, Tom Cullen, Emmet Dalton, Joe Guilfoyle and Joe Dolan joined us. They were jovial boisterous men who preferred horseplay to formalities. It was not long before they began throwing cushions at one another, then tangerine oranges, apples and nuts from the table, and finally coal from the coal-scuttles![45]

Some people took to such scenes with less indulgence than did Napoli MacKenna. Sean O'Hegarty, OC of Cork No. 1 Brigade, for instance, wrote[46] to Liam Lynch, OC of the 1st Southern Division purporting to be dismayed at the report of a Brigade officer after a visit to London. O'Hegarty relayed tales of 'rowdy and drunken conduct at Hans Place continuously'. Such conduct was 'particularly bad' when 'a dance or dances were held, or some form of entertainment ceremony'. These functions had been known to result in the 'smashing of a chair and door panels'. O'Hegarty notes 'the name of Michael Collins bandied about as central figure in alleged orgies'. But worse than all this a 'Fr. Dempsey had gone three times to see Michael Collins and discovered him "half cocked" on two occasions and "worse on the third".' A clear note of envy is struck as O'Hegarty grimly records that the drink bills from 'two houses' for one week were £300 and £200 and states that it is 'not clear whether the "two houses" means from two public houses for Hans Place establishment or has reference to the two establishments which I understand are being maintained in London for the delegation'.

When O'Hegarty, whom Mulcahy refers to as being 'always a snarly gob'[47] was pressed to substantiate his allegations, he replied that the officer who had supplied him with the information was 'not now available being despatched on a special mission'.[48] O'Hegarty believed it was 'his duty' to make such a report but having made it said 'the responsibility for the matter passes from me'.

Of course the reports also passed all round Ireland and very easily became intertwined with talk of treachery and espionage, especially when beautiful women could be mentioned (legitimately) in the same context. One of the most beautiful women in London at the time was Hazel Lavery, wife of the Belfast-born portrait painter, Sir John Lavery. She came from a branch of a well-known Galway family, the Martyns, which had settled in Chicago. In 1910 she married Lavery, who was nearly twice her age, and became one of London's most-talked-of society hostesses.

The writer Shane Leslie, first cousin of Winston Churchill, who was once in love with Hazel Lavery himself, said:

. . . of Hazel's achievement in bringing about the Irish Treaty of 1921 I know no historical comparison save the Princess Dorothea de Lieven's diplomatic cleverness amongst the statesmen of the drawing room in bringing about the Treaty of London in 1827 by which the Powers recognised the Independence of Greece. It was from her salon which was also her husband's studio that Hazel set out to inveigle English and Irish statesmen from the summits to descend and know each other personally as well as politically. Many such as Winston Churchill and Lord Birkenhead or Michael Collins and Arthur Griffith had reason to remember number five Cromwell Place (an ironical name for omen) during the twenties.[49]

This is an accolade indeed, but a more prosaic approach is taken by another authority on the period, Terence de Vere White,[50] in his biography of Kevin O'Higgins. He gives the then orthodox view amongst Collins' associates and admirers of the relationship between Hazel and Collins:

Lady Lavery developed a romantic attachment to Michael Collins which was notorious. Rumour gave colour and exaggeration and Lady Lavery, it must be confessed, gave rumour wings – to what was, after all a fancy on her part. Collins was unaware of the role which he played in the lively imagination of his hostess. He was engaged to be married . . . Lady Lavery persisted in the belief that Collins was unattached, and put on widow's weeds which only the firm tact of a friend prevented her from wearing at his funeral. Letters from Collins were shown to Lord Birkenhead by Lady Lavery and he noticed that the occasional romantic passages were interpolated in a woman's handwriting, valiantly, if unsuccessfully, disguised. It was all very odd, very unreal but not unpleasant, when one became accustomed to it and accepted the romantic convention. O'Higgins was destined to take the place of Collins in Lady Lavery's romantic imagination.[51]

But was it only a 'romantic imagination'? The truthful answer appears to be almost certainly not, however unconsummated the affair may or may not have been. The RTE documentary film, by Colm Connolly, shows close-up shots of her wearing deep mourning black and very obviously devastated by grief. Shane Leslie made a more complex analysis of the relationship of Hazel Lavery to both Collins and Kevin O'Higgins, whom Kathleen Napoli MacKenna termed 'the Irish Robespierre'.[52] Writing to Lady Audrey Morris about her proposed biography of Hazel he said that if their relationship

were truly portrayed there would be war in Dublin and much protestation. Both men were hopelessly in love with Hazel in the style of Tristan with the wife of King Mark because they had drunk a poisonous drug not intended for them. I had a sip myself so I know what it was like. The Republicans intercepted her letters to Collins and decided to shoot them both. Their three ambushes in August 1922 failed but Collins was shot a week later owing to those letters, as his enemies boast.

Collins' own letters to Hazel were of a type – full of half educated half romantic stuff but ending up with vital messages to the English Cabinet which were shown to Winston, Charlie [Lord Londonderry, Edith's husband] and others. It was on the strength of these letters that the Treaty was made. Hazel was proud of the letters and carried them about unwisely in a bag and was inclined to show Collins' love for her. Here she told me that she brought them on a party here and was convinced they were rifled by another guest called Dixon [a prominent Unionist]. This is given colour too by the names in the visitors' book. Every letter that would enable the Orange Party to frighten and blackmail the cowardly English Government had disappeared. John did not mind how much Collins and Kevin adored Hazel. He knew she was playing pityingly and ambitiously with men. He sent for me the night after Kevin was shot and took me for the first and only time to Hazel's bedroom. I held her for some hours while she shook and sobbed in my arms. She was aghast. She cried out that every man who loved her with true love was bound to die. She had killed her first husband and Collins and Kevin. She cursed herself as a curse to men.

She showed men's letters to each other. She actually gave me a copy of the pathetic love poems which Kevin wrote her. We all did! She showed one of my prose poems to Collins which he took and wrapped around her miniature. They were returned soaked with his blood after his death . . .

I think that as far as liaisons it was what the French call 'Le cas de Madame Recamier'. Do you know what I mean.[53]

It was all very different from the world in which Collins and O'Higgins were brought up and it is understandable that an unexpected draught of the sophisticated 'drug' which Leslie describes would have worked powerfully on young, idealistic men who had never before encountered such sophistication.

It says much for Hazel Lavery's alchemy that she should have captivated O'Higgins as well as Collins. Kevin O'Higgins, newlywed, was a devout Catholic, an austere, spiritual man who fasted for six months before his marriage in October of 1921 to Bridget Cole, a teacher and daughter of T. E. O'Sullivan, the man who wrote the song 'God Save Ireland'.

His best man was Rory O'Connor, whose execution he sanctioned in 1922. When assassins fatally wounded him in 1927, amongst his last words were 'I forgive my murderers', and he joked with his wife, picturing himself sitting on a damp cloud with a harp and arguing politics with 'Mick'.[54]

But no man can hold himself immune from love as one of the 'pathetic' poems Shane Leslie refers to indicates:

H   How can I tell you – I unskilled to sing –
A   All the deep nadirs of despair I know –
Z   Zeniths of joy that from remembrance flow
E   Evening may fall before our torches glow,
L   Love of my life, for time is on the wing.[55]

After Collins' death O'Higgins favoured Lady Lavery for the post of Governor General of Ireland. But by then the tide of revolution had ebbed and the thoughts of his colleagues were flowing in more mundane directions. The Laverys were not appointed to the old Viceregal Lodge[56] and Hazel's reward for her service to Ireland was to have her portrait printed on the Irish banknotes, where it appears to this day, although in recent designs, only as a watermark. Apart from helping to smooth the Treaty negotiations Hazel appears to have come to Collins' assistance on at least one other occasion. Although the precise date is not known it probably occurred in May or June of 1922 when relations between Collins and Churchill were particularly strained (see Chapter 11). Churchill was taking a tough line with Collins, for, amongst other things, the latter's North of Ireland activities and his refusal to crack down on former comrades whose activities were causing Churchill considerable embarrassment with the Die-hards.

Collins, who needed arms and continued British support at that stage, called with Hazel Lavery to Sir Philip Sassoon's home at Lympne where Churchill was painting. But Churchill refused to leave the easel. 'Young men must learn patience'[57] was his message to the butler. However, Hazel persisted. Shane Leslie, although he may have overstated its value, nevertheless authenticates her description of the situation at this juncture:

matters were looking desperate in the Irish troubles, so I arranged for a special meeting of Collins with Winston Churchill . . . at Sir Philip Sassoon's house at Port Lympne. At first Churchill was hesitant about coming to the meeting. But I impressed upon him the urgency of the situation, and he finally agreed . . . This meeting, arranged while Michael Collins was on a forty-eight-hours visit to England, really saved Ireland, and brought about the creation of the Irish Free State.[58]

A number of items concerning Hazel were found on Collins' body after he was killed. One was a transcript of a description by Shane Leslie of three portraits by Lavery in the Grosvenor Gallery, Collins, Hazel and Dennison Ross. Entitled 'To a Portrait of Hazel as Leda or Rose O'Grady' it included:

What feathered denizen of the sea or hills, what proud plumed lover from the mountain or the lake did Lavery suspect when he painted that flowing fluttering trembling view of your surprised and passionate Beauty? . . . or was it some amorous flamingo who broke through his bars at the Zoological Gardens or some dreadful nighthawk who clawed and dropped you ere he could carry you to his eyrie or was it some fierce 'wild goose' of Ireland that passed crying in the night.[59]

Others are fragments of letters which passed between them. One[60] is dated the day he was killed, 22 August 1922, and Hazel has written on it: 'Note written the day he was killed – found in his pocket – also small ruby brooch belonging to me which he wore in his scapular case. These and his note case were given to me after his death through his sister Johanna.' The Collins note says, 'must face realities . . . so goodbye – I read your letter again this morning before going to sleep. When I woke the pages were by my side. God bless you, I am *mombuirnin* [Irish term of endearment, 'my darling'] yours, M.' Another fragment[61] also said to be written by Collins but with a different pen from that used in the previous remnant, says, 'Hazel My Dear Dear Hazel I too wish it was "tomorrow" – with all my love, yours M.'

If Hazel did make romantic interpolations in Collins' letters in a disguised hand, as Birkenhead averred, it is not impossible that others may have done the same, perhaps to an even greater extent. A portion of a celebrated letter, said to be from Collins to Lady [Edith] Londonderry[62] which was quoted by Montgomery Hyde in his book *The Londonderrys*[63] raises the possibility that Collins may have had yet another relationship with a society figure. The quotation is as follows:

Forgive me. I bitterly regret my outburst at L. You are very kind to arrange the meeting and I am very well aware that I was miserably minded to listen to W. Churchill.

It is all very well to tell me as you do that he has no 'interest' in you. But how can you expect me to believe that, feeling as you know very well how I feel. So you must forgive my bitterness, and try to imagine what it means to be a man like myself entirely self-made, self-educated, without background and trying to cope with a man like Lord L., a man who has every advantage I lack . . .

I feel savage and unhappy, and so I blame you for a situation for which I alone am to blame, but I contrast myself with my uncouthness, with his distinction, my rough speech and his unconscious breeding, and the worst of it is I like and admire him, and feel he is brave and honest.

On one point alone I believe myself his superior.

Edith Londonderry was one of the great English political hostesses. From her Park Lane eminence, Londonderry House, far above the social torrent, she ran the Ark, a celebrated social grouping. She was married to Charles Stewart Henry Vane Tempest-Stewart, 7th

Marquess of Londonderry, a descendant of Castlereagh, father of the
Union which Collins had done so much to undermine. Educated at
Eton and Sandhurst, and a more enlightened figure than normally
found in Unionist circles, Londonderry was a reforming Minister for
Education. Lord Londonderry was a very proper person for a Catholic
Nationalist leader to get to know. But the Londonderrys never forgot
where the seat of their power and wealth lay, the British connection,
particularly the right wing of the Tory party, as we shall see in
Chapter 11. The Ark's membership included the Duke of York
(later George VI), the Prince of Wales (later Duke of Windsor) and the
Duke of Gloucester, to say nothing of Balfour, Carson, Lord
Hailsham, Ramsay MacDonald, Churchill, Neville and Mrs
Chamberlain, and a spattering of figures such as Elinor Glyn and Sean
O'Casey.

It was certainly all a long way from Woodfield. Would a conspirator
of Collins' calibre have written such a letter therefore? The first
answer is he might have, given the 'out of my country and myself I go'
atmosphere of London society that obviously affected both himself
and Kevin O'Higgins where Hazel Lavery was concerned. Also,
judging from notes accompanying it, the letter was regarded by the
Londonderry family as coming from Collins.

However, though the notepaper seems to be genuine, headed from
the Lavery's Cromwell Place home, it carries no date, no signature
and is written in pencil. Collins hated pencilled notes and I do not
remember seeing any from him in the vast number of his letters I have
gone through. The writing does not look like his. Nor is there any
signature. What does accompany the letter is a transcript in Lord
Londonderry's handwriting which, judging from the rusted paper
clip, was pinned to the pencilled original around the time both were
written. Was the letter shown to Lord Londonderry by his wife,
whose attitude to politics was swayed by the head, not the heart, out
of interest? Or to compromise Collins? If the former, it indicates a
greater degree of empathy between husband and wife than the
contents of the letter would suggest. The second would be in line with
the political antagonism of Collins and the Londonderrys where
Northern Ireland was concerned. Or, a third possibility, was the letter
copied from Lord Londonderry's transcript? The obvious way to
settle the question would be to consult a handwriting expert.
Unfortunately the North of Ireland Public Record Office would not
allow a photostat of the letter to be made under the rules governing the
collection. It must be said that if the Londonderrys ever did have plans
to 'set up' Collins these would not appear to have survived Londonderry's first meeting with him:

I can say at once that I spent three of the most delightful hours that I ever spent
in my life . . . and I formed a conclusion of the character of Michael Collins

which was quite different from the one I would have formed if I had only known him as I had heard of him before this particular interview.[64]

Both Hazel Lavery and Moya Llewelyn Davies openly claimed to have had sexual relations with Collins. Moya said that on the night he learned that de Valera was going to reject the Treaty: 'He was so distressed that I gave myself to him.'[65] And Hazel, who claimed that he rang her up the night he signed the document and said, 'I've signed your damned Treaty', wrote a letter about their last encounter which may have had fatal consequences. Certainly his last dinner party with Moya seems to have had. It was given in Furry Park, by Crompton and Moya, some days before Collins was killed.

The guests are said to have included George Bernard Shaw, the Laverys, Desmond Fitzgerald and his wife, Horace Plunkett and his wife, Piaras Beaslai and Joe O'Reilly. It was a pleasant, animated gathering. Bill McKenna was then fifteen years of age and the memory of the scene at Furry Park that night remained with him for the rest of his life.[66] McKenna had been sent to the house with a message for Joe O'Reilly. Word had been received of an assassination attempt on Collins. O'Reilly wanted Collins to move away from the windows while the grounds were searched but, careless of danger as ever, Collins refused. Both O'Reilly and Hazel Lavery then sat in the window to shield him. Eventually the search party in the grounds found a sniper, a man called Dixon, an ex-Connaught Ranger, perched in a tree. A number of attempts had been made on Collins' life shortly before this. Accordingly, as inside the house gaiety continued, outside it Collins' bodyguard took Dixon through the darkened fields, down to the sloblands and shot him dead.[67]

The shooting of the sniper sounds authentic; the problem is, when did it occur? Lennox Robinson wrote to Lady Gregory telling her about a dinner at Horace Plunkett's house, Kilteragh, in Foxrock on the Saturday before Collins was killed. Lady Gregory noted in her journals (pp. 180-1) that Robinson said: 'Kilteragh on Saturday. He came in Lady Lavery's train, or rather she in his, for she is his abject admirer. The Shaws were there too. G.B.S. was in great form on Sunday afternoon.' Shaw certainly met Collins that weekend, as a famous letter[68] he wrote to Hannie on his death shows. It is not impossible that he went to both houses on the same night, or that the dinners occurred on different nights, nor is it impossible that a number of the same guests were at the different houses. But the uncertainty leads one to be cautious about what is supposed to have been said at those dinner tables. In a letter to Collins Kitty Kiernan made a comment which is all the more relevant for having been made during the week in question. She had heard of 'a society woman – don't know if she's a girl – in London that her only idea in life now is to get spending a night with Mick Collins. One night will do her, just for the "notoriety" of it.'[69]

Hazel afterwards said that Collins asked her to go away with him that weekend.[70] According to her story, which she repeated widely, he stopped outside her bedroom window in a car. The horn sounded. She got out of bed and looked down at him and then at her elderly, sleeping husband. Her conscience smote her and, as she told it, 'the car drove away with a mournful sounding of the horn.' The story may or may not have been wishful thinking on Hazel's part.

Certainly Collins' busy schedule that weekend did not allow for any elopements. He left for the country at 6 am the following morning, Sunday. And as his correspondence shows he was in his office for at least part of the previous day[71] before spending a large part of Saturday evening at Furry Park and/or Kilteragh. At all events, the week after he was killed Hazel wrote a letter of sympathy to Emmet Dalton[72] telling him that Collins and she had been together at the weekend in terms which suggested intimacy and mentioning that he had been worried that the anti-Treaty forces were learning of his movements through opening her letters. She said that he suspected Noel Lemass, a prominent anti-Treaty intelligence officer, of being responsible. The contents of the letter became known to others. It was decided that the case called for more than a mere death threat. In July the following year, after the civil war had ended, Lemass was kidnapped and murdered by unknown men.

So much for the romantic web of fact and fiction woven around Collins and the circumstances leading to the signing of the Treaty and its aftermath. After Collins' funeral Oliver St John Gogarty told Lady Leslie: 'We had Lady Lavery in widow's weeds, full of confidences of Collins. Lady Fingall made her go home and leave the arena to Kitty Kiernan.'[73] It is time now for us too to leave the arena of romance to return to the political arena and the storm that burst over Ireland after de Valera learned of the signing of the Treaty.

The delegates were given a send-off as exuberant as their welcome on arrival in London to start the negotiations. At Euston, 'Mick was chaired, and lost his trilby in the delightful hurly-burly,' writes Kathleen Napoli McKenna. But when she got home herself the next day she found a very different atmosphere in Dublin. Gearoid O'Sullivan was amongst the group which met her party:

A strong dust-laden wind was blowing as they accompanied us to a waiting car. We at once noticed that O'Sullivan was black in the face with rage, and, while looking ahead, his eyes fixed on space, whistling between his teeth in an annoying fashion he had, we managed to gather from him: 'the fat's in the fire; the so-and-so and his so-and-so buddies, Stack and Brugha, won't accept what the Big Fellow signed; the Country will be quartered; nothing can prevent a split in the army, and the outbreak of civil war!' We were nonplussed.

Collins had not been sanguine leaving London. As Dr T. Ryle Dwyer has observed, 'He had realised that de Valera would oppose the agreement, if only on selfish grounds.'[74] It was a compromise, but it was not de Valera's compromise. As he prepared to preside at a Dante Commemoration ceremony in the Mansion House on the evening of 6 December, Austin Stack showed de Valera a copy of the *Evening Mail* with the terms. These should not have got out so soon as, according to the arrangements arrived at in London, neither side was to publish until eight o'clock, by which time the couriers, Duggan and Fitzgerald, would have had time to get an official copy to the President. They managed to get him a few minutes after he had read the *Evening Mail*. He was in a 'towering rage'. Duggan handed him the Treaty and, noticing that he was taking no interest in it, asked him to read it.

'Why should I read it?' was the reply. Taken aback, Duggan told him about the publication arrangement and pointed out that it was then nearly eight o'clock. 'What,' exclaimed de Valera, 'to be published whether I have seen it or not – whether I approve or not?' Beaslai, who was one of the speakers at the Dante Commemoration, says: 'I was astonished at the state of suppressed emotion under which he seemed to labour. And all this time he had not taken the trouble to study the Treaty. Apparently the fact that a Treaty had been signed without first being referred to him was the source of his agitation.'

The next morning de Valera summoned a Cabinet meeting of the members available in Dublin and announced that he was calling for the resignations of the three absent members, Collins, Barton and Griffith. Cosgrave stood up to him, saying he ought to wait to see what the three had to say first. 'This was the first indication that Cosgrave was not in agreement with him. Caution was necessary', says his official biography.[75] Realising that if Cosgrave went with Collins and the others he would be outvoted in the Cabinet, instead of calling for scalps he decided to issue a press statement. When Fitzgerald saw it he pointed out that it might be construed as meaning that de Valera was opposed to the settlement. He was surprised and puzzled, because at that stage, he, like a lot of other people judging de Valera on his published statements, regarded him as a moderate. He was soon disabused of his impression. 'That is the way I intend it to read. Publish it as it is,'[76] was the answer. The statement said:

In view of the nature of the proposed treaty with Great Britain, President de Valera has sent an urgent summons to the members of the Cabinet in London to report at once so that a full Cabinet decision may be taken. The hour of the meeting is fixed for 12 noon tomorrow, Thursday. A meeting of the Dail will be summoned later.

That was the first open step taken in the direction of civil war. By it the public learned, amidst a rapturous chorus of press approval for the

Treaty, that more ominous notes were being sounded. Peace was not assured. The IRB put on what Childers termed 'an organised Army reception'[77] for Collins and Griffith when they arrived at Dun Laoghaire. Collins took advantage of it to ask Tom Cullen, 'What are our fellows saying?' Cullen replied, 'What is good enough for you is good enough for them.' It was far from good enough for de Valera, Brugha and Stack. Childers arrived to find de Valera 'head in hands reproaching M.C. for signing'. De Valera was to speak at great length that day. He centred his opposition mainly on the fact that the delegates had not referred back to him before signing as Griffith had promised to do, claiming that he would have gone to London had it not been for Griffith's promise not to sign without referral back. And he recalled the fact that he had replied 'yes' when Childers asked him if the first three clauses should be scrapped.[78] His subsidiary argument was that he had always worked for Association which would not have given up the Republic and would have been acceptable to 'the Cathal party' as Childers termed it. But now all was thrown away without an effort, without permission of the Cabinet, or even consultation.

Barton 'strongly reproached the President'[79] and said the whole situation had arisen because of de Valera's 'vacillation'. He had had his chance of going to London and had refused. The disaster was that 'we were not a fighting delegation'.[80] There was much discussion as to whether or not the delegation had signed under 'duress'. Collins said that the position was that in a contest between a great empire and a small nation the settlement was as far as a small nation could go. Until the British Empire was destroyed Ireland could get no more. On that basis only was he intimidated. Kevin O'Higgins did not like the Treaty which he felt should not have been signed, but having being signed it should be supported. He stressed the absolute necessity for unity, unity being possible only on the Treaty. In the end Cosgrave decided the issue, voting with Collins, Griffith and Barton against Brugha, Stack and de Valera.

Diarmuid O'Hegarty made a strong appeal to the President not to oppose the decision publicly because of the consequences that would follow, but de Valera issued the following statement to the press:

The terms of this agreement are in violent conflict with the wishes of the majority of this nation, as expressed freely in successive elections during the past three years. I feel it my duty to inform you immediately that I cannot recommend the acceptance of this treaty either to Dail Eireann or to the country. In this attitude I am supported by the Ministers of Home Affairs and Defence . . . The greatest test of our people has come. Let us face it worthily without bitterness, and above all, without recrimination. There is a definite constitutional way of resolving our political differences – let us not depart from it, and let the conduct of the Cabinet in this matter be an example to the whole nation.

De Valera was back to his old tactic of taking an extreme course while sounding moderate. Beaslai[81] spoke for many when he said that the publication of the statement was akin to throwing a torch into a powder magazine. The Cabinet's example was followed, the country marched inexorably into civil war. De Valera's policy was quite deliberate. The next day he met the anti-Collins wing of the delegation, Gavan Duffy, Barton and Childers, in the Mansion House at three o'clock in the afternoon. Childers recorded in his diary that they discussed an 'alternative scheme' to the Treaty. It was a 'revelation' to Childers to discover that de Valera was not thinking of appealing to moderate opinion.[82] In order to defeat Collins and Griffith he intended to adopt a policy for which he would get 'extremist support' rather than 'moderate support'. Childers found 'his nerve and confidence are amazing. Seems certain of winning. Will put up a scheme productive of real peace . . .' At this remove de Valera's 'nerve' certainly does appear amazing. His courting of extremist support was to prove productive of the peace of the grave for many of his fellow countrymen.

For Collins that Christmas of 1921 was to prove only slightly less nervewracking than the previous year's when he had almost fallen into the clutches of the Auxiliaries. He literally had no home to go to and he stayed either in the Gresham, with friends, or in his old lodgings in Mountjoy St. Family considerations prevented him from going to Granard to spend Christmas with Kitty because Johnny was released[83] and there were details to be attended to, medical treatment for him, and the question of reuniting the family. But on the first occasion he met Batt O'Connor after the Treaty signing, 8 December, the night of the confrontation with de Valera in the Mansion House, he was so unnerved by the events of the day that he hesitated on the step after O'Connor had opened the door to him. Seeing him stand there 'with a strange expression on his face', O'Connor was puzzled and asked him, 'What are you waiting for?' Collins replied, 'I thought you would have no welcome for me, Batt.'[84] In the days that lay ahead there would be many who would agree with O'Connor who brought him in and told him:

You have brought back this Treaty. It is a wonderful achievement. The people want it. They must at least be given the chance to say what they think of it. Then if they reject it (only they will not reject it) you will have done your part, and will have no responsibility for the consequences.

That soothed Collins a little. He agreed that the people should have their say. 'I will accept their verdict.' But only a little. O'Connor describes him as being too filled with emotion to sit down. He strode up and down the room, the same room in which O'Connor had persuaded him to go to London in the first place, flailing his arms and threatening to leave Dublin and go back to Cork if the Treaty were defeated. 'If the fighting is to be resumed,' he said, 'I will fight in the open, beside my own people down there. I am not going to be chivvied and hunted through Dublin as I have been for the last two years.'

But for every comforting Batt O'Connor there were others like the woman who cut him dead in the street as he stopped to greet her and her husband.[85] When the Dail debate on the Treaty began, in University College, Earlsfort Terrace, because the Mansion House was occupied by a Christmas Fair, Collins knew he had the IRB behind him. But he literally had de Valera, Brugha and Stack in front of him, the division between the parties being brought into the open by the contestants sitting across the floor from each other. The subsequent debate calls to mind images from both Swift and Yeats. The former described a war fought over which end of an egg should be topped, the latter his hero Cuchullain being seized with madness, through the wiles of King Conchubar, so that he went out to spend his strength fighting the waves. Whether one sees Collins as Cuchullain and either de Valera or Lloyd George as Conchubar is really immaterial; the result was the same. The heroes fought the froth of the Oath and ignored the substantive flaw in the Treaty, which is still disturbing the peace of Ireland and bedevilling Anglo-Irish relations – the enshrinement of partition.

De Valera began[86] as he intended to continue, in Conchubar fashion. Speaking in Irish he explained that while he would like to deliver his speech in Irish he did not have enough command of the tongue to express himself properly and therefore he was going to continue in English. However when he spoke in English it was to begin by saying: 'Some of the members do not know Irish, I think, and consequently what I shall say will be in English.' What he had to say was said at enormous length. Apart from his formal speech of opposition his contributions to the debate came to a total of thirty-nine pages in the official reports. This compares with twelve for Collins and eight for Griffith. The debate lasted for thirteen days of private and public sessions during which de Valera behaved as if he were motivated, not by precepts of Republicanism, but by notions of the divine right of kings. One commentator has written: 'Whenever the President wanted to say something he seemed to act almost as if he had a right to determine his own procedure.'[87] In all he interrupted the proceedings more than 250 times.

His opening gambit was to try to convey the impression that the delegation had exceeded their instructions in signing. He read out the secret instructions with which they had been issued. At the same time he stressed that they did have plenipotentiary powers and while his audience was still trying to work out whether the signatories had or had not exceeded their instructions he moved that the press and public be excluded so that misunderstandings could be cleared up. Collins refused to let him get away with the ploy and read out the credentials which the plenipotentiaries had received, saying that the secret instructions should not have been read out without them. He objected to going into private session saying, 'I have been called a traitor . . . If I am a traitor, let the Irish people decide it or not . . . I do not want the issue prejudged. I am in favour of a public session here.' He pointed out that as with the British side, only the respective parliaments could ratify or reject the Treaty. However de Valera got his way with the private session suggestion.

He had two major objectives in following this course. One, he wanted Dail approval for the sort of draft treaty he felt should have been signed. Secondly, he returned to the charge of signing without permission:

I was captaining a team and I felt that the team should have played with me to the last and I should have got the chance which I felt would put us over and we might have crossed the bar in my opinion at high tide. They rushed before the tide got to the top and almost foundered the ship.

Collins' comment was: 'a captain who sent his crew to sea, and tried to direct operations from dry land'. He argued that as the document they actually signed was quite different from that rejected at the Cabinet meeting on 3 December, in fact Griffith had not broken his undertaking. This is stretching things somewhat, but de Valera could equally have been accused of exaggeration when he claimed that the only reason he had not gone over himself was a remark made not to him but to Cathal Brugha. However, he continued to use that argument not only in Cabinet but when trying to rally support outside the Dail, in the country and in America. In the end it was one of the few arrows he was left with in his quiver because his effort to win 'extremist support' with an alternative to the Articles of Agreement was a fiasco which turned hard-liners against him as being soft on the Republic and won no adherents from the Collins camp. Collins dubbed his proposal Document No. 2. It was a rehash of the proposals which the British had rejected on 4 December when Gavan Duffy provided the opportunity for a break.

Document No. 2 did not contain an oath. It provided that 'for the purposes of the Association, Ireland shall recognise his Britannic Majesty as head of the Association'. It resurrected External Association and practically replicated the Articles on partition, merely entering a demur that 'the right of any part of Ireland to be excluded from the supreme authority of the National Parliament and Government' was not recognised. On defence, the document proposed that after five years Ireland should be responsible for its own coastal defence 'unless some other arrangement for naval defence was agreed upon by both governments'.

Collins rejected these proposals, both for what they contained and because they had been tried before. For him, Document No. 2 was not worth fighting for.

However, his close friend and IRB colleague, the much-respected Sean Hales, very nearly let the cat out of the bag with his frank description of what he did think was worth fighting for, and, as we shall see in Chapter 11 secretly did continue to fight for. After pointing out that the people were for the Treaty and that for the moment the Volunteers were poor and exhausted, Hales went on to describe the situation he envisaged when the 'army of occupation' was withdrawn:

in a short time with the building up of the youth of the country, the training of their minds and the training of them as soldiers and the equipping, that day will soon be at hand when you could place Ireland to my mind in rightful place amongst the nations of the earth . . . when Sarsfield under duress signed that treaty with the English King foolishly enough . . . he honourably kept his word and they honourably broke it. Well the day is coming when we will pay that back . . . There is no fear that the soul of Ireland will die. Ireland's destiny is to be a Republic.[88]

Significantly, Hales did not use this argument in the public debate, confining himself merely to a declaration that he would support the Treaty. Whether he or Collins chose caution must be a matter of conjecture. The fact that de Valera was supported during the wearisome hours of public and private discussion (the Treaty debates fill two fair-sized books) by the women deputies and by Erskine Childers led to his support being dubbed the 'women and Childers party'. The women included Mary MacSwiney, Terence's sister, who was the most vociferous anti-Treatyite, Countess Markievicz, Tom Clarke's widow, Kathleen and Mrs Margaret Pearse, mother of Padraig and Willie. Sean Etchingham said of them, 'the women in the Dail will show they are the best men in it'. But de Valera realised that their support was not reflected by the public at large and he tried to have Document No. 2 withdrawn when the Dail returned to public session (on 19 December) having settled nothing in the private wrangle.

His manoeuvre drew from Griffith the icy and telling question: 'Am I to understand, Sir, that the document we discussed at the Private Session is to be witheld from the Irish people?' The document of course disclosed the fact that de Valera was not standing as 'the living symbol of the Republic' but as someone who favoured a compromise similar to the one on offer. A compromise, moreover, which Brugha and Stack had been prepared to accept. Griffith subsequently handed Document No. 2 to the press and resumed the public debate with a speech[89] in which he referred to 'the man who won the war' – Michael

Collins – and pointed out that not once was a demand made for recognition of the Irish Republic in the letters that preceded the negotiations. De Valera made a lengthy speech which never once mentioned partition, but it was Collins' reply which was regarded as the centrepiece of the day. He had a script before him but rarely used it. The press described him as 'passionate, forcible, and at times almost theatrical'.[90] Sometimes he stood erect, sometimes leaned forward to make a point. 'His flashing eyes, firm jaw, and thick black hair, through which he ran his fingers from time to time, were all revealed under the dazzling lights of the electroliers.' He drew applause when he dealt with the charge that he had been bluffed into signing. 'England put up quite a good bluff for the last five years here and I did not break down before that bluff.' He read out the correspondence between Lloyd George and de Valera which had preceded the negotiations and, having pointed out that Lloyd George had made it clear that they were not negotiating on a Republic, declared: 'If we all stood on the recognition of the Irish Republic as a prelude to any conference we could very easily have said so, and there would be no conference.' Recommending acceptance of the Agreement he said:

In my opinion it gives us freedom, not the ultimate freedom that all nations desire and develop to, but the freedom to achieve it . . . we have stated we would not coerce the North-East. We have stated it officially. I stated it publicly in Armagh and nobody has found fault with me. What was the use of talking big phrases about not agreeing to the partition of our country. Surely we recognise that the North-East corner does exist, and surely our intention was that we should take such steps as would lead to mutual understanding. The Treaty has made an effort . . . to deal with it on lines that will lead very rapidly to goodwill and the entry of the North-East under the Irish Parliament.

He wound up with a ringing declaration that he had stood over deeds which had caused excommunication, that he still stood over them, and appealed to people to stop quoting the dead. His objective was to achieve something which the dead, the living, and the children yet unborn would approve of.

Collins' speech had the impact he hoped for. Public and press reaction was clearly with him. The shrewd Tim Healy judged that his contribution was 'worthy of a lawyer as well as a politician. It was big enough for a trained statesman. I was surprised by its precision and detail, and rhetoric.'[91] However, in the emotional let-down that often follows such an effort Collins thought he had done badly and wrote to Kitty that 'it was the worst day I ever spent in my life . . . the Treaty will almost certainly be beaten.'[92]

The Dail recessed for Christmas on the 22nd. Between then and 3 January when the debate resumed Cosgrave as Minister for Local Government may have taken a hand in inducing no less than twenty

County Councils to pass resolutions of support for the Treaty proposals outside the Dail. Inside it, however, due in no small measure to the type of deputy whom Collins himself had been instrumental in getting selected by Sinn Fein, things were different. In Desmond Ryan's inspired phrase, there continued the 'long wrestle between ghosts and realities with all the stored-up spleens of five years flaming through the rhetoric'.[93] De Valera had also been active. He subjected deputies who announced their intention of voting for the Treaty to inquisitions for their threatened *lèse-majesté*.[94] In a letter to Joseph McGarrity, the Irish-American leader, who had originally hailed the Articles of Association until he learned of de Valera's rejection, he wrote of:

. . . an act of disloyalty to their President and to their colleagues in the Cabinet such as is probably without parallel in history. They not merely signed the document, but in order to make the *fait accompli* doubly secure, they published it hours before the President or their colleagues saw it.[95]

The reference to himself in the third person is indicative of the state of de Valera's ego at this period. Even though warned by close friends, such as Dr Farnan, that the country did not understand his alternative, Document No. 2,[96] he returned to the charge with it after the recess. Initially there had been hope that the contestants could bury their differences by means of a stratagem suggested by the Labour Party and supported by Collins. This would have involved the Dail passing legislation to set up a Provisional Government as a committee of the Dail. The Provisional Government would then proceed to draw up a Constitution, as would be necessary if the Treaty were accepted. But it would be an autochthonous constitution, one derived from the Irish people themselves, not an outside authority, such as the Crown. Thus those with reservations about taking the Oath could do so in the knowledge that they were swearing allegiance to the Free State's Constitution drawn up by Irishmen. De Valera however rejected the compromise.[97] He had revised Document No. 2 over Christmas and he proposed to put this as an amendment to the motion advocating Dail approval for the proposed Treaty. This manoeuvre was in fact an attempt at a filibuster. Had it been accepted, everyone in the house would have the option of speaking on the amendment, whether or not they had already spoken.

The ploy failed. Griffith revealed that de Valera's latest proposals were really Document No. 3[98] because he had materially altered the document from the one the Deputies had argued over for several days at the private session. De Valera tried to bluster his way out of this embarrassing revelation by saying, 'I'm going to choose my own procedure.' Griffith was outraged. He rose to his feet and said in a formal, even tone, 'I submit it is not in the competence of the President to choose his own procedure. This is either a constitutional body or it is not. If it is an autocracy let you say so and we will leave it.'

De Valera evidently considered it could be an autocracy when he saw fit. His answer was, 'In answer to that I am going to propose an amendment in my own terms.' It was after this scene that Griffith gave Document No. 2 to the press. Its publication cost de Valera a good deal of the hoped-for extremist support. Neither end of the egg, the Treaty or Document No. 2, appeared particularly appetising to the IRA. And the public at large could see so little difference between the two documents that it was hard to make out what all the fuss was about.

That night a group of pro- and anti-Deputies met at Sean T. O'Kelly's house to work out a peace formula. Again it showed the enormous respect de Valera was held in. The idea was based on the Labour Party initiative which he had already vetoed. In order that 'the active services of President de Valera should be preserved for the nation' eight of the Deputies (one, Liam Mellowes abstained) 'respectfully' recommended that de Valera 'might advise abstention from voting against the Treaty' provided: 'that President de Valera should continue as President of Dail Eireann. The Provisional Government would be permitted to function by the Dail, and would derive its powers from the Dail.' The Army and other services would also remain under control of the Dail. Griffith and Collins accepted the plan. Not so de Valera. According to one historian,[99] 'The whole nine Deputies then waited on de Valera, who, when he received it, flew into a passion, swore, and refused to accept the terms of the agreement, again urging the acceptance of his own pet document.'

His passion was added to by a broadside against him in the *Freeman's Journal* next morning (5 January) for his 'criminal attempt to divide the nation' by his Document No. 2 which the *Freeman* found 'much worse' than the Treaty. The editorial said that he 'had not the instinct of an Irishman in his blood'. The public were exhorted to 'put their fate in the hands of their own countrymen', that is, Collins, Griffith and Mulcahy. Collins wrote to the *Freeman*, protesting at the slur on de Valera. But the gesture had no effect on the Great Adamantine. For although, as one of the pro-Treaty members of the Committee, Joseph McGuinness, said in the Dail afterwards, 'the people on this side literally went on their knees to President de Valera to try and preserve the unity of the country,'[100] in private session the next morning (6 January 1922) de Valera thumped the table and said: 'There is no use in discussing it. The whole of Ireland will not get me to be a national apostate and I am not going to connive at setting up in Ireland another Government for England.'

When the Dail reconvened that afternoon in public session his reason for not accepting the joint appeal by the Deputies to avoid a split became clear. Gambling on the power of his own enormous prestige he moved the goalposts of the debate away from Treaty v. Document No. 2 to the question of his own resignation. He opened the afternoon session with a lengthy and oft-quoted speech[101] in which he portrayed himself as the Apostle of Unity who had for four years linked Sinn Fein, as represented by Arthur Griffith, to the Volunteers, as represented by Cathal Brugha. He read out his hard-line letter of 25 October to Griffith, thus making it abundantly clear that the letter had been written in the first place with an eye to the record. Dealing with the animadversions of the *Freeman's Journal* concerning Irish ancestry he said: 'I was reared in a labourer's cottage here in Ireland (applause) . . . and whenever I wanted to know what the Irish people wanted I had only to examine my own heart and it told me straight off what the Irish people wanted.'

What an examination of his heart on this occasion told him was required was his re-election so that he could pick a new Cabinet and 'throw out that Treaty'.

It may seem surprising at this remove that none of de Valera's opponents thought to ask the author of these republican-sounding propositions why he had not seen fit to mention the word 'republic' either in Document No. 2 or in its revised version, nicknamed Document No. 3. De Valera's stance appears very similar to his conduct at the Republican Convention in Chicago. There he was more concerned to show that he was the leader of Irish opinion than with the possible benefits to Ireland of the Cohalan-sponsored resolution. Now, on the second last day of the Dail debate as one authority[102] has described it: 'his attitude towards the Treaty was similarly influenced by his determination to show that he, not Collins, was the real Irish leader. Hence the President's refusal to accept the Treaty even under the terms urged upon him by Sean T. O'Kelly.'

The effect of de Valera's introducing the question of his resignation across the path of discussion angered Collins, as it prevented him analysing Document No. 2. He made a reference to 'Tammany Hall methods'[103] being employed by the Treaty's opponents and condemned the fact that the Sean T. O'Kelly initiative had not been pursued because the House had been prevented from getting a report on it 'by three or four bullies'. Asked to withdraw the term he paused for almost a minute before replying to the Speaker, Eoin MacNeill: 'I can withdraw the term, but the spoken word cannot be recalled. Is that right, sir?' At this Cathal Brugha, who had controlled himself well during the rest of the procedings, took offence:

I don't know to whom he referred when he mentioned this word 'bullies'. Possibly he may have referred to me as being one of them. In the ordinary way I would take exception and take offence at such a term being applied to me, but the amount of offence that I would take at it would be measured by the respect or esteem I had for the character of the person who made the charge. In this particular instance I take no offence whatsoever.

The atmosphere was further thickened when Harry Boland also took issue with the Tammany Hall reference. He had only joined the debate that day. He told Collins that 'if he had a little training in Tammany Hall, and reserved some of his bullying for Lloyd George we would not be in the position we are in today'.

Collins wrote to Kitty that night:

Saw H. last night. He was friendly, of course, and very nice. I'm afraid he was not so nice today, but not about you – I mean not on the subject of you. I'm afraid he wasn't fair in his homecoming in what he said about our side today. He's working like the very devil against us.[104]

The bitterness and the casuistry continued to the end. Seamus Robinson said that Collins' 'reputation and great deeds of daring were in existence only on paper'[105] and asked if there was 'any authoritative record of his having ever fired a shot for Ireland at an enemy of Ireland?' He thought that there was a prima facie case for 'the charge of treason' against the delegates, Arthur Griffith and Michael Collins. When Joseph MacGrath recalled that Harry Boland had been sent to America by the President to 'prepare the American people for something short of a Republic'[106] de Valera's reply was: 'Short of the *isolated* Republic.'

In general de Valera eschewed personalities, contending that the difference was purely one of principle. However the mask slipped during the course of one of his frequent protestations of high mindedness. Having declared that he was 'sick and tired of politics . . . I have only seen politics within the last three weeks or a month. It is the first time I have seen them and I am sick to the heart of them',[107] he went on to give another reason for wishing to resign: 'For instance there is the case in today's papers. Someone was kidnapped, and the Minister for Finance sent someone to make enquiries. He had no right to send anybody.'

A man who listened to him make this speech afterwards commented:

One of the most irritating features of Mr de Valera's behaviour at this time was, having used every device of a practised politician to gain his point, having shown himself relentless and unscrupulous in taking every advantage of generous opponents, he would adopt a tone of injured innocence when his shots failed, and assume the pose of a simple, sensitive man, too guileless and gentle for this rough world of politics.[108]

The wearing proceedings came to a conclusion insofar as a vote on the Treaty was concerned the following day, 7 January 1922, but not before Cathal Brugha delivered a particularly venomous attack on Collins.[109] He developed Seamus Robinson's innuendo about Collins not having taken an active part in the fighting, saying that he would not have done so had Griffith not made a reference to 'Mr Michael Collins as the man who won the war'. According to Brugha, Collins had merely been a 'subordinate in the Department of Defence', a seeker of notoriety, of whom the Press made 'a romantic figure, a mystical character such as this gentleman certainly is not'. He returned again to the charge that the British had selected their men during the negotiations.

Winding up for the Treaty side Griffith vigorously defended Collins:

He was the man that made the situation; he was the man, and nobody knows better than I do how, during a year and a half, he worked from six in the morning until two the next morning. He was the man whose matchless energy, whose indomitable will carried Ireland through the terrible crisis and though I have not now, and never have had, an ambition, about either political affairs or history, if my name is to go down in history I want it associated with the name of Michael Collins. Michael Collins was the man who fought the Black and Tans for twelve months until England was forced to offer terms.[110]

In theatrical terms he brought down the House. The psychological release, even on the anti-Treaty side, of being able to answer Brugha's invective by simple applause was amply availed of. It was some time before Griffith was able to continue. Yet the Collins reference only took up a fraction of an oration whose tone and content it is only possible to hint at in short extracts.

Although a procedural agreement between the pro- and anti-Treaty sides before the debate had given the last word to Griffith, de Valera tried to have the final say by making a melodramatic declaration that the 'document would rise up in judgement'[111] when compared to his 'explicit document'. Collins cut him off: 'Let the Irish nation judge us now and for future years.' And so the counting began, alphabetically. Ironically the first vote for the Treaty was cast by Collins himself on behalf of his Armagh constituency, a part of Ireland that was to be cut off from Dail Eireann by the terms of the Treaty. Neither he nor his colleagues who had been elected to more than one constituency voted twice. The result was sixty-four for and fifty-seven against. The Treaty had passed by seven votes. When the news filtered out of the chamber there was cheering in the streets, but little enough enthusiasm inside the House.

The first speaker after the announcement of the result was de Valera, saying that he intended to resign.[112] Collins appealed to his adversaries to help in preserving order, to form some sort of a committee to carry on because in times 'when countries change from peace to war or war to peace, there are always elements that make for disorder and that make for chaos'. For a moment there appeared to be a prospect that there might be a reaching out of hands and hearts but an obviously enraged Mary MacSwiney ended the moment:

This is a betrayal, a gross betrayal; and the fact is that it is only a small majority, and that majority is not united; half of them are looking for a gun and the other half are looking for the flesh-pots of the Empire. I tell you there can be no union between the representatives of the Irish Republic and the so-called Free State.

It was the authentic voice of those from whom he would require 'extremist support'. De Valera made no reply to Collins directly but called on his supporters to meet him the following day. Collins tried again for an 'arrangement' that would 'preserve the present order in the country, at any rate over the weekend'. But de Valera ignored the overture. He tried an oratorical flourish: 'I would like my last word here to be this: we have had a glorious record for four years; it has been four years of magnificent discipline in our nation. The world is looking at us now . . .' But his control failed him and he broke down. Brugha looked around the chamber, women crying, men trying not to, and then remarked: 'So far as I am concerned I will see, at any rate, that discipline is kept in the Army.' Collins gazed across at Harry Boland. There were tears in both men's eyes.

10

Wading Through Blood

'The Volunteers . . . in order to achieve freedom, will
have to march over the dead bodies of their own
brothers. They will have to wade through Irish blood.'

Eamon de Valera

Outside the encapsulated world of the Dail, preoccupied with Oaths
and formulae, the problem confronting both parts of the country was
not the difference between the Treaty and Document No.2, but the
growth of anarchy. The situation in the North was growing uglier by
the day. In the South, apart from the physical damage caused by the
war, there was the economic cost. Over 130,000 people were out of
work.[1] What industry there was, was in imminent danger of collapse,
and a million acres of land had gone out of cultivation. Commandeering and crime were rife in the country. The Volunteers, who should
have been policing the country, were wracked with dissension over
the Treaty. The people looked to the Dail for a restoration of peace and
progress towards prosperity. This was both the strength and the
weakness of Collins. A strength because, despite what was said in the
Chamber by the Treaty's opponents, outside it the people were
massively in favour of it. A weakness because, inevitably, to respond
to the feelings of the public at large meant a parting of the ways with
old friends in the IRA.
    By trying to maintain the freedoms and potential offered by the
Treaty, while at the same time avoiding taking action against the
elements who wished to smash it, he set up terrible tensions within
himself and those around him. Time after time he attempted to bridge
the unbridgeable; by doing deals with irreconcilable opponents; by
trying to uphold the Treaty while at the same time fathering a
Constitution which, had it not been vetoed by the British, would have
subverted Dominion status; by postponing taking military action as
the South slid further and further into chaos. And, over and above all
this, throughout virtually the entire period he was risking bringing
everything to a crash by sponsoring undercover military action
against the Six Counties. In the last eight months of his life Michael
Collins was a man on the rack.

He had four major spheres of contention: the Twenty-six County political arena in which de Valera continued to be his principal adversary; relationships with the British Government; the position of the Army; and Northern Ireland. (The last is best examined separately and is dealt with in some detail in Chapter 11.) The first major hurdle for Collins and Griffith after the Treaty vote was the vote three days later (10 January 1922) on de Valera's resignation, which in effect was another vote on the Treaty. The result was a further defeat for de Valera, though by a narrow margin, sixty votes against fifty-eight. He left the chamber in protest, followed by all his supporters, thus leaving the country without a government. Griffith was elected in his stead, appointing a six-man team of Ministers: Finance, Michael Collins; Foreign Affairs, Gavan Duffy; Home Affairs, Eamonn Duggan; Local Government, W.T. Cosgrave; Economic Affairs, Kevin O'Higgins; and Defence, Richard Mulcahy.

The atmosphere in the Dail caused by the de Valera walk-out may be gauged from the following exchanges, though Beaslai in 1937 disputes the record (p. 352):

Collins:	Deserters all! We will now call on the Irish people to rally to us. Deserters all!
D. Ceannt:	Up the Republic!
Collins:	Deserters all to the Irish nation in her hour of trial. We will stand by her.
Markievicz:	Oath-breakers and cowards!
Collins:	Foreigners – Americans – English.
Markievicz:	Lloyd Georgeites.

Later on, after de Valera had made a reappearance, Erskine Childers made some criticisms of Griffith which caused that normally phlegmatic man to lash out uncharacteristically, 'I will not reply to any damned Englishman in this assembly.'

Against that sort of background it is not surprising that Collins should write to Kitty around this time in the following terms[2]:

My dearest Kitty,
    I am absolutely fagged out and worn out and everything, but I send you this note to give my little remembrance of you. If you knew how the other side is 'killing' me – God help me – we had to beat them again today. Please come up as soon as you can . . . In awful haste and trying to catch a post so that you'd know I was thinking of you,
My fondest love,
Kitty dear,
Miceal.

The next major political development occurred a few days later at the Mansion House on 14 January when, under the terms of the Treaty, a Provisional Government was formed from the pro-Treaty members of the Dail and the four Unionists returned by Dublin

University. Until such time as the Free State Government contemplated by the Treaty was set up this was the body which would take over the administrative machine from the British. Collins became Chairman of the Provisional Government and Griffith remained President of Dail Eireann. De Valera refused to take any part in the setting up of the PG.[3] The Cabinet again included Duggan, Cosgrave and O'Higgins along with Joe McGrath, Eoin MacNeill, P.J. Hogan and Fionan Lynch. Collins thus took on responsibility for fourteen departments of Government; negotiations with the British, which entailed several journeys to London; the existing Dail Ministry of Finance; the explanation of Government policy to journalists and at public meetings all over the country; and a great deal of the negotiation over the increasingly troublesome IRA.

His first major task was to receive the hand-over of Dublin Castle on 16 January, a step of enormous practical and symbolic significance, tangible proof to the man and woman in the street that whatever might be said against the Treaty, it really had changed things. Characteristically there are differing accounts of what Collins actually said on this historic occasion. Two different anecdotes have an identical ring of truth. In one, a fussy official, perhaps the Viceroy, Lord FitzAlan, is supposed to have said, 'You're seven minutes late, Mr Collins.' Collins replied, 'We've been waiting 700 years, you can have the seven minutes.' In the other, James MacMahon, the helpful Under Secretary, said, 'We're glad to see you Mr Collins,' to which the West Cork accent responded, 'Ye are like hell boy!'

Collins probably took on so much administrative work himself at this stage that it had harmful effects on the day-to-day overseeing of the developing crisis in the Army. As so many of the significant IRA officers were also members of the Dail the political split over the Treaty was automatically replicated in the Army. Several of the most important GHQ and rural OCs were opposed to the Treaty. Liam Lynch stated, 'We have declared for an Irish Republic and will not live under any other law.'[4] Oscar Traynor said that the Treaty was 'not what the hungry and ragged men of the Dublin Brigade fought for'.[5] They were young, they were brave, they were fiery. Some felt they had beaten the British into conceding Dominion status in Round One. Round Two would bring the Republic. The Truce had been seen purely as a breathing space to gain strength before resuming the struggle. Many felt at the time they joined the Volunteers that they were taking part merely to keep alive the tradition of a 'rising in every generation', another gallant failure. They couldn't cope with the thought that they might have actually won something. It seemed dishonourable to stop now. For many, war had simply become a way of life.

The sheer size of the Army was another factor in the situation. It had probably comprised around 3,000 fighting men at the time of the coming of the Truce. But an unhealthy mushroom growth took place after that so that by 'the beginning of November 1921, nominal IRA strength was listed as 72,363'.[6] Many of these 'Trucilers' as they were called were poorly disciplined and (a great source of suspicion and tension to men who had fought all through the Black and Tan war) were former British Army men.

Within a few days all these sources of conflict had combined to make nonsense of Cathal Brugha's statement about maintaining discipline in the Army. The day after Mulcahy succeeded him as Minister for Defence (11 January 1922) a demand was served on Mulcahy that he should hold a Volunteer Convention, described as a Convention of the Irish Republican Army. Backing the demand were prominent IRA leaders like Rory O'Connor, Liam Mellowes, Oscar Traynor, Sean Russell and Liam Lynch. Eventually it was decided that a Convention would be held in two months' time. Meanwhile, at a meeting of both wings of the IRA in Parnell Square on 18 January, a watchdog Council comprising two from O'Connor's side and two from Mulcahy's was set up to ensure that 'the Republican aim shall not be prejudiced'.[7] By delaying the Convention – the proposed date had been 5 February –Mulcahy's side ensured that no open split occurred in the meantime, and that therefore there was no reason for the British to cease their evacuation. On the other hand the compromise of 11 January meant that from then on the British were handing over barracks to both pro-and anti-Treaty forces.

A similar rickety compromise was patched up on the political front at an Extraordinary Sinn Fein Ard Fheis held on 21 February to consider policy in the light of the Treaty's passing. Collins and de Valera came to an agreement whereby the Treaty was not put before the Ard Fheis,[8] and in return no change, that is, no split, would occur in the organisation and no election was to be held for three months. This last point was the important one. While the Ard Fheis, or Convention, would have gone overwhelmingly anti-Treaty, Collins' Provisional Government colleagues pointed out, correctly, that de Valera and his supporters would have been rejected by the public at large had an election been held. But against the forfeiture of this seemingly invaluable advantage Collins weighed up the possibility of staving off an open split and inevitable civil war. As we shall see shortly in the case of both the Army and the Sinn Fein Convention he was pinning his hopes on the same panacea for uniting pro- and anti-Treaty forces, the terms of the Constitution which, like the postponed general elections, was called for by the terms of the Treaty. He hoped that it would be possible to produce a Constitution which would be both acceptable to the British and Republican enough to prevent civil war.

The election would return party candidates to the new Free State Parliament wherein a government would be formed replacing both the existing Dail and the Provisional Government. Griffith was unhappy with the compromise at the outset and he and his colleagues soon had cause to be even more displeased, as the records of the Dail show. De Valera and his followers, while not recognising the Provisional Government, tried to have it both ways by putting down harassing questions for its members, who were also members of Dail Eireann, about PG activities.

Collins selected a Constitutional Committee which held its first meeting in Dublin on 25 January 1922.[9] Collins himself was its first Chairman though subsequently, because of his other commitments, he had to allow Darrell Figgis, who was the paid Secretary to the Committee, to act in his stead. However Collins laid down the guidelines for the Committee and all final decisions were taken by him. In a very real sense, 'Michael Collins was ultimately responsible for drafting the Constitution of the Irish Free State.'[10]

In many ways, the rarely illuminated story of the setting up and instructing of the Constitutional Committee[11] shows the nobler aspects of Collins' vision, the constructive thought for the future of a man who hoped it would be one of independence, democracy and peace. He told the Committee that what he wanted was 'a true democratic Constitution'; it was to contain 'not the legalities of the past but the practicalities of the future'. It was to be 'short, simple and easy to alter as the final stages of complete freedom were achieved'. He felt that the Constitution should omit anything already covered in the Treaty concerning Anglo-Irish relationships. Therefore the Oath should be left out. (His legal adviser, Hugh Kennedy, told him this was legal.) To put it in the Constitution would make it appear the Irish wanted it there. He further decreed that there should be no suggestion in the Constitution either of a Governor General, or that any power in Ireland derived from the Crown. The new Constitution 'must' be one which would guarantee Ireland's equality of status not only within the British Empire but amongst all the nations of the world.

Collins received regular progress reports from James Douglas, the Dublin businessman and humanitarian whom we encountered helping the activities of the White Cross in Chapter 7, an expert on constitutional matters, and from Kevin O'Shiel, a lawyer and expert on Northern Irish affairs.

Crompton Llewelyn Davies also gave advice and assistance. The first task for Davies and Hugh Kennedy, who afterwards became the Irish Chief Justice, was to go with Collins to London to get from Lloyd George the answers to two central questions raised by Douglas at the Committee's first meeting. Would the British ratify the Treaty before the Constitution was finalised? Would the Constitution have to be submitted to London for approval before being approved by Dublin? On the first, Collins succeeded in out-manoeuvring Lloyd George whose first instinct had been to tell him that prior ratification was impossible. Collins' reply was that he had not come to London to discuss the impossible but to inform the British Government that the Provisional Government was in imminent danger of collapse under anti-Treatyites' pressure and Lloyd George conceded on ratification but stipulated that the British would have to see the Constitution before Collins published it.

The British wasted no time in implementing promise number one. The Irish Free State (Agreement) Bill was introduced into the Commons on 9 February and, shepherded by Churchill in the House and Birkenhead in the Lords, passed all stages so swiftly that it received the Royal assent on 31 March. Whether one agrees or disagrees with the terms of the Treaty, it has to be conceded that Churchill's prowess in steering the ratification through his own constitutional and political minefields made a significant contribution to the creation of modern Ireland. But it was unrealistic of Collins to expect him to persuade Parliament a few months later to accept a Constitution which discountenanced all its symbols of authority. However, for the moment, Collins had bought time not only to bring his Constitution to fruition, but also in Churchill's phrase, to 'hold an election under favourable conditions at the earliest moment'. His Sinn Fein Ard Fheis agreement with de Valera was concluded in an attempt to create 'favourable conditions'. But militarily and politically the situation continued to develop inexorably towards a position which made the attainment of such conditions impossible.

Militarily, under the terms of the arrangement come to between the two wings of the IRA on 18 January, the 'watching Council' should in theory have prevented hostilities between those loyal to the Rory O'Connor faction and Collins' supporters, at least until the holding of the proposed Convention. But in fact the truce between the two wings was very like the truce between the IRA and the British the previous year; both sides used the lull in an attempt to improve their situation. As Collins and Mulcahy strove to consolidate their position from Beggar's Bush barracks, where Ginger O'Connell, who had American Army training, was trying to train up a new army as quickly as possible, the O'Connor forces were raiding for arms and transport all over the country. Figures like Ernie O'Malley and Seamus Robinson became virtual warlords in their own areas. Robinson, for instance, wrecked the offices and machinery of the pro-Treaty Clonmel *Nationalist* and threatened its editor with death.

From the end of February Limerick became a flashpoint. Sean Forde, an anti-Treaty IRA commander, issued a proclamation (on 18 February) repudiating Beggar's Bush and subsequently began arresting pro-Collins officers. Between 3 and 11 March, armed anti-Treaty forces took over buildings in the city. It seemed inevitable that the two wings would have to come into conflict, as figures like Griffith and

O'Higgins urged in Cabinet, but an agreement was hammered out, in the Mess of Beggar's Bush, largely through the mediation of Liam Lynch and Stephen O'Mara, the Mayor of Limerick, whereby in effect both sides withdrew from the city.

Although Mulcahy had calculated that the Army was simply not strong enough yet to dislodge the IRA from Limerick, some of his colleagues saw the Limerick compromise as little short of 'capitulation to mutineers'[12] and it was realised that a firmer line would have to be taken if the proposed Convention was not to result in an embarrassingly large vote for an anti-GHQ army. The Convention was banned. But O'Connor forced the pace. Asked at a press conference if he proposed to set up a military dictatorship he replied, 'You can call it that if you wish.' The banned Convention was then held despite GHQ on 26 March and a new Executive was set up with Rory O'Connor at its head. Underlying the sanguinary-sounding proceedings of the Convention there were two significant sub-texts. One, the same sort of disinclination Collins entertained against turning guns on old comrades and two, a lack of organisation and of political awareness.

But the public at large, knowing nothing of either factor, was understandably alarmed at reports of resolutions discussed at the Convention. These included 'the declaration of a dictatorship which would . . . overthrow the four Governments in Ireland opposed to the Republic – viz: Dail Eireann, Provisional Government, British Government and Northern Government.' Apart from this 'if there's a government we're against it', policy there was a great deal of talk about suppressing newspapers, drastically enforcing the Belfast boycott, and interfering with Provisional Government activities such as the building up of a police and courts system. The talk soon turned to deeds with the wrecking of the *Freeman's Journal*'s premises and presses on 30 March, because of its Convention reportage. From this there followed bank and post office raids, and the destruction of goods and sometimes premises in prosecution of the Six-County boycott, interference with mails, and seizures of state revenues such as excise duties and dog licence payments! Yet though the presence of two rival armies in the field made it inevitable that the guns would sometime begin to go off there was a reluctance on both sides to actually attempt to kill each other.

Watching the unresolved build-up of tension in Limerick, Churchill sent a telegram to Cope asking plaintively: 'Do you think there is any fighting quality in the Free State Government? Will anybody die for it or kill for it?'

Early in April a British naval vessel, the *Upnor*, allegedly en route to Portsmouth from Haulbowline Dockyard, was intercepted off the Cork coast by a ship commandeered by Cork IRA men and a large quantity of arms was landed at Ballycotton. Collins was convinced that there was collusion between elements on the British side and his opponents. Churchill rejected this charge but Collins accepted neither Churchill's denials, nor his estimates of the amount of arms seized.[13] There was speculation in London prior to the *Upnor* seizure, which was mentioned in the House of Commons, that the guns were to be made available to the IRA. Various reasons were advanced for this. Either it was intended simply to destabilise Collins' regime, with a view to facilitating a British return, or to strengthen forces held to be at the disposal of de Valera so that he could emerge as a strong man who, unlike the vacillating Collins, would restore law and order.

Collins cabled Churchill:

We do not charge collusion from high responsible authorities but we are convinced there has been collusion from subordinates. It is absurd to believe that a vessel containing such quantities of arms and ammunition be left open to seizure in an area where it is notorious our opponents are well armed . . . the fact that the Cork raid was talked of in London service clubs before it came off has been reported to us here. This corroborates Ward's statement [in a House of Commons query] and convinces us of collusion between some subordinates and our opponents.[14]

The War Office made an official estimate[15] of the strength of the *Upnor* haul as 381 rifles and 700 revolvers, which was much lower than that of the rumours current in Dublin. Churchill may have been deliberately misled. The War Office told him[16] that T. Barry and the Harbour Master, Cork Harbour Board, were responsible for the '*Upnor* business'. But Collins' sources of information were such that it is unlikely that he would have complained to Churchill if he thought that the *Upnor* affair was simply due to Tom Barry's outwitting him. 'Dirty tricks' departments are a familiar phenomenon in Ireland, as the collusion between some high-ranking British decision-takers and their Unionist confederates detailed in Chapter 11 illustrates.

Despite a universal urge towards restraint the first shots in the civil war were fired in April. Throughout that month, though casualties were light,[17] there were scores of clashes all round the country. The anti-Treaty forces attempted to seize barracks, commandeer lorries, and ambush rival troops for weapons. Speaking in Wexford, on 9 April, Collins described the situation bitterly but honestly: 'The humiliating fact has been brought home to us that our country is now in a more lawless and chaotic state than it was during the Black and Tan regime. Could there be a more staggering blow to our National pride, and our fair National hopes?'[18]

Then, on 14 April, O'Connor's men seized the nerve centre of Ireland's legal system, the Four Courts in Dublin, where they set up their headquarters. A number of other Dublin centres were also seized: the Fowler Hall, the Masonic Hall, Kilmainham Jail and the *ancien régime* Kildare St Club. These seizures conveyed sectarian overtones combined with a flouting of Provisional Government authority. But on this occasion, as on many others, Collins hesitated to assert his authority, even though he was personally involved in several potentially deadly incidents.

The military and political situations overlapped in his and Griffith's appearance at public meetings which the anti-Treatyites tried to prevent them addressing as a matter of set policy. Collins wrote to a friend around this time:

The opposition policy is making it almost impossible for us to hold useful meetings. The crowds assemble all right, but 20, or 30, or 40 interrupters succeeded in most places in preventing the speakers from being heard. That apparently is official policy accompanied by blocked roads and torn up railways to prevent the excursion trains from bringing the people to our meetings.[19]

He had first-hand experience of all the conditions he described. At Cork, on 14 March he was humiliated when a group of armed men refused him entry to the Republican burial plot. Subsequently he addressed a huge meeting in the city, possibly attended by as many as 50,000 people. Shots were fired throughout his speech. He told his listeners that those who accused him of betraying the national position could apply one simple test. Whoever ended in possession of the battlefield had won the war. The British were leaving, and would be gone altogether if de Valera and his friends would allow them to depart. Meanwhile outside the city a train bringing people to hear him was halted by armed men at Mogeely station. At Dungarvan a train he was actually speaking from was driven off in the middle of his address. He finally succeeded in speaking from a hotel balcony. At Castlebar he addressed a meeting which he had to get to over blocked roads and through cut railway lines. Many of his potential hearers were prevented from getting to hear him by armed parties on the roads, who held them up and sent them home. In Kerry, where his message was that neither the Treaty nor the Republic was worth the risk of civil war, he spoke in circumstances of great danger, as at both Tralee and Killarney his meetings were formally proclaimed by the IRA. He secured a hearing partly by negotiation with local commanders, partly through improvisation. At Killarney his platform was destroyed by fire but he obtained a brake. When the local anti-Treaty commander stepped in front of him, backed up by a force of armed men, as he strode towards the brake, he simply pushed past him and, turning his back on the gunmen, moved on to give his speech.

These were far from being his only brushes with gunmen. On the night of the Cork meeting in March he was on his way to the house of his sister, Mary Collins Powell, when a man with a revolver appeared in front of him shouting, 'Collins I have you now.' Before he could pull the trigger Sean MacEoin had him. After disarming him he asked Collins, 'Will I shoot him?'

'No. Let the bastard go,' was Collins' answer. The following month he drew his automatic on a party of riflemen who tried to seize his car outside Vaughan's Hotel. The pistol jammed but he grabbed one of the raiders and despatched him to Mountjoy.

Arthur Griffith showed similar, or possibly even greater courage in view of his age, and the fact that, unlike Collins, he had little experience of military confrontation. When it became known that he was going to address a meeting in Sligo on Easter Sunday, 16 April, it was proclaimed and the town was heavily invested by anti-Treaty forces. Bloody confrontation seemed inevitable. But Griffith did not flinch. He was already deeply critical of Collins' 'softly softly' approach and, Ernest Blythe recalled:

For the first and only time in my experience, he rose to his feet at a Cabinet meeting and made a formal speech. He spoke, I remember, under obvious stress and with a degree of passion I had never before known him to show. He wound up by saying that if we were not prepared to fight and preserve the democratic rights of the ordinary people and the fruit of national victory, we should be looked upon as the greatest set of poltroons who had ever had the fate of Ireland in their hands.[20]

The night before the meeting was due to be held he left his friends the Montgomery family with a letter to be opened in the event of his death. When some months later he did die the envelope was opened and the message was found to read: 'Let the people stand firm for the Free State. It is their national need and their economic salvation. Love to all the Irish people and to all my colleagues and friends.'

He arrived in Sligo in an armoured car surrounded by armed troops. At the eleventh hour the IRA commander, Liam Pilkington, who afterwards became a priest, stepped back from the prospect of fratricidal strife and the meeting passed off peacefully. But large-scale fighting broke out a few weeks later in Kilkenny where anti-Treaty forces made a Sligo-type investiture of strongpoints from which they were only driven after two days' fighting and the taking of 150 prisoners. Remarkably only two men were injured.

Cooler heads on both sides realised that that sort of luck could not last indefinitely and one last major effort at securing peace between the fighting men was made under the auspices of the IRB. Lynch and a number of top Cork IRA leaders including Tom Hales, Sean O'Hegarty and Florrie O'Donoghue were out of sympathy with the anti-democratic drift of the O'Connor-led Executive and, for their part, figures such as O'Connor, O'Malley and Mellowes were shrewd enough to realise that the prospects of military success without Lynch and the others were slim. Although an early proposal by Florrie

O'Donoghue failed, on 1 May an IRB-sponsored statement appeared, signed by Collins, Mulcahy, Gearoid O'Sullivan, Eoin O'Duffy for the pro-Treaty faction and for the other side by Dan Breen, Sean O'Hegarty, Florrie O'Donoghue, Tom Hales and Humphrey Murphy.

It called for a closing of ranks in the face of the 'greatest calamity in Irish history' and conceded that a majority of the people were for the Treaty. It called for an agreed election, Army unification and the forming of a government which would have 'the confidence of the whole country'. This was the last time the IRB played a major role in the developing crisis. It was largely unsuccessful. Rory O'Connor immediately issued a public statement repudiating the initiative as a 'political dodge intended to split the Republican ranks'.

But it did create a basis for a dialogue between the two sides. Lynch, Mellowes and Sean Moylan on behalf of the Executive agreed to a form of truce with three of Collins' nominees, O'Duffy, O'Sullivan and MacEoin. These six continued to meet and somehow, a truce more or less held between the sides until near the end of June, although raids and robberies directed by the Executive forces or their sympathisers continued all round the country. Then on 15 June O'Connor and O'Malley handed Mulcahy a document repudiating the six-man talks, which had been faltering over matters which the Cabinet obviously could not concede such as the Four Courts' men's demand that they appoint the Army's Chief of Staff. Three days later an Executive Convention was held in the Four Courts to consider the resolution, 'That this Executive Council of the IRA hereby decide . . . the only means of maintaining the Republic is by giving the English seventy-two hours' notice to evacuate the country.'

The Four Courts' men proposed:

The destruction of all barracks occupied by our troops, the attacking present port positions held by the English troops. The striking at English forces . . . wherever possible in areas which the pro-Treaty troops occupy so that they may be brought into collision with English troops.

O'Connor and his followers were in fact debating how best to embroil the two wings of the IRA in a renewed struggle against the British. The military path to civil war was now within a few days of its destination. At this stage we must turn to see how and by whom the political path to the same destination was constructed.

De Valera's decision not to go to London for the Treaty negotiations really rebounded on him and on the nation in the months following the vote on the Treaty. Certainly if he, Collins and Griffith had come back with their names on a document, opposition to it throughout the country would have been only a small fraction of what he stirred up against the Treaty. Even if he had gone without Collins,

as he did in July 1921, in the words of Tom Hales, the man in charge of
the ambush party that shot Collins, 'If Dev had come back with a
document that Collins didn't like, there'd have been no civil war.'[21]
The 'what might have been' tragedy for Ireland lay in the fact that in a
very real sense it was de Valera who later proved the validity of
Collins' 'stepping-stone' argument.

On the Irish scene, de Valera was a great figure, but the actions of
great men, particularly on a small stage, can sometimes have far-
reaching and harmful consequences, especially when they seek
extremist support. He began by founding a new party (on 15 March)
from amongst the anti-Treaty section of the Dail known as *Cumann
na Poblachta* (League of the Republic). Then in addition to the election
postponement of two months secured by the Sinn Fein Ard Fheis pact
between himself, Collins and Griffith, he attempted to gain further
postponement by trying to get the election held on a new register
which, as Griffith commented when rejecting the stratagem, would
have made 'an election impossible for the next six months'[22] and
would effectively 'muzzle the electorate'.

De Valera's 'extremist support' policy then led him to launch
himself on a course of inflammatory speech-making which became an
ineradicable blot on his reputation. At Dungarvan, on 16 March, he
said:

The treaty . . . barred the way to independence with the blood of fellow
Irishmen. It was only by civil war after this that they could get their
independence. If you don't fight today, you will have to fight tomorrow; and
I say, when you are in a good fighting position, then fight on.[23]

In Tipperary he marked St Patrick's Day with two speeches which
raised the spectacle of drowning the shamrock in blood. At Carrick-
on-Suir, where it was estimated his audience included several hundred
IRA men, he said:

If the Treaty was accepted the fight for freedom would still go on; and the
Irish people, instead of fighting foreign soldiers, would have to fight the Irish
soldiers of an Irish Government set up by Irishmen. If the Treaty were not
rejected, perhaps it was over the bodies of the young men he saw around him
that day that the fight for Irish freedom may be fought.[24]

He then went on to Thurles, where the composition of his audience
may be gauged from the fact that hundreds of his hearers carried rifles,
and repeated these statements, adding:

If they accepted the Treaty, and if the Volunteers of the future tried to
complete the work the Volunteers of the last four years had been attempting,
they . . . would have to wade through Irish blood, through the blood of the
soldiers of the Irish Government, and through, perhaps, the blood of some of
the members of the Government in order to get Irish freedom.

Next day in Killarney he said: 'If our Volunteers continue, and I hope they will continue until the goal is reached . . . then these men, in order to achieve freedom, will have, I said yesterday, to march over the dead bodies of their own brothers.'[25]

When he was condemned editorially by the *Independent* for these speeches de Valera riposted with a letter in which he said he had been misrepresented in a 'villainous' way that showed 'criminal malice'.[26] He said that his speeches were 'an answer to those who said that the London Agreement gave us "freedom to achieve freedom".'

After the seizure of the Four Courts, representatives of the Labour Party met him in an effort to avert the wading 'through Irish blood'. One of those who pleaded with him, Senator J. T. O'Farrell, afterwards told the Seanad that:

the only statement he made that has abided with me since as to what his views were was this: 'The majority have no right to do wrong.' He repeated that at least a dozen times in the course of the interview, in response to statements made to him to the effect that the Treaty had been accepted by a majority, and that consequently, it was his duty to observe the decision of the majority until it was reversed. He refused to accept it on the grounds that the majority had no right to do wrong.[27]

Far from repudiating the Four Courts' men de Valera greeted the seizure with a proclamation on 16 April which declared: 'Young men and young women of Ireland, the goal is at last in sight. Steady all together; forward, Ireland is yours for the taking. Take it.' At this stage Harry Boland was working for de Valera as his secretary and he was obviously relaying the thoughts of the Master when he wrote to Austin Stack: 'Civil war is certain unless Collins and Company see the error of their ways and come to terms with their late colleagues.'[28] Two days later (on 29 April) the Catholic Archbishop of Dublin, Dr Byrne, tried to bring the former colleagues together by convening a meeting at the Mansion House between Collins and Griffith and de Valera and Brugha. Brugha provoked a scene by telling Collins and Griffith that they were British agents. Collins jumped up and glared at him: 'I suppose we are two of the Ministers whose blood is to be waded through?' Brugha replied, 'Yes, you are two.' De Valera neither rebuked nor disowned him but, somehow, Dr Byrne managed to keep the peace.

Collins argued that 'every adult has a right to vote.'[29] But Brugha replied: 'No nation has power to part with its nationality or barter any part of national heritage.' Collins proposed a plebiscite but Brugha refused, saying no such issue should be put before the people while the threat of war was there.

De Valera did not want an election to be held either, but clothed his fear of facing any sort of national verdict on the Treaty in an objection to the 'stone age plebiscite' proposed. The idea was that people would congregate in certain areas, mainly at churches, and signify their preference by walking through gates or barriers. His real objection of course was that he was angling for 'extremist support' and the Four Courts' men were opposed to an election. So he had to follow the anti-democratic path, issuing a statement after the Mansion House débàcle[30] explaining his refusal by saying that 'Republicans maintain that there are rights which a minority may justly uphold, even by arms, against a majority.' He justified his refusal to co-operate in holding an intimidation-free election in June by counter-proposing a six-month postponement so that:

Time would be secured for the present passions to subside, for personalities to disappear, and the fundamental differences between the two sides to be appreciated – time during which Ireland's reputation could be vindicated, the work of national reconstruction begun, and normal conditions restored.

The 'fundamental differences' of course were those between the Treaty and Document No. 2, and as for the work of 'national reconstruction' it may be observed that the day before the statement appeared[31] the Four Courts' men organised countrywide swoops on Bank of Ireland branches – their section of the IRA was no longer being paid by Beggar's Bush – which netted more than £230,000. But far from appearing taken aback by this, de Valera, if anything, strengthened his hard-line approach in an interview with John Steele of the *Chicago Tribune* which he thought so highly of that it was reprinted in the paper published by his faction which Erskine Childers edited, *Poblacht na hEireann*. He assured Steele that: 'We all believe in democracy, but we must not forget its well known weaknesses. As a safeguard against their consequences the most democratic countries have devised checks and brakes against sudden changes of opinion and hasty, ill-considered actions.'[32] He pointed out that in America a Treaty needed a two-thirds majority to pass the Senate. As Ireland had not had 'an opportunity of devising constitutional checks and brakes', he said, 'The army sees in itself the only brake at the present time and is using its strength as such.' Looking back at this phase in his country's history the poet Yeats would one day write:

Had de Valera eaten Parnell's heart
No loose-lipped demagogue had won the day
No civil rancour torn the land apart.[33]

At this stage it becomes necessary for a moment to consider Griffith's attitude to de Valera. As these developments unfolded, his opinion of the 'Long Fellow' sank lower and lower. After the vote on the Treaty was taken he said, 'There is no man in Ireland I respect and love more'. Then he became a 'good man whom America spoiled'.[34] After the abortive Mansion House talks he told Ernest Blythe and others in private, 'that was the first time I really got after the "Long Fellow".'[35] In public he read out the following from *Poblacht na hEireann*: 'We'll not have this Treaty executed. Let us rather execute the man who signed it for us behind our backs.'[36] Griffith said of the article in which the foregoing occurrred: 'I say that is a deliberate incitement to the assassination of the plenipotentiaries and they won't get off with it . . . I know the atmosphere which is being prepared. You may assassinate us but you won't intimidate us.'

Griffith was sick and tired of the confusing two-hatted Dail/ Provisional Government position. He wanted an end to the make-believe and an election to a new, unambiguous parliament. Following the Sinn Fein Ard Fheis pact with de Valera this election was now scheduled for 16 June. But above all he urged Collins to take action to dislodge the Four Courts men. 'By God we will', Collins would say, thumping the table. But always he postponed the issue and tried to compromise.[37] We can image Griffith's dismay, therefore, when on 20 May 1922 his greatest compromise was unveiled. Under a formula devised by Harry Boland, Collins, acting independently of Griffith, entered into an electoral pact with de Valera.

The idea was that they should face the electorate together under an arrangement whereby the Treaty would not be an issue. However a coalition panel of candidates would be formed from both the pro- and anti-Treaty sections of Sinn Fein, each section having a number equivalent to its existing strength in the Dail. The Cabinet seats in the ensuing Government were to be apportioned on the basis of the election results.

It was a highly dubious arrangement, which, apart from anything else, cut across the interests of the other parties, the Farmers and Labour. Griffith was appalled when it was brought before the Cabinet. Asked if he would accept it, 'he spent three whole minutes reflecting, pulling nervously at his tie and wiping his glasses. The other ministers waited in silence for his answer for what seemed a long time, and when he did assent he no longer addressed Collins as "Mick", but with a noticeably formal "Mr Collins".'[38] In the few months of life left to the two men their former cordiality was not re-established. In London they had drawn close together because of de Valera; now they were driven apart because of him. Another admirer of Collins, Hugh Kennedy, the Law Officer, was also horror-struck when he learned of the pact's terms. He immediately sent him a 'lengthy memorandum in a spirit of helpfulness, and not of obstruction', setting forth the blatant illegality of the arrangement:

(a) The Provisional Government is, as far as the Treaty is concerned, the only Government with authority until the Parliament and Government of the Irish Free State has been established . . . until after the Constitution has been adopted.

(b) You cannot have a Coalition Provisional Government consisting of pro-Treaty and anti-Treaty members. Every member of the Provisional Government must accept the Treaty in writing.[39]

If that is how the pact seemed to an Irish friend of Collins' one can imagine how it looked to British critics. It is not generally known that Churchill had been well aware that something of the sort was likely and that he had written in very strong terms to warn Collins against concluding any such arrangement five days before the pact was announced:

I think I had better let you know at once that any such arrangement would be received with world-wide ridicule and reprobation. It would not be an election in any sense of the word, but simply a farce, whereby a handful of men who possess lethal weapons deliberately disposed of the political rights of the electors by a deal across the table . . . It would be an outrage upon democratic principles and would be universally so denounced . . . Your Government would soon find itself regarded as a tyrannical junta which having got into office by violence was seeking to maintain itself by a denial of constitutional rights.

The enemies of Ireland have been accustomed to say that the Irish people did not care about representative Government, that it was alien to their instincts, and that if they had an opportunity they would return to a despotism or oligarchy in one form or another. If you allow yourself to be misled into such an arrangement as is indicated, such action would be immediately proclaimed as justifying to the full this sinister prediction. As far as we are concerned in this country, we should certainly not be able to regard any such arrangement as a basis on which we could build.[40]

Collins ignored Churchill's letter and on 17 May began three days of negotiation with de Valera at University College, Dublin. Apart from hoping to secure an intimidation-free election, Collins had three other considerations in mind in going ahead with the pact in the face of the Churchillian warning.

First he still desperately hoped to avoid conflict with his former comrades with whom he still empathised to a greater degree than with many of his Cabinet colleagues. Sean O'Muirthle said of Collins at this period that he was not particularly worried about losing either de Valera's friendship or that of many of his political colleagues:

What troubled Collins was the split in the Army. There were men in the Army that he would go almost any distance to satisfy. He would rather, as he said to me more than once, have one of the type of Liam Lynch, Liam Deasy, Tom Hales, Rory O'Connor, or Tom Barry on his side than a dozen like de Valera. These were men of great energy and patriotic outlook down through the . . . Anglo-Irish War, and they had been faithful subordinates as well as personal friends, and the thought of turning the guns on such men was abhorrent to Collins.[41]

Secondly, he still hoped that his Constitution, now nearing

maturity, would bring peace. Judging from British intelligence reports analysed by Lionel Curtis it seems clear that he gave de Valera some indications that the Constitution would be sufficiently Republican to allow of the formation of a Coalition Government. Curtis commented: 'The possibility that this project may furnish the key to the Agreement cannot be ignored.'[42]

Thirdly, the hidden agenda to his pact with the anti-Treaty forces included agreement on a joint IRA offensive in Northern Ireland which was to commence a few days later.

How much either de Valera or British Intelligence knew of this component of the deal must be a matter for speculation. Apart from whatever Collins may have told him directly the former's relationship with Frank Aiken, the Northern IRA leader, who was central to the offensive, would certainly seem to indicate that he knew something of Collins' Six-County intentions. British Intelligence could hardly have gleaned as much as it did of Collins' constitutional scheming without picking up something of his military plotting also. On the other hand the fact that the gun-running which preceded the offensive was successful might indicate that the agents of his military plans were more security conscious than his political associates.

It must be conceded that the whole pact episode and its attendant manoeuvrings places Collins more in the light of a conspirator than a statesman. But though he might appear to have been merely either weak or simply attempting to throw a cloak of constitutionality over a preferred course of IRA activity, his vision of what he sought remained clear even in that maelstrom month of May. This was shown in a reply to a former close IRA associate in Liverpool whose letter of regret at parting from him well articulates the naive sincerity of many Republicans, both then and subsequently. Paddy Daly wrote to him saying:

I have put off writing this letter from day to day in the hope that some form of unity might be accomplished . . . Possibly you have already heard that I am against the Treaty. I needn't point out the path I have chosen is not an easy one and that my freedom could not last very much longer on this side . . . I want you to know I am following my conscience and am not influenced by any individual . . . believe me, I would rather be riddled a hundred times over than think I had helped in any way to harm you. On the contrary, I would defend you as your nearest friends would.

I say this because I know you are as sincere today as you were in Xmas 1920 when things looked black – sincere in the idea of an Irish Republic. I know also and believe that you are acting as you think in the best interests of Ireland . . . continue now and finish the fight . . . struggle for fifteen or twenty years, would be a forlorn consolation. The big businessmen and politicians will come forward when peace is established and perhaps after some years gain control. Their interests would never demand a renewal of war.[43]

The whole thing has given me more mental worry than I have ever experienced. . . .

Beannact De, a Naom muire leat, do cara, P.O'Dalaig, L'pool (The blessing of God and his holy mother on you, your friend P. Daly).

In the press of events Collins took nearly a month to reply:

Believe me the Treaty gives us the one opportunity we may ever get in our history for going forward to our ideal of a free independent Ireland. This cannot be gained without very much work yet – very hard work, *and perhaps more than hard work* [Author's italics]. And it is not by dissipation of the national energy that we can gain this. It is not by acts of suppression, and is not by denial of liberty that we can reach liberty.

At any rate I am perfectly conscious that you are influenced only by what you think right in the matter, and with an expression of very sincere appreciation of your past services, and a hope that we may work in the same company again, I leave the matter.[44]

Lloyd George and Churchill knew little of such partings of the ways, but they understood all too well that there was a strong likelihood of divergence from the Treaty's terms following the publication of those of the Collins–de Valera pact. The Treaty signatories were immediately invited to London and Cope was instructed to find out what was happening. Collins gave him a number of assurances[45]: (1) that Churchill would be quite happy when he heard what the delegation who were going over to London to explain the pact had to say; (2) that it would not breach the Treaty; and (3) that de Valera would not see the Constitution before the delegates, including Griffith, left for London. However he did not give Cope one important reassurance sought. He said there was as yet no decision as to whether or not the Constitution would be a Coalition measure. Most significantly of all he at first refused to go to London himself. It took a personal letter from Churchill in his own hand-writing to induce him to travel: 'I learn from Mr Cope with great apprehension that you may consider yourself unable to come . . . Your absence would I fear be misunderstood. Certainly it would be deeply regretted.'[46]

It was a meeting, or rather meetings, of 'great importance'. Between Saturday 26 May and 15 June whatever slight hope there was of avoiding the Irish civil war evaporated. The Constitution on which Collins had pinned such hopes ended up being so altered as to bring it back into conformity with the Treaty. Collins did not join the talks until Saturday 27th, having spent the previous Friday afternoon arguing with Darrell Figgis who objected to Collins' decision to include in the Draft Constitution provisions for four 'Extern' ministers to join the Government by appointment which would have allowed de Valera and Childers, for example, to have joined the Cabinet without taking either the Oath or being subject to collective responsibility. Figgis' opposition indicates that he was reflecting the views of his friend Arthur Griffith whom the British regarded as 'the only Irish leader who appreciates his real obligations under the Treaty'; a break between him and Collins was therefore speculated on as a real possibility.[47]

Churchill made use of Hazel Lavery to let Collins know how the Cabinet viewed the Irish situation. In a handwritten letter marked 'private', he said:

My dear Hazel,
   I had a very pleasant talk with M.C. this morning and hope to see him again on Monday. I am very glad he and his colleagues are dining with you tonight. I am sure your influence will be exerted in the cause of peace . . . I ought, I think, to let you know 'confidentially' that my colleagues take a most grave view of the Constitution.

The style of the Churchill–Collins meeting may have been 'very pleasant talk' but the substance of those May – June dealings was very tough. The gravamen of the British case on the pact and on the Constitution was as follows: the pact was a giving way to unconstitutional forces, '2% of the population' represented by 'Boland, de Valera's Secretary'.[48] Churchill developed the arguments contained in his letter of 15 May to Collins. The Provisional Government 'had made one surrender after another to the Republicans and had not obtained the free opinion of the Irish people' causing the British Treaty signatories to be subjected to a 'fierce scrutiny of our actions'. Churchill warned that: 'You will find that we are just as tenacious on essential points – the Crown, the British Commonwealth, No Republic – as de Valera and Rory O'Connor, and we intend to fight for our points.'

At first sight the Constitution struck Churchill as being of 'Bolshevik character'. After a more measured perusal Lloyd George termed it a 'complete evasion and complete negation of the Treaty'.[49] Adducing the opinions of Law Officers, the Lord Chancellor and the Lord Chief Justice, he told his increasingly depressed Irish listeners[50] that, amongst other things, the Draft Constitution was so far from its intended basis in the Canadian Constitution that it was

substantially a setting up of an independent Republic in Ireland. The Crown was only brought in under conditions very derogatory to its dignity. The Court, which constitutes the Empire, was expressly excluded . . . The British Empire was ruled out from the making of Treaties altogether . . . the Constitution was a complete going back on the provisions of the Treaty.

Days of frequently emotional exchange followed. At one meeting[51] Collins burst out at Lloyd George that during the Anglo-Irish war, the British had released Childers 'after half an hour because he was an Englishman', whereas had he fallen into English hands he would have been shot. The Prime Minister replied evenly that 'they would indeed have shot him'. Lionel Curtis was present at this meeting and after it he and Lloyd George discussed Collins. Lloyd George said that 'Collins was just a wild animal, a mustang'. Curtis compared negotiating with Collins to 'trying to write on water'. Lloyd George replied, 'Shallow and agitated water'.[52]

The Irish argued that without the pact[53] an election could not have been held, the British that the trouble came from Collins' failure to confront O'Connor. Collins' responses sometimes went to the outer limits of discretion. At one meeting he repeatedly told Lloyd George that he was willing to 'give Ireland back as a present'. Understandably, Lloyd George found this 'the most significant feature of the interview', which was described as being of 'great gravity and of a menacing character'.[54] Collins gave Lloyd George a dossier on atrocities perpetrated against Catholics in the North and demanded an inquiry. When he was asked if he got the inquiry he would disavow the IRA in Northern Ireland he replied that he was prepared to co-operate with Craig but that 'he was not prepared to hold up the hands of the Ulster Government while Catholics were being murdered'. One British Minister, Worthington Evans, took this as an outright indication that Collins was behind the IRA in the North.

One can say with certainty that few issues in the long, stormy history of Anglo-Irish relations produced such blunt speaking in Downing St, or so little positive result, as did Michael Collins' Constitution. On the question of an inquiry into the atrocities in the North of Ireland Lloyd George showed some sympathy with Arthur Griffith who had argued that arming the undisciplined Ulster Protestant Militia, the B-Specials, was like 'arming the East End'. He commented: 'The Fascisti in Italy would be a more exact analogy.'[55] Lloyd George told the Cabinet that he feared that Collins was manoeuvring him into a break over Ulster, not over the Constitution. He said that the British case on Ulster was bad in the eyes of world opinion. They had armed Protestants but Catholics had been murdered with impunity. If a break came on 'Republic versus Monarchy', England's case before the bar of world opinion was sure of 'solid support'. Accordingly it was decided to send for Craig with a view to setting up an inquiry. The futile outcome of this aspiration may be judged in Chapter 11.

The respective strengths of the two countries was symbolised by the attendance at the final meeting of the Irish and British negotiators at Downing St on 15 June, the day before the Irish General Election. Only Griffith and Kennedy were present on the Irish side. The British, by contrast, had strengthened their original nine-man team by the addition of Sir Frederick Liddell and Sir Francis Greer. The stronger side got the Constitution it wanted. Afterwards, Kennedy was congratulated by Churchill and the British Chief Justice, Lord Hewart, for his 'enormous service to the cause of the execution of the Treaty'.[56] Churchill was positively glowing in his 'admiration of Mr Kennedy's resource' and the speed with which he had been able to draft changes. In the legal sense the praise was well merited. The Irish Free State's Constitution *qua* Constitution was an admirable document. But in the eyes of Irish Republicans intent on armed defiance of the state it contained incitements to continue rather than inducements to change their minds. The word 'Republic' was so repulsive to contemporary British political thought that Kennedy noted amongst a list of British amendments he sent to Collins: 'They have also rendered "Uachtaran" as "President of the Executive Council"; the word "President" alone suggests a republic to their, at present, panicky minds.'[57]

When he got Kennedy's letter Collins made one last effort to get the Constitution through. He went immediately to London on the 12th, and tried without success to change Churchill's mind. He returned the next day in despair and went straight to Cork for solace. For there were many more concessions to 'panicky minds'. Collins' intention to keep the Constitution separate from the Treaty was frustrated. The preamble to the Constitution specifically stated that the Articles of Agreement were given the force of law and that any law passed or amendment made under the Constitution repugnant to the provisions of the Treaty was 'absolutely void and inoperative'. The Irish legislature was to consist of the King and two houses. Parliament was to be summoned and dissolved in the name of the King. His Representative, that is, the Governor General, was to sign any Bill passed by the two Houses, before it could become law. Right of Appeal to the Privy Council from the Irish Supreme Court was included, thus making it a superior court to any in Ireland. Above all the Oath of Allegiance contained in the Treaty was made mandatory on every member of the Irish Parliament.

The Southern Unionists were also unhappy with the Constitution. Agreement was not reached with their representatives[58] until 13 June. The Unionists argued that the Senate 'constituted as proposed by Popular Election and with powers so strictly limited' did not afford protection for minorities.

From Collins' point of view the only bonus emerging from the Constitution débâcle was the fact that it enabled him to outmanoeuvre de Valera on the eve of the election. On 6 June when the fate, though not the form, of the Constitution was already fixed, Collins and de Valera joined in a joint appeal to support the Pact because: 'many of the dangers that threaten us can be met only by keeping intact the forces which constituted the national resistance in recent years'.

De Valera was aware that the Constitution had run into trouble;

Poblacht na hEireann had printed speculation that it had 'been amended under British threats to suit British demands'.[59] On the same day the *Independent* carried a report that de Valera had been 'acquainted with matters requiring joint consideration and action'.[60] But he shrank from any repetition of the 'violent conflict with the wishes of the Irish people' proclamation with which he had greeted the return of the Treaty. That statement had sent a shock-wave through the country but his attempt to win extremist support had not impressed the Rory O'Connor faction and his 'wading through blood' speeches had cost him moderate support. So long as the Constitution was not published he did not have to take up a position on its terms. It was in his interest not to break with Collins as there might yet be electoral advantage in the pact. The mood of the public was such that any party standing against the Treaty would fare badly.

Accordingly he stayed silent. Collins, recovering in Cork from his unsuccessful encounter with Churchill, did not. Two days before the election, while de Valera was urging an audience in Kildare to support the pact,[61] Collins repudiated it in Cork. His speech, which was reprinted in all the major newspapers contained the following:

You are facing an election here on Friday and I am not hampered now by being on a platform where there are Coalitionists. I can make a straight appeal to you – to the citizens of Cork, to vote for the candidates you think best of, who the electors of Cork think will carry on best in the future the work they want carried on. When I spoke in Dublin I put it as gravely as I could that the country was facing a very serious situation. If the situation is to be met as it should be met, the country must have the representatives it wants. You understand fully what you have to do, and I depend on you to do it.

The Constitution was printed on the morning of the election, again too late for de Valera to be able to derive any advantage from its terms. Whether it would materially have affected the result in an atmosphere in which the issue was rapidly narrowing down to peace or war, is a matter of conjecture. Certainly the result was a severe blow to the de Valera faction which held only thirty-six seats, a loss of twenty-two. The Collins/Griffith party won fifty-eight seats, a loss of eight, but which taken with the pro-Treaty Labour Party's seventeen seats, the Farmers' Party seven, the six independents and the four Unionists represented a solid pro-Treaty majority. But the ending of the pact and the terms of the Constitution taken together clearly presaged a breach with the Four Courts Executive. The military paths and the political ones were fast converging. The convergence was completed by the assassination of Sir Henry Wilson on 22 June and the kidnapping of the Provisional Government General, J. J. 'Ginger' O'Connell, by the Four Courts men four days later.

The Wilson assassination and the reasons for it are dealt with in some detail in Chapter 11. Suffice it to say here that it caused consternation in London. The British considered a move against the Four Courts men who were, wrongly, held responsible for it. In the House of Commons Churchill, in the teeth of a howling gale of Tory outrage that would have intimidated anyone else, delivered a bellicose speech:

The presence in Dublin, of a band of men styling themselves the Head-quarters of the Republican Executive is a gross breach and defiance of the Treaty. The time has come when it is not unfair, premature or impatient for us to make to the strengthened Irish Government and new Irish Parliament a request in express terms that this sort of thing must come to an end. If it does not come to an end, if through weakness, want of courage, or some other less creditable reason it is not brought to an end and a speedy end, then it is my duty to say, on behalf of His Majesty's Government, that we shall regard the Treaty as having been formally violated, and we shall take no steps to carry out or legalise its further stages, and that we shall resume full liberty of action in any direction that may seem proper, or to any extent that may be necessary to safeguard the interests and the rights that are entrusted to our care.[62]

Collins' response to this was sulphuric. He 'spoke raging'.[63] Now whatever he did to enforce the mandate received at the election would be represented as being at the behest of the British. 'Let Churchill come over here and do his own dirty work,' he snarled.[64] He had come very near to deciding to dislodge the Four Courts men himself. A note of his for a Provisional Government Cabinet meeting, held the same day as Churchill spoke, reads as follows: 'Internal policy in our own area. The restoration of ordinary conditions. Arrangements for peace and order.'[65]

Collins was only too well aware that if he did not attack the Four Courts the likelihood of the British doing so was growing by the hour. This would mean a halting of troop evacuation with two very unlovely possible side effects. One, that they might not resume evacuation again. Two, that if the British did attack the Four Courts the situation might escalate to a point where the Provisional Government troops might end up fighting alongside the British.

Despite his anger at Churchill, Collins was finally prompted to act against his old comrades by these and two other additional, secondary, but precipitative considerations. One, he believed mistakenly that the Executive was split between the followers of Mellowes, O'Connor and O'Malley and those of Liam Lynch. A quarrel had taken place but had been patched up. The second consideration arose when the Provisional Government arrested a prominent Four Courts' man, Leo Henderson, on 26 June, while he was commandeering transport for the dual purpose of use in Northern Ireland and enforcing the Belfast boycott against the garage concerned, Fergusson's of Baggot St. Angered at this because they believed the shared Collins/Executive anti-Six-Counties policy to be still in place, O'Connor ordered the seizure of the popular Deputy Chief of Staff, Ginger O'Connell in retaliation.

Griffith, O'Higgins, and the rest of the Cabinet took the kidnapping as the last straw. Even Collins told Mulcahy that they would have to fight.[66] But then he agonised for one more day before agreeing that:

Notices should be served on the armed men in illegal occupation of the Four Courts and Fowler Hall that night, ordering them to evacuate the buildings and to surrender up all arms and property, and that in the event of their refusing to do so, the necessary military action should be taken at once.[67]

The ultimatum was received at about 3.40 am on Wednesday 28 June 1922 by a gentleman called 'Skinner' O'Reilly.[68] Given twenty minutes to surrender, the garrison decided not to send any reply but knelt down and said a decade of the Rosary in Irish.[69] Within minutes the Four Courts dome became a target for shells fired from across the Liffey by two eighteen-pound field guns borrowed from the British.

Arthur Griffith stood on the roof of Government Buildings watching the bombardment. As the smoke drifted up from the Irish Supreme Court he 'shook his fist at the clouds of gunsmoke and cursed de Valera'.[70] Ever practical, Collins realised that clean shirts would be hard to come by in the coming days. He called at Vaughan's Hotel to pick up his laundry and found someone else with the same idea, Harry Boland. It was the last time they met.[71]

The shells which the British supplied with the two howitzers were shrapnel, unsuitable for use against heavy masonry. Emmet Dalton, one of the few officers on the pro-Treaty side who knew how to fire the guns, was called back to his office, leaving an inexperienced gunner in charge of one gun. A short time later he received an urgent summons to Macready's HQ in the Royal Hospital. The Republicans were attacking. As his car screeched to a halt outside the HQ where Macready, very correct, very aloof in his full regalia awaited him, a shell burst a short distance away from the group. Aghast, Dalton hurtled back to the gun sites to find that the gunner was using the eighteen-pounder to fire at a sniper on the roof of the Four Courts dome. The shells were passing right through and exploding in the Phoenix Park.[72]

Apart from deficiencies in calibre, the stock of shells supplied by the British was too small and Macready delayed in sending Collins what he asked for to such an extent that Collins cabled Churchill on the 29th: 'Hampered by the continued lack of material . . . promised . . . but not available . . . Essential that action be taken immediately otherwise situation will become impossible.'[73]

Churchill was assuring Collins that 'ample quantities of ammunition are being despatched'.[74] In his eagerness to continue the attack successfully he cabled Collins that:

General Macready . . . has been told to place one of the six-inch howitzers at your disposal . . . can be fired from their positions in Phoenix Park . . . If necessary IFS officers can be by the howitzers and can actually fire them. It is absolutely vital not to break off the attack which having being started must surely be carried through in one way or another.[75]

The following day he urged 'essential to take the 60-pounder [*sic*], its gunners and its ammunition and most desirable to use the six-inch howitzer as well and all together'. He also cabled that 'aeroplanes manned by their own pilots will carry out any action necessary. They could be quickly painted Free State colours to show that they were an essential part of your forces.'[76]

However, without accepting Churchill's lethal largesse, Collins' assault succeeded to a point where at 3.30 pm on Friday, 30 June 1922, a white handkerchief was tied to a broom handle by the defenders. O'Connor had planned to take his men out through the sewers, but he had not allowed for the tidal Liffey.[77] O'Malley signed the unconditional surrender and threw his parabellum into the Liffey to show his contempt. Another, greater, demonstration of contempt resulted in two lorry-loads of gelignite exploding in the Public Records Office situated in the Four Courts complex. For hours after the explosion, the biggest ever recorded in Dublin, priceless manuscripts, some going back to the twelfth century, floated over the city. Miraculously no one was killed. Churchill's comment, contained in a most unwelcome message of congratulation to Collins, was: 'The archives of the Four Courts may be scattered, but the title deeds of Ireland are safe.'[78] The Free State was not safe yet; many casualties lay ahead, amongst them the shared anti-Six-County policy of Collins and the members of the Executive he had just blasted out of the Four Courts. Even while his men were shelling the Four Courts, Collins was securing governmental approval for protests to Churchill concerning two matters arising out of the Northern situation.[79] These were the British decision to give further assistance to the Protestant paramilitary force, the B-Specials, and the fact that an Irish officer, Commandant Hogan, attempting to negotiate with British counterparts over a crisis on the border had been: 'treated with the greatest discourtesy, and it was clear that the attitude of the British officers towards the inhabitants of the district was conducive to disorder rather than to peace.'

It is now necessary to examine how Collins' policy towards Northern Ireland arose and was implemented.

11

Setting up the Six

'Ulster will fight; Ulster will be right.'
Lord Randolph Churchill

One of the buzzwords in the Anglo-Irish dialogue is 'ambivalence'.
This is generally used by British or Unionist commentators to indicate
that Dublin and the Nationalists condemn the IRA in word but
condone it in deed. Viewed from the Unionist standpoint Michael
Collins, in the last months of his life, could be regarded as the supreme
practitioner of this policy. Janus-faced he stood in Dail Eireann,
arguing fiercely for the Treaty and the establishment of law and order
in a democratic, independent Irish State, while at the same time he
acted with the vigour, intent, and methodology of any chief of staff of
the Provisional IRA to wreck the other state enshrined in that Treaty,
'Ulster'. He told northern IRA men that although the Treaty might
appear to be the 'outward expression of Partition . . . Partition would
never be recognised even though it might mean the smashing of the
Treaty.'[1] However, the Nationalist also uses the term 'ambivalence'
when he or she points to the methods by which the Northern statelet
was set up and maintained. Collins was a Nationalist to the core. From
prison camp he had written to Susan Killeen after the Rising of 1916
'anything but a divided Ireland'. He had also been intimately
connected with the process by which Ireland was partitioned.
Ironically, his killing of Swanzy had probably helped to accelerate the
process, in which three fundamental steps had already been taken
before he became Chairman of the Provisional Government. As
Chairman he would encounter the final step, the refusal to introduce
proportional representation into the voting system.

  He resented each one of these steps, each one more bitterly than the
last. The first was that involving the fundamental question of the area
of the state itself. The Irish Committee unambiguously recommended
to the Cabinet, on 17 February 1919, that:

the whole of the Province of Ulster should be included in the Northern
Parliament. The Committee consider that a Northern Parliament consisting

of the nine counties in Ulster is more likely to lead to the ultimate union of the whole of Ireland than if the Northern Parliament was composed of six counties only.

That this viewpoint was accepted and widely supported by the Cabinet is evidenced by the fact that at the end of that year an unusually well-attended meeting held in Downing St on 3 December 1919 agreed that 'the general feeling was that the ultimate aim of the Government's policy in Ireland was a united Ireland with a parliament of its own'.[2] This was subject to various provisos about Ulster's consent, but throughout that December it was made crystal clear[3] that British Cabinet policy *as a whole* favoured a united Ireland as the ultimate goal. But somehow the goalposts were moved. On 15 December the Cabinet was informed that 'the Ulster leaders were doubtful whether the Northern Parliament of Ireland would be able to govern Northern Ireland where there was a Nationalist Majority, and greatly preferred that the scheme should be limited only to the six Protestant counties.' On the same day Worthington Evans reported that Craig had suggested:

the establishment of a Boundary Commission to examine the distribution of population along the borders of the whole of the Six Counties, and to take a vote in those districts on either side of and immediately adjoining that boundary in which there was no doubt as to whether they would prefer to be included in the Northern or the Southern Parliamentary area.

This suggestion is of course of great interest in view of Sir James' subsequent attitude to the Boundary Commission but the major point to be noted here is that while they had accepted the principle of partition for reasons of political expediency, the more far-seeing British statesmen, including Churchill and Birkenhead, had perceived that it was in Britain's and Ireland's best interests to have a peaceful united Ireland (Dublin after all lies closer to Liverpool than to Belfast) athwart the Western approaches, but that Orangism, and more importantly their Tory spokesmen, notably Balfour, had decided otherwise. Ulster would not be Ulster, but six Protestant counties and in fact these Protestant counties had Catholic majorities in the city of Derry, and the counties of Fermanagh and Tyrone.

Lloyd George personally confirmed Craig's views with him and reported to the Cabinet meeting of 19 December 1919 that Craig was 'strongly in favour of the proposed Boundary Commission in order to define the precise boundary of the Parliamentary Area'. At that meeting it was again 'strongly urged' that the new state include 'the whole of Ulster'. But Craig's allies at the table saw to it that *realpolitik* set in with a thud. It was acknowledged that: 'the jurisdiction of the Northern Parliament over the whole of Ulster as a geographical unit was more logical and in many ways easier to defend in Parliament.'

But it was 'generally felt that it was *even more important* [author's italics] to get a scheme which, even though theoretically less perfect, would meet with general acceptance.'

The more far-seeing imperialists saw it otherwise. Birkenhead later pointed out to Lord Londonderry 'the admitted circumstances that if the political considerations allowed it the economic and financial interests of Ireland would be greatly benefited by union, however long postponed.'[4] But ad hocery carried the day and, as we have seen, two years later the Boundary Commission surfaced again under the guise of a Tom Jones idea during the Treaty negotiations. By then Craig was declaring himself vehemently *against* his own proposal.

It is of course easier to speak of change being inevitable than to have to experience it. The assimilation, marriage, blending, call it what one will, of what the Unionists termed 'Ulster' and the Nationalists scornfully referred to as Carsonia or, more accurately, as the Six Counties, with the rest of Ireland in 1921 might not have been a pleasant experience at the time. It would certainly have been viewed with fear, hatred and hysteria by a large number of Northern loyalists. How far these feelings would have been translated into action without the money and support received from the Tories, and the almost equally valuable reluctance of the British Army to open a second front with loyalists as well as Nationalists are amongst the 'ifs' of history. Nevertheless a state, like a company, a tree, or a family either grows or it dies. The tragedy, for 'Ulster', and Michael Collins, is that 'Ulster's' philosophy of government was founded on trying to ignore this inevitability.

This was seen clearly in the second major step in enshrining partition. The Cabinet proposed that 'Ulster' should have a bicameral system so that an upper house would be an integral part of the parliamentary system, so weighted as to be capable of discharging its conceived duty of safeguarding Catholic interests. However a Cabinet meeting presided over by Lloyd George, at which Balfour and Bonar Law were also present, held on 3 November 1920, was informed that: 'Sir Edward Carson and the Ulster Members were strongly opposed to a Second Chamber for the Northern Parliament and would use the whole weight of their opposition to endeavour to defeat the proposal.'[5]

The Cabinet was somewhat exercised at this. Nevertheless the proposals for a second chamber vanished into a portmanteau Council of Ireland compromise in which if either side (North and South) 'did not approve the scheme there would be no Second Chamber'. There was no second chamber.[6] However, to ensure that, in Craig's words, Northern Ireland would continue to have 'a Protestant Parliament and a Protestant state',[7] two more safeguards were required, the withdrawal of proportional representation from the area and the formation of the militia, generally known as the 'B-Specials'.

While generally speaking the 'Specials' grew out of the pre-war Ulster Volunteer Force (UVF) set up to frustrate Home Rule, they took their formal shape from developments in 1920. Sir Basil Brooke began organising Protestant vigilante forces in his native Fermanagh in April of that year. He had visited Dublin, where his wife was having a baby, in the aftermath of the 1916 Rising. The visit decided him to fight any attempt at a Sinn Fein takeover in the North.[8] Also in April, Carson urged Bonar Law to back the idea of recruiting loyalists into a special force to combat the IRA. He used the familiar Unionist argument that if these forces were not organised there might be unorganised retaliation which could bring loyalists into confrontation with British forces.[9] Helped, *sub scriptum*, by the Unionist hierarchy and in particular by pre-war UVF leaders like Colonel Wilfred Spender, a central figure in the pre-war raising of the UVF, and by Fred Crawford, the principal architect of the Larne gun-running, the UVF continued to grow in strength. Captain Hardy established underground contact with the force for use in his counter-insurgency activities. By 23 July 1919, after renewed pressures by Carson and Craig for the introduction of loyalist recruitment, Churchill wanted to know: 'what . . . would happen if the Protestants in the Six Counties were given weapons . . . charged with maintaining law and order and policing the country'.[10] He got a good insight into the likely outcome in Craig's memorandum[11] on the subject to the Cabinet on 1 September in which he complained about Catholic influence in the RIC and demanded the formation of a Special Constabulary from the ranks of the UVF forthwith. Otherwise the Unionists would have to: 'see what steps can be taken towards a system of *organised* reprisals against the rebels, mainly in order to defeat them, but partly to restrain their own followers from acts which are regrettable and in a large measure ineffective.'

Balfour backed the idea[12] and a surprisingly small but strongly pro-Unionist meeting of the Irish Committee[13] decided that not only should the Ulster Volunteers be enlisted as Special Constables, the whole of Ireland should be offered a chance of enlistment. The decision appalled both Macready and Anderson. Anderson wrote to Bonar Law:

I sincerely trust there is no foundation for the rumour that the Government contemplate recognising the Ulster Volunteers in any form. Macready has said in the plainest terms more than once that to do so would not bring relief to the Forces of the Crown but the reverse and I am convinced that he is right. Not only would party and religious feeling be intensified all over Ireland, but sooner or later the Regular Forces would inevitably come into conflict with the Volunteers called to their aid.[14]

However the 'Tudor Tory' influence of Balfour, Bonar Law and the rest was sufficiently strong at Westminster to override the advice of Britain's two top experts, military and civil, on the ground in Ireland. The formation of the Specials was announced on 22 October 1920. There were three categories, A, B and C. The A-Specials were full-time and received the same arms, equipment and high pay as the RIC. The B-Specials were a part-time body whose duties were to patrol, man road blocks and conduct searches. They were intended to operate only in their own localities. The C category was for calling out in emergencies and was mainly used for intelligence purposes.

The Specials were specifically designed as a sectarian force and were not well received in British Liberal and Labour Party circles, coming as they did against the murderous reaping of what the *Daily Herald* of 31 August 1922 termed the 'bloody harvest of Carsonism'. In order to counter 'the opposition of the Labour Party in England' to the fact that the Specials were to be chosen by all-loyalist selection committees UVF leaders,[15] who admitted that 'it is fully recognised that, at first at any rate, no Roman Catholics will respond', suggested an appeal to all 'well- disposed citizens' as 'the only means whereby this scheme can be put through'.

How well-disposed some of the citizens who came forward were may be gauged from the Cromwell Clubs which eventually were subsumed into the Specials. The Clubs were but one of the groupings formed to take the 'organised reprisals' of which Craig wrote. They were located mainly in Belfast. Each Club was armed with a Lewis gun, service revolvers, automatic pistols, rifles and night glasses. Lists of suspects were supplied by the local military intelligence. A Sergeant William MacCartney of the RIC who operated under the Belfast Detective officer DI Harrison, from Musgrave St Police Barracks was a principal organiser of the Cromwell Clubs, which had 50 to 100 members each, drawn from the ranks of loyalist ex-service men. At one recruiting meeting[16] MacCartney said that the object of the Clubs was to establish a system of terror amongst Catholics by shootings, ambushes and midnight visits to ordinary houses.

Such reports had a marked influence on Collins who obviously felt for the Northern Nationalists very profoundly. He would appear to have approached his North-Eastern brethren in liberal terms at the outset. Sean MacEntee, later to be a Minister, successfully proposed at a meeting in Dail Eireann on 6 August 1920 that in view of the pogrom against Catholics which was raging at the time 'an embargo be laid upon the manufactures of the . . . city of Belfast'.

Collins spoke against 'the attempt which had been made by two deputies (Blythe had seconded MacEntee) from the North of Ireland to inflame the passions of members. There was no Ulster Question'. As MacEntee had given the most appalling record of outrage and atrocity against the Catholic community of Northern Ireland one can only speculate as to why Collins spoke thus. Perhaps he simply underestimated the strength of resistance to Dublin which existed in Northern Ireland. His experience of Protestantism in Cork was very different to that of the North. He wrote to Art O'Brien: 'There is really only one small question in Ulster and it has its pivot in the Belfast shipyards. They are the spot from which the strength of intolerance comes.' During a famous speech he made in Armagh on Sunday, 4 September 1921, he said that religious intolerance 'was the product solely and entirely of British policy operating in Ireland'. It had been widely forecast that his appearance in Armagh would lead to serious trouble. He wrote to Moya Llewelyn Davies on 2 September: 'This damned meeting is making me feel nervous already. I should more gladly look forward to an ambush. But perhaps I'll have that also. The unity of Ireland is going to be my main idea I think.'

In fact, with appropriate symbolism, Collins got more of a scare in Dublin than he did in Armagh.[17] His secretary Ally Lyons worked late for him the night before the meeting. As he walked with her to a taxi, gunmen accosted them. A shot was fired as Collins immediately tackled the pair. It subsequently turned out that the two were only Republican police on patrol, but Ally, not knowing this, fled. When she reached home in a panic, thinking him shot, he was there with her father, checking if she was all right. 'What kept you?' he asked.

In Armagh he was greeted by one of the biggest and most peaceful crowds of the period.[18] He delivered a serious, well-researched argument on the 'Unity of Ireland' showing how Ulster had declined under British rule and appealed to his Protestant listeners 'to join with us, as Irishmen to come into the Irish nation . . . to come in and take their share in the government of their own country'. While the meeting itself concluded peacefully, the stones which whistled around his car as he drove home were his answer and by the New Year of 1922, just a few months later, he had changed his approach. 'Non-recognition of the Northern Parliament was essential.'[19]

In thus setting out to negate an essential part of the Treaty which he had done more than anyone else in Ireland to have accepted, Collins, and the British ironically enough, took their precedent from the same source, though as is usual in Anglo-Irish relationships, the two sides interpreted it differently. The Cabinet feared that the term 'Treaty' implied 'recognition of an existing Irish Republic and which it might prove impossible to resist in the case of India'.[20] However as Sinn Fein preferred 'Treaty' to 'pact' the Cabinet had decided to proceed on the basis that a precedent existed since the seventeenth century for the use of the word Treaty, the Treaty of Limerick. Anyone with a knowledge of Irish history could have told the Cabinet that the Treaty of Limerick is notorious in Ireland for having been broken by the British, a fact which Collins secretly made use of with devastating

TOM BARRY'S WEDDING PHOTOGRAPH, VAUGHAN'S HOTEL, 22 AUGUST 1921

Seated on ground: (far right) Gearoid O'Sullivan. First row, seated: (second left) Harry Boland, (from sixth left) Liam Deasy, the bride Leslie Price, de Valera – who insisted on sitting between bride and groom – Tom Barry; (from right) Countess Marcievicz, Mary MacSwiney. First row, standing: (far left) Sean Lehane, (fifth left) Jim Hurley, Ted Sullivan, Collins – his head is lowered because he suspected the photographer was a police informer – (tenth left) Dick Mulcahy, (12th left) Eoin O'Duffy, (16th left) Emmet Dalton, (15th right) Tom Cullen, (13th right) Rory O'Connor. Last row: (second and third left) Sean Hales, Liam Devlin, (far right) Joe O'Reilly

(*Right*) November 1920: after the 'sack of Balbriggan'

(*Centre*) The Propaganda war: two stills from a British newsreel purporting to show Sinn Feiners shot and captured by Auxiliaries after a Kerry ambush. In fact they show Vico Road, Killiney; (*Right*) The British Tommy, who had no part in the intelligence war, was generally not disliked by the people and the IRA

Michael Collins and Harry Boland on the hurling field

(*Below*) Cathal Brugha

bove) Richard Mulcahy

ight) The 'Long Fellow' with Griffith, ndon 1921

The bodies of Catholic publican MacMahon, his three sons and a barman, murdered in a sectarian raid with the connivance of the RUC, March 1921 – the youngest son, aged twelve, survived and was later noted for flying a Union Jack every Armistice Day

Field Marshal Sir Henry Wilson, the Chief of Imperial General Staff effect. Eamonn de Barra described to me a highly significant incident which occurred at a moment when the Treaty was hanging in the balance. On 29 December 1921, he encountered Sean Hales, a staunch Republican, probably the most significant pro-Treaty figure in Cork after Collins himself. De Barra, who took the anti-Treaty side, dared to ask the legendary 'Buckshot',[21] who was several years older than he, why he had changed his mind. 'I agree with Mick. He says the British broke the Treaty of Limerick, and we'll break this Treaty too when it suits us, when we have our own army,' he replied. The de Barra incident was no isolated occurrence. Frank Aiken described Eoin O'Duffy[22] telling an IRA gathering in Clones around the same time that the signing of the Treaty with GHQ approval 'was only a trick' in order to get arms to continue the fight. Aiken demurred at the use of such tactics saying that if the Treaty went through the people who supported it would constitute an obstacle to independence. The attendance included some of the most senior IRA officers from the midlands and the north who realised O'Duffy was close to Collins (Collins told Batt O'Connor that he regarded O'Duffy as his successor[23]). They were impressed when O'Duffy repeated that he would never dream of taking an oath, or of asking anyone else to take it.

Collins didn't only use that argument in debate. He put it into practice. His 'stepping stone' was to be a jumping-off point for raids, kidnappings and gun-runnings into Northern Ireland. He also personally initiated policies of obstruction with every single Governmental agency through which the North dealt with the South. However before taking warlike action he gave peace a chance, or at least made an effort to find out what the North's government was thinking. A representative of the Provisional Government was given credentials and sent to ascertain the attitude of the Northern Government towards the South. The representative, Diarmuid Fawsitt, saw J.M. Andrews, the Minister of Labour, and reported his findings on 13 January 1922:

The official view and feeling is that understanding and co-operation with the South is desired by the Northern Government. The present mandate of the Northern Cabinet would not warrant a change in policy towards the South at the moment.

A meeting of the Ulster Unionist Council will be held on 27 January before which a full statement on the position of the Northern Parliament and Government will be laid, and a line of future political action will be submitted for consideration and adoption.

Pending a decision by the meeting of the Ulster Unionist Council on the programme, the Ulster Cabinet will take no steps towards an immediate arrangement with the Provisional Government of the Irish Free State.[24]

Despite this, Collins arranged to see Craig before the 27 January meeting in London, at the Colonial Office where Churchill was in charge of Irish affairs, having become Chairman of the Provisional Government of Ireland Committee which evolved from the Cabinet's earlier Irish Committee. Collins secured his own Cabinet's approval for his policy[25] of putting it to Craig that 'his Cabinet could stop all the outrages in the North if they set their hands to do so.'

His meeting with Craig was 'friendly' and resulted in a five-point agreement. It called for a conference of elected representatives 'for all Ireland' to draw up a constitution which would guarantee the North its autonomy. Most importantly, the Boundary Commission was to be scrapped and Collins and Craig were to work out the boundaries between them. Craig agreed to get the Catholic workers who had been driven out of their employment reinstated in their jobs and Collins promised to call off the Belfast boycott. The two men also agreed to meet again to thrash out the vexed question of Republican prisoners in Northern jails. It seemed that North-South relationships were improving.

But appearances were deceptive. Craig ran into such opposition to his boundary proposals at the Council meeting of 27 January that he had to assure the gathering that there would be no change that left 'our Ulster area any less than it is' and the all-Ireland conference was not even discussed. Yet when Collins and Griffith met a delegation of Northern Nationalists on 1 February, the day before he saw Craig for their progress report meeting in Dublin, he assured them that large transfers of territory from the Six Counties would be forthcoming under the terms of the Boundary Commission if that had to be invoked.

Collins was in an extraordinarily delicate situation, pulled between the machinations of de Valera to appeal to the increasingly militant Republicans on the one hand, and the British and Craig on the other. The bulk of the people in the twenty-six counties wanted a return to peace, not adventures across the border. This wish was amply reflected in the composition of his Cabinet, particularly in the views of figures like Griffith, MacNeill, O'Higgins, Hogan, Blythe and Cosgrave. Their priority was bringing the crisis in the South to a head so as to crush the 'Irregulars' as they both termed and thought of their opponents, before they grew too powerful. They were fully prepared to settle down to building what they could within twenty-six county confines, leaving the solution of partition to the future. Mulcahy was probably the only one at the Cabinet table who shared Collins' approach.

There is a tendency on the part of some contemporary historians to ascribe Collins' Northern policy merely to his desire to keep the South's Republicans in line. But it went deeper than that. Collins was not only the head of the newly formed twenty-six-county Irish state.

He was the head of the IRB, committed by conviction and by the oath administered to him by Sam Maguire to continue what was begun in 1916. He said as much publicly, and could hardly have been more explicit. Speaking at Wexford on 9 April 1922, he said:

the acceleration of cowardly and murderous violence in North-East Ulster allays an inexorable and unquestionable duty of every Irish patriot – a duty which is as definite and immediate as if the British were again violently threatening our Nation . . .
If the so-called Government in Belfast has not the power nor the will to protect its citizens, then the Irish Government must find means to protect them.

This is what he had to say about the Act which set up the six-county state: 'It is my own very strong view now that we should have refused to negotiate a Peace until that Act of Usurpation had been written off. But it is easy to be wise after the event. That Act is written into the Treaty.' And he then went on to speak words which we can see now contained a very ominous ring for Sir Henry Wilson:

We all know only too well the hopes and aims of Orange North-East Ulster. They are well expressed to the world with a lightly veiled brutality in the language of Sir Henry Wilson. They want their ascendancy restored . . . They want the British back . . .
British diehards and mischief makers of the Sir Henry Wilson breed are leaving no stone unturned to restore British domination in Ireland.

Collins' behaviour might well be termed duplicitous in his role as head of the fledgling Irish government, but those sentiments, and his subsequent actions, were entirely consistent with his position as head of the Irish Republican Brotherhood, the logic of attitudes inculcated by Santry and Lyons. After he had signed the pact with de Valera, on 20 May, Collins wrote a note to himself: 'Above all, Ulster'.[26] And certainly the appalling risks he took for the greater part of 1922 in attempting the impossibility of secretly conducting an aggressive policy against the new northern state indicate that he did in fact place this objective 'above all'.

Before meeting Craig for round two of their pact negotiations, and before meeting the Northern Nationalists with Griffith he laid down his policy to the Cabinet:

Non-recognition of the Northern Parliament was essential – otherwise they would have nothing to bargain on with Sir James Craig. He had suggested to Sir James that a meeting of all Irish representatives should be called to draft an Irish Constitution. He would put plainly to Sir James the advisability of the Northern people coming in under the Free State.[27]

But when he met Craig in Dublin on 2 February it was evident how far this approach was from the reality of Unionist sentiment. Collins produced maps showing how much of the Six-County area he felt would be restored to the twenty-six counties under the terms of the Boundary article of the Treaty. The meeting promptly broke down. The main purpose of the Cabinet in accepting the Treaty had been to remove Ireland from the British political agenda. Now, Collins' attempts to push the Treaty beyond its already unpopular parameters and bring 'Ulster' back centre-stage were anathema to the British Government. In his heart Collins had no faith in the Boundary Commission and was only using it as a ploy in his negotiations with the Unionists. Writing to Louis Walsh on 7 February 1922 he said:

You will have seen the map published in the papers yesterday. This map was the most argumentative map we used in conference, and it was for this reason I made use of the expression, 'forcing an open door'. I must confess, however, that I am no lover of partition, no matter in what form it appears. . . . It would be far better to fix our minds for a time on a united Ireland, for this course will not leave minorities which it would be impossible to govern.[28]

As he said to Walsh, Collins did have some faith in ending partition 'in an economic way. This intercourse will inevitably bring our views before the supporters of the others . . . people will wonder why they cannot agree on the bigger things.' But he also made it clear in his letter that he was pleased that in their recent conference Craig had angered British statesmen by sticking out for nothing less than a six-county state because 'we shall be in a much better position to resume the fight with them.' In a nutshell Collins' vision was of a united Ireland which if necessary would have to be fought for.

To the Unionists his activities were, inevitably, simply inflammatory. Carson had not conceded three Ulster counties and settled reluctantly for the six, which the Unionists knew they could control, to permit the precious six to be whittled down by any pact. Craig was not allowed to deliver on any of his five promises. The expelled Catholics were not re-admitted to their jobs. And the Unionist Council meeting stipulated that if relief payments were made to the destitute workers similar sums would have to be made available to unemployed loyalists.[29] There was no give whatever on the issue which was to precipitate the most drastic immediate response from Collins – that of Republican prisoners. But the initial reaction from the Republican side to the pact's breakdown was quite different. Mulcahy sent Collins a note the next day which is revealing of militant Nationalist sentiment in the North:

Mick,
Aiken was tremendously relieved yesterday at the Ulster hitch. Previously in the day he came to speak to me about the Ulster position generally and the following are points which he stressed very earnestly and asked me to stress with you:

A better consultative body regarding Ulster than whatever one at present exists is absolutely necessary for the Provisional Government . . . this body is absolutely necessary to preserve a link between a very strong body of Ulster Sinn Feiners and the Provisional Government.

In your future dealings with Ulster you should not recognise Joe Devlin or his clique . . . there can be no vigorous or harmonious policy on our part inside Ulster if his people occupy any position in our circle.[30]

Collins was to act on the Aiken suggestions in two important regards, the setting up of a North-Eastern Advisory Committee to advise the Provisional Government on Northern affairs, and the avoidance of Joe Devlin and his party. This was an inevitable but unfortunate development as Devlin, an able and intelligent politician, would have been a most useful ally for the Provisional Government. The old suspicion of Constitutional politicians was continuing.[31] Something else was continuing also: the old Collins preoccupation with IRA men in jail. On 14 January 1922 a group of Monaghan footballers including Major General Dan Hogan, OC of the 5th Northern Division, based in Monaghan, had been arrested in Dromore, County Tyrone, on their way to play in the Ulster Gaelic Football Championship. The party were carrying arms which they claimed they were entitled to do under the terms of the Truce. But the Unionists believed, rightly, that they intended to rescue three IRA prisoners in Derry Jail who were due to be hanged in early February.[32] The prisoners had been in jail since before the Truce and GHQ had sanctioned an escape attempt on 2 December 1921 stipulating that no firearms were to be used. Unfortunately chloroform was, and two warders were accidentally killed, one of them a friend of another warder, Patrick Leonard, who was assisting in the unsuccessful escape attempt. Fifteen prisoners were tried for murder and three, Leonard amongst them, were sentenced to hang.

Collins, who of course knew all about the escape plans, put pressure on both Churchill and Craig to have the Derry prisoners reprieved and the Monaghan men released. He wrote to Craig on 26 January 1922 reminding him that: 'I mentioned particularly to you the cases of these Co. Monaghan prisoners who were arrested at Dromore. I left you on the understanding that these cases would certainly be dealt with promptly with a view to release.'

On the face of it Craig responded reasonably and promptly, replying on the following day that if 'the prisoners will at once apply for bail, I will direct the Attorney General not to oppose . . . at the Assizes, the further necessary steps will be taken'. However this course raised the question of recognising the Northern courts. Collins wrote to Eoin O'Duffy, Chief of Staff of the newly formed Army, saying, 'I don't think it would do. Before I reply I would like a word with you.'[33] O'Duffy replied, 'No, Sir James's suggestion of bail will not do. I have written to you today at some length in connection with the action I propose to take in this matter, and hope to discuss it with you further tonight.'[34] O'Duffy had indeed set down his proposals, on official Army notepaper:

I have information from many sources this morning that there is grave consternation in the counties of Monaghan, Cavan, Fermanagh and Tyrone over the continued detention by the A-Specials of Commandant Hogan, and the Officers of the 5th Northern Division, and they demand authority from me to take immediate action to bring public opinion to bear on the situation . . .

You understand that I have arranged for the kidnapping of onè hundred prominent Orangemen in Counties Fermanagh and Tyrone. This was to take place last Tuesday, the 24th inst., but on account of the agreement arrived at between Sir James Craig and yourself I postponed action until tomorrow, Tuesday, 31st inst. and failing to hear from you to the contrary the kidnapping will commence at 7 o'clock tomorrow evening . . .

The North and South Monaghan Comhairle Ceanntair jointly demand that the Boycott be not lifted in Co. Monaghan until the men that did so much to secure the present measure of freedom be released from the custody of the pogromists. I am anxious to reply to my Monaghan friends tonight.

I should add that there are 54 affiliated Clubs in Co. Monaghan and each of them are sending two delegates to the Ard Fheis. This means 108 votes fore [sic] Monaghan for the Treaty . . .

Apart from squarely implicating Collins in cross-border hostilities the letter from the Chief of Staff speaks volumes for the attitudes amongst his own supporters with which Collins had to deal. O'Duffy was telling him in plain language that if he needed those hundred Monaghan votes to help him uphold the Treaty and, *ipso facto*, law and order in the South, then, in the North, illegality and disorder would have to be countenanced and the one hundred Orangemen would have to be kidnapped.

In the circumstances 'ambivalence' is a term which hardly covers the situation. But kidnapped a number of Orangemen duly were a week later, ironically enough on the night of 7 February, the day that the British reprieved the Derry prisoners, much to the disgust of the Orangemen.

In all some forty-two people were kidnapped in the cross-border raid well-described in the telegram that Craig sent to a startled Lloyd George apprising him of the situation:

Large bands crossed frontier at Derry, Tyrone and Fermanagh. They attacked and occupied houses of leading citizens on Ulster side of boundary. Numerous leading citizens including a High Sheriff were wounded or kidnapped and taken across border to the South. Bridges were blown up. Twenty Ulster Specials at Rosslea (Fermanagh) were kidnapped and taken across border. The Ulster police captured 11 men who were identified as members of the IRA from Longford and Leitrim. They were armed with bombs and revolvers and had transport. Sir J. Craig regards this as deliberate and organised attack on Ulster.[35]

Lloyd George, only too well aware of what the affair would do to a Coalition already creaking under the weight of the Treaty, reacted by sending a copy of the telegram to Collins accompanied by one of his own saying:

If anything approximating to this has happened H.M. Government take gravest view of the situation; such acts are a breach of the Truce and gravely imperil the Treaty. They will be glad to hear at once from you that you are taking immediate steps to ensure release of prisoners and to provide against any repetition of these grave outrages.[36]

Arthur Griffith, completely in the dark about what Collins and the IRB were doing, cabled Collins:

The diehards here are representing what appears to me to be the taking of hostages against the execution of political prisoners in Derry as an invasion of Ulster. I assume that since the 3 political prisoners have been reprieved – a decision which only reached me last night – every possible step will be taken to have these hostages released and to prevent the malign influences at work in England against the Treaty from scoring a success. Message from you to this effect will blunt widespread press attacks tomorrow.[37]

Collins in reply sent copies of his telegram to both Griffith and Lloyd George. To say that he economised with the truth is to understate the case very considerably:

Throughout yesterday I was extremely anxious as to what might happen in view of pending executions of the three men in Derry prison. I made special efforts to prevent acts of violence on the part of my people and as soon as I heard of reprieve last night I took steps to have information conveyed without delay to leading men on border in order to allay anxiety and to ensure against any untoward incident. The Provisional Government will do everything it possibly can to ensure the safety of the captured men and their early return to their homes.[38]

Whatever suspicions this response may have aroused in Griffith it convinced at least one influential observer of Collins' *bona fides*, Alfred Cope, on whom Lloyd George relied heavily. Cope joined in the fusillade of cables to implore that Craig and Collins be brought together again saying, 'Collins and his colleagues are doing their best but their difficulties are great . . . Collins has had great difficulty in holding in certain sections of the IRA who were out for hostages.'[39] The extent to which Collins had succeeded in masking his hand may be judged from another passage in Cope's telegram:

Please endeavour to get Craig to hold in check the special constables and also Belfast otherwise there will be pogroms. If he can do this there will be no more incursions from the South and Collins will have an opportunity of squaring up things. To think that the fruits of our long labours should be jeopardised by damn fools makes me sick. Let Griffith see Collins' statement. Could Griffith and Craig [Craig was also in London] meet at once and see what can be done . . . Collins has given very firm orders to his people against repetition . . .

To put it bluntly Collins was hoodwinking Cope. Far from making 'special efforts to prevent acts of violence' he had taken the most extraordinary steps to cause it. Prior to the Derry prisoners' reprieve he had called in two of his toughest Squad men, Charlie Byrne and Joe Dolan, and told them that 'at all costs' they were to shoot the two hangmen deputed to execute the Derry prisoners. Here, in his own stark terms, is Joe Dolan's description of what happened:

Charlie Byrne and myself were sent across to England to shoot Ellis and Willis, the two executioners, before they could reach Ireland. Mick Collins told us to get them at all costs, but if we were captured we could not expect any help from him, as we could not identify ourselves as part of the newly formed National Army.

. . . I went to Rochdale to get Ellis. . . . I saw Ellis' wife and made her come round the house with me while I searched it. She told me Ellis had gone to Ireland . . . I had to wait an hour for a train which was held up by a snowdrift, all the time expecting to have a fight for my life if the police came, but I think I frightened Mrs Ellis so much that she was afraid to leave the house. When I came back to Ireland I found out that the executioners had reached Ireland all right, but the prisoners had been reprieved.[40]

Much later in the year, on 12 July, Collins was still keeping up the fiction that someone else had done the kidnappings. He replied to a letter of Cope's on that day saying, 'Residents of the Six Counties alleged to have been kidnapped and were supposed to have been detained in the 26 Counties . . . I discovered that there were 10 Specials from Belcoo in custody (while on a visit to Athlone) Gearoid O'Sullivan also discovered 17 in Dundalk on 19th.'[41] But Craig too had his fiction of ferocity. He reacted to the kidnappings by demanding of Churchill whether there was any 'legal obstacle to our sending a flying column of 5,000 Constabulary to recover the kidnapped loyalists'. He wanted Churchill to reinvade the border area of the South and reoccupy a portion of territory for every person kidnapped until such time as they were all returned. Aghast, Churchill pointed out that such a policy would probably lead to the resignation of the Provisional Government, 'thus creating chaos and leaving the extremists in control'.

Reactions to the kidnappings were explosive. Three days after the O'Duffy raids a party of B-Specials travelled through County Monaghan in the South en route to Enniskillen in the North. During a stop at Clones Station a row broke out between the B-men and IRA Commander Fitzpatrick, who was shot dead. His colleagues retaliated by shooting four of the B-men and arresting the survivors. This precipitated a literal slaughter of the innocents in Belfast, where, amongst other ghastly incidents, a bomb was hurled into a group of Catholic children playing in a schoolyard, killing six of them.

The British responded by halting troop withdrawals from the South and by setting up a Border Commission on 16 February to monitor and control happenings along the border. Churchill told Collins that the Commission was an alternative to 'drastic steps which Parliament would otherwise expect me to take for securing the area of Northern Ireland'. Collins had little time for its mixture of IRA, British and B-Special observers and events bore him out; even Macready said the Commission was a farce.[42] The day after the Commission was set up he introduced a scheme whereby the Provisional Government assumed liability for the payment of teachers who refused to accept the authority of the six-county Government. In the preceeding fortnight he had also made it Government policy that local government councils in the North were also to be supported with funds if they refused to recognise the regime and he set in train a whole battery of minor obstructions. These included refusing to co-operate with the Northern Department of Agriculture, stipulating that trainee teachers from Northern Ireland who wished to take the customary examinations in Dublin would require a knowledge of Irish and stalling all requests from the Northern civil service for the transfer of files from Dublin to Belfast, as the Northern state set up its own departments and services.

All these dealings were unacknowledged at first. Dilworth, the Secretary of the Office of National Education, was instructed to reply to a query from his counterpart, McQuibban, at the Ministry of Education in Belfast, on 7 April, stating that he had 'no knowledge of the payment from Dublin of teachers in Northern Ireland'.[43] Dilworth was telling the literal truth. The £220,000 was paid from the Secret Service Estimate[44] 'not a penny' of which 'has been or is being spent on espionage . . . this money was required for a particular service.'[45]

Yet in correspondence with Lord Londonderry on the issue Collins blandly wrote on 10 April:

I fully agree with you that 'reasonable co-operation between the North and the South in educational matters' is very desirable. It seems to me that such co-operation on equitable terms could easily be arranged. For this purpose I suggest a conference between yourself and such others as you may desire.[46]

However, in education as in much else, 'reasonable co-operation' between Collins and the Northern Government could not 'easily be arranged'. The education issue in fact was almost a non-event compared to some of the happenings in Northern Ireland at the time.

In the conditions prevailing in Northern Ireland, the Truce between the British and the IRA overall, signed in Dublin in July 1921, was never closely observed by the Unionists in the North, to whom the mere existence of the IRA was a provocation and a threat. A threat made particularly fearful by the fact that with the coming of the Truce the British dispensed with the services of the Specials. There were several outbursts of sectarian rioting throughout the province and a particularly vicious outbreak in Belfast in August which escalated until it involved the IRA and the loyalist para-militaries directly. Each side killed ten victims. Nevertheless the liaison arrangement for the country as a whole obtained with varying degrees of success until 19 November 1921. GHQ continued to supply the various units in the North with arms, money and training from figures like Emmet Dalton, Dan Breen, Mulcahy and Eoin O'Duffy who actually set up an office in St Mary's Hall in Belfast from which he directed Republican activities. But in November, at a time of renewed rioting in Belfast, the British handed over responsibility for Justice and Security to the Six-County Government. Wilson was still Chief of the Imperial General Staff and he and Worthington Evans saw to it that Craig's government received considerable numbers of weapons and ammunition to assist in bringing the Specials back on to the stage. The new administration immediately put arms and men to use in cracking down on the IRA. GHQ was particularly incensed by a raid on an IRA training camp at Cranagh in the Sperrin Mountains on Christmas Eve, 1921. Until then no operations against Specials had been sanctioned but the Derry prisoners issue had been causing temperatures to rise and the pot boiled over with the arrest of the Monaghan footballers. At the end of February, following the expiry of the date for handing in all unauthorised arms, that is, those in Catholic hands, raiding by Specials intensified and during a ten-day period in March Collins sanctioned reprisal attacks against barracks at Pomeroy, Maghera, and Belcoo in which a number of Specials were killed.

Along with the covert activities of Prescott Decies (see p. 353) Collins also had cause for concern in the overt activities of Field Marshal Sir Henry Wilson who, on retiring from the Army, had been returned unopposed as the Unionist candidate for North Down on 21 February 1922 and was appointed Military Advisor to the Northern Government on 14 March. Craig was enraptured by Wilson, telling a group of businessmen[47] that he regarded him as 'my only guide as to what steps are necessary. Everyone else is brushed aside. All suggestions will be put before the Field Marshal, and if he recommends them I'll carry them out.' According to Wilson himself Craig 'put aside two millions to carry out my plan'.[48]

The plan involved disbanding the RIC and setting up a new force known as the Royal Ulster Constabulary and 'stringent regulations' concerning the carrying of arms. The law was to be 'strengthened in various ways for dealing with men found guilty of outrage'. The strengthening process included the introduction of flogging. Wilson got official British sanction for his plans. Macready promised to send in extra battalions of troops and Wilson's nominee, General Sir Arthur Solly-Flood, was put in command of the new force immediately after Wilson's appointment.

These developments coincided with the announcement by Dawson Bates that he had given instructions that there was to be no further liaison with the Border Commission and that the Government had ordered the police to refuse to recognise the IRA in any way. This announcement was underscored on the night of the circulation of Wilson's plans three days later, 18 March. The headquarters of the liaison committee, St Mary's Hall in Belfast, was raided, drawing a rebuke from the Provisional Government that 'the liaison arrangement between England and Ireland still holds good, and it is a pure breach of the Truce to take over the hall now.'

Both Churchill and Lloyd George had been strongly warned against issuing a political and military blank cheque to the Unionists before they allowed Wilson to take it to the bank. On 18 March 1922 two of the top civil servants concerned with Ireland, Lionel Curtis and Tom Jones, had drawn up a memorandum for the British Government on the Specials, following Craig's announcement that he was having nothing to do with the Boundary Commission. It said:

the whole of these Specials are Protestant . . . The British Government has armed and is paying for that force, but without question the Government of Northern Ireland controls it . . . The British Government has armed and is paying for forces which, it is told by the one who controls them, will in certain eventualities be turned against itself.[49]

Tom Jones followed this up with a note to Lloyd George saying, 'I feel strongly that you should not personally be drawn into conniving in the policy clearly hinted at . . . in Craig's speech when he implied his Government would resist any Boundary changes they did not like.'[50] But two days later Wilson presented his cheque by unveiling his plan for strengthening the North's forces. Next day it was announced in the Northern Parliament that the British would pay for the Specials. Collins was furious and wrote to Churchill saying that this made the British Government 'directly responsible for the situation in Belfast'. He warned Churchill that reaction in Dublin to what was happening in Belfast was generating pressures on the Provisional Government which were 'well-nigh overwhelming. In fact it is no exaggeration to say that the very existence of the Treaty will be gravely threatened.'[51]

As the split developed over the Treaty in the South it opened up in the North, with one important difference. In the North the debate

centred not so much on questions of the Oath and the terms of the
Treaty, but of whether Michael Collins or those opposed to him
would be more reliable in helping the Northerners to throw off the
yoke which still burdened them. Joe McKelvey (3rd Northern) and
Charlie Daly (2nd Northern) ultimately went anti-Treaty, being
subsequently executed by the pro-Treatites. They were replaced by
Seamus Woods and Thomas Morris respectively. The complexity of
the IRA's Northern organisation and the increasing pace of events
caused Collins to sanction the formation of a Northern Military
Council with Frank Aiken in command. Aiken, Commander of the
4th Northern Division, was a South Armagh man who had earned a
formidable reputation during the Anglo-Irish war. He made notable
efforts to avert the civil war before finally siding with the anti-Treaty
forces, eventually becoming Chief of Staff.[52] His Deputy on the
Military Council was Sean MacEoin. The objective of this Council
was twofold: to prevent the Stormont Government from consoli-
dating its position under the 1920 Government of Ireland Act and to
protect the Catholics of Northern Ireland. As Mulcahy put it in a
policy directive to the 4th Northern Division: 'The general aim
underlying all operations in Carsonia is to disorganise the economic
structure of the territory and to make the hostile inhabitants realise
that aiding and abetting the activities of the Enemy does not pay.'[53]

O'Duffy's official memo to Collins confirming the setting up of a
'Military Council for the North' is dated 10 March 1922. In the memo[54]
he also thanked Collins for sending him a letter from a correspondent,
'your Mr O'Driscoll', saying, 'I appreciate some of his suggestions
particularly that in connection with widespread incendiary fires.'
Other matters mentioned in the memo included the creation of a
'central dump in Cavan' for 'all supplies for the North'. In a sworn
affidavit describing these activities[55] Thomas Kelly, Divisional
Engineer of the 2nd Northern Division says: 'Michael Collins and
General O'Duffy took a staggering risk in supplying . . . weapons and
ammo because all were a part of the equipment handed over by the
British Forces to the Provisional Government.' Collins attempted to
minimise the risks involved in his clandestine operations by
exchanging the weapons held by men in the anti-Treaty Southern
Division, led by Liam Lynch, for the equipment he had received from
the British. The most hair-raising experience was that of the 3rd
Northern Division whose lorry broke down en route to Belfast
outside the home of a British Army officer, a genial type who gave the
IRA men tea and helped them to get the vehicle on its way again. The
smoothest gun-running operation was that of the 2nd Northern.
Thomas Kelly, who collected the consignment of 200 Lee-Enfield
rifles with 100 rounds of ammunition each from O'Duffy, says in his
affidavit:

These issues were made with the knowledge and approval of Michael Collins. The rifles and ammo were brought by army transport to Donegal and later moved into Co. Tyrone in a compartment of an oil tanker. Only one member of the IRA escorted the consignment through the Special Constabulary Barricade at Strabane/Lifford Bridge. He was Sean Haughey, father of Charles Haughey.[56]

O'Duffy was also authorised at a meeting at which Collins was present for the 'formation in Belfast of a Guard up to 60 men and the payment of £3 per week'.[57] Payments for the guard and twelve officers came to a total of only £216 per week. The rate of pay for officers in the province as a whole was Divisional officers £5 per week, Brigade officers £4. 10s and Battalion officers £4. In the 2nd Northern Division four Battalion officers were paid £2 a week instead of the £4 for two officers sanctioned by GHQ. An internal Free State civil service memorandum describing the conditions of the time says the decision to make payments was taken because:

the Volunteers were unable to carry on their daily work . . . and so as to obviate an exodus from the area. There was no organised attack on North of Ireland forces. The Volunteers [in Belfast] were daily however engaged in dealing with the riots or mob element . . . Orange mobs continually attacked the Catholic areas . . . Volunteers were almost exclusively confined to beating off these attacks. The police intervened when Volunteers pressed the attack into Orange areas and in that way Volunteers came into contact with them.[58]

During 1922 a Commission appointed by Belfast Catholics investigated some of the murders committed in Belfast.[59] Its report opened: 'there is little difference between these murders and the murders carried out in various parts of Ireland by the Black and Tans, except that in nearly all cases in Belfast, the bodies were mutilated.' One Head Constable[60] 'always used the bayonet on his victim' as he considered it prolonged his agony and 'he didn't believe in giving them an easy death.' The police murder gang had been active during the Black and Tan war. The Duffin brothers were murdered in their home in Clonard Gardens at 10.35 on the night of 23 April 1921. The gang included two District Inspectors, two sergeants and four policemen all of whom were identified. They used a silenced revolver, but ironically, says the report, left a dumb witness:

a dog belonging to the police barracks followed the Gang . . . In their hurry to fly the scene of their crime, the police slammed the door after them, leaving the dog in the kitchen. It was only next morning, about 9 o'clock, one of the police noticing the absence of the dog recollected what had happened.
. . . two of the police were in a sulky mood, and both demanded that as it was [the] DI who organised the murders it was up to him to go back for the dog . . . at 9.30 he came over for the dog . . . seen by numbers of people

coming in by the back way and taking the dog away. His doing so, far from destroying traces of evidence, only added to it.

After the Tans had gone the police continued the killings. While Collins was arguing with Craig on one hand and trying to damp down the fires of civil war on the other, one of the most revolting murders in the North's history occurred, the murder of the menfolk of the well-off family of publicans, the MacMahons on the morning of Friday 24 March. A statement given by one of the survivors, John MacMahon, in the Mater Misericordiae Hospital, on the evening of the attack tells what happened:

This morning about one o'clock I heard the hall door being smashed in. Five men rushed up the stairs and ordered my brothers and myself and Edward McKinney out on the landing. Four of the five men were dressed in the uniform of the RIC but from their appearance I know they are 'Specials' not regular RIC. One was in plain clothes. They ordered us downstairs. When we got down they lined us up in the room below, my father, my four brothers, Edward McKinney and myself, against the wall. The leader said, 'You boys say your prayers', and at the same time he and the others fired volley after volley at us. I think I lay on the floor for half an hour before the ambulance came. Three or four regular RIC came too.

John MacMahon suffered wounds to the head and body; his youngest brother, aged eleven, crawled under a table and survived also; the others did not. The man responsible for organising the MacMahon massacre and many other lesser-known killings was Detective Inspector Nixon. Nixon and District Inspector Harrison, head of the Belfast Detective Division, were given a free hand in organising Specials and RIC into a counter-insurgency unit in East Belfast which killed Catholics with impunity, either in reprisals for IRA activity or simply to cow others into fleeing or becoming unwilling to help Sinn Fein. Affidavits testifying to Nixon's active part in a number of killings, obtained from Catholic members of the police force who saw him in action, were made available to Collins.[61] He also had the testimony of figures like Bishop Joseph MacRory of Belfast who later became a cardinal and who was so friendly with Collins that the latter brought him to a meeting of the Provisional Government[62] at which Northern policy was formulated. MacRory told the North-Eastern Advisory Committee[63] that Brown St Barracks at the foot of the Protestant Shankill Rd contained a 'number of notorious murderers' who were 'immune' from discipline. Collins, however, knew better. While he agreed with the bishop about Brown St he pointed out that it was not a question of 'immunity'. The Brown St men and their ilk in other police barracks were acting in 'collusion with their superiors who were acting on even higher instruction'.

Collins knew what he was talking about. His intelligence service in Northern Ireland was not as widespread as in the South but he had

valuable sources nevertheless. Sergeant Matt MacCarthy was only
one of a number of informants in the RIC who included, amongst
others, the personal assistant to General Solly-Flood, the senior
British officer commanding North of Ireland police operations. He
knew that figures in the Northern establishment, including the
respected Secretary of the Cabinet, Colonel Spender and of course the
Minister for Home Affairs, Dawson Bates, were in favour of reprisals.
Men like Igoe and Prescott Decies, who opposed 'parley with
murderers' at the Liverpool Unionist Conference during the Treaty
talks, were at work in the North. Even before the truce, IRA
intelligence had established that Igoe had personally shot four Sinn
Fein sympathisers near Newry on 6 July.[64] Brigadier General Prescott
Decies, when he was a District Commissioner of the RIC in the Cork
area, so dismayed Macready that he wrote: 'Strickland will have to
watch the police very carefully for certainly Prescott Decies will think
that martial law means that he can kill anybody he sees walking along
the road whose appearance may be distasteful to him.'[65]

A background document prepared for Collins by the Catholic
Commission for the NEAC meetings said: 'The official position of
Prescott Decies in Belfast is a mystery. He is busying himself,
apparently with the Ulster Ex-Servicemen's Association and taking a
leading part in the anti-boycott campaign.' The ESMA was the para-
military body most associated with driving Catholics from the
shipyards in 1920 and with taking various actions against the
employment of Catholics throughout Belfast. The anti-boycott
campaign was directed at putting pressure on Catholics in retaliation
for their co-religionists' activities in the South. A crude method of
doing this was to burn out Catholic publicans, who were often found
in Protestant areas, and see to it that when the business re-opened it did
so in Protestant hands. The MacMahons appear to have fallen victim
to an extension of this policy.

Sinn Fein temporarily buried its differences on the day of the
MacMahon murders to hold a meeting in Dublin presided over by de
Valera at which Collins was represented by Kevin O'Shiel. It passed a
resolution:

That, just as when the nation was menaced by Conscription, common action
was taken by parties fundamentally in disagreement on other questions, the
Officer Board of Sinn Fein now appeal that common action be taken to bring
the outrages committed in North-East Ulster before the public opinion of the
world.

In London, on the same evening, the view that common action was
called for also prevailed and the Government reacted to the murders
by issuing a 'formal request' to Collins, Craig and their advisors to
come to London to confer on 'every aspect of the situation'. Both

parties accepted but there was a very acrimonious public exchange of statements between them before the Conference met in London on 29 March. Collins issued a lengthy point-by-point condemnation of Craig's failure to uphold the earlier pact saying that he 'had neither kept his undertakings with us nor done anything to meet us on the several points of controversy'. With the air of a man who had never even heard of a memo from O'Duffy about kidnapping Orangemen, never mind acting on it, he termed it an 'absolute fabrication' and an 'outrage' for Craig to have said in Parliament that the South was trying to 'coerce Ulster citizens and stir up strife here by bombing and sniping them'. Craig riposted by saying that Collins' interpretation of the Boundary Clause in the Treaty was a 'predatory attack' on Ulster and that Collins 'was not big enough to stick to his signature'. Collins drew attention to the provision of Clause 12 which stipulated that the boundary was to be determined in accordance with the wishes of the inhabitants 'so far as may be compatible with economic and geographical conditions'. He declared ringingly: 'I stand by my signature and the Treaty'.

Two points about the foregoing exchanges strike one.[66] One is that the strain of the Northern situation coming on top of his other problems can be guessed at from the emotional tone of Collins' language and the length of his public comments which are strikingly at variance with the terse style he used during the war. The second point is that, ironically in view of the great volume of publicity given to the terms of the Boundary Clause and its impact on the 'wishes of the inhabitants', this was the period in which the Northern Government introduced the deceptively styled Representation of the People Bill (No. 2). In fact its effect would be to gerrymander Counties Tyrone and Fermanagh so that the wishes of the Catholic inhabitants of those areas could not be electorally expressed.

But despite the background against which it took place the meeting was a success – on paper; so much so that Churchill caused Paragraph 1 of the Agreement, published on 30 March, to read: 'Peace is today declared.' It certainly sounded as though better days were coming. Both governments pledged themselves to co-operate in 'the restoration of peaceful conditions in the unsettled areas'. The police in Belfast trouble spots were to be Protestant, Catholic, or a mixture of both, depending on the area. An Advisory Committee of Belfast Catholics was to be set up to help select Catholic recruits to the Specials. There was to be a joint Committee of Protestants and Catholics set up in Belfast to investigate complaints of intimidation and violence. IRA activity was to cease. There were to be further meetings on the Boundary Commission. People expelled from their homes were to be encouraged back with the assistance of the Advisory Committee. The British Government was to vote £500,000 for relief works in Belfast, two-thirds for Protestants and one-third for Catholics. Subject to agreement between the parties, political prisoners were to be released, provided their crimes occurred before 31 March 1922, the day on which the terms of the pact were released to the press.

Privately Collins was far from optimistic. He wrote to Kitty Kiernan on 31 March:

We came to an agreement on certain things with Craig yesterday – I am not very sanguine about the future from any point of view. We have however secured release of all the prisoners – at least the agreement will mean that in the course of a few days and I am hopeful of getting the same result in favour of all the prisoners here. But the news from Ireland is very bad and 'the powers that be' here are getting very alarmed and there may be a burst up any moment. Were it not for the awful consequences I'd almost welcome it.

. . . When I think of how the position is given away behind our backs. Last week Belfast and the N.E. was dreadful to everyone here. A few things are done by our political opponents and all is changed they stand in with Craig again immediately.[67]

The reaction to the pact showed that Collins was right not to be too hopeful. Peace, though declared, was far from accomplished. Sir Henry Wilson, for one, was furious. He visited Ulster (14–22 April) and, at a Government meeting, he 'bit' his hearers by asking, 'Who is governing Ulster? You or Collins?'[68] Apart from the weight Craig attached to Wilson's opinions he knew from the reception that he had already received in Parliament[69] that the Field Marshal's views were widely shared by his followers. Some of these had shown their feelings in particularly grisly fashion the day after the Agreement was published.

A policeman was shot dead[70] at about 10 pm, at the foot of the Shankill Road and an hour or so later a group of uniformed police, led by DI Nixon, emerged from Brown St, the dead man's former barracks. They entered the nearby Catholic areas of Arnon St and Stanhope St, accompanied by a strong force of Specials and armoured vehicles, and broke into a number of houses. The occupant of one of them, Mrs Elizabeth Walsh, of No. 18 Arnon St, afterwards described what happened:

men broke in the front door of our house. My husband was in bed with two of the children. He was upstairs; I was sleeping downstairs with another child. They rushed upstairs . . . I heard the shots . . . When I went up I found my husband shot dead. His hands were over our two children. Bridget aged 1 year and 9 months and Michael aged 7 years; they too were shot.[71]

In all, three people were shot dead, one was battered to death with a sledgehammer and a child, one of a number wounded on the occasion, died some days later from gunshot wounds. Nixon and Harrison were folk heroes in Protestant East Belfast. In the atmosphere of the time neither Craig nor the British could or would prosecute or investigate such men without risk of a serious backlash amongst the Specials. Nixon, who had openly threatened the lives of his senior officers on occasion, was eventually dismissed on 29 February 1924. Collins telegraphed both Craig and Churchill pressing for an inquiry on two occasions (5 and 10 April) before meeting the North-Eastern Advisory Committee on the 11th and telling it that 'if we don't get an inquiry there is not very much use in going on with the pact', in other words pursuing the solution of the North-Eastern problem by political means. What other means should then be employed?

The proceedings of the inaugural Committee meeting,[72] which was held in private, and the status of those who attended it are important for an understanding of Collins' policy towards the North. The purpose of the Committee was to 'advise the Provisional Government' both on the Agreement and on 'all matters affecting the Six-County area'. On Collins' side the meeting, chaired by him, was completely representative of his Cabinet, with Griffith, Mulcahy, Fitzgerald, O'Higgins, McGrath and O'Duffy present. The Northerners included three bishops, a number of priests, Sinn Feiners of whom the most prominent was Cahir Healy, and some members of the IRA active in the Northern area. It did not include Joseph Devlin or any of his followers, which certainly left a gap in the representation of Nationalist opinion. The moderates, and the propertied Catholics, who tended to be found in the Devlin camp, were the very type Collins was depending on to push the Treaty through in the South. There were of course no Unionists present. The proceedings of the Committee were reflective of Catholic concerns only. How these impacted on Northern Protestants we shall see later.

It was open knowledge at the Committee that Nixon and company had refused to turn up for the identification parade at Brown St Barracks after Aron St. Collins proposed holding their own inquiry but Bishop MacRory told him that he would need a 'regiment of soldiers' to protect such an inquiry if it were held in Belfast. With characteristic truculence Collins replied, 'We could hold it all right!' He then read out his correspondence with Craig and said that he believed there would be no inquiry and that Craig would attempt to gloss over the pogrom and attempt to represent the situation as being a direct consequence of a Catholic invasion along the border. Griffith explained the dilemma of the Provisional Government:

We're sitting here as political cock-shots for our opponents and we are trying to defend the people of the North-East and our political opponents come along and call us traitors. We're quite prepared for that . . . I am quite prepared to advocate the breaking with Craig and take all the consequences. I want to know your views.

Views rather than policy were what he got. Bishop MacRory pointed out how helpless the Catholics were, hounded out of jobs and penned into their ghettoes with the Specials rampant, and suggested that if the state and the new police force were recognised to the extent of Catholics taking up the places allotted to them it would at least put arms in some 1,000 Catholic hands. Without the Treaty and the Agreement Catholics were totally defenceless and dependent on relief. At least under the Agreement the one-third of the £500,000 was available. Fears were expressed on all sides as to the debilitating effect of a split in the South over the Treaty in relation to the forces available for Northern Ireland. No one contradicted Mulcahy when he observed 'I take it that under the terms of the Treaty we recognise that Parliament in order to destroy it . . . to carry out all its terms will ultimately unify the country and destroy the Northern Parliament.' This was a strong underlying sub-text to the entire meeting, how to destabilise the Northern state rather than how to work with it, an approach which Devlin and his spokesmen would certainly have been expected to explore more fully.

Collins read out correspondence from Lord Londonderry which made it clear that he had lied point-blank on the payments to teachers.[73] He told him that as far as he was aware the Provisional Government was not responsible for the payments. The clerical representatives were not particularly enthusiastic about the payments policy. They were more concerned to have it understood that the schools would remain under Catholic church control. Archdeacon Tierney said firmly: 'We have come here *merely* to attend to the National aspect of things . . . What I would suggest is that schools under Catholic managers would get the right to adopt the programme and timetable of Southern Ireland. If we get that I would close with them at once.'

O'Higgins raised the uncomfortable point that the destruction of loyalist-owned property which was occurring in some areas in the South as an unsanctioned collateral of the Belfast boycott was giving the Orangemen a justification for their behaviour. Dr Russell MacNabb said, however, that the destruction of property made the other side 'uncomfortable' and remarked wistfully that there had been 'some beautiful fires in Belfast each night'. Collins said frankly, 'I know for a good many months we did as much as we could to get property destroyed. I know that if a good deal more property was destroyed . . . I know they think a great deal more of property than of human life. The whole thing again is what *is* proposed?' He did not get any clear answer. Nor was he able to give one to MacRory's fundamental query, 'Can you protect us?'

Collins decided on his own answer, a three-tier strategy of public, parliamentary and military pressure. In public, he continued his increasingly voluminous and acrimonious correspondence with Craig and, as the Provisional Government minutes for the time show, had little or no difficulty in carrying the Cabinet with him. On the 21st it was decided, because of the 'continuation of the outrages in Belfast', that Collins should wire Churchill informing him that unless Craig took immediate action 'to show his good faith' the Provisional Government would regard the Agreement as broken and it was also decided to tighten the screw of non-cooperation with the Northern educational authorities.[74] The Cabinet also backed him in preparing a tough reply to Churchill's answer asking Collins to meet Craig in London again. It would be 'useless' to meet Craig unless he showed 'some intention of abiding by the Agreement'.[75] He sent Craig a letter of almost six closely typed foolscap pages on 28 April, in which he found him guilty of 'the greatest want of courtesy', and went on to say:

Your entire letter has apparently been drafted with a view to keeping attention off the daily practice of atrocities and murders which continue uninterrupted in the seat of your Government. There is not space here to detail the abominations that have taken place in Belfast since the signing of our Pact, and I quite understand your desire to draw the attention of civilisation away from them.

Belfast was not of course the only place in uproar; the entire province was in convulsions, but Belfast was the worst-hit. In all twenty-four Catholics and eleven Protestants were killed in the city from 1 April to the date of Collins' broadside to Craig. On a day, 19 April, when Sir Henry Wilson was inciting an audience at Bangor, by drawing their attention to the dangers of Republican troops massing on the border 'while a supine British Government withdrew from Ulster,' the *Irish News* carried the following report of an attack on the Catholic Marrowbone area of Belfast, in which two women were killed, and fifteen houses burned down:

The match and petrol men operated with as much freedom as if they had happened upon as many deserted 'shanties' in the American backwoods 100 miles from the nearest civilised settlement, and all the time scores of men wearing the King's uniform were quiet witnesses of the scenes of destruction and many scores were within hailing distance, while the occupants of an armoured car could almost warm their hands at the flames.

The side-effects of the Northern convulsions on Catholic–Protestant relationships in the South were nothing like as horrific as in the North. The southern authorities actively worked to combat and overcome sectarianism. Nevertheless the South did have its share of atrocities. Ironically one of the worst outbreaks of sectarian killing was in Collins' own home district. It began when an anti-Treaty IRA officer, Commandant O'Neill, was shot dead when he called at a Protestant-owned farm near Bandon on 25 April. Three Protestants were shot at Dunmanway and over the next week the latent sectarianism of centuries of ballads and of landlordism (described in Chapter 1) claimed a total of ten Protestant lives. Tom Hales, Commandant of O'Neill's Brigade (3rd Cork), ordered all arms brought under control and issued a statement promising 'all citizens in this area, irrespective of creed or class, every protection within my power'.[76]

Speaking in the Dail, Griffith echoed the sentiments expressed by Hales, who was at the time actively engaged in armed opposition to Griffith's government. He said:

Dail Eireann, so far as its powers extend, will uphold, to the full extent, the protection of life and property of all classes and sections of the community. It does not know and cannot know, as a National Government, any distinction of class or creed. In its name, I express the horror of the Irish nation at the Dunmanway murders.

However, the effect of the killings on the Southern loyalists may be gauged from a letter from a Protestant lady in Crosshaven, County Cork, Alice Hodder, to her mother in England, which was forwarded to Lionel Curtis as Secretary of the Cabinet's Irish Committee:

For two weeks there wasn't standing room on any of the boats or mail trains leaving Cork for England. All Loyalist refugees, who were either fleeing in terror or had been ordered out of the country . . . none of the people, who did these things, although officially reported as the rebel IRA faction, were ever brought to book by the Provisional Government. And what is even more sinister is that the worst murders and roughest evictions took place in Clonakilty where Michael Collins comes from.

Then the murder of young Woods shook us all very much. Do you remember him last summer? He used to bring us up lobsters and mackerel. He was a bit of a ne'er-do-well and a bit mad but he'd done splendid work in the war and was recommended for a VC . . . his aunt and uncle had been subjected to a lot of persecution and feared an attack so young Woods went to stay with them. One night about 2.30 am armed men . . . broke in . . . Woods fired on the leader and shot him.

They . . . caught Woods . . . tried him by mock Court Martial and sentenced him to be hanged . . . The brothers of the murdered man then . . . gouged his eyes out while he was still alive and hanged him . . .

The letter went on to give details of Protestant farmers being turned out of their farms by anti-Treaty IRA parties as part of a policy 'got up by the Irish Transport Union, because all these people have brought down their labour, owing to the slump in prices and the workmen refusing to reduce wages.' Even though the pro-Treaty IRA always reinstated such people Hodder commented, not surprisingly, 'you never know when you've been reinstated what will happen next', and enquired: 'When will the British Government realise that they are really dealing with savages and not ordinary normal human beings?' Curtis' comment appended to the letter was, 'This is rather obsolete.'

But the file already contained too many such protests to be ignored.[77] For example Carson was eliciting considerable anger and sympathy amongst Conservatives and in the Press, particularly the *Morning Post*, over 'the worst thing that happened', the case of an 'outraged girl' in Tipperary, a Protestant, whom raiders had 'forced to submit seven times'.[78]

On 13 April 1922 Collins sent Desmond Fitzgerald copies of two telegraphed despatches which the Dublin Correspondent of the *Morning Post*, Bretherton, had filed, with a note saying: 'You will observe that portions are what would be described as fair newspaper comment, but the strain of certain parts is very objectionable', and he suggested that Fitzgerald get one of his people to interview Bretherton. 'It need only be a friendly interview.'[79] One of the despatches (5 April) stated that 'Dublin swarms with youths wearing leggings and faces that the kindliest hangman would be glad to get to work on.' The other, describing a resolution passed by Waterford workers concerning the Belfast situation said:

What the Southern Bosthoon thinks, if the word think can be properly used in this connection, of the trouble in Belfast is well illustrated by the resolution passed last night (March 21st) by the Waterford and District Workers Council STOP

The time for the massacre to begin is clearly now STOP . . . This attractive resolution proceeds to declare 'Unionists in Waterford and the South of Ireland must shoulder responsibility for what is happening in Belfast . . . should the Unionists . . . not take requisite measures to discharge their serious responsibilities in the matter the Workers Council will accordingly act immediately STOP

Probably no brighter example of the typical Southern Irish mentality could be provided than these truculent and ignorant bolshies every one of whom is awaiting his chance to murder and some of whom have doubtless already assisted in murdering with all the circumstances of filthy brutality the loyalists whom they hate not merely because they are loyalists but still more because they are clean decent and industrious and have something that Bolshies can steal STOP.

Apart from whatever results might have been expected from this type of coverage, and their many other sources of disagreement, Craig and Collins had been exchanging letters throughout April over the seizure by anti-Treaty forces of the headquarters of the Loyal Orange Institute of Ireland in Dublin, which they used to house homeless Catholic refugees from the North. The prosecution of the Belfast boycott by anti-Treaty forces also resulted in the destruction of some Protestant businessess, and in fines and threats which sometimes caused Protestants, particularly in border areas, to flee northwards. County Leitrim, with a particularly bad history of poverty and bad landlords, was harshly affected in the latter regard.[80] But there is no doubt that in many other parts of the country, the land-hungry and predatory element which emerges from any revolution tried to take advantage of the times to seize what did not belong to it.

It was a time in which the newspapers' daily list of Northern outrages, the bulk of them directed against Catholics, took 'from about half a column to a column each day'.[81] Defending the conduct of the boycott, Sean Moylan had no hesitation in telling the Dail:

> Raids and acts of obstruction have been enumerated and it was stated that this work has been done under cover of the Boycott. It has not been done under cover of the Boycott. It has been done as part of the Boycott work until this affair in the North – these murders and so on – is stopped.[82]

Accordingly, Curtis was instructed to write to the Provisional Government on 13 May inquiring about recompense for the relief expended by His Majesty's Government on 'the large and increasing number of persons who have been driven from their homes in Ireland by intimidation, or even by actual violence at the hands of men acting openly in defiance of the authority of the Provisional Government'.

Replying on 18 May, Diarmuid O'Hegarty accepted liability[83] in *bona fide* cases but warned that 'an organised movement' aiming at discrediting both governments was responsible for 'a considerable number of persons having left Ireland on the plea of compulsion without any justification whatever for that plea'. He urged the British to be vigilant in ensuring that only '*bona fide* cases' received assistance. O'Hegarty repeated guarantees already given to the Church of Ireland Synod that the Government would 'secure civil and religious liberty' and 'the restoration of their homes and property to any persons who have been deprived of them by violence or intimidation'.

This ecumenical approach was unquestionably Collins' also. But the Janus-faced approach inevitably led to perversions of it. At the Parliamentary level Collins privately explored every avenue open to him to bring down the Northern Administration. On 4 May he circularised every member of the Cabinet that they should:

> get the advice of your experts on the exact powers and limitations of the Northern Parliament in the British Act of 1920 . . . You will need to watch carefully to prevent any extension of these powers. You will also need to have a scheme prepared for non-co-operation in every possible way with the Northern Parliament. And in addition, a scheme towards making it impossible for them to carry on.[84]

To impress upon his colleagues that he was serious in this proposal he again circularised them on the 15th and 16th emphasising 'the importance of not losing sight of this matter'. On the 16th he wrote:

> I want a memo giving any points regarding the position of your Ministry in

relation to the Six-County Parliament ie any matter troubling you, any point you want raised, or that you have anything particular to say about. This matter should be treated as very urgent.[85]

He did not circularise his colleagues on the third strand of his policy of 'making it impossible for them to carry on', his pact with the IRA to use force against the Northern Parliament in flagrant breach of the Treaty he was so desperately trying to uphold in the Provisional Government area.

Collins' idea in mounting the Northern offensive had been to give the British the impression that it was in fact a defensive operation, a reaction against the activities of the Specials. This fig leaf lost a good deal of whatever credibility it possessed when at the beginning of May the 2nd Northern Division went into operation on its own, apparently through a confusion over orders from GHQ. Attacks were launched on barracks in Derry and Tyrone in which six RIC and Specials were killed. However any lingering qualms Collins might have had about launching a more co-ordinated campaign would certainly have been dissipated by the proceedings of the Catholic Advisory Committee provided for by the pact. The Committee did not hold its first meeting until 16 May, two days before the large-scale offensive was due to begin. Solly-Flood made it quite clear that he was not going to give the Committee any reforming role where the Specials were concerned. Some of its members were in the IRA and he regarded the Committee as a device to gain information about the security forces. At the last meeting of the short-lived Committee, held on 7 June 1922, it was pointed out that its members were being arrested and their homes, including those of priests, were being shot up by the Specials.

By 7 June the Collins-sponsored IRA campaign in Northern Ireland was well under way. It may be considered to have begun formally on the morning of 18 May when Seamus Woods led an attack on Musgrave Street police barracks in Belfast. It was marked by confusion and lack of co-ordination.[86]

However the overriding reality was that the forces against the IRA were overwhelmingly superior in numbers and material. One IRA officer described 'three train loads of Specials coming into Belfast every day'. His recollections are of daring incidents rather than of a campaign that seemed likely to win ultimate success. Ernie O'Malley records the OC of the Belfast Brigade and a companion being followed through the streets of Belfast as 'we ran from a job. We only had forty-five rounds between us.' The campaign was short and sharp, practically over by the end of June except for Belfast, where amongst other pieces of destruction the colleagues were responsible for raiding the Custom House and 'sledging' an estimated 500,000

gallons of whiskey. Though 50,000 seems more likely, it was said that
the aftermath was such that: 'the drains couldn't take it all. Men were
drunk on the fumes.' In some circles that particular raid probably did
more to set back Orange–Green relationships than anything else.

All told, the IRA managed to cause over a million pounds worth of
damage by burning Unionist property, roughly half of it in Belfast.
The war did not seriously discommode the loyalists' decision-takers,
though it touched some of them. Belfast's Twadell Avenue today
commemorates the Unionist MP, W. J. Twadell, shot because of his
inflammatory speeches and involvement with the para-military
grouping, the Imperial Guards, which also became subsumed into
the Specials. The homes of the Speaker of the Six-County Parliament,
Sir Hugh O'Neill, and the hard-line Conservative MP, Captain
Ronald MacNeill, were amongst the properties burned.

But the reaction fell heaviest on Catholics. For instance, May saw
sixty-three deaths in Belfast alone. Of these, forty were Catholics. In
an effort to balance the sectarian scales the IRA made things worse. On
19 May after three Catholics had been murdered two days earlier, an
IRA party entered a cooperage in York St and enquired, 'Who are the
Mickies here?' The three Protestants present obligingly pointed out
their Catholic workmates and were promptly themselves shot dead.[87]
Next day, out of a total of thirteen killings, Protestant retribution
claimed twelve Catholic lives. It was the same if not worse in the
countryside. This was part of settled B-Special policy. The British
General, Ricardo, a founder member of the UVF, who later became
disenchanted with the force, described the Specials' *modus operandi* in
a memorandum prepared for the British Government:

The 'B' Head Constable . . . goes to the leading local nationalist . . . He tells
him that they have arms and mean to patrol at nights . . . the nationalist is
shown a list with his name at the top and is told that if any 'B' man is touched
the list will be attended to from the top. This is not an effort of the
imagination but is not an uncommon arrangement.[88]

In reacting to the IRA onslaught the Unionists made other
'uncommon arrangements'. Internment was introduced, the hulk, the
Argenta, moored off Larne, being used as a prison ship. Although
murders were running at a rate of two Catholics for every Protestant,
only Nationalists were interned. All Nationalist and Republican
organisations were banned, but no loyalist groupings were proclaimed. Curfew was introduced in Belfast and Craig said (on 23 May)
that as far as the North was concerned the Boundary Commission was
now finished. In Dublin, the Cabinet, most of whom were unaware of
Collins' part in these developments, backed him in a statement saying
that as the Treaty was entered into between Great Britain and Ireland,
the interpretation of its clauses did not lie with Sir James Craig.[89]

Churchill was displeased with Craig's repudiation of the Boundary Commission which he termed 'little short of a defiance of the Imperial Government'. The defiance was particularly unwelcome because it came at the same time as Craig was seeking what Churchill accurately termed 'enormous' financial and military aid in order to strengthen the Specials along lines advocated by Wilson and Solly-Flood. In money, Craig sought £5 million sterling, in weaponry, 23,000 rifles, 15,000 bayonets, 242 Lewis guns, 50 Vickers guns, mortars, grenades and other equipment such as uniforms and tents.

However Churchill took the view that the troubles in the North stemmed from the fact that:

two so-called divisions of the Irish Republican Army were located in Ulster, and these divisions were most improperly maintained as organisations in spite of the truce, in spite of the Treaty . . . the prime and continuing cause of all the horrors which have taken place in Belfast is the organisation of these two divisions of the Irish Republican Army in Northern territory and the continuous effort by extreme partisans of the South, to break down the Northern Government and force Ulster against her will to come under the rule of Dublin.[90]

In these circumstances Churchill, though he claimed to believe in long-term Irish unity, decided like his father before him that Ulster would fight and Ulster would be right. After some quibbling Craig got almost everything he asked for plus a bonus of 3,000 surplus RIC revolvers and ten million rounds of ammunition. Units of the Navy and RAF were also sent to Ulster and ex-officers recruited to help train the Specials. By contrast it may be noted that less than two weeks earlier Wilson had observed with satisfaction[91] that Churchill had vetoed a request from Cope to supply Collins with arms, lest they be used in the North. That day, 10 May, Wilson had made a speech in the House of Commons demanding that the four battalions of British troops then in Cork should be sent to Ulster. They were, bringing the total of British troops in the area to some 9,000 and the Specials to approximately 48,000. Churchill told the Cabinet:

We could do no less, having regard to the gathering of the forces from the South and the ferocious steps used against Ulster . . . [Collins] having joined hands with avowed republicans we could hardly wonder that the North has gone back to its extreme and violent position. I think we have to give them assurances of help.

Churchill gave more than assurances. He took drastic action in support of the Unionists in two territorial disputes involving a triangular section of Fermanagh that ran a little way into Free State territory. At one end is Pettigo, largely in Free State territory, though the border runs through some of the houses. Belleek is in the Six-County area, overlooked by a fort on the Free State side. The Specials commandeered a house in the Pettigo area belonging to the parish priest. On 28 May there was an exchange of fire between the Specials and Provisional Government troops under Divisional Commander Joe Sweeney who earlier had had to run for his life when Specials opened fire on him. One Special was killed and the rest evacuated.

Churchill, who was coming to view Collins as a 'corner boy in excelsis'[92] saw the triangle incidents as an opportunity to teach him a lesson. On 3 June he ordered into Pettigo 1,000 British troops armed with a battery of howitzers, and a number of armoured cars. The troops were told 'to inflict the greatest possible loss on the enemy'. The village was shelled, the gunners succeeding in killing three Irish soldiers and one Special. The commander of the garrison and fourteen of his troops were captured, and newspaper reports make it clear that had the other Irish troops not fled with the civilian population casualties would have been much higher.

Collins sent a telegram to London demanding an immediate joint inquiry and protesting at 'unwarranted interference with our forces in our territory. An extension of the trouble will be disastrous and will certainly imperil the whole situation.'[93] Churchill's reply next day, 6 June, illustrates the confusions and tensions of the period:

On Wednesday last information was received that armed republican forces had invaded the Northern territory and had entered both Belleek and Pettigo . . . We immediately brought this to your notice . . . You told us that these forces were not your forces, that you disclaimed any responsibility for them. I announced this in Parliament in your presence the same afternoon.

It is with surprise that I received in the Communiqué issued from GHQ Beggar's Bush that there were 'no other Irish troops' than 'our troops', ie Free State Troops, 'in the district now or then' and I shall be glad if you will explain the discrepancy . . .

British troops have also been ordered to occupy the village of Belleek . . . It must not be supposed that any part of the border can be kept in a continuous state of disorder and alarm either by raids or by fire directed from your territory and all persons and armed parties over whom you have any control should be warned by you that they will certainly be counter-attacked . . . There can be no question of any inquiry into these operations.

Collins replied to him on the same day saying that his telegram 'had made the situation very much worse'. He protested at the lack of warning, repeated his demand for an inquiry and pointed out that while Belleek was in the North the Barracks was in the South's territory. He finished by telling Churchill: 'You misunderstand the position and only immediate inquiry can put it right.' The Belleek–Pettigo situation was exacerbated by an attack on the Mater Misericordiae Hospital in Belfast by Specials which occurred on the night of the 5th. The Specials sprayed the Catholic hospital with machine-gun

fire for some forty-five minutes. Then the hospital was raided by the
police 'in search of arms'. Pelion was piled upon Ossa in Collins' view
by the Northern Government which ordered the arrest of three
members of the Police Committee that night. They were lodged in the
Crumlin Road Jail alongside the Mater Misericordiae, for which he
demanded military protection.[94]

For once Lloyd George sided with Collins. He had come to think
that Collins had allowed himself to 'become obsessed with the Ulster
situation'. But he also saw himself being drawn into a war for which
he considered de Valera and Wilson responsible. He could see the
Treaty collapsing and hostilities resuming, not merely in the North
but with the Provisional Government. He warned Churchill that the
Oath or the Constitution were the only grounds on which they could
hope to carry public opinion for a break with Dublin. He said
privately that he thought 'there was a strain of lunacy in Churchill'.[95]
Nevertheless Churchill got his way by threatening to resign. All he
conceded to Collins was a promise to 'discuss the border situation
with Mr Griffith tomorrow in the light of your telegram'.[96]

Collins did not view the affair lightly. While he 'did not regard the
Belleek position as being so serious . . . the whole position is
unquestionably cause for gravest anxiety'.[97] In Dublin civil war
loomed. A general election was due to be held within a few days. The
last thing the Provisional Government needed or wanted was trouble
on the border. The tension between Collins' secret activities and the
views of his colleagues is reflected in the Minutes of a Provisional
Government meeting on 'The North East Question', on 3 June.
Paragraph 1 says:

It was decided that a policy of peaceful obstruction should be adopted
towards the Belfast Government and that no troops from the twenty-six
counties, either those under official control or attached to the Executive,
should be permitted to invade the Six-County area.

Obviously, from the reference to 'official control', some members of
the Cabinet had an inkling that their troops might have been used to
'invade the Six-County area'. Equally obviously, paragraph 2 is
undiluted Collins:

Any extension of powers on the part of that Government should be strongly
opposed and care should be taken to prevent it being granted powers other
than those conferred on it by the 1920 Act.

The same dichotomy of approach was noticeable after the Cabinet met
in agitation to discuss the Belleek incident. The first decision read:

It was arranged that the Minister of Defence should obtain daily reports from
every post on the twenty-six county side of the Border, and that particular
care should be taken to ensure that there would be no Border conflicts.[98]

From this it is evident that the other members of the Cabinet were unaware that the Minister of Defence, Mulcahy, was already receiving daily reports of what was happening in the North of a very different character from what was envisaged around the table.

The strain of these events was taking its toll on all concerned. Collins wrote to Griffith in London where he was attending one of the incessant meetings with Churchill, necessitated by the press of events, 'Duggan and O'Hegarty both laid up. I am a little better today.'[99] The object of the letter was to force an inquiry into the Pettigo attack from Churchill:

It appears to me that the position in the North-East gets steadily worse, and if we are ever to get anywhere there must be an enquiry about Pettigo. The whole incident must be gone into. All the incidents leading up to the final attack must be revealed.

But Churchill refused to concede any inquiry despite a particularly undiplomatic public call for one by Collins on 11 June in the course of which he said that while he would strain every nerve to avoid border clashes with the British it did not follow that his Government had not 'a very definite policy to put into effect as a last resort against that demoniacal barbarism which is aiming at the extermination of their people in the Six Counties'.[100] The two sides eventually came to an agreement to follow the practice 'adopted in Silesia with very great success'[101] and set up a sort of neutral buffer zone in the area. Churchill afterwards wrote that the triangle episodes:

gave me the opportunity of reassuring Ulster that if it came to an actual invasion they would certainly be defended. The IRA realised that we should not hesitate to levy open war and the Free State government knew that at any rate one line was drawn which would not be transgressed.

However there is a dimension missing from Churchill's policy considerations in this seemingly straightforward summation, that of the influence of Sir Henry Wilson on the growing disenchantment of 'Tudor Toryism' with the Coalition between the Conservatives and the Liberals. As Collins said in Wexford, plans were afoot for a new Die-hard party. Lady Londonderry had been canvassing the idea in the great houses of England for some time and as she plotted amongst the peers the right-wing backbencher John Gretton was taking similar soundings amongst his colleagues. As letters circulated amongst various lords[102] over Christmas, Northumberland had written to Lady Londonderry on 23 December asking her to stay with him to discuss the formation of the new party and the selection of a leader:

I quite agree about Salisbury. He has far more experience than anyone else in the Lords and would carry more weight . . . as to Horne I like him, and I think his instincts are Tory, but I'm afraid he has gone too far to turn back. He thinks Michael Collins is a very good fellow!!! He told me so the other day.

Wilson approved of these endeavours, noting after a lunch at Londonderry House in London at which only he and Lord and Lady Londonderry were present:

We discussed the possibility, necessity and probability of forming a real Conservative party. Lady Londonderry is working hard to this end with Salisbury, Northumberland, Carson, Ronald MacNeill and I am sure this is the right thing to do and I believe if they could get a fine leader it is a real possibility.[103]

The possibility had become considerably more real by mid-May 1922, when it was obvious that the Coalition was beginning to crack up. Wilson was addressing Die-hard meetings and more and more 'Tudors' were beginning to see him as the 'fine leader'. However he felt the time was not yet ripe for him to accept the leadership, and contented himself with attacks on the coalition for being 'increasingly inclined to work with the King's enemies'.[104] The Collins–de Valera pact played straight into his hands, Collins having said openly at the Sinn Fein Ard Fheis on 23 May that it would enable him to concentrate on the North-East. Churchill told a delegation of Catholic businessmen from Belfast on 2 June[105] that the pact adversely affected the relationship between Dublin and London. He said it also prevented Craig from working with a government in league with Republicans. Churchill described the pact as doubling the forces of evil and halving the forces of good. The power of Sir Henry Wilson was doubled he said, and told the delegation that 'you are being tortured by Wilson and de Valera'. Sir Geoffrey Shakespeare gives Churchill credit for 'keeping the Die-hards at bay and upholding Michael Collins'[106] but he was also concerned with upholding one Winston Spencer Churchill.

What Churchill did not tell the Catholic businessmen was that the previous day he had told the Committee of Imperial Defence's sub-committee on Ireland that 'in order to protect Ulster from invasion by the South' he wanted plans drawn up immediately whereby, when operations commenced, 'all our means of exercising pressure on Southern Ireland should be applied at once . . . we must act like a sledge-hammer so to cause bewilderment and consternation among the people in Southern Ireland.'[107] A version of the 'sledge-hammer policy' was duly applied over the Constitution and the Belleek–Pettigo area, but at this stage Churchill was still not sure whether Collins was going to break with de Valera or take steps to eject Rory O'Connor and his men from the Four Courts. 'Although the British could breathe a bit easier now, they could not abandon measures designed to conciliate the Provisional Government such as the proposed enquiry in Belfast.'[108] Accordingly, Churchill, having first got Balfour to test the waters, wrote to Craig on 10 June:

We gathered from Lord Balfour that at his interview with you last week you were not unfavourable to the setting up of a Commission of Enquiry on certain lines . . . such an enquiry would be of real value . . . show the provocation the Protestants have received and are continuously receiving as well as the bloody reprisals with which they repay it. I would not have been in favour of such an enquiry if the main constitutional issues which we have with the Irish Provisional Government were not now in a fair way of settlement.

Furthermore having shown quite clearly by the use of British military force our intention and our inability [sic] most faithfully to carry out our duty of defending your frontiers, and having supplied you with arms and financial aid for your own Police forces, I feel entitled in the general interest to make this request to you, and to make it seriously and definitely.[109]

However even in Craig had any real intention of holding an enquiry along the lines pressed for by Collins, Dawson Bates had not. He had a reputation for hostility to Catholics which included leaving them waiting for hours whenever they were forced to call on him on business. As Minister for Home Affairs, he had not attended any meeting of the Conciliation Committee set up by the Agreement. He had seen it purely 'as any voluntary committee'[110] without executive powers and had refused to grant it any expenses. Now he was even more opposed to the idea of an outside inquiry. He wrote to Craig:

It is impossible to agree to Mr Churchill's suggestion without gravely weakening the Government of Northern Ireland . . . the Executive of Northern Ireland and those who attempt to carry out the law must be supported at all costs. To set up an outside tribunal to enquire into the action which is found necessary from hour to hour, and to justify or condemn it would strike at the very roots of government.[111]

Armed with this, Craig was able to tell Churchill and Lloyd George, whom he met in Downing St on the 16th, that he was opposed to an inquiry the request for which did not come from Ulster. He was afraid that the new police force would get the idea that 'Dublin Castle methods' would prevail and that the identities of their secret service agents would be disclosed. Londonderry said that a public inquiry would only encourage the South to redouble their efforts to defeat partition. Instead, Craig proposed that some government official be sent over to decide whether or not an inquiry should he held. Churchill, who seems to have expected some such reaction, said that he wanted to have a Cope-like figure in Ulster and the meeting, which included Balfour, Chamberlain and Lord FitzAlan agreed to Craig's suggestion. The man suggested to the meeting to action Craig's proposal was Colonel Stephen Tallents, at the time a civil servant, private secretary to Lord FitzAlan, the Chief Secretary, with a record of achievement in organising food rationing and putting down Bolshevism in the Baltic. Now he was required, in effect, to put down the claims of Michael Collins for a public inquiry and to ration unpalatable truths.

Tallents very obviously got the message. In a letter accompanying his report[112] to the Under Secretary at the Colonial Office, Sir James Masterson Smith, he recommended that a permanent representative of the British Government should be appointed to Belfast. He was given the job in October 1922, Churchill having first got the report[113] he wanted in July. The stated brief was:

to enquire and report (for the information of Mr Churchill, as Chairman of the Irish Committee of the Cabinet) upon the extent to which effect has been given to the Agreement of 30th March signed in London by Representatives of the Government of Northern Ireland, and of the Provisional Government of Southern Ireland, and countersigned by representatives of the Imperial Government. In so far as effect may not have been given to that Agreement, you should report as to the reasons.

Tallents had high praise for the friendliness of the many and varied personages he met with in the Six Counties.[114] These were mainly Unionists, though he did meet MacRory. Interestingly enough, MacRory had just come back from a mission to the South which included calling on de Valera to intercede with him, Tallents said, in 'calling off the murder gang'. Obviously Collins had decided not to strain his relationship with the bishop by letting him know that he was better placed than de Valera to get the Northern campaign called off. Tallents did not attempt to see Collins or any representative of the Southern administration. He found that the 'failure to give effect to Clause 6 of the Agreement, which provided for the cessation of IRA activity in the Six Counties, was the major cause of its failure'. He deliberately lied in part of the report, Paragraph 26 of which stated: 'I am not aware of any responsible suggestion that the Provisional Government have promoted active measures by the IRA in Northern Ireland against the Northern Government.' The paragraph, in order to illustrate the difficulties confronting the Northern Administration, then went on to quote a document 'found in a Belfast house', and headed 'Headquarters 4th Northern Division' which stated: 'The immediate job which is up to us here in Ulster, no matter what happens in the rest of the country, is to get Ulster to recognise the principle of a united Ireland.' This document was part of a large and damning dossier supplied to him by Solly-Flood and other leading figures in the Northern hierarchy, proving conclusively that 'the Provisional Government is fully cognisant of the activities' of the IRA in Northern Ireland.

Tallents was welcomed by the Unionists, Spender writing[115] to him on 20 June to invite him to stay with him when he came to Belfast, referring to 'the pleasing rumour' that he was to be appointed liaison officer, the term used by Londonderry at the Downing St meeting. He got complete co-operation and it is quite evident from the material supplied to him in the form of captured IRA documents and intelligence reports that 'responsible suggestion' took the form of proof positive that Collins was implicated. Solly-Flood, for instance, supplied him with a breakdown of the 'connection between GHQ Beggar's Bush and the Northern Divisions'[116] and Spender, who was in charge of garnering the evidence from the various Departments, wrote to him on 29 June:

When you come to examine the facts you will have to admit that not only has there been a failure to co-operate but that the Southern Government has taken active measures to obstruct the Government of Northern Ireland in its normal functions and to undermine its actions . . .

Not only does our evidence show that the IRA in Northern Ireland is regarded as loyal to the Headquarters at Beggar's Bush, and, therefore, is presumably acting under the orders of the Provisional Government, but there is clear proof that there is active co-operation between the members of the IRA inside the Six Counties with members of that force outside the Six Counties who are undoubtedly representatives of the Provisional Government.[117]

Tallents therefore had all the relevant information but chose not to make use of it in the report proper, though he did make a vast amount of very revealing material available to his superiors. Churchill and his colleagues were under increased pressure from the Die-hards. To have produced a governmental report showing that Michael Collins, with whom the Treaty had been negotiated, was hand-in-glove with the IRA might have brought down the Government. Also, if a critical report had been published, the resultant spotlight would have shone not only on Michael Collins, but on the behaviour of the forces of law and order in the state he was trying to overthrow. Forces for which the British taxpayer had been committed unwittingly to writing a blank cheque, politically as well as economically.

The pressures of the Tories in London were however of greater moment to Churchill than those of Nationalists in Dublin on the Provisional Government. In the event Tallents wrote privately to Masterson Smith making a number of criticisms. He found that the 'Government has failed to perform the elementary duty of guaranteeing life and property.' Apart from that, however, he thought that it had 'made good progress'! He at first used the word 'disgusting' to describe the B-Specials' reputation but then substituted 'disquieting'.[118] And he was deeply critical of the manner in which Solly-Flood and Craig had been allowed to run up an establishment of 48,250 paramilitaries, costing nearly £5 million a year. 'A weapon is being forged which in time of crisis might be most dangerously used by other hands than those who now control it.' He thought Dawson Bates so bad that he was an 'asset' to the Republicans. He wrote wistfully,

If I had to choose a precise wish for immediate fulfilment in Northern Ireland,

my first selection would be the kindly removal of the present Minister of
Home Affairs to a less responsible Ministry. I am inclined to think that my
second would be his replacement by Lord Londonderry.

Where Collins was concerned he noted

for future consideration that the system employed in the Agreement of
inviting Mr Collins virtually to act as the representative of a minority in the
territory of another Government both encouraged the Catholics in the North
in their policy of non-recognition of the Northern Government and
exasperated Sir James Craig's supporters.

In the circumstances he felt

sure that the idea of holding an independent judicial enquiry into events in
Belfast, though it may have been feasible at one stage, should now be ruled
out. I do not think it could secure any advantage and I am sure it would lead to
a revival of propaganda about matters that are best forgotten.

Where his own report was concerned Tallents felt that 'Collins'
inclination to interfere in the Six Counties needs no encouragement'[119]
and that to send him either a copy of the report, or even a digest of it,
would 'supply such encouragement without any corresponding
advantage'. Churchill accepted this advice and the report was buried
as finally and completely as either the MacMahons or the victims of
Aron St. Churchill did allow a partial inquiry into one set of killings
which occurred while Tallents was conducting his investigations, the
shooting by B-Specials of three unarmed Catholic youths in
Cushendall[120] on 23 June. Because of the involvement of British
troops Churchill ultimately sanctioned an investigation by the
Recorder of Hythe, F. T. Barrington-Ward, the month after Collins
himself was killed. Barrington-Ward found that the Specials had
cold-bloodedly shot the three youths without provocation. But the
report was never published. The Unionists then conducted their own
inquiry which exonerated the Specials. Both reports were pigeon-
holed when the Unionists' allies, the Tories, were returned to
Government after the fall of the Coalition.

Collins' Northern policy caused the assassination which led to the
Cushendall deaths, that of Field Marshal Sir Henry Wilson. His name
had been placed on a death list by the IRB in June 1921 but the Truce
came shortly afterwards and the order was cancelled.[121] His shooting
can only be understood against the terrible backdrop of the times and
the bogey-man reputation which the former Field Marshal had built
up for himself in Nationalist circles. When de Valera heard the news he
said:

I do not know who they were who shot Sir Henry Wilson, or why they shot him . . . I know that life has been made a hell for the Nationalist minority in Belfast and its neighbourhood for the past couple of years. I do not approve but I must not pretend to misunderstand.

A colleague of Collins' was less circumspect: 'When Mick saw the pogroms he grew very angry and said: "We'll kill a member of that bunch".'[122] Wilson's involvement with every prominent anti-Nationalist and pro-Unionist cause from the Curragh mutiny to the foundation of the Specials would have been damning enough without his frequent attacks on Collins personally and the Treaty settlement in general.

The assassination was one of the most indefensible, inefficient, and hopelessly heroic deeds of its kind of the entire period. Wilson was shot on his own doorstep on the afternoon of 22 June by two ex-servicemen, Reggie Dunne and Joseph O'Sullivan, who had lost a leg at Ypres. Dunne was second-in-command to Sam Maguire in London, a friend of both Collins and Rory O'Connor, both of whom he had talked with on a visit to Dublin shortly before the shooting. The fact that he took a one-legged man with him on such a mission indicates what the split over the Treaty had done to the London IRA. One of the reasons for the shooting in fact was that it was 'hoped that it would bring about unity between the two sides'.[123] Dunne could easily have escaped, but he chose to stay with O'Sullivan and the pair were captured and beaten by an angry crowd in a fracas during which official tempers were worsened by a policeman being shot.

The Cabinet almost went into shock on hearing the news. Macready was told to confine his troops to barracks in Dublin (though not in Belfast) and ordered immediately to London. The revolvers used by Dunne and O'Sullivan and the documents found on them were brought to Lloyd George and his colleagues.[124] After examining these items the Prime Minister sent the following letter to Collins:

I am desired by His Majesty's Government to inform you that documents have been found upon the murderers of Field Marshal Sir Henry Wilson which clearly connect the assassins with the Irish Republican Army and which further reveal the existence of a definite conspiracy against the peace and order of this country.

The ambiguous position of the Irish Republican Army can no longer be ignored by the British Government. Still less can Mr Rory O'Connor be permitted to remain with his followers and his arsenal in open rebellion in the heart of Dublin in possession of the Courts of Justice, organising and sending out from this centre enterprises of murder not only in the area of your Government but also in the Six Northern Counties and in Great Britain. His Majesty's Government cannot consent to a continuation of this state of things and they feel entitled to ask you formally to bring it to an end forthwith . . .

I am to inform you that they regard the continued toleration of this rebellious defiance of the principles of the Treaty as incompatible with its faithful execution. They feel now that you are supported by the declared will of the Irish people in favour of the Treaty, they have a right to expect that the necessary action will be taken by your Government without delay.[125]

Collins was in Cork when the letter arrived, conducting an investigation into tampering with his votes which had raised the question of his seat being in jeopardy. In his absence Diarmuid O'Hegarty, as Secretary to the Provisional Government, replied with a masterpiece of instantaneous procrastination:

My Government have been profoundly shocked by the tragic and untimely death of Sir Henry Wilson and they hasten to place on record their condemnation of the assassination by whomsoever it was perpetrated.

The Provisional Government is gravely concerned with the statements in your letter as to information in the possession of His Majesty's Government revealing the existence of a conspiracy on the part of certain elements in Ireland to undertake attacks against life and property in England and in this country . . . It would appear however from your letter that your Government is in possession of information which leads them to conclude that a more serious state of affairs exists threatening serious consequences both in England and in Ulster.

The Provisional Government has no intention of tolerating such a situation of things and therefore requests your Government to assist them in dealing with the situation by placing at their disposal the information to which you refer. They will then be able to call upon the newly elected parliament which meets on the 1st proximo to support them in such measures as may be considered adequate.[126]

Churchill replied by wire, via Cope for Griffith: 'Information in our possession is at present of a highly secret character and cannot be disclosed. The Cabinet are awaiting the answer of Provisional Government to Prime Minister's letter.' The information Churchill referred to may have been secret intelligence reports concerning the IRA offensive against the North. It does not seem to have been given even to Macready at a crisis meeting on the 23rd. But I think I can say with certainty that the documents discovered on Dunne and O'Sullivan linking them to the IRA consisted principally of a lengthy letter smuggled out from an IRA prisoner in jail in England which could be construed as containing a fairly damning reference to Collins. After some coded references to guns and weaponry the following occurred:

Insist on a proper system. You are entitled to meeting. Now is the time to reorganise. If four of you go and see the Big Fellow he would arrange an election. And recruits – let 44 and 1 concentrate on the district around No. 1 and so on. The place Smith comes from needs attention. Put 84 and 85 there permanently . . . I shall write more later follow out *our old plan* of campaign if things recommence. Then all will be OK.[127]

For a few days after Wilson's death it appeared that war might break out again between the Irish and the English. Macready was instructed to draw up a scheme for attacking the Four Courts immediately. But he managed to delay matters until the Cabinet cooled down and reconsidered the consequences. On 25 June, 'word came through from London that the Government had reconsidered their original decision and that no action was to be taken against the Four Courts – I never ceased to congratulate myself on having been an instrument in staving off what would have been a disaster.'[128]

The Wilson assassination placed the Coalition under enormous strain. The *Morning Post* of 23 June said 'Mr Lloyd George, Mr Austen Chamberlain and Mr Asquith all shared in the murder of Sir Henry Wilson and are bedabbled with the stain of his blood.' When the House of Commons met to debate the issue on 26 June it did so, in William O'Brien's memorable phrase, 'hungry with anti-Irish fury'.[129] Had Collins not attacked the Four Courts garrison two days later the burden of probability is that the Conservatives would have either forced Lloyd George to do so, or moved to bring down the Coalition. In his death Wilson wielded more widespread influence than at any other time in his political career.

It was a foregone conclusion in the circumstances that Dunne and O'Sullivan would hang. They were sentenced to death at the Old Bailey on 18 July and executed on 16 August. Dunne was prevented from reading his reasons for their action during the trial. But their statement was subsequently published in the *Irish Independent* on 2 July. It said:

We took our part in supporting the aspirations of our fellow countrymen in the same way as we took our part in supporting the nations of the world who fought for the rights of small nationalities . . . the same principle for which we shed our blood on the battle-field of Europe led us to commit the act we are charged with. You can condemn us to death today, but you cannot deprive us of the belief that what we have done was necessary to preserve the lives and happiness of our countrymen in Ireland.

Sir Henry Wilson . . . was not so much the great British Field Marshal, as the man behind the Orange Terror . . . as Military Advisor he raised and organised a body known as the Ulster Special Constables who are the principal agents in his campaign of terrorism. You may, by your verdict, find us guilty, but we will go to the scaffold justified by the verdict of our own consciences.

Neither man ever went beyond that in explaining who or what motivated them.[130] But a deathbed crisis of conscience on the part of someone who played a small but vital part in the Wilson affair helped me to put together the hitherto unacknowledged details of the assassination.

The mother of a school friend of mine, Gearoid Johnston, as a girl worked for a small, elite group of couriers, whom Collins sometimes used for special missions. They were not allowed to join *Cumann na mBan*; the Women's Auxiliaries of the IRA, or any of the more obviously Sinn Fein-connected organisations. They operated from Leix House in Gardiner St, sometimes taking guns or ammunitions to country commanders, sometimes carrying messages. My friend's mother, Peig ni Braonain, before marriage, always knew when she was working directly for Collins, although no one ever specifically told her so. 'There seemed to be a tension in the air. Everyone took more care and something always seemed to happen afterwards', she told her son.

One day in June 1922 she was given an assignment in London by Pat Fleming, the famous jail escaper. She had never been out of the country before, but from the care taken with her instructions she sensed that they came from Collins. Fleming gave her a cover letter which purported to be the offer of a job as a waitress at Woburn House, a favourite London stopping place for Irish visitors. The real purpose of her journey was to bring a letter for someone who would meet her at Euston, 'a tall man called Tobin'. Peig duly carried out her instructions, and a week later Wilson was assassinated. She realised that she had brought the instructions for the killing. Years later as she came near death conscience assailed her, not for Wilson, but for Dunne and O'Sullivan. On her deathbed she told her son the story for the first time.

Liam Tobin, who was of course the 'tall man' of Euston, was back in Dublin when the news broke.[131] He received it with elation rather than remorse, and proceeded to tell Mulcahy 'that our lads had shot Wilson'. Mulcahy was far from elated. At first he refused to believe Tobin, then he reacted by saying he was 'going to resign'. At that Tobin began to realise the enormity of the situation and he made a beeline for Kingsbridge Station to intercept Collins as he returned from Cork. Worried as he was himself Tobin felt that Collins seemed even more so 'alone, carrying the weight of the Republic on his shoulders'. When he told him about Mulcahy, Collins replied, 'I'll make that all right,' and, said Tobin, 'It was all right, for it was never again mentioned.'

The Wilson shooting was in fact discussed by Collins on at least one other occasion that day, 23 June. One of his generals, Joseph Sweeney, remarked that he looked 'very pleased. The last time I had seen him look so pleased was when a DI was shot to his order in Wexford' (Lee-Wilson).[132] Sweeney asked, 'Where do we stand on the shooting?' and Collins replied, 'It was two of ours that did it.' Collins tried to have the 'two of ours' rescued and sent Tom Cullen over to make the attempt, but it was hopeless. Cullen reported back that rescue was impossible.[133] He did 'everything I possibly can' to secure a reprieve.[134] But the tragedy of what can happen to men caught up in large impersonal forces was highlighted in the result of his exhortation to Cosgrave to 'make an official representation that mercy be extended to these men'.[135] The law officer duly drafted the appeal but at 9.45 am the following day, we find Sinead Mason sending the draft to MacDunphy, the Government official who was to sign it, with a note saying: 'Draft was handed to me last evening at 6.40 pm to get off but as you were not present to sign the letter nor any typist available I could not possibly get it out. The matter is urgent as Thursday is fixed for the executions.'

However, Edward Shortt, Principal Secretary of State for Home Affairs, turned down the plea on behalf of the British Government, and Dunne and O'Sullivan were hanged the following morning in Wandsworth Prison.

The 4th Northern Division of the IRA, seeking a 'law-abiding and united Ireland' by means of the unacknowledged Collins-assisted offensive, carried out one of the worst atrocities of the period in June 1922. It occurred at a time of RUC activity in the area such as the murder of two Catholics whose bodies were subsequently found on a road deposited in holes which were originally dug by the IRA to plant mines. At the beginning of the offensive Aiken had issued the following directive to his men:

To all Brigade O/Cs – operations are to be continued all over the division until further notice. These operations are to be:
(a) General destruction of enemy property, wires, bridges etc.
(b) Destruction of property owned by prominent Orangemen living or having residence in your Brigade area.
(c) Reprisal – all reprisals must be taken at once. Reprisal must be six to one, so as to prevent the enemy from continuing same.
(d) Spies and informers to be shot on sight.[136]

On the night of Saturday 17 June 1922, in pursuit of (c), Aiken's men moved into the townlands of Altanaveigh and Lisdrumliska in South Armagh, less than a mile from the major town of Newry, mining the roads against interruption. In his unpublished memoirs John McCoy tells what happened:

Seven or eight farm houses belonging to Unionists were attacked with bomb and rifle fire and five of the inhabitants slain, two others dangerously wounded and the residences of some burned. The dead:
Thomas Crozier and his wife, James Heaslip, farmer (50), Robert Heaslip, his son (17), James Lockhart, farmer, single (21), James Gray (17).
Badly wounded: John T. Gray, William Lockhart, Joseph and Edward Little. The houses of Thomas Crozier, John Heaslip and William McCullagh were partly burned.[137]

Looking back on the period some sixty years later John McCoy wrote:

The record . . . should be an object lesson to the people in the North who are led to take offensive action against their fellow countrymen who have a different political outlook or who worship at a different church. The resort to force is a two-edged weapon which has a persistent habit of recoiling on the user and which in the last analysis seldom achieves anything that could not be obtained by reason and peaceful means.

The only people who have thrived on discord in the North are a select number of the trouble-making politicians who have climbed to office and are today engaged in the old device of creating the canard that men of a certain religious persuasion are *ipso facto* disloyal . . . their own 'loyalty' has always depended on how far they were able to dictate British policy here. When their power was in danger they preached sedition and sowed rebellion with uncomfortable results.

Apart from the rejection of his demands for an enquiry into the North's security methodology and issues such as the Derry prisoners and the Belleek–Pettigo affair 'discord in the North' involved Collins in major controversies with the British on other matters, at least two of which deserve examination. They concerned banking and proportional representation.

The second of these issues we shall come to shortly, the first dropped on his desk in the form of a letter from H.S. Guinness, the Governor of the Bank of Ireland on 11 June 1922, a date that leads one to speculate that it was part of the general British screw-turning policy of the time. It said that the Bank had just been informed from London that the Treasury proposed to transfer to London and Belfast from Dublin the Register of Stocks and:

at an early date to seek Parliamentary authority for the discontinuance of the Register of British Government Stock at present maintained at the Bank of Ireland in Dublin and for the establishment of a Register at the principal office of that Bank in Belfast.

Collins immediately wrote to Griffith in London asking him to consult Kennedy about this:

. . . typical instance of how they load the dice against us at every turn. It shows also the vital necessity of settling with them at once and finally so that we won't have to be thinking of their politics on every occasion. Equally it is another of these moves calculated to strengthen enormously the position of the N-E. Naturally there are several retaliatory measures we could take and in fact must take if things of this kind go on.[138]

The Bank of Ireland directors had a stormy meeting with Sir Basil Blackett at the Treasury on 16 June[139] and learned that the Treasury 'had acted in the first instance at the request of the Northern Ireland Government'. Guinness signed a protest from the Bank saying that the Treasury's action could:

certainly be attributed to a favoured nation treatment of Northern Ireland and would further embitter the present unfortunate relations between South and North and the removing of the remaining stocks to London would have the appearance of prejudging the financial arrangements between Great Britain and the Irish Free State, to the detriment of the latter state.[140]

Guinness kept up a stubborn rear-guard action and the issue was finally resolved in Dublin's favour after Collins' death through the intervention of Tim Healy, then Governor General of the Irish Free State. Collins must have been relieved as well as gratified at the Bank's attitude. During the Black and Tan war his intelligence network had intercepted letters from Captain Hall at the Admiralty, giving lists of the Captain's spies, one of which had stated, 'In the Cos. of Cork and Waterford there are several Agents who work to me through the Governor of the Bank of Ireland'.[141] Sean MacEoin used to tell a story about Collins' first dealings with the Bank[142] in January 1922. MacEoin accompanied him on a visit to the Bank's directors to seek a loan to finance the fledgling Provisional Government. The directors at first demurred and Collins sprang up and began to pack his briefcase, saying to MacEoin, 'Right so! General, when we get back to the office, make immediate arrangements to have the guard removed from this building.' As they made for the door the puzzled MacEoin whispered, 'What guard, Mick?' To which the reply was a sotto-voce growl, 'Shut up you fucking eejit, a large whiskey they'll be after us before we're well out the door.' The pair hadn't even reached the door when there came an embarrassed cough and a 'Mr Collins, can we discuss this matter a little further . . .' Collins got the loan, MacEoin got his whiskey and, as civil war spread, the Bank did actually get a guard.

Collins' commitment to the Catholics of Northern Ireland was deeply felt. In his last two weeks of life he continued to fight their cause over the proportional representational issue. Churchill replied to an earlier protest of his (made on 28 June) on 31 July saying that during the month's delay:

the Bill has been exhaustively examined by His Majesty's Government. As a result it appears very doubtful whether under the system of proportional representation, which the Bill abolishes, the Catholic minority in the six Northern counties would obtain a more adequate representation on the county councils and other municipal and local bodies than they may expect to obtain under the system by which under the Bill proportional representation is replaced.

In any event I feel bound to observe that the continuing refusal of the Catholic minority to recognise the Northern Government robs of much of their substance and possible validity the arguments urged in your letter against the passage of the Bill.

Collins noted on the first page of the letter: 'It is a sentence of death or expulsion on every Catholic in the North.'[143] He took time out from his increasingly successful prosecution of the civil war to reply to Churchill on 9 August:

I have been very seriously disappointed by the decision indicated in your
letter of 31st ultimo . . . The effect of this Bill is to prejudice the Catholic and
Nationalist position in the whole of the North Eastern Counties. It purports
to repeal the Local Government Act passed in the year 1919 against the most
strenuous opposition from the Orange Members at Westminster. Your
Government insisted upon that Act as a measure of justice for minorities
everywhere in Ireland, but particularly where they most needed it – in the
North-Eastern Counties.

Prior to the Act of 1919 (which Sir James Craig's Government has now
repealed) what with the gerrymandering of constituencies, the system of
direct voting produced a result which practically excluded Catholics and
Nationalists from their rightful position in these Counties. Take Tyrone
where there is an admitted Nationalist majority of over 15,000 – our people
could never get a fair show there, largely by being thrown into one huge area,
Omagh, which was treated as one constituency, while the Unionist areas
were divided up into a number of constituencies. The Act of 1919 went a long
way towards curing that state of affairs.

The Local Government Bill which has just been passed restores the bad
system prevailing before 1919. This is flagrantly so in Tyrone and
Fermanagh. Tyrone with its nationalist majority will now have an Orange
council with an Orange majority.

Do you not see, or have His Majesty's advisers not disclosed, the true
meaning of all this? Not merely is it intended to oust the Catholic and
Nationalist people of the Six Counties from their rightful share in local
administration, but it is beyond all question intended to paint the Counties
of Tyrone and Fermanagh with a deep orange tint.

I therefore urge upon you that this Bill should not be allowed to pass into
law.[144]

Cope backed him in his appeal as 'a necessary condition of a step in
conciliation being taken by either side'[145] but proportional representation was duly abolished and the results over the ensuing decades
more than bore out Collins' predictions to Churchill about gerrymandering.

After the triangle episode and the start of the civil war, which was
also causing divisions in the Northern IRA, Collins knew that the
Unionists could not be defeated by military means. Despite his brave
words about 'definite Government policy' he knew that his Cabinet
colleagues did not share his feelings on Northern incursions. The
position of the Northern units may be imagined from the following
report to GHQ concerning the state of affairs in Belfast, the only area
still able to put up any semblance of a fight two months after the May
offensive began:

Strength of Brigade – 800 men
Armament: 181 rifles and 11,600 rounds of ammunition. 308 service
revolvers and autos, 7,400 rounds of ammunition. 5 Thompson guns and
1,220 rounds of ammunition.

Engineering material: 156 detonators
                        12 stone war flour.
                        20 lbs cheddar. [Home made explosives]
                        12 lbs gelignite,
                        20 ft time fuse.
                        Enemy strength in area:
British military: 5,500
RUC: 2,650
Specials: 26,680
                        _____

    Total   34,830

For a period of three months previous to our resuming the offensive the enemy was running loose murdering and harassing our people, and as the Army was not very active the people were gradually losing the respect they had for the IRA. This respect had been won, not so much out of sympathy with our National aspirations, and our fight for National freedom, but more on account of the part the Army had played in defending the minority against organised attacks by uniformed and non-uniformed Crown forces.

When, however, we commenced a campaign of destruction of enemy property which hit the authors and promoters of the pogrom, and was having the effect of stopping the murder campaign, the sympathy and support of the people was slowly coming back to us.

As I have already reported to GHQ there was a small Executive following in Belfast and on the 31st May they attempted to shoot two Specials. Most of our officers . . . were attending a Brigade Meeting when this happened, and before they could get back to their areas the Specials ran amok, and shot up practically every Catholic area in the city; the death toll for that day was twelve and upwards of 50 were wounded. This was the hardest blow the civil population had got, and it almost broke their morale. Notwithstanding that we kept up our campaign of burning, and in a short time the enemy realised that they would require to change their tactics. They set about establishing a series of block-houses throughout our areas, and selected their men specially with a view to fraternising with the Catholic population.

This policy has met with great success as the people war-worn and long tired were glad of an opportunity of peace. Unfortunately however, the anti-Irish element of the population are taking advantage of the situation and are giving all available scraps of information to the enemy. Several of our dumps have been captured within the last few weeks, and in practically every case the raiding party went direct to the house.

. . . many officers and men are forced to go on the run, necessarily in their own restricted areas. They find it difficult to get accommodation with the people now and in a particular area, seventeen of our best officers and men had to sleep in a refugee home where they were all captured.

The enemy are continually raiding and arresting; the heavy sentences and particularly the 'floggings' making the civilians very loath to keep 'wanted men' or arms. The officers are feeling their position keenly. Recently a number of men were rounded up and detained in custody. The mother of one of the boys when bringing him food shouted out, in the presence of Crown forces, the name of local o/c and made a tirade against him for misleading her boy into this movement.

As I have mentioned before the economic position is very acute. To give a rough idea there are 171 married men with 405 dependants and 346 single men with 936 dependants. These figures are taken from cards returned by each company and where there were two brothers the number of dependants was divided. To relieve the situation it would require a grant of say £500 per week.

The men are in a state of practical starvation and continually making applications for transfer to Dublin to join the 'Regular Army' . . . under the present circumstances it would be impossible to keep our Military Organisation alive and intact, as the morale of the men is going down day by day and the spirit of the people is practically dead.

In the face of that report, from a brave man, not given to exaggeration, Collins knew that to attempt to continue the Northern activities with a civil war raging in the south would be disastrous. In the two years between 21 June 1920 and 18 June 1922, it was reckoned that 428 people had been killed in the North and some 1,766 wounded; 8,750 Catholics had been driven out of employment and, the object of the exercise, around 23,000 driven out of their homes altogether.[147] To have continued would certainly have made those figures worse. The one man in the Cabinet who shared his approach to the North, Mulcahy, said bluntly to Collins in a memo dated 24 July:

The people were for a peace policy and for a recognition of the Northern Government . . . They are even giving information to the Specials. Our officers seem to realise there is no other policy for the North but a peace policy of some kind, but the situation for peace or war has gone beyond them, none of them feel they are able to face the policy of one kind or the other.

By coincidence on the same day that Mulcahy wrote, Collins also heard from Markham in the Castle, who passed him an assessment of Carson by a senior Scotland Yard figure called MacBrien:

Carson dominates the British Administration and will continue to do so. He has Lloyd George, Churchill and Asquith in his power. All the monied classes are at his back. He has more to do with the dispensation of honours and jobs than any man in England. . . Carson is itching for an opportunity to lay Ireland in ruins.

How accurate the assessment was is a matter of opinion. But the continuation of the ineffective IRA campaign in Northern Ireland would certainly have given him an opportunity to vent any instincts he may have had towards laying Ireland in ruins. A meeting of officers of the Northern Divisions was convened in the Officers Mess in Portobello Barracks on 2 August to outline the new policy. It was to be a meeting of the defeated but, as Thomas Kelly's affidavit bears out, 'many and varied views were expressed, some quite heatedly'.

The only statement of importance now was the final summation and decision of Michael Collins. His final words remain clear and distinct in my mind to this day. He said: with this civil war on my hands, I cannot give you men the help I wish to give and mean to give. I now propose to call off hostilities in the North and use the political arm against Craig so long as it is of use. If that fails the Treaty can go to hell and we will all start again.

His intention to 'start again' communicated itself to everyone present as being sincere. The Belfast OC, Seamus Woods noted:

The late C-in-C outlined the policy we were to adopt – one of non-recognition of the Northern Government and positive resistance to its functioning. At the same time, from the military point of view we were to avoid as far as possible coming into direct conflict with the armed forces of the Northern Government, and any action on our part would be purely protective.[148]

The day after the Portobello meeting Collins was furious to hear news of the killing by the British military of two girls, one aged twelve and the other nineteen, in a raid at Edenappa, near the Jonesboro-Dundalk border on 23 July. He wrote to Cosgrave:

I am forced to the conclusion that we have yet to fight the British in the North-East. We must by forceful action make them understand that we will not tolerate this carelessness with the lives of our people. . . It is not individuals who are in charge of shooting parties or 'Hold-up' parties that are the guilty ones. The guilt lies with the high authorities, and we must face that.

He sent a memo to GHQ on 7 August which certainly indicated an intention to 'fight the British', rather than co-operate with them: 'at the present moment I think we ought to be making every possible effort to develop Intelligence system in North-East'.[149] However, Collins' Cabinet colleagues had no wish to 'fight the British' and by this stage were clearly making difficulties over aspects of his Northern policy. For instance there were problems in sustaining the payments to the teachers in the North and Cosgrave, who had taken over from Collins as Minister for Finance only two days earlier, noted on 14 July that

The question of payments in the Six-County area is in a pretty chaotic condition. . . There was no authority to spend money raised by taxing the South in the North. . .that the Northern Government may be enabled to avoid its own proper liabilities and this is done in such a manner that the Free State tax payer cannot tell that his money is being spent in this way.[150]

A change in policy was obviously taking shape as Collins became more and more immersed in the conduct of the civil war. More than a little disingenuously he had given an impetus to a policy shift himself by making peaceful noises in public while the IRA offensive he was sponsoring was still continuing. In an interview with the *Daily Mail* on 30 June he had said:

I think my attitude towards Ulster, which is the attitude of all of us in the Government, is not understood. There can be no question of forcing Ulster into union with the 26 Counties. I am absolutely against coer⁻ion of the kind. If Ulster is to join us it must be voluntarily. Union is our final goal that is all.

Kevin O'Shiel, the Government's civil service expert on the North, judged correctly when he wrote: 'The Army for a long time had one policy and the civilians another, or rather a series of policies that changed as quickly as the circumstances on which they were founded.' Collins, he said with massive understatement, 'tended to come to quick decisions without consulting many'.[151]

The Cabinet decided that there should be a civilian policy and that as many as possible should be consulted in its formulation. On 1 August a committee was set up 'to consider the question of the policy to be adopted towards the Belfast Government and with regard to the North-East Ulster question generally.' The Committee consisted of James Hogan, J.J. Walsh, Desmond Fitzgerald, Ernest Blythe and Michael Hayes. A copy of the governmental minute recording the fact of the Committee's formation was sent to Collins.[152] The two who actually prepared a report for the Cabinet were Blythe and Hayes. Blythe, an Ulster Protestant who had come south to learn Irish and join the revolution, had altered his views since he wrote in *An tOglach* that a British soldier 'merits no more consideration than a wild beast, and should be killed without mercy or hesitation.'[153] Hayes too was growing more constitutional by the hour. As Chairman of the Dail, it had been his duty to administer the Oath to its members. The joint report,[154] presented on 19 August, was in effect a condemnation and complete overturning of Collins' policy. The central recommendations were:

As soon as possible all military operations on the part of our supporters in or against the North-East should be brought to an end . . . The line to be taken now and the one logical and defensible line is a full acceptance of the Treaty. This undoubtedly means recognition of the Northern Government and implies that we shall influence all those within the Six Counties who look to us for guidance, to acknowledge its authority and refrain from any attempt to prevent it working.

The policy document set out at some length both the reasons for the *volte face* and the steps to be taken to achieve it:

The results of the General Election and the still more important results of the offensive against Irregulars put the Government for the first time in a position to decide freely upon its policy in regard to the North-East.
 . . . Nothing that we can do by way of boycott will bring the Orange party to reason . . . Their market is not in our territory. Our boycott would threaten the Northern ship-building industry no more than a summer

shower would threaten Cave Hill . . . the same may be said of the linen industry . . . pressure must be absolutely normal and constitutional. The use and threat of arms must be ruled out of the dispute . . .

The events of the past few months have done much towards fixing the Border where we cannot consent to its being fixed. It is full time to mend our hand. . . . Payment of teachers in the Six Counties should immediately stop. . . . We should stop all relations with local bodies in the Six Counties. Catholic members of the Northern Parliament who have no personal objection to the Oath of Allegiance should be urged to take their seats and carry on a unity programme . . . precautions should be taken to prevent border incidents from our side. Any offenders caught by us should definitely be handed over to the Northern authorities . . .

Catholics in the North . . . should be urged to disarm 'on receiving satisfactory assurances from the British'. Prisoners in the North should be requested to give bail and recognise the courts. The outrage propaganda should be dropped in the twenty-six counties.

Heretofore our Northern policy has been really, though not ostensibly, directed by Irregulars. In scrapping their North-Eastern policy we shall be taking the wise course of attacking them all along the line . . . The belligerent policy has been shown to be useless for protecting the Catholics or stopping the pogroms. There is of course the risk that the peaceful policy will not succeed. But it has a chance where the other has no chance. The unity of Ireland is of sufficient importance for us to take a chance in the hope of gaining it. The first move lies with us.

The Cabinet decided that 'a peace policy should be adopted in regard to future dealings with North East Ulster' and negotiations were authorised on outstanding educational matters, 'subject to . . . obtaining the approval of the Commander-in-Chief'. Collins was not present and may never have read the document. Notification of the 'peace policy' decision was sent to him on the 21st and he was killed the next day. The day after he was buried it was decided to circulate the memorandum 'to all Ministers'. It was adopted as Government policy both by the Provisional Government and, with minor alterations, by all administrations in Southern Ireland since. In practice the policy document was found to be erroneous in its judgement that 'the Treaty gives us a clear claim to at least two and a half counties of the Six. They can only dig themselves in if we help them by producing a state of turmoil and disorder'. The Northern authorities took full advantage of the opportunities presented by peaceful conditions after Collins' death to dig themselves in, using the mechanisms of law and legislature which they had fashioned expressly to achieve that purpose. The border remained unchanged and so until our day troubled 'Carsonia' remains a separate entity, neither properly in nor out of either England or Ireland. And now it is time to examine the final steps taken by Michael Collins to ensure the establishment of the Free State, and how these led to the two parts of Ireland acquiring the shape they still have today.

12

The Mouth of Flowers

What is that curling flower of wonder
As white as snow, as red as blood?
When Death goes by in flame and thunder
And rips the beauty from the bud.

They left his blossom white and slender
Beneath Glasnevin's shaking sod;
His spirit passed like sunset splendour
Unto the dead Fiannas' God.

Good luck be with you, Michael Collins,
Or stay or go you far away;
Or stay you with the folk of fairy,
Or come with ghosts another day.

Shane Leslie

(From poem written on seeing Sir John
Lavery's picture of the dead Michael Collins)

The worst fate that can befall a nation was about to strike Ireland: civil war. 'The safety of the Nation is the first law and henceforth we shall not rest until we have established the authority of the people of Ireland in every square mile under their jurisdiction.'[1] With these words Michael Collins took off the gloves and went to war with his former friends. Even though the new National Army was in a chaotic, disorganised condition, once he made up his mind to fight the result was practically a foregone conclusion. Many 'irregulars' joined in the shooting merely because the 'Free Staters' had fired on their comrades, or because of some friend's urgings or example. Sean Dowling, littérateur, dentist and lifelong Republican spoke for many when he said, 'against my struggling conscience, I found myself behind the barrel of a gun in Upper O'Connell St'.[2] They didn't have the people with them and they didn't have Michael Collins. They had neither the heart nor the expertise for firing on their fellow countrymen. Oscar Traynor, who like Dick McKee was a printer, had succeeded McKee as OC of the Dublin Brigade. He later became a long-serving minister under de Valera. A loyal, courageous man, Traynor lacked McKee's flair, and made the elementary mistake of seizing a number of buildings in O'Connell St on the side opposite the Four Courts so that there was no possibility of his linking up with the garrison. De Valera reported to his old unit as a private soldier. Years later Tod Andrews recalled his feelings of disgust at finding so much of the Republican leadership cooped up in the one block of buildings. After the Four Courts bombardment he made his way through the tunnelled buildings to the Gresham Hotel where he found Art O'Connor, de Valera, Robert Barton, Countess Markievicz, Austin Stack, Oscar Traynor and Brugha, 'all apparently without purpose'.[3] The anti-Treaty leaders were courageous, but woefully bad tacticians, disorganised and lacking any overall strategy.

The fighting in Dublin was over in a week, by 5 July, leaving the centre of the city in ruins for the second time in six years. Most of the group escaped the fighting, de Valera getting away in a Red Cross ambulance, but Brugha refused to flee or to surrender.[4] He was fatally wounded as he advanced on a Free State barricade manned by riflemen, revolver in hand, ignoring calls to surrender. The soldiers aimed low but a bullet severed a femoral artery. He died in hospital that night. Collins wept when he heard the news and wrote chidingly to a friend who had written to him after Brugha's death making disparaging remarks:

Many would not have forgiven – had they been in my place – Cathal Brugha's attack on me on January 7th. Yet I would forgive him anything. Because of his sincerity I would forgive him anything.

At worst he was a fanatic – though in what has been a noble cause. At best I number him among the very few who have given their all that this country – now torn by civil war – should have its freedom.

When many of us are forgotten, Cathal Brugha will be remembered.

Collins' magnanimity towards a man who had caused him so much trouble was entirely in character. What is surprising is that, not long before he died, Brugha was overheard 'saying all sorts of nice things' about Collins. Kitty Kiernan wrote to Collins telling him of a conversation, in which 'Cathal B. RIP' was reported as quoted, and then went on to say that 'he only said those things about you in the Dail to save the Republic etc, that you were one of the best men, full of energy, and that he'd like to see the man who could beat you in votes and several other things . . . it was a great surprise to them all . . .'[5] At the end of the month Collins had cause to weep again. He had written to Harry Boland in obvious distress saying:

Harry – it has come to this! Of all things it has come to this.

It is in my power to arrest you and destroy you. This I cannot do. If you will think over the influence which has dominated you it should change your mind.

You are walking under false colours. If no words of mine will change your attitude then you are beyond all hope – my hope.[6]

Boland was well aware who Collins was referring to as 'the influence which has dominated you'. Earlier that year Kitty had described how Boland had told her (in a burst of confidence) 'of Dev's dislike for you (Collins), because you are too anxious for power, that Dev likes Griffith, but Harry dislikes Griffith, and (of course) likes you, etc'.[7] Griffith had stood down for de Valera to allow him to become President of Sinn Fein. But there was no chance of Collins, a younger man, standing out of his way now and de Valera knew it. Collins seems to have taken on a new lease of life in the period following the Four Courts' shelling. Though in one part of his mind he was clearly heartbroken at the loss of personal friendships as his letter to Boland shows, in another he seemed to have clicked back into gear. The period of uncertainty and hesitancy was over. He was back doing what he could do best, soldiering. But Boland seems to have taken Collins' appeal to him as some kind of implied threat. He was certainly harbouring bitter feelings against Collins by then as a letter to Mrs Wyse Power protesting against the closing down of the Sinn Fein HQ at Harcourt St shows:

Altho' dictatorship is now the rule I hope you will not attempt to imitate 'Mick', 'Dick', and 'Owney' (O'Duffy) by arrogating to yourself the functions of the Ard Fheis as they have attempted to usurp the functions of the new National Government.[8]

He was well aware of the dark, loving, ruthless forces surrounding Collins – men who would act without hesitation or consultation to take a life if they thought it threatened 'The Big Fellow'. At any rate, during a meal with Anna Kelly at Jammet's restaurant the night after writing to Mrs Wyse Power he urged her to 'eat well, because it may be your last meal with me.'[9] The following night, 31 July, he was surprised in bed in a hotel in Skerries. Unarmed, he made a characteristic burst to get away but was shot down by an in-experienced soldier.[10] He lay wounded in Skerries for several hours before being taken to Portobello Barracks and from thence to St Vincent's Hospital. Collins immediately sought word of his condition:

Will you please send some good officer to St Vincent's Hospital and make a report on the exact condition of Mr Harry Boland. It is necessary to find out whether he has been operated on and what the doctors think of his condition.
There will not be a guard placed over him but we want to take some precaution to prevent escapes.[11]

Three nights later Boland died. As he lay dying his sister Kathleen asked him who shot him.[12] He would not tell. He asked instead that he be buried beside Cathal Brugha. Fionan Lynch was sleeping in his room in Mountjoy St when Collins burst in, weeping uncontrollably at the news.[13] Writing to Kitty he said:

Last night I passed Vincent's Hospital and saw a small crowd outside. My mind went in to him lying dead there and I thought of the times together and whatever good there is in any wish of mine he certainly had it. Although the gap of 8 or 9 months was not forgotten – of course no one can ever forget it – I only thought of him with the friendship of the days of 1918 and 1919. . . . I'd send a wreath but I suppose they'd return it torn up.[14]

That was the Soft Man, Michael Collins, the warm-hearted human being. The Hard Man, the soldier, was functioning efficiently, relentlessly. On a plane of broad strategy the story is simply told. From the signing of the Truce in July 1921 to the time of writing, the people of Ireland never again gave country-wide support and succour to the IRA at anything remotely approaching the Tan War levels. The difference between robbing banks, blowing up bridges, burning the homes and killing the sons of one's own people and those of a foreign enemy, is very great indeed. In six weeks the Provisional Government took Cahir, Cashel, Clonmel, Dundalk, Limerick, Sligo, Tipperary, Tuam and Waterford. Seaborne landings added Cork, Tralee and Westport to the total without much difficulty. The only really serious fighting occurred around Limerick City, at Kilmallock and New-castle West. Liam Lynch, who had assumed the leadership of the anti-Treaty, or Irregular forces, after the attack on the Four Courts, was forced to take to the hills. He and Liam Deasy had been captured in Dublin during the fighting but had been released by Mulcahy, because it was thought that, having been opposed to O'Connor and the others in the Four Courts, he would neutralise his forces. In fact he became the Provisional Government's principal adversary. As one reverse followed another he became less and less inclined to surrender and after being driven from the main centres the Irregulars' campaign became one of guerrilla warfare, which generated acts of destruction and viciousness on both sides that the nation did not recover from for fifty years.

Collins became Commander-in-Chief of the Army a week after Dublin fell, in circumstances which were still generating controversy and allegations of conspiracy sixty years later. As these circumstances were wrongly held to be directly linked to his death it is important in setting the record straight to examine both the allegations and the question of the appointment itself. An allegation which one meets with in Republican circles is that Collins had been out-manoeuvred by a 'junta within the Cabinet into accepting what appears to be a military post of great importance, but one which in fact was bereft of political power'.[15] The main source of this allegation was Sean MacBride who gave two controversial interviews to me in the *Irish Press* on 16 and 18 October 1982. One reason for his theory was Collins' Northern policy which MacBride correctly surmised was unwelcome to his Cabinet colleagues and of course to the British. MacBride reasoned that British

Intelligence would have another very compelling motive for wanting Collins dead. Quite apart from the question of what Collins had already done to their agents, not inconsiderable grounds for revenge, MacBride argued that there was considerable alarm at what he might yet do to 'Thorpe', the pseudonym given to the Castle's longest-serving and probably most important informer. The Burke and Cavendish murders in the Phoenix Park of 1882 which outraged England and dashed Home Rule from Parnell's grasp were carried out by a Fenian splinter group, the Invincibles, who were thought to have been sent to the gallows by an informer called Carey who was himself subsequently murdered. But then rumours began to circulate that the real informer was 'Thorpe'.[16] Collins asked Markham to check for clues to 'Thorpe's' identity on 21 April 1922.[17] On 4 August 1922, Markham seemingly found some evidence, for on that date, an entry occurs in a Collins diary 'Markham – Thorpe – Healy'. MacBride's theory was that Collins had learned that 'Thorpe' was in fact Tim Healy, a trusted advisor of his, an uncle of Kevin O'Higgins, and destined after Collins' death to be the first Governor General of the Irish Free State. If Healy was a spy he changed Irish history, being the most active of Parnell's opponents in the disastrous split of 1890. Had Parnell succeeded, Home Rule would have been conceded and a child born that year, Michael Collins, would probably have become a prosperous businessman in an un-partitioned Ireland.

MacBride's theory was that Healy, then a member of the IRB, with a Clan na nGael emissary, returned to the Clan man's hotel unexpect-edly one evening to find the proprietor, Captain Jury, a British agent, going through the Clan man's luggage. Somehow they managed to poison Jury. The Clan man got back safely to America but the Castle made Healy an offer he could not refuse. Either he went to work for them, or he faced a murder charge. According to MacBride, Healy then became an agent and remained one throughout his long career in law and politics. Obviously this is a highly speculative tale, scarcely to be given credit were it not for (a) the stature of its teller and (b) the fact that many people think that Collins was ousted from his position as Chairman of the Provisional Government and that this ousting was in some way connected with his death.[18] Therefore a biographer is called upon to make some effort at evaluation.

The limited research I was able to conduct did turn up some odd details. Working backwards from the Parnell split I found a death certificate for a Henry James Jury, hotel proprietor, who was certified as having died from 'typhus fever 5 days uncertified' on 29 May 1882 at Donnybrook in Dublin. Poisoning could produce symptoms which to a non-medical person might appear to be those of typhus. But the interesting thing about the certificate is that it bears three different dates. The death is registered on the 22nd. It is certified as having occurred on the 20th but there is a note on the certificate saying that the typhus was certified as having existed for 'eight days four hours' on the 29th. The fact that the certification of the disease somehow took place a week after the death was registered and nine days after it occurred apparently struck someone else as strange also, because the dates 22nd and 29th are circled and linked.

One would not have thought that a prosperous hotel owner would have been left with 'typhus fever 5 days uncertified'. The Jury death is also the only one with a date in the certification column. This could merely be attributed to nineteenth-century methods of record-keeping, but it is certainly a coincidence, if nothing else, that the Invincibles carried out the Phoenix Park murders on 6 May 1882. It could also be merely a coincidence that Collins himself in his memos to Art O'Brien, at the height of the Tan War, just before Bloody Sunday, was showing a curious interest in getting O'Brien to chase up a history of the Invincibles for him. It is also true that within hours of the news of Collins' death reaching Dublin someone opened his desk in Portobello Barracks and removed documents. But it is not clear to this day whether this removal was the official one ordered by 'direction of the Provisional Government',[19] on 23 August 1922, in which all Collins' papers were collected by his secretary, Gearoid McGann, and placed 'in the ground-floor Strong Room of the President's Department in Government Buildings'.

After Collins' death Markham did find some papers which had a bearing on his Healy enquiry. They passed into the hands of Frank Gallagher, the first editor of the Irish Press, who in turn gave them to Dr T.P.O'Neill, de Valera's biographer, who only gave them a preliminary investigation before placing them in the National Library where, alas, up to the time of writing they have not been discovered. Markham did tell Gallagher that Collins had specifically instructed him to try to find out if Healy was 'Thorpe'.[20] So, even leaving the question of the death certificate's strange dates to one side, MacBride's theory has at least the validity that Collins himself had suspicions of Healy.

However I am bound to say that the Cabinet documents of the time, far from proving that a 'junta' ousted Collins as MacBride asserted, tend to indicate the contrary. Collins was very much in control of the Government and took over the job of Commander-in-Chief because he wanted to lick the Army into shape and win the civil war quickly, quite possibly with at least one eye on the possibility of putting himself in a position 'to walk in on top of the Northern crowd one day', as an authoritative figure of the period assured me was his intention.[21]

MacBride's theory also overlooks the Frongoch/IRB factor. Though the IRB had not been able to bridge the gap in preventing civil war, the wing, by far the largest, that remained with Collins dominated every important position in the Army.[22] Interestingly enough de Valera himself did not subscribe to the junta theory. He told T. P. O'Neill[23] that he saw it as a tactical move on Collins' part. The IRA were so mistrustful of politicians of all sorts that Collins wished to establish himself in the minds of the fighting men as one of themselves and thus establish rapport. De Valera saw Cosgrave as merely a stopgap whom Collins would replace with ease when he wanted to. The relevant Cabinet minute records that a report on the military situation was submitted and noted, 'Mr Collins announced that he had arranged to take up duty as Commander-in-Chief of the Army and would not be able to act in his Ministerial capacity until further notice.'[24] That certainly has the ring about it of the Boss making an announcement. It was also Collins himself who announced to the Cabinet the formation of the War Council of Three with Mulcahy as Chief of Staff and Minister of Defence and O'Duffy as Commander of the South-Western Division. Two days later Collins wrote to Griffith:

It would be well, I think, if the Government issued a sort of Official Instruction to me nominating the War Council of Three, and appointing me to act by special order of the Government as Commander-in-Chief during the period of hostilities. It should contain a statement which could be directed to the Army by me as an Order of the Day . . . It should be pointed out that in the present fighting the men we have lost have died for something, that the wounded are suffering for something . . . for the same principle that we fought the British for – the People's right to live and be governed in the way they themselves choose.

This should go on to deal with the point that what the Army is fighting at present is . . . opposition to the People's will. What they are fighting for is the revival of the Nation. That this revival and restoration of order cannot in any way be regarded as a step backwards, nor a repressive, nor a reactionary step, but a clear step forward.

Griffith, in conjunction with Hugh Kennedy, duly produced the draft on the lines sought.[25] There was one big row in connection with the Cabinet decisions of 12 July, but this tends to show the power of the military wing as opposed to the political arm, rather than vice versa. Collins[26] had directed that the arrangements he had announced should be gazetted. These included four other Army postings: Fionan Lynch to be Vice Commandant of South-Western Division; Kevin O'Higgins to be Assistant Adjutant General; Joseph McGrath to be Director General of Intelligence; and Diarmuid O'Hegarty as Director of Organisation. But after the announcements appeared in the press (on the 14th) Gearoid O'Sullivan, at that stage the Adjutant General of the Army, rang up the Acting Secretary of the Provisional Government, Michael MacDunphy, to convey 'in strong terms an objection on behalf of the Army to the issue of the notices in the name of the

Provisional Government.[27] Cosgrave wrote to Collins on 25 July telling him what had happened and asking him whether he wanted the notices published in the official Government record, *Iris Oifiguil*. Collins died without replying and the result was that the appointments were never gazetted.

There was considerable feuding and jealousy over appointments and promotions at the time. And there was some very serious drinking being done also. These were young men who had lived three lifetimes of intensity in the space of a few years. The effects both of the strain they had gone, and were going, through, and of sudden access to the facilities of Officers' Messes, on young men hitherto hard-pressed to find the price of a pint, left many a noted figure of the time struggling with an alcohol problem for the rest of his life.[28] This background probably explains the reaction of O'Sullivan who had just acquired an Assistant AG he may not have been happy with, as O'Higgins was a strong critic of the Army's performance.[29]

Liam Tobin, who had been finding it difficult to adjust to his responsibilities under native Government, cannot have been greatly pleased either at being replaced by Joe MacGrath as Director of Intelligence. Collins personally directed that his appointment was not to be gazetted.[30] McGrath initially resigned but later took the job. Collins saw to it that Tobin went to Cork, with the rank of Major General, to take part in Emmet Dalton's successful campaign there. Certainly there would never be any question of O'Sullivan or Tobin opposing Collins, whom they idolised. But the failure to gazette the appointments that July day in 1922 were a contributory factor in fuelling the fires of gossip concerning Collins' death.

The 'bereft of political power' theory hardly survives a perusal of some letters that passed between Collins and Cosgrave after the Commander-in-Chief appointment was announced. Two days after Collins took over, Cosgrave, as Acting Chairman, wrote to him saying that at that day's Government meeting:

it was the general opinion that the Government should be kept in constant touch with the military situation throughout the country, and it was decided that the Army authorities should be asked to have reports forwarded regularly to me in my capacity as Acting Chairman, similar to those reports which were formerly supplied to you.[31]

Next day Collins agreed to supply reports but concluded: 'I cannot promise any definite date of starting as numerous command arrangements to receive similar reports are in hand at the present moment, and until I have these completed I cannot say precisely what my final arrangements are to be.'[32]

Cosgrave was still waiting for his reports nearly two weeks later. Writing to Collins on 27 July he says, 'I shall be glad to know whether you are yet in a position to let us have these reports, as the absence of official information at meetings of the Government is a considerable drawback.' Another letter of Cosgrave's on the same day replies to a communication in which Collins had raised the question of taking stern action against those responsible for incidents such as the ambushing of a train in County Wexford. The Government had agreed with him but before proceeding any further sought his views on the advisability of issuing a Proclamation and 'if you agree, a draft of the proposed Proclamation'. Cosgrave also wondered 'for the information of the Government' whether a Government proposal to have small undercover squads operating in Dublin 'meets with your approval'.[34] The tone and tenor of that exchange certainly does not sound as though Collins was in the grip of a 'junta'. A Government which has to plead with its Commander-in-Chief to let it know how he is conducting a civil war on their behalf sounds more as though it were controlled by the Commander-in-Chief rather than the other way around.

Certainly an important memo on propaganda which Collins wrote to Desmond Fitzgerald[35] is the work of a man who was thinking of the future, and quite confident of his standing with regard to his colleagues. It displays not only the time-honoured determination of all politicians to put their activities in the best light, but the overlay of a philosophy that, had matters turned out differently, might have helped to change the face of Ireland.

There is a constructive sense and a decency that transcends propaganda in the memo. The fact that it is addressed to Desmond Fitzgerald emphasises the fact that it is the letter of one elected representative to another. This is not simply Mick Collins sending a note to that '— stuffed shirt' Desmond Fitzgerald, whom he threw a bucket of slop water over because Dessie officiously stopped Nancy O'Brien going up to see the Great Man in Harcourt St simply because she had no appointment.[36] This is the work of a man who takes his responsibilities seriously. In the memo Collins showed a remarkable grasp of how the cinema was being used for propaganda purposes in Germany, and how Lloyd George used posters to get his message across. He proposed that all these and other methods should be used not only against the 'Irregulars' but also to rally the public behind a programme of investment and development in agriculture, fishing, forestry and industry, following the examples of countries such as Denmark, Germany and Holland.

Collins' interest in European examples extended beyond the economy to the Army. In his papers one finds references to a project for sending Ginger O'Connell and three other officers to Switzerland 'to make a report on the Swiss Army system for the Irish Government'.[37] He liked the idea of the Swiss Citizen Army model and he did not want the emerging Irish institutions to be mere slavish copies of their English counterparts. In May he had circulated his colleagues instructing them to 'outline policy to be adopted after the election, including reforms, economies, extensions and improvements'.[38] He stipulated that the new forms of Administration should be altered from the old so as to be 'thoroughly Irish . . . the use of the Irish language to be introduced wherever possible.'

Another set of military ideas he thought applicable to Ireland were those of T.E. Lawrence (Lawrence of Arabia), whom he tried unsuccessfully to attract to Ireland as a training officer.[39] Collins thought Lawrence would make a great Flying Column commander.

A combination of his Irish blood[40] and dissatisfaction with Britain's treatment of the Arabs seems to have inclined Lawrence towards the Irish cause. He is said to have met Collins first on 3 December 1921, but this is almost certainly the wrong date.[41] That they did meet during this phase of Collins' life is certain and Collins' influence may have led Churchill to intervene decisively in Lawrence's plans.

During the Treaty negotiations Lawrence was working under Churchill in the Colonial Office and growing increasingly embittered at the betrayal of British Governmental war-time promises made to the Arabs through him. He had decided to leave the Colonial Service and join the RAF as an aircraftman, under a false name, but Churchill, who regarded the idea as ludicrous, actively impeded his plans. The idea of Michael Collins and T.E. Lawrence teaming up struck Churchill as a far worse prospect than having Lawrence as an aircraftman. He withdrew his opposition and shortly afterwards 'John Hume Ross' joined the Air Force. Collins was killed five days later in circumstances which have generated even more controversy than Lawrence's own mysterious death.

One of the continuing accusations against Collins in Republican circles is that, particularly in his final phase, he drank too much. This may have been true on one tragic occasion, but overall, to paraphrase Lincoln's remark when Grant's drinking was reported to him, if Collins did drink as heavily as alleged I would seriously advocate that the cadets in the Irish Army Staff college be instructed to partake of a few glasses of his favourite John Jameson each night, because the amount of work he got through in the last days of his life was phenomenal. Apart from the overall conduct of the war he attended to a myriad details, of which the following examples of his activities form but a tiny fraction. The extracts also give some idea of the state of the country at the time:

To Director of Intelligence, 14/7/22:
It would be well to have looked up and definitely located, two brothers Greer, formerly with RIC and now residing at 86 Thomas St. Their movements are to be observed. It is thought they were with the British Secret Service.

To Lt Gen. O'Connell, Curragh Camp Operations area, 16/7/22, 7.30 pm:
Your despatch of yesterday's date, which was not timed, to hand.

You will note the following report received, check its accuracy and report the steps taken to deal with the possibility of a recurrence: BIRR: Barracks at Crinkle burned down by Irregulars Friday night, all roads blocked round locality and yesterday they occupied the three principal hotels in town. They took possession of Railway Station, and commandeered driver of train to reverse engine, and then they proceeded in direction of Roscrea. When they got about three miles out they broke up line and derailed engine and carriages. I think they are still in possession of the town.

Provisional Government Meeting, 19 July 1922:

The Minister for Agriculture reported he had instructions from the Commander-in-Chief to organise food supplies in Co. Mayo and he was making the necessary arrangements in the matter.

Collins to Government, 25 July 1922:

I wish to inform Government that in my opinion the absence of Courts will cause a very serious handicap to military action – to some extent it is causing it already, as every day cases are reported that are really not cases of the Irregulars, but cases of a criminal nature of one kind or another. What will be the procedure for bringing these men to trial before a Civil Court, and what Civil Courts are there to bring them to?

The extent to which drink was a problem for Collins in trying to instil discipline into the new army may be gauged from the following notice taken from the *Independent* of 27 July 1922:

MILITARY ORDER. It is prohibited to supply members of the National Army in uniform with intoxicating liquor. Where a member of the National Forces is found under the influence of drink in a licensed premises the licence of such will be immediately cancelled and a fine imposed.

Collins to Intelligence, 30 July 1922:

The Government say that peculiar-looking individuals were seen going in and coming out of these premises (offices in Suffolk St, Dublin). Government is good at making suggestions of this kind, but I think that constant observation would repay the trouble.

Collins to group of Northern IRA officers at Portobello Barracks, 1 August 1922:

The civil war will be over in a few weeks and then we can resume in the North. You men will get intensive training.[42]

Collins to QMG, 1 August 1922:

In going about the thing that has struck me the most is the untidiness and uncleanliness that comes from bad mattresses . . . This is of great importance from the health point of view.

Intelligence report to Collins:

Erskine Childers has been sighted in Liverpool (on 5 August) trying to get to U.S. aboard the *Carmenia*.

Cope and Kennedy proposed that he could be either kept there, charged with treason/sedition or returned to Ireland on a Dublin warrant. Collins however proposed that he be arrested merely as a 'stowaway'.[43] Unfortunately for Childers Collins' suggestion that he be held in England was not adopted and Childers escaped back to Ireland and was later executed.

A grimmer note is entering the struggle. Casualties and destruction are beginning to mount. On 4 August Collins sends Cosgrave the draft of a threatening statement he wishes to have issued 'as an official statement either now, or at some more suitable opportunity'. It contains the following:

The Government is aware of plots to murder the members of the Government who are carrying out the people's mandate to restore order to the country. They are further aware that certain Officers in the Army whose military services are well known are marked down similarly.

After stating that the reason for issuing the statement is to alert the public and enlist their assistance in scotching the plots, Collins goes on to say that 'in accordance with the precedents of all civilised countries' the prominent members of the organisation which plans and executes such outrages will, together with those personally taking part in them, be held responsible and brought to account. What part Collins himself played in the 'bringing to account' process as practised by certain members of the Squad and ASU who found themselves in a Special Branch capacity in the CID HQ in Oriel House can only be speculated on. But certainly the Squad's Tan war policy of shoot-to-kill was often indistinguishable from its activities during the civil war.

Collins to Mulcahy, 7 August 1922:

We are not in a position to repose confidence in the effectiveness of the Civic Guard as a body to maintain ordinary law . . . it is not necessary for me to illustrate this by pointing to the wretched Irish Republican Police system, and to the awful personnel that was attracted to its ranks . . . the lack of construction and the lack of control in this force have been responsible for many of the outrageous things that have occurred throughout Ireland.[44]

Collins to Kiernan, 8 August 1922 (After attending a Mass for nine soldiers who had been killed in action in Kerry):

I did not get back until very late last night, I was in Maryborough, the Curragh and so on. It was woefully cold and I was petrified when we arrived back in Barracks . . . we have had a few hard days here – the scenes at the Mass yesterday were really heartbreaking. The poor women weeping and

almost shrieking (some of them) for their dead sons. Sisters and one wife
were there too, and a few small children. It makes one feel I tell you.[45]

The day after the Requiem Mass[46] he wrote to the Director of
Intelligence concerning the activities of a group of men engaged in
robberies in County Wexford: 'Any man caught looting or destroying
should be shot on sight.' The following day he is looking to the future
again. In a note on the composition of a body to investigate Army pay
and conditions he recommends the inclusion of 'a representative who
would be in touch with rank and file – and sympathetic to the rank and
file – a junior line officer of a certain type would be ideal'.[47]

He was obviously looking to the future also, though for what
purpose we can only speculate, when in the midst of all the foregoing,
and much else besides, he wrote to the Director of Intelligence: 'At the
present moment I think we should be making every possible effort to
develop the Intelligence system in the North-East.'[48]

At this period of the civil war the members of the Provisional
Government were living as well as working in Government Buildings. Even to make a sortie onto the roof at night to light a cigarette
was to invite a sniper's bullet. Kevin O'Higgins, who was almost shot
in this way, would later describe the Government of the time as
'simply eight young men standing amidst the ruins of one administration with the foundations of another not yet laid, and with wild
men screaming through the keyhole!'[49] But not all the members of
Government were young men. The combined attrition from unseen
foes and only too omnipresent colleagues was appalling. Early in the
month it became evident that Griffith was near collapse. Although
ordered to a nursing home he insisted on carrying out Cabinet
business. On 12 August he suffered a brain haemorrhage and died.
Oliver St John Gogarty wrote of 'his poor Arthur':

> He made the loud tyrannical foe dumb-founded
> And to relax his yoke.
> Inglorious in the gap: by many a hater
> The scoffing word was said.
> He heard from those who had betrayed him, 'Traitor!'
> The cross-grained and cross-bred
> He shook from off him with grand impatience,
> The flesh uncomforted,
> And passed among the captains in whom nations
> Live when these men are dead.[50]

Collins was making a tour of inspection through Tipperary,
Limerick and Kerry when the news reached him in Tralee. He turned
for Dublin to face a funeral day of double mourning. For it was on the
day Griffith was buried, 16 August, that Reggie Dunne and Joseph

O'Sullivan were hanged. The strains he had caused Griffith, the fate he had brought upon Dunne and O'Sullivan, must have weighed upon him as he marched at the head of the funeral procession to Glasnevin, a fine soldierly figure of a man whose appearance at the head of the Army he had brought into being was still talked of in Dublin admiringly fifty years later. But apart from mental stress, pain was gnawing at him from what could have been either incipient appendicitis or an ulcer.[51] Seeing him gazing at the grave for an unusually long time his friend Bishop Fogarty said to him, with more solicitude than tact, 'Michael, you should be prepared – you might be next.' Collins looked at him, 'I know', he replied, and then, feeling the effects both of the long, slow, ceremonial march and his instinctive urge to attempt to joke his way out of serious moments, 'I hope nobody takes it into his head to die for another twelve months.'[52]

The one undisputed fact[53] concerning Collins' last week of life is that he was in bad physical and mental shape. Every account of those days speaks of misery to some degree or other. Frank O'Connor says:

He lived it in suffering, mental and physical. Though still full of ideas and enthusiasm, he found it hard to work. He sat at his desk, scribbled a few lines, then rose and left the room, not in the old dashing way but slowly and in dejection.

The shadow had begun to fall. To Cosgrave he said, 'Do you think I shall live through this? Not likely.' He turned to a typist and asked, 'How would you like a new boss?' It was so strange, coming from him that she repeated it to O'Reilly who worried over it. Next day, as the two of them were driving into town together, O'Reilly asked after his health. 'Rotten', replied Collins. There was a slight pause. 'How would you like a new boss?' O'Reilly's heart sank.

Collins set off on his last, ill-advised journey for a variety of reasons. He wanted to continue his tour of inspection, which was also a morale-boosting exercise, as he was the man who embodied the new State, particularly since Griffith had died. Possibly also he hoped to make some peace contacts with his native Corkonians. He certainly wanted to seize some Republican funds and he simply wanted to visit his native place. Clonakilty was calling and a glass at the Four Alls would taste better and have a more therapeutic effect than one anywhere else in Ireland.

His decision to go to Cork provoked a scene with Joe McGrath who thought he was crazy to run the risk of travelling through the area where the Irregular leadership was strongest. It is said[54] McGrath went to the extent of putting down his objections in red ink but Collins was adamant. He despatched Frank Thornton on a mission to Clonmel to ensure that the barracks there was manned only by pre-Truce Volunteers who could be trusted, if safe conducts were given, to recognise and respect the prominent Republicans to whom they were to be extended, probably figures of the calibre of Dan Breen. Thornton however ran into an ambush and was so badly shot up that he lay unconscious for days. With characteristic self-importance de Valera deduced that he had been sent by Collins from Dublin to murder him.[55] So whatever peace talks were intended for Clonmel never came off. The same fate befell over-vague arrangements which appear to have been set in train in Cork.

Mulcahy says that before he left Portobello on his last journey he was 'writhing with pain'.[56] He roused a friend to say goodbye and joined him in a farewell drink. Told by Joe Sweeney he was a fool to go he replied, 'Ah, whatever happens, my own fellow countrymen won't kill me.'[57] As he walked down the stairs to wait for his armoured car he tripped and his gun went off, an ill-omen.[58] Roused by the shot, Joe O'Reilly rushed to his window. He saw Collins outside, a small green kitbag on his back, his head bent in depression. The impression he formed of his mood caused O'Connor to say afterwards that 'he had never seen so tragically dejected a Collins as this man who, thinking himself unobserved, let himself fall slack in the loneliness and silence of the summer morning'.[59] O'Reilly pulled on his trousers and rushed downstairs. Too late; the Big Fellow was gone.

Collins first went to the Curragh Barracks where he carried out an inspection, then to Limerick and on to Mallow. There is some confusion over whether he paid a visit to Maryboro (now Port-laoghaise) Jail en route to talk to Tom Malone. Malone, alias Sean Forde, was a top East Limerick Brigade IRA officer in the Tan war who had gone anti-Treaty and was regarded as one of the most formidable fighting men in the country. However Tom Malone's own account[60] states that Collins visited him on his earlier southern tour, the one cut short by Griffith's death. Malone said: 'He asked me would I attend a meeting of senior officers to try to put an end to this damned thing. As he went out, he slapped one fist into a palm in characteristic fashion: "That's fine the three Toms will fix it." The other two Toms were Tom Barry and Tom Hales. His last words to Jack Twomey, the Governor, were to look after me. Within a few days however he met his death.'

Malone's version would account for sending Thornton to Clonmel and for Collins' taking the risk of going to Cork. But Malone was old and ill when he recorded the interview and his memory may have been faulty. However, another prisoner[61] told me that Collins did call at the prison on his last trip and ordered that a whitewashed stripe be painted all around the top of the prison walls so that any would-be escapers could be easily spotted. A timetable of Collins' journey from Dublin jotted down at GHQ in Dublin has him arriving in Cork, via Mallow, at 8.30 pm.[62] Another account has him arriving much later.[63] In favour of the second timing is the fact that it would also explain the report[64] that he visited an army dance in Cruises' Hotel, in Limerick, that weekend. At the bar a young priest called him a traitor. 'Immediately', says an eye-witness, 'a young officer from Dublin hit the priest who fell to the floor and rolled under some stools . . . Michael Collins never said a word. He left the dance and about midnight set out for Cork.' The second story would also explain how it was that, when he got to Cork, he found that the two young sentries on duty in the lobby of the Imperial Hotel were both fast asleep. He banged their heads together and strode on.[65]

These discrepancies and contradictions are important only inasmuch as they remind us that it was a time of extraordinary emotion, a time governed by fear, hatred, confusion, tiredness, inexperience and hard drinking that did not make for accurate record-keeping or precise recall. If there is conflict of evidence about the simple facts of how long it took Michael Collins to get from point A to point B, and what he did en route on a trip of secondary importance, it is easy to see, in a land of legend, how a journey that culminated in the death of such a mythic figure could spawn a thousand theories. The first question I was asked by almost everyone to whom I mentioned I was writing a life of Collins was, 'Did you find out who shot him?' As a writer[66] in the *Irish Times* put it: 'Who killed Michael Collins, was it friend or foe, accidental or otherwise? This question has fuelled the great Irish whodunnit industry ever since the fateful day during the Civil War in August, 1922. . .' It is a perversion of Collins' significance to Irish history that the circumstances of his death, important though they are, should have come almost to overshadow the significance of his life. In an effort to redress this imbalance somewhat I will therefore ask the reader to bear with me as I set out the facts of Collins' last hours of life, and particularly what followed, in a manner which I think should make it clear once and for all how he came to be killed. It was a very Irish ending and it appears that there was a lot less to the tragedy than met the eye of many a theorist.

Apart from his hopes for peace Collins had another important motive in making his trip to Cork. Before Emmet Dalton's seaborne landings drove the anti-Treaty men from the city their control had been so complete that it included taking over the *Cork Examiner* and entrusting its editorship to Frank Gallagher. They also took over the collection of Customs and Excise revenues – partly by sending armed men to the Cistercian Monastery at Mount Melleray where a Revenue official was 'drying out' on retreat, and forcing him to append his signature to drafts at the point of a gun.[67] This money may have been the source of the persistent rumour that one of the reasons for Collins' last journey was to recover a cache of IRB gold which he is said to have with him when he was killed.[68] There was a sizable sum involved, approximately £100,000,[69] in the revenue seizures, which in today's values would be worth well over £2 million sterling.

Even in the middle of civil war, monies of that scale alone might well have brought Collins to Cork, both to protect his struggling Government's revenues and to deny them to the State's enemies. He had already directed Joseph Brennan, the financial adviser of the Treaty negotiations, now the Auditor General, to go to London to try to trace any anti-Treaty monies in London accounts. The man who advised him on the Cork banking scene, H.A. Pelly, manager of the Hibernian Bank, Cork, warned him that 'time may be a big factor in trying to recover some of this money,'[70] and he spent a part of the Monday in consultation with Pelly, taking notes on Imperial Hotel notepaper[71] before writing to Cosgrave:

(1) The bank position is slightly obscure. It will require a full investigation and combined with that investigation there must be an examination of the Customs and Excise position . . . (2) It would be very desirable to mak‸ an examination of the destination of certain drafts on the London County, Westminster and Parrs, London. Childers (Mr and Mrs) kept and keep an account or several accounts at the Holborn (I think) Branch of this Bank . . . don't announce anything until I return.[72]

Some £38,000 was later recovered.[73]

Another interest of Collins' lay in getting normal policing restored. He also wrote to Cosgrave about this at 3.30 pm that day. 'It would be a big thing to get Civic Guards both here and in Limerick. Civil Administration urgent everywhere in the South. The people are splendid.'[74]

Contact with his own people seems to have given him a new lease of life. He met his sister, Mary Collins-Powell and sent her son Sean, his nephew, later to be Chief-of-Staff of the Irish Army, on an errand connected with the Pelly mission. It was a good example of his ability to choose unorthodox helpers. The lad was followed on his bicycle, but managed to shake off his trackers and the note got through. However, he refused to take him on his trip the next day. 'I've got my job to do and you've got yours,' he said.

He drove out later in the day as far as Macroom, inspecting military posts, visiting relatives and friends and got back to the Imperial Hotel in a far more cheerful frame of mind than he had entered it the previous evening. It is said[75] that an unidentified Frongoch friend called to urge him to make peace. Collins argued with him for some time and then made the significant reply: 'Very well, see me tomorrow night. I may have news for you.' Then the Commander-in-Chief of the new National Army challenged his friend to a 'bit of ear' and the pair ended up rolling around the floor to the alarm and perplexity of the sentries.

(above) 17 August 1921: Dail Eireann meets in public session to debate Lloyd George's proposals for talks on Dominion status

(above) The Irish Delegates during the Treaty talks: (left to right) Arthur Griffith, Eamonn Duggan, Erskine Childers, Michael Collins, Gavan Duffy, Robert Barton, John Chartres

(*Right*) Collins leaves Downing Street with relief during break from talks

(*Foot*) Collins at pro–Treaty rally, March 1922

The British team: (*left*) Lloyd George a[nd] Winston Churchill, [(*far left*) Austen Chambe[rlain] and (*above*) Lord Birkenhead

Commander-in-Chief Collins on day of Griffith's
funeral, and (*foot*) on his fateful journey through
Bandon and Skibbereen (back seat, left) on day
of his death, 22 August 1922
(*Below*) Mass card of Sonny O'Neill

"All I ask of you is to remember
me at Holy Communion."

Sacred Heart of Jesus,

HAVE MERCY ON THE SOUL OF

Denis O'Neill,

NENAGH,

DIED 5th JUNE, 1950.

Aged 62 years.

A light is from our household
gone,
A voice we loved is stilled.
A place is vacant in our home
Which never can be filled.

(*Top*) Collins' body in Shanakiel
hospital, Cork
Faces of grief: Joe O'Reilly
(*above*), and Liam Tobin and
Tom Cullen (*above right*) at
Collins' funeral
(*Right*) Collins' brother, Johnny,
the only mourner allowed at
the blessing of the monument
over Collins' grave, with a
gravedigger in Glasnevin
Cemetery, 1939

Collins set off at 6.15 pm on 22 August 1922 for a tour of West Cork. It was one of the dates he and Kitty had discussed for a wedding, along with that of 21 June, when he had planned a double wedding in Longford with Sean MacEoin. MacEoin indicates that there was something concerning peace talks in the hint Collins gave to his wrestling friend. He recalls that 'prominent Cork citizens' had communicated peace terms to Collins, via Emmet Dalton. Collins does not seem to have been overly impressed with comments made by some of the people involved. Nevertheless MacEoin's papers include the definite statement that:

General Collins agreed to a meeting on the night of 22nd of August. Republican forces supplied Dalton with details of laid mines, mined bridges etc and generally speaking assured a safe conduct for the Commander-in-Chief. As time would not allow the contacting of every outlying post, and for that reason only, an armoured escort was included to serve as it were both as deterrent to possible attack and as an identification.

This would help to explain, if not justify, the ludicrously small escort which accompanied Collins through the most strongly held Republican territory in Ireland, despite Dalton's objections and urgings that he should not go at all. All the published accounts[77] say that the escort consisted of a motor-cycle scout, followed by an open Crossley tender containing two former Squad men, Joe Dolan and Sean O'Connell, eight riflemen and, supposedly, two machine-gunners, though these last were not much heard from in the fatal ambush. Emmet Dalton sat with him in the next vehicle, an open tourer with two drivers, and bringing up the rear was the Slievenamon, a Rolls Royce armoured car. However an unpublished account which I was shown[78] says there was also another vehicle containing six unarmed members of the pro-Treaty IRA from Mayo who wanted to join the police force and were being given a lift to Dublin, on condition that they accompanied the convoy, to give a hand with removing any barricades encountered on the tour – felled trees and such-like.

The party headed first to Macroom, via Coachford, and some writers have read significance into the fact that he went back there a second time, the morning after he had visited the local army post at Macroom Castle. It is said that he went there to meet Florrie O'Donoghue. 'It seems to have been an important meeting and Collins gave O'Donoghue a safe-conduct pass. Its importance lay in the fact that it had bearing on Collins' whole outlook at this time on the civil war.'[79] Feehan's theory was that Collins was trying to make peace whereas the politicians who had ousted him wanted no truck with 'stepping stones to Republics' and were insisting on an unconditional surrender of arms by the Republicans. That is not the way O'Donoghue described the meeting[80] which seems to have occurred by sheer chance. O'Donoghue had borrowed a car to visit his mother, who was ill. Dalton, the officer commanding the area, had given him a safe-conduct pass. But he was stopped in Macroom 'by a fool' of a Free State Officer and lodged in a cell in Macroom Castle. He saw Collins through the window and managed to get a note to him via the sentry whose rifle he minded in the meantime. Collins came to his cell to let him out personally. O'Donoghue says: 'He was really talking big. I got the impression that he wanted to leave politics to take charge of the Army. He said "I've been all over this bloody county and no one has said a bloody word to me." ' He was surprised and pleased 'that no one could stop him.' It was this frame of mind, more than anything else, which caused Michael Collins' death.

The journey to Macroom was uneventful but from there on the route to Bandon was an obstacle course of blown bridges and trenched roads. Accordingly the party was provided with a guide, a local taxi driver, to direct them to Bandon. The vulnerability of the little convoy was underscored at Ballymichael Hill where the Slievenamon stalled on the hill and soldiers had to get out and push to get it to the top. Later that day the touring car also gave trouble, seemingly through overheating, and there are reports of water being required on at least two occasions, before it was finally abandoned.

The village of Kilmurry lies ahead of Ballymichael and the motor-cycle scout, Lieutenant Smith, a member of the Dublin Brigade, whether acting on orders or otherwise is not known, occupied himself during Operation Push by knocking on doors calling out, 'The Commander-in-Chief is coming.' Apart from the folly of alerting anyone who might have wanted to take a shot at Collins this was a provocative thing to do because several of the men in the area had been in the anti-Treaty party that had been beaten out of Limerick, suffering defeats also at Buttevant and Kilmallock. There was no reaction, however, and the convoy passed safely on to the cross-roads at the entrance to Bael na mBlath, an undistinguished little gap where hilly ground rises on either side of the road. Even with the guide, the maze of unsignposted little roads caused uncertainty and the party had to ask a man standing outside Long's public house for directions. Denny Long, 'Denny the Dane', as he was known locally, obligingly pointed out the road to Bandon. He was standing with one hand resting on the Wild West-style swing doors to the pub and, unknown to the Collins party, had carefully stood a rifle on its butt inside the door seconds before they appeared.

For 'Denny the Dane' was an IRA sentry. Several important IRA officers were in the pub because of a meeting of No.s 1 and 3 Cork Brigades at Murray's farmhouse up the hill behind Long's. Two days earlier, at a meeting in Ballyvourney, Liam Lynch had decreed that the war must go on, even though many of the men who were now meeting, including Tom Hales, had argued otherwise. The Ballyvourney gathering was so important that it had drawn to the area de Valera, Childers, Tom Hales, Liam Deasy and other top-ranking figures on the Republican side. One of its decisions was that the sort of conventional warfare in which the IRA had fared so disastrously in Limerick, Cork City and elsewhere should be abandoned and that the organisation would revert to its old-style 'target of opportunity', guerrilla warfare.

Denny the Dane's tip-off meant that their adversaries' prime target had just presented itself to the IRA men. Tom Hales directed that an ambush for Michael Collins and his escort be laid at Bael na mBlath on the Bandon road, a mile or so away from Long's. On a military plane the reasoning behind the ambush was that the patrol might come back the way it had gone. On an emotional level the words of Flor Begley, the man who piped through the fighting at Crossbarry, strike a more convincing note, that of the territorial imperative. Begley said:

It leaked out that Michael Collins was coming south and that some members of the Dublin Brigade were coming to protect him and that they didn't give a damn about the 3rd West Cork Brigade fellows. This 'got their goat' [that is, Kelliher, Hurley, Deasy etc], and they decided to have a go at the Dublin crowd.[81]

Deasy tends to corroborate this view in his valuable account of the civil war, *Brother Against Brother*. He regarded Collins 'as the greatest leader of our generation'. But he points to the fact that between the area around the ambush site and Bandon 'not one active Volunteer had joined the Free State Army'. He says he found it

hard to accept that the convoy was travelling merely on a social visit to West Cork. It is mere conjecture, but I rated it as the foolhardy act of a brave man who knew well the area he was driving through and the men there . . . This last expedition of his may have been the gesture of a man who felt that reconciliation was no longer possible with so many intimate friends and comrades in West Cork. Nobody knew better than Collins the area through which he would pass, and consequently he arranged to travel in full military convoy. As such there could be no question of any intention on his part, as was suggested elsewhere, of meeting us for discussions.

It seems reasonable to speculate that Collins, without the know-ledge of his Cabinet colleagues, may have been attempting to bring about peace through negotiating with some Republican activists who were prepared to defy Liam Lynch. De Valera would almost certainly have been made aware of such an initiative through Frank Aiken, and would have been eager to explore the possibilities of another Collins–de Valera pact. All that is certain is that, whether because of the Thornton ambush, or for some other reason, it is obvious that no word of Collins' peace intentions had reached Bael na mBlath. However it is believed[82] that Collins was expected at the house of Canon Tracey of Crookstown during his last visit. The reason for the visit, it is said, was to make contact with some intermediaries who may have included a well-known priest Fr W.P. Hackett and figures such as Alfred O'Rahilly and Sean O'Hegarty, the officer who complained about Collins' drinking during the Treaty negotiations. During the IRA discussions which took place at Ballyvourney, Hegarty was confirmed as OC of the Cork No. 1 Brigade, even though he was recognised as being a neutral and engaged in peace moves of some sort. A stop at Crookstown would explain the seemingly inexplicably circuitous Bael na mBlath route back to Cork from Bandon which Collins took. As a glance at the map will show, it is a straight run of some twenty-one miles to Cork from Bandon via Inishannon on a main road which is said to have been open at the time.[83]

Had Collins survived the ambush and either kept his appointment at the Canon's house or with another group of peace-makers who were said to be waiting for him at the Desmond Hotel in Cork that evening,[84] it is possible that Deasy and Hales would subsequently have been contacted. Possible, but not certain, because apart from the vagueness surrounding these arrangements another ambush was apparently laid for him on the route to Crookstown from Cork. The Canon's housekeeper is said to have talked indiscreetly in Crookstown when she went in to buy extra drink and groceries for 'some important visitors' the previous Sunday.

The shop was the old-fashioned type – pub, grocery, hardware shop combined. Standing at the bar were three Irregulars[85] who heard the housekeeper tell the owner whom the extra order was for. An ambush was laid at a wooded area near Crookstown, called Farran, with a view, not to killing Collins, but to kidnapping him. Trees overhanging the route were sawn through so that they were only held upright by wires, the idea being to drop the trees so as to isolate Collins' car from the rest of the convoy. When Collins did not show up on the 21st as expected the Crookstown IRA had enquiries made in Cork. A waitress in Hoskins Hotel, Prince's St, was despatched to the Imperial to learn what she could about his movements. Some of the escort party were drinking at the bar and the girl picked up the next day's route from them. This was telephoned to Crookstown and corroborated by the garrulous housekeeper during another visit to the all-purpose shop. She said she was expected to have lunch ready at four. The Farran ambush was reactivated and remained in place all day until long after dark. It seems, therefore, that had Collins managed to get through Bael na mBlath safely he could also have been in serious danger had he visited Crookstown and left by the Farran Road.

However, blissfully ignorant of all this, Collins continued on that morning through Bael na mBlath. En route to Bandon his driver took a wrong turning – his regular driver had been injured in the Stillorgan ambush and neither of his two replacement drivers, Corry and Quinn, had any knowledge of the countryside and very little of war-time driving – and his car became detached from the rest of the convoy and drove into Newcestown. When the rest of the party caught up with him they found him in Newcestown Churchyard examining names on the tombstones. Meanwhile back at Bael na mBlath an ambush party under Tom Hales lay in wait, the road blocked by removing a wheel from a dray seized from a carter employed by the Bandon Brewery. The major part of the ambush party occupied the high ground on the left-hand side of the road, past Long's pub on the way to Bandon. On the right-hand side of the road, across a small stream behind a tall hedge overlooking the roadway, a smaller group lay hidden. Mines were placed on the roadway.

An interested observer of these preparations was Eamon de Valera, who had spent the night in a farmhouse about two miles away. He is quoted as having made a number of observations. 'What a pity I didn't meet him,' and, 'It would be bad if anything happens to Collins, his place will be taken by weaker men.' An integral part of 'the great Irish whodunnit' mystery is that de Valera had a hand in Collins' death. This is true only in the sense that he was the principal architect of the overall civil war situation. My information is that he actively tried to to prevent the actual ambush. It comes from the account,[86] given by Jimmy Flynn, the ADC assigned to him while he was in the Cork area. De Valera learned about Collins' presence in the area before Denny the Dane did. His driver saw Collins pass through Crookstown that morning and went immediately to alert de Valera, who then made for Long's where he discovered the ambush preparations in train. According to Flynn he asked that Collins be not ambushed, saying that he was in the area to meet Collins, and that arrangements had been made to bring them together.[87] Though de Valera 'virtually pleaded with them' no one accepted his arguments that surrender was a real prospect and that they would get a better deal from Collins in his native county than when he was back in Dublin amongst his Cabinet colleagues. He was told that while he was in the area his status was that of a staff officer under the Area Commander, Liam Lynch. The pub party were on active service under Lynch and intended to carry out his wishes about switching to guerrilla warfare. De Valera then 'stormed out of the meeting in a rage' and made for Kilworth where he had a meal at the home of a friend, a local doctor, who provided him with a pony and trap to get through Fermoy, a garrison town. Once through Fermoy, de Valera linked up safely with his car – cars were still rare enough in the area to draw attention to him – and drove to Fethard where he spent the night with Jimmy Flynn's parents. Later that night he heard the news of Collins' death and was 'furious and visibly upset'.

While de Valera was travelling to Fethard Collins and his party had gone into Bandon and from thence to Clonakilty, where he joined his escort in sawing through a tree across the roadway. Then on to Sam's Cross, Rosscarbery and Skibbereen, returning in the evening to Bandon, after a second visit to Rosscarbery, several hours after he was said to have been expected at Crookstown. During the course of the day his presence in the towns he passed through caused a sensation. People turned out to wave and cheer. He met several of his relatives, including his brother Sean, many old friends, like Sean Hales, the senior Free State Army officer in the area, and the mother of an old friend of his, Gerald MacDonald of Rosscarbery, whose death he had just heard of. There were crowds and handshakes, food and drink in plenty. Collins, with his usual generosity, insisted on buying drink for the escort party. One biographer allows him a pint of 'Clonakilty wrastler' at Sam's Cross [Forester], another [O'Connor], a bottle of stout at Rosscarbery, although he is said to have disliked stout. Collins himself may have had less to drink than the others, but though there is, as usual, some conflict of evidence on this point a number of accounts say that the escort was well under the influence by the time they left Bandon for the last time. Emmet Dalton, a very heavy drinker in later life, denied that the party, including Collins, was drunk. 'It's a lie', he said.[88] But with true soldierly bluntness he privately told members of the crew that made the film about his life for RTE that 'we were all arseholes!'[89] Billy Powell, Captain of Lissarda Company of the IRA, said the members of the convoy were 'in no shape for fighting. They'd been on a bit of a spree all day. Mick Collins stood them drink wherever he stopped.'[90]

Another account[91] describes a scene in Callinan's pub in Rosscarbery while Collins was away, possibly visiting Mrs MacDonald. A row broke out between Dublin members of the convoy and local troops when the machine-gunner of the Slievenamon, John McPeake, took a bottle of whiskey from a shelf in the pub. McPeake himself later admitted that there was some drinking on the trip but firmly denied[92] that it was to excess. The pub affray may have been the reason that six soldiers are said to have been disarmed and locked up, though local legend has it that they were put away by the local Commander, Captain Sean McCarthy, because they were ex-British Army personnel who were thought to be plotting against Collins. When McCarthy told Collins of his suspicions, and warned him to be careful, Collins is said to have listened to him in silence and then shaken hands saying, 'I'm going to put an end to this bloody war as soon as possible.'[93]

Both at Sam's Cross and at Bandon before he left for the journey back through Bael na mBlath Collins was warned to be careful. He may even have been specifically told, in Rosscarbery, that an ambush party was in place at Bael na mBlath. It was an open secret[94] in the district that an ambush had been laid. The postman had coined a witticism that he repeated at each farm he called at that morning: 'Collins is gone wesht, but he won't go easth.'[95] It is said that two farmers who had been drawing lime from Castlemore Quarries near Bael na mBlath became involved in a row with the ambush party when they attempted to remove the cart barricade. One of the farmers is said to have been a relation of Collins. When he got home he sent his son to Callinan's pub to warn Collins at around six o'clock that evening. The pub owner, Paddy Callinan, took the message and passed it on to Collins. A first cousin, Captain Paddy Collins, of Castle Freke, said his reaction was to shrug and say, 'Yerra, sure they'd never attack me.'[96] Captain Collins described him on that last day as being 'the same old Mick, not under any strain'. The greatest figure produced by the area, or indeed the Ireland of his day, Collins was back with his own, away from the intolerable tensions of Dublin. Forget the war, relax, take a drink, have a chat and a joke. It was human but it was not wartime behaviour. Collins would not have lasted a day had he been so unguarded during the Black and Tan period. In Bandon he said goodbye to Sean Hales, laughingly shrugging off his warnings to be careful, and set off for Bael na mBlath where Sean's brother, his close friend Tom, was waiting to kill him.

The ambush party had been in place for so long that most of them had given up, gone home, or gone to the pub, leaving six[97] members in place on the left-hand side of the road, coming from Bandon. They were: Tom Hales, Tom Kelliher, Jim Hurley, Dan Holland, Sonny O'Neill and John O'Callaghan.

Tom Hales decided that the mines should be rendered safe so that farmers could go to the creamery in the morning. He was carrying one mine and had taken the detonation leads off the other when Smith, the motor-cycle scout, appeared around the corner behind him approaching from Bandon. It was now nearly eight o'clock. Two of the men on the hill, Kelliher and Sonny O'Neill, fired warning shots and Hales[98] 'boosted' the mine over the low fence on the side of the road nearest him, that beside the stream, and tumbled over after it. It was one of the most ill-prepared ambushes of the entire period. The one Thompson sub-machine-gun available to the party had been carried back to the pub. The mines were disconnected and the handful of men on the hill were not equipped to take on a convoy which included an armoured car and men of the calibre accompanying Collins. The party's objective at that stage was to get Hales clear and make good their own escape.

The light was failing and the roadsides were overgrown and much narrower than they are now, more suited to horse-drawn traffic than to motor vehicles. In fact, beyond the barricade there was an ass and cart, temporarily abandoned by its wrathful owner because of the ambush. The ass was grazing at the side of the road and Smith skidded into a ditch avoiding it. 'Just the sort of donkey and just the sort of cart they have at home . . .'⁹⁹ Dalton realised that the convoy was in a highly dangerous situation and yelled at the driver: 'Drive like hell!' But Collins, who had tackled and disarmed gunmen who confronted him in the past, was not going to flee from an ambuscade in his own territory. Indeed, since the warning in Rosscarbery, he may have been expecting it because Dalton remembers him picking up his rifle as they neared Bael na mBlath. When the shots rang out he put a hand on the driver's shoulder and called out, 'Stop! Jump out and we'll fight them.' Dalton's account speaks of a 'heavy fusillade of machine-gun fire' sweeping the road, but the attackers had no machine-guns that I could ever find evidence of. The firepower was on the side of the convoy, the handful of attackers possessing the advantage of surprise and better positioning. The armoured car moved up and down the road, several times passing over the unremoved, but harmless, mine while McPeake kept up a heavy fire from the Vickers machine-gun. Bullets were clipping the grass all round Kelliher and he reckoned that had the gun not jammed suddenly he would have been killed. The jamming was caused by one of the inexperienced passengers in the armoured car feeding the belt awkwardly into the magazine. The gun should have been manned by two trained machine-gunners, but in the disorganisation of the time only one, McPeake, had been allocated to accompany the Commander-in-Chief. The other occupants of the Slievenamon were the drivers and two members of the escort party who had got into the armoured car because it was warmer than the Crossley tender which may also have been overcrowded through taking on extra passengers during the afternoon.¹⁰⁰

The two Lewis guns in the Crossley do not appear to have greatly discommoded the ambushers. Survivors' reports speak of the Vickers only. When it ceased there was such a lull in the sound of firing that instinctively it was felt that the brief battle was nearly over.

However, both sets of riflemen continued to fire, the firing being augmented by some members of the ambush party who had re-emerged from the pub and were now firing from the top of the hill on Long's side of the road, too far away to have any bearing on the ambush. Incredibly enough it is thought that a small group of Kerry IRA men retreating back to Kerry were drawn to the scene by the sound of shooting and also loosed off a few shots at the convoy from the same side of the road as Long's party.¹⁰¹ Both these firing parties were thus above and behind Collins, to his right and that of his men. For most of the fight he had remained behind the car firing in the direction of Kelliher and company, above him and to his left. But then some of the Hales-Kelliher party began to retreat. Collins saw them and called out, 'Come on boys! There they are, running up the road.'

He is then said to have left the shelter of the car and moved back in the direction of Bandon for some fifty yards to gain a better view of the men moving up the hill on his left. All this time he was out in an open roadway, with no cover, while in front and behind him some of the toughest and most experienced flying column men in the country were firing at him and his party. Accounts differ as to what happened. Some say he went down into a prone firing position, others that he remained firing standing up. Years later, Florrie O'Donoghue said that Dalton had told him, 'Mick wouldn't keep his head down. If he'd ever been in a scrap he'd have learned to stay down. For I was flat down and Mick was killed standing up.'[102] The unpublished account given by the Mayo man, who claims he and his five colleagues accompanied the convoy, also says that Collins was shot standing up, though in the back of the head, and not more than fifteen yards from the vehicles. The shooting had begun to slacken off when, Dalton says, he fancied he heard a cry of 'Emmet' and he and Sean O'Connell rushed from their shelter behind the armoured car to find Collins lying on the roadway, 'a fearful gaping wound at the base of the skull and behind the right ear'. O'Connell said an Act of Contrition and thought that he was answered by a slight pressure of the hand.

On the hillside above him Sonny O'Neill, an ex-British Army marksman, made off into the gathering dusk. He had lingered for a last, long shot and instinctively felt he might have hit the tall officer, whoever he was, but now it was a time to retreat, not to hang around checking. The whole encounter had taken not much longer than an hour, in fact some reports say only twenty minutes. What is certain is that for those on the roadside below a time of nightmare had begun.

Light and life were fading rapidly as O'Connell, under covering fire from Dalton, dragged Collins to shelter under the armoured car. Lieutenant Smith helped him to bandage the hideous wound and carry the body to the tourer, even though he had been shot through the neck and could not ride his motor-cycle which had to be abandoned.[103] Dalton cradled the body in his arms in the back seat as the convoy drove back to Cork, a distance of nineteen miles. They did not arrive there until 1.30 am. Dalton subsequently explained this by reference to the condition of the roads and bridges.[104] If the party, earlier in the day, with morale high and the services of a guide, had had to ask for directions, it is reasonable to assume that they could have been confused in darkness, on a return journey which had suffered such a cataclysm. Nevertheless the drivers had already been over the route and people in reasonable control of their faculties would have been expected to have made better progress. Certainly if word had been sent back to Bandon a few miles away, along a road which the convoy had just traversed, Sean Hales would have provided guidance. This failure to seek help from the nearest point available is one of the strangest features of that whole awful night.

The convoy is said to have left Long's at 9.30, having procured water for one of the vehicles and a cloth to wipe the blood from Collins' face. At Long's members of the party revealed who the dead man was. There were some local Irregulars in the pub, not members of the ambush party, and word was sent up the hill to Murray's where the IRA meeting had resumed.

'We had barely started,' says Deasy,

when Sean Galvin of Crookstown rushed in and excitedly told us that Michael Collins had been shot dead in the ambush and the convoy had taken his body to Cork via Crookstown, Cloughduv and Killeeny. [This would suggest that the convoy had had to again ask for directions in the pub and thus the return route became known.] The meeting was adjourned immediately and many of us left Murray's with heavy hearts. To those of us who had known Collins personally, and there were many, his death was tragic: to Tom Hales, Tadhg O'Sullivan and myself who had known him intimately, our sorrow was deep and lasting. We parted without discussion of any kind . . . each of us all too conscious of the tragedy and the loneliness that only time could heal.

The convoy stopped again at Bellmont Mills, near Crookstown, looking for the road to Cork and asking for a priest. They were told where Canon Tracey lived, outside the village, but as this would have meant a detour, and as apparently none of them knew anything about a meeting between Collins and the Canon, it was decided to drive on to Cloughduv where the curate's house was pointed out by a civilian who escorted a soldier to the door. The convoy got to Cloughduv at around eleven o'clock, an hour and a half after leaving Long's. In considering this time span it might be worth noting that at the time of writing, admittedly in daytime, under no strain and over far better roads, the same journey took me less than ten minutes. The area is so small that Canon Tracey, who was also parish priest of the Bael na mBlath district, subsequently wrote: 'It was my misfortune to be listening to the dreadful firing when Michael Collins was done to death.'[105]

Dalton's description of what happened next is as follows:

On the way back we came upon a church – with a stretch of gravel and railings in front – along the road. One of my men went in asking for a priest. A priest came out as far as the railings, looked in at the dead Collins lying on my shoulder in the back seat of the car then turned on his heel and walked back in. One of my officers raised his rifle to shoot the priest and only that I struck up the barrel the priest would have been shot. The bullet was actually discharged.

Dalton commented, 'the incident left a grim impression on the minds of the entire party.'[106] He lodged a complaint with the priest's superiors the next day. However the priest, Fr Timothy Murphy, gave a very different account.[107] He says that he went with the soldier and the civilian to the car, not merely to the railings.

COUNTY CORK

0   20

miles

Fermoy

CORK

Coachford

Ballvourney

Macroom

Farrin

Crookstown

Beal na mBlath

Kilmichael

Newcestown

Innishannon

Bandon

Dunmanway

Lisavaird

Clonakilty

Woodfield

Skibbereen

Rosscarbery

Rabbit Island

Fastnet Rock

Killeeny

CORK

Coachford

Kilumney

Aherla

Cloughduv

Bellmont Mills

Crookstown

Beal na mBlath

0   2

miles

It was a dark night and the soldier carried in his hand an old carbide lamp which was giving a very bad light. I walked out to the roadway where the convoy had stopped. There was a soldier lying flat with his head resting on the lap of a young officer. The young officer was sobbing and crying and did not speak. There was blood on the side of the dead man's face. I said an Act of Contrition and other prayers and made the Sign of the Cross. I told an officer to wait until I got the Holy Oils. I went to the house but when I returned the convoy had gone . . . the civilian heard an Army officer say 'that priest is not coming back' and he ordered the lorries to drive away. Some of the soldiers were hysterical.

As readers will no doubt have observed the priest does not mention any rifle shot.

Bael na mBlath, Crookstown, Cloughduv, Aherla, Killeeny, nondescript little no-places, beads on a sorrowful decade of the rosary. The traumatised convoy passed through them all on their way back to Cork, but seems to have missed coming anywhere near the ambush said to have been laid at Farran, which would probably have been lifted with the onset of darkness anyhow. At a spot on the road near the townland of Kilumney the Macroom railway bridge was blown and again there are conflicting reports as to whether a warning from a man on the road, good driving or good luck saved one or all of the vehicles from a forty-foot drop. The convoy detoured and at Kilumney, near Kilumney House, turned into a cul-de-sac and entered a farmyard by mistake. It then took to the fields across country to rejoin a road. There followed a terrible interlude of shouting and skidding and pushing as the soldiers attempted to get the vehicles across the fields, sometimes using greatcoats and petrol tins to give the wheels a purchase. Eventually the touring car was abandoned and Collins' corpse was carried to the roadway, grey matter, from what a few hours earlier had been a brilliant brain, seeping onto the shoulders of its bearers. The party finally reached Cork at 1.30 am.

Here again there are different accounts of what happened next. Almost fifty years later it was put to Dalton by an interviewer that he 'left the corpse on the Western Road with orders that it was to be taken to a hospital belonging to the British Army'.[108] Dalton's reply was: 'So far as I can remember the entire party went to the Imperial Hotel [GHQ] and that Dr Leo Aherne took the body to the Bon Secours Hospital.' In fact the body was taken to Shanakiel Hospital. About this the record is clear. The convoy appears to have encountered two members of the Cork Civic Patrol at the corner of Washington St and Grand Parade who led them there. There was a wireless link between the Imperial Hotel and Valentia Island Cable Station. According to Dalton, news of Collins' death was transmitted by the link to the Island. In order to reach Dublin it had to be transmitted first to New York and then back across the Atlantic to London and across the Irish

Sea to Dublin. But the operator to whom he gave the telegram, Matt Quigley, was later reported[109] as saying that the message, to Mulcahy, was sent direct to Dublin, uncoded, though normally military messages were sent in code because of the presence of British warships in Cork Harbour. Possibly contacts in Dublin gave the tip-off, but both the London *Daily Express* and the *Freeman's Journal* reported the death next morning before the *Cork Examiner* had printed a word about the tragedy. The *Daily Express*, whose correspondent was particularly close to British official sources, seems to have been warned to hold its front page for the news.[110] And, during the morning, Dalton was incensed to receive a cablegram from Hearst newspapers offering £1,000 for the story.

However it was sent, Dalton's cable found its mark. Charlie Dalton, Emmet's brother, recalled his bedroom door at Portobello opening after the coded message arrived, and 'in walked the Adjutant General, Gearoid O'Sullivan. He did not greet me as customarily, but stood rather bewildered-looking for a second or two and then broke down weeping and spoke in a rather uncertain voice saying "Charlie, The Big Fella is dead." '[111] The first two they broke the news to were Joe O'Reilly and Tom Cullen. Cullen lit a candle as they entered his room and in its light looked at their faces and burst out, 'Something terrible has happened – I know what you have come to tell me – The Big Fella is dead! I've been dreaming about him.' They then went to break the news to Batt O'Connor: even sixty years later the memory of the consternation and grief caused in her home by the news made Sister Margaret Mary fall silent as she spoke to me about the telling. Messengers were sent about the city and all through the night shocked men were ushered through the sandbags and barbed wire guarding Government buildings. The shock was so palpable that Cullen and O'Reilly burst into tears when they saw the grey, taut faces. With finger raised, Cosgrave stepped forward. 'This is a nice way for soldiers to behave. . .'[112] Mulcahy slipped away to write a message to the Army directing how he thought soldiers *should* behave:

Stand calmly by your posts. Bend bravely and undaunted to your work. Let no cruel act of reprisal blemish your bright honour. Every dark hour that Michael Collins met since 1916 seemed but to steel that bright strength of his and temper his gay bravery. You are left each inheritors of that strength.

13

Honouring the Dead?

'We are losing many splendid men – many fine noble
friends. I hope someone will be left to pay due tribute to
their deeds and their memories – but only one tribute can
repay them – the freedom of this land and in God's good
time that will rest with us.'

Michael Collins

Rumours about Collins' death spread as the mourners went home to
the four corners of Ireland. His stature, the fact that he was the only
one killed in the ambush, all helped to fuel the gossip. Then, a few
months after his death, the rumours received a tremendous fillip. On
2nd December John McPeake, the machine-gunner, deserted to the
Republican side taking the Slievenamon, the armoured car, with him.
McPeake himself said the reason he left the Army was that he was
disgusted at the shooting of two prisoners by his Army comrades.[1]
Locally it is said that he was a great ladies' man who told a woman
friend that he was getting a bad time from his comrades over the
jammed gun and would have liked to get out. The girl, a Republican,
relayed this to the IRA who struck a bargain with him, promising to
look after him and get him back to Scotland, provided he would desert
with the armoured car. He was arrested in Glasgow the following
July, returned to Ireland and given six years for the theft, much of it
spent in solitary confinement. In Portlaoise Jail he joined some
Republican prisoners on hunger strike and for this and other breaches
of prison regulations had a bad time in jail. Those were harsh times
and it can be taken for granted that, had he had anything to do with
Collins' death, he would hardly have survived his arrest, never mind
his imprisonment.

On McPeake's release on 4 August 1928 a group of Dublin
Republicans took up a collection for him. It netted £60. Someone in
high places seems to have decided that he deserved more than this,
however, because after de Valera came to power, I am reliably
informed that McPeake received a Secret Service pension.[2]

The unfortunate Emmet Dalton was the target for the most
sustained allegations. He was held responsible for not ensuring a
better escort for Collins, not taking a safer route, not insisting that the
convoy 'drive like hell', accidentally shooting Collins through drink

or panic and, ugliest of all, deliberately killing him for British 'blood money'.[3] It is said that Sean Hales was shot by the British Secret Service because he was pressurising the Provisional Government into holding an inquiry 'as he did not accept Dalton's version'.[4] Sean Hales was in fact shot by the IRA and in reprisal for his death Rory O'Connor, Liam Mellowes, Joseph McKelvey and Dick Barrett were roused from their sleep in Mountjoy where they had been lodged since the fall of the Four Courts and told they would be shot at daybreak. The executions were carried out on the morning of 8 December 1922.

The facts of Hales' death are set out in a secret IRA communiqué initialled by Liam Lynch to the OC of the 1st Southern Division: 'Padraig O'Maille, Deputy Speaker, F.S. Parliament wounded, Sean Hales, F.S. T.D. and an officer of F.S. Army shot dead – unintentionally while in company with P. O'Maille. It was intended only to wound Hales, but he was mistaken for O'Maille.'[5] So far as Dalton was concerned, the disorganised and insufficient escort was a product purely of the times and, as I have indicated, of Collins' desire to go through his own county at will with a bodyguard of his own choosing. As to 'blood money', Dalton, a man of outstanding character and ability, would have shot himself sooner than have injured Collins. He found it difficult after the ambush to adjust to life, leaving both the Army through scruples about the harsh governmental measures taken against the Irregulars, and, subsequently, a comfortable post given to him by Cosgrave as Clerk of the Seanad, because of alcohol. Far from living comfortably on £10,000 blood money as alleged (the allegation is constant, only the sum changes), Dalton became so short of money that I have been told[6] that he offered Collins' Field Diary, which he had on him when he was shot, to the Government. Cosgrave is said to have phoned Johnny Collins to get him to buy it from him 'because otherwise he'll hold us up to ransom'. The diary certainly returned to the Collins family via Government sources years after Collins was killed. It is also true that Dalton was reduced to selling encyclopaedias – the set my father bought is still a treasured family possession – before pulling himself together and making a successful career in the film industry. At the outbreak of the Second World War he was approached by a racing friend, Lord FitzWilliam, to ask him to join an elite, SAS-type unit being set up by Lord Louis Mountbatten. The idea was to include men from Ireland, England, Scotland and Wales. But Dalton turned down the offer and spent the war working in the film industry, augmenting his income by travelling around to race meetings as a full-time professional punter, which, say the dedicated conspiracy theorists, was an ideal cover for intelligence work.

One of the most enduring theories is that Collins died from a Mauser pistol bullet, the implication being that the bullet came from

Dalton's gun. Commandant Frank Friel, the officer who brought Collins' body to Shanakiel Hospital, felt that a .303 rifle bullet could not have made the huge wound in the skull. I know that even some of the ambush party felt that Denis (Sonny) O'Neill must have inadvertently used a round of dum-dum. Another theory is that one of the rifles which was supposed to have been sent northwards in the undercover swap which Collins had arranged in order to arm the Northern IRA without implicating himself, was a particularly fine elephant gun. O'Neill is said to have been so taken with the weapon that he substituted another rifle for it and kept the elephant gun for himself. Thus, in a very real sense, Collins is said to have died as a result of his own Northern policy. However the Colm Connolly documentary which reconstructed the death with the aid of, amongst other experts, the Irish State Pathologist, Dr Harbinson, demonstrated that a high velocity rifle bullet, making an inconspicuous entry wound at or above the hairline could leave a gaping aperture on exiting. The bullet apparently drives not only particles of bone, but also an air pocket before it.

Obviously, had an inquest been held, such speculations might have been ended nearly seventy years ago. The fact that one was not held might be explained by a Provisional Government decision of 29 June 1922 which stated that 'Inquests should be held on all dead civilians and also on all military killed whose deaths did not occur in definite military action.'[7] Collins' death could be considered 'definite military action'. But it became known after de Valera assumed office in 1932 that the outgoing Government had issued a directive that documents relating to three classes of incident were to be destroyed, those dealing with courts martial, executions and – the death of Collins. Even though by then, in 1924, he had led what amounted to a mutiny against the Government, Liam Tobin, because of his unique Intelligence experience, was brought back from civilian life to supervise this operation and much documentation was destroyed. De Valera took a photostat of the directive (which was signed by Desmond Fitzgerald) into retirement with him, and Dr T. P. O'Neill[8] has a definite recollection of studying it during his biographical research. But there is nothing intrinsically sinister in the Collins cover-up. All three topics would have been fertile fields of propaganda in the climate of the time, and in addition, if any matters relating to a 'spree' preceding Collins' death were unearthed they would have been embarrassing for all concerned, including the Collins family.

What happened to Gogarty's post-mortem report is anybody's guess. It was said to have been placed in a safe at the Royal College of Surgeons in Dublin but, despite a diligent search, the librarian, Professor J. B. Lyons, who is also a biographer of Oliver St John Gogarty's, could find no trace of it.

And so we come to the story of the real cover-up. I am of course aware that the continuing suspicion is, and always will be, that Collins in some way fell victim to the British Secret Service. I know[9] that an account has been set down by a survivor of that day alleging that Collins was murdered and that the fatal shot was not fired by Sonny O'Neill. This account, I am informed at the time of writing, will become available on the survivor's death. Yet pending any such disclosure – and I have not been shown what proof the survivor intends to advance in support of his contention – at this stage the facts I have been able to collect and study force me to the conclusion that the cover-up was a far more benign affair than has hitherto been adverted and in fact reflects credit, not guilt, on those concerned. Initially both Free Staters and Republicans had every reason for damping down controversy. There was no glory in it for either side and much inducement to keep silent. The Government was in a weak and vulnerable position and had lost its greatest figure in circumstances which said little for its military prowess or its credibility generally. An army that could not protect Michael Collins could hardly be trusted to protect a country. The Republicans feared reprisals, and with good reason. Dalton has described how – at gun-point – he had to order some of his soldiers from the gates of Cork Jail where they were trying to get at the Republican prisoners. Joe McGrath told me that he intervened personally to prevent de Valera being shot as a reprisal and Vinnie Byrne, to give but one example, told me that for 'four or five days I'd have shot any bloody Die-hard [Irregular] I came across.' For a long time the Republican areas around the ambush site lived in dread of a Black-and-Tan-type reprisal raid by Free State troops.

But there was also, over and above all this, a 'decency factor' which accounted for a great deal of the mystery. Johnny Collins and Nancy were well aware of the details of how Michael died from within a year of the death. The ambush had been the work of men who were neighbours and friends before the civil war and they continued to be friends and neighbours after it. Tom Hales who 'cried his eyes out over the killing',[10] took the initiative in making his peace with Johnny and Nancy and then, through him, other members of the party did likewise. One of them, Jim Hurley, broke down and cried in their home when he first visited them in Dublin in 1923. 'How could we do it?', he sobbed. 'We were too young – I was only nineteen.'[11] The family was then living in Donnybrook. Many years later, when they had moved to Booterstown, and were rearing the children of the marriage, one of the children, a boy, Michael, was puzzled by the sight of a man walking up and down outside the house for a long time, glancing in and then turning away. At one stage Michael went out to him and the man asked him if that was the house Johnny Collins lived in. Michael said yes and invited him in. 'I'll go in all right, but in my

own time', was the answer. Johnny then came to the door, saw who it
was and exclaimed: 'Will you come in out of that.' It was Jim Hurley
paying his second visit to the family. He received a warm welcome
and he and Johnny became the closest of friends. But Johnny, like his
brother, respected confidences, and it was many years before Michael
was told the significance of Jim's visit.

Hales knew Sonny O'Neill had probably fired the fatal shot. He
told Johnny what had happened, in confidence. O'Neill, a deeply
religious man, had been fundamentally disturbed and upset by the
killing and had confided in his Commanding Officer that he had
calculated that it was probably his last shot that had killed Collins. But
he lived in the area and for neighbourly reasons, as much as reasons of
security, secrecy remained the order of the day, until one day, long
after the civil war was but an evil memory, Sonny O'Neill was
diagnosed as having a terminal heart condition. He enquired of Hales
what Johnny's attitude to the shooting was and Hales assured him it
was one of 'total forgiveness'. O'Neill may have been planning to visit
Johnny before his illness ran its course but he collapsed and died at a
railway station returning from a pilgrimage to Knock on 5 June
1950,[12] without ever having discussed 22 August 1922 with him, or
anyone else for that matter. When the Colm Connolly documentary,
'The Shadow of Bael na mBlath', was screened his family was
devastated. One result was that they sent me a transcript of an
interview with Tom Foley, a survivor of the ambush, conducted by Fr
Aidan O'Driscoll, on 2 September 1989. Foley discounted O'Neill's
involvement. I believe the facts of Collins' death are as I have given
them but, to make the record as fair and as complete as possible, here is
a relevant extract from the transcript:

Fr O'Driscoll: . . . this statement that Sonny O'Neill fired the fatal shot . . .
    You were there as a seventeen-year-old . . . what were you doing exactly
    on the day? What was your job?
Foley: I went for the mines and I went down for the cigarettes. And any
    fellow wanted anything, I'd get it for him.
Fr O'Driscoll: As to the claim that Sonny O'Neill shot Michael Collins, what
    do you think of that?
Foley: . . . It was raining in the evening . . . Before the ambush started it got
    wet and that's why the lads were going away. [Sonny O'Neill] . . . had left
    the ambush position an hour before it.
Fr O'Driscoll: Is it possible to know who fired that shot.
Foley: Not possible! Not possible . . . you weren't going to keep your head
    up while they shot, were you? And McPeake cleaning the briars off the top
    of the ditch with the machine-gun. Not a very safe place to put your head
    up at all, to see or otherwise. They were firing them shots now without
    ever seeing where they were going to, you can be sure of that. Oh life is
    sweet, but an ambush like that is still sweeter.

Fifteen years after Sonny O'Neill's death Johnny Collins also died, on 30 January 1965, just when Jim Hurley, who in his lifetime had become one of Cork's legends of hurling, was diagnosed as having cancer. He went to Mount Mellary on a two-day retreat and, on his return, finding that his case was worse than had been feared, and that he had only days to live, sent for Michael Collins, who as a boy had once told him where Johnny Collins lived. Hurley wanted Michael to go to the parish priest to get him to intercede with the man who owned the plot beside the one Johnny Collins was buried in to sell it to him. 'Tell him I want to be buried beside Shafter.'[13] Hurley got his wish and today lies in Clonakilty churchyard alongside Michael Collins' brother. No shadow from Bael na mBlath falls over those graves. It appears that 'The great Irish whodunnit' mystery was largely fuelled by a decent West Cork reticence.

And by an IRB reticence. It was not to be supposed that the Brotherhood would make no effort to find out how its President died. Despite civil war and subsequent Army divisions and dissolutions the inquiry was pursued. Finally in 1966, the fiftieth anniversary of the 1916 Rising, Collins' old friend, Sean McGarry, who was also a President of the IRB, persuaded the doctor who had examined Collins' body in Shanakiel Hospital to record his account of the examination. Dr Cagney (whose willingness to talk after a lifetime's silence may have been prompted by the fact that he had just retired) bore out Dr Harbinson's description of the effects of a high velocity rifle bullet. Dr Cagney, who had served through the Great War and had 'a wide knowledge of bullet wounds' told McGarry that Collins was killed by a .303 rifle bullet. The bullet entered behind the left ear, making a small entrance wound, and exited above the left ear making 'a ragged wound' on the left side of his head. Collins' long hair hid the entrance wound. It was his fate to die, almost accidentally, in his home county, at the hands of men who admired him, in one of the most avoidable, badly organised ambushes of the period. Any one of his assailants could have fired the fatal shot. None of them would have been proud to do so.

What would have happened if Collins had lived? This again is a question asked incessantly in Ireland and though I have already dealt exhaustively with questions of speculation, and hesitate to weary the reader any further with issues which, by definition, must be totally matters of opinion, some evaluation is called for. Obviously he had a greater grasp of economics than his contemporaries and would have brought more drive, efficiency and imagination to bear upon the task of building up the country after the civil war than did anyone in any government or party that came after him. My opinion, and it has to be purely based on speculation, is that Ireland would have benefited enormously had he lived. Unlike de Valera whose talent lay in getting and holding power, Collins asked himself the question, 'All this for what?', and tried to provide the answers. However practical or impractical his recorded ideas may have been they were the thoughts of a still-young man, capable of great development; a man who, in the eye of the storm, was able to take time to try to plot a course for his people and his country. Certainly he would not have been solely dependent on Department of Finance civil servants for his economic policies as was every leader of the country who came after him except Sean Lemass. And Lemass once told[15] Collins' nephew, Michael Collins, that his economic philosophy was derived from a study of *The Path to Freedom*, a compendium of Collins' thoughts on cultural and economic matters, published as a pamplet.[16]

His philosophy was an extraordinary mixture of Gaelic revivalism, *perestroika*, the Sinn Fein 'we ourselves' approach and an idiosyncratic common sense. Collins took his starting point from the differences between British and Irish culture. 'The Romans did not come to Ireland . . . Gaelic civilisation was quite different. Their unity was not of any military solidarity. It came from sharing the same traditions . . . They never exalted a central authority . . . The land belonged to the people . . . held for the people by the Chief of the Clan.' He wanted to restore a 'democratic social polity, with the exaltation of the things of the mind and character . . . the essence of ancient Irish civilisation . . . must provide the keynote of the new.' Some would dismiss this sort of thing as mere Gaelic revivalism but Collins gave examples of what he meant:

English civilisation . . . for us . . . is a misfit. . . . the Irish . . . qualities are hidden, besmirched, by that what has been imposed upon us, just as the fine, splendid surface of Ireland is besmirched by our towns and villages – hideous medleys of contemptible dwellings and mean shops and squalid public houses. We are now free in name. The extent to which we become free in fact and secure our freedom will be the extent to which we become Gaels again . . . The biggest task will be the restoration of the language.

Collins made it clear that he did not see the language being restored for generations and then as matter of political and economic necessity as much as out of cultural desirability, to enable people to act in an innovative Irish way: 'Economically we must be democratic, as in the past . . . The people must become again the "guardians of their law and of their land".' The peculiarly Irish form of democratisation would ensure capital was not 'allowed to be an evil'. A co-operative system would mean 'our countrysides would cease to be the torpid deserts they are now, giving the means of existence and nothing more'. Agriculture was to be 'improved and developed'. Transportation, water power, harbours too. Foreign trade was to be stimulated by 'making facilities for the transport and marketing of Irish goods abroad and foreign goods in Ireland'. Investors must be encouraged to invest Irish capital in Irish concerns. 'Taxation, where it hinders must be adjusted.' He advocated land reform, breaking up the big estates, 'the ranches' and studying Denmark's, Holland's, and Germany's farming methods so as to promote agri-business, specifically, meat processing, cheese-making and dairying and a range of downstream activities, including agricultural machinery. He recommended that factories should 'as far as possible' be dispersed about the country instead of being concentrated in a few areas, both to avoid congestion, improve the earning power of the rural population and 'enlarge their horizon'.

No potential area of development was left unconsidered, be it forestry, minerals, marketing, or the expansion of Dublin port. He drew attention to the vast amount of money (£194 million in banks and £14 million post office deposits) 'lying idle in banks', the huge capital outflows and forecast 'with scope for our energies, with restoration of confidence, the inevitable tendency will be towards a return of this capital to Ireland.' He had detailed plans for developing industry, using hydro-electric power – 'the white coal of Ireland'.[17] He wanted to avoid both State socialism which he saw as merely another form of monopoly, and industrial development along 'the old commercial capitalistic lines of the huge joint stock companies':

We all realise that the industrial status quo is imperfect . . . one of the most pressing needs – if not the most pressing – is the question of labour in relation to industry, and it is consequently vitally necessary for the development of our resources that the position of employers and employees should rest on the best possible foundation.

He proposed that: 'we must not have state Departments headed by a politician whose only qualification is that he has climbed to a certain rung in the political ladder.' Government should be democratic and 'carry out for them all, and only, what is needed to be done for the people as a whole. It must not interfere with what the people can do for themselves in their own centres.'

'Our external life,' he said:

has become the expression of all we have been deprived of – something shapeless, ugly, without native life . . . Irish art and Irish customs must be revived, and must be carried out by the people themselves, helped by a central Government, not controlled and managed by it; helped by departments of music, art, national painting etc. Everybody being able to contribute we would have a skilled audience criticising and appreciating, and not only, as in England, paying for seats to hear famous performers.

His development plans were all set in a united Ireland context. The rivers Erne and Bann lie in the Six Counties but in 1922 Collins was writing about methods which would 'utilise the water-power of the

Shannon, the Erne, the Bann and the Liffey. It is probable that the Liffey and the Bann, being closely connected with urban centres can be dealt with at once.' His abiding belief was that 'a prosperous Ireland will mean a united Ireland. With equitable taxation and flourishing trade our North-East countrymen will need no persuasion to come in and share the healthy economic life of the country.'

It is easy to scoff at these ideas, or to point out the difficulties of implementing such schemes when actually running a normal peacetime Government. But Collins was a unique combination of the visionary and the practical. Throughout the difficulties of the Black and Tan war he had tried, through the underground Dail, to further constructive projects such as fishery development. But (on 11 March 1921) he recommended that all work on fisheries should cease because 'it was too big a problem in present circumstances'. The fishing schemes had all been 'disastrous to the reputation of the Dail'. Their failure, he said, 'all arose from the dishonesty on the part of the fishermen'. The man who propelled his country into the Black and Tan war, so that she might win her freedom to carry out such plans, and who also, while on the run, showed the practical ability to float a successful national loan, would have tackled fishery and allied problems with renewed force and insight when circumstances permitted. As the remarkable, lengthy memorandum on propaganda, mentioned earlier, which he wrote to Desmond Fitzgerald[18] on 12 July 1922 (the same day that the War Council was announced), demonstrates, he had detailed, well-thought-out proposals for a campaign of films, posters and press publicity to win the people to these ideas.

Collins had political skills and powers of oratory of which the least that can be said is that he was better equipped than most men to make his dreams come true. Birkenhead was so impressed by a speech Collins gave in Cork (to the accompaniment of volleys fired over the heads of his hearers by a party of Irregulars who were trying to stampede them) that he paid him a remarkable compliment in the House of Lords (on 16 March 1922) when he told his peers that anyone who read

that speech delivered by a man without political education and, so far as I know, without very much other education will consider that it is a speech which, whether you examine the form of its literary expression, or its judgement of affairs, no member of this House need be ashamed of having delivered.

But the effect of the civil war has to be reckoned with in assessing the climate Collins would have had to work in. Estimates of the death toll vary[19] from around 1,000 to as many as 4,000 lives. The financial cost[20] was around £47 million, an appalling sum for those days. The cost in idealism, energy, and enthusiasm was probably higher.

Bitterness, cynicism, disillusionment, emigration, censorship, clericalism and stagnation became the hallmarks of Irish society until Lemass got control and age began to prise the civil war generation's fingers from the levers of power in the Sixties. And even then the spurt of prosperity was but short-lived. At the time of writing unemployment figures are nearly 100,000 higher than they were when the Labour Party made its appeal for alleviation in the days after the Treaty was first ratified.[21] For as the poets and the warriors fell by the wayside the bureaucrats took over.

The saga of poor Joe O'Reilly efforts to buy the meagre furnishings of his late Commander-in-Chief's bedroom at Portobello, is instructive. After much internal memo-writing Joe gave up in disgust. Then Collins' sister, Mrs Margaret O'Driscoll, learned of the story and made an offer. It was decided to give the furnishings to her at a reasonable figure, but someone in authority intervened. The articles had been offered to Colonel O'Reilly for a higher sum. He would have cause for complaint if they went to someone else for less. O'Reilly of course would have given them to any member of Collins' family for nothing, but more memo-writing followed before a formula was arrived at whereby Mrs O'Driscoll got the old bed, the battered wardrobe, and the washhand-basin stand at the price they were offered to Joe but 50 per cent more than she would have had to pay if the deal had not been interfered with. In all, the transaction generated a total of twenty-four letters, costing far more in civil servants' time than the furniture was worth. Just as Joe O'Reilly's face at the Collins funeral was a paradigm of Ireland's grief so does his attempt to buy some mementoes of his fallen Chief illustrate how the State that emerged from the civil war frustrated Ireland's imagination.

Collins himself might have been similarly frustrated, despite his mighty powers. The sheer strength of the forces massed against him in the North make it very hard to see how his efforts to achieve unity by force could have succeeded. He might have succeeded in destabilising the Northern statelet in the same way as the Provisional IRA have done, possibly to a greater extent, as the Catholics of all classes were more united in opposing partition then than now. But to have proceeded thus would inevitably have turned his Cabinet colleagues against him and left him dependent for support on the Army, and the more militant Republicans. This could have had harmful consequences for the development of that native Irish democracy which, despite all the problems Ireland has faced and is facing, is probably Michael Collins' most enduring testament. The evidence, however, appears to be inescapable that, the civil war won, his reaction during times of pogrom or rioting directed against Catholics would have been to turn to his Joe Dolans and Liam Tobins to deal with figures like Dawson-Bates or DI Nixon as he had with Wilson and nearly with the two hangmen. It does appear that had he lived he would certainly have made greater efforts to bring about unity than anyone who came after him. He would not have allowed an apartheid state to be erected in Northern Ireland without making serious, sustained, and perhaps violent protest. Writing about the IRB Sean O'Muirthle made what I feel is a highly significant comment: 'I think had Collins lived that he would have made further use of the Organisation towards achieving still further freedom.'[23] Collins would have had to resolve within himself the tensions of his dual role. Head of a democratic Government, head of a secret society which in fact regarded itself as a Government within a Government. Conspirator versus democrat. Destroyer versus builder. He might not have been able to resolve these conflicts and might have disintegrated in drink or disillusionment. On the other hand a period of rest and peace would have given him an opportunity to do many things himself, and to prevent others doing much that was harmful. Certainly it is reasonable to speculate on the basis of what is known of his character that he would have opposed executions such as those of Childers, Rory O'Connor and the others. It would be wrong to think he would not have prosecuted the war ruthlessly and vigorously. But merely by being there his personality and leadership would have provided a better rallying point for the forces in the country opposed to war's continuation than were his successors. Ironically it was his death and the leadership vacuum it created on the Provisional Government's side that helped to create the situation in which the Government felt it necessary to introduce a policy of reprisal executions, selecting firing squad victims from the ranks of men already in prison, either to make a point by shooting leaders, as in O'Connor's case, or to bring terror to a locality where some Irregular killings had occurred. Those who came after him had resolution but neither his charisma nor the military prowess whereby peace might have been had by other means.

With Collins gone the major political personality left in the Free State was on the other side, de Valera. His reaction to the news of Collins' death was reminiscent of his nervous attack during 1916. The leader of the eight-man escort party[24] which accompanied him across country from Fethard in County Tipperary to Callan, County Kilkenny, from whence he was smuggled to Dublin, has described how he behaved the day after Bael na mBlath. De Valera indicated that he wanted to travel alone and the party leader respected his wishes, keeping within earshot but not talking to him, while the other seven scouted well ahead:

Quite a lot of the 15 or so miles to Callan were done on foot across country and during that time de Valera seemed very distressed and he appeared to be talking or muttering to himself. Several times when he spoke out loud, not addressing me or anybody in the escort, I distinctly heard him say, 'I told them not to do it, even pleaded with them, but they wouldn't listen to me and now what will become of us all.' Dev was so distressed that when he spoke out I felt he was crying.

De Valera knew of course that news of his presence in Bael na mBlath might well seal his death warrant. In fact a local priest, Canon Cohalan of Bandon, preached a famous sermon in which he thundered: 'The day Michael Collins was killed where was de Valera? Ask the people of Bael na mBlath and they will tell you. There was a scowling face at a window looking out over that lonely valley and de Valera could tell who it was.' But he speedily recovered his composure. He had spent the night before the ambush with a family called O'Sullivan who got a letter from him a few days later asking for his binoculars to be sent on to him. Both letter and binoculars were retained.[25] But de Valera had better fortune in efforts to regain power. His pacific arguments of August had not found acceptance. A line more likely to secure extremist support was again espoused with such success that by January 1923 he had regained influence once more with the Republican military leadership to a point where he was in a position to draft a statement for Liam Lynch rejecting peace proposals. Liam Deasy, who had become increasingly disenchanted with the war, after capture had issued a statement to his fellow officers deploring the conflict which he thought had reached the stage where it might lead to British being welcomed back with more enthusiasm than was shown for their departure.[26] De Valera promptly drew up a statement rejecting Deasy's initiative with a covering letter in which he argued that peace without political advantage to his side would be 'awful'.[27] Lynch issued the statement verbatim and the civil war continued uselessly for four more months.

It ended in May 1923 leaving de Valera the undisputed leader on the Republican side. Persuaded by Sean Lemass that he should form a Constitutional Party, he did so and cut loose from his IRA following and the support of figures like Stack and Mary MacSwiney to form Fianna Fail in 1926. He then led his party into the Dail and took the Oath. Asked once[28] how he could square taking the Oath with his civil war position, he replied, 'I didn't really take an Oath. My fingers didn't touch the Bible'.

Worsening economic conditions, Kevin O'Higgins' murder in 1927 and the accidental death of Patrick Hogan, the Government's able Minister of Agriculture, combined with the hostility generated by the Government's repressive policy and the post-1929 global economic crash, all helped de Valera to oust Cosgrave at the general election of 1932, a contingency Cosgrave foresaw when he introduced legislation in 1927, after O'Higgins' murder, forcing elected representatives either to take the Oath or forfeit their seats.

Once in power, taking advantage of Britain's preoccupation with the Abdication crisis, de Valera introduced a more sectarian, but republican-sounding, Constitution which abolished the Oath and the Governor General, and stands to this day. He faced the issue of the Second Authority as ruthlessly as did his predecessors, using both internment and the death penalty to deal with the IRA. Under de Valera, Ireland continued to evolve as a sovereign, democratic state, very much as Collins had argued that it would, albeit far more inefficiently run and depending on emigration to supply de Valera's lack of an economic philosophy which Collins did have the ability to provide. The real scandal of the Treaty, partition, remained unaffected by his posturings and *volte face*. The Border was not altered by one millimetre throughout de Valera's long reign.

If one overlooks de Valera's behaviour over the Treaty and the civil war his sheer durability has to be acknowledged. His courage in controlling a nervous temperament and in fighting the blindness that affected him increasingly from the start of the Second World War, his successful struggle to maintain Irish neutrality, all speak of a man who contained within himself elements of greatness. In one area however, his attitude to Michael Collins, he consistently showed the small-mindedness of a guilty conscience.

In 1935 Joe McGrath, by then a millionaire through the operation of the Irish Hospitals Sweepstakes, mooted the idea to Johnny Collins of putting a marble cross over Collins' grave.[29] A similar proposal[30] had been put forward by Tim Healy, then Governor General, in the wake of the civil war. He said he was 'acting on behalf of an American lady who wished to remain anonymous'. Mulcahy, seeing Lady Lavery's Chicago origins looming behind the suggestion, discreetly declined the offer 'on behalf of the military Council', saying that as the grave was still in use for military casualties no plans for a memorial could be entertained at that time. McGrath had bought a quarter of a ton of Carrera marble and he offered both to donate this and defray the costs of shipping it from Italy for the memorial cross. As Collins was buried in a military grave, Johnny wrote on 13 February 1935 for the necessary permission to Frank Aiken, who was acting as Minister for Defence at the time:

The brothers and sisters of the late General Michael Collins intend to have erected, as soon as the necessary arrangements are completed, a monument over his grave in Glasnevin cemetery.

   The plot in which the remains have been interred was purchased by the late Government for the State and being now I understand, vested in and maintained by the Department of Defence, I would like to know if you as the Minister responsible for the administration of that Department would have any objection to the proposal referred to above. Hoping for a reply at your earliest convenience.[31]

The reaction to this proposal may be gauged both from the tone of the reply from Aiken's secretary and its date, 3 June 1935, which indicates how the term 'earliest convenience' was interpreted:

With reference to your letter of the 13th February last and your subsequent conversation with the Minister relative to the erection of a monument on the grave of the late General Michael Collins in Glasnevin Cemetery, I am directed by the Minister for Defence to inform you that generally the erection of monuments other than those erected by the State is not permitted.

In view of the representations made on behalf of your family, however, the Minister will offer no objection to the erection of a monument if it is still your intention to do so.

However, more than three years later, we find Johnny still writing to Aiken for help in cutting through red tape. The Dublin Cemeteries Committee had objected to the fact that the base proposed for the monument would encroach three inches on the space on either side of the grave:

The Collins grave plot is 4 ft in width and 8 ft in depth and the 'Celtic Cross' intended to be erected thereon will be 11°6' in height and the sculptor has specified for a minimum base of 4°6' x 3°0' x 1°3' high. While the plot in its present layout is fully that width the committee will not allow the foundation of the monument to exceed 4° without Government authority.[32]

On 4 March 1939 Aiken's secretary was authorised to write to the Secretary of the Dublin Cemeteries Committee as follows: 'The Minister appreciates that a base 4°6' wide will encroach on the paths on each side of the grave to an extent of 3', but as it is improbable that the paths will ever be used as a burial ground, he has agreed to the proposal.'[33]

But the foregoing correspondence, indicative of delay and reluctance though it is, does not reveal anything like the full extent of de Valera's vindictiveness and pettiness in the memorial saga. Firstly the letters do not reveal the fact that at one stage the Collinses considered legal action as a method of forcing the Government to abandon the delaying tactics. Katie, then Mrs Sheridan, normally the most pacific of the girls, had become outraged at the treatment of her 'Tom Tulliver'. But Johnny Collins persuaded Katie and his other sisters to be patient while he continued the negotiations personally. In 1938 he saw de Valera twice in connection with the project. During the visit he merely listened to the proposition and said he would consider it. When he sent for Johnny the second time he agreed to the erection of the cross but with a number of stipulations. He would not agree to the use of marble, but to a limestone cross and surrounds not exceeding £300 in cost. There was to be no public subscription and no publicity. The inscription was to be totally in Irish in front. The inscription on the back had to include 'M. Collins erected by his brother and sisters'. The inscription in Irish had to be approved by him. He then went on, 'I am sorry to have to say no member of your family may be present except yourself. The Cross can be blessed by the chaplain to the cemetery and an altar boy will be necessary to carry Holy Water.'

Johnny asked, 'What about Nancy and my sisters', to which the reply was, 'Nobody but yourself can be present.'

When Nancy heard the story she at first refused to believe Johnny and then commented: 'It's not Miceal who's being belittled. He's letting himself down.' I too found the story hard to accept at first (though of course the last of the illustrations in this book speaks for itself), but through the courtesy of the cemetery staff at Glasnevin I eventually discovered a certificate of authorisation, describing the cross's dimensions and inscription. It is dated 31 July 1939 and signed by Eamon de Valera. With a final Machiavellian touch, to cover himself against a charge of pettiness at having the Prime Minister of the country interest himself in such a matter on the eve of a new world war, he describes himself as 'acting Minister for Finance'.

The wording which de Valera agreed to and which appears on the cross is (front): '*I ndil-cuimne ar Miceal O'Coileain a rugad an 12ad la de mi deiread Fogmair, 1890, agus d'eag an 22ad la de mi Lugnasa, 1922.*' (In English this inscription says: 'In loving memory of Michael Collins who was born on 12 October 1890, and who died on 22nd August 1922'.) Below it, another inscription in Irish says: '*Go dtugaid Dia suaimneas Siorraide da anam* (May God give him eternal happiness).' At the bottom it says: 'Erected by his brothers and sisters'. On the back of the cross the wording is: 'Michael Collins' and then, in Irish, '*A Dia Dein Trocaire Orainn*' ('God have mercy on us').

The irony is that Johnny would never have allowed anything controversial to appear on the gravestone anyhow. Whenever memorials were erected to Michael in other parts of the country he insisted that the only wording to appear should be the name, and the dates of birth and death, nothing about the circumstances of the latter. However de Valera's stipulations were met. When the limestone cross was erected in 1939[34] the only persons present apart from Johnny, the priest and the altar boy were the foreman gravedigger, who had learned of the blessing, and a passing gravedigger. He asked, 'Where are the press?' and when he heard that none were allowed, exclaimed, 'Poor Mick, I've tended his grave since '22,' and got a passing tourist to take the picture reproduced in this book. Johnny's son, Michael, who was thirteen at the time told me: 'It was the first time my father looked old. He was terribly hurt.' However there was little Johnny could do by the way of protest. The injury to his hand meant that he had had to give up the farm at Woodfield and take a job as a civil servant in the Department of Lands where he, with a new family to rear, was in no position to fight de Valera. Later, when he had retired

and returned to live with Nancy at Clonakilty, Oscar Traynor called
on him. Traynor, who succeeded Aiken as Minister for Defence at the
outbreak of the Second World War, was the Minister whom Johnny
had approached in the first place; he had to see to it that de Valera's
wishes were followed. Traynor, who had also retired at the time
of his visit to Johnny and Nancy, said the cross decision had been the
hardest of his life to implement. To give an idea of the scale of
attendance which might have been expected at the erection of a cross
over Collins' grave, it might be noted that there were tens of
thousands from all over the country at the unveiling of a memorial at
Sam's Cross in 1965. Masses were said in over seventy churches in
West Cork alone.

The pettiness over the cross was no isolated incident. Representatives of the Army were forbidden to attend the annual commemoration service for their first Commander-in-Chief at Bael na mBlath as
late as 1971. And in 1965 an official guide book, *Facts about Ireland*,
produced by the Department of Foreign Affairs, had to be reprinted
after controversy broke out over the exclusion of Collins' picture.
Frank Aiken, then Minister for Foreign Affairs, was blamed for this
but the omission occurred after consultation with de Valera.[35] There
was no publicity, however, over a more significant example of de
Valera's rancour which occurred a year later in 1966, the 50th
anniversary of the Rising.[36] As late as 1990, there was controversy as
to whether or not the President would attend the ceremony for
handing over Woodfield, the Collins family home, to the nation.
There was further controversy and uncertainty as to whether the
Army would be allowed to attend at Woodfield or at the annual
commemoration ceremony this year at Bael na mBlath. Hitherto,
although under the Coalition Government an Army presence had
been allowed, Fianna Fail had only permitted the Army one appearance at Bael na mBlath, on the fiftieth anniversary of Collins' death.

Joe McGrath had wanted to forge ahead with his memorial project,
only on a far grander scale, at Sam's Cross. But when he consulted
Johnny in 1964 Johnny made a characteristic reply. 'Joe, you've still
more money than sense. Why not start a trust fund that would educate
some bright boys.' In 1966 McGrath was told that he had only a few
months to live and he sent for Johnny's son, Michael, by now one of
Ireland's leading chartered accountants, to develop the idea. It was
decided that Sean T. O'Kelly whom de Valera had succeeded as
President should be approached to be a patron and then de Valera
himself. O'Kelly subscribed five pounds, which was a notable gesture
for him as he had a legendary tight-fistedness. But the patronage was
of short standing. O'Kelly pulled out saying, 'He'd be furious if he
knew I agreed', immediately on hearing de Valera's reaction to the
proposal. McGrath had gone to him, telling him the state of his health,

and asking him to co-operate in the Foundation project by becoming a patron, saying, 'My days are numbered and there's no differences in the grave.'

De Valera paused before replying to the suggestion. It had been his Karma to live a long and distinguished public life. Although he was then in his eighty-fifth year he was looking forward to a second seven-year term as President of Ireland. But he knew that before the bar of history his name and fame were inextricably linked and threatened by a handful of years' association with a man whose allotted span had been destined to be but a third of his own. He knew that the story of Eamon de Valera could not be told without that of Michael Collins. Already he had embarked on what he knew in his heart was a futile effort to influence the record for the benefit of posterity. His newspaper and political empires had published innumerable favourable articles, histories and recollections. And in the years ahead he planned to ensure that much more favourable comment and chronology would be collated and set down. He had fashioned a vigorous dialectic of de Valerism that would bulwark him against critical re-appraisal long into the future. But de Valera was a realist, a man whose doodlings on the back of documents took the form of mathematical symbols. He realised only too well that his party, his newspapers, his Constitution even, had grown out of his opposition to Michael Collins and the resultant civil war. He knew that eventually, in the truthful telling of history, two and two would make four. Torn between his own clarity of vision and the myths he had spun around himself, de Valera struggled painfully for words to express himself. Then he said: 'I can't see my way to becoming Patron of the Michael Collins Foundation. It's my considered opinion that in the fullness of time history will record the greatness of Collins and it will be recorded at my expense.' He could be right.

Notes

Abbreviations

pps	papers
AUTHOR	Copy in author's possession
AUTHOR'S	Original in author's possession
BMH	Irish Bureau of Military History
CAB	Cabinet Minutes
CO	Cabinet Office
NG	National Gallery of Ireland
NL	National Library of Ireland
PG	Provisional Government Minutes
PRO	Public Records Office
PRONI	Public Records Office, Belfast
SPO	State Papers Office, Dublin
SO	Stationery Office, Dublin
TCDU	Dublin University, Trinity College archives
UCD	University College Dublin archives

NOTE: where diaries are quoted, which may be available in several editions, entry dates are given rather than page numbers.

Chapter 1 (pp. 3–31)

1. Major Sirr pps, Manuscripts Division, TCDU.
2. Mary Collins-Powell was a sister of Collins who helped him in both the Anglo-Irish and the Irish civil wars. Her memoir was compiled for her grandchildren and distributed by her granddaughter, Deirdre Collins-Powell. AUTHOR.
3. Details of Collins' early life compiled from family sources and earlier biographical works, notably those written by Piaras Beaslai, Frank O'Connor, Rex Taylor and Margery Forester: see Bibliography, p. 458.
4. Memoir of Collins' sister, Sister Celestine, known to the family as 'Lena, short for Helena, written in longhand. It was subsequently photostated and circulated within the family. AUTHOR.
5. Mary Collins-Powell memoir.
6. By Rex Taylor, in *Michael Collins*, Four Square, 1961, p. 24.
7. On microfilm, National Library Dublin.
8. Mary Collins-Powell memoir.
9. Mary Collins-Powell memoir.
10. *West Cork People*, the week after her death, 14/4/07.
11. Told to author by Michael Collins, nephew.
12. Sr Celestine memoir.
13. Margery Forester, *Michael Collins: The Lost Leader*, Sphere, 1972, p. 13.
14. At the time, 9/3/22, O'Brien was a magistrate in Kenya. Letter AUTHOR'S.
15. Sr Celestine memoir.
16. This is the quotation from Wolfe Tone's writings most favoured by republicans. For a more rounded view of Tone's work, see the authoritative biography, *Wolfe Tone*, by Marianne Elliot, Yale University Press, 1989.
17. In Frongoch internment camp, writing to Kevin O'Brien, 16/10/16. Quoted by Taylor p. 25.

18. Piaras Beaslai, *Michael Collins and the Making of a New Ireland*, Phoenix, 1926, Vol. I, p. 11.
19. Quoted by Forester, p. 12.
20. For a history of Bandon and account of life there during the period under review, *see There is a Bridge at Bandon*, by Kathleen Keyes McDonnell, Mercier Press, 1972).
21. J.B. Armour, *Against the Tide*, PRO, 1985.
22. 'Dublin', from 'The Closing Album', 1939, in *Louis MacNeice: Selected Poems*, (ed.) Michael Longley, Faber, 1988, pp. 74–5.
23. Quoted in Mary Collins-Powell memoir.
24. A fortnight before he died de Wet sent a message of congratulation to Collins, 21/1/22, in reply to Collins' letter to his boyhood hero.
25. Frank O'Connor, *The Big Fellow*, Corgi, 1969, pps. 52–3.
26. Collins family papers, quoted by Taylor, p. 27.
27. *Ibid.*
28. Quoted by Forester, p. 16.
29. Eoin MacNeill to A. MacBride, MacNeill pps, U.C.D.
30. '. . . . the printed sources were either vague, or differed in their information. We therefore opted for only recording those years for which we had some real evidence in the form, I think, of his name appearing in the voters' lists. He may very well have resided there over a longer period than that'. Letter to author, from Christopher Jeens, Borough Archivist, 24/4/89. The unveiling of the plaque was marked by a stage presentation commemorating Collins' life and death, commissioned by Hammersmith and Fulham Libraries Department. It was described as 'being very well attended.'
31. *West Cork People*, obituary and report of Marianne Collins' funeral, 16/4/07.
32. AUTHOR'S.
33. Beaslai, Vol. I, p. 16.
34. AUTHOR: original in N.L. MS 13329.
35. Collins also became a member of the Chancery Lane Club of Sinn Fein. Further details of his life at this stage are available in the MacEoin pps, Franciscan Archives, Killiney; O'Muirthle memoir, Mulcahy pps, UCD; in P.S. O'Hegarty's *The Victory of Sinn Fein* and in biographies by Beaslai, O'Connor, Taylor and Forester.
36. P. 2 of undated letter to unnamed friend. Quoted by Taylor, p.32.
37. Quoted by Forester, p. 30.
38. O'Connor, p. 19.
39. Collins to Susan Killeen, 28/8/16, from Frongoch, AUTHOR'S.
40. Robert Mackey, Assistant Manager of the Guaranty Trust. Quoted by Brendan O'Reilly in Beal na mBlath Oration, 24/8/80. Also available in full, Collins pps, SPO.
41. O'Connor, p. 19.
42. O'Hegarty, *The Victory of Sinn Fein*, Talbot Press, 1924, p.23.
43. Collins to Susan Killeen, AUTHOR.
44. O'Hegarty, p. 139.
45. Dorothy Macardle, *The Irish Republic*, 4th edition, Irish Press, 1951, p. 50.
46. John McCoy memoir, AUTHOR'S.
47. W.S. Churchill, *Lord Randolph Churchill*, 2 vols, Odhams, 1906, vol. II, p. 59.

48. *Ibid*, p. 65.
49. A.T.Q. Stewart, *The Ulster Crisis* Faber, 1967, p. 55.
50. Quoted by Patrick Buckland, *Ulster Unionism*, Gill & Macmillan, 1973, p. 54.
51. O'Connor, p. 57.
52. Quoted by A.T.Q. Stewart, *Edward Carson*, Gill & Macmillan, 1981, p. 39.
53. Buckland, p. 55.
54. Quoted by Stewart, *Edward Carson*, p. 27.
55. *Ibid*, p. 26.
56. Quoted by Bucknell *op. cit.*, p. 85.
57. Major the Hon. Gerald French, *The Life of Field-Marshal Sir John French, First Earl of Ypres*, Cassell, 1931, p. 193.
58. A.T.Q. Stewart's *Ulster Crisis* gives a first-class account of the entire gun-running saga.
59. Quoted by Stephen Gwynne, *Life of John Redmond*, Harrap, 1932, p. 211.
60. Quoted by Macardle, p. 92.
61. Forester, p. 29. However a note in the MacEoin pps, Franciscan Archives, Killiney, states that in 1913 Edward Lee proposed Collins for command of the company of Volunteers which Collins helped to found at 28 Princes Rd, Notting Hill – an appropriate address for a man who told William Darling (Quoted by O'Broin pp. 82–3) that one of his favourite books was Chesterton's *Napoleon of Notting Hill*.
62. Macardle, p. 92.
63. The 1916 Rising preparations are described in several works: *see* especially Leon O'Broin's *Dublin Castle and the 1916 Rising*, Helicon, 1966; Diarmuid Lynch's *The I.R.B. and the 1916 Rising*, (ed.) O'Donoghue, Mercier Press, n.d. Lynch was a senior member of the I.R.B. Max Caulfield's *The Easter Rebellion*, Four Square, 1965; Tim Pat Coogan's *Ireland Since the Rising*, Greenwood Press, Connecticut, 1976, or is *The I.R.A.* Fontana, 1970 and subsequent editions.
64. Collins pps, SPO.
65. Quoted by T. Ryle Dwyer, *Michael Collins and the Treaty*, Mercier Press, 1981, p. 5.

Chapter 2 (pp. 32–57)

1. P. S. O'Hegarty, *The Victory of Sinn Fein*, Talbot Press, 1924, pp. 24–5.
2. 'The Path of Freedom,' Talbot Press, 1922, p. 130.
3. Mulcahy pps, UCD.
4. Margery Forester, *Michael Collins: The Lost Leader*, Sphere, 1971, p. 38.
5. C. Desmond Greaves' *The Life and Times of James Connolly*, Lawrence & Wishart, 1961, or Emmet Larkin's *James Larkin*, Routledge & Kegan Paul, 1965 are both recommended for their graphic, authoritative portraits of the Dublin of the period.
6. Coogan, *Ireland Since the Rising*, Greenwood Press, 1976, p. 19.
7. Forester, p. 32.
8. See Stephen Gwynne's *Life of John Redmond*, Harrap, 1932 for the effect of the conscription crisis on Redmond's authority.
9. David Lloyd George, *War Memoirs*, new edition, 2 vols, Odhams, 1934, Vol. I, p. 417.
10. *Ibid*, p. 453.

11. Birrell's role in the 1916 crisis is well drawn by O'Broin in *Dublin Castle and the 1916 Rising* and particularly so in *The Chief Secretary*, Sidgwick & Jackson, 1969, a biography of Birrell.
12. MacCullough to author: *see Ireland Since the Rising*, p. 10.
13. Col Pat Collins, Nancy's stepson, to author.
14. Forester, p. 48.
15. *Ibid*, p. 42.
16. Dorothy Macardle, *The Irish Republic*, 4th edition, Irish Press, 1951, p. 37.
17. Frank O'Connor, *The Big Fellow*, Corgi, 1969, p. 27.
18. Desmond Fitzgerald, Memoirs, UCD, 1969.
19. Rex Taylor, *Michael Collins*, Four Square, 1961, p. 49.
20. Eamon de Valera to Sinead, dated Easter Saturday, 1917, AUTHOR.
21. Max Caulfield's account of what happened under de Valera's command is especially vivid: *see The Easter Rebellion*, Four Square, 1965, pp. 270–77.
22. *Ibid*, p. 277.
23. Mulcahy pps, UCD.
24. Caulfield, p. 280.
25. O'Connor, pp. 31–2.
26. Desmond Ryan, *Michael Collins and the Invisible Army*, Anvil, n.d., p. 24.
27. To Sean Deasey, undated, quoted by Taylor, p. 33.
28. O'Connor, p. 32.
29. This officer's activities are well described in Ryan, p.34, and in Liam Tobin's unpublished memoir, prepared for BMH, AUTHOR.
30. Caulfield gives good descriptions of both the behaviour of the British troops in general and of Bowen Colthurst in particular.
31. Tobin memoir, AUTHOR.
32. Thornton memoir, BMH.
33. Piaras Beaslai, *Michael Collins and the Making of a New Ireland*, Phoenix, 1926, Vol.1, p. 106.
34. Taylor, p. 51.
35. O'Connor, p. 33.
36. Thornton memoir.
37. For the importance of prison in the lives of Republican prisoners and to the Republican movement generally, *see*: Tom Clarke's *Leaves from an Irish Felon's Prison Diary*, Maunsel, 1962; Tim Pat Coogan's *On the Blanket*, Ward River, 1980 and *The I.R.A.*, Pall Mall, 1970; and Sean O'Mahony's first-class *Frongoch: University of Revolution*, FDR, 1987.
38. Quoted by Forester, pp. 50–51.
39. Ryan, *Remembering Sion*, Barker, 1934, p. 215.
40. Forester, p. 51.
41. Collins to Susan Killeen, Stafford Jail, 27/5/16, AUTHOR.
42. *Ibid*, 1/6/16, AUTHOR.
43. The letter is undated, but mentions that it was written the day he arrived in Frongoch. So Susan's place in his affections obviously merited one of the first letters he wrote there.
44. Collins to Sean Deasey, n.d, quoted by Taylor, p. 55.
45. O'Mahony, pp. 100–101.
46. O'Connor, p. 108. Collins' wrestling prowess brought the IRA one of its most valuable recruits. Sean MacEoin (MacEoin pps, Franciscan

Archives, Killiney) tells how he at first refused to join the Volunteers when Collins approached him, having got his name from Tom Clarke's list provided by Mrs Kathleen Clarke. He had promised his dying father that he would look after his widowed mother and her young family. After hours of argument Collins offered to settle the issue by a wrestling bout with MacEoin, a blacksmith. Collins won.
47. Roberts memoir, AUTHOR.
48. *Ibid*.
49. Collins to Susan Killeen, Frongoch, 21/9/16.
50. 3/8/16.
51. Macardle, pp. 160–1.
52. Caulfield, p. 362.
53. *Ibid*, p. 366.
54. Quoted by Freida Kelly, in *A History of Kilmainham Jail*, Mercier Press, 1988, p. 107. Also in 'The Last Words', (ed.) P.F. MacLouchlain, Kilmainham Jail Restoration Committee, 1971, p. 28.
55. Collins to Kevin O'Brien, Frongoch, 6/10/16 quoted by Taylor, p. 58.
56. O'Mahony, p. 66.
57. Coogan, *The I.R.A.*, p. 26.
58. Quoted by Forester, p. 54.
59. Collins to Hannie, 25/8/16 quoted by Forester, p, 54.
60. Collins to Susan Killeen, n.d., addressed as from Frongoch, AUTHOR.
61. Collins to Sean Deasey from Frongoch, 22/10/16, quoted by Taylor, p. 58.
62. O'Connor, p. 37.
63. Quoted by O'Mahony, p. 124.
64. O'Mahony, p. 125.
65. O'Connor, p. 37.
66. O'Connor, p. 30.

Chapter 3 (pp. 58–93)

1. Collins to Susan Killeen, 31/12/16.
2. On 20/9/13.
3. 27/5/16.
4. 30/5/16.
5. William O'Brien, *The Irish Revolution & How It Came About*, Allen & Unwin, 1923, p. 308.
6. The report by Fisher and his team, and subsequent appalled comments of Cabinet members, are recorded in the Leon O'Broin pps, NL.
7. 'The Path to Freedom' Talbot Press, 1922, p. 73.
8. In 1965, about the approaching fiftieth anniversary of the Rising.
9. 'The Path to Freedom', p. 74.
10. Brighid Lyons Thornton, quoted in Timothy O'Grady and Kenneth Griffith, *Curious Journey*, Hutchinson, 1982, p. 108. Further insights into Collins-Kiernan relationship are in MacEoin to Kevin McClory, MacEoin pps, Franciscan Archives, Killiney, and O'Connor, p. 158.
11. Lord Longford and T. P. O'Neill, *Eamon de Valera*, Gill & Macmillan, 1970, p. 57.
12. Authenticated by Mr Josh Honan, a son of de Valera's principal political worker in Clare, who was present when the incident occurred. Letter, 1/2/88, AUTHOR's.
13. Broy O'Malley, O'Malley pps, UCD.
14. What began as a series of interviews for my book

on the I.R.A. ultimately blossomed into his writing his own fascinating story, *The Spy in the Castle*, McGibbon & Kee, 1968.
15. David Neligan, *The Spy in the Castle*, p. 71.
16. *Ibid*, p. 74.
17. Piaras Beaslai, *Michael Collins and the Making of a New Ireland*, Phoenix, 1926, Vol. I, p. 212.
18. Mulcahy pps, UCD, AUTHOR.
19. Story told to author by Michael Collins, Nancy's son.
20. Beaslai article, 'Collins Memorial Supplement', *Irish Independent*, 20/8/66.
21. Details supplied to author by Liam O'Donnachadcha.
22. 15/2/21.
23. Report of meeting of Cork Commissioners, *Cork Examiner*, 11/10/66.
24. No minutes were issued for the ten meetings between 13/11/20 and 12/12/20. CAB 27, PRO, London.
25. 17/10/19, CAB 24, No. 89, PRO, London.
26. 11/11/19, CAB 24, No. 193, PRO, London.
27. Wilson's Irish anxieties are well documented in *American Opinion and the Irish Question* by Francis M. Carroll (Gill & Macmillan, 1978).
28. Wilson Diaries (Cassell, 1927), quoted by Dorothy Macardle, *The Irish Republic*, 4th edition, Irish Press, 1951, p. 253.
29. Sturgis Diaries, NL, 27/10/21.
30. CAB 27/69, PRO, London.
31. Collins to Stack, quoted by Margery Forester, *Michael Collins: The Lost Leader*, Sphere, 1972.
32. Michael Collins' election address, published by the *Southern Star*, Skibbereen, November 1918.
33. *Ibid*.
34. Shortt to PM, 4/7/18, Leon O'Broin pps, NL.

Chapter 4 (pp. 94–119)

1. In letter to Liam Tobin, 2/4/60, AUTHOR'S.
2. Murphy describes this and many other incidents involving Collins, in his unpublished autobiography, 'Murphy Beaucoup', AUTHOR.
3. Mulcahy pps, UCD, P7 D/38.
4. Michael Collins (nephew) to author.
5. Sr Margaret Mary and Liam O'Donnachdcha, a friend and relation of Nancy's, to author.
6. Barton pps, PRO, Dublin. Collins' concern for prisoners is well exemplified by correspondence with Barton's sister concerning Barton's welfare. In one letter (11/2/21) Collins asked her to 'please give him my fondest love – tell him I am constantly thinking of him and that he is no end of a loss to us', AUTHOR'S.
7. He was said to have offered a soldier £10 for a rifle. The court martial was evidently unaware that the tommies were only asking between five shillings and £2 for their weapons at the time.
8. Both Beaslai and Loughlinn McGlynn (in the authoritative *Sworn to be Free*, a compendium of IRA jail-breaks 1918–1921, Anvil, Tralee, 1971) give accounts of his imprisonment.
9. Frank O'Connor *The Big Fellow*, Corgi, 1969.
10. Piaras Beaslai, *Michael Collins and the Making of a New Ireland*, Phoenix, 1926, Vol. 1, p. 241.
11. *Ibid*, Vol. I, p. 267.
12. Collins is also credited with being the chief architect of the escape in *Sworn to be Free*.

13. Beaslai, Vol. I, p. 269.
14. Lord Longford and T. P. O'Neill, *Eamon de Valera*, Gill & MacMillan, 1970, p. 87.
15. Eamon de Valera to Sinead, Lewes jail, Easter 1917, AUTHOR.
16. De Valera to Sinead, 24/8/18, AUTHOR.
17. An English reporter who asked him, 'what are Sinn Fein's objectives on reaching power?' received the immortal reply, 'Vingince, bejasus'! O'Keefe anecdote preserved in Collins family.
18. Lord Longford and T. P. O'Neill, p. 90.
19. Beaslai, Vol. I, p. 239.
20. Darrell Figgis, *Recollections of the Irish War*, quoted in *Arthur Griffith*, by Padraig Colum, Browne & Nolan, 1959, p. 193.
21. *Ibid*, p. 194.
22. Collins pps MS 1 17090, NL.
23. Minutes of Proceedings, Dail Eireann 1919–21, SO.
24. This is hardly surprising, as one of those who had a hand in its drafting was his fellow Frongoch graduate, the Labour leader, William O'Brien.
25. M. Goblet, *Irlande dans la crise universelle*, Félix Alan, Paris, 1921, pp. 356–7, quoted by Macardle, p. 276.
26. Brennan memoir, BMH.
27. Beaslai, who took part, refers to 'feeling disgusted with the atmosphere of mutual admiration' (Vol. I, p. 300).
28. Minutes of proceedings, Dail Eireann, 10/4/19, SO.
29. Dail proceedings, *op cit*.
30. *Ibid*.
31. Beaslai, Vol. I, p. 303.
32. Quoted by Margery Forester, in *Michael Collins: The Lost Leader*, Sphere, 1972, p. 101.
33. Barton letter to Margery Forester, 2/11/64, Barton pps, PRO, Dublin.
34. Quoted by Kathleen Napoli MacKenna, in Memoir, AUTHOR'S.
35. Uinseann MacEoin (ed.), *Survivors*, Argenta Press, 1980, 2nd edition 1987, p. 516.
36. Forester, p. 101.
37. Dorothy Macardle, *The Irish Republic*, 4th edition, Irish Press, 1951, p. 280.
38. AUTHOR'S.
39. CAB 27/69, PRO, London.
40. Dail Debates, 9/4/19.
41. Dail Eireann, 9/4/19, SO, p. 61, col. 2.
42. Un Uctbth, 1921, quoted by Leon O'Broin, *In Great Haste*, Gill & Macmillan, 1903, p. 23.
43. O'Connor, p.55.
44. Eamon de Valera to Sinead, 2/6/19, AUTHOR.
45. The fact that Collins acquired this position is attested to by his fellow IRB Supreme Council member, Sean O'Muirthle, in his unpublished memoir (Mulcahy pps, UCD) and by authoritative contemporaries such as Beaslai.
46. Collins to Stack, 20/7/19, AUTHOR.
47. Daly memoir, BMH, copy in Mulcahy pps, UCD.
48. Interview with author, 14/1/88.
49. Broy to O'Malley, O'Malley notebooks, UCD.
50. CAB 24/92, PRO, London.
51. CAB 103, *ibid*.
52. Leon O'Broin pps, NL.

Chapter 5 (pp. 121–156)

1. 20/6/21 Original in O'Donoghue pps, NL, MS 31, 280 series.
2. The Flying Column idea has been variously attributed to Dick McKee, Dan Breen and Sean Treacey of Tipperary.
3. Michael Brennan memoir, BMH, AUTHOR.
4. Mulcahy pps, UCD.
5. Ibid.
6. Quoted by Beaslai, *Michael Collins and the Making of a New Ireland*, Phoenix, 1926, Vol. I, p. 429.
7. Collins to MacSwiney, 22/3/20, 'D/E' series, SPO.
8. O'Donoghue pps, NL, MS 31, 313.
9. Quoted by Dorothy Macardle, *The Irish Republic*, 4th edition, Irish Press, 1951, p. 432.
10. Lord Riddell in his *Intimate Diary of the Peace Conference*, Gollancz, 1933, p. 147, quotes French as saying that administration was 'as bad as can be . . . There is no proper control. It is impossible to make a satisfactory alteration under existing conditions.'
11. Quoted by Tom Jones, *Whitehall Diaries*, (ed.) K. Middlemass, Oxford University Press, 1971.
12. Cope to MacMahon, O'Broin pps. NL. After the end of hostilities and setting up of the new State, Cope wrote to MacMahon saying that without him the Free State would not have been set up, *see* Leon O'Broin's *No Man's Man*, Institute of Public Administration, 1982, p. 103.
13. Wilson Diaries, Vol. II, p. 222.
14. Frank O'Connor, *The Big Fellow*, Corgi, 1969, p. 103.
15. Kathleen Napoli MacKenna, in *Capuchin Annual*, 1970.
16. Thornton memoir, from which much of what follows is taken.
17. Collins to O'Brien, 9/12/19, Collins pps, NL.
18. Ibid, 20/1/20.
19. Sr Margaret Mary, daughter of Mrs O'Connor, in interview with author.
20. Thornton memoir, BMH.
21. Dave Neligan, *The Spy in the Castle*, McGibbon & Kee, 1968, p. 120.
22. Paddy Daly statement, Mulcahy pps, UCD.
23. Anna FitzSimons, subsequently Anna Kelly, the first woman editor of the *Irish Press*.
24. The relevant files in the PRONI, are closed to researchers since Michael Farrell was discovered to have gained partial access to them while researching *Arming the Protestants*, Brandon, 1983.
25. Collins to Art O'Brien, 12/5/21, Collins pps, NL.
26. 24/2/20, 'D/E' series, 2/530, SPO.
27. Thornton memoir.
28. Liam Devlin to Col Pat Collins (nephew), as told to author.
29. O'Connor, pp. 108–109.
30. Ernie O'Malley, *On Another Man's Wound*, Anvil, 1979, p.114.
31. Frank O'Connor, *My Father's Son*, 1966, pp. 122–4. O'Connor did not mention the incident in his Collins biography, saving it until O'Reilly's death, for his autobiography, completed after his own death by Maurice Sheehy. O'Reilly's daughter corroborated the incident.
32. Oscar Traynor, in O'Malley Notebooks, UCD.
33. Noyek to O'Malley, O'Malley Notebooks, UCD.
34. Related to author by his daughter, Dr C. O'Reilly.
35. Patrick Daly memoir, Mulcahy pps, UCD.
36. The story is given as O'Connor tells it, (p. 138) though Mulcahy, in his papers, adds that Collins suggested to the policeman that he mind a bicycle for them.
37. Mulcahy pps, UCD.
38. 31/3/21.
39. Uinseann MacEoin (ed.), *Survivors*, Argenta Press, 1980, p. 404.
40. In 'Sean Lemass Looks Back', a lengthy series of interviews in the *Irish Press* with political correspondent Michael Mills, between 20/1/69 and 6/2/69.
41. Montgomery's Irish Campaign is well described in 'Montgomery in Ireland', *Irish Historical Review*, Spring 1985.
42. Wilson Diaries, 29/9/20.
43. Thornton Memoir.
44. Flor Begley to Liam O'Donnachadcha, notes AUTHOR's.
45. Tom Barry, *Guerilla Days in Ireland*, Anvil, 1962. In *On Another Man's Wound*, O'Malley also refers to reports of casualness over evidence where some IRA shootings of informers were concerned.
46. Mulcahy pps, UCD.
47. Traynor interview with O'Malley, O'Malley Notebooks, UCD.
48. Lecture by Col Joe Leonard, 9/3/48, Mulcahy pps, P7D/104, UCD.
49. I had taken him into the area on one of the few recorded visits he ever made to a cinema, to see Jane Fonda's 'China Syndrome', which interested him not as cinema, but as anti-nuclear propaganda.
50. CAB 23/21, PRO, London.
51. Charles Townshend, *The British Campaign in Ireland 1919–21*, OUP, 1975, p. 121.
52. Letter to Lloyd George's Secretariat, quoted by Townshend, p. 113.
53. Wilson Diary, quoted by Townshend. p. 116.
54. Macardle, p. 419.
55. Ibid.
56. Daithi O'Connell, a nephew of one of the Kerry pike victims, later became a leader of the Provisional IRA and is alleged to be the inventor of the car-bomb although no proof exists. The ensuing descriptions of shootings and atrocities were all first highlighted by the *Irish Bulletin* and later cited by both Beaslai and Macardle. Other cases may be found in Brigadier Crozier's work *Ireland for Ever* (Cape, 1932).
57. They were in the private collection of Mr W. O'Brien, former active Republican and Assistant Art Editor of the *Irish Press*.
58. *On Another Man's Wound* (pp. 247–52) details the tortures O'Malley experienced. MácEoin generally agrees with these accounts though his papers in the Franciscan Archives, Killiney, suggest that he and others were locked in their cells on the morning of the armoured-car rescue, not because of his temperature, but because the warders wanted members of a new guard to have

an opportunity of studying the prisoners. He also confirms that Collins travelled to Longford after the rescue attempt failed to assure his mother that the next time he came 'we'll have him with us.'
59. Thornton memoir.
60. This was attested to by witnesses at the time. The subsequent account of the tortures is based on a sworn affidavit by Hales, quoted by Kathleen Keyes McDonnell, *There is a Bridge at Bandon*, Mercier Press, 1972, pp. 160–61.
61. Collins to O'Brien, Collins pps, NL.
62. Kavanagh describes the incident in the winter edition of *An tOglach*, 1967, reprinted *Irish Historical Review*, summer 1987.
63. All foregoing correspondence taken from O'Donoghue pps, MS 31, 192, NL.
64. McCorley statement on Swanzy shooting. O'Donoghue pps, MS 31, 313, NL.
65. *Ibid*, MS 31, 223.
66. Report of shooting taken from Beaslai, Vol. 11, p. 33.
67. Among those who took part in agitation for their release, which Sir Henry Wilson opposed, were General Bryan Mahon, Col Morris Moore and Capt. Stephen Gwynne. Their appeal was supported by Irish officers and ex-officers of the British Army.
68. *My Fight for Irish Freedom*, Talbot Press, Dublin, 1924, p. 225.
69. 15/10/20, Mulcahy pps, UCD.
70. Beaslai, Vol. 11, p. 213.
71. Llewelyn Davies told this to Lord Longford who informed the author, 12/4/89.
72. CAB 23/23, PRO, London.
73. In a biography of *Kevin Barry* by Donal O'Donovan, Glendale Press, 1989.
74. Margery Forester, *Michael Collins: The Lost Leader*, Sphere, 1972, p. 167.
75. Beaslai, Vol. 11, p. 54–5.
76. CAB 23/22, PRO, London

Chapter 6 (pp. 157–184)

1. Two of his books at least were inspired by his Irish experiences, *Recoil* and *Never in Vain*. The quotations used here are from *Never in Vain*, Doubleday, New York, 1936.
2. Joe McGuinness and George Nolan, members of the ASU, Joe McGuinness memoir, BMH, AUTHOR.
3. Thornton memoir, BMH.
4. In his biography (*Michael Collins*, Four Square, 1961), Rex Taylor quotes a letter to Dick McKee from Collins, dated 17th, since vanished, that says 'Lt. G. is aware of things.' He suggests the 21st. A most suitable date and day I think.' Dave Neligan however both told me that there was no Lt. G. and categorically said so in his book. The name may be a cover for someone else, perhaps Major Reynolds. Markham, for example, one of Collins' most important Castle informants was known as Donovan until after the war.
5. Anna FitzSimons' recollection, quoted by Taylor, p. 105. She had just got out of prison and gone to the house next door 'for a good sleep'.
6. Mattie MacDonald, O'Malley Notebooks. UCD.
7. *Ibid*.
8. O'Hanlon's son, Rory, was Minister for Health in the Irish Cabinet at time of writing.
9. Tod Andrews, *Dublin Made Me*, Mercier Press, 1979, p. 153.
10. Charles Dalton, *With the Dublin Brigade*, Peter Davies, 1929, pp. 106–8.
11. Frank O'Connor, *The Big Fellow*, Corgi, 1972, p. 124.
12. Quoted by T. Ryle Dwyer, *Michael Collins and the Treaty*, Mercier Press, 1981, p. 18.
13. *Op cit*.
14. Sr Margaret Mary to author.
15. Wilson Diaries, 25/11/20.
16. Childers Diaries, 25/11/20, TCDU.
17. Chief Secretary's report, CAB 27/108, PRO, London.
18. CAB 23/23, 29/12/20 PRO, London.
19. Rex Taylor, p. 104.
20. At Cabinet meeting, 29/12/20.
21. Quoted by Taylor, p. 106.
22. O'Donoghue pps, MS 31226, NL.
23. Collins to O'Brien, 6/6/21, Collins pps, NL.
24. David Neligan, *The Spy in the Castle*, MacGibbon &Kee, 1968, p. 83.
25. The foregoing account of the MacGrane raid and its aftermath was given to me at different times in conversations with both Broy and Neligan. A description of Collins' stratagems to save Broy can also be found in Broy's interviews with O'Malley (O'Malley Notebooks, UCD).
26. Piaras Beaslai, *Michael Collins and the Making of a New Ireland*, Phoenix, 1926, Vol. II, p. 212.
27. Collins to I.O. East Clare Brigade, quoted by Beaslai, Vol. II, p. 212.
28. Tom Jones, *Whitehall Diaries*, (ed.) K. Middlemass, OUP, 1971, Vol III, p.60.
29. Mulcahy pps, UCD.
30. J. Bowyer Bell, 'The Thompson Submachine Gun in Ireland, 1921', *The Irish Sword*, Vol VIII, no. 31, pp. 98–108.
31. Tom Barry, *Guerilla Days in Ireland*, Anvil, 1962, p. 164.
32. *Ibid*.
33. Collins to Hales, 15/12/20, AUTHOR.
34. *Ibid*, 13/8/20.
35. Collins to Art O'Brien, 21/9/20, Collins pps, NL, dispatch no. 479, no. 4.
36. Leahy memoir, O'Donoghue pps, NL *op. cit.*
37. Collins to Hales, 7/8/21, AUTHOR.
38. Hales to O'Donoghue, 11/6/53, O'Donoghue pps, NL.
39. Collins to Hales, 7/7/21, AUTHOR.
40. Michael Brennan memoir, BMH, AUTHOR'S.
41. *Ibid*, published by Michael Collins Association.
42. Beaslai, Vol. II, p. 202.
43. 7/6/21.
44. Mary Collins-Powell memoir, AUTHOR'S.
45. Correspondence in 'D/E' series, 2/500, SPO.
46. Childers pps, TCDU.
47. Quoted by Uinseann MacEoin, *Survivors*, 2nd edition, Argenta Press, 1987, p. 405.
48. Collins to O'Daly, 8/3/21 and 9/3/21, Mulcahy pps, UCD.
49. Mulcahy to Mellowes, 22/3/21, Mulcahy pps, UCD.
50. O'Connor, p. 141.
51. 7/D/60, F2/35, Mulcahy pps, UCD.
52. MacEoin, p. 405.

53. Mulcahy pps, UCD.
54. Collins to Sr Celestine, 5/3/21, AUTHOR.
55. Collins to Hales, 1/8/21. Genoa, AUTHOR.
56. Anecdote repeated to author by Liam O'Donna-chadcha.
57. Instruction to 16th Infantry Brigade, Fermoy, 17/6/21, O'Donoghue pps, MS 31, 2231, NL.
58. Childers pps, Ms 7808, TCDU.
59. Thornton memoir, BMH.
60. Ibid.

Chapter 7 (pp. 185–235)

1. CO 704/188, PRO, London.
2. Ibid.
3. CO 704/100, PRO, London.
4. Moylette to Rex Taylor, quoted by Taylor, in Michael Collins, Four Square, 1961, p. 106.
5. T. Ryle Dwyer, Michael Collins and the Treaty, Mercier Press, 1981, p. 18.
6. CAB 23/23, PRO, London.
7. The writer adopted the initials after his nom de plume, Aeon, was once shortened accidentally through printer's devilry.
8. Francis M. Carroll, American Opinion and the Irish Question, 1910–1923, Gill & Macmillan, and St Martin's Press, 1978, p. 11.
9. According to his papers in the Franciscan Archives, Killiney, de Valera made a distinction between 'big money' and 'small money'. Overall he aimed at getting funds to run an underground Irish Government from the interest of capital invested in the US. Both interest and capital were to be repaid if the Nationalists won. While the small subscribers, commented on scornfully by the Wall Street Journal, were plentiful, he felt that to attract the 'big money', it would be necessary to have as much capital as possible invested in the US.
10. De Valera to Cohalan, 20/2/20, quoted by Piaras Beaslai, Michael Collins and the Making of a New Ireland, Phoenix, 1926. Vol. I, p. 8.
11. Quoted by T. Ryle Dwyer, p.13.
12. Quoted by Beaslai, Vol. II, p. 2.
13. De Valera to Cohalan, quoted in Eamon de Valera, by Lord Longford and T.P. O'Neill, (Gill & Macmillan, 1970.)
14. Cohalan to de Valera, op. cit.
15. De Valera to Griffith, Beaslai, Vol. II, p. 6.
16. Collins to Griffith, 20/7/20, 'D/E' series, SPO.
17. The originals of this letter from Collins, 14/8/20, and of the correspondence alluded to between Sinead de Valera and Kathleen O'Connell are in the de Valera papers in the Franciscan Archives, Killiney. Both this collection and others (NL, SPO) contain several letters from Collins giving de Valera news of the children, their health, studies, how he played with them regularly and so on. The Franciscan Archives also hold many letters from de Valera to Sinead indicating solicitude for her welfare and that of the children.
18. Lord Longford and T.P. O'Neill, p. 113.
19. Gaelic American, 21/8/20 to 11/9/20.
20. Collins to Boland, 15/10/20, copy in possession of T.P. O'Neill.
21. W. Field (Collins) to J. Woods (Boland), 19/11/20.
22. Collins to Devoy, 30/9/20.
23. February 1922.
24. Quoted by Carroll, p. 161.
25. Father, later Monsignor, MacMahon, both kept a diary and wrote about the Clune initiative in 'The Cream of their Race', published as a pamphlet by the Clare Champion, 15/11/21.
26. Ireland for Ever, Cape, 1932, p. 104–5. He also detailed his charges in a letter to the press, 14/5/21, and the Irish Press, 13/4/36.
27. Ibid, 15/10/20.
28. Quoted by Leon O'Broin, Michael Collins, Gill & Macmillan, 1980, p. 65.
29. Collins to Irish Independent, 7/12/20, The full version of his statement is published in Beaslai, Vol. II, p. 116.
30. Collins to Griffith, 14/12/20, quoted by Beaslai, Vol.II, pp. 126.
31. Griffith to Collins, 13/12/20, quoted by Beaslai, Vol. II, pp. 123–5.
32. Collins to Art O'Brien, 15/11/20, 'D/E' series, 2/234, SPO.
33. CAB 23/23, 24/12/20, PRO, London.
34. CAB 23/23. PRO, London.
35. Copy also in O'Donoghue pps, 31,22391, NL.
36. Described by Dermot Keogh, The Vatican, the Bishops and Irish Politics, CUP, 1986, p. 64.
37. Msr Hagan, Rector, Irish College, to Archbishop Walsh, 23/1/21. Dublin Diocesan Records, Archbishop's House, Dundrum.
38. Art O'Brien to Collins, 17/2/21. Collins pps, 'D/E' series, SPO.
39. Ibid, 17/2/21.
40. Hagan to Walsh, 14/2/21, original: Archdiocesan archives, Dublin.
41. D.H. Akenson and F.P. Fallin, 'Drafting of the Irish Constitution', Eire Ireland, Irish American Cultural Institute, Minnesota, Spring 1970, p. 19.
42. Harding to O'Brien, 26/3/21.
43. F.M. Carroll, 'The American Committee for Relief in Ireland, 1920–1922', Irish Historical Studies, Vol. XXIII, No. 89, May 1982, p. 47.
44. Collins to Griffith, 21/12/20, 'D/E' series, 2/85, SPO.
45. Related to author as told to Michael Collins by his father who heard the story from Batt O'Connor, who may also have been sent by Collins to welcome de Valera home.
46. There are conflicting accounts as to who met de Valera. His official biography (Longford and O'Neill) only mentions Cullen, however Collins family sources - based on O'Connor's recollections - are adamant that O'Connor was present. There is no mention of the Big Fellow/Long Fellow exchange in the de Valera biography.
47. Quoted by T. Ryle Dwyer, p. 1.
48. T. Ryle Dwyer, p. 31.
49. See O'Broin and Frank O'Connor, The Big Fellow, Corgi, 1969.
50. Mulcahy, Mulcahy pps, UCD.
51. Ibid.
52. Ibid.
53. Minutes of Proceedings of Dail Eireann, 25/1/21, pp. 241 and 247.
54. O'Broin, p. 79, quoting Mulcahy, Studies, autumn 1978, and An Cosantor, 1980.

55. McGuinness memoir, BMH, AUTHOR.

56. Michael Brennan memoir, BMH.

57. Ernie O'Malley, *On Another Man's Wound*, Anvil Press, 1979, pp. 293–4.

58. O'Connor to Lloyd George, 16/1/21, Leon O'Broin pps, NL.

59. McCoy to O'Malley, O'Malley Notebooks, UCD.

60. Hamar Greenwood to Lloyd George, 26/1/21, quoted by O'Broin, p. 69. Greenwood's optimism was based on the fact that 20 Sinn Feiners were facing execution. With appropriate symbolism O'Connor's letter was addressed from 58 Northumberland Road, Dublin, while Greenwood's – 'the man on the spot' – notepaper was headed Irish Office, Old Queen St, London.

61. O'Hegarty to de Valera. 9/5/21, SPO, Dublin.

62. CO 904/188, PRO, London.

63. Charles Townshend, *The British Campaign in Ireland 1919–21*, OUP, 1975, p. 80.

64. Collins to O'Kelly, 28/4/22, 'D/E' series, 2/514, SPO.

65. O'Kelly to Collins, 1/5/22, 'D/E' series, SPO.

66. Collins to O'Kelly, 6/5/22, 'D/E' series, SPO.

67. O'Malley Notebooks, UCD.

68. Sturgis Diary, 12/8/22.

69. Philadelphia Public Ledger, 22/4/21.

70. Emmet Dalton in interview, Radio Telefis Eireann, 6/1/78.

71. Elections called for by Better Government of Ireland Act, which took place on 19/5/21 (in the South) and 24/5/21 (in the North).

72. Collins to de Valera, 15/1/21, 'D/E' series, SPO.

73. Wilson Diaries, Vol. II, p. 293.

74. 'D/E' series, 2/262, SPO.

75. *General Smuts* by Sarah G. Millin, London, 1936, Vol. II, pp. 319–33.

76. CAB 22/107, PRO, London.

77. Casement Diary, 23/6/20, SPO, Dublin.

78. Sturgis Diary, 26/6/21, NL.

79. The last recorded incident prior to the Truce was an attack on the RIC barracks at Kingscourt, County Cavan.

80. Report of the O.C., H Company, Cork No. 1 Brigade, 10/7/21, Mulcahy pps, UCD.

81. Liam Deasey, *Brother against Brother*, Mercier Press, 1982, p. 21.

82. Collins to Moya Llewelyn Davies, 8/7/20, quoted by Margery Forester, *Michael Collins: The Lost Leader*, Sphere, 1972, p. 201.

83. De Valera referred in the Dail to the Collins plan, without naming its author, as official policy, 26/8/21, *see* Private Sessions, Dail Eireann, 1921–22 SO, p. 77.

84. Dorothy Macardle, *The Irish Republic*, 4th edition, Irish Press, 1951, p. 460.

85. It is dated 13/7/21 and appears to have formed part of an unsent letter, quoted by Taylor, p. 112.

86. O'Connor, p. 155.

87. *Ibid*.

88. P.S. O'Hegarty, *Sunday Independent*, 3/11/46.

89. T. Ryle Dwyer, p. 31.

90. *Gaelic American*, New York, 19/2/21.

91. O'Mara pps, NL, MS 21, 549.

92. Wilson's Diary, 17/10/21, quoted by Ryle Dwyer, p. 52. Griffith used the same argument, 19/12/21, pointing out that Ireland had never sought a Republic in the correspondence with Lloyd George which had preceded the Treaty negotiations, because they knew such a request would have been refused.

93. Tom Jones, *Whitehall Diaries*, (ed.) K. Middlemass, OUP, 1971, Vol. III, p. 60.

94. Lord Riddell, *Intimate Diary of the Peace Conference*, Gollancz, 1933, p. 238.

95. CAB 23/26, PRO, London.

96. Collins in Treaty Debates, Dail reports, SO, p. 32.

97. Robert Barton 'Notes for a Lecture', PRO, Dublin, MS 1093/14.

98. Collins to Hayden Talbot, quoted by T. Ryle Dwyer, p. 46. He dates the interview as 2/8/22. De Valera may have begun to try to influence Collins into going to London earlier than 20/8/21, the date on his papers in the Franciscan Archives, Killiney, but he does not appear to have brought Boland into the argument before then.

99. Batt O'Connor, *With Michael Collins in the Fight for Irish Independence*, Peter Davies, 1929, p. 136.

100. Private Sessions, Dail Eireann, 14/9/21, p. 95.

101. De Valera to Lord Longford, 25/2/63, Childers pps, 7848/302, TCDU.

102. Private Sessions, Dail Eireann, 14/9/22, p. 95.

103. Collins to Joe O'Reilly 11/11/21, quoted by Taylor, p. 120.

104. McGarrity was the principal Irish-American leader to back de Valera during the Devoy-Cohalan row. He later split from de Valera, charging him with abandoning the Republican ideal.

105. De Valera to McGarrity, by Sean Cronin, *The McGarrity Papers*, Anvil, 1972, pp. 109–11.

106. Quoted by Macardle, p. 530.

107. P.S. O'Hegarty, *The Victory of Sinn Fein*, Talbot Press, 1924, pp. 86–7.

108. 14/10/21. 'D/E' series 2/304, SPO. Griffith of course remained unaware that some two months earlier (the document, in the de Valera papers in the Franciscan Archives, Killiney, is undated but appears to have been compiled in either late July or early August) de Valera had decided against sending the External Association proposal to the British over his own name.

109. Quoted by Mrs Tom Clarke, Private Sessions, Dail Eireann, 17/12/21, p. 262.

110. O'Muirthle memoir, Mulcahy pps, UCD.

111. Collins to Boland, quoted by Taylor, p. 113.

112. Collins to Tobin, 29/7/21, Mulcahy pps, UCD.

113. Brugha to Mulcahy, 13/9/21, Mulcahy pps, UCD.

114. At the home of Mrs Humphries, Ailesbury Rd., Dublin.

115. Mulcahy pps, UCD.

116. Beaslai, Vol. II, p. 292.

117. The letter was quoted by Taylor as addressed to John O'Kane, a London-based Irish businessman. The person alluded to did exist and was close to Collins throughout the Treaty

negotiations. However I have reason to suppose that 'O'Kane' was a pseudonym.
118. Taylor, quoted by O'Broin, p. 90.
119. He was born 31/3/1871.
120. I have relied particularly on Kathleen Napoli MacKenna's unpublished memoir and Padraig Colum's biography, *Arthur Griffith*, Browne & Nolan, 1959.
121. Collins to O'Dalaigh, 5/10/21, Mulcahy pps, UCD.
122. *Ibid*, 29/9/21.
123. It forms part of an untitled set of documents relating to the Treaty talks, memoranda, records of conferences, descriptions of disagreements, etc, compiled by Robert Barton and kindly loaned to the author by Dr T.P. O'Neill.
124. A contemporary of Collins, the authoritative Leon O'Broin, historian and former Secretary of the Department of Posts and Telegraphs, who worked with my father in local government at the time, told me he had first-hand knowledge of these meetings.
125. This is made clear in the O'Muirthle memoir, Mulcahy pps, UCD.

Chapter 8 (pp. 236–276)

1. Captured in one of the classic studies of the Anglo-Irish relationship, *Peace by Ordeal*, Sidgwick & Jackson, 1972, by Lord Longford. Birkenhead's son was at Oxford with Longford and on visits to Birkenhead's home, where a portrait of Collins hung in an honoured place, Longford was suggested by Birkenhead's daughter as the ideal person to chronicle the struggle. He subsequently co-authored de Valera's authorised biography.
2. Lord Longford, *Peace by Ordeal*, p. 106.
3. Padraig Colum, *Arthur Griffith*, Browne & Nolan, 1959, p. 282.
4. Leslie's mother and Churchill's were sisters.
5. The title of a major series of nine articles by Henry Mangan (6), Dr Nancy Wyse Power (2) and Piaras Beaslai (1), which appeared in the *Irish Independent* between 14/10/35 and 4/11/35.
6. A detailed exposition of this theory appears in *Survivors* (p. 400 *et seq*), the most important published (The O'Malley Diaries are unpublished) compendium of Republican views and reminiscences in existence: (ed.) Uinseann MacEoin, Argenta Press, 1980.
7. Collins to O'Brien, 6/8/21, Collins pps, NL.
8. Collins to Hales, 15/2/19, AUTHOR.
9. Dr Wyse Power, *Irish Independent*, 1/11/35.
10. *See* Blythe and Kennedy pps, UCD.
11. The memoir was originally conceived as a lecture, but he later expanded his notes. These, with some other relevant material, are in PRO, Dublin, nos. 1093/12 and 1093/14.
12. Compiled by Capt. C.J. O'Kelly, 12/10/21, and circulated three days later, CAB/243, PRO, London.
13. Pen portraits taken from The Earl of Birkenhead, *The Last Phase*, Thornton Butterworth, 1959, p. 150.
14. Barton memoir, PRO, Dublin.

15. Lloyd George, quoted by Longford, *Peace by Ordeal*, p. 121.
16. *Op. cit.*
17. To 'O'Kane', quoted by Rex Taylor, *Michael Collins*, Four Square, 1961, Chapter 4.
18. Erskine Childers said of Collins: 'It was he who prevented a break several times suggesting delay when it had been practically decided to break, coats on etc.' Childers Diary, Childers pps, TCDU, p. 70.
19. Barton says in his memoir that Jones arranged a meeting between Lloyd George and Chamberlain at which the Prime Minister said that better progress would be made if he could shed Greenwood and Worthington Evans and the Irish also dispense with part of their team. Longford gives much the same version of a 'ten minutes conversation' initiated by Lloyd George, though he credits Duggan with bringing back the suggestion from Cope.
20. Tom Jones, *Whitehall Diaries*, (ed.) K. Middlemas, OUP, 1971, Vol. III, p. 141.
21. 'D/E' series, 2/304:2, SPO, Dublin, quoted by Ryle Dwyer, *Michael Collins and the Treaty*, Mercier Press, 1981, p. 67. *See also* Ulick O'Connor's, *Oliver St John Gogarty*, (Cape, 1964) in which the author analyses Childers' character sympathetically, though not uncritically.
22. Churchill, in *The Aftermath*, Butterworth, 1929, and Sturgis in his Diary, are but two of the chroniclers of the period on the British side who regarded Childers as a malign influence on the Conference. His previous role as editor of the *Irish Bulletin* was also remembered.
23. de Valera to Griffith, 16/10/21, this and following letters in compilation of Barton documents on Treaty negotiations, AUTHOR.
24. de Valera to Griffith, 19/10/21. Barton Treaty compilation, AUTHOR's.
25. de Valera to Griffith, 14/10/21, *ibid*.
26. Correspondence between de Valera and Griffith, 10–12/10/21, Barton compilation, AUTHOR's.
27. de Valera to Griffith, 22/10/21, *ibid*.
28. The following quotations from the Sixth Plenary Session are taken from a transcript of the proceedings, AUTHOR's.
29. Later an Irish Foreign Minister and a Nobel Peace Prize winner.
30. Note by Barton on de Valera letter and its sequel in Barton Treaty compilation, AUTHOR's.
31. Barton compilation, AUTHOR's.
32. Ministry of Defence Archives, NL.
33. *Ibid*.
34. The inside story of the Windsor Barracks raid was told by Brennan in his memoir, BMH.
35. Leon O'Broin, *Michael Collins*, Gill & Macmillan, 1980, pp. 100–103.
36. Recounted to author by Michael and Pat Collins (nephews).
37. Collins to Mulcahy, 23/11/21, Mulcahy pps, UCD.
38. O'Broin, p. 103.
39. British memorandum, Barton compilation, AUTHOR.
40. *ibid*.

41. Longford, *Peace by Ordeal*, p. 158.
42. According to official records of the period, such as Griffith's letters to de Valera, and informed sources such as Longford.
43. Margery Forester, *Michael Collins: The Lost Leader*, Sphere, 1972, p. 231.
44. Griffith to de Valera, 31/10/21, Barton compilation.
45. Barton, note in Treaty compilation.
46. Barton, 'Notes for a Lecture'; PRO, Dublin.
47. Barton, in Treaty compilation.
48. *Ibid.*
49. Barton, note in Treaty compilation.
50. Possibly as early as 26/10/21. After this date there is a '?' and then, in pencil, '29th'. Original in CAB 21/243, PRO,
51. As it was, Brugha created a scene which almost disrupted the final Cabinet meeting in Dublin (3/12/21) at which terms of the proposed Treaty were discussed, by suggesting that the British had opted for a sub-conference methodology in order to have Collins and Griffith selected as principal negotiators.
52. Collins to 'O'Kane', 23/11/21, quoted by Taylor, p. 125.
53. C.P. Scott, quoted by Margery Forester, p. 230.
54. The original formed part of the Collins family collection, which was loaned to a researcher, but never returned. It was undated, typed, initialled by both men, and quoted by Taylor, pp. 142 and 143.
55. Quoted by O'Broin, p. 114.
56. Birkenhead to Collins, Griffith, 3/11/21, Barton compilation.
57. Griffith to de Valera, 3/11/21, *ibid.*
58. Longford, p. 167.
59. Longford, p. 169.
60. Griffith to de Valera, 9/11/21, Barton compilation.
61. Griffith to de Valera, 9/11/21, *ibid.*
62. Craig to Lloyd-George, 11/11/21, *ibid.*
63. Griffith to de Valera, 12/11/21, *ibid.*
64. Longford, p. 177.
65. The visit and Birkenhead's forceful advocacy are described by Salvidge's son, Stanley, in *Salvidge of Liverpool*, Hodder & Stoughton, 1934.
66. CAB 23/27. PRO, London.
67. CO 904/188, PRO, London.
68. Michael Farrell, *Arming the Protestants*, Brandon, 1983, p. 76.
69. Griffith to de Valera, 16/11/22, Barton compilation.
70. Collins to 'O'Kane', 29/11/21, quoted by Taylor, p. 140.
71. Note in Barton compilation.
72. Barton compilation.
73. Earl of Birkenhead, *(F.E.) The Life of F.E. Smith: First Earl of Birkenhead*, Eyre & Spottiswoode, 1959, pp. 382–3.
74. Griffith to de Valera, 29/11/22, Barton Treaty compilation, AUTHOR.
75. Longford, p. 203.
76. O'Muirthle memoir, Mulcahy pps, UCD.
77. Childers Diary, 3/12/21, TCDU.
78. Despite de Valera's pressure, O'Hegarty had been retained in London. He came over with

the delegation for these discussions and may have kept notes. But, these, along with his records of a lifetime in public service, were probably destroyed when, towards the end of his life, he burned his papers.
79. Private Session. Dail Eireann, p. 187.
80. O'Murchadha notes.
81. Childers Diary, TCDU.
82. Private session, Dail Eireann, p. 176.
83. O'Murchadha notes.
84. Anthony Gaughan, *Austin Stack*, Kingdom Books, 1971.
85. Private Session, Dail Eireann, p. 177.
86. Barton, 'Notes for a Lecture'.
87. CAB 23/27.
88. Collins, Report of Conference, 5/12/21, Barton Treaty compilation, AUTHOR.
89. Longford, p. 216.
90. Tom Jones, *Whitehall Diaries*, (ed.) K. Middlemas, OUP, 1971, p. 180.
91. *See* Longford, Ryle Dwyer.
92. Collins memorandum, written immediately after seeing Lloyd George, 5/12/21, Collins pps, AUTHOR.
93. In *Peace By Ordeal*, Lord Longford (pp. 220–21) says, 'Collins yielded at last' to repeated efforts by Jones, made through Griffith.
94. Jones, Vol III, p. 180.
95. CAB 23/27, PRO, London.
96. Barton account of Sub-conferences, Barton Treaty compilation, AUTHOR.
97. Churchill, *The Aftermath*, quoted by Longford, p. 239.
98. Austin Chamberlain, *Down the Years*, London, 1935, quoted by Longford, p. 239.
99. Barton's recollection, quoted by Longford, p. 239.
100. Churchill, *The Aftermath*, quoted by Longford, p. 241.
101. Barton, 'Notes for a Lecture.'
102. Childers' Diary, TCDU.
103. MacKenna memoir, AUTHOR.
104. Sir Geoffrey Shakespeare, *Let Candles be Brought In*, MacDonald, 1949, p. 89.

Chapter 9 (pp. 277–307)

1. Well summarised by O'Broin in *In Great Haste*, Gill & Macmillan, 1983, p. 92.
2. Treaty Debates, 3/1/22, p. 190.
3. Kiernan to Collins: 1/12/21, *In Great Haste*, p. 68.
4. Michael Collins, *The Man Who Won the War*, Mercier Press, 1990, pp. 13, 14.
5. Film screened 6/1/79, the day he died.
6. Confidential source.
7. 'In the Shadow of Bael na mBlath', produced, narrated and written by Colm Connolly.
8. Dr Arthur Schlesinger, Chair in the Humanities, City University of New York.
9. Schlesinger to author, 21/2/89, AUTHOR's.
10. Schlesinger Jr. to author, 6/12/89. Alexandra Schlesinger has an interest in Irish history, being a direct descendant of Thomas Addis Emmet, Robert Emmet's older brother. She once did some research on Collins for a file, most of it during a visit to England 'of some months'.
11. Her father, Michael Mick O'Brien of Carri-

groc, Clonakilty, was a cousin of Collins' grandfather, James O'Brien. Michael Mick married twice. His second wife was a first cousin of Collins' mother, Marianne. Nancy was the youngest daughter (of five) of this marriage.

12. Liam O'Donnachadha to author, 22/02/89.
13. To mark Collins' centenary, Liam Collins led the family in having Woodfield refurbished and given to the nation as a museum in October 1990.
14. Collins to Killeen, 02/02/20, AUTHOR.
15. Boland to Kiernan, 5/10/21, In Great Haste, p. 22.
16. Boland to Kiernan, 10/1/22, ibid, p. 99.
17. Collins to Kiernan, 30/12/21, ibid, p. 62.
18. Collins to Kiernan, 12/12/21, ibid, p. 62.
19. Kiernan to Collins, 10/2/22, ibid, p. 117.
20. Received 7/6/22, ibid, p. 176.
21. 26/6/22, ibid, p. 185.
22. Received 15/7/22, ibid, p. 196.
23. 2/8/22, ibid, p. 210.
24. 15/7/22. ibid, p. 197.
25. Told to author's parents by O'Sheil.
26. The eldest was christened Felix, after his father.
27. 17/8/22.
28. AUTHOR. Original in O'Brien pps, NL.
29. Fr P. P. Maguire, Newbliss, County Monaghan, to Collins, 4/10/21, AUTHOR'S.
30. Collins to Maguire, 15/10/21, AUTHOR'S.
31. Collins to Art O'Brien, 1/4/21, Collins pps, NL.
32. This was the sum Llewelyn Davies mentioned to Art O'Brien, O'Brien to Collins, 13/5/21, Collins pps, SPO.
33. Hansard, Vol. 143, 14/7/21. p. 203.
34. Collins to O'Connor, 29/5/21, Collins pps, SPO.
35. O'Connor to Collins, 3/6/21, ibid.
36. Collins to O'Brien, 4/5/21, ibid.
37. Author's note: I have found speech drafts headed 'From C.Ll.D. in Collins' papers.
38. Collins to O'Brien, 21/3/21, Collins pps, SPO.
39. Napoli MacKenna memoir, AUTHOR'S.
40. In his home at Blackrock, County Dublin, 12/1/88.
41. Hutchinson, 1958, and Four Square, 1961.
42. Lord Longford showed her a typescript of Peace by Ordeal, Sidgwick & Jackson, 1972, which she felt showed 'a strong bias for the viewpoint of de Valera, Barton and Childers', and she wrote to Frank Thornton, 8/8/34 (AUTHOR) asking him to 'confirm . . . that Mick never "persuaded his extremists of the I.R.B. to vote for the Treaty".'
43. Uinsean MacEoin (ed.), Survivors, Argenta Press, 1980, p. 507.
44. Ibid, p. 406.
45. Napoli MacKenna memoir.
46. O'Hegarty to Lynch, 22/11/21, Mulcahy pps, UCD.
47. Mulcahy pps, UCD.
48. 2/12/21.
49. Shane Leslie memoir of Hazel Lavery, Leslie pps, Georgetown University Library, Washington DC.

50. Methuen, 1948; Anvil 1966.
51. O'Broin reproduces the de Vere White assessment in his Michael Collins, Gill & Macmillan, published as late as 1980.
52. Napoli MacKenna memoir.
53. Shane Leslie to Audrey Morris, 18/6/21, Leslie pps, Georgetown University.
54. See last page of Kevin O'Higgins, by Terence de Vere White, Methuen, 1948.
55. Acrostic poem to Hazel Lavery, by Kevin O'Higgins, Kilmainham Museum, Dublin, MS 864 J.
56. Now renamed Arus an Uachtaran and home to the Irish President.
57. Confidential source.
58. Shane Leslie commentary on Lavery anecdote as told to Derek Patmor, Leslie pps, Georgetown University.
59. Original, Kilmainham Museum, Dublin, MS 964F.
60. Kilmainham Museum, Dublin, MS 964A.
61. Ibid.
62. Londonderry pps, 15/3/52, File No. D3099. PRONI.
63. H. Montgomery Hyde, The Londonderrys, Hamish Hamilton, 1979, p. 151.
64. Ibid.
65. Confidential source.
66. Quoted in Furry Park House, pamphlet by Seamus Cannon, Furry Park Preservation Committee, 1985.
67. Report of shooting as told by Bill MacKenna to Cannon.
68. Shaw to Hannie Collins, 24/8/22, quoted by Taylor, Michael Collins, Four Square, 1961, p. 209.
69. Kiernan to Collins, received 15/8/22, In Great Haste.
70. Confidential source.
71. One of the letters he wrote that Saturday, 19/8/22, timed 12.30 p.m., was a complaint to Desmond FitzGerald, Director of Publicity, about the fact that no publicity had been given to an attempt on his life at Stillorgan the previous day, Collins pps, SPO.
72. Dalton showed the letter to members of an RTE TV crew, who made a film of his life in 1978. After his death, it passed into the possession of his son, Mr Richard Dalton of Weybridge, Surrey, but at the time of writing, Mr Dalton said it had been mislaid. Noel Lemass was also suspected by Collins' former associates of having been responsible for shooting Sean Hales (see Chapter 13).
73. Quoted by J.B. Lyons, Oliver St John Gogarty, Blackwater, p. 125.
74. Ryle Dwyer, Michael Collins and the Treaty, Mercier Press, 1981, p. 106.
75. Lord Longford and T.P. O'Neill, Eamon de Valera, Gill & Macmillan, 1970, p. 168.
76. Ryle Dwyer, p. 106.
77. Childers Diary, 8/12/22, TCDU.
78. Ibid.
79. Ibid.
80. Ibid.
81. Piaras Beaslai, Michael Collins and the Making of a New Ireland, Phoenix, 1926, Vol. II, p. 312.
82. Childers Diary, 9/12/21, TCDU.
83. 23/12/21, In Great Haste, p. 90.

84. Batt O'Connor, *With Michael Collins in the Fight for Irish Independence*, Peter Davies, 1929, pp. 180–2.
85. Frank O'Connor, *The Big Fellow*, Corgi, 1969, p. 173, see also Margery Forester, *Michael Collins: The Lost Leader*, Sphere, 1972, p. 272.
86. Public Session Treaty Debates, Dail Eireann, 14/12/21. col. 1, p. 7.
87. Ryle Dwyer, p. 112.
88. Sean Hales, Treaty Debates, Private Session, 17/12/21, p. 263.
89. 10/12/21.
90. *Irish Times*, 20/12/21.
91. Tim Healy, *Letters and Leaders*, Thornton Butterworth, 1928, p. 645.
92. Collins to Kiernan, 20/12/21. The letter is not included in *In Great Haste*, but was quoted by Margery Forester, p. 271.
93. Desmond Ryan, *Remembering Sion*, Barker, 1934, pp. 278–9.
94. Joseph Sweeney describes such an interview in O'Malley Notebooks, UCD.
95. de Valera to McGarrity, 27/12/21, McGarrity pps, NL.
96. Childers Diary, TCDU, 28/12/21.
97. Described in *Irish Times* and *Freeman's Journal*, 4/1/22.
98. Treaty Debates, Public Session, 4/1/22, p. 217.
99. Beaslai, Vol. II, p. 332.
100. Public Session, Dail Eireann, 5/1/22, p. 277.
101. Treaty Debates, Public Session, pp. 271–5.
102. Ryle Dwyer, p. 138.
103. Treaty Debates, Public Session, p. 277.
104. Collins to Kiernan, 6/1/22. *In Great Haste*, p. 194.
105. Treaty Debates, Public Session, 6/1/22, pp. 290–2.
106. *Ibid*, p. 307.
107. *Ibid*, p. 281.
108. Beaslai, Vol. II, p. 335.
109. Treaty Debates, Public Session, pp. 324–5.
110. *Ibid*, pp. 235–44.
111. *Ibid*, p. 344.
112. *Ibid*, p. 346. De Valera's papers apparently do not contain answers to such key questions as: Exactly what policy did he intend to follow if he succeeded in destroying the Treaty; what forces did he intend to use to enforce his policy; what was his assessment of Michael Collins? It is clear from Dorothy Macardle (p. 672), whose work he regarded as the main repository of his ideas until his own official biography was published, that de Valera was aware in February and March 1922 that Collins intended to move towards a Republic if he got co-operation from his opponents. She says: 'others believed that he [Collins] was rather inviting his countrymen to co-operate with him in deceiving the British and would presently declare the Republic again. Had he received such co-operation on a large scale, [author's italics] *there is little doubt that he would have thrown all his great energies into achieving progress on those lines.*'

Chapter 10 (pp. 308–332)

1. Statistics quoted in Labour Party submission to Dail, 10/1/22, Dail Debates, SO.
2. Collins to Kiernan, 9/1/22, *In Great Haste*, (ed.) Leon O'Broin, Gill & Macmillan, 1983, p. 95.
3. T. Ryle Dwyer, *Michael Collins and the Treaty*, Mercier Press, 1981, p. 142.
4. The quotation provides the title for Florrie O'Donoghue's biography of Diarmuid Lynch, *No Other Law*, (Irish Press, 1954).
5. Traynor to O'Malley, O'Malley Notebooks, UCD.
6. Michael Hopkinson, *Green Against Green*, Gill & Macmillan, 1988, p. 16.
7. Piaras Beaslai, *Michael Collins and the Making of a New Ireland*, Phoenix, 1926, Vol. II, P.372.
8. Literally 'High Conference', usually meaning Annual General Conference.
9. The Drafting Committee met at the Shelbourne Hotel, in a large room still known today as 'The Constitution Room'.
10. Quotation from an important series, 'The Irish Civil War and the Drafting of the Free State Constitution', by D.H. Akenson and J.P. Fallon, in the quarterly, *Eire Ireland*, Irish-American Cultural Institute, Minnesota, 1970.
11. The members of the Committee were: Darrell Figgis, James Douglas, James MacNeill, C.J. France, Kevin O'Shiel, Hugh Kennedy, John O'Byrne, James Murnaghan and Alfred O'Rahilly. Douglas and France, an American lawyer, had been involved with the American Relief activities (Irish White Cross) during the Tan war. Kennedy and O'Shiel, both lawyers, were active in politico-legal affairs and O'Byrne and Murnaghan were prominent Dublin barristers; MacNeill, a brother of Eoin MacNeill, was a retired Indian Civil Servant who had also worked with the White Cross. Alfred O'Rahilly, a Professor of Mathematics, was a leading Catholic intellectual. Figgis was the only paid member of the Committee.
12. Michael Hopkinson, p. 65.
13. 'Sandow' Donovan, the Irregular officer in charge of landing the *Upnor* arms, gave an account to Ernie O'Malley from which it appears that the haul was many times greater than Churchill's estimate. O'Malley Notebooks, UCD. Hopkinson, p. 74, says it took 200 lorries to carry the booty, which is nearer to the description given by Donovan, who, at that stage, in private conversation, had no reason to lie to his old comrade.
14. Collins to Churchill, 5/4/22. AUTHOR.
15. CAB 16/42, PRO, London.
16. *Ibid*.
17. Eight dead and some sixty injured.
18. Copy of original speech, AUTHOR.
19. Collins to McGarrity, 5/4/22, AUTHOR.
20. Quoted by Padraig Colum, *Arthur Griffith*, Browne & Nolan, 1959, p. 339.
21. Tom Hales to Liam O'Donnachadcha; account, AUTHOR'S.
22. *Irish Independent*, 7/3/22.
23. *Ibid*, 17/3/22.
24. *Ibid*, 18/3/22.
25. *Ibid*, 20/3/22.

26. *Ibid*, 23/3/22.
27. *Seanad Reports*, 20, 1876, quoted by Donal O'Sullivan, *The Irish Free State and its Senate*, Faber, 1940, p. 19.
28. Boland to Stack, 27/4/22, Stack pps, quoted by Ryle Dwyer, p. 145.
29. Notes taken by Archbishop Byrne, originals, Diocesan records, Archbishop's House, Dublin.
30. 1/5/22.
31. 30/4/22.
32. *Poblacht na hEireann*, 18/5/22.
33. 'In Parnell's Funeral', Gill & Macmillan, 1934.
34. Colum, p. 343.
35. Quoted in Blythe letter to Padraig Colum, Griffith's biographer.
36. Dail Debates, 27/4/22, p.303.
37. O'Broin, p. 128.
38. Sean O'Luing, *Art O'Griofa*, Sairseal agus Dill, 1953, p. 396.
39. Kennedy to Collins, 20/5/22, Kennedy pps, UCD.
40. Churchill to Collins, 15/5/22, AUTHOR.
41. O'Muirthle memoir, Mulcahy pps, UCD.
42. *Ibid*.
43. Daly to Collins, 3/4/22, Mulcahy pps, UCD.
44. Collins to Daly, 5/5/22, *ibid*.
45. Cope to Churchill, 23/5/22. CAB 43/1, PRO, London.
46. Churchill to Collins, 22/5/22, AUTHOR.
47. Lionel Curtis, who made the assessment, was at the time (6/6/22) Secretary of the British Government's Provisional Government of Ireland Committee, see CAB 27/154. PRO, London.
48. Churchill to Irish delegates, CAB 21/249, *ibid*.
49. Downing Street, 27/5/22. CAB 21/249, *ibid*.
50. Collins, Griffith, Duggan, Cosgrave, Hugh Kennedy and Diarmuid O'Hegarty, Secretary. The British team was Lloyd George, Chamberlain, Birkenhead, Churchill, Worthington Evans, Hamar Greenwood, Tom Jones, Lionel Curtis and Quentin Hill. The last three were Secretaries.
51. Downing Street, 1/6/22, CAB 21/257, PRO, London
52. Tom Jones, *Whitehall Diaries*, Vol III, (ed.) K. Middlemass, OUP, 1971, 1/6/22.
53. CAB 23/30, PRO, London.
54. *Ibid*.
55. *Ibid*.
56. CAB 21/249, PRO, London.
57. Kennedy to Colum, 11/6/22. Kennedy pps, UCD.
58. Lord Middleton, Andrew Jamieson, Dr J.H. Bernard and the Earl of Donoughmore.
59. *Poblacht na hEireann*, 5/6/22.
60. *Irish Independent*, 5/6/22.
61. De Valera speech, *Irish Independent*, 5/6/22.
62. *Hansard*, 26/5/22.
63. Margery Forester, *Michael Collins: The Lost Leader*, Sphere, 1972, p. 319.
64. Frank O'Connor, *The Big Fellow*, Corgi, 1969, p. 207.
65. Collins pps, quoted Forester, p. 320.
66. O'Connor, p. 207.
67. P G, 27/6/22. S. 1322, PRO, Dublin.
68. Baroon Bardon, Jonathan B. and Conlin, Stephen C., *Dublin: 1000 Years of Wood Quay*, Blackstaff, 1984, p. 26.
69. Fr Albert's Diary, Dublin Diocesan Records, Archbishop's House, Dublin.
70. O'Connor, p. 208.
71. *Ibid*.
72. Dalton, on RTE TV film, 'The Shadow of Bael na mBlath', 1989.
73. AUTHOR.
74. Churchill to Collins, 28/6/22, AUTHOR.
75. *Ibid*.
76. AUTHOR.
77. Bardon and Conlin, p. 26.
78. O'Broin, p. 137.
79. PG, 28/6/22. PG 39, SPO.

Chapter 11 (pp. 333–385)

1. Second Northern Division report, NL, MS 17143.
2. CAB 23/83, PRO, London.
3. *Cf* Cabinet meetings: 15, 19 and 22 December, CAB 23/18, PRO, London.
4. Birkenhead to Londonderry, Londonderry pps, PRO, Belfast.
5. CAB 23/23, PRO, London.
6. There was a Senate, but this, heavily representative of the land-owning lords, had little or no relevance to Catholic grievances.
7. Speaking in Stormont, 24/4/34.
8. Brookeborough to author, see Coogan, *The I.R.A.*, Fontana, 1987, p.58.
9. Carson to Bonar Law, Carson pps, PRONI D 1507/1/1920/16.
10. CAB 24/109/1693, PRO, London.
11. Craig to Cabinet, CAB 5/1, PRONI.
12. CAB 23/22/53, *ibid*.
13. CAB 22/107, PRO, London.
14. 1/9/20, Anderson to Bonar Law, CO/904/188, PRO, London.
15. Gen. Ricardo, Col. McClintock and Major Stevenson, D 1678/6, PRONI.
16. Intelligence Report, 3rd Northern Division, 26/10/21. Mulcahy pps, UCD, p. 7/a/26.
17. Mulcahy pps, UCD, p. 7d-1.
18. *Morning Post*, 5/9/21.
19. PG, 30/1/22, SPO.
20. 20/7/21, CAB 23/26, PRO, London.
21. The nickname derived from the frequently proposed Hales formula for dealing with Black and Tans and their allies: 'give 'em the buckshot!'
22. Aiken to O'Malley, O'Malley Notebooks, UCD, p. 17b/193.
23. Batt O'Connor, *With Michael Collins in the Fight for Irish Independence*, Peter Davies, 1929, p. 181.
24. Copy of Fawsitt's Confidential Report to Provisional Government, 3/1/22, original, SPO, AUTHOR's.
25. PG, 20/1/22, SPO.
26. Mulcahy pps, UCD.
27. PG, No. 45, 30/1/22, SPO.
28. AUTHOR.
29. Michael Farrell, *Arming the Protestants*, Brandon, 1983, p. 91.
30. Mulcahy to Collins. 3/3/22, Mulcahy pps, UCD.
31. It exists today in the division of nationalist ranks in the Six Counties and the existence of

two separate nationalist parties, Sinn Fein, and the Social Democratic and Labour Party. (SDLP).

32. Documents allegedly proving these were found. Hopkinson, p. 79.

33. Collins to O'Duffy, 28/1/22, SPO.

34. O'Duffy to Collins, 30/1/22, SPO.

35. Craig to Lloyd George, 8/2/20, CAB 21/254, PRO, London.

36. Lloyd George to Collins, 8/2/22, CAB 21/254, PRO, London.

37. Griffith to Collins 8/2/22, CAB 21/254, PRO, London.

38. Collins to Lloyd George, 8/2/22, CAB 21/254, PRO, London.

39. Cope to Jones, 8/2/22, CAB 21/254, PRO, London.

40. Dolan memoir, BMH. Sean O'Muirthle in his memoir also mentions taking part in an attempt to call off the shooting of the hangmen, but gives different dates.

41. AUTHOR.

42. Quoted by Hopkinson, p. 81.

43. Ed. 13/1/400, PRONI.

44. Blythe pps, UCD, p. 4/386 9(15).

45. Minister for Finance, William Cosgrave, Dail Eireann, 9/11/22.

46. Ed 32/B/1/2/52, PRONI.

47. 3/4/22, At the Assembly Hall, Belfast.

48. Wilson Diaries, 15/3/22.

49. CO 906/30, PRO, London.

50. Tom Jones, Whitehall Diaries, Vol III, (ed.). K. Middlemass, OUP, 1971, p. 195.

51. Collins to Churchill, 24/3/22, CAB 6/75, PRONI.

52. In 1968, as Irish Foreign Affairs Minister, he pursuaded the United Nations General Assembly to adopt a resolution on nuclear arms limitation, which he devised. It remains the only international statutory instrument for curbing the spread of nuclear weapons.

53. Mulcahy pps, UCD, p7/1A/47 L.

54. AUTHOR.

55. AUTHOR.

56. Charles Haughey was himself dismissed from a Fianna Fail Cabinet in 1970 and unsuccessfully charged with 'illegal importation of arms into the State', after the North had again erupted in 1969.

57. Copy of formal letter of authorisation dated 22/2/22, AUTHOR'S.

58. Blythe pps, UCD, p. 24/554.

59. Statements collected by the commission's lawyers and the evidence given at the Northern Advisory Committee, which first met 11/4/22, are scattered through the several boxes of the bulky collection of Committee documentation, notably S. 10111 and S 11195, SPO.

60. Named in confidential Intelligence Report to Free State Government, 20/2/24. Blythe pps, UCD, p. 24/176.

61. Farrell, pp. 114–150.

62. PG, 30/1/22, SPO.

63. ´12/4/22.

64. McCoy to O'Malley, O'Malley Notebooks, UCD, b76 and 116.

65. Macready to Jeudwine, 10/12/20, quoted by Charles Townshend, The British Campaign in Ireland, 1919–21, OUP, 1975, p. 138.

66. Collins' statements, the text of the Sinn Fein Resolution and the British invitation to talks, Freeman's Journal, 25 and 29 March, and Craig's speeches can be found both there and, in a more approving setting, in the columns of the Belfast Newsletter.

67. AUTHOR.

68. Wilson Diaries.

69. On 4/4/22 the Agreement was strongly criticised by a number of the more extreme Unionists, notably Messrs Coote, Lynn and M'Guffin.

70. The Free State Government Intelligence Document of 24/2/22, already quoted, says the killing was done at Nixon's instigation to give a pretext for what followed.

71. The information on the Arnon and Stanhope St killings is taken from 'Memos for Mr Michael Collins: Extracts from Statutory Declarations, re Arnon St and Stanhope St massacres', Collins pps, AUTHOR.

72. Complete transcript available, SPO, S. 1011.

73. Londonderry to Collins, 5/4/22, PRONI, Ed. 13/1/400.

74. PG, 21/4/21, SPO, 9.

75. PG, 25/4/22, SPO, 10.

76. Dorothy Macardle, The Irish Republic, Irish Press, 1951, p. 705.

77. See CO 739, 14, 15, 16 and CO 906/23, PRO, London.

78. CAB 739.16, PRO, London.

79. SPO, AUTHOR.

80. See D.H. Akenson, The U.S. and Ireland, Harvard UP, 1973, and by the same author, Education and Enmity: The Control of Schooling in Northern Ireland, Institute of Irish Studies, 1973.

81. Sean Moylan, Dail Debates, 28/4/22.

82. Ibid.

83. Correspondence in CO 739/16, PRO, London.

84. Available SPO, AUTHOR.

85. Ibid.

86. McCorley interview, O'Malley Notebooks on Northern campaign, UCD, Nos. 176 and 30.

87. Described to the author by an eyewitness, while researching The I.R.A.

88. Ricardo to Tallents, PRO, CO 906/27.

89. PG, 23, 24/5/22.

90. House of Commons, 26/6/22, Hansard.

91. Wilson Diaries, 10/5/22.

92. CO 739/16.

93. CAB 21/254. PRO, London.

94. Collins to Churchill, 6/6/22, telegrams nos 72, 75, AUTHOR.

95. See Jones, pp. 195, 198, 206 and 211.

96. Churchill to Cope for Collins, 7/6/22. AUTHOR.

97. Collins to Churchill, 8/6/22, ibid.

98. Minute No. 31, 9/6/22.

99. Collins to Griffith, 9/6/22, AUTHOR.

100. Morning Post, 12/6/22.

101. Churchill to House of Commons, 26/6/22.

102. These included Asquith, Londonderry, Selbourne, Salisbury, Carson, Erskine, Stanhope and Sumner, PRONI, Londonderry.

NOTES **447**

103. Wilson Diaries, 14/1/22.
104. Speech to Die-hards at Caxton Hall, 9/5/22.
105. CO 906/25, PRO, London.
106. Geoffrey Shakespeare, *Let Candles Be Brought In*, Macdonald, 1949.
107. CAB 16/42. PRO, London.
108. Michael Farrell, p. 139.
109. Churchill to Craig, CO 906/29, PRO, London.
110. Dawson Bates to Belfast Conciliation Committee, 13/4/22, CO 906/23, *ibid.*
111. Dawson Bates to Craig, 15/6/22, CO 906/29, *ibid.*
112. Tallents to Masterson Smith, 4/7/22, CO 906/30, *ibid.*
113. Tallents Report, 6/7/22, CO 906/30, *ibid.*
114. Tallents Report, p. 2.
115. Spender to Tallents, CO 906/24, PRO, London.
116. Solly-Flood to Secretary, Minister for Home Affairs, 27/6/22, CO 906/23, *ibid.*
117. Spender to Tallents, 29/6/22, *ibid.*
118. Tallents to Masterson Smith, 4/7/22, CO 906/30, *ibid*, p. 4.
119. 18/7/22, CO 739/16, *ibid.*
120. The Cushendall affair is documented at some length in Farrell, pp, 162–3.
121. O'Malley Notebooks, UCD, pp. 171 and 31.
122. *Ibid.*
123. Tobin to O'Malley, Notebooks 17b and 94, UCD.
124. CAB 21/255, PRO, London.
125. Original in S1570, SPO.
126. CAB 21/255, PRO, London.
127. AUTHOR.
128. Gen. Sir Nevil Macready, *Annals of An Active Life*, Hutchinson, 1924, Vol. II, p. 652.
129. Quoted by Macardle, p. 740.
130. Dunne subsequently wrote accounts of the beatings meted out to himself and Sullivan, which together with other details of the Wilson shooting and its aftermath, were later collected by Florrie O'Donoghue. *See* index to the O'Donoghue Collection, NL, and in particular, MS 31, 256.
131. Tobin to O'Malley, O'Malley Notebooks 17b and 94, UCD.
132. Sweeney to O'Malley, *ibid.*
133. P.A. Murray to O'Malley, *ibid.*
134. Collins to O'Sullivan, 7/8/22, SI 570, SPO.
135. Collins to Cosgrave, 6/8/22, SI 570. PRO, Dublin.
136. Printed in Raymond P. Watson, 'Newry's Struggle', Cath Saoirse an Iuir, n.d. p. 62.
137. AUTHOR.
138. Collins to Griffith, 11/6/22, Kennedy pps, UCD, p. 237.
139. (ed.) Lyons, F. S., *Bank of Ireland Centenary Essays*, Gill & Macmillan, 1983, p. 70.
140. 6/7/22, quoted from *Bank of Ireland Centenary Essays*, p. 72.
141. O'Donoghue pps, NL, MS No. 31, 223.
142. Related to author by Michael Collins, Collins' nephew, as told to him by MacEoin.
143. Actual letter in possession of Kevin O'Sheil's daughter, Mrs Eda Segarra.
144. Collins to Churchill, CO 906/31, PRO, London.

145. Cope to Masterson Smith, *ibid.*
146. Report to CoS of situation in No.1 (Belfast) Brigade, 20/7/2, by Seamus Woods, O.C. 3rd Northern Division, Mulcahy pps, UCD.
147. Statistics quoted by Macardle p. 730.
148. Woods to Mulcahy, 2/10/22, Mulcahy pps, UCD, AUTHOR
149. Mulcahy pps, UCD.
150. Teachers' payment references taken from Department of Finance files Nos 76/53, 118/19 and 150, PRO, Dublin.
151. O'Shiel's comments in a memo he circulated to the Cabinet on 6/10/22, Kennedy pps, UCD, p. 4/V/1.
152. PG, No. 78, 1/8/22.
153. Piaras Beaslai, *Michael Collins and the Making of a New Ireland*, Phoenix, 1926, Vol. 1, p. 211.
154. PG 94, 19/8/22.

Chapter 12 (pp. 386–415)

1. *Irish Independent*, 29/6/22.
2. Uinseann MacEoin (ed.), *Survivors*, Argenta Press, 1980, reprinted 1987, p. 406.
3. C.S. Andrews, *Dublin Made Me*, Mercier Press, 1979, p. 234.
4. Some accounts say that he had a Thompson sub-machine gun; that he pushed away a St John's Ambulance officer, Col A. J. MacCarthy, who was attempting to get him to surrender, threatening him with a weapon. However, all accounts agree that he advanced on a heavily armed position with the obvious intent of going down fighting.
5. Kiernan to Collins, 15/7/22, *In Great Haste* (ed.) Leon O'Broin, Gill & Macmillan, 1983, p. 198.
6. Collins to Boland, 28/7/22, quoted by Rex Taylor, *Michael Collins*, Four Square, 1961, p. 194.
7. Kiernan to Collins, 28/4/22, *In Great Haste*, p. 169.
8. Boland to Wyse Power, 29/7/22, Mulcahy pps, UCD.
9. Taylor, p.195.
10. Like Brugha, accounts of his shooting vary. Anna Kelly, *Irish Press*, 1/8/38, said that he moved towards his bedroom door, saying 'I want to see your officer', a gun went off and he was shot in the stomach.
11. Collins to Director of Intelligence, 31/7/22, SPO.
12. Taylor, p. 195.
13. Margery Forester, *Michael Collins: The Lost Leader*, Sphere, 1972, p. 329.
14. Collins to Kiernan, quoted by Forester, p. 329.
15. John Feehan, *The Irish Press*, 18/10/82, p. 3.
16. MacEoin, p. 409.
17. *Irish Press*, 18/10/82.
18. Feehan, *The Shooting of Michael Collins*, Royal Carberry Books, 1988, p. 84.
19. MacDunphy, 2/9/36, SPO, 5.3708.
20. T.P. O'Neill quoting Gallagher to author.
21. Confidential source.
22. A list of these is given in Sean O'Mahony's *Frongoch: University of Revolution*, FDR, 1987, p. 219.
23. O'Neill to author.

24. PG Decision, 12/7/22, PG 57.
25. AUTHOR'S.
26. PG 58, No. SI. 318, SPO.
27. MacDunphy memo 1/10/22, SPO.
28. Mulcahy pps, UCD, contain an alarmed memo from Mulcahy to Collins about 'irregularities' in the mess accounts of Tobin and Cullen.
29. Mulcahy pps, UCD, contain several references to Mulcahy's difficulties with O'Higgins over the Army.
30. S. 03/09/22, SPO.
31. Cosgrave to Collins, 14/7/22 SPO.
32. Collins to Cosgrave, 15/7/22 SPO.
33. Cosgrave to Collins, S. 1336/22, SPO.
34. Ibid, S. 1376/22.
35. Collins to Fitzgerald, 12/7/22, Fitzgerald pps, UCD.
36. Pat Collins to author.
37. Collins to London contact, quoted by Piaras Beaslai, Michael Collins and the Making of a New Ireland, Phoenix, 1926, Vol. 11, p. 422.
38. Collins to each minister, Provisional Government, SPO.
39. The writer, Maurice Hennessy, vouches for the story, which was told to him by Hannan Swaffer, the journalist, a friend of Lawrence's who was present when Collins made the offer.
40. Lawrence was the illegitimate son of Sir Thomas Chapman and Sarah Turner, who took the name Lawrence when she became Chapman's housekeeper. The couple left Ireland after she became his mistress.
41. Collins was in Ireland that day for crucial discussions on the British Treaty proposals. Thomas, who contributed an important article on the Collins/Lawrence connection to the Irish Historical Review, spring 1985, published by the Michael Collins Association, says their first meeting occurred on this day. However, Collins' secret activities lend themselves to many such discrepancies, and the rest of the article is both illuminating and interesting in its own right.
42. MacPartland, Mulcahy pps, UCD.
43. Mulcahy pps, UCD.
44. Ibid, quoted Michael Hopkinson, Green Against Green, Gill & Macmillan, 1988, p. 91.
45. In Great Haste, p. 213.
46. Collins to Director of Intelligence, 9/8/22, SPO.
47. Collins' recommendation on setting up a commission on Army pay, 10/8/22, Mulcahy pps, UCD.
48. Collins to Director of Intelligence, 7/8/22, Mulcahy pps, UCD.
49. Quoted by O'Broin, In Great Haste, p. 90.
50. Quoted by J.B. Lyons, in Oliver St John Gogarty, Blackwater Press, 1980, p. 124.
51. Various writers have suggested both. Forester refers several times, as does Frank O'Connor, The Big Fellow, Corgi, 1969, to his suffering acutely from stomach pains. Eileen O'Donovan also told me he had severe stomach trouble.
52. Forester, p. 331.
53. To name but one example of conflicting reports, John Lavery has Hazel sitting in front of a window to shield Collins from the sniper in a Dun Laoghaire Hotel, rather than in Furry Park. O'Connor has him going to bed at 7.30 pm on his last night in Dublin, without going to dinner in either Clontarf or Dun Laoghaire, and John A. English gave a convincing account of meeting him at a dance in Cruise's Hotel in Limerick that night to the Limerick Weekly Echo on 26/8/72.
54. Forester, p. 333.
55. Hopkinson, p. 76.
56. Quoted by O'Connor, p. 211.
57. Ibid.
58. Col Charlie Russell, an ex-member of the Squad, told Hales about the gun incident. Hales repeated it to Liam O'Donnachadha.
59. O'Connor, p. 211.
60. MacEoin, p. 99.
61. Confidential source.
62. NL, MS 22, 77. Leon O'Broin favours this version, p.141.
63. Forester, p. 334.
64. Limerick Weekly Echo, 26/8/72.
65. Told to author by Lt Gen Collins-Powell (nephew).
66. Dick Hogan, 13/5/88, Irish Times.
67. Collins family anecdote.
68. Again, a Sean MacBride-sponsored theory.
69. Leon O'Broin, No Man's Man, Institute of Public Administration, 1982, p. 116.
70. Pelly to Collins, 21/8/22, see O'Broin, p. 115.
71. AUTHOR.
72. Brennan pps, NL, quoted by O'Broin, p. 117.
73. O'Broin, p. 119.
74. Original in possession of Michael Collins' nephew, quoted by Forester, p. 334.
75. O'Connor, p. 212.
76. Forester, p. 344.
77. These, based on statements by survivors of the ambush, were exhaustively reviewed for Colm Connolly's film, 'The Shadow of Bael na mBlath', RTE. I have also checked them against newspaper accounts of the time, biographies and discussions with Irish Army experts and works such as Feehan's re-creation of the shooting. MacEoin's hitherto unpublished insights are contained in his papers in the Franciscan Archives, Killiney.
78. On condition that I did not publish its author's name or the full details of the report.
79. John Feehan, p. 50.
80. O'Donoghue to O'Malley, O'Malley Notebooks, UCD.
81. Begley to O'Donoghue, O'Donoghue's notes, AUTHOR'S.
82. Garda Hickey, a member of the newly formed Garda Siochana, or police force, was one of a three-man team which was assigned to gather whatever details there were to be had about Collins' last trip. The topic became of life-long interest to him. He was stationed for years in Crookstown and knew Canon Tracey well. When he had retired from the force, Hickey, a major proponent of the Tracey peace visit story, gave his version of the day's happenings to the Limerick Weekly Echo, in a series of articles, 26/8/72 – 16/9/72.
83. Feehan, p. 114.

84. Feehan, p. 86.
85. Hickey's account, *Limerick Weekly Echo*.
86. Flynn's account, supplied to the author by a confidential source, 26/3/90.
87. On this point, however, Dr T.P. O'Neill assures me that in later life de Valera used to say that no such meeting was arranged. 'Collins was a realist. He'd go where the power was. He knew I had no power at that stage', was the burden of his comment.
88. *Sunday Independent*, 23/8/22.
89. Confidential source.
90. Account given to author by Liam O'Donnachadha.
91. Hickey's account, *Limerick Weekly Echo*.
92. In series of interviews with Raymond Smith and Jim Nicholl, in the *Irish Independent*, 1971.
93. Feehan, p. 56.
94. Edward O'Mahony, a native of the district, wrote an authoritative account of the day of Collins' death in *Magill* magazine, May 1989.
95. Hickey's account, *Limerick Weekly Echo*.
96. Liam O'Donnachadha to author.
97. One writer, O'Mahony, says seven. The number given by a survivor, Tom Kelliher, who accompanied Eamonn de Barra on a tour of the area, 20/9/70 says six. De Barra took down an account of the ambush from him, which he gave to Liam O'Donnachadha, who knew Kelliner well, and accepted his figure.
98. Liam Deasy in *Brother Against Brother*, Mercier Press, 1982, p. 78, says Hales accompanied him back to the pub. I am using the version given by Hales to O'Donnachadha.
99. Dalton's descriptions are taken from the official report he made to the Government, quoted by Beaslai and other biographers.
100. There are conflicting reports on this. Liam O'Donnachadha told me Collins was quoted as saying 'blasht yiz, don't you think we have enough trouble as we are,' when six would-be Garda recruits presented themselves, looking for a lift on their way to Dublin. Other accounts say they were the Mayo men already mentioned. Dalton's account of the last trip does not mention them at all. I have been reliably informed that extra passengers, from whatever county, were present on the return journey.
101. Fr Twohig, a local historian, of Mallow, County Cork, was told the identity of the man who is thought to have killed Collins from amongst that group by a penitent (*Sunday Press* 23/8/87) Robert O'Doherty, who went to live in Florida.
102. O'Malley pps. UCD. The re-creation in the Colm Connolly documentary, based in part on Dalton's information, also shows him being shot standing up.
103. Collins' cap was found the following day, washed, and buried in a biscuit tin in a local farm yard. The farmer, who was worried about the possibility of any human particles being buried in unconsecrated ground, because they might attract ghosts, mentioned its presence to a priest, who visited the house a little later on a 'station', the country custom whereby Mass is said in a house. The priest then took the tin either to pass it on in strict confidence to the authorities or otherwise dispose of it as he saw fit. The uniform Collins was wearing was later taken to Argentina by a doctor from the hospital his body was first brought to, Shanakiel, in County Cork. The story of the cap was given to Liam O'Donnachadha by Tom Hales. O'Donnachadha pointed out to the author the farm where the cap was buried.
104. Dalton to MacCartaigh, *Sunday Independent*, 23/8/70.
105. Undated letter, Collins pps, AUTHOR.
106. *Sunday Independent*, 23/8/70.
107. Garda Hickey to Frank Hamilton, *Limerick Weekly Echo*, 26/8/72, and to Martin Brennan, *Evening Herald*, 12/9/70, quoted by Fr Anthony Gaughan, 'Letters to Editor', *Irish National Daily*, January and February 1990.
108. MacCartaigh, *Sunday Independent*, 23/8/70.
109. Feehan, p. 96.
110. *Ibid.*
111. *Sunday Independent*, 25/8/46.
112. O'Connor, p. 213.

Chapter 13 (pp. 416–432)

1. McPeake interviews, *Sunday Independent*, 1971.
2. This is not necessarily sinister; the Secret Service fund is a time-honoured method of coping with embarrassing government expenditures.
3. Micheal O'Cuinnegain, *Partition, from Michael Collins to Bobby Sands*, O'Cuinnegain, 1986.
4. John Feehan, *The Shooting of Michael Collins*, Royal Carberry Books, 1988, p. 112. An abstract of the tape-recorded discussion may be studied in Sean MacEoin's papers in the Franciscan Archives, Killiney. MacEoin tried to copy the McGarry tape, but the experiment was not a success. The whereabouts of the master tape is not known.
5. AUTHOR. Original, dated 27/1/23, held by Eamonn de Barra.
6. Confidential source.
7. PG 41, SPO.
8. Conversations with author in course of writing.
9. Confidential sources.
10. Description given by Nancy Collins to Liam O'Donnachadha, notes, made over a period of twenty years, AUTHOR.
11. *Ibid.*
12. Michael Collins (nephew) to author.
13. Johnny was nicknamed Shafter after making a winning throw in a weight-throwing competition at a local sports contest. Delightedly he had exclaimed, 'I'm a better weight-thrower than Shafter'. Shafter was, at the time, a world shot-putting champion.
14. Written not long before Devlin's own death from cancer on the eve of Collins' anniversary, 21/8/59.
15. Michael Collins (nephew) to author.
16. Collated after his death and published in 1922 by Talbot Press under the title of *The Path to Freedom*.
17. The phrase was first used by Lord Northcliffe in a speech in London on St Patrick's Day, 1917.
18. Fitzgerald pps, UCD.

19. In the Tan War (June 1920 – Truce, July 1921) 405 police and 150 military killed, 682 police and 345 military wounded. Official Irish civilian deaths are c. 150, but estimates vary between British and Irish sources, Overall a figure of 750, including Volunteers, is accepted by Irish historians such as Macardle, and probably between 800 and 1,000 wounded, but many Volunteer casualties were never reported.

20. Leon O'Broin, No Man's Man, Institute of Public Administration, n.d., p. 118.

21. Official statistics, published Irish Times 8/3/90, put the unemployment total at 220,000, and emigration running as high as 50,000 annually.

22. Correspondence in Department of Finance files, to inspect which I had first to sign the Official Secrets Act.

23. O'Muirthle memoir, Mulcahy pps, UCD.

24. A man called Philips, who gave the story to Col Pat Collins (nephew) towards the end of his life while a patient in the Meath Hospital, Dublin, Related to author, 21/10/89.

25. Account given by Ms A. Brennan, Rosscarbery, in letter to Mr Liam Collins, 1/5/22, AUTHOR. Ms Brennan also says that a son of the O'Sullivan family was told to leave the house and not to come back after he had burst in excitedly to announce 'we shot Mickeen'.

26. Michael Hopkinson, Green Against Green, Gill & Macmillan, 1988, p. 230.

27. Originals of both letters in the possession of Mr Eamonn de Barra.

28. On a visit to the Carmelite Convent in Dublin, of which Sister Margaret Mary is a member.

29. The account is given as it was told to me by Mr Michael Collins (nephew).

30. Correspondence in the Department of Finance files.

31. Johnny Collins to Frank Aiken, 13/2/35, AUTHOR's. Original in Department of Finance archives.

32. Ibid, 22/12,38.

33. M.J. Beary to Secretary D.C. Committee, 4/2/39. AUTHOR. Original in Department of Defence Archives.

34. Johnny and his sisters paid for the cross. Margaret and P.J. O'Driscoll, the sister and brother-in-law with whom he lived in Clonakilty are buried a few metres away.

35. Department of Foreign Affairs source.

36. Told to author by Michael Collins (nephew).

NOTE

The little boy smiling after Collins in the picture on the back cover of this book provided one of the few living links with Collins as the book was being written. Alphonsus Culliton was then fourteen. He had been brought to Collins' attention after being taken to Portobello Barracks in Dublin, having been caught up in a civil war shoot-out between Free State troops and Irregulars in New Ross, County Wexford.

When Collins discovered that Alphonsus had run away from a violent, drunken home in Liverpool, he falsified his age as sixteen so that the lad could join the Army. Collins left written instructions that in the event of anything happening to him the lad was to be brought up by Tom Keogh, a former Squad member of Collins' elite hit-team, the 'Squad'.

On the day the picture was taken, Collins was in a grim mood, striding past his protegé as he returned from a Requiem Mass for a party of his soldiers killed in a civil war engagement in Kerry. Keogh too was fighting for his life in a Limerick hospital, after being blown up by a landmine. Two weeks after the picture was taken, Alphonsus, disobeying orders, ran away again – this time to Limerick where he visited the hospital to inform Keogh that Collins himself had been killed in an ambush. Keogh died shortly afterwards and the use of landmines subsequently led some of his surviving Squad comrades to participate in some of the worst atrocities of the civil war. In Kerry captured Irregulars were tied together and forced to dismantle mined barricades.

Deprived of both his protectors, Alphonsus was brought up in the Army, and, like Collins himself, began his working career in the post office. He later emigrated to America. After his wife's death he returned to Ireland and lived in a retirement home.

Appendix

ARTICLES OF AGREEMENT AS SIGNED

on December 6th, 1921

1. Ireland shall have the same constitutional status in the Community of Nations known as the British Empire as the Dominion of Canada, the Commonwealth of Australia, the Dominion of New Zealand, and the Union of South Africa, with a Parliament having powers to make laws for the peace, order and good government of Ireland and an Executive responsible to that Parliament, and shall be styled and known as the Irish Free State.

2. Subject to the provisions hereinafter set out the position of the Irish Free State in relation to the Imperial Parliament and Government and otherwise shall be that of the Dominion of Canada, and the law, practice and constitutional usage governing the relationship of the Crown or the representative of the Crown and of the Imperial Parliament to the Dominion of Canada shall govern their relationship to the Irish Free State.

3. The representative of the Crown in Ireland shall be appointed in like manner as the Governor-General of Canada and in accordance with the practice observed in the making of such appointments.

4. The oath to be taken by Members of the Parliament of the Irish Free State shall be in the following form:

I . . . . do solemnly swear true faith and allegiance to the constitution of the Irish Free State as by law established and that I will be faithful to H.M. King George V, his heirs and successors by law, in virtue of the common citizenship of Ireland with Great Britain and her adherence to and membership of the group of nations forming the British Commonwealth of Nations.

5. The Irish Free State shall assume liability for the service of the Public Debt of the United Kingdom as existing at the date hereof and towards the payment of war pensions as existing at that date in such proportion as may be fair and equitable, having regard to any just claims on the part of Ireland by way set-off or counter-claim, the amount of such sums being determined in default of agreement by the arbitration of one or more independent persons being citizens or the British Empire.

6. Until an arrangement has been made between the British and Irish Governments whereby the Irish Free State undertakes her own coastal defence, the defence by sea of Great Britain and Ireland shall be undertaken by His Majesty's Imperial Forces. But this shall not prevent the construction or maintenance by the Government of the Irish Free State of such vessels as are necessary for the protection of the Revenue of the Fisheries.

The foregoing provisions of this Article shall be reviewed at a Conference of Representatives of the British and Irish Governments to be held at the expiration of five years from the date hereof with a view to the undertaking by Ireland of a share in her own coastal defence.

7. The Government of the Irish Free State shall afford to His Majesty's Imperial Forces:

(a) In time of peace such harbour and other facilities as are indicated in the Annex hereto, or such other facilities as may from time to time be agreed between the British Government and the Government of the Irish Free State; and

(b) In time of war or of strained relations with a Foreign Power such harbour and other facilities as the British Goverment may require for the purposes of such defence as aforesaid.

8. With a view to securing the observance of the principle of inter-national limitation of armaments, if the Government of the Irish Free State establishes and maintains a military defence force, the establishments thereof shall not exceed in size such proportion of the military establishments maintained in Great Britain as that which the population of Ireland bears to the population of Great Britain.

9. The ports of Great Britain and the Irish Free State shall be freely open to the ships of the other country on payment of the customary port and other dues.

10. The Government of the Irish Free State agrees to pay fair compensation on terms not less favourable than those accorded by the Act of 1920 to judges, officials, members of Police Forces and other Public Servants who are discharged by it or who retire in consequence of the change of Government effected in pursuance hereof.

Provided that this agreement shall not apply to members of the Auxiliary Police Force or to persons recruited in Great Britain for the Royal Irish Constabulary during the two years next preceding the date hereof. The British Government will assume responsibility for such compensation or pensions as may be payable to any of these excepted persons.

11. Until the expiration of one month from the passing of the Act of Parliament for the ratification of this instrument, the powers of the Parliament and the Government of the Irish Free State shall not be exercisable as respects Northern Ireland and the provisions of the Government of Ireland Act, 1920, shall so far as they relate to Northern Ireland remain of full force and effect, and no election shall be held for the return of members to serve in the Parliament of the Irish Free State for constituencies in Northern Ireland, unless a resolution is passed by both Houses of the Parliament of Northern Ireland in favour of the holding of such election before the end of the said month.

12. If before the expiration of the said month, an address is presented to His Majesty by both Houses of the Parliament of Northern Ireland to that effect, the powers of the Parliament and Government of the Irish Free State shall no longer extend to Northern Ireland, and the provisions of the Government of Ireland Act, 1920 (including those relating to the Council of Ireland) shall, so far as they relate to Northern Ireland, continue to be of full force and effect, and this instrument shall have effect subject to the necessary modifications.

Provided that if such an address is so presented a Commission consisting of three persons, one to be appointed by the Government of the Irish Free State, one to be appointed by the Government of Northern Ireland and one who shall be Chairman to be appointed by the British Government shall determine in accordance with the wishes of the inhabitants, so far as may be compatible with economic and geographic conditions, the boundaries between Northern Ireland and the rest of Ireland, and for the purposes of the Government of Ireland Act, 1920, and of this instrument, the boundary of Northern Ireland shall be such as may be determined by such Commission.

13. For the purpose of the last foregoing article, the powers of the Parliament of Southern Ireland under the Government of Ireland Act, 1920, to elect members of the Council of Ireland shall after the Parliament of the Irish Free State is constituted be exercised by that Parliament.

14. After the expiration of the said month, if no such address as is mentioned in Article 12 hereof is presented, the Parliament and Government of Northern Ireland shall continue to exercise as respects Northern Ireland the powers conferred on them by the Government of Ireland Act, 1920, but the Parliament and Government of the Irish Free State shall in Northern Ireland have in relation to matters in respect of which the Parliament of Northern Ireland has not power to make laws under that Act (including matters which under the said Act are within the jurisdiction of the Council of Ireland) the same powers as in the rest of Ireland, subject to such other provisions as may be agreed in manner hereinafter appearing.

15. At any time after the date hereof the Government of Northern Ireland and the provisional Government of Southern Ireland hereinafter constituted may meet for the purpose of discussing the provisions subject to which the last foregoing article is to operate in the event of no such address as is therein mentioned being presented and those provisions may include:

(a) Safeguards with regard to patronage in Northern Ireland:
(b) Safeguards with regard to the collection of revenue in Northern Ireland:
(c) Safeguards with regard to import and export duties affecting the trade or industry of Northern Ireland:
(d) Safeguards for minorities in Northern Ireland:
(e) The settlement of the financial relations between Northern Ireland and the Irish Free State:
(f) The establishment and powers of a local militia in Northern Ireland and the relation of the Defence Forces of the Irish Free State and of Northern Ireland respectively:

and if at any such meeting provisions are agreed to, the same shall have effect as if they were included amongst the provisions subject to which the Powers of the Parliament and Government of the Irish Free State are to be exercisable in Northern Ireland under Article 14 hereof.

16. Neither the Parliament of the Irish Free State nor the Parliament of Northern Ireland shall make any law so as either directly or indirectly to endow any religion or prohibit or restrict the free exercise thereof or give any preference or impose any disability on account of religious belief or religious status or affect prejudicially the right of any child to attend a school receiving public money without attending the religious instruction at the school or make any discrimination as respects state aid between schools under the management of different religious denominations or divert from any religious denomination or any educational institution any of its property except for public utility purposes and on payment of compensation.

17. By way of provisional arrangement for the administration of Southern Ireland during the interval which must elapse between the date hereof and the constitution of a Parliament and Government of the Irish Free State in accordance therewith, steps shall be taken forthwith for summoning a meeting of members of Parliament elected for constituencies in Southern Ireland since the passing of the Government of Ireland Act, 1920, and for constituting a provisional Government, and the British Government shall take the steps necessary to transfer to such provisional Government the powers and machinery requisite for the discharge of its duties, provided that every member of such provisional Government shall have signified in writing his or her acceptance of this instrument. But this arrangement shall not continue in force beyond the expiration of twelve months from the date hereof.

18. This instrument shall be submitted forthwith by His Majesty's Government for the approval of Parliament and by the Irish signatories to a meeting summoned for the purpose of the members elected to sit in the House of Commons of Southern Ireland, and if approved shall be ratified by the necessary legislation.

<table>
<tr><td>On behalf of the British
Delegation.
Signed</td><td>On behalf of the Irish
Delegation.
Signed</td></tr>
<tr><td>D. LLOYD GEORGE.
AUSTEN CHAMBERLAIN.
BIRKENHEAD.
WINSTON S. CHURCHILL.
L. WORTHINGTON-EVANS.
HAMAR GREENWOOD.
GORDON HEWART.</td><td>ART Ó GRÍOBHTHA (ARTHUR GRIFFITH).
MICHEÁL Ó COILEÁIN.
RIOBÁRD BARTÚN.
EUDHMONN S. Ó DÚGÁIN.
SEÓRSA GHABHÁIN UÍ DHUBHTHAIGH.
December 6th, 1921</td></tr>
</table>

ANNEX

1. The following are the specific facilities required:

Dockyard Port at Berehaven

(a) Admiralty property and rights to be retained as at the rate hereof. Harbour defences to remain in charge of British care and maintenance parties.

Queenstown

(b) Harbour defences to remain in charge of British care and maintenance parties. Certain mooring buoys to be retained for use of His Majesty's ships.

Belfast Lough

(c) Harbour defences to remain in charge of British care and maintenance parties.

Lough Swilly

(d) Harbour defences to remain in charge of British care and maintenance parties.

Aviation

(e) Facilities in the neighbourhood of the above Ports for coastal defence by air.

Oil Fuel Storage

(f) Haulbowline   To be offered for sale to commercial companies under
       and   guarantee that purchasers shall maintain a certain
    Rathmullen   minimum stock for Admiralty purposes.

2. A Convention shall be made between the British Government and the Government of the Irish Free State to give effect to the following conditions:

(a) That submarine cables shall not be landed or wireless stations for communications with places outside Ireland be established except by agreement with the British Government; that the existing cable landing rights and wireless concessions shall not be withdrawn except by agreement with the British Government; and that the British Government shall be entitled to land additional submarine cables or establish additional wireless stations for communication with places outside Ireland.

(b) That lighthouses, buoys, beacons, and any navigational marks or navigational aids shall be maintained by the Government of the Irish Free State as at the date hereof and shall not be removed or added to except by agreement with the British Government.

(c) That war signal stations shall be closed down and left in charge of care and maintenance parties, the Government of the Irish Free State being offered the option of taking them over and working them for commercial purposes subject to Admiralty inspection, and guaranteeing the upkeep of existing telegraphic communication therewith.

3. A Convention shall be made between the same Governments for the regulation of Civil Communication by Air.

			A. G.
D. LL. G.	B.	W. S. C.	M. O C.
A. C.		E. S. O. D.	R. B.
			S. G. D.

DOCUMENT NUMBER TWO

The Counter-proposal drafted by de Valera.

'That inasmuch as the "Articles of Agreement for a treaty between Great Britain and Ireland", signed in London on December 6th, 1921, do not reconcile Irish National aspirations and the Association of Ireland with the Community of Nations known as the British Commonwealth, and cannot be the basis of an enduring peace between the Irish and the British peoples, DAIL EIREANN, in the name of the Sovereign Irish Nation, makes to the Government of Great Britain, to the Government of the other States of the British Commonwealth, and to the peoples of Great Britain and of these several States, the following Proposal for a Treaty of Amity and Association which, DAIL EIREANN is convinced, could be entered into by the Irish people with the sincerity of goodwill':

Proposed Treaty of Association Between
Ireland and the British Commonwealth

In order to bring to an end the long and ruinous conflict between Great Britain and Ireland by a sure and lasting peace honourable to both nations, it is agreed

Status of Ireland.

1. That the legislative, executive, and judicial authority of Ireland shall be derived solely from the people of Ireland.

Terms of Association

2. That, for purposes of common concern, Ireland shall be associated with the States of the British Commonwealth, viz: —The Kingdom of Great Britain, the Dominion of Canada, the Commonwealth of Australia, the Dominion of New Zealand, and the Union of South Africa.

3. That when acting as an associate the rights, status, and privileges of Ireland shall be in no respect less than those enjoyed by any of the component States of the British Commonwealth.

4. That the matters of 'common concern' shall include Defence, Peace and War, Political Treaties, and all matters now treated as of common concern, amongst the States of the British Commonwealth, and that in these matters there shall be between Ireland and the States of the British Commonwealth 'such concerted action founded on consultation as the several Governments may determine.'

5. That in virtue of this association of Ireland with the States of the British Commonwealth, citizens of Ireland in any of these States shall not be subject to any disabilities which a citizen of one of the component States of the British Commonwealth would not be subject to, and reciprocally for citizens of these States in Ireland.

6. That, for purposes of the Association, Ireland shall recognise His Britannic Majesty as head of the Association.

Defence

7. That, so far as her resources permit, Ireland shall provide for her own defence by sea, land and air, and shall repel by force any attempt by a foreign Power to violate the integrity of her soil and territorial waters, or to use them for any purpose hostile to Great Britain and the other associated States.

8. That for five years, pending the establishment of Irish coastal defence forces, or

for such other period as the Governments of the two countries may later agree upon, facilities for the coastal defence of Ireland shall be given to the British Government as follows:–

(a) In time of peace such harbour and other facilities as are indicated in the Annex hereto, or such other facilities as may from time to time be agreed upon between the British Government and the Government of Ireland;

(b) In time of war such harbour and other naval facilities as the British Government may reasonably require for the purposes of such defence as aforesaid.

9. That within five years from the date of exchange of ratifications of this Treaty a Conference between the British and Irish Governments shall be held in order to hand over the coastal defence of Ireland to the Irish Government, unless some other arrangement for naval defence be agreed by both Governments to be desirable in the common interest of Ireland, Great Britain, and the other Associated States.

10. That, in order to co-operate in furthering the principle of international limitation of armaments, the Government of Ireland shall not

(a) Build submarines unless by agreement with Great Britain and the other States of the Commonwealth;

(b) Maintain a military defence force, the establishments whereof exceed in size such proportion of the military establishments maintained in Great Britain as that which the population of Ireland bears to the population of Great Britain.

Miscellaneous

11. That the Governments of Great Britain and of Ireland shall make a convention for the regulation of civil communication by air.

12. That the ports of Great Britain and of Ireland shall be freely open to the ships of each country on payment of the customary port and other dues.

13. That Ireland shall assume liability for such share of the present public debt of Great Britain and Ireland, and of payment of war pensions as existing at this date as may be fair and equitable, having regard to any just claims on the part of Ireland by way of set-off or counter-claim, the amount of such sums being determined in default of agreement, by the arbitration of one or more independent persons, being citizens of Ireland or of the British Commonwealth.

14. That the Government of Ireland agrees to pay compensation on terms not less favourable than those proposed by the British Government of Ireland Act of 1920 to that Government's judges, officials, members of Police Forces and other Public Servants who are discharged by the Government of Ireland, or who retire in consequence of the change of government elected in pursuance hereof:

Provided that this agreement shall not apply to members of the Auxiliary Police Force, or to persons recruited in Great Britain for the Royal Irish Constabulary during the two years next preceding the date hereof. The British Government will assume responsibility for such compensation or pensions as may be payable to any of these excepted persons.

15. That neither the Parliament of Ireland nor any subordinate Legislature in Ireland shall make any law so as either directly or indirectly to endow any religion or prohibit or restrict the free exercise thereof, or give any preference or impose any disability on account of religious belief or religious status, or affect prejudicially the right of any child to attend a school receiving public money without attending a religious instruction at the school, or make any discrimination as respects State aid between schools under the management of different religious denominations, or divert from

any religious denomination or any educational institution any of its property except for public utility purposes and on payment of compensation.

Transitional

16. That by way of transitional arrangement for the Administration of Ireland during the interval which must elapse between the date hereof and the setting up of a Parliament and Government of Ireland in accordance herewith, the members elected for constituencies in Ireland since the passing of the British Government of Ireland Act in 1920 shall, at a meeting summoned for the purpose, elect a transitional Government to which the British Government and Dáil Eireann shall transfer the authority, powers, and machinery requisite for the discharge of its duties, provided that every member of such transition Government shall have signified in writing his or her acceptance of this instrument. But this arrangement shall not continue in force beyond the expiration of twelve months from the date hereof.

Ratification

17. That this instrument shall be submitted for ratification forthwith by His Britannic Majesty's Government to the Parliament at Westminster, and by the Cabinet of Dáil Eireann to a meeting of the members elected for the constituencies in Ireland set forth in the British Government of Ireland Act, 1920, and when ratifications have been exchanged shall take immediate effect.

ANNEX

1. The following are the specific facilities referred to in Article 8 (a):

Dockyard Port at Berehaven

(a) British Admiralty property and rights to be retained as at the date hereof. Harbour defences to remain in charge of British care and maintenance parties.

Queenstown

(b) Harbour defences to remain in charge of British care and maintenance parties. Certain mooring buoys to be retained for use of His Britannic Majesty's ships.

Belfast Lough

(c) Harbour defences to remain in charge of British care and maintenance parties.

Lough Swilly

(d) Harbour defences to remain in charge of British care and maintenance parties.

Aviation

(e) Facilities in the neighbourhood of the above Ports for coastal defence by air.

Oil Fuel Storage

(f) Haulbowline and Rathmullen   To be offered for sale to commercial companies under guarantee that purchasers shall maintain a certain minimum stock for British Admiralty purposes.

2. A Convention covering a period of five years shall be made between the British and Irish Governments to give effect to the following conditions:

(a) That submarine cables shall not be landed or wireless stations for communications with places outside Ireland be established except by agreement with the British Government; that the existing cable landing rights and wireless concessions shall not be withdrawn except by agreement with the British Government; and that the British Government shall be entitled to land additional submarine cables or establish additional wireless stations for communication with places outside Ireland.

(b) That lighthouses, buoys, beacons, and any navigational marks or navigational aids shall be maintained by the Government of Ireland as at the date hereof and shall not be removed or added to except by agreement with the British Government.

(c) That war signal stations shall be closed down and left in charge of care and maintenance parties, the Government of Ireland being offered the option of taking them over and working them for commercial purposes subject to British Admiralty inspection and guaranteeing the upkeep of existing telegraphic communication therewith.

(The following addendum concerning N.E. Ulster was to be proposed as a separate resolution by the President.)

ADDENDUM

NORTH-EAST ULSTER

Resolved:

That, whilst refusing to admit the right of any part of Ireland to be excluded from the supreme authority of the Parliament of Ireland, or that the relations between the Parliament of Ireland and any subordinate Legislature in Ireland can be a matter for treaty with a government outside Ireland, nevertheless, in sincere regard for internal peace, and in order to make manifest our desire not to bring force or coercion to bear upon any substantial part of the Province of Ulster, whose inhabitants may now be unwilling to accept the national authority, we are prepared to grant to that portion of Ulster which is defined as Northern Ireland in the British Government of Ireland Act of 1920, privileges and safeguards not less substantial than those provided for in the Articles of Agreement for a Treaty between Great Britain and Ireland signed in London on December 6th, 1921.

Bibliography and Sources

PRIMARY SOURCES

Collins' Diary, and information concerning Collins' career and other matters, from nephew, Mr Michael Collins.

Collins' memorabilia and material concerning Bael na mBlath ambush and aftermath, from nephew, Col Pat Collins.

Collins' papers, from nephew, Mr Liam Collins.

Collins' letters to Donal Hayes (unpublished), from Dr Dermot Keogh.

Collins' letters to Kitty Kiernan (unpublished), from her son, Mr Felix Cronin.

Collins' letters to Susan Killeen, from her daughter, Mrs Maire Mulloy.

Collins/Churchill correspondence, from Professor Edith Sagarra.

Sister Celestine, unpublished memoirs, from Collins family.

Collins-Powell, Mrs Mary, unpublished memoirs, from Collins family.

de Valera, Eamon, letters to Sinead de Valera, from anonymous source.

Foley, Thomas, transcript of interview, conducted by Fr A. O'Driscoll.

IRA and RIC documents concerning liaison activities of Sean Haughey and others in Derry around time of Derry prisoners' escape attempt (2/11/21) in author's possession.

McCoy, John, unpublished memoir; and documents relating to pension claims made under Military Service Pensions Act 1934, from Mr Harold O'Sullivan.

MacKenna Napoli, Kathleen, unpublished memoirs, from Fr P. Brennan.

Tobin, Liam, memoirs, letters and other material, from daughters, Ann Thornton and Marie Tobin.

Documents and reminiscences supplied by Mr Eamonn de Barra.

'Notes' and reminiscences concerning Collins and his associates, compiled by Mr Liam Donnachadcha.

Information and material supplied by Collins' nephew, Col Pat Collins, and by Ms Mary-Clare O'Malley.

Compilation of documents relating to Treaty signing and its aftermath; original drafts of MSS for de Valera biography dealing with de Valera's Irish-American controversies, including correspondence with Harry Boland and Collins; and memoir by Gerry Boland, from Dr T. P. O'Neill.

At some stage the author has interviewed almost all the chief actors in the Irish drama of the years circa 1916–22, and he has amassed a correspondingly large amount of documentation concerning Irish Republican activity which has been drawn on for background information in the present work. Some specific conversations which were particularly helpful include those with figures who have since passed on: Gerry Boland, Michael Brennan, Eamonn Broy, Vivion de Valera, Sean MacBride, Richard Mulcahy, David Neligan, and Peadar O'Donnell. Three survivors, still alive as this was being written, who were particularly illuminating, were Eamonn de Barra, Vinnie Byrne, Sr Margaret Mary and Ms Eileen O'Donovan.

ARCHIVES CONSULTED

ARCHDIOCESAN RECORDS
(Dublin) Archbishop Byrne papers; Archbishop Walsh papers.
(Perth) Archbishop Clune papers.

ARMY ARCHIVES, Cathal Brugha Barracks, Dublin
Originals of Collins military despatches (also available on microfilm, National Gallery of Ireland, pp.911–22) and correspondence with various contacts; miscellaneous material, including Liam Lynch's despatch on Collins' death and some commemorative articles by contemporaries.

DEPARTMENT OF FINANCE, Dublin
Collins' files containing correspondence from Gen. Richard Mulcahy, Joe O'Reilly, Tim Healy and others relating to erection of Collins Memorial and disposal of effects.

DEPARTMENT OF DEFENCE, Dublin
Correspondence between Johnny Collins, Frank Aiken and others relating to Collins Memorial.

DUBLIN UNIVERSITY (TRINITY COLLEGE)
Erskine Childers Diaries and papers; Frank Gallagher papers; Major Sirr papers.

GLASNEVIN CEMETERY, Dublin
Certificate of authorisation for cross on Collins' grave, signed by Eamon de Valera.

GEORGETOWN UNIVERSITY LIBRARY, Washington D.C.
Shane Leslie papers.

H.M. STATIONERY OFFICE, London
Hansard, both for House of Commons and House of Lords throughout period under review, especially for developments such as those in November 1920 (Bloody Sunday and other incidents), the Irish Treaty debates (December 1921– March 1922), and the Beleek/Pettigo and Sir Henry Wilson controversies of June 1922.

IRISH BUREAU OF MILITARY HISTORY
Memoirs of Michael Brennan, Paddy Daly; Joe Dolan; Joe McGuinness; Jim Slattery; Frank Thornton; Liam Tobin.
Catalogue of Events 1898–1921, 3 Vols.

IRISH STATIONERY OFFICE, Dublin
Dail Debates: First Dail 1919–21 (Private sessions); Second Dail 1921–22.
Treaty Debates (Public sessions) 1921–22 and subsequent proceedings of the Dail until June 1922.

KILMAINHAM MUSEUM, Dublin
Collins correspondence.
Material on Lady Lavery and Collins, Kevin O'Higgins, Shane Leslie.

NATIONAL LIBRARY OF IRELAND
Papers of F.S. Bourke; Michael Collins; Frank Gallagher; Thomas Johnson; Sir John and Hazel Lavery; Joe McGarrity; Kathleen Napoli MacKenna; Leon O'Broin; Art O'Brien; William O'Brien; Florrie O'Donoghue; Austin Stack.
RIC records (microfilm).
Mark Sturgis Diary (microfilm).

NATIONAL MUSEUM OF IRELAND
Collins memorabilia, including 'Collins' cap', almost certainly wrongly claimed to be the cap he was wearing at the moment of his fatal wounding.
PUBLIC RECORDS OFFICE, BELFAST
Londonderry papers.
Col Spender material relating to Collins' Northern Ireland Education and Trades Union policy, B-Special activities and other matters.
PUBLIC RECORDS OFFICE, DUBLIN
Robert Barton's expanded 'Notes for a Lecture' and replies to Margery Forester's questionnaire, and other miscellaneous material.
Department of Finance material for 1922.
PUBLIC RECORDS OFFICE, LONDON
Correspondence from figures such as Churchill, Andrew Cope, Lionel Curtis, Tom Jones, Lloyd George, Gen. Macready, Lord Middleton, Mark Sturgis.
STATE PAPER OFFICE OF IRELAND, DUBLIN
Collins papers and correspondence (including 'D' and 'S' series dealing with Provisional Government, Dail Cabinet, and Executive Council material). Proceedings of North Eastern Advisory Committee.
Material relating to police activities in Northern Ireland, to the Derry Prisoners' affair, the condition of nationalists in Northern Ireland, the Collins/Craig pacts. Proceedings of the Catholic Advisory Committee.
Accounts of the Beleek/Pettigo affairs, the Boundary Commission and the Sinn Fein Funds case.
UNIVERSITY COLLEGE DUBLIN
Earnan O'Malley Notebooks and papers.
Papers of Ernest Blythe; Desmond Fitzgerald; Hugh Kennedy; Eoin MacNeill; Richard Mulcahy; Ginger O'Connell.

NEWSPAPERS AND PERIODICALS

Belfast Newsletter; Daily Herald; Evening Herald; Freeman's Journal; Gaelic American; Irish Bulletin; Irish Independent; Irish News; Irish Press; Irish Times; Irish World; Limerick Weekly Echo, Magill Magazine; Manchester Evening Guardian; Morning Post; Northern Whig; Poblacht na hEireann; Sunday Independent; Sunday Press; The Times.

PAMPHLETS AND ARTICLES

AKENSON, D.H. and Fallin, F.P., 'The Irish Civil War and the Drafting of the Irish Constitution', *Eire Ireland*, Irish American Cultural Institute, Minnesota, Vols. I, II, IV, 1970.
BARTON, Robert, 'The Truth about the Treaty', Republican Press, n.d.
BOYCE, D.G., 'British Conservative Opinion, the Ulster Question, and the Partition of Ireland', *Irish Historical Studies*, Vol. XVII, No. 65, 1970-1, pp. 89-112.
BUREAU OF MILITARY HISTORY, *Chronologies*, Dublin, vols I-III.
CARROLL, F.M., 'The American Committee for Relief in Ireland, 1920-1922', *Irish Historical Studies*, Vol. XXIII, No. 89, May 1982.
COLLINS, Michael, 'Arguments for the Treaty', Martin Lester, 1922; 'Free State or Chaos' (Pamphleted version of speech delivered Waterford, 24/2/22).
CURTISS, L.P., 'Anglo-Saxons and Celts', *Studies in British History and Culture*, Connecticut Conference on British Studies, 1968; 'The Anglo-Irish Predicament', *20th-Century British History and Culture*, Ireland, Vol.II, 1970, pp.37-93.
'DALTA', 'National Land Policy', Talbot Press, Dublin, 1920.
DE VALERA, Eamon, 'The Alternative to the Treaty, Document No. 2', Irish Nation Committee, Dublin, 1923.
'The Anglo-Irish Treaty and de Valera's Alternative', Irish Nation Committee, Dublin, 1924.

GALLAGHER, Frank, 'The Partition of Ireland', Gill & Macmillan, Dublin, 1947.
HAYES, Michael, 'Dail Eireann and the Irish Civil War', *Studies*, Dublin, Spring 1969.
MACREADY, Gen. Sir Nevil, 'Churchill and Lloyd George', Dublin, n.d. (probably 1922).
O'BEIRNE, John Ranelagh, 'The I.R.B.: Treaty to 1924', *Irish Historical Studies*, Vol. XX, 1976.
O'HIGGINS, Kevin, 'The New de Valera', Dublin, 1922.
O'MULLANE, Michael, 'Noel Lemass', Joe Clarke, Dublin, n.d.
O'RAHILLY, Alfred, 'The Case for the Treaty', n.d.

TELEVISION DOCUMENTARIES

CONNOLLY, Colum, (dir.), 'The Shadow of Bael na mBlath', Radio Telefis Eireann, 1989.
O'SHANNON, Cathal, (dir.), 'Emmet Dalton', Radio Telefis Eireann, 1978.

SELECT BIBLIOGRAPHY

AKENSON, D.H., *Education and Enmity: the Control of Schooling in Northern Ireland, 1920–50*, Newton Abbot, 1973; *A Mirror to Kathleen's Face*, David & Charles, 1975; *The U.S. and Ireland*, Harvard University Press, 1973.
ANDREWS, C.S. *Dublin Made Me*, Mercier Press, Cork, 1979.
ARTHUR, Sir G., *General Sir George Maxwell*, John Murray, 1932.
ASH, B., *The Lost Dictator*, Cassell, 1968.

BARRY, Tom, *Guerilla Days in Ireland*, Anvil, Tralee, 1962; *The Reality of Anglo-Irish War*, Anvil, Tralee, 1974.
BEASLAI, Piaras, *Michael Collins and the Making of a New Ireland*, 2 Vols, Phoenix, Dublin, 1926.
BEAVERBROOK, Lord (Max Aitken), *Decline and Fall of Lloyd George*, Collins, 1963.
BENNETT, Richard, *The Black and Tans*, New English Library, 1970.
BIRKENHEAD, Earl of, *(F.E.) The life of F.E. Smith: First Earl of Birkenhead*, Eyre & Spottiswoode, 1959.
BOURKE, Marcus, *John O'Leary*, Anvil, Tralee, 1967.
BOWMAN, John, *De Valera and the Ulster Question, 1917–1973*, Oxford University Press, 1982.
BOYCE, D. G., *Englishmen and Irish Troubles*, Cape, 1972; *Nationalism in Ireland*, Gill & Macmillan, Dublin, 1982; *Separatism and Irish Nationalist Tradition*, ed. C.H. Williams, University of Wales Press, 1982.
BOYLE, Andrew, *The Riddle of Erskine Childers*, Hutchinson, 1977.
BREEN, Dan, *My Fight for Irish Freedom*, Talbot Press, 1924, Anvil Books, Tralee, 1964.
BRENNAN, Robert, *Allegiance*, Irish Press, Dublin, 1950.
BROMAGE, Mary C., *de Valera and the March of a Nation*, Hutchinson, 1956; *Churchill and Ireland*, University of Notre Dame Press, Indiana, 1964.
BUCKLAND, P., *Irish Unionism 1, The Anglo-Irish and the New Ireland*, Gill & Macmillan, 1972; *Irish Unionism 11, The Origins of Northern Ireland 1886–1922*, Gill & Macmillan, Dublin, & Barnes and Noble, 1973; *James Craig*, Gill & Macmillan, Dublin, 1980.

CALLWELL, C.E., *Field Marshal Sir Henry Wilson: His Life and Diaries*, 2 Vols, Cassell, 1927.
CARROL, Francis, *American Opinion and the Irish Question*, Gill & Macmillan and St Martin's Press, Dublin, 1978.
CAULFIELD, Max, *The Easter Rebellion*, Frederick Muller, 1964, (paperback) Four Square, 1965.

CHURCHILL, Winston, *Lord Randolph*, Odhams (2 Vols), 1906, and Heinemann, 1 Vol: 1966; *The Aftermath*, Butterworth, 1929.
CLARK, Wallace, 'Guns in Ulster', *Belfast Constabulary Gazette*, 1967.
COLLINS, Michael, *The Path to Freedom*, Talbot Press, Dublin, and T. Fisher Unwin, 1922.
COLUM, Padraig, *Arthur Griffith*, Browne & Nolan, Dublin, 1959.
COOGAN, T.P., *Ireland Since the Rising*, Pall Mall, 1966; *The I.R.A.*, Pall Mall, 1970, and Fontana 1970, new editions 1980 and 1985; *On the Blanket*, Ward River, Dublin, 1980.
CORFE, Tom, *The Phoenix Park Murders*, Hodder & Stoughton, 1968.
COXHEAD, Elizabeth, *Lady Gregory*, Macmillan, 1961.
CRAWFORD, Robert, *Loyal to King Billy*, Gill & Macmillan, Dublin, 1987.
CRONIN, Sean, *Ideology of the I.R.A.*, Ann Arbor University Press, 1972; *The McGarrity Papers*, Anvil, Tralee, 1972; *Washington's Irish Policy, 1916–18*, Anvil, 1987 and Irish Books & Media, Minnesota, 1987.
CROZIER, Brig. F.P., *Impressions and Recollections*, Laurie, 1930; *Ireland for Ever*, Cape, 1932.
CURRAN, Joseph, *The Birth of the Irish Free State, 1921–23.*, Alabama University Press, 1988.

DALTON, Charles, *With the Dublin Brigades 1917–21*, Peter Davies, 1929.
DE BURCA, Padraig and Boyle, John F., *Free State or Republic?*, Talbot Press, Dublin, and T. Fisher Unwin, 1922.
DE VERE WHITE, Terence, *Kevin O'Higgins*, Methuen, 1948.
DONNELLY, J., *Landlord and Tenant in 19th-Century Ireland*, Gill & Macmillan, Dublin, 1973; *19th-Century Land and People of Cork*, Routledge & Kegan Paul, 1975; with S.Clarke, *Irish Peasants*, Manchester University Press, 1983.
DRIBERG, Tom, *Study in Power and Frustration*, Weidenfeld & Nicolson, 1956.
DUDLEY EDWARDS, Ruth, *Patrick Pearse, The Triumph of Failure*, Gill & Macmillan, Dublin, 1981.
DWANE, David T., *Early Life of Eamon de Valera*, Talbot Press, Dublin, and T.Fisher Unwin, 1922.
DWYER, T. Ryle, *Eamon de Valera*, Gill & Macmillan, Dublin, 1980; *Michael Collins and the Treaty*, Mercier Press, Cork, 1981; *de Valera's Darkest Hour, 1919–32*, Mercier Press, Cork, 1982; *Michael Collins: The Man Who Won the War*, Mercier Press Cork, 1990.

ERVINE, St John, *Craigavon, Ulsterman*, Allen & Unwin, 1949.

FANNING, Ronan, *Irish Department of Finance*, Institute of Public Administration, Dublin, 1978; *Independent Ireland*, Helicon, Dublin, 1983.
FARRELL, Michael, *Arming the Protestants*, Brandon, Kerry, and Pluto Press, 1983.
FEEHAN, Sean, *Michael Collins, Murder or Accident*, Mercier Press, Cork, 1981.
FITZPATRICK, David, *Politics and Irish Life 1913–21*, Gill & Macmillan, Dublin, 1977.
FORESTER, Margery, *Michael Collins – The Lost Leader*, Sidgwick & Jackson, 1971, Sphere, 1972.
FOSTER, Roy, *Modern Ireland, 1600–1972*, Allen Lane, 1988, Penguin Paperback, 1989.

GALLAGHER, Frank, *The Indivisible Island*, Gollancz, 1957, *The Anglo-Irish Treaty*, Hutchinson, 1965.
GAUGHAN, Anthony, *Austin Stack*, Kingdom Books, Tralee, 1971; *Constable Mee*, Anvil, Dublin, 1975; *Thomas Johnson*, Anvil, Dublin, 1980.
GEARY, Laurence, *Plan of Campaign*, Cork University Press, 1986.
GILBERT, Martin, *Winston Churchill, Vol. III* 'The Challenge of War 1914–1916', Heinemann 1971; *Companion*, Heinemann, 1977; *World in Torment, W.S.Churchill, 1917–22*, Minerva, 1990.

GLEESON, James, *Bloody Sunday*, Peter Davies, 1962.
GOLDRING, Maurice, *Faith of Our Fathers*, Repsol, Dublin, 1982.
GREAVES, Desmond C., *The Life & Times of James Connolly*, Lawrence & Wishart, 1961; *Liam Mellowes and The Irish Revolution*, Lawrence & Wishart, 1971.
GREELEY, Andrew, *That Most Distressful Nation*, Quadrangle, Chicago, 1972.
GRIFFITH, Kenneth & O'Grady, Timothy, *Curious Journey*, Hutchinson, 1982.
GWYNN, Denis, *De Valera*, Jarrolds, 1933.
GWYNNE, Stephen, *The Life of John Redmond*, Harrap, 1932.

HAMBRO, C.J., *Newspaper Lords in British Politics*, MacDonald, 1958.
HARKNESS, D.W., *The Restless Dominion*, New York University Press, 1970.
HOLT, E., *Protest in Arms, 1916-21*, Putnam, 1960.
HOPKINSON, Michael, *Green against Green*, Gill & Macmillan, Dublin, 1988.
HYDE, Montgomery, *The Londonderrys*, Hamish Hamilton, 1979.

JENKINS, Roy, *Asquith*, Collins, 1965.
JONES, Tom, *Whitehall Diaries*, Vol. III: *Ireland 1918-25*, (ed.) K. Middlemas, Oxford University Press, 1971; *Lloyd George*, Harvard University Press, 1951.

KEE, Robert, *The Green Flag*, Weidenfeld & Nicolson, 1972.
KILFEATHER, T.P., *The Connacht Rangers*, Anvil, Tralee, 1919.
KITSON, Brig. F.E., *Low Intensity Operations*, Faber, 1971.

LAFFAN, Michael, *The Partition of Ireland*, Dundalgan Press, Dundalk, 1983.
LARKIN, Emmet, *James Larkin*, Routledge & Kegan Paul, and MIT Press, Cambridge, Mass., 1965.
LEE, Joseph and O'Tuathaig, Gearoid, 'The Age of de Valera', Ward River and RTE, Dublin, 1982; Lee, Joseph (ed.) *Towards a Sense of Place*, Cork University Press, 1985; Lee, Joseph, *Ireland 1912-1985*, Cambridge University Press, 1989.
LE ROUX, Louis N., *Tom Clarke and The Irish Freedom Movement*, Talbot Press, Dublin, 1926; *Patrick H. Pearse*, Trans: Desmond Ryan, Phoenix, Dublin, 1932.
LESLIE, Anita, *Edwardians in Love*, Hutchinson, 1976: *Clare Sheridan*, Hutchinson, 1976; *Gilt and the Gingerbread*, Hutchinson, 1981; *Cousin Randolph*, Hutchinson, 1985.
LLOYD GEORGE, David, *War Memoirs*, 2 Vols, Odhams, 1934;
LONGFORD, Lord and O'Neill, T.P., *Eamon de Valera*, Gill & Macmillan, Dublin, and Hutchinson, 1970. Lord Longford (Frank Pakenham), *Peace by Ordeal*, Sidgwick & Jackson, 1972 (First published Cape, 1935).
LUCEY, Charles, *Ireland and the Irish*, Doubleday, New York, 1970.
LYNCH, Diarmuid, (ed.) *Florence O'Donoghue*, Mercier Press, Cork, 1957; *The IRB and the 1916 Rising*, Doubleday, n.d.
LYONS, F.S.L., *Ireland Since the Famine*, Weidenfeld & Nicolson, 1971; (ed.) *The Bank of Ireland 1783-1983*, Gill & Macmillan, Dublin, 1983.
LYONS, J.B., *Oliver St John Gogarty*, Blackwater Press, Dublin, 1980; *Tom Kettle*, Glendale, Dublin, 1983.

MACARDLE, Dorothy, *The Irish Republic*, Gollancz, 1937, and Irish Press, Dublin, 1951.
MACREADY, Gen. Sir Nevil, *Annals of an Active Life*, 2 Vols, Hutchinson, 1924.
MACCARTAN, Patrick, *With de Valera in America*, Brentano, New York, 1932.
MACDONAGH, Oliver, *Ireland: The Union and its Aftermath*, Allen & Unwin, 1977.
MCDONNELL, Kathleen Keyes, *There is a Bridge at Bandon*, Mercier Press, Cork, 1972.
MACEOIN, Uinseann (ed.), *Survivors*, Argenta, Dublin, first published 1980, reprinted and enlarged 1987.

MACLOCHLAINN, Piaras F., *Last Words*, Kilmainham Jail Restoration Society, Dublin, 1971.
MACMAHON, Sean, *Rich and Rare*, Ward River, Dublin, 1984.
MACMANUS, M.J., *Eamon de Valera*, Talbot Press, Dublin, 1944.
MCCAFFREY, Lawrence J., *The Irish Diaspora in America*, Indiana Press. Bloomington, 1976.
MCCANN, John, *War by the Irish*, The Kerryman Ltd, Tralee, 1946.
MCCRACKEN, J.P., *Representative Government in Ireland*, Oxford University Press, 1958.
MARJORIBANKS, Edward, *Life of Lord Carson*, Gollancz, 1932.
MANSERGH, Nicholas, *The Irish Question 1840–1921*, Allen & Unwin, 1965.
MARTIN, F.X. (ed.), *The Irish Volunteers 1913–15*, Dublin, 1963; (ed.)*Howth Gun-Running*, Browne & Nolan, Dublin, 1964; *Leaders & Men of the Easter Rising: Dublin 1916*, Methuen, 1965.
MIDDLEMASS, Keith & Barnes, John, *Baldwin*, Weidenfeld & Nicolson, 1969.
MILLER, David, *Queen's Rebels*, Gill & Macmillan, Dublin, 1971.
MITCHELL, & O'Snodaigh, *Irish Political Documents, 1916–49*, Irish Academic Press, Dublin, 1985.
MOODY, T.W., *The Ulster Question, 1603–1973*, Mercier Press, Cork, 1974.

NEESON, Eoin, *The Civil War in Ireland 1922–1923*, Mercier Press, 1967; *The Life and Death of Michael Collins*, Mercier Press, Cork, 1968.
NELIGAN, David, *The Spy in the Castle*, McGibbon & Kee, 1968.
NI DHERIG, Isold, *The Story of Michael Collins*, Mercier Press, Cork, 1978.

O'BROIN, Leon, *Dublin Castle and the 1916 Rising*, Sidgwick and Jackson, 1966; *The Chief Secretary*, Chatto & Windus, 1969; *Fenian Fever*, Chatto & Windus, 1979; *Michael Collins*, Gill & Macmillan, Dublin, 1980; *Revolutionary Underground – The Story of the I.R.B. 1858–1924*, Gill & Macmillan, Dublin, 1976; *No Man's Man*, Institute of Public Administration, Dublin, 1982; (ed.) *In Great Haste*, Gill & Macmillan, Dublin, 1983; *Protestant Nationalism in Ireland*, Gill & Macmillan, Dublin, 1985.
O'CONNOR, Batt, *With Michael Collins in The Fight for Irish Independence*, Peter Davies, 1929.
O'CONNOR, Frank, *The Big Fellow*, first published, US, 1937. Revised and reprinted, Clonmore and Reynolds, 1965 and 1966. Corgi paperback, 1969.
O'CONNOR, Sir James, *History of Ireland, 1798–1924*, 2 Vol.s, Arnold, 1925.
O'CONNOR, Ulick, *Oliver St John Gogarty*, Cape, 1964 and NEL paperback, 1967.
O'DONOGHUE, Florence, *No Other Law: The Story of Liam Lynch and the Irish Republic, 1916–23*, Irish Press, Dublin, 1954; (ed.) *Complete Book of IRA Jailbreaks, 1918–21*, Anvil, Trailee, 1971.
O'FAOLAIN Sean, *De Valera*, Penguin, 1939.
O'FARRELL, Patrick, *Ireland's English Question*, Schocken, New York, 1971.
O'HALLORAN, Clare, *Partition and the Limits of Ideology*, Gill & Macmillan, Dublin, 1989.
O'HANLON, Thomas J., *The Irish*, Deutsch, 1976.
O'HEGARTY, P.S., *The Victory of Sinn Fein*, Talbot Press, Dublin, 1924; *The Indestructible Nation*, Maunsel, Dublin, 1918.
O'HEGARTY, P.S., and O'Hegarty, Mrs E., *A History of Ireland Under The Union, 1801–1922*, Methuen, London, 1952.
O'MAHONY, Sean, *Frongoch: University of Revolution*, FDR Teoranta, Dublin, 1987.
O'MALLEY, Earnan, *The Singing Flame*, Anvil, Dublin, 1978; *On Another Man's Wound*, Anvil, Dublin, 1979; *Raids and Rallies*, Anvil, Dublin, 1982.
O'SULLIVAN, Donal, *The Irish Free State and its Senate*, Faber, 1940.

O'SULLIVAN, Harold, with Joseph Gavin, *Dundalk, a Military History*, Dundalgan Press, Dundalk, 1987.

RIDDELL, Lord George, *Intimate Diary of the Peace Conference*, Gollancz, 1933.
RIDDLE, Patrick, *Fire over Ulster*, Hamish Hamilton, 1970.
ROSKILL, S,.W., *Hankey, Man of Secrets*, Vol. 11, Collins, 1972.
RYAN, Desmond, *Remembering Sion*, Barker, 1934; *Unique Dictator*, Barker, 1936; *Michael Collins and the Invisible Army*, 1932, reprinted Anvil, n.d.
RYAN, Meda, *The Day Michael Collins Was Shot*, Poolbeg, Dublin, 1989.

SALVIDGE, Stanley, *Salvidge of Liverpool: Behind the Political Scene, 1890–1928*, Hodder & Stoughton, 1934.
SCOTT, C.P. (ed.) T. Wilson, *Political Diaries, 1911–28*, Collins, 1970.
SENIOR, Hereward, *Orangism in Ireland and Britain*, Routledge & Kegan Paul, 1966.
SHAKESPEARE, Sir Geoffrey, *Let Candles be Brought In*, MacDonald, 1949.
SHANNON, William, *The American Irish*, Collier Macmillan, New York, 1963.
SHAW, G.B., *How to Settle the Irish Question*, Talbot Press, Dublin, 1917; *Autobiography 1898–1950*, Reinhardt Books, 1970; *Collected Letters*, Vol. 111, Reinhardt Books, 1985.
STEVENSON, Francis (ed.), *Lloyd George: A Diary*, Hutchinson, 1971.
SHERMAN, Hugh, *Not an Inch*, Faber, 1942.
STEWART, A.T.Q., *The Ulster Crisis*, Faber, 1967; *Edward Carson*, Gill & Macmillan, Dublin, 1981.
STREET, Major C.J., *The Administration of Ireland, 1920*, Philip Allen, 1921; *Ireland in 1922*, Philip Allen, 1922.

TALBOT, Hayden, *Michael Collins' Own Story*, Hutchinson, 1932.
TAYLOR, A.J.P., *War by Timetable*, MacDonald, 1969; *Churchill, Four Faces and the Man*, Allen Lane, 1969; *Beaverbrook*, Hamish Hamilton, 1972.
TAYLOR, Rex, *Michael Collins*, Hutchinson, 1958, and Four Square paperback, 1961; *Poems*, Hutchinson, 1959; *Assassination: The Death of Sir Henry Wilson*, Hutchinson, 1961.
TOWNSHEND, Charles, *The British Campaign in Ireland, 1919–21*, Oxford University Press, 1975; *Political Violence in Ireland*, Oxford University Press, 1983.

WINTER, Sir Ormonde, *Winter's Tale*, Richard's Press, 1955.

YEATS, Padraig and Wren, Jimmy, *Michael Collins*, Tomar, Dublin, 1989.
YOUNGER, Calton, *Ireland's Civil War*, Frederick Muller, 1968, and Fontana 1970; *A State of Disunion*, Frederick Muller, 1972; *Arthur Griffith*, Gill & Macmillan, Dublin, 1981.

Index

Tim Pat Coogan is a native of Dublin. He was the editor of the *Irish Press* for twenty years and, as a leading commentator in Irish affairs, has contributed to several international newspapers. His previous books include *Ireland Since the Rising*, which was hailed as a pioneering work; and the definitive history, *The IRA*.

Dedicated to all of our clients who we teach and from whom we learn.

With heartfelt thanks and appreciation to our personal and business families: to Alex and Richard Berg, Dianne Rudo and Chloe, Anthony Garcia, Chris Tomasino, Barbara Feinman, Danielle Caldwell, Kay Peters, Greg Coram, Jerry Michaels, Pat Collins, Lou Hampton.

To Ted Stevenson, it's clear we couldn't have done this without you. It was far better and more enjoyable to do with you. Thank you.

Table of Contents

1

The Five-Minute
Guide to this Book

A high proportion of adult Americans view the prospect of speaking in public quite literally as a *fate worse than death*.

Several years ago, in a now-famous study, a market research organization conducted a poll on the question "What do you fear most?" The results were included in *The Book of Lists*. As you might expect, "heights" was high on the list, along with "financial problems," "flying," "serious illness," and "death." But *topping* the list—the number one fear—was "speaking before a group."

Yet this is a prospect more and more of us face every day. We may be living in the "electronic communications age," when a great deal of information is transmitted via computers, but the operative word here is *communications*. For while electronics make many kinds of communications possible, in *most situations* the *most effective* means of communication is human being to human being.

It is in direct, face-to-face presentations that we have the best opportunity to get our message across—to *get to the point*.

We'd like to make it clear at the outset that we're not talking about formal speeches. Very few of us ever need to give speeches. Rather, we are referring to the relatively short and informal talks with clearly defined objectives that take place most often in a work-related context. Although there are different types of talks, each with unique goals, for our purposes let's simply call them *presentations*.

Presentations—and therefore presentation skills—are more important in the business world than they have ever been before. Every passing day swells the ranks of people who need to be able to present effectively in order to do their jobs effectively. In particular, presentation skills are vital to any person who ever has to *sell, persuade, motivate, inform,* or *represent*.

Our Bottom Line

The purpose of *Get to the Point* is to teach those skills. If you read this book and follow our program, it will reduce your presentation anxiety to a manageable level. (In fact, it may actually make the experience almost enjoyable.) But more to the point, it will *make you a better presenter*.

Who Do We Think You Are?

From our vantage point as corporate consultants and trainers in this field, the audience for this book is quite broad. A few examples may suffice to indicate the range: the book editor *presenting* the spring list to the publishing house sales force; the advertising account manager *outlining* an ad campaign for a prospective client; the engineer *instructing* a manufacturing team; the consultant *updating* a client on project status; the law associate *briefing* a senior partner on research for an important case; the college graduate *interviewing* for a new job; the unhappy consumer *complaining* to a store manager; all these—and many more—fall within our definition of *presenters*. All of these need to know how to get to the point.

Who Are We?

Karen Berg and Andrew Gilman are the principals of Comm-Core, a New York–based communications consulting firm. We prepare business people and public officials for the full range of communications challenges. Among others, our clients include AT&T, General Foods, the American Lung Association, Chase Manhattan Bank, Eastdil Realty, Goldome, and G. D. Searle. Most of our work involves teaching the specific skills we will discuss in this book: how to make better, stronger presentations.

We also prepare clients for media appearances—from trade and consumer press to radio and television interviews, including programs such as *60 Minutes* and *20/20*. We frequently prepare expert witnesses for sworn testimony before congressional committees, administrative agencies, and public utility commissions. Other seminars we offer include sales skills, stress management, writing, and crisis communications.

Getting Ahead

How important are presentation skills? In today's competitive business world, highly developed presentation skills add up to a bankable career advantage that you won't want to be without.

The ability to make successful presentations has become a prerequisite in business.

A generation ago, skillful presentation was a nice plus for a manager, but back then it was the possession of technical job-related skills that helped you get ahead. Today, things have changed; today the edge goes to those with highly developed communications skills. Because while technical skills are important, communication is ultimately what business is about.

It makes sense, doesn't it? Put yourself in the position of an employer. Assume you are considering two equally qualified candidates, with good references and experience. Which one would you hire? Probably the one with the better communications skills because the one who is better able to *communicate* the needs and demands of the job is more likely to do the job successfully.

Presentation skills are becoming a direct link to promotion and success. In many companies today, good verbal presentation ability is a *specific requirement* for advancement. In companies such as AT&T and Citibank, a significant factor in personnel evaluations is an employee's ability to present well. In fact, one executive at General Electric told us why he came to work on his presentation skills: "My manager, the division vice president, told me what it would take to get any higher up the ladder. He said, 'You have the right training, have made the right moves within the company, and have proven yourself by your performance. How you look, act and talk will determine where you go from now on.'"

Training: A Competitive Edge

Every person brings natural strengths and weaknesses to the challenge of public presentation; each of us instinctively handles some aspects well and, after practice, will learn from experience. But given the pace and intensity of life today, few of us can afford to rely on our natural gifts or the accumulation of experience to acquire this edge.

Consider an analogy: A tennis player gets ahead by learning to hit the ball accurately and assertively, by learning to reach any ball hit to him and return it authoritatively. That's how points are made.

A weekend player can rely on natural talent plus a few pointers from fellow players. After all, in the long run there is rarely money or a career at stake. A *professional* tennis player, however, learns winning skills by training with a professional coach virtually every day, until these skills become second nature.

It's no different for a communicator: The ability to serve a clean and assertive message, to field a challenge or question from any position and play it back with strength and authority, is the essence of effective public presentation.

With the competitive edge professional training provides, you can learn to make *your* points—and that means selling your organization, your products, your services, your point of view with confidence.

That's what *Get to the Point* is all about.

Bottom Line—Again

Let us reiterate our goal. (As you will shortly see for yourselves as you read on, we don't mind repeating ourselves—it's a sound communications strategy.) If you acknowledge the importance of presentation-making and you feel your skills could be stronger, *Get to the Point* will improve your skills. If you're a beginner, *Get to the Point* will turn you into a capable, confident presenter. If you're already experienced, *Get to the Point* will make you better.

As skilled presenters and communicators, we use the techniques we teach nearly every day. And they work, for us and for our clients.

Our wide experience allows us to teach you basic skills of presentation making and to train you in advanced skills as well. We'll explore numerous situations that we and our clients have faced—print and media interviews, legal and legislative testimony, panel discussions, media appearances, meetings, job interviews, and more. As your presentation powers grow, *Get to the Point* will continue assisting you.

Caveat

We must point out that *Get to the Point* is not a quick, magical program. For it to work, you have to work. And the *harder* you are willing to work, the *better* it will work.

The Capsule Version

In keeping with our goal-oriented approach, we want to give you the basics of the *Get to the Point* program. Here's our approach to presentation making, reduced to its bare essentials:

- Know your audience.

- Decide on your bottom line message or action plan and say it early. If possible, pull in your audience with a strong attention-getter.
- State your supporting points with clarity, focus, and emphasis.
- Anticipate listeners' questions and concerns.
- Make your points again while answering questions.

Background

Here is some of the research that forms the foundation of our program, which will be discussed in the chapters that follow.

Ebbinghaus. Much of the basis for our approach to communications is drawn from research about *retention*, the ability of the human mind to remember what it has taken in. The basic facts are condensed from the work of Hermann Ebbinghaus, pioneer researcher on the psychology of human memory, around the turn of the century.

Ebbinghaus's research tells us that the typical listener will forget 40 percent of what he or she has heard during a presentation within half an hour. By the end of the day, 60 percent will be gone. A week after hearing a presentation, the average listener *retains* only about 10 percent of what was said.

Our whole approach is designed to maximize retention; to increase that 10 percent. One key to improved retention is *focus*. Clearly focused messages are easier to remember than unfocused ones. We have a lot to say about focusing on your overall purpose, on your specific point, and on your audience.

The other keys to retention are *repetition* (the more frequently a message is heard, the more likely it is to be remembered) and *proximity* (the more recently a message is heard, the better it will be remembered). We are great believers in the rule for verbal communications propounded by the late journalist, Edward R. Murrow: "Tell 'em what you're gonna tell 'em. Tell 'em. Then tell 'em what you told 'em." In keeping with this principle, you'll find us deliberately repeating ourselves quite a bit.

Nonverbal aspects of verbal communication. More recent research by Albert Mehrabian on the nonverbal elements of communication tells us that words are not the whole message. Far from it: One important study concludes that only 7 percent of interpersonal communication is traceable to words; about 55 percent is the result of facial expression and other body language; and the remaining 38 percent comes from "paralanguage," or how we use our voices. We give extensive coverage to the nonverbal elements of delivery: physical gestures, eye contact, vocal inflection, and phrasing.

Other research tells us that presentations are more persuasive if they are supported by *visual materials*. We have a lot to say about the selection, design, and use of visual aids.

A Chain Is Only as Strong . . .

To draw these elements together—focus, repetition, body language, use of visuals—is to create powerful communication. There is no single key to better and more convincing presentations. Think of these elements as a chain forged from a series of links, and only as strong as the weakest of them.

One Last Time

Get to the Point offers you a wealth of practical suggestions. We hope you'll read the book, and say, "Ah-ha! That makes sense. This will help me make my point more clearly and more directly."

We designed the book to be flexible. If you have a five-minute presentation to give this afternoon, go right to our Quick Points section on the Talking Memo in Chapter Twenty-three. If you have a fifteen-minute presentation to give tomorrow, see our Quick Point 'In-Flight' Presentation Writing Technique. If you already know how to organize a presentation, skip to Chapter Seven on visuals; if you are familiar with the use of visuals, you might want to concentrate on Q & A (question and answer) techniques, covered in Chapter Nine. Once you've mastered all the fundamentals, you will want to learn our advanced techniques. Whatever aspect of presentation-making you want or need to improve, we can help.

But the book will work only as hard as you are willing to work. If you follow our suggestions and put in the time, you'll make better presentations. It's that simple.

Get to the Point is a complete presentation training program. And it works. We know because we teach it, day in and day out, to people whose success proves it.

Quick Reference Summary

- Public speaking is America's number one fear.
- Face-to-face verbal presentations are the most effective way to make your point to others.
- This book will reduce public-speaking fear and make you an expert presenter.
- Presentation skills are a requirement for success in business, vital to anyone who ever has to sell, persuade, motivate, inform, or represent.
- Our training will help you improve your skills quickly and dramatically.
- The basic components of strong presentation-making are:
  - Know your audience; anticipate their needs.
  - Know your bottom line message and say it early.
  - Anticipate listeners' questions and answer them during the presentation.
  - Make your key point again in a summary statement.
- The typical listener forgets 40 percent of what he or she has heard in the first half hour; 60 percent by the end of the day; 90 percent after a week.
- Clarity, focus, and repetition help build listener *retention*.
- Visual aids help increase comprehension *and* retention.
- How you look, move, and speak can outweigh the content of what you say.
- If you follow the program and *do the work,* this book can teach you the basics and the fine points of presentation making, turning you into a confident presenter.

2

Game Plans:
The Audience Profile

Knowing your audience is the first and most crucial step in giving a presentation. You'll always have an audience, but each audience is different. Your content, style, and delivery will vary depending on the group.

There is a distinction between "speaker-centered" and "audience-centered" messages.

Speaker-centered messages are the points that the presenter wants to make. They reflect the speaker's perceptions and needs. Audience-centered messages reflect the needs, concerns, attitudes, beliefs, and understanding of the people addressed.

Skilled presenters understand that messages need to be audience-centered and design their presentations accordingly. This does not mean that their messages are *not* speaker-centered, but that they

strike a balance. What the audience needs to hear and what you
have to say are *both* important. Therefore the most powerful message is one that integrates the two. This approach to message building is fundamental to the art of *getting to the point*. And it is true no
matter what audience you are addressing.

> **Case Study:** In 1985, a young upstart company, MCI, playing
> David to the communications industry's Goliath, AT&T,
> brought suit for antitrust violations. Like David, MCI won, but
> the victory was muted in the subsequent damage suit. The bil-
> lions of dollars sought by MCI ended up as an award of only
> millions.
>
> After a trial in Chicago in 1985, a member of the jury com-
> mented that one important factor in determining the amount of
> damages was that the precise meaning of crucial MCI evidence
> was *"never made clear to the jury."* (Emphasis added.) Had the
> jury clearly understood MCI's complex statistical argument, he
> implied, the damages could have been significantly higher.
>
> The MCI attorneys apparently had fallen into a classic com-
> munications trap: not identifying and addressing their real au-
> dience. Instead of speaking to the jury *in language they could
> understand*, they were drawn into an intricate, high-tech statis-
> tical debate with the opposing counsel. MCI won the debate,
> but the practical, dollars-and-cents cost of their failure to cor-
> rectly identify and speak to their audience might have been as
> high as billions of dollars.

The Audience Profile

To create audience-centered messages, the speaker must know the
audience—their knowledge, needs, concerns, interests, attitudes,
beliefs, and in many cases even their personalities. The *better* the
speaker knows them, the more finely tuned his or her messages can
be. That is why the first step in preparing for any presentation is an
accurate and detailed audience profile. It is the strategic foundation
for a successful presentation. It's your game plan.

Defining your audience is parallel to the process a football team goes through in preparing for a game. In the big leagues, it's not enough to be good; the winning edge comes from knowing your opponent's game as well as you know your own. Professional football teams hire scouts to watch other teams. They analyze each opposing player's strength, speed, stamina, and spirit. Based on this information, the coaches work out a game plan that adapts their team's strengths to best meet the challenge of the opposing team. That's what the audience profile does for a presenter.

This preparation is both offensive and defensive. In football, the goal of the offense is tailoring plays to gain yardage and score points. In a presentation the objective is tailoring *messages* to make your point. In football, the job of the defense is turning back challenges mounted by the opposition. In a presentation, similarly, the speaker's goal is to meet any challenges or resistance from the audience, usually by anticipating and answering questions.

Questions, questions. Doing an audience profile is a process of questioning. Different questions shed light on different facets of your audience.

If you know your audience personally, for example, your questions will relate to the power levels, specific turfs, subject matter expertise, and personal idiosyncrasies of individual participants. We'll discuss presentations to specific audiences later. For the moment, we'll stick with general audiences.

If your audience is a complete unknown, you really need to start at the beginning.

Question: Who's going to be there; who *are* these people?

Basic demographic information can give you the overview that serves as the background for a more detailed picture. Basics include:
- Age
- Sex
- Income level
- Occupation or professional status
- Political affiliation
- Ethnic identity

> Gather basic audience profile information even if you *think*
> you know it. Assumptions can get you into trouble.

Don't assume you know this basic information—find someone who
does. If you are an invited speaker, for example, and you're going in
cold, the contact person in the organization who issued the invitation would be a logical source to tap.

> **Case Study:** Not long ago, an editor from a major metropolitan
> newspaper was invited to fill in at the last minute for the sched-
> uled speaker at a weekly luncheon gathering of public relations
> professionals. The editor knew that the people who usually at-
> tended these meetings were entry-level and junior account exec
> types and therefore thought it wasn't a very important event.
> Her talk was aimed at such an audience; it had the tone of wis-
> dom talking to inexperience and could be summarized along
> the lines of, "You people will have to learn to write a proper
> press release if you want to get along with us. . . ."
>   What she *didn't* know was that the speaker she replaced was
> a very important industry figure. As a result, the crowd that
> day actually contained a lot of executive VPs and CEOs; people
> who had the power to decide when she got a story—or if she got
> one at all. They were *not* accustomed to being addressed in this
> tone, nor was the message appropriate to this group. Simply
> taking the time to ask the basic audience profile questions could
> have avoided this debacle.

As the story shows, accurate audience identification will influence
things as fundamental as your choice of subject matter or content.

Question: What do you want to tell *these* people; what do *they*
need to hear?

Just as you would design one sort of message for CEOs and another
for assistant account execs, you would want to present different
kinds of material to a consumer watchdog group than you would to
the Lions Club. And the Lions Club in Cincinnati will be different

from the Lions Club in Philadelphia. The same holds true in other settings.

Getting inside their heads. The goal of the basic audience profile is understanding the audience's point of view and providing answers to the questions everyone carries around in the back of their mind:
- "So what?"
- "Who cares?"
- "What's In It For Me?" (WIIFM).

A good way of getting at the answers to these questions is to focus on the audience's relationships.

Question: What is the audience's relationship to itself?

What defines this particular group? What is their common thread? What issues, attitudes, concerns, or backgrounds forge this diverse collection of individuals into a unified group?

These questions will tell you where the group's attention will be focused, providing you with an accurate index to your audience's interests and concerns.

Question: What is your relationship to the audience?

Are they customers? Colleagues? Your boss (or bosses)? Stockholders? Neighbors? Potential followers? Or simply fellow citizens? Are you appearing as an authority? An informer? An advocate? An apologist?

Question: What do you have in common with your audience?

What natural points of alliance do you see? What threads can you weave into your presentation that will continually reaffirm those connections, binding you together and counteracting any natural antagonisms? The range of possibilities is quite broad. It might be goals—personal, professional, social, or political; interests—common or opposing; a business or occupation; an affiliation; a skill; or an occasion (such as a retirement party or a sales awards banquet).

Question: How knowledgeable would you expect this group to be in your area of expertise; what level of interest can you anticipate?

Answers to these questions can provide clues to the appropriate *depth* of your presentation. Gauging depth can be important. You certainly don't want to talk down to people; it's deadly. Nor do you want to talk over their heads.

Case Study: A client of ours who manages a major company's research lab once took a group of new employees on an indoctrination tour of the facility, supplying a running commentary about blood chemistry, hemoglobin, and platelet research. When the tour was finished, he asked if anyone had any questions. One man raised his hand and asked, "What's a platelet?"

Question: What are the potential areas of conflict and confrontation with the audience?

In spite of tailoring a message based on an audience profile, nearly every presenter raises issues that may be possible sources of dispute. Every message has the potential for conflicts, and identifying these is the second crucial goal of the audience profile process.

The strongest presentation is one in which you, the presenter, invite questions, but in many situations a question and answer session may be mandatory. If you haven't anticipated the inevitable tough questions and have not prepared good answers, the strength of the presentation may be completely undermined. We will discuss this more fully in Chapter Nine.

Here's a final question you should ask before any presentation where the speaker is unfamiliar with the attendant conditions:

Question: Are there any special circumstances surrounding this presentation?

The question about circumstances is really about anticipating your audience's frame of mind, and together with consideration of your relationship to the audience, bears on the *tone* your presentation takes. It's always worth a discreet question to your contact person on the day of the presentation: "Is there anything going on that I should know about?" If the president of the foundation died of a heart attack earlier in the week; if the company's local plant recently released massive amounts of toxic chemicals into the local water supply; if the sales force just landed a substantial government contract for portable computers; these are things you need to know *before* you make your presentation. This kind of knowledge can spare you the embarrassment of being lighthearted or flippant in somber circumstances or will enable you to focus on positive developments.

The Inside View

The approaches to the audience profile we have outlined thus far are applicable primarily to *public* presentations. For what we call *internal* presentations—those that take place within a company or organization—the focus is generally quite different. The principle is the same, but there are two significant ways in which internal presentations differ from public ones.

First, you are much more likely to be working with a preestablished agenda; the subject matter is usually determined by others. As a result, goals are likely to be clearly defined and results easy to evaluate: Did you accomplish your purpose? Was your budget approved? Was your task force recommendation accepted? Did you get authority to hire the five new people you need?

Second, since companies are hierarchically structured, a specific focus of the message must be persuading key people and placating others. Individual personalities must be taken into account during preparation. The audience will be a complex mixture of human factors: people with a vital stake in the outcome and those with none; staunch supporters and inveterate opponents; friends, mentors, protégés, enemies, potential allies, and everything in between.

Personality profile. Your preparation for an internal presentation should profile each important audience member—as a personality, and in terms of job function and power. Here are some of the questions you should consider:

Question: Who are the key people you have to persuade in order to accomplish your goal?

Question: Have you developed a WIIFM (what's in it for me—pronounced "wiffum") for each of these people?

Question: What personal idiosyncrasies or habits might affect your presentation?

For example, if there is a key person who has a reputation for arriving late for meetings or leaving early, do you arrange the agenda to accommodate that person?

Focusing on the individual. What are the overriding personal concerns of each key person?

Question: Who's bottom-line oriented; who goes for the broad overview? Who's concerned with pricing, timing, human resources, environmental issues?

Question: How do you and your message relate to any or all of these concerns?

Rather than compete with these players, can you find a way to form a tennis doubles team and play on the *same* side of the net?

Question: From whom can you expect opposition as a matter of course?

Is there a tough-minded executive who likes to grill *everybody*? Is there someone who just doesn't *like* you?

Question: From whom can you expect *real* (substantive, as opposed to personal) opposition?

Who is likely to genuinely disagree with your plan? This part of the profile is essentially no different from that for public presentations.

Question: What are your answers to this opposition?

Question: With whom might you build alliances before presentation time?

Question: Who among the participants is important enough to require acknowledgment (usually a special WIIFM message), even though not a key player in this scenario?

That is, are there any VIPs present whose feathers would be ruffled if they were left out of the discussion despite the fact that they don't have a decision-making role in the issue at hand?

Also consider the organization's political climate of the moment (who is receptive to particular types of moves, projects, or approaches, and who is not) and the organizational "culture" (in this connection, primarily a question of what kinds of positions or stances can be taken by people in different levels of the organizational power structure without violating the group sense of "good form").

If you have any doubts about the political mood, sample opinion in one-on-one sessions before the meeting. If the climate is clearly hostile to the kinds of ideas and approaches you wish to set forth, you may want to reconsider your position for now.

A sensitivity to "culture" can help you avoid the pitfall of calling attention to yourself in the wrong ways—of offending higher-ups by overstepping your position. The same awareness can guide you in making your point without violating corporate canon.

Here are two real-life examples that demonstrate the value of a detailed audience profile for internal presentations:

Case Study 1: Twice a year the sales force of a major U.S. corporation gathers for a meeting with corporate management for a review. Sales figures are discussed, as are projections and goals for the rest of the year. At this meeting, management asks questions, seeks clarifications and explanations, probes, examines, and picks at details. It's potential "on the carpet" time for the sales reps, and they have to be prepared to deal with any matter the brass wants to raise—and try to come out looking good.

Also on the agenda are any problems, suggestions, complaints, or special projects that sales personnel want to bring before corporate management.

From a tactical point of view, the salespeople have three goals at these meetings:

- To present their track record as positively as possible
- To anticipate and develop answers to questions and problems managers are likely to raise
- To create a favorable climate for their own agenda

Sales personnel felt they could make considerably better use of these meetings, so they invited us to help them prepare. We held a two-day planning and training session in which every part of the presentation agenda was examined carefully.

One of our real skills is helping people see the significance of information they already have in their heads—such as the company's sales figures—and shaping such information into messages aimed at particular persons and their interests. To do this effectively, it is necessary to understand the people and interests at which the messages are aimed—to do an audience profile.

Accordingly, we spent 10 percent of the entire preparation time—over an hour and a half—clearly identifying and analyzing the top executives who were to be the audience for this event.

What we needed to know was each person's:

- Background
- Corporate rank
- Relationship with sales
- Personal as well as managerial interests
- Personality and temperament

We talked these things over with our presenters, wrote down the findings on large pieces of paper, and tacked them to the walls where they could be seen by all as we developed our strategies.

The managers involved in the meeting were:

- Group vice president of sales
- Vice president of sales
- Vice president of marketing

- Director of advertising
- Regional sales managers

Group discussion produced the following information that profiled the key players:

Group vice president of sales. He was respected by the reps for his intelligence and was liked for his genial personality. He was also new to the company and to the industry—having recently moved from another, quite different consumer products company—and therefore was not fully aware of corporate history or culture, or the specific problems of the business. Because of this, he was something of an unknown quantity. Also, although he carries the highest title, his function in the meeting was not one of direct authority or responsibility. In essence, his concerns reflected those of his immediate subordinate, the next man on the list.

Vice president of sales. He was the executive head of the sales department, the sales reps' bosses' boss. This was really *his* meeting. He was well known to the reps and, though demanding, was thought to be reasonable, fair, and competent.

Vice president of marketing. He was considered by the reps to some extent an adversary—for two reasons. First, there had been tension between the marketing and sales departments for some time, marketing contending that sales wasn't doing a good enough job pushing the product line, sales maintaining that they needed better products with lower prices. Second, he was by nature a challenging and nit-picking person, more numbers- than people-oriented.

Director of advertising. He was pleased with the sales force. Once his ad campaign was launched, the reps really went out and hustled the products that were advertised, making him look good. Further, the company did a lot of cooperative advertising (that is, it shared the cost of ad campaigns run by retailers who sold the company's products), so the sales team was a vital link in the overall advertising strategy. He was basically an ally.

Regional sales managers. These were the immediate bosses of the salespeople with whom we were working. They were, of course, 100 percent behind the reps, since they worked together closely. But the culture of this particular company dictated that in these semiannual review sessions the reps were on their own; sales managers were not expected to intervene on their behalf. For that reason, they were not likely to make much substantive contribution to the proceedings.

Using this detailed audience profile as a foundation, we went on to consider content and the structuring of the six individual presentations that would be given by selected sales reps. Each of these contained a primary selling point, and within the group of presentations we were careful to include several WIIFM messages, carefully tailored to speak to the interests of each of the principal audience members.

In particular, having identified the vice president of marketing as a potential trouble source, we were able to reduce his antagonism by:

- Anticipating many of the issues he might raise and preparing to respond to them
- Addressing his interests within the messages
- Understanding that resolving the ongoing tension between marketing and sales was not the responsibility of the salespeople, but of the respective vice presidents (in other words, no matter how tough this guy was, the reps weren't working for him; it was their boss, the vice president of sales, that they had to satisfy)
- After clearly identifying the personality type, anticipating expected behavior and taking it in stride

Case Study 2: This example shows the value of premeetings with key players

Our client was a manager at a pharmaceutical company and was representing a study group that had been given the task by senior management of making recommendations on whether the company should enter another line of business. She would be presenting the group's findings to the corporate management committee, which consisted of the president and CEO, the CFO, and vice presidents for marketing, finance, legal, licensing, corporate human resources, planning, and research.

The group's bottom line message was that the company *should* enter this line of business, and they were proposing three possible means: outright purchase of an existing company, internal development of a new company with products and sales force, or developing a line of business by comarketing with an existing company.

Knowing that she would be presenting to very important corporate executives, our client knew she needed to do a very thorough audience profile. Each of these officers had his or her own business priorities.

Here are the significant findings:

- The vice president of marketing, having established the study group, was the pivotal power person, the main person who needed to be satisfied that the study group's findings were valid.
- The vice president of finance had a reputation for asking tricky questions about numbers.
- There was some ongoing tension between the presenter and the vice president of licensing, who as a result had confronted her with some rather testy questions in other, similar circumstances.

This audience profile suggested to our client that in addition to including WIIFM messages for all the principle players, she had better lay down a prepresentation foundation:

- As a courtesy (since he was the spark plug of the project) and to make sure there were no surprises, she made a preliminary presentation to the VP of marketing.
- She did the same with the VP of finance, since she hadn't

done a complete financial analysis. This eliminated the possibility of embarrassing numbers questions in the full presentation and effectively made an ally of a potentially
dangerous opponent.
- She approached the VP of research, who agreed to deal
with the difficult questions the presenter anticipated from
the VP of licensing.

With the help of these preliminary maneuvers, the presentation went quite well. The group's recommendation was only
partially adopted, but its work won general approval.

The Personal Touch

Before we leave the audience profile, there's one more aspect of
audience identification you should give some thought to—
personalization.

The more often you can make reference to concrete aspects of your
listeners' lives—names, places, events, situations—the more you create in them a feeling that you share these things, that you are "one of
them." This subtle change in your status—you're not just a speaker,
you're a community member on some level—diminishes the barrier
of separateness that naturally exists between strangers, so you are
heard more clearly.

This may mean doing research or simply putting to use information you may already have. Whatever the effort involved, personalization adds a valuable dimension to your presentation.

If, for example, you're in Springfield to talk about developments
in microcomputer marketing, instead of talking about retailers in
the abstract, why not use Mike's Megabyte Computer Store down
the block, a company many of your listeners may do business with,
as an example in your discussion.

If you're a senior at Carnegie Mellon interviewing for a job at
Anheuser Busch, you will naturally do enough research to sound as
if you're familiar with the company. Why not go the extra yard and
find out something about Purina and some of the other large companies headquartered in St. Louis, not to mention the city itself. You

want to sound as if you are familiar with the company's community and using this information in your presentation will help you make points effectively.

If your presentation opens with a futuristic fantasy about a homeward-bound commuter calling on his wrist-radio telephone to tell his preprogrammed oven to start dinner, why not set the stage on the "five fifty-seven out of Penn Station," or whatever train your listeners have been taking home from the office most of their working lives? Touches like these create a picture your listeners can easily step into.

This personalization technique works for internal audiences as well. Opening lines might be: "Gary asked for an update on Delta project" or "Following Beth's overview of marketing plans, I was asked to isolate the twenty-one- to forty-year-old segment." The personal touch draws others in, makes it *us*, not just *you*.

To add the personal touch you need to think about the people in your audience. Do you share a common experience with them? Maybe an affiliation, a career path, a boss? Perhaps it's worth the time to visit the manufacturing plant, the sales office, the downtown area. The little bits of information you pick up in this way, the little touches you add, can make all the difference.

Quick Reference Summary

- Effective presenters are both speaker- and audience-centered.
- Satisfying the WIIFM (What's In It For Me?) syndrome of your audience is crucial.
- Know your audience—their agenda, personal biases, level of knowledge on subject, level of interest.
- What is your message to the audience?
- What do they need or want to learn?
- Create a bond by using common threads that run through the group.
- Analyze your relationship to the people you're presenting to, such as boss, peers, or community members.
- Be aware of special circumstances: press conference, awards, etc.

- Who are the particular people in your audience who need to be persuaded?
- What are their habits (such as consistently late arrival or challenging attitude)?
- What are their attitudes toward the issues?
- Who will opposition and support come from?
- What are the "hot button" points—issues on which you can expect controversy?
- Know the answers to likely questions.
- Try to foresee problems and work them out before the presentation.
- Use what you know about your audience to personalize your presentation. If necessary, do a little research into your listeners' lives.

3

When, Where,
What . . . and Why:
Times, Places, and Things

"To every thing there is a season; a time to every purpose under heaven" (Ecclesiastes 3:1). This includes presentations.

If you ever have the choice, the best time to schedule an important presentation is Tuesday morning at ten or eleven o'clock.

Why? The key to the answer is *attention*. Tuesday mornings are the point in the five-day-work-week cycle when people's minds are least likely to be occupied with other matters. Wednesdays around the same time are a good second choice. Third choice is midafternoon between two-thirty and four o'clock on either of these days.

Earlier or later in the week, people are preoccupied with the weekend, past or approaching. Early in the work morning, their minds are occupied with the transition from home to work: the rigors of the commute, the mail, and starting the daily schedule. After eleven-thirty or so, lunch begins to loom large. After lunch, the digestion process literally takes oxygen away from the brain and concentration suffers. If lunch involves drinks, concentration may be shot for the rest of the day. If not, there is a period in the middle of the afternoon when people can focus clearly on business—before the mind turns to going home.

These are not cynical observations, but facts about human beings; facts that you need to take into consideration when planning your presentation.

If You Can't Plan, Adjust

Very often we don't have control over the time of a presentation. So why raise the issue? While you may not be able to pick your time, you *can* anticipate the quality of attention you are likely to encounter from your audience and structure your presentation accordingly.

For example, if you find yourself appearing at the Breakfast Club on Monday morning or addressing the sales force at four-thirty on Friday afternoon just before they're about to leave to catch a plane to Boca Raton for the semiannual sales conference, you can adjust your approach and maximize the possibility of getting *something* useful across.

Most often, this means *simplifying;* zeroing in on one or two clear-cut points and making them as forcefully and as frequently as you can in the time available.

There are other factors that affect listener attention and should be taken into consideration in your presentation planning.

Meals. Sometimes your presentation may take place in conjunction with a meal. In this situation, you will be competing with the digestive process, which favors the stomach over the brain. People are usually fairly alert first thing in the morning, even after a good breakfast. But following a lunch or dinner, your audience is likely to be at least 25 percent asleep. (If alcohol has been served—something you should always try to find out beforehand—it may be more like 75 percent.)

> **Tip:** If your audience is sleepy, one of your few chances to wake them up is to try to get them to stand up or move around a little. You might come prepared with some simple survey question: "How many of you have two or more television sets in your home? Please stand up, so we can see you. Now, how many of you standing have *more* than two? Just raise your hands. Thank you. . . ."

Numbers. Another circumstance that arises frequently is being one of a number of speakers or presenters. At many companies, for example, the budget review process involves meeting after meeting, presentation after presentation, a marathon of facts and figures.

Knowing where you *fit into the parade* can help guide your preparation. If you know you're the fifth presenter—meaning that you will begin long after people's normal attention span is exhausted—you can at least try to compensate.

When you are scheduled to present after the audience's attention has dissipated, your choices are to use an especially striking opening to rekindle their attention (see discussion of "grabbers," p. 48) and/or to hone your presentation to its bare essentials, concentrating exclusively on key messages.

Site Survey

To plan effectively, you need to know the physical location of your presentation. If you don't know what to expect, you're likely to be in for some surprises, and surprises of this kind are almost always unpleasant.

Find out:
- Room size
- Layout
- Lighting
- Equipment

Information about presentation site is likely to be of most concern to those giving public presentations in unfamiliar locations. If most of your presentations take place in your living room, the community center conference room, or the company boardroom, you'll already be familiar with the basic setup. But taking things for granted is taking unnecessary risks. We suggest that you use our checklist and eliminate all uncertainty, whatever the location.

Presentation Site Checklist

Space, Layout, and Seating

☐ How big is the room? (Smaller rooms are more conducive to audience participation.)

☐ What is the seating arrangement?
   · Conference table
   · Chevron
   · Auditorium

☐ How visible will you be when not speaking? Will you be "on stage" for the whole proceeding, or will you enter and exit? Is there a room where you can warm up?

☐ How are the sight lines? Will you be able to see everyone? Will they be able to see you? Will you be blocking anyone's view of the screen when you show visuals?

☐ What does the speaker's platform or area look like from the audience's viewpoint?

☐ What is the visual background? Can you alter it (draw a curtain, for example) or dress to harmonize with it?

☐ Is there a lectern? How tall is it? If you stand behind it how much of you will the audience be able to see?

Lighting and Temperature Control

☐ Is the lighting at the speaker's platform adequate for you to see your notes?

☐ Will *you* be able to adjust this lighting?

☐ Is the room lighting variable (as opposed to on/off)? If you need to show slides, will the room be so dark that you will be invisible?

☐ Will you be able to adjust room lighting without leaving your speaking position?

☐ Will you need to turn on air-conditioning or adjust the room temperature since lights, equipment, and a certain number of human bodies tend to raise the room temperature level?

Audiovisual and Sound Equipment

☐ Does the room contain the audiovisual equipment you need?

☐ Do the projectors, if needed, actually work? How about backups? Are spare bulbs nearby?

☐ How and on what are projectors positioned? Are they handy to the lectern? Are they easily moved?

☐ Will you need amplification? If so, what kind of microphone is available? (Your best choice would be a wireless mike or, if that's not available, a clip-on. These restrict your physical mobility much less than a fixed lectern or "goose-neck" mike.)

☐ If refreshments are to be served:
  · Is the necessary equipment available?
  · Are you responsible for ordering food and setting up?
  · Is there adequate space?
  · Are there enough electrical outlets to plug in the coffee urn *and* whatever audiovisual equipment you plan to use?

If It's Worth Doing . . .

The attention to equipment and other physical arrangements can take a good deal of time, but it needs to be done well. If these elements aren't completely invisible to the audience, they're getting in the way of your message. If the event is very important, you may find it worthwhile to follow the example of theatrical directors and hold a technical rehearsal, in which every aspect of lighting, sound amplification, and visuals presentation is run through *exactly as it will be in your actual presentation*—whether by you or an assistant. This means actually using the microphone you will be using (and if it is a clip-on, practicing putting it on quickly and properly; see

p. 169). It means actually projecting your slides to verify that the projector is working, that you or your assistant know how to operate it smoothly, and that your slides are properly set up. It means setting lighting and sound levels and making sure these are easily replicated by marking the necessary controls and switches. You should be able to run through all the necessary checks in ten minutes or so.

Whether or not you decide to run a full tech rehearsal, checking and using the physical setup well before presentation time pays a huge dividend in peace of mind. It eliminates potential surprises, and ensures that, mechanically at any rate, things will go as smoothly as possible. This will leave you free to do what you're there to do—make your point.

Tip: To ease the process of setting up and checking out the presentation site it's a good idea to approach the person in charge of the premises directly. In a public facility this would be the manager or custodian. For the boardroom, it might well be the CEO's assistant. Whatever the case, the person with responsibility for room scheduling and accommodations can be invaluable in helping you make sure things are properly set up.

Quick Reference Summary

- Best time to make an important presentation: ten to eleven A.M. Tuesday. You're more likely to have listeners' *attention*.
- If you're in the middle of a group of presenters, find a way to make your presentation stand out.
- If you can't control the circumstances, you may have to adjust your goals and *simplify* your message.
- Check presentation site for size, seating, audiovisual facilities, lighting, and temperature control.
- Rehearse at the site *with the equipment:* Use the sound system, make all the lighting changes, run the projectors.

4

Building Strong Messages:
Selling Points
and Word Power

It is now time to be speaker-centered—time to consider *your* message and how to express it in the most powerful way possible.

Strong messages use vivid, unambiguous language. They rest on a foundation of information presented in a package that we call a *selling point,* which makes a positive statement and then gives an illustration.

Background: Some Thoughts on Selling

The word *selling* may strike you as odd or inappropriate in this context. So, before we turn our attention to selling points and persuasive language and their roles in building strong messages, we'd like to take a moment to clarify our thinking in this area.

As we see it, nineteen times out of twenty, when making a presentation you're really there to sell. Not necessarily a product or a service; it might be an image or idea, a course of action, a point of view—even yourself.

When we ask our workshop clients what their presentation goals are, we get a pretty standard array of answers. The list generally includes: to educate or inform, to solve problems, to arrive at decisions, to agree on a course of action, to persuade, and, yes, to sell.

You'll notice that most of these—all but the first, really—have a clearly active component. We want people to *do something*, based on what we are saying. We want our listeners to agree with us, to approve the recommendations we are making, to make the decision we are supporting. Those of you who have some experience in sales understand not only the obvious—that a sale is persuasion—but also that a sale *is* agreement, that a sale *is* arriving at a decision, that, very often, a sale *is* the solution to a problem.

And even those of you who present to inform or educate might consider for a moment whether there isn't a more active purpose to your presentations than simply to impart information. You probably also want your listeners to *do something*.

Suppose that you are giving a presentation about cardiopulmonary resuscitation. Aren't you are there to do more than simply inform your listeners of the existence of this life-saving technique? Certainly you're there to give them some insight into how it works, but more importantly you want to convince your listeners to *learn* CPR so they can save lives.

Many of us are uncomfortable with the idea of selling. We feel that selling "isn't nice." Perhaps this comes from our experience with certain types of salespeople. Who knows? But the reality is that our society is built on selling; it goes on *all the time* in our culture. Calvin Coolidge put it this way: "The business of America is business." And that means *selling*.

Our point here is not that you should become a slick, fast-talking, hard-sell artist, rather that conscious awareness of your underlying goal can provide *focus* to your presentations. And a focused message is a strong message. The more conscious you are of an *active* goal, the more powerfully your message will be communicated. You want your listeners to *do* something; you want, in effect, to close the sale.

Retention Factors

In addition to making your point powerfully, focus contributes to retention. You want people to remember your message long enough to act on it. Unfortunately, this is not so easy to accomplish. Here's one key fact for you to remember about communications:

People don't remember much

As we mentioned in Chapter One, the classic research of psychologist Hermann Ebbinghaus tells us that half an hour after a presentation, the average listener has forgotten 40 percent of what was said. By the end of the day, 60 percent. By the end of a week, 90 percent will have been forgotten. The significance of this cannot be overstated.

If you really want to make your point—if you want it to be *remembered*—you had better make it *clear*, you had better make it *simple*, and you had better make it, as an anonymous wit once put it, "the way they used to vote in the Windy City—*early* and *often*."

Clarity, simplicity, and *repetition*—the words a successful presenter lives by. A message that is not clearly and emphatically stated will quickly be forgotten. A complicated message—or too many messages—may not be absorbed by listeners. A message presented once—as the conclusion of a closely reasoned argument—may not even be recognized as a message!

Selling Points

Creating selling points is a particular way of crafting information into an instrument of persuasion. We've already asserted that it is the foundation of a strong message, but what *is* a selling point?

Example: It's very rewarding being part of the Jaycees; we're a people organization. Seeing Mary Foster win the wheelchair sprint at the Millbrook Special Olympics was worth all the time I've put in over the years.

Notice that this selling point consists of two elements: a positive statement or assertion (the Jaycees is a rewarding organization to be involved with), which we call a *headline*, and an illustration that backs up the assertion (this experience was worth all the time given), which we call a *specific*. A headline can be any positive statement about your company, service, product, program, project, or research. The specific can take many forms: statistics, examples, anecdotes, third-party proof, visualizations, and analogies, to name a few.

Both components—headline and specific—are necessary. Without the specifics, you can't justify the headline. Without the headline to act as a pointer, the significance of the facts may be overlooked. When you use these elements together, your message becomes focused.

Most people just give the general statement—such as, "Our company is a reliable, high-quality service organization." They fail to go the extra step and provide a specific—"Did you know that the city government just hired us to maintain all of Springfield's police and fire alarms?"—that *demonstrates* the validity of the headline. It's the specific, not the headline, that actually gets most of the attention. And the more a specific can capture a listener's attention, the better it makes your point.

Case Study: The research director for a large corporation was making his presentation at the annual budget review. To justify his budget allocation, he needed to allay general management's concern that research wasn't contributing materially to the corporation. His contention was that although the department would never be a profit center in itself, it contributed to virtually every other division.

His *headline*: "Research *is* important." His *specific*: "One of our researchers developed a substitute for a high-priced ingredient in a food product that saved the brand over *nine million dollars* per year."

Empowering Language: Put a Tiger in Your Talk

The strongest selling points are the ones that appeal to people's "gee whiz" or "I didn't know that" response—and/or hit them in one of three other vital areas: the heart, the tummy, or the pocketbook. The more vividly they do this, the more likely your listeners are to remember your messages. Perhaps not the actual words, but at least the point.

Our primary tool as presenters is the spoken word. But there's another important tool that's often overlooked: our listeners' imagination. If we can use our speaking to engage the audience's imagination, we can get our messages across powerfully. If people can *visualize* your point they become active listeners. The key to powerful language in presentations is really quite simple. Don't tell, *illustrate*.

This approach is especially effective when applied to statistics or numbers. Though we use numbers a lot as communications tools, they can be quirky. Since Western science describes the world and its events primarily in numerical terms, as a culture we have a very high regard for numbers, almost a reverence. We equate numbers with *facts*. On a personal level, we're able to reject numbers as abstractions and tune them out.

If you have a statistic that you feel makes your point, find a vivid way of *illustrating* it and you will multiply its impact several times over.

Case Study: The American Lung Association had come up with a very powerful number that they were trying to impress on the public: Every day nearly one thousand people in this country die prematurely of smoking-related diseases. That's disturbing, but it's just a number; easy for most people to tune out. "Almost a thousand people a day" isn't enough to really get the average person's attention, so we helped them explore alternate ways of presenting the same information.

Almost a thousand people a day adds up over time; it's equivalent to about 320,000 people a year. That has a bit more impact; it's harder to mentally exclude yourself from a group that size. But it's still just a number. To give it power we needed to relate it to something, to make it concrete.

"That's like Giants Stadium filled five times over . . ." was one idea we came up with. Not bad, but it had two problems. First, for anyone who doesn't know how big Giants Stadium is it doesn't mean much. Second, it fails to underscore the main idea: death on a large scale.

Finally we came up with a presentation that would hit home to just about everybody: "Almost one thousand people in this country die each day from smoking-related illnesses. Imagine it. That's as if two fully loaded jumbo jets collided over your hometown *every day*—and everyone aboard was killed. We would do something about the air traffic problem that was responsible. Likewise, we should do something about the smoking problem."

You can almost see that scene of the planes crashing and the wreckage and carnage on the ground. This is a painful image, but it is the type of image the ALA wants people to have—to *actively* see in their minds' eyes, and perhaps be motivated to take action.

This selling point was so impressive that U. S. Surgeon General C. Everett Koop began using it for his own presentations .

Selling Point File

Creating good selling points doesn't require a consummate literary gift, but it does take thought, attention, and imagination. We suggest that you keep an active selling point file—especially if you present to "external" audiences. In external presentations your listeners often have little or no real stake in you or your message; there is no common task orientation, as there is in a business meeting. This means your messages have to be stronger to make your point.

Good headline material—points you might need to communicate—comes up all the time. Write these points down in a notebook or on file cards along with whatever statistical evidence substantiates them. Don't ignore newspapers and magazines as potential sources of material.

Then spend some time creating supporting illustrations, analogies, or visualizations that really bring them to life. Don't go too far; some analogies work, others stretch the imagination beyond the point of receptivity. If you do your work conscientiously, you may come up with several compelling specifics for any given headline. This gives you the option of remaking the same point in a fresh way.

This approach works for "internal" presentations, of course. For example: "The new personnel policies and regular staff meetings have improved productivity. George Smith says that lateness is down 15 percent. More importantly, George told me that Felix Jones is working harder and said he felt like he had more of a stake in the organization."

Keep adding points and working with the ones already in your file. You can't have too many selling points. The opportunity to deliver a selling point can come up at any time in a presentation. The better yours are worked out, the more impact they will have. And the more you practice the art of creating selling points, the easier it gets.

Well-Chosen Words

Communicating clearly is not an easy matter, even when all parties have the best intentions. Words can convey meaning with intricate precision, but they have an equal capacity to mislead. Carefully chosen words are more likely to carry the meaning you intend than carelessly chosen ones. Here are our two principles of presentation language:

Use simple, everyday language as much as possible. Use
strong, active, and, above all, *positive* words.

Keep It Simple

In general, try to use one word, preferably a short one, where
several might do. If you must use technical jargon or industry
buzzwords, define your terms.

It would be foolish to let your vocabulary make your point un-
intelligible. If your message hangs on one or two key terms and those
terms aren't understood, then your message is wasted. Assuming
that your listeners share your special vocabulary is a pitfall—you
can't be sure.

Acronyms are particularly problematic because they are ambiguous. "OTC," for example, may mean "over the counter" to both a
stockbroker and a pharmaceutical manufacturer, but to a travel
agent it means "one stop charter." In the telephone business it means
"operating telephone company," which is also known as a "LEC"
(local exchange company) or a "BOC" (Bell operating company).
Compound that ambiguity by the number of acronyms we encounter every day and the potential for misunderstanding is astonishing.

For clear communications, don't use esoteric, trendy, and highly
technical words and terms—especially acronyms. If you're absolutely sure that the people you're talking to speak the same private
language, go ahead and use them. But *can* you be sure?

Case Study: We once gave a session with people from two different telephone companies, both of which sold an alarm monitoring service. The companies marketed the same product
under different names—one called it "Scan Alert," the other
"React." We discovered during the session that people from
each company were unaware of the trade name of the other
company's product.

The point of this illustration is not that you must avoid using a
trade name in your talk. When you do use a trade name or any other

term that listeners *might* be unfamiliar with, add a brief explanation (e.g., "Scan Alert—that's our alarm monitoring service . . ."). It's simple to do, and it can make the difference between the success or failure of your presentation.

Make It Strong and Positive

There is another dimension of message building we want to cover here. Modesty, which many of us are taught as a cultural value in childhood, dictates that we refrain from "blowing our own horns." As a consequence we often refer in neutral terms to accomplishments that we are proud of. Modesty, however, is out of place in selling.

We want you to look at each of your selling points and notice your wording. Can you find a word that says it more positively? More emphatically? This means using affirmative terms like "I believe," "I know," or "I recommend" instead of the relatively neutral terms "I think" or "it seems."

For example, if your company has to meet federal standards in doing business with the government, this may be a fact you mention in your presentations as an indication of product quality. But compare these statements: "We meet federal standards in this area" and "We *exceed* federal standards." The latter statement sends a much more powerful message.

Instead of a colorless statement like "I think this proposal should be approved . . ."—assuming you truly believe it—an emphatic phrase like "The research really convinces me . . ." leaves listeners in no doubt about exactly where you stand.

Signal Words, Themes, and Triplets

There are three more specific ideas we'd like to cover before we leave the topic of words.

Signal words. As a presenter you want your listener's undivided attention, and you may come close to that goal at times. Realistically, you should realize that people's attention does wander, but that it can be summoned back when it's especially important for you to have it. You have to send out a signal that says, "Pay attention!"

Signal words like "What's significant here," "I want to stress," "Let me underscore," "What's important here," or "This *can't* be overemphasized" send that kind of a message. Review or summation phrases like "In conclusion," "To summarize," or "Let's review" do the same. These words put the audience's attention back where it should be—on the speaker.

Themes. As you create the powerful images that give life to your messages, look for a phrase that might serve as a theme; a special idea or image that sums up your message. An image like this can be woven through your talk, building power and retention through repetition and remaining in the listener's memory long after the rest of your message has disappeared.

Case Study: Benjamin Lambert, chairman and CEO of Eastdil Realty, Inc., a major real estate investment organization, was preparing for an industry conference talk in San Francisco when he came up with the image of the amber light.

The traffic light analogy is an investment business cliché. Investors and brokers are always talking about investment red lights and green lights. One of Ben's fundamental points, however, was that in the real estate market, the light is almost never either green or red. In real estate, one is virtually always proceeding on the amber light of caution.

We liked the analogy and suggested that he make it his lead, work it into the body of the speech, and use it again as a close. We even helped create a little anecdote for the opener about the country's first traffic light, erected in Cleveland in 1914. And so was born the Amber Light Theory of real estate investment. The image got such a strong response that within a week the idea had made it from one coast to the other, by word of mouth. A potential client in New York, who had not attended the session, later told one of Lambert's executives that he had heard the theory—and agreed with it.

Triplets. Experienced speakers, writers, broadcasters, and others whose livelihoods depend on effective use of language have long been aware that three words are often better than one. (Please allow us this exception to the "one word where several will do" advice, above.)

There's something mystically powerful about grouping words in triplets. It's one of the oldest tricks in the book of rhetoric and memorable examples abound, especially in oratory and advertising: "blood, sweat, and tears . . ."; "government of the people, by the people, and for the people . . ."; "round, firm, and fully packed . . ."; "snap, crackle, and pop. . . ."

Learn to think in threes. It can add punch to your selling points and your key messages.

Quick Reference Summary

- Think of your presentation as if you were selling; it will help you focus your message.
- Your message should ask your listeners to *do* something: to vote, to decide, to act.
- Clarity, simplicity, and repetition aid retention.
- Selling points are the foundation of a persuasive presentation—whether or not you are literally selling.
- A selling point consists of a positive statement—a *headline*—backed up by a supporting illustration or *specific*.
- Look for vivid, visual ways of illustrating your selling points—images that make your listeners *see* your point.
- Use simple, everyday words; avoid technical jargon and acronyms.
- If you must use technical language, jargon, or industry buzzwords, explain them.
- Use strong, active, positive words, not guarded or negative ones.

- Use signal words and phrases to keep the audience tuned in: "The real issue is . . ."; "What's important here . . ."; "This is critical . . ."
- Look for visual themes that can tie a presentation together.
- Use words in groups of three to increase audience interest and retention.

5

The Three-Minute Presentation Writing Technique

Somebody once asked Abraham Lincoln how long it took him to prepare a speech. "It takes me about two weeks to write a good twenty-minute speech," he said, "but I can write a *forty*-minute speech in *one* week. And," he added, "I can give a two-hour talk on almost any subject right now." Or, as a correspondent of ours once put it: "If I'd had more time, I'd have written you a shorter letter."

The point? It's hard to be concise.

With our three-minute presentation writing technique, however, we give you a way to cut the job down to size. Once you are proficient with it, you should be able to draft your presentation in three minutes or less, regardless of length. Our technique works whether you make thirty-second, five-minute, or two-hour presentations.

Not only is it fast, our writing technique also gives you an important psychological edge. Think of the times you've sat down to write a presentation, a memo, or a report and gotten stuck trying to come up with a lead. Remember the days before word processors, how those crumpled pages piled up on the floor? Our method relieves you of all the frustration of getting started because the lead will come later.

The technique centers on two easy steps:

1. Stating your conclusion
2. Listing your arguments

These elements comprise the core of your presentation. Almost the entire structure flows from them. A third element is often necessary to complete the scheme, and that has to do with the "lead" we just mentioned. We'll discuss that later.

The first step is the key, but it rests on doing something that does *not* come naturally to most people. The natural tendency in formal communications seems to be to save the conclusion—recommendation, action plan, sales pitch—for the end. Our writing technique, however, reverses that process.

Step One. Make a succinct, one-, two-, or three-line statement of your message; the bottom line of your presentation.

By the time you're ready to start writing you should be able to do this fairly easily. If you can't, the chances are you're not ready to write.

This point of departure acts like a mental funnel, channeling your whole thought process into a tightly focused output. It makes for a stronger presentation because it forces you to focus on your *message* rather than your argument.

In communications, arguments are secondary. The first priority is to make clear what is being proposed; then the supporting facts can be introduced to bolster the conclusion.

Case Study: A client of ours, a research scientist with a pharmaceutical firm, provides an excellent illustration of why this is so important. She came to us to improve her presentation skills following her first experience in presenting to senior business management.

True to the scientific method in which background and data precede the conclusion, our scientist launched into an hour's worth of data related to her projects. After about three minutes, the president of the company slammed his hand on the conference table and demanded, "Do we have a new drug here, or *don't* we?"

For him, this was the bottom line. If the answer was *yes,* then he wanted to hear the details; if it was *no,* the details were irrelevant. If it was *maybe,* he could decide, but without knowing the point of the message, a lengthy exposition was unacceptable.

The principle illustrated by this example is true even when it's not a go/no-go situation, as in the preceding case study. Look at it from a listener's point of view: When you know where an argument is leading, you can judge how well the points substantiate the conclusion as the argument unfolds.

In a sense, the facts that make up the argument are just packaging; they usually won't be remembered.

Another thing to consider is that in many informal presentation situations (in the hall, in the elevator) you may be cut off at any moment. Even in formal meetings you never know what key figure may have to leave early. So, whatever the circumstance, give them your message early.

Where to start. Begin. Grab a pad and a pencil; you're ready to start creating your presentation. First state your conclusion, your recommendation, and your action plan. Most often this should take the form of a direct call for action.

You'd be surprised how many presenters never really tell their audience what they want from them. This is true even of salespeople: According to Hank Trisler (*No Bull Selling,* Bantam Books, 1985), 63 percent of sales calls end without the salesperson ever asking for the order. We want you to formulate your message so that you make it absolutely clear what it is you want them to do. Here are a few examples:

- "Lease a car from us. It will give you convenience, flexibility, and reliability."
- "I recommend that we reorganize our materials supply system and keep this plant open."
- "Volunteer some of your time to the United Way; you'll feel better about yourself and our community will be stronger."
- "My committee's recommendation is that the management invest four-point-seven million dollars in this new line of business. We'd like your approval."

What's *your* conclusion? Write it down. Say it out loud. How does it sound to you? Make it clear and strong. You're off and running. Once your conclusion is set, the rest of your presentation should fall into place.

Step Two. List the selling points that support your conclusion.

These two elements—your *conclusion* and *action plan* and your list of *selling points*—form the backbone of your presentation. Here's how it works:

Conceptually, we divide presentations into three sections:
- Beginning
- Middle
- End

in which you:
- Tell 'em what you're gonna tell 'em
- Tell 'em
- Tell 'em what you told 'em

The beginning and ending essentially mirror each other, stating your conclusion and briefly summarizing the supporting material. The middle, the body of the presentation, consists of discussing that material in detail.

Let's look at the specific structure of each segment of the presentation.

Beginnings

The function of your opening is to clearly state your message, to outline the argument that supports it, and to prepare listeners for the detailed discussion that will follow. It has another function as well. In addition to introducing your message, your opening is your big chance to really get your listeners *listening*.

Perhaps you know the story about the old farmer who came upon a neighbor one day, trying to get his mule to go. The man was shouting and cursing and pulling on the bridle—all to no avail. Picking up a handy piece of two-by-four, the farmer whacked the mule between the ears with all his might. The mule shook its head. The farmer shouted, "Gee-up!" The mule blinked for a moment and then started forward. "The problem is," explained the farmer, "you first got to get his attention."

Think of the attention span of today's Zippers and Zappers. (Zippers are those who fast forward through the commercials on programs they have taped on videocassette recorders. Zappers change TV stations with their remote controls.) Few listeners or viewers give a station much time before flicking the dial. It's often a matter of seconds. And the producers of programs and commercials don't want us to fast-forward or change the channel or station. In the presentation arena, you have a little more time—about 30 seconds before people tune you out. If they don't leave the room, they think about errands they have to run, the weather, work piling up on their desk, the movies. If we admit to being Zippers and Zappers, then you can see why it's important to have a strong opening or grabber in a presentation.

Attention is a prerequisite to communication. The more of the audience's attention you have, the more communicating you can do.

Here is the third element in the three-minute writing technique, relating to the "lead."

Step Three. An introduction that captures your listeners' attention is a necessity.

It doesn't matter *when* this element gets created. Despite the fact that it will be used in your introduction, it can be the last step in your preparation.

The Grabber. Since audiences can be quite mulelike, a presenter needs a verbal equivalent of the two-by-four in our story. You want not merely to capture your listeners' attention but to really engage their minds. We call this kind of attention-getting kickoff the *grabber*.

The appropriate degree of "grab" will vary from one type of occasion to another. Generally, your grabber doesn't have to make the stars fall from the sky or shake the pillars of the temple. It should introduce the topic in a catchy, arresting, or amusing manner, or it should introduce *you*, creating a connection between you and your listeners. If it can do both, even better.

We use three types of grabbers:

- The anecdote
- The prop
- The bottom line

At its very simplest, your grabber can be something as transparent as relating a pertinent thought, insight, or observation that "occurred to me as I was driving out here this morning." Or perhaps "I was talking to Amy just before the meeting, and she was telling me some of her concerns about test market results on the product." Personal references like these help break down barriers between you and the audience by establishing a connection, even if it's a small one.

The Anecdote. Humor is good bonding material, which makes it a valuable ingredient in openings. We don't recommend jokes as grabbers, because even seasoned pros like Johnny Carson fall on their faces about 30 percent of the time. But almost any humorous anecdote such as a personal story with a laugh—or just a smile—can do the job. Good material of this sort is often close at hand.

Case Study: A woman in one of our workshops had compiled a comprehensive report on what in the telecommunications business is called "corridor traffic" (that is, phone calls between major markets that cross state lines, say from Camden, New Jersey, to Philadelphia). Her presentation about the report was interesting and informative, but it lacked a distinctive opening.

In a casual conversation with us, she mentioned that she had become a minor celebrity around the office as a result of her efforts. Her colleagues had dubbed her the "corridor queen." We pointed out that this would make a terrific opener: "Let me tell you how I came to be called the corridor queen. . . ." She'd had it in her head all the time; it just hadn't seemed relevant to a public presentation.

Personal, whimsical touches like these pull an audience in. You wouldn't necessarily use this type of grabber for the chairman of the board, but it would work fine for a group of peers.

Even an amusing play on words can make a good grabber.

Case Study: A new vice president of marketing at a midwestern phone company who was new to the telephone business was convinced an acronym describing Local Access Transport Areas (LATAs) would never be understood by the public. He wanted it changed.

The company's advertising director, however, had studies that indicated that LATA had gained a high recognition factor within the industry and that changing the terminology at this point would be extremely costly. Her message was, "Let's keep things the way they are"; and status quo can be a lot harder to sell than innovation. She wasn't going to astound anyone with what she had to say, so in keeping with her low-key message, she came up with an effective grabber: "Good morning. We're here today to discuss the LATA matta'. I believe that LATA is here to stay, and in support of this I'm going to give you some

LATA data . . ."—which she then proceeded to do. And recognizing a good thing, she mirrored the opening in her conclusion: "I hope that now we'll be able to lay the LATA matta' to rest."

The Prop. There are times when you'll really wish you had a two-by-four for an attention-getter. We really don't recommend this, but sometimes the right prop will do the job.

Case Study: A product manager we know was once the fourth of six scheduled presenters at a morning sales meeting held in Montevideo, Uruguay. To begin with, a lot of salespeople don't want to be bothered with information. Their attitude is, "All I need to know is what's the price and what's my cut?" And in this particular setting, their minds were mainly on the sightseeing they would be doing as soon as this meeting was over.

His topic was the chemical properties of the company's new shrink wrap—a subject the salespeople would need to know when they talked to customers. How to get their attention? This was his solution:

"You will notice that I have placed on your desks two oranges. One is shrink-wrapped, the other is not. I want you to take these home and put them on your kitchen windowsill. Call me in a month and tell me how they're holding up. I guarantee that the orange that isn't wrapped will be a shriveled wreck. The one that *is* wrapped will look just about the way it does now.

"Then take a knife and cut into the shrink-wrapped orange. You'll find it as fresh and sweet as any orange you could buy at the store that morning. Now. Let's talk about the chemical properties of this improved shrink-wrapping. . . ."

The prop helped to penetrate; it got a "gee whiz" response by graphically and dramatically *illustrating* something significant about the product. It was interesting enough to hold their attention for the time he needed to make his point.

The Bottom Line. The stunt with the oranges is really a *dramatization* of a selling point. Very often a strong selling point makes an excellent grabber. Especially effective selling points are those that stimulate the intellect, provoke our "gee-whiz" response, appeal to our sense of self-interest or well-being, or touch one of our emotional buttons—hitting us in the heart, the tummy, or the pocketbook.

Case Study: Probably one of the toughest audiences any presenter could face, in terms of attention-getting, are the passengers on the New York–Washington, D.C., air shuttle. These people are busy and stressed. They've heard the air safety instructions scores of times.

Knowing this, the stewardess on one recent flight began her spiel with the following: "Did you know that flying is the safest form of transportation? Safer than riding a bicycle or a train?" With this grabber, she caught the attention of the normally blasé passengers.

She continued: "But safety is everybody's responsibility, so please take out the card from the seat pocket in front of you and read along as I review the information. . . ."

Our rough estimate was that about one-half of the passengers did indeed reach for their instruction cards and seemed to be following along—about a tenfold increase over a normal shuttle flight.

Case Study: A client of ours was involved in marketing an order processing software package. In her presentation, she mentioned one implementation in which this system had reduced 350 days of order processing time to 5 working days. We suggested she make this her grabber: "If we could help you boil down an entire year's order processing work into *one week*, wouldn't you be interested in learning something about our services?" This selling point was so strong we encouraged her to use it in her closing as well.

We could go on about grabbers, but we've certainly given you some ideas to work with. Whatever opening gambit you hit upon, it should lead directly and naturally into the statement of your bottom line (if your grabber does not, in fact, contain your message), after which you can briefly outline the body of your talk. And that's your beginning.

Once you have worked out the beginning of your presentation, we strongly recommend that you commit it to memory.

During the first moments of your interaction with the audience, you want to be able to mobilize all your communications skills, which means making eye contact with your listeners and having your hands and arms free to gesture (see Chapter Seven for a detailed discussion of delivery skills). Memorizing your opening lets you concentrate fully on your delivery.

A final thought on openings and grabbers: Although you may think we're pushing you to become vaudeville performers with all this razzle-dazzle, we really just want you to be strong presenters. We actually welcome the opportunity to tell presenters to tone it down. If you have doubts about any of this, think for yourself how you respond to presenters who drone on and on, or take a long time to come to the point. We feel strongly that it's better to *challenge* your listeners than to leave them to their daydreams.

Middles

The middle of your presentation is the guts. It's where the information is imparted and the persuasion takes place. It may contain:

- Supporting data
- Statistics
- Evidence
- Research
- Findings
- Proof

Without good, hard information in the middle, all the audience profiling and message tailoring in the world isn't going to mean much. Paradoxically, information is the part of your talk people are most likely to forget, but it is still a vital element. It is the material the audience needs to make decisions. If it's not there—or it's not convincing—you are *not* going to succeed in making your point.

Likewise, a ho-hum approach to the structure and the wording of the middle of your presentation can lose you the whole ball game. Strong visual imagery in your selling points, colorful or surprising illustrations and examples, and well-planned visuals can all add sparkle to the middle of your talk. They will help sustain interest and attention, but they are no substitute for solid facts.

Don't fall into the trap of putting all your time and effort into the ending and beginning and leaving the middle to take care of itself. If the body of your talk is boring or ponderous, it will completely undermine even the strongest opening. And it doesn't matter how stirring your closing is if you've already lost your audience.

There are four basic ways to structure the middle of a presentation. We call them:

- Question and answer (Q & A)
- Problem/solution
- Time/sequence
- Topical

Question and Answer. The Q & A approach analyzes a problem or task and puts it into a series of questions that needs answers. For example, "The questions we need to explore in our marketing plan are: What type of media support do we have? What are our sales objectives? and, Where does the sales force tie in?" After setting this agenda, the presenter then covers the individual questions and answers in detail.

Problem/solution. This scenario works well for reporting results and generally goes something like this: "As you know, we've been facing a serious and unanticipated cash-flow problem, stemming ultimately from a troublesome deterioration in accounts receivable. We were asked to study the situation and develop some measures to correct it. We found that both the average age of receivables and percentage of overdue accounts had risen sharply in the first quarter. We also found that our reporting system made it extremely cumbersome to track down the specific information that would help us take appropriate action. . . ."

In other words, the problem/solution scenario involves a concise statement detailing the elements of the problem, followed by an outline of how solutions were developed, leading into a detailed discussion of the significant stages and findings. This kind of a middle would naturally culminate in an emphatic selling point something like: "With our new reporting system up and running we have been able to reduce the average age of receivables from sixty-one to forty-seven days, which is far below industry standards. And we're happy to report that cash flow is looking better than it has for years."

Time/sequence or 'timeline.' This approach stresses the history or chronology of a process, problem, or issue.

Case Study: Marc Chodorow, vice president of public relations for Goldome Bank, a national banking company, uses the timeline approach when representing Goldome to the press or to securities analysts. A thumbnail version goes roughly like this:

"Between December 1981 and March 1982, the former Buffalo Savings Bank, whose assets were three billion dollars, acquired three troubled thrift institutions. Assets grew to nine billion dollars. In early 1983, the organization became Goldome (named after the gold-domed building that had been the institution's home since 1901). The year 1983 also saw the creation of our mortgage banking company and insurance agency, and the acquisition of two savings and loans in Florida. In 1983–84, we created a merchant banking group. In 1985–86, the new corporate headquarters were completed in Buffalo, incorporating the original building and thus symbolizing the progress from a regulated savings bank to a diversified national banking concern. In 1986, we recorded our highest profits ever, and in 1987, Goldome went public."

Another time/sequence example would be the pharmaceutical product manager explaining to new management recruits the process of getting a new product to market; running down the sequence of events from preclinical testing through application for FDA approval, product design, tooling up, clinical testing, packaging design, advertising and promotion development, to actually getting the drug to the sales force and into hospital formularies and onto pharmacy shelves.

Topical. This method is probably the most common. Basically, it says, "Here are the topics that need to be dealt with or resolved in situation X." As with all these approaches, it is important that you provide your listeners with a good road map. For example, you might begin, "There are several topics we need to explore in evaluating this acquisition. . . ." But instead of proceeding to exploring them one by one, take the time to list them first: "The topics include the Dependable Company's product line, the cost and payment terms of the acquisition, and the synergies between our two companies." Then go through the list. This way, each topic is like fitting a brick into place; listeners anticipate the structure of the argument and watch it take shape.

If there are many facts in the middle of your presentation, it is a good idea to summarize your progress from time to time.

It's like erecting signposts for your listeners. "Now that we've covered the issues of cost and product lines, let's discuss the topic of synergies. . . ." If you've given a good clear opening statement of your objective you can reinforce that objective as you move through your points by explicitly referring back to it. For example, "Keep in mind that these numbers and statistics help prove the overall soundness of the marketing plan and should be considered when you vote later on. . . ."

Endings

You've told 'em what you're gonna tell 'em and you've told 'em. Now it simply remains to tell 'em what you told 'em—and to drive it home.

Briefly summarize the points of your argument and restate your message. To get the maximum impact from your restatement, you need to introduce or set off the ending with a signal phrase like "Let me summarize what I've said . . ." or "In conclusion. . . ." "Flagging" your conclusion increases its impact by focusing your listeners' attention; it alerts them to the fact that you are about to tell 'em what you told 'em. If they weren't paying close attention before, they will respond to this signal and pay attention.

The whole ending should take no more than a minute.

Like the opening, your ending should be memorized.

The reasoning here is the same as for the beginning: The end of your talk is the last thing your audience will hear, and the last thing heard is the thing most likely to be remembered. The more clearly and forcefully it is stated the greater the likelihood that it will be remembered accurately. Memorizing your ending lets you concentrate on clear and emphatic delivery.

Recap

Here's our three-minute writing technique in a nutshell:

1. Write your conclusion.
2. List the supporting material—your selling points: data, facts, statistics, research, examples.
3. Find an appropriate grabber.

Once you're familiar with the process you can go through it quite quickly—three minutes or less—when you need to. The technique works whether you're sitting in your office using a dictaphone, or in an airplane seat using pencil and paper.

In fact, the technique can be condensed into the "down and dirty thirty-second writing technique." And there are people who can use this. Pharmaceutical sales reps come to mind. They catch a doctor coming out of the elevator or the hospital cafeteria and very often they have literally thirty seconds to make a pitch. Something like

"Hey, Doctor Smith, I know you're just out of surgery and you haven't slept in four days and you have to go on rounds, but let me tell you the four reasons why our new drug is a better preoperative sedative. . . ."

Even if you don't normally work under these conditions, you may find the thirty-second technique comes in handy once in a while. You never can tell when you're going to find yourself in the elevator with the president of the company—that never-to-be-repeated opportunity to let the boss know—in person—what you've done for the organization lately.

Quick Reference Summary

- The three-minute writing technique begins with two primary steps:
    1. Write your conclusions, including an action plan.
    2. List your supporting arguments (selling points).
  These elements form the core of your presentation: beginning, middle, and end.
- Writing the conclusion first helps clarify and focus your thoughts.
- It is vital to gain an audience's attention within thirty seconds of beginning. Think "What's in it for them?"
- Develop a grabber to pull in audience. Grabbers are pertinent thoughts, insights, observations, analogies, personal experiences.
- Avoid jokes; they fall flat too often.
- Props dramatize points.
- After the grabber, the beginning of the presentation will mirror the ending. The key point goes *up front*.
- The middle of a presentation contains hard evidence; data, statistics, research.
- Presentation of the middle is vital to your credibility; take the time to do it well.
- Visual imagery of selling points, colorful or surprising information, and well-planned visuals add sparkle to middle of presentation.

- Presentation middle can be designed in one of four ways:
    1. Q & A—asking and answering vital questions on issue.
    2. Problem/solution—posing problems; offering solutions.
    3. Time/sequence—chronological orders of events to make your point.
    4. Topical—listing topics one by one, addressing them individually.
- Ending contains two elements: summary of key points and call for action. Tell audience what you want them to do.
- Set off your ending with signal words, summarize your arguments, and leave them with your action plan ringing in their ears.

6

Noteworthy Notes

You may or may not want to write out your entire presentation as you develop it, but you'll almost certainly want to have some sort of written material with you as you deliver your talk.

We feel very strongly that a presenter should use notes, rather than a full transcript. It is much harder to achieve the spontaneous conversational tone that is appropriate to presentations when reading from a full transcript. You almost inevitably sound like you're "giving a speech," which feels wrong to the audience in most presentation situations. Notes support the conversational mode, prompting and reminding you of what you want to say.

The most frequent question we get is, "How extensive should my notes be? What do I put down and what do I leave out?" Actually, the two questions, "how much" and "what," are not the same.

How much? Clearly, we can't give you a specific answer to this. It's going to depend on such factors as how long your presentation is, whether you give it once or often, and how much factual or numerical detail it contains. But we can offer a *general* answer—which is, "Probably a lot less than you think."

Notes should be a reminder, not a transcript.

Especially when people are new to presenting, they will begin by writing out a talk fully and then whittling it down to a few sparse notes. Others prefer to start with a detailed outline and pare that down. It may take a few presentations to get an accurate feel for what is important to have in front of you and what isn't.

Less is more. The more material that goes into your notes, the harder it will be for you to extract what you need.

The art of note making lies in achieving a balance between completeness and accessibility. As you include more information in your notes, either the word density increases to the point where your eye has trouble finding what it's looking for or you end up with too many pieces of paper.

What to write. Start with the idea that your notes should at least reflect the organization of your talk. This means at a minimum they should clearly list, in order, the points or topics you wish to cover. This will make sure you don't leave out anything you planned to say. Or, if time gets short, it lets you *choose* what to skip over and what to include.

You can use "bullets" (heavy black dots) to list your points or, if you prefer, number them. Numbering will be especially helpful if you open with a remark like, "There are really only four things that this committee needs to know about enzyme detergent additives."

Stay away from complete sentences. Generally, a word or two or a short phrase, will be sufficient to suggest each point you wish to cover.

In general, list facts, not principles.

Under stress, we tend to forget "facts"—specific references, numbers, examples. The facts listed on note cards will always lead us to the larger point, but it does not work the other way. If their accuracy is crucial, the details in your notes should be things like exact numbers or statistics, and lengthy quotations. Other things included will be cues for particular stories or anecdotes, cues for visuals, and personal reminders.

> **Tip:** Some experienced presenters dispense with notes altogether by working the information that would otherwise be on note cards into their visuals. This is not a bad idea unless it pushes you to include more visuals than taste and reason would otherwise dictate. Further, if your equipment malfunctions, you can be up a creek. Play it safe and have a hard copy of any notes you'll really need.

How to write. Print clearly, preferably in block capitals. Or type your notes. Keep notes sparse; leave as much blank space as is practicable to maximize legibility. You've probably all seen presenters who made their notes too small or wrote too much and had to squint to make out the key words. We don't want this to be you.

Make sure your notes are readable.

> **Tip:** You can use colored pens or highlighters to make crucial facts or cues virtually jump off the page. Red is the most visible for writing or underlining, but other colors work well, too. In fact, you can "code" your notes by using more than one color: for example, red for reminders, blue for statistics, green for quotations, and orange for anecdotes. Yellow isn't very read-

able, so you won't want to write with it; on the other hand, it is excellent for highlighting (marking over words to make them stand out).

Another possibility is using colored index cards to code the different sections or areas of your presentation. One color each for beginning, middle, and end, perhaps. A colored card for your facts and figures. A colored card for your final summary points. The possibilities are limited only by your needs and ingenuity.

What to write on. You can make notes on virtually anything. Legend has it that Abraham Lincoln wrote the Gettysburg Address on the back of an envelope. If that's all you have available, fine; but other things work better.

Five-by-seven-inch file cards make the best note cards.

File cards are best because the heavy paper stock stands up to normal wear and tear. We recommend the five-by-seven size because, in our experience, that is the best compromise between legibility and manageability (smaller and you either have to write small or you can't get much on one card; larger and they become awkward to handle—and conspicuous). They are best used in the vertical or "portrait" orientation, perpendicular to the way the lines are printed, so you will want to use the blank side. Writing across the short dimension of the card helps keep notes short and concise.

Tip: If you plan to follow your talk with a question and answer session, make a separate card listing important selling points you made during your talk, points important enough to be repeated.

Glance over the card before you begin your Q & A, and refer to it from time to time as you field questions. You can also jot down on this card any vital numbers, facts, or statistics you need to have at your fingertips for answering questions.

Case Study: Here's a concrete example of how a set of presentation notes might look. Six sparsely worded five-by-seven note cards were all Andy needed for a forty-minute presentation to an audience of eighty lawyers in a course designed to improve their courtroom skills and techniques.

The message of the presentation was that *how* a lawyer communicates can be as important as what he or she says. The talk referred primarily to opening and closing arguments during a trial, but was also applicable to questioning of witnesses before a judge or jury. Andy's action message was to ask the lawyers to be aware of this aspect of trial work and to practice the techniques he would demonstrate to improve their skills.

The stated assumption in the talk was that there was no substitute for a good case with good witnesses and the facts and/or the law on your side. But all things being equal, it is very often the better presenter or communicator who convinces a judge or a jury.

But the question here is: What did Andy put on the cards?

```
                                          Note Card 1

    1.—AG
       CCI

    2.—NOTICE ME
            SUIT
            LIMP
            TIE


       TENN.
       IDAHO
       FDA
```

Andy's first remarks concerned his name and a brief statement about CommCore and our business.

Next, Andy asked people what they noticed about him as he walked to the front of the room. The points, in case he didn't get much response, were that these lawyers, or members of a jury (their audience) would notice a suit, the fact that Andy was limping due to a recent injury, and maybe that he had a red "power" tie on.

The third set of points were grabber points (see our discussion of "grabbers," p. 48) to convince the lawyers that judges and jury members still wanted to be entertained. The notes were Andy's cues for short anecdotes about events in Tennessee, Idaho, and the Food and Drug Administration. These anecdotes all led to the conclusion that judges, commissioners, and other decision makers are supposed to base their judgments on the facts a presenter gives, not how it is presented. These anecdotes also let Andy's audience know that these decision makers are also human beings influenced by how things are communicated. What's important about his notes is that he wrote down the anecdotal note, not the conclusion. From the anecdote, he could always get to the conclusion. However, if he'd just written a note about the conclusion, he might have forgotten to mention Tennessee or one of the other examples.

Andy concluded his opening with a statement about the purpose of the talk.

Note Card 2

3.—Ct. Room Scenes
        Inherit the Wind
        Pat & Mike
        Perry Mason
        The Verdict
        LA Law
        (Imperfect)

4.—CONTRAGATE
        Brendan Sullivan

John Niels
Arthur Liman

Andy next asked the lawyers to name some of their favorite courtroom scenes. This was part of an attempt to make the talk interactive. His note card list of movies and TV shows was in case the lawyers didn't come up with suggestions, or in case he wanted to bridge to a point.

The "(Imperfect)" point was to remind the lawyers that part of their comments related to impression, but they should not be thrown off by the "perfect" world of the tube or the silver screen. The courtroom is a more "imperfect," real-world environment.

Point four related to several comments Andy wanted to make about the Iran/Contragate congressional hearings, which were then going on. His comments were more about the lawyers involved than the key witnesses.

Note Card 3

<u>IMPRESSION</u>
40
60
90

7
35
58

<u>FDA</u>
<u>TENN.</u>
<u>IDAHO</u>

Remember the statistics we've talked about concerning what an audience retains and what makes up the entire impression? Andy quoted them and applied them to courtroom situations, where a jury can always ask for testimony to be read back to them.

"FDA," "TENN.," and "IDAHO" had been on card 1. However, in case Andy forgot to mention them early on, he wanted to get the points in during the talk. And that illustrates an important point about notes: In some ways, Andy didn't even need the cards. He probably could have used one card with several points. However the cards are a good crutch, as well as a reminder in case he forgot something. During the talk, he referred to them several times. Even at the end of the talk, he bought a moment before his conclusion by saying, "Give me a moment; let me check my notes to make sure I covered everything."

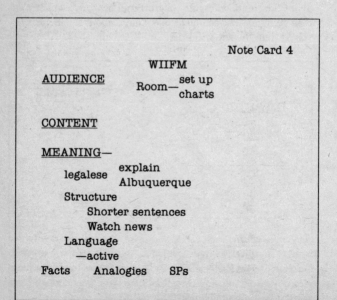

With the note "AUDIENCE," Andy asked the lawyers to be aware of the audience, whether it was a judge or a jury. Clearly, the audience profile would have been done during jury selection. But the point was to be aware of the appropriate WIIFMs. The other point was to be aware of the physical environment and to use the room effectively.

"CONTENT" was Andy's statement that the facts had to be right. However, given facts and content for a statement or questions, the lawyer should be mindful not to use too much legalese with a jury lest they not understand all the information. Andy illustrated this with an anecdote about an Albuquerque lawyer.

"STRUCTURE" cued Andy to mention using shorter sentences in important oral communications and that a good way to learn oral communications skills is to watch good commentators on television.

The "LANGUAGE" notes refer to many of the elements we just covered in the writing chapter. The specific words— "Facts," "Analogies," and "SPs"—were points Andy wanted to make.

Note Card 5

VOICE
GESTURES
EYES
DRESS
NERVES
PAUSES

As you read further in *Get to the Point* you will learn what we have to say about all these elements. Andy used the cue words to be sure to cover each element and how it relates to communications, impressions, and retention. One word was enough for a one- to two-minute chunk of his talk.

```
                                           Note Card 6
        PRACTICE
        EXERCISES
        LISTEN to TV, RADIO
        SMILE
        ENJOY                               Marion
        NERVES                              Seltzer
        JACK LALANNE
```

These were Andy's final notes about how to apply and use the information in his talk. Each word was a cue. Again, this is much of what we have covered and will cover in *Get to the Point*.

The name on the right was written in at the last minute and was a reference to one of the course instructors Andy met just before he spoke. This was a way to personalize the talk. In fact, he had mentioned Ms. Seltzer earlier in the talk, but the note was here just in case he forgot.

The "JACK LALANNE" note was to remind himself to get the audience members up on their feet and to show them exercises that would loosen them up before a presentation. (You'll find these exercises on p. 154.) Everyone present indeed did rise and do the exercises, including a federal and a state judge who were sitting on the dais.

Since doing closing statements and answering questions have long since become second nature to him, Andy made no cards for these parts of the talk. So that's it. Six cards, forty minutes. Try making note cards; they'll work for you, too.

Note choreography. Walking to the lectern or speaker's platform with a handful of papers can add a distracting element to the beginning of your presentation, a transition that you want to go as smoothly and unobtrusively as possible. If you have to put on a microphone, empty hands are necessary. What do you do with your notes? If you use the five-by-seven cards we recommend, they will usually fit neatly in either an inside breast pocket or an outside jacket pocket.

If you like to use large sheets, for whatever reason, solving the problem is trickier. You can fold your notes and put them in a pocket, but this means you will have to carefully unfold the pages before you begin speaking, which can be quite noisy when amplified. Further, once folded, paper has a tendency to fold back up, so unless you go through the cumbersome process of reverse-creasing them, your pages probably won't lie flat and may be difficult to read.

A solution is to leave your notes on the lectern before the proceedings begin. But this creates another hazard: It will be very easy for someone else to inadvertently walk away with them. A covering sheet that says something like "Speaker's Notes—Do Not Remove on Pain of Death" should prevent this. Even safer would be to use the cover sheet *and* tape the notes to the lectern with removable tape.

If you work without a lectern, you will have to hold your notes. Five-by-seven (or smaller) cards work best in this situation. Letter-size note pages are a distraction—a visual distraction to the audience and a physical distraction to you.

Quick Reference Summary

- Speak from notes, not from a complete transcript. The talk is in your head; your notes function as a written agenda including vital reminders.
- Five-by-seven file cards held vertically work best for notes.
- Keep notes succinct; a word or two per item.
- Write *facts* on notecards, not general overview statements. Stress reduces the ability to remember specifics. You can always get the statement from the fact, not vice versa.
- Visual aids can serve as notes.
- Use colored pens, highlighters, and cards to help make important information stand out.

7

Show and Tell:
Visual Aids

Even an accomplished presenter can become better by using visual aids. Visual materials—whether they consist of flip charts, overhead transparencies, color slides, films, videotapes, or three-dimensional models or other physical props—can be of tremendous help in making a point. Their skillful and judicious use can add dimensions to your presentation that no amount of extra speaking can contribute.

A recent study by the University of Minnesota and the 3M Corporation (which updates an earlier study by the Wharton School) finds that an audience is *43 percent more likely to be persuaded by presenters who use visuals*.

As useful as visuals are, however, we would like to emphasize that they are best used in moderation. Notice that we use the words "visual *aids*." While we want to enhance our communication by letting our audience see as well as hear, the visual material should be there to assist—*not* to control or dominate.

We make this point because it is easy to get carried away with visuals, to include so many that they overshadow the main attraction—which is you. Visuals are rather like icing: a pleasing complement to cake but cloying if too thickly spread.

You should follow these three rules:

- KISS (Keep It Short and Simple)
- Color
- Pause

If you do, visuals will add focus to your presentation. But beware: As visuals proliferate, they lose their impact and dull your listeners' attention.

Case Study: One company we know invested in the latest technology, a computer-generated graphics device that produces quite professional-looking images, highly detailed and very colorful—images that can grow and evolve right on the screen. A consulting client of ours in that company was among the first to get his hands on this device, and he received many compliments on the fine graphics in his presentations. The problem was that few people could recall the content of his message.

The University of Minnesota/3M study put it this way: " Image-enhanced graphics are effective only when selected and used carefully."

What is the optimum number of visuals to use? We obviously can't give you a specific answer, but we do have a recommendation: Keep them to a minimum. A good rule of thumb is, "When in doubt, leave it out."

Limit your visuals to those points that will have more impact visually than verbally and you'll be on safe ground.

Never begin or end your presentation with a visual unless it is absolutely compelling. Remember, they came to see *you*, not a media show.

We all sense the truth in the old saying, "A picture is worth a thousand words," but make sure it's the *right* picture in the right place. The very thing that makes good visuals so powerful is, in a word, *simplicity*.

A picture that conveys a complete idea or set of relationships in a single visual image is the proverbial thousand-worder.

One of our all-time favorite ads is the familiar Coppertone billboard, with the little girl and the puppy who's playfully pulling down her swimsuit bottom. It communicates a simple message, uncluttered with extraneous information like the price or the sun-block number. All it really says is "suntan product"—and that's all it needs to say.

Good visuals work in the same way as a strong verbal selling point—by illustrating, not explaining. And the simplicity and vividness of the imagery add up to *high retention*.

Busy and cluttered visuals—complicated charts and graphs, screens full of words—can actually decrease retention. There are two seemingly contradictory reasons for this. First, complex or cluttered graphics present a task—a dense mass of visual fodder for the eye to munch through and digest—that the brain naturally resists. Second, though the brain resists digesting the visual, it will continue to try, and will be distracted from your message. It will return to this annoying challenge and "worry" it. The problem is that while this is happening what you are saying will not be heard.

The Basics

We have distilled the treatment of visuals down to three basic rules:

- The first, *KISS*, relates to content.
- The second, *color*, relates to execution.
- The third, *pause*, relates to delivery.

KISS. It's the rule seen at work in the Coppertone ad. Apply it when you design your visuals. When in doubt, simplify; eliminate extraneous material. If necessary, use an additional visual rather than burdening one with more information than it can efficiently transmit.

Different industries use this rule in various imaginative ways. The print advertising business, for example, gives us the "six-pack rule": A presentation visual should contain no more than six lines of copy and a "package" or headline on top. The art director of a television news broadcast team put it this way: A visual should contain no more information than what a motorist can absorb from a billboard, driving past at forty miles an hour.

You can bet that billboard ad designers have this down to a science, and they give us thousands of superbly produced examples to study—along the sides of every street and highway. Instead of ignoring billboards, you would do well to give them some attention. They can give you valuable ideas for your own visuals.

Color. Since color movies became standard in the forties and color television—and all its advertising—became the standard in the sixties, we have come to expect the stimulation of color and so have our audiences. The University of Minnesota/3M study confirms that "color is more persuasive than black and white." If possible—and wherever possible—use color in your visuals.

The same communications media—movies and TV—have also conditioned us to be more receptive to pictures than to words. If you can, use a picture. Above all, take the time and trouble to design visuals that are as attractive as you can make them. Your visuals will be judged, unconsciously at least, by the standards of commercial TV production.

The touches you add to breathe life into your visuals can be quite simple; as simple as adding a picture to relieve the severity of type.

Case Study: A telephone company executive was presenting basic information on a service program they were selling called "Linebacker." He had prepared a viewgraph that consisted of a bulleted list of his main selling points, but he enhanced the communications value of this list immeasurably by taking the extra time and trouble to set the words inside the brightly colored image of a football helmet. This not only gave the audience an image to relate to, it *united* the selling points in a concrete way with the program's clever name: Linebacker.

You can add touches of color to your black and white flip charts and overhead transparencies without getting into complex artwork. Write, underline, circle, or even fill in columns or other areas with transparent colored markers. We'll go into greater detail as we discuss these types of visuals separately.

Pause. Whenever you present a new visual . . . pause. If necessary, count, "One hippopotamus, two hippopotamus," to yourself. Here's why: The moment you display a visual, that's where your audience's attention goes. If you are talking while this process is taking place, either you won't be heard or your visual won't be seen. Without the pause, you'll be competing with your own visual.

Many people are afraid to pause, because they're afraid that no communication is going on during the silence. In fact, there is a great deal of communication going on; it's just not *spoken* communication. Sportscasters Vin Scully and Joe Garagiola have won praise and recognition in the broadcasting industry for the way they use silence in their World Series telecasts. When excitement explodes or tension builds, they let the picture tell the story instead of competing with it.

Do the same when you display a visual. Don't compete with it; give your audience time to absorb it.

A pause of two or three seconds is generally enough if you designed your visual according to our advice. Then you can resume talking.

Say what you have to say about your visual. Then, when you're done, *get rid of it*. Turn off the projector, flip the page, cover the model, and return to the lectern. As long as the visual remains on view, some or all of your audience will be paying attention to it, not to you. Also, the action involved in getting rid of the visual serves as a demarcation line. It tells the audience, "We're on to the next point."

Choreographing Visuals

Poorly planned or executed visuals can harm your presentation more than they help. If they are ugly, confusing, or too numerous, they will turn off your audience. By the same token, if they are handled ineptly and if they are not smoothly integrated into the overall performance, they can weaken it more than they strengthen it.

The process of dealing with the physical objects involved in presenting visuals can interrupt the flow of the presentation.

The cure for this is planning and preparation. During the presentation, have your equipment set up where you intend to use it. Dragging the flip chart or projector to where you are speaking, or making an excursion to the other side of the room to operate your equipment takes too much time. It makes you look and feel hurried and unprepared. If your equipment is set up in advance, when you are ready to use it the minor pause that will naturally occur as you reach over to turn on the projector or walk over to the flip chart will help "frame" the visual rather than create a major distraction.

Tip: If you follow another speaker, take the time you need to reset the room for your presentation. A simple statement, "I'll be with you in a moment, I'm just setting up the equipment . . ." will buy you the few moments you need.

Mixing media. A common question is: Should I use more than one type of visual aid? Our general answer is that it's better—certainly safer—not to. It just multiplies the possibilities for mistakes and other disasters. It's one more thing you have to prepare in advance, keep under control, and remember how to operate.

That's not an absolute answer, of course. Suppose the sales force is making a presentation to management and everyone agrees to use color slides, but one salesman wants to show the television spot that one of his retail accounts is running. Maybe it's justified, but it will entail turning off the slide projector, adjusting the room lighting, moving the VCR into position, and making sure beforehand that the tape is properly cued up. It can be done and may make a nice change of pace. But unless it is well choreographed and deftly handled, the mechanics may result in slipups and general disruption of the pace of the presentation.

Pointer pointers. If you have things to say about your visual, politeness and practicality dictate that you face the audience as you speak. Many people reach across their bodies to point or actually face away from the audience as they speak, lessening the impact of the visual.

If you use a pointer, you must hold the pointer in the hand that allows you to both point and face the audience: If your visual is on your left as you face the room, the pointer goes in your left hand; and conversely.

When you are through using the pointer, it's best to get it out of the audience's view. Set it down or, if it is the telescoping kind, collapse it and return it to your pocket. Having a pointer in your hand can turn the simple act of turning off a projector into a moment of high drama. If you forget to put away the pointer, it becomes a prop. You've probably seen someone absentmindedly brandishing the pointer like a sword, bending it like an iron bar, conducting the *1812 Overture;* generally creating quite a lot of distraction, if not amusement. So, when the pointer has served its purpose, retire it, like the visual, from the scene.

Specific Visual Aids Guidelines

Flip Chart

This is the easiest of the visual aids to use. It is effective for groups of up to twenty-five people or so, and is an excellent way to present simple text or graphs.

In planning your chart, think in terms of key words, like the bulleted points in your notes.

Less is more; be terse; use single words or short phrases. Let your commentary amplify the words on the chart. Your audience sees the key word or phrase; you provide the explanation. If you must use complete sentences, or simply prefer it, that's okay. But be consistent; stick to one style. If you use a sentence to start a chart, do the same for all the items on that chart.

Make your writing as legible and as attractive as you can.

Unless your calligraphy is above average, it's a good idea to stick with block capitals. Magic marker is probably the best writing tool for this job. Because markers are available in a wide variety of colors, it is an easy matter to introduce color into your charts. Even the simple use of a bright accent to underline helps flip charts come alive.

Writing on a flip chart during a presentation automatically creates a pause, but unless your addition to the chart is quite concise, this pause can be too long.

The simplest solution to this problem is to prepare your flip charts in advance and flip or tear off sheets as you go.

Preparing charts in advance, rather than creating them as you present, has the added virtue of letting you do the job beforehand more slowly and carefully.

This idea suggests completely prefabricated flip charts, perhaps produced by the art department. But studies indicate that higher retention occurs if the chart is not actually completed in advance—leaving the presenter to fill in several key blanks, write the last line, or underline key words on the spot. This provides an air of spontaneity, and watching the presenter in the act of creating the visual has special significance for the audience. It is a process; it's an expression of you, not just prepackaged information.

> **Tip:** While doing your charts beforehand, you can lightly pencil in the words or elements you plan to fill in during the actual presentation. The audience won't be able to see them, but they're good cues for you. Whatever you decide to write on the spot—be it much or little—when you are finished, you still need to stand back and . . . *pause*. Really give your listeners a moment to take in the finished product.

Many presenters feel limitations in terms of picture possibilities with flip charts—unless they draw well. Actually, unlike with some of the other kinds of visual aids, audiences tend to be quite forgiving of less-than-professional graphic quality in flip charts. The audience sees you making them and they don't expect you to be a professional calligrapher, designer, or illustrator. We encourage you to think in terms of picture possibilities and not worry too much about living up to a professional graphic's standard.

> **Case Study:** A marketing professor was lecturing students on the concept of "hard goods promotion": the selling of such items as soap powders, cereal, or nails. Rather than simply use written words to enumerate the features and benefits of her product examples, she created a visual with the simple outline of a box of detergent, within which she enumerated the key selling points. This provided a clear, albeit simplified, visual frame of reference for the verbal information.

When you plan to use flip chart visuals, be sure to find out in advance whether anyone else will also be using the chart. If the answer is yes, you will need a way to locate your prefab charts or blank pages quickly. You can easily mark your pages by dog-earing them or by affixing a paper clip. Then, instead of flipping page after page, you can simply leaf through the stack from the side till you

find your marker and flip all the pages at once. This not only eliminates a potentially distracting and time-consuming muddle, it will
spare you the embarrassment of inadvertently displaying other people's visuals in the middle of your talk.

When you are finished with a particular page, don't leave it there
where it will compete with your continuing presentation; tear it off
or flip it over.

Be sure to include blank sheets between your prepared
charts so that you *can* get rid of them—by flipping to the
blank.

Overhead Projector

This familiar device is useful for displaying visuals to groups of up
to fifty people or so. The overhead, or "viewgraph," projects eight-
by-ten-inch transparencies best shown when mounted on cardboard
frames. These require some specialized equipment to produce: either a "dedicated" transparency machine or a photocopier that will
print on some sort of transparent film. Most of today's "plain paper"
copiers will handle this job. (See the sidebar in this chapter on making your own transparencies.)

Those who don't have direct access to the necessary equipment
can use the services of graphics houses that can handle any stage of
the process, from setting type, to artwork, to layout, to transferring
a finished layout to transparent film and mounting it on a projection
mask.

Like any equipment, the overhead projector requires some prepresentation setup. First, you must be familiar with the equipment
you will be using. This doesn't mean knowing how to use an overhead projector; it means knowing how to use the overhead projector
that's there. Know where the controls are as well as how to operate
them. Always make sure during setup that the machine is actually
functioning—which will also require you to determine that there is
a working electrical outlet where you need it, or the required extension cords.

Most important of all, *always* make sure there is a spare bulb
on hand—and that you know how to replace the bulb—or
that a *working* backup projector is available.

You don't want to find yourself in the position of one Ph.D. candidate who blew a bulb in the middle of a major presentation of his
dissertation and had no backup—whereupon one member of the review committee was heard to murmur, "Now we'll see what he
really knows."

To set up, position the machine, turn it on, and focus it, using
your first slide as a test. To minimize the muss and fuss of moving it
into position during your talk, leave the projector as close to where
you will be operating it as you can. (If you can't leave it in the exact
position, take a cue from professional stagehands and mark the correct position on the floor with tape.) Assuming no one else will be
using the machine before you, you can leave your first transparency
on the projection glass, ready to go. Then when the time comes for
your first visual, all you have to do is step over to the machine, move
it into position if necessary, and flip the switch.

Tip: If you use viewgraphs a lot, you should consider making
a guide to help in positioning slides. Two simple blocks of
wood—or in an emergency, even a couple of pencils—fastened
to the projection glass in an *L* configuration with strips of tape
should virtually eliminate those awkward moments of looking
back over your shoulder, trying to get the image straight and
centered. ("Gaffer's tape," used by filmmakers, or duct tape,
available at any hardware store, are the best choice for this.)

There aren't many rules about the specific treatment of overhead
transparencies, but one of the most important ones we teach is:

However tempting it may be, avoid beginning or ending your
presentation with a viewgraph or slide. It kills the human element.

As with any visual, remember to *pause* after displaying an over-head; let the audience absorb the information before you begin to talk about it. When you're through discussing the visual, turn the projector off (or change to a neutral logo slide) so the attention of the audience is not divided.

In general, if you have things to say in connection with your graphic, you should step back and talk near the screen, not the pro-jector. Remember to face the room and hold your pointer, if used, in the hand next to the screen. If you speak near the projector, there is a tendency to look down at—and thus talk down to—the slide rather than the audience.

If you have a number of graphics to present, especially if they come together in a cluster, try to introduce some variation in your presentation technique to avoid lulling your audience into inatten-tion. You can do this by occasionally introducing the material ver-bally *before* you present the image. Subtle as it may seem, this is an effective variation on the technique of showing the image and then talking after the pause.

> **Example:** "This next graphic will show anticipated first-quarter sales for the new SuperWidget." Turn on projector. Pause. Continue. "You can see in column two, which is outlined in blue, that we expect a 4.7 percent increase over the same period last year." Just remember, whichever order you use for a particular visual, what you *don't* want to do is present and talk simultaneously.

> **Tip:** To minimize the number of pieces of paper or props you have to handle, why not put the white cardboard borders of your viewgraph transparencies to work? They make a conve-nient place for notes relating to your next graphic or your next point.

One advantage of viewgraphs is that they are relatively easy to re-turn to. This comes in handy at Q & A time. If you *plan* to return to a particular visual or visuals, you can save the trouble of searching by creating duplicates. If you have only a few transparencies you may not feel the need to do this.

Making Your Own Transparencies

For those of you without an art department, but with access to a plain-paper, enlarging/reducing photocopier, here's our quick and easy home viewgraph production recipe:

Step 1: Type your text neatly according to your layout. If your typewriter or printer can boldface, consider using this design element. You can "paste up" the final arrangement if you choose. (In general, a pasted-up layout gives greater flexibility, but of course it's a bit more work.) Cut out the various elements and carefully position them on a clean sheet of paper. Rubber cement is a standard material for pasteup as it allows for some repositioning and is easy to clean up. Photocopy the finished layout onto a clean sheet (normal size or "100 percent") and white out any hairlines created by the edges of the cut-and-pasted elements.

Step 2: Enlarge your text to the desired size by running it through the enlarging photocopier.

Step 3: Photocopy your completed visual onto transparent film and mount it in a cardboard frame.

Step 4: You now can easily add touches of color by boxing, underlining, or adding exclamation points or other punctuation in brightly colored transparency markers. In fact, if you're willing to use a transparency only once, you can consider adding text or underlining or other colorful touches while you're projecting the visual—just like writing on a flip chart!

One special technique you can use with the viewgraph is to reveal your graphic gradually. (We call this the "striptease effect.") If, for example, you have a list of bulleted points or headlines, you can set up the slide with all but the first one masked off with a large file card or other opaque object. Then, as you get to the next point, move the mask down to expose the next headline, and so on. This adds something of the element of motion and participation that flip charts provide. If you use this technique, remember to remove the mask altogether when you reveal the last element. If you leave the mask there, at least half the audience will be wondering what's still hidden under the file card instead of listening to what you are saying.

Tip: A sophisticated alternative to typing/word processing is "press type." Readily available at art supply stores, press type comes in a wide variety of typefaces and sizes and rivals professional typesetting in quality. Best of all, it's relatively inexpensive and easy to work with. Anyone with a steady hand and a little patience can produce professional-looking results. Ask your art supply dealer for more information and basic instruction.

Photographic Color (35 mm) Slides

Color slides are a popular visual medium and are useful for groups of between ten and several hundred people.

It takes careful design and execution to produce top quality slides—the kind of expertise provided by corporate graphics departments or professional third-party vendors. Since slides are more likely to be judged by professional standards than charts or viewgraphs, they have not been the medium of choice for presenters without access to these resources.

Producing professional-looking slides has recently become easier, thanks to developments in microcomputer-generated graphics. It's easy now; the art department has been eliminated. Just remember: *Easy* does not necessarily equal *good*, and less is often more.

In terms of presentation to your audience, slides are not really very different from viewgraphs, and virtually all of what we have said about the latter applies here (including *not* beginning or ending your presentation with projected images). There are, however, a couple of comparative advantages and disadvantages to consider.

The main disadvantage of slides is having to darken the room. This creates a disruption in the flow of your overall presentation. Since it tends to be troublesome, there is a tendency to cluster all your visuals together so that you only have to go through this once. This does not necessarily work to the advantage of your presentation.

For best effect, the lighting should be adjusted so that the audience can see you as well as the images. This can be tricky; work it out carefully in advance. Figure out exactly which lights to turn off and mark the switches with tape; or, if there is a dimmer, place a piece of tape next to the dial and mark the correct position so that you or whoever is adjusting the lighting can do it with one motion instead of fumbling around, trying to gauge if you've got it right. This will help minimize the disruption.

> **Tip:** In halls where slide projection necessitates complicated lighting adjustments, it is a good idea to enlist the aid of an assistant who can handle the lighting and/or the projection duties. The less you have to cope with physically, the more you can concentrate on making your presentation.

Another minor drawback with slides is that the possibility of physically interacting with the graphics—as in underlining or adding text to a flip chart or viewgraph—is virtually eliminated. You can, however, create essentially the same effect as either the revealed graphic or the overlay technique in successive slides. And probably with graphically superior results.

The main advantage to slides is that the sophisticated design of slide projectors makes slides physically simpler to present. It's been reduced to simple button-pushing, which is not to say that it can't be fouled up. As with any projection system, you must *always* check out the equipment beforehand. While slide projectors are fairly standard, it is essential that you or your assistant know how to operate the projector that is actually there. Make sure the projector is working and that there is a spare bulb or a *working* backup projector of the same type close at hand.

During setup, check the projector by *running through all your slides*. Be sure they are in the correct order—and position. You can then leave the projector set up with your first slide ready to go. Fumbles at the slide projector—upside down and reversed images and frantic scrambling to get slides into the right order while the audience stares at the blinding glare of the blank screen—are a classic presentation error. Let it be someone else, not you.

Tip: If you are changing your own slides, taping the remote control to the side of the podium or lectern allows you to keep both hands free to point or gesture. (Again, gaffer's tape or duct tape is excellent for this.) When you want to bring up the next slide, all you need to do is step over—or lean over—and tap the button. It is also a good idea to put a piece of tape over the backup or reverse button, to spare yourself the muddle and embarrassment of inadvertently showing slides you've already presented.

Film and Videotape

Although used less frequently than any of the foregoing visual media, film and video work well for certain kinds of presentations. Films can be shown to groups of almost any size. Video is useful for groups up to twenty-five people per monitor. Except for a few details relating to the physical setup, they are essentially the same visual aid.

Our information and precautions for slide presentations (including the desirability of an assistant) are virtually the same for film, adding that you will need to darken the room even more. Know how to operate the projector—which should be carefully set up and tested, including the sound system. Carefully set focus and sound levels. The film should be carefully cued up and ready to go at the flip of a switch. We're all familiar with the Academy Leader (the strip that heads a movie: "Five—four—three—two—one"); don't make it part of your presentation. As we said, your audience has been conditioned to the standards of commercial television, so slipups like this are likely to lose you points.

Setting up a video requires similar care. You don't necessarily have to darken the room for short tapes, though for tapes of longer than two minutes you should, bringing the lights back up immediately after the tape finishes. Adjust the color and sound levels ahead of time. Clean the monitor screen if necessary. Every VCR and playback machine cues up a little differently. Leave your video accurately cued up with a second or two of black before the picture comes on. It should be left ready to go. If the playback unit has a remote control, know how to use it and make sure to locate it conveniently for easy use.

There's not much for you to do during the film or videotape presentation, but these media require careful introduction so that they support your presentation rather than take it over. Set up your audience using "flag" words to direct their attention: "Pay close attention to . . ." or "You'll notice about thirty seconds into this clip that . . ." These flag words cue the viewers in to what you want them to notice instead of randomly focusing on what interests them.

Tip: Be aware that your audience will subconsciously judge film and video by the standards of commercial television—so they'd better be good.

Handouts

Distributing printed copies of your presentation to the audience can help build retention. Handouts should reflect the shape of your presentation in content, and might well resemble your notes in form. As with any visual, take the trouble to execute them well. Make them clean and uncluttered; keep information to a minimum. Leave lots of white space around your key words or major points.

Unless it is absolutely necessary for people to follow along, don't pass out written material until you are finished. Anything they have in their hands—or in front of their eyes—competes for their attention, which you want focused on you. Of course, you don't have to literally pass out materials. It is certainly easier—and perhaps more dignified—to have the materials placed on a table at the exit door.

If you *do* decide to pass out your handouts before the presentation, you can make them an interactive part of your presentation—by creating space for listeners to make notes. If people are taking notes, remember to slow down so they can get all the information.

Tip: One way to encourage people to take your handouts is to include something they might want to *use* later, such as the phone number of a particular public service you offer.

Quick Reference Summary

- A presentation with visuals is 43 percent more persuasive than one without.
- Keep visuals simple and uncluttered with a maximum of six lines per page.
- When in doubt, use fewer visuals rather than more.
- Phrases or words are better than sentences. Be consistent with structure throughout the visuals.
- Use color; it makes your visuals stronger.
- Try to limit visuals to one medium.
- Pause before referring to information on visuals to allow the audience to absorb the visual.
- Put down the pointer when you're finished pointing out items. It's distracting to the audience if you hold it.
- When through explaining a visual, remove it.
- Flip charts are useful for small groups.
  - Write charts in block capitals beforehand and use adequate spacing between lines.
- Overheads are useful for groups of up to fifty people.
  - Use white borders for additional notes.
  - Use the "striptease" technique when referring to lists on overhead. Show one point at a time to keep your audience focused.

- 35-millimeter slides work well for ten to several hundred people.
  - When using slides, tape the remote control to the side of the podium or lectern rather than holding it; this frees your hands to gesture. Tape over the reverse button to prevent hitting it accidentally.
- Film is good for any sized group; twenty-five people per video-tape monitor is the maximum.
- Prefocus projectors for smooth performance.
- Make sure there's a spare bulb for any projector.
- Film and videotape quality is judged by what is done commercially, so make it good.
- Use signal words to introduce tape or film, such as, "Watch for . . ." or "You'll notice thirty seconds into this . . ."
- Provide hard-copy handouts to increase audience retention.
  - Distribute handouts *after* the presentation so audience is not distracted, or if necessary to distribute handouts during the presentation, integrate them into the session and leave white space on handouts for audience to make notes.

8

Perfecting Delivery

In one important sense, a presentation is like a symphony: It may exist as notations on paper, but it really comes into being only through performance. And it's possible to perform a great work badly, just as it's possible to perform a mediocre one well. Beethoven's Fifth Symphony played by the New York Philharmonic is quite different from the same symphony played by the Springfield High School orchestra.

Performance has an impact quite apart from the quality of the "work itself."

The point here is that the *delivery* of your presentation, in a practical sense, *is* your presentation.

Think about it. When you walk up to the front of that room you're a lot like an orchestra conductor stepping onto the podium. The unfolding of the event is in your hands. The content of your talk is already there in your notes—the musical score, so to speak—but without your skilled and sensitive execution it won't really work.

There's a cartoon we often share in our workshops: The drawing is of a little man in a tailcoat looking down at a large book laid out on the podium. There are no musical notes on the page, only an instruction telling the man to wave the baton until the music stops—then turn around and bow. We get a lot of laughs with this. That's how we all *wish* it were. In reality, however, it matters a lot what you do with the baton while you're up there. That's what this chapter is all about: the delivery skills you need to turn out a polished performance.

Like it or not, how you look and sound has more impact on listeners than the actual words you speak.

People don't carry away from a speech or presentation primarily information. They carry away an *impression*.

Let's look back for a moment to Chapter One. Among the studies we quoted there is one that analyzes the dynamics of verbal communication. The findings:

- 55 percent of interpersonal communication comes from facial expression and other body language.
- 38 percent relates to "paralanguage," or vocal quality.
- The remainder—approximately 7 percent—is derived from the meaning of the words: the content.

How you look and sound add up to 93 percent of the impression you make. And if those factors aren't working for you, they're working against you.

We're not suggesting that content is unimportant. Skillful preparation of content is essential, which is why we've spent four chapters discussing it. But remember our chain analogy? The communications chain is no stronger than its weakest link. Like Beethoven's

Fifth, your first-rate presentation content can be seriously undermined by poor delivery.

Case Study: We once undertook to prepare an expert witness for testimony in a product liability lawsuit. The plaintiff in the case was a high school athlete who had injured his spine in a sports accident and was paralyzed as a result—possibly for life. There were three defendants: the high school coach, the school board, and the manufacturer of the sports equipment the boy had been wearing. Our expert witness was an engineer testifying for the equipment manufacturer.

Juries like to award monetary "damages" in accident cases. In this case, the defendant most likely to be found responsible was our client, the equipment manufacturer. Not because they *were*, in fact, responsible, but because they had money—they were the "deep pocket."

The job of our key witness was to make the jury understand that the equipment was very carefully engineered and was as safe as it could possibly be. In his lab at the plant, the engineer was quite convincing about the careful design of the equipment. He made it quite clear to us that the equipment did an excellent job of protecting the head, but that it did not and could not protect the rest of the anatomy (in this case, the neck). Like many people who do not regularly testify, he was not comfortable in the courtroom, and despite his unquestionable expertise, he struck us as a potentially ineffective witness.

As might be expected of an inexperienced testifier, he spoke in a careful monotone: his voice was flat and evenly paced. He never gestured and he rarely looked at anybody while he spoke. He looked above everyone's head or down at the floor rather than meeting people's eyes.

He also used a lot of technical language in his answers. Although he was professionally correct in not wanting to oversimplify, we suggested he clarify his terms. It is important to understand that facts are facts, but in a court of law, facts are facts only if a jury (or judge) understands and believes them.

Once he accepted the idea that his role as a witness carried more importance than just conveying facts, he began to work on the presentation side of his testimony, as well. In any trial, it is up to the judge or jury to ultimately decide conviction or acquittal; however, as a result of our consulting, the witness and others from the company did come across better on the stand by improving eye contact, voice modulation, gestures, and using layman's English.

Content aside, what distinguishes the effective speaker is looking good and being intelligible.

The two really cannot be separated. "Looking good" involves acting:
- Confident
- Animated
- Relaxed

These qualities are communicated through:
- Facial expression
- Eye contact
- Posture
- Physical gestures

"Being intelligible"—expressing yourself clearly and persuasively—involves sounding:
- Confident
- Animated
- Relaxed
- Articulate

These qualities are communicated through the elements of vocal inflection:
- Pace
- Pauses
- Pitch
- Volume

This, in turn, builds:
- Phrasing
- Emphasis

We'll discuss the role each of these elements plays in getting your message across, but first we'd like to offer some general facts and suggestions relating to appearance and impressions.

Looking Good

Whether we're aware of it or not, we begin communicating with our listeners even before we actually begin to speak. We think of communicating primarily as a process of moving our mouths, but how we move our bodies also speaks to our audience. How we stand, how we carry our head, where we rest our gaze, what we do with our hands—these are all components of language.

The impression-building process begins the instant a person becomes the focus of attention. The moment the image strikes their eyes listeners will start forming impressions: "How attractive (unattractive) this man or woman is." "How authoritative (confident, intimidated, disorganized) he or she looks." "Look how tall (or short) he or she is, how trim (overweight)." "Look how much weight Leslie has lost since I last saw her." "What a nice blouse she's wearing." "Carl's tie is a little loud for this company." And so forth. All these impressions will have an effect on how the audience *listens*. To the extent that you can control the impressions you create, it is important to start on the right foot. (In this connection, see our discussion of presentation dress in Chapter Thirteen.)

If you're at a lunch or a dinner, finish eating well before your presentation. Have your jacket buttoned; check your makeup; make sure your notes are ready; make whatever last-minute checks you need. If you're being introduced, be aware that the audience will not be concentrating on the person who's performing the introduction, they will be looking for the person being introduced.

So *be ready*. Model the behavior you would like others to display when you're up there; look at the person who's introducing you; give that person the kind of attention you would like listeners to give you.

When the moment arrives to go on, stand up smartly—with good posture. Walk to the front of the room with a sense of purpose.

When you arrive, don't immediately begin speaking. Pause. Arrange your notes and visual aids. Get settled. Give the audience a moment to get used to you. Make eye contact. Smile. *Then* you can begin. This all adds up to an *impression* of conviction, authority, and self-assurance.

This nonverbal communication process continues for your entire presentation. It's subtle stuff, mostly taking place at the subconscious level. But it is powerful—and important enough to merit a detailed discussion of each of its elements.

When you're smilin' . . . The old song underlines an old truth: Smiling is infectious. So are the feelings it expresses. A smile from you, the presenter, is a positive signal to which your audience responds positively. It tells them you're comfortable—which makes them comfortable.

"Suppose I'm *not* comfortable?" Smile anyway. Two reasons. First, the reverse of what we said above is also true: If you communicate your discomfort to your listeners, it will make them uncomfortable. Second, and perhaps more important, *smiling will make you feel better*. This may strike you as absurd, but psychologists have discovered that while our faces naturally express what we're feeling inside, the reverse is also true to some extent. Our facial expressions—particularly the smile—can actually alter our emotional chemistry. If you are afraid of flying, a smile will make you less uncomfortable in an airplane. If presentations make you nervous, a smile will make you feel more at home.

So we heartily recommend smiling. By "smile" we don't necessarily mean the expression used by actors in toothpaste commercials. A sphinxlike smile with the corners of the mouth turned up slightly is just fine—though you might want to flash a stronger version from time to time.

What the eyes tell. An image we like to use in teaching presentation skills is that communication is like a game of catch. When you throw a ball in a game of catch, you generally don't turn your back or bury your face in your hands, you look to see if the ball is caught. In the same sense, each time you toss out a thought or idea in your presentation, you should look to see if it is caught. You do this with eye contact. The catch is indicated by responses from individual audience members in the form of returned eye contact, a nod, a smile, or a generally attentive look. These responses let you know the ball has been caught and returned, and that the audience is awaiting the next toss. A good rule of thumb is that each thought, sentence, or idea is a separate throw and catch with another individual.

Eye contact will also tell you if your ball has *not* been caught (blank stares, no reaction, quizzical or uncomprehending looks) and thus will alert you to stop and "throw again" (in other words, clarify your point) so that the game can continue.

Television has conditioned most of us to expect strong eye contact. The people who talk to us over the tube—be they newscasters, advertisers, or political speakers—look us straight in the eye (through the camera). So deeply are we conditioned that we subconsciously question the honesty and integrity—or at least the conviction—of anyone who will not or does not look us in the eye. This is basic practical psychology. By making *conscious* use of eye contact we can enhance the overall credibility and effectiveness of our presentation. Certainly, if we *fail* to make eye contact, we definitely limit the potential impact of our presentation.

If you doubt that people rely on eye contact to make impressions, think about your own personal experience. When you have something to say that you are consciously uncomfortable about in some way—if you're embarrassed or if you aren't telling the truth, for example—you tend to avoid the gaze of the person you're speaking to. And how do you know when children are lying? They won't look you in the eye.

Conversely, in a one-on-one situation where you have something earnest and important to convey, something you really want to get across—perhaps something as urgent as "I love you"—you actively seek out the other person's eyes.

It's not much different for public communication. Strong eye contact conveys an impression of confidence, conviction, openness, honesty, enthusiasm, even urgency. Poor eye contact may suggest anything from simple nervousness to embarrassment or furtiveness to outright mendacity.

Like smiling, eye contact says, "I'm comfortable with myself and with what I'm telling you." Avoidance of eye contact says, "There's something wrong here," leaving some part of the listener wondering, "Why doesn't this add up?"

This means not keeping your eyes glued to your notes—which suggests you are speaking from your own private bubble. It means not looking over the heads of the audience or off into the far reaches of space—which suggests that you are afraid of being with them. It means looking at the people you are talking to—at least a good part of the time. This may be somewhat unnerving at first. Why? For the very reason that it is important: It really is a gesture of intimacy.

Eye contact with whom, specifically? It generally doesn't matter a great deal with *whom* you make eye contact, simply that you look at *someone*. Exceptions are the question and answer session (see page 123), one-on-one presentations, and presentations in which a specific "power person" takes precedence over others. So it makes sense to pick a person who is giving you positive feedback such as a supportive nod or a smile. This should help to alleviate any discomfort you feel at fostering intimacy with utter strangers.

Here are three basic eye contact principles:

- In general, hold eye contact with a single person for at least a full thought, phrase, or sentence.
- In a group situation (except where you are obliged to play to a specific individual) divide the audience into several sections—like a tic-tac-toe board—in order to spread your eye contact around the group. The number of sections depends upon the size of the group. Pick a friendly face in each area. These people serve as your contact points. You can then literally "work the room," moving from a friendly eye in one sector to a friendly eye in the next, returning as necessary. This grid solution works well for audiences of as few as six or as many as a thousand.
- In a one-on-one session, or when you're responding to a "power person," look directly at him or her and don't worry about the others very much.

> **Tip:** If meeting people's eyes is a problem for you, try this trick: Rest your gaze on a person's forehead just above the eyebrows and visualize the Radio City marquee with the words of your text running across in lights.

Winning Moves

Physical gestures are a vital ingredient in verbal communication. Gestures do the following:

- Add emphasis to our words
- Animate the voice
- Provide an outlet for nervousness

If the words are the meat of communication, gestures are the spices. Gestures add flavor to our speech—the accents that make the difference between bland and stimulating.

Try a little test: Visualize yourself making an impassioned plea, speaking out urgently on a subject that you care about deeply . . . *without* gesturing—standing motionless with your arms at your sides. It's hard to picture, isn't it? Without gestures, half the message is lost. The same principle holds true for less impassioned utterances as well.

In addition, gestures have a direct effect on the voice, lubricating and animating it, making your speech more conversational and hence more accessible and more credible. You can actually "hear" your gestures when you listen to a tape recording of your presentation. Gesturing also tends to open up the upper body physically, promoting good breathing and muscular relaxation, both of which exert a further positive influence on the voice.

Perhaps most important of all, gesturing gives us a great way to burn off nervous energy. If we *don't* gesture, our nervousness finds other ways to express itself, usually ways that call attention to the nervousness, distracting our listeners and detracting from the impact of what we are saying.

> **Tip:** Learn to gesture and you will live longer. We have seen
> studies that report that orchestra conductors live longer than
> the average citizen. Why? Because in their work, the physical
> gesture is their sole means of communication. They are con-
> stantly using the arms and the upper body; more blood is
> pumped by the heart, taking more oxygen to the rest of the
> body. The result is better health and longer life—in addition to
> effective communications. We've already suggested, at the be-
> ginning of this chapter, that you think of yourself like an or-
> chestra conductor; why not in this way as well?

Helping gestures happen. Starting out in an appropriate stance can facilitate gesturing, and we recommend the "ski pole position." For those of you who don't ski, this means standing straight, forearms held at about waist level, with the hands apart, relaxed, and open. Most people find this a comfortable position from which it is easy and natural to gesture.

Stand up and try it. How does it feel? If having your hands "just hanging in space" feels awkward (which in itself should encourage you to gesture), try the "professorial" position, in which the hands are brought together with the fingertips lightly touching.

Problem postures. There are a number of postures that severely inhibit gesturing. An act as simple as clasping your hands together, for example, breeds a whole category of problem postures: the "firing squad" position—hands behind back, body often rocking forward and back; the "lower anatomical protective" position—hands anchored over the crotch; the "higher anatomical protective" position, with arms crossed firmly over the breasts. There is nothing wrong with clasped hands, but having found something to hold on to (each other), the hands tend to remain firmly fastened together, effectively eliminating the possibility of gesturing.

Grasping the lectern creates similar problems. You've probably seen the "white knuckler," who appears to be holding on for dear life, and the "ship captain," who leans into the lectern and steers it first one way, then the other. Again, the problem is not that they grasp the lectern, but that they never let go. If you speak from a lectern, start with the hands resting *lightly* on it.

Whatever position you find yourself in, watch out for "sticky elbows," a position that is another serious inhibitor of gestures. Like hands, elbows seem to be provided with their own adhesive. If you start out with your elbows stuck to your sides, they are likely to remain there throughout your presentation. You will still be able to move your hands and forearms, but the gestures will tend to have a nervous, truncated quality.

Give it a try. Feels awkward, doesn't it? Your motions tend to be stunted and ungainly, as if you had flippers like a seal. Now unstick your elbows; immediately, your gestures become more fluid and expansive.

Some of you, of course, may be self-conscious about gesturing. Big, expansive gestures may feel quite unnatural. With all due respect, we feel that *not* gesturing is unnatural and that it's worth investing some of your time and energy to overcome your discomfort in this area. This is especially true if you are likely to be presenting to large groups in large spaces. In a big hall, the listeners at the back can't really see your face at all, but if you can make big gestures, they'll feel some sense of connection, even way back there. The bigger the room the bigger your gestures need to be.

With practice, gesturing will come to feel more natural. One good way to practice gesturing is to slip into your orchestra conductor persona and gesture on key words as you read dialogue from a book. If you have trouble remembering to gesture, put a little reminder symbol, perhaps a stick figure with arms upraised, or the word *gesture* next to key words in your notes.

More body problems. Two common unconscious physical habits that you should strive to avoid or eliminate are swaying or rocking back and forth and wagging your head from side to side, keeping time like the pendulum of a metronome. It's fine to shift your weight and to gesture with your head for emphasis, but the rhythmic repetition of either movement is distracting. It tends to give your speech a singsong cadence and conveys an overall impression of nervousness.

To combat swaying, try placing your feet either slightly closer together (to reduce your leverage), or slightly farther apart (to widen your base and stabilize the body), or with one foot slightly in front of the other. To combat head wagging, watch videotapes of your presentations and practice until you break the habit.

Tip: To remind yourself to gesture, use eye contact, watch for any bad habit, and pick a person in your audience to cue you for a certain thing. You might say, "When I look at Marge, I'll check to see if I'm swaying; when I look at Bill, that's a cue to check for eye contact."

Sounding Good

If you have something to say that you believe in—if you are enthusiastic about what you do, your products, your research, the company you work for—your enthusiasm should be reflected in the *way* you speak as well as in the words you choose. Which brings us to "paralanguage"—vocal quality or how we use our voices.

What most of us associate with the term *vocal quality* is the characteristic sound of an individual's voice—its unique tone or timbre: high, low; smooth, scratchy; breathy, resonant; nasal, guttural. These vocal characteristics are largely based on physical factors, but they can be changed far more than most of us realize. If you do not have a naturally pleasant voice and presentations are a necessary part of your life, you might consider devoting some time and effort to improving it by finding a voice teacher. There are many fine ones that teach speaking as well as singing.

In any case, there's a lot more to consider about vocal quality than timbre. Here we will explore the elements of *inflection* and their use to create *phrasing* and *emphasis*.

Inflection. The literal meaning of this word is "to bend, to alter." *Vocal inflection,* specifically, refers to voice variables:
- Pace
- Pauses
- Pitch
- Volume

We use these to make our verbalizations more expressive.

In comparison with that of other English speakers, American speech is characteristically deficient in inflection. Richness of inflection is one of the qualities that makes British (and other non-American) English so distinctive—and so attractive. Fortunately, inflection is easy to improve, and once mastered will make your speech pleasant to listen to and easy to understand.

Pace. Fast, slow, or in between, words spoken at a steady, even pace take on a sameness, like driving through a prairie landscape. They blur together and soon lull the listener into inattention. Varying the pace of your words and phrases adds contour, creating interest.

It can be helpful to begin your talk at a somewhat slower pace than normal, especially if you are addressing people who are unfamiliar with your voice. This gives the audience time to "learn" your voice and speaking mannerisms. Once they have had a minute or two to get the hang of your style, you can step up the overall pace. This is a technique that Henry Kissinger uses for public speaking. He gives his listeners time to get used to his accent, then accelerates to his normal speaking pace.

In some cases, speaking faster can actually *increase* comprehension.

The brain can absorb information at rates up to approximately eight hundred words per minute—which is about four times faster than normal speech. Like a mainframe computer, the mind is spending only a small proportion of its time with the task of comprehension and tends to fill in the remaining time with other tasks. In other words, it wanders, and concentration suffers. Dealing with a higher "word density," the mind of the listener is less likely to be distracted. The catch here, of course, is that if you want to speak quickly and be understood, you have to speak very clearly.

Another aspect of pace to consider is the changing of pace from phrase to phrase. We're not talking about anything contrived here, just using the natural rhythms of ordinary speech: Close your eyes and listen to any trained speaker, or even to an informal conversation. You'll discover that people—both professional speakers in their professional settings and nonprofessionals in casual ones—group words together in "meaning clusters". They push together groups of relatively unimportant words and slow down to give emphasis to the key words and phrases that carry important information. It makes the words live.

We do this naturally, but when we get into a situation that's uncomfortable—speaking in front of a group of people, for example—we tend to freeze up and *un*naturally even out our speaking pace. We can all spot an untrained or inexperienced person (like owners of small businesses who insist on doing their own television commercials) reading off a TelePrompTer. The flat, mechanical singsong is unmistakable.

Pauses. Many presenters, especially inexperienced ones, are afraid to pause while speaking, even for a moment. To these people, two seconds of silence seems like an eternity. When asked to explain their reluctance to pause, our workshop clients often cite the fear that no communication is going on during the silence. This is simply not the case.

Pauses are a vital element of nonverbal communication and are essential to strong delivery.

We can't overemphasize this fact. Pauses contribute to communication in at least four ways:

1. They carry a message of their own ("I'm relaxed, thoughtful, confident").
2. They serve as a catalyst for verbal comprehension by "ventilating" the flow of words. This gives the speaker time to catch his or her breath, and for the listeners to absorb what has been said.

You should *always* pause following the introduction of a new key term or idea, and especially after displaying a visual.

With terms or ideas, the pause can be brief; with a visual, it must be long enough for listeners to become readers and really take it in. This means two to three seconds.
3. Pauses also signal transitions. They say "Okay, we've finished that thought or topic; here comes the next point." Referring to your notes at these transition points seems natural and reinforces the message of the pause.
4. A brief pause in the middle of a phrase or sentence—in the "wrong place"—is a very effective way to call attention to what follows (see example, page 104).

Pitch and volume. We have a special word for people whose speech lacks this quality: *monotone* (literally, "one pitch"). It is clearly a pejorative term; we don't refer to someone's "stirring monotone." Used as an adjective, the word is *monotonous*—which means "boring" or "expressionless." Clearly, the rise and fall of vocal pitch is a key element in clear, communicative speech.

Always speaking at the same volume level is equally drab and expressionless.

Both faults rob us of the opportunity to enhance the meaning of our words by directing the listeners' attention to what's important.

Phrasing and emphasis. In written communication, punctuation and typography are used as expressive devices to help to bring out the meaning of the words. In oral communication, clarity of expression is achieved through vocal inflection, as it creates *phrasing* and *emphasis*. And these add up to a *much more powerful* tool than commas, semicolons, and italics.

By the term *phrase* we don't mean quite the same thing a grammarian does. To a speaker, a phrase is an organizational unit, a "meaning cluster"—a group of words expressing a unified idea that is spoken in one breath. One *thought* equals one *breath* equals one *phrase*.

The natural lift that occurs after each phrase as we pause to take our next breath signals the listener that we have completed one idea or thought element and are about to start another. This creates what we call a "thought rhythm."

As an illustration, here's how the opening of Abraham Lincoln's celebrated Gettysburg Address might be phrased:

> FOURSCORE AND SEVEN YEARS AGO [breath]
> OUR FATHERS BROUGHT FORTH ON THIS
>   CONTINENT [breath]
> A NEW NATION [breath]
> CONCEIVED IN LIBERTY [breath]
> AND DEDICATED TO THE PROPOSITION [breath]
> THAT ALL MEN ARE CREATED EQUAL.

Try it yourself. Read it out loud. For contrast, try running the phrases together without the lifts. (You should be able to read the lines in two breaths without much trouble.) Do it several times each way until you feel comfortable with the words. Which way do you prefer? Record your readings on tape and play them back. Which do you think would be easier for an audience to follow? We're betting on the shorter phrases. It is a documented fact that people speak in shorter word groupings than they write. The typical written sentence runs fifteen to twenty-three words; the average spoken sentence, eight to ten.

Emphasis. The complement to skillful phrase shaping is the careful placement of emphasis. To emphasize is, of course, to call attention to selected words or groups of words—to point to their special importance. But emphasis can *add* meaning as well.

> **Tip:** If you're uncomfortable with short detached phrases, and feel unsure about how they really come across, rent a videotape of an old Bette Davis movie. Her phrasing really makes you pay attention—and you are never in doubt about what she's saying.

Try this exercise. It is designed to make you aware of the subtleties of meaning that you can impart through emphasis. Say "I will not go" out loud four times, each time stressing a different word:

<u>I</u> will not go.
I <u>WILL</u> not go.
I will <u>NOT</u> go.
I will not <u>GO</u>.

Each reading conveys a slightly different message. The first is about the identity of who will go; maybe somebody else but not me. The rest are variations on an emphatic statement, but with different connotations. The second suggests stubbornness in the face of urging. The third is a flat contradiction. The last, a defiant proclamation—the most emphatic of all.

Emphasis can be achieved by means of any or all of the elements of vocal inflection we examined earlier:

- *Changing pace.* One simple and effective way to emphasize an important word is to pause briefly before enunciating it. For example: "The plan that has been proposed this morning is . . . a disaster." This is especially effective when combined with changes in pitch and volume.
- *Changing pitch.* Just as monotone signals the listener that there is nothing of special importance in what you are saying, inflecting your vocal pitch clearly creates interest. It doesn't much matter whether the pitch change is upward or downward, except at the end of sentences, where consistent downward inflection suggests a lack of conviction.

- *Changing volume.* Speaking louder is perhaps the most obvious way to create emphasis, but *decreasing* the volume is actually just as effective. It is the contrast that creates the emphasis. A whispered phrase can be very dramatic.

As you prepare a presentation, you can plan your phrasing and placement of emphasis in portions of the talk that are important enough to write out. Expand on the technique we used earlier in our Gettysburg Address example: Write or type each phrase on a separate line; then simply underline the words you wish to emphasize. *Which* words should you emphasize? The active, emotional ones; these will generally be verbs, nouns, and adjectives.

> FOURSCORE AND SEVEN YEARS AGO
> OUR FATHERS <u>BROUGHT</u> <u>FORTH</u> ON THIS
>   CONTINENT
> A <u>NEW</u> NATION
> CONCEIVED IN <u>LIBERTY</u>
> AND <u>DEDICATED</u> TO THE PROPOSITION
> THAT <u>ALL</u> <u>MEN</u> ARE CREATED <u>EQUAL</u>.

Tip: We don't want to leave the subject of emphasis without extending an urgent plea: Try to avoid the cliché, now solidly embedded in our aural culture by second-rate television news broadcasters and public officials, of stressing the prepositions (such as *of, to, for, in, among*). It is a verbal affectation that adds nothing useful to your speech. Also, don't stress conjunctions (*and, but, because*) and articles (*a, an, the*).

Here are a few general rules about delivery:
- Any time you pose a question—even a rhetorical one—make a real pause. Whether or not you expect listeners to answer, it lends emphasis and gives them time to consider the implications.
- Avoid the habit of letting the ends of your sentences drop. If you have this problem, practice deliberately emphasizing the final

two or three words of every sentence until this becomes second nature.

To listeners this mannerism suggests a lack of conviction. It often *occurs* for an entirely different reason: either because your mind is already onto the next sentence or thought, or because you are running out of breath. If the former, remember to pause and slow down; if the latter, practice speaking in shorter phrases, remembering to pause and *breathe*.

- Never undermine your selling points by glossing over them vocally. Be fully aware that you are delivering a selling point and stress it. "Signal" words, like *proud* or *excited*, can help to add appropriate emphasis.

- If you feel a verbal fumble coming on, ask your audience's permission to stop and think. You can cover with a phrase like, "Let me consider how best to say this . . ."

- Take care to enunciate key words clearly, especially trade names and terms, and most especially if there's any ambiguity. If you're discussing UNIX (an operating system for computers), for example, you don't want half your audience to be wondering why on earth you are talking about emasculated harem attendants *(eunuchs)*. If any such verbal gremlin is lurking in *your* presentation, make sure the audience sees the word written down right off the bat.

Practice Guidelines

All the elements of vocal quality can be readily improved through practice. The first step is to attune your ear. You can build your awareness of pace, pitch, and volume inflection just by carefully listening. Many study materials are readily available, from television and radio to the conversation going on behind you in a restaurant. Close your eyes, and don't even listen to the words. Just hear the speeding up and slowing down, the placement of pauses, the rise and fall of the voice, the changes from loud to soft, the emphasis of an important phrase.

Then practice. Take a section of your presentation that's well worked out—your opening, for example. Write it out as we suggested above—in short phrases divided into logical units of meaning. Decide which words to emphasize in order to best express your message, and underline them. Read the lines out loud using different types of emphasis: upward inflection and downward, louder, softer. Mark your pauses.

Once you begin to be comfortable with your expanded range of expression, record yourself on tape. While this will probably increase your self-consciousness at first, the direct feedback will be invaluable in helping you fine-tune your handling of inflection and emphasis. Eventually it will become second nature, and in time it will evolve into a distinctive personal speaking style.

Quick Reference Summary

- Good delivery or performance can enhance content. *Poor* delivery or performance can *undermine* content.
- An audience carries away an impression of you that can outweigh the content of what you say.
- How you look and sound constitutes 93 percent of the impression you make.
- Three components of effective delivery are:
  - Confidence
  - Animation
  - Relaxation
- The audience begins judging and evaluating you the minute you're introduced—before you even open your mouth. Be ready.
- Walk to the front of the room with dignity and authority. Posture is critical in making a good impression.
- Pause and survey the room before you begin speaking; pick out friendly faces.
- Smile as you begin your talk.
- Look at the audience as you speak. Stop talking to look down at your notes, then look up and resume.
- Keep your eyes on one person for a full thought, or a complete sentence.

- If you have trouble meeting people's eyes, look at a person's nose or forehead; this creates the illusion of eye contact.
- Making eye contact with the audience helps relieve your own anxiety.
- Gestures are important in presentations. They burn off tension naturally, animate your face, and lubricate your voice.
- When using a lectern, don't lean on it in order to press tension away. Keep your hands at waist level and allow yourself to gesture naturally.
- Use variety in your voice; pause, alter your pitch for emphasis and phrasing.
- Speak important phrases slowly.
- Pause to let the audience absorb information. This lets you emphasize a point nonverbally.
- Use signal words to introduce an important phrase. Deliver the phrase, then pause. This helps people remember.
- Vary your pitch for emphasis.
- Speaking in a quiet, confidential tone is a strong way to occasionally make a point.
- Keep phrases short, so you can deliver them in one breath. Eight to ten words per sentence is appropriate.
- Analyze your text to mark for emphasis. Stress can alter the meaning of your content.

9

Tough Questions, Good Answers

Usually, the most effective format for making your point is a brief talk or presentation *followed by a question and answer period*. The experienced presentation-maker knows this well and will insist on a Q & A whenever possible.

Properly handled, a Q & A session gives you an opportunity to make your point *again*—often several times.

Furthermore, in many situations—internal presentations, witness appearances, and interviews, for example—answering questions is mandatory. The personnel manager, customer, divisional vice president, regulatory commissioner, concerned community member, opposing counsel, or reporter will ask *any* question. Their questions may be tough—and your answers had better be good. That's what this chapter is about: tough questions and good answers.

You can see that the art of handling questions is a crucial component of the presenter's craft. Although many people find the prospect intimidating, rest assured that it consists of a set of skills that you can learn.

If you do the considerable amount of work involved in mastering Q & A skills, you can transform a potentially terrifying prospect into an *important opportunity*.

Mastery of Q & A doesn't mean you can entirely eliminate the risks involved in facing questions. Mastery is primarily a matter of preparation, and you can never be prepared for *every* question. You may still get a zinger or a dumb, off-the-wall question from time to time. But if you've been through our Q & A training and are comfortable with the techniques of handling questions, you'll have a huge advantage. You'll be equipped to handle these situations with equanimity and, frequently, to *turn them to your advantage*.

If we haven't already made it clear, we believe that the Q & A is the most important part of the presentation process. There are four reasons, all of them related to retention.

1. This is the first time listeners have had an opportunity to actively participate in an exchange of ideas or information.
2. You can reemphasize important points.
3. You can introduce new, positive information.
4. The last things heard are remembered best.

The first reason Q & A helps you make your point is that interacting with the speaker is stimulating to the audience; it makes them *focus their attention* better. They will actually remember your message better when it's presented as an answer to their questions than when you make the same point in your prepared talk.

The second is that it gives you an opportunity to repeat. Repetition is one of the factors that increases *retention*. The more often your listeners hear a message, the more likely they are to remember it.

The third reason is that a question often creates an opportunity for you to deliver a selling point that didn't quite fit in with your talk, thus allowing you to make one of your main points again in a different way.

Point four really speaks for itself. But there's one final benefit of the Q & A. It gives you an opportunity to display *you*. In the context of a Q & A, your energy, confidence, conviction—and in the face of difficult or hostile questioning, your courage and compassion—have a better chance to come through than they do from behind the lectern. All of which helps you *get to the point*.

The Control Factor

A lot of people find the idea of the Q & A unnerving. The reason? They feel that in taking questions they relinquish control. With the opening portion of your presentation—the "prepared text"—you are in command. You choose the words and the pictures, and direct the flow of ideas. But when the time comes to throw the floor open to discussion—if you know that the vice president, the comptroller, or whoever, may interrupt you at any moment—you may feel like a tiny boat on a storm-tossed sea, completely at the mercy of the elements. In reality, you can retain a considerable degree of control when the presentation becomes interactive.

Case Study: During his White House years, Henry Kissinger, undoubtedly one of the most successful communications manipulators of recent times, once reportedly opened a press conference by asking the press corps, "Does anyone have questions for my answers?" His quip made explicit what he knew and the reporters knew: For Henry Kissinger a press conference was more than a place to answer questions; it was an opportunity to deliver prepared policy statements on issues of his own choosing. They did ask questions, and he did provide answers, but he in no way relinquished the agenda to the press. He went in knowing what points he wanted to make—and he made them.

Skilled Q & A handling is a process of turning questions—as often as possible—into a platform for remaking your points.

Mr. Kissinger's press conferences illustrate the basic point we wish to make—that you don't have to relinquish control. However, we don't suggest that you imitate Mr. Kissinger's outspoken style of handling the matter. When you're in that powerful a position, go right ahead. Meanwhile . . .

The best overall effect is achieved when you are responsive to the questions and keep your awareness of the control factor in the background.

Be Prepared

The Q & A technique we will outline is one of answering the questions and then finding a connection between that question and one of your selling points. The key to Q & A control is *preparation*. This point can't be overstressed. So before we work through the technique let's spend some time preparing.

In Q & A, there's virtually no such thing as being *overprepared*.

Phase One of preparation is, specifically, preparation for *difficult questions*. This begins back where we started—with the audience profile. Remember our potential conflict analysis? That's the part of the audience profile that relates specifically to Q & A. It's a clue to the kinds of questions you can expect.

If you're prepared for a question, you're obviously going to do a better job of handling it.

Case Study: Former President Reagan's press secretary, Marlin Fitzwater, has said the White House staff can anticipate roughly four out of five questions reporters will pose at any given press conference. This means that during the press conference, the President is ready for 80 percent of the questions that come from the floor.

If the President of the United States can anticipate four out of five questions in an unrestricted presidential press conference, then with preparation the rest of us ought to be able to anticipate nine out of ten questions.

This means that roughly one time in ten someone will throw you a curve when you were looking for a fastball, and you will have to think on your feet. It also means that the rest of the time you'll have an answer prepared. You'll know what's coming—maybe not the exact words or all the nuances, but at least the specific area or issue. And you'll be able to step into the pitch and hit a line drive up the middle.

In other words, contrary to appearances, a skilled handler of Q & A is never very far from his or her "prepared text," because that text includes answers for every question that might come up.

The first step in your preparation is to anticipate, write down, and think through every question that might come up in the context of your topic. Look especially for difficult, tricky, or belligerent ones. Then prepare answers as far in advance as possible.

This is the most rigorous work you will have to do in the course of your presentation training. But, like a lot of what a recruit does in boot camp, it will pay off under fire. Walking into a Q & A without doing this homework is like walking into battle without a weapon.

For this exercise, we recommend you make a *Difficult Questions Worksheet*. The worksheet is essentially a four-part list containing:

- Questions you have found difficult to answer in the past
- Questions on matters you would prefer not to have exposed in public, to other departments, to your superiors, or to interviewers
- Issues that are particularly critical to your position, department, business, industry, or organization
- Your primary selling points

After making out your Difficult Questions Worksheet, spend some time mulling over the contents. This is not a process you want to hurry through. If possible spread it out over several days. Try to expand your thinking. Don't always be linear; let your mind associate freely. Consider every possible ramification of your business, of related public concerns, and of your positive program. Continue this process—letting ideas percolate and integrate—until you feel you *really* know your way around all the issues, pro and con.

> **Tip:** Try the technique known as "mind mapping," in which you write the central thought of the question in the middle of the page and write down ideas all around it.

By the time you've completed this phase of preparation, you should be pretty comfortable with a broad spectrum of questions. *Part* of your job in the Q & A will be to answer those questions, but it's not your whole job. Along with your answers, you also want to work in your selling points. That's what makes the Q & A an *opportunity*.

Phase Two of preparation is the forging of *connections* between the issues raised by the *questions* you studied in phase one and your selling points. For help in this second phrase of preparation, we have designed the *Plus/Minus Worksheet* (see next page).

On the left side of the page, list all the negative issues; on the right side, list all your positive selling points. As you study the material in this format, your aim is to bridge the rhetorical space that separates the two sides with concepts that create a connection between one side and the other. Look for logical paths that lead from items on the negative side to items on the positive side and draw actual lines *connecting* issues that relate conceptually.

Sometimes you can answer a minus question with a plus word and specifics. For example, **Question:** "Isn't this promotional plan unnecessary?" **Answer:** "It's *absolutely* necessary. Let me give you our specific objective and our anticipated results."

Sometimes you need to answer the negative and use a "but" or a "however" to get to your plus side. For example, **Question:** "Isn't the anticipated expense figure one-point-five million dollars with only a

PLUS/MINUS WORKSHEET

– – – – –   + + + + +

_____

three hundred thousand dollar sales figure the first year?" **Answer:**
"Yes, that's true. *But* this is an investment that will make us competitive in the long run. The numbers show us turning a profit in the
fourth year."

_____

> Work out a connection from *every* item on the minus side to
> *some* point on the plus side. It's much more important for all
> the minuses to be covered than for every plus to make an
> appearance.

_____

You will probably begin to notice that certain concepts crop up more
often than others (the cost of living or the importance of customer
service, for example). These are your "higher" or "broader" issues;
take special note of them because they are important.

Q & A Architecture: Building Bridges

After analyzing in detail how "their" questions and "your" answers *connect*, you're now ready to meld these two elements into the powerful rhetorical device we call the *bridging technique*.

As the name suggests, the technique consists of building a verbal bridge between the point raised by the questioner and the selling point *you wish to emphasize*.

Case Study 1: A classic example of skillful bridging is drawn from the 1980 presidential campaign when candidate Edward Kennedy appeared on a television interview program.

The senator's pet campaign issue was his health care program for the elderly and it was a popular issue. His selling points were bankable votes for him, so naturally he wanted to make the audience aware of it. Twenty minutes of the thirty-minute program had gone by and the senator hadn't had an opportunity to talk about health care. The next question was: "Senator, what is your view on the MX missile?"

Think for a moment what you would do in this situation. You need to answer the question, but you also need to get in some of your selling points. Is there any way that you can answer the question and find a connection that will allow you to bridge to health care? How about the issue of costs?

Senator Kennedy's answer went something like this: "My staff and I are against the MX. We don't think it is the right weapons system for this country. First of all, we are adequately covered by our existing systems. Second, you can't look at the MX—or any other weapons system—without focusing on its cost. We have only so much money in our national budget, and I believe that more funds should be spent on domestic priorities such as rebuilding our roads or in areas such as national health care . . ." With this bridge, Kennedy was off and running. "In this country today, the average American senior citizen spends about one-third of his or her income for health care maintenance. With my bill, we can bring this down to one-fifth or less, and each elderly person in this town could save as much as four hundred dollars a year."

At this point, the reporters might follow up with further questions on the health care issue, or they might come back to the MX missile. The point is that the smooth transition gave the senator a chance to make his selling point and left him in a position where it was even odds he would be able to make others.

That's the technique in a nutshell. Here was a smooth, logical, persuasive path from the *issue* of a weapons system, to the *broader issue* of costs and the national budget, to a *specific economic issue*— the high cost of health care. And finally the *selling point*—the Kennedy-sponsored bill and its benefits for the elderly.

Case Study 2: Moving to the private sector, Marc Chodorow, vice president in charge of public relations for Goldome, was talking to a reporter on the subject of KWIKLINE, the bank's telephone banking service.

"Twenty-five to thirty percent of our 'platform' transactions [at a desk, with an officer] are now being handled by phone . . ." he was saying when the reporter broke in: "Does this mean that old-fashioned, face-to-face human services are going down the tubes?"

"Not at all," said Chodorow. "We still believe in personal banking services, and we always will, but [*but* is often a very important word in bridging] we find that using the phone works better for us—it's cheaper and more efficient. And frankly, it often works better for our customers as well.

"Here's an example. Last April 15, just hours before the last possible minute to file a tax return, we got a call from a customer who was out of town but who wanted to fund his IRA. The added complication was that he needed to take out a loan to do so. We were able to take care of *both* transactions for him over KWIKLINE in time for him to meet the IRS filing deadline."

The story makes another textbook example of skillful bridging: Chodorow answered the question (we aren't abandoning walk-in banking services), bridged (but) to his selling point (we think it works better—for us and for the customer), and added a memorable supporting specific (look what this service can do for you in a pinch).

Bridging is a flexible and adaptable technique that can be used one way or another in almost any Q & A situation. The more you do it, the better you'll be at it.

Practice, Practice, Practice

We have a whole chapter on practicing, but practice is particularly crucial for Q & A, so we need to say a few things about it here.

Skillful Q & A always requires specific preparation. Former President Reagan, for example, spent approximately six and a half hours preparing for every press conference. That's the kind of commitment that produces results. But before you get into that league, you're going to have to devote some time to mastering the pivotal Q & A technique, bridging.

Your practice at this stage has three primary goals:
- Perfection of your command over the issue-bridge-selling point links
- A spontaneous conversational tone
- Conciseness

The more closely you can approximate real presentation conditions, the more effective your practice will be. This means responding to real questions. Getting a friend, spouse, or colleague to scan your worksheet and fire tough questions at you would be most effective.

If you don't have access to a practice partner, you will have to frame questions for yourself—just as you imagine they might come from the audience:
- Write your questions down on slips on paper.
- Put the slips in a paper bag and pull them out one by one to simulate random questions from an audience.
- Do *not* write down your answers. Say them out loud, in your own words, just as you would in any conversation or discussion.

As you practice, *strive to refine and simplify your answers*. The more succinct they are, the more likely they are to be understood and retained. Work at getting the main message of your selling point as close to the front of your answer as possible.

Repeat each answer until it goes smoothly. This will probably take you about three tries per answer in the beginning. As you develop skill, you'll do better and better on your first try.

To really help yourself improve, record your practice sessions on audio tape. Listening to yourself speak is the most effective feedback.

As you listen to the tapes of your practice session, we suggest that you first make notes on what you *like*, then concentrate on what needs improvement.

More Q & A Techniques

You've prepared for the tough questions and spent time practicing the bridging technique. You're probably feeling pretty confident about the prospect of facing a question and answer session.

We've got some good news and some bad news. The bad news is that you're not quite ready yet; there are more question-handling techniques for you to master. The good news is that they're easy— and they will make your performance that much stronger.

The following rules and guidelines will keep the Q & A session running smoothly and under your control. They will help you steer clear of serious pitfalls, and generally help to make your Q & A a success.

Keep in mind that these are generalities and must be filtered through experience and common sense. Some points are more applicable to one situation than another. The list is most useful in the more formal presenter/audience situation. In the one-on-one meeting with your boss, or in a job interview, you are much more restricted in the range of appropriate techniques.

Set ground rules. In small presentations, this is not usually possible. In large meetings, however, this is highly recommended to establish your authority in the Q & A setting.

You may, for example, ask that questioners raise their hands or stand and identify themselves and their affiliations. You will probably want to save questions until after you have completed your presentation. If so, ask listeners to hold their questions until the end. If you want to limit questions to one per person, say so; you can always graciously make an exception to this or *any* ground rule on an ad hoc basis. If you forget to ask members to hold their questions and some-one interrupts, either suggest that he or she write down the question and save it until the end, or you can answer it and ask everyone else to please hold further questions until you have finished your presen-tation.

Be prepared to get the ball rolling. When preparing for a Q & A session, you should always write a question or two *for yourself.* Au-diences are sometimes slow to begin asking questions and you must start the ball rolling or the whole Q & A may fall flat.

"One question that is frequently raised about this subject is . . ." is one way to handle it. Another is, "Just before we started this eve-ning, Marty asked me . . ." There are many possibilities. Once you have primed the pump, the audience will generally warm up and begin asking their own questions.

Tip: You can help stimulate questions from the audience while you set your ground rules: As you explain how you'd like mem-bers of the audience to seek recognition, raise your arm to illus-trate; you'll find that this tends to elicit an arm-raising response. If this doesn't do the trick, proceed to your fall-back questions.

Answer all questions. Only personal questions, questions relating to proprietary information, and questions to which you don't have an-swers (see our discussion of "don't-know" questions on page 127) are exceptions. The rest are fair game.

Try to look at difficult questions as an opportunity to demonstrate your strength. If questions have been submitted in written form, you might consider tackling one or two of the tough ones first just to demonstrate your willingness to face all issues. Here is an opportu-nity to head off anticipated questions raising particular problems. If you have prepared conscientiously, you should be able to offer a rea-sonably strong answer to the occasional unpredictable zinger. And even if you don't handle a question brilliantly, the courage and commitment you show by taking it on in good faith will ultimately work in your favor.

Always **pause before answering a question.** Pausing gives you time to collect your thoughts. It takes the brain more than two seconds to formulate a well-considered answer, and when the question is a difficult one, you really need that think time. The pause helps you avoid the pitfalls of "having your tongue drive your brain" and unconsciously repeating the negative language in a hostile or inflammatory question (which we will discuss presently). Just remember: Listen, think, and answer.

Not all questions are brain-crunchers, but there are two good reasons to pause *even on easy questions*.

First, the pause conveys an attitude of respect both for the questioner and for the question itself. It tells the audience that you are relaxed and that you regard each question as worthy of serious reflection. It also shows that you are *listening*. Jumping on the question before it is out of the questioner's mouth is likely to send the message either that you are anxious or that you have glib, ready-made answers for everything.

Second, if you pause before *every* question, the audience quickly assimilates this as an aspect of your style. Then when you are asked the tough question and you *need* the time, your pause doesn't telegraph to the audience the message that you find the question a problem.

For difficult questions, in addition to pausing, it is a good idea to have a small repertoire of phrases prepared to extend your time to think. This will also allow you to launch into your answer unobtrusively. ("Well, let me tell you how we view that issue. . . .") Try to avoid the response, "I'm glad you asked that question," which often comes across as defensive. On the other hand, an acceptable answer, even on the witness stand, is, "I've never thought about the issue that way. Give me a moment to consider it in that light."

Bridge answers whenever possible. With innocuous questions, bridge *to* your selling points. With tricky or embarrassing questions, after dealing with at least part of the substance, bridge *away* to more comfortable ground. Respond to the specifics of the question and move to the realm of the larger issues that it raises. Once there, you can almost always reiterate your message.

Don't repeat negative language. A natural response to a tough question is to buy time to think by repeating the question verbatim. This is the worst thing you can do. In mindlessly repeating the question, you will be emphasizing the negatively charged language. ("Are we ripping off the public with our new pricing structure? . . .")

Coming full circle to repeat a question at the end of an answer is a natural impulse. If you do not check it, especially with a hostile or otherwise difficult question, you may undo a lot of skillful work you did in bridging away from it in the first place. You may well end up where your questioner began—with a negative statement. ("So, no, in answer to your question, I don't think we're ripping off the public. . . .") You want to end with the positive. It might help to *visualize* a bridge—a structure that leads from one side of the river to the other, not around in a circle.

Anticipate the brain-crunchers. To defuse a potentially volatile issue—if you suspect or know that someone in the group is going to hit you with a tough question—you can meet it head on by raising it yourself. It certainly is better for you to do this than for you to be surprised with it from the floor. And the audience may respect you for your courage and candor.

Keep it moving. Make an effort to be crisp and concise with your answers. In general, aim at keeping your answers between thirty seconds and a minute. Answer the question; if appropriate, bridge to a selling point; take another question.

Disengage eye contact and move to another questioner. This helps you include more people in your answers and also discourages follow-ups. Establish eye contact as you field a question. Maintain that contact for the first few moments of your answer. Then shift to one or more other members of the group, perhaps settling on the next questioner even as you finish your current answer.

This technique obviously doesn't apply when you're dealing with a power person. You must stick with that person until he or she is done dealing with the question or issue.

Leave on a high note or with a brief summary. Nothing looks worse than dutifully droning on until the audience has no more questions. After the Q & A time you have allotted, or when you feel you've reemphasized your selling points, you should wind up the session. An effective technique is to ask for "one or two more questions." If the first is an easy one and you have made a positive bridge on your answer, you can use that as an opportunity to exit. If you don't manage to handle the first question smoothly, take a second. If neither goes particularly well, give a prepared thirty-second summary of your presentation so that you can leave the audience with a positive message. You might actually say, "Although I didn't handle that question particularly well, let me finish strongly with a brief summary."

Close with dignity. Following your final answer or your summary statement, pause for a count of two or three, take off your microphone, gather your papers, and walk off with the same purpose and dignity with which you approached the lectern.

Quick Reference Summary

- "Q & A session" doesn't mean "inquisition"; use it to your advantage.
- Preparation is the key to feeling in control of the Q & A.
- Analyzing the audience is the number one priority.
- Anticipate and practice difficult questions.
- Use the bridging technique to turn negative questions into positive answers.
- Try "mind mapping"—free association of ideas emanating from the central thought of a question—to allow you to bridge to a selling point.
- Develop the discipline of using the Plus/Minus Worksheet. It

will help you create transitions from negative questions to positive answers.

- By bridging you can (1) narrow the focus of interest of a question to a specific issue within the issue raised, or (2) expand the focus of interest to the broader issue, which may allow you to bring in selling points.
- Bridging can diffuse an adversarial question.
- It is important to answer a question first, then bridge.
- To practice Q & A, have a friend ask tough questions. If no help is available, write questions on slips of paper, and draw them at random.
- *Always* pause before answering a question. Take time to think.
- First thought when a question comes is "What's my selling point?" Second thought: "What's my bridge?" Pause. Then answer.
- In many cases, you can set ground rules. When possible, make things as comfortable for yourself as you can.
- To stimulate questions, ask one of yourself.
- Don't dodge or evade questions. If you don't know the answer, say so and volunteer to get the information to the questioner.
- When you don't know the answer to a question, try to bridge back to something pertinent that you *do* know.
- Watch for negative language in questions. Never repeat negative language in your answer.
- Don't repeat questions—unless the audience really can't hear them.
- In an adversarial encounter, move your eyes to another questioner as you finish your answer. This prevents follow-ups.
- If possible, keep answers short. Thirty seconds to a minute is appropriate.
- Leave on a high note. Always summarize key points in a positive manner.

10

Tricky Questions, Difficult Questioners

Most questions are straightforward, inviting equally straight-forward answers. But there are several types of questions containing rhetorical pitfalls that come up frequently enough so that every presenter needs to learn to recognize them immediately.

The same holds true for several types of questioners (or styles of questioning) that have a disruptive effect on the smooth flow of your Q & A.

In examining these problems, we will concentrate on two separate but related areas:

- *Awareness:* Learning to clearly identify the specific types of problems
- *Tactics:* Learning how to deal with them smoothly, maintaining focus and control, and turning potential problems into *opportunities* to make your point

Tricky Questions

The "Don't Know" Question

For some reason, many of us feel when we get up in front of a group we have to be omniscient; as a result, we are often reluctant to acknowledge our occasional ignorance.

Sometimes, the best answer you can give to a question is, "I don't know."

If you don't know the answer, don't make it up. Trying to fake an answer is a mistake for several reasons:
- It's hard to be convincing when you're not convinced yourself.
- If there is someone present who does know the answer, you're likely to be shown up on the spot.
- If anyone in the audience later learns that your answer was incorrect, you may look bad forever in that person's view, no matter how well you handled yourself during the Q & A.

If you don't know, *step one* is be candid; say so.

But don't leave matters there. *Step two* is to amplify; offer whatever explanation or justification you can: "I'm sorry, that just isn't my area of expertise" or "Those figures won't be available for another few days."

Step three is *always* to offer to remedy the situation: "I'll find out that information and get back to you. When will you need that by?"; "See me afterward and I'll tell you who to contact about this"; or, to a reporter, "What's your deadline?"

Step four, having demonstrated your integrity and good faith, is to transform this into an *opportunity*. By bridging back to what you *do* know, you create an opportunity to deliver a selling point: "But I *can* tell you that in this general area we've been making an effort to . . ." This response is like a negotiation where you say, "I can't give you that, but will you take this instead?"

The Loaded Question

Confrontational questions that contain highly charged negative language ("rip-off," "monopoly," "profiteering," "endangering public health") can be very disconcerting. Saying little is your best tactic in response.

Never reinforce negative or highly charged language in a question by repeating it.

You may not be able to neutralize the effect of such a question entirely, but don't lend credence to the charge by expanding on it.

Take your time. Pause. Use your own words. Above all, be concise. Don't overanswer and don't allow yourself to get drawn in or distracted by the emotionality of what's been said.

If you need to buy a little extra thinking time, use a phrase like, "I certainly wouldn't use those words" or "I strongly disagree with your characterization. . . ."

The Forced Choice (AKA the False Choice)

This is the situation in which the questioner poses two alternatives as if they were mutually exclusive ("Do you walk to school, or do you carry your lunch?") and invites the presenter to endorse one or the other.

The *real* answer to an "A or B" question may well be "*neither* A nor B, but C." Or it may be "*both* A and B."

("Are lower earnings the result of mismanagement or employee theft?" Quite possibly neither one. "What do you want, high profits or a clean environment?" Without question, both.)

The defense against the forced choice is simple: Awareness. As long as you recognize the critter when it turns up, it is easy enough to deal with: Remember to pause thoughtfully, then use the word *both* or *neither*, as the occasion requires.

The Multiquestion

Often when people get an opportunity to ask a question they sense that this may be their only chance. Typically, they then turn all the various questions on their mind into one lengthy run-on question. Trying to log in, remember, and respond to a whole list of questions can be confusing, taxing, and time consuming.

This is one situation in which it is okay *not* to be 100 percent responsive.

If you ask the questioner which question he or she wants you to answer first, it invariably turns out to be the toughest.

Instead, simply pick out the one question that you most want to answer and do it. Everyone is generally satisfied with this. A second option is to respond along these lines: "Well, you've asked me several questions; I think the issue that covers all of them is . . ."

The situation where these tactics don't work is the small management meeting or any other one-on-one situation where you're being grilled by your superiors. In this type of Q & A session it's best to take notes as questions are asked, then try to answer them succinctly. If you need to buy a little think time, you can ask for a restatement of one or more questions, or a confirmation of specific items asked for. It is okay to be human in this situation; if you forget one of the questions, it's all right to ask: "What was your third question again?"

In terms of the order in which you answer multiple questions from your boss, if there is a particularly tough one, you might choose to tackle that one first. This allows you to move on to more comfortable territory and end your multianswer on a positive note.

The Hypothetical Question

Many questioners begin their queries with "Suppose that . . ." or "What if . . ." and then, describing some particular set of circumstances, invite you to speculate about their effect. The temptation to wrestle with the problem may be strong, but resist. Buying into another person's speculative scenario creates the impression that you are endorsing it, even though *you* understand that it is hypothetical.

In dealing with hypothetical questions, above all, never accept the premise out of hand.

Begin your response by verbally flagging the question as "a hypothetical" or "an 'if' question." You then have three options:

1. You can respectfully decline to speculate.
2. You may choose to answer, *making it absolutely clear that you are speculating*.
3. You can respond with a reality-based answer.

Whether you choose to provide an answer or merely indicate your unwillingness to speculate, make sure you have clearly identified the problem *to the audience*, so they don't think you are being arbitrarily unresponsive.

Case Study 1: Reagan administration Defense Secretary Caspar Weinberger did a fine job of this in an interview following the U.S. bombing of Libya in 1986. Chris Wallace of NBC News asked, "If this does not deter Colonel Qaddafi and terrorism continues, what then?" Weinberger responded, "That gets us into hypotheticals, and you know I try not to deal with those. . . ."

Having flagged the hypothetical, Secretary Weinberger then used the opportunity to deliver a selling point when he added, "But I think it will send an unmistakable signal, and I think it will go very far towards deterring future acts."

Case Study 2: During the Iran-Contra hearings in 1987, we recall many hypotheticals posed to witnesses. When congressional investigators framed speculative scenarios to Lt. Col. Oliver North, his attorney, Brendan L. Sullivan, was always quick to flag them in no uncertain terms. At one point he said about an "if" question, "That's so hypothetical it's dreamland."

On the other hand, when it was in his interest to do so, North answered such questions: "That's a hypothetical, but let me tell you that if those events had occurred, it would have been a very positive development."

Tip: If you are confronted with hypothetical questions on the witness stand (as in an administrative hearing), you can sometimes be forced to speculate. In such a case, be sure to qualify *each* answer ("This is speculation, of course, but if I must, I'd have to say . . ." or "In answer to your hypothetical . . ."). This makes for a clearer transcript and a minimum of ambiguities later on about what part of your testimony was asserted as fact and what was forced speculation (see our discussion of being a witness in Chapter Sixteen).

Tip: Hypothetical questions crop up frequently in job interviews. Here again, flagging the question type is a good tactic. It lets the interviewer know that you're listening and that you're careful. For example: "If you're a product manager for Brand X and your market share drops by two points, what would you do?" It's a fair answer to flag the *if*: "Well, you're asking me to speculate on a matter I don't believe will come to pass. However, if that were to occur, let me state . . ."

Difficult Questioners

We identify four problem questioner "types" who crop up fairly frequently:
- The Supporter
- The Detailer
- The Negator
- The Filibusterer

The key to understanding these questioners is to remember that in a sense they aren't really questioners at all. The problems arise from the fact that each type is functioning for the moment as a speaker. The speech may be a generous statement of appreciation, a criticism or grievance, or a self-serving rhetorical orgy.

In dealing with troublesome personalities in the presentation situation, *you must take control.*

While there are exceptions, in most presentations it is your privilege to set the agenda. Although you don't want to be rigid about it, it is up to you to keep to that agenda: your message.

Dealing firmly and politely with those who seek to usurp the floor helps present *you* as a confident and assertive person, lending conviction to your message indirectly.

Bonus: It is almost always possible to use even troublesome encounters as opportunities to deliver additional selling points.

Let's look at problem questioners one by one.

The Supporter

You may be surprised to find support listed as a problem. It is, but only in one sense. Because of our cultural notions of modesty, it is hard for most of us to accept praise, directly and wholeheartedly expressed. It makes us uncomfortable and we want to make the situation go away as quickly as possible. In a presentation, this tends to result in, at best, a hasty word of gratitude, at worst, a piece of embarrassed self-effacement.

If we are aware of the problem, however, we can use supportive comments to our advantage:

- Openly and sincerely thank the speaker for the kind words.
- Tell why the appreciation is gratifying. You strive to do good work and appreciation adds to the satisfaction.
- Then add a selling point, a further example of achievements you

feel are praiseworthy: "Thanks for your kind words, John. We do try to be good corporate citizens, and it's nice to know that our efforts are appreciated. One of our latest projects in a related area is . . ."

Tip: You won't always be able to add the selling point, but it's nice to be prepared. At several points in this book we have suggested that the presenter make up a note card listing points he or she wants to score in the Q & A. In this situation it is usually pretty easy to bridge to one of the points on your card.

The Detailer (AKA the Nit-Picker)

This is the person who likes to quibble with facts and figures. A natural response to this provocation is to get into a debate. This is also the worst response. The point raised by the detailer is usually minor and often insignificant. If you pursue it too far you can completely lose the rest of your audience.

The problem here is the competing claims of one individual versus the whole group. Politeness requires that you spend time with the questioner, but if you spend too much time, you lose everybody else. Tactically, your main goal is to deal with the question as expeditiously as possible.

If you are sure of your facts and figures, stand by them. If there is legitimate room for disagreement, volunteer to see the person after the meeting and resolve the matter then: "George, I'm not 100 percent sure of those figures. Why don't you see me after we finish here. I'll get all the information from you and then get back with the answer. . . ."

Be absolutely sure you follow through on any pledges to "get back" with information or contacts.

You can certainly include others, and again, this is a good *opportunity* to bridge to one of the larger issues and deliver a selling point.

"Anyone else who is interested is welcome to join us. Now the *issue* that George raises here is one I *can* discuss . . ." In this way you can deal with the question in a reasonably short time without getting bogged down in a lot of nit-picking. You come out looking good: friendly, courteous, tolerant, concerned, helpful.

The Negator

This is the questioner with a personal problem or a negative statement that is clearly not a question at all. In this case you are being cast more in the mold of arbitrator or ombudsman than as a source of information. You would like to be helpful, if possible; at the very least you would like to *appear* concerned. But you don't want to take up the entire audience's time with one person's problem, which may be only marginally relevant to your agenda. You need to respond, but not to get sidetracked and lose your audience.

The solution is to take the problem where it belongs: outside the bounds of your Q & A.

- First, be responsive, if possible, to the issue being raised, if only to validate or acknowledge it: "I just don't *know* what happened to your brother-in-law. . . ."
- Next, indicate your willingness to help—and the restrictions you are operating under in this situation: ". . . and we don't really have time to discuss it *here* as fully as I would like."
- Then, offer to put yourself at the person's disposal outside of presentation time: "See me after the meeting and I'll be glad to do what I can to clarify this for you."
- Finally, try to use the incident in a positive way by addressing an issue that encompasses the point or problem raised by the negator: "But I'd like to point out—on the broader issue of jobs in general—that for the past two and a half years we've been striving . . ."

By expressing compassion and/or a willingness to help, you make a favorable impression. By offering to deal with the issue or problem outside of the presentation context, you regain control of the proceedings. By addressing the larger issue, you are able to make a selling point. This is turning a problem into an opportunity; getting to the point.

The Filibusterer

This is the most flagrant variety of "problem nonquestioner": the person who launches into a rambling, run-on statement that may show early promise of becoming a question but never does. It's an aggravated form of thinking out loud. Since the statement is almost always negative or critical in tone and is without any explicit statement to come to grips with and address, it tends to make both you and the audience uncomfortable.

The source of the discomfort here is the issue of control. You have nothing concrete to respond to; the "questioner" has seized control of the proceedings. This makes you anxious, and *it has the same effect on your audience.* Like it or not, they look to you to take and maintain control—which is your primary task here.

A natural impulse would be to interrupt and challenge the filibusterer, asking, "Well, are you going to ask a question or not?" Unfortunately, appropriate as this may seem, it is likely to seem rude and confrontational; it is better to avoid this kind of impression.

If he or she gives you an opening you can jump in and regain control by "answering": Well, Chris, *if I understand what you're asking . . ."*

If not, as is often the case, your only recourse is to use what we call the "relay race baton-pass" technique. After listening politely for a while—twenty-five to thirty seconds is quite sufficient—you figuratively reach out and grab the baton (i.e., the monologue) from the filibusterer and run with it.

1. Look directly at the person.
2. Address him or her by name, if you know it (which generally causes the speaker to pause for a second or two).
3. Pick up on a few key words, and then start talking.

Begin by literally echoing the speaker's last few words. Talk a little louder and more forcefully than your filibusterer, and as you do so, move your eye contact to another member of the audience. *Keep talking* as you bridge to the general issue. This assertive technique is quite effective, and the audience will appreciate your taking control.

There are a few additional personality types that cause problems specifically in the context of *meetings*. We cover these fully in Chapter Seventeen.

A Final Note: You may feel that we're a little rabid about pushing you to get your selling points in at every opportunity. In reality, it's a rare individual who actually turns the Q & A to advantage. We asked a person in one workshop, "How did you do on the Q & A?" He said, "Well, I had my answers ready, but they didn't ask the right questions!" If you really want the Q & A to work for you, you have to be like the notorious "Boss" (William Marcy) Tweed, grand sachem of Tammany Hall, who said about his career, "I seen my opportunities and I took 'em."

Quick Reference Summary

- Watch for the "A or B" dilemma: being forced to chose between presented alternatives. A third choice may be the right one.
- With multipart questions, answer the part of the question that lets your selling point come through. It's generally your choice if you want to go on to another part of the question.
- In internal presentations, especially to your boss, you may have to answer all parts of a question. In this case, tackle the toughest part first, then easier parts, and end on a positive note.
- "Flag" hypothetical questions: "You're asking me to speculate . . ." or "That's a hypothetical . . ."
- Be prepared to express pride in project or company in response to a Supporter's questions or remarks.
- In response to a Nit-Picker, stick to your guns if the point is important; if it isn't, concede that the fact may be true and offer to talk with the person after the session.

- Be aware of Negators. Stay calm. Don't buy into the person's negative tone or words. Don't get caught in a fight.
- Offer to see a Negator, and any other interested parties, after the presentation to deal with the related issue.
- Once you know you've got a Filibusterer on your hands (thirty to forty seconds should be long enough to tell), intervene by using the person's name (if you know it), and expressing concern over issues being raised. If you don't know the person, "take back the floor" by echoing the Filibusterer's words and bridging to another point.

11

How Do I Get
to Carnegie Hall?

You'll probably recognize that question as the opening line of an old joke. The punch line is *"Practice!"* Which is what you need to do if you truly want to become an accomplished presenter. You've learned enough just by reading *Get to the Point* to improve, but if you really want to be *good*, you must practice. Practice alone, practice with family, with colleagues, or with professionals—but practice!

Here's a whole chapter filled with advice and techniques to help you practice efficiently and enjoyably and get the most out of your effort.

General Practice Concepts

We'd like to start by giving you some general maxims about practice; how to make the most effective use of your time.

Don't work on too much at once. Like playing the piano, giving a presentation requires us to integrate a number of complex processes into one seamless performance. Especially in the early stages of practice, avoid trying to do it all at once. Break things down into discrete components, mastering each separately before putting them together.

By concentrating on one factor at a time, you will master the process more quickly than if you try to "do it all."

Feel free to be free. Practice time is the time to take chances. We strongly encourage you to try everything; any zany idea that comes into your head. Later on, you'll have time to weed out things that don't work, but some of the things you discover this way will become invaluable components of your personal style.

If you don't take chances in a training session, you'll never do it in "real life."

For peak performance, make it tough. Once you've mastered the fundamentals, make practice harder than the real thing; you'll perform better. Call it the "on-deck" principle: The batter waiting in the "on-deck circle" swings a heavily weighted bat so that when he gets to the plate the bat he swings at the oncoming pitch will feel light.

Case Study: Len Dykstra, one of the New York Mets' batting heroes of the 1986 World Series, credits his success to just this kind of approach: making the practice task harder than the real thing. Dykstra set out to learn to hit a major league fastball by batting against "Iron Mike," the pitching machine. He began at the normal distance—sixty feet, six inches from the pitching mound. Once he was comfortable hitting what the machine threw from this distance, he began to move closer to the machine, effectively reducing the time the eye and brain had to track the ball's trajectory and set the bat on a collision course. Eventually he got as close as forty-five feet to the Iron Mike and was hitting balls that were faster than anything a human being could possibly throw.

If you design your practice to be tougher than the real thing, you too can have that performance edge. If you know you have ten minutes to give your presentation, make sure you can do it in eight—without rushing. When you practice for your Q & A, really dig deep and look at *every* embarrassing, malicious, or underhanded question that your worst enemy might raise. Prepare for the toughest presenting slot: Assume that you're going to be the fourth of six speakers, so you'll find a way of launching your talk that will really wake up the audience.

Whatever practice devices you come up with, challenge yourself. Your efforts will pay off.

The more closely you can approximate real presentation conditions, the more your practice will pay off.

Presentation Practice

Out loud, please. Most of the work we've done so far in *Get to the Point* has been in terms of the written word. Presentation making, however, is a spoken skill, and to master it you have to transfer your skills into the speaking mode.

When you're actually making a presentation, your mind, your body, and your voice all have to work together. Therefore, they all need to be used in practice workouts.

Thought patterns and sentence structures differ radically between writing and speaking. The average spoken sentence, for example, contains nine words; the average written sentence, twenty-three. What looks good on paper may sound unnatural and therefore unconvincing delivered vocally. Listeners tend to detect—even if only subconsciously—a "reading quality," which diminishes your overall credibility.

Perhaps the primary reason is that verbal speech dances to the rhythm of the breath; written speech has its own, quite different rhythms. Working from written text, you may find it hard to breathe properly. (This is one reason we encourage using notes rather than a full transcript.) So, to be effective, your practice must be done out loud.

> **Tip:** Stretch physically and vocalize a bit before practicing in order to get into the habit before the real presentation. (See Chapter Twelve for recommended exercises.)

Get it on tape. By recording your practice sessions you increase their effectiveness immeasurably. The direct feedback of listening to your own voice, watching your own face and body is more valuable than a dozen critiques. In the early stages of practice, audio recording is fine; later on, you'll want to do videotaping, if at all possible.

> **Tip:** With the accessibility and portability of cassette and microcassette recorders, you can make use of "dead" time like commuting time for presentation practice. In the privacy of your car you can both record and listen. On public transportation you may feel inhibited about speaking into your recorder, but with a tape player and headphones, you can certainly listen discreetly.

Practice Plan

Divide and conquer. As we suggested above, practice pays off better if, instead of attacking the whole presentation at once, you divide it into brief segments and work on each segment separately.

A logical place to start would be with your opening, which you'll memorize. Practice the *whole process* of beginning your talk. If using a lectern, literally walk up to a lectern (a box on a table will do) and put down your notes. Pause. Visualize the room you'll be in and the people you'll be addressing; actually look at them in your mind's eye. Make mental eye contact, take three deep breaths, and launch into your grabber. Once you've finished, turn off the recording machine, rewind the tape, and listen.

Self-critique. Your first assignment on playback is to notice what you did well. This may not be easy. We humans tend to be hypercritical of our own performances, wincing at every little imperfection and remaining deaf and blind to our strengths.

The key to effective self-criticism is detachment.

Try to be like another person while you listen. This may be tough at first, but it makes a big difference in what you're able to hear.

So, from as objective a point of view as possible, what did you like about your performance? Was your voice animated? Did you sound confident? Conversational? Whatever it was that you felt good about, dwell on it awhile; feel that strength, let it sink in, reinforce it. Then move on to considering what needs improvement.

The 'Rule of Three.' Don't be afraid to do "retakes" as you practice your segments. Generally, it takes at least three tries to achieve a suitably polished, confident, and convincing rendition. However, if you feel additional run-throughs would strengthen your performance further, by all means do them.

Audio checklist. Go through the playback–self-critique process for each segment of your talk. Here's a list of things for you to listen for:
☐ Is your voice clear?
☐ Are your selling points strong and clear?
☐ Do you sound audience-centered?
☐ Did you use signal words to continually pull the audience in?
☐ Is there any phrase or image that might be developed as a theme throughout your talk?
☐ Do you need to:
    ☐ Slow down?
    ☐ Speed up?
    ☐ Vary your pace?

☐ Did you take time to breathe?

☐ Did you pause occasionally?

☐ Was your voice flexible in pitch? Did it move up and down the musical scale, or did it hover within a limited pitch area?

☐ Did you make effective use of emphasis, giving life to the emotional words, the action words?

☐ Are you unconsciously stressing the prepositions and/or conjunctions?

☐ Did you ever emphasize by *lowering* your voice?

☐ Did you keep phrases short and crisp, or did you ramble on and on and on, gasping for breath?

Record, play back, study, and rerecord each segment of your talk until you no longer find any major problems, until you've bolstered all your strengths to the maximum.

Once each segment is working smoothly, put them all together and practice the presentation as a whole. (If yours is a long presentation, you may want to assemble short segments into intermediate sized sections before practicing the whole thing.)

Skill drills. In addition to working on your presentation section by section, you should devote some time to practicing specific skills. Listening to yourself and going through the vocal checklist should quickly reveal the areas that need work.

If you're a natural monotone, for example, practice—especially with feedback from your tape recorder—can change this. This is a situation where you really need to give yourself permission to take some chances—even to feel silly for a while, if necessary. Keep it firmly in mind that this is only practice; you've got nothing to lose but your inhibitions.

For working to change monotone, choose a short selection of material as a practice piece. It could be from your presentation or it could be something else, but in either case it should have some excitement to it, some emotionality. Pick out the active words, then work on making them come alive. Try out different effects. Move the voice higher and lower—to the very top and bottom of your range. Exaggerate. Be outrageous. Explore your limits.

You'll soon find it doesn't sound so outrageous. You might even like your new vocal expressiveness. In any case, you can always tone it down when you're in front of an audience if you need to.

Another psychological technique to improve your vocal expressiveness is to imagine that you are giving your presentation over the radio—that your voice is the only tool you have to make your points. Treat your tape recorder like a broadcast microphone as you tape your practice session; then imagine it is a radio as you play back your tape. Would you tune in to hear this commentator again?

What you can hear on a tape if you're listening carefully is amazing. You should even be able to hear where you gestured. You can't hear the actual gesture, of course, but you can hear where your voice got animated. If that didn't happen very often, practice can help here, too. Find a private practice space and read or act out a practice piece, gesturing emphatically on the thoughts or ideas you want to stress. As with your previous vocal practice, really exaggerate and be expansive. Read newspapers, poetry, lines from a play, speaking faster and slower. Try for effective delivery at a variety of tempos.

If you rarely or never paused and were out of breath, you need to work on your phrasing. Again, working out loud with written material, your own or others', is the best regimen. Use a copy you can mark up. Divide the text into short, crisp phrases. Indicate your pauses and word stress, and phrase groupings in the manuscript with our script marking symbols (or invent your own):

- / for a brief pause; // for a longer pause
- —————————— or = = = = = = = for emphasis
- ⌒ to tie groups of words together
- ᵛ to indicate a breath

Mark on your notes anything you need to remember. Inflection, pace, pauses, and gestures can all be indicated on your note cards. It can be a symbol—like an upward or downward arrow to indicate pitch or a stick figure with arms upraised to remind you to gesture—or a word—"SLOW DOWN," "FASTER," "BREATHE," "SMILE," "EYES."

Don't worry that you shouldn't be looking at your notes often enough for this kind of reminder to help much. This is practice, remember? At this stage, look at your notes as much as you need to. As you practice, you will learn to do these things naturally. Any that remain stubborn can be marked in your final notes.

Listening is learning. Here's a supplementary assignment for you: Listen to others as you go through your day. Listen to the way people speak. Listen with real attention. Material is everywhere, and we suggest you concentrate on:

- Professional actors and announcers (television and radio news broadcasters, especially the better known ones, are often very good models)
- Nonprofessional communicators in informal circumstances; that is, any conversation in which the parties are at ease and un-self-conscious

Listen for all the elements of inflection, phrasing, and emphasis that we covered in Chapter Eight.

If you hear something you like, something that stimulates your listening attention, work it into your own delivery.

The video eye. Once you've worked through your presentation segment by segment and practiced all the skills you felt needed improvement, it's time to try to gain the use of a videotape system. Videotaping yourself is not indispensable; but it is quite valuable. Everything an audio recording can tell you about your verbal presentation, a video recording will tell you about your expression, gestures, and body language.

Set the camera up to record a full-length view of you. You don't want to be a talking head here, because that's not what people will see. For rehearsal purposes you need to be able to observe your face *and* your upper body, particularly your arms and hands.

Video checklist. Tape your delivery. Play it back. As with the audio taping, your first assignment is to notice what you liked about it. Notice *everything* you did well. Then look for spots or aspects that need improvement.

☐ Was your face expressive?

☐ Or a frozen mask?
☐ Did you remember to smile?
    ☐ Before you began?
    ☐ From time to time during your talk?
☐ Was your body loose and mobile?
    ☐ Or did you stand like a wooden Indian?
☐ Were your gestures full and fluid?
    ☐ Or were your shoulders immobile?
    ☐ Or were your elbows frozen to your sides?

If you had a lot of trouble with one specific aspect of delivery—
gestures, for example—tape your delivery several times, concentrating on that one skill. Keep taping it until the embarrassment—that
feeling of "this can't be *me* doing this"—goes away.

As with your audio tape practice, record, play back, study, and
rerecord until you've eliminated all the problems and maximized
your strengths. Plan to videotape your entire presentation two or
three times.

Once your delivery is smooth, add your visuals. Actually observ-
ing the orchestration of your visuals on video can help tremendously
in polishing this aspect of your presentation. The audience's point of
view really lets you learn from experience how long a pause is
needed to absorb each image. (It also reveals how good your visuals
are. If they're too complicated or are poorly designed or laid out,
you'll see it better on the video playback than you will looking at the
visual itself. This is the time to make any improvements.)

Q & A practice. If your talk will include a question and answer
session—or if it is an internal presentation in which you will be subject to questions, either at the end or throughout—you will need to
do some Q & A practice. If at all possible, have other people help
you out on this. If not possible, you can do quite a bit on your own.
Refer to our Q & A practice suggestions in Chapter Seven. As you
review your audio tapes and/or videotapes of Q & A practice, be
alert for the following basics:

☐ Did you answer the question?
☐ Did you recognize tricky question forms?

□ Did you clearly flag tricky questions when you recognized them?
□ Did you bridge to a selling point?
□ Did you shift your eye contact?

Critiques from others. Once you feel you have derived all the benefit you can from the direct feedback of practicing with recording devices, see if you can enlist a volunteer audience to view your presentation. If you have friends, colleagues, or mentors who are experienced in presentation techniques or public communication in general, solicit their advice and criticism. Even if you don't have experts at your disposal, invite anyone you can get to sit still long enough and listen—friends and family will usually help. If you can coax some candid comments from them, so much the better. Even without feedback at this point, just presenting in front of an audience will help make you that much more comfortable when the actual presentation time comes.

Quick Reference Summary

- Divide your presentation into components to avoid frustration.
- Take chances; go beyond what is usual for you in voice, tone, pitch, and gestures.
- Breathing exercises will help calm your anxiety.
- Practice out loud. Use a tape recorder—video or audio.
- Stretch physically and vocalize a bit before practicing in order to get into the habit.
- If using lectern for presentation, use lectern (or some semblance) for practice. A box on a table will do.
- Listen and/or watch your tapes as if the taped performance were someone else's; be objective.
- Always note what is good before dwelling on what needs improvement.
- Retape segments again and again, trying variations in your voice—in the sound level and enunciation.
- When you pinpoint areas to work on—pacing the voice, for

example—devise exercises to correct the problem. Read newspapers, poetry, lines from a play, speaking faster, slower, trying for effective delivery at a variety of tempos.

- Don't worry about referring to notes in practice; use them as much as you need to.
- Spend the bulk of your practice time working with audio tape. You can actually hear more—breathing, inflection, voice-dropping at ends of sentences—than on video, since you aren't distracted by the visual element.
- Do plan to videotape your presentation at least two or three times if at all possible.
- Once comfortable with speaking, add your visuals.
- Remember to pause when you show a visual. Turn to the audience and talk.
- Remember to summarize after your talk—even in practice. Leave on a high note.

12

Performance Anxiety: Dealing with Nerves and Tension

There's more to being a polished performer than mastery of technique. All the technique in the world won't guarantee a great presentation if you're so tense that your body conveys discomfort to a degree that overshadows your words. Indeed, nervousness and physical tension are the things people fear most about public speaking.

Almost everybody experiences nervousness in front of a group or audience.

This chapter deals with nerves and physical tension. And the bottom line is that both are natural *and* controllable.

Actress Helen Hayes, "first lady of the American theater," was asked in an interview late in her career whether she still got nervous before a performance. "Sure," she replied, "I still get butterflies before *every* performance. But over the years, I've managed to teach them to fly in formation."

For some people nervousness is an affliction that goes away over time, or that disappears when they are making a lot of appearances—only to reappear when they haven't been in the spotlight for a while.

For others, in some degree it is always there. And this group includes quite a number of professional performers—like Helen Hayes.

Some nervousness is perfectly natural. There are two types of nervousness. "Fight or flight" most often stems from inadequate preparation. The other is a more positive anxiety, the kind a racehorse feels at the starting gate. It's a positive adrenalin flow. You should feel thoroughly prepared if you've followed the *Get to the Point* program, so we hope you won't experience the first type of nervousness. You really *ought* to have the second kind. If you don't feel an excited anxiousness at all, it means you really don't care. Even so, nerves are nerves. When your knees are shaking it doesn't matter what the source of the problem is. The objective here is to give you the tools to keep nervousness to a manageable minimum.

Teach *Your* Butterflies to Fly

If you understand that nerves are natural and can accept a certain amount of nervousness as normal, you are well on the way to getting it under control. Nervousness, like other forms of fear, feeds on itself. Without awareness, that little voice inside your head saying, "Look how nervous you are! What a terrible, inadequate person you are!" will go unchecked. This will put you at a real disadvantage.

Accepting your nervousness is the first step in reducing it. After you've done that there are a number of other measures you can take to keep it under control. Since nervousness is both a mental and a physical phenomenon—it originates in the mind but is expressed by the body—we need to address both the body and the mind to deal with it.

Psych-ups: The Mind

Your concepts, attitudes, and mental images are the sources of your nervousness. These are often unconscious, which makes them tricky to deal with.

The bugaboo of formality. If you simply start with the idea "speech" at the back of your mind, you're already in trouble. If you can intercept this thought and counter it by consciously picturing yourself in a conversational situation, you've won half the battle.

The fear of fear itself. Another problem is the fear that the audience will see your nervousness. This is actually two fears: one, that your listeners *do* perceive your feelings; and two, that they think badly of you for having them. Your unconscious mind thinks, "They know how nervous I am," and then, "They must think I'm terrible." You're likely to be wrong on both accounts.

The fact is, audiences are largely unaware of a speaker's nervousness. They've got lots of other things to pay attention to. Make yourself a big note in red at the top of your first note card: "I FEEL CONFIDENT!" It should help reduce your anguish.

The other thing to keep in mind is that even if some of your nervousness does communicate itself, audiences tend to be forgiving, not judgmental. Evidence of your human fallibility will often evoke an empathetic response. Sounds unlikely? Look at your own experience as a member of an audience. Have you been to a presentation where the speaker really blew it? Just plain got lost and had to start over? What was the reaction? Usually it's forgiving and supportive. The typical listener's feeling is, "There but for the grace of God go I."

Keep in mind, though, that this isn't a free pass to blunder your way through a presentation. Especially in a business meeting setting there's an impatient attitude lurking right behind the forgiving one. That audience sits through a lot of meetings and will be empathetic to a point, but they want to get something *useful* from each one.

Get the audience involved. Making the presentation interactive as soon as possible is another technique that helps many presenters get over their nerves. Interaction—give and take—is like conversation: familiar and comfortable.

One simple way to introduce an interactive element is to poll the gathering on some preselected questions; ask for a show of hands. A similar technique is to pose a specific question and field an answer. Be prepared to bridge to the right answer if you don't get the one you were looking for.

It might go something like this: "Given our present market position, who can suggest a merchandising scheme for our new self-adjusting widget?" One member of the team might suggest, "How about a drive-time radio contest?" You now bridge to your answer: "Well, Jack, I know how well that worked for the high-performance miniwidget, but what we've been looking at for SuperWidget III is a direct mail/store coupon offer."

Mental imaging. Many people—including a number of world-class athletes—use the powerful techniques we call mental imaging to combat nervousness and improve concentration. One imaging approach involves creating a strong mental picture of the result you want to achieve. This can be as simple as seeing yourself walking away from the lectern feeling great after a successful presentation. Or it might be more specific: the committee voting to accept your recommendation, for example. Whatever the desired outcome, bringing a positive mental image of it to the presentation should help make things go well.

A different approach to mental imaging is used by many speakers to overcome persistent "audiophobia." Sir Winston Churchill is reputed to have been petrified in front of an audience—until he hit on the idea of imagining his listeners sitting naked in the audience! He mentally turned the tables, "projecting" (in psychoanalytic jargon) onto his audience the sense of vulnerability he felt himself.

If you like Sir Winston's image, use it; we're sure he'd be delighted. If that one doesn't suit your personality, here are a couple that we have found useful: Instead of unconsciously wondering, "Will they like me?" reverse the positions; ask yourself, "I wonder if I will like *them*?" Or say to yourself as you approach the lectern,

"Okay, now I'm going to do everything I can to make *them* comfortable." Be on the lookout for an image all your own; it will be the most effective of all.

Reminders; breaking the cycle. Since nervousness begins in the unconscious and automatically reinforces itself once begun, one of the practical problems in combating it is finding a way to break the cycle. As we suggest elsewhere, you can use your notes as an aid in refocusing your awareness. Write in an occasional reminder key. It could be as simple as "SMILE" or "BREATHE" or "MAKE THEM COMFORTABLE," written in big, easy-to-read letters. Notes like this can be a lifeline to grab when the nerves start to buzz. These techniques probably won't make your butterflies go away, but they should help you to keep them in formation.

Warmups: The Body and the Voice

Nervousness usually manifests itself physically in the form of muscular tension. In order to give our bodies the best opportunity to perform well, we need to release as much of the tension as possible beforehand and then continue to channel it out of the body as we go along.

If circumstances permit, do a real physical warmup before your talk—bending and stretching.

If tension is a particularly big problem for you, you might want to do some fairly strenuous exercise. If you're a jogger, jog. If you play racketball and the facilities are available, do that. You can do this as much as an hour or two beforehand and you'll still feel the beneficial effects at presentation time.

Most of the time, of course, a major physical workout won't be possible. But if you have access to a reasonably private room before you are scheduled to appear, you can do some of the less strenuous kinds of warmups that singers use.

The *Get to the Point* Warmup Program

The Body

For the following warmups, stand in a comfortable position.

Fingers, wrists, and arms. Start by wriggling your fingers; then shake your wrists; finally, the arms. You should feel all the joints loosening up.

Shoulders. Stand tall, feet apart, as if you were supported by a string attached to the very top of your head. Let your shoulders hang naturally. Then draw the shoulders up high; try to touch your ears. Hold that position for a slow count of three. Then relax the shoulders and let them hang again. Repeat this several times. A variation on this is the "shoulder roll": First shift your shoulders forward as far as they will comfortably go. Hold. Then move them up—and hold. Then all the way back—and hold. Finally, press them down as far as they will go—and hold. Reverse the direction if you wish. Repeat the cycle until your shoulders feel loose.

Neck and surrounding muscles. Stand in a relaxed posture and gently let your head drop forward. Feel the neck muscles stretch. Then, very slowly, like an elephant swinging its trunk, roll your head sideways. To give you an idea of how far, imagine a clock face: In the head-down position you're at six o'clock; you want to roll your head up past nine o'clock, then counterclockwise to six and up past three o'clock. Continue this gentle rolling-stretching two or three times in each direction—or until all the kinks are out.

Warning: Don't roll all the way around the back. This can hurt both the neck muscles and the larynx (what we usually call the "vocal chords," although there are no "chords").

The mind. Calm yourself before presentation time by listening to soft music. If you need to get psyched up, rock and roll or other more spirited music can be helpful.

The Voice

The jaw. Follow these steps:
- Loosen the lower jaw by moving it from side to side.
- Work the jaws in a chewing motion.
- Stretch your mouth W-I-D-E open. Feel the jaw and facial muscles loosen.

The lips. Relax the muscles in and around your lips by making the sound we make when we are cold. (We usually spell it "Brrrr," but it doesn't really sound like that.)

The voice. Start on a low pitch and softly hum. Let the voice move up and down as high and as low as you comfortably can. Remember, keep it *soft*; this is literally a stretching exercise for the larynx, and gentle is better than forceful. A minute or two of humming should leave your voice feeling clear and flexible.

The chest. Whether or not you had the opportunity to do any of the foregoing, always take a few deep, deliberate breaths just before you go on. The technique is straight out of self-hypnosis: Inhale slowly through the nose, letting your chest expand, filling your lungs to capacity. Hold the breath for a moment before exhaling slowly and quietly through the mouth.

These are a good basic set of loosening up techniques. Of course you may add others that work for you.

Tip: Do not consume alcohol or caffeine just before a presentation. Alcohol can dull your senses. Caffeine can make you too jumpy.

Once you begin speaking, you need to *stay* loosened up. And the best way to accomplish this is . . . yes, to *gesture*. Don't hang on to the lectern or clasp your hands. These positions not only prevent you from making gestures, they give the muscles something to tense against. And tense they will; it's almost like doing isometric body-building exercises. If you can keep your arms and upper body moving, however, you burn off your muscular tension.

Quick Reference Summary

- It's natural to be nervous. Some natural anxiety *helps* your presentation.
- Channel tension out of your body through gestures.
- Calm yourself by breathing correctly and deeply.
- Prior to presentation time, if you need to calm down, try listening to soft music. If you need to get psyched up, listen to rock and roll or other more spirited music.
- Think of your presentation as a chat; this makes it less stiff.
- Make your presentation as interactive as possible. Ask questions of the audience early in the presentation or invite questions from the audience as you go along.
- Use mental imaging—see the process through to the end in a positive way.
- Use your note cards to remind yourself to "SMILE," "STAND STILL," "PAUSE," etc.
- If possible, do a real physical workout—running, swimming, racketball—a couple of hours before presentation time to get your body loosened up.
- Do warmup/relaxation exercises on pages 154 and 155 or find your own to get physically relaxed.
- Do not consume alcohol or caffeine just before a presentation.

13

Clothing:
What the Well-Dressed
Presenter Wears

Carefully and thoughtfully chosen, your clothing can lend powerful support to your physical presence. Generally this support should be unobtrusive, so you might save the sartorial spectaculars for the weekends and nonpresentation days.

You should dress well, but your clothing should not call attention to itself.

Clothing that captures the audience's attention interferes with the message you want to deliver. Remember that *you* are there to make a statement, not your clothes.

For virtually everyone, presentation dress means "business dress."

For men, this means business suits (or shirtsleeves in some companies, if the meeting is around the conference table); for women, suits, dresses, or skirt-blouse ensembles. The only exceptions to business dress would be uniforms for military personnel and possibly police or other uniformed public officials and perhaps a lab coat or hard hat for a scientist, engineer, technician, or plant manager giving a media interview in the workplace.

We used to counsel conservatism in presentation dress: When in doubt, go for a more conservative look. Today we are happy to report a real trend away from the *ultra*conservative dress mode in most industries. Without going too far out on a limb, we can say there is greater flexibility—a greater range of acceptable styles and modes—today than in the recent past, particularly for women. The key factor is knowing your business and following the prevailing political dictates regarding clothing choice.

Know your industry.

Dress codes differ markedly from industry to industry, profession to profession. Bankers do not dress like entertainment industry executives. We trust that you are familiar with the traditions operating within your organization and your industry. You should also be aware that dress standards vary from region to region.

Case Study: A New York City–based executive was called to testify at a regulatory hearing in a small New England town. He wore what he thought was appropriate clothing; what he was accustomed to wearing at such hearings in New York. This consisted of a dark blue pinstriped suit with vest, white shirt, and dark tie. As he walked into the hearing room, he overheard one of the commissioners whisper to a colleague, "The only time we dress like that in these parts is when we're carried out in a box."

Adjusting dress to conform to regional preferences is a complicated issue. It certainly isn't simply a question of "when in Rome, do as the Romans do." Your audience knows you're *not* a Roman, and pretending to pass yourself off as one may be seen as patronizing—you may thoroughly alienate your audience. A Yankee wearing new cowboy boots in El Paso is what we call an "easy mark."

The best counsel we can offer on this aspect of presentation dress is that you seek specific advice from someone in the place you will be making your presentation. Remember that this advice needs to take into account the image you wish to project and the nature of the proceedings as well as your regional identity.

If, for example, you're a financial officer from the Boston office going to handle a tax audit at corporate headquarters in Houston, find someone in Houston who can help you work out a dress approach that fits in rather than calling attention to any aspect of regional identification. In other words, you may want to make some adjustments in your clothing.

Quality Shows

Although most of what follows has to do with specifics of style, color, patterns, and fabrics, something perhaps more important than these is the question of quality. With clothing, more than many things in this world, you get what you pay for. A superior quality suit communicates an image of confidence and authority to those you address. The fact that you will *feel* more confident and authoritative is an important reason for wearing fine clothes. We suggest that money spent on fine clothes for your presentation appearances is money well spent. Even if it seems extravagant at the time of purchase, it will pay off in overall presentation effectiveness.

Remember, your clothing can give you strong, unobtrusive support for your image—and your message. Buy the strongest support you can find.

> **Tip:** When you're making an important presentation, wear something that you like and that makes you feel good. If your clothes put you in a positive mood, chances are you'll make a more effective presentation.

Guidelines for Men

Suits:

- Fabric: Wear wool. Although we think of wool as winter wear, its properties really make it the fiber of choice for all seasons. Tropical-weight wools are nearly as cool as any other hot-weather fabric, they tend to breathe better, and they unquestionably look better. Besides, rooms are air-conditioned in the summertime.
- Colors: The darker tones—navy, gray, even black—can generally be worn in all seasons. The darker the shade, the greater the sense of formality and authority. The turn away from conservatism in dress is reflected in the fact that lighter colors are now a possibility in the summertime. A rich beige works especially well with a light blue shirt.
- Patterns: Pinstripes, especially subtle ones, are acceptable in many industries and regions and virtually required in some. Save checks for the country club. If you are a professor, you may wear tweeds.
- Vests: Except on television where they add roughly fifteen pounds to your looks, vests look fine. But we recommend they be avoided because they tend to constrict your breathing. If you feel you must wear a vest, make sure it is loose enough for you to breathe easily and deeply. Also, if you wear a vest, it's fine to leave your jacket unbuttoned; if not, we recommend buttoning the jacket. In a seated presentation leave your jacket open.

Shirts:

- Fabric: Wear cotton or cotton blends.
- Colors: Wear white, off-white, pastel, light grays, or neutrals. For television appearances, white shirts are generally out. Their brightness causes the cameras' automatic exposure control to overcompensate, resulting in underexposure of your face. If you are unable to consult wardrobe or other production people, stay on the safe side and wear a standard pastel—blue, yellow, or pink—or an off-white.
- Patterns: Another area in which clothing conservatism has re-

laxed is shirt fabric patterns. At the time of writing, there are some very nice patterned shirts. Stripes are generally fine, especially the more traditional pinstripes. Avoid busy, loud patterns and strong colors.

- Sleeves: Wear long sleeves for a finished look.
- Details: Wear button-down or classic pointed collars. Trendy or unusual collar styles and other shirt details are out of place.

Ties:
- Fabric: Silk is best.
- Patterns: Solids or simple patterns are best. Foulards, paisleys, and flowers are not recommended for presentations. One dress consultant recommends that you choose ties from one of the familiar categories that can be described in a single image such as solid, polka dot, "repp" (i.e., stripe), or club.
- Color: The range of acceptable colors is wide. If in doubt, tone it down. Red ties—or ties with a strong red component—are very popular with television news broadcasters not only because they show up well on camera, but also because the color reflects and adds flattering warmth to facial coloring.

Jewelry:
- Style: Avoid anything that calls attention to itself—unless you wish to refer to it. You might, for example, wish to wear a Kiwanis tie tack or a twenty-five-year service pin in your lapel. Gold watch fobs and other such adornments are best left at home.

> **Case Study:** We once asked an executive whom we were preparing for testimony before a presidential commission in Washington, D.C., to remove his ID bracelet. We try not to overdo dress rules when working with clients, but in this case we were concerned that people would be distracted by this sparkler on his wrist rather than listening to his words. While ID bracelets were in vogue in his home state, in the hearing room in Washington the adornment was just in the way.

Shoes:

- Style: Any style of shoe you would normally wear to work should
  be fine for presentations. Any shoe that says "sport" should be
  avoided.

    Principle: Whatever style of shoes you choose, make sure
    they are *polished*.

- Color: Black should be appropriate in any setting. Browns
  should be on the dark side. In some localities, brown shoes have
  negative connotations and should be avoided. If you are going to
  be presenting in an unfamiliar place, try to get an idea of the
  local attitude to brown—or settle for black.

Guidelines for Women

As we suggested in our opening remarks, the what-to-wear question is considerably more open for women than for men. Women
have gained sufficient acceptance in corporate culture that
they can express their femininity a little more freely than was possible five or ten years ago. What we call the "deaconess" look—dark
navy suit, white, high-collared blouse, and navy silk bow tie—is
blessedly dead. Increasingly, women in executive positions are finding they can dress more in their own tastes without interfering with
their career progress. We're happy to report that even in some very
conservative areas (in certain investment banking companies, for example) it is a woman's ability, not her conformity to a strict, conservative dress code, that makes her promotable.

You know your working environment; suits may still be *de rigueur*
in your industry. But even so, you may be able to cultivate little
touches that lead away from the deaconess look. We feel you'll be
more comfortable—more yourself—with your business (including
presentation) wear, if you have a little fun with it.

Suits:

- Fabrics: Wear wool, silk, and look-alikes. One of a number of
  options that exist for women but not for men is knits. Suit, skirt,
  or dress, knits are perfectly acceptable presentation wear (subject to industry or regional exceptions). They offer the advantage
  of moving with your body more easily than in woven fabrics.

Make sure that they fit well and that the skirt lays smoothly over the hips.

- Style: Designers are finally becoming more sensitive to the needs of working women and are making some stylish business-oriented suits, giving you a direction to move in—away from the prim, straitlaced look. There is also more of a spectrum now, so you can test the waters a little at a time.

- Cut and fit: These are very important. A garment that really follows the contours of your body and moves with you when you move makes you look good. When you raise your arm to point at the screen, does the shoulder seam pull, the armhole bind? Can you button the jacket comfortably? (Actually, women don't need to keep suit jackets buttoned, but it's nice to have the option.)

- Skirt length: Hem lines rise and hem lines fall. Even if miniskirts are in vogue for street wear, we suggest you consider knee-length or below the knee as standard for presentation dress.

- Colors: There is a very broad palate of acceptable colors these days. It's easier for us to cover the unacceptables: Avoid anything truly bright, garish, or loud. (Again, keep in mind the basic principle: You are the main attraction, your clothing is part of the supporting cast.) In conservative industries, you may be limited to the more traditional navies and grays, with the possible inclusion of browns, rusts, tans, beiges, or dark greens.

Blouses:

- Fabrics: Wear cotton, silk, or fine synthetics.
- Patterns and colors: Generally, keep them simple. Subtle stripes or other unobtrusive patterns are okay. Quite a range of color is possible, from traditional whites and pastels to vivid, jewellike hues (best in silk and best under darker colored suits). Ruffled fronts are fine if not extreme.

Dresses:

- Fabrics: Wool (including knits), silk, or fine synthetics.
- Patterns: Avoid busy patterns, extreme styles, plunging necklines, and anything that will actively distract from your presentation.

Ties: Ties are becoming more of an optional accessory for women. The day of the obligatory dark-toned club pattern bow tie is over. Designers are coming up with new, more imaginative, more feminine ties like those fashioned in a rose at the throat. A tasteful silk scarf or a brooch are possible alternatives.

Hose: Wear neutral to dark tones. Subtle textures and patterns may work, depending on your business.

Shoes: Avoid boots, open toes, and sling-backs. By all means choose colors to coordinate with your outfit. Black patent leather, the ultra-conservative choice, is always safe. Even if you normally wear flats, we suggest you wear at least a little heel for presentations.

Hair: Careful grooming, not length or cut, is the issue. Keep your hair pulled away from your face. Nothing is more distracting than watching a woman constantly flicking hair out her eyes—or not being able to see the eyes because of all the hair.

Jewelry: Avoid dangling earrings or necklaces. Leave your diamonds and other sparklers at home. Pearls or other matte finish pieces that don't reflect too much light are best.

Makeup: Every woman over the age of twenty-five should wear at least a little makeup for presentations; a little blush, mascara, and light lipstick. For presentations where you will be brightly lit—which includes television appearances—makeup will need to be heavier than your usual to create the same effect. Bright lights wash out skin tones.

Quick Reference Summary

- Your choice of clothing can enhance your image as a presenter, making your message stronger.
- You should dress well, but your clothing should not call attention to itself.

- For virtually everyone, "presentation clothing" means "standard business clothing."
- Be aware of dress standards in your region and in your business or industry.
- While business dress standards are less conservative than they used to be (especially for women), avoid flamboyance.

14

Some Final Practicalities:
Interruptions
and Choreography

A few practical presentation matters that are not directly connected to any of the larger conceptual areas we have dealt with do nevertheless need to be covered. The two broad areas are the problem of interruptions and the choreography of microphones and the lectern.

Interruptions

Interruptions can come from a number of sources. Someone may bring you a message, a person may wander into the meeting room by mistake, some members of the audience may carry on their own loud conversation, a truck driver outside may lean on his horn. The list is as long as the possibilities life brings. And you can be sure that some interruption or other distraction will plague your presentations from time to time.

Minor distractions—people occasionally walking in or out, a minor cough, a message handed to someone in the room—are fairly normal occurrences in meetings and presentations and can generally be taken in stride. After all, the show doesn't stop when one person arrives late to the theater. But major disturbances do call for action. The criterion for deciding whether or not to take action is *the degree to which it is likely to capture the attention of the listeners and interrupt communication*.

If you try to compete with a distraction, you invariably lose.

Acknowledge major interruptions immediately. Because no communication is going to take place, you might as well stop talking the very second you become aware that "something is going on." And that is precisely what you *ought* to do.

It's very simple. Stop speaking and wait for external or nonhuman distractions to pass. The dogfight outside the window will eventually wind down; the truck driver will stop honking; the airplane noise will die away enough to allow you to continue.

With human disruptions, however, your listeners will expect you to take control. If thoughtless colleagues are holding a private conversation, for example, generally all you need to do is stop and look over at them. The silence will most likely get their attention, and your eye contact will clearly communicate your feelings about the interruption.

Occasionally, this tactic will fail to work. Then you will have to take appropriate action to regain control of the proceedings. If it is a case of rudeness or insensitivity—people are talking and don't pick up your polite signals or simply won't shut up—you may have to say something. Responses vary with the person interrupting, so the specific approach you take is a judgment call. Let's consider some possibilities.

If an aide walks in with a note for a member of a meeting—let it go. If they engage in extended conversation, a pause would be appropriate. If the people interrupting are your equals in rank, you might ask them to keep it down or even to go outside the room to finish their conversation. If the disruption involves people senior to you, try extended silence. If that doesn't work, you might *politely* ask if they want you to wait until they complete their discussion. Sometimes well-meaning people are unaware of the disruptive effect they are having on a group.

If your disruption is a natural disaster—a member of the audience having a coughing fit, for example—try to alleviate the problem by handing the afflicted person a glass of water or some similar action. In such a case it is a good idea to offer an expression of concern, whether or not you actively intervene. A simple "Are you all right over there?" or "Do you think you'll be okay now?" will suffice.

Tip: Any time someone delivers a note to *you* while you are presenting, you need to give the audience *some* indication of the contents or they'll wonder what it was about—and not pay attention to what you're saying. If it's for you, say so. If it concerns someone else in the room, pass on the message: "For the person who drives a blue Buick with Colorado plates: You left your lights on"; or "Sarah, you just received an urgent phone call. Go ahead; we'll fill you in on anything you miss."

Choreography

Like a ballet, a presentation contains movements—usually interaction with the physical setup—that need to flow smoothly if the performance is to be successful. We covered one such area, the choreography of visuals, in the context of our general discussion of that subject. Here we cover the other major areas of choreographic concern, relating to microphones and lecterns.

Microphones. Generally, if a meeting room or auditorium is large enough to require a sound system, it will have one. From the speaker's point of view, one sound system is pretty much like another, except for microphones. There are three types commonly in use:
• Fixed
• Wireless
• Clip-on

A fixed or "gooseneck" mike that's attached to the lectern attaches you to the lectern as well.

If you have a choice, always request a nonfixed microphone, one that attaches to you.

The wireless microphone, technologically the most up-to-date, is actually a tiny radio transmitter that sends your voice to the amplification system without any wires to encumber you. This gives you worry-free mobility—and makes the wireless mike your first choice. To "mike up," just clip the unit to your lapel, shirt, blouse, or necktie, about one hand's span (six inches) from your mouth.

Since wireless systems are relatively expensive, however, not every hall is so equipped. Midway between the fixed mike and the wireless, in terms of convenience, is the "clip-on" or lavaliere. This is a very small pickup that either hangs around your neck or fastens to your clothing with an alligator clip, like the wireless.

The clip-on gives you almost as much mobility as the wireless, but there *is* a cord to contend with—which adds one important step to the process of "miking up." First, attach or hang the mike about six inches from your mouth, as with the wireless. Then, to keep the wire out of the way of your hands and feet, lead it inside your jacket (if you're wearing one) and around to the back. Tuck a loop into the waistband of your skirt or trousers, making sure to leave some slack, and (for men) rebutton your jacket.

Tip: Women who wear dresses can tuck the mike wire into a belt or sash. If your dress is beltless, you'll have to do without this safety net.

Aside from getting the wire out of the way, both physically and visually, this procedure gives you a safety net: If you walk away from the lectern without removing the mike—and it is easy to forget about these tiny mikes—what happens? The mike crashes to the floor, sending an amplified thunderclap through the room. If you've tucked the cord into your waistband, then rather than jerking the microphone off your lapel, your motion simply pulls out the loop of cord and disaster is averted.

Lecterns. Inexperienced presenters often use a lectern as a crutch. Or perhaps "security blanket" is a better way to put it. The lectern provides the thing a drowning person desperately longs for: something to hold on to. But this proves to be a liability as well as an asset. The same mentality that craves something to hold on to won't let it go. This results in some postures you probably recognize: the "white-knuckler," who seems quite literally to be "hanging on for dear life"; the "ship captain," who leans in and grasps the lectern in a bear hug, listing first to one side, then to the other as he steers his ship through the perilous waters of his presentation. They may feel safer for their physical contact with the lectern, but they sacrifice their ability to move and gesture. The security blanket becomes a straitjacket.

Another reason to avoid grabbing or clinging to the lectern is that it tends to diminish your energy and results in shortness of breath and muscle tension. Gesturing will relieve the tension and help your breath supply.

Some presenters avoid the trap of physically grasping the lectern but instead use it as a sort of psychic shield or fortress; something to hide behind. Unseasoned presenters tend to stay firmly rooted behind the lectern, in effect imprisoned in their fortress. Others—we call them the "space walkers"—are able to get out from behind and drift a short distance, but they can get no farther away than the length of their arm, which acts like the hose that connects them to their life support system.

The lectern as psychic shield or fortress protects you, but conversely it acts as a barrier between you and your audience. Without the obstruction of a lectern, you simply have more presence; you're communicating more directly.

To the extent that you can free yourself from the lectern, your presentation stands to gain in liveliness and credibility.

Learn to move away from the lectern. Think of it as a place to park your note cards: Walk out from behind it as you develop a point; then, when you need to refer to your notes, simply walk back. If eventually you can do without the lectern altogether, so much the better. Presenting without a lectern doesn't fall under the heading of cardinal rules, but it's one of those subtle but significant factors that add up to making points.

Quick Reference Summary

- Ignore minor distractions—someone walking into the room, a cough or sneeze. If a distraction affects audience attention, pause until it passes.
- If you try to compete with major disruptions in a presentation setting, you'll lose.
- Step one in responding to major interruptions or disruptions is to *stop speaking*. If the disturbance is human, look at talkers in silence. If not, simply wait for it to abate.
- If people are talking and don't respond to your silence, ask them to "keep it down" or finish their conversation outside.
- For coughing, sneezing, or choking fits, offer assistance, if possible, and make sure the person is okay.
- How long to wait during an interruption is a judgment call. Go with your feelings.
- Listeners expect you to manage the group. Take action when necessary.
- If *you* receive a message when presenting, always let your audience know if it is for you. If it isn't, pass it along to whomever it is for.
- If your voice is to be amplified, choose a clip-on or wireless mike to give you mobility.
- Clip the mike one hand-span from your mouth and tuck the cord, if there is one, behind you in your belt or waistband.
- If you need to cough or clear your throat while wearing a mike, turn your head away from the mike.
- Don't lean on the lectern. It diminishes breath supply.

- Don't cling to the lectern; it creates muscular tension and prevents you from gesturing.
- A lectern is a barrier. The more you can get out from behind it and face your listeners, the more "presence" and impact your presentation will have.

15

Media Interviews

We have prepared people for *60 Minutes*, *20/20*, *MacNeil/Lehrer*, *Business Week*, *The Today Show*, *MIS Weekly*, *Health Magazine*, and *Live at Five*, as well as for numerous live radio call-in shows, so we know media interviews. We can tell you that, with the exception of the brief, spontaneous hallway or "deadline" interview, ninety-five times out of a hundred media interviews provide an excellent opportunity to make your points—and usually to a very large audience.

Essentially, a media interview is a presentation in question-and-answer format. Like any Q & A session, you do have to answer questions put to you, but you can almost always get around to making—and emphasizing—the points you want to leave with the audience. All the basic presentation skills come into play in the interview, including writing or content-organizing, but most especially the question-preparation and bridging skills.

A reporter *wants* to hear your selling points; you're the "source," the expert, the person who can make him or her look good.

Most of the time a reporter calls you because you have information he or she *needs* for a story. You are a subject matter expert. The caveat of media interviews is that if you are *not* the expert, don't fake it. Your obligation is to refer the reporter to whomever is the expert. Learn the ways that we will presently describe to gracefully say, "I don't know" or "I can't talk about that matter," and give them a source who can help them.

Before the Interview

When the reporter calls step one is to get his or her name and affiliation (paper, magazine, broadcast show) and ask, "Have you spoken to public relations?" That's the rule in most companies. In fact, several of our clients have a rule printed on their daily news summaries: "If you get a call from a reporter, or you have a news-worthy story, call _____ in media relations, at _____-_____." The public relations people will generally determine if you are the proper person to be talking to this reporter.

Ground rules. Once an interview has been set, the first thing to do is gain control by setting some ground rules. The most crucial thing to establish is the topic or purpose of the interview. Open-ended in-terviews have a way of getting out of hand. If for any reason you don't feel comfortable dealing with the topic the reporter is pursu-ing (or, as we mentioned, if you're not the expert), don't agree to do the interview. If you have no problem with the topic, you can proceed—and don't hesitate to keep the interview confined to the agreed subject. Be sure to find out when the interview will appear (print *or* broadcast).

If the interview has not been set up by the public relations depart-ment, you may wish to set other criteria or ground rules, such as arranging the date and time and/or location to suit your convenience, establishing a time limit for the interview, or imposing certain restrictions on subject matter. The latter will avoid "no comment" situations.

Audience profile. Your next step is to do an audience profile. Remember that the reporter is just a vehicle. Ultimately, your communication is not with the reporter but with the reporter's audience—the reader, listener, or viewer. The reporter, however, is your means of reaching your audience; in this case, the only means. So, read the paper; watch the show; find other articles by this reporter. See what kinds of approaches and quotes he or she tends to showcase. Also find out all you can about the demographics of the media's audience; call their ad sales department. All of this will prepare you to make the most of the interview opportunity.

During the Interview

Following are the most important rules to be aware of during interview time.

Be alert for 'difficult' questions. Review the question types we covered in Chapter Ten: the hypothetical, the false choice, the multipart, and the loaded questions. Reporters wield questions all day long—this is their stock in trade—so they are masters of all of these.

Case Study: Also be on the alert for confused, uninformed, or general questions that are an invitation for you to explain more of your material. Sometimes these are outrageous, as on one occasion when a New York area computer company executive was being interviewed by a reporter from a trade journal and was asked in the middle of the interview, "Excuse me, is this hardware or software we're talking about?" The point is that you, like the executive in the story, should be mindful of the *opportunity*, not the inappropriateness of the question. Use such questions as occasions to explain or even teach.

Flag your selling points. You know what your selling points are but neither the reporter nor the reporter's audience does. Underscoring the points you consider vital with phrases like, "What's important here is . . ." or "I'd like to stress the following . . ." helps focus the audience's attention.

Never go 'off the record.' A reporter's job is to gather—and publish or broadcast—information. If you don't want the public to be privy to it, keep it to yourself. "Not-for-attribution" comments are tricky stuff; we suggest you steer clear.

Never say 'No comment.' This doesn't mean you have to answer every question thrown at you in an interview, but it does mean you have to learn to decline gracefully. "*No comment*" has a combative, confrontational tone to it. It brings to mind television coverage of events like a drug bust where the suspect shields his face from the camera with his coat. You create a much more positive impression when you offer an explanation of *why* you decline to answer a question.

There are three areas of questioning that clearly violate the bounds of the "interview compact": Questions that fall outside of the agreed topic, personal questions, and questions relating to proprietary information. You can set firm limits and still appear fully cooperative if you cover your refusal with a clear explanation. This works particularly well if you then bridge to related information you *are* prepared to discuss. For example, "That's really outside the bounds of what we agreed to talk about, but here's what I *can* say about the general issue you raise . . ."; "The FCC hasn't ruled on our petition, but I can tell you what we argued"; "It's a matter under litigation and we can't talk about it until the courts have ruled. But our position is . . ."; or "I'm sure our competitors would *love* to have that information, but we won't discuss this until we make our formal announcement. But if you'd like some general information . . ."

End the interview after a reasonable length of time. Presumably, if you set a time limit you will adhere to it unless the interview is going very well and you think you can make a few more points by continuing. If it's going the other way, by all means terminate it after a "decent interval."

Facilitate follow-ups. Let the reporter know where and when you can be reached for follow-ups and make yourself available as promised. Having taken the time to talk to a reporter, take the extra time to give him or her the opportunity to call you so that if they do have questions, the information will be right when it's printed or broadcast.

Special Rules for Different Settings

Prearranged interviews. In cases where you know about the interview in advance, you can prepare fully. Find out both the topic and the format. You can research the general topic, which will give you an overall perspective, much as gathering an audience profile adds to your perspective in a standard presentation. This can guide you in preparing solid, well-developed selling points focused on the subject matter, with strong headlines and vivid supporting specifics.

Always be prepared to summarize your most important points. Remember, repetition builds retention. If a reporter hears one of your points three or four times, the chances are three or four times as great that it will be broadcast or turn up in print. Feel free to bring notes or a summary card just to make sure you don't forget any key points. For radio and print interviews—and certainly for interviews held over the phone—you should refer to your notes at any time. For on-camera interviews, you might carry a file card and refer to it discreetly from time to time—only during commercial breaks and *only* if you're a skilled spokesperson.

It is also a good idea to send background information to the reporter. The worst that can happen is that he or she doesn't read it. If the first question doesn't lead to a general statement of the background information, you can take a moment to provide it to the audience: "Well, Clare, I can give you those figures in a moment. However, let me first take a little time to give you an idea of what this product means to us—its features and how we've positioned it. . . ."

If appropriate, have props—products or books, for example—on hand to demonstrate one or more aspects of what you're discussing. If you're doing the interview at the studio, tell them in advance you're bringing something to show; they will then set up the best shot for viewing it.

Spontaneous on-camera interviews. These can be quite intimidating. After establishing the basics—primarily credentials and topic, as discussed above—ask for a few minutes to compose your thoughts. You should use this time to pull together a hasty but coherent agenda. Jot down your bottom line and your two or three main selling points if you can. You may or may not get a chance to refer to them, but even if you don't, writing them down helps fix them in your memory.

In addition to basic ground rules discussed above, get as comfortable as possible in a difficult situation: Ask that cameras, lights, and microphones be kept at a reasonable distance. To give yourself the same lifeline the reporter would take for himself or herself, ask for a retake on any fumbled answer. You may not get the retake, but generally reporters want you to look and sound good, so they might allow you to do a retake.

Interviews in your office. The main advantage to holding an interview on your own territory is that you will at least feel at home with the surroundings. Make the physical environment as pleasant as possible—get out from behind your desk and into a living room setting. All of this tends to diminish the natural atmosphere of tension.

Two other steps we suggest you consider taking are to invite your public relations representative to be present (if you have one) and to arrange to make your own tape of the interview. The former will help keep you and the reporter on track; the latter will serve as a "file copy" of the entire interview—not just the reporter's edited version.

Television Appearances

Aside from straight reporting, which is covered in spontaneous on-camera interviews, virtually all television appearances for presenters fall into the broad category of talk shows. Appearing on television can be nerve-racking, but most people feel it's worth whatever discomfort it entails because it's great exposure. You really can't buy the kind of coverage you get free from a guest appearance on television—the "third party endorsement effect"—even with a no-expense-spared advertising budget.

To make your television appearance go as smoothly as your presentations, follow the basic training precepts we've discussed throughout this book: Get to know the show, host, and format—preferably by watching. Prepare a list of strongly delineated selling points. Arm yourself for difficult questions. Make a Plus/Minus sheet to guide you in bridging answers. Find out if there is a topic or theme; if so, slant your selling points and plan your bridges accordingly. Find out who else will be on the show; consider what topics and directions are likely to result. Plan bridges as appropriate.

If you plan to use props—a good idea to illustrate your points—or to give a toll free phone number for further information, be sure to mention it to the producer prior to your studio appearance.

Dress. The first principle really goes without saying: Look your best. For the rest, our basic presentation dress principle applies: Your clothes should not call attention to themselves. It's you, not your wardrobe that people are interested in. White shirts cause photographic exposure problems with television cameras; they're too bright. Avoid this problem by wearing soft off-white or pastel colors. Ties or blouses containing some red reflect a flattering warmth to facial tones.

Arrival. Get to the studio well ahead of the scheduled time. Introduce yourself to the producer, makeup and wardrobe people, and, if possible, to the host. Don't be intrusive, but if you have an opportunity to chat with the host or anyone who helps determine content, use it. The more you can get across about yourself and your topic before things get under way, the more likely the interview will go smoothly and be interesting.

Even if you don't get a chance to speak with the show host beforehand, you can use the "mike check"—the part of the preshow setup where your microphone level is balanced with that of the host—to get a little information across. When the sound person asks you to speak into the microphone so they can get an accurate level, instead of following the traditional "Testing, testing; one, two, three, four . . ." we suggest you simply identify yourself and your company or other affiliation and mention one of the points you'd like to make during the show.

This may seem outré, but think about it. First, these are busy people who don't get a chance to do all the preparation they'd like. Second, they want the same thing you do: to get an interesting interview. Third, indicating that there are certain things you want to talk about is an immediate stimulus to the host to follow up on those points. The more of a sense the interviewer has of the areas in which you are interested and able to speak to, the greater the likelihood that the interaction will be entertaining—which means viewers will be less likely to flip the channel.

On camera. All the impression factors are doubly important on television. Here are some vital tips that should help make your appearance a success:

- *Posture*. You will generally be seated for most of your time on-camera. Sit forward in your chair and sit up straight. You don't have to sit literally on the edge of your seat, but definitely avoid lounging. *Important:* Lean in toward the host when you answer. This demonstrates energy and conviction.

- *Eye contact*. Maintain eye contact with the host even when the host looks at the camera. Don't worry about the cameras. You communicate to the audience through the host. In fact, keep your eye contact and posture until you hear an "All clear" or "We're off the air" signal so you don't drop your on-camera demeanor prematurely.

- *Smile*. Even when the show is on a sensitive issue, smile when you're introduced and when the show—or your segment—ends.

- *Gesture*. Keep your hands resting lightly on your thighs. From this position, it is easy and natural to gesture.

- *Be concise*. Try to keep your answers between twenty and thirty seconds.

- *Be dramatic.* Use visual images and analogies to help dramatize your points for the audience.
- *Offer tips,* if appropriate. The American public *loves* tips, and if they believe they have learned something useful from you, they may in fact remember your product, service, or message better.
- *Don't lose sight of your audience.* Never forget that you're really talking to the show's listeners, not the host or other guests.
- *Enjoy yourself!*

Quick Reference Summary

- Media interviews are like presentations in question-and-answer format.
- Preparation is the key; have your selling points ready.
- Do an audience profile: Familiarize yourself with the program or publication, and *who they view as their audience.* If possible, get to know the interviewer's style and point of view.
- Keep in mind that your ultimate audience is those who watch, read, or listen to the interview.
- Remember, you are the expert, the "source." Your input is valuable; you can make the reporter look good.
- Take control whenever possible: Find out the topic and stick to it; set ground rules.
- Be on the alert for "tricky" questions. (Review the types in Chapter Ten.)
- Learn the art of the graceful "No comment." (That is, never actually say "No comment," but offer an explanation for *why* you must decline to answer a question.)
- Never go "off the record." If you don't want to see it broadcast or in print, don't say it.
- Remember to bridge to your selling points.

16

Being a Witness:
The Presentation
That's All Q & A

Being a witness—whether in a civil or criminal trial, before a congressional or legislative panel, at a regulatory hearing or an administrative proceeding—may be the most difficult communications environment you will ever encounter.

Why? The setting is often intimidating. The stakes are generally high. You're sworn to your testimony. Most of all, it's the questioner's forum, not the answerer's, so your ability to get *your* message across may be restricted.

Believe it or not, though, giving testimony is still basically a presentation, and with the proper preparation, you can maintain some degree of control and usually *get to the point*.

Case Study: One of our clients was invited to appear at a congressional hearing on pharmaceutical pricing. There was a real question whether the company even wanted to send a representative, since it was anticipated that the hearing was going to be something of an inquisition. In addition, it was feared that the legislator sponsoring the hearing was not really investigating anything. Rather, he had already made up his mind and was merely using the hearing as a forum for making *his* points to his constituents and the media—very likely at the expense of our client. We were able, however, to convince management that, although it wouldn't be easy, such a hearing, properly handled, could be a valuable communications opportunity. The company decided to put in an appearance and make the best of it.

The best of it, of course, meant making some points of their own. The company president himself decided to testify, and he took our number one rule seriously. He prepared. As a result, he succeeded in communicating some real selling points, about research and development costs, and about the economics of the business. A few of the more important comments were reflected in television and print coverage. As a result of his willingness to take the risks and then prepare properly, our client fared much better than the competition who shunned the hearing altogether.

Perhaps the main point to draw from this story is that, however difficult the witness stand may be as a communications forum, you should not be intimidated. There's always a way to prepare and make a point or two. Sometimes you can do quite a lot better than that.

Whatever your opinion might have been of the political actions of former national security advisor Lt. Col. Oliver North, when he took the stand in the Iran-Contra hearings he was prepared and took advantage of the opportunities that arose.

Each type of witness environment—law court, legislative hearing, regulatory proceeding, investigative panel—has its own rules and procedures. If you're familiar with these, you can pretty accurately anticipate the restrictions you will be facing, and thus you can have a pretty good idea of the points you'll be likely to make. Let's look at each of these environments individually.

Courts of Law

This is, of course, the scene most of us think of in connection with the notion of witnessing. While most of us have rarely if ever been in a courtroom, we have watched countless dramas on television and in the movies. In a sense, we all have a little preliminary training for this venue. It can be rather confusing, though, because in a real courtroom the story doesn't unfold in a smooth or natural way; it unfolds in pieces.

Trial testimony road map. Since the average television script doesn't take the trouble to explicitly set forth the rules of trial conduct, we shall give an overview here. Here's how the Q & A usually works: After jury selection (if any) and opening arguments, each side in the trial—prosecution (or plaintiff) and defense—calls its own witnesses.

Direct examination. The attorney for the prosecution or plaintiff calls witnesses for that side and conducts "direct examination." In the proper turn the attorney for the defense does likewise with defense witnesses. Direct examination is usually friendly questioning, in which your lawyer guides you through the unfolding of your story. "Please tell us, in your own words, what happened on the night of . . ." In other words, in "direct," you will usually be able to give quite full answers and get your selling points in, although a careful judge and skilled opposing counsel may keep your comments confined to the facts and will try to keep you from drawing conclusions and making judgments—which are part and parcel of good selling points. We suggest that you be prepared to try to get in as much of this information as possible. The jury can be instructed to disregard it, but having heard it, they can't *entirely* disregard it.

Cross-examination. The picture changes dramatically with cross-examination. In "cross," the opposing attorney will have a chance to question you about your direct testimony. They will pick at details, and attempt to frame narrow questions that elicit a strict yes-or-no or other brief answer. You may have no idea what points the lawyer is trying to score. The main problem with cross-examination from the witness's point of view is that you rarely get a chance to explain or to repeat any of your selling points. A good lawyer will cut you off the instant you say the words *but* or *however*.

Our cross-examination advice is that you listen to each question carefully, pause for a moment, then answer. If you can't or don't want to answer *yes* or *no*, say so. A determined lawyer, however, may force you into a yes-or-no choice. In such a case try starting your answer, "Although the answer is yes [or no] . . ." This answer allows your qualification. Another tactic to consider is using the word *and* as a bridging device. If you can anticipate a question or issue in cross-examination, you can sometimes take advantage of a small opportunity to slip in information that is not directly responsive to the question. The examining attorney may ask to have it stricken from the record, but the jury will have heard it.

Coaching. A good lawyer will thoroughly prepare his witnesses for both direct and cross-examination. When the stakes are high, this will involve careful rehearsal and videotape analysis. The film *The Verdict*, with Paul Newman, was not an accurate look at the workings of the law, but as an example of witness preparation it was superb. In a key scene, the defense attorney, played by James Mason, used videotape to prepare a physician for testimony. The firm staged a mock trial and let the witness see and hear what he sounded like. Direct testimony was rehearsed and the questions for cross-examination were anticipated.

If you ever have to testify in a trial, you should go through a drill for difficult questions, just as for any presentation. Keep in mind that in this situation you have a professional adversary—opposing counsel—who will search out any weaknesses in your testimony and probe them. So make your practices good ones. And make sure *your* lawyer is aware of all the tough questions you believe you will get. Your lawyer should then take you through the whole preparation process—direct and cross. If the stakes are high, this should include videotape feedback. As one lawyer we know put it, there should be no surprises from an opposing counsel, either on questions or on their witnesses' answers on cross-examination.

Legislative Hearings

Legislative hearings are presumably held for the purpose of collecting information that will help legislators enact laws. In reality, they often serve other purposes, including providing publicity for individual legislators and their programs. In this sense, they are often "theater pieces," set up to realize a preexisting "script," and in which each witness is a sort of guest artist, playing a role.

There are rarely any surprises. Staff researchers have usually determined the positions of the witnesses beforehand, and thus the content of their testimony. This doesn't keep legislators from registering carefully rehearsed *expressions* of surprise for the television cameras.

In short, events at a legislative hearing are often staged and carefully choreographed for television coverage, down to details like choosing a room small enough that it will appear crowded even with only a few people present.

All this might lead us to the conclusion that testimony at such hearings is a pro forma affair at best. You appear to set on the record what the legislators already know, and answer questions, if they're asked. In keeping with what they understand these hearings to be, most companies and organizations prepare a written statement to enter into the record, and a chosen representative then reads a portion of the prepared remarks. It's all "for the record." In this boring situation, you will often find legislators reading their mail, talking to their aides, or working on other matters. No communication is taking place, and apparently no one *expects* any.

Our position is: Use legislative hearings as an *opportunity*; a chance to really make your points *forcefully* and *dramatically* in a public arena. As pointed out by Arthur Liman, chief counsel to the Senate in the Iran-Contra hearings, in criminal trials, "You sometimes leave the best story untold because of the rigid rules of evidence." However, in a congressional hearing, "You try to tell a full story so the American people know what happened and Congress can take appropriate corrective action."

So by all means appear. Let your words underscore the well-researched written position statements that you submit. Try to figure out how your company or organizational interests dovetail or coincide with those of the legislators (this is basic audience profile work). Find a way to play on the same side of the net—at least part of the time. Then dramatize your testimony. Think about vivid, visual selling points. Practice your delivery. You can make an impact.

Regulatory Proceedings

Witness-stand testimony in this type of proceeding invariably follows prefiled direct testimony. In other words, it is essentially cross-examination (with occasional redirect and recross), although compared to a court of law there is generally much more room for a witness to explain or amplify his or her answers. In light of this, many witnesses at regulatory hearings view their job as merely defending the written statement. Again, we take the view that such hearings, even though conducted on a cross-examination basis, are an opportunity to educate—and make points.

In practice, this means a lot of bridging. Preparation for a regulatory hearing should concentrate on the plus/minus analysis. The key bridges are areas where your company or organization shares concerns and issues with the public; it's the dovetailing principle again. It is also important to be clear about who your real audience is. Although you will be responding to the questions of a commission attorney or "intervenor," you may in fact ultimately be addressing the legislators' constituents, the public.

Special Points for the Witness Stand

Fundamentally, the rules for testimony presentations are the same as for more typical presentations, but often with a twist or qualification.

For example, it is essential that you know what you want to say and be prepared to say it forcefully, but as a witness you also need to be aware of how and when circumstances will make it possible for you to do so. That is, you need a clear understanding of the rules and procedures for information exchange and how these may restrict your ability to make your point. Above all, you should be prepared to bridge when you can, especially if you have reason to believe you will not be able to make your point without doing so. See your opportunities and take 'em.

You need to know your audience, but the audience you really wish to reach may not be the person or persons you actually address. In a trial, you are questioned by a lawyer, but you need to make your points to the jury or judge. In a legislative hearing, it is the legislature or the committee as a whole that you address, not the legislators or staff members holding the hearing. This audience can be expanded to include the public at large, through the media.

And of course all the basics of delivery apply here, too, only perhaps more so: Make good eye contact. Lean in when you answer questions; if there's a microphone, "embrace" it with your presence. Gesture with your hands and arms. Project and animate your voice. Keep your language simple; if you have to use technical language, industry jargon, or acronyms, explain them. Use signal words and phrases wherever possible. These are effective emphasizers, both as they are delivered and when written transcripts are reviewed.

The one overriding rule for all types of testimony is, "Be prepared." It relates most clearly, perhaps, to the content and style of difficult questions.

Case Study: Several years ago, we saw an important government witness reveal a weak spot in the context of a congressional hearing. Seated behind a table in the stately conference room, the senior official appeared relaxed and confident. He was handling questions well: His voice was strong and animated, he was leaning in to make his points, making effective gestures. Then on the next question, his whole demeanor stiffened: His voice flattened out; his hands went flat on the table. He answered the question, but his reaction clearly signaled that the legislator had hit a tender spot in his testimony. His reaction made the congressman continue to probe this area. Staff members made little checkmarks in the margins of their transcripts as reminders to investigate this area further. So, while the witness didn't "say anything wrong," he still gave away the game.

You can take two steps to prevent this happening to you:

1. Anticipate all the tough questions and be waiting for them. Do the difficult-questions drill and the Plus/Minus analysis; do them as thoroughly as you can.
2. Take our advice (see Chapter Nine) and pause before every answer you make. This way, whenever a question does take you by surprise, you have a little built-in recovery time.

Also, review the tricky question types we covered in Chapter Ten. The one you're most likely to encounter in your witness role is the hypothetical. Be careful and methodical and qualify each hypothetical with a phrase like, "That's an *if* question"; "In answer to your hypothetical"; or "I'm continuing with your hypothetical line of questioning. . . ."

The following are more specialized tips:

Listen. The full routine is Listen, Think, Answer. Experts can often be fast on the draw, anticipating the direction of a question. As you testify, keep in mind that there is a written record of the proceedings. If you listen to the entire question, you'll answer what is asked, not what you think is about to be asked. You will also make life easier for the court reporter or stenographer, who will not make as many mistakes and who will not have to stop you to slow you down.

Don't argue. This is for your attorney to do with the judge or hearing officer. You should try to remain calm and cooperative. But don't allow yourself to be trapped by a questioner's tactics, either. If you are asked a question that demands a yes-or-no answer and you can't answer that way, say so. If totally boxed in, try this response: "Although the answer is yes [or no], I would like to qualify . . ." With this tactic you have alerted those in the hearing room that you wish to qualify your answer and the written transcript will reflect this.

Be polite. When you take the stand, take the trouble to say "Good morning" or "Good afternoon" or some other civilized pleasantry. Try to be conversational in your responses, no matter how rigorous the questioning gets.

Flag the hypotheticals. On the witness stand, it's appropriate to call attention to hypothetical or "if" type questions. Unlike a general presentation or media interview, responses that we covered in Chapter Ten, on the witness stand you may be forced to answer such questions.

Our suggestion is that each time you are forced to answer a hypothetical, start your answer with a phrase like: "Well, counselor, in answer to your hypothetical . . ." or "In answer to your speculative question . . ." or "In response to your supposition, let me state . . ." Make sure that if the follow-up question continues the hypothetical premise, that you continue to flag the answer. The result will be a signal to the questioner and the court that you are being a careful witness, you will continue to think clearly, and most important the written transcript will be very clear as to the nature of the questions and the responses.

Be prepared for the media. The news media, particularly the trade press, is usually aware of public and administrative hearings. Reporters may approach you for a statement. Review the suggestions in the "Quick Reference Summary" for Chapter Fifteen. In particular, avoid saying "No comment." Give them at least a general selling point statement that reiterates the major elements of your testimony.

Bring a 'crib sheet.' Prepare a card or sheet with three or four of the points you want to make at any regulatory or legislative hearing. (These are not allowed in a court of law.) It's like the plus side of the Plus/Minus Worksheet.

We learned this lesson from a woman who testifies frequently in public utilities hearings. She is well qualified, being an accountant and a lawyer. And she is always well prepared. She always brings a sheet of paper summarizing the points she wants to communicate. On one occasion, an attorney noticed that the witness kept referring to her notes. (Keep in mind here that anything you bring to the witness stand is "discoverable" and can be introduced into the record.) The attorney swooped down on her accusingly: "You appear to be referring to a piece of paper that I do not have. What is it? We would like to have it introduced into the record; please tell us what it is."

Without skipping a beat, the witness responded, "Sure, counselor. The paper contains some of the points I wanted to communicate here today. One of them is . . ." And before he could cut her off, she had scored one of her points. A great example of taking advantage of your opportunities.

Two final thoughts we'd like to leave with you. The first is an idea we got from another seasoned witness: Treat the experience like a job interview. Think about it. When you go for a job interview, you must be *positive;* you must think about the points you want to get across; you have to anticipate the questions, answer them, and bridge to positive information; you must be enthusiastic and sell yourself. All these points apply to the witness.

The second thought is one of our themes and a suggestion that often turns the experience around for people who are dreading it: Have a good time!

Quick Reference Summary

- Sworn testimony can be the most intimidating of all presentation settings because it's the questioner's forum—and frequently an adversarial situation. However, with proper preparation, you can usually maintain enough control to make your point.

Court of Law

- The rules of evidence would seem to make it tough to make *your* points, especially on cross-examination.
- The attorney for "your" side should rehearse you thoroughly and should give you the opportunity to make all the points you feel are important.

- In cross-examination, be prepared for all "difficult questions." Have answers.
- Anticipating the line of questioning in cross-examination can help you to score points.
- You can sometimes be forced to answer hypothetical questions on cross-examination. Always be sure to qualify your answers: "In answer to your hypothetical question . . ." or "If I must speculate, I would say. . . ."

Legislative Hearings

- Although often pro forma, legislative hearings provide an opportunity for *you* to make your points, often to a very large audience.
- Live testimony generally supplements presubmitted written testimony.
- Often, you are given wide scope to make your own statement. Take advantage of this: Prepare. Have strong selling points. Practice your delivery.
- Remember that your audience is "the people."

Regulatory Proceedings

- Witness-stand testimony in regulatory hearings almost invariably follows prefiled direct testimony. Hence it is, in essence, cross-examination.
- Hearings, however, do not run under strict rules of evidence. As a witness you have a wide range of opportunities to make your point *by means of bridging*.

For All Types of Testimony

- Know what you want to say and be prepared to say it forcefully.
- Remember, it is almost never the person asking the questions who is the ultimate audience of your communication. In

a trial it is the judge or jury. In a legislative or regulatory hearing, it is generally the public.

- All the rules of delivery apply to testimony: Gesture; keep your voice animated; make eye contact, especially with cameras.

- As with all Q & A, remember: Listen, Think (which also means "pause"), Answer.

17

Meetings, Meetings, Meetings

The one thing all business people know about meetings is that there are too many of them.

Generally, meetings are necessary when you need the input of several people, when a decision is required from a group, or when you need the synergy of group interaction, as in brainstorming.

You'll be wise to eliminate as many as possible by asking the key question: Is this meeting truly necessary? Perhaps a phone call, a letter, or an office visit would be more efficient or productive.

If the answer to this key question is no, or you're not sure, decide whether your meeting can be postponed or rescheduled, or your business handled in some other fashion.

If the answer to the key question is yes, then you've got some preparation to do. Since you're this far in reading *Get to the Point*, you're already familiar with much of what you have to know. In this chapter, we'll discuss the similarities between meetings and other types of presentations and tell what else you'll need to know to conduct a successful meeting.

What *is* a successful meeting? In our experience, if you can discuss and take action on all of your agenda items and start and conclude on time, ninety-five times out of a hundred you can consider your meeting a success. It's the kind of success that enhances your value to your company or organization; the kind of success that gets you ahead.

Purpose, Planning, and Agenda

Once you have established the need for a meeting, it is up to you, the chairperson, to plan it or at least to supervise its planning. It is important for the purpose of the meeting to be clear. Presumably, since you carefully weighed the need for the meeting, its purpose is clear to you. Be sure it is equally clear to those who will be attending. You might want to give the meeting a title. When meeting announcements are sent out, a clear statement of purpose and/or a catchy title can focus attention on the objectives and help ensure good attendance.

All meetings require an agenda.

Agendas need not be set in stone, but without at least a loose structure, meetings wander. An agenda provides the chairperson a legitimate reason to move the meeting along.

If your meeting requires consensus on the agenda, you may want to reach agreement on a written agenda before the actual meeting takes place. This may mean preliminary phone calls, letters, or memos to solicit discussion items, opinions, and premeeting materials.

For more formal meetings, the agenda may include ground rules such as the length of time for opening statements and discussion, as well as rules for such issues as submission of materials and voting. Depending on the circumstances, even physical objects like tables can become items for discussion and even contention. Remember the Paris peace talks during the Vietnam War?

Usually you'll want attendees to have some sort of written agenda to refer to. If you don't distribute a sheet to each individual, put the agenda on a flip chart or a slide. At the very least, give an oral review before the meeting starts.

Tip: Whatever form your agenda takes, *never* include a minute-by-minute time schedule. It's fine to be organized, but meetings need a feeling of flexibility and you don't want a group of people constantly checking their wristwatches.

Audience profile. Unlike any other presentation situation, the audience profile for a meeting begins with deciding who should be there. Sometimes these decisions are quite simple. It may be obvious whose input is needed to adequately discuss a given issue or problem. Often you will want to invite the entire marketing committee, or all the members of a particular organization. At other times, the decisions are more subjective and will reflect political concerns.

Once you have decided on the list of attendees, you should go through the standard audience profile. As we made clear in Chapter Two, while you wish to accomplish the agenda and basic tasks of the meeting, most people who attend the meeting will be judging it according to their *personal* question: What's in it for me?

Facilities planning. The goal of physical planning is to create an environment in which those attending your meeting can concentrate on the subject matter without undue distraction. A smooth-running meeting depends on coordinating all the elements in your presentation "theater." Basically, this means choosing the right room. The following considerations apply:

- *Size.* The room should seat approximately the number of people you will bring together.

- *Seating arrangement.* Depending on circumstances, different configurations of seating—table, theater style, amphitheater, or chevron—may be preferable.
- *Lighting.* Aside from basic adequate lighting, the facilities should be capable of lighting the speaker well even while visuals are being presented.
- *Visual aids.* Make sure the equipment you will need—overhead and slide projectors, flip chart, videotape players and monitors, and spares—will be available.
- *Amplification.* If the room is large, check the public address system and microphone availability.
- *Lectern.* If you anticipate needing a lectern, make sure one is present.
- *Food and beverage.* Make sure that there is room and equipment for any refreshments you are planning to serve, or that appropriate catering facilities are located nearby and have been notified.

Even with small meetings, it is important to do a little house-cleaning and/or setting up beforehand. This may be as simple as cleaning up the coffee cups from the last group that used the conference room, or just tidying up and straightening the furniture and laying a photocopy of the meeting agenda at each place. Do something that says, "This is a serious working/communications environment; we appreciate your being here and will do all we can to make it a productive occasion."

Conference centers. To make sure that all these details are taken care of—without having to take care of them directly—many companies and organizations prefer to hold important meetings at conference centers, establishments that generally offer excellent facilities and can handle virtually any sized group. These centers are run by professionals who can provide valuable planning assistance. Just getting people away from the office and constant interruptions and phone calls may be worth the added expense.

A word of caution here, however: While conference centers generally provide excellent facilities, this is no substitute for doing your homework. You will still need to check out the meeting room, do a tech rehearsal, and practice with the equipment.

Meeting Management—Handling the Interaction

The entire tone of a meeting can be set by a strong opening statement. Opening statements should be short and to the point. Set yourself a time limit and stick to it.

If you want a model, think of a good opening statement you have heard in a political debate. At a meeting, the opening statement should always include a word of welcome, a review of the agenda, a statement of any ground rules you wish to establish, and the expected closing time.

If the participants don't know each other, make introductions.

This is an often-overlooked matter of protocol. In a small meeting you might ask participants to introduce themselves and perhaps to say a word or two on their expectations of the meeting. In a larger meeting, you should introduce the people who will be presenting.

Record keeping. Decide in advance what kind of records will be kept for the meeting. The chairperson should never be responsible for taking the official notes or minutes. In a small, informal meeting, you can ask for a volunteer. Usually, though, you should arrange beforehand for someone to serve as recording secretary. If you want a verbatim transcript, tape record the meeting. Most conference centers are set up to make full video transcripts of any meeting.

You may also want someone to list meeting items on a blackboard or flip chart. Appoint a separate person to fulfill this function.

In brainstorming meetings, record *all* suggestions, no matter how outlandish.

You can weed the list later on, but don't cut off suggestions unilaterally during the meeting.

Ground rules. Preestablished ground rules are vital to the orderly conduct of the discussion. Let the members know how much time is allotted to the overall discussion and how long each individual should expect to speak. If people run overtime, your job is to diplomatically cut them off. If Barbara Walters could cut off Ronald Reagan and Walter Mondale in their televised debates, you should be able to enforce agreed-upon time limits for your discussion.

Summarize or offer clarifying comments from time to time during the discussion, as appropriate. This will often help to refocus a discussion that has wandered. Generally this commentary, along with your "parliamentary" functions, will constitute your contribution to the body of the discussion. (It is generally considered inappropriate for the leader to be a contributing participant in the substantive discussion.) If the agenda calls for a decision to be made, and it is clear that it cannot be made at the current meeting, the leader should make sure there is agreement on the next steps, such as whether the matter will be resolved by further correspondence and a follow-up vote by telephone, mail, or another meeting.

People Management

Particularly in smaller meetings, personalities play an important role. We covered the common types of difficult questions and difficult questioners in Chapter Ten. As promised there, we will now cover some additional personality types that sometimes create difficulties in meetings.

The Silent Type. Silence is usually golden, but meetings are an exception. In a meeting, you often want to build consensus. Other times, the opinion or contribution of a particular individual is crucial—especially when you know it will be voiced to others outside the meeting. That's when silence becomes a problem. Silent people are not necessarily unimportant people. In fact, the silence may be an expression of power. If you single out the silent type by explicitly requesting input on a given topic you risk intimidating or alienating this person. A better approach is to ask a question of the group collectively and then follow up by polling members individually, placing the silent person somewhere in the middle.

The Objectionist. This person sees the negative side of every issue, plan, or proposal. He or she is much like the Nit-Picker or Detailer we discussed in Chapter Ten. Don't confront this person during the meeting. A better approach is to present your ideas or objectives and seek consensus from this person prior to the actual meeting session. If the Objectionist tries to dominate your meeting, do not take this personally or show irritation. Offer to consider certain points and revert to the agreed-upon agenda.

The Monopolist. This personality bears some resemblance to the Objectionist but is not as negative. Like the Filibusterer we met in Chapter Ten, this person just likes to talk and contribute, but finds it hard to come to the point. Enforcing time limits and being sure to elicit the opinions of others will help keep the Monopolist under control. "Henry, I'll get back to you in a moment. But let me first get the views of some of the other people who are here."

The Inadequate. The person who manifests the Inadequate personality may be vital to the group but, like the weakest performer on a sports team, needs support and a sense of belonging. Encourage this person to participate by helping him or her feel more adequate and powerful. Often, allowing this person to do small, easy-to-accomplish tasks will make him or her more productive at future meetings.

The Idealist. This person may be angry and belligerent or simply overly zealous about some cause peripheral to your meeting agenda. An effective leader will try to find common ground without necessarily subscribing to the idealist's full program. "Yes, this company does have many environmental concerns. . . ."

Decision Time

When it is time to make decisions at a meeting, the chairperson is responsible for ensuring that the decision-making process is fair, efficient, and accurate. Again, planning and advance preparation will make any vote taking easier. For internal meetings, the voting procedures are usually well established. For an external group, you should check the organizational or departmental rules, corporate bylaws, or constitution.

Other decisions include how voting should be done—by secret ballot, by voice, or by a show of hands—and whether the result should be determined by plurality, majority, two-thirds, or unanimous consent. Voice votes can generally be conducted by the chair. Be sure to ask someone to confirm your findings. A show of hands should be counted by two separate individuals. When you plan a secret ballot, prepare ballots in advance and plan a method for distributing and collecting them and counting the vote. Ballots should be rechecked and if necessary retained in a secure location.

Closing Time

As the meeting winds down, people often begin to leave. At this point you need to take control. Often a clear statement of the remaining time and business will accomplish this. If you don't take control, the early departures will distract the rest of the attendees and often make them feel as if they are being kept after school.

The closing of a meeting can be your most important moment in terms of input.

The last things said in a meeting are remembered longest, so use your closing statement to stress the points you feel are most important. As with a more standard presentation, nearly all of your statement can be prepared in advance.

In addition to your observations, a good closing statement can include:

- A recap of important action items and decisions, so that all attendees leave with a sense of accomplishment and agreement (and will be more likely to attend future meetings).
- A general word of thanks for all who attended and special thank-you's to people who accomplished tasks, presented information, and took on responsibilities.
- A clear statement of when and where any follow-up meeting or event is to be held or, barring that, a statement of how people will be informed.

Follow-Up

Meetings need follow-up, and this involves attention to details. As chairperson, you should always review the minutes before they are sent to the other attendees. Make sure the minutes are distributed. Also see that key commitments have been fulfilled. People sometimes make promises during a meeting and then delay or even fail to fulfill their promises. A polite note or phone call is often all it takes to do the trick. If this gentle prodding doesn't work, don't be afraid to use the legitimacy of the chairperson's position to encourage people to complete jobs they have undertaken.

Remember, if you have accomplished your agenda and have finished on or before your scheduled time, you can generally consider your meeting a success. Participants will consider their time well spent and they will be more willing to attend meetings you call in the future. Leading meetings effectively is a valuable skill that can lay a red carpet down the middle of your career path.

Quick Reference Summary

- Key question: Is this meeting necessary, or will a call, memo, or one-on-one conversation accomplish my purpose?
- Meeting success criteria:
  - Start and end on time
  - Cover your agenda points
- Meeting planning checklist:
  - ☐ Audience profile

☐ Agenda
☐ Site preparation
☐ Ground rules
☐ Voting procedure

- Problem personalities to be prepared for:
  - *The Silent Type*. Don't confront this person directly. Rather, solicit input from each group member and include the silent member somewhere in the middle.
  - *The Objectionist*. If possible, seek consensus with this person before the meeting. If objections are raised *in* the meeting, offer to consider certain points and revert to the established agenda.
  - *The Monopolist*. Keep this well-meaning person under control by enforcing time limits and encouraging others to offer views.
  - *The Inadequate*. Encourage this person's participation by assigning him or her meaningful but manageable tasks.
  - *The Idealist*. The best way to deal with the missionary zeal of this meeting type is to find some common ground.
- Guide, clarify, and summarize as the meeting progresses.
- Make sure follow-up operations are carried out.

18

The Job Interview

The job interview is the ultimate one-on-one selling presentation. Given two candidates with equal credentials on paper, almost invariably the better presenter or communicator will get the job.

Job interviews involve virtually all the main elements of presentation making.

Included are the audience profile, content preparation, selling points, preparation for difficult questions, bridging—and practice. And depending on the job, even visual aids may come into the picture.

Your goal for the job interview, as for any presentation, is to be focused, prepared, and positive. One important thing to keep in mind about this presentation is that although it is billed as an interview—which suggests the potential employers ask the questions, you give the answers—it's actually an interactive event, a two-way process. You're there so the hiring company can find out about you; you're also there to find out about the company, the position, and the people in the company.

Although you should certainly plan on asking questions at the interview, don't wait until then to begin gathering information about the company. Do your own audience profile, as you would for any presentation. This is important for three reasons:

1. It makes sense for you to gather as much information about the organization and the position as you can so you can judge whether this is the right situation for you.
2. Personnel officers and recruiters tend to be favorably impressed by the thoroughness and foresight demonstrated by a candidate's having researched the position in advance. It makes you look good.
3. If you do like what you see, then like any audience profile, your research helps you create more "audience-centered" messages. If you really understand what the organization is like, you can stress the ways you fit in with it.

It is generally not difficult to gather relevant information about a company, even a specific position. Corporate annual reports, stock and brokerage analysis reports, electronic data bases, trade and consumer articles, and former employees are all viable sources of information. Perhaps more specifically helpful will be the executive recruiter (if any) who told you about the job and your own personal network of friends and associates. If you can't get information any other way, call the company public relations or investor relations department and ask for some background.

Try to get a basic job description, including responsibilities and salary. Other key areas of advance information relate to the management and decision-making style of the department you would be joining and the personalities of the key managers. If, for example, you are a real go-getter being interviewed for a position in a department with a very laid-back management style, you should be aware of this and have some idea of why they would want to hire you.

You already have a list of your personal selling points. It's
called your résumé.

The accomplishments you list there are the headlines; the specifics
will be provided by you during the interview. Your preparation
should include pulling together at least one strong anecdote or other
specific for every point you have listed. If you can come up with two
or three, you'll look that much stronger. Try to make your selling
points as visual as possible; let the interviewer see the examples in his
or her mind's eye.

Their Questions

Preparing for a job interview is similar to preparing for any other
question and answer session. Keep in mind that in this case the questioner is an official representative of the organization you hope to
work for and that the basic message you want to communicate is the
corporate or organizational WIIFM: What's in it for us to hire *you*?
What's the significance of your accomplishments and experiences for
this job?

Those are the questions to keep at the back of your mind as you
make out your Difficult Questions Worksheet and your Plus/Minus
Worksheet. With some reflection, you should be able to anticipate
virtually all the questions the interviewer will ask. Naturally, this
will include questions about your past work history, which may well
contain some tender spots you would prefer not to have someone
probing. In other words, like any presentation, the job interview is
likely to involve questions you would prefer not to answer. And, as
in any presentation, you will need to be prepared to deal with them:
Respond to the question and bridge to more positive information.

In addition to questions you'd rather not answer, you need to be
alert to the other types of tricky questions we covered in Chapter
Ten, particularly hypotheticals. Job interviews frequently involve
speculative or hypothetical questions of the type, "Where do you see
yourself ten years from now?" or "If you were running this division,
given this set of facts, how would you respond?" You are almost re-

quired to answer these. Just flag them as hypotheticals before you do so. (*Note:* The question, "Would you be willing to relocate?" may not be hypothetical.)

What you don't have to say. Lest we leave you with the impression that you are at the mercy of all the interviewer's questions, be assured that there *are* questions you shouldn't feel obligated to answer.

As always, personal questions fit into this category. With the rising concern over individual rights, some of these areas of personal information have been declared off limits by law. This doesn't always stop interviewers from asking the questions, however. The best policy is to be polite and state firmly that the question is personal and can have no bearing on your work performance. If necessary, negotiate a little and offer other information that may be relevant.

> Example:
> *Question:* "Do you plan to have children?"
> *Answer:* "Can you explain why that is relevant to this interview?" or "I don't see how that is relevant, but if you're concerned about my commitment . . ."

You should also avoid answering questions that delve into proprietary information relating to your present position. Sometimes these questions are posed in an effort to gain information, sometimes just to test your reaction—since most employers don't want to hire somebody who's ready to give away information. Don't fall into this trap; just politely decline to reveal proprietary information and suggest that they would be unhappy if their employees did so in the course of job interviews they might have.

Some questions that come up in job interviews are just plain dumb. These could be anything from "Who do you think will win the World Series?" to "What did you think of that ugly sculpture in the lobby?" We suggest that you resist any impulse to be flippant or sarcastic. Just answer the questions, and treat them as a way for you to make another point (i.e., bridge to another selling point).

Your Questions

Your audience profile probably won't answer all your questions about the job and company, and the interview is the time to ask them. We suggest you prepare a list of questions or points that you wish to bring up. Realistically, there are a lot of things you *should* find out about. Some of your questions may just confirm information you gathered elsewhere. Having the list with you doesn't obligate you to ask all the questions on it, but the notes will be living proof of your preparedness. It's not unlike going to the doctor's office with a list of symptoms, concerns, and questions. In the pressure of the moment we tend to forget, and a list helps us remember.

Demeanor and Deportment

All of the skills we discussed in the core of the book apply equally to job interviews—only more so, since the stakes are higher. The impressions you make are crucial, from your clothes to the way you walk in and greet the interviewer to the way you sit, gesture, make eye contact, and use your voice.

- Good eye contact is crucial. Let your gaze rest on the interviewer's face rather than letting your eyes roll skyward or look down at the floor.
- Remember to *pause* before answering questions (see pages 102 and 103).
- Lean in to answer questions.
- Show your enthusiasm. Enthusiasm, or at least a good energy level, is important for any interview. Don't be a corporate cheerleader, but let your interviewer know you are capable and have an energetic, positive attitude.

Specific Job Interview Tips

Drinks. If your interview involves going out for a meal, you may have to decide whether or not to have a drink. This question is less likely to be a test of character than in days past. If you are inclined to have a drink, you may wish to follow the lead of your hosts: Do if they do, don't if they don't. On the other hand, it is also becoming more socially acceptable *not* to drink, so if you are inclined not to, don't. If the drink is a rite of passage or congratulatory gesture, on the other hand, it is best to go along.

Warmups. Clients tell us their best interviews are the ones where they are a little relaxed. (Not *totally* relaxed; a bit of adrenaline is helpful.) You may want to find the time and place to do the kind of relaxation warmup we recommended in Chapter Twelve (see page 154).

Decisions. Try to be clear about your motives in attending any given job interview. Is this really a job you want? Or are you just testing the waters, checking opportunities, or simply strengthening your job interview skills? Don't get tense over an interview for a job you don't really want and then agonize if the job is offered—or if it isn't.

Visuals. For some kinds of jobs—advertising, public relations, or design, for example—it may be appropriate for you to bring samples of your work such as ads or press releases. If you do bring samples, please remember our cardinal rule about the presentation of visuals: If you have preliminary remarks or explanations, make them. Then present the visual—and *pause*—long enough for the material to be absorbed and evaluated.

Quick Reference Summary

- Job interviews should be interactive and conversational.
- Do an audience profile on the company or organization.
- Be prepared to relate the selling points on your résumé to the objectives and outlook of the organization for which you are interviewing.
- Prepare for Q & A with the Plus/Minus and Difficult Questions Worksheets.
- Practice bridging to your selling points.
- Always ask your own questions.
- Be aware of your body language, eye contact, and energy.

19

How to Prepare
and Read a Speech

We feel that delivering a speech from notes is almost always preferable to using a fully prepared text. With notes, your eyes aren't glued to words on paper. Your performance has more spontaneity and you can look at the audience. Nonetheless you may at some time feel the need to work from a prepared text. Some of the occasions when you will want a prepared speech are: when the rules for all presenters are the same; when copies of the talk will be distributed to attendees; for more formal events such as annual meetings, very precise introductions, an explanation of rules and procedures, or if you don't have the time to rewrite the prepared speech from the company speech writers into your own words and thoughts. Here are some guidelines that will help you maintain eye contact and generally enliven your speech.

Typing the Speech

Use large type. Have your speech typed in uppercase letters, preferably in an oversized typeface. Most electric typewriters and daisy
wheel computer printers have an element (daisy wheel or type ball)
available for just this task. The typeface is often named something
like "Orator." Most dot matrix printers can print double height
and/or double width characters. If possible, use the double height–
double width combination.

Type phrases, not lines. Divide each sentence into thought or meaning units, then type only one thought or phrase per line. Double or
triple space between lines. For example, the beginning of Lincoln's
Gettysburg Address would become:

> FOURSCORE AND SEVEN YEARS AGO
> OUR FOREFATHERS BROUGHT FORTH ON THIS
>   CONTINENT
> A NEW NATION
> CONCEIVED IN LIBERTY
> AND DEDICATED TO THE PROPOSITION
> THAT ALL MEN ARE CREATED EQUAL.

Use only two-thirds of the page. Leave at least the bottom one-third
of the page blank. If you fill the page, by the time you read to the
bottom, you are looking down at quite a sharp angle. This tends to
make your voice drop and certainly makes eye contact difficult.
Leaving the bottom blank also reduces text density, making it easier
for your eye to pick up words and phrases. In combination with the
improved reading angle, this encourages you to make eye contact.

Don't jump paragraphs. Always try to finish a paragraph on the
same page on which you started it. This eliminates confusion as you
move to the following page; you'll have a natural pausing point and
can give yourself ample time to move the page and continue.

Number pages. Clearly.

Fine-Tuning the Speech

Mark up your text. Read your speech aloud, listening for the points where you will want to pause, emphasize words, and group words together. You can use the markup found in Chapter Eleven on page 144. Consider using colored pens to make your notations extra legible. Be neat.

Pauses: Put a slash (/) after a completed thought or sentence. Use a double slash (//) when changing thoughts or for dramatic impact.

Emphasis: <u>Underline</u> words to be emphasized. For extra emphasis, use double underlines. Generally, *emotional* and *action* words get this treatment.

Joining: Use a connecting line (⌒) to join words that should flow together and be spoken in one breath.

Here's how our example might look, marked up for delivery:

> FOURSCORE AND SEVEN YEARS AGO /
> OUR FOREFATHERS <u>BROUGHT</u> <u>FORTH</u> ON THIS
>   CONTINENT
> A <u>NEW</u> NATION //
> CONCEIVED IN <u>LIBERTY</u>/
> AND <u>DEDICATED</u> TO THE PROPOSITION
> THAT <u>ALL</u> <u>MEN</u> // ARE CREATED <u>EQUAL</u>.

Make marginal notes. At the beginning of your speech—and wherever you need reminders—give yourself marginal instructions such as "SMILE," "GESTURE," and "SLOW DOWN." Some people prefer symbols: A stick figure might mean "gesture"; upward or downward arrows could serve as inflection cues; eye glasses for eye contact. Use whatever works for you.

Don't staple pages. When delivering your talk, lay your pages on the lectern and move the first page to the left of the pile. As you finish reading the first page, reach with your left hand and move the second page to the left, on top of the first page. Continue in the same fashion. This is something like the way a page turner handles the problem for a musical performer. The idea is that it's what's coming that's important, not what's past.

Pause. Use pauses liberally in your talk. As we've said at every opportunity, pauses give your audience time to digest and appreciate what you've said. Pausing also gives you reading time, so you can then look up and make eye contact with the audience as you begin each new paragraph.

Practice, practice, practice! Generally, do a *minimum* of three runthroughs—out loud, with a tape or video recorder and/or an audience. Listen for clarity of phrasing and good vocal inflection. For the full story on practice, see Chapter Eleven. See also the section on lectern techniques, in Chapter Fourteen.

Quick Reference Summary

- Type your speech in large type or all capital letters.
- Type in phrases, not sentences or paragraphs.
- Mark your script with symbols to help you with pace and inflection.
- Practice, practice, practice.

20

Using a TelePrompTer

The TelePrompTer is a standard tool used when delivering a speech on television or videotape. In many ways it is ideal, since it enables you to read text while you appear to be looking directly into the camera.

But the benefits of the TelePrompTer can be liabilities as well. Because you are reading your text and generally have no audience present, it is difficult to maintain the energy and enthusiasm you would bring to a live audience when speaking from notes. Hence these guidelines.

The Machinery

Basically, there are two types of TelePrompTers: One is a video monitor, usually placed just below the camera lens, to which a copy of your text is transmitted. The other is a flat glass screen—usually placed *over* the camera lens, onto which your text is projected. The glass prompter is also suited to speaking before live audiences and is commonly used at political conventions and similar gatherings.

Remember the Basics

Although you will be speaking to a machine, remember that you are addressing an audience—through the camera. Use pauses liberally to give your audience time to digest and appreciate what you've said. Gesture to burn off tension and animate your voice. Maintain eye contact with the camera to avoid looking uncomfortable or insincere. If possible, put an easel stand next to the prompter with notes reminding you to "SMILE," "GESTURE," and "PAUSE."

Prepare Your Text for a TelePrompTer

Type and mark your script just as we described above for a live speech, except that you may, of course, use the whole page. The problems of reading angle and eye contact have been eliminated by the technology.

Get Comfortable

Do as much as you can to make yourself at home. Arrive early at the studio. Get to know the technicians and crew.

When you're in a studio looking at a camera, you want to appear as if you're talking to a real audience. There are several of ways to do this:

- Visualize someone behind the lens who you know or want to know, and talk to that person.
- Actually talk to the technician behind the camera, or have someone stand next to the camera who you can talk to.
- Bring a picture of someone you know—your kids, a loved one, your dog, whatever works for you—and tape it next to the camera lens or prompter screen to help you relax.
- Mentally recreate another setting in which you have given your speech.

Case Study: This last approach worked well on one occasion when we were coaching an executive who was new to the videotape process and the studio atmosphere.

He was a few minutes into his speech and it frankly wasn't going very well. He was stiff, wooden, and flat. We stopped him. "Where did you originally give this speech?" we asked. Colorado Springs, he told us, at a sales meeting. "All right," we said, "we want you to put yourself back there in that sales meeting." As soon as his mind returned to that setting, his reading became very natural, as if he were talking to that audience and not to the camera. The rest of the taping went beautifully.

The cardinal rule to remember with TelePrompTers is lead, don't follow!

There is a TelePrompTer operator whose job is to adjust the flow of copy to accommodate your reading pace. Remember that *you* set the pace; don't ever feel that you have to wait for the copy, or have to keep up with its flow.

What You'll See

About six lines of copy will be visible on the screen at one time. As you read, the text will scroll upward, revealing the next lines. Again, set your own pace. You drive the system, it shouldn't drive you.

Practice

We've said it earlier in this book, we've said it elsewhere; we say it again. With television, it's more important than ever. You are about to be a classic "talking head." Which means that your audience is going to be listening—and watching—*close up*. If at all possible, practice with videotape, in a studio. If this is not possible, use an audio recorder and practice in front of a mirror, or have someone observe you and comment on your performance—or both. Listen carefully to be certain your sentences are not too long to be easily understood. Generally, at least three out-loud rehearsals will be required before you will begin to feel comfortable with your speech.

If you think it doesn't take practice to deliver a speech, consider the case of one actress who did endless "takes" of her role in a television commercial before she was satisfied with the reading. Her lines? Just two words!

Quick Reference Summary

- Lead the TelePrompTer, don't follow.
- Relate to the audience through the camera lens.
- Visualize a real audience or real presentation situation or create a substitute to speak to, either a real person or a picture of someone.

21

Give and Take:
The Panel Discussion

As a communications environment, the panel discussion offers a nice mix of elements. It's more spontaneous than a speech or one-on-one interview. It is inherently interactive and offers both audience and participants the stimulation of an immediate contrast of views. The environment can be adversarial, though not to the extent that a trial or hearing is, so this too can be stimulating.

In a panel discussion you know your speaking time will be limited—but you have no way of knowing *how* limited. Hence panelist profile preparation is critical. In order to have the best chance of getting your points in, you must anticipate opposing positions and arguments:

- For ease of reference, list your key points on a five-by-seven index card.
- Always be ready to bridge.
- Also, be ready to jump in and make your points based on other panelists' statements.

- Try to repeat your key message two or three times during the course of the discussion.

The Split Audience Factor

One factor that complicates the preparation process for panels is that you're dealing with a "split" audience. This creates an unusual amount of audience profile work.

On one hand, there is your "true" audience, the people in the auditorium or those who are watching or listening to the broadcast. These are the people you're trying to sell your points to, so you'll need to do the normal audience profile: Get a firm understanding of who they are and center your messages on their concerns and their awareness (WIIFM).

On the other hand, you can't forget the moderator and the other panelists, the people with whom you will be interacting directly. Realistically, you're not there to convince them or win them over to your point of view, but you must be ready to respond to the issues and points of view they will raise, to anticipate the challenges they will present. To be effective, you need to know who's going to be there and what their areas of expertise are, along with their points of view and prejudices. So, given all of these players—audience, moderator, and other panelists—and the time constraints, set realistic, limited objectives. Concentrate on a few important selling points that you'll have on your note cards.

Here are a number of techniques and tactics that will help you make your point in panel discussions.

What to Find Out Ahead of Time

- Know the themes and subthemes of the event. How is it being billed or promoted?
- Who is the moderator? What is his or her perspective and/or agenda?
- Will you have an opportunity to make an opening and/or closing statement? Always make these statements, if at all possible.
- What is the physical environment—the panel setup, micro-

phones, water pitchers, audience seating? If you can influence the seating arrangement, get yourself located at one end of the table. These are the "seats of power."

- Can you appear with a colleague? It's usually more effective if two people can represent the same organization.
- Can you bring handouts, brochures, or other reading material to leave with the audience? If you can, this is an excellent way to reinforce your message.

At the Panel

- Arrive early. Introduce yourself to the moderator and the other panelists. If not prearranged, find the best seating positions.
- Set up any charts or other visual aids you have brought (after first making sure this is appropriate).
- Take a few moments to relax before the panel begins. Stretch and limber your muscles and your voice (see pages 153–156).
- Review your key points just before things get under way. Keep your note card in front of you during the proceedings. Take a few deep breaths just before it is your turn to speak (see page 155, Chapter Twelve).

During the Discussion

- Be sure to address the audience, not the panelists, during your opening and closing statements.
- Sit up and lean slightly forward when you speak. This demonstrates energy and commitment—and allows for better breathing.
- When others talk, keep your eyes on them. When responding to another panelist, begin your answer by looking at him or her, then shift your eye contact to the audience. This includes them in your answer, reduces the likelihood of a rebuttal from the panelist, and cues you to bridge your answer to an issue of interest to the entire group.
- Don't try to control the course of the discussion, but be sure to jump into the dialogue at any appropriate point and bridge to your selling points. If a colleague is appearing with you, decide

in advance which of you will address which issues and which of you will take on the responsibility of responding to unfocused questions or those not directly in your area of expertise. It's important not to look confused or unprepared.

- Most important, be constantly on the lookout for opportunities to add your points when your colleague or another panelist has finished talking. Unless strict rules of order have been set up, you don't have to wait your turn. If you have an important point that addresses the audience's needs, try to make it. Signal the moderator with a hand gesture or use a word or two to make a natural transition. Key words to use: "I'd like to add . . ." or "From our perspective . . ." or "Here's another point. . . ."

- When your colleague/copanelist is talking, your job is to think of selling points or specifics that drive home the general answer. This ability to have both of you answer shows a team approach and helps build audience retention of your message.

- Keep your sense of humor. Don't take comments personally, particularly in an adversarial discussion. Enjoy the opportunity to deliver a message to an audience.

After the Panel

- Make yourself available for informal conversation with members of the audience.
- Leave reading material or handouts with a contact telephone number or address so interested persons can reach you.
- Tell the panel organizers that, subject to your schedule, you are willing to appear at other discussions.
- To evaluate your own performance (as a guide to possible improvement for future panels), check your note card or other list of crucial points. How many of your selling points did you get in? Did you get your key message across two or three times?

Quick Reference Summary

- Prepare for two audiences: the listeners, and the moderator and other panelists. You want, ultimately, to communicate to the first, but you must do so by addressing the second.

- Keep your objectives limited; concentrate on a few important points.
- Jump in after other panelists' points and bridge to your message.
- Don't be afraid to repeat yourself. Try to make your key point two or three times.

22

How to
Introduce a Speaker

Introducing a speaker is one of those jobs that doesn't get much attention—if it's done right. It's when it is done badly that everyone notices.

An introduction is a minipresentation, with its own shape and choreography, and as such contains most of the elements that by now should be familiar. In fact, the only presentation elements that *don't* come up are the Q & A and visuals.

Audience Profile

Like any presenter, to prepare a good introduction you need to know the audience. Generally, you already do. If not, you need to do enough of a profile to understand what about the speaker will appeal to them. You are the connecting link between audience and speaker.

Your Message

Essentially, your bottom line message is, "Here's a great speaker." Your selling points are details about his or her background, qualifications, current activities—whatever compelling information you can gather to pull the audience in. Your call to action will be something like, "Please join me in giving a rousing welcome to So-and-So."

The speaker's name should be the very last words out of your mouth.

Here's why. First, it's your show only until you pronounce the name; then the audience's attention goes instantly and directly to the speaker. Once that transition occurs, you no longer have an audience. Second, the speaker generally takes his or her name as the cue to get up and walk to the lectern. A premature introduction can cause considerable confusion and embarrassment.

In addition, saving the speaker's name until last sometimes adds a bit of suspense—a touch of showmanship that is actually not out of place in an introduction. Why showmanship? In one sense, as an introducer you have a function similar to the warmup band at a rock concert or the kickoff person at a political rally. You are there to generate enthusiasm for what follows.

Beginning

To create enthusiasm you need to start with a high level of energy. The first words out of your mouth tend to set the tone. Accordingly, a good grabber is particularly important in introductions. Much of what we said earlier about grabbers (see Chapter Five) applies here, except that personal connections established should be between speaker and audience. Humor is a good ingredient if it comes naturally to you and is not inappropriate in terms of subject matter or occasion. Current events often provide a meaningful tie-in.

Middle

The main body of the introduction consists of information about the speaker (selling points) that will whet the audience's appetite. Social rules require us to be modest about ourselves in public, so your job as an introducer is to be *immodest* on behalf of the speaker, just as you would be about your company's product; hype his or her accomplishments, credentials, and stature. Like any other presenter, you're there to make a sale, to sell the speaker to the audience.

Selling Points

All too often, "introducers" limit their selling points to a thumbnail biography accompanied by a dry list of books and papers written, titles and degrees earned, affiliations, and/or other credentials that reveal very little about the person involved. The more you can convey a sense of knowing the person, however, the better you motivate the audience to do the same. This kind of connectedness comes from mentioning personal involvements, current projects and activities, something about the contents of books or papers. In fact, another device that often adds a touch of suspense is to foreshadow some aspect of what the speaker is actually going to say. Find out what the speaker is going to say and set up the talk without stealing his or her thunder.

As with all selling points, try to illustrate facts about the speaker and information about his or her work and accomplishments in dramatic terms. This means translating your points into words and images the audience can relate to intuitively. Your linking task becomes much easier if you have an opportunity to talk with the speaker beforehand, so take the time to get to know the speaker if you can. If you don't get a chance to speak about *anything else*, check the factual accuracy of all your information with the speaker before the event. It is embarrassing to all when the speaker feels compelled to correct academic or professional background information.

Ending

Once you've finished your remarks, deliver your call to action: "Please join me in welcoming . . ." If applause is appropriate, lead the applause. At this point, you have two options. You can leave the speaker's platform, which is often the simplest logistical choice, or you can stay to physically welcome and "install" the speaker. If you choose to stay, you will need to *step back* as the speaker nears the lectern, to let him or her pass in front of you. Generally, you will shake hands and "turn over" the lectern. Once he or she gets settled in, you will probably get a word or two of thanks, which is your cue to quickly exit.

As with any presentation, the more preparation and practice you put in, the more successful the introduction will be.

Awards Choreography

If the occasion is an awards ceremony, the person performing the introduction will generally be the one to physically present the award. In some circumstances, especially where a number of awards are being given, you may want to keep your remarks quite brief. In other cases, especially where only one recipient is to be honored, you will probably want to speak at greater length. When you have concluded your remarks and announce the recipient's name, you will step back, *holding the award in your left hand*, shake hands with the recipient when he or she arrives, hand over the award, and depart unobtrusively.

Quick Reference Summary

- Remember that you're the link between the speaker and the audience.
- Find personal notes, relevant anecdotes, or a WIIFM (What's In It For Me) message in addition to the standard listing of honors and accomplishments.
- Save the speaker's name for last.

23

Quick Points:
Presentation
on a Time Budget

#1: The Instant Presentation

The setting: An elevator, at the water cooler, leaving the cafeteria, at your desk.

The situation: A boss or peer stops you or phones you and demands an on-the-spot opinion, evaluation, update, or progress report.

The need: A clear, concise, convincing thirty-second response.

The strategy: Listen, Think, Answer.

  Step 1: Pause. That's right; pause. At all costs, resist the temptation to engage your mouth and let it drive the brain.

  Step 2: Think:
  • Who is this person? What's his or her relationship to me?
  • What is his or her concern or relationship to the issue raised?
  • What is the most succinct, bottom-line-oriented message I can deliver in a relaxed, conversational manner?

· Is there a specific fact or example that supports my message?

Step 3: Answer. Deliver your statement with the most conviction and confidence you can muster.

Step 4: Follow up and close. Don't be upset if you can't answer any follow-up questions that may be forthcoming. Try to answer them, but don't let the impromptu encounter go on too long. You can excuse yourself with a remark like, "I'm on my way to an important meeting . . ."; "You've caught me in the middle of something that can't wait . . ."; or "I've got someone sitting in my office . . ." Generally, it is prudent to offer to fulfill the request at your earliest convenience: "When would you need the rest of this information? I'll put it together for you . . ." whenever.

The instant presentation occasionally turns into a longer conversation. But focus on the first thirty seconds. If the encounter does run longer, try to develop a good closing line before you break it off.

#2: The Two-Minute Talking Memo

It happens all the time in business: You've been asked to make a presentation—sometimes couched as an "update" or a "status or progress report"—in your boss's office or at a staff meeting in *ten minutes*.

Here are guidelines that will enable you to pull off this assignment with style.

Put this kind of a presentation together the way you typically *read* a memo (as opposed to the way memos are usually *written*): *Get straight to the bottom line*.

You do this by determining and delivering *the information that this person or group really needs to know*.

Here's the simple, four-step technique:

1. Write your bottom-line message first. (This is the same as the information this person or group really needs to know.) It should consist of no more than two or three sentences.

2. Pull out two or three essential facts, or pieces of data that support your conclusion or bottom line. As you select your supporting points, consider *how* they support the conclusion. Ask yourself the questions: "So what?"; "Who cares?"; "What's the significance of this fact or data?"

3. Write a strong opening for your two-minute talk. This opening could be:

   · A relevant anecdote or personal note.
   · A prop that helps people visualize your point.
   · The strongest possible bottom-line message.

   Example: "If we increase production and authorize overtime, we can reduce our two-week backorder problem." This avoids the more standard (and boring) opening: "I want to give you an update on our order situation. . . ."

4. Review your material. Make sure you can deliver the basic message in two minutes or less. Anticipate any questions.

When you actually deliver your talking memo, the elements appear in the following order:

1. Opening
2. Bottom-line message, if different from the opening
3. Supporting points
4. Bottom line message—again—as conclusion message

#3: 'In-Flight' Presentation Writing

Here's a game plan f~ making the most of your time when you have to prepare a presentation in a limited—but not severely limited—amount of time (for instance, on the flight from Kansas City to Seattle). It is really an expansion of Quick Point #2, bridging the gap between the real shorties and a full-fledged presentation, adding the possibility of visuals, more and clearer selling points, and more time for Q & A.

Tools required are an airplane (or other) seat, a note pad, and a pen or pencil.

Audience profile. As in a full-length presentation, the first step is taking stock of who will be there. If you know the people, visualize them. What is each person's role in the proceedings, each person's personal concern? Who are likely to be supporters of your position? Who are likely to be opponents? What are the personality types? What "What's In It For Me" message can you formulate for each person or position represented within the group you will be presenting to? Jot down this information on your pad.

Your roles and goals. Using your audience profile, make a quick mental review of the stated reason for your appearance in this presentation setting. This should help you assess the basic expectations of those you will be addressing. In other words, what's your role here? Next, jot down a simple, clear statement of what your message is in the presentation:

- Consensus?
- Data?
- Ideas?
- A Sale?

(The object of this segment of preparation is to make sure your messages are both audience- and speaker-centered.)

Gee whiz points. What new, startling, amusing, unusual, or thought-provoking fact, statistic, or anecdote can you use to get the attention of your listeners and/or dramatically illustrate your selling points?

Problem-solution sheet. On one side of your page, quickly list all the problems, challenges, or negative aspects of your subject that occur to you. Don't worry about ordering or ranking them. Across from the negative points, list all the solutions, recommendations, or positive selling points that come to mind.

Identify your key issue. Look over your list of solutions and recommendations and pick the one that best keys in to the WIIFM needs of your audience. This is your key audience-centered issue. Your task is now to link it firmly to your personal bottom-line message with one or more strong bridges. This is the core of your presentation.

As with all bottom-line messages, you will state your positive point at the outset. Then you will examine the problem or negative. Finally, you will restate the solution or recommendation. (Tell 'em, tell 'em, tell 'em.)

Plus/Minus Sheet. Using your problem-solution sheet as a guide, make a real Plus/Minus Worksheet, listing every possible negative question or issue that might come up in the context of your talk, and indicate bridges to positive information. Make sure you have a bridge and a positive answer for every negative point on your sheet. Study your Plus/Minus Worksheet and rehearse your bridges.

Select visuals. Look over your material and decide what points would make good visuals. (In this scenario, you need to think in terms of flip chart visuals, since there is no time to create slides or overhead transparencies.)

Notes. Make notes if you feel you will need them. Keep them concise. List details and specifics, not general principles.

Run-through. If you have an opportunity (in the cab ride from the airport, for example), rehearse your talk—out loud. Spend some time visualizing tough questions, and practice bridging from these to your selling points.

ABOUT THE AUTHORS

KAREN BERG and ANDREW GILMAN are the principals in CommCore, Inc., a communications consulting and training firm based in New York. Their clients include AT&T, Chase Manhattan Bank, Campbell's Soup, the American Lung Association, and G.D. Searle. Edward P. Stevenson is an experienced business writer.

For 1990,

BANTAM MEANS BUSINESS!

**Turn the page for
a preview of the
newest business books
now available in
Bantam paperback
wherever you buy books.**

From:

THE PERFECT SALES PRESENTATION
by Robert L. Shook

Advice From:

MARY KAY ASH, Founder and Chairman of Mary Kay Cosmetics, Inc.

JOE GANDOLFO, The world's #1 life insurance agent

BETTYE C. HARDEMAN, America's #1 residential real estate agent

FRANCIS G. "BUCK" RODGERS, Marketing Consultant and former Vice President of worldwide marketing for IBM

MARTIN SHAFIROFF, Managing Director of Shearson/Lehman Brothers and the #1 stockbroker in the world

Mary Kay Ash believes that a salesperson gets only one chance to make a good first impression. For this reason, she thinks that the initial approach to a prospect is the most crucial part of the sales presentation. "All the selling skills in the world won't matter if you don't get your foot in the door," she claims.

The five sales experts agree that the way in which Baker immediately identifies himself to the prospect is professional and effective. "I like his directness," Hardeman says. "Up front, Baker states his name, the company he represents, and that it specializes in men's custom clothing. Unlike a lot of salesmen, he doesn't beat around the bush."

"He does what I used to do when I first got started in the insurance business." Gandolfo says. "I represented a company called Kennesaw Life Insurance Company, and after I'd introduce myself, I'd say, 'I'm sure you're familiar with Kennesaw Life.' Most people automatically nod their heads in agreement, especially when a salesperson's head is bobbing up and down. Now, I know that the vast majority of people never heard of the company, but by the way I said it, they thought they were *supposed* to know who Kennesaw was."

Gandolfo also likes Baker's appearance and the fact that he wears a Winchester suit. "It's a big mistake for a salesperson not to use the product he sells," the insurance agent states. "It's paramount to a Mercedes salesman driving a Caddy or a Chevy. Unless you believe in your product one hundred percent, you're simply not going to be effective. And I'll tell you something. Before I owned a million dollars of life insurance, I couldn't sell a million-dollar policy because I couldn't understand how anyone could afford so much coverage. Once I was insured for a million, and several more later on, I had the conviction to convince others that they, too, should be insured for those amounts. People sense this kind of conviction the very moment a salesman opens his mouth—whether he's in the same room or on the telephone."

Gandolfo, Shafiroff, and Rodgers are strong advocates of "concept selling" and like the way Baker tells the prospect, "I would like to share an idea with you." Gandolfo, for instance, initially tells a prospect, "I'm in the insurance and tax-shelter business, and I'm assuming that you pay more than four thousand dollars a year in taxes, personal or corporate. If so, you're paying too much and I'd like to run some ideas by you." This statement is a big attention-getter and opens the door with Gandolfo capturing immediate interest. "Who wouldn't be interested if they're paying more than four thousand a year in taxes?" he says. "Of course, I have to substantiate that statement in my presentation."

Likewise, in Shafiroff's initial approach he emphasizes that he deals in values. He stresses, "Wherever those values may be, and in whatever markets those values may be, my main concern is finding them for you. I also concentrate on special situations, seeking out companies with low multiples, high dividends, significant book values, and the possibility of realizing substantial capital gains." Shafiroff explains that he doesn't sell a specific stock during his first contact with a prospect. "I merely introduce myself and talk to him about my investment philosophy to see if it's in harmony with his. If we're not conceptually on the same wavelength, then I don't have anything to sell him."

Rodgers points out that the IBM cold-call approach creates initial interest by making a statement: "We're in the business of trying to provide solutions to a variety of different problems. Technology is moving very fast today, and I deal with many companies similar to yours, Mr. Prospect, where the use of our equipment has improved their profits. All we're trying to do at IBM is enhance productivity. For instance, our machines may accomplish this by enabling your volume to grow without having to increase your manpower. However, in order to take advantage of our equipment, there are a few things I have to know about your company." Then, soon into the presentation, a fact-finding session occurs.

During his initial approach, Baker mentions the names of several of his satisfied customers. This is done to establish credibility that his product has been well received by prominent people in the community. The five sales experts agree that this is an important procedure because it lets the prospect know that your product has benefited leading businesspersons who have good judgment. Shafiroff, who still makes it a practice to make six calls every day, claims that his best receptions are from those prospects referred to him by his existing clientele. When he mentions, "So-and-so told me to call you, Mr. Prospect," it's like having an introduction that gives him an immediate endorsement. The prospect knows that Shafiroff must have a fine reputation and expertise, because he respects the opinion of the third party.

From:

GET TO THE POINT: HOW TO SAY WHAT YOU MEAN AND GET WHAT YOU WANT
by Karen Berg and Andrew Gilman

The Three-Minute Presentation Writing Technique

Somebody once asked Abraham Lincoln how long it took him to prepare a speech. "It takes me about two weeks to write a good twenty-minute speech," he said, "but I can write a *forty*-minute speech in *one* week. And," he added, "I can give a two-hour talk on almost any subject right now." Or, as a correspondent of ours once put it: "If I'd had more time, I'd have written you a shorter letter."

The point? It's hard to be concise.

With our three-minute presentation writing technique, however, we give you a way to cut the job down to size. Once you are proficient with it, you should be able to draft your presentation in three minutes or less, regardless of length. Our technique works whether you make thirty-second, five-minute, or two-hour presentations.

The technique centers on two easy steps:

1. Stating your conclusion
2. Listing your arguments

These elements comprise the core of your presentation. Almost the entire structure flows from them. A third element is often necessary to complete the scheme, and that has to do with the "lead" we just mentioned. We'll discuss that later.

The first step is the key, but it rests on doing something that does *not* come naturally to most people. The natural tendency in formal communications seems to be to save the conclusion—recommendation, action plan, sales pitch—for the end. Our writing technique, however, reverses that process.

Step One. Make a succinct, one-, two-, or three-line statement of your message; the bottom line of your presentation.

By the time you're ready to start writing you should be able to do this fairly easily. If you can't, the chances are you're not ready to write.

This point of departure acts like a mental funnel, channeling your whole thought process into a tightly focused output. It makes for a stronger presentation because it forces you to focus on your *message* rather than your argument.

Case Study: A client of ours, a research scientist with a pharmaceutical firm, provides an excellent illustration of why this is so important. She came to us to improve her presentation skills following her first experience in presenting to senior business management.

True to the scientific method in which background and data precede the conclusion, our scientist launched into an hour's worth of data related to her projects. After about three minutes, the president of the company slammed his hand on the conference table and demanded, "Do we have a new drug here, or *don't* we?"

For him, this was the bottom line. If the answer was *yes*, then he wanted to hear the details; if it was *no*, the details were irrelevant. If it was *maybe*, he could decide, but without knowing the point of the message, a lengthy exposition was unacceptable.

The principle illustrated by this example is true even when it's not a go/no-go situation, as in the preceding case study. Look at it from a listener's point of view: When you know where an argument is leading, you can judge how well the points substantiate the conclusion as the argument unfolds.

In a sense, the facts that make up the argument are just packaging; they usually won't be remembered.

Another thing to consider is that in many informal presentation situations (in the hall, in the elevator) you may be cut off at any moment. Even in formal meetings you never know what key figure may have to leave early. So, whatever the circumstance, give them your message early.

Where to start. Begin. Grab a pad and a pencil; you're ready to start creating your presentation. First state your conclusion, your recommendation, and your action plan. Most often this should take the form of a direct call for action.

- "Lease a car from us. It will give you convenience, flexibility, and reliability."
- "I recommend that we reorganize our materials supply system and keep this plant open."
- "My committee's recommendation is that the management invest four-point-seven million dollars in this new line of business. We'd like your approval."

What's *your* conclusion? Write it down. Say it out loud. How does it sound to you? Make it clear and strong. You're off and running. Once your conclusion is set, the rest of your presentation should fall into place.

Step Two. List the selling points that support your conclusion.

These two elements—your *conclusion* and *action plan* and your list of *selling points*—form the backbone of your presentation. Here's how it works:

Conceptually, we divide presentations into three sections:

- Beginning
- Middle
- End

in which you:
- Tell 'em what you're gonna tell 'em
- Tell 'em
- Tell 'em what you told 'em

The beginning and ending essentially mirror each other, stating your conclusion and briefly summarizing the supporting material. The middle, the body of the presentation, consists of discussing that material in detail.

From:

PAY YOURSELF WHAT YOU'RE WORTH: HOW TO MAKE TERRIFIC MONEY IN DIRECT SALES
by Shirley Hutton and Constance deSwaan

Motivation and Goals

Don Bosson, a top division manager based in Joliet, Illinois and number one in the Fuller Brush company, is the quintessential committed salesman with strong values and valuable ideas about how to succeed in sales. He's been with the Fuller Brush company for nearly thirty years after a brief career as a luncheonette manager for W. T. Grant. He found his way to sales serendipitously.

"A friend told me he was selling for Fuller Brush and that it was a great thing to do. I thought I'd take a look at the business," he explained. "Since it was okay with the company for me to go out in the field with my friend. I did, and that clinched it. He was so *bad*—he did *everything* badly—that I thought, if this guy can make money selling door-to-door, so can I. As it turned out, I joined the company and he quit two months later."

Don excelled at sales and was promoted to field manager after two years, where he mostly recruited dealers. "At that time, twenty-four years ago, we just looked for men who wanted full-time sales jobs. It was company policy. Now that's all changed. We have mostly part-timers, and both men and women."

Over the years, he moved up to the top slot with Fuller Brush. What does he have that's special? How did he do it? What keeps him motivated? "It takes drive and desire. That's the start. You have to want to excel," he said. "When you excel, you think in terms of being a leader, not a follower. And if you want to be a leader, you'll be willing to put the effort forward that's good old-fashioned drive, to compete and be number one," he told me.

Don firmly believes that being a self-starter is "a must" in direct sales. However, many people will disagree with him. Though it's an asset to be a self-starter, many are not. They get their "push" through motivation by talking to or learning from others. Don felt differently and it worked for him. He advises. "Don't wait for someone to show you how to do anything. Just go and do it! Learn from your mistakes, but do it. Then do your best. It doesn't matter if you want the excitement that comes from the money or moving ahead. Take a chance on yourself."

These days, he's at his office at five-thirty or six in the morning, often putting in an eleven- or twelve-hour day. Don has made a lifetime commitment to his career, getting satisfaction from his achievements while still setting and meeting new goals.

Don and other outstanding direct sellers share an understanding of the qualities it takes to achieve: persistence, energy, enthusiasm, goal-setting, and being self-starting. No one has actually come up with a formula describing the ideally successful salesperson. The formula will always vary because each one of us is unique—not only in terms of our strengths and weaknesses, but because of timing, location, and what we want. Also, we all don't aspire to being number one or number ten (or even number one hundred) in a company.

But *why* we want to achieve is another matter—and an individual one. Many of us need and crave recognition, and approval. Others are content with the more tangible rewards—high income, jewelry, cars, overseas trips—and might even shy away from public attention. Still others labor long and hard working for work's sake—they're intimately involved in being productive, needing to accomplish as much as they can in a lifetime. And yet others appreciate and enjoy dollops of each—a little recognition, some money, the pleasure of spending a day doing what one *likes*.

The day you sign up with a direct sales company, you're automatically an enterpreneur. This means you are on your own, running your own "shop" in the manner that suits you best. It will operate by your own set of rules and goal-setting strategies, and of course there'll be changes to deal with and information to decipher. Each day will call for *effort* to keep going, especially when things look confusing or bleak. When you're an entrepreneur, you clock in and out at your chosen hours and your company operates almost entirely on *your own steam*! No boss will check up on you, there's no traveling to an office, and there's no gauranteed check on Fridays. The company you build at your desk reflects who you are and how you think. You decide the limits and how much money you'll earn. You've got to be *motivated*!

When you're an entrepreneur, you'll be taking a number of risks. Risk taking may reward you with *success* when your efforts pay off. But taking risks can also bring rejection, teasing, and discouragement. In tougher times, you must call on your stronger self, shrug off negativity, and believe you're worthy and that what you're doing is worthwhile. I bring this point up again because it's so critical to winning in sales—you've got to roll with the punches and be guided by the force of your high *self-esteem*!

Surprisingly, many people think their self-esteem is *lower* than it is. I've listened to thousands of stories over the years of successful women and men who joined the sale business originally believing they'd fail. Barbara Hammond, the Home Interiors vice president mentioned earlier, told me, "Sometimes I meet women who've signed up with us and I discover that we are the *only ones* to have ever encouraged them to achieve something for themselves," she said. "I found there are so few women who *believe* in themselves, or think they even *have* potential."

From:

CASHING IN ON THE AMERICAN DREAM: HOW TO RETIRE AT 35
by Paul Terhorst

Part 1 of this book reveals the formula that can turn your early retirement dream into a here-and-now reality. The formula has three parts. First, you'll find out how much money you need, how to invest, and how to spend. Next, you'll see how to kick the work habit. Finally, you'll get some ideas about what's out there and how to get started in your new life. Follow the formula and you'll never snooze through lukewarm coffee and bad cognac at your retirement dinner.

The rules you need to follow aren't conventional; neither is retiring after only ten or fifteen years of work. But they're simple rules, far more simple than the rules you've followed up to now. I've set out the rules in big block letters so you won't miss them. The three-part formula in part 1 is:

Do your arithmetic
Do some soul-searching
Do what you want

Part 2 expands on this formula. It tells how to make the formula come alive for you. It presents real-life case studies, tells how to save on taxes, looks at retiring with kids, and suggests a few lifestyle changes that can save hundreds of thousands of dollars. Someone once said it's not ideas that change things, but tactics. Part 2 of this book helps you come up with tactics that fit your style. All that's required on your part is a little imagination.

Later on, when you're 55 or 65, if you want to you can

"unretire" and go back to work. We used to work and then retire. This book suggests you work, then retire, then consider going back to work. Under this plan you devote your middle years to yourself and your family. During those years your mental and physical powers reach their height. You can explore, grow, and invest your time in what's most imporant to you. You can enjoy your children while they're still at home. Later, after you've lived the best years for yourself, you can go back to work if you want to. The choice will be up to you.

Pro athletes never plan forty-year careers. Martina Navratilova, Fernando Valenzuela, and Magic Johnson know their playing years are numbered. My work life lasted twelve years. To me, twelve years seems the minimum for a solid, proper career. But for football players, twelve years is the brilliant career of a superstar. Bob Griese, Herschel Walker, and Walter Payton may play twelve years. But most athletes burn out before they ever hit their Thirties Crisis. They may continue to dream of a chance to play in a Super Bowl, haggle over one more contract, or enjoy another headline. But their bodies scream at them to quit.

A tackle graduates from Ohio State and gets a signing bonus from the Raiders. For two years he draws a six-figure salary to play preseason games, beat up on special teams, and learn the playbook. In his third year he begins to start. Al Davis connects the name with the face, the fans and press talk about his quickness, and opposing players respect his talent. Our man plays three or four more years. During that period his salary doubles and then doubles again. He also makes big money on promotions and endorsements. But the travel, late nights, long workouts, mental strain, and injuries slow him by a fraction of a second. He begins to dread that inevitable Sunday when a younger player starts in his place. A season later he's washed up, as useless as a water boy without a pail.

But our man hired an agent to help him make deals, invest, and prepare for retirement. When his playing career ends he can live the rest of his life on interest and dividends from his investments. He may choose to buy a car dealership or open a saloon. But he may also choose to travel, relax on the beach, or organize a Special Olympics for retarded children.

We executives probably think we're smarter than the average jock. Most of us handle our own investments. But who's to tell *us* when to retire? Should we retire in our early 30s, like Sandy Koufax? In our 40s, like Pete Rose? Or in our 60s, like our fathers, grandfathers, and great-grandfathers? If a washed-up Raider can't decide to retire, Al Davis decides for him. Do you want your company to decide for you? Or do you want to step down on your own, with dignity, when you're still young and clearly in command?

This book is the first attempt to do for executives, screenwriters, models, stock jockeys, whiz kids, and mad marketeers what agents like Irving Marks do for highly paid jocks. Start thinking like athletes and you may wind up retiring at the same age they do. And you've got a big advantage. Their legs are shot. You can go back to work if you feel like it.

"A Penny for Your Thoughts,"

Peter said softly.

"Oh!" Torey exclaimed, suddenly aware she had been staring at him. "Well . . . two weeks ago I never dreamed I'd be traveling on the Orient Express, having dinner with a perfect stranger."

A perfect stranger . . . suddenly Angela's words came back to haunt her. Remembering Angela's outrageous suggestion that she have a fling, Torey felt uneasy.

To get her mind off the delicate subject, Torey looked up at Peter and said, "A penny for *your* thoughts."

He turned the full force of his compelling brown gaze on her and said with quiet intensity, "I'd like to spend the night with you."

PAMELA WALLACE
is a professional writer who has written numerous works of fiction, as well as for TV and magazines. Her spirited characters come alive on every page as she weaves a thought-provoking story of true-to-life romance. Ms. Wallace lives in Fresno, California.

Dear Reader,

Silhouette Special Editions are an exciting new line of contemporary romances from Silhouette Books. Special Editions are written specifically for our readers who want a story with heightened romantic tension.

Special Editions have all the elements you've enjoyed in Silhouette Romances and *more*. These stories concentrate on romance in a longer, more realistic and sophisticated way, and they feature greater sensual detail.

I hope you enjoy this book and all the wonderful romances from Silhouette. We welcome any suggestions or comments and invite you to write to us at the address below.

Karen Solem
Editor-in-Chief
Silhouette Books
P.O. Box 769
New York, N. Y. 10019

PAMELA WALLACE
Love With a
Perfect Stranger

Silhouette Special Edition
Published by Silhouette Books New York
America's Publisher of Contemporary Romance

Other Silhouette Books by Pamela Wallace

Come Back, My Love

 SILHOUETTE BOOKS, a Simon & Schuster Division of
GULF & WESTERN CORPORATION
1230 Avenue of the Americas, New York, N.Y. 10020

ISBN: 0-671-53563-3

First Silhouette Books printing December, 1982

10 9 8 7 6 5 4 3 2 1

Map by Ray Lundgren

SILHOUETTE, SILHOUETTE SPECIAL EDITION
and colophon are trademarks of Simon & Schuster.

America's Publisher of Contemporary Romance

Printed in the U.S.A.

Love With a
Perfect Stranger

Chapter One

Torey Jenson stepped out of the gondola onto worn stone steps. For a moment she paused to take one final look at Venice. It was a hot, still June evening. The sun was setting and the water of the Grand Canal was tinted with reddened light. The final, brilliant rays of the sun bathed everything in a golden glimmer. The walls, delicate pinnacles, and balconies of the *palazzi* that rose sheer from the water's edge shone with a special light that radiated into the clear sea air.

But what was especially magical about Venice, Torey thought, was the comparative silence. She knew that just a short distance away was the bustling train station. But here, as the gondolas glided serenely past, all Torey could hear was the dashing of oars, the liquid tinkle of the water, and the occasional cries of the *gondolieri*.

For a fleeting moment Torey felt mesmerized by the beauty and the low, muted sounds. In that moment, she was suffused with an inexpressible happiness, with a profound joy of living. Venice was enchanting and life was wonderful.

Reluctantly, Torey forced herself to turn away and head toward Santa Lucia Station. This was Wednesday evening; by Friday morning she would be back home in San Francisco. And though it would be nice to be home again, she knew that soon she would be eager to return to Venice.

A few minutes later Torey was in the middle of the station, where her baggage had been sent on ahead from her hotel. Arriving passengers, yawning from long train trips, pushed past her, while embarking passengers searched for the right platform. Torey pushed into the surging throng, trying to find her train, the Orient Express.

It had been an act of pure impulse, taking this famous train. Agatha Christie wrote about it. Rich, famous, dangerous people traveled on it. Lady Chatterley's husband took it; so did James Bond. To Torey, it was like something out of a dream, evocative of a bygone era of glamour and elegance. When she'd seen a poster advertising the Venice-Simplon Orient Express with the words, "An adventure in time and space and splendor," she was irresistibly drawn to it. She had quickly decided that the run from Venice to London would be a pleasant break between her buying trip in Venice and the flight home from London. And a perfect way to get on with her new life as a single, unencumbered woman after her recent divorce.

As she made her way through the hurrying people, Torey suddenly saw the train by a far platform. The gleaming black *Wagons-Lits* coaches and British Pullmans, dating from the 1920s, were trimmed in baroque gold filigree. The legend, *Compagnie Internationale Des Wagons-Lits,* was written in bold letters. Porters dressed in the traditional blue-and-gold livery carried luggage onto the train.

Torey's face broke into a huge, childishly gleeful grin. It was exactly as she had hoped it would be— opulent, luxurious, a fantasy on wheels. As she looked at it, Torey almost felt carried back in time to a period half a century earlier, when life was simpler and infinitely more romantic. Steam puffs, mystery, and the aroma of romance seemed to fill the air. . . .

"Torey!"

The high, lilting voice was unmistakable.

Surprised, Torey turned. "Angela! What on earth are you doing here?"

"Seeing you off, of course," Angela Montessori said, laughing gaily as she hurried up to Torey. Like many Northern Italians, Angela was a blue-eyed blonde with honey-colored skin. Nearly as tall as Torey, she had a voluptuous figure and an uninhibited attitude that, like a magnet, drew men to her.

Torey and Angela still made as striking a pair as they had when they were roommates at San Francisco University six years earlier. In contrast to Angela's gold-tinted coloring, Torey had gleaming blue-black hair that fell past her shoulders in thick natural waves. Wispy bangs lightly brushed her straight dark brows, accenting her finest features, her eyes. They were as deep, dark blue as a Norwegian fjord, and fringed

9

with long black lashes. In contrast, her skin was like porcelain, pale and smooth.

The unusual combination of such fair skin, such deep blue eyes, and hair as black as a moonless night, made for a striking effect. Only her short, upturned nose and round face made her look cute rather than classically beautiful.

Thrusting a small basket of fruit into Torey's hands, Angela explained, "I know it's customary to give fruit baskets to people traveling by ship. I hope the custom applies to train journeys also."

"Thank you." Torey smiled, taking the basket. "It was nice of you to come all the way down here."

"As usual I had an ulterior motive," Angela admitted with disarming frankness. "I was dying to see this train. Isn't it quaint? So old-fashioned."

"Isn't it," Torey agreed eagerly. "It's going to be a marvelous trip. I've been so busy this week I've hardly had time to visit with you, much less relax. By the time I catch the plane in London, I'll be thoroughly rested."

"Rested?" Angela's pale blue eyes widened in mock horror. "But how *dull!* This is not a time for rest. It's a time for adventure! It took you long enough to get rid of that *bastardo* husband of yours, but you're finally a free woman!"

"Angela, Mason left *me*," Torey reminded her frankly. The thought of her ex-husband brought a stab of regret for mistakes made, but not for losses sustained. When Mason, a professor at San Francisco University, left her for one of the many pretty young students he'd had affairs with, Torey's pride was badly dented. But her heart wasn't shattered. Her original love for Mason had long since died because of a complete lack of nurturing. The divorce was almost a relief.

But Angela insisted firmly, "No matter, the important thing is you're going to have some fun for a change."

"Angela . . ." Torey began, exasperated. They had been over this subject several times during the last week, as they caught up on one another's lives.

"No." Angela interrupted with an expressive wave of her lovely, slender hands. "Listen to me. You have been hurt by that terrible husband of yours. And so you build a wall around yourself. But you are much too young to lock yourself into a convent. And, besides, the *bastardo* isn't worth it. Meet other men, go out with them—"

"I've dated other men," Torey broke in firmly. "I've had some skirmishes in the battle between the sexes. And you know something? None of it seems worth it. Once I thought I was in love, but I don't believe in love anymore. And I'm definitely not looking for it."

"The way you look, *bella,* love will find *you.*"

"Then it will be disappointed," Torey insisted. "I've had six months of the dating game, putting up with men who are boring or crude or both. I'm through with all that."

"You're not through with it, you're just afraid of it."

"Perhaps," Torey admitted reluctantly. "But I just can't play the game according to today's rules. People don't form lasting relationships any more. There's no *real* intimacy, *emotional* intimacy. People get to know each other's bodies, but they don't know anything of each other's minds and hearts. No one falls in love anymore, they fall in and out of bed. And that isn't for me."

"Don't take life so seriously, Torey. Let yourself go for a change. Have a fling, as you Americans call it," Angela suggested slyly.

Torey sighed, shaking her head. "You're incorrigible."

"I'm simply realistic. We Italians know all about *amore.* Romance, especially when it's fleeting, adds zest to life. It brings color and texture to what is otherwise a drab existence. You have a fine appreciation of art, you should be able to understand that. Don't worry about finding true love so soon. Just let yourself have some fun for a change."

"I think I'll concentrate my energy on my business," Torey said pragmatically.

"So, you want to spend all your time being a businesswoman?" Angela spoke as if she were discussing a social disease.

"And what's wrong with that? *You* devote a good deal of time to earning a living."

"Of course, I have a healthy love of money. But I don't forget that I am a woman. And that I have other needs besides a nice apartment and designer jeans."

Grinning, Torey responded drily. "I see, Doctor. Your prescription is a mad, passionate affair with a perfect stranger."

"*Definitely.* Some of my most pleasant memories

are of brief, stolen moments with men I knew I would never see again. Try it, *bella*. It will do wonders for your complexion. You're looking much too pale and drawn."

Laughing, Torey finished, "I must board the train now. *Ciao, bella.*"

Angela hugged her affectionately, then turned and was quickly swallowed up by the platform bustle.

Torey was about to step onto the train when a commotion nearby stopped her. A short, plump, elderly woman burdened with a large purse and a brightly wrapped package was trying unsuccessfully to control a small dog on a leash. The dog, a nervous, yelping Skye terrier, clearly frightened by the noise and bustle around him, broke free.

Torey saw that the dog, with the woman calling frantically after him, was running straight toward her. Without thinking, she scooped him up in her arms, dropping her basket of fruit in the process.

"Oh, thank you, my dear," the woman said in an aristocratic English accent as she hurried up to Torey. Turning to the dog, she said reproachfully, "Winston, you wretched, disobedient little beggar! You made this nice young woman drop her parcel."

"That's quite all right," Torey said, laughing and scratching the dog's ear reassuringly. She bent carefully to pick up her basket while maintaining a firm hold on the now-quiet dog. "You've obviously got a great deal to handle, why don't you let me carry him to your compartment?"

"Why thank you, my dear, I would appreciate that. He'll calm down there. It's just all these people who are making him nervous. Unfortunately, Winston tends to be rather neurotic, like most of the people I know nowadays."

Torey smiled. The woman was endearing in a dithery sort of way, with her bright, youthful hazel eyes and flustered manner.

As they made their way down the narrow aisle, she continued her nonstop monologue, "I could have handled things except that at the last minute a friend insisted on giving me this going-away gift, which is where I imagine you got that lovely basket of fruit. Friends are well-meaning but sometimes they don't realize that one has enough to deal with on a trip without added encumbrances. And I was so eager to get on board to see if the train has changed at all. I traveled on it during the 1930s, you see, and this is rather in the nature of a sentimental journey for me. Dust off old memories, that sort of thing." She stopped at a compartment. "Ah, here we are."

"Where would you like me to put Winston?" Torey asked politely.

"On the seat here," the woman said, motioning behind her. "He'll be quiet as a lamb with no one else around to distract him." The woman went on dreamily as she surveyed the compartment. "It's just as I remember, so opulent and sinfully comfortable. And it was just this kind of evening too. Later there was a thin sliver of moon shining over the countryside. A promise of a moon . . ." Her voice trailed off and her soft eyes misted slightly.

"Well, I must be finding my compartment," Torey said gently.

"Of course, my dear." The woman smiled, recovering from her reverie. "Are you traveling alone?"

"Yes."

"And I imagine this is your first trip on the Orient Express?"

Torey nodded. She was anxious to get to her compartment but she didn't want to be rude; the woman obviously wanted to talk.

The woman looked at her carefully, and something in the shrewd way her pale eyes examined her made Torey think she wasn't quite the dithery old lady she appeared.

"I'm sorry if I went on a bit a moment ago, but I was remembering a particular night." Her voice softened and she smiled at Torey. "I would wish such a night for you, filled with romance and the promise of much more." Then she squeezed Torey's hand and said briskly, "Thank you again, my dear, for rescuing poor silly Winston. And I hope we run into each other again on the train. I'm Elizabeth Eaton."

"Victoria Jenson. Well, goodbye then," she said and stepped back into the aisle, the door closing behind her. She shook her head ruefully at the bizarre conversation. Well, she thought, what would a trip on the Orient Express be without colorful strangers?

Her single-berth compartment turned out to be small but beautifully decorated with polished wood and gleaming brass. Large windows were shaded in silk moire. A brass reading lamp with a rose silk shade sat on a polished mahogany drop-leaf table by the windows. Beside it was a delicate silver-plated bud vase of white freesias and a heavy brass ashtray.

There were little velvet pillows and, after a moment's confusion, Torey finally realized they must be to hold jewelry at night.

The seat was richly upholstered in a flame-stitch tapestry, and crisp white slipcovers protected the headrests. Marquetry panels on the walls featured brilliantly colored flowers in Art Deco designs and coats of arms. In the center of one wall was a small beveled-glass mirror in a gold frame.

Dropping her purse and the basket of fruit on the seat, Torey sat down and relaxed against the comfortable cushions. As she sat there, she glanced out the window and suddenly the old lady's words came back to her: "I would wish such a night for you. . . ."

Torey's thoughts were abruptly interrupted by an aging, white-haired porter who entered through the door she had left open. Thick, white terry towels were draped over his arm.

"Pardon, *mademoiselle,* I bring you fresh towels," he explained in a thick French accent. Hanging the towels carefully in the tiny lavatory, he turned and continued easily. "My name is Alfonse. I will be your cabin attendant. If you need me, simply press this call button." He pointed to a small button. "I can telephone the kitchen or the bar for room service, if you wish."

"Thank you, Alfonse. That sounds marvelous."

Smiling, Alfonse responded, "We wish our guests to feel thoroughly pampered, as they were when the Orient Express ran during la Belle Epoque."

"Well, the idea of being pampered is definitely appealing," Torey said with an impish grin. "Tell me, how do I open the windows if I want some fresh air?"

Alfonse showed her how to work the brass levers that opened the windows. "But much of the trip will be through cool mountains and the heat will be on," he cautioned.

"What is that door, by the way?" Torey asked, pointing to a door in the center of the wall opposite the seat.

"That door connects to the next cabin, *mademoiselle*. In the old days, often the very rich would book two cabins so that one could be a bedroom and the other a sitting room, especially on the long journey to Istanbul. The door is bolted on each side so you need not worry about someone entering without your permission."

"I see."

"And you will find there is only a washbasin in the lavatory, *mademoiselle*. The toilets are at the end of the corridors. Unfortunately, there are no showers."

Alfonse looked as if it pained him deeply to admit the Orient Express might be lacking in anything. Glancing at his watch, he finished, "I must go now. We depart momentarily."

Seconds after he left, a whistle blew shrilly. There was a long, melancholy cry from the engine, a sudden jerk, and then the long platform slid past as the Orient Express departed. Looking out the window, Torey watched as the train moved west along the great causeway which connects Venice with the mainland. Quickly, the twinkling lights of Venice were left behind. They passed buildings of spaghetti-colored stucco with red-tile roofs covered by flocks of pigeons and swallows. Then came the industrial flatlands, crisscrossed with black sewer troughs, and dotted with

17

refineries and factories spewing smoke into the clear evening air.

Finally, all Torey could make out in the darkening countryside were vague, shadowy shapes.

As the train moved rapidly through the night, Torey felt she was leaving behind her everyday life. It was as if she were entering another world, one of fantasy and luxury. Safe in the cocoon of her small compartment, she felt thoroughly relaxed and happy, and excited in a pleasant, expectant way. For a day and a night, she would be protected from the cares of the world by the doting ministrations of Alfonse and the unparalleled comforts of the Orient Express.

Suddenly, Torey caught the muffled sounds of someone moving around in the cabin next to hers. Through the connecting door came the unmistakable bump of a suitcase being firmly set down on the floor. Footsteps moved back and forth heavily, then stopped. Idly, Torey wondered who might be in the connecting compartment. It could be anyone, she knew, judging from the train's colorful history. Kings, emperors, tycoons, and spies had traveled on this train.

But Torey's curiosity about her fellow traveler was fleeting. She had learned to be cautious about whom she became friendly with while traveling, for obvious reasons. She had enjoyed meeting Elizabeth Eaton—and Winston—but she knew she needed this quiet, private time to collect herself. Once back in San Francisco, her life would become very hectic again.

Torey opened her overnight case and began unpacking. Taking out what little make-up she used, she set it on the marble washstand in the tiny lavatory. It was a delightful little alcove, brightened by a stained glass window done in vivid tones of orange and gold. The floor was inlaid wood.

Turning back to the cabin, Torey opened the small suitcase that was the only other luggage she had directed to be left in her compartment. As she unpacked, she heard the door next to hers open and close. The person next door had left, she realized, probably to go to dinner. When she booked this trip, Torey was assured that dinner would be prepared by the great chefs of the Hotel Cipriano in Venice. Now, as her stomach rumbled slightly, reminding her that she hadn't eaten since a hurried, early lunch, she looked forward to dining. Tonight, she decided, she would indulge herself shamelessly.

But first, a drink would be nice. A glass of white wine in the bar-salon car sounded extremely pleasant.

Checking her appearance in the mirror, Torey admitted that Angela was right about one thing, anyway: she was looking much too pale lately. She knew it was a result of throwing herself too vigorously into her work, trying to fill the void left by Mason.

Torey washed her face, feeling invigorated by the rush of cool water. Then she lightly brushed some blush over her cheekbones, and quickly brushed her thick, silky hair. Slipping out of the boldly striped cotton sundress she had worn all day, she hung it in the closet. From her suitcase, she took out a form-fitting sheath of blue silk, beguilingly slit up one thigh. Taking off the plain gold chain she had worn all day, she replaced it with a silver chain holding a heart-shaped diamond pendant that had been a gift from her parents for her twenty-first birthday. She added tiny diamond earrings, a gift from herself when her shop began to show a profit.

Slipping out of the bare little leather sandals that were so comfortable for walking through factories and showrooms, Torey put on silver heels with a thin strap that circled her ankles. At five feet eight inches, she was conscious of her height. But she'd learned to appreciate being tall and no longer slumped as she had done as an adolescent.

Surveying what little she could see of herself in the mirror, Torey decided she was satisfied with her transformation from critical buyer to lady of leisure. She grabbed a small silver evening bag that held a mirror and comb, then left the compartment.

In the bar-salon, a pianist was playing softly in a corner. Rich red drapes and upholstery, and subdued lighting from Lalique crystal lamps, gave the carriage a romantic, opulent air. Art Deco mirrors made it seem larger than it actually was. It was packed with well-dressed, happily chatting people. Looking around, Torey finally spotted a small, empty table in a corner. A minute later, she was sitting down, and almost immediately a waiter attended her.

"What may I bring you?" he asked politely.

"Chablis," Torey answered.

Nodding, the man left, returning in less than a minute with a glass of exquisite cut-crystal filled with cold, sparkling white wine.

Torey knew this was a fine vintage. It was smooth, not too sweet, and filled her with a pleasing warmth. She leaned back against the chair, sipped the wine, and tried to make out the song the pianist was playing. It was vaguely familiar, intriguing. . . .

Suddenly it came to her—"Some Enchanted Evening."

Smiling, Torey thought, This is an enchanted evening. The hypnotic murmur of the train, the pleasurable warmth of fine wine, soft music. All that's missing is the proverbial stranger. . . .

"May I join you? There doesn't seem to be another empty chair."

Startled, Torey looked up to meet the most compelling brown eyes she had ever seen. They were flecked with gold, ringed with a darker, chocolate brown. And the corners crinkled slightly in a friendly, engaging way. Pulling herself away from that riveting gaze wasn't easy.

"Of course," she responded. "Please do. It *is* awfully crowded in here."

As he sat down, Torey quickly took in his entire appearance. He was impeccably dressed in a well-cut tan linen suit with a sky-blue shirt. His features were strong and clean-cut: a straight nose, firm chin, and wide mouth. There was something especially appealing about his mouth. It was turned up slightly now in an expectant half-smile.

He was so tall that he had difficulty folding his long legs under the table. As he did so, he rocked the small table and Torey's evening bag slipped to the floor. Both he and Torey automatically bent down to retrieve it, and their heads bumped slightly. Torey laughed softly as they straightened up.

The man's slight smile became open, engaging, utterly devastating in its effect. It lit his face with a

21

boyish charm that was all the more potent for being seemingly uncalculated. "So much for first impressions," he said with a self-deprecating laugh.

Torey felt herself drawn to this man in a way that had never happened before—at least not with such sudden intensity. Her breath quickened and her pulse raced.

"So, you're American, too," he continued easily in a cultured but definitely American accent. "Somehow, I had the impression just from looking at you that you were European."

His words broke the spell. Feeling foolish and embarrassed, Torey told herself that she'd been watching too many late-night movies where the heroine fell in love at first sight with the handsome stranger. This was just another man. If his smile did strange things to her, it was merely a result of the romantic background—the train, the music, the soft lights.

"I'm from San Francisco," Torey explained, keeping her tone carefully neutral.

"Now I see why I thought you were European. San Francisco women tend to have an unmistakable flair that's very cosmopolitan."

"Do you know the city, as well as its women?" Torey couldn't resist asking. His facile compliment had made her even more wary and her curt tone reflected that wariness.

"Well enough. I live in Los Angeles, the city that San Franciscans love to hate. I fly up when I get desperate for that delicious sourdough bread." Then, clearly sensing what was bothering Torey, he continued with disarming directness. "This isn't a pickup, though I confess I wasn't unhappy that the only available chair was at the table of a beautiful girl."

With deceptive ease he had countered her unspoken but obvious cautiousness.

Before Torey could reply, the waiter appeared.

"I'll have the same," the stranger ordered with a swift glance at Torey's half-empty glass.

A moment earlier Torey had felt as if she could look into his brown eyes forever. Now, conversely, she couldn't quite meet their penetrating gaze.

Looking down at her glass, she said slowly, "I'm sorry if I seemed unfriendly."

"Don't be silly. After all, you can't be too careful on the Orient Express. We're traveling on the same train that once carried crown princes, demimondaines, and diplomatic couriers with valises handcuffed to their wrists. I might very well be a spy. I understand that you have to consider the implications of a conversation with a possibly dangerous stranger."

He was grinning openly now, teasing her in a mocking yet not unkind way.

Looking directly at him once more, Torey guessed that he was in his early thirties, though he had the sophistication and confidence of an older man. She suspected that he was quite experienced. Certainly he was far more at ease in this encounter than she was. He made her feel as if she were fifteen again, with that awful awkwardness that young girls feel around young men. She didn't know what to say or do; sophisticated flirtation wasn't something she'd ever been especially good at.

This is ridiculous, she finally told herself firmly. After all, I'm a twenty-seven-year-old divorced woman who has traveled a great deal and who knows more than a little of the world. Even if he is just looking for an easy pickup, I can deal with that.

Regaining the composure that had abandoned her so abruptly earlier, she replied, "It's just that I was lost in thought when you came. You startled me," she admitted.

As the waiter set down a glass of wine in front of the stranger, the man thanked him and picked it up. His hands were especially attractive, Torey couldn't help noticing, with long, sensitive fingers like those of a pianist or a surgeon.

"I have to admit that I was looking for you. I saw you outside on the platform before we departed. I watched you catch that little dog for the old lady. You seemed so charmingly unconcerned with how you looked, dropping everything to catch him."

Torey felt herself blush furiously. She wondered now exactly how she *had* looked. She suspected that she had appeared ridiculous. Trying to regain her composure, she said, "Do you know, that dog's name is Winston."

"Winston?"

"And the woman is Elizabeth Eaton. Somehow, it struck me as appropriate that she would name him that."

"And what else did you learn about her so quickly?" he asked, smiling.

"Well, she told me about the last time she traveled on this train. I got the distinct impression that she—" Torey stopped abruptly. Somehow, she didn't want to get into that story.

In the silence, the man gave her a direct, definitely

interested look. "I stood at the door of this car watching you for a minute before I approached you. You were obviously far away. There was a distant look in those remarkable blue eyes. It was *very* intriguing."

"I was trying to remember the words to that song."

"'Some Enchanted Evening.' It's nice, isn't it? I grew up with the Beatles and the Stones, but for some reason I like old songs like that. My favorite is that song from *Casablanca*. What's it called?"

"'As Time Goes By.'"

"Yes, that's it. Every time I hear it I picture Humphrey Bogart and Ingrid Bergman saying good-bye in all that swirling fog. Actually, they probably both immediately headed for their dressing rooms," he finished wryly.

Torey returned his smile. She felt her guard relaxing but told herself it was just the mellowing influence of the wine. Despite Angela's urging, she wasn't about to get involved with a romantic stranger on an over-night trip. She finished the last sip of wine in her glass.

"I'm sorry, but I do have to go now," she said, glancing at her watch. "My dinner reservation's for nine o'clock. It was nice talking with you. Please don't get up," she insisted as he started to rise.

As Torey walked away, she sensed somehow that he was watching her intently. When the door of the bar-salon closed behind her, she breathed a sigh of relief. A tiny voice inside her whispered, "Coward." Yes, she admitted, she was afraid. Afraid of a brown-eyed stranger who brought out feelings in her that were very disturbing.

Well, I probably won't see him again, she told

herself reassuringly. After dinner, I'll go back to my cabin, and tomorrow . . . well, it's a big train. I doubt that we'll run into each other again. And besides, if what he's looking for is just someone to warm his bed for this one night, he won't have any trouble. A man who's that attractive never does.

But she wasn't at all sure if the thought made her feel relieved or disappointed.

Chapter Two

The restaurant car was as sumptuously decorated as the rest of the Orient Express. Brass lamps glowed softly. Ornate wooden marquetry panels covered the walls between velvet-curtained windows. The brocade-draped tables were covered with crisp white damask linens that had the *Wagons-Lit* logo woven into them. And the tables were set with crystal, silver and fine white China. Silver bud vases held miniature white carnations. It was every bit as luxurious as the finest restaurants Torey had eaten in. And somehow, the low rumble of the wheels only made it more special.

The coolly efficient maître d' showed Torey to a table set for two.

"Will *mademoiselle* be dining alone?" he asked politely as Torey sat down in the velvet-covered seat.

"That remains to be seen."

The low, resonant, distinctly masculine voice came from behind Torey but she recognized it immediately.

The stranger, as Torey thought of him, slid into the seat opposite her, while the maître d' looked on in puzzlement. Leaning slightly forward and flashing that dazzling smile that was both impudent and engaging, he whispered to Torey, "The truth is, I *hate* eating alone. So . . ."

The word trailed off suggestively as he cocked one golden brown eyebrow quizzically.

His manner was almost arrogant; yet there was something about the boyishly hopeful look in his eyes that took the edge off that arrogance. Torey sensed that in spite of his confident manner, he wasn't at all sure of her response.

In spite of herself, Torey smiled a slow, indulgent smile. Without taking her eyes off the stranger, she answered the maître d', "No, *mademoiselle* will *not* be dining alone."

The look the stranger gave her out of those beguiling brown eyes was unabashedly grateful.

Picking up her menu, Torey concentrated on making her selection. The stranger did the same, and for several minutes neither said anything. The silence was intensely pleasurable, tinged with a delicious suspense. Somehow, fate—or the stranger himself—had taken matters out of Torey's hands. And this magical evening was proceeding along its own course.

The waiter arrived, took their order, then left, tucking the menus under his arm.

Torey looked up at the stranger once more. "To tell you the truth, I hate eating alone, too."

"I'm glad. When you ran out of the club car, I wasn't sure what to think. It seemed likely that either you found me repulsive or you're simply the kind of woman who requires a bit of persistence. Since I don't like to think I'm repulsive, I decided to try being persistent."

His tone was wryly self-mocking but Torey was convinced that he was aware just exactly how magnetic he was.

"By the way, I'm Peter West."

"Victoria Jenson. But I've always been called Torey."

"I can understand why," he responded in his direct, open manner. "The softer name suits you."

His long, studied appraisal in the bright light of the dining car was frankly appreciative. Torey noticed that he smiled with his eyes as well as his mouth, and there was nothing superficial in the effect. He liked what he saw of Torey and was open in his appreciation. To her chagrin, Torey felt another blush spread across her cheeks. She hadn't blushed so much in years, since the night Mason took her to see an X-rated movie in an effort to "liberate" her from what he called her "repressive upbringing." To Mason's intense anger, she had found the movie silly.

Torey told herself now that it was ridiculous to let this man's mental inventory of her bother her. She was used to frank stares from men on the street, and even bolder appraisals from dates. So there was absolutely no reason why it should be any different with Peter West.

But deep inside her, the same tiny voice that had accused her of cowardice responded irritatingly that perhaps she was so unsettled now because *this* time she found the man as attractive as he found her. Torey was honest enough to accept the truth of this, though it was distinctly unnerving.

The waiter brought the wine Peter ordered, a white varietal, light and faintly fruity. "I visited the village where this is made," Torey said, sipping the wine appreciatively as she eyed the label.

"Oh? What's it like?" Peter asked, interested.

"There's a beautiful old castle that overlooks the town. And vineyards that have been there forever. It's almost too quaint. The Italian tourist board might have created it. All it needs is a sign that says, 'We feature peasants and wine casks.'" Peter chuckled. "But I have to admit I liked it." Torey smiled.

"Well, they do make marvelous wine," Peter said, sipping the pale golden wine slowly.

"Yes," Torey agreed. The wine really was delicious but Torey wasn't sure whether the warmth suffusing her came from the wine or from Peter's penetrating look. If his gaze is this electrifying, what would his touch be like? Torey wondered.

That thought was so fraught with dangerous possibilities that Torey shied away from it immediately.

Suddenly Peter leaned forward and whispered, "I'm not sure, but I think Elizabeth Eaton just winked at me."

Torey turned to look behind her in the direction that Peter indicated. She saw the elderly woman sitting at a distant table, smiling back at her knowingly, as if to say, "I'm glad you're no longer alone."

Turning back to Peter, Torey laughed. "I could explain that but I don't think I will."

"So you're going to be mysterious, eh? Well, I have to admit that's not inappropriate in the setting. But you can at least tell me a little about yourself. Jenson is a Swedish name, isn't it?"

"Yes. My father was Swedish though he eventually became an American citizen."

"I can see you must have gotten your blue eyes and fair skin from him. But that black hair?"

"My mother was Mexican-American," Torey explained. "They made quite a striking pair. He was so fair and she was so dark. She always used to say that they were proof of the old saying that opposites attract. They were so different in every way—he was quiet and methodical, while she had the classic fiery Latin temperament. Whether she hated a thing or loved it, she did it wholeheartedly, without reservation. And she always acted impulsively without thinking first."

"Which of them do you take after?" Peter asked, his tone carefully neutral.

"Both," she said with a bland smile, secretly gratified at the momentary confusion her equivocal answer produced on Peter's face.

But he seemed genuinely interested in her parents. "How on earth did they get together?" he asked after a pause.

"They met in San Francisco when my father was serving at the Swedish Embassy there. My mother always said it was love at first sight, but it took her a while to make him realize it."

"They must have had an interesting relationship."

"Actually, they got along perfectly. To my knowledge, they never had an argument." Peter gave her a skeptical look, but she insisted, "I know, it's amazing. Their families apparently expected it to be a disaster. They had absolutely nothing in common. I asked my mother once how they did it and she just smiled enigmatically."

"From your use of the past tense, I assume they're no longer alive." It was a statement, not a question, and spoken with surprising sensitivity.

"They died in an automobile accident. They were visiting relatives in Sweden. It was four years ago," Torey explained, not really wanting to open that door in her past. Even now the memory of their loss still hurt. At the time the pain had been so profound, so unbearable, that it had propelled her into Mason's arms. That was the only excuse she could find now for a marriage that was so obviously a mistake from the very beginning.

Trying to lighten the conversation, Torey continued smoothly, "I inherited an old Victorian house from them that originally belonged to my maternal great-grandmother. It's on Union Street in San Francisco. A lot of the other old houses had been turned into shops and I decided to do the same. My gift shop is on the ground floor, my workshop is on the second, and I live on the third."

"What do you sell?"

"A wide variety of things. Lace and glassware from Venice, pottery from Mexico, paintings by unknown Bodega Bay artists. Anything I think I can sell, basically."

At that moment the waiter brought a relish tray filled with crisp cauliflower buds and other sliced raw vegetables. In the middle was a small bowl of spicy dip.

As Torey nibbled on an appetizer, Peter said, "I wish we'd run into each other in Venice. How long were you there?"

"Just a week. It was my first buying trip there, actually. And I was visiting a friend of mine, Angela Montessori. I fell in love with Venice immediately."

"I see." He smiled. "Love at first sight. Then you do take after your mother."

"Not so fast," said Torey, enjoying the banter. "Love at first sight with cities, perhaps, but not with people. People are entirely too complicated."

"And a harsh realist besides," Peter teased. "So what was it particularly about the city that charmed you?"

"*Everything.* The exotic little bridges, the archways, the palazzi, the streets of market stalls, and the bustling squares with musicians, minstrels, and sidewalk cafes." Torey stopped to catch her breath, then smiled, aware of how giddy she sounded. "I could go on and on."

"Did you feed the pigeons in San Marco square? That's a duty for every first time visitor."

"Of course. I was the consummate tourist. I was determined not to miss anything, because it will be at least several months before I can afford to return."

"And what did you like best? Don't tell me: the Ponte dei Sospiri—the Bridge of Sighs."

Torey laughed. "I admit I was charmed by it. But what really got to me was the light. The way it played on the filigree stonework of the palazzi and shimmered on the dark green water was enchanting. It was like a glimmer of incessant brightness. For a moment this evening, as I looked at Venice bathed in that radiant light I felt . . . completely happy."

She stopped, suddenly embarrassed. Peter looked at her intently. "I know," he said softly. "I know just how you felt."

The look that passed between them was filled with the intimacy of shared feelings. A moment during which words were superfluous. Suddenly Torey felt close to Peter, as if, in a way, she had always known him.

After a moment he said, "Why did you leave so quickly when I approached you in the bar?" His gold-flecked brown eyes were watching Torey intently, like the tawny eyes of a lion.

Torey decided that by now polite white lies were a social convention that could be dispensed with. "Because I didn't want to be picked up," she answered frankly.

"By me, or by anyone?"

"By anyone. When you approached me I assumed the usual—that you were looking for another notch on your headboard."

Peter laughed. "Touché." Then he went on, "And if I said that I was merely interested in friendly conversation?"

After the briefest hesitation, Torey admitted with a smile, "My ego would be insulted."

"Well, if I said that it would be a lie," Peter responded with equal frankness. "I read once that the average man makes up his mind in about six seconds whether or not he wants to get to know a woman better. I knew well within that time that I wanted to know you."

Things were moving far too quickly and suddenly Torey felt a need to slow them down. Only minutes earlier she had been lost in her own private fantasy. Now this persistent, intriguing, unsettling man had brought her back to the real world of people and relationships and the constant possibility of disappointment and heartbreak.

"Is that one of your more successful lines?" she asked bluntly, determined to deflate him.

"No, my usual line is more to the point," Peter responded amiably. "When I meet a woman I want to take to bed immediately, I say something like, 'I can't help feeling you've never been truly satisfied sexually.'"

"And it works?" Torey asked skeptically.

"Often enough. What usually happens is that the lady ignores me at first. Eventually her curiosity gets the better of her and she asks me exactly what I mean. From then on things are basically . . . inevitable."

Torey smiled. "Then why didn't you use that on me?"

"Because I didn't think it would work. There's something just a little intimidating about you, you know. Your expression. It signals, 'Stop! Don't pass Go. Don't even roll the dice.'"

Torey was a bit taken aback. "Oh? I wasn't aware of that."

"Aware or not, it's there. But if it's intimidating, it's also an irresistible challenge." He leaned forward and looked deeply into Torey's eyes. "So, I'm rolling the dice."

The moment was electric. Peter's brown eyes bore into Torey's blue ones. The message was unmistakable. It was as old as time itself.

Torey's immediate nervous reaction was to make a joke to diffuse the charged atmosphere. She almost said, "Can you at least wait until we've finished dinner?" But one look at Peter and all thought of humor disappeared.

The hum of the wheels, the passing countryside cloaked in darkness, the clink of crystal and silver, and the low murmur of conversation around them faded to a distant background blur. Torey's breath caught in her throat and her heart seemed to stop. In that explosive moment, Torey was no longer so sure of herself or of what lay ahead for her on this strange and wonderful night.

It's just chemistry, Torey told herself pragmatically, trying to regain her self-control. Infatuation, whatever I want to call it. A physical reaction like $E = MC$ squared. For some reason, Peter's molecules set mine spinning. But it's transitory. Nothing more than an illusion. Probably a combination of potent wine and a background that's all romantic fantasy. We don't even know each other, for heaven's sake.

Yet when she looked at him all of her careful pragmatism seemed to fly out the window. It might all be an illusion but it was an extremely seductive one.

Just then the waiter brought their soup, a clear consommé, and the atmosphere changed as sharply as if a curtain were rung down on a stage. As Torey sipped the hot liquid, she considered Peter's words. He was either being wonderfully honest or cleverly manipulative. She had absolutely no idea which.

"You're trying to make up your mind about me, aren't you?" Peter asked, the smile still playing at the corners of his mouth.

Why, he's laughing at me, Torey thought, suddenly infuriated.

In a remarkably short time he had gotten around her carefully structured defenses, and the knowledge definitely nettled her. If he expected her to succumb so easily to his practiced charm, he was due for a disappointment, she decided.

"Let's talk about *you* for a change."

"I'm a spy, of course. Who else would travel on the Orient Express, even if it doesn't originate in Istanbul anymore?" His voice sank to a whisper. "My mission is top-secret, but I warn you, lives and fortunes hang in the balance." His eyes twinkling, he deftly turned the game around. "And you must be a princess traveling incognito on her way to regain her lost throne in some mysterious Balkan country."

Despite her resolve, Torey couldn't resist his teasing. She smiled. "And I shall marry a prince and live happily ever after in a drafty old castle filled with moldy old ghosts and vampires."

Peter chuckled. "That's better. See, you *do* believe in fairy tales. I'm really not out to discover your most guarded secrets, you know. At least, not yet," he finished.

The sexual chemistry between them had been unmistakable for some time now. But Peter's banter made it seem less threatening now. Torey could consider it without feeling so defensive. Her physical response to this attractive man was all too human and understandable, she told herself. She had been alone for several months. In that time she had dated both amorous clients and the blind dates that her cousin, a determined matchmaker, kept arranging.

There was no lack of desire on her part. She was a healthy young woman with a natural interest in sex. But her interest wasn't piqued by casual, meaningless encounters with men she found only mildly attractive.

Peter West, however, was something else entirely. He made her conscious of her femininity, and pleased with it, in a way that Mason, with all his freewheeling attitudes, had never done. Her body responded to him in a disturbing way, as if for once all that mattered was the pure physical need involved. Despite her sophisticated veneer, Torey was inexperienced with this sort of thing and had no idea how to handle it.

"Tell me, what do you do in L.A.?"

"I'm an art consultant with the Hettinger Museum. I'm on an extended buying trip for them right now. In fact, I'll be traveling around Europe for several months looking for acquisitions. But before we get too involved with me, there's something else about you I'd like to know. Are you married?"

The direct question startled Torey. She bristled. "Would it matter?"

He met her look. "Yes, it would."

"I'm divorced," she finally answered.

To Torey's surprise, Peter's response was genuinely sympathetic. "I'm sorry. I imagine that wasn't very pleasant."

Not very pleasant. Torey considered the words as the waiter removed the soup bowls. Unpleasant wasn't exactly the word she would have chosen to describe her marriage and divorce, but it was surprisingly apt. It had been unpleasant watching the slow death of something that had started out with such bright promise and innocent hope, at least on her part.

But Torey had no intention of discussing her marriage with Peter. Determined to change the subject to something less personal, she looked at the food the waiter was setting before them—veal cutlet Milanese, sautéed zucchini and boiled young potatoes. After placing a basket of crisp French rolls on the table, the waiter said, "Enjoy, please," and left.

Torey grinned. "I think it's safe to say I'll enjoy this. It looks marvelous, doesn't it?"

"Yes. I understand the chef is a Venetian, and I have a terrible weakness for Northern Italian cooking."

"Do you always indulge your weaknesses?" Torey couldn't resist asking.

Peter smiled. "Whenever I'm given a chance."

If this were a game of tennis, the score would be "Advantage West," Torey thought, amused in spite of herself. When it came to verbal sparring, Peter was a formidable opponent because he was utterly direct and without pretense. It was a refreshing change from Mason's lies and manipulativeness. Torey realized that she was very vulnerable just then to such a reassuringly straightforward approach.

She decided to make a strategic retreat from the game.

For a few minutes they both ate in silence. The atmosphere was still tinged with a heady sexuality, the effect heightened by the image in her mind of the glamorous Orient Express plunging ahead through the night toward Paris. Nevertheless Torey felt surprisingly comfortable eating quietly with Peter. He didn't make unnecessary conversation, as most of the men she knew did out of nervousness. Sharing delicious food with him while the night-shrouded Italian countryside raced by outside their window seemed somehow natural and easy.

Torey found herself wishing their game of resistance and conquest could continue indefinitely. Peter was that rarity, a man who took the time to play the game of romance, not rushing things. He understood that the prelude was just as important as the main event. But Torey knew that the point of any game is its outcome.

When they finished eating, the waiter cleared the table, then brought dessert.

"Oh, Peter, look. Strawberries in wine," Torey said happily. It was her favorite dessert. Smiling slyly at Peter, she added, "I might almost suspect you bribed the chef to prepare this particular treat."

"Why would I do a thing like that?" Peter asked innocently.

"To get me tipsy, of course, thereby removing my inhibitions."

"I didn't resort to that even as a teenager when I needed all the help I could get. And besides, lovemaking is best when the senses aren't dulled in any way."

Before Torey could reply, he continued, "I like the way you say my name, Torey."

Once again Torey felt her cheeks flush warmly. She could handle his teasing banter much more easily than his quiet—and extremely effective—sincerity. She started to say something, then bit her lip. Sighing, she shook her head hopelessly. He got to her. It was as simple as that. It was useless to pretend otherwise.

The strawberries were cold and fresh and sweet, the wine chilled and light. Torey thoroughly enjoyed every sinful morsel.

The waiter appeared once more and Peter ordered coffee for both of them. When it came a moment later, he leaned back in the seat and looked at Torey directly.

"I don't believe in mixing fine food and serious conversation. But now that dinner's over, there's a great deal more I'd like to know about you."

"Such as?" Torey couldn't keep the wary tone from her voice.

"Ah, the wall comes up again. Don't worry, I'll start out with harmless questions. What do you like to do when you're not working?"

Relieved at the innocent question, Torey responded easily, "I visit local museums, take the ferry to Sausalito, walk in the Muir Woods, watch old movies on TV. Different things. But I especially enjoy art exhibits. I was an art history major in college."

"Why didn't you pursue that as a career?"

"Come now, Peter, you work in the field, you *must* know how hard jobs are to find. Most of the people I knew who majored in art history ended up working as bank tellers or real estate salesmen. I would have been lucky to get a job working in the basement of some museum, cataloguing acquisitions. Eventually, after several years, if I were lucky, I might be promoted to crating art. A gift shop might not sound like much to you, but it does keep me connected in some small way with art. And it has the definite advantage of allowing me to be my own boss."

"You don't like being told what to do?"

"Not any more," Torey answered with a thinly veiled reference to her marriage. Immediately she regretted the slip.

Peter was quick to seize the opportunity to discuss Torey's marriage. "Was your ex-husband the domineering sort?"

Trying to be flip, Torey answered, "He was a professor of psychology. He thought he knew everyone better than they knew themselves and he assumed people should accept his direction. Anyone who disagreed with him was repressed or, at the very least, unenlightened."

"I know the type well. Into the latest fads in pop psychology. I can't imagine you with someone like that."

"I was very young when I met him," Torey said defensively, "just a senior in college. And youth is a good excuse for a multitude of sins." She was determined to end the discussion then and there, but Peter was nothing if not persistent.

"How did you meet him?"

Torey hesitated, then said, "I took one of his classes." She didn't add that Mason had pursued her from the first day of that class and that she had firmly resisted him. He was married, though he insisted that his marriage was empty and meaningless. It wasn't until she had graduated and he was divorced that she consented to go out with him. When her parents died and suddenly she seemed so terribly alone, Mason was there, offering what she thought was love and security.

What an illusion, Torey realized now. What he was actually offering wasn't anything as true as love or as permanent as security.

"You're a million miles away again," Peter observed gently.

"Oh, I'm sorry." She hadn't realized she was being so pensive.

"For a moment you looked terribly hurt."

"That was just my battered pride showing," Torey explained, hoping the half-truth would satisfy Peter. "My husband left me for a very pretty, very young student who looked up to him as a god. He preferred that to being seen as a mere human. Though there was very little feeling left between us at that point, rejection is always hard to take."

She was still trying to sound flip and not managing it very well, she realized. Glib, sophisticated conversation wasn't her thing. Determined once and for all to change the subject, she continued, "It really is my turn now. Tell me about you."

"Everything?" Somehow, Peter managed to make the word sound like a sexual double entendre.

Exasperated, Torey answered curtly, "Why don't you start with your childhood and work your way up from there?"

Laughing, Peter responded, "Okay. But you don't know what you're letting yourself in for. My childhood was very happy and quite boring."

"Were you born in L.A.?"

"Yes, a native, believe it or not. One of the few you'll ever meet. Everyone else in L.A. comes from somewhere else. But my birth certificate actually reads Santa Monica, California."

"Is that where you were raised?"

"No, my parents have always lived in Pacific Palisades. You know, the suburb where President Reagan used to live. The closest hospital is in Santa Monica. My parents' house is near the beach. I grew up your average Southern California beach bum. I was pampered by my mother and my two older sisters, and indulged by my father. He grew up during the Depression and wanted me to have all the things he never had. I'd say my life was so easy that it really wasn't good for me. I coasted through high school, barely opening a book, and I thought surfing was the only truly worthwhile activity in life. Aside from girls, of course."

"What did your parents think about that?"

"My father is a lawyer but he has remarkably liberal attitudes. He saw so many of his friends' and clients' kids get into trouble with drugs and the law. I think he was relieved that I chose such a harmless mania. My mother's different, though. She spoiled me rotten, but she expected things of me. She's French. In fact, she comes from a rather old, aristocratic family in Paris who have always been patrons of the arts. She thought I should be aware there was more to life than waiting for the perfect wave."

"How did your parents meet?"

"It was rather romantic, actually. My father was a pilot during World War II. His plane was shot down near the country estate of my mother's parents. They hid him from the Germans for several months. By the time Paris was liberated and my father could come out of hiding, he and my mother were engaged. After the war, they married and he brought her back to Los Angeles."

Torey smiled. "That *is* a romantic story."

"True," Peter said thoughtfully, "but there were certain repercussions for me, all romance aside. As I said, my mother had a very cultured background and she wasn't about to sit back and watch her only son turn into a cretin. So, when I graduated from high school with vague notions of becoming a 'frat rat' at USC, she packed me off for a visit with her brother, Henri, in Paris. The idea was that I would soak up some culture. And to everyone's surprise, it worked. For the first time in my life my horizons were broadened from beach parties and surfing to museums and galleries. I ended up attending the Sorbonne."

"Obviously, you enjoyed it," Torey suggested.

"I did. I fancied myself an artist at first. I rented a tiny garret to work in because the studio my uncle offered in his house was far too grand. You see, I was convinced that I would have to suffer for my art."

"And?"

"*And* I suffered, to Uncle Henri's enormous amusement," Peter said ruefully. "And finally I accepted the fact that I would never be as good as I wanted to be. And then I stopped painting and started studying other artists. After getting my master's degree in art history, I returned to L.A. and was lucky enough to get a job at the Hettinger Museum."

"Isn't that the place that recently received a huge windfall?" Torey asked, remembering a headline she had seen in a newspaper recently.

"Yes. Oscar Hettinger was an enormously wealthy

businessman. As far as I can see, the one worthwhile thing he did in his life was to leave his entire fortune to the museum he founded some years ago. One hundred and fifty million dollars, all to be spent on art."

"That *is* impressive," Torey responded, shaking her head at the awesome figure.

"It's hard to believe sometimes. Here I am spending several months in Europe, with practically a blank check to make purchases for the museum. Considering my misspent youth, I can't believe I'm so lucky."

What a charmed life he leads, Torey couldn't help thinking as she looked at Peter. A background of wealth and privilege and love, a career that anyone interested in art would kill for, and an engaging charm that made it impossible to resent him for all his advantages.

Peter said softly, "A penny for your thoughts."

"Oh!" Torey ejaculated, suddenly aware she had been staring at him. "Well . . . two weeks ago I never dreamed I'd be traveling on the Orient Express, having dinner with a perfect stranger."

A perfect stranger. Suddenly Angela's words came back to haunt her. Remembering Angela's outrageous suggestion that she have a fling, Torey felt uneasy. Reality was turning out to be too close to what had seemed at the time nothing more than silly conversation.

To get her mind off the delicate subject, Torey looked up at Peter and said, "A penny for *your* thoughts."

For a long moment he was pensive, looking out the window instead of directly at her. This aloofness was unlike him and Torey wondered what was bothering him.

Then he turned the full force of his compelling brown eyes on her and said with quiet intensity, "I'd like to spend the night with you."

Torey was stunned by his directness. She had expected them to reach this point sometime during the evening, but she wasn't quite prepared for it yet. The fact that she was no longer sure in her own mind what she wanted to do, made the situation even more difficult.

Before she could answer, Peter continued in a more relaxed tone, "I just wanted to get that out into the open instead of springing it on you suddenly when I walk you back to your compartment."

His mouth curved in a slight smile, and Torey knew that he was trying to lighten the suddenly potent atmosphere between them. He clearly didn't want her to feel pressured, and she appreciated that.

Returning his smile, Torey said, "Why don't we return to the bar-salon for a drink?"

"Good idea," Peter agreed. He rose and helped her from her seat.

But as they walked back to the bar-salon, Torey was a mass of conflicting emotions. She felt torn as she never had in her life, between what was the safe, sensible thing to do, and the dangerously tempting alternative. Not answering Peter's unspoken, but obviously implied, invitation, was a play for time. However, time was something they had very little of.

Chapter Three

In the bar-salon car, the pianist was still playing softly. Peter and Torey found a small table in a corner and ordered cognac from the same waiter who had served them earlier. Conversation and laughter blended with the soft background music.

As Torey looked out the window at the dark countryside, she asked idly, "I wonder where we are?"

"We've passed Verona and are almost in Milan," Peter answered. "After Milan we'll be going through the twelve-mile Simplon Tunnel. That should be interesting."

"Ah, a long, dark tunnel. Isn't that the point when a shot rings out, the maid faints, and a body is discovered when the lights come back on?" Torey teased.

"Obviously, you've read Agatha Christie," Peter

commented, smiling. "You know, *Murder on the Orient Express* is one of my all-time favorites. That's what gave me the idea to make this trip. When I heard everything was being done as it had been in the '30s when she wrote the book, I couldn't resist. In a way, I thought, I could pretend I was in the middle of her story."

"You must be a romantic adventurer at heart," Torey said, "if you like to see fantasy come alive."

"And so must you," Peter responded meaningfully, "or you'd have taken a plane instead of a slow train."

"No, I'm a realist," Torey insisted. "I no longer see things as I'd like them to be but as they really are. Facing up to reality can be painful, but in the long run it saves a lot of time and wasted emotion."

"So now you go through life a hard-eyed realist," Peter scoffed, "no longer allowing yourself to have illusions."

"Illusions, by their definition, aren't real. I don't intend to be fooled by them again." Torey's tone was harsher than she had intended. She wondered how the conversation had suddenly turned so serious. To cover the self-consciousness she suddenly felt, she took a sip of cognac. It burned slightly in a pleasurable way.

It occurred to her that she knew none of the intimate details of Peter's life, while he was becoming disturbingly knowledgeable about her own. He had a talent for eliciting information from her, even details that she preferred to keep to herself. At the same time, he gave away very little personal information about himself. She didn't even know if he was married.

"Before you continue playing armchair psychoanalyst, it's only fair that I do some probing," she said lightly, but with an undertone of determination.

"Shoot," Peter responded. "My psyche is at your disposal. What would you like to know?"

"Are you married?"

"Do you think I would be pursuing you if I were?" he asked curiously.

"I don't know. That's just the point, you see. I don't really know you at all."

"Well, I'm not married. Never have been, though I came close once."

"What happened?" Torey asked, unable to hide her curiosity.

"That was during my starving artist period. The young lady was very beautiful and very sensible. She married someone older and wealthier."

Peter was trying to make light of it, but Torey sensed that his feelings still ran deep. Why else would he have remained single since then? she asked herself musingly.

"We're entering the outskirts of Milan now," Peter observed, pointing to the scattered lights becoming visible through the window.

Torey suspected he was trying to change the subject, as she had done earlier when he told her frankly that he wanted to sleep with her. But she wasn't about to let him get away with it. "I'm beginning to get a picture of your life," she said wryly. "The footloose and fancy-free bachelor, roaming the world, a girl in every city."

"That sounds wonderful. The only problem is that it doesn't take into account the fact that I spend most of my time in museums, galleries, and auction houses where the women tend to be either ancient and wealthy or middle-aged and devoted to restoring fine art."

"Somehow, I don't believe you lead the life of a monk."

"I didn't say that, exactly," he responded, getting the best of her once more. "Would you like to get out in Milan? We'll only be there for a few minutes, but it might be nice to stretch our legs."

"That does sound nice," Torey agreed. "In fact, there's an Italian magazine I'd like to buy before we leave the country. I meant to get it earlier and forgot."

The train was pulling into the station now. The soft glow of the brass lamps in the car was overwhelmed by the glare of the bright lights in the station.

"I'll have to stop at my compartment to get my purse," Torey said. "This evening bag only has nonessentials."

"I'll go with you."

As they reached the door of Torey's compartment a minute later, Torey pulled out her key.

"You're in B5?" Peter asked slowly. There was a curious tone to his voice that intrigued Torey.

"Yes."

"That's interesting," he said. As Torey opened the door, he finished. "You see, I'm next door."

For a moment, Torey paused. Then she continued into her room. Peter leaned on the doorway, his hands in his pockets, his expression studiedly innocent. But Torey knew that the same thought was going through both their minds. While they slept tonight, they would be separated only by a door that could easily be opened. *If* they both chose to do so.

The knowledge brought a flush to her cheeks. She pretended to take a minute to look for her purse to give herself a chance to recover. She told herself sternly, it's absolutely unimportant which compartment he's in. But try as she might, she couldn't escape the intriguing possibilities this new twist brought to mind.

Finally picking up her purse, Torey said, "We'd better hurry. The train won't stop long."

Peter remained standing in the doorway for a moment, watching her shrewdly. As she brushed past him, he said easily, "I heard you moving around in here earlier. I wondered who you might be. It never occurred to me you would turn out to be so wonderful."

The fact that his thoughts had mirrored her own was both uncanny and unsettling. Without responding, Torey moved past him.

The huge Milan station was nearly deserted at that late hour. Modeled on a cathedral, with high, vaulted ceilings, it had balconies with brooding stone eagles.

"Rather a grim place," Peter commented.

"Yes."

It was well past midnight and the man running the newsstand was sleepy-eyed and gruff when Torey paid him for the magazine she quickly selected.

"We may as well get back to the train," Peter said matter-of-factly.

Nodding, Torey accompanied him back inside the Orient Express.

Without thinking, Torey automatically returned to the bar-salon. As she and Peter sat down at the table they had left only minutes earlier, Peter asked, "Would you like another cognac?"

"No, thanks. I've drunk far more than usual tonight. And I'm beginning to feel it."

"Are you getting tipsy?" Peter asked teasingly.

"No." Torey laughed. "But as we walked outside I felt a bit wobbly."

The train whistle blew suddenly and a moment later the train began to move. In a matter of seconds, the bright lights of the station were gone and the atmosphere inside the train became once more subdued and romantic.

When the waiter appeared, Peter said, "Nothing, thanks," and the man left.

Their banter had been surprisingly easy and casual earlier, Torey thought. Now, as she thought of retiring to her compartment, she felt awkward with Peter.

Obviously trying to make reassuring small-talk, Peter asked, "Are you going all the way to London?"

"Yes. I'll catch a flight there for San Francisco. And you?"

"I get off in Paris. I have some work to do there and I want to visit my uncle."

"Oh." Torey's voice was small, disappointed. They had even less time together than she had imagined. She finished tiredly. "It's awfully late and I've had a long day. I think I'll retire now."

"I'll see you to your door. After all, it's on the way."

The train was quiet now as they made their way

back to their car. Most people had retired, and the only noise now was the hum of the wheels on the rails.

When they reached her door, Torey pulled her key out of her purse once more. Peter leaned against the wall, his hands in his pockets, his attitude casual. Torey opened her door, then turned back to Peter.

"Thank you for a lovely evening," she said, trying unsuccessfully to keep the nervousness out of her voice. She knew that in their game of seduction the next move was up to Peter. And she had absolutely no idea what he would do.

"May I ask you something personal?" he said unexpectedly.

"That depends on the question. You can ask anything you like, but I may not answer."

"Fair enough. Are you resisting me because of your husband? I don't know how long you've been divorced," Peter explained simply. "Are you still in love with him?"

Whatever Torey had expected, it wasn't this. None of the men she had dated since her divorce had seemed concerned about her emotional state. Though it was a very personal question, she didn't mind answering.

"No, he doesn't matter to me now. It bothers me a lot that I failed at something as important as marriage. But I don't wish I were still with him."

"From what you've said, it was his failure, not yours."

"Unfortunately, I think I have to share the responsibility for what happened. If nothing else, I chose the wrong person. That doesn't show tremendous judgment. But aside from the self-doubts that has left me with, I'm over it now. Whatever is going on with you and me isn't affected by him. It's strictly between the two of us."

"Are you telling me, then, that I may kiss you?" Peter asked abruptly.

"Why, no, I—"

"Because I'm going to."

He pulled her toward him gently but firmly, his arms circling her back. He bent his head and his mouth found hers. Without thinking, Torey slid her arms around his neck, meeting him eagerly. The question that had hovered at the back of her mind all night was finally answered—what was it like to touch him? It was bliss. It was even more wonderful than she had imagined. Her body seemed to melt, become lighter than air, almost unreal. She couldn't think, couldn't move, was utterly incapable of resisting him.

There was desire, passion, all the things she had missed with Mason by the end of their marriage, all the intense, profound feelings that she knew existed somewhere but couldn't find with the other men she dated. Her suspicion that Peter would be heaven to kiss was confirmed in one blinding moment. The confirmation was so sudden, so intense, that she reeled under it.

There was nothing in the world but the two of them, together. Neither time nor place had any reality because the train enveloped them in its own world. It was a dream from which Torey never wanted to awaken.

But dreams always come to an end. Slowly, Peter pulled back. His golden brown eyes looked surprised, shaken. Torey realized with a rush of exultation that he, too, was deeply affected. More so than he'd expected.

For a long moment neither spoke. Torey's level gaze met his, unflinching. She had pulled her arms away and stood apart from him now. She wondered curiously what he would say when he finally spoke.

"Your ex-husband is a fool," he said quietly.

Torey laughed.

Peter continued more seriously. "I think I've made it plain enough how I feel about you, Torey. I wanted you the first moment I saw you. It was all I could do to wait as long as I did before telling you. And now . . . well, I'm going to find it rather difficult to sleep tonight. But I won't pressure you into something you might regret in the morning. I know things are moving very quickly for you. I'll just tell you good night and say that the door will be unbolted on my side."

He didn't reach for her again. With one last lingering glance, he turned and walked the few feet to his own door. Pulling his key out of a pocket, he opened the door and went in, closing it gently behind him.

Torey went into her compartment. Just as she was closing the door, she heard a low click. She knew that the sound was Peter unlocking his side of their connecting door.

So, he was leaving it up to her. It must be *her* decision, made thoughtfully, with an awareness of the reality involved. That was so much more difficult than simply allowing herself to be swept away by the passion he aroused in her. He could have taken her into his compartment and she wouldn't have resisted. But she might very well have regretted it later, when he got off the train in Paris. And he didn't want that.

Whatever happened between them, however brief their relationship, he wanted her to be glad of it.

He was sensitive enough not to take advantage of her, to want her to come to him willingly, knowingly, or not at all.

In a way, Torey thought with a deep sigh of frustration, it's too bad he's so much a gentleman and not more a rogue.

Slowly, Torey took off her jewelry and set it on the small table by the window. Her mind was in turmoil, thought rushing upon thought.

I've never wanted a man so desperately in my life, but it's just a one-night stand, the sort of meaningless encounter I've always resisted. There's no commitment, no future. He'll be in Europe for several months while I'll be working in San Francisco. We couldn't see each other again for a long time, even if we wanted to. . . .

Torey realized that all her life she had been taught to avoid this kind of situation, never to lose herself in pure physical enchantment. It was, normally, too dangerous. Its butterfly-quick effect was, by its very nature, fleeting, and could leave behind sad longing.

Feeling angry and frustrated, Torey turned away from the window and began undressing. Hurriedly, with impatient fingers, she unbuttoned the dress, stepped out of it, and hung it in the tiny closet. Her shoes and the rest of her clothing followed. A moment later, she pulled on a nightgown. For this warm Italian night she had packed a white silk gown that was cut on the bias, with thin straps, and a tiny red silk rose centered in the deep V of the neckline. It had been a casual choice, made for comfort, without thinking that this was obviously a gown made more for love-making than sleeping.

Moving into the tiny lavatory, Torey tied her hair back with a ribbon, then bent over the marble wash-stand and washed the make-up from her face. The water was cool and invigorating. Looking up into the oval mirror, she saw that her eyes were bright, lit by a secret fire that had never been there before. Her cheeks were no longer pale but flushed with excite-ment. Everything about her suggested a startled doe, poised for flight, filled with a rush of adrenaline.

She was no longer tired. Every fiber of her being tingled pleasurably.

In the compartment once more, she glanced at the bed Alfonse had made up in her absence. One corner of the blanket and crisp white linen sheet were turned back invitingly. On the table where she had dropped her jewelry, Torey noticed the book she had taken out of her overnight case earlier. She had planned to read awhile before falling asleep. Now, she knew, she had absolutely no interest in the story, though it was the latest best-selling political thriller.

Torey stood for a moment, lost in thought. She was reminded of her parents, for some obscure reason. Now, with an adult's awareness and experience, she knew what she had sensed as a child and not under-stood. They were deeply in love, both emotionally and physically. Their desire for each other was far stronger than their many differences. It forged a bond between them that overcame all obstacles except death.

Then Torey remembered something her mother had

told her. It was shortly before her parents left on the ill-fated trip to Sweden, and Torey and her mother were discussing the pain and joy of growing older. Her mother had said, "As you grow older, it's the things you didn't do that you regret, not the things you did."

Torey realized now that she would always wonder what it would have been like with Peter.

She was in the throes of the hardest decision of her life. She tried to exert her will upon her desire, but it was hopeless.

The feelings Peter had awakened in her were still so new, so surprising. To think that she could have had such feelings—and all it took to trigger them was his kiss. But that one kiss had shown her that her mind could become totally subservient to her body. That was both frightening and exhilarating.

Moving to the window, Torey gazed out at the passing darkness. In the sky, the moon was a sliver of gold against a starry sky. "A promise of a moon . . ." Vividly, Elizabeth Eaton's words came back to haunt Torey. "I should wish that kind of night for you. . . ."

But it isn't forever, Torey reminded herself forcefully. It's only a promise of love until dawn.

Finally, relinquishing the last thread of self-control, Torey admitted what she had known from the moment Peter kissed her. She wanted him. Even if it was only to be for one night, then that would have to be enough. Their brief time together was like a gift from capricious gods who said "This much you may have, but no more."

Torey had gone into her marriage with her eyes

closed to the obvious problems. She was going into this affair with Peter with her eyes open, facing the hard realities and not hiding from them.

She turned off the lamp, then in one quick, sure movement, unbolted the door. Moving to the bed, she curled up in a corner of it, and waited.

Chapter Four

Though only seconds passed, Torey felt it was much
longer before the door slowly opened. For a moment,
Peter stood in the doorway, hesitating. Torey couldn't
see him very clearly in the darkness, couldn't make
out his expression. What little moonlight was filtering
through the windows revealed that he was wearing a
dark-colored robe that came to his knees. It was
obvious that he wore nothing under it.

Silently, he walked toward her, and the only sound
seemed to her to be the furious beating of her heart.

Peter eased himself onto the bed. One arm reached
across Torey, supporting his weight, while the other
reached out tentatively to touch her cheek. His face
was only inches from hers now and she could see his
expression clearly. She saw the hunger in his eyes and
knew that it was mirrored in her own.

As his fingertip lightly stroked her cheek, he said

huskily, "You've no idea how hard I was listening for the door to open. I could have heard a pin drop."

It was the mildest sort of humor. Yet somehow it relaxed Torey. The corners of her mouth turned up in a slow, provocative smile.

"Are you nervous?" Peter asked gently.

"No," Torey whispered.

She felt many things, not least a delicious sense of suspense. But she was no longer nervous. She wanted this experience, and somehow she was confident that Peter would make it entirely pleasurable. Nevertheless, she was glad that he wasn't rushing it, wasn't immediately caressing her intimately. She had made her decision and had no wish to back off from it now. But she *did* want to ease into things, to feel completely relaxed with him before they began exploring each other's bodies.

"Why did you change your mind about being with me?" Peter asked frankly, his voice low and quiet in the darkness.

Torey hadn't expected him to wonder about that. She had simply assumed he would be relieved that she'd given in. Now, she thought about why she had changed her mind, when all evening she'd been determined to resist him. She could say it was his kiss, but that wasn't entirely true. That kiss had awakened a storm of emotion in her, but that wasn't what had propelled her to this moment.

Haltingly, she explained as much to herself as to Peter, "At first, I assumed if I gave way to you I would burst into flame and go up like straw. Like most properly brought-up young women, I was taught to fear this sort of encounter. I assumed I would end up being quite hurt. But I finally realized that as long as I had no illusions about it and kept the reality of the situation firmly in mind, I needn't be hurt. In fact, for a woman, surrender doesn't have to mean defeat."

Peter laughed softly, a husky, masculine sound that was incredibly pleasant. If they could laugh together, Torey realized at that moment, then everything would be all right.

Peter responded. "I'm not overly religious, but there is one thing I believe strongly. Passion is a sin only when it is joyless. I mean for you to enjoy this as much as I will, Torey. I wouldn't be with you if I thought it was going to be otherwise. And I'll tell you one more thing, Victoria Jenson. If anyone has been conquered tonight, it's *me*."

As he looked down at her intently, his brown eyes shining with barely suppressed desire, Torey felt a rush of exultation. He was hers—for this one night, he was entirely hers. And that was enough.

"Have you ever read John Donne's poems?" Peter asked.

The question startled Torey. "No."

"You should. You'd like him, I think. There's one poem of his that I like particularly. It's called 'Elegie 19: To His Mistris Going to Bed.'" Smiling down at Torey with a mixture of controlled excitement and wry amusement, he continued, "I don't remember the whole thing. But I *do* know a few lines. 'Your gown going off, such beauteous state reveals . . .'"

The fingertip that had been lightly stroking her cheek wandered to her lips, tracing their outline with a feather-light touch. Torey could feel him tremble slightly, and the knowledge that she affected him so deeply made her giddy with power.

His fingertip continued to explore her body, tracing her small, firm chin, then sliding down the curve of her throat. Lightly, he pushed aside the narrow strap of her gown. Then he lowered his head and nuzzled her neck and shoulder, his lips tantalizingly close to her half-bare breasts.

Something had happened to her breath. It seemed caught in her throat as she waited for him to continue. He was proceeding with provocative, maddening slowness, arousing her, teasing every inch of her skin. He had barely begun, yet already Torey felt impatient with desire.

Peter slipped a finger through her other strap and pulled it down slowly. The top of the thin silk gown barely covered her nipples now. Her full, gently rounded breasts rose and fell heavily under his careful scrutiny. Then gently, with both hands, he pulled the gown down to her waist, so that she lay half naked before him.

"'. . . such beauteous state reveals,'" he repeated softly.

The spark that Torey had seen in his eyes earlier was glowing brighter now and she knew that it was an effort for him to continue with such careful deliberation. He caressed her breasts freely, cupping them in his powerful hands, flicking the nipples lightly until they were rigid. Bending down, he nuzzled her neck again, but this time his lips continued down to her breasts. His tongue was warm and moist as it made a slow circle around each nipple.

Torey could no longer lie passively. Reaching up, she pulled awkwardly at his robe, bringing it down over his shoulders. He reached up and took it off in one deft motion so that he was completely naked. Torey could see the outline of his long, hard body. It was lean, taut. The broad chest tapered to a narrow waist and hips, then long, muscular legs.

Torey slid her fingertips down his shoulders and arms, luxuriating in the way his muscled flesh felt.

Peter continued quoting softly, "'License my roving hands, and let them go,/Before, behind, between, above, below . . .'" His hands pulled the silk gown over her hips and tossed it on the floor carelessly. Then his eyes boldly raked her body in one long, slow, provocative gaze. And after a moment, his hands cupped her breasts, holding them gently.

"'How blest am I in this discovering thee . . .'" Peter whispered, his voice growing husky. "'To enter in this bonds is to be free;/Then where my hand is set, my seal shall be.'" His hands slid down to the curve of her waist, moving in tantalizing circles over her flat stomach.

Arching against Peter, Torey whispered, "Please, please . . ."

At her barely audible words, Peter's head came up and he looked at her intently. Then his lips found hers finally and it seemed to her that it had been an eternity since she had last felt them. This time his kisses were quick, hard, fleeting, teasing her with the sweetest kind of torture that left her desperate for more.

She pushed herself against him, in the insistent way a cat does when it wants to be stroked. Above all else she wanted to be close to him, to be part of him, to lose herself in his strength.

Responding, he forced her mouth open, almost brutally now, and his tongue probed it, demandingly, insistently. Then his body moved on top of her as she stretched out beneath him. The movement was both gentle and dominating. At that moment Torey knew she had passed the point of no return. His passion was no longer checked. Though he wouldn't hurt her, he would definitely possess her.

Torey knew a split second of fear at the thought of being possessed by this powerful, passionate man. Then her fear was drowned in a wave of desire so fierce that she was left reeling. Slowly, she wound her arms around his neck, her fingertips playing with the hair that curled softly there. She returned his urgent kisses, lost in her own hunger and need.

Torey couldn't think, couldn't speak, could only react to his expert love-making. Nothing had ever been like this, not the first time with Mason, nor any other time.

By now, both Peter and Torey were breathing heavily. Torey could feel her breasts quiver against his broad chest. It was smooth, muscled, hard against her softness. There was only the most slender thread of control remaining now, and Torey knew that would soon break.

Peter pulled Torey close against him as he moved over onto his side. They lay facing each other, legs and arms entwined, eyes meeting. There was a question in his glance. Torey understood it and answered it immediately, confidently.

"I want you, Peter. I never knew I could want

anyone so much." Her voice was a hoarse whisper but there was no embarrassment or reluctance in it.

Just as she finished, Peter cut off her words with a kiss that seemed to sear her very soul. He was no longer gentle, but insistent. Only the intense passion Torey felt for him kept his kiss from being brutal. She moved against him with a seductive demand, her body arched, eager. Her eyes looked at him through a heavy veil of desire.

His caresses rapidly became more intimate until every inch of her bare flesh burned with desire. She had no secrets from him now. He knew her intimately. The hollow of her throat, the tiny indentation at the base of her back, the soft underside of her breast.

And she knew him. The hard chest, the flat plane of his stomach, the smooth area between his shoulder blades.

Though the compartment was cool, Torey was suffused with a penetrating warmth. She moaned softly. She wasn't aware she had made a sound until Peter looked up at her abruptly. His mouth turned up slowly in a pleased half-smile.

"God, you're lovely! You have no idea how you make me feel." His voice was husky, impassioned.

He kissed her again, and the kiss was so breath-taking that Torey could only hold onto Peter tightly and return it. She was overpowered by him, and knew that he, too, felt overpowered by what was between them. She had suspected they would be good togeth-er, but she hadn't been prepared for *this,* this losing of herself in physical responses that were so intense they were almost animalistic. She wondered if Peter had expected this, or if he, too, was made half-crazy by it.

But her thoughts were immediately dissolved by caresses that were hotly demanding now. Torey no longer held back in any way but offered herself to him freely, completely.

"'Where my hand is set, my seal shall be,'" Peter repeated, running his strong hands down the full length of Torey's body. Torey breathed a long sigh as her body melted under his touch. And when he moved on top of her, his weight pressing her down against the cool linen sheet, she welcomed him. . . .

Afterward, they lay in each other's arms, pressed closely together in the narrow single bed. The movement of the train was only partially responsible for Torey's lingering feeling of dizziness. Her mind slowly stopped spinning as her body gradually relaxed. In three years of marriage, she had never known such fulfillment, such utter contentment. Peter had taken her to a strange, wonderful place where all thought was extinguished, and her only awareness was of a raging fire deep inside that engulfed her in its hot, sweet flames.

That was the reason, she realized now, that her marriage had quickly grown so empty. Mason couldn't bring her to this plateau of pleasure. He didn't care enough to bother arousing her to this fever pitch. Her own passion was enough to make sex enjoyable at first, but the fire was quickly banked by Mason's self-centeredness. When she ventured they would each enjoy their love-making more if he would listen to what she wanted and needed, he said they were each responsible for their own satisfaction. If she wasn't satisfied, it was her fault, not his. After that, Torey didn't even attempt to communicate her feelings to him. And her original ardor rapidly cooled until sex became an obligation.

Without looking at Peter, Torey whispered, "Thank you."

Rising up on one arm, Peter looked down at her, his expression gentle and teasing. "That's my line, lady."

Torey smiled. She felt thoroughly at ease with him, unselfconscious about her naked body. All of it—the love-making and now the quiet closeness—seemed natural and right.

"Your ex-husband must have been clumsy as well as a fool," Peter continued.

"Well, you are certainly neither of those things, Peter. You are graceful and sensitive and . . ." She stopped. What she wanted to add was "and I love you." The thought had come into her mind unbidden, unexpected. It wasn't something she consciously decided. It simply *was*. But as quickly as it came, she repressed it firmly. She wasn't about to complicate things by introducing a subject that was so out of place in the scheme of things. What was between them was passion, not love, she reminded herself forcefully. Hadn't she said only brief hours earlier that she didn't believe in love at first sight?

Remember, she told herself, no illusions.

"And I'm awfully glad there was the promise of a moon tonight," Torey finished instead.

Peter looked at her quizzically. "I don't understand you at all. In fact, you're a lovely enigma." He bent down and kissed her lightly, affectionately. "I'm just glad you decided to travel on the Orient Express."

"And I'm glad you read Agatha Christie," Torey

responded, grinning. "Or I might never have met you."

"I have a confession to make, Torey."

His tone was suddenly so serious that Torey felt a stab of fear. Was he going to tell her he was married, after all. Or engaged? Or otherwise remind her that what they had was nice but she shouldn't forget it was purely temporary?

"What is it?" Torey felt her body tense and withdraw from Peter.

"I'm absolutely starving. How about if we buzz Alfonse and order room service?"

The relief was so overwhelming that Torey burst out laughing. "Terrific!"

"What shall it be? Champagne and eggs? It's not that far from breakfast."

"Sounds marvelous," Torey agreed.

Rising, Peter put on his robe, then moved through the open door into his own compartment. Torey lay back, her hands clasped behind her head, watching him appreciatively. He moved with such grace, in a way that said he was sure of himself. He was handsome, compelling, powerful. Arrogantly male, yet surprisingly gentle and sensitive.

In his compartment, Peter pressed the call button, and a moment later there was a discreet knock at his door. Torey couldn't see what was happening, but she could hear Alfonse's voice.

"Yes, *monsieur?*"

"I'd like a bottle of Dom Perignon and scrambled eggs for two, please."

"Certainly, Monsieur West." Alfonse's tone was neither surprised nor questioning. If he was at all intrigued by the fact that Peter was ordering for two, he didn't let on.

A moment later, Peter returned to the bed. His robe had fallen open slightly, revealing a glimpse of his enticing chest.

Torey had slipped into a powder-blue velour robe, and sat curled up in a corner.

"Alfonse has remarkable control. It sounded as if he didn't bat an eyelash when you ordered for two."

"Considering the history of the Orient Express, I imagine tact is instilled in the porters early on," Peter answered, smiling. "From what Alfonse was telling me earlier, they've seen some pretty wild things on this train."

"I can imagine."

"There was one guy with the rather sinister name of Sir Basil Zaharoff. His origin was uncertain, according to Alfonse, but he apparently made a fortune in munitions during World War I. One night a young woman ran into his cabin, wounded and hysterical. It was her wedding night. She was a Spanish duchess and her groom was insane. He was locked up forever. Sir Basil formed a life-long attachment to the lady. They finally married when she was quite old and her husband had finally died. Sir Basil gave her the casino at Monte Carlo as a wedding present."

"Ah, I like the gentleman's style," Torey commented, grinning.

"Do you, now. Well, I can't quite match *his* gift, but I *can* give you something," Peter responded intriguingly. He returned to his cabin for a moment, then came back with a sketch-pad and pencil. "No, don't move," he ordered as Torey started to rise. "I want to capture you just as you are, delightfully disheveled."

"Oh, Peter, I must look a mess."

But he was already making quick, bold strokes on the paper as his eyes kept flitting from the pad to Torey and back again.

"I keep this with me in case I get a sudden urge to play artist," Peter explained as he continued drawing. "I was always better at drawing than painting."

"Peter, I feel ridiculous."

"You should feel quite serious. I'm capturing you for posterity. Try to imagine how La Giaconda felt when da Vinci was painting her."

Torey smiled broadly. "Is this right?"

"A bit too happy and not quite mysteriously subtle enough. But then I imagine she hadn't just been making love."

"Are you sure? Personally, I always thought her smile was very suggestive."

Peter laughed. "You may be right." Then he signed his name in one bold scrawl across the bottom of the paper and turned the pad around so that Torey could see it.

It was quickly, carelessly done, yet it was an amazing likeness. Peter had captured Torey's soft beauty and much more besides. There was the strength, the independence, and something more now—a womanly awareness that Torey had never seen in her expression before tonight.

"Peter, it's *very* good."

"Thanks." Ripping off the sheet from the pad, he handed it to Torey. "It's yours. So that you'll never forget me."

Torey almost said, "I could never do that," but stopped herself. There was no point in letting him see just how much he had come to mean to her in so short a time. Accepting the drawing, she laid it carefully on the small table by the bed.

"I wish I had something wonderful to give you in return."

"You already have," Peter said soberly.

For a long moment they looked into each other's eyes intently. Torey sensed there was something crucial in the air between them but she wasn't sure what it was. Peter looked as if he wanted to say more. He opened his mouth and began hesitantly, "Torey . . ."

The knock at his door interrupted him. Immediately the charged atmosphere became less electric.

Rising, Peter returned to his cabin and took the tray that Alfonse brought. Pulling out some francs from his robe pocket, he handed them to Alfonse, who responded gratefully, *"Merci, monsieur."*

In a moment the door had closed and Peter had returned to Torey. He deposited the tray on the bed between them. There were two covered dishes of scrambled eggs, two crystal champagne glasses, and a bottle of champagne in a silver bucket filled with ice. With one sure movement, Peter uncorked the champagne, then poured a generous amount into each glass.

Handing Torey a glass, he picked up his own and held it for a moment. "A toast," he said, smiling. "To the Orient Express. I think that for both of us it's been a real adventure."

As he touched Torey's glass with his own, there was a clear, tinkling sound. After the briefest hesitation,

Torey took a long sip. Peter watched her, then he, too, drank some of the golden liquid.

The champagne tickled as it went down, making Torey feel pleasantly silly. And it complemented the creamy scrambled eggs perfectly. Peter ate with gusto, and Torey was amazed at her own appetite. Only minutes earlier she had felt sated and lazy, without the energy to do more than loll against the pillows. Now, she felt wide awake and eager.

When they finished the eggs, they leaned back against the pillows, sipping champagne. Torey lay comfortably in the crook of Peter's arm, utterly content and happy. She was beginning to feel the champagne now. It was surprisingly potent. Combined with the very late hour, it was having a definite effect on her. She felt less and less inhibited as her mind moved in new, sensuous ways. Peter had opened up a whole new world of sensation to her; he had made all her most secret fantasies come true. She knew she would never love this way again.

As she nestled next to Peter, sipping the champagne, she began exploring his body with her free hand. She traced the firm, hard contours of his mouth and chin, then pushed aside his robe and lightly kissed his smooth, hard chest. When they had made love earlier, Peter had taken the initiative and he'd been very much in charge as he led her to realms of unimaginable ecstasy. And it had taken place in the dark where Torey could only half see him.

Now, Torey wanted to seduce him, and to see him clearly while she was doing it. She wanted to catch his every reaction, both emotional and physical, to enjoy every nuance of their love-making. Setting down the empty glass of champagne, she turned to face him. She kissed him lightly, teasingly, nibbling at his lower lip, then pushing her tongue between his lips to explore his mouth. It was warm and moist and tasted of champagne.

Torey pulled one leg up to rest easily against his leg as she continued to explore his body with her hands and her lips. She roamed over him freely while he lay back and abandoned himself to the pleasure of her touch. He had long since set aside his glass.

As Torey explored Peter, she talked softly. She found herself saying things she had never dreamed of saying to any man. She was explicit about what she longed to do to him and what she wanted from him in return. She goaded, teased, demanded.

Peter responded with growing eagerness, sometimes with delighted laughter, sometimes with a deep moan of intense pleasure.

Finally, when he could restrain himself no longer, Peter grabbed her hands and pulled her to him roughly, kissing her deeply and hard. He pulled her onto him, holding her tightly, demandingly. Torey had thought she could go no further than she had done when they made love earlier. Now, she discovered there were even more delights than she had suspected, a hundred ways to please and to be pleased.

Together, she and Peter explored them all as the Orient Express drove headlong into the dark night.

Chapter Five

Torey awoke at dawn. Before she opened her eyes, she was aware of cool linen sheets against her naked skin, and a strange rocking sensation. In that confused state of half-wakefulness she wondered idly why she wasn't wearing her nightgown. Then it all came back to her—where she was, the night, the passion, the ecstasy, and, finally, falling asleep exhausted in Peter's arms.

Opening her eyes, she turned to look at Peter. But he wasn't there. She was alone. It might all have been a particularly vivid dream; there was no evidence now that it had really happened. The connecting door between the two compartments was closed. For a moment Torey wondered if it *had* all been a dream. Then her eyes fell on a sheet of paper lying on the table by the bed. It was the drawing of her that Peter had done.

Torey picked up the drawing and looked at it carefully. It was a remarkable likeness, but what caught her eye was the bold scrawl at the bottom— Peter West. He *had* been here last night. It was no dream. But he was gone now, leaving her to face the morning alone.

Rising, Torey slipped into the nightgown that was lying in a crumpled heap on the floor. Then she looked out the window. The train was passing through the Swiss Jura Mountains now. The low mountains were dappled with light and covered with pine forests, lush pastureland, and deeply cleft and craggy valleys. It was some of the most beautiful scenery Torey had ever seen, yet she was barely aware of it. She was thinking of Peter, wondering why he had left. Obviously, she told herself, he didn't care to spend the night with her, once their love-making was over. Now, in the cold, clear light of dawn, Torey faced reality. It was a one-night stand, nothing more. The romance of the night before had evaporated in the sun's glare. And though Torey couldn't regret it, she found it hard to live with what she had done.

She had made herself *easy,* the worst epithet in the world, she felt at that moment. Of course, Peter would leave once he was satisfied. After all, sex was the only basis for such a brief relationship.

Torey felt tears stinging at the corners of her eyes. Fighting them back, she reminded herself that she was a grown woman, not a child who still believed in fairy tales. Only Prince Charming and Cinderella live happily ever after. Peter hadn't lied to her or led her on. He had given her only what he promised; and if she hoped for more, that was her fault, not his. If she had fancied herself falling in love with him so quickly, it was purely a result of too much champagne and his admittedly magnetic charm.

After all, she thought bitterly, her failed marriage was proof enough of her poor judgment.

Returning to the rumpled bed, Torey lay down, pulling the blankets up to her chin. It's over, she insisted to herself. Face it and put it behind you. You indulged yourself in a way that was thoroughly enjoyable, even if it was just a bit self-destructive. It's childish to cry "foul" now that the fun is over and the piper has to be paid.

But as Torey was gradually lulled back to sleep by the soft clicking of the wheels, she couldn't erase the memory of Peter's burning touch.

When Torey awoke again, it was nearly seven o'clock and bright sunlight poured through the windows. It was a gorgeous day, warm and clear. In a couple of hours, she knew, they would be arriving in Paris. In spite of herself, Torey felt her spirits lift. On a day such as this, it was good to be alive, even if her heart was yearning for something briefly found and irretrievably lost.

Well, rise and shine, she told herself wryly. There's a great deal of France to see today, and I don't intend to miss one square mile of it.

Glancing out the window, she saw that they had passed through Dijon, which meant they were in the Côte d'Or, the source of France's great Burgundian wines. The scenery was severe, with large fields spreading over the hills. There were isolated farms, woods, and pastures. In the distance, Torey caught a brief glimpse of a massive feudal château.

Torey didn't feel particularly hungry but she was determined not to stay in her compartment, pining uselessly. She would go to breakfast. And if, by chance, she ran into Peter, she would be casually friendly.

In the washroom, Torey stripped and gave herself a sponge bath. As the warm water trickled down over her breasts and hips, she tried not to remember how Peter's sensitive hands had explored her body only hours earlier. Then she washed her face, applied make-up sparingly, and brushed her hair until it shone with blue-black highlights.

Back in the compartment, Torey opened the tiny closet and pulled out the clothes she would wear today. First, a high-necked ruffled white blouse with puffed sleeves that stopped at her elbows. Then a full, flowered skirt, mid-calf length, over white boots.

Checking her appearance in the mirror, she saw that she looked rather gypsy-ish this morning, which was fine, since she felt decidedly less prim today than she had felt yesterday.

She packed her bags so she would be prepared to board the ferry at Boulogne. As she grabbed her purse to leave for breakfast in the dining car, she thought about Peter again. It wouldn't be as easy as she was trying to pretend. Just the thought of seeing him, brought a rising panic.

Just be cool, she reminded herself. Smile, be pleasant, but make it clear that you understand what's over is over. He won't want a clinging vine.

Her pep talk was interrupted by a firm knock at the door. Torey knew it would be Alfonse, letting her know that Paris was coming up.

Opening the door, Torey came face to face with Peter.

He stood there nonchalantly, looking absolutely wonderful in a cream-colored, open-neck shirt and tan slacks.

"Good morning, sleepyhead. I thought you'd never get up. I've been waiting for you for half an hour. And I'm absolutely starving. How on earth can you run a business if you keep such self-indulgent hours? By the way, you look *very* beautiful this morning," he finished, kissing the tip of her nose affectionately.

"I thought . . ." Torey stopped, flabbergasted. She simply didn't know what to say.

"Why don't we discuss it on the way to the dining car?" Peter suggested, taking her arm and leading her down the passageway.

Five minutes later they were seated at a table for two, drinking fresh orange juice and buttering piping hot croissants.

Sensing what was on Torey's mind, Peter explained, "Your single bed was meant for one person, not two. Especially not two tall people. After you fell asleep, I decided that we'd both be far more comfortable, if a bit lonelier, if I returned to my own cabin. Then, this morning, I wanted to give you a chance to get yourself together without me in the way. I thought you might feel more at ease getting dressed by yourself."

Torey knew he was right. Both of them simply couldn't fit comfortably into a single bed. And it would have been intensely awkward getting herself together in front of this man whom she knew intimately in only a physical sense. He was, after all, still a stranger really.

"I listened to hear you moving around, then gave you a few minutes before knocking at your door," Peter finished, taking a sip of juice.

"I appreciate your thoughtfulness. Like most women, I would rather be seen *after* I've gotten myself together, and not first thing when I wake up with messy hair and creased skin."

"I'm sure you looked lovely," Peter disagreed. "You certainly did last night when I left you. If that bed had been six inches wider, I would have stayed and chanced embarrassing you this morning."

Torey grinned and replied teasingly, "I'll have to suggest to Alfonse that the Orient Express management look into wider beds."

They had finished the croissants by now, and the waiter took their plates away. A moment later, he returned with *omelettes piperade,* omelettes garnished with tomatoes, peppers, onions, and ham, accompanied by a basket of hot brioches.

"Mmm, I think I'm hungry after all," Torey said happily.

"You've got quite an appetite this morning," Peter commented, smiling at her meaningfully.

Returning his smile, Torey replied, "I do seem to have worked up quite an appetite somehow. Must be the motion of the train."

"Must be," Peter agreed, then they both laughed.

Torey couldn't believe how comfortable she felt with Peter now. Only minutes earlier she had worried about how she would react if she saw him. Now they were eating breakfast and teasing each other as if they did it every morning. And it was all due to Peter. His frank, open attitude dispelled whatever feelings of awkwardness and embarrassment Torey had been feeling. However he felt about their brief affair, he wasn't making her feel cheap, as if she had been used and discarded.

Inwardly, Torey breathed a tremendous sigh of relief. They would have a pleasant time together as the train moved toward Paris. And though it would be painfully hard to leave Peter in Paris, at least she would feel no lingering regret at her behavior.

They would part friends, as well as lovers. And though she knew that Peter would be spending the next several months in Europe, Torey allowed herself the fragile hope that when he returned to Los Angeles, he might call her. As she leaned back and sipped hot coffee, Torey felt that this was, indeed, a glorious day.

As the waiter cleared away their breakfast dishes, Peter suggested, "Why don't we return to my cabin? Alfonse straightened it up earlier. There's going to be some fantastic scenery to look at before we get to Paris."

"Great," Torey agreed happily. "You know, I've never traveled through France before. I've only flown over it."

Peter took her arm and led her back to his cabin. "You've been missing something, then," he responded as they moved down the narrow passageway.

Suddenly, Torey saw Elizabeth Eaton coming toward them, pulling Winston on a leash.

"Good morning," the woman said brightly, her shrewd hazel eyes taking in the proprietary way Peter held Torey's arm.

"Good morning," both Peter and Torey responded together.

"Lovely trip so far, isn't it?" Elizabeth said politely.

"Yes, indeed. Last night was especially pleasant," Torey agreed, giving Peter a sly glance. He smiled at her warmly and his brown eyes twinkled merrily.

"Ah, yes, last night. There was a promise of a moon, wasn't there?" Elizabeth asked, raising one eyebrow quizzically.

"I believe there was," Torey answered, meeting her look.

"Well, I hope you young people have a marvelous day. It looks as if it's going to be really beautiful. Goodbye," she finished.

"Goodbye," Torey said warmly.

Peter looked at her curiously as they entered his compartment. "Somehow I got the feeling there were more than a few double entendres flying around during that conversation," he said as they sat on the seat.

"Maybe," Torey admitted. "But then, what would a trip on the Orient Express be without just a bit of mystery?"

"And romance," Peter added, kissing her lightly.

It was an innocent kiss, and Torey was too satisfied in every way to be as affected by it as she had been before. Still, even that fleeting brushing of the lips stirred something in her. And she knew that being near Peter today without making love to him again would be difficult.

"So tell me about France," Torey said, determined to quell her disturbing thoughts with conversation.

"I love it. It's my second home. I spend almost as much time here as in L.A. because one of the areas the Hettinger Museum specializes in is sixteenth- and seventeenth-century French furniture. When I'm in Europe, I make my uncle's house my base. I enjoy traveling, but I like to have a familiar place to return to."

"Where does your uncle live?"

"In a beautiful, rambling old house on the Ile Saint-Louis, an island in the Seine. He also has the country estate that I mentioned earlier."

"The one where your parents met during the war?"

"Yes. My uncle's head of the family now, so it all belongs to him. Both places are quite old, especially the château. Part of it dates from the twelfth century. When I complain about the plumbing or the lack of central heating, he reminds me that some day it will all belong to me. And then I'll have to deal with the headaches of repairs and maintenance."

"But, Peter, how wonderful. To have something like that that has been passed down through the generations. Things change so rapidly nowadays, it must be very reassuring to know that some things, at least, will stay the same."

"Although I tease Henri about it, the fact is I agree with you, Torey. Los Angeles will always be my primary home, but I appreciate the château and the Paris townhouse. The sense of history that I feel in them is incredible."

"My house is only ninety years old, yet I feel something of that, too," Torey responded fervently. "When I was cleaning it up at first I stripped off the paint and found beautiful wood underneath layers of awful colors. I thought, This must have been how it looked when my great-grandmother lived here. Sometimes I look out the windows on the top floor and see the ocean in the distance and wonder if she watched ships coming into the harbor from those same windows. It makes me feel close to her in a way, though I never knew her."

Peter smiled gently at Torey. "It's nice to know that you understand how I feel. My friends in L.A. tend to think I'm crazy for preferring charm to modern conveniences."

Torey returned his look. She realized they were making the same kind of emotional connection they had made the night before when they talked about the light in Venice. The intimacy they had known when they made love was quite different from this emotional union. In a way, this was even stronger. Knowing someone's body wasn't nearly so difficult and complicated as knowing his heart.

Suddenly, Torey felt very awkward. What was the point of becoming close, she thought, when they would be parting soon?

Sensing Torey's withdrawal, Peter said, "Tell me about your business."

Torey suspected he was just trying to make conversation and wasn't really interested in her small gift shop. But she obligingly answered, "It started out very small. I did everything from buying the merchandise to cleaning the store at night. I have some distant relatives in Mexico, cousins of my mother, who deal in pottery. They allowed me to sell some things on commission instead of having to pay for them up front. That helped a great deal because I started with so little money. Now, I make buying trips to Mexico several times a year, as well as coming to Europe."

"Who watches the store while you're gone?"

"My cousin, Elena. Her mother and mine were sisters. She's older than I am, with four teenage sons and a very demanding husband. Every time I leave, she tells me to stay away as long as possible, because for her working in the shop is like a vacation. It gives her an excuse not to cook and clean."

"Would you like to have children some day?" Peter asked unexpectedly.

"Why . . . yes," Torey answered slowly. This was something she had thought about a good deal, but she felt awkward discussing it with Peter. Mason had refused even to consider the possibility of having children, and it had been a source of constant disappointment to Torey. Since the divorce, she hadn't felt that she would ever want to marry again. And that meant never having children. As independent and self-sufficient as she was, she couldn't imagine having a child outside of marriage.

'I've always thought I would be missing something important if I didn't have children," Torey continued thoughtfully. "But, on the other hand, I definitely want a career. I love running my own business and I could never do as Elena has done, completely subordinating her own needs to those of her husband and children."

"Can't you have both a career and children?"

"Spoken like a typical male," Torey teased. "You have no idea how complicated that is. It would only work if the man was willing to accept a lot of the responsibility for the children. That could be a problem."

"It doesn't have to be. Compromises are always possible."

Torey looked at Peter, wondering if he would be willing to make such compromises. Somehow, she suspected he would find it difficult to curtail his freewheeling lifestyle to help care for children. "I suspect it's easier to talk about compromises than it is to make them," Torey finally said.

Peter laughed. "You're right. Deep inside, I think I've always assumed that when I married my wife would handle the actual drudge work of raising kids."

"*You* are a chauvinist, Peter West."

"Of course. After all, I've spent a lot of time in France, where the word came from in the first place."

Torey smiled, reminding herself that the conversation was all academic anyway. Soon she and Peter would part, perhaps never to see each other again. It didn't matter whether they agreed on such important subjects as raising children.

Then Torey noticed something she hadn't seen before—Peter's suitcases, standing near the door. Presumably, they were packed and ready for his departure in Paris. It was a depressing reminder of how little time remained to them now. Indeed, before she knew it, they were passing through the suburbs of Paris.

Torey realized they would be arriving at Austerlitz Station soon, and there was something she wanted to say before then. But she didn't know how to do it without sounding rather stupid. Finally, she said haltingly, "Peter, I . . . there's something I've been wanting to say to you."

"Yes?" His expression was interested.

Gathering her courage, Torey forged ahead, unable to quite meet his gaze. "I'm glad I met you. I'm glad for . . . what we had last night. You probably think I do that sort of thing all the time . . ."

She felt herself blushing furiously, and knew she was making an awful fool of herself. Before she could decide how on earth to continue, Peter lifted her chin gently with one hand and looked at her intently. His light brown eyes were infinitely kind and understanding. "I don't think you do that sort of thing all the time. Believe it or not, neither do I. And I'm *very* glad we met, too."

He kissed her then, gently but with a stirring of that passion that had completely engulfed both of them during the night. Torey wanted to draw him close to her, to explore his body once more, to give herself up to the sweet oblivion that his caresses could bring.

Instead, she summoned all the control she possessed and slowly pulled back.

The train had arrived at the busy, crowded station now, and stopped.

"I'd better return to my own compartment now," Torey said evenly. She was surprised at how light she was able to keep her voice. Later, she knew, there would be all the time in the world to indulge herself in sadness. Right now, she just wanted to end their affair on a positive, upbeat note.

"Torey . . ." Peter hesitated, his mouth compressing into a rare frown.

For a moment Torey's heart leapt as she thought he

was going to ask for her address and phone number. She couldn't offer it to him, that would be pressing too hard. But if he asked, that was entirely different.

Then, to her intense disappointment, he finished, "Goodbye."

"Goodbye, Peter. Take care."

In a moment she was back in her own cabin, with her back turned to the window. She didn't want to watch Peter walk out of her life.

When someone knocked at her door, Torey opened it quickly, hopefully. But it was only Alfonse.

"As I'm sure you know, *mademoiselle,* we have arrived in Paris. If you would like to step outside, I would remind you that we will only be here for approximately twenty minutes."

"Thank you, Alfonse. But I think I'll stay inside."

"Certainly, *mademoiselle.* We will arrive in Boulogne in about four hours and from there it is but a short trip across the channel to England. Tea will be served this afternoon before we arrive in London."

"Thank you."

Torey closed the door, then sat down heavily on the seat. Clasping her hands behind her head, she closed her eyes and tried to imprint Peter's face on her memory. There were so many things about him that she didn't want to forget. The way his eyes crinkled at the corners when he smiled. The wry way his mouth turned up slightly when he was teasing her. His expression during the throes of passion, when his eyes were hooded with desire.

Torey wanted to remember it all.

Chapter Six

Peter made his way slowly through crowded Austerlitz Station. It was especially busy at this time on a summer morning, as Parisians left on vacation and tourists arrived in the city. Shouldering his way through the teaming mass of travelers, he finally reached the sidewalk outside. Setting down his valise and larger suitcase, he paused for a moment.

The view here was spectacular: the wide Seine curving away, the old houses on the nearby Ile Saint-Louis, the fuzz of trees along the embankment, and on the skyline the towers of Notre Dame on the Ile de la Cité. No matter how many times he had seen it, he never ceased to be impressed with Paris. Seeing it after a long absence brought a rush of especially profound emotion.

But something was wrong this time. Peter looked at the line of waiting taxis, strangely reluctant to hail one. Something held him back. He'd felt it all morning. He knew what it was, but he'd been unwilling to face it.

Torey. With those beguiling blue eyes that looked at him in a way that made him feel more of a man than many far more experienced women had done. With her shy, disarming smile that made him want to wrap his arms around her protectively. With her stubborn independence and determination that made her more than just another pretty girl.

Torey. Last night she was just a woman who had awakened his deepest sexual instincts. This morning she was a face, a voice, a personality he couldn't get out of his thoughts.

"Damn!" Peter muttered under his breath, compressing his mouth into a tight line. Maybe all he'd been looking for last night was a one-night stand. Maybe he felt no need to get involved in a serious relationship right now. But despite all that, the fact was he couldn't walk away from her. He didn't know what more he wanted from her; he only knew that he couldn't let it end here.

Striding to the nearest taxi, he said quickly, "Put my bags in the trunk. I'll be right back."

Without waiting for the driver's reply, he turned and headed back into Austerlitz Station.

Two minutes later, after shoving his way rudely through the crowd, Peter knocked on Torey's door.

"Peter! What on earth . . ." Her expression was stunned, disbelieving.

"I don't want to leave you," he said simply. Then, entering her compartment, he said, "Where's your luggage?"

"There," Torey answered, pointing to the corner. "But . . ."

"Is there more in the baggage compartment?"

"Well, yes, but—"

"Then we'd better ask Alfonse to get it. The train's leaving in three minutes."

"Peter, will you please let me finish a sentence!" Torey said, exasperated. Facing him squarely, her hands on her hips, she finished, "What are you doing here?"

"I told you. I can't leave you. So I've decided that you should get off the train and spend some time with me in Paris."

"*You* decided," Torey flared.

Peter knew she was angry at his peremptory attitude, but there wasn't time for detailed discussions now.

"We've got to hurry—" he began.

But she cut him off curtly. "It may interest you to know, Peter West, that I have plans of my own that I will *not* change on a whim of yours."

It hadn't occurred to him that she might be reluctant to stay. Assessing the situation quickly, he said logically, "There's no reason why your plans can't be changed. Just call Elena and tell her she's going to have a longer vacation. That's all. From what you've said, she won't mind at all."

"Peter—"

"Torey, there isn't time to argue. We have less than three minutes now to get you, me, and your luggage off this train."

"Why should I get off the train to be with you?" Torey asking bluntly. "What are you offering, Peter?

A slightly longer affair in Paris instead of a one-night stand on the train?"

Her voice was calm, her expression carefully neutral. But he knew what it had cost her pride to ask that question. Unfortunately, there wasn't time to go into it.

"I don't know what I'm offering," he finally admitted.

"Then why should I get off with you, disrupt my life for you?"

Peter hesitated. Might as well get right to the point, he decided. There wasn't time for anything else. "Because there's so much more of you I want to know," he answered honestly.

Torey stood utterly still for a moment. Peter felt the awful pressure of the precious seconds ticking away. But he couldn't rush her now. She had a decision to make and he had to let her make it in her own way. He knew very well what was in her mind. They both had so much more to learn about each other, but that journey to knowledge might well end in disillusionment. More time with each other might spoil the fantasy of the night they had shared. They might end up disliking each other and wishing they had let it end at Austerlitz Station.

But on the other hand, they might not.

Peter had been watching Torey's expression carefully. Now he smiled tentatively, engagingly, and said, "How are you at rolling the dice, Torey?"

Torey smiled slowly in understanding. Peter saw the doubt, the fear, leave her face.

"Well . . . I'm not sure. But I'd like to find out."

Peter's tentative smile turned into a huge grin.

There was no time for a kiss or even a quick hug. Grabbing Torey's luggage, and Torey, he pulled her out of the cabin, calling for Alfonse loudly.

When Alfonse appeared, looking startled, Peter explained that they needed the rest of Torey's luggage. Quickly.

"But, *monsieur, mademoiselle*, we are leaving momentarily," Alfonse protested.

"I know. Mademoiselle Jenson has decided to take advantage of the optional stopover. So, move fast, *vite, vite*," Peter ordered, handing Alfonse a wad of francs.

"Mais oui, monsieur," Alfonse responded energetically.

In a matter of seconds, Torey and Peter were standing on the platform. Two minutes later, Alfonse delivered Torey's other luggage. Then the familiar whistle blew. Alfonse stepped back onto the train, with a quick tip of his hat and a heartfelt, *"Au'voir, mademoiselle, monsieur. Merci mille fois. Vois êtes très gentille."*

As the train pulled out, Peter turned to Torey and took her in his arms. "Welcome to Paris, love," he said softly.

Torey's answer was lost in his kiss.

Chapter Seven

$\mathcal{M}$y uncle's townhouse is here, on the Ile Saint-Louis," Peter explained, as the taxi crossed a narrow bridge onto a small island in the Seine.

Torey looked out at a world of tree-shaded quays, aristocratic townhouses and courtyards, sidewalk cafes, and antique shops.

"It's absolutely charming, Peter. It has a sort of sleepy, provincial air."

"It's a self-contained community with its own shops and cafes. Some residents haven't been on the main-land for years."

"I can understand why," Torey replied excitedly as she strained her neck to look out the window.

"It's the most exclusive neighborhood in Paris now. But when the Delacroix first moved here centuries ago it was little more than a cowfield," Peter explained. As the taxi made its way through the perfect symmetry of the checkerboard streets, he continued, "When it was still a field, duels were fought here. One foreigner wrote home, 'There isn't a Frenchman worth his salt who has not slain a man in a duel.'"

"Would *you* fight a duel for a lady, Peter?" Torey asked, grinning impishly.

"Afraid not. Remember, I'm only *half* French."

They passed broad, calm riverbanks, lushly shaded by tall poplars. The island and the water near it were powdered with cottonseed from the trees. The quays were crowded with an assortment of people—fishermen, sunbathers, and gaily scampering children.

"You find all kinds here," Peter continued. "Card players, fishermen, and, of course, *les amoureux.*"

Torey didn't have to ask him to define the last term. Couples strolled hand in hand all around them, stopping to embrace passionately with a total disregard of onlookers. Torey found the ecstatic, unabashed display of love refreshing.

Looking at the surroundings—the gently flowing river, the tiny green island, the colorful inhabitants—Torey said, "It almost seems like a scene from a fairy tale."

"It *is* an unusually charming place," Peter agreed wholeheartedly. "A lot of famous people have been drawn here. Madame Curie lived somewhere around here. And Voltaire lived there," he continued, pointing to a towering old mansion with elaborate wrought-iron balconies. "He lived with his mistress, the Marquise du Chateley. She was married but had an 'understanding' husband. Apparently the couple were famous for their quarrels. It seems the Marquise didn't believe in confining her charms either to her husband or her lover."

"A truly liberated woman," Torey commented slyly.

Shooting her a quick smile, Peter retorted, "Or an insatiable one."

"A typically male view," Torey replied, returning his smile.

"Ah, here we are," Peter said.

The taxi stopped in front of a house that was small only in comparison to the larger mansions surrounding it. After paying the driver, Peter led Torey through a delicate ironwork gate and into a courtyard garden brilliant with a colorful variety of flowers. An ancient well sat in the center, with wisteria hanging over its crumbling sides. The air was scented with lilac and lime blossoms, and filled with the twittering of songbirds. Plants in stone pots sat on the uneven pavement of brown, beige, and light gray.

The house itself opened onto the courtyard with many-paned long windows. The white shutters on the windows were open, letting in the clear, still air.

"Oh, this place is enchanting," Torey breathed softly.

"And so are you," Peter responded, looking at her soberly and squeezing her arm.

Turning to look at Peter, Torey saw the undisguised emotion in his eyes. For a moment, she felt overwhelmed—by Paris, by this charming old house, but most of all by Peter. She knew then that she had made the right decision on the train. No matter what happened to them in the future, there was something here worth pursuing.

Then the front door opened. A plump, elderly woman wearing a black dress and a lace-edged white apron, came out to greet them with outstretched arms.

"Mon petit Pierre," she exclaimed happily, hugging Peter affectionately.

"Elise, you get more beautiful each time I see you," Peter said warmly.

"You mean, there is more of me each time you see me," she laughingly answered in a thick accent. "And who is your lovely friend?"

"Elise Jobert, I'd like you to meet Miss Victoria Jenson. She'll be our guest for a few days."

"Bonjour, Mademoiselle Jenson," Elise said, extending her hand to Torey.

"I'm very pleased to meet you," Torey replied, grateful for the warm welcome.

"But do not stand out here in this hot sun. Come in, come in," Elise urged. "Oh, Peter, your uncle will be so pleased. He has been looking for you all this week," she finished as they came into the entryway.

It was tiled in a blue-and-white mosaic pattern, and the white walls were covered with paintings of Paris.

"Is Henri at home?" Peter asked.

"Yes, but he hasn't come down yet for breakfast. He grows lazy, that one."

"Well, don't wake him. We'll get settled in and perhaps by that time he'll be awake."

"Your room is ready, as always. Would you like me to put Mademoiselle Jenson in the green room?"

"That sounds fine."

The staircase they ascended was of polished oak, the steps covered with a blue carpet. Torey could see little of the house from the entryway. She caught glimpses of white walls covered by paintings, and simple, modern furniture upholstered in white and accented by colorful pillows.

On the second floor, they walked down a wide hallway before stopping at a door. Opening it, Elise said, "I hope you find this room comfortable, Mademoiselle Jenson."

The room was large, with French doors that opened onto a balcony with an ironwork railing. It was furnished with a brass bed, a small table flanked by two chairs, and a desk and chair in the corner. In front of the small green-tiled fireplace was a loveseat upholstered in the same pale green fabric that the drapes and bedspread were made of.

Torey thought the room was much more than comfortable. It was the incarnation of her fantasy of the perfect bedroom.

She said so to Elise, who beamed happily.

"I am so glad you like it. Now, if you will excuse me, I must see to breakfast. Would you like it served in the garden, Peter?"

"Yes, please. But just bring coffee for Torey and me. We've already eaten."

"Well, some croissants and perhaps some fresh fruit will not hurt," Elise insisted as she left.

When Elise had gone, Torey walked over to the French doors, opened them, and stepped out onto the narrow balcony. Below, she could see the garden. In a corner, near a trellis covered with sweet peas, was a round table and four chairs. That, she thought, must be where breakfast would be served.

"What do you think?" Peter asked, walking up to her and putting one arm lightly around her waist.

"I think you're tremendously lucky to live in such a place."

"I think so, too. I'm glad you like it. By the way, my room happens to be directly across the hall."

"Oh? Is that why Elise suggested this particular room for me?"

"She's far too old-fashioned to ever admit it. But I think she's much too French not to have thought of it."

Below, Torey saw Elise enter the garden and spread a bright red tablecloth over the table. Then she returned into the house.

"Is this where all your female guests stay, Peter?" Torey asked, trying to keep her tone light and teasing.

"Since you are the only female guest I have ever invited to stay here, I suppose the answer is yes," Peter replied, kissing her cheek and nuzzling her neck. Then he turned Torey to face him, and lifted her chin with his fingertip. "This is my uncle's house and I wouldn't insult him by inviting a string of girls here. When I asked you to stay with me in Paris, it wasn't a decision that I made lightly."

"Peter . . ." Torey hesitated. There was something that needed to be said; she decided to simply come right out with it. "When the Orient Express comes through Paris next Thursday, I'll be on it. I really can't stay away from my business any longer. And, besides . . ."

"You don't want to overstay your welcome," Peter finished for her tersely.

He was clearly irritated and Torey thought she knew why. He undoubtedly wasn't used to the women in his life telling him when a relationship would end. That had probably always been *his* prerogative, at least since the girl who had rejected him so many years earlier.

"We've been pretty honest with each other up to now," Torey replied evenly. "Let's not stop now. We both know what we have, let's not try to pretend it's anything more. I'm sure that deep inside, you're relieved there'll be no question of how to send me packing without being rude."

This bright, sophisticated reply masked Torey's true feelings. As she said the smart, liberated lines with practiced ease, she realized she had fallen in love. She had sensed it from the very beginning but had fought it, afraid that she was letting herself in for a heartache.

Now, as she looked at Peter standing only inches from her, she longed to admit her love, her fear, her fragile hope. But that was against all the rules in a relationship like this, where the word "love" was never mentioned, no matter how intimate they might become.

Torey had been around enough since her divorce to know that it was possible to go to bed with someone purely out of sexual attraction. But that wasn't how she felt about Peter. She hoped for much more from him than a sexual relationship with no strings attached.

However, she couldn't rush things. She had to play

it Peter's way, honest and open but without commitment. In a way, that cautiousness suited her at the moment. She'd made one youthful mistake with Mason out of ignorance and inexperience. She knew now that she needed to wait, to know herself as well as Peter.

Below them, Elise had come into the garden once more with a large tray filled with dishes.

"Breakfast is about ready. We'd better go now," Peter said. "I hope you're at least a little hungry, because Elise makes the most delicious croissants."

"Actually, I am a little hungry," Torey admitted as they walked down the hallway, then turned and descended the stairs.

"Me, too," Peter said. "And since you're so insistent that we be honest, why don't we admit that neither of us was entirely satisfied by breakfast on the train because we were so nervous about parting."

Torey laughed. "Very well. You're right. Now, tell me more about these croissants. My mouth is watering with expectation."

Before Peter could answer, a door opened and a man came into the hallway. Torey knew immediately that this must be Henri Delacroix. He was tall, like Peter, with slightly darker hair streaked with silver. His eyes were the same light golden brown as his nephew's, with that same mischievous glint. And his smile, as he spotted Torey, was nearly as charming as Peter's.

"Ah, Elise has just told me that we have a guest," he said, walking up to them. After hugging Peter warmly and kissing him quickly on both cheeks, he turned back to Torey. "I must confess, *mademoiselle,* that I did not expect someone so *très jolie*. Your taste, Peter, is improving with age."

"Thank you, Henri," Peter replied, grinning impudently. "Henri Delacroix, this is Victoria Jenson," he finished.

Henri took Torey's hand and kissed it lightly. "Welcome to my home, *mademoiselle*. May I say, you brighten it greatly by your presence."

The Gallic charm was overwhelming. "Thank you," Torey finally managed to respond.

"Before this lecherous uncle of mine tries to sweep you off your feet before my very eyes, let's have breakfast," Peter said. He steered Torey through the open French doors that led into the garden.

But it was Henri who skillfully managed to bypass Peter and take Torey's arm to escort her to the table.

The table was laid for an elaborate breakfast, with plates of croissants, slices of ham, and soft-boiled eggs in small silver cups. There were tiny dishes of butter and jam, and a lovely old silver coffee service.

"Elise has outdone herself, I see," Peter commented. "For *your* benefit, Torey, I suspect."

"She likes to impress guests with her cooking. It is her one vanity," Henri explained, smiling at Torey. "Please try a croissant. They are especially delicious."

Torey bit into the buttery, flaky pastry. It was so flavorful that it made the croissants she had tried back home pale in comparison. "Well, I'm definitely impressed. After a week of this, none of my clothes will fit."

"A week? Are you staying such a short time?" Henri asked, throwing Peter a quick, questioning glance.

"Torey is catching the Orient Express for London when it comes through Thursday," Peter explained.

"I am so sorry your visit will be such a short one, Mademoiselle Jenson," Henri said gallantly as he poured coffee for Torey.

"Please, call me Torey."

"Very well. And I would like you to call me Henri. It will make me feel much less my age than if you call me Monsieur Delacroix. Later, I will take you for a walk down to the quay. When my neighbors see me with a beautiful young woman who calls me by my first name, they will assume I have made a conquest. They will be scandalized and envious, and it will do wonders for my dwindling reputation."

Torey laughed softly. Henri was charming and she couldn't help wondering why he wasn't married. He must have been very attractive when he was younger for he was still a handsome man.

"I had planned to go to the château next week," Henri said to Peter. "Perhaps we could go sooner so that Torey might see it."

"That's a very good idea, Henri. We'll stay in Paris for a few days, then go to the château."

Turning to Torey, Henri explained, "It's a rather drafty old place, and quiet to the point of boredom. Especially in the winter when it rains constantly. But it's quite beautiful right now, with the flowers blooming in the gardens. And this is the perfect time of year to ride through the park that surrounds the house. Do you ride, Torey?"

"Barely," Torey admitted ruefully. "I took some lessons as a child, but there didn't seem to be much time to pursue it as I grew older."

"Well, we shall find a docile mount for you, then. Now, Peter, tell me about this business of yours. I hope you intend to be terribly busy while you're in Paris so that I may have the opportunity to escort Torey."

"I'm sorry to disappoint you, Henri, but I only have some minor business to take care of here. And I plan to take Torey with me for that. She knows a great deal about art and I thought she'd enjoy accompanying me."

"You mean on a buying excursion?" Torey asked.

"Yes, there's a painting the museum is particularly interested in that's available through a local dealer. I thought we'd look at it tomorrow."

"I'd love to," Torey replied enthusiastically.

"This is a Cézanne. One of his earliest works."

"A still life?" Torey asked.

"Why, yes," Peter replied, impressed by her knowledge.

"I prefer his later works, during his Impressionist phase. But his still lifes are interesting, too."

"Do you know a great deal about art?" Henri asked.

"Torey was an art history major in college, too," Peter answered for her.

Henri looked at her with renewed interest. The quick look he shot Peter seemed to say, "So she's not only pretty, but intelligent, too." To Torey, he said, "You must meet a good friend of mine, Margot Fulbert. She has a fine collection of Impressionist works—a Monet, a Van Gogh, a Matisse, among many others."

"A Van Gogh?" Torey responded eagerly. "Oh, I'd

love to see that. He's my favorite. I don't get a chance to see many of his paintings in San Francisco." Suddenly Torey broke into an embarrassed grin. "I'm sorry, I must sound silly. Like a groupie running after a movie star."

"You do not sound at all silly, my dear," Henri said warmly. "Your love of art is to be admired. I will make a point of introducing you to Margot."

A few minutes later when breakfast was over, Peter said, "We'd better begin our sightseeing as soon as possible. Why don't we go for a walk around the island? It isn't very big and we could see most of it this afternoon."

"That sounds marvelous. Henri, will you join us?" Torey asked.

"I would love to, but unfortunately I have a luncheon engagement that will probably last quite late. However, tomorrow I will come with you. As I said, you will do wonders for my reputation."

"I'd better change into something more comfortable," Torey said. "I'll just be a minute, Peter."

"I'll wait here."

As Torey walked back into the cool house out of the warm June sunlight, she felt irrepressibly light and happy. In fact, she felt almost like a princess in a fairy tale. And though she knew the spell of enchantment would end soon, she intended to enjoy every magical moment. Paris, like the Orient Express, was a fantasy. Soon she would be back in the real world of San Francisco, her business, and life without Peter. Until then, she wasn't going to dwell on anything but the pleasure of the moment.

* * *

When Torey had gone, Henri turned to Peter. "She's enchanting, Peter. So lovely and so refreshingly exuberant. How did you meet her?"

"On the train."

"Ah, how romantic. I thought that sort of encounter ended years ago when I was still young."

"Henri, don't read too much into this. In a week, she'll be gone."

"I see. And is that how you want it?" Henri asked, his brown eyes piercing and shrewd.

"Of course," Peter replied, twirling his empty coffee cup. He didn't meet his uncle's look. Then, he continued defensively, "After all, it's a perfect arrangement. No strings attached, no expectations. She doesn't want to get seriously involved and neither do I. I like my life just the way it is."

"Perhaps *she* doesn't want to get involved. She strikes me as a very independent young woman. But are you so sure *you* do not want involvement, Peter?"

"You're the last person who should be asking me about getting serious, Henri. Remember Chantal? You didn't think I should get serious then."

"That was ten years ago. You were too young and did not know yourself so well then. And I don't know what you expected to do with a wife who clearly had neither brains nor character."

"Henri!"

"Ah, Peter, do not get annoyed with me, *s'il te plaît*. I know that you thought the sun rose and set around that girl."

"Well, Chantal and I are just friends now."

"I know that. Let us change the subject."

"Fine."

But the irritated note hadn't gone out of Peter's voice. It bothered him even now to remember his affair with Chantal. He thought back to when he was twenty-three, struggling to become an artist, but enjoying the struggle. When he met Chantal Montand, everything in his life seemed to come together. She was exquisitely beautiful, and from the beginning their affair was deliriously passionate. How lucky he thought himself, to be loved by such a girl. All his friends were envious. As Peter walked around Paris that spring, he felt as if he were walking on air.

Then came the jolting pain. He made the mistake of sharing with Chantal his plans for their future— getting married and living together in the loft studio where he painted. When she told him firmly, but not unkindly, that she had other plans, he was stunned. She admitted that she found him charming, and enjoyed their affair, but that was all it was. And besides, she intended to marry someone wealthy.

Peter felt the loss keenly; but what he felt even more profoundly was the sense of humiliation. He had already told everyone—Henri, his friends, his family—that he was going to marry Chantal. He felt such a fool. He'd thought himself a man of the world, living in Paris, painting, having an affair with a gorgeous creature. Until that moment he'd never realized what a romantic he was.

It was a hard lesson in reality, but one he never forgot.

Now, as he sat quietly at the table with Henri, his expression was sober.

His uncle watched him with tolerant affection. "Your French half is showing, Peter. Your Latin temper is overwhelming your God-given intelligence. The curse of the French is a chronic irritability. I think it springs from our native pride. We are convinced we are more civilized and talented than any other race. On top of that, you have an arrogance that seems to come naturally to Americans. All of which makes it difficult for you to accept even the possibility of failure." As Peter thawed under Henri's good-natured teasing, the older man finished. "This girl has gotten to you, hasn't she?"

"I don't know what you mean," Peter insisted. But he did know. Earlier he had tried to walk away from that train—and Torey—but he couldn't do it. He told himself he was only buying a little more time with her. But he wasn't quite convinced of that.

He'd been with many women, some of them more beautiful than Torey, and some almost as charming as she. But none had found a chink in the armor he'd put on after Chantal. Also, the hard climb in his career had been an excuse not to get too involved. He enjoyed his work, was dedicated to it, and determined to succeed. The field of art was more ruthless than most, and it had taken all of his energy to reach his goal.

This buying trip, in fact, was his first on his own. Before, he'd always been someone else's assistant. Now, he was the head buyer. Suddenly, it occurred to him that perhaps this was why he found himself so wrapped up in Torey. Finally, he had enough time to sit back, relax, and think about his life without the pressure of striving for promotions.

As Peter considered this intriguing new thought, Henri commented, "You've never invited any other girl to stay here. And you've never looked quite so preoccupied, not since Chantal at any rate. If Torey can dominate your thoughts to this degree, then I say she is getting to you."

"You're the one who's making me angry, Henri. You're an unreconstructed romantic, like all the French."

"That is our reputation, true. But we are actually quite pragmatic, Peter. As you well know. Especially when it comes to something as important as marriage."

"No one has said anything about marriage. Torey is divorced and has no desire to get married again. And *I* certainly haven't thought about it."

"Haven't you?" Henri asked mischievously. Before Peter could respond angrily, he continued, "Well, never mind, I will accept your word for it. Neither of you is seriously interested in the other, and after this week you will probably never see each other again. You will go back to your totally satisfying life as a carefree bachelor. And Torey will merely be a smile that lights your face at unexpected moments. And what do you suppose you will be to her?"

"The man who showed her Paris. That's *all*."

"*Bien*. Though it sounds to me as if you are underestimating yourself, Peter. And that certainly isn't like you. Now, may I take the two of you to dinner tonight? Margot and I have reservations at Lassere. I could easily make them for four instead of two. And Margot would love to see you again."

"Okay," Peter replied coolly. Then, more politely, "Thanks, Henri. It's nice of you to offer."

"Not at all. You know that Margot is extremely fond of you."

"How is she?"

"Ah, the same. Beautiful and witty and exasperating. I used to pride myself on the clever way I kept her dangling. Lately, it has occurred to me that perhaps I am not so much in control. One day she will decide she has dangled long enough and we will marry."

"Are you serious?"

"Yes. I have not all the time in the world, you know."

"It would be good for you. I know how much you've missed Aunt Gabrielle. . . ."

"But it has been many years since she died," Henri finished for him. "Yes, I know. When she first died, I thought I would never marry again because I was so happy with her. Now, I realize that I want to marry again precisely because I was so happy before. I cannot ever again recapture what she and I had. But I can have something that will, perhaps, be just as good in its own way."

He finished his coffee, then set down the cup. "Well, enough of this serious talk, Peter. You and I are both definitely growing older if we talk of women in terms of marriage instead of in terms of conquests."

Peter laughed and looked at his uncle with a deep and abiding affection. "You have taught me most of what I know about women, Henri. I used to think you had taught me everything there was to know."

"And now?"

"Now, I don't believe it's possible to know everything about them," Peter finished drily, thinking about Torey.

"That is true, Peter. You see, women themselves are the teachers. From our cradles, they teach us about themselves. But they only let us know what they wish us to know. They are like chameleons. Just when you think you understand them, they change, and reveal facets of their personalities you never suspected. Tell me about your lovely young lady, Torey. You say she is divorced. I cannot imagine a man letting such a gem slip through his fingers."

"Her husband was a fool," Peter said emphatically. "He left her for someone younger, apparently."

"Ah, *les Américains,*" Henri breathed a long, sad sigh of understanding. "They value only youth and completely miss the advantages of age. It is a cliché, but true—women are like fine wine. They definitely improve with age. The young girl has only smooth skin and taut muscles to offer. The older woman has a wealth of knowledge that adds many layers to pleasure."

"At any rate, the experience left her feeling a bit defensive. Understandably so."

"It would, of course. She is so young herself. To be replaced by someone even younger must have been a great shock as well as an insult. What was she doing on the Orient Express?"

"She was taking a short vacation before returning to her home in San Francisco."

"Yes, she mentioned San Francisco. That is conveniently close to Los Angeles, is it not?"

"You know very well that it is."

"Why so touchy? I was merely commenting on California geography, which you know so much better than I. You read too much into my words, Peter."

Henri feigned hurt innocence so well that Peter laughed. "Well, she owns a gift shop there and she just finished a buying trip in Venice."

"I see. A *very* independent young woman, indeed, if she has her own business. No wonder she would not want to bother with you."

"Henri!"

"I am merely repeating what you have already said, Peter. Really, you are so touchy today. Is it the sun, do you think?"

"You are impossible."

"Of course. It is one of the few advantages of growing old. I can be impossible and people dare not reprimand me."

Just then, Torey returned to the garden. She was wearing a shirred-neck camisole in pale blue silk, with a full matching skirt over a white linen petticoat dotted with tiny blue flowers. Bare little white sandals, comfortable for walking, laced up her legs. The brilliant Paris summer sunlight drenched her in its special golden glow, making her dark hair even glossier and her blue eyes an even deeper blue.

Peter thought she looked utterly enchanting and rather innocent with her air of childish excitement. To her, he realized, being in Paris was an exciting adventure. He felt his heart leap. She was quite, quite special. And she would be his for only one week.

Suddenly a week seemed like the shortest time in the world.

Chapter Eight

Torey and Peter walked side by side along the rue Saint-Louis-en-L'Ile. A long, straight street, it ran down the length of the island with occasional side streets branching off at right angles.

"The plan of the island is simple," Peter explained, as they made their way through the crowd of shoppers, strollers, and children. "The whole island was built up during the same period in the seventeenth century. It was designed as an architectural whole by the king's architect, Louis Le Vau."

"That's why it almost looks like a page from a fairy tale," Torey said. "It all fits together so perfectly."

"Yes. The houses differ in size and shape, but they blend in their style and proportions. The only rebuilding was done at the downstream end of the island. So most of the Ile Saint-Louis remains intact, a perfect example of seventeenth-century grace."

"You're a terrific guide, Peter. Knowledgeable, enthusiastic, and not at all bored-sounding," Torey teased.

"Thank you. I won't even charge for the service."

They were at the corner of the rue de Bretonvilliers now. Pointing at an imposing mansion, Peter said, "That house once belonged to the Duc de Richelieu, a great-nephew of Cardinal Richelieu. He was renowned for his military accomplishments, especially against the British. But his greatest accomplishments were in bed."

"A typical Frenchman?" Torey asked, grinning.

"An exceptional one, apparently. His crowd of womenfolk were distinguished not only by their number but their variety—duchesses, servant girls, actresses. And apart from the time he spent with the ladies themselves, he spent a lot of time planning how to get at them, in dealing with their husbands, in duelling, and occasionally in marrying."

"He must have led a very hectic life."

"And a long one. He died at ninety-two, with a final score of three wives, forty-four official mistresses, and an uncounted number of more informal seductions."

"I suppose he had what the French call *joie de vivre*," Torey commented wryly.

"Apparently."

"You sound slightly envious, Peter."

"Not at all." Peter smiled good-naturedly. "The gentleman's record is one I would never even attempt to equal. I don't think I have his stamina."

"I don't know about that. Your stamina seems remarkable to me," Torey replied, glancing up at him seductively through her long, dark lashes.

For a moment there was a spark of that sexual magnetism that had drawn them together on the train the night before. Then Peter threw back his head and laughed deeply.

"Come on, minx," he finally responded, hugging Torey quickly, then taking her hand.

Soon they were passing small shops, cafés, and hotels.

"Some of these tradesmen have lived on the island all their lives," Peter explained, "like their fathers and grandfathers before them. They go as rarely as possible to the mainland."

"It's almost like a country village, in a way, isn't it?" Torey asked.

"Yes. It's cut off from the rest of the city by the Seine. Ah, here's the stern of the island."

Peter led Torey to a gravelly garden area full of screaming children clambering over benches. This point of the island was a paved sunny triangle with wide horizons. People were sunbathing, the men with their shirts off and their eyes closed sleepily.

"What a marvelous view," Torey exclaimed, looking out at the flowing Seine and, beyond it, the rest of Paris.

"Yes, the houses around the quays, like this one, are much finer than those in the interior of the island. The very rich, the titled, even movie stars, live on these outside quays."

"I can imagine." Torey turned her back on the river to look at the nearby houses. They were a fascinating jumble of terraces and towers, with broad bays of windows burnished with light from the river.

"This is called the Quai de Bethune," Peter explained. "As you can see, it's especially popular with sunbathers. I guess because it faces south, sort of drinking in the sun. Somehow, it's a bit livelier, less secluded than the other quays. There's less of that air of expectancy that seems to pervade the rest of the island. Some residents seem to be waiting for the return of something that will never come again."

"You mean *noblesse oblige* and 'Let them eat cake,' and all of that gaudy, decadent, seductive way of living?"

"Yes. *Exactly.*" Peter looked at Torey soberly for a moment. "You have an odd way of connecting with exactly what I'm feeling and thinking sometimes."

Torey knew what he meant. She experienced it herself when he seemed to look past the façade with which she protected herself to the real woman underneath. She had felt it especially when they made love and Peter had seemed to know, as if by magic, what she needed and wanted.

She felt awkward, as she did when Peter looked at her in just that particularly unnerving way. "Perhaps it's ESP or reincarnation or something," she responded lightly, trying to cover her discomfort. "We probably knew each other well in a past life."

Peter smiled. "You know, I almost think that might be true."

As they walked away, he pointed to the far side of the river. "By the way, that's the Left Bank. The houses there are more picturesque than the ones on the Right Bank, and only slightly less expensive. And this bridge we're passing is the Pont de la Tournelle."

"And that must be Notre Dame," Torey exclaimed excitedly as she noticed the famous silhouette rising out of the trees, floating above the river and the city, held down by the flying buttresses, like guy ropes.

"Would you like to see it later? There's a small, rather ugly footbridge that connects the Ile Saint-Louis to the Ile de la Cité, the island that the cathedral's on."

"Oh, yes, I want to see everything. The Tuileries, the Louvre, the Eiffel Tower . . ."

"Not that towering monstrosity? It's really pretty ugly, you know."

"I don't care. I can't go back to San Francisco without being able to say I saw the view from the Eiffel Tower."

"You *are* a tourist. And you show a dreadful lack of imagination. But I'll humor you."

"Thank you." She gave him a sidelong smile as they walked hand in hand. "And I'll bet the first thing you did when you came to Paris originally was visit the Eiffel Tower."

"No, the first thing I did was try to get into a really sleazy strip show at a Left Bank nightclub."

Torey laughed. "You're hopeless, Peter."

"And you're adorable," he replied, bending down to kiss her lightly.

Sighing happily, Torey decided that the Ile Saint-Louis was a charming place to live, a lovely place for a stroll, and a really nice place to be kissed.

They passed the Quai d'Anjou, where the island was joined to the mainland by the Pont Marie, a graceful bridge of mellow golden stone. Then they came to the Quai de Bourbon, the most peaceful part of the island. The houses here stood eave to eave and were grayish-white, ocher, pure gray, green, and a muddy buff—colors as subtle as the river or the Paris sky.

"They shine huge electric lights here at night," Peter said. "On warm summer nights it's a wonderful place for a midnight stroll. I'll bring you back here tonight and show you." Then he went on quickly, "Come on, I'll show you my favorite view of Paris."

He led Torey out onto the Pont Louis Philippe. As they stood in the center of the bridge, Torey could see the Quai de Bourbon behind its trees, the Pont Marie downstream, and the curving Seine. Nearby, small boats rocked up and down in the wash of the sightseeing boats, the *bateaux-mouches*. And the bank was crowded with flickering rods as fishermen silently plied their trade.

The scene was indescribably charming, like something out of a painting by Manet, timeless, in sun-ripened colors. Torey didn't know what to say. It fairly took her breath away. She leaned her head against Peter's shoulder, and he slipped his arm comfortably around her shoulder, holding her in companionable silence.

They stood there, neither feeling the need to speak, for a long while.

Chapter Nine

That night, Torey dressed with special care. Fortunately, she had brought one really dressy dress with her on the trip, because Angela had invited her to a very formal party. The dress was made of sheer black silk, knee-length, with a fuchsia silk band that provided a splash of color at the waist. The low, round neckline had a deep ruffle, and the sleeves were short and puffed. With it, Torey wore the same silver heels and diamond jewelry she had worn at dinner the previous night.

She pulled her hair back in a simple chignon and secured it with an ivory pin that she had bought in Venice. Looking at her reflection in the mirror in the bathroom, she decided she would do. There was a heightened color in her cheeks and a sparkle in her eyes that hadn't been there yesterday. Angela would certainly approve, Torey thought wryly, remembering

Angela's criticism of her pale complexion. She had to admit that she felt and looked much more attractive now, and it was all the result of meeting Peter.

Tossing some make-up and a comb into her silver-beaded evening bag, Torey left the bedroom and made her way downstairs to the sitting room. Peter and Henri were waiting for her there. Both were dressed in black tuxes, and looked quite handsome. But it was Peter, especially, whom Torey couldn't take her eyes off. Formal evening wear suited him. Unlike many men, he looked completely comfortable in it. The white, ruffled shirt contrasted nicely with his deep tan.

"Vous êtes jolie à ravir," Henri said, rising and kissing her hand warmly.

Turning to Peter, Torey said, "That sounds very nice, whatever it means."

"He said you look heartbreakingly lovely," Peter explained. "And he's right." His voice was deep with some emotion that Torey couldn't quite understand, and his brown eyes were bright with barely suppressed desire.

For a moment, as Torey was caught in his searing gaze, the room, Henri, everything seemed to fade away. There was only Peter.

Then Henri spoke. "Come, children, we must be off. I think we all look most impressive tonight and we should promenade ourselves for the rest of the world to admire."

Peter and Torey both grinned. "The French have no modesty, Torey. You'll have to get used to that."

As he took Torey's arm and led her outside, she replied, "I think Henri's right. We all look terrific."

"Terrific enough for dinner at Lassere?" Peter asked.

"Is that where we're going? I've heard of it."

"I should hope so. Though there is tremendous debate about these things, it's generally considered the best restaurant in Paris."

"And therefore, the best in the world," Henri added.

Torey and Peter looked at each other and laughed.

"What did I tell you?" Peter said, shaking his head. "An incorrigible race."

A few minutes later, they were driving down the Champs-Elysées in Henri's classic Daimler. The famous boulevard was brightly lit with street lamps and the lights of countless cars streaming beneath the golden glow of the floodlit Arc de Triomphe. In the darkness, the ghostly gray Eiffel Tower rose high above the Paris rooftops. This was Torey's first good look at it, and in the soft light of the nearby floodlit fountains, it looked like a work of lacy filigree.

"It might almost have been spun by spiders," Torey said softly, overwhelmed by its beauty as it dominated everything around it.

"In the daylight, you'll see that it's made of dark steel girders. In fact, it's actually ugly, as I said earlier. It's been called the 'iron monster,'" Peter commented bluntly.

"Then I prefer the way it looks tonight," Torey replied firmly. For this one brief interlude in her life, she preferred fantasy to reality. She had no illusions about her relationship with Peter. She knew what the end would undoubtedly be. But until that time when the Orient Express carried her out of his life, she wanted to forget reality and enjoy herself.

Margot Fulbert lived in a sumptuous apartment on the Avenue Kléber. A maid answered the door and led them into an exquisitely furnished sitting room. The furniture was all antiques from the Louis XV and XVI periods. Lovely porcelain figurines graced the marble mantel above the large fireplace, and the red walls were covered with fine examples of Impressionist art. An oriental carpet in deep shades of red, beige, and black covered the floor. Though everything about the room bespoke money and exceptional taste, somehow the atmosphere was cozy and warm. When Margot entered a moment later, Torey understood why.

A tall, elegant woman, she effortlessly projected Parisian chic in a white satin dinner suit trimmed in ermine. With smartly styled white-blonde hair, she looked just slightly younger than Henri. Her classic bone structure made her the sort of woman who is forever beautiful. She had artfully applied a touch of rouge on the eyelids to bring out the sheen of her eyes. She didn't try to look young, but definitely looked undiscouraged by the passing of time. When she was young, Torey knew, she must have been stunning. Even now, well into middle age, she was very attractive.

But her glamour and sophistication were matched by a friendly, down-to-earth personality. And that personality was reflected in the atmosphere of her home.

"*Bonsoir*, Henri, Peter," she said breezily, kissing

them both on the cheeks. Then, turning to Torey, she said, "And you must be Peter's friend, Torey Jenson. Do you mind if I dispense with the formalities and call you Torey?"

"Please do."

"And you shall call me Margot, because I am sure we are going to be great friends." She smiled winningly, then turned to Henri, "Do we have time for a glass of wine, Henri?"

"Certainly," he replied.

"Geneviève, bring the wine that I asked you to chill, please," Margot said to the maid. The young woman nodded and left. Margot continued, "Let's sit down and relax then, I'm so glad we don't have to rush right off to the restaurant."

The maid returned with a tray holding four crystal wine glasses and a carafe of sparkling white wine. She set the tray on a table in front of Margot and left. As Margot poured the wine and handed the glasses all around, she said to Torey, "Henri tells me you know something of Impressionist art. Come, let me show you one or two pieces that I think you will find interesting."

Taking Torey's hand, she led her to a wall that featured the Van Gogh Henri had mentioned. "Not one of his finest works, I'm afraid. But in my opinion, anything by Van Gogh is interesting," she finished breezily.

"I think it's *marvelous!* I could look at it for hours," Torey said eagerly as she took in the bold colors and broad, rough strokes of the painting of peasants in the fields at harvest time.

"Shall I tell you how it came into my family? It's a rather scandalous story, but then, what family doesn't have a few skeletons in its closet? The proprietess of a local . . . how do you call it?" She searched for the right word. Finally she smiled and went on, "Well, a 'house of pleasure,' shall we say. Anyway, she befriended many starving artists, including Van Gogh. He gave her this painting as a gift. She didn't think much of his work; of course, no one did at that time. So she gave it to one of her girls. This girl was a particular favorite of my grandfather. He liked the painting and bought it from her. I'm not sure what story he told my grandmother. Somehow I doubt that it was the truth. At any rate, the truth came out when he died and my grandmother found the receipt for the painting."

Torey smiled. "Your grandfather had excellent taste in paintings."

"Yes. And in women, too, so I hear."

"Before you ladies waste any more time with old gossip," Henri admonished with an indulgent smile, "we'd better be getting to the restaurant."

"Very well," Margot agreed. "Come, Torey, we'll have the rest of the evening to talk without this old sourpuss interrupting us."

The restaurant, Lassere, wasn't very far from Margot's apartment. They passed through the beautifully lit entrance, then were escorted by one smiling attendant after another, each offering a carefully measured smile and a *"Bonsoir, messieurs-dames."* Then they entered a small elevator entirely padded with cut velvet which took them to the restaurant itself. The dining area was very crowded, but the waiters adroitly negotiated their way among the tables.

As the maître d' led them to a quiet table in a corner, Torey took in the impeccable Louis XVI decor: fresh pink and red flowers in crystal vases at each table, richly upholstered chairs, and walls covered with ornate patterned wallpaper.

Red-jacketed busboys bustled about them as they were seated, and Peter asked with a smile, "Do you like it?"

"Of course. It's incredible."

"Wait till you taste the food. It's almost worth the obscene prices."

"We French have a natural talent for good living," Henri interjected with a chuckle. "Unfortunately to indulge it, one also needs a natural disregard for thrift."

Margot gave Peter a sly look. "And you, Peter, have a talent for secrets. I must reprimand you for not letting me know earlier that you would be having such a charming house guest. I would have planned a party, something *très intime.*"

"Well, Torey and I . . ." Peter paused and Torey could tell that he wasn't sure how to explain the situation. "It was all rather sudden and unexpected," he finally finished.

Torey knew that Peter was being careful in the way he described their meeting because he didn't want to give the impression that Torey was merely a girl he had picked up on the train. As she met his quick, concerned look, she smiled warmly, grateful for his consideration. If she'd had doubts before, she knew now that he didn't consider her just another conquest to boast about.

Margot's hazel eyes looked at Torey shrewdly, measuring her without being rude. "I see. Well, I believe there is a word in English for such unexpected good luck. It is serendipity, isn't it? My niece, who attends school in New York, told me that recently."

Glancing at Torey, Peter agreed softly, "Yes, serendipity is the right word."

For a moment their eyes locked. As they looked at each other they connected in the same profound way they had done when they first met.

Then Henri coughed discreetly, and Torey remembered they were in the middle of a conversation. When the waiter handed menus all around, Torey concentrated on reading hers.

"You'll have to translate for me, Peter. I can only make out part of this. My two years of French in high school didn't include a course in how to read a menu."

"No problem," Peter smiled. "I can honestly recommend just about everything here. Is there anything you particularly like or dislike?"

"I'll tell you what, you order for me. It will be fun to be surprised."

"Ah, an old-fashioned girl lurks beneath that modern façade," Peter teased. "Letting a man decide."

"Don't be fooled by a temporary lapse into tradition," Torey countered. "I'm a complete feminist."

"You are far too charming and feminine to be a feminist," Henri interrupted.

"Don't be silly, Henri. True feminists have always been charming and feminine," Margot insisted.

Henri argued with her briefly, but it was clear he

was only teasing her. For the entire evening he and Margot kept up a lively banter interspersed with sly, flirtatious looks. It was obvious they were romantically involved and Torey wondered if they were considering marriage.

After they ordered their meal, the *sommelier* appeared with their wine selection. He decanted the bottle of Batard Montrachet with expert care, examining the contents against a candle as he poured to ensure no dregs reached the silver and crystal decanter.

Dinner followed soon after; the first course was John Dory, a delicious light white fish from Australia steamed with watercress and accompanied by a watercress dressing. The main course was breast of chicken with light cream and lemon juice, cooked with snow peas and topped with flecks of bacon. That was followed by a lusciously textured salad with *radicchio,* a crisp red lettuce from Italy, and emerald-green *masche.* Tossed with hazelnut oil and a raspberry vinegar, it was topped with a hot *feiullete* of Gruyere, goat and Brie cheeses.

By the time dessert came, Torey was sure she couldn't eat another bite. But when she saw the raspberry cream with vanilla rounds, she couldn't resist. However she did resist the grapefruit and orange sorbet with pear liqueur that followed; she would have loved to have tried it, but there simply wasn't any room left in her stomach.

"Oh, Peter," she groaned good-naturedly. "I can't believe how much I ate."

"We'll go for a walk when we get home," he said. "That will work off a bit of this dinner."

"You just want to show Torey the Seine by moonlight," Henri said slyly.

"Well, that sounds marvelous," Torey replied, grinning.

Margot asked, "Would you like to go to the powder room with me, *chérie*, while the men order coffee and brandy?"

"Yes, thank you."

"Why is it," Henri asked, his eyes twinkling merrily, "that women always go to the powder room in groups, never alone?"

"So we may discuss you men, of course," Margot replied, bending to kiss him lightly on the cheek as she passed him.

In the large, beautifully decorated powder room, Margot and Torey sat next to each other on satin-covered chairs. As Torey carefully reapplied her lipstick, Margot said, "I shall have to order willow-wreaths for half the eligible young ladies in Paris. It's obvious that Peter has been smitten and won't be in circulation for long."

"I don't know what you mean," Torey began firmly.

"Don't you? Then you are a great deal more modest than is good for you, child. Peter is in love with you. It's that simple. And I must say I can understand why. You're just what he's needed, someone who is a match for him."

"Margot, you misunderstand," Torey insisted.

"Do I? I thought, from the way he has looked at you all evening, that this was a serious affair. But, of course, you know better than I do."

It was clear to Torey that Margot didn't accept her heartfelt denial. But she didn't know how to make the older woman believe her without sounding as if she were protesting too much. Finally she asked hesitantly, "Is Peter so sought-after, then?"

"Oh, *la,* yes. Well, he is so handsome, as the Delacroix always seem to be, and he has that American ruggedness that is *so* appealing. And, of course, some day he will inherit all of Henri's holdings, which will make him quite wealthy. Since we French are more avaricious than most, that is almost as important a consideration as his rather shattering charm. And he has a pleasant, foolish habit of keeping to one woman at a time. That is a quality to be valued nowadays when it is so hard to find."

Though Torey knew Margot meant her last comment in a positive way, she couldn't help interpreting it differently. If Peter did only go after one girl at a time, perhaps Torey was only "the girl of the month." Like a *Playboy* centerfold, next month she would be forgotten, replaced by someone else.

"Have you known Peter long?" she asked, after a long pause to cover her discomfort.

"About fifteen years . . . since he first came to Paris," Margot said. Her eyes twinkled with amusement as she recalled, "You should have seen him then, Torey. He had the offhand arrogance of the young that is so adorable. He didn't know how much he had to learn then, you see. A failed attempt at art, and rejection in love, tempered him though. It made him more sensitive and, therefore, even more attractive. Women have chased him shamelessly since. For a while I wondered if he would ever settle down. Then, tonight, you two seemed so close. . . ."

Her voice trailed off suggestively. Finally she added

dryly, "But, as you say, there is nothing between you."

"Margot, I know you don't believe me, but neither Peter nor I are looking for love right now."

"Aren't you? Perhaps you believe it too dangerous. Do you know what Richard de Fournival said in the thirteenth century?"

Torey shook her head.

"So long ago he said, 'Love is a folly of the mind, an unquenchable fire, a hunger without surfeit.' Rather an extreme view, but worth keeping in mind, I think."

Torey laughed. "Perhaps you're right. In fact, sometimes I wonder if real love even exists anymore. Maybe life has gotten too modern for such an old-fashioned ideal."

"I did hear a psychologist say recently that romantic love, like smallpox, is practically extinct today," Margot said pragmatically. "He insisted that the death of romantic love was a healthy development. It meant that marriages would no longer be founded on passionate illusions and end in inevitable divorces."

"Perhaps he was right," Torey said pensively, thinking of her own history.

"Oh come now," Margot said firmly. "Psychologists are fools, always writing books and papers about things they should be *living*. You don't believe that any more than I do. If anything, romantic love is stronger than ever today because marriages are not so economically or socially motivated. For most people nowadays, marriage is just one of many options. You marry because you want to, not because you have to."

"Obviously, *you* believe in love," Torey commented.

"Yes. I have felt it, therefore I know it exists. It's a marvelous feeling. Love is a euphoric state for a woman. We feel lighter, colors are brighter, the world sparkles." Margot laughed. "It is as if there is champagne in our veins instead of blood. We bubble with happiness." She eyed Torey carefully, "But then, perhaps you have never felt this."

Torey looked away, embarrassed. She *had* felt it. Every moment she was with Peter. And she knew that Margot could see that. As Margot looked at her, her soft hazel eyes perceptive yet infinitely kind, Torey decided to risk the truth. "You know how much I love him, don't you?"

"I'm afraid it's touchingly obvious, my dear. When you look at him your whole face lights up."

Torey bit her lip. "Oh, that sounds so unsophisticated. . . . I wish I could hide it better."

"Why? Love is nothing to be ashamed of, Torey."

"But I don't know that Peter loves me. He hasn't said so. You see, everything's gone so fast. I was divorced recently. My marriage was miserable for such a long time. I was just beginning to be happy again, to enjoy my independence. Then I took the Orient Express and met Peter. And all of my careful plans flew out the window."

"But sometimes it happens that way. For most of us love is a gradual building up of feelings. But occasionally, when two people are *very* right for each other, it happens all at once, in a burst of fireworks."

Impulsively, Torey reached out to touch Margot's hand. "Oh, I do hope you're right."

Margot laughed softly. "Of course I am." Then she briskly rose to her feet. "We'd better rejoin the men."

As they started out she added reassuringly, "Do not worry so much about things, *chérie*. Believe it or not, men feel love even more deeply than women do. Everything will be well with you. Somehow, I feel certain of it."

Torey looked at her for a moment, then smiled. "You're very wise and very kind."

"Why thank you, child. But don't tell Henri that. In my generation we have to let the man believe he is superior intellectually. It is a subterfuge that, luckily, women of your age can dispense with."

Back at the table, the men rose and helped the women into their seats. Then Margot asked Torey if she'd had a chance to do any shopping yet.

"No, this afternoon Peter took me on a tour of the Ile Saint-Louis."

"So like a man," Margot chided good-naturedly, "to think a woman prefers sightseeing. They never understand that we cannot wait to get to the shops. What are a few old moldy museums and landmarks compared to the latest fashions?"

Torey laughed. "I *would* like to buy a few things."

"Let me recommend a marvelous little boutique on the Left Bank," Margot said, pulling out a small notepad and pen from her purse and quickly jotting a name and address. She handed it to Torey, adding, "The owner's name is Danielle. Tell her you are a friend of mine and she will not overcharge you quite as much as she usually does Americans."

Turning to Peter, Margot said firmly, "Peter, I want you to promise to let Torey find her own way around Paris and not force anything boring on her."

"Promise." Peter smiled. "I won't drag her through

the Tuileries or Versailles or the Louvre. I'll let her run completely amok in the shops. However, we leave in two days for the chateau, so that doesn't allow a great deal of time."

"Then you must be careful where you shop, Torey," Margot continued. "The really interesting shops are on the Left Bank now. But the Right Bank still has the famous designers' showrooms, of course. Were you interested in anything besides clothes?"

"I'd like to look at some items for my shop back home," Torey replied. "Country French is *very* in, you know. I've been thinking for quite some time about importing some things."

"You mean such as *faïence?*" Margot asked.

"Why yes, exactly," Torey said, thinking of the lovely porcelain objects.

"There is a marvelous place in a village called Quimper. They make the most charming *faïence*. The owner is a friend. I'm sure he could help you."

"Thank you, Margot. I'll call him."

"Here is the phone number," Margot responded, writing it down for Torey.

"Well, ladies, shall we depart?" Henri asked.

They left the restaurant and a few minutes later were back at Margot's apartment. Peter and Torey waited in the car while Henri walked Margot to her door.

"I really like Margot," Torey said.

"She's great. She's been like a second mother to me."

"She and your uncle are adorable together. I love the way they tease each other. You'd think they were teenagers."

"They've known each other most of their lives. Margot was a good friend of Henri's wife, Gabrielle. Then, when they were both widowed at about the same time, they began seeing each other. It's been interesting watching their friendship turn into a romance."

"Do you think they'll ever marry?"

"Yes. In fact, I wouldn't be surprised if it happens soon. They've both lived alone for several years now, and I think they feel it's time to get married again. I know that Henri feels that way, at any rate."

"I think Margot does, too."

"Well, at their age, marriage *is* the logical thing," Peter said blithely.

Torey glanced up at him sharply. She wanted to ask, "Only at their age?" But she didn't.

Just then Henri returned, and for the rest of the drive home, both Torey and Peter were rather silent.

When Henri went up to bed, Peter and Torey went for a walk down to the river. The Quai de Bethune was deserted, but it wasn't dark. Floodlights lit the area, turning the huge poplars black and silver. The trees, the stone façades, the towers of the bridges and buildings were transfigured with the artificial light. Torey could see the spires of Notre Dame, gilded by light, soaring high into the black night sky. The river was especially beautiful on this summer's night. During the day it was a shining ribbon, but at night it became a soft, broad mystery, laced with silver and gold.

"This is the romantic vision of Paris," Peter said wryly. "Contrived, beguiling, French, and somehow utterly real."

Torey looked out onto the Pont Marie in the distance, and the shimmer of the lights on the mainland. Those lights shone on the water, and in the pathways of reflected light, the river seemed to fizz like champagne.

"It's magical," Torey said softly.

"And artificial," Peter replied. "The floodlights make everything look different than it really is. It's all an illusion."

"But a beautiful one," Torey insisted.

Looking at her, his eyes warm with affection, Peter teased, "I thought *you* were the realistic one."

"I'm taking a brief respite from reality. Right now I'm simply enjoying things. There will be plenty of time later to worry about business and . . . and everything," she finished awkwardly, looking away.

Peter looked at her silently for a long moment. Then he said slowly, "You know, Torey, I'm very glad we both took the Orient Express when we did."

"It's funny, isn't it, that we both happened to be there at the same time. It must have been fate," Torey finished, teasing.

"I really didn't plan on meeting anyone," Peter admitted. "I took the train to give myself time to think about this buying trip. It's the first one I've made on my own. I was recently promoted," he added with a note of pride in his voice.

"That is a coincidence. Both of us were just looking for some quiet time to think, and then . . ."

"And then I happened to glance out my window and saw you catching that silly little dog. And I thought how attractive you were. Then I saw you in the bar-salon, and I decided that you weren't just attractive, but downright beautiful. And I had to get to know you."

"That was fate again. After all, I was sitting at the table with the only empty chair."

"So we've been pawns of fate all along?"

"Exactly," Torey replied, smiling up at him. But something in his expression made her breath catch in her throat. And when he bent to kiss her, she responded eagerly, wrapping her arms around his neck and molding her body against his.

Finally, reluctantly, they pulled away from each other.

"The combination of that lovely gown revealing so much of your enticing body, and the moonlight, and the seductive glint in your eyes is too much, my love," Peter said huskily. "I think I've had enough walking for one night."

"Have you now? And just what did you have in mind, instead?" Torey asked, throwing back her head and eyeing him in a direct, challenging way.

"What I have in mind, *mon adorée*, is bed. But not to sleep."

And they didn't sleep until dawn bathed the city in its golden glow.

Chapter Ten

*T*he next morning, both Torey and Peter came down to breakfast late. It was served in the dining room, where Henri was finishing his final cup of coffee and folding up the newspaper.

"*Bonjour*, Torey, Peter," he said brightly.

"*Bonjour*," Torey responded gaily.

"Ah, very good. You almost have the accent down just right."

"Peter's been helping me polish my rusty French," Torey explained, with a quick smile at Peter.

"Well, what are you two up to today?" Henri asked, as Peter poured coffee for himself and Torey.

"I'm going to show Torey a bit of Paris this morning, then this afternoon I'm going to have a look at that Cézanne."

"Will you have time to go over some business matters later?" Henri asked.

"Can they wait till tomorrow? I've promised to leave Torey completely free then to do some shopping. So I'll be available all day."

"Fine. Well, I must be off. You children enjoy yourselves. By the way, Peter, Elise has planned your favorite dinner tonight."

"I see. We'll be sure to get back early, then."

"Good. By the way, Torey, you look enchanting this morning. That is a *very* pretty dress."

"Thank you," she smiled.

She was wearing a red sundress with bare shoulders, an elasticized top, a tiny cinched waist and a flounced skirt over a white eyelet petticoat. She'd found it in Venice and this was the first time she'd worn it. The appreciative smile Peter gave her when he first saw her earlier told her she made a good choice.

Now, she basked in Henri's compliment. She felt irrepressibly happy this morning. It was a beautiful, clear day, she was wearing a lovely new dress, and she was going to see Paris with the man she loved to distraction. As long as she concentrated on the present, and didn't think about the future, she felt she was the luckiest girl in the world.

When Henri was gone, Elise came out with two covered plates.

"You will need a good breakfast to give you the energy to go sightseeing today," she said pragmatically.

Peter smiled at her broadly. "You spoil me, Elise."

"You expect it, Peter, so do not pretend otherwise," Elise replied tartly. "Now eat your breakfast." Turning to Torey she said pleasantly, "If there is

139

anything else you wish, Mademoiselle Jenson, please let me know."

"Oh, thank you, but this looks like quite enough," Torey said as she uncovered the plate and found scrambled eggs dotted with green herbs, sausage, and croissants fresh from the oven.

A half hour later, Torey was full to the bursting point, and already thinking about dieting when she returned to San Francisco. As she pushed away her coffee cup, she asked Peter, "Will we be walking a lot today? I hope so, because I definitely need the exercise."

"We'll be taking my car, but we'll still end up walking quite a bit. Ready to go?"

"You keep a car here?" she asked as he helped her from her chair.

"Just a small sports car. It was a gift from Henri for my twenty-first birthday and I never bothered to ship it home. It comes in handy when I'm here."

A moment later they were in Peter's white Triumph speeding down the rue Saint-Louis-en-L'ile. Then they turned onto the Pont de la Tournelle and soon were in the city itself.

"Where are we going?" Torey asked.

"To my favorite shop in Paris. You'll notice I'm taking Margot's advice and not dragging you around to all the magnificent but boring monuments, churches, and museums."

Torey laughed. "Spoken like a true American. Why waste time on culture when I can spend some money?"

"Well, this time *I'll* be the one spending the money. I want to buy you something."

"Peter . . ."

"Don't argue, woman," he said with mock gruffness. "And don't worry. I'm not going to embarrass you with jewels or furs or $500-an-ounce perfume."

"Why not?" Torey asked teasingly.

"Only because I can't afford it, actually. But I think you'll find something you'll like almost as well in this store."

Rigodon, the shop in question, sold only puppets and dolls Torey discovered. It was for children, or those who are still children at heart, and Torey fell in love with it immediately. Hanging from the ceiling were a varied and sophisticated collection of puppets of all sizes, characters, and prices. There were donkey-headed women, Madame Pompadour, ducks, angels, witches on broomsticks, and even Mistinguette with a cluster of feathers in her hair.

"Oh, Peter, I'm reverting to my childhood," Torey exclaimed.

"I know, I always feel about ten years old when I come here. Whenever I have to buy a gift for a child, I come to Rigodon. I'm not necessarily sure that my nieces and nephews like getting puppets, but I love giving them."

This was a side of Peter that Torey hadn't seen before and would never have suspected. His sophistication made it hard to imagine him being charmed by these childishly simple puppets. Yet clearly he was, for he happily scrutinized almost every puppet in the store with Torey. Her mind boggled at the wide selection, and she thought she would never make up her mind which one to choose.

"You were right," she finally told Peter. "I'd much

rather have one of these puppets than furs or jewels or perfume."

Kissing her quickly on the forehead, he smiled. "The amazing thing is, I think you mean that. Now, come on, you've got to choose *something*. We've got a busy day ahead. You can't go back to San Francisco and tell everyone you spent all your time in Paris in a puppet store."

Torey laughed. "All right. But it's so hard to choose. I want them *all*."

"Now the truth comes out," Peter teased. "You're not such a cheap date after all." Then he suggested, "How about this Madame Pompadour? Or the duck there—"

"The ducks are nice, but . . ." Torey hesitated. Then she saw something that made her eyes light with excitement. "Oh Peter, look!"

"What is it?"

"A unicorn!" Torey hurried over to a corner where a unicorn puppet hung. It was white, with a tall, spiraling gold horn. "My shop's called The Sign of the Unicorn. This would be a perfect mascot."

"You've got it, then," Peter said quickly, grabbing the puppet and taking it immediately to the cashier.

As they left the shop, with the carefully wrapped unicorn under Torey's arm, she put her hand on Peter's shoulder, stopping him.

"Thank you," she said warmly. And she kissed him deeply, happily oblivious to the irritated pedestrians who had to make their way around them.

The rest of the morning was spent visiting one interesting shop after another. At a store called François Girand, Torey bought prints of old cars and railway engines for her nephews. At Carnavalette, she bought an old engraving of the Montmartre as a gift for Henri.

Afterward, she and Peter drove to the end of the rue de Seine, an area on the banks of the river where vendors sold an incredible variety of wares. They walked past flower vendors, including one elderly woman dressed in an old-fashioned black dress, who stood behind a flower-filled black barrow on high, bright red wheels. Torey selected a bouquet of multi-colored tulips to take back to Elise.

"How did you know Elise loves flowers?" Peter asked as Torey paid the woman.

"It wasn't hard to guess, with all the fresh bouquets around the house. Obviously Elise was the one responsible for them."

"Well, it's very thoughtful of you. I know she'll appreciate it."

Torey laughed, "Considering how well she's fed me, it's the least I can do."

They walked on, hand in hand amid the sun-splashed stalls of the marketplace that lined the parapets, past cages of trilling, multicolored birds, and sidewalk artists, and *bouquinistes*, or booksellers. The human bustle of vendors hawking their wares, the small children racing helter-skelter underfoot, and the warm summer sun overhead shimmering on the wide, slow-moving dark surface of the Seine gave texture to an atmosphere that was almost intoxicating for Torey.

The *bouquinistes* sold everything from postcards and second-hand books, to prints. Torey happily lost all track of time as she looked through the merchandise. Most of the prints were cheap and unimpressive, aimed at the tourist trade. But a few were actually signed, limited editions by fairly well-known artists. While Peter browsed nearby, thumbing through books, Torey searched through the prints for just the right thing.

And she found it. It was a print of a drawing of a boy by Leonardo da Vinci. The boy was no more than a year old, and what appealed to Torey immediately was his air of innocent mischievousness. Da Vinci hadn't tried to make the child cherubic, as most artists of his time did. Instead he had captured the soul of a very real little boy. Torey had always thought of da Vinci in regard to his big works—Mona Lisa, his drawings of helicopter-like machines and other futuristic devices. She was amazed at his sensitivity in capturing the sweet promise of this man-child.

It was a small print, no more than six inches by four, and not even very expensive. But it was exceptionally fine, and something about it touched Torey emotionally.

Well, it solves a sticky problem, she told herself. What do I give a man who obviously has more money than I do? An inexpensive print of a very beautiful drawing. . . .

Looking up, she saw that Peter was engrossed in a book nearby. Quickly Torey paid the vendor, who put the print in a small tissue bag.

"*Mademoiselle* has very good taste," the man said in heavily accented English.

"*Merci*," Torey smiled, grateful for the reinforcement, whatever the degree of its sincerity.

She tucked the bag under the tulips she'd bought for Elise, then joined Peter at a book counter.

"Ready to go?" she asked.

"Sure," he said, putting down the book he'd been thumbing through. "I couldn't find anything to tempt me today." As they strolled on, he glanced at her, "Don't tell me you didn't buy anything either?"

"Actually I did find one thing. But it isn't for me." As he opened the door of his car for her, she smiled up at him. "It's for you, Peter. I hope you like it."

She handed him the bag.

"You didn't have to get me anything, Torey."

"Don't be selfish. Let me have the pleasure of being as generous as you were."

"Okay." He laughed, drawing the print out of the bag. For a moment he looked at it silently.

Torey felt her heart sink; he doesn't like it, she thought. He probably thinks it's silly.

Then Peter looked up at her, and the expression in his eyes made her sigh with relief.

"Torey, it's *beautiful*." His voice was deep with emotion. "Nothing could have pleased me more."

For one brief, shining moment, he looked at her with such transparent adoration that Torey felt her heart would burst with happiness. He loves the print, she told herself. And he loves me.

Then he took her in his arms and held her tightly. Snuggled against his chest, Torey smelled his now familiar scent, a pleasant mixture of after-shave and other things. But as his arms held her securely, protectively, her euphoria began to ebb. Don't count on too much, she told herself sternly, forcing reality to intrude. Because that way lies heartbreak.

But she couldn't entirely suppress a sense of exultation. He *did* love her. He'd shown it clearly in that one unguarded instant. Whether or not that feeling would last was something else again.

The art gallery was on the Champs-Elysées. Part of this famous street, Torey discovered, was a drive through a chestnut-lined park; the other was a commercial avenue of sidewalk cafes, auto showrooms, offices, cinemas, and shops. Peter found a parking place near the gallery, and a moment later he and Torey were inside. The atmosphere was hushed, exclusive, with deep carpeting on the floor, and exquisite paintings on the walls. Peter asked a clerk to tell the owner he had arrived. When the young man disappeared into the back of the gallery, Torey asked, "Why are they offering this painting to your museum? Wouldn't it normally be sold through an auction?"

"Normally, yes. But I suspect they're giving me first refusal because they know how much money the Hettinger Museum has now. They're assuming we'll pay generously for such a piece—which we will—and they can avoid any delays."

A moment later the owner appeared. A well-dressed, rather portly man in his late forties, he beamed happily at Peter. "Welcome, Monsieur West. I am so happy to see you."

"How do you do, Monsieur Valmy. This is Mademoiselle Jenson," Peter said by way of polite introduction.

"*Enchanté, mademoiselle.* Now, I am sure you are most anxious to see the Cézanne," Valmy said, turning back to Peter.

"Of course."

"Please come this way. It is in my private office.

146

Naturally so priceless a creation could not be displayed out here," he explained as they walked to the rear of the gallery. Peter gave Torey a small smile at Valmy's use of the word priceless, but said nothing. Unlocking a door, Valmy added, "Our security is good, but not infallible."

The painting stood on an easel in the office. It was a still life, painted by Cézanne in the mid 1870s. Torey was disappointed; it was conventional in its adherence to the style of the period. Torey preferred Cézanne's later works, when the Impressionist influence lightened his palette and made his mature style what he became famous for—artfully distorted perspective and complex composition.

Peter studied the painting closely, then stood back a few feet to survey it for several long minutes.

When Peter still said nothing, Valmy said confidently, "It's a bargain at seventy-five thousand dollars, Monsieur West. And it would be a tremendous asset to the Hettinger."

Without thinking, Torey broke in. "But a similar work from the same period sold for half that price in Manhattan only a few months ago."

Valmy's friendly countenance hardened perceptibly. "Obviously, *mademoiselle*, you do not understand Cézanne's importance."

Torey felt her hackles rise, "I understand perfectly, *monsieur*," she responded tartly, with growing irritation at the man's superciliousness. "I studied art, the Impressionist School in particular. This is hardly a good example of Cézanne's work. And it *is* overpriced."

"That's up to *me* to decide," Peter said suddenly,

surprising Torey with the barely veiled irritation in his voice.

She looked at him, startled and hurt.

When Valmy shot her a satisfied look that clearly said, "Well, you've been put in your place, haven't you," she felt anger welling up inside her. She knew she was right in her opinion and she couldn't understand why Peter simply didn't agree with her.

"I'll wait in the car, Peter," she said, only barely managing an icily courteous nod at Valmy. Then she turned and strode out of the office and the gallery.

She sat in the car for fifteen long minutes. The heavy traffic moving past in the fading late afternoon sunshine, the outline of the Eiffel Tower in the distance, might all not have existed for all the attention Torey paid to them. She was growing angrier by the minute. How *dare* Peter dismiss her so summarily in front of that odious man? Obviously he found her acceptable as a bedmate, but not so acceptable in an intelligent debate. The toe of her sandal began to tap angrily against the floorboard, and she twisted and untwisted a strand of hair irritably.

You've been put in your place, she told herself coldly. And if you don't like that place, you've only yourself to blame. You fell into his bed so readily, naturally he thinks you're nothing but an empty-headed little fool.

Her diatribe against herself was picking up steam, her anger rapidly turning to bitterness, when Peter interrupted her.

"I'm sorry I was so long," he said as he got into the driver's seat. "Valmy is very talkative." When Torey said nothing, but stared ahead rigidly, he went on defensively, "Come on, Torey, I wasn't *that* long."

"No," Torey replied, but her voice was cold.

"Then what's wrong?" Peter asked, genuinely taken aback.

"*Nothing.*" Her tone was sharp to the point of rudeness. And Torey's blue eyes were dark with anger.

"Okay," Peter said, expelling a long sigh. "Nothing's wrong. Then why do you look like you'd gladly throw me to the alligators?"

"Why did you treat me like a child who crashed a party for grownups?" Torey asked furiously, turning to face him for the first time.

"So that's it," he said with a knowing nod. "Well, I didn't mean to treat you like a child, if that's what it seemed like. But you were getting more involved in the situation than I thought was appropriate."

"You brought me along because you said you were interested in my opinion," Torey reminded him bitingly.

"So I did. But it's up to me to make a decision about buying that painting. If you and Valmy get into an argument, that merely clouds the issue. It certainly doesn't help matters."

His reasoning did little to mollify Torey; Peter removed the keys from the ignition and suggested, "Let's go for a walk."

Reluctantly, Torey allowed him to help her out of the car. Then she walked beside him as he headed toward the Tuileries gardens nearby. The gardens, with their elevated terraces that looked down along the length of the Champs-Elysées, were a masterpiece of orderliness. Even the clustered chestnut trees were arranged according to design, and the paths were straight pebbled lengths. But merrily bubbling fountains broke the sense of rigid order, and there were surprising hidden glens and unexpected stairways. On thie early summer afternoon, the gardens were crowded with people listening to the chirping birds and admiring the yellow daffodils and red tulips. Mothers pushed baby carriages while children sailed toy boats on a pond.

But Torey was too irritated to enjoy the lovely tableau. As she and Peter sat down on a bench near a magnificent Maillol statue of a reclining nude, her mouth was set in a tight line and she avoided looking at him.

"So what is it really?" Peter asked, watching her closely.

"I *told* you," Torey snapped.

"Somehow I don't think you're angry just because I didn't automatically accept your opinion at the gallery," he said slowly. "I think there's something else bothering you."

When Torey said nothing, he took her chin in his hand lightly and turned her to face him. "I thought we could talk to each other, Torey."

Her icy wall of anger couldn't withstand the warmth and concern in his brown eyes. She said haltingly, "I guess . . . I wanted you to accept me as your intellectual equal. And not simply as a bed-partner."

He nodded and said, "I thought it was something like that. You know, darling, what happened back there had nothing to do with my opinion of your intelligence." He stroked her cheek lightly, then continued, "You're obviously a very sharp lady and you do know a great deal about art. Everything you said to Valmy was true. But it was *my* place to tell him those things, *not* yours."

"I see. I should stay in my place," Torey said bitterly.

"Now don't get all huffy on me. You know what I mean."

Torey knew what he meant. She even knew that he was right. But there was something deeper going on here than merely a disagreement about professional protocol. When Peter asked her to go with him, to participate in his business, she felt he was saying he wanted her to be a more integral part of his life. Now, she felt he was putting her in her place, reminding her that she was only a temporary diversion.

But Torey knew she had no right to expect so much of Peter. If she didn't like the terms of their relationship, she could leave. It was that simple.

"I don't want to argue anymore, Peter," she finally said softly, her voice devoid of emotion.

"Good. Neither do I. Let's go home now."

Torey realized that, in typical male fashion, Peter assumed that if she was dropping the argument, she had forgiven him. He didn't realize how deeply hurt she still was.

Back on the Ile Saint-Louis, Peter suggested a walk along the Seine before dinner. A few minutes later, he and Torey stood on a quay, watching the river, the fishermen, the barges and the patterns of bridges and trees and water. The water was greenish-brown and low, exposing the sides of the quay and the river rocks. Canoes full of children and sailing skiffs passed by. A cool breeze gusting off the water lightly ruffled Torey's hair.

As the boats skimmed by, the ripples on the river became deep folds. It was twilight on the Seine now, a slow, sad and sweet summer evening. As Torey and Peter stood quietly on the parapet, they watched the evening sky close slowly on a last strand of daylight, fading quietly like a sigh.

Torey felt that just as this day was ending, something was also ending between her and Peter. This was a turning point in their relationship. She had to admit what she had known from the beginning but had tried to hide—she loved Peter desperately and wanted more from him than a week's idyll. That was why she wanted him to think of her as more than just a girl he was having a fling with. That was why it meant so much to her when he dismissed her so summarily at the gallery.

From now on, playing Peter's game—being cool, not talking of commitment—would be difficult. Just in this brief time they'd shared in Paris, she'd seen what their life together could be like. They had so much in common, a need for roots, love of art, a shared way of looking at life and people.

Her thoughts were interrupted by Peter. "You're very quiet. Are you still angry?"

"No," Torey said honestly. She was no longer angry. She was the last thing she'd promised herself she would ever be again: deeply hurt.

"I see," Peter said slowly. It was clear he didn't believe her. He sensed that something was still wrong, and he assumed it was the argument they'd had. He took a last look over the water. "We'd better be getting back. Elise will have dinner ready."

Back in her bedroom, Torey changed into the blue silk sheath she'd worn the night she met Peter. And she freshened her make-up, trying to look as bright and sparkling as possible.

At dinner she kept up a steady stream of conversation with Henri, occasionally including Peter, to make it appear that all was well. But it was an effort, and she found herself barely tasting the delicious stuffed quail in rich cream sauce that Elise had prepared with such care.

After dinner, Torey excused herself, saying she was exhausted from the train trip and two days of sightseeing around Paris. Henri seemed to accept her excuse without question. But Peter looked at her thoughtfully for a moment before finally bidding her good night. "I'll see you in the morning. Sleep well."

In her room, Torey undressed and put on her gown and robe. But she was restless, and not nearly sleepy enough yet to go to bed. For a long time she stood by the open French doors on the balcony, looking out at the stars in the clear summer sky.

Now that she had faced the fact that she loved Peter, what could she do about it? Her thoughts were soon interrupted by the sound of someone walking past her bedroom door. The footsteps stopped; she knew it was Peter, for Henri slept at the other end of the floor. For a split second Torey held her breath, waiting, hoping Peter would come to her. If only he would apologize, or perhaps simply sweep her off her feet, smothering her anger with his touch, his kiss. But after a moment he went on to his own room, and

Torey heard his door close firmly. She sighed deeply in disappointment, then went to bed.

Torey lay in bed for a long while, unsuccessfully trying to put it all out of her mind. But her thoughts raced from one disturbing subject to another—being here in this interesting household, in this fabulous city, with Peter . . . her success at her business . . . she could lose it all if she didn't continue to work hard and stay abreast of trends . . . the glassware she had bought in Venice . . . would her customers like it or would it sit on the shelves, gathering dust, a financial loss she couldn't afford . . . the men she had known and how Peter compared to them . . . now that she knew Peter, she didn't understand how she could ever have thought herself in love with Mason. . . .

Her mind was racing furiously from subject to subject. Everything seemed so complicated, and suddenly she had absolutely no confidence in her ability to handle any of it.

This is ridiculous, she told herself. Everything's getting out of proportion. I need to forget about all of it and go to sleep.

But she couldn't sleep.

Finally, after tossing and turning for what seemed like hours, she decided that what she needed was a glass of warm milk. Lying in bed and trying to force sleep to come obviously wasn't working.

She put on her robe and slippers, then padded softly down the stairs to the first floor. She hadn't been in the kitchen, but she knew where it was. As she entered the bright yellow room, she was surprised to find the lights on. Then she saw Peter standing by the stove, pouring milk into a saucepan.

He flashed a quick, wry grin, and said, "I'd better make it a double."

Torey sat down at the small butcher-block table and said quietly, "I couldn't sleep either."

The milk was warm now and Peter poured it into two tall mugs that he took from a nearby cupboard. Handing one to Torey, he sat down opposite her at the table.

Raising his mug in a mock toast, he said, "Here's looking at *you,* kid."

Torey smiled. It was amazing, she thought, how comfortable she and Peter were with each other right now, considering the argument they'd had. He obviously wasn't the sort of man to pout, or draw out a disagreement. And she certainly was anxious to get back to their easy camaraderie. But there were problems that just wouldn't go away. Reality had reared its ugly head, intruding on their romantic fantasy. But just at this moment, Torey didn't want to get back into all of that.

Torey thought how close she felt to Peter now, as they sat at the table. The house was utterly still and quiet at this midpoint between late night and early morning. They were the only two awake, and somehow this made the moment more intimate than all the elegant, sophisticated outings they'd been on.

"I'm glad you were awake too," Torey said. "I feel like talking, but not about what happened today."

"I know," he said. "I feel the same way. I almost came to your room earlier, but I didn't want to press you. You were obviously upset. So for now let's just be friends and talk about things friends talk about."

"Such as?"

"People we've liked and disliked, values, politics . . . whatever you like."

"Who was your very first crush, Peter?" Torey asked suddenly.

Peter grinned. "That's easy. I've never forgotten her. Her name was Jennifer and she developed very early, as they say. Every boy in my eighth grade class was crazy about her. When I asked her to the big Christmas dance, I was more nervous than I've ever been in my life, before or since. And when she said yes, I was stunned. I don't think I've ever felt such pure elation in my life. It was an absolutely perfect moment. Even actually taking her to the dance wasn't quite as wonderful as the moment when she said she'd go with me." Peter paused, clearly lost for a moment in nostalgia. Then he looked at Torey and asked, "Who was your first love?"

"Randy Johnson." Torey smiled, as a misty image of a boy's face full of freckles and topped by a thatch of red hair surfaced in her mind. "He was a bit pudgy so it wasn't the purely physical attraction you felt with Jennifer," Torey teased. "But he had a jar full of coins and every day when the ice cream truck came by, he bought me something. Usually my favorite—chocolate ripple in a sugar cone. I guess I was a pretty practical little girl, putting wealth above good looks."

"A little gold digger." Peter smiled. Then he said softly, "I wish I could have seen you then. I'll bet you were adorable."

Torey smiled, sipping her milk. She didn't really feel she needed it now, though. The tension she had been feeling was quickly leaving her as she talked easily with Peter. That was the amazing thing about him; she always felt perfectly comfortable with him, as if he were a very old friend who knew her so well that she didn't have to bother with pretense.

They talked for a long time, until the milk grew cold. Finally, when they both started yawning, Peter said, "I think it's time for bed."

Torey smiled and nodded, and together they went back up the stairs. At her door Peter kissed her tenderly good night.

"By the way, my door will be unlocked," he said, looking into her eyes. "Just in case . . ."

Torey smiled slowly in understanding. He wasn't forcing himself on her. He was leaving the issue in her hands, the same way he had that first night on the Orient Express.

Then he went into his room, closing the door gently behind him.

In her own room Torey sat down on the edge of her bed and thought about Peter. He was a real find, she knew, in more ways than one. A very unusual man, confident without being arrogant or overbearing, sensitive yet strong.

I'd like a great deal more than just one week in Paris with him, she thought soberly. But if that's all I'm going to have, then I'm going to make the best of it. I'll worry about getting over him when the time comes.

She rose and slipped from her own bedroom, closing the door after her. She tapped lightly on Peter's door, then opened it quickly and entered.

The room was in darkness but moonlight was streaming through the open windows. Torey could see Peter, lying in his bed, the sheet pulled up to his waist, his chest bare. His eyes were wide open, his hands locked behind his head.

His eyes roamed over Torey's silken robe, which had fallen open to reveal the scanty gown beneath. "Did you come here to seduce me?" he smiled.

"Mais naturellement," Torey said in a sly, husky tone.

As Peter laughed, a deep, quiet sound, Torey leaned forward and lightly kissed his temples, his earlobes, and finally his lips. His mouth opened, his tongue meeting hers eagerly. His hands pulled her toward him, pressing her breasts against his bare chest.

He removed her robe and gown deftly, then pulled her into the bed with him. She was locked in his arms, feeling the tantalizing sensation of her bare skin against his. And she knew there was nowhere else she wanted to be.

They caressed each other gently at first. Then, as their passion grew, they each became more demanding, arousing each other more quickly than either had intended. Soon they were joined in a passionate, tumultuous union that completely obliterated the unhappiness they'd felt earlier.

Chapter Eleven

$\mathcal{T}$he next morning Peter dropped Torey off at the boutique that Margot had recommended. It was small but crammed full of exquisite things, especially silk and lace lingerie. Torey found a provocative little silk teddy that she especially liked. Cream-colored, covered with finely embroidered lace, it was ingeniously made so that it was held together by one pink rosebud-covered snap. When that was undone, the whole thing fell away. The thought of Peter unsnapping it was enough to persuade Torey to buy it. She also selected a black teddy for Elena that was only slightly less risque.

"*Mademoiselle* will find this very enjoyable, I think," the salesgirl said in heavily accented English as she wrapped the lingerie.

"I believe I will," Torey replied, smiling.

Outside she quickly caught a taxi and gave the

driver the name of the largest department store in Paris, Au Printemps. It turned out to be huge indeed, consisting of three stores and a supermarket connected by bridges on the second and third floors.

Torey browsed through it happily, picking up some gifts for friends back home and some perfume for herself.

Then she made her way with only slight difficulty to the Faubourg St. Honoré quarter where many of the *haute-couture* houses were located.

For hours she browsed through the showrooms of such famous designers as Lanvin, Dior, Hermès, Courrèges, Chanel, and Pierre Cardin, imagining that she was wealthy and could buy whatever she chose.

And then in a small but exclusive boutique that specialized in dresses by English designers, Torey found the dress of her dreams. It was made of yards and yards of cream-colored chiffon over a silk underskirt. The neckline was a long, low curve from shoulder to shoulder, with a deep, flat ruffle that was embroidered along the hem by seed pearls. The sleeves were layer upon layer of clear chiffon ruffles, ending just below the elbow in a tiny lace band. At the waist was a huge cream-colored silk bow, and along the full, sweeping hemline were more seed pearls in tiny clusters.

Cinderella might have worn it. Or Princess Diana. Torey didn't even look at the price before trying it on. And when she discovered that it would cost her entire clothing allowance for the next six months, she still wanted it desperately. She had no idea where she would wear such a dress, but that didn't matter. Just owning it was enough.

As she left the boutique, the box with the dress securely under her arm, Torey felt that she had been ridiculously extravagant. But she knew also that it was one extravagance she would never regret.

Later, when Peter picked her up and drove her home, she leaned her head against his shoulder.

"I have a surprise for you," she teased, thinking of the lace teddy with the provocative snap.

"And what might that be?"

"Ah, you'll see."

"Can't you show me now?"

"I could," Torey laughed, "but the nearest *gendarme* would arrest me." Then she nuzzled his neck and whispered, "But just wait until tonight."

Peter gave her a look that told her he was satisfactorily intrigued. Then he pulled her even closer to him.

Completely content, Torey snuggled warmly against him.

Margot came to dinner that night. Throughout the evening, Henri kept mentioning that they were leaving for the chateau in the morning for a short stay. Torey suspected there was an underlying reason for these hints, but she didn't understand what it might be.

Then, when Margot was preparing to leave, Henri finally asked openly, "Why don't you come with us? You love it there at this time of year."

Margot gave him a direct, no-nonsense look, and responded firmly, "I told you, Henri, that I have other plans. I cannot drop everything to accompany you when it is convenient for you."

Her tone was far from sharp, yet Torey sensed that she was making an important point to him.

Admitting defeat gracefully, Henri said, "You are right, of course. It is just that I will miss you."

"I will miss you, too, *mon cher,*" Margot replied with obvious affection. Then she turned to Torey. "Goodbye, *chérie.* You must promise me you will come by to see me before you leave Paris."

"Of course, Margot. I'll make a point of it."

Margot kissed her warmly on both cheeks, then left, accompanied by Henri who walked her to her car out on the street.

"I'm going to have a nightcap with Henri when he gets back," Peter said to Torey, as they turned away from the door and went back into the sitting room. "But I won't be long."

"Okay, I'll show you your surprise then."

"Oh, yes, *that.* I definitely won't be long, then," he said, giving her a quick, teasing kiss.

A few minutes later, Torey sat in a corner of her bed, waiting expectantly. Peter entered the dark room which was lit only by the pale moonlight streaming in through the tall windows. He crossed to her quickly, his eyes wide with pleased surprise. But they narrowed speculatively as he took in the sensuous teddy.

"Does this snap do what I think it does?" he asked, his fingers lightly exploring the tiny fastener.

"Yes, but . . ." Torey began.

Before she could finish he had flicked open the snap with one finger and the teddy fell away to reveal her high, rounded breasts, narrow waist, and gently curving hips.

"But, Peter," she protested half-heartedly as he pulled her down onto the bed. "I think, considering the small fortune it cost, you should enjoy it a bit longer."

"Believe me," he said huskily, "I enjoyed it." Then he silenced her protest with his searing kisses.

Chapter Twelve

Torey and Peter left for the château early the following morning. Henri had gone ahead, with Elise.

When they had left the city and had traveled some distance on a broad highway, Torey asked, "Are we far from the château?"

"No, it's only about fifty miles southeast of Paris. It's in the Ile de France, the green belt surrounding the city. You'll probably recognize much of it. It's been painted by all the great ones, Renoir, Monet, Cézanne. . . ."

"It must be beautiful."

"*Very*. It's really the heart of France. Caesar's armies marched through the area. There are Roman-esque ruins, Gothic cathedrals, castles, forests, sleepy villages. And, of course, châteaus."

"Are you near a town at the château?"

"Yes, Provins. A charming little place, with medieval cobbled streets. The upper town, *ville-haute,* is perched on a promontory, and the lower town, *ville-basse,* is crossed by two rivers, the Durteint and the Voulzie, which both flow into the Seine."

"Sounds beautiful," Torey said. "And romantic."

"It is, with ancient stone towers and bastions. And way back in the thirteenth century there were ramparts protecting it from the vast plains of Brie. You can still see some of those old battlements." He smiled, anticipating Torey's next question. "And yes, I will take you on a guided tour of the whole place."

Torey laughed, then leaned back against the seat and relaxed. The day was fine so Peter had lowered the top of the car, and Torey luxuriated in the warm wind blowing through her hair. Occasionally she glanced at Peter, sitting near her in the small car. A careful driver, he was intent on the road, only rarely flashing her a quick glance.

As she watched him surreptitiously, she thought how hard it was to believe that she had only known him four days. Four short days, filled with one surprise after another. Four nights filled with bliss.

It was incredible how abruptly life could change. On Wednesday afternoon, all she had been thinking about was her business. She was uninvolved, at loose ends emotionally, not sure she would ever experience real love. Then that night she met Peter. And by breakfast on Thursday she knew that she was capable of feeling love more deeply than she ever would have suspected.

The thought was reassuring in a way. She was happy at this moment, glad to be in love and not to have missed the experience. But she was also frightened. Such love was inherently dangerous, for it held the possibility of pain as well as pleasure, especially with a man like Peter, and with a relationship such as theirs. Peter's life was perfect; he had no reason to change it. And from the beginning their relationship had been a mad, impulsive affair, led by their hearts and not their heads. If there had been time to develop a friendship first, would things be different? Would Peter talk to her of love and marriage, and would she feel more sure about her own sense of judgment?

She felt ambivalent about their relationship. She wanted Peter to feel all this as deeply as she did. She wanted to mean something to him. Yet she was unsure of marriage, and especially of her own ability to make a commitment to it, after she had been so hurt once by the experience. Part of her wanted Peter to speak to her of love and marriage. But if he did, she wasn't at all sure how she would respond.

I want it both ways, she finally admitted to herself. I want to be loved but I don't want to risk being hurt again.

Suddenly Peter turned and caught her pensive look. "Penny for your thoughts," he said, smiling at her quickly before returning his attention to the road.

For one giddy moment Torey thought about telling him honestly what was occupying her mind. My thoughts are in turmoil. I love you, but I don't know if you love me. And even if you do, how do we know if we're really right for each other? This is really just a fantasy we're living.

Instead, Torey smiled slowly and said, "They're not worth the price."

Peter laughed and pulled her closer, keeping one

and furnish
elegant seve
"Has it a l
as Peter op
"Always
generations
land was o
confessor to
till you see
nese bridge
flowers."
"How ca
"It isn't
wonder wh
really love
about it. F
were too
Gabrielle,
been spend
must be a
Just the
ing happily
crossed the
"Welcom
cheeks. "
country ho
"Henri,
it."
"Wait til
led her ins
the hallwa
ued, "Pete
and I'll as

hand carefully on the leather-covered steering wheel. "All right, minx. You can have your thoughts. But your body belongs to me."

"Yes," she agreed in a whisper. And my heart, she added to herself.

"Here's the drive," Peter said with barely contained excitement.

He turned up a long, forested drive. The romantic, mysterious woods obscured the château itself for several minutes.

"There were stag and boar running wild here ages ago," Peter said as they drove along the narrow, paved lane. "They provided many a feast for celebrating Delacroix. Now there's only a few rabbits and squirrels. You'll be able to see the house in a moment."

When the château finally did come into view, its sheer magnificence left Torey breathless. Built of cream-colored brick, it was three stories tall in the center, with flanking two-story wings. Tall windows with gray shutters looked out on the sweeping grounds. The design was simple, devoid of ornamentation—in a word, classic. A stone esplanade ran the length of the house, with broad steps leading down to carefully manicured lawns. An artificial lake reflected the house.

"Peter, it's incredible. You didn't tell me it was so . . . so imposing."

"There's no way I could have prepared you for it. It has to be seen to be believed. It amazes me each time I see it, and I've been here a hundred times."

As he stopped the car near the front steps, he said blithely, "House by Mansart, gardens by Le Notre, and furnishings by Jacob. A splendid example of elegant seventeenth-century living."

"Has it always been in your family?" Torey asked, as Peter opened the door and helped her out.

"Always. That's the really amazing part. Seventeen generations of Delacroix have lived here, since the land was originally given to *Père* Delacroix, father confessor to Louis XIV. It was finished in 1676. Wait till you see the gardens in back—a marvelous Japanese bridge hung with wisteria amid thousands of flowers."

"How can you ever bear to leave?"

"It isn't easy. Sometimes as I'm driving off, I wonder why on earth I don't just stay forever. Henri really loves it here, despite the casual way he talks about it. For a while he stayed away because there were too many painful memories of his wife, Gabrielle, who died a few years ago. But lately he's been spending more and more time here again. Which must be a sign that he's getting over her loss."

Just then Henri appeared at the front door, beaming happily at them. As they mounted the steps, he crossed the broad esplanade to greet them.

"Welcome," he said, kissing them both on the cheeks. "Well, Torey, what do you think of our country house?"

"Henri, it's magnificent. There's no other word for it."

"Wait till you see the interior." Taking her hand, he led her inside, and Peter followed with her luggage. In the hallway lined with marble columns, Henri continued, "Peter, why don't you leave Torey's bags here and I'll ask one of the servants to deliver them to her room." Turning back to Torey, he explained, "We keep no permanent servants here. Whenever I'm in residence, as they say, I hire some villagers from Provins. Elise has a field day, supervising a kitchen staff instead of doing it all herself. Come, let me show you around the house."

They went first into the sitting room that opened off the entryway. It was a large room, richly paneled in golden brown, and made sunny and cheerful by the numerous floor to ceiling windows. A large fireplace with a carved wood mantle was the focus of the room, and most of the furniture was arranged around it. Torey immediately noticed Elise's touch in the many bowls and vases of fresh flowers that brightened the room. The raised white ceiling was ornately carved and the polished wood floors were covered with oriental carpets in shades of red, blue, and brown.

"The furniture was hand-carved by the great cabinetmaker, Georges Jacob," Henri explained. "My wife found it in the attic, gathering dust, and had it refinished and upholstered. In fact, Gabrielle renovated the entire house," he continued as they left the sitting room. "It was rather run-down and some modern decor had been added that clashed with the old-fashioned ambience. Gabrielle researched every scrap of fabric, every fitting and fixture from the doorknobs to the fireplace plates that needed replacement. She wanted it to be absolutely authentic."

"She did a marvelous job," Torey said with complete sincerity. "It looks as if it were always this way."

"Yes," Henri agreed, his brown eyes twinkling merrily. "Sometimes I can almost imagine I see the ghosts of my ancestors, dressed in breeches and long gowns, walking about these rooms, nodding approvingly."

"If there are any ghosts walking about this place, they've got to be right here in this spot," Peter said as they entered a spacious, richly decorated room.

"This is the *chambre du Roi*," Henri explained. "During the reign of Louis XVI, every château was required to have a room in which he could be received at any time. We use this as a guest room now. Even today it's rather impressive, I think, with that Tiepolo ceiling."

The vaulted ceiling, with intricate designs and reliefs of naked male and female figures carved into it, was stunning. It was truly a room fit for a king. The walls were covered in peach-colored silk wallpaper, and peach-colored velvet drapes hung at the tall windows. An oriental carpet in shades of peach and blue covered the floor. The furniture was all antique and obviously costly. Yet, somehow, the room was too formal—too frankly overpowering—to be comfortable, and Torey found herself hoping this was not to be her room.

As if reading her thoughts, Peter smiled and said, "Don't worry, we're not sticking you away in here. Over the years we've found that most guests prefer something a bit cozier. Come on, we'll show you to your room."

Torey was shown down a long hallway from the *chambre du Roi,* and into a bedroom. "This room once belonged to Peter's mother," Henri explained as they entered. It was relatively small, compared to the formal guest room, but large enough to include a small sitting area in front of the fireplace. The mood here was entirely different, and much more warm and comfortable. A lovely floral print in shades of pale rose and beige covered the chairs, the draperies, and the bed. The carpet covering the gleaming wood floor was plain beige. Light streamed in through the open French doors, reflecting off the cream-colored walls. It was bright, cheerful, and thoroughly enchanting, and Torey knew she would love staying there.

"Judging by your expression"—Henri smiled—"it is clear you prefer the simple pleasures to the magnificence of a king's chamber."

"This is a lovely room. Even lovelier than my room at your house in Paris."

"There's a bathroom through that door," Peter said, pointing to a door in a far corner. "We *do* have some modern amenities here."

"I can tell Elise has been here," Torey said, crossing to a vase of roses sitting on a small round table in front of a window.

"Yes, the first thing she did this morning was go out into the flower gardens and pick several bouquets. The very first one came to this room. You've made a conquest there, Torey," Henri said warmly.

Torey smiled at him appreciatively.

Suddenly a young maid wearing a simple, short black dress and white apron, appeared in the doorway. *"Pardon, monsieur,* but Madame Jobert asked me to tell you that luncheon is being served on the terrace."

"Merci, Ginevre," Henri replied.

The maid smiled in a friendly, curious way at Torey, then left.

"We'd better go. Elise becomes absolutely apoplectic if we let her food grow cold," Henri continued. "We can finish the tour another time."

"The terrace overlooks the gardens," Peter said, as they made their way back along the hallway. "They are truly beautiful at this time of year."

Access to the terrace was through French doors in the sitting room. The terrace was unadorned, save for the traditionally French boxed orange trees. But the view was stunning. Peter hadn't exaggerated when he said there were thousands of flowers. There were, and of every imaginable variety and color. The elegant lines of the carefully designed garden only served to accent the riot of color. In the distance, Torey saw the Japanese bridge Peter had mentioned, and beyond it a dreamy setting of weeping willows and rhododendrons in vivid red and pink. It was a setting meant for romance, and Torey vowed that before she left this house, Peter would walk with her across that bridge and kiss her in that lovely glade.

As they sat down at the table that was set with a white linen cloth and simple yet pretty country pottery, Torey said, "It's another world here. The twentieth century might never have happened."

"Nor the revolution," Henri added, "that sent Marie Antoinette to the guillotine."

It was a light lunch of salad with cucumber dressing and crepes stuffed with chicken and broccoli, and during the meal Henri talked to Torey about the history of the château. It was apparent how much it meant to him, and to Peter as well. Though Peter said little, he was very much at home here, more relaxed than he had seemed earlier. Both on the train and in Paris, Peter had been full of nervous energy, in a way that was natural for a young, ambitious man on his way to the top in a highly charged profession. But here at the château, he let himself relax completely.

As she looked around at the house and the beautiful grounds spreading out to the thick forest in the background, Torey envied Peter. It occurred to her that Peter's basic self-confidence probably came, at least in part, from having all this—knowing not only where he came from, but where his ancestors came from. Behind Peter West were centuries of privilege, as well as responsibility, and he wore it well.

"Let's go for a ride," Peter suggested as they finished lunch.

"All I have to wear are jeans," Torey said doubtfully.

"That's okay. We're not riding to hounds."

"And I don't have any boots," Torey further protested, although a bit lamely. The fact was, she was afraid of making a fool of herself in front of Peter, who was bound to be an excellent rider. Torey thought horses were fine creatures, but she had absolutely no confidence in her ability to stay up on one if it broke into anything faster than a mild canter.

"Don't worry," Peter reassured her. "I'm sure we can find some around here that will fit. And we'll find you a nice, gentle mount."

"The mare, Violette, is a good mount, not at all likely to run off with Torey," Henri suggested.

Torey gave in. "All right. But if I take a spill you've got to promise not to laugh."

"Of course," Peter said with mock seriousness. "Not even a chuckle."

"Peter," Henri suggested, "why don't you take

173

Torey back to her room to change, and meanwhile I'll try to find some boots for her."

Back in her room, it only took Torey five minutes to change. She was just pulling her hair back in a pony tail when there was a knock at the door. Opening it, she found the young maid, Ginevre, standing there, holding three pairs of boots.

"Pardon, *mademoiselle,* but Monsieur Delacroix said that he hopes you will find something suitable in this group."

"Merci. I'm sure I will." She took the boots from Ginevre rather awkwardly and dumped them on the bed. Then she sat down and began trying them on. None was a perfect fit, but one pair was only slightly too large. Torey was just getting into them when Peter stopped at her open door and looked in. He had changed into a plain blue shirt, open at the throat, and faded jeans tucked into riding boots.

"Find something that will do?"

"Yes, now if only the horse will cooperate." Torey smiled.

"Don't worry," he said. "I have no intention of letting anything happen to you."

Torey suddenly frowned. "Oh, Peter, do you mind if I make a quick phone call before we leave?"

"Of course not. There's a phone in my room. I'll show you."

Peter's room was only slightly larger than Torey's. It was clearly a man's room, furnished simply, almost sparingly. A simple checked and fringed blanket covered the bed. There was a leather-tufted chair for reading and roomy armchairs at the writing desk and a small tea table. The wall-coverings and draperies were done in an oriental tree-of-life pattern that Torey knew had been popular in the country style of the 1700s.

"This *is* nice," Torey said admiringly.

"Henri let me choose the decorations myself," Peter said. "That was considerate of him, since my taste tends to be a bit more rugged than his."

"Well, you have *very* good taste," Torey said, seating herself at his desk where the telephone was. "I'm afraid this is going to be a long distance call. I want to repay Henri for it, but . . ."

"Don't be ridiculous. You're our guest. Who are you calling, if you don't mind my asking."

"The man who makes that *faïence* Margot told me about. I thought if he isn't too far away I could take a train and visit his factory."

"You shouldn't be thinking about business right now. This is a vacation," Peter admonished gently.

"I have a living to make, Peter," Torey reminded him, a little annoyed that he should take her business concerns so lightly.

"Sorry," Peter replied briefly. Then, clearly trying to make amends for stirring up trouble, he added, "But don't worry about taking the train. I'll drive you there and we'll make a day of it. It'll give you a chance to see the countryside. You can't go back to San Francisco thinking that all France is châteaus and Paris."

"Marvelous," Torey said, grinning happily.

The call went quickly. The manager was more than willing to meet with a prospective American buyer, and gave Torey detailed instructions on how to get to Quimper.

When Torey hung up, Peter said, "That's in Brittany, on the northwest coast. It's rather a long drive, four hours or so. But if we leave early we can do it in a day. And you'll see some interesting country."

"Oh, Peter, you don't know how much I appreciate this. I'm very excited about going there. The manager, Monsieur Poterat, said Quimper is the headquarters for *faïence*. They've been turning it out since the seventeenth century."

"Well, enough business for one day. Let's go riding," Peter insisted.

Torey agreed happily. She was so excited about the trip the following day that she was no longer very concerned about her riding ability.

At the ancient stone stables, Henri was waiting with two saddled horses. Torey was given the smaller, more placid mount, an aging buttermilk-colored mare, while Peter took the spirited roan gelding.

As they headed off on a path that led into the forest, Torey quickly relaxed. It was obvious the mare had no intention of going any faster than she was absolutely required to go.

Save for the chattering of birds high in the branches of the trees, it was quiet as they rode; the stillness was broken only by the crack of the horses' hooves snapping twigs, or the low plopping sound of them on the dirt of the path. The sunlight filtering through the tall trees made patches of dancing light on the forest floor. The woods were cool, dim, and lovely. Occasionally they passed tiny, bubbling streams and small glades.

After an hour or so, Peter suggested they dismount at a clearing. It was secluded and cozy, and carpeted with soft green grass. Trees made a circle around the tiny glen and Torey could hear the trickle of a brook somewhere nearby. Tiny yellow and white wildflowers grew in small clumps in the lush green grass, gilded by spangles of sunlight from above.

Torey dismounted and stretched out on the grass while Peter tied the horses to a tree. Then he joined her.

"You and Violette seem to be doing fine," he said, sitting on the grass beside her.

"Yes, we're becoming fast friends—in the sense that she doesn't want to go fast and I don't want her to go fast."

Peter laughed, "Feeling sore yet?"

"Not at all."

"Well, you will if I keep you out too long. We'll head back soon, by a different route, so you can see a bit more of the country."

"I love what I've seen so far," Torey replied happily, stretching out fully on the grass with her head in Peter's lap. As she looked up, she could see the pattern of branches and leaves and flaring points of sunlight high above her.

Peter looked down at her, brushing tendrils of hair away from her cheeks.

"Enjoying yourself?"

"Yes. I haven't felt this happy since . . . since my parents were alive," Torey said quite truthfully. Lying there with her head cradled on Peter's lap, listening to the muted forest sounds and breathing the rich aroma of the earth, Torey could honestly judge it to be an absolutely perfect day.

They talked and laughed for several long, lazy minutes, then Torey said, "Tell me about Gabrielle."

"I only knew her for a short while," Peter said thoughtfully. "She died several years ago. But she was a wonderful person. I don't recall ever hearing her say a harsh word about anyone."

"Henri loved her very much, didn't he?"

"Yes. He's only recently begun to get over her loss. I think that's what attracted him to Margot at first. Having been Gabrielle's friend, she was able to share with him the pain and loss of her death. Now, though, I'm sure Henri loves Margot only for herself."

Pain and loss. Torey knew she, too, would be feeling those same emotions when this week was over. Suddenly there was a special poignancy to the beauty of this day, for it was ephemeral; it wouldn't last.

After a moment of watching her closely, Peter said, "You look as if you belong here, somehow."

"I feel that way." She turned to face him, smiling up at him. "I've been imagining what it must have been like here centuries ago."

"Maybe that's the previous life you mentioned." Peter smiled. "I was the arrogant aristocrat and you were . . ."

"And I was the village maiden whom you shamelessly took advantage of," Torey laughed.

"Well, there *was* feudal privilege, you know," Peter chuckled.

"You don't need *droit du seigneur* now," Torey said, now no longer teasing, but in a voice low and soft with desire. The intensity of her feeling about the fleeting quality of her happiness made her want Peter urgently. Suddenly there seemed so little time and so much of him she wanted to know.

She reached up to stroke his cheek lightly, then her fingertips moved down to his shoulders and his smooth chest. They stopped at his stomach. It was flat and hard, and the muscles contracted at her touch.

Peter looked startled, then pleased. Torey watched his brown eyes darken with desire. She smiled a slow, pleased smile. "Just how private is this little corner of the forest you've brought me to, Peter?"

"Private enough. It's Delacroix land. We won't be interrupted."

Slowly he pulled her into a kiss. Just before his mouth found hers, she caught his special scent. Then all awareness beyond the feel of him was blocked out. As his lips insistently parted hers, his thumb gently stroked the tiny hollow behind her ear, moving down her throat sensuously.

Torey felt herself arching toward him, pressing her body closer to him. She wrapped her arms around his neck, and returned his kiss wholeheartedly. Whatever slight hesitation she felt about their trysting place disappeared in the intensity of her desire for him.

The eagerness of her response, her wanton abandonment to passion in the glade, brought an immediate response from Peter. His kiss was demanding. now, communicating his raw hunger for her. His tongue penetrated her softly yielding lips and probed the warm moistness of her mouth.

He shifted position then, moving onto his side and

pulling her with him, so that they lay facing each other, their bodies pressed tightly together from head to toe.

Neither of them wanted the barrier of clothing now. With consummate ease, Peter unbuttoned her blouse and slipped it from her shoulders. Her silky, lacy bra followed, then the boots and jeans. Finally she lay naked against him. Then she undressed him, letting her hands roam freely, boldly over his body. She explored the contours that were becoming so familiar, and felt a secret exultation at the response her touch elicited from him.

The grass felt cool and soft, tickling her skin in a pleasant way. The slight breeze was whisper-soft as it caressed her nakedness. She felt free and natural, and knew that this was the way love-making was supposed to be, with no barriers of any kind.

"You're a wood nymph," Peter whispered huskily, pulling her to his hard, naked body. "And you've enchanted me."

"You're my lord and master," Torey whispered slyly in response, her lips nibbling at his ear. "And you may have your wicked way with me."

His arms held her tightly, one hand pressed between her shoulder blades to hold her as close to him as possible. Kissing her wasn't enough now. His lips traveled from the base of her throat where her pulse was wildly racing, to her high, rounded breasts.

Torey threw back her head, glorying in the exquisite pleasure of his touch. When his lips found her taut nipples, she moaned, a low animal sound deep in her throat. Instinctively, her hands slipped around his neck, pulling him against her. Her sensitive palms felt the tiny, soft curling hairs on the back of his neck, then she let them run down his back, loving the feel of rippling muscles beneath her fingertips.

Peter moved, allowing his lips and tongue to move in tantalizing circles over her quivering stomach, drawing her inexorably into eddying currents of desire.

The passion she'd felt was now a raw ache that needed desperately to be assuaged. Torey was past thinking; she was in the iron grip of elemental impulses and age-old instinct. When Peter brought his lips back to hers, she kissed him deeply, her hands continuing to explore his body. Her hips began to move in a rhythm against him that rapidly grew more urgent.

Torey wanted Peter to take her *now,* forcefully, while she was at a feverish pitch of excitement.

"Peter," she whispered, making the gasp an urgent plea.

His brown eyes were heavy-lidded with desire for her. Then as he entered her, she closed her eyes, obliterating everything but the sensation of being possessed by him. The feel of the grass, the soft sigh of the wind—all of it disappeared as Torey fell head-long into a dark, yawning chasm from which she never wanted to return.

Holding Torey close against him, Peter lay on his back, staring up at the patches of sky he could see between the branches of the trees. Torey sighed, then rested her cheek against the hardness of his chest. There were tiny beads of sweat glistening on his body and his golden brown hair was damp to her touch. She could feel her own hair hanging damply against her neck.

They had just coupled with unthinking, unreasoning abandonment, yet she felt her love for him more profoundly than ever. She had given herself to him totally, in the open, hiding behind nothing, not even the emotional barriers she'd once used. There was nothing more of herself she could give him.

She was so sated, so completely relaxed, that it startled her when he moved. He sat up, bringing her with him. Then he crooked one finger under her chin and lifted her face to his. He looked at her, an expression of wonderment in his eyes, and kissed her gently, without passion now, but with infinite tenderness.

Torey wanted desperately to know what he thought of her at this moment, if he was pleased with her, if what had just happened meant as much to him as it did to her. A doubt hovered at the back of her mind. What if he thought her too wanton, too easily taken?

"That was . . ." He stopped, clearly searching for the right words. Torey's mind was in an agony now. She could never regret what had happened—she could never regret anything that she and Peter shared. But if he didn't feel the love that had been at the center of their passion . . . that would greatly diminish her happiness at this moment.

"I don't have the words to say," he finally whispered, shaking his head impatiently.

"All I want to know is what you feel," Torey encouraged him. But her stomach was tight with anxiety.

"What I feel is that . . ." he said, turning to look

deeply into her eyes, ". . . you are the softest, loveliest thing I've ever known in my life. And what I feel is that what we just had was absolutely unique, that it could never possibly be that good again." The "never" made Torey's heart almost stop, and then he smiled. "And yet I also feel that it will be that good every time I'm with you."

Torey wasn't aware she'd been holding her breath until it came out in a huge sigh of relief. And then, because she had absolutely no idea what to say to him, and because she felt giddy with happiness, she laughed. She laughed deeply, joyfully, and then Peter was laughing with her, until they collapsed in each other's arms in exhaustion.

"We're very silly, you know," Torey said finally, wiping tears of laughter from her eyes.

"Because we made love in the middle of a forest?"

"Because we laughed about it."

"Well, I wouldn't want it any other way," Peter said, kissing her again gently.

She wrapped her arms around his neck and leaned her cheek against his broad chest once more. Then she kissed him there, enjoying the salty taste of his skin.

"I am the maid, and you're the master," she teased.

Peter kissed the top of her head and stroked her hair. "I think that might be turned around. I feel entirely under your enchantment right now."

Torey looked up at him and he cupped her face in his hands. His brown eyes looked at her with such love that for a moment she expected him to say "I love you."

Then the horses moved restlessly, a flock of birds

fluttered out of a nearby tree and the moment passed. He pulled her head against his chest and wrapped his arms around her.

Torey wasn't really disappointed. The look in his eyes had been enough.

"Why don't we stay here forever?" she suggested half-seriously. "We could run wild through the trees and eat nuts and berries. It would do wonders for my figure."

Peter chuckled. "True. But would you really be willing to give up Elise's cooking?"

"Absolutely not." Torey laughed, standing up and dusting off the grass and leaves from her body. "And speaking of that, I'm suddenly ravenous. Why don't we go back?"

Peter laughed deeply, then he also rose and began dressing. When they mounted the horses a few minutes later, he turned to Torey and said, "You're an enigma, Victoria Jenson. You can look delightfully innocent and proper, then behave in a way that an experienced courtesan would envy."

Torey laughed. "I'll take that as a compliment." Then she urged on the reluctant Violette and followed Peter down the path.

He called over his shoulder. "You should. It was meant to be."

"If I'm sore tonight, it won't be entirely due to the horseback ride," Torey said, rubbing her back. It was beginning to feel a bit stiff already. "I think I'll soak in a hot bath before dinner."

"Need someone to wash your back?" Peter asked with a mock leer.

"I believe I can manage by myself," Torey said

archly, but she flashed a warm smile that acknowledged their recent intimacy.

They continued to chat amiably for a while, before Peter turned off from the path. Making their way carefully through a thin stand of poplars, they quickly came to a paved road. Torey recognized it as the winding drive that led to the château.

"This will be faster than going back through the forest," Peter explained. "It'll give you more time for that bath."

They were just coming up to the château when Torey saw a rider approaching them at a canter. It was a woman on a magnificent black gelding. She was dressed in formal riding attire: knee-high, shiny black boots, tight white riding breeches, and a loose white silk blouse. With her flaxen hair pulled back into a tightly coiled bun at the nape of her neck, she looked the picture of the perfect equestrienne. She controlled the prancing, snorting horse with an ease that belied the skill behind it.

"Peter!" she exclaimed happily, pulling her horse up beside his. "I heard you were staying at the château and I came to see you. But Henri said you were riding. What a lucky coincidence." She spoke in a low, throaty voice with a thick French accent.

Somehow, Torey guessed who she was before Peter spoke. "Chantal, what a surprise. I didn't know you were here."

As Torey's eyes took in Peter's former lover, she felt her own appearance was sadly lacking. Her faded jeans and borrowed boots hardly compared to Chantal's equestrienne wardrobe. In contrast, Chantal was perfectly groomed. Her luminous green eyes and honey-colored skin went well with her pale, spun-gold hair. Slim and fragile-looking, there was an ethereal quality about her that Torey suspected men found irresistible.

She glanced quickly at Peter, who was smiling at Chantal in a friendly, yet not overly interested way.

"Chantal Fabre, this is Torey Jenson," Peter said. "Torey is our houseguest."

Houseguest. The term jolted Torey. It was so impersonal and could have implied that she was a guest of Henri, not Peter. After the intimacy they had known, how could Peter dismiss her so casually? Suddenly she felt cold inside. Houseguest. With that one word Peter had hurt her more profoundly than he could ever know. She looked at him more in puzzlement than in anger.

Chantal favored Torey with a brilliant smile and said easily, "Pleased to meet you, Mademoiselle Jenson. Is this your first visit to the area?"

"Yes. It's very lovely," Torey replied slowly.

Turning once more to Peter, Chantal continued, "I came over to invite you to a tennis party the Marchants are having tomorrow afternoon, Peter. It will be great fun. The Floquets will be there. They're thinking of selling their art collection, you know. When I told them you lived here, they were most anxious to meet you. They'd like your advice."

Peter's look sharpened with interest. "They're selling all of it?"

"Yes. With the political climate the way it is, they are considering selling everything and moving to Monaco. No taxes, you know."

"I'd be happy to talk to them. I know they have one

or two pieces my museum would be interested in bidding on."

Torey listened with near disbelief. This man who was so eagerly discussing business was the same man she'd made love to only minutes before. As he talked to Chantal, he seemed to have forgotten Torey's very existence.

"That should work out well, then." Chantal smiled. "Perhaps you can do some business between sets of tennis." Turning to Torey, she made her goodbye, "It was so nice meeting you, Mademoiselle Jenson. I'll look forward to seeing you tomorrow."

Before Torey could reply that she wouldn't be able to make it, Chantal kicked her horse's flanks and was off.

Pulling herself together, Torey said in a deceptively calm voice, "Peter, we can't go to the party tomorrow. We're going to Quimper, remember?"

"Oh." The look on his face clearly indicated that he had completely forgotten their plans. "Well," he said, "we can go the next day."

"I made a very definite appointment with the manager," Torey explained slowly. "This is a business trip, not a pleasure jaunt that can be canceled at the last minute. Surely this tennis party isn't that important."

"No, although it will be fun. The Marchants are very nice people. I always enjoy their company. But more importantly, I want to talk to the Floquets. If they are seriously considering selling their collection, I might be able to make some important purchases for the museum. They have some remarkable pre-Raphaelite art."

"Peter, *my* business is important, too."

"It can't be that important," Peter insisted.

"It is," Torey replied, growing angrier by the minute. The hurt she felt at his nonchalant treatment of her hadn't disappeared. But it was masked now by this argument over business. It was easier and safer somehow to let him think this was what was bothering her. "I don't know when I'll be back in France again. If I don't take care of this now, it could be quite a while before I get a chance to do it again."

"Torey, it can't be that crucial."

"A tennis party can't be that crucial either," Torey said. She wanted to add, "Unless, of course, you're so anxious to see Chantal." But with admirable restraint, she stopped herself. It would make her sound too much like a jealous girl friend, as if she had some claim on Peter. Bitterly she realized that despite the closeness, the intimacy they'd shared earlier, she had no real hold on him at all. His behavior had made that perfectly clear.

"It's ridiculous to argue about this, Torey. Believe me, you'd really enjoy the party. And we'll go to Quimper another time."

"My business has to come first, Peter," Torey said matter-of-factly. "Just as your business comes first with you."

"You can hardly compare some ceramic geese and rabbits with fine art," Peter said dryly.

"Those geese and rabbits will help support me," Torey said with no little heat. "To *me*, they're every bit as important as any work of art is to *you*."

"Torey, you're making this difficult when it doesn't have to be."

"You're right," she snapped. "It doesn't have to be. So I'll go to Quimper alone, and you'll go to the party. I'm sure I'll have no problem finding my way."

"Torey."

Torey prodded her mount. "We'd better be going, Peter. There isn't much time before dinner."

With a skill that surprised her, she kicked the reluctant Violette into a canter and headed off toward the château. The magic of the afternoon had compeletely evaporated now. Once more reality had intruded and left its ugly mark.

Dinner was miserable. Torey said little. She could tell Henri was puzzled by the change in the atmosphere between her and Peter, but he asked no direct questions. For his part, Peter tried to keep up a pretense that there was really nothing wrong, but his carefree manner rang false. Torey knew that he felt the depth of her disappointment.

Afterward she excused herself, saying she had some calls to make, and then wanted to retire early. She explained that she was tired from the traveling, sightseeing and shopping she'd done. Neither Henri nor Peter questioned her.

Later, as Torey dressed for bed, then sat at the vanity table brushing her hair, she thought about Peter being at the party with Chantal—laughing with her, talking with her, touching . . .

There was a soft knock at the door. Torey went to the door and opened it, still holding the brush in her hand.

Peter stood outside. "May I come in?" he asked.

"Yes," Torey replied. It flashed through her mind that this was the first time Peter had asked permission to enter her room. And it was the first time he wasn't welcome.

She wasn't at all happy to see him just then. Only one thing would mend their relationship at that point —if he offered to go with her to Quimper after all. And she was certain he wasn't going to do that.

Torey sat down on the small sofa in front of the fireplace, curling her legs up beneath her. Peter sat down next to her. He ran one fingertip lightly down her cheek to the soft underside of her chin.

"This fight is a ridiculous waste of time," he said, smiling. "There are many much more enjoyable things we could be doing."

He leaned over to kiss her, but Torey pulled away. She couldn't respond to him right now. She was still too hurt by his behavior earlier.

"I'm sorry, Peter," she said. "I'm very tired and I think I'll just go to bed, if you don't mind."

After a moment's hesitation, Peter replied, "Of course. I understand." Then he continued, "About tomorrow . . ."

"I'm taking the train. I called the information number and got the schedule. I also arranged for a taxi to pick me up in the morning to take me to the station."

"I see. So your plans are all made, then."

"I told you this is important to me."

"Has anyone ever told you how exasperatingly stubborn you are?" Peter said irritably.

"I think I would grant *you* pride of place in that regard," Torey responded, her anger flaring.

Peter rose stiffly. "Have a nice trip, then."

He left, shutting the door just a bit harder than was absolutely necessary.

For a long while, Torey sat on the sofa, barely moving. Her mind was in turmoil. She wanted to throw things. She wanted to scream. She wanted to cry. She wanted to do all three at once.

Finally, she said furiously, *"Damn* you, Peter West!"

She went to bed then, but she didn't go to sleep for a long, long time.

Chapter Thirteen

$\mathscr{P}$eter sat in a lawn chair in the shade of a chestnut tree. Nearby, a refreshment tent had been set up on the well-manicured lawns of the Château de Baynard, and servants circulated with trays of drinks and hors d'oeuvres. Peter was sipping a delicate chilled white wine and watching a tennis game on the nearby court. Henri and Claude Marchant were teamed against Chantal and Patricia Marchant.

Peter had dressed for tennis, in white shorts and a blue and white striped T-shirt. But somehow he didn't feel like playing. He also didn't feel like chatting sociably with the numerous people who kept stopping to say hello. In fact, he didn't really feel much like being at a party at all.

He should be having a good time, he told himself repeatedly. He liked most of the people here, it was a beautiful day for tennis, and the food and drink were great. In short, there were all the ingredients for a really good time. But something was missing. The smile that Chantal flashed at him wasn't the smile he was looking for.

He wanted Torey. It was that simple. Without her, none of this was at all enjoyable.

Why the hell couldn't she be reasonable? he asked himself angrily. She didn't have to go to Quimper today. She could have been with him. After all, they only had a few more days together.

But that line of thought left him feeling inexplicably guilty, and he quickly abandoned it.

When the game ended, Henri joined Peter, sitting down next to him and mopping his sweating brow with a small towel.

"Do not believe what they say about women being the weaker sex, Peter," Henri said tiredly. "They have an amazing amount of stamina." When Peter didn't respond, Henri looked at him carefully. "You're surprisingly quiet today. Is anything wrong?"

"Of course not. What could be wrong?" Peter snapped.

Henri leaned back in the chair and gratefully accepted the lemonade that a servant offered. After taking a long sip, he answered Peter's rhetorical question. "What could be wrong? Why, nothing of course. It's a beautiful day. We are in congenial company. All around us are lovely ladies of all ages to flatter us with their attention."

Peter smiled dryly and said, "All right, Henri, out with it. What's on your mind?"

"I was just thinking that I am not having a good time. And the reason I am not is that Margot isn't here. I miss her, Peter. I miss her very much. And I think I shall have to do something about it."

"Finally admitting that you need her?" Peter asked gently, his irritation with Henri gone.

"And why not? It is not so very difficult to admit we need women."

"Why are you including me in this discussion, Henri? I don't need anyone."

"Don't be so damned proud, Peter. Of course you do. You need Torey. And you're just as lost as I am because she isn't here."

"Henri . . ."

"Don't bother to deny it, Peter. I'm in a mood to be brutally honest right now. It was obvious from her behavior last night that you hurt her somehow."

Peter responded defensively, "I simply suggested she put off her business trip. After all, we don't have very much time together."

"And whose fault is that?" Henri asked pointedly. When Peter sat back, lost for a reply, Henri continued, "If you must have such a short time together, why should it be spent just as *you* wish?"

Peter smiled sheepishly. "Because I prefer to have my way, of course," he answered. Then he finished, "Why can't Torey be more amenable, like Chantal? Chantal knows how to defer to a man. I've been watching her today."

"Torey is American, not French," Henri replied. "Which is perfectly obvious, and I should think you'd be able to see it. She has her own identity and independence in a way that Chantal will never have. Chantal defers to men because she depends on them for support. But Torey is different. If she turns to a man it is because she loves him, not because she needs him financially. And that should be a great deal more flattering to you, Peter."

"It isn't."

"Personally, I like an old-fashioned woman like Margot, who tells me I'm wonderful and flatters me with the idea that whatever I do is infinitely more important than anything she might do. But that's because I grew up in a different age and am too old to change now. In the past a man married to have heirs and a woman married to have someone to support her. That is the system I am used to."

"Well, things have changed," Peter said dryly.

"I am aware of that. The marriage contract no longer provides sex and services in exchange for support. Marriage has a new meaning now and only those who can adàpt, who can adjust to change, can make a success of it."

"Why am I getting this lecture on contemporary sociology, Henri? I'm not getting married."

"Not yet, perhaps. But you are thinking about it, whether you will admit it or not. And you are frightened by it. That is because, like most of us, you hate change and are worried about having to do it."

Out of the corner of his eye, Peter caught Chantal smiling at him from several yards away. He smiled back, half-heartedly.

Noticing the exchange, Henri continued, "Torey is a much finer person than Chantal, Peter. If I were your age, I would try to make the changes necessary to be with a woman like her."

"Why have you suddenly decided that Torey is the one for me?"

"For many reasons. She is lovely, of course. That is nice, but it isn't really crucial. She has a quality that you lack, Peter. She wasn't born with a silver spoon in her mouth. She had to earn her place in the world. Oh, I know how hard you've worked to get where you are. But Torey has learned how to be a survivor. You've never had to cultivate that ability. She's tough in the best possible way, tough without being hard. And she is honest. I think it was her quality of guilelessness that first appealed to me. You can depend on her, Peter. And when you are looking for someone to spend your life with, that is crucial."

"I'm not looking for someone to spend my life with. And I'm certainly not looking for someone who gets so angry over a simple disagreement about social engagements."

"That isn't what is bothering Torey, and you know it. You are simply using that as an excuse to avoid the real issue."

"Are you becoming a psychologist now as well as a sociologist?"

"It doesn't take a psychologist to see that you and Torey have fallen in love. And that frightens both of you."

"Torey doesn't love me."

"Doesn't she? Does she make a habit of running off with men she has just met on trains?"

"Of course not. But . . ." Peter's words trailed off helplessly.

"Face it, Peter. You love the girl to distraction. And she absolutely worships you, though she is very angry with you right now. I understand that you are both afraid of being hurt. Torey is especially wary because she has gone through a divorce. Love can be painful; it can be short-lived. But it can also last forever. When you are lucky enough to love someone truly, that love increases over the years."

"You feel that way because you had such a wonderful marriage with Gabrielle. But it doesn't necessarily turn out that way."

"Do you think Gabrielle and I never disagreed? That we were always blissfully happy? Well, we weren't. There were problems, times when we each wondered if it was worth it. But by the end, we both knew that we'd had the best of it. And I'll tell you something else. It has been the same with your parents."

"I've never heard my parents have a serious disagreement," Peter protested.

"That is because they chose to do their fighting in private. Personally, I think that is a mistake because it has given you the impression that marriage is supposed to be without disagreements."

"Are you saying that my parents aren't as happy as I've always assumed they were?"

"Definitely not. They have a very strong, happy marriage. But I *am* saying that they have disagreed with each other. And that is healthy."

Peter thought back to his relationship with Chantal. They had never disagreed. That was why he'd presumed she reciprocated his feelings. Chantal's temper was always even. She never frowned or scowled.

As Peter sat in the beautiful setting that he knew Torey would have unabashedly admired, he could see her face: the way her eyes lit up when she laughed; the way her mouth curved sweetly when she smiled, just before she kissed him. She wasn't afraid, he knew, to let her feelings show. She didn't worry about laugh lines.

Shaking himself out of his reverie about Torey, Peter said, "You and Gabrielle, and my own parents, knew each other for years before you married. Torey and I have known each other for six days. Not even a week."

"That can be remedied. All it requires is time."

Peter stared thoughtfully off into the distance.

"I don't know what you will do, Peter. But I *do* know what I shall do. I am going home. I am going to call Margot and tell her it is time for us to be married. And I hope that she does not say no."

He rose, finished his lemonade, and set the glass down on a glass-topped, wrought-iron table. "If you have the good sense you should have inherited from me, you will do the same with Torey."

When Henri had gone, Peter continued to sit quietly for a long while. His thoughts were interrupted when Mr. and Mrs. Floquet sat down beside him and began discussing the pros and cons of selling their art collection. Though Peter tried to discuss the matter intelligently, his mind wasn't really on it. It was on Henri's provocative parting remark.

Torey felt the trip to Quimper was a complete success, from a business standpoint. She arranged to import some *faïence:* lovely white porcelain rabbits with glistening black eyes and pale pink ears, geese with bright red kerchiefs, and fat pigs with curling tails. Considering how popular Country French items were becoming, she felt sure these decorative pieces would sell well in San Francisco.

But, try as she would, she couldn't concentrate on business. Her mind kept returning to Peter and the complete disregard for her feelings that he had shown. By the time she arrived back in Provins, she had reached a difficult decision. She couldn't pretend everything was all right with Peter. She couldn't play the game anymore. The clever repartee was getting strained. When Peter had come to her the night before, expecting to make love, she was stunned. Surely, she thought, he must have sensed how hurt she was. But if he did sense it, he simply didn't care.

That was something she couldn't accept.

She knew it would be awkward telling Henri she was leaving at such short notice. And she would miss Peter terribly, in spite of everything. But at least she would no longer suffer the strain of keeping up a facade of breezy noncommitment.

When Torey returned to the château, it was nearly midnight. She expected to find it dark and quiet. Instead, all the lights on the first floor were blazing, as if a party were going on. As she entered the front door and came into the hallway, Torey heard laughter and talking in the sitting room. Intrigued, she went in.

She was surprised to see Margot sitting on a sofa, laughing with Henri. Peter stood by the fireplace, one arm leaning casually on the mantle, a glass of white wine in the other hand. A bottle of champagne in a silver bucket filled with ice, sat on a table. Obviously, a party of some sort was going on, but Torey had no idea what the occasion was.

"Torey! I'm so glad you've finally returned," Henri said happily, jumping up and taking her hand. "Come, sit down, we have a great deal to tell you."

"Henri, let the poor child relax for a moment," Margot chided him gently. "She's had a long trip. Look at her, she's exhausted."

"Have a glass of champagne, then. That will revive you," Henri insisted, pouring a glass for her.

As Torey took it, she glanced up at Peter. He said nothing, but he was watching her intently.

Unable to contain himself any longer, Henri said excitedly, "Margot, if you don't tell Torey the news, I will."

"Very well." As Margot turned to Torey, her pale eyes were alight with happiness. "To come straight to the point, my dear, Henri has proposed and I have accepted."

"After keeping me in an agony of suspense about your answer," Henri added teasingly.

"Don't be so dramatic, Henri. I took exactly five minutes to make up my mind."

"Oh, congratulations to both of you," Torey said, surprise and approval in her voice. Impulsively, she hugged both Henri and Margot, and said warmly, "I know you'll both be very happy."

"But you haven't heard all of it, yet," Henri went on. "We've decided that at our age a long engagement is a ridiculous waste of precious time. So we are going to be married here at the château on Saturday afternoon. I've moved heaven and earth to make the necessary arrangements so quickly."

"I would like you to be my maid of honor, Torey," Margot said. "If you will. And, of course, Peter will stand with Henri. You two are a part of our happiness."

"I'm very flattered, Margot, but I was going to leave on Thursday," Torey said doubtfully, not mentioning that she had just decided to leave even sooner. She was dismayed at the thought of being part of someone else's wedding when she was so sad.

"I don't want to make difficulties for you, but if you could rearrange your schedule and stay for just two more days, I'd be very happy."

Margot turned to Peter and continued, "Peter, you must persuade Torey to stay."

"The Orient Express will be stopping in Paris again on Sunday morning," Peter said, speaking to Torey for the first time. "I could drive you back to town in time to catch it."

Torey looked at him for a moment, trying to decide if he seemed to want her to stay. But she couldn't tell.

Then she looked back at Margot, who was watching her hopefully. She decided she should do this for Margot's sake, even if it meant spending several more uncomfortable days with Peter.

"I'll stay," she said. Then she added worriedly as a sudden thought occurred to her. "But I haven't a thing to wear."

Margot laughed, then responded. "I said the same thing when Henri proposed. But don't worry. It will be a very simple ceremony. There isn't time for anything else. I'm going back to the city tomorrow to shop for my dress. Why don't you come with me? I want to give you the dress you will wear."

"Margot, I couldn't possibly . . ."

"*Non*, do not argue. It is truly my pleasure."

"I think a toast is in order," Peter said, raising his wine glass. As the others raised theirs, he said, "To Henri and Margot. May you always be as happy as you are at this moment."

They sipped the wine, then Henri said, "Another toast. To love. At my age it is especially nice because it is a surprise." He looked at Torey and Peter, then finished meaningfully, "But at any age, it is a gift to be treasured."

Peter looked at Torey, his expression direct and intense. "To love," he repeated softly, then took a slow sip of champagne.

For a moment, Torey hesitated, still held by his look, then she lowered her eyes and sipped the champagne.

Torey saw Henri and Margot exchange a conspiratorial glance. Then Margot said, "I think I'll retire now. Tomorrow will be a long day, driving to town and shopping."

"I think I will retire, also," Henri said, setting down his glass. "Good night, Torey, Peter."

When Henri and Margot had gone, Torey set down her glass. "I think I'll go to bed, too. It's been a long day."

As she rose, Peter came up to her and placed a hand gently on her shoulders, stopping her. His touch sent a shiver down her spine. Whatever she might be feeling emotionally, her body still responded to his touch.

"Wait, please," he said. When she didn't look at him, he went on, "We have to talk, Torey."

"There's nothing to say, Peter," she replied, finally meeting his look.

"There's a great deal to say. And we'd better say it, or the next few days are going to be miserable for both of us."

She knew he was right. For everyone's sake, it was important that they resolve their differences, even if it meant agreeing that the affair was over.

"All right," she relented, feeling a tightening in the pit of her stomach. She knew very well how this discussion was bound to end. She and Peter would go their separate ways, behaving in as friendly a manner as possible for Henri and Margot's sakes.

"It's a warm night. Let's walk outside," Peter suggested.

They went out through the open French doors onto the terrace. The gardens were lit by a full moon that hung low, like a huge orange ball, in the star-studded sky. Peter led Torey down to the gardens and over the Japanese bridge. Finally, he stopped at a stone bench in the beautiful little glade that Torey had admired earlier. A cool breeze rustled gently through the drooping branches of a weeping willow, and Torey could smell the sweet, heavy scent of roses.

"Did your business go well today?" Peter asked politely.

"Yes. Very well." Torey said nothing further for she was sure Peter wasn't really interested.

"Torey . . . from the beginning of our relationship, we've been able to talk to each other pretty honestly. Yet last night we weren't communicating at all. I thought at first it was just a disagreement over our plans for today."

"That wasn't really the problem, Peter."

"I know that now. Henri said the same thing to me,

and I realized he was right. Something more is wrong. But whatever it is, it started when we ran into Chantal."

He paused, obviously waiting for Torey's response. But she had no intention of telling Peter what her feelings were about that encounter. They went too deep and were too private to share with someone who was only a temporary part of her life.

When she said nothing, Peter continued gently, "I see now that I hurt you badly, somehow." His voice was low, gentle, genuinely confused and touchingly vulnerable. "Torey, whatever it was, I'm sorry."

She hadn't expected an apology, certainly not one that was so clearly sincere and full of heartfelt contrition. Even though he didn't understand what he had done to hurt her, he didn't want to continue hurting her.

For the first time in twenty-four hours, Torey felt a faint stirring of hope. Maybe—just maybe—everything wasn't over, after all.

She turned to face him, and the profoundly worried look in his eyes made her breath catch in her throat.

"Oh, Peter." She didn't know what to say. She still couldn't open her heart to him, reveal her most secret feelings.

"I know I'm arrogant and willful and a damn fool at times," Peter responded. "But there hasn't been a moment since I met you that I haven't cared deeply about you. I wouldn't have hurt you for the world."

In the silence of the night, Torey heard her heart beating wildly. He cared about her. Suddenly the world wasn't such a wretched place after all.

"You don't have to talk about it, if you don't want

to," Peter went on. "But I would like it very much if we could start over again and just forget the past twenty-four hours."

Torey realized then that she would have to open up to him, to tell him what had hurt her and why. It was the only way to wipe the slate clean and put the agony of their estrangement behind them.

And besides, she didn't want to forget everything that had happened over the last twenty-four hours. Their forest tryst was very, very special to her, a memory that she would keep within her heart always. She didn't want to have to bury it along with the unhappy memories of this painful time.

Haltingly, feeling embarrassed, yet knowing she must say it all, Torey began, "Peter, you told Chantal I was your houseguest. It was that word . . . so impersonal . . . after what we had just shared."

"My God," Peter exclaimed, "I didn't mean . . ." He stopped, forcing himself to calm down. "I deserve a good swift kick right now. I'm guilty of terminal stupidity. But, Torey, I never meant that the way it must have sounded to you." He looked at her with a new understanding and awareness in his eyes. "What you must have thought . . ."

"Then, on top of everything, you seemed to ignore me, to concentrate on Chantal, as if . . ."

"As if I'd gotten what I wanted from you and was dismissing you," Peter finished candidly.

"Yes."

"Let me explain something to you about Chantal. The fact is, I don't really like her very much. And that makes me feel uncomfortable around her. Fortunately, I don't run into her too often, but when I do, it's always the same. I have to try very hard to be polite. Her husband is a good friend of Margot's and it would be awkward if I insulted her. When you thought I was concentrating on Chantal, I was actually concentrating on being polite. And in the process, I obviously forgot to be considerate toward you."

Torey felt as if a weight had been lifted from her chest. She felt lighter than air. She remembered what Margot had said. "When you're in love, the world sparkles. You bubble with happiness." Now, Torey began to feel the champagne she had drunk. It seemed to go straight to her head, making her giddy with happiness.

"I'm sorry," Peter began again.

Moving close against him, Torey placed her fingertips lightly on his lips, silencing him. "No more apologies. I should have told you what was bothering me instead of moping around. But that's all over and done with. We wasted one precious night, Peter. I don't want to waste another."

He kissed her then, with all the pent-up passion of twenty-four hours of loneliness.

Torey felt an overpowering sense of relief. From the beginning, they'd only had a week. Last night they lost even that. Now, they had it back again.

Chapter Fourteen

$\mathscr{T}$he days passed in a frenzy of activity. On Tuesday, Torey went shopping with Margot. For herself, Margot found a knee-length, sleeveless dress in lavender silk. Torey chose an equally sophisticated dress in lilac linen that complemented Margot's. It was one of those timeless "little" dresses of exquisite taste that would stay fashionable for years. And it was her first Dior.

Wednesday and Thursday were spent in making the final arrangements for the wedding. Even for an informal affair, there were a thousand details to be taken care of. Then on Friday night there was a pre-nuptial party.

Torey dressed with special care that night. She pulled her hair back in a knot at the nape of her neck, and wove a braided gold ribbon through it. She wore more make-up than usual so that her eyes stood out like deep blue sapphires on white velvet. And she put on the exquisite gown she had bought in Paris on Saturday. That day seemed so long ago now as Torey thought back over all that had happened during the intervening week.

In a way, she felt that she and Peter had lived a lifetime in that week. It was almost over now. And she was determined that her fantasy would end on an appropriate note, with her looking like a princess at a ball.

When Torey walked out onto the terrace, she found a small band playing old-fashioned dance tunes. Guests were dancing, strolling through the gardens that were lit by a hundred brightly colored paper lanterns, and choosing hors d'oeuvres from a table laden with food. Elise had outdone herself with delicacies of every imaginable variety.

Torey saw Margot and Henri dancing cheek to cheek. They looked wonderful together. But it wasn't they whom Torey was looking for. Suddenly, from behind her, came the familiar voice.

"Have you, by any chance, lost a glass slipper?"

Torey turned and smiled happily at Peter. "You must be Prince Charming."

"At your service, milady," Peter responded, giving her a low bow. "May I have this dance?"

Torey nodded and he swept her into his arms. As he held her, he said, "By the way, that is the loveliest gown I have ever seen."

Torey immediately decided that the dress was worth every hard-earned penny she'd paid for it. If she never wore it again in her life, it wouldn't matter. For she would always remember this night, when she'd felt like a princess in a fairy tale, dancing on the terrace of this magnificent old house, with Peter.

Looking back on it later, Torey remembered the lanterns swaying in the slight breeze, the sound of the music drifting over the gardens, and the profound happiness on Margot and Henri's faces. But what she remembered most was the feeling of being enveloped in Peter's arms.

When the last guest had finally gone, and Torey and Peter had drunk one last toast to Margot and Henri, Torey retired to her room. But she didn't undress. She stood by the window, waiting expectantly. Peter came to her immediately.

He undressed her with great care, showing infinite patience with the many tiny buttons that fastened at the back of the dress. When the dress fell in soft folds at Torey's feet, she reached up and clasped her arms around Peter's neck.

"I thought you would never finish," she whispered wickedly, her voice thick with desire.

"I was in no hurry," Peter responded, placing his hands on her bare back and pulling her against him. "Half the pleasure is in getting there."

And then he kissed her.

The day of the wedding was utterly perfect. It was warm but not hot, and there wasn't a cloud in the sky.

Chantal came with her husband. But Torey knew that today she was every bit as sophisticated as Chantal. And, besides, Chantal was no longer a source of jealousy.

The moment Torey saw Peter, he smiled and his eyes lit with pleasure.

"You're a chameleon," he said lightly. "One minute you're in jeans, the next you're in a dress right out of a Gainsborough painting, and now you're as sophisticated as any Frenchwoman. Which is the real Torey Jenson?"

"All of them. And today, they're all yours," Torey answered, slipping her arm through his.

"Then that's all that matters," Peter said, brushing her cheek provocatively with his lips.

During the ceremony, which was held beneath a bower of yellow roses in the garden, Torey stood to the left of Margot and Peter stood to the right of Henri. As the minister spoke of love and devotion, Peter looked at Torey thoughtfully. Torey caught the look, but didn't know quite what to make of it.

The remainder of the late afternoon and evening passed in a daze of numerous toasts, dancing, eating, laughing, and happy conversation. When Torey went to bed late that night, she felt surprisingly wide awake. Her mind raced and every nerve in her body seemed on edge. Yet she didn't feel like making love. And when Peter came into her room, she wasn't sure how to tell him.

Discarding his robe, he crawled into bed beside her.

"What a wedding. When the last guest finally left, Henri told me he was afraid the party might go on forever. He was getting anxious to retire with his bride."

"I think Margot felt the same way. Did you notice they only had eyes for each other all evening?"

"Yes. It was nice, wasn't it? They both seemed so young today."

Slipping an arm around Torey, he pulled her against him. For a long moment neither said anything.

Then Peter said quietly, "I think I'd just like to hold you tonight."

Torey reached an arm across his chest and hugged him tightly. "I think I would like that, too."

And they fell asleep in each other's arms.

Chapter Fifteen

Torey felt that Paris was beginning to seem very familiar as she and Peter drove into the city the next morning in his little white Triumph. They had left the château early, after a hurried breakfast and a warmly affectionate goodbye from Henri and Margot. Now, as they drove through the crowded, winding streets, Peter asked, "Would you like to stop at the Eiffel Tower? We have enough time for a quick visit before we board the train."

"We? I thought . . . I thought you were just dropping me off at the station," Torey responded, surprised.

"I'm going to London with you. I have some business to take care of there at Sotheby's, and that way I can see you off at the airport tomorrow morning. That is, if you don't mind," he added, suddenly realizing that he had sprung this change of plans on her with no notice.

"Of course, I don't mind," she said happily. It would give them one more night together. A little more time before the final leave-taking. "And I would *love* to see the Eiffel Tower," Torey admitted, grinning.

A few minutes later, Torey saw the tracery of the tower rising out of the low, broad cloud of trees on the Boulevard St. Michel. Peter parked the car in the parking lot of the Palais de Chaillot. Then he and Torey crossed the Pont d'Iena and reached the tower. Behind it, the gardens of the Palais de Chaillot swept down to the Seine.

The tower had just opened on this early Sunday morning and there were few people there yet. As they took the elevator to the second stage, Peter read to Torey bits of information from a guide book they had purchased on the ground floor. " 'The tower was built for the Exhibition of 1889 by Gustave Eiffel, a French engineer, and was never meant to be permanent. It weighs about 700 tons but exerts about the same pressure on the ground as an average-size person sitting in a chair.' "

"Peter, that's fascinating."

"You are a true tourist. No number of dull facts bores you."

When they left the elevator and stepped out onto the windy landing, Torey gasped as she saw the panoramic view. "It's incredible. You can see for miles. How high up are we?"

"I'm not sure how high we are, but the tower itself is 1056 feet high."

As Torey looked out at the spectacular view, her hair blew across her cheeks softly in the wind. Below, the quaint rooftops of Paris seemed to spread out forever.

Peter continued dryly, "You have to admit that up close it's rather ugly."

"I admit it was more beautiful when I saw it from a distance the other night, all lit up. That's the difference between romantic image and reality, I guess. But then, as the book says, it wasn't meant to last forever."

She was joking, but when she turned to look at Peter, she saw that something in her words had struck him forcefully. He was watching her intently, all trace of humor gone now. "No, it wasn't meant to last forever," he repeated slowly. "But it has."

"Obviously, Eiffel fooled them all," Torey teased.

As she smiled up at Peter, he brushed away the hair blowing across her eyes and cupped her face in his hands. "I love you, you know," he said as if he'd just thought of it.

The smile faded from Torey's lips. Suddenly it was no longer a game. It was real. Below, she could hear the sounds of the city, the blaring of horns and screeching brakes. Finally, she whispered, "No, I didn't know."

"When we were apart Monday, I realized how much you meant to me. Then yesterday at the wedding, as I watched Henri and Margot repeating those vows, making a commitment to each other, I knew that was what I wanted for us."

He finished thoughtfully. "I think I loved you from the very beginning, but I didn't want to admit it to myself. I had grown complacent about my life, and the thought of changing it, especially to meet someone else's needs, was frightening."

Nearby, a middle-aged couple who looked like American tourists, were listening with unabashed curiosity. Feeling stunned and shaken and happy, Torey said, "Why don't we go somewhere more private."

Glancing at the tourists, Peter answered, "Right. I guess this isn't the most private place in the world to make a proposal."

They went down to the gardens that ran between the tower and the Seine. As they walked along the paths, Torey could smell the sweet aroma of numerous flowers. Finally, they sat down on a bench. No one else was near.

"You haven't said anything," Peter pointed out, a note of uncertainty in his voice.

"That's because I'm stunned. I feel as if a passing fairy had just granted me one wish."

Peter grinned happily. "Then I suggest we follow Henri and Margot's example and have a *very* short engagement. Let's turn around and go back to the château. We could be married right away," he said excitedly.

Torey suddenly felt frightened by the abrupt turn of events, as if she were being swept along in an irresistible tide. Things were moving too quickly, they had been moving too quickly since the moment she met Peter.

"We've only known each other ten days," she said.

Turning her to face him, Peter said emphatically, "You're being logical and objective, but everything you're saying is completely beside the point. I love you, Torey. It may have started out as a temporary affair, but I don't want it to end that way."

"Oh, Peter, neither do I. I love you. You don't know how good it feels to be able to say that. I love you so much, just the thought of getting back on that train without you has been almost more than I could stand."

"Then let's do it, Torey! There's no reason to wait. This isn't a decision I've made lightly. I've thought about it all week. But now the decision is made and I want to get on with it. I want you with me."

"You don't understand. There are practical problems. I live in San Francisco, you live in Los Angeles. Which one of us is willing to move? I have a business that means a great deal to me, and I know how much your career matters to you. Who's going to make a sacrifice?"

Peter said thoughtfully, "I guess I assumed you would come with me."

"I've worked very hard to make a life for myself that is happy and fulfilling. I can't give that up for what may turn out to be a pipe dream."

Torey was throwing caution to the wind and being totally honest. There was no time to be anything less.

Peter's expression was serious but not discouraged. "I know I've been an absolute ass at times, and I haven't been as sensitive to your needs as I should have been. But I'm not completely incapable of compromise, Torey. You wouldn't have to give up anything. L.A. is only an hour's flight from San Francisco. You could keep your shop and fly up there whenever you like. Leave the day-to-day running of it

216

to your cousin. We could travel together, on my business and yours. Both of us have schedules that are flexible."

When Torey still looked doubtful, Peter continued, "We're right for each other, Torey. We can have it all, everything we've both always wanted—careers, children, each other."

Torey knew he was right. They *were* right for each other. Her objections about career conflicts and the difficulties of compromise masked her true feelings. Finally, she admitted what was really bothering her.

"We've been living in a fantasy world, Peter, first on the train, then in Paris, and at the château. It isn't the real world. The few times that real problems did come our way, our relationship got rocky. What happens when we have to deal with problems constantly—like who's going to do the laundry and how do we handle finances? We've been carried away by an attraction that may be purely physical. We're great together when we're making love, but in the real world, love-making is only a small part of living together."

"You think we'll discover that we don't really love each other."

"Yes . . . no . . . oh, I don't know. I thought I was in love with Mason, but eventually I realized I wasn't. I was in love with the person I thought he was, but it was all false. It was the same with you and Chantal."

"What I feel for you isn't false, Torey," Peter insisted with quiet confidence. "And I don't think that what you feel for me is false, either."

"But how can we be sure? I don't want to make another mistake, Peter. Going through a divorce is devastating, even when there's no love left in the marriage. I don't want that upheaval in my life again."

"Torey, in my business I have to make decisions about spending millions of dollars on art. Of course, I worry about whether I'm doing the right thing. But once the decision is made, I put it behind me. I don't walk around worrying about it, once it's done. You can't live your life out of fear. There's always the possibility of failure. That's part of life. You just have to take chances. But I don't think our relationship is very chancy, actually. I'm sure what we feel for each other will remain the same whether we're in Paris or Los Angeles or Outer Mongolia."

"Nothing remains the same," Torey responded slowly. "Even the continents drift."

Peter took Torey's face gently in his hands and looked deeply into her worried blue eyes. "You took a chance with me once, Torey, on the Orient Express. I think you're brave enough to do it again. But you don't have to make up your mind now. We can talk about it again later."

"Would you mind if we just think it over for a while, then talk about it in London? I'll give you an answer there, I promise."

"All right. Until London, then. Come on, love."

They arrived at the station just in time to catch the Orient Express. After settling into comfortable seats in the British Pullman car, they relaxed and enjoyed the scenery as the train crossed northern France. Neither mentioned Peter's proposal again.

At Boulogne, Torey and Peter, along with the other

passengers from the train, gathered on the veranda-deck saloon of the Sealink ferry for the ninety-minute crossing to Folkestone. There, they boarded the train once more. They continued with their tacit agreement to shelve any serious discussion until London. Both wanted to enjoy this trip on the train where they had first met.

At one point, Peter teasingly reminded Torey of the poster they had both seen, advertising the Orient Express as "An adventure in time and space and splendour."

"It was certainly an adventure," Torey agreed as they passed through the deep green English countryside.

Afternoon tea was served, and Torey thoroughly enjoyed the summer pudding with fresh fruit.

Then they passed through the hop fields of Kent. The scenery was pastoral, with Jacobean farmhouses, open meadows, pawing horses, kneeling sheep, and country lanes. Torey knew they were getting close to London and she began to think once more about Peter's proposal.

She was genuinely torn about whether or not to marry him. Part of her wanted to say yes, to claim him as her own, and to hell with any problems that might arise later. But another part, the part that had been so hurt by Mason, wanted to be absolutely sure before committing herself once more.

Then the train entered a tunnel and came out on the other side to rows of semi-detached houses and the playing fields of a college. They were coming into London now. And when they passed the brick terraces, coal yards, and narrow back gardens of the

South London suburbs, Torey knew that her time was almost up. In only a few minutes they would be at Victoria Station, and she still didn't know what to tell Peter.

The train rumbled through Clapham and into Victoria Station.

As they stepped out into the vast, cavernous station, with its throng of travelers, Torey felt as if she were a character out of an old movie: the heroine, seeing her lover off at the staion, wondering if he would come back to her. And then suddenly Torey knew what she would tell Peter. It was a wild idea, though to her it made perfect sense. She had no idea how Peter would take it.

"I made reservations for us at the Dorchester," Peter said, as they made their way to the waiting line of taxis. "Is that all right?"

"Yes, fine," Torey replied absently. She was familiar with the hotel, one of the finest in London, located across from Hyde Park. It didn't really matter to her where they stayed. What mattered was how Peter would react to her plan.

They checked into the Dorchester, a sedate, elegant, old-fashioned hotel, with obsequious clerks and an imposing doorman dressed in bright red livery. Before they went up to their room, Peter bought a bouquet of tiny white carnations for Torey at the flower stall in the lobby.

In their room, he phoned room service for a bottle of champagne. They were unpacking what little they would need for this one night, when the champagne arrived.

"A toast is in order, I think," Peter said, popping the cork on the champagne and pouring a generous amount in their glasses. "To the Orient Express. We began an adventure on it that I hope will never end."

Smiling up at Peter, Torey slowly sipped the champagne.

As they looked at each other, suddenly they both knew that the unpacking could wait. . . .

Later that night they had dinner on the terrace of a centuries-old restaurant overlooking the Thames. As the lights sparkled on the water and boats slid silently past, Torey and Peter made small talk. But Torey knew that it was time for the serious discussion they had put off all day. They had made love, they had eaten. Now it was time to talk about their future together.

Finally, when the waiter had cleared away their dishes and brought coffee, Peter said quietly, "I can't wait any longer, Torey. I must know what it's to be."

"I understand. I love you, Peter, and I'll marry you. But on one condition."

The smile that had begun to crease Peter's face, died. "What do you mean? What condition?"

"I think we need time to make sure how we feel about each other. When we return to our normal lives, apart from each other, we may decide that it was all just a fantasy after all. Without the romantic atmosphere of the Orient Express and Paris, maybe we'll feel that what we've known is infatuation, not love. I think we should test our feelings before making a commitment that might end in unhappiness."

"How do you suggest we do that? There are no tests for love, Torey. It can't be proven with a strip of litmus paper and a beaker of acid."

"You're going to be traveling through Europe for several months. I won't be coming back here on another buying trip until September. We can't see each other all summer anyway. I think it might be a good idea if we didn't contact each other during that time. It would give us both a chance to think, to sort out our feelings, to see if we miss each other as much as we think we will."

"That's ridiculous!" Peter exploded, causing heads to turn in the restaurant. Lowering his voice, he continued in a still-angry tone, "We'll be miserable without each other, and you know it."

"If we are, then we can meet in September. And all we will have lost is three months when we couldn't be together anyway. Giving up a few letters and phone calls isn't a huge sacrifice. And if either of us decides that this is a mistake, that we're not really in love after all, then we simply won't come. And there'll be no recriminations, no hard feelings."

"There's just no point in that," Peter argued stubbornly.

"If we love each other, Peter, three months won't make any difference. If this has all been a mirage, a romantic fantasy, we'll realize it and avoid the disappointment of divorce."

"Let's go," Peter said curtly, motioning to the waiter for their bill.

When he paid it and they left, Torey watched him tensely. Everything depended on whether or not he would go along with her plan. If he wasn't willing to

222

give her these three months, then there was simply no hope for them. This meant enough to her that she wasn't willing to compromise about it. If Peter couldn't put his own impatience aside to meet her needs this time, then their relationship wouldn't work anyway. He had talked about being sensitive to her needs. Now was the time to prove it.

Outside, Peter said, "Let's walk for a while."

As they set off along the embankment, Torey could tell by the stiff set of his broad shoulders that he was angry. Angry and disappointed. For one anxious moment she thought she'd ruined everything. Peter was furious with her, she knew. So furious, in fact, that he might very well call the whole thing off.

For a moment Torey thought of taking it all back, of saying it was a silly plan after all and she would do as he wished. But she knew if she did that, she would never forgive herself. And so she said nothing.

Then Peter reached out and put his arm around her, pulling her against him. He continued to walk in silence, not even looking at her. But she sighed inwardly with relief. He wasn't so angry that he no longer wanted her. He just needed time to think.

Darkness cloaked the buildings they were passing, but across the river Torey could see the medieval Tower of London and adjacent Tower Bridge brightly floodlit. Where the floodlights hit the water, the river glinted silver and gold.

Finally, Peter stopped. Looking down at Torey, he asked, "Is this really important to you?"

"Yes," she answered, the word a whisper in the darkness.

"I don't agree with it. I don't want to do it. But if it's really what you want, then I'll go along with it."

"Oh, Peter."

He bent down and kissed her gently. Then he asked, "Now, where shall we meet in September?"

"I thought, possibly, Victoria Station. At the Orient Express platform."

For the first time all night, Peter laughed. And his eyes, which had been dark with anger earlier, were lit by points of dancing light.

"You're an incurable romantic, you know that? You may pretend to be pragmatic, but I know better."

"Peter, it's really very logical . . ." Torey protested.

"Don't bother denying it," Peter interrupted her, smiling. "Very well, Victoria Station it shall be. When?"

"I'll be in London the first week in September."

"Okay. The Orient Express leaves London on Fridays and Sundays in the late morning. I can't remember the exact time. Let's say, the first Friday in September at the time of departure."

"Yes."

Peter looked at her intently. "I love you, Torey. I'll love you three months from now. I'll be waiting for you at Victoria Station. But after that, I warn you, I'll never let you out of my sight again."

As he kissed her again, deeply, Torey hoped in her heart that he meant what he said.

Later, back at the hotel, they made love again with a special urgency. Torey knew that despite Peter's reassurances, it was possible this might be the last time they would lie in each other's arms. The uncertainty added a depth, a poignancy to their passion.

The next morning Peter took Torey to Heathrow Airport to catch her flight to San Francisco. As she stood at the gate, the last thing he said to her was, "I'll see you in September."

And then he walked away.

Chapter Sixteen

Torey hurried down Union Street, past the charmingly renovated nineteenth-century houses that were now boutiques, restaurants, and galleries. Her mind wasn't on the quaint wrought-iron railings or sidewalk gaslights that she normally found so appealing. She was precariously balancing a paper bag containing two hamburgers with French fries, her purse, and an armful of dry-cleaning she'd just picked up.

When she came to her own shop, she called out, "Elena, help!"

Her cousin came to the door and opened it for her. There was no one else in the shop, so Torey simply dumped everything on a desk at the rear, instead of going on up to her living quarters on the third floor.

"Anything happen?" she asked, as she spread out lunch on the desk.

"Nothing. It's been quiet. I think I'll go home after I eat."

Elena was short and dark and inclined to plumpness. She had Torey's black hair, but there the resemblance stopped. Her eyes were brown, her skin olive. She sat down at the desk, biting into a hamburger hungrily. As Torey did the same, Elena said, "You still haven't told me about the trip. Did it go well?"

Torey had been back for a week. During that time she had been too busy catching up on things, and dealing with the normally heavy summer tourist crowd, to chat with Elena.

In a way, Torey used her hectic schedule as an excuse. She knew Elena was curious about her extended stay in Paris. But she didn't want to talk about it. Not yet. She was still adjusting to what had happened to her.

"The trip was . . . all right. I found some new things. Country French. They should do well."

"Is that why you stayed over in Paris?" Elena asked pointedly.

"More or less," Torey replied noncommittally, watching Elena scrutinize her carefully.

Then, taking another bite of hamburger, Elena let it pass.

"So how are things at home?" Torey asked, changing the subject. "Did the boys like their gifts?"

"They loved them. They put them up on their walls along with all their other posters. Personally, I think it looks a little strange to have posters of antique cars and trains next to Bo Derek, but they seem to think it makes sense. By the way, thanks for the lace teddy. I think it's single-handedly revived my sex life."

Torey laughed. "I'll bet your sex life didn't need reviving."

"Anyway, Joe *loved* it. He wanted me to ask you if the store where you got it has a mail order catalog."

"I'll find out."

"This morning a customer wanted to buy that little unicorn. She was very disappointed when I told her it wasn't for sale."

Torey looked over at the puppet hanging by the door. No, it *definitely* wasn't for sale.

"Where did you get it?" Elena asked.

"At a store called Rigodon," Torey answered, carefully leaving out the fact that Peter had given it to her. "They had an incredible variety of puppets."

"Well, I'll be going," Elena said, finishing the last French fry. "If you need any help, just call."

"I will. And thanks again for holding down the fort."

"No problem. I really enjoyed it. When will you be leaving again?"

"September." Just saying the word made Torey's pulse beat a little faster. So many things were wrapped up in that one word.

As Elena picked up her purse and slung it over her shoulder, she said thoughtfully, "You know, Torey, you look different since you got back."

"Different?"

"Yes. I don't know exactly what it is. I guess you don't look as drawn as you did before. You're more bright-eyed, somehow."

"The vacation did me good," Torey agreed deceptively.

"Well, I'll see you Sunday. Don't forget, you're coming to dinner."

"I won't forget. Bye."

When Elena had gone, Torey straightened up the desk, then dealt with the customers who came in. For the rest of the afternoon she was too busy to dwell on Peter.

That evening as she was locking the door, she glanced at the unicorn. She wondered what time it was in Paris, or whatever city Peter was in, and if he was thinking of her. Good night, Peter, love, she thought softly, then went upstairs to her living quarters.

Later, as Torey sat on a chintz-covered window seat by a big bay window in her living room, looking out at the sparkling lights of San Francisco, Peter filled her thoughts. She had only been away from him for a week, and already their time together seemed more like a dream than reality. It all seemed long ago and far away. How would it seem, she wondered, by the end of this long summer?

For a moment, panic rose inside her as she felt the vividness of his memory slipping away. She rose and hurried over to a desk drawer. Rummaging through it, she found the sketch Peter had done of her on the train. The sight of his bold scrawl reassured her. He was real. What they had shared was real. She mustn't let herself lose sight of that.

She put the sketch back in the drawer then and went to bed. That night she dreamed of a magical train that carried her through the clouds to a smiling lover.

At first, as the summer passed and Torey settled into the familiar routine of her life, she thought of Peter less and less. There were so many other things to do, so many other things to worry about. Then the long, lonely days and nights stretched into weeks. June became July, and July became August, and she began to wonder if he would be at their rendezvous. Her confidence in their love grew less and less as her mental image of him became dimmer.

Once, when she was standing at a newsstand, leafing through foreign magazines, she saw a picture of Peter at an art auction. After recovering from the unexpected shock, Torey scrutinized the picture carefully. She tried to connect the man in it with the man she had laughed with, talked with, made love with. Somehow, her memories and this picture didn't quite connect. It was then she began to doubt her own feelings.

After all, we only had ten days together, she reminded herself. What could we possibly really know about each other in such a short time? And we were in such romantic settings. What if it was the ambience I fell in love with and not the man?

Now, instead of worrying about whether Peter would come to their rendezvous, Torey began to doubt that *she* should go. What if she went and he didn't show? What if he did show but she looked at him and felt absolutely nothing?

Torey suspected that if she really loved him, she wouldn't have these doubts.

And then one day while she was taking inventory, she heard the tiny bell over the shop door tinkle. Looking up, she was stunned to see Mason standing there. She hadn't seen him since they appeared in court together for their divorce proceedings, nearly a year before. He looked absolutely the same—of middle height, lean, with brown hair slightly graying at the temples. His face had a craggy sort of handsomeness that Torey had always found attractive. Even now, as his cool gray eyes looked at her intently, she felt an involuntary twinge of attraction for him.

"Hello, Victoria," he said simply. He was the only person in her life who called her that. It sounded strange hearing it again after all this time.

"Hello, Mason."

She put down the pencil and notepad she'd been writing on. "Can I do something for you?"

"I was just in the neighborhood and thought I'd drop by." He cast a quick glance over the shop. "This place is really looking nice. You must be doing well."

"Fairly well."

"You know, I haven't been on Union Street in two years or more. It's certainly changed, all these gaslights and everything."

"Yes." She wasn't surprised Mason visited the area so rarely. Even when they were married and Torey spent a great deal of time renovating the house, Mason took no interest in it.

"I probably should have called first. But as I said, I happened to be close by and thought I'd drop in. I thought we'd have dinner, say at Houlihan's."

The mention of their favorite restaurant in Sausalito brought back a flood of memories to Torey—taking the ferry across the bay, walking around the tiny, quaint village, eating Oriental shrimp at the restaurant overlooking the water.

"Mason, I don't think . . ." Torey began.

But he interrupted her. "There are a lot of things I'd like to say to you. And rather than stand here, in the middle of your shop, and say them, I'd like to do it over a pleasant dinner at a place that holds a lot of nice memories for us."

Torey's determination to be civil but cool wavered. She couldn't help being curious. Looking at Mason now, after not seeing him for so long, she remembered why she'd found him attractive. One dinner couldn't hurt anything, she finally decided. At the worst, she would end up spending a boring evening remembering all the reasons she'd fallen out of love with him.

"All right. It's about closing time. I'll lock up the store and then change."

A few minutes later, she had changed into a brightly flowered silk skirt and matching peasant blouse. She threw a light sweater over her shoulders. It was cool on the bay at night, even in midsummer.

As they crossed the bay on the ferry, Mason said, "Remember how often we used to do this? I've missed you, Victoria."

"What about Cindy?" Torey asked bluntly, referring to the young student that Mason had left her for.

"That's all over," Mason answered tersely.

"She left you, didn't she." It was a statement, not a question. That was why Mason looked as if he were at loose ends. He had been dumped as unceremoniously as he had dumped her. Torey couldn't help feeling a twinge of satisfaction.

Mason looked as if the conversation were headed in

a different direction than he had planned. When the ferry docked and they walked over to the colorfully decorated restaurant, he continued more confidently. "Let's talk about *us*, not the past."

"There is no 'us,' Mason," Torey replied as they sat down at a table.

"But there could be," he answered, stroking her hand as it lay on the table.

She pulled her hand away.

The waiter took their order. When he had gone, Mason continued, "Haven't you missed me, just a little?"

Torey almost replied, "Not at all," but she stopped herself. She couldn't help being a little bit glad that Mason had suffered the same rejection that he'd inflicted on her. But she had no desire to be cruel or hurtful. Instead, she said honestly, "I've adjusted to the divorce."

"I can see that. You look . . . more together somehow. In fact, you look better than ever. You've grown, Victoria. You've . . . blossomed, I guess is the word I'm looking for."

"Thank you," Torey answered, smiling in a secretive way. First Elena, now Mason, had noticed the change in her. She had Peter to thank for it, she realized.

The waiter brought steaming bowls of thick clam chowder, and from that point on Torey tried to concentrate on the food. But Mason was determined to talk to her about "re-evaluating their relationship and re-thinking their options." As he used the same old pop psychology terms that he'd thrown at her constantly while they were married, she felt herself pulling back from him inexorably.

By the end of the main course, she was wondering why on earth she'd ever agreed to go out with him in the first place. Curiosity was a poor excuse.

When Mason ordered coffee and looked as if he was settling in for a long conversation, Torey said, "I'm afraid I'll have to be going. I have a lot to do tomorrow and I want to get to bed early tonight."

"But—"

"Sorry, Mason," Torey said firmly.

A few minutes later they were back on the ferry, headed toward the city.

Torey stood by a window, watching the salt spray glisten in the moonlight. The play of light on the water reminded her of another night in another city. . . . She and Peter were standing on a quay, looking out at the Seine. The memory was so unexpectedly vivid that Torey was startled when Mason spoke.

"Victoria . . ." His arm came around her shoulders. "God, you've become a lovely woman now."

His words trailed off as he pulled her toward him, kissing her deeply. She didn't resist but neither did she respond.

When he let her go, she looked up at him curiously. For in the moment when he kissed her, she remembered what it felt like to be kissed by Peter. She remembered his touch, so gentle and yet so tantalizing . . . the way his brown eyes crinkled at the corners when he smiled at her . . . how very much she loved him.

The doubts she'd begun to feel disappeared as if

they'd never existed. All it took was being with someone else to remind her of what it felt like to be with Peter.

A slow, mysterious smile spread across her face. "Thank you, Mason. You'll never know what this night has done for me."

Encouraged, he reached for her again.

"No," Torey stopped him as the ferry docked, bumping gently against the pier. "Don't say another word. Everything is absolutely perfect just as it is. Now, if you don't mind, I think I'll take a taxi home."

"But, Victoria, I don't understand."

"Of course you don't, Mason. Goodbye."

As Torey joined the disembarking crowd, she felt lighter than air. Remembering Margot's words about being in love, she thought, you're right. She strode jauntily down the pier, her hair swinging against her shoulders. The night was crisp and cool and clear. In the distance, she could see Coit Tower thrusting up into the sky, lit by floodlights. San Francisco was beautiful, the whole world was beautiful, for she, Torey Jenson, was in love. There was no longer any doubt at all in her mind.

It was the end of August and her rendezvous with Peter was only one week off, when Torey told Elena about it. She was at Elena's house, having Sunday brunch. The meal was over and Torey was helping Elena wash the dishes while the boys and their father watched a baseball game on television. Through the open kitchen door, Torey heard the sounds of the four males cursing the umpire and arguing vehemently about the game. But in the kitchen, it was quiet.

"Joe and the boys sound like they're having a good time," Torey said, skirting the subject she really wanted to discuss.

"Of course. *They're* having fun and *we're* doing the dishes. I'm surrounded by chauvinists, Torey."

Torey smiled. "Well, they're lovable chauvinists."

"Yes. And I have to admit that Joe does a lot of things for me. It isn't all one-sided. Last week I mentioned that I wanted to paint the bedroom, but I hated the thought of all that nuisance. When I got home last night from the shop, I discovered that he'd done it all himself, with a little help from the boys. He waited until I left for work in the morning, then did the whole thing before I got home, to surprise me. The room was a mess, of course, with the furniture all piled in the middle of it. But he looked so proud of himself."

Elena's expression was so loving when she talked about her husband that Torey commented, "You really love him, don't you?"

"Yes. After eighteen years, I still love him. In a way, I love him more now than the day I married him. I know him better now, you see. And I like what I know."

"It's reassuring to know some marriages work," Torey said teasingly.

Elena looked at her curiously. "Why are you suddenly so curious about marriage? That's one topic you haven't wanted to discuss for a long time."

Torey hesitated for just a moment before slowly, carefully telling Elena about Peter, the Orient Express, Paris, and their rendezvous at Victoria Station.

"Oh, Torey, I thought *something* happened to you

in Paris, but I never suspected . . ." She stopped, excited but worried. "You're supposed to meet him next week?"

"Friday."

"But it's been three months since you've seen him. Are you sure you should go?"

"Of course I'm not sure. I'm afraid he won't show up, and if he doesn't, I'll be deeply hurt. But, oh, Elena, if I don't go I'll never know if he was there. And I can't spend the rest of my life not knowing."

"But, Torey, you said yourself that it was like a fantasy. Maybe it would be safer to let it end now, while you have lovely, romantic memories. What if you're just chasing rainbows. You know, rainbows can't be caught."

Her words jolted Torey. Rainbows weren't real. But then, The Eiffel Tower hadn't looked real either as it traced a pattern of lacy filigree in the Paris night sky. Yet she and Peter had stood on it. It was entirely possible Elena was right. She was sure of her love for Peter, but what if he didn't love her? What if he didn't come to Victoria Station?

Torey said slowly, "I know what a chance I'm taking. He may not show up. And even if he does show, he may take one look at me and decide that all we had was an affair that should have ended in Paris. If that happens, I'll survive. I can handle the pain. What I can't handle is never knowing how it would have turned out if only I'd gone."

Elena was silent for a moment, her expression thoughtful.

"You think I'm crazy, don't you?"

"Yes. Crazy in love."

"Do you understand why I have to go?"

"Yes. I may have been married for eighteen years, but that doesn't mean I've forgotten what it felt like when I first fell in love. I just don't want to see you hurt."

"I know."

"Well, I guess there's just one thing to do then."

"What?"

"Go for it!" Elena said firmly.

Torey smiled a soft, bittersweet smile. That was just what she intended to do—*go* for it.

Chapter Seventeen

$\mathcal{A}$s Peter rode in a gondola down the Grand Canal, he took out a handkerchief and mopped his brow. It was a typically hot day at the end of August. Even the ocean breeze couldn't mitigate the sizzling heat.

It had been hot everywhere he went this summer, he reflected, from the Documenta art show in Kassel, Germany, to the auctions at Sotheby's in London, and the Basel Art Fair. Peter was in Venice now for the Biennale art show. For three days he had scrutinized the latest in contemporary art, and attended parties in the glittering palazzi.

He hadn't found anything for the museum; he didn't expect to. Contemporary art wasn't a favorite at the Hettinger. He was using the Biennale as an excuse to visit Venice and meet Angela Montessori.

He was on his way to meet her now, at a sidewalk cafe overlooking the Grand Canal. As he thought about this meeting with a woman he'd never seen before, he felt rather stupid. When they talked briefly on the telephone, Angela sounded a little reluctant, obviously wondering why Peter wanted to meet her when all they had in common was a friend, Torey Jenson.

Peter knew that Angela would think it even more odd when she realized why he wanted to meet her. He wanted to talk to her about Torey. After nearly three months, Torey's face was merely an indistinct blur in his memory. He needed to talk about her with someone who knew her well. In a very real sense, he needed to prove to himself that Torey wasn't just a figment of his imagination, but a flesh-and-blood woman who was as wonderful as he remembered.

The gondolier pulled up beside some stone steps, and Peter stepped out. The cafe was close by, and Peter spotted Angela immediately. She had described herself and said she would be wearing a red dress. The moment Peter saw the voluptuous blonde in the bright cherry-red dress, he knew it must be Angela.

After introducing himself, he sat down and ordered white wine for both of them.

"I appreciate your meeting me," he began awkwardly.

"It was no trouble," Angela replied, sizing him up quickly. Her frankly appreciative gaze revealed that she found him attractive. But her reticent attitude obviously meant she wouldn't go for a man who was somehow involved with a friend. "You said you met Torey in Paris?"

"Yes. She mentioned you and since I had to be in Venice for the Biennale, I thought I'd look you up."

The waiter brought the wine, and Peter said absently, *"Grazie."*

They talked for a few minutes about Peter's buying trip and Angela's work in the import-export business. Then Peter asked casually, "Have you known Torey long?"

"Since we were roommates at college. I attended San Francisco University while my father worked as a visiting conductor with the San Francisco Symphony. Torey was my first friend in America and we've remained close. I just saw her in June when she was here on a buying trip."

"Yes, she told me on the train."

"The Orient Express?" Angela asked, interested.

"Yes. That's actually where we met. Then she stayed with my uncle and me in Paris for a while."

Angela's ice-blue eyes looked at Peter with renewed interest. "I see. So she took my advice, after all."

"I don't understand."

"I told her to have a fling. Obviously, she did," Angela finished, smiling.

Angela's careless words shook Peter. Could she be right? Had Torey merely been taking her friend's flippant advice to have a fling when she met him? Had she suggested the September reunion as the most graceful way to end an affair that was dragging on too long?

Suddenly Peter felt that he'd had enough of Venice. He forced himself to talk politely to Angela for a while longer, then excused himself. Returning to his hotel, he packed quickly and made a reservation on the next flight to Paris. It was time to go home, he decided. He had a lot of thinking to do before next Friday.

On Thursday night Peter was sitting quietly in the sitting room of the house on the Ile Saint-Louis. He was holding a glass of brandy, which he absently twirled in his hand. Across the room, Margot and Henri sat together on a sofa, leafing through a photo album.

Margot looked up at Peter. "You're awfully quiet tonight."

"I was just thinking about business," Peter lied.

"Well, I'm glad your business has finally allowed you to come back to Paris. We've missed you this summer, Peter."

"It's good to be back, Margot."

"By the way, I meant to ask you, have you heard from Torey?"

"No," Peter said, looking away.

"We received the nicest note from her when she got home."

When Peter said nothing, Margot shot Henri a glance, then said, "I think I'll leave you two to finish your brandy. I'm rather tired this evening."

Rising, she kissed Henri, then said good night to Peter before leaving the room.

When she had gone, Henri put down the photo album and looked at Peter carefully. "Anything wrong?" he asked casually.

"Nothing," Peter replied, but this time it was obvious he was lying.

"It couldn't possibly be Torey, could it?"

"Why do you ask?"

"Well, it just seems strange that she has dropped out of your life so suddenly. You two seemed to be getting rather serious."

Peter hesitated. He hadn't told anyone about the arrangement he and Torey had made to meet in London. Since he had spoken with Angela, he couldn't get over his doubts that Torey would show up.

Henri continued lightly. "I thought you would at least have heard from her."

Finally, feeling rather embarrassed, Peter told Henri the truth. To his surprise, Henri nodded approvingly and responded, "Torey is careful. She does not want to be impulsive about something as important as marriage. That shows a great deal of sense."

"It's stupid!" Peter exploded, giving vent to a summer's worth of frustration. "We should have gotten married and taken our chances. The worst that would have happened is divorce."

"Yes, but Torey has gone through that. You haven't. Naturally, she does not want to go through it again. The end of a marriage, whether through divorce or death, is traumatic."

Peter rose and poured himself more brandy. Then he walked over to the window and looked out at the garden.

"If you will look at it logically, Peter, you will see that Torey's caution is well-founded," Henri continued. "I suspect you wanted to rush into things, did you not?"

When Peter still didn't respond, Henri finished, "But that isn't all that is bothering you, is it? There is something more."

"I haven't seen her in three long months," Peter finally answered slowly. "I can't even remember what her face looks like anymore. I only have a dim recollection of lovely blue eyes."

"What really bothers you is the thought that she might be right—that this summer apart may reveal you didn't really love her. Is that so?"

"Yes," Peter finally admitted. "For three months I told myself that we loved each other. That we'd both go to Victoria Station. And everything would be fine. Then something happened in Venice to make me doubt it all. Now, I just don't know. It happened so fast between us, neither of us was looking for love."

"We all look for love constantly," Henri corrected him gently. "But we don't always admit it to ourselves. In a way, it is better that you met the way you did. It was spontaneous. You didn't say, 'I am ready to marry, so let me select a suitable person.' You were simply attracted to each other and that attraction grew into real love."

"Did it?" Peter asked. "Torey said we were living in a fantasy world, and once we returned to the real world we might realize we didn't love each other."

"You keep repeating what Torey said. Is she alone responsible for this situation? I suspect, Peter, that what bothers you is your own doubts, not Torey's."

"What if she was right? What if I meet her tomorrow and I feel nothing for her? What can I possibly say?"

"You will not have to say anything. She will read it in your eyes immediately. It will be awkward but that will pass. Torey struck me as the sort of person who is strong enough to handle even such a delicate situation as that. The question is, can *you* handle it?"

"What?"

"Do not pretend you do not know what I mean. What if Torey does not come tomorrow? Or does come but does not feel the old passion for you? What if *you* are the one who is rejected?"

Peter smiled ruefully. "The thought *had* occurred to me."

"And your ego, which is as frail as any man's, cannot handle that, *n'est-ce pas?*"

"Well, I didn't handle it too well with Chantal. And I didn't love her, I realize now. If the same thing should happen with Torey . . ."

"I will tell you something, Peter. You are contemplating not going tomorrow. And that is not worthy of you. To run away is not like you. Do you know what I liked about you when you first came to live with me? Not your fine mind or your appreciation of art. Those are special qualities but they are not so rare. What I liked about you was your brave spirit. You were never defeated by anything."

Peter looked back out at the garden, then took a sip of brandy. Henri was right, he admitted guiltily. He was thinking of not going tomorrow.

"I would like to see that brave spirit now, Peter," Henri urged. "What you and Torey had together is worth risking pain for. So many people go through life knowing only physical passion, which is fleeting, or a companionable sort of affection which is pleasant but not exhilarating. You and Torey had a bond strong enough to last a lifetime. You should . . . oh, what is the phrase I'm searching for?"

"Go for it," Peter said softly. The phrase, a vivid reminder of his youth, brought a wave of nostalgia. He remembered paddling on a surfboard, watching a giant wave building, feeling that mixture of fear and expectation that left his mind reeling. Alone in the water, he would whisper to himself, "Go for it!"

"What?" Henri asked.

"Go for it," Peter repeated thoughtfully.

Chapter Eighteen

In September, London wasn't nearly as full of tourists as it had been in June, Torey thought, as she wandered around the city. She was trying to enjoy the sights. But as she strolled through Hyde Park, and walked along the Chelsea embankment, her mind kept returning to Peter. Would he come to their rendezvous? And if he did, would he be disappointed in her?

She was sure of her own feelings now. But she had no way of knowing what a summer apart had done to his feelings. He might very well have met someone else in that time, someone prettier, more charming, less demanding of him. Absence doesn't necessarily make the heart grow fonder; it can make the heart forget.

Thinking back on it now, Torey realized that she

had asked a great deal of this man whom she had only known for ten days. She had asked him to understand her, to consider her feelings and occasionally subordinate his own needs to hers. She had asked him for commitment. And though she was willing to give back in full measure the same thing, she knew commitment was something many men couldn't give.

As she was walking along a picturesque, winding street in Knightsbridge, Torey suddenly caught her reflection in a shop window. She looked at herself critically. What would Peter think when he saw her? She looked basically the same. The only difference was a slight tan from Sundays at the beach. She had dressed with special care in a peach-colored silk blouse and white linen skirt.

Despite the fact that she was very much the same person Peter had fallen in love with in June, Torey was afraid that he might be disappointed when he saw her now. His memory could have built her up to the point where he was bound to find reality less than he expected.

Then Torey smiled at her folly. It didn't matter what she wore or how she looked. Either Peter's love for her was true or it wasn't. She could do nothing about that. She could only hope that he would come.

As Torey walked on, she felt a slight tinge of fall in the air. The weather was still warm but it was the kind of warmth that wouldn't last much longer. The change of the seasons was evident in the slight breeze that sprung up unexpectedly and in the warm woolen clothes in the shop windows. Everywhere, there was a feeling of imminent change. Torey knew that soon, one way or the other, her own life would change forever.

Checking her watch, she decided that it was time to make her way to Victoria Station. A long summer of waiting was almost over.

At the station, Torey stood waiting nervously on the platform where the Orient Express was due to depart in only a few minutes. The train was just as Torey remembered, splendidly romantic. As she remembered that blissful night she had spent on it with Peter, Torey wished she could step back onto it and lose herself once more in a world of luxury and fantasy. But she couldn't. The fantasy was over. Now it was time for reality, and if she was lucky that would be even better than fantasy.

At first, the platform was crowded with travelers— youths with backpacks, returning Continentals with Harrod's shopping bags, well-dressed couples. But they soon disappeared into the train. And when the whistle blew and the train started to slowly move out, only one or two people remained on the platform.

Torey waited, holding her breath, as the seconds ticked away. When the train was completely out of sight and she was the only person left on the platform, she still waited. But the minutes passed and she began to feel rather foolish standing there alone. Finally, she faced the awful truth. Peter hadn't come. Instead of feeling his strong arms holding her lovingly, all she would know for the rest of her life was a memory of a romantic idyll.

She remembered the words she had spoken so

confidently to him three months earlier—"If either of us doesn't come, there won't be any hard feelings."

It was so easy to sound brave then; it was much more difficult now.

I won't cry, she told herself sternly, holding her head high. Elena was right. You can't catch a rainbow. You can only enjoy it for a fleeting moment, until it fades away.

In spite of everything, the empty ache of disappointment, she was glad she had come. She would always have regretted not taking this chance.

Slowly, feeling heavy and wooden, she left the platform and made her way through the crowded station.

"Torey!"

Torey stopped, for a moment unsure.

"Torey!"

This time she heard her name clearly. She turned, looking back at the Orient Express platform, and saw a lone figure standing on it.

Peter.

Slowly, feeling unaccountably shy, she began to walk toward him. Finally, she stopped at arm's length from him.

He looked the same, wonderfully so. His hair had just a touch more gold and his skin was just a bit darker after the summer. But he was the same Peter, with soft brown eyes and a mouth she could kiss forever.

It was his eyes that Torey concentrated on, trying to read their expression. He had come, but that didn't mean everything was all right. As Torey looked at him intently, she couldn't quite grasp what he was feeling.

"I thought you weren't coming," she finally said.

"I almost didn't come," he admitted.

The sound of his voice, so familiar yet unheard for so long, jolted Torey. She felt her heart skip a beat.

Peter continued. "I told myself that you probably wouldn't show up, so why come and make a fool of myself? But that wasn't the real problem."

He hesitated, and somehow Torey sensed what was coming.

"I know," she said softly. "You were afraid we would look at each other and feel nothing."

"Yes. I couldn't remember your face, you see, and somehow that made me doubt what I felt for you. Then I was driving down the Champs-Elysées and I happened to look up and see the Eiffel Tower. And for a split second I could see you vividly in my mind, the way you looked that day. Suddenly, I knew I *had* to come."

"That's why you were late."

"I almost didn't make it. I drove furiously to Orly Airport and barely caught a plane to London. Then my taxi was held up by traffic." He smiled the old heart-stopping smile that took Torey's breath away. "I gave the driver fifty pounds to get here on time. When he pulled up at the curb, I bolted out the door, and as I ran I heard him shout, 'Hope you catch yer train, guv'nor.'"

Torey smiled at Peter's expert imitation of a Cockney taxi driver. *At least we can still talk to each other,* she thought. *Whatever happens, that hasn't changed.*

"I knew I was late and it was then I realized how desperately I wanted to see you," Peter continued. "When I got to the platform and you weren't here,

God, I felt . . . then I caught just a glimpse of you moving through the crowd."

"And you called my name."

"You turned and I saw your face. And suddenly you were no longer a dream but the real woman I remembered. I love you, you know."

The words were even more wonderful now than when Peter had said them on the Eiffel Tower.

The expression in his golden brown eyes was so full of love that Torey felt giddy with relief. What they'd had before was no fantasy, no impossible dream, but real and true and lasting.

"I'll never leave you again," Peter said emphatically. Then he added angrily, "That was the most harebrained idea I ever agreed to . . ."

Before he could finish, Torey placed her fingertips gently on his lips to stop him.

"We have the rest of our lives to argue, Peter. Kiss me."

And he did, holding her tightly as if he would never let her go.

MORE ROMANCE FOR
A SPECIAL WAY TO RELAX

$1.95 each

1 □ TERMS OF SURRENDER Dailey

2 □ INTIMATE STRANGERS Hastings

3 □ MEXICAN RHAPSODY Dixon

4 □ VALAQUEZ BRIDE Vitek

5 □ PARADISE POSTPONED Converse

6 □ SEARCH FOR A NEW DAWN Douglass

7 □ SILVER MIST Stanford

8 □ KEYS TO DANIEL'S HOUSE Halston

9 □ ALL OUR TOMORROWS Baxter

10 □ TEXAS ROSE Thiels

11 □ LOVE IS SURRENDER Thornton

12 □ NEVER GIVE YOUR HEART Sinclair

13 □ BITTER VICTORY Beckman

14 □ EYE OF THE HURRICANE Keene

15 □ DANGEROUS MAGIC James

16 □ MAYAN MOON Carr

17 □ SO MANY TOMORROWS John

18 □ A WOMAN'S PLACE Hamilton

19 □ DECEMBER'S WINE Shaw

20 □ NORTHERN LIGHTS Musgrave

21 □ ROUGH DIAMOND Hastings

22 □ ALL THAT GLITTERS Howard

23 □ LOVE'S GOLDEN SHADOW Charles

24 □ GAMBLE OF DESIRE Dixon

25 □ TEARS AND RED ROSES Hardy

26 □ A FLIGHT OF SWALLOWS Scott

27 □ A MAN WITH DOUBTS Wisdom

28 □ THE FLAMING TREE Ripy

29 □ YEARNING OF ANGELS Bergen

30 □ BRIDE IN BARBADOS Stephens

31 □ TEARS OF YESTERDAY Baxter

32 □ A TIME TO LOVE Douglass

33 □ HEATHER'S SONG Palmer

34 □ MIXED BLESSING Sinclair

35 □ STORMY CHALLENGE James

36 □ FOXFIRE LIGHT Dailey

37 □ MAGNOLIA MOON Stanford

38 □ WEB OF PASSION John

39 □ AUTUMN HARVEST Milan

40 □ HEARTSTORM Converse

41 □ COLLISION COURSE Halston

42 □ PROUD VINTAGE Drummond

43 □ ALL SHE EVER WANTED Shaw

44 □ SUMMER MAGIC Eden

45 □ LOVE'S TENDER TRIAL Charles

46 □ AN INDEPENDENT WIFE Howard

47 □ PRIDE'S POSSESSION Stephens

48 □ LOVE HAS ITS REASONS Ferrell

49 □ A MATTER OF TIME Hastings

50 □ FINDERS KEEPERS Browning

51 □ STORMY AFFAIR Trent

52 □ DESIGNED FOR LOVE Sinclair

53 □ GODDESS OF THE MOON Thomas

54 □ THORNE'S WAY Hohl

MORE ROMANCE FOR
A SPECIAL WAY TO RELAX

55 ☐ SUN LOVER Stanford

56 ☐ SILVER FIRE Wallace

57 ☐ PRIDE'S RECKONING Thornton

58 ☐ KNIGHTLY LOVE Douglass

59 ☐ THE HEART'S VICTORY Roberts

60 ☐ ONCE AND FOREVER Thorne

61 ☐ TENDER DECEPTION Beckman

62 ☐ DEEP WATERS Bright

63 ☐ LOVE WITH A PERFECT STRANGER Wallace

64 ☐ MIST OF BLOSSOMS Converse

65 ☐ HANDFUL OF SKY Cates

66 ☐ A SPORTING AFFAIR Mikels

**LOOK FOR *SEASON OF SEDUCTION*
BY ABRA TAYLOR AVAILABLE IN FEBRUARY
AND *AN ACT OF LOVE* BY BROOKE HASTINGS
IN MARCH.**

SILHOUETTE SPECIAL EDITION, Department SE/2
1230 Avenue of the Americas
New York, NY 10020

Please send me the books I have checked above. I am enclosing $_____
(please add 50¢ to cover postage and handling. NYS and NYC residents
please add appropriate sales tax). Send check or money order—no cash or
C.O.D.'s please. Allow six weeks for delivery.

NAME _____

ADDRESS _____

CITY _____ STATE/ZIP _____

Silhouette Special Edition

Coming Next Month

After The Rain by Linda Shaw

One man had already hurt Patrice Harrows
and she was not yet ready to trust Madison Brannen. But
there was one thing the lady lawyer couldn't argue away:
her love for him.

Castles In The Air by Tracy Sinclair

Mike Sutherland was determined to buy Morgan
Construction but the owner, Sam Morgan, to his surprise
was a woman—all woman—and equally
determined not to sell!

Sorrel Sunset by Gena Dalton

Dynah Renfro and Reed Harlan struck a bargain
to be co-owners of a race horse . . . but Reed soon had full
ownership of Dynah's heart and her future.

Traces Of Dreams by Jane Clare

Art historian Pia Martell and photographer
Jules d'Archachon seemed made for each other. Would
love be strong enough to hold them together when
jealousy threatened to tear them apart?

Moonstruck by Christine Skillern

Until Caroline Conal set sail with Jake St. Simon she had
never known real work—or real love. Beneath the starry
Pacific sky they lost themselves in a love without regrets.

Night Music by Kathryn Belmont

Carla Santucci tried to remind herself that Harrington
Bates was her boss—but on one special evening she saw a
side of him that refused to leave her memory.